WOMEN
IMAGES AND REALITIES

A Multicultural Anthology

Fifth Edition

Suzanne Kelly
State University of New York, New Paltz

Gowri Parameswaran
State University of New York, New Paltz

Nancy Schniedewind
State University of New York, New Paltz

McGraw Hill

Connect
Learn
Succeed™

WOMEN: IMAGES AND REALITIES, A MULTICULTURAL ANTHOLOGY, FIFTH EDITION

Published by McGraw-Hill, a business unit of The McGraw-Hill Companies, Inc., 1221 Avenue of the Americas, New York, NY 10020. Copyright © 2012 by The McGraw-Hill Companies, Inc. All rights reserved. Previous editions © 2008, 2003, 1999, and 1995. Printed in the United States of America. No part of this publication may be reproduced or distributed in any form or by any means, or stored in a database or retrieval system, without the prior written consent of The McGraw-Hill Companies, Inc., including, but not limited to, in any network or other electronic storage or transmission, or broadcast for distance learning.

Some ancillaries, including electronic and print components, may not be available to customers outside the United States.

This book is printed on acid-free paper.

1 2 3 4 5 6 7 8 9 0 DOC/DOC 1 0 9 8 7 6 5 4 3 2 1

ISBN 978-0-07-351231-0
MHID 0-07-351231-1

Vice President & Editor-in-Chief: *Michael Ryan*
Vice President & Director of Specialized Publishing: *Janice M. Roerig-Blong*
Publisher: *William Glass*
Senior Sponsoring Editor: *Debra B. Hash*
Marketing Coordinator: *Angela R. FitzPatrick*
Project Manager: *Erin Melloy*
Design Coordinator: *Brenda A. Rolwes*
Cover Designer: *Studio Montage, St. Louis, Missouri*
Cover Image: © *Stephanie Miller Corfee*
Buyer: *Kara Kudronowicz*
Media Project Manager: *Sridevi Palani*
Compositor: *Laserwords Private Limited*
Typeface: *10/13 Palatin*
Printer: *R. R. Donnelley*

All credits appearing on page or at the end of the book are considered to be an extension of the copyright page.

Library of Congress Cataloging-in-Publication Data

Women : images and realities : a multicultural anthology / Suzanne Kelly, Gowri Parameswaran, Nancy Schniedewind.—5th ed.
    p. cm.
    ISBN 978-0-07-351231-0
    1. Feminism—United States. 2. Women—United States—Social conditions. 3. Women's studies—United States. I. Kelly, Suzanne M., 1969. II. Parameswaran, Gowri, 1963. III. Schniedewind, Nancy, 1947-
HQ1421.W653 2012
305.420973--dc23   2011038725

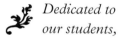 *Dedicated to
our students,*

*our mothers: Mary Kelly
Sulochana Parameswaran
Grace Douglass Schniedewind (1912–1995)*

*our sisters: Jeanne Kelly
Bhuvana Parameswaran (1936–2010)
Carol Schniedewind*

*and: Mickey Haggerty and Cassandra Levey
Ajit Zacharias, P. Parameswaran, Adityan Gowri Ajit
and Ananthan Gowri Ajit
Dave Porter and Jesse and Daniel Schniedewind*

Preface

This fifth edition of *Women: Images and Realities* has emerged from a process of reflective teaching and research that builds upon the first four editions. The book originally grew out of the experiences of the initial editors—Amy Kesselman, Lily McNair, and Nancy Schniedewind—as teachers of introductory courses in women's studies and psychology of women. Dissatisfied with the available texts, they spent many years foraging among journals and anthologies to bring students a view of feminism that reflected their diverse experience and spoke in a language that was accessible and compelling. While they wanted to include some of the fruits of feminist research, they felt it was most important that students' first encounter with women's studies be one that engages them and evokes the flash of recognition and connection that has long drawn women to feminism. Although two of the editors have changed, the fifth edition of *Women: Images and Realities* continues in that tradition.

The introductory women's studies course at State University of New York at New Paltz, called *Women: Images and Realities*, provided both the inspiration and structure for this anthology. Since it was first offered in 1974, the course has developed to reflect the responses of thousands of students who have taken it. Instructors still find that students are more adept at analyzing social structures after they have discussed ideas about gender and its effect on individual women's lives. Therefore we have continued to structure the book to move from the more visible manifestations of sexism in our culture to the forms of discrimination that are embedded in social institutions.

NEW TO THE FIFTH EDITION

The new edition includes 35 new selections, 15 selections that have been updated, and 11 boxes that are new or revised. Like previous editions, we have included a great many first-person and fictional accounts. In order to address issues that emerge from discussions of the lives of women with diverse backgrounds, we have included pieces about not only a variety of female experiences, but also, in Chapter VI, those that directly address some of the systems of oppression that interact with gender in women's lives.

This fifth edition also reflects the experiences of students and faculty who have used this book in the past 16 years. In response to students' enthusiasm for the young voices in the fourth edition, we have included more in the new edition. Because we live in an ever more interdependent world and in a world where solidarity between women transnationally will greatly influence all women's freedom and survival, this revision includes more transnational articles, even though the text remains focused on the United States. Reflecting political and social changes in the last few years, the chapters on social institutions, health care, and reproductive justice include many new and updated essays. Because of the importance of developing a transnational consciousness and awareness of the effects of citizenship on women's lives, we have added a new section, "Nations, Boundaries, and Belonging: Citizenship in Women's Lives" in Chapter VI. The final chapter, "Changing Our World" also has many new pieces reflecting the renewed vigor of feminist activism in the past few years.

This fifth edition brings together a broad array of perspectives and experiences from contributors and editors. We are all academics. Gowri has done research on liberatory pedagogy, social conflicts, and peace education, and worked with children in the Global South. Nancy's work is in the areas of multicultural/social justice education, feminist pedagogy, and resistance to market-driven educational policies. Suzanne's research draws largely on feminist philosophies of the body and the environment.

Our interest in women's studies and feminism, however, is not merely academic; we are all deeply committed to feminist social change. We have tried, in *Women: Images and Realities,* to stimulate an intellectual interest in women's studies by presenting a wide variety of women's studies topics. In addition, by demonstrating the ways that women have been able to make significant changes in our society and culture, we hope to encourage a political commitment to creating a just and generous world.

ACKNOWLEDGMENTS

The fifth edition of this book, like the first four, has truly been a collaborative effort. Our cooperative working arrangements and consensual decision-making process, characteristic of feminist process, have been both stimulating and arduous. We appreciate each other's patience and commitment.

Many people have made important contributions to this fifth edition. David Ryan Solomon and Kelly Collins have been resourceful in gathering needed material for this edition. We are, once again, grateful to Emily Caigan, who helped us to locate the cover art. Thank you to Dan Schniedewind, who provided valuable ideas and feedback. This edition has also benefited from the ongoing contributions of Ajit Zacharias, David Porter, and Mickey Haggerty.

For their thoughtful reviews in preparation for the fifth edition, we would also like to thank Barbara Hawthorne, University of Northern Colorado; Linda

Weinhouse, Community College of Baltimore County; Kristyan Kouri, California State University at Northridge; Laurie Fuller, Northeastern Illinois University; Swift Stiles Dickison, Montgomery College; Sharon Fodness, Minneapolis Community and Technical College; Becky Lewis, University of South Carolina; Gabriela Diaz de Sabates, Kansas State University; Shelley Bannister, Northeastern Illinois University; Jeannette Riley, University of Massachusetts at Dartmouth; Bettina Aptheker, University of California at Santa Cruz; and Michelle Rowley, University of Maryland at College Park.

For their extremely important support, we are grateful to our sponsoring editor, Debra Hash; our developmental editor, Janice Wiggins-Clarke; our project manager, Erin Melloy; and our permissions editor, Kayrn Morrison. Finally, we especially thank all the contributors to this volume, some of whom rewrote earlier pieces for this book.

Contents

CHAPTER II: BECOMING A
WOMAN IN OUR SOCIETY   45

No attn in book to Women's mental health

CHAPTER VII: VIOLENCE AGAINST WOMEN 492

Violence in Intimate Relationships 496

Introduction

Inspired by the very positive responses to the previous four editions of *Women: Images and Realities: A Multicultural Anthology*, we are pleased to bring updated information and an even wider range of voices and issues to the fifth edition. While *Women: Images and Realities* remains largely focused on women's struggles in the United States, this fifth edition better recognizes the connections between the feminist movement in the United States and a growing transnational women's movement, the impact of globalization, and the place of nation and citizenship in women's lives. We have also worked to gather into this book, once again, readings that will be meaningful to you and challenge your thinking about what it means to be female in the United States. You will hear the voices of women of different racial, cultural, and socioeconomic backgrounds who have made various choices in their lives. Because the selections reflect a wide variety of female experience, some parts of this book will resonate for you while others will not. We hope the book will enable you to understand what women have in common as well as the ways women's lives are shaped by other systems of inequality such as race, class, sexual orientation, age, and citizenship.

The structure of this book is inspired by the consciousness-raising process that has been a central part of contemporary feminism. The goal of consciousness-raising is to use insights from personal experience to enhance a political critique of the position of women in society. Echoing this process, the book moves back and forth between personal experience and social realities, illuminating the way sexism in society affects women's lives. We hope the selections in this book will stimulate your thinking about your own life.

ORGANIZATION AND USE OF THIS BOOK

Women: Images and Realities is divided into eight chapters. We begin by introducing the subject of women's studies, an approach to knowledge that emerged as part of the contemporary feminist movement. Because a feminist perspective provides the groundwork for women's studies, Chapter I explores the meaning of feminism and women's studies for different groups of women and for male supporters of feminism. It also examines the impact of women's studies and feminist scholarship on other academic disciplines.

Chapter II presents prevailing ideas about what it means to be female in our society and describes the way we learn and internalize these ideas. Chapter III explores the effects of these ideas on women's attitudes toward our bodies and our sexuality. Because this anthology is designed to enable you to make connections between your personal life and social realities, it moves from a focus on individual experience in Chapters II and III to an examination of the social institutions that shape women's lives in Chapter IV. Articles in this chapter demonstrate the ways that the subordination of women is deeply embedded in social institutions such as the legal system, the workplace, the family, and religion. Chapter V examines the sexism in the medical-care system and women's efforts to control their health. This includes women's ongoing struggle for reproductive rights, including access to birth control, abortion, and protection from sterilization abuse.

While all chapters in *Women: Images and Realities* include accounts by women from diverse social groups, Chapter VI directly addresses the ways that socially defined differences among women have been used to divide us from each other. Examining the ways that inequities in our society based on race, class, sexual orientation, age, and citizenship have often separated women, it analyzes how these differences manifest in institutional discrimination, create both divisions and connections among different groups of women, and intersect in the lives of women in ways that are often made invisible.

Chapter VII explores violence against women in various forms, particularly battering, rape, and incestuous sexual abuse. Chapter VIII reviews ways that women have worked together to make social and political change. By reminding us of the rich tradition of female resistance both within and outside an organized feminist movement, the selections in Chapter VIII provide inspiration and hope for changing our lives and the world around us. The resurgence of political activism on college campuses in the twenty-first century reinforces a renewed sense of the possibility of change both in the United States and throughout the world.

We have tried to create a rich brew—a mixture of short stories, poems, autobiographical accounts, and journal excerpts as well as analytical and descriptive essays from a variety of disciplines. We hope this mixture will engage you intellectually and emotionally. Introductions to sections provide a framework that places the selections in the broader context of the chapter. While most of the material is current, some articles provide a historical perspective. Those written in the earlier years of the contemporary feminist movement are important because they laid the conceptual groundwork for further research and analysis.

There are theoretical insights in *Women: Images and Realities,* but this book does not provide a theoretical introduction to women's studies in all the various disciplines. Theory is discussed in those women's studies courses that explore feminist issues and particular disciplines in depth. Here, you will hear the words of a wide variety of writers, some prominent feminist writers and some students like yourself. Because the emotions provoked by this material can sometimes be unsettling, you may find it useful to discuss your responses outside of class as well as in the classroom. These discussions might take place with friends, family members, or a counselor, depending on the intensity of the personal connection with the issue.

This book may raise specific questions for African-American, Asian-American, Latina, Arab-American, Native American, Muslim, and Jewish women. Women of color are struggling against the sexism in their communities and the particular ways that sexism and racism interact in their lives. The different priorities and emphases that emerge from various cultural and racial contexts complicate and enrich a feminist perspective. An expanded transnational focus also deepens that perspective, stressing the differences among women as much as the connections between them in our ever-changing global world. Men who have taken women's studies courses have often found it intellectually and emotionally challenging to be in a course focused on women, taught by women, and usually including a majority of female students. By listening to women's experiences and sharing the experience of being a male in a sexist society, men can both benefit from and contribute to a women's studies course.

Many students will use this book in the introductory women's studies course, an interdisciplinary course that familiarizes students with the field of women's studies and the feminist perspectives that shape women's studies scholarship. In such a course, you may also read *Our Bodies, Our Selves:* written by the Boston Women's Health Book Collective (Simon and Schuster, 2011). Even if the book is not assigned in your course, it is an excellent complement to *Women: Images and Realities*, and we recommend it.

HOW WE SEE FEMINISM

Because *Women: Images and Realities* is informed by a feminist perspective, we want to describe what feminism means to us. We see gender as a central fact of all women's lives, even though it wears many different faces. The life of a single mother struggling to support her family on the wages she earns doing domestic work is very different from the life of a woman struggling to succeed in a scientific establishment dominated by men. But both survive in a world where women are paid less than men on all levels, both live in a society in which one woman is raped every three minutes, and both face the possibility of losing their jobs if they resist their employer's sexual advances. Feminism is a social movement whose goal is to eliminate the oppression of women in all its forms. This means making major social, economic, political and cultural changes in our society—changes so fundamental and numerous that the task sometimes seems overwhelming. Yet feminists have succeeded in making changes that would have appeared unthinkable 50 years ago—and such accomplishments give us hope and courage.

One of the most important ideas that contemporary feminism has generated is that "the personal is political"—what happens in our private lives reflects the power relations in our society. This book examines the inequities both in women's personal lives and in the world. The belief in our right to determine our lives empowers us to expand our choices: to develop relationships based on equality and mutual respect, to choose when and if to have children, to work toward career goals that are meaningful to us.

Because of the connection between personal and political life, our ability to control our own lives is limited by the environment in which we live. We cannot, for example, choose when and if we have children unless safe, effective, and legal birth control and abortion are available and accessible. Feminism is more than an individual lifestyle. It involves a commitment to social change, which can take a variety of forms. It might mean working to make your campus safer for women; forming a support group for women in your school, department, or office to discuss the conditions of your lives and ways to improve them; organizing a forum about sexual harassment at your workplace or on your campus; or establishing a cooperative child care center in your community. Feminism means making changes wherever you are.

THE AUTHORS: THREE FEMINIST JOURNEYS

Because this book affirms the differences among us, we want to tell you who we are and what feminism means to each of us.

Suzanne   In 1969, the year of my birth, the United States was undergoing radical social and political transformation. By the time I entered school, a range of civil rights legislations had been passed, including new laws that extended rights and protections to women. Growing up in a white, working-class family, the language of equality was everywhere. I was told by my parents, teachers, and friends that I could be and do anything. I would later learn that those new laws could not have been changed without a fight. But as a child, I was relatively unaware of the activism and struggles that led to this new language of equality, and how those hard-won victories had made my life much more free of the institutionalized sexism that was commonplace just years before.

When I reached adolescence, however, I started to become fairly skeptical of the idea that, as a girl, I shared the same freedoms and liberties as the boys around me. While some of the laws had changed, many attitudes had not. The message—that if I just tried hard enough, I could seize my equality and cast myself into a future where I was on equal footing with men—began to feel more and more like a lie. In those years I grappled with the prevailing sexual double standard, feeling pressured by peers, teachers, and the Catholic Church to adhere to being a good girl. I was born a stubborn child, and had long before learned to speak up for myself. And, yet, I knew that if I was to be accepted, it was safer to remain quiet. Even though speaking up gave me a sense of power, I still felt powerless in the face of boys who asserted their dominance through gestures and comments. I witnessed friends violated in their intimate relationships with boys, and found myself an accomplice to their silence and shame.

Upon entering college, these unsolved inequities were, to my great benefit, suddenly legitimate questions to be worked out. I found answers to these questions in classes that placed women at the center of their inquiry, that interrogated relationships of power, and that saw women's problems, like those I had experienced, as not just my own, but shared by other women and shaped by forces larger than my own life. Feminism gave me a language and a means to engage in actions toward change, both individually and collectively. And teaching women's studies has given me the added strength to endure.

Gowri I was born and spent most of my childhood in a small town in South India. The British had been forced to give up their jewel in the crown, as India was referred to, a decade before I was born, and the possibility of change and transformation was everywhere. At the time of India's independence, a constitution based on democracy and representative government had been drafted, with every citizen being granted one vote, men and women, rich and poor. In the process of organizing for the struggle against the British, the traditionally hierarchical society in India had grown a new consciousness about equality. Centuries of unequal laws actively tolerated and even encouraged by the British conquerors were erased, replaced by a constitution that was aimed at leveling the playing field. Yet, in the town where I grew up, you would never know that India had changed.

I grew up in a privileged Brahmin family; Brahmins were a privileged caste into which you had to be born. India has a very hierarchical caste system where the upper castes control all the reins of power and wealth in society. We had a little army of servants and gardeners in my house, but few were allowed in the kitchen or the room where the gods were displayed, because of caste-related taboos. During my early teens, as I read and understood firsthand the many barriers to equality that people from the lower castes faced, I became aware that laws were not enough to transform society. In order to make change, there has to be collective action from people at all levels of society, especially those who bear the brunt of the oppression. It was through understanding caste oppression that I also discovered that as a woman I was less valued than the men in my community. Sexism became a significant paradigm through which I began to understand my experiences.

My parents were a great inspiration. They taught me that I can lead a very fulfilling life if I am willing to stand up for truth and justice. In college I was exposed to feminist theory and writings by women from around the world. After my move to the USA, there was a deepening of my commitment to positive social change through activism. In my teaching, I help facilitate a safe environment in the class, where students can think of themselves as agents of change toward justice. Teaching about sexism and other forms of social discrimination is central to my philosophy and engagement with society.

Nancy   Growing up as a white female in a semi-rural New England community, I was not aware of the price I was paying for being female. I did not wonder why I hated science. No one called my attention to how few females appeared in my textbooks or discussed the ways that the absence of role models inhibits learning and stunts expectations. I never wondered why no one encouraged me to become a scientist despite my aptitude for science. Though I knew I loved sports, I never connected my failure to take myself seriously as an athlete with the fact that the high school athletic budget and programs for boys' sports were extensive, while those for girls were nonexistent.

I was also unaware of the privileges I received by being white. I didn't realize that because we were white my family was able to move to our town by taking advantage of the government's Fair Housing Act (FHA) after WWII to obtain a mortgage to buy a home, thereby benefiting from better public schools. I didn't know that the program was discriminatory, denying mortgages to most applicants of color. I didn't wonder why there were only two African-American families in our town. I never thought about the comfort of being in the racial majority in my school and how my sense of being "normal" enhanced my ability to learn. I didn't ask why I had the privilege to go home to play when my African-American classmates went home to help their mothers do the laundry they took in to support their families.

I saw my life as my own. Even throughout my master's degree program, I failed to see patterns of discrimination and privilege. I thought the sexual harassment I experienced was my own problem, not part of a pattern experienced by millions of women. There were no women's studies courses in the late 1960s, and it was only through long talks with friends and co-workers that I opened my eyes to sexism. Subsequently, I read much of what the burgeoning women's movement was producing. Looking back at my life, I saw how I had been affected by gender, race, and class, and look to the future with a renewed commitment to work for change.

Feminism offers me the support, values, and ideas for living an authentic life. It provides me a way to understand women's experience and a vision of a more just and humane future. Feminism contributes to my role as an educator by helping me understand how sexism limits men's and women's educational potential. Its values underlie my feminist approach to teaching, which is more equitable, cooperative, and empowering that traditional approaches. As a family member, feminism gives me the consciousness and strength to encourage more equitable family relations. Finally, feminism sustains my faith in women's collective power to transform our individual lives and social institutions.

As our own stories demonstrate, the experience of integrating feminism into one's life can be both challenging and exhilarating. We hope this book makes you feel stronger and better able to both make choices in your own life and participate in the process of creating a more just and generous world.

C H A P T E R I

What Is Women's Studies?

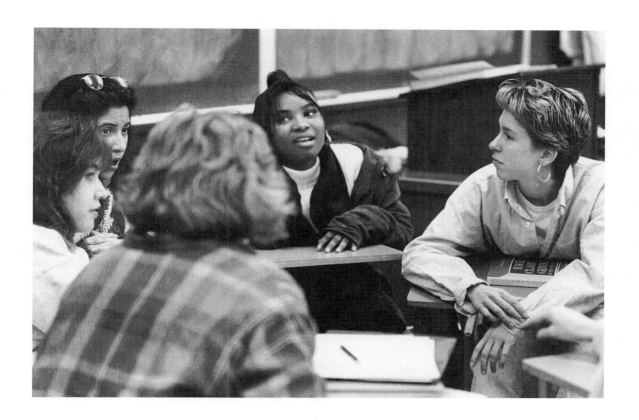

Before the late 1960s there were no women's studies courses. Most college courses focused on male experience, and women were shadowy, marginal figures. The resurgence of feminism in the late 1960s led students and faculty to ask "Where are the women?" and work to establish courses that focused on women's experiences. Today there are women's studies programs throughout the world, close to 1,000 of them in the United States.

What is women's studies? You will probably hear this question often when you tell people that you are taking women's studies classes. Despite the spectacular growth in women's studies programs and courses in the past four decades, some faculty members and students still view women's studies as marginal to the main business of the university. Yet to countless others, women's studies is an important and exciting experience that introduces new ways of seeing both the world and oneself. Women's studies courses investigate women's experiences, perspectives, and contributions, placing women at the center of inquiry.

As Barrie Thorne has pointed out, women's studies has been a two-pronged project: it has created courses within disciplines, such as women and literature or sociology of women, that seek to incorporate the experiences of women into the subject matter of the disciplines. But the boundaries that separate the disciplines begin to blur and appear arbitrary when we seek to answer questions about women's lives. The second prong of the women's studies project, therefore, is to create interdisciplinary courses and lines of inquiry. The introduction to women's studies courses in most colleges is an example of an interdisciplinary course that draws on theory and approaches from a variety of disciplines to render women's lives visible.[1] Women's studies scholars working both within and across disciplines have generated new concepts and approaches to understanding the world. A basic premise of women's studies is that we cannot understand the world without understanding women's experiences, perspectives, and contributions.

A women's studies approach to education emphasizes an interactive learning process that challenges students intellectually and emotionally. Women's studies emerged from the questions women asked about their own experiences as well as about the subjects they were studying, and this process remains a central part of a women's studies education. Women's studies instructors usually encourage students to ask questions of the material and to bring their own experiences to bear on the material they are studying. Learning to ask such questions is part of crafting what Cynthia Enloe calls a "*feminist* curiosity." "Using a *feminist* curiosity," she explains, means "asking questions about the condition of women—and about relationships of women to each other and about relationships of women to men." While asking such questions can be difficult, Enloe also tells us it can be "energizing," as it "motivates one to treat as puzzling the relationships of women to any aspect of social life and nature that other people take for granted."[2]

---

[1]Barrie Thorne, "A Telling Time for Women's Studies," *Signs: A Journal of Women in Culture and Society* 25, no. 4 (2000), p. 1183.

[2]Cynthia Enloe, *Globalization and Militarism: Feminists Make the Link* (Lanham, MD: Rowman and Littlefield, 2007), p. 10.

Women's studies instructors see themselves as resources and guides in this process, not as authorities who are handing down knowledge to passive recipients. The values of feminism, including a critique of all forms of domination, an emphasis on cooperation, and a belief in the integration of theory and practice, have shaped an approach to teaching termed feminist pedagogy, which makes the women's studies classroom an interactive learning environment. The realities of schooling in the United States contradict these approaches to learning. Education has often been a bittersweet experience for women. We expect that knowledge of our world can be empowering, enabling us to change our lives and our communities. For many women, particularly those of us who have experienced racial or ethnic discrimination, educational achievement assures greater access to resources and opportunities. But the educational institutions of our society have too often been limiting, rather than empowering, for women. The practices of educational institutions frequently encourage girls and women to pursue occupations in traditionally "female" areas rather than in traditionally "male" domains such as math and the sciences. Schools and teachers tend to reinforce girls' compliance and passivity rather than their assertiveness and inquisitiveness. Men have historically exercised authority in institutions of higher learning, determining "valid" areas of inquiry and "legitimate" methods of analysis and research. In sum, the dominant message is that human experience equals male experience. Sometimes this message is overt, but it is sometimes so subtle and deeply embedded in the educational experience that we are not aware of it. There has been some progress in the past four decades, but for the most part the massive outpouring of research by women's studies scholars has not been integrated into mainstream education.

Women's studies was born out of the conviction that women are worth learning about and that understanding women's experiences helps us to change the condition of women. Emerging from the feminist movement of the late 1960s and 1970s, women's studies courses and programs were deeply political. The Buffalo Women's Studies Program asserted, for example, "This education will not be an academic exercise; it will be an ongoing process to change the ways in which women think and behave. It must be part of the struggle to build a new and more complete society."[3] From their beginnings in the 1960s, women's studies courses spread rapidly across the country. By 1989, over 500 colleges in the United States had women's studies programs. In the past 40 years, thousands of books and articles about women have been published, challenging old assumptions and charting new territory. Today, women's studies has become part of the academy and offers majors, minors, master's degrees, and, at a more than a dozen universities, doctorates in women's studies. Women's studies flourishes in conferences, workshops, journals, and research institutes and in countless Internet sites and discussion lists.

As feminist scholars began to chart female experience, they sometimes found the available vocabulary inadequate and confusing. As a result, feminist scholarship has generated several new words or has endowed familiar words with new meaning.

---

[3]Quoted in Florence Howe and Carol Ahlum, "Women's Studies and Social Change," in *Academic Women on the Move*, ed. Alice Rossi and Ann Calderwood (New York: Russell Sage, 1973), p. 420.

The word *gender*, for example, used to pertain only to grammar but has come to mean the socially constructed behaviors and characteristics that are associated with each sex. While gender is a social category, the word *sex* applies to the physiological identities of women and men. The distinction between sex and gender enables us to see that the particular expectations for women and men in our culture are neither immutable nor universal. Recently, however, feminist scholars have argued that sex itself is not a purely biological category but has been powerfully shaped by gender. For many years, for example, doctors have insisted that sexually ambiguous genitalia be surgically altered so that they fit into the prevailing divisions between male and female, thereby showing the power of gender to constitute sex.[4] In addition, scholars have pointed out that the social construction of gender is a complex process in which individuals and groups sometimes challenge gender norms. Tina Chanter suggests that we think of sex and gender as always a dynamic relation and the distinctions between the two realms as not fixed or rigid but malleable and flexible.[5]

The word *sexism* appeared because the available phrase *sex discrimination* did not adequately describe the pervasive bias against women in our culture. Sexism therefore has come to mean behaviors, attitudes, and institutions based on the assumption of male superiority. The term *patriarchy* refers to "power of the fathers" and is used by feminists in two ways: (1) to describe a society in which older men are in positions of power; and (2) to describe a male-dominated society. This new vocabulary has been instrumental in shaping the ways in which we now think about the experiences of women and girls in our society.

Over the past four decades women's studies has developed and changed as it seeks to more effectively understand the lives of all women. Initially women scholars endeavored to address the absence of women in the literature of varied academic areas by uncovering women's achievements. For example, psychology has benefited from the work of scholars who focused on the important contributions to psychological research made by women such as Mamie Phipps Clark, Carolyn Sherif, and Margaret Harlow. It quickly became apparent, however, that the central concepts of many academic disciplines excluded women or assumed women's inferiority to men. Even the language used to describe these concepts and ideas is often laden with assumptions about female inferiority. Some 20 years ago, the anthropologist Emily Martin, for instance, exposed how "scientific" descriptions of the egg and the sperm relied on stereotyped notions of male and female roles, while also reinforcing widely held myths about male and female power.[6] But as Gowri Parameswaran points out, over the past few decades women have reshaped the field of biology to question these assumptions by pointing to the egg's active role in fertilization.

---

[4]Ann Fausto-Sterling, *Sexing the Body* (New York: Basic Books, 2000).

[5]Tina Chanter, "Gender Aporias," *Signs: Journal of Women in Culture and Society* 25, no. 4 (2000), p. 1241. See also Judith Butler, *Gender Trouble: Feminism and the Subversion of Identity* (New York: Routledge, 1990); and Ann Fausto-Sterling, *Sexing the Body.*

[6]Emily Martin, "The Egg and the Sperm: How Science Has Constructed a Romance Based on Stereotypical Male-Female Roles," *Signs: Journal of Women in Culture and Society* 16 (1991), pp. 485–501.

In the field of history, for example, subject matter was traditionally limited to the public arena, such as political parties, wars, and the economy. The domestic world, where many women spent a great deal of their time, was considered trivial or irrelevant, and the relationship between the domestic and public worlds was ignored. In literature, the very definition of great literature, or "the canon," was based on standards that white male authors generated. Feminist anthropologists have demonstrated the important contributions women make in forging societies and have examined the status of women in relationship to public and private activities. Some fields have been more resistant to the influence of feminist scholarship. By emphasizing the contributions of women, critically challenging the conceptual frameworks underlying traditional scholarship, and presenting theory and research focusing on women's experiences, women's studies is transforming the terrain of human knowledge. When women are placed at the center of inquiry, everything changes dramatically, as if a kaleidoscope has been turned.

As Michael Kimmel points out, "Women's studies has made gender visible."[7] Thus, examining gender is more than examining women's lives; it also includes acknowledging the enormous influence of gender on all of our lives. Boys' and men's experiences are powerfully affected by ideas about masculinity and femininity. Women's studies has, as a result, generated the broader field of gender studies. Gender studies examines the ways that ideas about the social relations of women and men structure our politics and culture and the way we all experience our world. By reaffirming the significance of gender in our lives, gender studies is very much related to women's studies in its content. Elizabeth Minnich aptly describes this complementary relationship: "Gender Studies requires Women's Studies, just as Women's Studies requires the study of gender. One does not substitute for the other; they are mutually enriching."[8]

The ideas of feminism have inspired the development of women's studies theory and courses. The term *feminism* refers to the belief that women have been historically subordinate to men as well as to the commitment to working for freedom for women in all aspects of social life. Though feminist beliefs, values, and practices are continually evolving, reflecting new ideas, movements, and historical research, it is clear that similar values have informed the lives and work of many different groups of women, even when they may not have identified their beliefs as "feminist." Paula Gunn Allen, a Native American writer, pointed out that roots of contemporary feminism can be found in many Native American cultures.[9] Some of these societies were gynarchies (societies governed by women) that were egalitarian, pacifist, and spiritually based. These values and practices are comparable to those of

---

[7]Michael Kimmel, "Men and Women's Studies: Premises, Perils, and Promise," in *Talking Gender: Public Images, Personal Journeys and Political Critiques,* ed. Nancy Hewitt, Jean O'Barr, and Nancy Rosebaugh (Chapel Hill: University of North Carolina Press, 1996), p. 154.

[8]Elizabeth Minnich, *Transforming Knowledge* (Philadelphia: Temple University Press, 1990), p. 139.

[9]Paula Gunn Allen, *The Sacred Hoop: Recovering the Feminine in American Indian Traditions* (Boston: Beacon Press, 1986), p. 213.

present-day feminism, such as cooperation and respect for human freedom. As we understand the varied ways in which women have worked toward self-determination in different contexts and cultures throughout history, the definition of feminism becomes broader and richer.

The word *feminism* originated in France and was introduced into this country in the early 1900s after efforts to expand women's political rights had been flourishing throughout the world for many decades.[10] The women who first identified themselves as feminist in the early twentieth century believed that the "emancipation of women" required changes in the relations between women and men and between women and the family, as well as between women and the state.

For many women, the goal of freedom for women was inextricably linked with the end of all forms of domination. Women of color, in particular, saw the connections between sexual and racial oppression. African-American activists like Anna Cooper argued for a women's movement that challenged all forms of domination and made alliances with all oppressed peoples.

U.S. historians often refer to the movement that began in the nineteenth century and culminated with the Nineteenth Amendment, granting women the right to vote, as the first wave of feminism. The legal, educational, and political achievements of the movement were considerable, despite the fact that it faced enormous opposition to every demand. Yet the organizations that led the movement did not speak for all women and often refused to seriously consider the concerns of African-American and immigrant women. The history of the suffrage movement demonstrates how race and class divisions can prevent a movement from working effectively to achieve freedom for all women.

In the decades after women won the right to vote in 1920, the organized women's rights movement in the United States dissipated, and the word *feminism* fell into disuse and ill repute. In the 1960s, a new generation revived the fight for what they now called "women's liberation" and a vision of a world free of domination and subordination. This movement struck a responsive chord for countless women. The feminist movement grew rapidly throughout the 1970s, permeating every aspect of social, political, and cultural life. The new feminist movement has argued that reproductive rights are essential for women's freedom. It has criticized the disadvantaged position of women in the workplace and the subordination of women in the family, pointing out the connection between the place of women in the labor force and in the family. By declaring that "the personal is political," contemporary feminists have brought into the open subjects that previously had been discussed only in whispers, such as sexuality, rape, incestuous sexual abuse, and violence against women. Lesbian and bisexual feminists have pointed out that freedom to love whomever one chooses is an essential element of self-determination. For feminists, all of these struggles are inextricably connected, and changes in all of them are necessary to attain freedom for women.

---

[10]Nancy Cott, *The Grounding of Modern Feminism* (New Haven, CT: Yale University Press, 1987), p. 14.

Feminism is continually developing a more multicultural and inclusive perspective, reflecting the lives of women of all races, ethnic groups, and classes. Feminists of varied races and ethnicities are generating theory and practice that address their particular experiences and consciousness, broadening and deepening the scope of feminist analysis. It is important to recognize that although gender affects all of us, these effects are powerfully shaped by other aspects of our experience.

Black feminist thought, for example, reflects the unique position of African-American women in American society. As eloquently expressed by Alice Walker, black feminism, or "womanism," draws on the historical strength of black women in their families and communities and the rich African-American tradition of resistance, persistence, and survival. By describing "womanist" with a broad brush that celebrates the everyday lives of black girls and women as well as the political implications of their activism, Walker's definition resonates with the experiences of many black women. African-American feminists have also emphasized the concept of "multiple consciousness" or "intersectionality": the idea that the distinct systems of racism, sexism, and class oppression interact simultaneously in the lives of women of color in the United States. They have also suggested an African-centered rather than a Eurocentric perspective on the history of women, allowing for an appreciation of the powerful roles that women have played in some African societies.

Jewish feminists have also reclaimed their tradition of Jewish female resistance and have reexamined insulting stereotypes like "pushy Jewish mother" and "Jewish American Princess" to express the legitimacy of female assertiveness. They have revived Rabbi Hillel's question "If I am not for myself, who will be? If I am only for myself, what am I?" to explore both the meaning of anti-Semitism for Jewish women and the importance of the connections between different groups of suppressed people. Reflecting on this project, Melanie Kaye/Kantrowitz has pointed out, "What is best in people is a sturdy connection between respect for the self and respect for the other: reaching in and out at the same time."[11]

Asian and Latina feminists have pointed out the tensions between immigrant and U.S. cultures, and the concurrent need to affirm their cultural heritage and reject its sexism. Traditional Japanese culture, for instance, expects women to be docile and to put family honor ahead of their own needs. One's self is inextricably tied to one's family; to break away is often viewed as an act of betrayal. Asian-American feminists have also confronted the myths about Asian women's sexuality, myths that have emerged from an interplay between Western stereotypes and the expectations of women in Asian cultures. Latina feminists have demonstrated the need to negotiate a path between the sometimes conflicting demands of the Latino community's expectations and female self-determination. Feminism for Latina women, and women of other oppressed groups, means simultaneously working with Latino men against their common oppression and challenging sexist or "macho" attitudes and behavior.

---

[11]Melanie Kaye/Kantrowitz, "To Be a Radical Jew in the Late Twentieth Century," *Sinister Wisdom* 29–30 (1986), p. 280.

Contemporary American Indian feminists carry many of the traditional values and practices of women-centered Native American cultures into the present. In addition, Native American women's vision of connectedness to the earth and spiritual world, along with a legacy of responsibility toward the environment, are emerging as important concerns for many feminists. For example, ecofeminism addresses the connection between women's oppression and the exploitation of the earth's natural resources, and emphasizes women's role in confronting these environmental issues.

One of the most exciting developments of the past few decades has been the emergence of a powerful transnational feminist movement that has worked throughout the world to challenge violence against women, defend women's rights as human rights, expand the education of girls, champion women's sexual and reproductive freedom, and support women's access to economic independence. The activities and ideas of women throughout the world have enriched and broadened feminist theory and practice contributing to a transnational multicultural feminism aimed at the liberation of all people. To emphasize the diversity within feminism, some scholars have begun to refer to "feminisms."

Speaking up for ourselves is an essential first step for women taking an active role in their education. In the first selection in this chapter, bell hooks writes from the context of the Southern black community in which she grew up, where "talking back" as a girl was an act of daring. It often takes courage for women to speak up for themselves in an educational setting, where male-oriented norms, curricula, and classroom processes often silence women's voices. Mai Kao Thao echoes this message in her essay, "Sins of Silence," as she describes the pain she and other "good Hmong women" have endured when they have kept silent about the realities of their lives.

Adrienne Rich, feminist author and poet, wrote the next selection as an address to a primarily white, female graduating class in 1977. Its message, about the importance of women "claiming an education" that is meaningful to them, continues to be relevant today in any educational setting. Rich provides a personal context for understanding the role of women's studies courses in shaping such an education.

Just as feminism has become more inclusive of women from diverse backgrounds, so too has the content of women's studies expanded over the years, embodying the experiences of women from varying racial, ethnic, and class groups. In their classic essay, Akasha (Gloria) Hull and Barbara Smith place the development of black women's studies in a political and historical context. By highlighting the legacy of black women's struggles to obtain an education during and after slavery, Hull and Smith show us the connection between black women's studies and the politics of oppression.

Originally delivered as a lecture by Michael Kimmel at an anniversary of the women's studies program at a major university, the next essay focuses on men and women's studies. Kimmel begins by stating that "many readers are wondering . . . what I'm doing in such a volume of essays."[12] A sociologist who studies men's relation to

---

[12]Michael Kimmel, "Men and Women's Studies," in *Talking Gender: Public Images, Personal Journeys and Political Critiques,* ed. Nancy Hewitt, Jean O'Barr, and Nancy Rosebaugh (Chapel Hill: University of North Carolina Press, 1996), p. 153.

feminism, Kimmel gives us another important example of the relevance of women's studies for all students. That relevance extends outside of the borders of the United States. As Heather Hewett observes in the next article, by removing the United States from the center of feminism and reorienting women's studies in terms of transnational questions new stories begin to emerge.

In the next six selections, women's studies students and one instructor speak of the value of a women's studies education to their intellectual, political, and personal lives. Because the authors of each piece come from varied backgrounds, women's studies took on different meaning for each of them.

We end this section with an essay examining the history of women's studies' spectacular growth within American colleges and universities within the last four decades. Marilyn Boxer's essay celebrates this growth and calls for the continued integration of feminist research and teaching into institutions of higher learning.

 1

Talking Back

BELL HOOKS

In the world of the southern black community I grew up in, "back talk" and "talking back" meant speaking as an equal to an authority figure. It meant daring to disagree and sometimes it just meant having an opinion. In the "old school," children were meant to be seen and not heard. My great-grandparents, grandparents, and parents were all from the old school. To make yourself heard if you were a child was to invite punishment, the back-hand lick, the slap across the face that would catch you unaware, or the feel of switches stinging your arms and legs.

To speak then when one was not spoken to was a courageous act—an act of risk and daring. And yet it was hard not to speak in warm rooms where heated discussions began at the crack of dawn, women's voices filling the air, giving orders, making threats, fussing. Black men may have excelled in the art of poetic preaching in the male-dominated church, but in the church of the home, where the everyday rules of how to live and how to act were established, it was black women who preached. There, black women spoke in a language so rich, so poetic, that it felt to me like being shut off from life, smothered to death if one were not allowed to participate.

It was in that world of woman talk (the men were often silent, often absent) that was born in me the craving to speak, to have a voice, and not just any voice but one that could be identified as belonging to me. To make my voice, I had to speak, to hear myself talk—and talk I did—darting in and out of grown folks' conversations and dialogues, answering questions that were not directed at me, endlessly asking questions, making speeches. Needless to say, the punishments for these acts of speech seemed endless. They were intended to silence me—the child—and more particularly the girl child. Had I been a boy, they might have encouraged me to speak believing that I might someday be called to preach. There was no "calling" for talking girls, no legitimized rewarded speech. The punishments I received for "talking back" were intended to suppress all possibility that I would create my own speech. That speech was to be suppressed so that the "right speech of womanhood" would emerge.

Within feminist circles, silence is often seen as the sexist "right speech of womanhood"—the sign of woman's submission to patriarchal authority. This emphasis on woman's silence may be an accurate remembering of what has taken place in the households of women from WASP backgrounds in the United States, but in black communities (and diverse ethnic communities), women have not been silent. Their voices can be heard. Certainly for black women, our struggle has not been to emerge from silence into speech but to change the nature and direction of our speech, to make a speech that compels listeners, one that is heard.

Our speech, "the right speech of womanhood," was often the soliloquy, the talking into thin air, the talking to ears that do not hear you—the talk that is simply not listened to. Unlike the black male preacher whose speech was to be heard, who was to be listened to, whose words were to be remembered, the voices of black women—giving orders, making threats, fussing—could be tuned out, could become a kind of background music, audible but not acknowledged as significant speech. Dialogue—the sharing of speech and recognition—took place not between mother and child or mother and male authority figure but among black women. I can remember watching fascinated as our mother talked with her mother, sisters, and women friends. The intimacy and intensity of their speech—the satisfaction they received from talking to one another, the pleasure, the joy. It was in this world of woman speech, loud talk, angry words, women with tongues quick and sharp, tender sweet tongues, touching our world with their words, that I made speech my birthright—and the right to voice, to authorship, a privilege I would not be denied. It was in that world and because of it that I came to dream of writing, to write.

Writing was a way to capture speech, to hold onto it, keep it close. And so I wrote down bits and pieces of conversations, confessing in cheap diaries that soon fell apart from too much handling, expressing the intensity of my sorrow, the anguish of speech—for I was always saying the wrong thing, asking the wrong questions. I could not confine my speech to the necessary corners and concerns of life. I hid these writings under my bed, in pillow stuffings, among faded underwear. When my sisters found and read them, they ridiculed and mocked me—poking fun. I felt violated, ashamed, as if the secret parts of my self had been exposed, brought into the open, and hung like newly clean laundry, out in the air for everyone to see. The fear of exposure, the fear that one's deepest emotions and innermost thoughts will be dismissed as mere nonsense, felt by so many young girls keeping diaries, holding and hiding speech, seems to me now one of the barriers that women have always needed

and still need to destroy so that we are no longer pushed into secrecy or silence.

Despite my feelings of violation, of exposure, I continued to speak and write, choosing my hiding places well, learning to destroy work when no safe place could be found. I was never taught absolute silence, I was taught that it was important to speak but to talk a talk that was in itself a silence. Taught to speak and yet beware of the betrayal of too much heard speech, I experienced intense confusion and deep anxiety in my efforts to speak and write. Reciting poems at Sunday afternoon church service might be rewarded. Writing a poem (when one's time could be "better" spent sweeping, ironing, learning to cook) was luxurious activity, indulged in at the expense of others. Questioning authority, raising issues that were not deemed appropriate subjects brought pain, punishments—like telling mama I wanted to die before her because I could not live without her—that was crazy talk, crazy speech, the kind that would lead you to end up in a mental institution. "Little girl," I would be told, "if you don't stop all this crazy talk and crazy acting you are going to end up right out there at Western State."

Madness, not just physical abuse, was the punishment for too much talk if you were female. Yet even as this fear of madness haunted me, hanging over my writing like a monstrous shadow, I could not stop the words, making thought, writing speech. For this terrible madness which I feared, which I was sure was the destiny of daring women born to intense speech (after all, the authorities emphasized this point daily), was not as threatening as imposed silence, as suppressed speech.

Safety and sanity were to be sacrificed if I was to experience defiant speech. Though I risked them both, deep-seated fears and anxieties characterized my childhood days. I would speak but I would not ride a bike, play hardball, or hold the gray kitten. Writing about the ways we are traumatized in our growing-up years, psychoanalyst Alice Miller makes the point in *For Your Own Good* that it is not clear why childhood wounds become for some folk an opportunity to grow, to move forward rather than backward in the process of self-realization. Certainly, when I reflect on the trials of my growing-up years, the many punishments, I can see now that in resistance I learned to be vigilant in the nourishment of my spirit, to be tough, to courageously protect that spirit from forces that would break it.

While punishing me, my parents often spoke about the necessity of breaking my spirit. Now when I ponder the silences, the voices that are not heard, the voices of those wounded and/or oppressed individuals who do not speak or write, I contemplate the acts of persecution, torture—the terrorism that breaks spirits, that makes creativity impossible. I write these words to bear witness to the primacy of resistance struggle in any situation of domination (even within family life); to the strength and power that emerges from sustained resistance and the profound conviction that these forces can be healing, can protect us from dehumanization and despair.

These early trials, wherein I learned to stand my ground, to keep my spirit intact, came vividly to mind after I published *Ain't I A Woman* and the book was sharply and harshly criticized. While I had expected a climate of critical dialogue, I was not expecting a critical avalanche that had the power in its intensity to crush the spirit, to push one into silence. Since that time, I have heard stories about black women, about women of color, who write and publish (even when the work is quite successful) having nervous breakdowns, being made mad because they cannot bear the harsh responses of family, friends, and unknown critics, or becoming silent, unproductive. Surely, the absence of a humane critical response has tremendous impact on the writer from any oppressed, colonized group who endeavors to speak. For us, true speaking is not solely an expression of creative power; it is an act of resistance, a political gesture that challenges politics of domination that would render us nameless and voiceless. As such, it is a courageous act— as such, it represents a threat. To those who wield oppressive power, that which is threatening must necessarily be wiped out, annihilated, silenced.

Recently, efforts by black women writers to call attention to our work serve to highlight both our presence and absence. Whenever I peruse women's bookstores, I am struck not by the rapidly growing body of feminist writing by black women, but by the paucity of available published material. Those of us who write and are published remain few in number. The context of silence is varied and multidimensional. Most obvious are the ways racism, sexism, and class exploitation act to suppress and silence. Less obvious are the inner struggles, the efforts made to gain the necessary confidence to write, to re-write, to fully develop craft and skill— and the extent to which such efforts fail.

Although I have wanted writing to be my life-work since childhood, it has been difficult for me to claim "writer" as part of that which identifies and shapes my everyday reality. Even after publishing books, I would often speak of wanting to be a writer as though these works did not exist. And though I would be told, "you are a writer," I was not yet ready to fully affirm this truth. Part of myself was still held captive by domineering forces of history, of familial life that had charted a map of silence, of right speech. I had not completely let go of the fear of saying the wrong thing, of being punished. Somewhere in the deep recesses of my mind, I believed I could avoid both responsibility and punishment if I did not declare myself a writer.

One of the many reasons I chose to write using the pseudonym bell hooks, a family name (mother to Sarah Oldham, grandmother to Rosa Bell Oldham, great-grandmother to me), was to construct a writer-identity that would challenge and subdue all impulses leading me away from speech into silence. I was a young girl buying bubble gum at the corner store when I first really heard the full name bell hooks. I had just "talked back" to a grown person. Even now I can recall the surprised look, the mocking tones that informed me I must be kin to bell hooks—a sharp-tongued woman, a woman who spoke her mind, a woman who was not afraid to talk back. I claimed this legacy of defiance, of will, of courage, affirming my link to female ancestors who were bold and daring in their speech. Unlike my bold and daring mother and grandmother, who were not supportive of talking back, even though they were assertive and powerful in their speech, bell hooks as I discovered, claimed, and invented her was my ally, my support.

That initial act of talking back outside the home was empowering. It was the first of many acts of defiant speech that would make it possible for me to emerge as an independent thinker and writer. In retrospect, "talking back" became for me a rite of initiation, testing my courage, strengthening my commitment, preparing me for the days ahead—the days when writing, rejection notices, periods of silence, publication, ongoing development seem impossible but necessary.

Moving from silence into speech is for the oppressed, the colonized, the exploited, and those who stand and struggle side by side a gesture of defiance that heals, that makes new life and new growth possible. It is that act of speech, of "talking back," that is no mere gesture of empty words, that is the expression of our movement from object to subject—the liberated voice.   [1989]

 ## 2

Sins of Silence

MAI KAO THAO

My mother used to tell me that I should always be a good, obedient woman, and smile silently as I swallow the bitterness that others give me. "Nod your head and say yes even if you don't agree. It's much easier. No trouble," she would say. Through these words, I heard, "Silence is power! It is a woman's strength." I remember hearing my father criticize my mother, even about the smallest things. "The rice doesn't taste good enough! Now the meat is too hard! You are a bad woman, a stupid woman! No good." And all the while, my mother would go about fixing what she did "wrong" without uttering a word, just wearing her usual, invisible mask of sadness. Oh well. At least there was no trouble.

I was trained to avoid conflict. When my brother lectured me, I'd reply "uh" and shake my head in agreement. I was punished with harsh reprimands and scorching displeasure if I talked back or offered an opinion, so I was silent. I was declared insolent if I spoke a little louder than I should have, so I learned

to whisper. My voice was soft, sweet, and so delicious to the ear of authority. Yes. I was a good girl. Wordless. Humble. Obedient. A perfect Hmong woman.

Sexism laid comfortably on top of my silent submission. I smiled politely when older men gave me kisses on my cheek, more like wet, slow licks that made my innocent skin crawl. Hands grappled my body. Was that a bad touch or a good touch? Must have been a good touch. Relieved. No one will say that I was wrong in thinking that it was a bad touch, because it wasn't, and no one will call me stupid girl. There will be no trouble. Yes, it must be a good touch! Racism grinned at my passivity, while I, the "damned chink," gave it my pride, tears, and forgiveness. But no matter! I was stone. Silent. Hard. Emotionless. Nothing was going to hurt me!

In reality, I wasn't stone. I was flesh and blood. I was a cup, continuously filled, half with anger, dissatisfaction, and anxiety, and the other half with emptiness. My silence had killed my Self, the essence which holds and molds an individual together in order to form one complete organism. Without it, I was but an empty shell; a bird without the courage to fly. I suppressed my ideas of independence and ignored my innate disposition to feel and need. I had not learned to listen to the voice within, and so I did not know how to express these feelings or needs to others. Sadly, not only did I alone deprive my Self of its necessary nutrients, but I also allowed others to do it. And I wondered why no one understood me or gave me the respect I hungered for.

With love, my mother gave me her legacy, a shield of silence to protect me from pain and to prevent me from troubles. It gave me a source of inner strength, but it also barred inner peace from reaching the premises of my soul. Although my mother's words are wise, they are in some cases unsuitable to deal with problems which I faced in the context of my experiences in this new country. Back in Laos, my mother's life consisted of devotion to others, her parents, her husband, her children, because she was never expected to go beyond the role of the traditional Hmong woman. Here in America, opportunities are more plentiful. Education delivers knowledge. Employment offers financial independence. Women's support groups give an identity not solely in relation to men, but within the boundaries of our own person. And I can possess all of this!

In addition, I realized that I could not avoid every dragon or retreat from every problem. I was tired of running, of being voiceless, of being afraid, and I no longer wanted to be stepped on, suppressed, or taken for granted. I couldn't continue pretending that I was less than others. I craved to belong in the world, not as a silent observer, but as a human being; shaping, creating, questioning, reforming, or advocating. I wanted to exist!

Silence is power? In my silence, I was the sacrificial lamb. I was the martyr, like my mother. We suffered pain in the name of obedience just so no one will accuse us of being insolent or naughty, and in the struggle for harmony, loving the people around us. These can be good causes, but when we are silent even in the face of injustice, then I cannot in all fairness pronounce them good ones. As a Hmong woman, I am expected to perfect the art of hiding the painful reality of sexual, physical, or mental abuse. These conflicts cannot be resolved with silence, only deepened and catalyzed through it. If to be a good Hmong woman means to ignore my identity, to swallow my pride so others can abuse me, or to shut my eyes in the face of injustice by turning the other cheek, I do not want to be a good Hmong woman.   [1996]

 3

Claiming an Education

ADRIENNE RICH

For this convocation, I planned to separate my remarks into two parts: some thoughts about you, the women students here, and some thoughts about us who teach in a women's college. But ultimately, those two parts are indivisible. If university education means anything beyond the processing of human beings into expected roles, through credit hours, tests, and grades (and I believe that in a women's college especially it *might* mean much more), it implies an ethical and intellectual contract between teacher and students. This contract must remain intuitive, dynamic, unwritten; but we must turn to it again and again if learning is to be reclaimed from the depersonalizing and cheapening pressures of the present-day academic scene.

The first thing I want to say to you who are students is that you cannot afford to think of yourselves as being here to *receive* an education; you will do much better to think of yourselves as being here to *claim* one. One of the dictionary definitions of the verb "to claim" is: to take as the rightful owner; to assert in the face of possible contradiction. "To receive" is to come into possession of; to act as receptacle or container for; to accept as authoritative or true. The difference is that between acting and being acted-upon, and for women it can literally mean the difference between life and death.

One of the devastating weaknesses of university learning, of the store of knowledge and opinion that has been handed down through academic training, has been its almost total erasure of women's experience and thought from the curriculum, and its exclusion of women as members of the academic community. Today, with increasing numbers of women students in nearly every branch of higher learning, we still see very few women in the upper levels of faculty and administration in most institutions. Douglass College itself is a women's college in a university administered overwhelmingly by men, who in turn are answerable to the state legislature, again composed predominantly of men. But the most significant fact for you is that what you learn here (and I mean not only at Douglass but any college in any university) is how *men* have perceived and organized their experience, their history, their ideas of social relationships, good and evil, sickness and health, etc. When you read or hear about "great issues," "major texts," "the mainstream of Western thought," you are hearing about what men, above all white men, in their male subjectivity, have decided is important.

Black and other minority peoples have for some time recognized that their racial and ethnic experience was not accounted for in the studies broadly labeled human; and that even the sciences can be racist. For many reasons, it has been more difficult for women to comprehend our exclusion, and to realize that even the sciences can be sexist. For one thing, it is only within the last hundred years that higher education has grudgingly been opened up to women at all, even to white, middle-class women. And many of us have found ourselves poring eagerly over books with titles like: *The Descent of Man; Man and His Symbols; Irrational Man; The Phenomenon of Man; The Future of Man; Man and the Machine; From Man to Man; May Man Prevail?; Man, Science and Society; One-Dimensional Man—*books to describe a "human" reality that does not include over one-half the human species.

Less than a decade ago, with the rebirth of a feminist movement in this country, women students and teachers in a number of universities, began to demand and set up women's studies courses—to *claim* a woman-directed education. And, despite the inevitable accusations of "unscholarly," "group therapy," "faddism," etc., despite backlash and budget cuts, women's studies are still growing, offering to more and more women a new intellectual grasp on their lives, new understanding of our history, a fresh vision of the human experience, and also a critical basis for evaluating what they hear and read in other courses, and in the society at large.

But my talk is not really about women's studies, much as I believe in their scholarly, scientific, and human necessity. While I think that any Douglass student has everything to gain by investigating and enrolling in women's studies courses, I want to suggest that there is a more essential experience that you owe yourselves, one which courses in women's studies can greatly enrich, but which finally depends on you, in all your interactions with yourself and your world. This is the experience of *taking responsibility toward yourselves*. Our upbringing as women has so often told us that this should come second to our relationships and responsibilities to other people. We have been offered ethical models of the self-denying wife and mother; intellectual models of the brilliant but slapdash dilettante who never commits herself to anything the whole way, or the intelligent woman who denies her intelligence in order to seem more "feminine," or who sits in passive silence even when she disagrees inwardly with everything that is being said around her.

Responsibility to yourself means refusing to let others do your thinking, talking, and naming for you; it means learning to respect and use your own brains and instincts, hence, grappling with hard work. It means that you do not treat your body as a commodity with which to purchase superficial intimacy or economic security; for our bodies and minds are inseparable in this life, and when we allow our bodies to be treated as objects, our minds are in mortal danger. It means insisting that those to whom you give your friendship and love are able to respect your mind. It means being able to say, with Charlotte Bronte's Jane Eyre: "I have an inward treasure born with me, which can keep me alive if all the extraneous delights should be withheld or offered only at a price I cannot afford to give."

Responsibility to yourself means that you don't fall for shallow and easy solutions—predigested books and ideas, weekend encounters guaranteed to change your life, taking "gut" courses instead of ones you know will challenge you, bluffing at school and life instead of doing solid work, marrying early as an escape from real decisions, getting pregnant as an evasion of already existing problems. It means that you refuse to sell your talents and aspirations short, simply to avoid conflict and confrontation. And this, in turn, means resisting the forces in society which say that women should be nice, play safe, have low professional expectations, drown in love and forget about work, live through others, and stay in the places assigned to us. It means that we insist on a life of meaningful work, insist that work be as meaningful as love and friendship in our lives. It means, therefore, the courage to be "different"; not to be continuously available to others when we need time for ourselves and our work; to be able to demand of others—parents, friends, roommates, teachers, lovers, husbands, children—that they respect our sense of purpose and our integrity as persons. Women everywhere are finding the courage to do this, more and more, and we are finding that courage both in our study of women in the past who possessed it, and in each other as we look to other women for comradeship, community, and challenge. The difference between a life lived actively, and a life of passive drifting and dispersal of energies, is an immense difference. Once we begin to feel committed to our lives, responsible to ourselves, we can never again be satisfied with the old, passive way.

I have said that the contract on the student's part involves that you demand to be taken seriously so that you can also go on taking yourself seriously. This means seeking out criticism, recognizing that the most affirming thing anyone can do for you is demand that you push yourself further, show you the range of what you *can* do. It means rejecting attitudes of "take-it-easy," "why-be-so-serious," "why-worry-you'll-probably-get-married-anyway." It means assuming your share of responsibility for what happens in the classroom, because that affects the quality of your daily life here. It means that the student sees herself engaged with her teachers in an active, ongoing struggle for a real education. But for her to do this, her teachers must be committed to the belief that women's minds and experience are intrinsically valuable and indispensable to any civilization worthy of the name; that there is no more exhilarating and intellectually fertile place in the academic world today than a women's college—*if* both students and teachers in large enough numbers are trying to fulfill this contract. The contract is really a pledge of mutual seriousness about women, about language, ideas, methods, and values. It is our shared commitment toward a world in which the inborn potentialities of so many women's minds will no longer be wasted, raveled-away, paralyzed, or denied.   [1977]

 4

The Politics of Black Women's Studies

AKASHA (GLORIA T.) HULL
and BARBARA SMITH

Merely to use the term "Black women's studies" is an act charged with political significance. At the very least, the combining of these words to name a discipline means taking the stance that Black women exist—and exist positively—a stance that is in direct opposition to most of what passes for culture and thought on the North American continent.

To use the term and to act on it in a white-male world is an act of political courage.

Like any politically disenfranchised group, Black women could not exist consciously until we began to name ourselves. The growth of Black women's studies is an essential aspect of that process of naming. The very fact that Black women's studies describes something that is really happening, a burgeoning field of study, indicates that there are political changes afoot which have made possible that growth. To examine the politics of Black women's studies means to consider not only what it is, but why it is and what it can be. Politics is used here in its widest sense to mean any situation/relationship of differential power between groups or individuals.

Four issues seem important for a consideration of the politics of Black women's studies: (1) the general political situation of Afro-American women and the bearing this has had upon the implementation of Black women's studies; (2) the relationship of Black women's studies to Black feminist politics and the Black feminist movement; (3) the necessity for Black women's studies to be feminist, radical, and analytical; and (4) the need for teachers of Black women's studies to be aware of our problematic political positions in the academy and of the potentially antagonistic conditions under which we must work.

The political position of Black women in America has been, in a single word, embattled. The extremity of our oppression has been determined by our very biological identity. The horrors we have faced historically and continue to face as Black women in a white-male-dominated society have implications for every aspect of our lives, including what white men have termed "the life of the mind." That our oppression as Black women can take forms specifically aimed at discrediting our intellectual power is best illustrated through the words of a "classic" American writer.

In 1932 William Faulkner saw fit to include this sentence in a description of a painted sign in his novel *Light in August*. He wrote:

> But now and then a negro nursemaid with her white charges would loiter there and spell them [the letters on the sign] al.oud with that vacuous idiocy of her idle and illiterate kind.[1] [Italics ours]

Faulkner's white-male assessment of Black female intellect and character, stated as a mere aside, has fundamental and painful implications for a consideration of the whole question of Black women's studies and the politics that shape its existence. Not only does his remark typify the extremely negative ways in which Afro-American women have been portrayed in literature, scholarship, and the popular media, but it also points to the destructive white-male habit of categorizing all who are not like themselves as their intellectual and moral inferiors. The fact that the works in which such oppressive images appear are nevertheless considered American "masterpieces" indicates the cultural-political value system in which Afro-American women have been forced to operate and which, when possible, they have actively opposed.

The politics of Black women's studies are totally connected to the politics of Black women's lives in this country. The opportunities for Black women to carry out autonomously defined investigations of self in a society which through racial, sexual, and class oppression systematically denies our existence have been by definition limited.

As a major result of the historical realities which brought us enslaved to this continent, we have been kept separated in every way possible from recognized intellectual work. Our legacy as chattel, as sexual slaves as well as forced laborers, would adequately explain why most Black women are, to this day, far away from the centers of academic power and why Black women's studies has just begun to surface in the latter part of the 1970s. What our multilayered oppression does not explain are the ways in which we have created and maintained our own intellectual traditions as Black women, without either the recognition or the support of white-male society.

The entry entitled "A Slave Woman Runs a Midnight School" in Gerda Lerner's *Black Women in White America: A Documentary History* embodies this creative, intellectual spirit, coupled with a practical ability to make something out of nothing.

[In Natchez, Louisiana, there were] two schools taught by colored teachers. One of these was a slave woman who had taught a midnight school for a year. It was opened at eleven or twelve o'clock at night, and closed at two o'clock a.m. . . . . Milla

Granson, the teacher, learned to read and write from the children of her indulgent master in her old Kentucky home. Her number of scholars was twelve at a time and when she had taught these to read and write she dismissed them, and again took her apostolic number and brought them up to the extent of her ability, until she had graduated hundreds. A number of them wrote their own passes and started for Canada. . . .

At length her night-school project leaked out, and was for a time suspended; but it was not known that seven of the twelve years subsequent to leaving Kentucky had been spent in this work. Much excitement over her night-school was produced. The subject was discussed in their legislature, and a bill was passed, that it should not be held illegal for a slave to teach a slave. . . . She not only [re]opened her night-school, but a Sabbath-school. . . . Milla Granson used as good language as any of the white people.[2]

This document illuminates much about Black women educators and thinkers in America. Milla Granson learned to read and write through the exceptional indulgence of her white masters. She used her skills not to advance her own status, but to help her fellow slaves, and this under the most difficult circumstances. The act of a Black person teaching and sharing knowledge was viewed as naturally threatening to the power structure. The knowledge she conveyed had a politically and materially transforming function, that is, it empowered people to gain freedom.

Milla Granson and her pupils, like Black people throughout our history here, made the greatest sacrifices for the sake of learning. As opposed to "lowering" educational standards, we have had to create our own. In a totally antagonistic setting we have tried to keep our own visions clear and have passed on the most essential kind of knowledge, that which enabled us to survive. As Alice Walker writes of our artist-thinker foremothers:

They dreamed dreams that no one knew—not even themselves, in any coherent fashion—and saw visions no one could understand. . . . They waited for a day when the unknown thing that was in them would be made known; but guessed, somehow in their darkness, that on the day of their revelation they would be long dead.[3]

The birth of Black women's studies is perhaps the day of revelation these women wished for. Again, this beginning is not unconnected to political events in the world outside university walls.

The inception of Black women's studies can be directly traced to three significant political movements of the twentieth century. These are the struggles for Black liberation and women's liberation, which themselves fostered the growth of Black and women's studies, and the more recent Black feminist movement, which is just beginning to show its strength. Black feminism has made a space for Black women's studies to exist and, through its commitment to all Black women, will provide the basis for its survival.

The history of all these movements is unique, yet interconnected. The Black movements of the 1950s, '60s, and '70s brought about unprecedented social and political change, not only in the lives of Black people, but for all Americans. The early women's movement gained inspiration from the Black movement as well as an impetus to organize autonomously both as a result of the demands for all-Black organizations and in response to sexual hierarchies in Black- and white-male political groupings. Black women were a part of that early women's movement, as were working-class women of all races. However, for many reasons—including the increasing involvement of single, middle-class white women (who often had the most time to devote to political work), the divisive campaigns of the white-male media, and the movement's serious inability to deal with racism—the women's movement became largely and apparently white.

The effect that this had upon the nascent field of women's studies was predictably disastrous. Women's studies courses, usually taught in universities, which could be considered elite institutions just by virtue of the populations they served, focused almost exclusively upon the lives of white women. Black studies, which was much too often male-dominated, also ignored Black women. Here is what a Black woman wrote about her independent efforts to study Black women writers in the early 1970s:

> . . . At this point I am doing a lot of reading on my own of Black women writers ever since I discovered Zora Neale Hurston. *I've had two Black Lit courses and in neither were any women writers discussed.* So now I'm doing a lot of independent research since the Schomburg Collection is so close.[4] [Italics ours.]

Because of white women's racism and Black men's sexism, there was no room in either area for a serious consideration of the lives of Black women. And even when they have considered Black women, white women usually have not had the capacity to analyze racial politics and Black culture, and Black men have remained blind or resistant to the implications of sexual politics in Black women's lives.

Only a Black *and* feminist analysis can sufficiently comprehend the materials of Black women's studies; and only a creative Black feminist perspective will enable the field to expand. A viable Black feminist movement will also lend its political strength to the development of Black women's studies courses, programs, and research, and to the funding they require. Black feminism's total commitment to the liberation of Black women and its recognition of Black women as valuable and complex human beings will provide the analysis and spirit for the incisive work on Black women. Only a feminist, pro-woman perspective that acknowledges the reality of sexual oppression in the lives of Black women, as well as the oppression of race and class, will make Black women's studies the transformer of consciousness it needs to be.

Women's studies began as a radical response to feminists' realization that knowledge of ourselves has been deliberately kept from us by institutions of patriarchal "learning." Unfortunately, as women's studies has become both more institutionalized and at the same time more precarious within traditional academic structures, the radical life-changing vision of what women's studies can accomplish has constantly been diminished in exchange for acceptance, respectability, and the career advancement of individuals. This trend in women's studies is a trap that Black women's studies cannot afford to fall into. Because we are so oppressed as Black women, every aspect of our fight for freedom, including teaching and writing about ourselves, must in some way further our liberation. Because of the particular history of Black feminism in relation to Black women's studies, especially the fact that the two movements are still new and have evolved nearly simultaneously, much of the current teaching, research, and writing about Black women is not feminist, is not radical, and unfortunately is not always even analytical. Naming and describing our experience are important initial steps, but not alone sufficient to get us where we need to go. A descriptive approach to the lives of Black women, a "great Black women" in history or literature approach, or any traditional male-identified approach will not result in intellectually groundbreaking or politically transforming work. We cannot change our lives by teaching solely about "exceptions" to the ravages of white-male oppression. Only through exploring the experience of supposedly "ordinary" Black women whose "unexceptional" actions enabled us and the race to survive, will we be able to begin to develop an overview and an analytical framework for understanding the lives of Afro-American women. [1982]

NOTES

1. William Faulkner, *Light in August* (New York: Modern Library, 1932), 53.
2. Laura S. Haviland, *A Woman's Life-Work, Labors and Experience* (Chicago: Publishing Association of Friends, 1889; copyright 1881), 300–301; reprinted in Gerda Lerner, ed., *Black Women in White America: A Documentary History* (New York: Vintage, 1973), 32–33.
3. Alice Walker, "In Search of Our Mother's Gardens," *Ms.* (Magazine 1974), 64–70, 105.
4. Bernette Golden, Personal letter, April 1, 1974.

 5

Men and Women's Studies: Premises, Perils, and Promise

MICHAEL KIMMEL

What does women's studies have to do with men? For one thing, it clears an intellectual space for talking about gender. I am not suggesting that among all the other things women's studies has to do, it must now also drop everything and take care of men in some vaguely academic version of the second shift. (I have heard arguments from men suggesting that women's studies must provide us with "a room of our own" within the curriculum, to appropriate the words of Virginia Woolf—and make sure that room has a rather commanding view of the traditional campus!)

When I say women's studies is about men, I mean that *women's studies has made men visible*. Before women's studies, men were invisible—especially to themselves. By making women visible, women's studies also made men visible both to women and to men themselves. If men are now taking up the issue of gender, it is probably less accurate to say, "Thank goodness they've arrived," the way one might when the cavalry appears in a western film, than to say, "It's about time."

Of course, making men visible has not been the primary task of women's studies. But it has been one of its signal successes. The major achievement of women's studies, acting independently and as a force within traditional disciplines, has been making *women* visible through the rediscovery of long-neglected, undervalued, and understudied women who were accomplished leaders, artists, composers, and writers and placing them in the pantheons of significance where they rightly belong. In addition, women's studies has rediscovered the voices of ordinary women—the laundresses and the salesgirls, the union maids and the union organizers, the workers and the wives—who have struggled to scratch out lives of meaning and dignity. For this—whether they know it or not, whether they acknowledge it or not—women all over the world owe a debt.

But in making women visible, women's studies has been at the epicenter of a seismic shift in the university as we know it. Women's studies has made *gender* visible. Women's studies has demonstrated that gender is one of the axes around which social life is organized, one of the most crucial building blocks of our identities. Before women's studies, we didn't know that gender mattered. Twenty-five years ago, there were no women's studies courses in colleges or universities, no women's studies lists at university presses across the country. In my field of sociology, there were no gender courses, no specialty area called the Sociology of Gender. We had, instead, a field called Marriage and the Family—to my mind the Ladies' Auxiliary of Sociology. By making women visible, women's studies decentered men as the unexamined, disembodied authorial voice of the academic canon and showed that men, as well as women, are utterly embodied, their identities are as socially constructed as those of women. When the voice of the canon speaks, we can no longer *assume* that voice is going to sound masculine or that the speaker is going to look like a man.

The problem is that many men do not yet know this. Though ubiquitous in positions of power, many men remain invisible to themselves as gendered beings. Courses on gender in the universities are populated largely by women, as if the term applied only to them. "Woman alone seems to have 'gender' since the category itself is defined as that aspect of social relations based on difference between the sexes in which the standard has always been man," writes historian Thomas Lacquer.[1] Or, as the Chinese proverb has it, the fish are the last to discover the ocean.

I know this from my own experience: women's studies made gender visible to me. In the early 1980s I participated in a graduate-level women's studies seminar in which I was the only man among about a dozen participants. During one meeting, a white woman and a black woman were discussing whether all women were, by definition, "sisters" because they all had essentially the same experiences and because all women faced a common oppression by all men. The white women asserted that the fact that they were both women bonded them, in spite of racial differences. The black woman disagreed.

"When you wake up in the morning and look in the mirror, what do you see?" she asked.

"I see a woman," replied the white woman.

"That's precisely the problem," responded the black woman. "I see a *black* woman. To me, race is visible every day, because race is how I am *not* privileged in our culture. Race is invisible to you, because it's how you are privileged. It's why there will always be differences in our experience."

As I witnessed this exchange, I was startled, and groaned—more audibly, perhaps, than I had intended. Someone asked what my response meant. "Well," I said, "when I look in the mirror, I see a human being. I'm universally generalizable. As a middle-class white man, I have no class, no race, no gender. I'm the generic person!"

Sometimes, I like to think it was on that day that I *became* a middle-class white man. Sure, I had been all those before, but they had not meant much to me. Since then, I have begun to understand that race, class, and gender do not refer only to other people, who are marginalized by race, class, or gender privilege. Those terms also describe me. I enjoy the privilege of invisibility. The very processes that confer privilege to one group and not another group are often invisible to those upon whom that privilege is conferred. American men have come to think of ourselves as genderless, in part because gender privilege affords us the luxury of ignoring the centrality of gender. But women's studies offers the possibility of making gender visible to men as well and, in so doing, creating the possibilities of alliances between women and men to collaboratively investigate what gender means, how it works, and what its consequences are.

In *Fire with Fire*, Naomi Wolf returns often to her book's epigraph, that famous line of Audre Lorde, "the Master's tools cannot dismantle the Master's house." Wolf believes that her book is a refutation of that position, and when one considers the impact of women's studies on the university and the culture at large, it seems that on this score at least, Wolf is quite right—that passionate, disciplined scholarship, inspired and dedicated teaching, and committed, engaged inquiry can contribute to the reorientation of the university as an institution. All over the country, schools are integrating "gender awareness" into their first-year curricula, even orienting the entire curriculum around gender awareness. Within the professional organization of my discipline, sociology, the Sex and Gender section is now the largest section of the entire profession. Gender has moved from the margins—Marriage and the Family—to the center and is the largest single constituency within the field.

Most commentators laud the accomplishments of women's studies programs in transforming women's lives, but it is obvious that women's studies programs have also been transformative for men. The Duke case is a particularly successful one: the popular house course "Men and Gender Issues" has been offered under the umbrella of Women's Studies for five years. Men Acting for Change (MAC), the campus group for pro-feminist men that has become a model for similar groups on campuses around the country, found a supportive harbor in the Women's Studies Program. The first time I came to lecture at Duke three years ago, my lecture was jointly sponsored by the Women's Studies Program and the Inter-Fraternity Council—the first time, I'm told, that those two organizations had cooperated on anything. Women's studies can—and does—forge creative alliances!

Essentially, however, the program at Duke and women's studies in general has centered around the same two projects as any other discipline: teaching and research. And to speak personally, the perspectives of women's studies have transformed both my research and my teaching. Women's studies made it *possible* for me to do the work I do. And for that I am grateful. Inspired by the way women's studies made gender visible, I offered a course called "Sociology of the Male Experience" in 1983 at Rutgers University, where I was then a young assistant professor. This was the first such course on men and masculinity in the state of New Jersey, and I received enormous support both from my own department and from the Women's Studies Program at Rutgers, then chaired by Catharine Stimpson. Today, I teach that course as well as a course entitled "Sex and Society" at Stony Brook to over 350 students each semester. Now, as then, the course is cross-listed with women's studies. But I also teach our department's classical sociological theory course, the course on the historical development of social and political theory. In that course, students traditionally read works by Hobbes, Locke, Rousseau, Smith, Marx, Durkheim, Tocqueville, Weber, and Freud. This is probably the most intractably canonical "Dead White European Men" course we offer in the social sciences. But it has become impossible for me to teach the works of those "great men" without reference to gender—without noting, for example, the gendered creation myths that characterize the move from the state of nature to civil society in the thought of Locke or Hobbes, or the chronic anxiety and loss of control attendant upon modern society documented by Tocqueville, Marx, Weber, or Freud. Moreover, I find that I cannot teach about the rise of nineteenth-century liberal individualism without including Frederick Douglass or Mary Wollstonecraft; nor can I teach about the late nineteenth-century critiques of individualism without references to W. E. B. Du Bois or to Charlotte Perkins Gilman.

If women's studies has made gender, and hence *men*, visible, then it has also raised a question about men: where are they? where have they been in women's struggles for equality? Taking my cues from women's history, I began to research men's responses to feminism. *Against the Tide* tries to provide part of the answer, a missing chapter from women's history: the chapter about the men who supported women's equality.[2] When I began *Against the Tide*, I mentioned to Catharine Stimpson, then dean of the Graduate School at Rutgers, what I intended to do. "A book about men who supported feminism?" she asked. "Now that will surely be the world's shortest book!" she joked. Of course, she knew better, but I did not really know what I would find. It turns out that in every arena in which women have struggled for equal rights—education (the right to go to college or professional school, the right to go to college with men), economic life (the right to work, join unions, receive equal wages), social life (the right to own property, have access to birth control, get a divorce), or political life (the right to vote, to hold elective office, to serve on juries)—there have been American men, some prominent, many unheralded, who have supported them: men such as Thomas Paine, who sat before the Declaration of Independence in 1776 and recognized that women would not be included under its provisions, although women had, as he put it, an "equal right to virtue." Men such as famed abolitionists William Lloyd Garrison and Frederick Douglass, who campaigned tirelessly for women's rights from Seneca Falls onward. Men such as Matthew Vassar, William Alan Neilson, and Henry Durant, founders of Vassar, Smith, and Wellesley colleges. It was Durant, founder of

Wellesley, who in 1877 called the higher education of women a "revolt": "We revolt against the
slavery in which women are held by the customs
of society—the broken health, the aimless lives, the
subordinate position, the helpless dependence, the
dishonesties and shams of so-called education. The
Higher Education of Women is one of the great
world battle cries for freedom; for right against
might. It is the cry of the oppressed slave. It is the
assertion of absolute equality."[3]

Pro-feminist men have included educators such
as John Dewey, who urged that women be admitted to the University of Chicago and was one of
the founders of the Men's League for Woman Suffrage, the nation's first pro-feminist men's organization. The group of pro-feminist men included
W. E. B. Du Bois, Ralph Waldo Emerson, and
Eugene Debs among the most vigorous supporters of woman suffrage. And there have been
academic men such as Lester Ward and George
Herbert Mead, to name but two, who pointed
toward the scholarly study of women and opposed
gender inequality. In one of his major treatises,
Applied Sociology, Ward provided an epigraph for
the advent of women's studies, arguing that "the
universal prevalence of the androcentric worldview acts as a wet blanket on all the genial fire of
the female sex."[4] Pro-feminist men are also poli-
cymakers such as Robert Reich, secretary of labor
in the Clinton administration, who wrote a furious letter (reprinted in *Ms.* magazine) to a college
president when his wife was denied tenure, and
Representative Don Edwards of California, who
has introduced the ERA in every session of Congress since 1974, as well as former Supreme Court
justice Harry Blackmun, that vigilant defender of
women's right to control their own bodies.

Supporters of women's equality have also
included the less-celebrated men who simply lived
out their principles of equality without fanfare.
Men such as James Mott (married to Lucretia),
Theodore Weld (married to Angelina Grimké),
and Wendell Phillips, ardent abolitionist and suffrage supporter. In 1856, Lucy Stone called her
husband, Henry Brown Blackwell, "the best husband in the world. In the midst of all the extra care,

hurry and perplexity of business, you stop and look
after all my little affairs," she wrote, "doing everything you can to save me trouble."[5] More than a
half a century later, Margaret Sanger quotes her
husband, William, as telling her to "go ahead and
finish your writing, and I'll get dinner and wash the
dishes."[6] (She also comments that she drew the
curtains in the kitchen of their first-floor Greenwich
Village apartment, lest passersby see her husband
wearing an apron.) It appears that long before Ted
Kramer and Mr. Mom, real men did housework!

Men *have* been there supporting women's equality every step of the way. And if men have been
there, it means that men *can* be there and that they
will be there. This legacy of men who supported
women's equality allows contemporary men to join
what I like to think of as the Gentlemen's Auxiliary of the Women's Movement. Neither passive
bystanders nor the front-line forces—and especially
not the leaders of those troops—men still have
a pivotal role to play. Men can join this epochal
struggle and provide support both individually and
collectively. This strikes me as an utterly honorable
relationship to feminism, quite different from an
impulse I've encountered among newly enlightened
men that goes something like, "Thanks for bringing
all this to my attention, ladies. We'll take it from
here." It also serves as an important corrective to
many men's fears, which often boil down to "How
can I support feminism without feeling like—or
being seen as—a wimp?" To be a member of the
Auxiliary is to know that the cental actors in the
struggle for gender equality will be, as they always
have been, women.

But women's studies has done more than make
the study of gender possible; it has made it *necessary*. The issues raised by women in the university
and outside it have not "gone away" or subsided
now that women have been offered a few resources
and an academic room of their own. Women's studies has not been content with one room while the
rest of the university goes about its androcentric
business, any more than the women's movement
has been convinced of its political victory because
100 percent of the U.S. senators from California
in 1993 are women. Think about the shockwaves

that rippled outward from Clarence Thomas's confirmation hearings over two years ago. Remember how the media responded to that event; recall the shameful way Anita Hill was treated by the Senate Judiciary Committee. The phrase the media used, as if with one voice, was that Thomas's confirmation would have a "chilling effect" on American women—that women would be less likely to come forward to describe their experiences of sexual harassment in the workplace, that women would be less likely to speak of the inequities and humiliations that permeated their working lives. Have the media ever been more wrong? Not only was there no "chilling effect," there was a national thaw. Women have been coming forward in unprecedented numbers to talk about their working lives. And they have not gone away. On campuses and off all across the country, women's studies students and faculty have joined in this virtual national seminar about men, masculinity, and power.

Gender as a power relation is the "it" that men "just don't get" in the current discussion. Women's studies scholars have demonstrated that masculinity and femininity are identities that are socially constructed in a field of power. Gender, like race and class, is not simply a mode of classification by which biological creatures are sorted into their respective and appropriate niches. Gender is about power. Just because both masculinity and femininity are socially constructed does not mean that they are equivalent, that there are no dynamics of power and privilege in operation. The problem with bringing men into this discussion about gender and power is that these issues are invisible to men.   [1996]

NOTES

1. Thomas Lacquer, *Making Sex: Body and Gender from the Greeks to Freud* (Cambridge: Harvard University Press, 1990), 22.
2. Michael S. Kimmel and Thomas Mosmiller, eds., *Against the Tide: Pro-Feminist Men in the United States, 1776–1990. A Documentary History* (Boston: Beacon Press, 1992).
3. Thomas Paine, "An Occasional Letter on the Female Sex," 1775, and Henry Fowle Durant, "The Spirit of the College," 1877, in *Against the Tide,* ed. Kimmel and Mosmiller, 63–66, 132.
4. Lester Frank Ward, *Applied Sociology: A Treatise on the Conscious Improvement of Society by Society* (Boston: Ginn and Company, 1906), 232.

 6

Women's Studies and Transnational Feminism

HEATHER HEWETT

More often than not, the story we tell about the discipline of women's studies is a story that starts with the first wave of feminist organizing in the United States and England during the nineteenth and early twentieth centuries. But what kinds of stories might we tell about feminism and women's studies if we were to examine the diverse range of women's movements in *all* countries and cultures? A global perspective on feminism reveals how ideas about women's rights and feminism have originated and developed in many different places, and how these ideas have traveled between individuals living in very different circumstances. This perspective removes the United States from the center of feminism and asks us to place the U.S. women's movement in a broader context. As Aili Mari Tripp observes, "Regardless of the common perception in the West that ideas regarding the emancipation of women have spread from the West outward into other parts of the world . . . in fact, the influences have always been multidirectional" (Tripp, 51). This global viewpoint, which many feminist scholars identify as *transnational*, is challenging the field of women's studies to rethink basic concepts and reorient feminist activism in ways that respond to a rapidly changing world.

THE WORDS WE USE AND THE IMAGES THEY CREATE

In the social sciences, many researchers argue that the term *transnational* provides the most accurate description for our globalized, and rapidly globalizing, world—more accurate, they argue, than the more familiar term, *international*. They argue that the world of the early twenty-first century has changed dramatically: as a result of new information and computer technologies, increased travel, and the growth of the global economy, we are more connected and integrated than ever before. As a result, individual activists and organizations can increasingly work with other individuals or organizations *across* national borders without the sanction of international institutions such as the United Nations, whose structure enables cooperation and dialogue *between* nations and their representatives. In addition, many issues cut across national borders, requiring activists to rethink how to address planetary issues such as environmental degradation, poverty and hunger, or sex trafficking. Social scientists who study globalization and contemporary activism frequently observe that there has been a significant growth of "transnational feminist networks" around the world, in which women from multiple countries come together around a common agenda or issue, such as violence against women (Moghadam, 4).

Many feminists also prefer the term *transnational* for philosophical reasons. The term originated in the U.S. academy and stems from concerns that earlier manifestations of "global feminism" tended to assume that women worldwide should embrace a "Western model of women's liberation that celebrates individuality and modernity" (Grewal and Kaplan, 17). Other feminists further critiqued the idea of a "global sisterhood," the assumption that all women share similar experiences, oppressions, and perspectives simply because they are women, and that simply being a woman was enough for a unified, global women's movement (Alexander and Mohanty, "Introduction," xviii; Mohanty, 110). Women can have a vast range of experiences based on the many other dimensions of their identity: race/ethnicity, class, sexuality, culture, nationality, religion, and so on.[1] Indeed, these differences can lead to vastly dissimilar needs and priorities when it comes to activism and social change. Given this diversity, perhaps the term "transnational feminisms" more accurately conveys the plurality of women's perspectives and activisms globally.

A transnational feminist perspective has particularly deep ties to the research, writing, and activism of women in the third world and women of color throughout the world. Many of these women have pointed out that it is not just terms

such as *global feminism, sisterhood,* or *international* that require rethinking. In fact, quite a few of the categories we use to divide up the world (such as "West"/"East," "first world"/"third world," or "Global North"/"Global South") are binaries that, while at times useful, can also lead to simplified views of the world and distortions of complex realities.[2] ("Global North" and "Global South," which may be unfamiliar terms, are used by social scientists to describe the Northern and Southern Hemispheres.) For example, the category "third world" (used to refer to economically underdeveloped countries) might suggest that everyone living in the third world lives in poverty, thus failing to convey the presence of a class of wealthy elites in many third-world nations. Likewise, an uncritical categorization of the United States as "first world" might lead some to assume that poverty does not exist within U.S. borders.

In a media-saturated world, binary categories (such as the dichotomy "first world"/"third world") that describe unfamiliar places and people can be easily influenced by visual images and unexamined stereotypes. Many scholars have examined how publications such as *National Geographic* and Hollywood films have deeply influenced how we perceive "other" cultures and countries.[3] Well-intentioned researchers, journalists, and activists have not been immune, either. As a consequence, a powerful and pervasive image of certain women has emerged: the oppressed third-world woman. Although it is true that many women living in third-world or Global South nations struggle with poverty, the images we have of this woman tend to erase the nuances of the variety of women's lived experiences. We are left with a flattened stereotype. Chandra Talpade Mohanty unpacks this stereotype as follows:

> This average Third World Woman leads an essentially truncated life based on her feminine gender (read: sexually constrained) and her being "Third World" (read: ignorant, poor, uneducated, tradition-bound, domestic, family-oriented, victimized, etc.). This, I suggest, is in contrast to the (implicit) self-representation of Western women as

educated, as modern, as having control over their own bodies and sexualities and the freedom to make their own decisions. (Mohanty, 22)

Feminist scholars such as Mohanty have examined how these stereotypes have even become embedded in the assumptions underlying international development projects and social science research. Other scholars have examined how some very diverse groups of women—such as Muslim women—tend to be viewed as a single, homogeneous group with only one story told about them. Mohja Kahf's examination of several centuries of English literature leads her to remark that "'the Muslim woman is being victimized' is the common axis undergirding a wide variety of Western representations" (Kahf, 1). Likewise, Marnia Lazreg observes that frequently, Muslim women find that one element of their identity—their religion—becomes identified as the sole source of their victimization as well as the only reason for their country's underdevelopment (Lazreg, 86). Often, any understanding of the vast range of Muslim women's experiences becomes reduced to one item of clothing—the veil—which comes to symbolize "the Western narrative of Islam as oppressor and the West as liberator" (Ahmed, 167).

Many women have also participated in the creation and reproduction of these images. Özlem Sensoy and Robin DiAngelo argue that the image of the oppressed Muslim woman helps to "prove" to Western women that they themselves are liberated and free, thus creating a binary that reduces the complexities of women's lived experiences (Sensoy and DiAngelo). Kahf makes this point in her short poem "*Hijab* Scene #2":

"You people have such restrictive dress for
      women,"
she said, hobbling away in three-inch heels and
      panty hose
to finish out another pink-collar temp pool day.

Examining how women worldwide have acted to influence the circumstances of their lives can help provide a broader picture of the challenges facing women and the changes feminists continue to work for globally.

CHALLENGING AND CHANGING THE DISCIPLINE

Teachers, scholars, and students in the field of women's studies continue to grapple with how to develop a transnational feminist perspective, particularly in college and university courses. Clearly we need to learn more about women around the world, acquainting ourselves with their particular histories, socioeconomic contexts, and activisms, so that we might dispel false notions about how all women are helpless or in need of being saved. Yet at the same time, women worldwide struggle with many issues, particularly with the processes of globalization and the resulting "economic and social dislocations" that have impacted poor women, and women of color, in particular (Naples, 11). How can feminists living in different places find common interests and concerns that can provide the basis for solidarity and working together?

Even beyond this, however, scholars such as Alexander and Mohanty remind us that a transnational feminist perspective does not define the "global" as "elsewhere" but rather seeks to draw new maps that reveal how the "local," including our own, is interconnected with the "global" (Alexander and Mohanty, "Cartographies," 35). In drawing these maps, we need to include the universities where we teach and learn, so that we can unpack one final binaristic category: the "academic"/"activist" binary (ibid., 26). A transnational feminist perspective challenges us to examine not only what we think we know, but also how we know it, for what purpose, and to whose benefit. In this way, reflecting upon our individual perspectives, locations, and journeys can provide an important first step toward imagining a better world and working with others to make this world a reality.

NOTES

1. In particular, see chapter 6, "The Differences Among Us."
2. See Naples, p. 5, and Mohanty, pp. 226–227. As both point out, terms such as *third world* emerged at earlier historical moments.
3. For example, see Lutz and Collins; Steet; Shaheen; and Mayer.

WORKS CITED

Ahmed, Leila. *Women and Gender in Islam: Historical Roots of a Modern Debate.* New Haven, CT: Yale University Press, 1992.

Alexander, M. Jacqui, and Chandra Talpade Mohanty. "Cartographies of Knowledge and Power: Transnational Feminism as Radical Praxis." In *Critical Transnational Feminist Praxis*, ed. Amanda Lock Swarr and Richa Nagar. Albany: State University of New York Press, 2009.

———. "Introduction: Genealogies, Legacies, Movements." In *Feminist Genealogies, Colonial Legacies, Democratic Futures*, ed. M. Jacqui Alexander and Chandra Talpade Mohanty. New York: Routledge, 1997.

Grewal, Inderpal, and Caren Kaplan. "Introduction: Transnational Feminist Practices and Questions of Postmodernity." In *Scattered Hegemonies: Postmodernity and Transnational Feminist Practices*, ed. Inderpal Grewal and Caren Kaplan. Minneapolis: University of Minnesota Press, 1994.

Kahf, Mohja. "Hijab Scene #2." In *E-Mails from Scheherazad.* Gainesville: University Press of Florida, 2003.

———. *Western Representations of the Muslim Woman: From Termagant to Odalisque.* 1st ed. Austin: University of Texas Press, 1999.

Lazreg, Marnia. "Feminism and Difference: The Perils of Writing as a Woman on Women in Algeria." *Feminist Studies* 14, no. 1 (1988): 81–107.

Lutz, Catherine A., and Jane L. Collins. *Reading National Geographic.* Chicago: University of Chicago Press, 1993.

Mayer, Ruth. *Artificial Africas: Colonial Images in the Times of Globalization.* Hanover, NH: Dartmouth College Press, 2002.

Moghadam, Valentine M. *Globalizing Women: Transnational Feminist Networks.* Baltimore: Johns Hopkins University Press, 2005.

Mohanty, Chandra Talpade. *Feminism Without Borders: Decolonizing Theory, Practicing Solidarity.* Durham, NC: Duke University Press, 2003.

Naples, Nancy A. "Changing the Terms: Community Activism, Globalization, and the Dilemmas of Transnational Feminist Praxis." In *Women's Activism and Globalization: Linking Local Struggles and Transnational Politics*, ed. Nancy A. Naples and Manisha Desai. New York: Routledge, 2002.

Sensoy, Özlem, and Robin DiAngelo. "'I Wouldn't Want to Be a Woman in the Middle East': White Female Student Teachers and the Narrative of the Oppressed Muslim woman." *Radical Teacher* 8, no. 1 (2006). Available online.

Shaheen, Jack G. *Reel Bad Arabs: How Hollywood Vilifies a People.* New York: Olive Branch Press, 2001.

Steet, Linda. *Veils and Daggers: A Century of National Geographic's Representation of the Arab World.* Philadelphia: Temple University Press, 2000.

Tripp, Aili Mari. "The Evolution of Transnational Feminisms: Consensus, Conflict, and New Dynamics." In *Global Feminism: Transnational Women's Activism, Organizing, and Human Rights*, ed. Myra Marx Ferree and Aili Mari Tripp. New York: New York University Press, 2006.

 7

Have You Ever Heard of Asian-American Feminists?

STACEY G. H. YAP

I can say that I stumbled into women's studies accidentally. I had no intention in my younger days to choose this area. It's true that there were few to no courses offered in women's studies in the early 1970s when I first arrived at college on the East Coast, and it's also true that I stereotyped women's liberation as a group of white women gone mad! I didn't see myself identifying with "them" even if I had seen courses offered in the women's studies area then. It was only when I went to graduate school and unintentionally selected a course about "men and women in corporations" that I was first introduced to the research in women's studies without ever knowing it. And from then on, my life was transformed.

Today I am a faculty member and chair of the women's studies (minor) program in my college, and teaching a course in women's studies, I cannot help thinking how much my life has changed from an undergraduate business major to a women's studies/sociology college teacher. My students must wonder about the irony of any Asian (American) teacher teaching them about women's studies and the American women's movement. The unexpected role that I play in influencing my students' lives will probably help them remember how much common ground we share even though we are ethnically different. What will transform my life and my students' lives is the complete element of surprise that women's studies can offer. It is the story of our lives, our mothers' and our grandmothers' lives, and the conditions and experiences we women have gone through and are going through now. Feminist scholars have researched experiences in great detail and told stories of our lives that have never been told before in colorful and powerful language.

What is more surprising are the uncharted territories women's studies offers, and what is not documented. Particularly, since I look and speak differently from my students, women's studies presents an opportunity for my women students to ask me more questions about me: How do I feel about American white men? What do I think about American black women? Do I think that the socialization process they learn is different in the Asian context? What is different about mother-daughter relationships among whites and those that are written by Chinese Americans like Amy Tan and Maxine Hong Kingston? The fact that Asian-American women are not represented in the mainstream of women's studies literature made my students and myself more intense in our search to wonder about their absence. As a feminist, I acknowledge their absence but do not feel upset nor angry by their lack of recognition. This neglected treatment by white American women who dominated this field in producing women's anthologies for women's studies courses is understandable. I try to remedy this by teaching my students and my friends about Asian-American women and their experiences. I center my research in the "unearthing" of Asian women's experiences. Whether they are Asian-born women or American-born Asian women, I recognize that their experiences have helped shape the history, politics, and literature of this country.

Women's studies has taught me that women must be studied on their own terms and not judged by male-defined standards. Similarly, Asian women must be allowed to speak for themselves because, while we share a great deal with other women, our experiences are unique, and women of other backgrounds can't speak for us. Asian women come to feminism in a variety of ways. Some of us stumbled into politics through fighting against unfair wage practices, and others protested against the Vietnam war. Including Asian women's experiences in women's studies courses is important, for we, like most women around the world, do not passively or silently accept the oppression we share with all women.   [1992]

 8

Voices of Women's Studies Students

Women's Studies as a Growth Process

DANISTA HUNTE

I remember trying to fit Introduction to Women's Studies into my schedule for five semesters and feeling frustrated each time that chemistry or some other requirement took precedence. Finally, first semester senior year, I was able to fit it into my schedule. After three years at Vassar College, I thought my feminist development was far beyond the introductory level and there would not be much for me to learn from the class. I was wrong. My politics were challenged daily. It seemed that everything that was changing and developing could be linked to a reading or discussion in women's studies. I learned life lessons that take some people all of their lives to learn. The most important lesson was that the many parts of myself—black, female, feminist, Caribbean, pro-choice, working class, etc.—could coexist as one healthy individual. I gained a better understanding of how our society consistently seeks to "divide and conquer" or to squash any possible coalition among oppressed individuals. I confronted a lot of the anger I felt toward white society. I do not know whether I will ever resolve that anger, but identifying its source and understanding the way in which it can stifle my own growth and development are valuable lessons. I gained a better understanding of the environment and the culture in which my mother was raised and in turn how she raised me. I realized how difficult it is to be someone's mother, and I appreciate my mother even more. Although I left some class sessions feeling confused and schizophrenic, by the end of first semester I felt empowered and confident that I could handle anything.

On the first day of class, I counted the number of women of color in the class. There were two of us. I had a reputation of being a vocal student, and nothing less was expected of me in this class. I also knew that I would be the official spokeswoman of color and the voice of all black women on campus. Initially I resented having to occupy the "speaker" role, and I was even angry at the other sister in class who never spoke in concert with me. As a matter of fact she never spoke at all, which may tell another tale altogether. There was no support or comfort upon which to depend.

These feelings were not new. For the three years prior to women's studies, my being was fueled by anger and the thrill of battle. I craved the opportunities for combat with the administration of the college. I enjoyed sitting on committees with faculty and feeling confident about what I had to contribute or debating with a white man who presumed to know "who I was and what my life was about" based upon his proficiency in two Africana studies courses! These encounters excited me and made me feel powerful; however, by the time I had reached senior year, I was *tired* and did not want to fight anymore. After reading Audre Lorde's "The Uses of Anger: Women Responding to Racism" in *Sister Outsider,* those feelings of anger and resentment began to subside. Through Lorde's writings I identified some of the reasons for the anger I was feeling about the class, my experiences at Vassar College, and toward myself. Lorde warns black women not to let our justified anger eat away at our compassion to love ourselves and others. She advocates that black women must find ways in which to channel their anger into *healthy* and *productive* actions that will hopefully transform our situations. Anger should not be denied, but explored and used to produce something positive that will move the individual forward.

Introduction to Women's Studies was painful, but I learned a lot. There is *much* work to be done on the part of all women, and especially by women of color. The class offered very little feminist theory by African-American women, Hispanic women, Asian women, or Native American women, which angered me. From my own personal readings I had found a wealth of writings by women of color on issues of motherhood and parenting, male domination, and the portrayal of women in film, etc. There

are time constraints when developing a syllabus. However, when the theoretical and critical analyses that comprise the syllabus are written by white feminists, this conveys only one perspective. This imbalance facilitates the myth that black women do not theorize or are not capable of critically analyzing their own situations or of offering criticism of their society. We as black women need to pursue fields in which we can create and command our own destinies and have an impact upon our lives and the lives of our sisters.

Lorde says that, "for survival, Black children in America must be raised to be warriors."[1] Unfortunately, that often means we grow up justifiably paranoid and untrusting of anyone who is not like us. Women's studies rejuvenated my spirit and reassured me that people can grow and things can change. As a result of the class, I try not to build walls around myself and I want to be more inclusive in my politics. Each new experience, whether categorized as "good" or "bad," facilitates growth. I look upon my experience in Introduction to Women's Studies as a growth process—and, for the record, it was "good." [1991]

NOTE

1. Audre Lorde, "Man Child: A Black Lesbian Feminist's Response," *Sister Outsider* (Freedom, CA: Crossing Press, 1984), 75.

Finding My Latina Identity Through Women's Studies

LUANA FERREIRA

Taking a women's studies course entitled Women: Images and Realities helped me to become the person that I am today. It enabled me to share both my experience as a woman and my experience of Latino culture with other women and understand more fully the position of women in society.

When I lived in the Dominican Republic, I'd see the same scene over and over, especially around the holidays: women were in the kitchen cooking and setting the table while the men were in the living room discussing sports or politics. My grandmother always told me that once a woman learned how to do house chores, she was ready for marriage, and that a woman should always depend on a man because a woman will always need the *strength* of a man. At this point in my life I was beginning to feel frustrated and anxious. I asked myself why at the age of 17 I still was not engaged, or in a relationship, and what would happen if I never got married.

Once I arrived in the United States and enrolled in college, I began to see male-female relationships differently. I saw that women were indeed more career-oriented and independent. However, as a college student, I thought that the women's movement, womanism, and feminism were a little too radical for me. The word "feminist" to me meant "man hater."

The course taught me a great deal about women in the United States and around the world. I could not believe how much I had been missing out! I must admit that I was biased in choosing the teacher. Looking in the catalogue, I saw three different names, but one stood out: Delgado. Since I am Latina, the idea of having a teacher I can relate to pleased me. Professor Linda Delgado, a proud Puerto Rican woman, taught me how to detach myself from traditional ideas about women without losing my cultural values and awareness. At the same time, having a Latina teacher for this course has helped me to become more involved in my community. I learned about sexism in religion and in the labor force, and I became more aware of issues such as rape, abortion, and sexual harassment.

In my traditional family, my parents always taught me "where a woman's place in society is." According to them, rape victims deserve to get raped because of the way they were dressed, pregnancy is a punishment for the irresponsibility of a woman, virginity is a proof of purity and decency and is the best wedding gift to a man, a spouse can be found through one's cooking, and so forth. I can go on forever with these myths and taboos.

The course made me realize that clothing should not determine the reputation of a woman, that women have the right to make their own decisions about sex, and that both men and women should be concerned about pregnancy. I also learned that one should learn to do chores for survival, not to please someone else. I have become more secure

about myself. I am able to make my own decisions because I am using my own judgment, *not* doing what my parents expect or what society dictates. I am also more firm in my decisions. Before, if I were involved in a discussion with a male, I always worried that if I opened my mouth he would lose interest in me. I cannot believe that I used to think this way! I operated on the assumption that if I were too articulate or too much of an activist, I would lose the relationship of my dreams. I thank my teacher and the course for making me understand that standing up for your rights and for what you believe in will raise your self-confidence and self-esteem. Now I find myself having interesting discussions with many colleagues, males and females, and I am more open with my female friends.

Today I am happy to say that I am a woman striving for a career. I am very involved in my community, and I am not afraid to state my beliefs and ideas. Now I know that being a feminist, far from being a man hater, is rather fighting for equal rights, struggling against discrimination, and educating one's self and others about women's issues.

[1992]

What Women's Studies Has Meant to Me

LUCITA WOODIS

I had no understanding of what women's studies meant when I first looked through the spring catalogue at the University of New Mexico, but it sounded intriguing. So I went to the Women's Studies Center on campus and asked lots of questions: What is women's studies? What can I gain from a course like this? Can I use the information from women's studies courses outside the university? Can I use this for a certain area of my life?

Well, my questions were answered in such a positive way that the very same day, I stepped into the Women's Center and signed up as a women's studies minor.

Now that I've been introduced to the curriculum, I believe that women's studies means empowerment for women. We as women want equality in our lives—in areas such as the workplace, where we want to have acknowledged that people should be paid on the basis of their experience, not their sex; that regardless of sex, we are human. As women, we need respect for making our choices and decisions. We need power and control—not power over others, but shared power with other human beings who work together cooperatively. This is especially meaningful to me as a woman of color, a Native American artist who grew up on the Navajo Reservation.

I have never experienced a more close, supportive, nurturing, and expressive multicultural group of women as I did in the Women in Contemporary Society class at the University of New Mexico. Our bond as women enabled us to break through the barriers of race, creed, and color to interact as human beings and discover a common ground. In our class discussions, we were able to express our intolerance at being victims of pornography and sexual abuse, knowing that with every issue there has been some change for the better. We saw how we as women have bonded together through self-help groups, have opened up shelters for battered women, and in a sense have been saying that we do have power—power to overcome these intolerable abuses and survive as powerful women into the 1990s.

The knowledge I gained through the course came from the classroom, my classmates, and my professor, Deborah Klein. Ms. Klein was very avid in our discussions and presentations, as we bonded together through our openness. She helped the class evolve to an intimate level. With no remorse or self-consciousness, we created an atmosphere of acceptance, shared a great deal of ourselves, and enhanced each other's lives. As a sister to women of color, I experienced support, nurturing, and the embrace of other women as we expressed our experiences openly and individually.

I used part of my class experience to take the group on a journey about the meaning of sexual abuse in a woman's life, particularly in mine. I chose to present my journey as a narrative. I told my story with the visual images of my artwork, as well as with my words. My goal was to convey to others that confronting one's self can be a positive

path toward strength, confidence, and the ability to be true to one's self.

Exploring women's issues has truly been a journey for me, a spiritual journey filled with healing and cleansing and enlightenment. My explorations have led me toward harmony and balance and enable me to feel peaceful, calm, and serene.

As a Native American (Navajo), I can only stress that women are powerful. We are a maternal society, the bearers of children. We are patient yet very strong in our decision making. I can say I have benefited from the women's studies program and won't be silent long. I will be verbally expressive as well as visually expressive, because that is who I am—an artist. I share a very intimate part of myself through my art. I will always be a Native first, as I am from a traditional family, and I'm proud to know my clan through my ancestors. Yet I can also say that I'm from the Navajo Nation *and* part of the larger women's experience in our society.

Today, I understand that I am not alone. I am important. I am not a second-class citizen, I am a capable, strong, and independent Native American Navajo woman. I will always carry my culture and traditions in my heart whether on the Reservation or in the outside world. Through my spirit, I will carry a message visually and verbally that to survive and heal from abuse is to come full-circle to contentment, that we are all part of a larger whole.

Nishtinigíí shit beehozin   (Navajo)
I know who I am   (English)   [1992]

Women's Studies: A Man's Perspective

EVAN WEISSMAN

Bob Marley once sang, "Don't forget, no way, who you are and where you stand in your struggles." Because I was interested in examining my role in society as a young man and exploring what I could do for women's struggles for freedom and equality, I registered for the course "Women: Images and Realities." I have always been aware of the feminist fight for equality; I grew up surrounded by feminists, but I never had the opportunity to take a class focused on women and was eager to learn more about the struggle today.

Although most of the reactions of my friends and family were positive and encouraging, some men ridiculed me for taking a women's studies class. I remember one individual who constantly challenged my "manliness" by saying things like "My, Evan, you look very feminine today; is that class rubbing off on you?" I often felt hopeless in the face of such ridicule, but I realized the mockery came from ignorance. Rather than becoming defensive, I would ask him whether he was insecure about his manhood, since anyone secure in themselves could easily take a women's studies class. Men are often unfamiliar with the facts of women's subordination, the extent to which it is practiced, and the role we can play in changing it. From my experience, it is often easier for people to joke about things they are scared to face or know nothing about. It is much easier for a man to criticize women's studies than to take a critical look at one's self and the advantages given to men in a society based on gender hierarchy.

Because the media portray feminists as "dykes who hate men," I brought into my first women's studies class a fear that my female classmates would hate me because I was a man, I was the oppressor. I learned in the course the difference between acting against men and acting against the actions of men. My classmates judged me by my beliefs and actions, not by what I have between my legs. Feminism, I learned, does not call for men's subordination but for the fair and equal treatment of women.

I learned in "Women: Images and Realities" that sexism is far deeper than I had previously thought. I also came to realize that I have many privileges as a white man. I learned that my skin color and gender give me an unfair advantage in American society, a realization that was extremely difficult to deal with. These privileges make life easier for me than for those who do not benefit from their skin color or sex. Without these privileges, my life goals and dreams would be more distant and difficult to achieve. Once I acknowledged this fact, I had to figure out what I could do with this information. It

is not possible for me to divest myself individually of these privileges simply because I now recognize them. But I can work to change the system while being conscious of what these privileges have done for me.

Through "Women: Images and Realities," I became more aware of the prevalence of sexism in everyday life and the many small, seemingly insignificant ways in which men keep women in subordinate roles. I decided to stand up for my beliefs at all times, even when they were not popular. I wanted to contribute to women's struggles by dissenting from sexism in groups of men, but I soon learned that men don't always welcome such intervention.

A few months after the class ended, I was at a party and got into an argument with an acquaintance, who I'll call Bill, who was talking about how "pussy" needed to be "fucked." None of the other guys around had anything to say, so I asked him to clarify himself. When he repeated his statement, I asked him whether his mom had a "pussy" that needed a good "fuck." He replied, "Yeah, for someone else." I was disgusted and tried to explain to him how disrespectful his comment was. I argued that he could never make that comment to a woman's face. After a while I walked off, realizing that I could not make him take his comment back, especially with all of his friends around. I went up to my cousin and told her about what Bill had said. She immediately went over to him and said "I don't have a pussy that needs to be fucked." In a few minutes Bill approached me ready for a fistfight. "Why did you do that?" he asked. "I was making the point that you couldn't make your comment to a woman's face because it is disrespectful," I responded and walked off.

To this day Bill holds a grudge against me, but I don't regret my action. It was important to me to let Bill know that I would not tolerate sexist behavior. I have to be true to myself and stand for what I believe in. I must fight against injustice whenever possible, even when it is difficult. My male friends seldom say insulting things about women in my presence, and I feel good about this even though they probably continue to say these things when I'm not around. At least I've made them think. I now see myself as a feminist, making the struggle for women's equality my own, and I will not forget who I am and where I stand in this struggle. [1998]

Jump-Starting My Future: The Force of Women's Studies in My Life

ELEANOR JAILER-COLEY

I was given a rude awakening when I enrolled in my first women's studies course. Even though I was raised by a feminist mother and internalized many of her values, I was unaware of a range of issues that affected women's lives on a daily basis. Some of those issues—like the unhealthy media portrayals of women and the rampant epidemic of violence against women—came as a shock. As I learned about the suppressed history and realities of women's lives and the movements that have struggled to recover them, I began to feel a deep need to join with other women to work toward change. My first step in that process was declaring a women's studies major.

My women's studies classes ignited in me a hunger to understand how both individual and systematic oppression affect my own life, not only because I am a woman, but because of my other identities as well. I learned that being Deaf and queer and female have all worked against me in a culture that privileges men, heterosexuality and the hearing. For example, because I still sometimes worry about coming out of the closet in casual conversations, I often play the pronoun game when speaking about my female significant other. The pronoun game is where nonspecific gender pronouns are used. This is surprisingly easy to do in sign language.

Women's studies also gave me the means to understand why I needed to work harder to get to where I want to be. By society's definition I am not "normal," and I often experience interactions with people who are unable to understand my background. While this remains a challenge, becoming aware of my oppression through women's studies has not discouraged me in the slightest. In fact, it has only made me feel more empowered. Women's studies gave me the tools to see that knowledge is power. Instead of hiding myself, I now feel a great

need to educate others who are ignorant about women's oppression as well as queer and Deaf culture.

Still, I often struggle with the intersections of my identities. While the feminist and queer communities are quite intertwined, the Deaf community tends to be much more separate. Also, Deaf issues are often invisible to these other communities. A good example of this is that while there are several domestic violence shelters that are accepting of lesbians, there is only one Deaf-specific violence shelter in the United States.

Despite my differences, my women's studies classes all took the time to address the importance of recognizing various kinds of oppression. Because I was able to talk about my experiences, I never felt isolated or alone and this, in turn, made me feel supported. Being able to speak openly was liberating and exhilarating, but it was also a way of connecting with other women. Sometimes I would hesitantly share my intimate experiences only to be relieved by an expression of encouragement or someone else in the class who went through the same thing.

This sense of connection and solidarity inspired me to become an activist and that is where I found my community. Various activist clubs on campus, such as the queer group and the feminist collective, became my home. I was rarely just a member in these groups. Instead, I took the initiative to facilitate and organize events. Many of the events that I worked on were political, such as the National Equality March in Washington, D.C., that encouraged Lesbian, Gay, Bisexual, and Transgender rights. The march left me feeling inspired, alive and ready for more. Other events had an educational focus, like the National Day of Silence—a day of protest against anti-LGBTQ name-calling. That event allowed for people to become aware of the effects of anti-gay slurs. We held signs that spoke directly to people's experiences and the weight of our everyday language. The National Day of Silence was written about in the college paper, and started a ripple effect of people becoming more conscious of their word usage.

What ignited my passion for women's studies also sparked my desire to go into the field of social work. Empowering others is one of the core values found in both the Social Work Code of Ethics and feminist activism and theory. Fortunately, feminists and social workers dovetail as agents of change. I am currently working toward my master's in social work for Deaf clients. Because foundational concepts found in feminist theory can be directly applied to social work, I actively implement all different kinds of women's issues (i.e., gay adoption, LGBTQ teenager identity formations, and positive identities of feminists) into my new academics.

Once I graduate, I plan to pursue a career where I will have the opportunity to work with Deaf women. Stepping foot into that first women's studies class awakened a thirst to understand my own life, the lives of other women, and the systems of oppression that bear down on us in sometimes very different ways. But because I could have never predicted where I would be today, my introduction to women's studies was so much more than just a class—it jump-started my future.

 9

Women's Studies as Women's History

MARILYN J. BOXER

Thirty years after it was institutionalized in the U.S. academy, women's history now has a secure place in American higher education. The history of women's studies, however, remains mostly lost amid the politics that deny it legitimacy, both within and outside academic feminism. Philosopher Jane Roland Martin in her recent memoir declared, "Had women in the 1970s been aware of the gendered underpinnings of the academy, let alone known how powerful and persistent our education-gender system is, the women's studies movement might never have been launched" (109). How was it possible? What mixture of hope, energy, courage, and perhaps naïveté can explain the success of the scattered and motley contingent of feminist activists, students, faculty, staff, and community supporters who launched and sustained the women's studies

movement through its founding years? What conjuncture of developments in the history of higher education in the United States can account for its initial acceptance and rapid growth across the country in institutions of all kinds, defying predictions that it was "just a fad"? Where does women's studies fit into the larger story of American women's history? Does this tale offer any insight into possible futures for women's studies as an academic field? What can we learn from the history of women's studies? Is Martin right?

I think not, for the generation of women who founded women's studies acted out of intellectual and emotional needs too powerful to repress, whatever the nature of the institutional "beast" we faced. (An early women's studies publication at San Diego State University bore the imprint "Inside the Beast.") Women's studies developed at a particular period in the history of the United States, of American higher education, of feminism, and in the lives of women brought up to believe in the reality of the opportunities we were promised. To contextualize the beginnings of the academic feminist movement, it is useful to follow the scheme laid out by Florence Howe, Barbara Miller Solomon, and others, according to which women's studies can be viewed as a third phase in American women's struggle for equal access to higher education (Howe, *Myths of Coeducation*; Solomon). In the pre–Civil War era, women such as Lucy Stone demanded and sometimes won admission to institutions of higher learning, but generally they had to settle for special programs of study deemed suitable for their sex. In a second phase, in the later decades of the nineteenth century, women such as M. Carey Thomas called for admission to the "men's curriculum," both in new colleges for women that aimed to equal the private Ivy League institutions that educated men of the elite, and in state-supported, land-grant universities that promised "coeducation." Thomas wanted to set to rest allegations regarding the inferiority of the female mind by requiring of women a curriculum as rigorous and challenging as any offered at the men's colleges. Beginning in the mid-1960s, enterprising women with feminist consciousness launched a third phase. Declaring coeducation a myth, they challenged the content of higher education as well as academic structures and procedures that taught a hidden curriculum of women's second-class status. In this view, courses that ignored women's experiences and perspectives subtly reinforced old ideas about female intellectual deficiencies while also perpetuating women's social, economic, and political marginality.

This third phase originated in broad historical developments including the postwar expansion of higher education through the G.I. bill; the proliferation of institutions needed to serve the children of the G.I. generation (the "baby-boomers"); governmental assumption of a central role in expanding access to higher education through funding bricks and mortar, awarding research grants to faculty, providing financial aid to students; and so forth. Across the country, as statewide systems were established to accommodate new constituencies, teachers' colleges were transformed into state universities and student populations mushroomed. Unlike the governments of other countries (such as France, for example) where national ministries of education set educational policies, establish professorial chairs, and sometimes determine curricular decisions, for the most part legislative bodies in the United States exerted minimal influence on the content of university curricula—a fact of major salience in the expansion of women's studies. Spared powerful external forces governing academic content, many local faculties and administrators readily agreed, frequently under pressure from activist students, to add the new coursework on women.

Sociopolitical currents of the 1960s—the civil rights, antiwar, free speech, and student power movements, and the New Left—constituted an equally powerful influence on the history of women's studies. As revolts against tradition and authority, they laid the basis for wholesale rejection of standard academic requirements such as Western civilization courses, and for a concomitant demand by students for coursework they deemed "relevant" to their lives. For feminists this meant seeking a useable heritage and a useful ideology. The first new courses on women in history, literature, and society, taught in cities around

the country in community settings as well as colleges and universities, fulfilled these needs. The first new "programs" augured a future in which women would seek a permanent place in the curriculum and in virtually all aspects of university life. Concurrent increases in the proportion of female students at all levels, and of women faculty and administrators, facilitated by affirmative action, all encouraged support for women's studies programs (Chamberlain; Pearson et al.).

The early history of women's studies reveals rapid expansion from one integrated program in 1970 to 150 in 1975, 300 in 1980, 450 in 1985, and 600 in 1990. (A recent list of programs, departments, and research centers that maintain Web sites extends the number to more than 650.) This growth attests to the passion and intellectual energy brought by feminists to the academy (Boxer, "For and About Women"; "Women's Studies: A World View"). It is worth emphasizing how critical a role students played in this history. They demanded classes at a time when student voices carried major influence in university forums, and they enrolled in massive numbers in the new courses, especially in enrollment-budgeted state institutions such as the California State University system where many "firsts" in feminist education took place.[1] As graduate students they also initiated and taught many of the early courses, for minimal cost to dollar-strapped institutions. To university administrators struggling to meet both activist student challenges and legislative demands for "productivity" measured in enrollment numbers, women's studies offered a bargain.[2] It also served at times as a proxy for affirmative action. By adding women's studies to the curriculum, universities might meet the spirit if not the letter of government mandates, as well as some academicians' desires to include women more fully in institutional life.

The role played by women's studies in the economics of higher education became clear in the 1980s. During the Ronald Reagan era, students flocked toward business and professionally or vocationally oriented programs. Attracted by career opportunities newly opened to women, often thanks to successful feminist-inspired lawsuits, female students comprised a large component of the increased enrollment in both undergraduate and graduate degree programs in accounting, finance, marketing, and related fields. A president of the American Academy of Collegiate Schools of Business (AACSB) once remarked in my presence that the explosive growth in his field in the 1980s could be attributed to women students; male enrollment had remained steady while female numbers soared. The new careers, of course, paid much more than the traditional "women's" professions of teaching, nursing, and social work.

As students deserted fields of study long favored by women such as history and literature for newer pastures, and universities eliminated graduation requirements that formerly sustained enrollments in the social sciences and humanities, the pressure of reduced demand in those fields helped boost support for women's studies. Students who declined to take History 101 or Literature 101 often signed up for Women's Studies 101 or disciplinary courses focused on women. In addition, in the curriculum revisions that many universities undertook to adjust to new campus and student priorities, women's studies faculty began to win approval for their courses in the new and generally less prescriptive general education programs that faculties adopted. Undergraduate minors and majors, masters' degrees, and Ph.D. concentrations gradually enriched traditional curricula. As more women faculty, including many interested in women's studies, attained tenured positions, they could exert greater influence in academic affairs. Women's studies was well placed by the 1990s both to survive the adverse environment that came with pervasive fiscal retrenchment and to respond to an increasing emphasis, sometimes economically motivated, on crossing disciplinary borders within universities and between universities and local communities. Newly established endowments provided program support and professorial chairs at the University of Cincinnati, Indiana University, Stanford University, the University of South Carolina, and the University of Southern California, among others. The label "department" attached to women's studies began to appear across the educational landscape,

increasing rapidly in recent years from about twenty in 1997 to thirty-six or more by 2001.[3]

How can we account for the success of the women's studies movement, in personal as well as institutional terms? From my perspective, generational analysis offers a useful interpretive framework. The founders of women's studies belonged to the post-1950s generation of mothers and daughters. The older contingent had experienced, albeit as children or youth, a war fought for the "American way"; then they struggled against the hypocrisies and fallacies of the culture of "togetherness" that, in the 1950s and early 1960s, sought to limit their roles outside the family. Wives of "men in gray flannel suits" and "organization men," some of us were also daughters of Philip Wylie's smothering "moms," targets of Freudian-imbued misogyny, cruelly caricatured in popular postwar novels, diagnosed as sick, neurotic, destructive. Thanks to the new historians of women, we came to understand the 1950s as the worst decade in American history for women who aspired to personal achievement outside familial roles.[4]

The daughters of these 1950s mothers grew up along with the new ideas of the mid- and late 1960s. Like the "ideas of the 1860s" that sparked the rebellion of privileged young people in Russia a century earlier, new currents of thought about the social condition of other oppressed groups—serfs in 1850–1860s' Russia, Blacks in the 1950s–1960s' United States—elicited awareness among many women of the need for political action to liberate themselves from constricted societal roles.[5] Some of us resisted our parents, even (or especially) our mothers, as agents of repression, and set out to work actively with men in liberation movements, until we began to see the latter—at least some of them—as also the source of our problems. We needed feminist awareness to see ourselves as primary agents and to recognize that women matter. We began to ask new questions about our foremothers and ourselves. We wanted to study about women.

It is useful to recall just how audacious it was circa 1970 to proclaim that women should be the central focus of a college course. Is there enough material for a whole course, we were asked. Perhaps the most remarkable aspect of the curriculum initiated at San Diego State College (now University) in the fall term 1970 and publicized in *Female Studies I* was that it included *ten* whole courses, plus supervised field experience in the women's community (Tobias).

That was then. Now we have that many freestanding, multidisciplinary Ph.D. programs in women's studies, a development scarcely imaginable thirty years ago ("Established and Proposed Women's Studies Ph.D. Programs"). It is a history not likely to be repeated, for the context has utterly changed. Today a rapidly growing frontier for women's studies lies abroad where women's studies also serves to produce women leaders and to spur development of gender equity more generally (Howe, "Women's Education"). Instructional programs and research centers abound around the world and their numbers are growing ("Women's Studies: A World View"). According to a 1993 "international handbook" of women's studies, more than one hundred countries house educational programs, research centers, or training institutes focused on women, including many founded in the 1990s following the collapse of the Soviet Union (Brown et al.). A 1997 "international list-in-progress" encompasses more than five hundred such centers ("Centers for Research and Teaching on Women"). Feminist scholars, many thousands of whom have produced dissertations focused on women, now debate such issues as the relative merits of departmentalization, integration into gender studies, infusion into general education programs, and free-standing doctoral degrees. Some praise while others deplore shifting terminology in program and department rubrics (Boxer, "Remapping the University"). Definitions of women's experiences continue to expand as scholars with "transnational" feminist perspectives undertake new research, create new courses, and produce new instructional materials, enriching women's studies and drawing in ever more diverse students and faculty (Grewal and Kaplan).

Some things never change: Witness recent, lengthy discussions in meetings and online about student resistance to feminism and faculty vulnerability to burnout.[6] Some scholars of note continue to ignore women's studies altogether or to deplore feminist scholarship, often without ever bothering to read any of it.[7] The content of women's studies scholarship remains marginal to some disciplines where it has much to offer. In some places, instruction and administration in women's studies still depend on volunteer labor, and faculty contributions of time and talent go unrecognized and unrewarded.

But the cup is, I think, more than half full. Women's studies grew out of the needs and experiences of women and reflected the spirit of a certain time in history. Times have changed but the justification for feminist scholarship remains as valid now as then. Asserting newly developed "intellectual confidence," feminist scholars still find in abundance unanswered, important questions to research. Many errors remain to be corrected; many lacunae to be filled; new thinking to be encouraged. Each generation finds new questions to ask and pressing issues to pursue. Today, economic globalization profoundly affects the content of research and teaching, conferences and publications in all areas of women's studies. Social consciousness and behavior will be altered on the basis of the new knowledge thus produced. If some students still come to class resisting feminist awareness, they do come. Others enter with new knowledge, for insights inspired by women's studies have spread into mainstream vocabularies. A girl today may learn at two, three, or four to name parts of her body that went unrecognized by some of us until, at twenty, thirty, or forty, we read of them in *Our Bodies, Ourselves*.[8] In the aggregate, institutional support for women's studies is strong in the United States and elsewhere, and it continues to spread into new fields. For example, the Ford Foundation, long a mainstay of academic feminism, recently provided a six-figure grant to a group of Chinese scholars for the purpose of developing women's studies curricula, training faculty, and translating women's studies materials, largely from English, into their language.[9]

One task today is to pursue cultural authority commensurate with our expertise on topics related to women and human relationships (Boxer, *When*

Women Ask the Questions, 242–45). Women's studies has fared badly with the media. Like feminists in society, proponents of women's studies in academia have yet to convince our opponents that we represent more than a special interest, that our work is grounded in both ethical and intellectual imperatives. We have often, alas, failed even to engage the resistance in debate; we must seek dialogue with the opposition. Today we can claim as feminist few "public intellectuals." More of us might follow the example of Ruth Rosen, professor of American women's history, who for years has contributed to the press op-ed pieces that translate feminist scholarship into lively and accessible prose. Like Professor of English bell hooks, we might voice our views in strongly provocative, personal essays that elicit variously admiration, agreement, and opposition—but are heard by a large public. We should join her in "talking back" in forums and media outside the academy.[10]

Whatever the forces of resistance, another vital task is to assure the continuing survival of women's studies in U.S. higher education in the absence of a strong feminist movement. The way to do that, even while countering dominant intellectual trends, is to integrate as fully as possible into academic structures. The trend toward departmentalization is, in my view, a good thing, as are doctoral programs. The more institutionalization, the better. We must highlight the scholarly mission of women's studies. Excellence in research and teaching are the keys to maintaining and increasing the value of the feminist educational enterprise launched a generation ago. That teaching should include the various histories of women, of feminisms around the world, and of women's studies as an educational movement.

Today we have occasion to celebrate. Rather than lament our shortcomings, we must continue to work as long, as hard, and as smartly as we can. We must demonstrate that women's studies is not only an important chapter in women's history but also, thanks to the knowledge it creates, an essential part of women's future, inside the classroom and beyond, everywhere in the world. Just as women's rights constitute human rights, so women's studies forms an integral and transformative part of the history of humanity.   [2002]

NOTES

Earlier versions of this paper were presented at the Berkshire Conference in Women's History, University of Rochester, 4–7 June 1999, and at the conference on "Then and Now: The Politics of Women's Studies," at the Graduate Center of the City University of New York, 1 December 2000.

1. In addition to the first program at San Diego State and a program at Humboldt State that dates from 1972, pioneering programs in the California State University system soon appeared at San Francisco State (which incorporated racial diversity from the start), San Jose State (which developed one of the first women's studies master's degrees in the country), Sonoma State (where the celebration of a national women's history day was launched in a women's studies class), and Sacramento State (which in 1973 hosted the first national conference on women's studies). The founding meeting of the National Women's Studies Association in 1977 was sponsored by women's studies at San Jose State.

2. My success as department chair in building faculty lines from 2.4 to 8.1 at San Diego State between 1974 and 1980 reflects a male feminist dean's need to satisfy his superiors by increasing enrollment. Typically, during the first week of classes he would call and ask whether we could fill another class or two if given additional salary funds. We never failed to do so.

3. On endowments, information on the University of Southern California is from former director Lois Banner, personal communication, 29 April 1997; on Stanford, from former director Iris Litt, personal communication, 30 April 1997. On the University of Cincinnati, see Strumingher; on Indiana University, see Allen; on the University of South Carolina, see Rosser and Mille. In 1997 I counted 20 departments; by 2001, 36; my count was based on authors' affiliations listed in journal articles and books as well as messages contributed by e-mail to WMST-L, a women's studies e-mail discussion list.

4. "Togetherness" was a slogan promoted by *McCall's* magazine to romanticize family life. Terms are borrowed from Sloan Wilson, *Man in the Gray Flannel Suit* (1956); William H. Whyte, *Organization Man* (1956); and Philip Wylie, *Generation of Vipers* (1955). Representative novels include Philip Roth, *Goodbye Columbus* (1959), and Herman Wouk, *Marjorie Morningstar* (1955), as well as anything by Norman Mailer. For depiction of Wollstonecraft and feminists as neurotic, see Lundberg and Farnham. Flexner's pathbreaking 1959 history, *Century of Struggle*, began the revisionist project in American women's history; it was reprinted six times between January 1968 and April 1971.

5. On Russia, see Turgenev and Engel and Rosenthal.

6. In an extended thread on "women's studies burnout" that appeared on WMST-L during October and November 2001, many correspondents repeated old laments,

often attributing to current events attitudes that seem to be endemic in women's studies.

7. See, for example, the journal of the American Academy of Arts and Sciences, which purported to review "transformation" in the fields of economics, literary studies, philosophy, and political science for the period 1945 to 1995, with scarcely a mention of women's studies: *Daedalus* 106, no. 1 (winter 1997).

8. Personal observation of my granddaughter, born 1996.

9. Personal communication from Wang Zheng, formerly of Stanford University's Institute for Research on Women and Gender, now at the University of Michigan, Ann Arbor, 2000. The grant is providing for translation into Chinese of my book *When Women Ask the Questions*, among many others.

10. A list of 100 "public intellectuals" that appeared in the *New York Times* on 20 January 2002 included second-wave feminists Betty Friedan and Gloria Steinem, along with Camille Paglia and Christina Hoff Sommers, both authors of widely cited attacks on women's studies. Rosen recently left her professorship to become a full-time journalist with the *San Francisco Chronicle*. Her columns have been reprinted in the *Los Angeles Times* and elsewhere. For bell hooks's call for black women "to change the nature and direction of our speech, to make a speech that compels listeners, one that is heard," see hooks, especially 6–9.

WORKS CITED

Allen, Judith. "Fund Raising for Women's Studies." Paper presented at "The Next Twenty-Five Years," Women's Studies Program Administrators Conference, Arizona State University, February 1997.

Boxer, Marilyn J. "For and About Women: The Theory and Practice of Women's Studies in the United States." *Signs: Journal of Women in Culture and Society* 7, no. 3 (1982): 661–95.

———. "Remapping the University: The Promise of the Women's Studies Ph.D." *Feminist Studies* 24, no. 2 (1998): 387–402.

———. *When Women Ask the Questions: Creating Women's Studies in America*. Baltimore, MD: Johns Hopkins University Press, 1998.

Brown, Loulou, Helen Collins, Pat Green, Maggie Humm, and Mel Landells, eds. *W.I.S.H.: The International Handbook of Women's Studies*. New York: Harvester Wheatsheaf, 1993.

"Centers for Research and Teaching on Women: An International List-in-Progress." *Women's Studies Quarterly* 25, no. 3–4 (1997): 249–86.

Chamberlain, Mariam K., ed. *Women in Academe: Progress and Prospects*. New York: Russell Sage, 1988.

Engel, Barbara Alpern, and Clifford N. Rosenthal, eds. *Five Sisters: Women Against the Tsar*. New York: Schocken, 1987.

"Established and Proposed Women's Studies Ph.D. Programs in North America: A Current Listing." *Feminist Studies* 24, no. 2 (1998): 326.

Flexner, Elanor. *Century of Struggle: The Woman's Rights Movement in the United States*. 1959. New York: Atheneum, 1971.

Grewal, Inderpal, and Caren Kaplan, eds. *Scattered Hegemonies: Postmodernity and Transnational Feminist Practices*. Minneapolis: University of Minnesota Press, 1994.

hooks, bell. *Talking Back: Thinking Feminist, Thinking Black*. Boston: South End, 1989.

Howe, Florence. *Myths of Coeducation: Selected Essays, 1964–1983*. Bloomington: Indiana University Press, 1987.

———. "Women's Education: Policy Implications for the New Century." *Women's Studies Quarterly* 27, no. 3–4 (1999): 169–84.

Lundberg, Ferdinand, and Marynia F. Farnham. *Modern Women: The Lost Sex*. New York: Grosset and Dunlap, 1947.

Martin, Jane Roland. *Coming of Age in Academe: Rekindling Women's Hopes and Reforming the Academy*. New York: Routledge, 2000.

Pearson, Carol S., Donna L. Shavlik, and Judith G. Touchton, eds. *Educating the Majority: Women Challenge Tradition in Higher Education*. New York: AAC/Macmillan, 1989.

Rosser, Sue V., and Katherine W. Mille. "A Grass-roots Approach to Funding Women's Studies." *NWSAction* 1, no. 4 (1988): 1–3.

Solomon, Barbara Miller. *In the Company of Educated Women: A History of Women and Higher Education in America*. New Haven, CT: Yale University Press, 1985.

Strumingher, Laura S. "The Birth and Growth of 'Friends of Women's Studies' at the University of Cincinnati." *Frontiers* 8, no. 3 (1986): 83–86.

Tobias, Sheila, ed. *Female Studies I*. Pittsburgh: KNOW, 1970.

Turgenev, Ivan. *Fathers and Sons*. 1862. New York: Norton, 1966.

"Women's Studies: A World View." Special issue of *Women's Studies Quarterly* 22, no. 3–4 (1994).

Feminists Transform Science

GOWRI PARAMESWARAN

In the last few decades, there has been an influx of women scientists into the field of biology. Many of them have questioned traditional ways of thinking about sex roles, especially with regard to sexuality and mating. They have pushed fellow biologists to examine a wider array of animal species and abandon predetermined frameworks to understand behavior. One of the earliest ideas questioned by many was the notion that traits associated with each sex are fixed. Instead, they argued that nature favored species that exhibited enormous inter-individual diversity. Because feminist biologists reject the notion that science is objective, they have shone a torch on the politics that has driven science from its earliest period. With all the new technology that is now at the disposal of biologists, these feminist scientists have taken a second look at events that seemed to confirm stereotypes based on biological sex, while also calling for more research on species and events that do not conform to the prevailing frameworks of a predominantly male-dominated discipline.

One example of a very significant influence that feminists have had on biology is the remarkable shift in the portrayal of the process of fertilization and the role that eggs and sperms play before, during, and after the moment of conception. Traditionally biology texts attributed feminine qualities to the egg, describing it as big, sluggish, and passive as it is pushed through the fallopian tube. The sperms were pictured as agile and active warriors competing with each other to penetrate the egg. Twenty years ago, Emily Martin pointed out that this scientific language used to describe the fertilization process was indeed gendered, where the sperm "propelled" itself toward and "penetrated" the egg and the egg "drifted" or was "transported" to the sperm through the fallopian tubes. This language brings to mind the countless fairy tales written about women and girls needing to be rescued by men and boys. By the end of this process of fertilization, the woman's reproductive tract was often depicted as a battlefield with millions of dead sperms and only one "fearless" sperm getting the prize.

With the influx of women into the field as well as newer discoveries, a less gender-biased view of the process of fertilization has emerged. Today scientists recognize that despite the fact that both gametes are essential for fertilization, the role that the egg plays is central to fertilization and to our understanding of developmental biology. The egg is documented to exert powerful influences in the form of biochemical secretions that prevent defective sperms from getting close to it. When a viable sperm reaches the egg, the egg secretes softening chemicals that allow the sperm to enter and deposit its DNA contents inside of the egg. In this new paradigm, the egg's genetic contribution (e.g., egg proteins, mRNA, mitochondria) is dominant over the sperm's contributions, as is evident from the size disparity between the egg and the sperm to the developing zygote.

REFERENCES

Birkhead, T. R., D. J. Hosken, and S. Pictnick. (2009). *Sperm Biology: An Evolutionary Perspective.* Oxford: Elsevier.

Gowaty, P. A. (1997). *Feminism and Evolutionary Biology: Boundaries, Intersections and Frontiers.* New York: Chapman and Hall.

Martin, Emily. "The Egg and the Sperm: How Science Has Constructed a Romance Based on Stereotypical Male-Female Roles," *Signs* 16 (1991).

C H A P T E R   I I

Becoming a Woman in Our Society

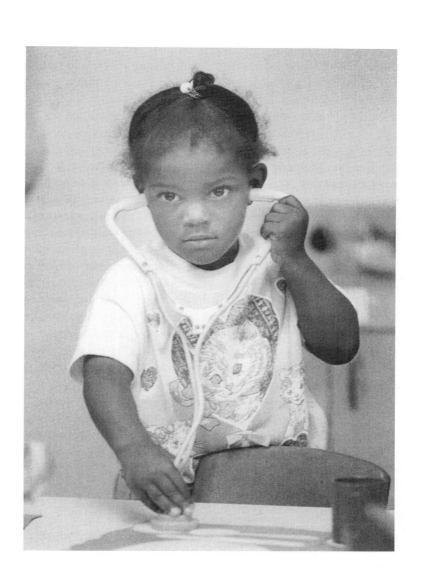

Images of women convey powerful beliefs about what is considered appropriate behavior for girls and women. Regardless of the context of these images, they tend to illustrate prevailing norms. From the adorable and delicate baby girl, to the seductively attractive young woman, such images are part and parcel of our culture's portrayal of girls and women. What does it mean to be a woman? Ideas about what it means to be a woman permeate all cultures, powerfully shaping the way that women are perceived and treated. These ideas vary from culture to culture, yet they are presented as if they were ordained by either God or nature. In this chapter we explore the notion of "femininity and masculinity" as social constructs: a prevailing set of ideas, myths, stereotypes, norms, and standards that affect the lives of all women and men in a variety of ways. In recent years, there has been an increased recognition among both feminists and biologists that sex is fluid. There are so many biological and social determinants that contribute to an individual's sex and sexuality that it is impossible to firmly classify people as completely female or male. Some biological determinants are one's sex chromosomes which can take the form of more than two possible arrangements, hormonal influences that vary from individual to individual from birth, anatomical changes and prenatal influences. Life experiences and societal expectations add to the fluidity of experienced sex and gender.

Western concepts of femininity include a combination of ideas about female good and evil that feminists have identified as the madonna/whore dichotomy. Female virtue has traditionally been presented as pure, selfless, and maternal while female evil has been presented as deceitful, dangerous, and sinful. In a society which is racist as well as sexist, it is frequently the white woman who appears as pure and selfless while women of color are seen as deviant. In the United States, ideas about femininity have been inextricably linked with ideas about race and class. In the nineteenth century, for example, urban, white, middle-class women were told it was "woman's nature" to be frail and demure while slave women worked alongside men in the fields. For these reasons, women's studies scholars often describe gender norms as racialized. Thus, we often hear of the African-American woman's "domineering" and "matriarchal" nature; the exotic, mysterious sensuality of the Asian-American woman; the Chicana as evil, sexually uncontrollable, and betrayer of her race; and the status-conscious Jewish American princess.

Although they vary among different racial and ethnic groups, these images of women reflect the negative half of the madonna/whore and good girl/bad girl stereotypes that have historically defined standards of behavior for all women. One learns very early—from peers, family, educational institutions, and the media—what are acceptable behaviors, attitudes, and values. For females, this means that from infancy on, young girls are bombarded with messages about what "good" girls do and, even more insistently, what they don't do.

Consider the many ways in which American society communicates expectations of females and males from the moment of birth. Gender markers immediately differentiate female infants from male infants: pink gowns with frills and bows convey a feminine gentleness, purity, and fragility while blue sleepers decorated with animals, trains, and sports scenes evoke strength, vigor, and activity. From the family outward to the community, children are continuously exposed to direct and indirect messages regarding appropriate behavior. For example, different household chores are typically assigned to boys and girls at home: dishwashing and housecleaning for girls, and washing cars and yard work for boys. Such divisions in responsibility reinforce the notion that the domestic world is girls' domain while the world outside the home is reserved for boys. This dichotomy further supports the idea that girls' and women's roles are primarily reserved for nurturing while boys and men are expected to exercise control and power in the outside world. Prevailing norms also influence the ways women's behavior is judged.

Women have traditionally been defined in relation to male standards and needs. Man is seen as strong, woman weak, and the resulting dichotomy perpetuates the superiority of males. A woman has historically been viewed as a man's subordinate, someone different from and inferior to him. "Masculine" traits are socially desirable and valued while "feminine" ones are not. In one of the most frequently cited studies of sexism in psychotherapy, Broverman and her colleagues asked mental health professionals to rate the behavior of a psychologically healthy woman, man, and adult.[1] The results indicated that the standard for mental health reflected attributes considered characteristic of men (e.g., independent, intelligent, aggressive) while women's mental health was described as a deviation from the male norm. The findings of this study forcefully demonstrate the pervasive use of male behavior as the norm, with "femininity" carrying negative connotations for perceptions of women. In a more recent replication of the study, the authors found that little had changed over almost three decades since the original study was published.[2]

As we explore the experience of being female, we call attention to the ways in which society has limited and trapped women through myths and stereotypes. In American culture, ideas of success are associated with male traits. Women's self-perceptions are often distorted, reflecting cultural values about women rather than realistic appraisals of women's worth. All too often, these self-images take the form of diminished notions of ability and strength and exaggerated ideas of inferiority and weakness. Ultimately, many girls and women begin to question themselves and feel powerless, whether they are in the classroom, at work, or in relationships with others. To begin to value oneself beyond these limiting expectations can be an arduous task when the majority of society's messages are undermining one's self-respect.

Stereotypes about girls and women make it easier for individuals to think they can predict behavior, allowing a quick evaluation and categorization of behavior. For example, adhering to stereotypes leads people to (erroneously) evaluate

---

[1] I. K. Broverman, D. M. Broverman, F. E. Clarkson, P. S. Rosenkrantz, and S. R. Vogel. "Sex Role Stereotypes and Clinical Judgments of Mental Health," *Journal of Consulting and Clinical Psychology* 34 (1970), pp. 1–7.

[2] Inge K. Broverman, Susan Raymond Vogel, Donald M. Broverman, Frank E. Clarkson, and Paul S. Rosenkrantz, "Sex Role Stereotypes: A Current Appraisal," in *Caring Voices and Women's Moral Frames: Gilligan's View*, ed. Bill Puka (New York: Garland, 1994).

attractive, blonde women as unintelligent. Stereotypes of women's mental capability give rise to snap judgments that women are not as qualified as men for certain positions requiring what are presumed to be masculine attributes (e.g., intelligence, decisiveness, logical reasoning skills, leadership, and financial acumen). Stereotypes are tightly woven into the social fabric of this culture and reinforce dichotomous notions of "femininity" and "masculinity."

In her classic work in psychology, Naomi Weisstein detailed the ways in which psychologists have lent a mantle of scientific "authority" to these ideas by promoting the concept of a "female essence" and ignoring the powerful influence of social context and environment on behavior.[3] Weisstein exposed the ways that scientists, rather than pursuing evidence, have created theories on the basis of the ideas of femininity they inherited from the culture. A more effective way of understanding the behavior of both women and men, she argued, would be to study the power of social expectations to influence behavior.

There are few cultural institutions and practices that do not promote and reinforce the stereotyping of women. Through language, for example, maleness is the standard (consider the terms *mankind, chairman, policeman, postman,* and so on). From subtle uses of language to more overt messages transmitted through the media, advertisements, and the classroom setting, girls are bombarded with sexist views of the world and of themselves. The dynamics of the classroom often reinforce existing power relationships between males and females. These patterns are so pervasive that we don't usually notice them. However, studies of classrooms reveal that teachers call on female students less frequently than on male students and discourage females' classroom participation, thus eroding their self-confidence. Ultimately, we see females literally tracked into "feminine" fields such as literature, art, education, and nursing and males into "masculine" fields such as science, math, and engineering.

In the second section of this chapter, selections focus on family and cultural norms, educational experiences, nonverbal communication, and the media, which have all had powerful effects on the way women and girls see themselves and their world. The lyrics of many mainstream contemporary songs, from rock to rap, as well as images in the music videos accompanying them, promote sexist notions of women that emphasize women's sexuality and subordination to men. The power of these images is so strong that girls as young as five and six who are exposed to constant messages of women's sexual objectification, often desire the "Britney Spears" or "Beyoncé" look in fashion: a look that is revealing and sexually suggestive. When girls and women are constantly exposed to messages of male superiority, they will inevitably feel powerless and insignificant. However, a growing number of contemporary young women musicians are defying these stereotypes by portraying women as strong and assertive, active and rebellious. By challenging restrictive norms and practices, these women provide more realistic and positive models of "what it means to be a woman."

---

[3]Naomi Weisstein, *Kinder, Küche, Kirche as Scientific Law: Psychology Constructs the Female; Or, the Fantasy Life of the Male Psychologist* (Cambridge, MA: New England Free Press, 1968).

Dominant Ideas About Women

Images of femininity, while powerful in our culture, vary according to class, ethnic group, and race and have been manipulated to serve the needs of those in power. Precisely because these portrayals of women interact with specific stereotypes, it is critical to examine the ways they affect the experiences of different groups of women. Betty Friedan exposed the myths and realities of the "happy middle-class housewife" of the 1960s in her book *The Feminine Mystique.* This book represented a pivotal point in the consciousness of many white middle-class women, who identified with Friedan's characterization of many women's discontent and frustration with the decorative supportive roles glorified in the popular culture of the 1950s and 1960s. Marge Piercy echoes this theme in her poem "A Work of Artifice," as she equates the fragile beauty of the bonsai tree with traditional expectations of femininity. Piercy suggests that women pay a price for complying with these social norms, as does the bonsai tree, which is artificially stunted for ornamental purposes.

Danzy Senna shares her experiences as an adolescent "growing up mixed in the racial battlefield of Boston," where she struggles to become clear about her identity and what kind of woman she wanted to be. Torn between her observation of the real-life power dynamics between men and women and her desire to conform to the racialized gender norms of popular culture, Senna shows us that young women with multiple racial and ethnic backgrounds negotiate a complex path as they consider conflicting messages of what they "should" be.

Another widely held misconception is that women with physical disabilities do not have sexual lives. Debra Kent challenges the assumption that women have to be attractive and perfect in order to be sexual. In doing so, she shows us that the struggle of women with disabilities to claim their sexual lives reflects "everyone's battle against the binding rules of conformity."

Naomi Wolf criticizes how the ritual surrounding weddings preserves traditional notions of femininity, even while increasing numbers of women see themselves as independent individuals who are not becoming their husband's property. This section concludes with three pieces that challenge the ever-present image of the sweet innocent girl who grows up and becomes the passive helpless woman. Elisa Dávila describes how she learned to be a "good girl" in a patriarchal and sexist society. Developing an understanding of the different standards imposed for men's and women's behavior, Dávila challenged them, creating a life in the United States that resonates with her own needs for self-fulfillment. However, she reminds us that regardless of where she is or what she does, she is still subject to being judged by artificial ideals of womanhood. Ana Grossman and Emma Peters-Axtell, both fourteen years old, are determined to make a difference in the world by challenging stereotypic notions about girls. In "Not a Pretty Girl," Ani DiFranco squarely defies the idea of women as decorative, fragile, and in need of rescuing.

🌿 10

The Problem That Has No Name

BETTY FRIEDAN

Gradually I came to realize that the problem that has no name was shared by countless women in America. As a magazine writer I often interviewed women about problems with their children, or their marriages, or their houses, or their communities. But after a while I began to recognize the telltale signs of this other problem. I saw the same signs in suburban ranchhouses and split-levels on Long Island and in New Jersey and Westchester County; in colonial houses in a small Massachusetts town; on patios in Memphis; in suburban and city apartments; in living rooms in the Midwest. Sometimes I sensed the problem, not as a reporter, but as a suburban housewife, for during this time I was also bringing up my own three children in Rockland County, New York. I heard echoes of the problem in college dormitories and semi-private maternity wards, at PTA meetings and luncheons of the League of Women Voters, at suburban cocktail parties, in station wagons waiting for trains, and in snatches of conversation overheard at Schrafft's. The groping words I heard from other women, on quiet afternoons when children were at school or on quiet evenings when husbands worked late, I think I understood first as a woman long before I understood their larger social and psychological implications.

Just what was this problem that has no name? What were the words women used when they tried to express it? Sometimes a woman would say "I feel empty somehow . . . incomplete." Or she would say, "I feel as if I don't exist." Sometimes she blotted out the feeling with a tranquilizer. Sometimes she thought the problem was with her husband, or her children, or that what she really needed was to redecorate her house, or move to a better neighborhood, or have an affair, or another baby. Sometimes, she went to a doctor with symptoms she could hardly describe: "A tired feeling. . . . I get so angry with the children it scares me. . . . I feel like crying without any reason." (A Cleveland doctor called it "the housewife's syndrome.") A number of women told me about great bleeding blisters that break out on their hands and arms. "I call it the housewife's blight," said a family doctor in Pennsylvania. "I see it so often lately in these young women with four, five and six children who bury themselves in their dishpans. But it isn't caused by detergent and it isn't cured by cortisone."

Sometimes a woman would tell me that the feeling gets so strong she runs out of the house and walks through the streets. Or she stays inside her house and cries. Or her children tell her a joke, and she doesn't laugh because she doesn't hear it. I talked to women who had spent years on the analyst's couch, working out their "adjustment to the feminine role," their blocks to "fulfillment as a wife and mother." But the desperate tone in these women's voices, and the look in their eyes, was the same as the tone and the look of other women, who were sure they had no problem, even though they did have a strange feeling of desperation.

A mother of four who left college at 19 to get married told me:

I've tried everything women are supposed to do—hobbies, gardening, pickling, canning, being very social with my neighbors, joining committees, running PTA teas. I can do it all, and I like it, but it doesn't leave you anything to think about—any feeling of who you are. I never had any career ambitions. All I wanted was to get married and have four children. I love the kids and Bob and my home. There's no problem you can even put a name to. But I'm desperate. I begin to feel I have no personality. I'm a server of food and putter-on of pants and a bedmaker, somebody who can be called on when you want something. But who am I?

A twenty-23-old mother in blue jeans said:

I ask myself why I'm so dissatisfied. I've got my health, fine children, a lovely new home, enough money. My husband has a real future as an electronics engineer. He doesn't have any of these feelings. He says maybe I need a vacation, let's go to

New York for a weekend. But that isn't it. I always had this idea we should do everything together. I can't sit down and read a book alone. If the children are napping and I have one hour to myself I just walk through the house waiting for them to wake up. I don't make a move until I know where the rest of the crowd is going. It's as if ever since you were a little girl, there's always been somebody or something that will take care of your life: your parents, or college, or falling in love, or having a child, or moving to a new house. Then you wake up one morning and there's nothing to look forward to.

A young wife in a Long Island development said:

> I seem to sleep so much. I don't know why I should be so tired. This house isn't nearly so hard to clean as the cold-water flat we had when I was working. The children are at school all day. It's not the work. I just don't feel alive.

In 1960, the problem that has no name burst like a boil through the image of the happy American housewife. In the television commercials the pretty housewives still beamed over their foaming dishpans and *Time*'s cover story on "The Suburban Wife, an American Phenomenon" protested: "Having too good a time . . . to believe that they should be unhappy." But the actual unhappiness of the American housewife was suddenly being reported—from the *New York Times* and *Newsweek* to *Good Housekeeping* and CBS Television ("The Trapped Housewife"), although almost everybody who talked about it found some superficial reason to dismiss it. It was attributed to incompetent appliance repairmen (*New York Times*), or the distances children must be chauffeured in the suburbs (*Time*), or too much PTA (*Redbook*). Some said it was the old problem—education: more and more women had education, which naturally made them unhappy in their role as housewives. "The road from Freud to Frigidaire, from Sophocles to Spock, has turned out to be a bumpy one," reported the *New York Times* (June 28, 1960). "Many young women—certainly not all—whose education plunged them into a world of ideas feel stifled in their homes. They find their routine lives out of joint with their training. Like shut-ins, they feel left out. In the last

year, the problem of the educated housewife has provided the meat of dozens of speeches made by troubled presidents of women's colleges who maintain, in the face of complaints, that sixteen years of academic training is realistic preparation for wifehood and motherhood."

There was much sympathy for the educated housewife. ("Like a two-headed schizophrenic . . . once she wrote a paper on the Graveyard poets; now she writes notes to the milkman. Once she determined the boiling point of sulfuric acid; now she determines her boiling point with the overdue repairman. . . . The housewife often is reduced to screams and tears. . . . No one, it seems, is appreciative, least of all herself, of the kind of person she becomes in the process of turning from poetess into shrew.")

Home economists suggested more realistic preparation for housewives, such as high-school workshops in home appliances. College educators suggested more discussion groups on home management and the family, to prepare women for the adjustment to domestic life. A spate of articles appeared in the mass magazines offering "Fifty-eight Ways to Make Your Marriage More Exciting." No month went by without a new book by a psychiatrist or sexologist offering technical advice on finding greater fulfillment through sex.

A male humorist joked in *Harper's Bazaar* (July 1960) that the problem could be solved by taking away women's right to vote. ("In the pre-19th Amendment era, the American woman was placid, sheltered and sure of her role in American society. She left all the political decisions to her husband and he, in turn, left all the family decisions to her. Today a woman has to make both the family *and* the political decisions, and it's too much for her.")

A number of educators suggested seriously that women no longer be admitted to the four-year colleges and universities: in the growing college crisis, the education which girls could not use as housewives was more urgently needed than ever by boys to do the work of the atomic age.

The problem was also dismissed with drastic solutions no one could take seriously. (A woman writer proposed in *Harper's* that women be drafted for compulsory service as nurses' aides and baby-sitters.) And it was smoothed over with the age-old panaceas: "love is their answer," "the only answer is inner help," "the secret of completeness—children," "a private means of intellectual fulfillment," "to cure this toothache of the spirit—the simple formula of handing one's self and one's will over to God."

The problem was dismissed by telling the housewife she doesn't realize how lucky she is—her own boss, no time clock, no junior executive gunning for her job. What if she isn't happy—does she think men are happy in this world? Does she really, secretly, still want to be a man? Doesn't she know yet how lucky she is to be a woman?

The problem was also, and finally, dismissed by shrugging that there are no solutions: this is what being a woman means, and what is wrong with American women that they can't accept their role gracefully? As *Newsweek* put it (March 7, 1960):

> She is dissatisfied with a lot that women of other lands can only dream of. Her discontent is deep, pervasive, and impervious to the superficial remedies which are offered at every hand. . . . An army of professional explorers have already charted the major sources of trouble. . . . From the beginning of time, the female cycle has defined and confined woman's role. As Freud was credited with saying: "Anatomy is destiny." Though no group of women has ever pushed these natural restrictions as far as the American wife, it seems that she still cannot accept them with good grace. . . . A young mother with a beautiful family, charm, talent and brains is apt to dismiss her role apologetically. "What do I do?" you hear her say. "Why nothing. I'm just a housewife." A good education, it seems, has given this paragon among women an understanding of the value of everything except her own worth. . . .

And so she must accept the fact that "American women's unhappiness is merely the most recently won of women's rights," and adjust and say with the happy housewife found by *Newsweek:* "We ought to salute the wonderful freedom we all have and be proud of our lives today. I have had college and I've worked, but being a housewife is the most rewarding and satisfying role. . . . My mother was never included in my father's business affairs . . . she couldn't get out of the house and away from us children. But I am an equal to my husband; I can go along with him on business trips and to social business affairs."

The alternative offered was a choice that few women would contemplate. In the sympathetic words of the *New York Times:* "All admit to being deeply frustrated at times by the lack of privacy, the physical burden, the routine of family life, the confinement of it. However, none would give up her home and family if she had the choice to make again." *Redbook* commented: "Few women would want to thumb their noses at husbands, children and community and go off on their own. Those who do may be talented individuals, but they rarely are successful women."

The year American women's discontent boiled over, it was also reported (*Look*) that the more than 21,000,000 American women who are single, widowed, or divorced do not cease even after 50 their frenzied, desperate search for a man. And the search begins early—for 75 percent of all American women now marry before they are 24. A pretty 25-year-old secretary took 35 different jobs in 6 months in the futile hope of finding a husband. Women are moving from one political club to another, taking evening courses in accounting or sailing, learning to play golf or ski, joining a number of churches in succession, going to bars alone, in their ceaseless search for a man.

Of the growing thousands of women currently getting private psychiatric help in the United States, the married ones were reported dissatisfied with their marriages, the unmarried ones suffering from anxiety and, finally, depression. Strangely, a number of psychiatrists stated that, in their experience, unmarried women patients were happier than married ones. So the door of all those pretty suburban houses opened a crack to permit a glimpse of uncounted thousands of American housewives who suffered alone from a problem that suddenly everyone was talking about, and beginning to take for granted, as one of those unreal problems in American life that can never be solved—like the hydrogen bomb. By 1962 the plight of the trapped American housewife had become a national parlor game. Whole issues of magazines, newspaper columns, books learned and frivolous, educational conferences, and television panels were devoted to the problem.

Even so, most men, and some women, still did not know that this problem was real. But those who had faced it honestly knew that all the superficial remedies, the sympathetic advice, the scolding words and the cheering words were somehow drowning the problem in unreality. A bitter laugh was beginning to be heard from American women. They were admired, envied, pitied, theorized over until they were sick of it, offered drastic solutions or silly choices that no one could take seriously. They got all kinds of advice from the growing armies of marriage and child-guidance counselors, psychotherapists, and armchair psychologists, on how to adjust to their role as housewives. No other road to fulfillment was offered to American women in the middle of the twentieth century. Most adjusted to their role and suffered or ignored the problem that has no name. It can be less painful, for a woman, not to hear the strange, dissatisfied voice stirring within her.   [1964]

11
A Work of Artifice

MARGE PIERCY

The bonsai tree
in the attractive pot
could have grown eighty feet tall
on the side of a mountain
till split by lightning.
But a gardener
carefully pruned it.
It is nine inches high.
Every day as he
whittles back the branches
the gardener croons,

It is your nature
to be small and cozy,
domestic and weak;
how lucky, little tree,
to have a pot to grow in.
With living creatures
one must begin very early
to dwarf their growth:
the bound feet,
the crippled brain,
the hair in curlers,
the hands you
love to touch.   [1973]

12
To Be Real

DANZY SENNA

Growing up mixed in the racial battlefield of Boston, I yearned for something just out of my reach—an "authentic" identity to make me real. Everyone but me, it seemed at the time, fit into a neat cultural box, had a label to call their own. Being the daughter of both feminist and integrationist movements, a white socialist mother and a black intellectual father, it seemed that everyone and everything had come together for my conception, only to break apart in time for my birth. I was left with only questions. To Be or Not to Be: black, Negro, African-American, feminist, femme, mulatto, quadroon, lesbian, straight, bisexual, lipstick, butch bottom, femme top, vegetarian, carnivore? These potential identities led me into the maze of American identity politics, and hopefully out the other side.

When I was 11 years old, an awkward child with knobby knees and a perpetually flat chest, I was preoccupied with questions of womanhood and what kind of woman I would become. Even then, I was aware of two kinds of power I could access as a female. There was the kind of power women got from being sexually desired, and the kind women got from being sexually invisible—that is, the power in attracting men and the power in being free of men. I also noticed that women fought one another for the first kind and came together for the second. Even as a child, I knew people craved power. I just wasn't sure which kind I wanted.

I liked the power of looking pretty, but wasn't certain men were worth attracting. I didn't like the effect they had on the women around me. Like most of my friends, I lived in a female-headed household. My mother raised us with the help of other women, a series of sidekick moms who moved in and out of our lives. In the evenings, we all converged in the kitchen, an orange-painted room on the second floor of our house. In the kitchen, laughter, food, and talk formed a safe space of women and children. On those occasions when men did enter the picture—for dinner parties or coffee—the fun of wild, unabashed laughter and fluid gossip seemed to float out the window. In walked huge, serious, booming creatures who quickly became the focus of attention. The energy of the room shifted from the finely choreographed dance of womentalk, where everyone participated in but no one dominated the conversation, to a room made up of margins and centers. The relative kindness of men didn't change the dynamic of their presence. From my perspective, it appeared that they immediately became the center of the kitchen, while the women were transformed into fluttering, doting frames around them. The women who had a moment before seemed strong, impenetrable heroines, became, in the presence of men, soft and powerless girls.

My confusion about which kind of power I wanted to have—which kind of woman I wanted to be—is reflected in a diary entry from that year. In round, flowery script I wrote vows. "Always wear lipstick. Never get married." The prospect of being able to turn heads, to be asked out on dates—to be desired—was an aspect of my impending adolescence which looked thrilling. Lipstick became the symbol of this power in my mind. At the same time, I noticed that once Lipstick Women had attracted men, often they became old and beaten, pathetic, desperate creatures, while the men remained virile and energized. At 10, I hoped there was a space in between the two extremes—a place where I could

have both kinds of power—a place where I could wear lipstick and still be free.

My mother and her friends seemed to have settled for only one of these forms of power—the power of feminism—and their brazen rejection of the "lipstick world" insulted and embarrassed my burgeoning adolescent consciousness. I remember one dusky evening in particular, when a group of women from the local food cooperative came banging on our door. They wanted my mother's support in a march protesting violence against women. She liked these tough, working-class women and what they stood for, so while other mothers called their kids into dinner, ours dragged us into the streets. My sister, brother, and I were mortified as we ran alongside the march, giggling and pointing at the marching women chanting "Women Unite— Take Back the Night!" The throngs were letting it all hang out: their breasts hung low, their leg hair grew wild, their thighs were wide in their faded blue jeans. Some of them donned Earth shoes and T-shirts with slogans like "A Woman Needs a Man Like a Fish Needs a Bicycle." They weren't in the least bit ashamed. But I was. I remember thinking, "I will never let myself look like that."

Shortly after the march, I began to tease my mother. "Why can't you be a *real* mother?" I asked. It became a running joke between us. She'd say, "Look, a real mother!" pointing at prim women in matching clothes and frosted lipstick at the shopping mall. We'd laugh together, but there was a serious side to it all. I wanted my sixties mother to grow up, to stop protesting and acting out—to be "normal." I loved her, but at the same time craved conformity. In my mind, real mothers wore crisp floral dresses and diamond engagement rings; my mother wore blue jeans and a Russian wedding ring given to her from a high-school boyfriend. (She had lost the ring my father gave to her.) Real mothers got married in white frills before a church; my mother wed my father in a silver lamé mini-dress which she later donated to us kids for Barbie doll clothes. Real mothers painted their nails and colored their hair; my mother used henna. And while real mothers polished the house with lemon-scented Pledge, our house had dog hair stuck to everything.

My mother scolded me, saying I wanted her to be more "bourgeois." Bourgeois or not, to me, *real* equaled what I saw on television and in the movies, whether it was the sensible blond Carol Brady or the Stephen Spielberg suburban landscape—a world so utterly normal that the surreal could occur within it. At night, visions of white picket fences and mothers in housedresses danced in my head. I dreamed of station wagons, golden retrievers, and brief case-toting fathers who came home at five o'clock to the smell of meat loaf wafting from the kitchen. But *real* was something I could never achieve with my white socialist mother, my black intellectual father who visited on Sundays, and our spotted mongrel from the dog pound, because most of all, real was a white girl—and that was something I could never, ever be.

I was 14 when I first sat perched on a kitchen stool and allowed a friend to put an iron to my head—a curling iron, that is. She wasn't pressing my hair straight. Just the opposite. She was trying to give my straight, chestnut-brown hair some curl, and I wasn't taking no for an answer. So far, I had been mistaken for almost everything—Italian, Greek, Jewish, Pakistani—but never for black. My features and hair brought me forever short of Negritude. In a 1980s twist on the classic tragic mulatta, I was determined to pass as black. And if that wasn't possible, at least with my hair-sprayed "crunchy curls" I could pass as Puerto Rican. I remember lying in bed at night and smelling Spanish cooking from the apartment downstairs; I would close my eyes and fantasize that I was actually Puerto Rican, that everything else had been just a bad dream, that my name was Yolanda Rivera, and that I lived in the barrio.

I had dropped my quest for a "real mother" and yearned for something within my reach: a real ethnicity, something other than the half-caste purgatory to which I had been condemned. Now I yearned for Blackness, which, like femininity, was defined by the visible signifiers of the times. In my father's era, these had been a daishiki, an Afro, a fisted pik. No longer. This was still Boston in the 1980s and to be authentically black meant something quite different. Now you had to wear processed hair and Puma sneakers. I remember gazing at my best friend's straightened black hair, at the sheen of the chemicals and the way it never moved, and thinking it was the most beautiful hair I had ever seen. I believed the answer to that ubiquitous question "How can I be down?" lay in cultural artifacts: a Louis Vuitton purse, a Kangol, a stolen Ralph Lauren parka.

On my first day of high school, I went decked out in two-toned jeans, Adidas sneakers, and a red bomber with a fur-lined collar. My hair was frozen in hard curls all over my head and I wore frosty pink lipstick. I snapped my bubblegum and trailed after my sister. She is a year older than me and like most firstborn children, had inherited what I saw as the riches: kinky hair and visible blackness. We sauntered into the cafeteria where everyone hung out before class began. Doug E. Fresh beats boomed from someone's radio. Old friends greeted my sister with hugs; she introduced me and, to my relief, everyone smiled and commented on how much we looked alike. A dark-skinned boy with a shaved-bald head asked my sister where she had been hiding me, and I blushed and glanced away from his steady brown-eyed stare. There, across the cafeteria, my gaze fell on a girl, and we stared at each other with that intensity that could only mean love or hate.

She looked a little like me, but right away I knew she was more authentic than I would ever be. With an olive complexion, loose dark curls, and sad brown eyes, she sat in a cluster of pretty brown-skinned girls. She was smoking and squinting at me from across the hazy cafeteria.

I whispered to my sister: "Who's that girl?"

"That's Sophia."

Sophia whispered something just then to the girls at her table and they giggled. My cheeks began to burn.

I nudged my sister. "Why's she staring at me?"

"Cause David, her boyfriend, has been eyeing you ever since you came in here."

The bald-headed boy—David—winked at me when our eyes met and I heard my sister's voice beside me warn: "Just keep your distance and it'll be okay."

It wasn't. As the year progressed, the tension between me and Sophia escalated. It was as if we took one look at each other and said, "There ain't room in this school for both of us." From her point of view, I threatened her position not only with David, who had a fetish for light-almost-white girls, but also her position in the school. She, like me, had gotten used to her role as "the only one." Her "whiteness" had brought her status within the black world, and she didn't want that threatened by anyone, and certainly not by me with my crunchy-curls.

In a strange way I idolized Sophia, though I would have never admitted it at the time. To me, she was a role model, something to aspire to. She represented what I had spent my whole life searching for: she was the genuine article. While I lived with my white mother in a rambling brown-shingled house, Sophia lived with her black mother in an inner-city townhouse. While my curls were painstakingly acquired, Sophia's were natural. While I was soft, Sophia was hard core. And of course, while I was the tragedy trying to walk-the-walk and talk-the-talk, Sophia didn't need to try.

David became our battleground. I told my friends and family that I was in love with him and that I despised Sophia. The truth is that Sophia was the real object of my desire. I wanted to be her. But it was just dawning on me that certain things could not be manufactured. By curling my hair, wearing heavy gold hoop earrings, and a bomber jacket, I could not re-create her experience. My imitation of her life could only go skin deep. So my desire for her was transformed into an obsessive envy. If I couldn't be her, I would beat her.

One day I discovered obscenities about me splattered on the girls' room wall—just the regular catty slander, nothing too creative, saying I was a bitch and a ho. But there was a particular violence to the way it had been written, in thick red marker around the bathroom mirrors. In tears, I went to find my big sister. Always my protector, she dragged me to the girls' room after lunch period to set things straight with Sophia once and for all. We found her in there with her girls, skipping class and preening in front of a mirror.

Sister: "Did you write this about my sister?"

Sophia: "She been trying to get with my man all year. That bitch had it comin' to her."

Sister: "I asked you a question. Did you write this about my sister?"

Sophia: "Yeah, I did. And what are you gonna do about it?"

Soon, in the bright spring sunshine, my sister and Sophia came to blows while I stood on the sidelines with the rest of the black population of our school. I had been warned by Sophia's rather hefty cousin that if I jumped in the fight, she would whip my ass. I didn't jump in. And after all was said and done, my sister ended up with a broken nose, Sophia with two black eyes and a scratched up face. The war was over and I got out without a scar. My sister had protected me, and I knew I was a coward, a fake. And as I sat holding my sister's hand in the hospital waiting room, I knew it wasn't blackness I had failed in. It was sisterhood.   [1995]

 13

In Search of Liberation

DEBRA KENT

When I joined a women's consciousness-raising group a few years ago, I'm not quite sure what I expected—to discover some bond of understanding with other women, perhaps, to feel myself part of the growing sisterhood of the liberation movement. But through session after session, I listened in amazement and awe as the others delivered outraged accounts of their exploitation at the hands of bosses, boyfriends, and passersby. They were tired of being regarded as sex objects by male chauvinist pigs. All their lives, they lamented, they had been programmed for the confining roles of wife and mother, roles in which their own needs were submerged by those of the men they served.

I had to admit that their indignation was justified. But it was impossible for me to confess my own reaction to their tales of horror, which was a very real sense of envy. Society had provided a

JAP: The New Anti-Semitic Code Word

FRANCINE KLAGSBRUN

Isn't it odd that the term *JAP*, referring to a spoiled, self-indulgent woman, should be so widely used at a time when women are working outside their homes in unprecedented numbers, struggling to balance their home lives and their work lives to give as much of themselves as they can to everybody—their husbands, their kids, their bosses?

Jewish women, like women throughout society, are trying to find their own paths, their own voices. And, along with other changes that have taken place, they have been finding themselves Jewishly. And yet we hear the term *JAP* being used, perhaps almost more now than ever before. Why?

The new-found, or rather newly-accepted, drive of women for achievement in many arenas threatens many men. What better put-down of the strong woman than to label her a "Princess"? She is not being attacked as a competitor—that would be too close to home. No—she's called a princess, and that label diminishes her, negating her ambition and her success.

One may note, and rightly so, that there *are* materialistic Jewish women—and men too. But are Jews the only people guilty of excesses in spending? Why should the word "Jewish" be used pejoratively to describe behavior we don't approve of?

I think the answer is that there is an underlying anti-Semitic message in that label. Loudness is somehow "Jewish." Vulgarity is somehow "Jewish." All the old stereotypes of Jews come into play in the use of the term *JAP*. In this day, polite Christian society would not *openly* make anti-Jewish slurs. But *JAP* is O.K. *JAP* is a kind of code word. It's a way of symbolically winking, poking with an elbow, and saying, "well you know how Jews are—so materialistic and pushy."

What is interesting is that this code word can be used in connection with *women*—the Jewish American *Princess*—and nobody protests its intrinsic anti-Semitism.   [1980]

place for them as women, however restricting that place might be, and they knew it.

Totally blind since birth, I was seldom encouraged to say, "When I grow up I'll get married and have babies." Instead, my intellectual growth was nurtured. I very definitely received the unspoken message that I would need the independence of a profession, as I could not count on having the support of a husband.

For myself and for other disabled women, sex discrimination is a secondary issue—in life and in the job market. To the prospective employer, a visible handicap may immediately connote incompetence, and whether the applicant is male or female may never come under consideration at all. In fact,

the connotations that disability holds for the public seem, in many ways, to negate sexuality altogether. In a culture where men are expected to demonstrate strength and dominance, the disabled man is regarded as weak and ineffectual. But in social situations he may have an advantage over the disabled woman.

Our culture allows the man to be the aggressor. If he can bolster himself against the fear of rejection, he can make overtures toward starting a relationship. At least he doesn't have to sit home waiting for the telephone to ring.

According to the stereotype, women are helpless creatures to be cuddled and protected. The disabled woman, however, is often merely seen as helpless. A man may fear that she will be so oppressively dependent upon him that a relationship with her may strike him as a terrifying prospect. To prove him wrong she may strive for self-sufficiency, only to have him say that she's too aggressive and unfeminine.

People may pity the disabled woman for her handicap, or admire her for her strength in overcoming it, but she is too unlike other females to be whistled at on the street. Somehow she is perceived as a nonsexual being. If men don't make passes at girls who wear glasses, what chance does a blind girl have, or one in a wheelchair, or a woman with spastic hands?

American culture still pictures the ideal woman: slender, blonde, blue-eyed, and physically perfect. Of course, there is plenty of leeway, and not every man is worried about these cultural stereotypes when choosing a mate. But as long as a woman remains a status symbol to the man who "possesses" her, the living proof of his prowess, the woman with a disability will be at a severe disadvantage. The man who is not completely secure will be afraid to show her off with pride because she is too different.

The worst period for most disabled men and women is probably adolescence, when conformity to the group's norms is all-important. Then, even being overweight or having a bad case if acne is enough to brand one as a pariah. Things may become easier later on, as emphasis on outward appearances gradually yields to concern with qualities as well. But it is hard to shake off the sense of being an outcast.

Even when she establishes a healthy relationship with a man, the disabled woman may sometimes find herself wondering, "Why does he want me unless there is something wrong with him? If someone else comes along, won't he leave me for her?"

But why, I ask myself, should it ever make a difference to society whether people with disabilities are ever accepted intact—as human beings with minds, feelings, and sexuality? Though we have become more vocal in recent years, we still constitute a very small minority.

Yet the Beautiful People—the slender, fair, and perfect ones—form a minority that may be even smaller. Between these two groups are the average, ordinary citizens: Men who are too short, women who are too tall, people who are too fat or too thin, people with big noses, protruding ears, receding hairlines, and bad complexions. Millions of people go through life feeling self-conscious or downright inadequate, fearing that others will reject them for these physical flaws. Perhaps the struggle of disabled people is really everyone's battle against the binding rules of conformity, the struggle for the right to be an individual.

As I sat in that consciousness-raising group, I realized that disabled women have a long and arduous fight ahead. Somehow we must learn to perceive ourselves as attractive and desirable. Our struggle is not unlike the striving for self-acceptance of the millions of nonhandicapped who also fall short of the Beautiful People image.

Our liberation will be a victory for everyone.

[1987]

14

Brideland

NAOMI WOLF

Brideland exists primarily in the bridal magazines, which conjure up a fantastic, anachronistic world that really exists nowhere beyond itself. It is a nineteenth-century world, in which major late-twentieth-century events, like the sexual revolution and the rise of the financially self-supporting woman, seem to have transpired only glancingly, to be swept away by a dimity flounce like so much unsightly grit. It is a theme park of upward mobility; in Brideland, in the events surrounding The Event, everyone is temporarily upper middle class: everyone routinely throws catered events and hires musicians and sends engraved invitations and keeps carriages or vintage cars awaiting. At the ceremony itself, things become downright feudal: the bride is treated like a very queen with her court of "maids." She has, perhaps, a child to lift her train, a child to bear her ring, and a sparkling tiara upon her hair. Cinderella is revealed in her true aristocratic radiance at last, and, in the magazines, she is perpetually arriving at the ball.

Brideland has very little to do with the relationship or even the marriage: it is, like any theme park, eternally transient: you enter, you are transformed completely, and then, presumably, you depart. It is a world of lush feminine fantasy, eerily devoid of men, who appear, if at all, as shadow figures retrieving luggage or kneeling before the bride in a state of speechless awe. Brideland has an awful lot to say about what women want that they are not getting, and it taught me a thing or two about myself.

My own initiation was abrupt. Shortly after we made our announcement, I picked up one of those magazines, mostly to find out what the rules were that I was bound to be breaking. As I turned page after page, I started to change. Long-buried yearnings surfaced, a reminder, which little else gives me, that until I was six, I inhabited a world unchanged by the 1970's women's movement. Somehow, I had picked up atavistic feelings about The Bride that I would never have recognized in my conscious, feminist, and more skeptical mind.

By page 16 my capacity for irony was totally paralyzed. I tried hard to activate it but, as in a dream, I was powerless; it wouldn't budge. By page 32 I was hypnotized; by the time I reached the end, the honeymoon section—for the magazines are structured chronologically, as if they want to be sure you know what comes first—I had acquired new needs; blind, overwhelming, undeniable needs. The fantasies I had put away in 1966 with Bridal Barbie resurfaced with a vengeance. I needed . . . garters! And engraved stationery—engraved, not printed! And fetching little lace mitts; and a bouquet that trailed sprays of stephanotis! And heavens, maybe a veil or mantilla of some kind—down my back, of course, not over my face—would not be as unthinkable as I had thought.

You must understand: this is coming from a woman who had viewed all traditional wedding appurtenances as if they represented death by cuteness. While I am the product of an egalitarian marriage, and fervently believe in the possible goodness of life partnership, I have had such a strong resistance to all things matrimonial that when I pass Tiffany's I break out in a cold sweat. I could imagine eloping; or a civil ceremony; or even an alternative ceremony, so creatively subversive that it would be virtually unrecognizable for what it is. But not—never—a wedding.

Part of my aversion comes from my ambivalence, not about the man—about whom I have no doubts—but about the institution. How can I justify sealing such a private, precious relationship with a legal bond that lets a man rape his wife in 14 states? How can I endorse an institution that, in the not-too-distant past, essentially conveyed the woman over to her husband as property, denying her even the right to her own property? How can I support a system that allows me to flaunt my heterosexual relationship brazenly, but forbids deeply committed gay and lesbian friends of mine to declare their bonds in the same way? How can I ask my love to be sanctioned by a legal order that leaves divorcing women to struggle in a desperately unevenly matched battle in sexist courts for money and custody of children? And, less profoundly, but no less urgently, if I were to do it, what on earth would I wear?

Brideland lulls the reader into a haze of romantic acquisitiveness that leaves most such political considerations firmly outside the threshold. The magazines' articles about the origins of different rituals leave no doubt as to the naked patriarchalism of the ceremony's origins. Bridesmaids were originally dressed similarly to the bride so as to confuse marauders who would wish to abduct the woman. Groomsmen were warriors whose role was to help the bridegroom fight off the would-be kidnapers. The cedar chest and mother-of-the-bride embroidered handkerchiefs—even the beading and faux-pearling and glitter down the bodices of many dresses—are all vestigial reminders that brides and their trousseaus were essentially chattel to be bartered, bearing a specific value. Even the word *honeymoon* derives from the Old English custom of sending the couple off for a month to drink honeyed ale, as a way to relax sexual inhibitions and, presumably, ease the anxieties of virginal teenage brides who most likely had had little contact with their mates, and whose attraction to them was generally considered an irrelevance. But in the glossy pages, these fairly unnerving details fade into quaintness.

The centerpiece of Brideland is, of course, the dress, and it is this that has elicited my deepest buried fantasies. For a reason that for a long time was mysterious, I felt that I had to, but absolutely had to, create a wedding dress that had an eighteenth-century bodice, three-quarter-length sleeves, and an ankle-length skirt with voluminous panniers. I have since homed in on the trace-memory, and realize that the transcendentally important look of my dress on the critical day was predetermined by a drawing of a milkmaid in the A. A. Milne (creator of Pooh) children's book, *Now We Are Six*.   [1995]

🌿 15

On Being a "Good Girl": Implications for Latinas in the United States

ELISA DÁVILA

I am an immigrant Latina. My gender, my ethnicity, and my status as an "émigré," shape and define my life and the work I do. I was born in Colombia, a beautiful but violent country. The early years of my life were marked by the horrors of civil war.[1] I grew up not only witnessing the desolation left by civil war but also experiencing the inner devastation forced upon women by the socially constructed demands of *good-girlism*.[2] As a woman, I have had a major struggle to overcome the senseless impositions of a patriarchal and sexist society, which has established different standards of behavior for men and women. This is particularly relevant for Latina women living in a *machista* society and having to conform to the dictates of *marianismo*.

The origins and ideology of *marianismo* and how it affects women were first discussed by Evelyn Stevens in 1973. In the essay "Marianismo: The Other Face of Machismo in Latin America," she writes:

> Latin American mestizo cultures—from the Rio Grande to the Tierra del Fuego—exhibit a well-defined pattern of beliefs and behavior centered on popular acceptance of a stereotype of the ideal woman. This stereotype, like its *macho* counterpart, is ubiquitous in every social class. There is near universal agreement on what a "real woman" is like and how she should act. Among the characteristics of this ideal are semidivinity, moral superiority, and spiritual strength. This spiritual strength engenders abnegation, that is, an infinite capacity for humility and sacrifice. No self-denial is too great for the Latin American woman, no limit can be divined to her vast store of patience with the men of her world. Although she may be sharp with her daughters—and even cruel to her daughter-in-law—she is and must be complaisant toward her own mother and her mother-in-law for they, too, are reincarnations of the great mother. She is also submissive to the demands of the men: husbands, sons, fathers, brothers.[3]

As a young woman, I realized that I did not like being what was considered a *good girl* in my culture. I was aware of the different treatment given to the males in the family (brothers, cousins, friends). While men were allowed the freedom to go alone into town, to stay up late, to party all night long, and particularly to wait around to be served by the women around them, my sisters and I were held to different standards.

Being a *good girl* meant denying big chunks of myself such as the freedom to choose a career over a husband, to work and live away from home, or the basic right to know my feelings and to experience my own body. In a patriarchal society like Colombia's, a woman is expected to conform to a set of rules that dictate the manner by which she can act, dress, talk, have sex, even think. A woman is supposed to accept domesticity and motherhood as the two guiding forces of her life.

> Home. Family. Honor. These are the guiding principles of female-male relations that have remained constant from 1492 to the present. The typical Latin American family is portrayed as patriarchal

in structure with an authoritarian male head, bilateral kinship, and a submissive mother and wife concerned with the domestic sphere.[4]

To survive under *good-girlism,* a woman undergoes a major displacement or disconnection inside her own self. Caught between the expectations of family and community and her individual needs and desires, a Latina is at war with herself. The rewards given to her by society for conforming—protection, security, relationships, alliances, and all the other status-related goods and benefits of a good woman—do not serve to end the war. For in the long process of adjustment to the imperatives of *machismo* and *marianismo,* a woman suffers from emotional alienation from her own feelings, physical and aesthetic estrangement from her body, social isolation, betrayal of her own gender, and silencing of her own voice.

As an adolescent, I also realized that in order to be other than the ideal subservient, suffering, and chaste woman, destined for motherhood and domesticity, I had to be different from the women in my family, from the women in the large household where I grew up, and from the women around me at school, at church, in the neighborhood. It was a painful realization, for I had to reconcile the expectations of my family and community that were at odds with my own inner imperatives.

It is in the process of reconciling these contradictory messages that a Latina may find the roots of her inner strength and the driving impetus for change. I did not come to these realizations alone or in a vacuum, nor did I arrive at the place where I am now without the example and encouragement of other women, many of them ignored by the recorders of history. Since the early days of European colonization, women's presence in the larger social structure and their universe have been ignored. Historians have traditionally excluded such experience from their writings, except for some notable examples (mostly notorious ones), such as queens, courtesans, mistresses, and nuns. The norm has been to ignore women (women as absence) or to portray them as obstacle, as the other, as atavism, or as foible.

In my own life, I have been inspired by teachers, union organizers, women fighting for human rights in Argentina, Chile, Guatemala, El Salvador, and immigrant women working in sweat shops and maquiladoras in New York City and the Mexican-American border to understand their strength and to emulate their courage to change. These women have some character traits in common: they all have aspired to be *other than* the externally imposed cultural model of the *good woman,* and they do it with unabashed dignity and great courage.

To become *other than,* which means, unlike many of the women in my household, or in my neighborhood, or in my school, I had to cross many borders: educational, sexual, national, linguistic, cultural. With each crossing, I was breaking familiar, many times, psychological bonds that tethered me to the extended family structure and the community.

After crossing national and linguistic borders and immigrating to the United States, I began living away from the expectations and demands of the family core and the extended family of friends and acquaintances. I entered the realm of being the *alien/other.* A major displacement took place. In a *machista* society, like Colombia where I was born and raised, a woman is the *other* in terms of intergender and class relations. As the *other* she is the object of sexual and sexist oppression and dominance on the part of the males of the society, condoned, of course, by the *marianista* female culture. But, as a Latina immigrant in the United States, one becomes the *other* in terms of ethnic and linguistic categorizations. Also, within the prejudicial male chauvinism of Anglo culture, a Latina becomes either a desirable *other,* objectified and used as a sensuous and passionate being, or an undesirable "illegal" with no rights.[5]

Married to an Anglo man who brought into my life a new set of expectations and ideas of the concept of a "good American wife" and striving to acculturate and function in the new environment, I began to feel at the margins of society, and on the edge of disintegration. With my hyphenated name that caused a severe rift with my mother-in-law, I became no more than a hyphen to the new family.[6] This *otherness* made me long for what I had left behind. In this new environment, lacking recognition from the family I had married into and not quite understanding its cultural norms and social transactions, I began to idealize my past and my background (family, traditions, friends, etc.). I needed my "cultural security blanket."

Patriarchy offers some rewards to the women who conform. Among others, there is social recognition, stability, financial security, and "machista gallantry." There is some attraction to the discourse of family unity and support, motherhood and domestic security. Being a *good girl* seemed attractive to the lonely, newly married woman walking the empty streets of a suburban American neighborhood. Homesickness and silence fueled the desire to return, to give up, to find refuge under the normative system of male oppression and Catholic patriarchy I had left. After all, cultural and familiar oppression and gallant machismo seemed better than the cultural exile I was experiencing in the new country.

To survive, I plunged into working and learning English, as well as the language of acculturation. Alongside my new skills came a divorce, different jobs, other lovers, and a new identity. One family rejected me, the other wanted me to go back to Colombia and be protected by the extended family. I refused to go back with the excuse of finishing my Ph.D., which I could not have done in Colombia. But guilt and solitude made me doubt my decision to stay in the United States. Was I becoming a *bad girl?*

In the eyes of the society where I grew up, I am successful and, perhaps, secretly admired. But I am also the object of pity and compassion for being a failure as a woman, for not having procreated, and particularly for not having a male at my side. When I travel home or to other Latin American countries, invariably men and women ask me not about my work, or the articles and poems I write, but about husband and children. My responses usually elicit some pitiful comments by women that go more or less like the following:

• "Y no te sientes solita, mi hijita?" (And, don't you feel very alone, my child?)
• "Y dónde está tu familia?" (And where is your family?)

• "Pero, de verdad, no piensas volver donde tu familia?" (But, tell me the truth, don't you want to go back to your family?)
• "Si, mi hija, está bien estudiar, pero también hay que hacer la casa." (Yes, my dearest, it is good to study, but it is also important to make a home.)
• "Y, eso del Ph.D., te va a cuidar cuando estés viejita?" (And that thing called the Ph.D., is it going to take care of you when you are old?)

Men's responses can be very aggressive because either they interpret my divorced status as an invitation to sexual advances or they feel some unstated discomfort about my sexuality that does not include them.

No matter how far I have traveled, the powerful ideological force of sexism that determines the behavior of men and women, and the ways in which girls are raised, or the manner in which women are expected to act, dress, talk, have sex, continues to haunt me. The basic and culturally constructed definers of the female condition are still the parameters by which I am judged and accepted.   [2011]

NOTES

1. Colombia's history, like that of so many Latin American countries, can be described as a relentless unsuccessful attempt to define and practice democracy. For almost two decades, beginning in the mid-1940s, the traditional conservative forces, supported by the Catholic church and the military, unleashed a bloody period of civil strife in Colombia. Liberal forces made up primarily of intellectuals, union workers, students, poor farm laborers, and the disenfranchised masses of urban centers fought against the military and the police. As in the case of the Mexican Revolution of 1910, the Bolivian and Guatemalan Revolutions of the 1950s, and many other revolutionary movements in Latin America, a popular uprising with political overtones and civil rights goals resulted in indiscriminate killing and devastation. A military coup and dictatorship ended the civil war, but not the abuse of the poor by the rich or the poverty and illiteracy of the masses. The dream of equality and freedom was crushed.

2. In 1995, for about eight months, a group of college professors at SUNY–New Paltz (Drs. Sue Books, Ann V. Dean, and Elaine Kolitch), a pastoral counselor (Rev. Kathy Brady), and I worked on trying to understand what it meant to be a *good girl* in different cultures. We presented a panel discussion on this topic at the April 1996 American Educational Research Association (AERA) Conference in New York, "A Cross-Cultural Autobiographical Excavation of *Good-Girlism*." The following was the group's definition of *good-girlism*. *Good-girlism* ". . . is a powerful ideology, often invisible to

us in our everyday practices and relations, that can be used to monitor female identity in private and public spheres . . . is a historical, cross-cultural phenomenon, constantly reified by institutions (family, school, church, state, etc.) that benefit from having oppressed members . . . thrives in discursive practices that mediate moral selfhood . . . is bred and nurtured in the moral /emotional tyranny that threatens to render us illegitimate should we opt out of the unspoken agreement: protect me and I will legitimate/love/protect you."

3. Evelyn P. Stevens. "Marianismo: The Other Face of Machismo in Latin America," in *Female and Male in Latin America*, ed. Ann Pescatello (Pittsburgh: University of Pittsburgh Press, 1973).
4. Gertrude Yeager. "Introduction," in Pescatello, *Female and Male in Latin America*, p. xi.
5. I recommend the film *Carmen Miranda: Bananas Is My Business* by Helena Solberg (New York: Noon Pictures, 1994) to understand some of the issues of exploitation, discrimination, and stereotyping of Latin American women in the United States.
6. My former mother-in-law could never understand why I did not want to be just Mrs. Smith and preferred to be called Mrs. Dávila-Smith.

🌿 16

Girls: "We Are the Ones Who Can Make a Change!"

ANA GROSSMAN and
EMMA PETERS-AXTELL

What is the girls' movement? Well, we're girls. But we—and most other girls—don't talk about a "Girls' Movement." We just think life should be fair, and things should be equal between girls and guys. And we still have a long way to go to reach that goal.

So, who are we? And who are we to tell you what the Girls' Movement is to girls? We're Ana and Emma; we're both 14 years old as we write this; and we've been friends since—forever! We're also both editors for *New Moon: The Magazine for Girls and Their Dreams*. That means we hear from a lot of girls. We hear about what girls are doing and thinking. We hear girls' opinions on what they find unfair, and on what they do to change things in their daily life.

We don't actually *call* ourselves "The Girls' Movement," because we just don't feel there is a

large organized girls' movement going on, like there is with adult feminism. Also, even though we know there's a long way to go, we feel we've already come a long way, *because* of feminism. Compared to how things were thirty years ago, we feel very lucky to be girls *now*.

We define feminism in terms of our everyday actions: how we react to unfair situations and what we do to change them.

Here are a few stories from girls we are in touch with. These stories show why we still need feminism and how it helps us.

- *"I love sports and play baseball, but since I'm a girl, I always play outfield. I'm pretty good. There are a lot of other girls who play outfield, too. But the boys play infield—where the ball goes."—Kay, from Brussels, Belgium.*

Sports is one area where things have really gotten better for girls (because of Title IX). But there's still unfairness.[1] Last year, Emma's soccer team was discriminated against because they're girls. Her school has one good playing field and the girls weren't allowed to scrimmage there—while boys' teams *were* allowed. The female coach didn't fight the decision because she was worried about retaliation later from the Director of Athletics. Even though we were inspired by our country's huge excitement about the U.S. Women's Soccer Team triumphs in 2000, when it comes closer to home, we're still struggling.

- *"I think things are pretty equal right now, but some aspects of equality need work."—Olya, 14, from Duluth, Minnesota.*

One thing that is still unequal is how people think about "women's jobs" and "men's jobs." Ana's goal is to be a lawyer and one day run for president of the United States. Right now there really are too few women leaders in politics.[2] But when Ana tells people her goals, they sort of laugh and say "Ohhhh . . ." But in their voices it sounds like they are really saying, "She's just a kid, and she doesn't know what she wants, and that goal is *way* too high." In fact, Ana has thought a lot about the process of getting there (lawyer and later president) and she knows what it involves to reach the goal.

Also, many people automatically assume that she wants to be the *first* woman president—which she doesn't. She says, "It will be twenty-three years before it is even *possible* for me to run for president, and that is *way* too long for this country to wait for a woman president!!!"

• *"Recently, a girl in my class was assaulted. She didn't want the adults to find out. But I told a teacher and he got her some help from the school nurse."*— *Molly, 13, from Compton, Rhode Island.*

It's terrible that many girls experience harassment, assault, or date rape.[3] But we can help each other deal with these things. A friend of Emma's was being verbally harassed at school. The things that were said to her made her suffer a great deal. She became self-conscious and withdrawn. But her friends helped her, and with their extra encouragement she felt courageous enough to take the problem to the principal.

• *"I wish the media would realize that girls should be recognized for being talented and healthy-looking."*—*Justine, 12, from Chicago, Illinois.*

Media image—that's a *huge* issue for girls.[4] When we see unrealistic, "perfect" images over and over, telling us that looking *that* way will make us popular, we start to think those images are the "right" ones. And if that isn't enough, the faces and bodies of models and celebrities are airbrushed to make them even *more* perfect! Many girls then see these impossible images, and strive to be just like them. This creates self-consciousness and low self-esteem. Some girls even end up hurting their bodies, trying to become thinner or look different, in order to fit those images.

We think that's awful—and at *New Moon,* we're *doing* something about it. In 2000, we created the international "Turn Beauty Inside Out" (TBIO) Campaign. Thousands of people have joined it. TBIO protests the narrow way media portrays girls and women. We put the focus on Inner Beauty instead. In 2001, we went to New York to meet with advertising executives. We told them what we thought was good *and* bad in ads, and we developed the "Best Practices for Advertising and Girls." In 2002, we went to Los Angeles, California, to protest Hollywood's images of girls and women. We should not be treated as objects and should not be judged based on our appearance! We should be seen for who we are as *people!*

These stories show what feminism means to us—and that we still need it. But things are better for girls and women than they were, and we thank feminism for that. It shows that real change *can* happen—*and that women and girls can make it happen.*

In the future, we want women and girls to be treated equally with men and boys; to get the respect men and boys get. We want girls to be encouraged to become scientists and mathematicians. We want girls to be allowed to play any sport a guy can. We want equality in the workplace, at school, and in sports. We want equal opportunity and equal pay. We also want equal representation. Women should be expected and encouraged to take political positions. We want to walk down the halls at school and the streets of our city and feel safe from violence against us. We want to end stereotypes against girls and women.

Equality will not only improve society's view of girls and women; equality will also help us speak up—for ourselves *and* for other people.

We have great dreams for how the world can be a better place. Together, we can make these dreams real.

As Catlyn, 13, of Seattle, Washington, says, "The world would be a better place if girls understood that *we are the ones who can make a change!"*　　　[2003]

NOTES

1. See Barbara Findlen, "Women in Sports: What's the Score?" in *Sisterhood Is Forever: The Women's Anthology for a New Millennium,* ed. Robin Morgan, p. 285 (New York City, NY: Washington Square Press, 2003).
2. See Pat Schroeder, "Running for Our Lives: Electoral Politics," in Morgan, *Sisterhood Is Forever,* p. 28.
3. See Anita Hill, "The Nature of the Beast: Sexual Harassment," p. 296, and Andrea Dworkin, "Landscape of the Ordinary: Violence Against Women," p. 58, in Morgan, *Sisterhood Is Forever.*
4. See Gloria Steinem, "The Media and the Movement: A User's Guide," p. 103, and Carol Jenkins, "Standing By: Women in Broadcast Media," p. 418, in Morgan, *Sisterhood Is Forever.*

🌿 17

not a pretty girl

ANI DI FRANCO

i am not a pretty girl
that is not what i do
i ain't no damsel in distress
and i don't need to be rescued
so put me down punk
wouldn't you prefer a maiden fair
isn't there a kitten
stuck up a tree somewhere

i am not an angry girl
but it seems like
i've got everyone fooled
every time I say something
they find hard to hear
they chalk it up to my anger
and never to their own fear
imagine you're a girl
just trying to finally come clean
knowing full well they'd prefer
you were dirty

and smiling
and i'm sorry
but I am not a maiden fair
and I am not a kitten
stuck up a tree somewhere
generally my generation
wouldn't be caught dead
working for the man
and generally I agree with them
trouble is you got to have yourself
an alternate plan
i have earned my disillusionment
i have been working all of my life
i am a patriot
i have been fighting the good fight
and what if there are
no damsels in distress
what if i knew that
and I called your bluff
don't you think every kitten
figures out how to get down
whether or not you ever show up

i am not a pretty girl
i don't really want to be a pretty girl
i want to be more than a pretty girl   [1995]

Learning Gender

We learn about gender—ideas about what it means to be female and male—in a variety of overt and subtle ways. Images of women are communicated through the language we use, media depictions of women, direct messages from family, friends, and teachers, and many other sources.

Judith Lorber explores the many ways in which groups exert domination and power through the construction of social practices that heighten, exaggerate, and mark gender. Robert Jensen encourages both men and women to think about the public and private constructions of masculine ideals in society and its implications for men's behavior. Gender differences are constructed by the institutional structures and processes that we take for granted. Murielle Minard's poem, "The Gift," describes a doll given to a girl on her seventh birthday. Beautiful and perfect, the fragile doll symbolizes the essence of femininity. The doll is to be admired for her beauty, never played with lest she be damaged. Susan Jane Gilman considers the powerful influence that Barbie has on young girls' emerging sense of femininity. She recalls that although many women have a nostalgic reaction to Barbie, she and her friends realized that "if you didn't look like Barbie, you didn't fit in."

School experiences are another powerful socializing force. In a variety of ways, female students learn more than academic material in the classroom. Here, they also learn about the norms for appropriate behavior in our culture and begin to consider how well they will measure up to those standards. Karen Zittleman and David Sadker explore sexism in schools today, pointing out that over the course of schooling girls receive less instructional time and fewer resources than boys. In the final analysis, all children lose in schools that do not value their unique gifts.

Accepted patterns of interpersonal and nonverbal communication reinforce traditional power relationships between men and women. The ways in which women and men address one another, disclose personal information, and even look at each other during conversations communicate messages about differences in status and power. Nancy Henley and Jo Freeman's classic article, written in 1979, was instrumental in calling attention to subtle yet powerful patterns of sexism in male–female communication. In a review of recent research, the authors find that power imbalance in interpersonal behaviors between men and women is still as relevant as when they first published their study.

One of the most influential purveyors of social norms is the media. From television to print and electronic media, norms projected through these avenues shape our views of what it means to be female. Anastasia Higginbotham addresses the impact of fashion and beauty magazines on teenage girls. Through both advertising and editorial materials, these magazines encourage their readers to pursue strategies for "getting a guy, and dropping 20 pounds." Jennifer Pozner comments on the negative portrayal of women in "reality TV," citing the pervasive stereotypes that fuel the profits garnered by the media. In a companion piece, Pozner cites the pervasive nature of anti-women reporting on TV and in print news. She guides us through how to write an effective protest letter that will get the attention of editors, without getting their defenses up. She makes sure to remind us to offer positive reinforcements to newspapers when they do provide pro-women coverage to news stories.

Johnetta Cole and Beverly Guy-Sheftall discuss the gender politics of hip-hop, addressing the implications of misogynist images of Black women in hip-hop for the future of African-American communities. Aya de Leon paints a picture of a world where women ran hip-hop. It would be a world without violence. Hip-hop performances would take place in arenas that are child- and women-friendly. These authors show us that despite the pervasive sexist images of women in our culture, young women are finding new and exciting avenues for creatively expressing themselves in a positive and empowering way. This is illustrated in the song "Video," as India.Arie forcefully asserts, "I'm not the average girl in your video, my worth is not determined by the price of my clothes. . . ." India.Arie is part of a movement of young Black women musicians telling the story of their lives as African-American women defying traditional expectations of femininity. Along with artists such as Mary J. Blige, Queen Latifah, and Jill Scott, she is forging a powerful new direction in contemporary music.

This chapter closes with two articles that challenge our notions of the dichotomous nature of gender. The first reading is a fictional exploration of what might happen if society abandoned all traditional gender expectations of girls and boys. In "X: A Fabulous Child's Story," Lois Gould tells the story of Baby X, a child whose gender is unspecified as part of a social experiment on the effects of gender typing. This engaging account highlights the many seemingly insignificant ways children and adults learn sexism, giving us a glimpse of what might occur if we risked examining and changing our ideas about traditional sex roles. As a transgender person, Barb Greve describes his lifelong struggle with gender, and his need to be honest about his whole self and "not being willing to put part of me aside to make others feel comfortable."

🦎 18

Night to His Day: The Social Construction of Gender

JUDITH LORBER*

Talking about gender for most people is the equivalent of fish talking about water. Gender is so much the routine ground of everyday activities that questioning its taken-for-granted assumptions and presuppositions is like thinking about whether the sun will come up.[1] Gender is so pervasive that in our society we assume it is bred into our genes. Most people find it hard to believe that gender is constantly created and re-created out of human interaction, out of social life, and is the texture and order of that social life. Yet gender, like culture, is a human production that depends on everyone constantly "doing gender" (West and Zimmerman 1987).

Gender is such a familiar part of daily life that it usually takes a deliberate disruption of our expectations of how women and men are supposed to act to pay attention to how it is produced. Gender signs and signals are so ubiquitous that we usually fail to note them—unless they are missing or ambiguous. Then we are uncomfortable until we have successfully placed the other person in a gender status; otherwise, we feel socially dislocated. In our society, in addition to man and woman, the status can be *transvestite* (a person who dresses in opposite-gender clothes) and *transsexual* (a person who has had sex-change surgery). Transvestites and transsexuals construct their gender status by dressing, speaking, walking, gesturing in the ways prescribed for women or men—whichever they want to be taken for—and so does any "normal" person.

*Judith Lorber, "Night to His Day: The Social Construction of Gender," from *Paradoxes of Gender* (New Haven, CT: Yale University Press, 1994), pp. 13–15, 32–36. Copyright © 1994 Yale University. Reprinted by permission of Yale University Press.

For the individual, gender construction starts with assignment to a sex category on the basis of what the genitalia look like at birth.[2] Then babies are dressed or adorned in a way that displays the category because parents don't want to be constantly asked whether their baby is a girl or a boy. A sex category becomes a gender status through naming, dress, and the use of other gender markers. Once a child's gender is evident, others treat those in one gender differently from those in the other, and the children respond to the different treatment by feeling different and behaving differently. As soon as they can talk, they start to refer to themselves as members of their gender. Sex doesn't come into play again until puberty, but by that time, sexual feelings and desires and practices have been shaped by gendered norms and expectations. Adolescent boys and girls approach and avoid each other in an elaborately scripted and gendered mating dance. Parenting is gendered, with different expectations for mothers and for fathers, and people of different genders work at different kinds of jobs. The work adults do as mothers and fathers and as low-level workers and high-level bosses, shapes women's and men's life experiences, and these experiences produce different feelings, consciousness, relationships, skills—ways of being that we call feminine or masculine.[3] All of these processes constitute the social construction of gender.

To explain why gendering is done from birth, constantly and by everyone, we have to look not only at the way individuals experience gender but at gender as a social institution. As a social institution, gender is one of the major ways that human beings organize their lives. One way of choosing people for the different tasks of society is on the basics of their talents, motivations, and competence—their demonstrated achievements. The other way is on the basis of gender, race, ethnicity—ascribed membership in a category of people. Although societies vary in the extent to which they use one or the other of these ways of allocating people to work and to carry out other responsibilities, every society uses gender and age grades. The process of gendering and its outcome are legitimated by religion, law, science, and the society's entire set of values.

GENDER AS PROCESS, STRATIFICATION, AND STRUCTURE

As a social institution, gender is a process of creating distinguishable social statuses for the assignment of rights and responsibilities.

As a *process*, gender creates the social differences that define "woman" and "man." Members of a social group neither make up gender as they go along nor exactly replicate in rote fashion what was done before. In almost every encounter, human beings produce gender, behaving in the ways they learned were appropriate for their gender status, or resisting or rebelling against these norms. Resistance and rebellion have altered gender norms, but so far they have rarely eroded the statuses.

Everyday gendered interactions build gender into the family, the work process, and other organizations and institutions, which in turn reinforce gender expectations for individuals.[4] Because gender is a process, there is room not only for modification and variation by individuals and small groups but also for institutionalized change (J. W. Scott 1988, 7).

As part of a *stratification* system, gender ranks men above women of the same race and class. Women and men could be different but equal. In practice, the process of creating difference depends to a great extent on differential evaluation. From society's point of view, one gender is usually the touchstone, the normal, the dominant, and the other is different, deviant, and subordinate.

In a gender-stratified society, what men do is usually valued more highly than what women do because men do it, even when their activities are very similar or the same. In different regions of southern India, for example, harvesting rice is men's work, shared work, or women's work: "Wherever a task is done by women it is considered easy, and where it is done by [men] it is considered difficult" (Mencher 1988, 104). A gathering and hunting society's survival usually depends on the nuts, grubs, and small animals brought in by the women's foraging trips, but when the men's hunt is successful, it is the occasion for a celebration. Conversely, because they are the superior group, white men do not have to do the "dirty work," such as housework; the most inferior group does it, usually poor women of color (Palmer 1989).

Societies vary in the extent of the inequality in social status of their women and men members, but where there is inequality, the status "woman" (and its attendant behavior and role allocations) is usually held in lesser esteem than the status "man." Since gender is also intertwined with a society's other constructed statuses of differential evaluation—race, religion, occupation, class, country of origin, and so on—men and women members of the favored groups command more power, more prestige, and more property than the members of the disfavored groups. Within many social groups, however, men are advantaged over women. The more economic resources, such as education and job opportunities, are available to a group, the more they tend to be monopolized by men. In poorer groups that have few resources (such as working-class African Americans in the United States), women and men are more nearly equal, and the women may even outstrip the men in education and occupational status (Almquist 1987).

As a *structure*, gender divides work in the home and in economic production, legitimates those in authority, and organizes sexuality and emotional life (Connell 1987, 91–142). As primary parents, women significantly influence children's psychological development and emotional attachments, in the process reproducing gender. Emergent sexuality is shaped by heterosexual, homosexual, bisexual, and sadomasochistic patterns that are gendered—different for girls and boys, and for women and men—so that sexual statuses reflect gender statuses.

THE PARADOX OF HUMAN NATURE

To say that sex, sexuality, and gender are all socially constructed is not to minimize their social power. These categorical imperatives govern our lives in the most profound and pervasive ways, through the social experiences and social practices of what Dorothy Smith calls the "everyday/everynight world" (1990, 31–57). The paradox of human nature is that it is *always* a manifestation of cultural meanings, social relationships, and power politics; "not biology, but culture, becomes destiny" (J. Butler 1990, 8). Gendered people emerge not from physiology or sexual orientations but from the exigencies

Masculine, Feminine or Human?

ROBERT JENSEN

In a lecture on masculinity I ask my college students to imagine themselves as parents whose 12-year-old son asks, "Mommy/daddy, what does it mean to be a man?" The list they generate is not hard to predict: To be a man means being strong, responsible, loving, weathering tough times, providing for your family, and never giving up. I then ask the women to observe as the men answer the second question: "What do you say to each other about what it means to be a man in all-male spaces" (in the locker room, for instance)? Initially, there is nervous laughter and then fumbling from the men as they begin to offer a list that defines masculinity not in terms of what it is, but in terms of what it isn't. In the vernacular: Don't be a girl, a sissy, a fag. To be a man is not to be too much like a woman or to be gay. This list expands to other descriptions: To be a man is to be a player, someone who does not take shit from people, who can stand down another guy if challenged, who does not let anyone else get in his face.

One revelation from reflecting on the responses to these two questions is that the answers in response to the first question are not really distinctive traits of men, but rather traits of human beings that we value, what we want all people to be. The masculinity that men routinely impose on each other when they are alone is quite different. The locker room values are in fact dominant and toxic conceptions of masculinity that all men in the USA are exposed to.

It is obvious that there are differences in the male and female human body, most obviously in reproductive organs and hormones. Given our limited understanding of the implications of these differences, it is hard to draw conclusions about intelligence, morality, or emotionality associated with these biological gender differences, especially after thousands of years of patriarchy where men have defined themselves as superior. We would benefit from a critical inquiry of the categories of gender itself, no matter how uncomfortable they may be.   [edited, 2008]

Source: R. Jensen, "Masculine, Feminine or Human?," in *Doing Gender Diversity,* ed. Rebecca F. Plante and Lis M. Maurer (New York: Westview Press, 2008).

of the social order, mostly from the need for a reliable division of the work of food production and the social (not physical) reproduction of new members. The moral imperatives of religion and cultural representations guard the boundary lines among genders and ensure that what is demanded, what is permitted, and what is tabooed for the people in each gender is well known and followed by most (C. Davies 1982). Political power, control of scarce resources, and, if necessary, violence uphold the gendered social order in the face of resistance and rebellion. Most people, however, voluntarily go along with their society's prescriptions for those of their gender status, because the norms and expectations get built into their sense of worth and identity as [the way we] think, the way we see and hear and speak, the way we fantas[ize], and the way we feel.

For humans, the social is the natural. Therefore, "in its feminist senses, gender cannot mean simply the cultural appropriation of biological sexual difference. Sexual difference is itself a fundamental—and scientifically contested—construction. Both 'sex' and 'gender' are woven of multiple, asymmetrical strands of difference, charged with multifaceted dramatic narratives of domination and struggle" (Haraway 1990, 140).   [1994]

NOTES

1. Gender is, in Erving Goffman's words, an aspect of *Felicity's Condition*: "any arrangement which leads us to judge an individual's . . . acts not to be a manifestation of strangeness. Behind *Felicity's Condition* is our sense of what it is to be sane" (1983:27). Also see Bem 1993; Frye 1983, 17–40; Goffman 1977.
2. In cases of ambiguity in countries with modern medicine, surgery is usually performed to make the genitalia more clearly male or female.
3. See J. Butler 1990 for an analysis of how doing gender is gender identity.
4. On the "logic of practice," or how the experience of gender is embedded in the norms of everyday interaction and the structure of formal organizations, see Acker 1990; Bourdieu [1980] 1990; Connell 1987; Smith 1987.

REFERENCES

Acker, Joan. 1990. "Hierarchies, jobs, and bodies: A theory of gendered organizations," *Gender & Society* 4:139–158.

Almquist, Elizabeth M. 1987. "Labor market gendered inequality in minority groups," *Gender & Society* 1:400–14.

Bem, Sandra Lipsitz. 1993. *The Lenses of Gender: Transforming the Debate on Sexual Inequality*. New Haven: Yale University Press.

Bourdieu, Pierre. [1980] 1990. *The Logic of Practice*. Stanford, Calif.: Stanford University Press.

Butler, Judith. 1990. *Gender Trouble: Feminism and the Subversion of Identity*. New York and London: Routledge.

Connell, R. [Robert] W. 1987. *Gender and Power: Society, the Person, and Sexual Politics*. Stanford, Calif.: Stanford University Press.

Davies, Christie. 1982. "Sexual taboos and social boundaries," *American Journal of Sociology* 87:1032–63.

Dwyer, Daisy, and Judith Bruce (eds.). 1988. *A Home Divided: Women and Income in the Third World*. Palo Alto, Calif.: Stanford University Press.

Mencher, Joan. 1988. "Women's work and poverty: Women's contribution to household maintenance in South India," in Dwyer and Bruce.

Palmer, Phyllis. 1989. *Domesticity and Dirt: Housewives and Domestic Servants in the United States*, 1920–1945. Philadelphia: Temple University Press.

Scott, Joan Wallach. 1988. *Gender and the Politics of History*. New York: Columbia University Press.

Smith, Dorothy. 1987. *The Everyday World as Problematic: A Feminist Sociology*. Toronto: University of Toronto Press.

West, Candace, and Don Zimmerman. 1987. "Doing gender," *Gender & Society* 1:125–51

19

The Gift

MURIELLE MINARD

On my seventh birthday
A beloved uncle

Gave me a doll.
She was a beautiful creature
With blue eyes
That opened and shut,
Golden curls
And a blue velvet dress.

Once a week,
On Sunday afternoon,
My mother would sit me
In a chair
And place the doll in my arms.
I was not to disturb its perfection
In any way,
I would sit there
Transfixed
By its loveliness
And mindful
Of my mother's wishes.

After a time
She would take the doll from me,
Rewrap it carefully
In tissue,
Put it back into its own
Long, gray box
And place it
High on the closet shelf,
Safe from harm.

To this doll
Nothing must happen.   [1984]

20

klaus barbie, and other dolls i'd like to see

SUSAN JANE GILMAN

For decades, Barbie has remained torpedo-titted, open-mouthed, tippy-toed, and vagina-less in her cellophane coffin—and, ever since I was little, she has threatened me.

Most women I know are nostalgic for Barbie. "Oh," they coo wistfully; "I used to *lôôoove* my Barbies. My girlfriends would come over, and we'd play for hours. . . ."

Not me. As a child, I disliked the doll on impulse; as an adult, my feelings have actually fermented into a heady, full-blown hatred.

My friends and I never owned Barbies. When I was young, little girls in my New York City neighborhood collected "Dawns." Only seven inches high, Dawns were, in retrospect, the underdog of fashion dolls. There were four in the collection: Dawn, dirty blond and appropriately smug; Angie, whose name and black hair allowed her to pass for Italian or Hispanic; Gloria, a redhead with bangs and green eyes (Irish, perhaps, or a Russian Jew?); and Dale, a black doll with a real afro.

Oh, they had their share of glitzy frocks—the tiny wedding dress, the gold lamé ball gown that shredded at the hem. And they had holes punctured in the bottoms of their feet so you could impale them on the model's stand of the "Dawn Fashion Stage" (sold separately), press a button and watch them revolve jerkily around the catwalk. But they also had "mod" clothes like white go-go boots and a multicolored dashiki outfit called "Sock It to Me" with rose-colored sunglasses. Their hair came in different lengths and—although probably only a six-year-old doll fanatic could discern this—their facial expressions and features were indeed different. They were as diverse as fashion dolls could be in 1972, and in this way, I realize now, they were slightly subversive.

Of course, at that age, my friends and I couldn't spell subversive, let alone wrap our minds around the concept. But we sensed intuitively that Dawns were more democratic than Barbies. With their different colors and equal sizes, they were closer to what we looked like. We did not find this consoling—for we hadn't yet learned that our looks were something that required consolation. Rather, our love of Dawns was an offshoot of our own healthy egocentrism. We were still at that stage in our childhood when little girls want to be everything special, glamorous and wonderful—and believe they can be.

As a six-year-old, I remember gushing, "I want to be a ballerina, and a bride, and a movie star, and a model, and a queen. . . ." To be sure, I was a disgustingly girly girl. I twirled. I skipped. I actually wore a tutu to school. (I am not kidding.) For a year, I refused to wear blue. Whenever the opportunity presented itself, I dressed up in my grandmother's pink chiffon nightgowns and rhinestone necklaces and paraded around the apartment like the princess of the universe. I dressed like my Dawn dolls—and dressed my Dawn dolls like me. It was a silly, fabulous narcissism—but one that sprang from a crucial self-love. These dolls were part of my fantasy life and an extension of my ambitions. Tellingly, my favorite doll was Angie, who had dark brown hair, like mine.

But at some point, most of us prima ballerinas experienced a terrible turning point. I know I did. I have an achingly clear memory of myself, standing before a mirror in all my finery and jewels, feeling suddenly ridiculous and miserable. *Look at yourself,* I remember thinking acidly. *Nobody will ever like you.* I could not have been older than eight. And then later, another memory: my friend Allison confiding in me, "The kids at my school, they all hate my red hair." Somewhere, somehow, a message seeped into our consciousness telling us that we weren't good enough to be a bride or a model or a queen or anything because we weren't pretty enough. And this translated into not smart enough or likable enough, either.

Looks, girls learn early, collapse into a metaphor for everything else. They quickly become the defining criteria for our status and our worth. And somewhere along the line, we stop believing in our own beauty and its dominion. Subsequently, we also stop believing in the power of our minds and our bodies.

Barbie takes over.

Barbie dolls had been around long before I was born, but it was precisely around the time my friends and I began being evaluated on our "looks" that we became aware of the role Barbie played in our culture.

Initially, my friends and I regarded Barbies with a sort of vague disdain. With their white-blond hair, burnt orange "Malibu" skin, unblinking turquoise eyes and hot-pink convertibles, Barbie dolls represented a world utterly alien to us. They struck us as clumsy, stupid, overly obvious. They were clearly somebody else's idea of a doll—and a doll meant for vapid girls in the suburbs. Dawns, my friend Julie and I once agreed during a sleepover, were far more hip.

But eventually, the message of Barbie sunk in. Literally and metaphorically, Barbies were bigger than Dawns. They were a foot high. They merited more plastic! More height! More visibility! And unlike Dawns, which were pulled off the market in the mid-'70s, Barbies were ubiquitous and perpetual bestsellers.

We urban, Jewish, Black, Asian, and Latina girls began to realize slowly and painfully that if you didn't look like Barbie, you didn't fit in. Your status was diminished. You were less beautiful, less valuable, less worthy. *If you didn't look like Barbie, companies would discontinue you.* You simply couldn't compete.

I'd like to think that, two decades later, my anger about this would have cooled off—not heated up. (I mean, it's a *doll* for chrissake. Get over it.) The problem, however, is that despite all the flag-waving about multiculturalism and girls' self-esteem these days, I see a new generation of little girls receiving the same message I did 25 years ago, courtesy of Mattel. I'm currently a "big sister" to a little girl who recently moved here from Mexico. When I first began spending time with her, she drew pictures of herself as she is: a beautiful seven-year-old with café au lait skin and short black hair. Then she began playing with Barbies. Now she draws pictures of both herself and her mother with long, blond hair. "I want long hair," she sighs, looking woefully at her drawing.

A coincidence? Maybe, but Barbie is the only toy in the Western world that human beings actively try to mimic. Barbie is not just a children's doll; it's an adult cult and an aesthetic obsession. We've all seen the evidence. During Barbie's 35th anniversary, a fashion magazine ran a "tribute to Barbie," using live models posing as dolls. A New York museum held a "Barbie retrospective," enshrining Barbie as

a pop artifact—at a time when most human female pop artists continue to work in obscurity. Then there's Pamela Lee. The Barbie Halls of Fame. The websites, the newsletters, the collectors' clubs. The woman whose goal is to transform herself, via plastic surgery, into a real Barbie. Is it any wonder then that little girls have been longing for generations to "look like Barbie"—and that the irony of this goes unchallenged?

For this reason, I've started calling Barbie dolls "Klaus Barbie dolls" after the infamous Gestapo commander. For I now clearly recognize what I only sensed as a child. This "pop artifact" is an icon of Aryanism. Introduced after the second world war, in the conservatism of the Eisenhower era (and rumored to be modeled after a German prostitute by a man who designed nuclear warheads), Barbies, in their "innocent," "apolitical" cutesiness, propagate the ideals of the Third Reich. They ultimately succeed where Hitler failed: They instill in legions of little girls a preference for whiteness, for blond hair, blue eyes, and delicate features, for an impossible *über*figure, perched eternally and submissively in high heels. In the Cult of the Blond, Barbies are a cornerstone. They reach the young, and they reach them quickly. *Barbie, Barbie!* The Aqua song throbs. *I'm a Barbie girl!*

It's true that, in the past few years, Mattel has made an effort to create a few slightly more p.c. versions of its best-selling blond. Walk down the aisle at Toys-R-Us (and they wonder why kids today can't spell), and you can see a few boxes of American Indian Barbie, Jamaican Barbie, Cowgirl Barbie. Their skin tone is darker and their outfits ethnicized, but they have the same Aryan features and the same "tell-me-anything-and-I'll-believe-it" expressions on their plastic faces. Ultimately, their packaging reinforces their status as "Other." These are "special" and "limited" edition Barbies, the labels announce: clearly *not* the standard.

And, Barbie's head still pops off with ease. Granted, this makes life a little sweeter for the sadists on the playground (there's always one girl who gets more pleasure out of destroying Barbie than dressing her), but the real purpose is to make it easier to swap your Barbies' Lilliputian ball gowns.

Look at the literal message of this: Hey, girls, a head is simply a neck plug, easily disposed of in the name of fashion. Lest anyone think I'm nit-picking here, a few years ago, a "new, improved" Talking Barbie hit the shelves and created a brouhaha because one of the phrases it parroted was *Math is hard.* Once again, the cerebrum took a backseat to "style." Similarly, the latest "new, improved" Barbie simply trades in one impossible aesthetic for another: The bombshell has now become the waif. Why? According to a Mattel spokesperson, a Kate Moss figure is better suited for today's fashions. Ah, such an improvement.

Now, I am not, as a rule, anti-doll. Remember, I once wore a tutu and collected the entire Dawn family myself. I know better than to claim that dolls are nothing but sexist gender propaganda. Dolls can be a lightning rod for the imagination, for companionship, for learning. And they're *fun*—something that must never be undervalued.

But dolls often give children their first lessons in what a society considers valuable—and beautiful. And so I'd like to see dolls that teach little girls something more than fashion-consciousness and self-consciousness. I'd like to see dolls that expand girls' ideas about what is beautiful instead of constricting them. And how about a few role models instead of runway models as playmates? If you can make a Talking Barbie, surely you can make a Working Barbie. If you can have a Barbie Townhouse, surely you can have a Barbie business. And if you can construct an entire Barbie world out of pink and purple plastic, surely you can construct some "regular" Barbies that are more than white and blond. And remember, Barbie's only a doll! So give it a little more inspired goofiness, some real *pizzazz!*

Along with Barbies of all shapes and colors, here are some Barbies I'd personally like to see:

Dinner Roll Barbie. A Barbie with multiple love handles, double chin, a real, curvy belly, generous tits and ass and voluminous thighs to show girls that voluptuousness is also beautiful. Comes with miniature basket of dinner rolls, bucket o' fried chicken, tiny Entenmann's walnut ring, a brick of Sealtest ice cream, three packs of potato chips, a T-shirt reading "Only the Weak Don't Eat" and, of course, an appetite.

Birkenstock Barbie. Finally, a doll made with horizontal feet and comfortable sandals. Made from recycled materials.

Bisexual Barbie. Comes in a package with Skipper and Ken.

Butch Barbie. Comes with short hair, leather jacket, "Silence = Death" T-shirt, pink triangle buttons, Doc Martens, pool cue and dental dams. Packaged in cardboard closet with doors flung wide open. Barbie Carpentry Business sold separately.

Our Barbies, Ourselves. Anatomically correct Barbie, both inside and out, comes with spreadable legs, her own speculum, magnifying glass and detailed diagrams of female anatomy so that little girls can learn about their bodies in a friendly, nonthreatening way. Also included: tiny Kotex, booklets on sexual responsibility. Accessories such as contraceptives, sex toys, expanding uterus with fetus at various stages of development and breast pump are all optional, underscoring that each young women has the right to choose what she does with her own Barbie.

Harley Barbie. Equipped with motorcycle, helmet, shades. Tattoos are non-toxic and can be removed with baby oil.

Body Piercings Barbie. Why should Earring Ken have all the fun? Body Piercings Barbie comes with changeable multiple earrings, nose ring, nipple rings, lip ring, navel ring and tiny piercing gun. Enables girls to rebel, express alienation and gross out elders without actually having to puncture themselves.

Blue Collar Barbie. Comes with overalls, protective goggles, lunch pail, UAW membership, pamphlet on union organizing and pay scales for women as compared to men. Waitressing outfits and cashier's register may be purchased separately for Barbies who are holding down second jobs to make ends meet.

Rebbe Barbie. So why not? Women rabbis are on the cutting edge in Judaism. Rebbe Barbie comes with tiny satin *yarmulke,* prayer shawl, *tefillin,* silver *kaddish* cup, Torah scrolls. Optional: tiny *mezuzah* for doorway of Barbie Dreamhouse.

B-Girl Barbie. Truly fly Barbie in midriff-baring shirt and baggy jeans. Comes with skateboard, hip hop accessories and plenty of attitude. Pull her cord, and she says things like, "I don't *think* so," "Dang, get outta my face" and "You go, girl." Teaches girls not to take shit from men and condescending white people.

The Barbie Dream Team. Featuring Quadratic Equation Barbie (a Nobel Prize–winning mathematician with her own tiny books and calculator), Microbiologist Barbie (comes with petri dishes, computer and Barbie Laboratory) and Bite-the-Bullet Barbie, an anthropologist with pith helmet, camera, detachable limbs, fake blood and kit for performing surgery on herself in the outback.

Transgender Barbie. Formerly known as G.I. Joe.

[2000]

🦎 21

On Language: You Guys

AUDREY BILGER

Oprah says it. My Yoga instructor says it. College students around the country say it. The cast of *Friends* says it, as do my own friends, over and over again. At least ten to twenty times a day, I hear someone say "you guys" to refer to groups or pairs that include and in some cases consist entirely of women. I get e-mail all the time asking after my (female) partner and me: "How's everything with you guys?" or "What are you guys doing for the holidays?" In informal speech and writing, the phrase has become so common in American English that it's completely invisible to many who use it. In response to my post on the topic, participants on WMST-L, a listserv for women's studies teachers and scholars hosted by the University of Maryland, report that it's not confined to young people,

nor is it an altogether recent development (some of the participants' older relatives used it in the '50s and '60s). Furthermore, the usage is beginning to spread to Canada, England, and Australia, largely through the influence of American television.

What's the problem? people ask when I question this usage. The language has evolved, and now "guys" is gender neutral, they say. Even those who consider themselves feminists—who conscientiously choose "he or she" over "he"; use "flight attendant," "chairperson," and "restaurant server"; and avoid gender-specific language as much as possible—seem quite willing to accept "you guys" as if it were, generic. But let's do the math: One guy is clearly male; two or more guys are males. How does a word become gender neutral just by being plural? And then how do you explain something like Heyyouguys.com, "The Man's Search Engine"? Can the same culture that says "it's a guy thing" to refer to anything that women just don't get about male behavior view a woman as one of the guys?

Current dictionaries, such as *Merriam-Webster's Collegiate Dictionary,* eleventh edition, tell us that "guys" may be "used in plural to refer to the members of a group regardless of sex"; but then, we need to keep in mind that dictionaries are not apolitical. They record the state of language and reflect particular ways of seeing the world. (This same tome offers the word "wicked" as one synonym for "black.") My 1979 ninth edition of *Webster's* includes no reference to gender-free guys, an indication that "you guys" had not yet become a standard form of address.

In "The Ascent of Guy," a 1999 article in *American Speech,* Steven J. Clancy writes, "Contrary to everything we might expect because of the pressures of 'politically correct' putative language reforms, a new generic noun is developing right before our eyes." Although Clancy doesn't take issue with the development (as you could probably guess from his disparaging tone on the whole idea of feminist language reform), his report ought to make us stop and think. During the same decades in which feminist critiques of generic uses of "man" and "he" led to widespread changes in usage—no mean feat—"you guys" became even more widely accepted as an informal and allegedly gender-free phrase. What Clancy concludes is that English contains a "cognitive framework in which strongly masculine words regularly show a development including specifically male meanings (man, he, guy) along with gender nonspecific forms . . . whereas in English, feminine words do not undergo such changes." In practice, that is, terms signifying maleness have been more readily perceived as universal than those signifying femaleness. Or, to put it another way, if you call a group of men "you gals," they're not going to think you're just celebrating our common humanity.

And this should trouble us. After all, haven't we been largely pleased by the way the media has worked to adopt at least a semblance of nonsexist language? Newscasters and other public figures make an effort to avoid obviously gender-biased words, and major publications such as *The New York Times* and *The Wall Street Journal* do the same. In spite of vocal criticism from those who view such shifts as preposterous, genuine feminist language reform has gained some ground. But as is the case with all advances brought about by feminism and other progressive movements, we need to stay on top of things—or else we may wake up one day to find them gone. This seemingly innocent phrase may be operating like a computer virus, worming its way into our memory files and erasing our sense of why we worry about sexism in language to begin with.

Up until a couple of years ago, I used the phrase as much as anyone, and I never gave it a thought. "You guys" sounds casual, friendly, harmless. When two female friends told me one day that it bothered them to be called "you guys," my wounded ego began an internal rant: *I'm* a literature and gender studies professor, *I* know about language, *I* spend much of my time teaching and writing against sexism, and here were people whose opinions I valued telling me that *I* was being patriarchal. Impossible! And then I started listening. I listened first to my own defensive indignation. Clearly, my friends had touched a nerve. Deep down I knew that they were right: Calling women

"guys" makes femaleness invisible. It says that man—as in a male person—is still the measure of all things.

Once I copped to being in the wrong, I started hearing the phrase with new ears. Suddenly it seemed bizarre to me when a speaker at an academic conference addressed a room full of women as "you guys"; when a man taking tickets from me and some friends told us all to enjoy the show, "you guys"; and on and on. It was as if these speakers were not really seeing what was before their eyes.

Alice Walker, a vocal opponent of this usage, recounts how she and filmmaker Pratibha Parmar toured the U.S. supporting the film *Warrior Marks* and were discouraged to find that in question-and-answer sessions audience members continually referred to them as "you guys." "Each night, over and over, we told the women greeting us: We are not 'guys.' We are women. Many failed to get it. Others were amused. One woman amused us, she had so much difficulty not saying 'you guys' every two minutes, even after we'd complained" (from "Becoming What We're Called," in the 1997's *Anything We Love Can Be Saved*). Because it took me the better part of a year to eradicate this usage from my own speech, and after hearing friends—whom I've encouraged to follow suit—apologize when they slip back into it, I feel like I understand the problem from the inside out. Most of us are familiar with the idea of internalized oppression the subtle process by which members of disenfranchised groups come to accept their own lesser status. We need to recognize that accepting "guys" as a label for girls and women is a particularly insidious example of that process.

Many people on WMST-L have offered alternatives, ranging from the Southern "y'all" or less regionally marked "you all," to the Midwestern "yoonz" or "you-uns," to the apparently unhip "people," which is associated, it seems, with nerdy high-school teachers and coaches. "Folks" received the most support as a truly gender-free option. Some suggested "gyns" as a playful feminist variant. A more radical solution might be to use a word like "gals" as generic and get men used to hearing themselves included in a female-specific term.

Although the majority of those who posted and wrote to me privately viewed the spread of "guys" as something to resist (with many noting how they sometimes regressed), others expressed hope that the phrase would indeed free itself from masculine connotations over time. One professor writes, almost wistfully, "I, for one, have always liked the formulation 'you guys' and wholeheartedly wish it were gender neutral. English could use a gender-neutral term to refer to a group of people (or even to individuals for that matter) . . . I've had students (female) be offended when I've used 'you guys' to them, but I still like it for some reason." I think many feminists who find "you guys" acceptable would similarly like to believe that it is indeed nonsexist. It's a powerful phrase precisely because it seems so warm and cozy. But we ought to ask what we are protecting when we claim that "you guys" is no big deal.

Sherryl Kleinman, professor of sociology at the University of North Carolina in Chapel Hill, has dedicated herself to eliminating the usage. She argues, in "Why Sexist Language Matters" (published in *Center Line,* the newsletter of the Orange County Rape Crisis Center), that male-based generics function as "reinforcers" of a "system in which 'man' in the abstract and men in the flesh are privileged over women." With the help of two former students, Kleinman developed a small card to leave at establishments where "you guys" is spoken (it's available to download at www.youall2.freeservers.com). The card succinctly explains what's at stake in this usage and suggests alternatives. She reports that distributing the card has aroused some anger. After dining with a group of female friends and being called "you guys" several times by the server, Kleinman left the card along with a generous tip. The server followed the women out of the restaurant and berated them for what he perceived to be an insult. Christian Helms, who designed the card's artwork, comments, "It's interesting how something that is supposedly 'no big deal' seems, to get people so worked up."

Most of us have probably had the experience of pointing out some type of sexist expression or behavior to acquaintances and being accused of being "too sensitive" or "too PC" and told to "lighten up." It's certainly easier just to go along with things, to avoid making people uncomfortable, to accept what we think will do no harm. If you feel this way about "you guys," you might want to consider Alice Walker's view of the expression: "I see in its use some women's obsequious need to be accepted, at any cost, even at the cost of erasing their own femaleness, and that of other women. Isn't it at least ironic that after so many years of struggle for women's liberation, women should end up calling themselves this?"

So open your ears and your mouth. Tell people that women and girls aren't "guys." Stop saying it yourself. Feminist language reform is an ongoing process that requires a supportive community of fakers. The more we raise our voices, the less likely it is that women and girls will be erased from speech.   [2002]

❦ 22

Gender Inequity in School: Not a Thing of the Past

KAREN ZITTLEMAN and DAVID SADKER

"I heard that girls are doing fine now in school, really better than the boys. Is sexism really still a problem?" Many teachers, parents, and students are confused about gender equity in schools. They are not alone. We recently received a call from a young reporter who wanted to speak about our work "in making women superior to men." The reporter viewed gender bias in school as males versus females. We do not. Gender bias short-circuits both boys and girls, and both move forward when gender restrictions are removed.

In the past decades, we have seen great progress in battling gender bias and discrimination. Females comprise more than 40 percent of high school athletes; they enroll in biology, chemistry, and pre-calculus courses at rates equal to or greater than males, and they have access to virtually all colleges. Boys are making impressive progress as well. More boys are scoring higher on standardized tests, taking advanced placement exams, graduating from high school, and going on to college.

It should be noted, however, that for poor students and students of color the situation is far less encouraging. They are more likely to drop out and far less likely to go on to college. When making gender comparisons, it is important to consider race, economic class, ethnicity, and other relevant demographics. When people say "boys are in crisis" or "girls are struggling in science," one needs to remember that poor children and children of color have faced race and class discrimination for many decades, and for these students the challenges are more profound and persistent.

So is gender bias a relic of a bygone era? Hardly. Consider the following:

Boys and schools. Boys are still plagued by lower grades, overdiagnosis, and referral to special educational services, too many preventable athletic injuries, bullying, peer harassment, disciplinary problems, and violence. The way we socialize boys too often teaches them that reading and academics are for girls, that "real boys" need not focus on schoolwork.

Girls and schools. Gender socialization teaches girls to please others, and working hard at school is part of that. Teachers appreciate students who follow directions and do not cause problems, part of the reason girls receive better report card grades than boys. But these higher grades carry a large hidden cost as docile and compliant children may grow into adults with lower self-esteem and less independence. In fact, even today more than one-third of students in 3rd–12th grades report "people think that the most important thing for girls is to get married and have children."

Test scores. In the early years, girls are ahead of or equal to boys on most standardized measures of achievement. By the time they graduate from high school or college, girls have fallen behind boys on all the key exams needed to gain entrance to and scholarships for the most prestigious colleges and graduate schools, including the SAT, ACT, MCAT, LSAT, and GRE.

Instruction. Perhaps one reason female test scores tumble is that from elementary school through higher education, studies show that female students receive less active classroom instruction, both in quantity and quality. Girls' grades may be less a sign of academic gifts than a reward for following the rules, being quiet, and conforming to school norms.

Curricular bias. No matter the subject, the names and experiences of males continue to dominate the pages of schoolbooks. Current elementary and high school social studies texts include five times more males than females; elementary reading books and award-winning Caldecott and Newbery children's books include twice as many males.

Math and science enrollment. Female enrollment in most high school and college mathematics and science courses has increased dramatically. Girls are the majority in biology, chemistry, algebra, and precalculus courses. Unfortunately, the connection between girls and science and math remains tenuous. A survey by the Society of Women Engineers found that 75 percent of American girls have no interest in pursuing a career in science, math, or technology. Why? They perceive these subjects as cold, impersonal, and with little clear application to their lives or to society.

Parental perceptions. Researchers at the University of Michigan followed more than 800 children and their parents for 13 years and found that traditional gender stereotypes greatly influence parental attitudes and behaviors related to children's success in math. Parents buy more math and science toys, and spend more time on these activities with their sons. Simply put, parents expect their sons to do well in math, and not surprisingly, over time, girls get the message, and their interest in math decreases.

Sexual harassment. You may be surprised to learn that boys are the targets of sexual harassment almost as frequently as girls: nearly four out of five students (boys and girls) in grades 8 through 11 report they have been harassed. Nine in 10 students (85 percent) report that students sexually harass other students at their school, and almost 40 percent of students report that school employees sexually harass as well. The most common sexual harassment against boys takes the form of "gay-bashing" or questioning their sexuality, while girls experience verbal and physical harassment, including unwanted touching.

Athletics. Male high school athletes outnumber female athletes by more than a million, and male athletic participation is now growing at twice the rate of female participation. Although girls constitute 49 percent of the students in the nation's high schools, they receive only 41 percent of the opportunities to play sports. Girls' teams typically have less visibility and status than male teams, and are often denied the same benefits, like adequate facilities and financial support.

College and careers. Men had been the majority of college students from the colonial period to the early 1980s. Today, women are the majority, especially at two-year colleges. Put into perspective, there is a higher percentage of both women and men attending all college today than ever before. What is often missed in these attendance figures is that many college majors and careers are hypersegregated. Teaching, social work, and nursing are overwhelmingly female. Engineering, computer science, and physics are overwhelmingly male. Although women comprise almost half of the associates at law firms, they are less than 20 percent of the partners. Women are an underwhelming 20 percent of our leading journalists. Men constitute about 97 percent of the top executives at Fortune 500 companies. Female representation in the U.S. House of Representatives ranks a disheartening 69th in the world, behind Iraq and North Korea.

Although women are the majority of U.S. paid workers, they are still discriminated against in wages, benefits, pensions, and social security. Workers still do not have paid family medical leave guaranteed nationwide (although numerous countries do) and there is only very limited publicly funded child care. In fact, half of all women employees do not have one paid sick day. Women who work full-time and year-round earn on the average 78 cents for every dollar men earn. For Asian-American women, the figure is 87 cents; for African-American women, 62 cents; and for Latinas, 53 cents (National Women's Law Center report, *Falling Short in Every State: The Wage Gap and Harsh Economic Realities for Women Persist,* April 2009).

These statistics reveal that gender bias is alive and well in our schools and society.

HELP ALL CHILDREN REACH THEIR POTENTIAL

If we want males and females to value fairness and justice for others, and reach their potential whatever choices they want to make, we must create schools in which they experience justice—in their classes, relationships, school experiences, and outcomes. Here are a few activities to help parents and teachers uncover the hidden messages they send and start working toward gender equality in schools and at home:

1. *If These Walls Could Speak*—Walk down the hallway of your child's school. Look at the displays, exhibits, photographs, athletic trophies, and other awards. What gender lessons are being taught to the students who travel those halls?

2. *Famous Men and Women*—Ask your child to list famous men and women from history, excluding the wives of presidents. Do their lists indicate more women or men? Does the list include individuals of diverse racial and ethnic backgrounds? What does it mean when children see one gender as movers and shakers, and the other gender as spectators? Discuss with them what might be done to learn more about those missing pages of American history.

3. *Honor the Unique Gifts of All Children*—Parents and teachers who focus on human qualities, on how children treat one another, on how the world can become a better place, on opening all careers to everyone, are saying that each child is unique and accepted. When boys and girls hear the other sex described in terms of their human and individual strengths, instead of a stereotypical gender yardstick, they learn important lessons that can help undo gender stereotyping. Applauding the special talents of each child develops what is most important in all of us: our inner humanity.

4. *Check out Title IX:* You are not alone. The weight of the law is on your side. Title IX protects girls and boys, teachers, and staff, from gender bias in schools. Visit http://www.titleix.info/ for information, activities, and suggestions. [2009]

NOTE

This article is adapted from material in *Still Failing at Fairness: How Gender Bias Cheats Girls and Boys in Schools and What We Can Do About It*, by David Sadker, Myra Sadker, and Karen Zittleman (New York: Scribner's, 2009).

Reality Versus Perception

JO SANDERS and SARAH COTTON NELSON

Daniel Brown, an AP physics teacher, reported that he had initially been skeptical of any gender inequity in his classroom. "Maybe in other teachers' classrooms," he insisted, "but certainly not in mine." He set out to prove the statistics wrong for his classroom by conducting an experiment.

He asked a teacher to observe his class and time his responses to both his male and female students. This was a gender issue that one of the earlier workshops had tackled. Just knowing that someone was clocking him during that period made him extra aware; he was all the more certain that his time allocation would be fair. At the end of the class, his colleague showed him the results: Taking into account the class's gender representation, the teacher had spent 80 percent of his time responding to boys and 20 percent to girls. "It absolutely bowled me over," Brown said.

He worked hard the next month on implementing strategies presented in the workshops to make the classroom environment more gender-equitable. Making changes in his teaching practice meant becoming aware of a number of gender-based patterns that are below most teachers' level of conscious awareness. He paid attention to which students he called on, how much time he spent waiting for their responses, how much eye contact he maintained, which types of questions he asked specific students, and whether he accepted or refused called-out answers.

Once again, he asked his colleague to observe him in class. During that period of observation, he felt that he had gone overboard in his attention to the girls. He was sure that the observing teacher would tell him that he had swung the pendulum completely back the other way—that he was now spending 80 percent of his time responding to girls and 20 percent to boys. At the end of the period, the observing teacher told him the results: "Fifty-fifty, dead on."

Jo Sanders and Sarah Cotton Nelson, "Closing Gender Gaps in Science." *Educational Leadership*, November 2004, pp. 74–77.

Checklist for Inclusive Classrooms

MERCILEE JENKINS*

How have teachers' choices of materials and patterns of classroom interaction affected you?

TEXTS, LECTURES, AND COURSE CONTENT

1. Are your texts' language sex-neutral, using words with relation to both sexes whenever this is the author's intent?
2. Is course content addressed equitably to men, to women, people of color?
3. Do your texts portray equitably the activities, achievements, concerns, and experiences of women and people of color?
4. Do your texts' examples and illustrations (both verbal and graphic) represent an equitable balance in terms of gender and race?
5. Do your texts and lectures reflect values that are free of sex and race bias?
6. Does your course content incorporate new research and theory generated by feminist and ethnic scholarship?
7. Do your texts and materials make it clear that not everyone is heterosexual?

CLASSROOM INTERACTIONS

1. What is the number of males versus females or of various cultural and racial groups called on to answer questions?
2. Which of these categories of students participate in class more frequently through answering questions or making comments?
3. Do interruptions occur when an individual is talking? If so, who does the interrupting? Is one group of students is dominating classroom interaction?
4. Are verbal responses to students positive? aversive? encouraging? Is it the same for all students? If not, what is the reason? (Valid reasons occur from time to time for reacting or responding to a particular student in a highly specific manner.)
5. Is one section of the class addressed of the classroom more than others? Is eye contact established with certain students more than others? What are the gestures, postures, facial expressions, etc., used, and are they different for men, women, people of color?

[2011]

*Edited version of Mercilee Jenkins's "Checklist for Inclusive Teaching."

🌿 23

The Sexual Politics of Interpersonal Behavior

NANCY HENLEY and JO FREEMAN

Social interaction is the battlefield on which the daily war between the sexes is fought. It is here that women are constantly reminded what their "place" is and here that they are put back in their place, should they venture out. Thus, social interaction serves as the locus of the most common means of social control employed against women. By being continually reminded of their inferior status in their interactions with others, and continually compelled to acknowledge that status in their own patterns of behavior, women may internalize society's definition of them as inferior so thoroughly that they are often unaware of what their status is. Inferiority becomes habitual, and the inferior place assumes the familiarity—and even desirability—of home.

Verbal, nonverbal, and environmental cues aid this enforcement of one's social definition. Formal education emphasizes the verbal message but teaches us little about the nonverbal one. Just how important nonverbal messages are, however, is shown by the finding of Argyle et al.[1] that nonverbal cues have over four times the impact of verbal ones when verbal and nonverbal cues are used together. Argyle also found that female subjects were more responsive to nonverbal cues (compared with verbal ones) than male subjects. This finding has been confirmed in the extensive research of Rosenthal and his colleagues.[2] In studies of people of all ages and from a variety of occupations and cultures, they found consistently greater sensitivity to nonverbal communication among females than among males. If women are to understand how the subtle forces of social control work in their lives, they must learn as much as possible about nonverbal cues, particularly how they perpetuate the power and superior status enjoyed by men.

THE WORLD OF EVERYDAY EXPERIENCE

Even if a woman encounters no one else directly in her day, visual status reminders permeate her environment. At work, male bosses dictate while female secretaries bend over their steno pads. Newscasts show gatherings of senators, heads of state, economic ministers, business leaders—all predominantly men. At lunchtime, restaurants are populated with female table servers who wait on men. When a woman is introduced to others or fills out a written form, the first thing she must do is divulge her marital status, acknowledging the social rule that the most important information about her is her legal relationship to a man. Her spatial subordination is shown in ways parallel to that of other animal and human subordinates: women's "territory" (office space at work, individual rooms, or space at home) tends to be less extensive and less desirable than men's. Women are not as free to move in others' territory or "open" territory (e.g., city streets) as are men.

Advertisements form a large part of our visual world, and their subtle messages suggest that the way the genders are shown in them is the usual and appropriate arrangement. Sociologist Erving Goffman[3] describes six themes involving gender distinctions in advertising pictures: *relative size*, symbolizing the greater importance of men; *feminine touch*, not fully grasping; *function ranking*, with males directing the action; *the family*, in which fathers are linked with boys (and are distant) and mothers with girls; the *ritualization of subordination*, in which women, by lower spatial position, a broken body line, smiles, and clowning, display subordinate status; and *licensed withdrawal*, in which women are relatively less oriented to the situation and dependent on men.

ASYMMETRY IN SOCIAL INTERACTION

Environmental cues set the stage on which the power relationships of the genders are acted out and the assigned status of each gender is reinforced.[4] Goffman has delineated many ways in which status affects interpersonal behavior:

> Between status equals we may expect to find interaction guided by symmetrical familiarity. Between

superordinate and subordinate we may expect to find asymmetrical relations, the superordinate having the right to exercise certain familiarities which the subordinate is not allowed to reciprocate. Thus, in the research hospital [in which Goffman conducted his research], doctors tended to call nurses by their first names, while nurses responded with "polite" or "formal" address. Similarly, in American business organizations the boss may thoughtfully ask the elevator man how his children are, but this entrance into another's life may be blocked to the elevator man. . . .

Rules of demeanor, like rules of deference, can be symmetrical, typical of equals, or asymmetrical, typical of unequals:

> . . . at staff meetings on the psychiatric units of the hospital, medical doctors had the privilege of swearing, changing the topic of conversation, and sitting in undignified position; attendants, on the other hand . . . were implicitly expected to conduct themselves with greater circumspection than was required of doctors. . . . Similarly, doctors had the right to saunter into the nurses' station, lounge on the station's dispensing counter, and engage in joking with the nurses; other ranks participated in this informal interaction with doctors, but only after doctors had initiated it.[5]

A status variable that illustrates rules of symmetry and asymmetry is the use of terms of address, widely studied by Brown and others.[6] In languages that have both familiar and polite forms of the second person singular ("you"), asymmetrical use of the two forms invariably indicates a status difference: the person using the familiar form is always the superior to the person using the polite form. In English, status differences are similarly indicated by the right of first-naming: the status superior can first-name the inferior in situations in which the inferior must use the superior's title and last name.[7]

According to Brown, the pattern evident in the use of forms of address applies to a very wide range of interpersonal behavior and invariably has two other components: (1) whatever form is used by a superior in situations of status inequality can be used reciprocally by intimates, and whatever form is used by an inferior is the socially prescribed usage for nonintimates. Thus friends use first names with each other, whereas strangers use titles and last names. (2) Initiation or increase of intimacy is the right of the superior; for example, students may not use a professor's first name unless specifically invited to.

We have seen this pattern in Goffman's rules of deference and demeanor. The social rules also say that moves to greater intimacy are a male prerogative: it is boys who are supposed to call girls for dates, men who are supposed to propose marriage to women, and males who are supposed to initiate sexual activity with females. Females who make "advances" may be considered improper, forward, aggressive, brassy, or of loose morals. By initiating intimacy, they have usurped a status prerogative; the value of such a prerogative is that it is a form of power. Thus in interactions between the genders, as in other human interactions, the one who has the right to initiate greater intimacy has more control over the relationship.

DEMEANOR, POSTURE, AND DRESS

Like the doctors in Goffman's research hospital, men are allowed such privileges as swearing and sitting in undignified positions, but women are denied them. Although the male privilege of swearing is curtailed in mixed company, the body movement permitted to women may be circumscribed even in all-female groups. It is often considered "unladylike" for a woman to use her body too forcefully, to sprawl, to stand with her legs widely spread, to sit with her feet up, or to cross the ankle of one leg over the knee of the other. Many of these positions are ones of strength or dominance.

Henley has reviewed the research evidence for gender differences in nonverbal behavior, linking it with evidence for differences due to power, status, or dominance.[8] She concludes that the symbols and gestures used by males tend to be those of power and dominance, while the gestures of females tend to be those of subordination and submission. Wex reached similar conclusions through her examination of the public postures of women and men photographed in Germany.[9] Depending on her clothes, a woman may be expected to sit with her knees together, not to sit cross-legged, or not even to bend over.[10] Although these strictures seem to have lessened in recent years, how much so is unknown, and there are recurring social pressures for a "return to femininity."

Because women's clothes are contrived to cling and reveal women's physical features, rather than to be loose as men's are, women must resort to purses instead of pockets to carry their belongings. In a time of otherwise blurred gender distinctions in clothing and hairstyles, purses have become one of the surest signs of gender, and thus have developed the character of a stigma, for example, when they are used by comics to ridicule both women and transvestites.

PERSONAL SPACE AND TOUCHING

One way to indicate acceptance of one's place and deference to those of superior status is to follow the rules of "personal space." Sommer has observed that dominant animals and human beings have a larger envelope of inviolability surrounding them—i.e., they are approached less closely—than those of lower status.[11] Various authors have subsequently shown that this rule applies between men and women, with women both having smaller personal space than men and tending to yield space to men when the two sexes come into proximity.[12] And women's time, like their space, can be invaded more readily.[13]

Touching is one of the closer invasions of personal space, and in our low-contact culture it implies privileged access to another person. Even the figurative meanings of the word convey a notion of access to privileged areas—e.g., to one's emotions (one is touched by a sad story), or to one's purse (one is touched for ten dollars). In addition, the act of touching can be a subtle physical threat.

Remembering the patterns that Brown found in terms of address, consider the interactions between persons of different status, and picture who would be more likely to touch the other (put an arm around the shoulder or a hand on the back, tap the chest, hold the arm, or the like): teacher and student; master and servant; police officer and accused; doctor and patient; supervisor and worker; business executive and secretary. Again, we see that the form used by the status superior—touching—is the form used between intimates of equal status. It is considered presumptuous for a person of lower status to initiate touch with a person of higher status, as it is in first-naming.

Observational and self-report studies indicated that females are touched more than males are, both as children and as adults. In observations of incidents of touch in public urban places, higher-status persons have been found to touch lower-status persons significantly more than vice versa, and men touched women more, even when other pertinent variables were held constant.[14] In one observational study in public places, researchers found that when mixed-gender couples walked together in public, the female was most often on the side of the male's dominant hand. These researchers speculated that such "strong-arming" reflected male dominance and would allow more convenient male touching of the female.[15]

There is also evidence that people's interpretations of touching associate power/dominance with touch; as Hall notes, "People's beliefs, anecdote, self-report, [and] observational studies of socio-economic status and age, and one true experiment favor either the power-privilege idea or the idea that relative dominance increases as a consequence of touch initiation."[16]

GAZE AND DOMINANCE

The most studied nonverbal communication among humans is probably eye contact, and here too we observe a gender difference. Researchers have found repeatedly that women look more at another person in a dyad than men do.[17] This may be a sign of greater sociability, but also is related to dependency and subordination: Rubin suggests that gazing "may allow women to obtain cues from their male partners concerning the appropriateness of their behavior."[18] This interpretation is supported by the data of Efran and Broughton, who found that male subjects too "maintain more eye contact with individuals toward whom they have developed higher expectancies for social approval."[19]

However, looking can also be an aggressive and dominant gesture, when it becomes a stare. Dovidio and Ellyson write:

> In humans as in other primates, the stare widely conveys messages of interpersonal dominance and control. Research conducted over the past 60 years

suggests that, in general, staring at another person is a dominance gesture while breaking eye contact or not looking is a sign of submission.[20]

How can the same gesture—looking at another—indicate both dominance and deference? Perhaps women may watch men when they are not being looked at, but lower or avert their gaze when a man looks at them, as submissive animals do when a dominant animal looks their way.

Also, as Dovidio and Ellyson point out, the meaning of gaze depends on the context, and on the patterning of looking with other behaviors, most notably with speaking. A series of experiments by Ellyson, Dovidio, and their colleagues has developed a measure of "visual dominance": the ratio of [looking at another while speaking] to [looking at another while listening]. In peer interaction, we tend to look while listening more than we look while speaking; however, visually dominant people, both men and women, have a greater proportion of look/speak to look/listen than do non dominant people. People with higher status, expertise, or an orientation to interpersonal control all showed higher visual dominance ratios than did people without those characteristics. Gender also affects visual dominance behavior: in an experiment with mixed-gender pairs, both female and male experts showed greater visual dominance in interaction with non-experts; when there was no differential expertise, men still showed greater visual dominance than did women.[21] Like other tiny habits of which we are scarcely aware, women's "modest" eye lowering can unintentionally signal submission or subordinate position.

VERBAL CUES TO DOMINANCE

Gestures of dominance and submission can be verbal as well as nonverbal. Gender differences are to be found in phonological, semantic, and grammatical aspects of language as well as in word use.[22] Subtle verbal cues—especially paralinguistic features, such as emphasis, inflection, pitch, and noncontent sounds—are often classified with nonverbal ones in the study of interpersonal interaction, because they have similar regulating functions aside from the traditional verbal content. Other features of verbal interaction, such as frequency and length of utterance, turn-taking patterns, interrupting, and allowing interruption also help to regulate interaction and to establish dominance.

A major means of asserting dominance is to interrupt. Those who want to dominate others interrupt more; speakers generally will not permit interruption by social inferiors, but will give way to those they consider their superiors. Zimmerman and West found, in natural conversations between women and men, that forty-six of the forty-eight interruptions were by males; other research on interruption consistently finds men interrupting more than women.[23]

Female voices are expected to be soft and quiet, even when men are using loud voices. Women who do not fit this stereotype are often called loud—a word commonly applied derogatorily to other minority groups or out-groups.[24] One of the most popular derogatory terms for women is *shrill*, which, after all, simply means loud (applied to an out-group) and high-pitched (female).

As noted earlier, status superiors are allowed to be less circumspect in behavior to others. In verbal communication, we find a similar pattern of differences between the genders: men may not only be louder, but also have the privilege of swearing, and access to a taboo vocabulary less available to women.

EMOTIONAL EXPRESSION AND SELF-DISCLOSURE

Women in our society are expected to reveal not only more of their bodies than men but also more of their minds. Whereas men are expected to be stolid and impassive and not to disclose their feelings beyond certain limits, women are expected to express their feelings fully. Female socialization encourages generally greater expression of emotion than does male socialization, although expression of anger is permitted more to men than to women.

Hall's review of thirty-eight studies of females and males as nonverbal communicators showed females to be more expressive than males in almost two-thirds of the studies surveyed.[25] Differences in emotional expression do not necessarily mean that the actual emotions are felt differently. Women and men have different "display rules" for feelings. One study attempting to separate felt emotion from display rules found no gender differences in *emotional state* experienced by participants in response to emotional stimuli, but did find women to show more *facial activity* than men.[26]

Research studies frequently find that females are more self-disclosing to others than males are, both of emotion and of other personal information.[27] One psychological study found that men who were very self-disclosing, and women who were not very self-disclosing, were considered by others to be more psychologically maladjusted than were nondisclosing men and disclosing women.[28] Knowledge is power: self-disclosure gives away knowledge about oneself, thus women are put at a disadvantage relative to men. The inverse relationship between disclosure and power has been reported in Goffman's earlier cited observations in a research hospital and in other studies.[29]

Another factor adding to women's vulnerability is that they are socialized to care more than men, especially about personal relationships. Ross articulated in 1921 what he called the Law of Personal Exploitation: "In any sentimental relation the one who cares less can exploit the one who cares more." The same idea was stated more broadly by Waller and Hill as the Principle of Least Interest: "That person is able to dictate the conditions of association whose interest in the continuation of the affair is least."[30] Women's caring, like their openness, gives them less power in a relationship.

GESTURES OF SUBMISSION

Henley and LaFrance compare the nonverbal asymmetry of male and female to the asymmetry of racial/ethnic/cultural dominance.[31] In any situation in which one group is seen as inferior to another, they predict, that group will be more *submissive*, more *readable* (nonverbally expressive), more *sensitive* (accurate in decoding nonverbal expressions), and more *accommodating* (adapting to another's nonverbal behaviors). We have seen that these characteristics are among the nonverbal behaviors of females; research by Snodgrass supports the contention that decoding sensitivity is associated with dominance and authority, rather than with gender per se.[32]

Other verbal characteristics of persons in inferior status positions are the tendencies to hesitate and apologize, often offered as submissive gestures. If staring directly, pointing, and touching can be subtle nonverbal threats, the corresponding gestures of submission seem to be lowering the eyes from another's gaze, falling silent when interrupted or pointed at, and cuddling to the touch, all familiar as traits our society considers desirable "feminine" characteristics. There is even a word for this syndrome that is applied predominantly to females: *coy.*

SEXUAL INTERACTION

Sexual interaction is widely expressed through nonverbal communication: the caress, the gaze, coming close to each other, the warm smile, smelling the other, provocative postures and inviting gestures. Much sexual contact, unlike other forms of human interaction, is purely nonverbal. Sexual interaction, like all interaction, is conditioned by the social context in which it takes place, and the fact that males have more power, prestige, and status than do females cannot but affect heterosexual interaction.

Applying the findings presented earlier in this article, when gestures are not mutual (or not balanced over time), one person may dominate by initiating touching, hand-holding, and kissing; maintaining gaze; putting an arm around the other's back when sitting; initiating moves to greater intimacy in the course of a relationship or a single encounter; exerting more influence over the couple's spacing, postures, and walking pace; getting to hold hands using the preferred hand; having the hand in front when walking holding hands; and terminating as well as initiating hand-holding, kissing, and sexual activity. Subordination may be expressed by the person who is more emotionally expressive, is more self-disclosing, accommodates timing and action to the other, and exhibits the reciprocal behaviors of those described as dominant.

Although heterosexual custom prescribes male leadership and dominance, many people today do not wish to have unequal sexual relationships or to express gender inequality unconsciously. Nevertheless, since we do not attend much to our body language, it may be hard to change: nonverbal expressions may lag behind changes in attitudes, values, and ideas.

DIFFERING INTERPRETATIONS OF THE SAME BEHAVIOR

Status differences between female and male mean that many of the same traits and actions are interpreted differently when displayed by either gender. Female office, restaurant, and factory workers are quite used to being touched by their male bosses and coworkers, but they are expected not to misinterpret such gestures as sexual advances. However, women who touch men are often perceived by the men as conveying sexual intent.

Research confirms that, when women display dominance gestures to men, they are rated higher on sexuality and lower in dominance than men are rated when making the same gestures to women.[33] Because our society's values say that women should not have power over men, women's nonverbal communication is rarely interpreted as an expression of power. If the situation precludes a sexual interpretation, women's assumption of the male prerogative may be dismissed as deviant (castrating, domineering, unfeminine, or the like). Women in supervisory positions thus often have a difficult time asserting their power nonverbally—gestures that are socially recognized as expressions of power when used by male supervisors may be denied or misinterpreted when used by women.

CHANGE

Knowledge of the significance of nonverbal communication can help us to understand not only others' gestures but also our own. There has been growing pressure on women to alter their verbal and non-verbal behavior[34] to the words and movements of "power," that is, to those associated with men. But it would be mistaken to assume that such gestures are automatically better and that it is only women who should change. Revealing emotions rather than remaining wooden-faced and unexpressive, for example, may be seen as weak when only one person in an interaction is doing it; but, in the long run, openness and expressivity— by all people—may be better for the individual, the interpersonal relationship, and the society. [2011]

NOTES

1. M. Argyle, V. Salter, H. Nicholson, M. Williams, and P. Burgess, "The Communication of Interior and Superior Attitudes by Verbal and Non-Verbal Signals," *British Journal of Social and Clinical Psychology*, 9 (1970), 222-31.
2. R. Rosenthal, J. A. Hall, M. R. DiMatteo, P. L. Rogers, and D. Archer, *Sensitivity to Nonverbal Communication: The PONS Test*, (Baltimore: Johns Hopkins University Press, 1979); J. Hall, *Nonverbal Sex Differences: Communication Accuracy and Expressive Style*, (Baltimore: Johns Hopkins University Press, 1984).
3. E. Goffman, *Gender Advertisements*, (New York: Harper and Row, 1979).
4. The term *power* is used here to mean social power, the ability to influence the behavior of others based on access to and control of resources; *status* refers to acknowledged prestige rankings within the social group; *dominance* is used to refer to a psychological tendency (desire to dominate) and immediate pairwise influence (rather than general social value or influence).
5. E. Goffman, "The Nature of Deference and Demeanor," in E. Goffman, *Interaction Ritual*, (Garden City, N.Y.: Anchor, 1967), 47-95; quotations 64, 78-79.
6. Several studies are described in R. Brown, *Social Psychology*, (Glencoe, Ill.: Free Press, 1965), 51–100.
7. For discussion of these rules vis-à-vis women and men, see S. McConnell-Ginet, "Address Forms in Sexual Politics," in D. Butturff and E. L. Epstein (eds.), *Women's Language and Style*, (Akron, Ohio: University of Akron Press, 1978), 23–35.
8. N. M. Henley, *Body Politics: Power, Sex, and Non-verbal Communication*, (Englewood Cliffs, N.J.: Prentice-Hall, 1977).
9. M. Wex, *Let's Take Back Our Space: "Female" and "Male" Body Language as a Result of Patriarchal Structures* (Hamburg: Frauenliteraturverlag Hermine Fees, 1979).
10. See also S. J. Frances, "Sex Differences in Nonverbal Behavior," *Sex Roles*, 5 (1979), 519–35; I. H. Frieze and S. J. Ramsey, "Nonverbal Maintenance of Traditional Sex Roles," *Journal of Social Issues*, 32, no. 3 (1976), 133–41; M. LaFrance and C. Mayo, "A Review of Nonverbal Behaviors of Women and Men," *Western Journal of Speech Communication*, 43 (1979), 96–107; C. Mayo and N. M. Henley (eds.), *Gender and Nonverbal Behavior* (New York: Springer-Verlag, 1981); S. Weitz, "Sex Differences in Non-verbal Communication," *Sex Roles*, 2 (1976), 175–84.
11. R. Sommer, *Personal Space*, (Englewood Cliffs, N.J.: Prentice-Hall, 1969), Chapter 2.
12. For example, see Frieze and Ramsey, "Nonverbal Maintenance of Traditional Sex Roles"; Henley, *Body Politics*, Chapter 2; N. M. Henley and M. LaFrance, "Gender

as Culture: Difference and Dominance in Non-verbal Behavior," in A. Wolfgang (ed.), *Nonverbal Behavior: Perspectives, Applications, Intercultural Insights,* (Lewiston, N.Y.: C. J. Hogrefe, 1984), 351–71.

13. Henley, *Body Politics,* Chapter 3.

14. Henley, *Body Politics,* Chapter 7. See also B. Major, A. M. Schmidlin, and L. Williams, "Gender Patterns in Social Touch: The Impact of Setting and Age," *Journal of Personality and Social Psychology,* 58 (1990), 634–43.

15. R. J. Borden and G. M. Homleid, "Handedness and Lateral Positioning in Heterosexual Couples: Are Men Still Strongarming Women?" *Sex Roles,* 4 (1978), 67–73.

16. Hall, *Nonverbal Sex Differences,* 117.

17. Henley, *Body Politics,* Chapter 9; J. A Hall and A. G. Halberstadt, "Smiling and Gazing," in J. S. Hyde and M. C. Linn (eds.) *The Psychology of Gender: Advances Through Meta-Analysis,* (Baltimore: Johns Hopkins University Press, 1986); J. F. Dovidio and S. L. Ellyson, "Patterns of Visual Dominance Behavior in Humans," in S. L. Ellyson and J. F. Dovidio (eds.), *Power, Dominance and Nonverbal Behavior,* (New York: Springer-Verlag, 1985), 129–49.

18. Z. Rubin, "Measurement of Romantic Love," *Journal of Personality and Social Psychology,* 16 (1970), 265–73; quotation 272.

19. J. S. Efran and A. Broughton, "Effect of Expectancies for Social Approval on Visual Behavior," *Journal of Personality and Social Psychology,* 4 (1966), 103-7; quotation 103.

20. Dovidio and Ellyson, "Patterns of Visual Dominance Behavior," 129.

21. Dovidio and Ellyson, "Patterns of Visual Dominance Behavior." See also J. F. Dovidio, C. E. Brown, K. Heltman, S. L. Ellyson, and C. F. Keating, "Power Displays between Women and Men in Discussion of Gender-Linked Tasks: A Multichannel Study," *Journal of Personality and Social Psychology,* 55 (1988), 580–87; J. F. Dovidio, S. L. Ellyson, C. F. Keating, K. Heltman, and C. E. Brown, "The Relationship of Social Power to Visual Displays of Dominance Between Men and Women," *Journal of Personality and Social Psychology,* 54 (1988), 233–42.

22. See, for example, M. R. Key, *Male/Female Language,* (Metuchen, N.J.: Scarecrow, 1975); see also C. Kramarae, *Women and Men Speaking,* (Rowley, Mass.: Newbury House, 1981); Thorne, Kramarae, and Henley (eds.), *Language, Gender and Society;* R. Lakoff, *Language and Woman's Place,* (New York: Harper and Row, 1975); S. McConnell-Ginet, R. Borker, and N. Furman (eds.), *Women and Language in Literature and Society,* (New York: Praeger, 1980); and B. Thorne and N. Henley (eds.), *Language and Sex: Difference and Dominance,* (Rowley, Mass.: Newbury House, 1975).

23. D. Zimmerman and C. West, "Sex Roles, Interruptions and Silences in Conversation," in B. Thorne and N. Henley (eds.), *Language and Sex: Difference and Dominance,* (Rowley, Mass.: Newbury House, 1975), 105–29. See also C. West and D. Zimmerman, "Small Insults: A Study of Interruptions in Cross-Sex Conversations between Unacquainted Persons," in B. Thorne, C. Kramarae, and N. Henley (eds.), *Language, Gender and Society,* (Rowley, Mass.: Newbury House, 1983), 102–17.

24. W. M. Austin, "Some Social Aspects of Paralanguage," *Canadian Journal of Linguistics,* 11 (1965), 31–39.

25. J. A. Hall, *Nonverbal Sex Differences,* (Baltimore: Johns Hopkins University Press, 1984), 53.

26. P. D. Cherulnik, "Sex Differences in the Expression of Emotion in a Structured Social Encounter," *Sex Roles,* 5 (1979), 413–24.

27. E. P. Gerdes, J. D. Gehling, and J. N. Rapp, "The Effects of Sex and Sex-Role Concept on Self-Disclosure," *Sex Roles,* 7 (1981), 989–98.

28. V. J. Derlega, B. Durham, B. Gockel, and D. Sholis, "Sex Differences in Self-Disclosure: Effects of Topic Content, Friendship, and Partner's Sex," *Sex Roles,* 7 (1981), 433–47.

29. For example, see D. I. Slobin, S. H. Miller, and L. W. Porter, "Forms of Address and Social Relations in a Business Organization," *Journal of Personality and Social Psychology,* 8 (1968), 289–93.

30. E. A. Ross, *Principles of Sociology,* (New York: Century, 1921), 136. W. W. Waller and R. Hill, *The Family: A Dynamic Interpretation,* (New York: Dryden, 1951), 191.

31. N. M. Henley and M. LaFrance, "Gender as Culture: Difference and Dominance in Nonverbal Behavior," in A. Wolfgang (ed.), *Nonverbal Behavior: Perspectives, Applications, Intercultural Insights,* (Lewiston, N.Y.: C. J. Hogrefe, 1984), 351–71.

32. S. E. Snodgrass, "Women's Intuition: The Effect of Subordinate Role upon Interpersonal Sensitivity," *Journal of Personality and Social Psychology,* 49 (1985), 146–55; S. E. Snodgrass, "Further Perceptual Study," in S. L. Ellyson and J. F. Dovidio (eds.) *Journal of Personality and Social Psychology,* 62 (1992), 154–158.

33. N. M. Henley and S. Harmon, "The Nonverbal Semantics of Power and Gender: A Perceptual Study," in S. L. Ellyson and J. F. Dovidio (eds.), *Power, Dominance, and Nonverbal Behavior,* (New York: Springer-Verlag, 1985), 151–64.

34. For example, Lakoff, *Language and Woman's Place;* L. Z. Bloom, K. Coburn, and J. Pearlman, *The New Assertive Women,* (New York: Dell, 1976).

🦎 24

Teen Mags: How to Get a Guy, Drop 20 Pounds, and Lose Your Self-Esteem

ANASTASIA HIGGINBOTHAM

I used to be the teen magazine market's ideal consumer: vain, terribly insecure, white, and middle class. I craved affection and approval from boys (often at the expense of meaningful relationships with girls), spent far too much time staring at myself in the mirror, and trusted the magazines' advice on all sorts of really, really important issues, like lip gloss and *luv.*

I plastered my family's refrigerator with pictures of models I'd torn out of *YM, Seventeen, Sassy,* and *'Teen,* and also *Vogue, Cosmopolitan,* and *Mademoiselle*—a strategy I used to remind me not to eat. I hoped they would inspire me to do great things, like be in a David Lee Roth video. I wish I were kidding.

Though this characterization might lead you to believe I was kind of a doorknob, I assure you I was merely acting like most girls my age at whom these magazines are directed, aspiring to an ideal that I knew would bring me much success in the social world. In my first 14 years, I learned that the pretty girl who knows how to play the game wins the prize. The "prize" being older, cooler, all-star boyfriends, multiple mentions and pictures throughout the school yearbook, and seasonal dubbings as makeshift teen royalty (Homecoming Queen, May Queen, blow-job queen, and so on). And so I absorbed the rules of the game, with teen magazines serving as a reliable source of that information.

Ten years later, I pore over these magazines to see what they're telling girls today. As I flip through the pages of *YM, Seventeen, Sassy,* and *'Teen,* my blood begins to boil and my eyes cloud with anger; teen magazines make millions off of girls by assuming that girls need improving, and then telling girls how to make themselves prettier, cooler, and better. Has anything changed?

As horrified as I am by these magazines, I cannot deny their raging success. *Seventeen* and *YM* (which used to stand for *Young Miss* and now stands for *Young and Modern*) rake in nearly two million subscriptions each from their teen-to-early-twenties market. *'Teen* and *Sassy,* with readerships of 1.3 million and 800,000 respectively, cater to the younger end of the spectrum.

In each of the magazines, cover lines offer the girls "Model hair: how to get it," "Boy-magnet beauty," "Your looks: what they say about you," and "Mega makeovers: go from so-so to supersexy." Their image of the ideal girl is evidenced by the cover models: white, usually blond, and invariably skinny.

When I asked why this is, Caroline Miller, editor in chief of *Seventeen,* explained, "There's a traditional expectation that African-Americans don't sell magazines." *Seventeen* has recently tested this proposition (which, by the way, fails to address the invisibility of Asian and Native American models) by featuring pop star Brandy on its April cover and another African-American model on October's cover (both months are normally hot sellers). October sold just as well as the typical white-model cover, while the Brandy cover was possibly *Seventeen*'s best- selling April issue ever. Despite *Seventeen*'s success, rather than jeopardize newsstand sales and advertising dollars, well-intentioned editors at other magazines like *'Teen* and *Sassy* compromise by featuring some white-looking black model in a month that typically has the worst sales. Meanwhile, *YM* would probably be satisfied with a different shot of Drew Barrymore each month.

In the wake of *Sassy*'s transmogrification from bold, feminist teen mag into dumbed-down, superficial teen rag (*Sassy* was sold to Peterson Publishing, the same company that owns *'Teen,* in December 1994 after years of controversy with advertisers and parents over its content), *Seventeen,* under Miller, has taken up the *Sassy* mantle with smart stories about interracial dating, student activists, and African-American girls' body image. *YM,* on the other hand, offers nothing more than bullshit and bad advice, and *'Teen* is not much better. The new *Sassy* lacks much of the brains, courage, and wit of the old *Sassy;* something that its editors, tragically, see as a good thing.

Just what are the messages in the teen magazines? A series of catch-22s—ugliness is next to nothingness and a girl with insufficient interest in boys is referred to as a "deserted island," yet one who is too sexy is also in trouble. For instance, April 1995 *Sassy* warns girls to watch who they flirt with because men cannot distinguish between harmless flirting and a full-on pass. According to *Sassy,* while a girl is flirting, "there's always a chance [men are] wondering what you look like without your clothes on." This mentality is used to justify the behavior of grown men who "get a little carried away sometimes" and harass, insult, and assault young women. A girl bears the responsibility of attracting every "hottie" (hot guy) on the beach, but if one of them jumps her, well then, it sucks to be her. Using *Sassy*'s logic, that girl should have known she was dealing with a potential psychopath.

YM echoes this sentiment in the July 1995 episode of "Love Crisis," a column in which Editor in Chief Sally Lee solves "agonizing love problems." A girl reveals that she was invited by her boyfriend to a party that turned out to be just him and his two male friends. They got her really drunk and she "ended up . . . having sex with all of them!" She writes, "I feel so dirty. . . . How could I have been so stupid?" The letter is signed "Mortified." *YM* apparently wonders the same thing: a caption on the page with her letter reads "Wake up and face the facts: you made a pretty big mistake." Lee then chastises the girl for underage drinking and not asserting herself.

Even if the girl has not actually been gang-raped, Lee's complete disregard for a girl who was tricked and humiliated by her boyfriend and his friends is unforgivable. *YM* shamelessly promotes boy-catching tactics with articles like "the ultimate get-a-guy guide," then acts surprised, even judgmental, when the tricks actually work. Girls are bombarded with messages about the thrill of catching boys, so why is it shocking when a girl's pursuit includes a little creative compromise, like forgiving her boyfriend for lying about the party, drinking when he tells her to drink, and being too drunk to care (or too drunk to resist) when he and his friends fuck her? *YM* shows girls 100 asinine ways to be super-sexy and then provides them with no follow-up skills, self-defense, or self-esteem—as if ignorance will keep them from going all the way. If *YM* ever changes its name again, I suggest *Dicktease*.

Likewise, when it comes to body image, teen magazines send a convoluted message. Girls are encouraged to love their bodies, no matter what they look like, by magazines with fashion spreads featuring only stick-thin, flawless-faced white models in expensive outfits. Granted, there is that one light-skinned black girl in every fashion layout. But she's just as thin as the white girl standing next to her, and that white girl is *always* there—like a chaperone. Like it's the white girl's responsibility to keep the black girl in line, make sure she doesn't mingle with other black folks, start a riot or something. The black model doesn't have any black girlfriends; she's lucky if she gets a similarly non-threatening black boyfriend for the prom. Maybe they think if they surround her with enough white people no one will even notice she's black.

The thin factor is equally dismaying. While the old *Sassy* strictly enforced a no-diet policy, forbidding publication of any and all diet advice (including the kind masquerading as a fitness article), the new *Sassy* eats it up. Catherine Ettlinger, until recently the editorial director of the new *Sassy*, rejects the connection between articles offering diet tips and girls' obsession with thinness: "We present them with options. 'If you want to eat more low-fat stuff, here's some information; if you don't, fine.'"

If it were that simple, girls would not be getting sick. In a culture that all but demands that a women weigh no more than 120 pounds, girls do not want for diet advice. Girls do not need more low-fat options, nor do they need to learn how to shed or hide "excess fat." Similarly, when *'Teen, YM*, and *Seventeen* take a turn on the self-love/body-pride trip, they tend to fall flat on their faces. Photos that accompany the stories typically depict a model—who isn't the least bit fat. Readers are supposed to empathize with girls who weigh 125 pounds but who are afraid to put on a bathing suit, exposing what they perceive to be huge thighs and bulging stomachs. Girls are reminded that because of their "low self-esteem" (certainly not because of patriarchy), they imagine their bodies to be much larger than they actually are. So, if they can get over that self-esteem thing and realize that they're not fat, they have nothing to worry about.

While body hatred of this type is epidemic, presenting body image as being about thin girls who think they're fat does nothing to undermine the essential prejudice against fatness, especially fat women. Is a fat girl beautiful? Should she worry? If she relies on these magazines for affirmation of her self-worth, yes, she should. And so should we.

Teen magazines' glorification of boy-focused, looks-based, prom-obsessed idiocy reinforces every negative stereotype that has ever been used to justify—and ensure—women's second-class status. But as a woman with very clear memories of high school, I understand the trauma associated with fitting in and finding love. I was not prepared for a feminist revolution at 16; I could barely deal with what the humidity did to my hair.

I wanted to find out what girls think about teen magazines nowadays, so I staged an informal survey with a group of teenagers and showed them issues of *'Teen, Sassy, Seventeen,* and *YM.* Some girls criticized the magazines for being too white, too into skinny, and too superficial, but readily admitted to delighting in them anyway.

Kate Stroup from Philadelphia subscribes to *Seventeen,* as well as to various "adult" fashion magazines. "I like the ads," she says. Stroup and her friends can spend hours looking at the pictures, talking about the articles, "even talking about how bad it is." She explains, "It gives us something to bond over."

Girls looking for something easy and entertaining are sure to find it within the pages of teen magazines. Just as I lapped up celebrity gossip while researching this story, the girls I spoke with see no harm in learning a stupid hair trick.

Some girls read them for tips on navigating the social scene and dealing with relationships. "Sometimes I like to read about what guys say, not saying that I would actually follow their advice," says Kenya Hooks of Memphis.

But Roshanda Betts from Dallas no longer reads teen magazines. "I can't relate to them and I don't really think that they're made for me," she says, referring to the unrealistic size requirements for girls, racist definitions of beauty, and what she sees as the magazines' self-contradictions. "They have articles talking about, 'You should love yourself for who you are,' and then they have the seven-day diet."

The girls all like *Seventeen*'s "School Zone," which each month features six pages of photos and quotes from a different high school and which, according to Betts, "shows the spectrum of what's really happening." It's the only place in any of the magazines where kids from various racial and ethnic backgrounds, with "imperfect" shapes and "flawed" complexions, are portrayed in all their splendor. "School Zone" puts the rest of the images in the magazine to shame merely by providing a glimpse of truth.

In the articles, reality often comes in the form of "real-life stories" injected into each magazine, it seems, to scare the hell out of the girl reading it. We can choose from "one girl's battle with depression," another's physically abusive relationship, the story of a woman who sank to 55 pounds, a girl who was "raped, shot, and left for dead," and many more. Without some analysis or a context in which to place these stories (Why did she starve herself? How can we avert these tragedies?), they are nothing more than tales of tabloid horror.

Several months' worth of *'Teen, Seventeen, YM,* and *Sassy* left me with a blur of contradictory messages about how to navigate life as an adolescent girl. The sum of it is this: be pretty, but not so pretty that you intimidate boys, threaten other girls, or attract inappropriate suitors, such as teachers, bosses, fathers, and rapists; be smart, but not so smart that you intimidate boys or that, god forbid, you miss the prom to study for finals; be athletic, but not so athletic that you intimidate boys or lead people to believe that you are aggressive, asexual, or (gasp!) a lesbian or bisexual; be happy with yourself, but not if you're fat, ugly, poor, gay, disabled, antisocial, or can't at least pass as white.

The creators of teen magazines claim to reflect the reality of girls' lives; they say that they're giving girls what the girls say they want and, I'm sure that sometimes what girls want is, in fact, a new hairstyle and a prom date. But filling girls full of fluff and garbage—under the pretense that this is their reality—is patronizing, cowardly, and just plain lazy. Magazines that pride themselves on teaching girls beauty tips to "hide what they hate" ought to stop reflecting a reality marred by heterosexist double standards and racist ignorance and start changing it.

I understand the tremendous pressures that editors deal with from parents and advertisers who hold pristine ideas about teendom and girlhood and impose those ideas backed by the mighty dollar. But it's very clear where these editors and advertisers draw their lines. If they really wanted girls to love their bodies, they'd give them a few more shapes and colors to choose from, they'd provide articles exploring some of the real reasons why a girl might plow through a box of Oreos one moment, yak her guts out the next, and then zone in front of the television for 16 hours a day. If they can be so brazen about teaching a girl how to kiss the boy of her dreams, they can teach her how to kiss a girl. They just won't.   [1996]

 25

Gender in the Media

MARIELENA ZUNIGA

MEDIA: NOT A GIRL'S BEST FRIEND

Whether it's barely dressed women displayed in magazines, the treatment of women in the political arena, or the "bitches and ho's" portrayed in rap and hip-hop music—sexist ideas and imagery abound in the mass media. In magazines, film, TV, radio, and even within the field of print and broadcast journalism itself, women either are portrayed in sexist or stereotypical ways or are missing in great numbers.

In a Dolce & Gabbana magazine ad, for example, a scantily clad woman with spike heels is pinned on the ground by her wrists by a bare-chested man while four other men look on. Public outcry eventually forced Dolce & Gabbana to pull its "fantasy gang rape" ad. But it served its purpose—publicity and sales, which are key to advertisers who want to grab the public's attention and pocketbooks.

The connection between the economics and the messages women and girls and men receive can't be separated, says Carolyn M. Byerly, Ph.D., department of journalism, Howard University in Washington, D.C.[1] "The pattern we see, then, is that women are told they need to be thinner, wear certain kinds of clothing, which in Western countries

helps sexualize women," Byerly says. "It tells them there's something wrong with them, with the person they are and the body they were born into. If you have a strong, intelligent woman who wants to make her own way through life, who wants to be head of her class or government, who wants to exert her intelligence in some way—these things are downplayed when women are emphasized for their sexuality and allure."

And when it comes to the media's coverage of female politicians, the treatment is blatantly sexist. When Secretary of State Hillary Rodham Clinton took the step of becoming a viable female candidate for president in the United States' 232-year history, this incredibly accomplished woman was reduced to sexist stereotypes.

She was slammed for wearing a perceived low-cut blouse. Her legs were too fat. Her suits too boring. Her voice too screechy. News pundit Tucker Carlson portrayed Clinton as castrating, commenting, "Every time I hear Hillary Clinton speak, I involuntarily cross my legs."

Many other examples exist of powerful women leaders being defined by sexist stereotypes. Condoleeza Rice, when chosen by U.S. President Bush as national security advisor, was featured in a front page *New York Times* story about her clothing selection—that she preferred comfortable pumps and conservative jewelry and even had two mirrors on her desk to check the front and back of her hair.[2]

"The problem is that the media covers female politicians as if they're ladies first and leaders a distant second," says Jennifer Pozner, executive director of Women in Media & News (WIMN), a media analysis, education, and advocacy group in Brooklyn, New York. "What that does in terms of shaping public opinion is very damaging to the notion that women are competent, effective leaders."[3]

WHERE THE GIRLS AREN'T

The flip side of the media's sexist treatment of women and girls is their lack of representation. In early 2008, researchers from all over the U.S. and the world gathered in California for a conference presenting research about the representation of females in films and television. The event was sponsored by the Los Angeles-based Geena Davis Institute on Gender in Media (GDIGM), a nonprofit working to increase awareness of gender imbalance in the media and develop strategies to change media portrayals of women and girls.[4]

Academy Award winner Geena Davis (who played the first female U.S. president in the now-defunct TV series *Commander in Chief*) founded the Institute after watching children's television and videos with her then two-year-old daughter and noticing a remarkable imbalance in the ratio of male to female characters. At that conference, Davis said: "Whatever environment we're in on TV, it's nothing near the 50 percent we are in the world. Girls see this imbalance and realize 'I'm not important.' Women have presence and space in this world."

A conference overview of female portrayals on U.S. television pointed to more recent programs with stronger female characters, such as *Cold Case*, *Grey's Anatomy*, and *Law and Order*. Even with progress, however, research studies from the GDIGM show that both TV and film suffer from an underrepresentation of females. Today, the on-screen ratio of females to males is still only one in three, up from one in five two decades ago.

According to recent research by the USC Annenberg School for Communication and Journalism, only 29.9 percent of the 4,379 speaking characters identified in films were female, while 83 percent of all directors, writers, and producers were male.[5] "Our findings show a representational roadblock for females in film," said Stacy L. Smith, communication professor who led the study. "They do not occupy 'half of the cinematic sky'— far from it. There is a dearth of females working in the movie industry no matter which way you look at the data."

When girls are represented, they are valued first for appearance, and second for inner character, if at all, says Crystal Cook, the GDIGM's former director. These were the findings in a GDIGM study of 13 top-grossing children's films with female leads produced between the mid-1930s through 2005, many of them from Disney. Plots of the extreme makeover and romance were strong in movies such as *Cinderella*, *Sleeping Beauty*, *Anastasia*, and *The Little Mermaid*. Only one character wasn't looking for "happily ever after" with a prince charming— and that was Dorothy Gale from *The Wizard of Oz*.[6]

The GDIGM's studies also found that females are more than five times as likely as males to be shown in alluring apparel. The institute is not only concerned about how these messages affect women and young girls, but young males as well. It's just as important for males to see females as capable, valued for their character, and their stories as being worthwhile, Cook says.

"Males grow up to be the companions, employers and employees of women," she adds. "As young children, they are the playmates and schoolmates of girls. Patterns for lifelong behaviors begin when we are very young children and it's important for both girls and boys to see girls taking up space and being important from the youngest ages forward."

MULTIPLICITY OF IMAGES MISSING

Complex portrayals of both genders in film and TV are also important, Cook adds, because males can also be "stereotyped into being bumbling, ineffective, as distant dads or as overly aggressive." However, television has always portrayed a multiplicity of men in various characters, such as fathers and workers of all kinds, says Amanda D. Lotz, Ph.D., of the department of communication studies at University of Michigan, Ann Arbor, and author of *Redesigning Women: Television After the Network Era*.[7]

What's still missing on television is a multiplicity of images that show the diversity of women, such as characters that are lesbian, not white, in stable relationships or lacking rewarding careers, she says. "In some ways we've come 180 degrees with women portrayed overwhelmingly in career roles, but we don't see working-class women on TV very often," she says.

The lack of substantial roles for women of a certain age in Hollywood also concerns women's rights advocates. A documentary, *Invisible Women* sponsored by a grant from the Screen Actors Guild Foundation, spotlights the diminished careers of female actors who find themselves "pink-slipped" at 40, and includes interviews with, among others, Susan Sarandon and Christine Lahti.[8] "If characters in pop culture are not reflecting women over 40, it makes it even easier for employers to express biases—to put you into a little box based on gender stereotypes," Janice Grackin, a social psychology professor at Stony Brook University, New York, stated in a *Newsday* article.[9]

WOMEN OF COLOR

In addition, women of color are scarce in female leads, especially in film, says Cook. They also are "virtually invisible as experts and news sources," Pozner adds, and whether in news or entertainment, they are "deprived of any kinds of roles that speak to positions of power."

In film, radio, and television, women of ethnic backgrounds continue to be blatantly missing. According to a 2010 study released by the Motion Picture Association of America, women go to the movies more than men. Despite that fact, Hollywood continues to be a male-dominated industry, with actresses of color faring the worst. Only one movie released by Paramount in 10 years starred an actress of color—Queen Latifah in *Last Holiday* (2006). Out of 30 lead actresses, only one actress— Queen Latifah—was a person of color.

In Hollywood and many other areas of the mass media, Asian women are often portrayed as "China dolls" and as exotic, subservient, compliant, and eager to please. This stereotype is epitomized by the self-effacing title character of the opera *Madame Butterfly*, but it can also be seen in works like *Teahouse of the August Moon*. Another major female stereotype views Asian women as inherently scheming, untrustworthy, and back-stabbing. This portrayal is often named the "dragon lady," after the Asian villainess in the vintage comic strip *Terry and the Pirates*.

On prime-time cable new programs, more than three-quarters of the hosts are white men and less than a quarter are white women. None of the hosts are people of color. Latinos were particularly underrepresented. Though they now comprise 15 percent of the American population, they made up only 2.7 percent of cable news guests, according to Media Matters for America.

At daily newspapers, women and people of color remain under represented. Nearly 90 percent of reporters/writers and newsroom supervisors are white and about two-thirds are male. Women make up only one-third of the top 100 syndicated opinion columnists in the U.S. Just three of the top 10 op-ed writers are women.

GENDER/MEDIA PICTURE WORLDWIDE

The situation isn't much better globally. At the United Nations Fourth World Conference on Women in Beijing in 1995, the Platform for Action declared that "the print and electronic media in most countries do not provide a balanced picture of women's diverse lives and contributions to society in a changing world." In addition, it stated that "violent and degrading or pornographic media products are also negatively affecting women and their participation in society."

Despite the Platform for Action, women's voices are still largely absent from mainstream media. A media monitoring study carried out by 12 southern African countries found that stereotypes abound and are actively promoted by the media. The worse culprits, however, are in the Middle East where 98 percent of stories uphold gender stereotypes.[10]

Another report titled "The Gender of Journalism" found that even in a female-friendly nation such as Sweden, "journalism as a field has remained male-dominated." And in Spain, women are far from achieving equality "even in the most 'feminized' sectors of culture, such as literature," according to another report about women and culture.[11]

In 2009, volunteers in 108 countries across the world as part of the Global Media Monitoring Project (GMMP) spent much of the day pouring over national newspapers, listening to radio newscasts and watching television news to provide a snapshot of the representation and portrayal of women and men in news media.[12]

The report revealed that the agenda of the news media was not very different from information recorded in 2005. Women are still five times as likely to be portrayed in their roles as wives, mothers, etc., with women continuing to be under-represented as experts providing comments based on specialist knowledge of experience and spokespersons on behalf of organizations. In other words, 11 years into the new millennium, news stories are six times more likely to reinforce gender stereotypes than to challenge them, according to the GMMP.

The media in Asia, for instance, continue to focus on an idealized version of beauty. When Fabienne Darling-Wolf, Ph.D., lived and taught in Japan in 1995, more than 50 percent of models in Japanese magazines were white, she says. A professor in the department of journalism at Temple University in Philadelphia, Darling-Wolf focused her dissertation on Japanese women and their representation of attractiveness in the media. Her research found that in Japan's media-saturated society, magazines and "trendy dramas" (the equivalent of Latin America's telenovelas) all portrayed white and Westernized versions of beauty and appearance.[13]

"When I conducted interviews about this for my research, all the women were quite assertive about not liking the fact that there were White models in their magazines. They said, 'This does not fit us.' They were very adamant it was a bad thing," she says. "Since 1995, you look at Japanese magazines and you have fewer Western models but you have Japanese models who look Western."

The Japanese media also are notorious for pushing the starving beauty trend, where ideals of thinness and weight have become an obsession. Research points to the media-weight connection in the United States as well. One study found the amount of time adolescent girls watch soap operas, movies, and music videos is associated with their degree of body dissatisfaction and desire to be thin. In another study, 10-year-old girls told researchers they were unhappy with their bodies after watching a music video by Britney Spears.

"Many women feel they have these unrealistic standards the media has set to live up to in order to be wanted by a man," wrote another blogger on Ask Amy. "It's no wonder anorexia and depression affects so many young girls these days!"

One Canadian report, however, found that not all young women and teens were so easily influenced. They voiced everything from disappointment to annoyance and disgust at the media's portrayal of their gender. "As I get older, I'm trying to be a lot more comfortable with myself rather than trying to look at the images and say, 'I wish I was like that,'" a 21-year-old Ottawa student told CanWest News Service. "You're trying to figure out who you are, but there are some girls still trapped in that mindset—they're trying to be what the image on TV is telling them."

BEHIND THE SCENES, ON THE SCREEN

One reason women and girls suffer from negative portrayals in the media—if they're portrayed at all—has to do with whether women have access to authority and ownership levels in media. "We have to really understand how news is made, how TV programs are made, how films are made, and we have to look at the politics and economics of these," says Howard University's Byerly. "We have to understand that public policy has an awful lot to do with that."

More media mergers means fewer people are setting policies and their values trickle down through their main industries. In December 2007, the Federal Communications Commission (FCC) in the U.S. voted to allow greater consolidation in media ownership, despite vocal opposition from consumer groups and women's rights organizations.

Whenever the FCC allows big media conglomerates to gobble up more stations, it leaves fewer outlets for women to purchase, and the voices and viewpoints of women and people of color are even further marginalized. Today, women own only 6 percent of commercial broadcast television stations and full power radio stations.

There is also a dearth of female ownership in the entertainment industry, adds Cook, formerly of the GDIGM. "Although there are many more women in executive positions than before, women still lag greatly behind men in creative positions that hold power, such as writer, director and producer." Of the 150 films nominated for best picture from 1977 to 2006, only a handful were directed by women, including *Awakenings* by Penny Marshall, *The Piano* by Jane Campion, and *Little Miss Sunshine* by Valerie Faris.

In 2010, however, a woman broke new ground at the Academy Awards. Kathyrn Bigelow became the first woman in Oscar history to win the Best Director Award for her film *The Hurt Locker,* about a bomb-disposal team in Iraq. Bigelow called it "the moment of a lifetime." In total, the film garnered six Academy Awards, including Best Picture.

If anything, Byerly would like to see concerned women of all perspectives refocus or shift their attention to those who produce content in media. "It's important to keep writing and documenting and complaining about what we don't like," she says. "But I can tell you these things aren't going to change until we restructure industries and until women move into more decision-making positions in media."

And it will be up to women to make that happen. Dismayed at the way Hillary Clinton had been portrayed, supporters drafted language into the Democratic platform standing up against sexism and all intolerance. It reads, "Demeaning portrayals of women cheapen our debates, dampen the dreams of our daughters and deny us the contributions of too many."   [2011]

NOTES

1. Carolyn M. Byerly, interview, March 2009.
2. L. Flanders, 2004, *Bushwomen: How They Won the White House for Their Man.* Verso.
3. Jennifer Pozner, interview, March 2009.
4. Geena Davis Institute on Gender in Media, *GDIGM Major Findings Overview based on Gender Stereotypes: An Analysis of Popular Films and TV* (2008).
5. USC Annenberg School of Communication and Journalism, *USC Annenberg Study Shows Recent Top Films Lack Females on Screen and Behind Camera.*
6. Crystal Cook, interview, March 2009.
7. Amanda D. Lotz, interview, March 2009.
8. Invisible women productions.
9. *For Women of a Certain Age,* Newsday.com, April 1, 2005.
10. ILGA, *Gender and Media Misrepresentation in the Global South,* July 23, 2010.
11. IPS-InterPress Service, *The Untold Stories of Violence Against Women,* November 26, 2009.
12. The Global Media Monitoring Project, *Executive Summary,* September 2010.
13. Fabienne Darling-Wolf, interview, March 2009.

 26

Bitches and Morons and Skanks, Oh My!: What Reality TV Teaches Us About "Women"

JENNIFER L. POZNER

Women are bitches. Women are stupid. Women are incompetent at work and failures at home. Women are gold diggers.

How do we know? Because reality TV tells us so.

Media is our most common agent of socialization, shaping, and informing our ideas about people, politics, and public policy. Just ask Mike Darnell, the bottom-feeder suit at Fox who brought us such classy celluloid concoctions as *Who Wants to Marry a Multi-Millionaire, Joe Millionaire,* and *Temptation Island.* The secret to his ratings success, he once told *Entertainment Weekly,* is that his series are all "steeped in some social belief."

If you, like most people, think reality TV is harmless fluff, Darnell's admission should give you pause. When it comes to women, the "social beliefs" that reality producers, writers, and editors exploit are both anachronistic and toxic. According to a decade of "unscripted" (but carefully crafted) television, women are desperate, pathetic losers who can never possibly be happy without a husband—and it's hilarious when they get mocked, dumped, or punched in the face. We've learned that women of color are violent, ignorant, "ghetto" whores; bisexuals and lesbians only enjoy making out in view of horny male onlookers; and men must always beware of manipulative, money-grubbing gold-diggers. Meanwhile, fresh-faced teens, hard-working moms, and professional powerhouses alike all received the same memo: the only thing that *really* matters is how you look in a bikini.

That's just the beginning. What else do reality TV producers, writers, editors, and advertisers want us to believe it means to be a "real" woman today?

What do contemporary women think, how do they behave, who *are* they, at their core?

Here are three of the genre's most troubling answers.

1. CATTY, MANIPULATIVE BITCHES

From "frenemies" on lifestyle series such as *The Real Housewives* and *The Hills* to flat-out enemies on dating and modeling shows such as *The Bachelor* and *America's Next Top Model*, reality television presents women as being in constant competition for romantic love, professional success, and personal fulfillment. Like the crabby villains in those old Scooby Doo cartoons, everything a woman is supposed to want could be available to her . . . if not foiled by some meddling bitch.

"We're all enemies, vying for the same prize," one *For Love or Money* dater says of her sexed-up competitors. As proof, we're treated to endless scenes of love-starved ladies badmouthing one another to the lone Y chromosome in their midst. "Women tend to be jealous and catty and bitchy," one of *Joe Millionaire's* so-called "gold-diggers" insists. One angry *Bachelor* babe rants, "Girls can be conniving, deceiving and just vicious!" while another gestures a mock-punch and grumbles, "I want to kick her ass. I want to wring her neck. I want to so bad!" The lunkhead princes of such shows hardly hold their harems in higher esteem: "There's nothing like a good catfight!" Flavor Flav smirked on *Flavor of Love;* second season *Bachelor* Aaron grumbled, "The vindictive nature of all the women is starting to show."

That's right—*all* the women. It's not unusual for the genre to reduce an entire gender to a few insulting adjectives. Women's inherent cattiness is coded into promo commercials plastering the phrase "BACK STABBING!" in big, bold captions, while images of pretty babes are accompanied by feral hissing soundtracks. "The claws were *bound* to come out," announcers promise. Feline madness was also promised on *Age Of Love*, which pit "kittens" in their twenties against "cougars" in their forties to win the momentary affections of a doltish 30-year-old hunk. In the premiere, the 20-somethings hung around their apartment hula hooping in bikinis, while the "decrepit"

older women sewed needlepoint and did laundry (because that's what worn-out old crones do, yes?).

Women's antagonism toward one another is portrayed as innate even when a man isn't in the mix—and, we learn, it starts early. A *Toddlers & Tiaras* promo announces, "If competition had a face, it would be hers," over B-roll of a tot made up like a Gabor sister. Editing plays up regional and ethnic stereotypes. Stuck-up snobbery and betrayal among wealthy white women is a major theme of *The Real Housewives of Orange County*. In contrast, Italian-American women throw "low-class" tantrums on *RHO New Jersey*, accusing each other of prostitution, kidnapping, and drug dealing while flipping over banquet tables, while the African-American *RHO Atlanta* are called "ghetto," get into verbal brawls, and even hit one another.

Producers ensure that women dutifully perform their bitch-tastic roles by egging them on with techniques that would make PSY-OPS intelligence officers proud. After all, the same tactics used to produce the genre's oh-so-important "drama"— sleep deprivation, misinformation, constant surveillance, isolation from the outside world, minimal food, and constant alcohol—are often used as elements of torture. And so, they snipe away. They attack each other in antagonistic confrontations ("You are all a bunch of catty-ass bitches!"—*Flavor of Love*), conspire like high school Mean Girls ("[She's] a ho and she's got to go. She's a total bitch!"—*Joe Millionaire*), mouth off in bleep-filled "confessionals" ("You f★cking worthless c★nt. You are so . . . wasteful, bitchy, stupid . . . you're worthless. Your parents must be ashamed of you!"— *America's Next Top Model*). Whether sloshed and overtired or sober and alert, such angry outbursts are stoked and edited to "prove" that no matter how sophisticated or sweet her façade, nearly every woman is a selfish schemer deep down.

The moral of these sorry stories? If you don't want to get stabbed in the back, heed this canny *Bachelor* babe's advice: "I know better than to trust women."

2. STUPID, DITZY BIMBOS

Across unscripted subgenres, the female half of the population is portrayed as cringe-inducingly stupid. After all, we learn from *Bridezillas'* Karen, "Thinking is a waste of time. Thinking is for people who have no brains."

When the genre's gender templates were first being created, reality TV taught us that "dumb blondes" exist for our comedic pleasure. In 2002, the original reality TV train wreck, *The Anna Nicole Show*, encouraged us to snicker at the steady mental and physical decline of a buxom, addle-brained, and seemingly stoned former *Playboy* Playmate, whose slurred speech and erratic behavior fueled the show's tagline, "It's not supposed to be funny. It just is." One year later, MTV welcomed *Newlyweds'* star Jessica Simpson, who boggled our minds with how little seemed to be in hers. She told the U.S. secretary of the interior, "You've done a nice job decorating the White House," and couldn't tell the difference between chicken and tuna. Her every confused quote became proof that, as a *Dateline* newscast announced, "Saying something really dumb was now 'pulling a Jessica.'" Her presence on television was harkened as proof that the stereotype of the "'dumb blonde' won't go away" because "Maybe it's true."

Reality producers cut their teeth on "dumb blondes," but they want viewers to believe female stupidity knows no racial limits. On *The Real Housewives of Atlanta,* NeNe Leakes was portrayed as a simpering idiot, unable to help her son with his math homework because she doesn't know if one third is bigger or smaller than one half. While NeNe couldn't pass grade-school algebra, the sole white woman on the show, Kim Zociak, couldn't pass elementary English: asked, "How do you spell cat?" she replied: "K-A-T." Producers pounce on such moments to paint their stars as intellectually inferior, yet during *RHOA's* entire first season viewers never learned about original castmember DeShawn Snow's postgraduate divinity studies. Why? Because filming a competent, intelligent African-American woman pursuing a masters degree would have broken their preferred narrative: that Black women (and their wealthy white lady friends) are gossipy idiots.

Casting directors seek out female participants who are, lets just say, in no danger of being recruited to join Mensa. Producers pair them with male counterparts who expect to exploit their assumed

stupidity to get off—reality TV dudes act as if the less intelligent their conquest is, the more easily they can bed her—or to get over, as when *Survivor: Samoa* castaway Russell Hantz bragged about "my 'dumbass' girl alliance." Meanwhile, female scholars, business leaders, community advocates, and other high achievers are left off the dial.

While we don't get to see shows highlighting women's brilliance, sometimes their inherent idiocy is the concept around which an entire series is built. On Ashton Kutcher's *Beauty and the Geek,* dim-witted hotties paired with brainy but socially awkward boys are instructed to "teach" each other "valuable" life skills. The men instruct the women in math, science, grammar, geography, technology, and how to not be stuck-up bitches. In return, the "beauties" (code for "bimbos") teach the boys how to find the right pair of good-ass jeans, construct the perfect pickup line, and dazzle at cocktail parties with breaking news about Brangelina. The point of this "social experiment"? One gender's knowledge is vital to the workings of the world, while the other has a lock on all things superficial. Where the triumphant men emerge as smart, well-rounded individuals with oh-so-much-better haircuts, fashion sense, and confidence, the jiggly, giggly girls' "transformation" is limited to gushing about how they've looked *deep inside* and learned that *even geeks* can be good people. Wait, let me get that Harvard application.

Dating shows, too, bend over backward to convince us that women are dumb as a pile of rocks. On NBC's early reality series *Meet My Folks,* nubile young things were given a patronizing "smarts test" (sample question: "When was the war of 1812?"). When a ditzy dater thought there are 346 days in a year, the host snapped, "Are you blushing because you're embarrassed? Because if you're not, you should be!" Yet in a horrible catch-22, when reality TV women aren't embarrassingly dumb, they're condemned for *that,* too. This is what Tyra Banks told bony medical student Elyse, favored to win the first season of *America's Next Top Model,* just before eliminating the frontrunner:

> "Elyse, your look is really strong for the fashion world. . . . I admire your intelligence. I think you are so smart. But one thing with that intelligence is

that it can intimidate people, and there's a way to use that intelligence in a way that doesn't feel like you're maybe putting down other people or sounding derogatory."

After a long, silent pause for dramatic effect, Tyra sending Elyse packing. Her tiny couture bod made the grade, but her big, fat brain cost her the title, and the $100K that came with it. Get that, girls? Your mind is a terrible thing to use.

If we're supposed to assume that no one wants to see a brainiac in a bikini, we're also meant to understand that mental acuity isn't cute in the quest for love. Thinking for a living is seen as a romantic handicap. "I'm a rocket scientist," 25-year-old Natasha said by way of introduction to bachelor Luke on the opener of plus-size dating series *More to Love*. "My goodness. That's a little bit intimidating," he blurted in response. "Oh! Sorry!" she tittered self-consciously. He sent her home at the end of the first episode. As if there was ever any doubt.

3. WEAK WORKERS, WICKED WIVES, MEDIOCRE MOMS

The logical extension of women's stupidity is women's incompetence—the notion that we are inequipped to function effectively in the "real" world (not to mention *The Real World*).

Reality TV has very clear, archaic notions about what a "woman's place" is, and what it isn't: as one *Wife Swap* husband put it, fathers shouldn't do housework or cook for their children because "cave men, the dad would go out there, work, and mom would stay home, cook, clean, and take care of the kids." Women, the genre suggests ad nauseam, should be confined to their rightful realms of hearth and home (and, of course, hot tubs and strip clubs). But a funny thing happened on the way to prime time: even when we've shed any last indicators of pesky ambition for the confinement of reality-TV-approved domesticity, we still can't perform our "natural" roles with any efficacy.

We're losers while we're single, and especially pitiful if unmarried after 35, cautionary tales such as *Who Wants to Marry My Dad?* and *The Cougar* tell us.

We're terrors before we wed: "There's three kinds of Bridezillas stalking the streets of America: the Princess Bride, the Neurotic Bride, and the Obsessive Bride," warns a *Bridezillas* narrator in horror movie tones.

If we work outside the home for fulfillment or from economic necessity, we're slovenly housekeepers and bossy tyrants to wimpy husbands, or so says *Wife Swap*, a televised version of the news media's trumped-up "Mommy Wars."

We're piss-poor parents to our out-of-control children on *Super Nanny* and *Nanny 9-11*, where "experts" from central casting can accomplish more with our kids in just a few days of parenting-book platitudes than we can in all the years since we birthed them.

And as *The Real Housewives* are meant to illustrate, women with money are horrid human beings who care more about our implants, mansions, galas, and feuds than our kids, husbands, families, or communities.

Taken together, the reality TV landscape paints us as failures in the domestic domain that we're supposed to believe is our sole responsibility. If the genre insists women can't even perform well in their rightful realms of hearth and home—often described on family shows as our "God-given roles"—imagine how much worse its messages are about female performance in professional and public life.

Boob-power, not brainpower, is the key to women's success on *The Apprentice*, where ambitious (and always gorgeous) female executives are often shown relying on their sexuality to compete against men's supposedly inherent problem-solving abilities. They flirt with clients to raise donations for charity, flash their bellybuttons and drop their skirts to sell lemonade and M&Ms, and are depicted as inept when unable to coast on their feminine wiles. What Donald Trump presents as standard business practice is a recipe for a class action sexual harassment suit.

Excelling in sales negotiations is just one of many things reality TV tells women we just can't do. We can't wait tables, milk cows, or manage not to desecrate cremated ashes (*The Simple Life*). We can't inseminate pigs, sling fast food burgers, or avoid getting drunk as a nudist colony staffer (*New York Goes to Work*). We can't serve and protect ("Female officers put people's lives at risk," a husband tells his "new wife," a cop, on *Wife Swap*). We can't work construction, or even assemble an out-of-the-box children's playground safely (*Charm School*). We can't cook as delectably as men (only one *Top Chef* winner in six seasons has been female). We can't write or sing hip-hop (*Ego Trip's The [White] Rapper Show*). We can't even dress ourselves appropriately for work, play, or the simple task of not embarrassing our loved ones (*What Not to Wear*).

THE BOTTOM LINE ABOUT REALITY TV'S "BITCHES," "BIMBOS," AND "INCOMPETENT SKANKS"

Reality shows can be addictively amusing—but make no mistake, they are also deeply political. Their ideology mirrors *Mad Men* minus the cool clothes, and their producers have routinely glorified *and tried to revive* archaic gender stereotypes most of us assume died away 50 years ago.

As any advertising executive can attest, media images impact our desires, our beliefs, and our behavior—often dramatically. For example, more than one 1,000 viewers preordered the Pontiac Solstice *sight unseen* within 41 minutes of GM launching the car on a commercial masquerading as a storyline on *The Apprentice*.

Long-term exposure to tropes about women as stupid, incompetent, gold-digging bitches may begin to affect the way we see ourselves, our relationships to friends, loved ones, and co-workers, and our own place in public and private life. Damning portrayals of women's incompetence at home and at work can send messages that are truly toxic to women's rights. If women are generally flakier, less talented, and less capable than men, why hire us, support our artwork, elect us as politicians, pay attention to our concerns as citizens, or respect us as equal life partners? Likewise, the reign of the reality TV Ditz Queen is an attempt to reinforce a deeply held social belief (here's looking at you, Mike Darnell!) about women's inherent intellectual inferiority that we have struggled for centuries

to overcome. And depictions of women as inherently at war over female beauty and male booty put an entertaining spin on decades of corporate news coverage pitting women against one another socially and economically, diverting attention from true problems we could be allying to solve. If millions of TV viewers come to believe that sisterhood is not powerful but spiteful, it becomes all that much harder for women to achieve any further social, economic, or political progress.

Young women and men who reached voting age this year would have been just eight years old when reality shows such as *Who Wants to Marry a Multi-Millionaire* arranged an on-air wedding between an unsuspecting bride and a groom with a secretly violent, restraining-order-tainted past. If they've had TVs in their homes (or on their computers), they've potentially consumed a steady diet of thousands of hours of programming claiming that in "reality," female solidarity doesn't exist, women's inequality in the workplace and government is the result not of structural bias but individual weakness, and the most important thing a girl can do is look pretty. How can this help but poison their worldview?

So the next time *The Bachelor* asks, "Will you accept this rose?"—consider the thorns.   [2011]

NOTE

Jennifer L. Pozner is a journalist, a lecturer, and the director of Women In Media & News. This essay was adapted from *Reality Bites Back: The Troubling Truth About Guilty Pleasure TV*. You can read additional excerpts, watch a satirical media literary webisode series "Reality Rehab," and find information about multimedia lectures and workshops at RealityBitesBackBook.com.

 27

Words of Protest: How to Write an Effective Letter to the Editor

JENNIFER L. POZNER

When an 11-year-old girl is brutally gang raped by 18 boys and men ranging from middle school attendees to a 27-year-old, the *New York Times* reports that the victim wore inappropriate clothing and was known to hang out with older boys, and laments that, in the words of quoted sources, "These boys have to live with this the rest of their lives."

You flip through the cable news dial and on seemingly every network, all-male panels of politicians and pundits are discussing conservatives' latest attempts to restrict women's access to birth control, abortion, and ob-gyn care—and few bother to allow any women (not to mention feminists) a voice in the debate.

More than a million feminists and their allies gather in Washington, D.C., for a March for Women's Lives in 2004, then the largest-ever protest in the nation's capital—bigger than every civil rights and anti-war protest in the 1960s. America's top print and broadcast news outlets significantly undercount protestors' numbers and frame their demands as having little to no impact . . . when they don't ignore the march entirely.

California Democrats Loretta and Linda Sanchez become the first sisters ever to serve together in Congress, and the *Washington Post* devotes 1,766 words in its style section to inform readers about the representatives' preferences regarding housekeeping, hairstyles, and "hootchy shoes." (Number of paragraphs focusing on the congresswomen's political viewpoints: one.)

In the year 2000, just as Condoleeza Rice becomes the first African-American National Security Advisor, Fox rolls out "Who Wants to Marry a Multi-Millionaire," which advances the notion that women can only achieve success by proxy, as arm candy to rich husbands. By 2009, Senator Hillary Rodham Clinton is the Democratic front-runner for president and Sarah Palin is the GOP nominee for VP—but on "reality" TV, "The Millionaire Matchmaker" and "The Real Housewives of New York City" showcase women who aspire mostly to lives of leisure.

So, what else is new? Sexist and biased fare is business as usual for all too many media outlets—but what do you do when hurling household objects at Bill O'Reilly's head just isn't enough? These tips from Women in Media & News (WIMN), a New York-based media-monitoring, training, and advocacy group, can help you make the leap from righteous indignation to effective critique.

BE FIRM BUT POLITE

Make your case sans insults, rants, and vulgarity. Nothing makes it easier for editors and producers to dismiss your argument than name-calling. Good idea: "Your discussion of the rape survivor's clothing and makeup was irrelevant, irresponsible, and inappropriate. Including those details blames the victim and reinforces dangerous myths about sexual assault." Bad idea: "Your reporter is a woman-hating incarnate of Satan!"

BE REALISTIC BUT OPTIMISTIC

Calling for the *New York Times* to transform itself into a socialist newspaper will get you nowhere; suggesting that quotes from industry executives be balanced by input from labor and public-interest groups is more likely to be taken seriously.

CHOOSE YOUR BATTLES

While we'd all like to see fewer exploited female bods used to sell beer, asking the networks to reject such ads is a waste of time. (A letter-writing campaign to the companies that produce those ads is another matter.) However, it's worth the effort to pressure news corporations to strictly uphold the wall between advertising and editorial, and to lobby the Federal Communications Commission to demand disclosure of product placement every time stealth advertising appears on screen. After all, imagine how different your viewing experience would be if the words "This is an ad!" or "Commercial!" appeared on screen every time a rejected bachelorette sobs into her name-brand cell phone on a reality TV dating show, or an unhealthily skinny girl is belittled while filming a TV ad for CoverGirl in a product placement infomercial masquerading as program content on "America's Next Top Model."

CORRECT THE RECORD

For example, remind media outlets discussing "partial birth abortion" that this imprecise and inflammatory term doesn't refer to an actual medical procedure but is, rather, a political concept fabricated by conservative groups to decrease public support for abortion rights. Focusing on facts is more persuasive than simply expressing outrage: "Christina Hoff Sommers's quote contained the following inaccuracies" or "It is irresponsible to quote sources who are widely known to lie about matters of public record" are better than "Antifeminists like Christina Hoff Sommers should not be quoted in your newspaper."

EXPOSE BIASED OR DISTORTED FRAMING

Look at whose viewpoint is shaping the story. Does a news report about economic policy quote only representatives of corporations or government, without featuring any substantive input from labor advocates or economic justice experts? Does a piece about foreign policy describe war as inevitable, without including perspectives of experts in diplomacy?

KEEP IT CONCISE AND INFORMATIVE

If your goal is publication on the letters page, a couple of well-documented paragraphs will always be better received than an emotional three-page manifesto. Sticking to one or two main points will get a busy editor to read through to the end.

AVOID OVERGENERALIZATION

Don't complain that your local paper "never" reports on women's issues or "always" ignores poor people. Even if stories on topics like workfare are infrequent or inaccurate, their very existence will serve as proof to editors that your complaint doesn't apply to their publication.

ADDRESS THE APPROPRIATE PERSON

Letters about reportorial objectivity sent to editorial columnists or opinion-page editors will be tossed in the circular file.

PROOFREAD!

Nothing peeves an editor faster than typos or bad grammar.

FINALLY, GIVE 'EM CREDIT

Positive reinforcement can be as effective as protest. Be constructive whenever possible, and commend outlets when they produce in-depth, bias-free coverage.   [2011]

 28

No Respect: Gender Politics and Hip-Hop

JOHNNETTA COLE and BEVERLY GUY-SHEFTALL

WHAT'S LOVE GOT TO DO WITH IT?

At the core of the gender politics of hip-hop is a pervasive and profound ambivalence toward Black women and the portrayal of relations between the sexes as primarily conflictual. In an important study of gangsta rap's influence on college students' actual attitudes, and potentially their behavior, Professor Bruce Wade and his student Cynthia Thomas-Gunnar present a compelling argument that "explicit [rap] lyrics are generally inappropriate and harmful to society."[1] They discovered that contemporary Black college students, especially men, believe that rap music accurately portrays gender relations. Is it any wonder then, since the music frequently communicates a general hostility, distrust, and disregard for Black women as anything other than atomized body parts and sex objects, that the study concluded that men who listen to rap music favorably were more likely to harbor attitudes that could be described as rape-prone?

Given the enormous popularity of hip-hop and gangsta rap, this is certainly a frightening and explosive finding. It confirms many critics' beliefs that rap music has an undeniable and adverse influence on its young listeners. Certain rap music lyrics, particularly gangsta rap, are apparently effective at communicating a dangerous message: that the enemy of Black urban youth is not just the police or poverty, not only an unjust system, but Black women and girls as well. Songs like "Trust

No Bitch, Trust No Hoe" and "Bitch Betta Have My Money" portray Black women as predatory, untrustworthy, and worthless.

In many of these music videos, women are stripped of any humanizing subjective identity, since the viewer observes only body parts, and the script is usually what social critic Michael Eric Dyson refers to as the rappers' "subterranean, pornographic fantasies."[2] Often described as "booty rap," this form of rap is "characterized by an obsession with sex and perverted eroticism, visually backed by scantily clothed women mimicking sex and sometimes actually performing it on stage," according to Perkins.[3] As evidenced by the lyrics of Underground Kingz (UKG), even pedophilia becomes fair game in this distorted and unreal world of rap, sex, and violence. In an *Essence* article, "Are Music Videos Pimping Our Girls?" self-described hip-hop feminist Joan Morgan believes "it's up to us to identify these videos for what they are—adult content that shouldn't be shown in prime time."

THE VIRGIN/WHORE SPLIT

Given mainstream culture's simple classification of women as virgins or whores—or, as Dyson puts it, angels or demons—it is not surprising, although it is disappointing, that contemporary African American culture has internalized a general animosity and ambivalence toward women. We believe strongly that the overwhelmingly sexist representations of Black women in gangsta rap and hip-hop are linked to persistent negative images of Black womanhood in mainstream American culture. While African American culture is distinct in many ways from white culture, it is not immune to external influences. To be sure, the misogyny in hip-hop/gangsta rap is not entirely different in its impact from the woman-hating messages of the dominant culture. As one critic of hip-hop rightly points out, "The misogynist lyrics of gangsta rap are hateful indeed, but they do not represent a new trend in Black popular culture, nor do they differ fundamentally from woman-hating discourses that are common among White men."[4] To understand this hostility, we have to begin with an analysis of the larger American

cultural framework. A consideration of the legacy of slavery is a good place to begin a serious examination of the root causes of the gender conflicts that can be highlighted in hip-hop.

Under slavery, Black women's bodies were viewed as commodities, and used as a breeding ground for the reproduction of a slave population. Enslaved Black women were also raped for the illicit pleasure of predatory white slave masters. Lacking control of their sexuality and unable as mothers to protect their children from being sold, Black women have always occupied a precarious social space in American society.

Paradoxically, Black women have long represented the asexual, caretaking "mammy"; the seductive and licentious siren; as well as the long-suffering or emasculating matriarch. The deeply held belief that Black women are less valuable than women of other races/cultural groups—a legacy of slavery—pervades all aspects of American culture. Because their bodies have been devalued and unprotected, it is appalling but not surprising that exploitative surgical procedures were perfected using the bodies of enslaved women in the American South. Anthropologist and writer Zora Neale Hurston captures the devalued status of Black women in her famous novel *Their Eyes Were Watching God* (1937). Here, she creates a strong female protagonist, Janie Crawford, who struggles to assert her personal and sexual independence in the face of criticism from a visible Black community and an invisible white world. As Janie comes of age, her grandmother cautions her against trying to establish her own identity and place in the world because "Black women is de mules of deh earth."

. . . As long as female hip-hop artists are willing to break down barriers and challenge misogyny in hiphop culture, there is reasonable hope for progress. And when a lone male dares to go against the pack, there is cause for celebration as well. Writer and cultural critic Kevin Powell asserted in his "Confessions of a Recovering Misogynist": "These days I am a hip-hopper-in-exile. I dress, talk, and walk like a hip-hopper, yet I cannot listen to rap radio or digest music videos without commenting on the pervasive sexism. . . . I constantly 'pick on the men' and myself, because I truly wonder how many men actually listen to the concerns of women."[5]

The range of gender ideologies in hip-hop, whether deployed by men or women, requires much greater scrutiny as well as a commitment by hip-hop artists and producers to healing the rift between the sexes that is becoming harder-edged and more mean-spirited than ever before. We hope that rap artists who create this powerful music, which is now exported around the globe, can be persuaded to respond positively to critiques about its potentially negative impact on young people. The historic hip-hop summit that took place in New York City in June of 2001 and brought together hip-hop artists with influential leaders, mostly male, from many segments of the Black community, was a welcome intervention. Organized by rap music mogul Russell Simmons (Rush Communications/Def Jam Recordings), the summit participants included Kweisi Mfume (NAACP), Minister Louis Farrakhan (Nation of Islam), Representative Cynthia McKinney (Democrat-Georgia), scholars Manning Marable, Cornel West, and Michael Eric Dyson, as well as hip-hop artists such as Sean (Puffy) Combs (Bad Boy Records).[6] Rap music has the artistic space to accommodate competing and complementary views. But if the more positive, progressive voices are to be heard and have an impact, rap artists must gain greater control over the production of their work and the dissemination of their messages. This is a challenge when the mostly white, greedy corporate world controls the production and distribution processes with no regard for promoting positive social values or healing the social rifts between Black men and women.

To be sure, the ultimate responsibility for shifting the language and images now pervasive in some strands of rap music lies within Black communities. Several African American leaders are committed to continuing meeting with leading hip-hop producers and superstar performers with hopes of persuading them to use the power of their lyrics to communicate more positive, empowering messages. The most prominent leader to wage war on rap music while also calling for dialogue with rap artists has been the Reverend Calvin Butts, pastor of Harlem's famous Abyssinian Baptist Church. An outspoken organizer at the 1993 protest rally in New York City during which he called for censorship, the Reverend Butts continues his advocacy efforts for major reforms in the rap community despite their First Amendment rights to free speech. More of us, on an individual and collective level, must challenge degrading images of women, boycott music that perpetuates hate and gratuitous violence, and talk, talk, talk with one another in our schools, universities, churches, mosques, and community centers about how we can move a more solution-oriented gender debate into the public arena. We must continue to dialogue with artists and producers of rap about creating more affirming, socially conscious messages. We must demand that songs with countermessages get more air time, such as BWP's "NO means NO!" and A Tribe Called Quest's "Date Rape," which assails acquaintance violence. We must address ways of countering the low self-esteem that plagues many of our young people to the point where they demean themselves with words and images as powerful as shackles, whips, and nooses.

We must engage in active resistance to the more toxic aspects of hip-hop. At the annual NAACP conference in Houston, Texas, during the first week of July 2002, President Kweisi Mfume denounced "song lyrics [that] defame our struggle, demean our ancestors, denigrate our women, and disrespect our culture.[7] Of all the problems facing Black America that he delineated—incarceration, breast cancer, prostate cancer, HIV/AIDS—his reference to hip-hop received the most rousing response from the audience, suggesting that many Black people are fed up with certain aspects of this music. It is imperative that we seriously consider that the negative consequences of our young people being exposed to a steady stream of antisocial messages, pornographic images, and destructive behaviors will continue to erode our communities from within. And the ticking time bomb of corrosive gender relations will inevitably explode in our faces.

In the October 2002 issue of *Ebony*, editor Lerone Bennett Jr.'s hard-hitting article, "Sex and Music: Has It Gone Too Far?," labels this sexually explicit music "macho-macho," and articulates the ways in which it is harmful to Black communities. He is also clear about what we must do: "We also need a new understanding—in the media, in the entertainment industry, in our churches, schools and organizations—that popular songs are as important as civil rights bills and that a society that pays pipers to corrupt its young and to defame its women and mothers will soon discover that it has no civil rights to defend and no songs to sing" (150).

The power of words—and the attitudes they reflect—cannot be ignored. The hateful and harsh gender talk in too much of rap music and American popular culture must be addressed by socially conscious women and men who deplore violence and misogyny, and understand the damage it does within our communities and around the world.   [edited, 2003]

NOTES

1. Bruce Wade and Cynthia Thomas-Gunnar, "Explicit Rap Music Lyrics and Attitudes Toward Rape: The Perceived Effects on African American College Students' Attitudes," *Challenge: A Journal of Research on African American Men* (October 1993), 58.
2. Michael Eric Dyson, *Holler If You Hear Me* (New York: Basic Books, 2001).
3. William Eric Perkins, ed., *Droppin' Science: Critical Essays on Rap Music and Hip Hop Culture* (Philadelphia: Temple University Press, 1996), 24.
4. Leola Johnson, "Rap, Misogyny and Racism," *Radical America* 26, no. 3 (1992), p. 10.
5. Kevin Powell, "Confessions of a Recovering Misogynist," *Ms.*, April/May 2000, p. 77.
6. See Kevin Chappell, "Hip-Hop at the Crossroads: Will Lyrics and Perceptions Change?," *Ebony*, September 2001, pp. 111–114.
7. The Honorable Kweisi Mfume, Keynote Address, 2002 NAACP Annual Convention, Houston, Texas, July 2002. Quoted in *The Atlanta Journal-Constitution*, July 9, 2002, p. A3.

 29

If Women Ran Hip Hop

BY AYA DE LEON

If women ran hip hop
the beats & rhymes would be just as dope,
but there would never be a bad vibe when you
    walked in the place

& the clubs would be beautiful & smell good
& the music would never be too loud
but there would be free earplugs available anyway
& venues would have skylights and phat patios
and shows would run all day not just late at night
cuz If women ran hip-hop we would have nothing
    to be ashamed of
& there would be an African marketplace
with big shrines to Oya
Yoruba deity of the female warrior & entrepreneur
and women would sell & barter & prosper
If women ran hip hop
there would never be shootings
cuz there would be onsite conflict mediators
to help you work through all that negativity &
    hostility
& there would also be free condoms & dental dams
in pretty baskets throughout the place
as well as counselors to help you make the
    decision:
do I really want to have sex with him or her?
& there would be safe, reliable, low-cost 24 hour
    transportation home
& every venue would have on-site quality
    child care
where kids could sleep while grown folks danced
& all shows would be all ages
cause the economy of hip-hop wouldn't revolve
    around the sale of alcohol
If women ran hip hop
same gender-loving & transgender emcees
would be proportionally represented
& get mad love from everybody
& females would dress sexy if we wanted to
    celebrate our bodies
but it wouldn't be that important because
everyone would be paying attention to our minds,
    anyway
If women ran hip hop
men would be relieved because it's so draining
to keep up that front of toughness & power
    & control 24-7
If women ran hip hop
the only folks dancing in cages would be
    dogs & cats
from the local animal shelter

excited about getting adopted by pet lovers in the
    crowd
If women ran hip-hop
there would be social workers available to refer
    gangsta rappers
to 21-day detox programs where they could get
    clean & sober
from violence & misogyny
but best of all, if women ran hip hop
we would have the dopest female emcees ever
because all the young women afraid to bust
would unleash their brilliance on the world   [2007]

 30

Video

INDIA.ARIE

Sometimes I shave my legs and sometimes I don't
Sometimes I comb my hair and sometimes I won't
Depend on how the wind blows I might even paint
    my toes
It really just depends on whatever feels good in my
    soul

I'm not the average girl from your video
And I ain't built like a supermodel
But I learned to love myself unconditionally,
Because I am a queen

When I look in the mirror and the only one there
    is me
Every freckle on my face is where it's supposed
    to be
And I know my creator didn't make no mistakes
    on me
My feet, my thighs, my lips, my eyes, I'm loving
    what I see

Am I less of a lady if I don't wear pantyhose?
My momma said a lady ain't what she wears but
    what she knows
But I've drawn the conclusion, it's all an illusion
Confusion's the name of the game

A misconception, a vast deception,
Something's got to change

Now don't be offended this is all my opinion
Ain't nothing that I'm saying law
This is a true confession
Of a life-learned lesson
I was sent here to share with y'all
So get in when you fit in
Go on and shine

Clear your mind
Now's the time
Put your salt on the shelf
Go on and love yourself
'Cause everything's gonna be alright

Keep your fancy drink, and your expensive minks
I don't need that to have a good time
Keep your expensive cars and your caviar
All's I need is my guitar

Keep your Cristal and your pistol
I'd rather have a pretty piece of crystal
Don't need no silicone, I prefer my own
What God gave me is just fine.

I'm not the average girl from your video
And I ain't built like a supermodel
But I learned to love myself unconditionally,
Because I am a queen.   [2001]

 31

X: A Fabulous Child's Story

LOIS GOULD

Once upon a time, a baby named X was born. This
baby was named X so that nobody could tell whether
it was a boy or a girl. Its parents could tell, of course,
but they couldn't tell anybody else. They couldn't
even tell Baby X, at first.

You see, it was all part of a very important Secret Scientific Xperiment, known officially as Project Baby X. The smartest scientists had set up this Xperiment at a cost of Xactly 23 billion dollars and 72 cents, which might seem like a lot for just one baby, even a very important Xperimental baby. But when you remember the prices of things like strained carrots and stuffed bunnies, and popcorn for the movies and booster shots for camp, let alone 28 shiny quarters from the tooth fairy, you begin to see how it adds up.

Also, long before Baby X was born, all those scientists had to be paid to work out the details of the Xperiment, and to write the *Official Instruction Manual* for Baby X's parents and, most important of all, to find the right set of parents to bring up Baby X. These parents had to be selected very carefully. Thousands of volunteers had to take thousands of tests and answer thousands of tricky questions. Almost everybody failed because, it turned out, almost everybody really wanted either a baby boy or a baby girl, and not Baby X at all. Also, almost everybody was afraid that a Baby X would be a lot more trouble than a boy or a girl. (They were probably right, the scientists admitted, but Baby X needed parents who wouldn't *mind* the Xtra trouble.)

There were families with grandparents named Milton and Agatha, who didn't see why the baby couldn't be named Milton or Agatha instead of X, even if it *was* an X. There were families with aunts who insisted on knitting tiny dresses and uncles who insisted on sending tiny baseball mitts. Worst of all, there were families that already had other children who couldn't be trusted to keep the secret. Certainly not if they knew the secret was worth 23 billion dollars and 72 cents—and all you had to do was take one little peek at Baby X in the bathtub to know if it was a boy or a girl.

But, finally, the scientists found the Joneses, who really wanted to raise an X more than any other kind of baby—no matter how much trouble it would be. Ms. and Mr. Jones had to promise they would take equal turns caring for X, and feeding it, and singing it lullabies. And they had to promise never to hire any baby-sitters. The government

scientists knew perfectly well that a baby-sitter would probably peek at X in the bathtub, too.

The day the Joneses brought their baby home, lots of friends and relatives came over to see it. None of them knew about the secret Xperiment, though. So the first thing they asked was what kind of a baby X was. When the Joneses smiled and said, "It's an X!" nobody knew what to say. They couldn't say, "Look at her cute little dimples!" And they couldn't say, "Look at his husky little biceps!" And they couldn't even say just plain "kitchy-coo." In fact, they all thought the Joneses were playing some kind of rude joke.

But, of course, the Joneses were not joking. "It's an X" was absolutely all they would say. And that made the friends and relatives very angry. The relatives all felt embarrassed about having an X in the family. "People will think there's something wrong with it!" some of them whispered. "There *is* something wrong with it!" others whispered back.

"Nonsense!" the Joneses told them all cheerfully. "What could possibly be wrong with this perfectly adorable X?"

Nobody could answer that, except Baby X, who had just finished its bottle. Baby X's answer was a loud, satisfied burp.

Clearly, nothing at all was wrong. Nevertheless, none of the relatives felt comfortable about buying a present for a Baby X. The cousins who sent the baby a tiny football helmet would not come and visit any more. And the neighbors who sent a pink-flowered romper suit pulled their shades down when the Joneses passed their house.

The *Official Instruction Manual* had warned the new parents that this would happen, so they didn't fret about it. Besides, they were too busy with Baby X and the hundreds of different Xercises for treating it properly.

Ms. and Mr. Jones had to be Xtra careful about how they played with little X. They knew that if they kept bouncing it up in the air and saying how *strong* and *active* it was, they'd be treating it more like a boy than an X. But if all they did was cuddle it and kiss it and tell it how *sweet* and *dainty* it was, they'd be treating it more like a girl than an X.

On page 1,654 of the *Official Instruction Manual,* the scientists prescribed: "plenty of bouncing and plenty of cuddling, *both.* X ought to be strong and sweet and active. Forget about *dainty* altogether."

Meanwhile, the Joneses were worrying about other problems. Toys, for instance. And clothes. On his first shopping trip, Mr. Jones told the store clerk, "I need some clothes and toys for my new baby." The clerk smiled and said, "Well, now, is it a boy or a girl?" "It's an X," Mr. Jones said, smiling back. But the clerk got all red in the face and said huffily, "In *that* case, I'm afraid I can't help you, sir." So Mr. Jones wandered helplessly up and down the aisles trying to find what X needed. But everything in the store was piled up in sections marked "Boys" or "Girls." There were "Boys' Pajamas" and "Girls' Underwear" and "Boys' Fire Engines" and "Girls' Housekeeping Sets." Mr. Jones went home without buying anything for X. That night he and Ms. Jones consulted page 2,326 of the *Official Instruction Manual.* "Buy plenty of everything!" it said firmly.

So they bought plenty of sturdy blue pajamas in the Boys' Department and cheerful flowered underwear in the Girls' Department. And they bought all kinds of toys. A boy doll that made pee-pee and cried, "Pa-pa." And a girl doll that talked in three languages and said, "I am the Pres-i-dent of General Mo-tors." They also bought a storybook about a brave princess who rescued a handsome prince from his ivory tower, and another one about a sister and brother who grew up to be a baseball star and a ballet star, and you had to guess which was which.

The head scientists of Project Baby X checked all their purchases and told them to keep up the good work. They also reminded the Joneses to see page 4,629 of the *Manual,* where it said, "Never make Baby X feel *embarrassed* or *ashamed* about what it wants to play with. And if X gets dirty climbing rocks, never say 'Nice little Xes don't get dirty climbing rocks.'"

Likewise, it said, "If X falls down and cries, never say 'Brave little Xes don't cry.' Because, of course, nice little Xes *do* get dirty, and brave little Xes *do* cry. No matter how dirty X gets, or how hard it cries, don't worry. It's all part of the Xperiment."

Whenever the Joneses pushed Baby X's stroller in the park, smiling strangers would come over and coo: "Is that a boy or a girl?" The Joneses would smile back and say, "It's an X." The strangers would stop smiling then, and often snarl something nasty—as if the Joneses had snarled at *them.*

By the time X grew big enough to play with other children, the Joneses' troubles had grown bigger, too. Once a little girl grabbed X's shovel in the sandbox, and zonked X on the head with it. "Now, now, Tracy," the little girl's mother began to scold, "little girls mustn't hit little—" and she turned to ask X, "Are you a little boy or a little girl, dear?"

Mr. Jones, who was sitting near the sandbox, held his breath and crossed his fingers.

X smiled politely at the lady, even though X's head had never been zonked so hard in its life. "I'm a little X," X replied.

"You're a what?" the lady exclaimed angrily. "You're a little b-r-a-t, you mean!"

"But little girls mustn't hit little Xes, either!" said X, retrieving the shovel with another polite smile. "What good does hitting do, anyway?"

X's father, who was still holding his breath, finally let it out, uncrossed his fingers, and grinned back at X.

And at their next secret Project Baby X meeting, the scientists grinned, too. Baby X was doing fine.

But then it was time for X to start school. The Joneses were really worried about this, because school was even more full of rules for boys and girls, and there were no rules for Xes. The teacher would tell boys to form one line, and girls to form another line. There would be boys' games and girls' games, and boys' secrets and girls' secrets. The school library would have a list of recommended books for girls, and a different list of recommended books for boys. There would even be a bathroom marked BOYS and another one marked GIRLS. Pretty soon boys and girls would hardly talk to each other. What would happen to poor little X?

The Joneses spent weeks consulting their *Instruction Manual* (there were 249½ pages of advice under "First Day of School"), and attending urgent special conferences with the smart scientists of Project Baby X.

The scientists had to make sure that X's mother had taught X how to throw and catch a ball properly, and that X's father had been sure to teach X what to serve at a doll's tea party. X had to know how to shoot marbles and how to jump rope and, most of all, what to say when the Other Children asked whether X was a Boy or a Girl.

Finally, X was ready. The Joneses helped X button on a nice new pair of red-and-white checked overalls, and sharpened six pencils for X's nice new pencilbox, and marked X's name clearly on all the books in its nice new bookbag. X brushed its teeth and combed its hair, which just about covered its ears, and remembered to put a napkin in its lunchbox.

The Joneses had asked X's teacher if the class could line up alphabetically, instead of forming separate lines for boys and girls. And they had asked if X could use the principal's bathroom, because it wasn't marked anything except BATHROOM. X's teacher promised to take care of all those problems. But nobody could help X with the biggest problem of all—Other Children.

Nobody in X's class had ever known an X before. What would they think? How would X make friends?

You couldn't tell what X was by studying its clothes—overalls don't even button right-to-left, like girls' clothes, or left-to-right, like boys' clothes. And you couldn't guess whether X had a girl's short haircut or a boy's long haircut. And it was very hard to tell by the games X liked to play. Either X played ball very well for a girl or played house very well for a boy.

Some of the children tried to find out by asking X tricky questions, like "Who's your favorite sports star?" That was easy. X had two favorite sports stars: a girl jockey named Robyn Smith and a boy archery champion named Robin Hood. Then they asked, "What's your favorite TV program?" And that was even easier. X's favorite TV program was "Lassie," which stars a girl dog played by a boy dog.

When X said that its favorite toy was a doll, everyone decided that X must be a girl. But then X said that the doll was really a robot, and that X had computerized it, and that it was programmed to bake fudge brownies and then clean up the kitchen.

After X told them that, the other children gave up guessing what X was. All they knew was they'd sure like to see X's doll.

After school, X wanted to play with the other children. "How about shooting some baskets in the gym?" X asked the girls. But all they did was make faces and giggle behind X's back.

"How about weaving some baskets in the arts and crafts room?" X asked the boys. But they all made faces and giggled behind X's back, too.

That night, Ms. and Mr. Jones asked X how things had gone at school. X told them sadly that the lessons were okay, but otherwise school was a horrible place for an X. It seemed as if the Other Children would never want an X for a friend.

Once more, the Joneses reached for the *Instruction Manual*. Under "Other Children," they found the following message: "What did you Xpect? *Other Children* have to obey all the silly boy-girl rules, because their parents taught them to. Lucky X—you don't have to stick to the rules at all! All you have to do is be yourself. P.S. We're not saying it'll be easy."

X liked being itself. But X cried a lot that night, partly because it felt afraid. So X's father held X tight, and cuddled it, and couldn't help crying a little, too. And X's mother cheered them both up by reading an Xciting story about an enchanted prince called Sleeping Handsome, who woke up when Princess Charming kissed him.

The next morning, they all felt much better, and little X went back to school with a brave smile and a clean pair of red-and-white checked overalls.

There was a seven-letter-word spelling bee in class that day. And a seven-lap boys' relay race in the gym. And a seven-layer-cake baking contest in the girls' kitchen corner. X won the spelling bee. X also won the relay race. And X almost won the baking contest, except it forgot to light the oven. Which only proves that nobody's perfect.

One of the Other Children noticed something else, too. He said: "Winning or losing doesn't seem to count to X. X seems to have fun being good at boys' skills *and* girls' skills."

"Come to think of it," said another one of the Other Children, "maybe X is having twice as much fun as we are!"

So after school that day, the girl who beat X at the baking contest gave X a big slice of her prize-winning cake. And the boy X beat in the relay race asked X to race him home.

From then on, some really funny things began to happen. Susie, who sat next to X in class, suddenly refused to wear pink dresses to school any more. She insisted on wearing red-and-white checked overalls—just like X's. Overalls, she told her parents, were much better for climbing monkey bars.

Then Jim, the class football nut, started wheeling his little sister's doll carriage around the football field. He'd put on his entire football uniform, except for the helmet. Then he'd put the helmet *in* the carriage, lovingly tucked under an old set of shoulder pads. Then he'd start jogging around the field, pushing the carriage and singing "Rockabye Baby" to his football helmet. He told his family that X did the same thing, so it must be okay. After all, X was now the team's star quarterback.

Susie's parents were horrified by her behavior, and Jim's parents were worried sick about him. But the worst came when the twins, Joe and Peggy, decided to share everything with each other. Peggy used Joe's hockey skates, and his microscope, and took half his newspaper route. Joe used Peggy's needlepoint kit, and her cookbooks, and took two of her three baby-sitting jobs. Peggy started running the lawn mower, and Joe started running the vacuum cleaner.

Their parents weren't one bit pleased with Peggy's wonderful biology experiments, or with Joe's terrific needlepoint pillows. They didn't care that Peggy mowed the lawn better, and that Joe vacuumed the carpet better. In fact, they were furious. It's all that little X's fault, they agreed. Just because X doesn't know what it is, or what it's supposed to be, it wants to get everybody *else* mixed up, too!

Peggy and Joe were forbidden to play with X any more. So was Susie, and then Jim, and then *all* the Other Children. But it was too late; the Other Children stayed mixed up and happy and free, and refused to go back to the way they'd been before X.

Finally, Joe and Peggy's parents decided to call an emergency meeting of the school's Parents' Association, to discuss "The X Problem." They sent a report to the principal stating that X was a "disruptive influence." They demanded immediate action. The Joneses, they said, should be *forced* to tell whether X was a boy or a girl. And then X should be *forced* to behave like whichever it was. If the Joneses refused to tell, the Parents' Association said, then X must take an Xamination. The school psychiatrist must Xamine it physically and mentally, and issue a full report. If X's test showed it was a boy, it would have to obey all the boys' rules. If it proved to be a girl, X would have to obey all the girls' rules.

And if X turned out to be some kind of mixed-up misfit, then X should be Xpelled from the school. Immediately!

The principal was very upset. Disruptive influence? Mixed-up misfit? But X was an Xcellent student. All the teachers said it was a delight to have X in their classes. X was president of the student council. X had won first prize in the talent show, and second prize in the art show, and honorable mention in the science fair, and six athletic events on field day, including the potato race.

Nevertheless, insisted the Parents' Association, X is a Problem Child. X is the Biggest Problem Child we have ever seen!

So the principal reluctantly notified X's parents that numerous complaints about X's behavior had come to the school's attention. And that after the psychiatrist's Xamination, the school would decide what to do about X.

The Joneses reported this at once to the scientists, who referred them to page 85,759 of the *Instruction Manual*. "Sooner or later," it said, "X will have to be Xamined by a psychiatrist. This may be the only way any of us will know for sure whether X is mixed up—or whether everyone else is."

The night before X was to be Xamined, the Joneses tried not to let X see how worried they were. "What if—?" Mr. Jones would say. And Ms. Jones would reply, "No use worrying." Then a few minutes later, Ms. Jones would say, "What if—?" and Mr. Jones would reply, "No use worrying."

X just smiled at them both, and hugged them hard and didn't say much of anything. X was thinking, What if—? And then X thought: No use worrying.

At Xactly nine o'clock the next day, X reported to the school psychiatrist's office. The principal, along with a committee from the Parents' Association, X's teacher, X's classmates, and Ms. and Mr. Jones, waited in the hall outside. Nobody knew the details of the tests X was to be given, but everybody knew they'd be *very* hard, and that they'd reveal Xactly what everyone wanted to know about X, but were afraid to ask.

It was terribly quiet in the hall. Almost spooky. Once in a while, they would hear a strange noise inside the room. There were buzzes. And a beep or two. And several bells. An occasional light would flash under the door. The Joneses thought it was a white light, but the principal thought it was blue. Two or three children swore it was either yellow or green. And the Parents' Committee missed it completely.

Through it all, you could hear the psychiatrist's low voice, asking hundreds of questions, and X's higher voice, answering hundreds of answers.

The whole thing took so long that everyone knew it must be the most complete Xamination anyone had ever had to take. Poor X, the Joneses thought. Serves X right, the Parents' Committee thought. I wouldn't like to be in X's overalls right now, the children thought.

At last, the door opened. Everyone crowded around to hear the results. X didn't look any different; in fact, X was smiling. But the psychiatrist looked terrible. He looked as if he was crying! "What happened?" everyone began shouting. Had X done something disgraceful? "I wouldn't be a bit surprised!" muttered Peggy and Joe's parents. "Did X flunk the *whole* test?" cried Susie's parents. "Or just the most important part?" yelled Jim's parents. "Oh, dear," sighed Mr. Jones.

"Oh, dear," sighed Ms. Jones.

"Sssh," ssshed the principal. "The psychiatrist is trying to speak."

Wiping his eyes and clearing his throat, the psychiatrist began, in a hoarse whisper. "In my opinion," he whispered—you could tell he must be very upset—"in my opinion, young X here—"

"Yes? Yes?" shouted a parent impatiently.

"*Sssh!*" ssshed the principal.

"Young *Sssh* here, I mean young X," said the doctor, frowning, "is just about—"

"Just about *what?* Let's have it!" shouted another parent. ". . . just about the *least* mixed-up child I've ever Xamined!" said the psychiatrist.

"Yay for X!" yelled one of the children. And then the others began yelling, too. Clapping and cheering and jumping up and down.

"*SSSH!*" SSShed the principal, but nobody did.

The Parents' Committee was angry and bewildered. How *could* X have passed the whole Xamination? Didn't X have an *identity* problem? Wasn't X mixed up at *all?* Wasn't X *any* kind of a misfit? How could it *not* be, when it didn't even *know* what it was? And why was the psychiatrist crying?

Actually, he had stopped crying and was smiling politely through his tears. "Don't you see?" he said. "I'm crying because it's wonderful! X has absolutely no identity problem! X isn't one bit mixed-up! As for being a misfit—ridiculous! X knows perfectly well what it is! Don't you, X?" The doctor winked. X winked back.

"But what *is* X?" shrieked Peggy and Joe's parents. "*We* still want to know what it is!"

"Ah, yes," said the doctor, winking again. "Well, don't worry. You'll all know one of these days. And you won't need me to tell you."

"What? What does he mean?" some of the parents grumbled suspiciously.

Susie and Peggy and Joe all answered at once. "He means that by the time X's sex matters, it won't be a secret any more!"

With that, the doctor began to push through the crowd toward X's parents. "How do you do," he said, somewhat stiffly. And then he reached out to hug them both. "If I ever have an X of my own," he whispered, "I sure hope you'll lend me your instruction manual."

Needless to say, the Joneses were very happy. The Project Baby X scientists were rather pleased, too. So were Susie, Jim, Peggy, Joe, and all the Other Children. The Parents' Association wasn't, but they had promised to accept the psychiatrist's report, and not make any more trouble. They even invited Ms. and Mr. Jones to become honorary members, which they did.

Later that day, all X's friends put on their red-and-white checked overalls and went over to see X. They found X in the backyard, playing with a very tiny baby that none of them had ever seen before. The baby was wearing very tiny red-and-white checked overalls.

"How do you like our new baby?" X asked the Other Children proudly.

"It's got cute dimples," said Jim.

"It's got husky biceps, too," said Susie.

"What kind of baby is it?" asked Joe and Peggy.

X frowned at them. "Can't you tell?" Then X broke into a big, mischievous grin. *"It's a Y!"* [1972]

 32

Courage from Necessity

MR. BARB GREVE

"Are you going to change your name?" he asked.

"No," I responded.

"I admire your courage."

I knew he meant it as a compliment, but I had a hard time accepting it as such until a friend of mine reminded me that sometimes courage is born of necessity. That is certainly the case here. "Courage" is the last word I would have used to describe my actions.

My decision to ask people to use masculine pronouns in reference to me comes from a feeling of need. I need to be honest about my whole self and am not willing to put part of me aside to make others feel comfortable. I realize this will challenge and scare a lot of people and that it already has.

As a friend so aptly wrote after I told hir about my pronoun change, "I have to admit, I felt kind of unsettled by this news when I was thinking about it last night. I thought about it a lot, actually. I came to the conclusion that it feels this way because it's kind of scary. I mean, before, your transgenderism seemed like a totally internal thing. Now you're challenging the rest of us to completely change our mindsets, to step outside our safe boxes and

see the world completely different from what is as ingrained in us as responding to our own names. And that's scary . . . you bet it's scary."

I think the most frustrating part for me and probably the scariest for you is that I can't clearly explain the "why." I can tell you this change feels right, and for me, this is enough. But I fear that by my using masculine pronouns and keeping the name Barb, I will confuse the issue for you and make life harder for others who identify as transgendered. I know human instinct is to try to group like people together, but like so much of life, two people who appear to be alike on the outside may be entirely different. For this reason I want to say clearly that I am speaking only about my experience and no one else's. I've found the most comfortable combination I can imagine for myself but there are many people, transgendered and not, who will make other choices.

I choose to keep the name Barb because it has great significance to me. I was named Barbara because my adoptive mother always wanted the name for herself. The meaning used in our family is "stranger in a foreign land." As an adoptee, I can't think of any name with a more appropriate meaning. While I have tailored the original name to fit my personality, I still consider it a precious gift from my parents.

My father asked me if I was intentionally trying to confuse people by keeping my name. The simple answer is no. But I've come to the realization that in order for me to be comfortable with myself, I may need to confuse others. Many people have asked me why I can't just identify as a butch woman since that is what I am . . . really. But they fail to realize I don't understand myself to be a woman. When I was younger, I thought I was really a boy and some mistake had been made with my body. Ever since kindergarten I've understood that I would grow up to be a guy.

When I hit puberty in junior high, I discovered I was attracted to girls. One day a girl in my class called me a lesbian. I went home from school that day and looked up the word in the dictionary to discover it meant "women who love women." I decided this must be who I am. After all, I had the same type of body the other girls in my class had, so I must have just gotten confused somewhere along the line.

I came out publicly as a lesbian in college. My friends encouraged me to join women-only meetings. They thought I would enjoy being in women-only spaces more than hanging out with the guys. I tried hard to find my place during those years. I surrounded myself with all types of women, many who were working to redefine women's roles in the world. Yet the more I hung out with them, the less I felt I belonged. Other than our attraction to women, we had very little in common.

I've since learned that gender is not as simple as biological sex (which can be altered); nor can we simplify and limit gender's definition to social constructs. I believe gender to be a combination between biology and social roles. We all choose to express our gender in different ways—our styles of dress, how we show emotions, what hobbies we enjoy, and who we hang out with are just some of them. For some people, this means limiting how they are in the world; for others, it means challenging stereotypes.

I struggled with my gender for years. I wanted more than anything to blend in and fit a stereotype. My only problem was, I couldn't find one. I looked to the men in my life to be my role models. I

accepted their standards of behavior as my own. As I grew older, I discovered some of the limitations I had put on my behavior were uncomfortable. I then began to look to the women in my life for help. But I ran into the same types of problems. I realize I wasn't comfortable expressing my gender as either one.

Most people think gender expression is the same as gender identity, but for me, it isn't. My understanding of my gender identity is the same today as it was 20 years ago. The differences between then and now are (1) the words I use to describe myself and (2) the way they express my identity. As a child I never heard the word "transgender." No one ever told me it was OK to identify as something other than male or female. Alone, I struggled with how to describe what I knew inside was a truth: I was not going to grow up to be either a man or a woman. I had already spent many years trying to make myself into one or the other and had been unsuccessful. Society's need to make gender one or the other sacrifices the life experiences of people like me. We are forced to choose between a man and a woman. For me, this would mean denying a large part of who I am. My journey is not about transitioning into one of the two acceptable genders. It is not about making a political statement. My journey is about becoming a whole person. It is about being the best person I can be: a transgendered guy named Barb.   [2002]

CHAPTER III

Gender and Women's Bodies

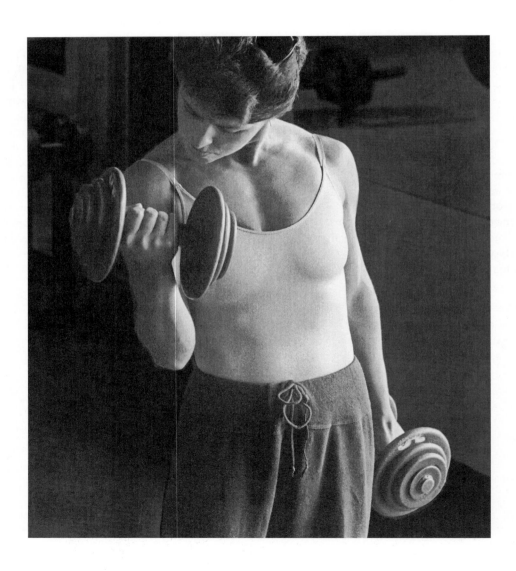

For women and girls in our culture, "Learning to care about looks is a lifelong process."[1] Our value has been defined by our bodies, and we quickly learn that our worth derives from our physical appearance more than from our intelligence, skills, or talents.

Although women's attitudes about their bodies are changing, reflecting a greater appreciation of athleticism, strength, and health, most girls and women still find fault with their physical appearance. One study found that by the time they reach 13 years old, 53 percent of girls express dissatisfaction with their bodies; this increases to 78 percent for 18-year-olds. Additionally, losing weight is cited as the top "wish" of adolescent and adult women.[2] In a more recent international survey that included teens from 24 countries, the authors found that significantly more girls than boys were dissatisfied with their bodies in every country.[3] Bombarded with messages of ideal beauty and body size, many physically maturing adolescent girls struggle to meet these unrealistic standards. Weight and appearance become the guiding focus of many women's lives—focal points for achieving control, social acceptance, and self-worth.

A constant barrage of messages and subtle cultural expectations regarding physical attractiveness form the dominant standard: thinner is better, fat is bad, dieting is good—even for girls as young as seven and eight. The advertising world contributes more than its share to the notion of "classic beauties"—a notion that excludes nearly all women, particularly those who depart from the "ideal" of white, Anglo-Saxon, young, and thin. Striving to fit this standard, women can often fail to appreciate their own uniqueness, undertaking numerous (and sometimes dangerous) beauty enhancements such as plastic surgery, chemical injections, aggressive diets, and dangerous appetite suppressants to achieve the "right look." When these attempts do not succeed, many women end up feeling defeated, often blaming themselves for their "imperfections."

For women of color, white definitions of beauty are less pervasive now than they were 30 years ago. The shift to celebrating the African roots of African-American culture has expanded the definitions of female beauty, providing many possibilities for self-expression through fashion and hairstyle. Similarly, resurgence in urban hip-hop culture presents alternatives to traditional norms for young people. Unfortunately, despite these changes, the waif-like white woman remains the dominant image of female beauty promoted in the media. In addition, the beauty norms prevalent in U.S. society forces girls and women of color to go to great lengths financially and emotionally to conform to dominant beauty standards. The cosmetic surgery

---

[1]Rhoda Unger and Mary Crawford, *Women and Gender: A Feminist Psychology,* 2nd ed. (New York: McGraw-Hill, 1996), p. 317.

[2]Jo Ann Deak, with Theresa Barker, *Girls Will Be Girls: Raising Confident and Courageous Daughters* (New York: Hyperion, 2002).

[3]Haleama Al Sabbah et al., "Body Weight Dissatisfaction and Communication with Parents Among Adolescents in 24 Countries: International Cross-Sectional Survey," *BMC Public Health* 9 (2009), pp. 1–10.

industry grew by a phenomenal 725 percent over the last decade.[4] The pressures that men face in terms of their bodies have also increased in recent years, though they are nowhere as narrow and constraining as these pressures are for women.[5]

Expressions of sexuality are closely related to how women view themselves and their bodies. Powerful myths and stereotypes about women's sexuality have had damaging effects on women's sexual experiences and have historically defined women's sexuality, prescribing only certain behaviors and expressions of sexuality as appropriate.

Reflecting shifts in social and cultural norms about sexuality and the role of women in society, attitudes about female sexuality have changed radically over the years. In Europe, from the 1400s to the 1700s, women were seen as sexually insatiable; female sexuality was viewed as dangerous, evil, and in need of control. The embodiment of this uncontrollable sexuality was the "witch," who was thought to consort with the devil to satisfy her lustful desires. During the 1800s these attitudes changed dramatically, reflecting the Victorian values of nineteenth-century Europe. White women were now regarded as pure, genteel, and passionless, but darker-skinned women were cast as embodiments of lust. During the years of slavery in the United States, this double standard for white and black women was played out in the continued sexual exploitation and rape of slave women, often by the same white slave-owners who viewed their own wives as sexually pure and innocent.

Contemporary stereotypes about women's sexuality continue to reflect the ways racism and sexism interact in our culture. Viewed as "other," relative to white women, Latinas are cast as "hot-blooded," and Asian women as exotic and geisha-like. Oddly, their hypersexuality verges on the unfeminine: to be hot-blooded, seductive, and erotic is the opposite of being pure and genteel.

In the 1960s, restrictions on sexual behavior loosened for women, although the double standard has nevertheless persisted. And even though the cultural climate of the United States is now more conducive to women's sexual expression, we continue to see men's sexuality described mainly in positive terms and women's sexuality in negative ones. Thus, a sexually active man who has several partners is a "stud," but a woman who has several partners is a "ho."

Sexual "scripts" are messages about expected behavior in sexual interactions that derive from stereotypes. In our culture, these scripts refer to women's heterosexual behavior, totally excluding the sexual expressions of lesbian and bisexual women. And when lesbian and bisexual women's sexuality is considered, it is often compared to the heterosexual "norm." For example, the definition of "sex" that is often used to survey couples' sexual behavior typically assumes heterosexual behavior, that is, penile-vaginal intercourse. For lesbian couples, this definition

---

[4]T. S. Liu and T. A. Miller, "Economic Analysis of the Future Growth of Cosmetic Surgery Procedures," *Plast Reconstr Surg.* 121, no. 6 (2008), pp. 404e–12e.

[5]Diane Prusank, "Masculinities in Teen Magazines: The Good, the Bad, and the Ugly," *Journal of Men's Studies* 15, no. 2 (Spring 2007), pp. 160–77.

is meaningless and fails to capture the range of emotional and physical aspects of sexual relations between two women. As the old saying goes, "What men call 'foreplay,' women call 'sex.'"

The sexual script for young women today is markedly ambiguous in that they are expected to be sexually available while at the same time women's chastity is still prized as a virtue. There are common terms that capture the contradictory pressures regarding sexuality for women. The terms "hooking up" and "friends with benefits" (sexual encounters between friends without any expectation of commitment) imply that men and women are equal partners in a sexual encounter. In contrast, the term "the walk of shame"—when a woman walks out of a room the morning after a "hook up"—reveals the demeaning way in which society still regards women's control and enjoyment of their sexuality.[6]

Sexual scripting can also take the form of taboos. Shaped by cultural ideology and mythology, taboos directly affect a woman's experience of her own sexuality. It is not unusual to hear women discuss ambivalent feelings about their sexual desires and relationships or to wonder whether "something is wrong" because they do not experience sex the way they think they "should." A feminist perspective suggests that for women living in a sexist culture, sexuality can encompass both pleasure and danger. Women have a right to sexual pleasure and desire, but they must also make their own choices in order to balance the pursuit of sexual pleasure with a concern for their safety and health. Thus, it is important for women to take control of their sexual interactions, learning to be comfortable and assertive with their partners while addressing issues of safe sex and pregnancy.

Our attitudes about beauty, body image, and sexuality begin developing early in life. Unrealistic expectations created by a society that objectifies women restrict our choices and limit our growth. As the selections that follow reveal, understanding how gender socialization and sexism create damaging stereotypes and expectations will help us create our own standards of personal beauty and our own ideas about sexual intimacy.

---

[6]Cheryl Wetzstein, "Hip-Joined or Hooked Up?" *Insight on the News*, September 3, 2001.

Female Beauty

"The beauty myth," as Naomi Wolf calls it in her book by that name, is omnipotent and far-reaching. It consists of the belief that women must possess an immutable quality, "beauty," in order to be successful and attractive to men. In fact, standards of beauty vary greatly from culture to culture and have changed radically over time. In our culture, prevailing notions of beauty emphasize being young, thin, white, and Anglo-Saxon. Naomi Wolf questions the foundation of this myth and states that "the beauty myth is not about women at all. It is about men's institutions and institutional power."

Images of beauty vary across ethnic groups, demonstrating how racism and sexism interact to shape expectations of women. Nellie Wong, Inés Hernandez-Avila, Aishe Berger, and Lucille Clifton describe the effects of stereotyped notions of beauty on Asian-American, Latina, Jewish, and African-American women. As these selections demonstrate, such standards create anguish and confusion for most women and particularly women of color who are outside the prevailing "norms" of beauty.

In addition to affecting a woman's sense of self-worth, ideals of physical beauty often have destructive effects on a woman's physical health. The increasing rate of eating disorders in the United States is just one example of the unhealthy consequences of rigid standards of beauty. Abra Fortune Chernik captures the intensity of a woman's experience with anorexia, drawing the connection between dramatically losing weight and "starving away my power and vision, my energy and inclinations." Graciela Rodriguez tells a similar story, as she recounts her experience with anorexia and bulimia. Rodriguez's account shows that Latinas are not immune to eating disorders; in fact, she states that "the media's and society's images of women . . . promised acceptance and happiness if I could only look like them." The pervasive pressure to be thin goes hand in hand with a fat-hating attitude in our culture. Viewed as "the other," many big women face hostility from a culture that considers them, as July Siebecker writes, "too loud and too laughing, too big for our britches." In "The Fat Girl Rules the World," Siebecker praises the resilience and strength of fat girls and women, who have to contend with unrelenting negative attitudes toward them in our society.

When women begin to defy social scripts for physical beauty, they can begin to see the beauty within themselves and define beauty in a more meaningful way. Lucille Clifton's poem "Homage to My Hips" reflects contemporary women's new standards of beauty. Like many of the selections in this section, this poem conveys important messages for women of all racial and ethnic backgrounds who are freeing themselves from restrictive standards of beauty. In "Double Life," Lisa Latham, through her exploration of societal meanings attributed to women's breasts, highlights the objectification of women's bodies. While the display of women's breasts as sexual objects is socially permitted, the natural function of breasts as sustenance-giving to infants is like a dirty secret that women are supposed to keep hidden. Women who breastfeed in public are chastised and made to feel as though they have violated public decency rules.

🌿 33

The Beauty Myth

NAOMI WOLF

At last, after a long silence, women took to the streets. In the two decades of radical action that followed the rebirth of feminism in the early 1970s, Western women gained legal and reproductive rights, pursued higher education, entered the trades and the professions, and overturned ancient and revered beliefs about their social role. A generation on, do women feel free?

The affluent, educated, liberated women of the First World, who can enjoy freedoms unavailable to any women ever before, do not feel as free as they want to. And they can no longer restrict to the subconscious their sense that this lack of freedom has something to do with—with apparently frivolous issues, things that really should not matter. Many are ashamed to admit that such trivial concerns—to do with physical appearance, bodies, faces, hair, clothes—matter so much. But in spite of shame, guilt, and denial, more and more women are wondering if it isn't that they are entirely neurotic and alone but rather that something important is indeed at stake that has to do with the relationship between female liberation and female beauty.

The more legal and material hindrances women have broken through, the more strictly and heavily and cruelly images of female beauty have come to weigh upon us. Many women sense that women's collective progress has stalled; compared with the heady momentum of earlier days, there is a dispiriting climate of confusion, division, cynicism, and above all, exhaustion. After years of much struggle and little recognition, many older women feel burned out; after years of taking its light for granted, many younger women show little interest in touching new fire to the torch.

During the past decade, women breached the power structure; meanwhile, eating disorders rose exponentially and cosmetic surgery became the fastest-growing medical specialty. During the past five years, consumer spending doubled, pornography became the main media category, ahead of legitimate films and records combined, and 33,000 American women told researchers that they would rather lose 10 to 15 pounds than achieve any other goal. More women have more money and power and scope and legal recognition than we have ever had before; but in terms of how we feel about ourselves *physically*, we may actually be worse off than our unliberated grandmothers. Recent research consistently shows that inside the majority of the West's controlled, attractive, successful working women, there is a secret "underlife" poisoning our freedom; infused with notions of beauty, it is a dark vein of self-hatred, physical obsessions, terror of aging, and dread of lost control.

It is no accident that so many potentially powerful women feel this way. We are in the midst of a violent backlash against feminism that uses images of female beauty as a political weapon against women's advancement: the beauty myth. It is the modern version of a social reflex that has been in force since the Industrial Revolution. As women released themselves from the feminine mystique of domesticity, the beauty myth took over its lost ground, expanding as it waned to carry on its work of social control.

The contemporary backlash is so violent because the ideology of beauty is the last one remaining of the old feminine ideologies that still has the power to control those women whom second wave feminism would have otherwise made relatively uncontrollable: It has grown stronger to take over the work of social coercion that myths about motherhood, domesticity, chastity, and passivity, no longer can manage. It is seeking right now to undo psychologically and covertly all the good things that feminism did for women materially and overtly.

This counterforce is operating to checkmate the inheritance of feminism on every level in the lives of Western women. Feminism gave us laws against job discrimination based on gender; immediately case law evolved in Britain and the United States that institutionalized job discrimination based on women's appearances. Patriarchal religion declined; new religious dogma, using some of the mind-altering techniques of older cults and sects, arose around age and weight to functionally supplant traditional ritual. Feminists, inspired by Friedan, broke the stranglehold on the women's popular press of advertisers for household products, who were promoting the feminine mystique; at once, the diet and skin care industries became the new cultural censors of women's intellectual space, and because of their pressure, the gaunt, youthful model supplanted the happy housewife as the arbiter of successful womanhood. The sexual revolution promoted the discovery of female sexuality; "beauty pornography"—which for the first time in women's history artificially links a commodified "beauty" directly and explicitly to sexuality—invaded the mainstream to undermine women's new and vulnerable sense of sexual self-worth. Reproductive rights gave Western women control over our own bodies; the weight of fashion models plummeted to 23 percent below that of ordinary women, eating disorders rose exponentially, and a mass neurosis was promoted that used food and weight to strip women of that sense of control. Women insisted on politicizing health; new technologies of invasive, potentially deadly "cosmetic" surgeries developed apace to re-exert old forms of medical control of women.

Every generation since about 1830 has had to fight its version of the beauty myth. "It is very little to me," said the suffragist Lucy Stone in 1855, "to have the right to vote, to own property, etcetera, if I may not keep my body, and its uses, in my absolute right." Eighty years later, after women had won the vote, and the first wave of the organized women's movement had subsided, Virginia Woolf wrote that it would still be decades before women could tell the truth about their bodies. In 1962, Betty Friedan quoted a young woman trapped in the Feminine Mystique: "Lately, I look in the mirror, and I'm so afraid I'm going to look like my mother." Eight years after that, heralding the cataclysmic second wave of feminism, Germaine Greer described "the Stereotype": "To her belongs all that is beautiful, even the very word beauty itself . . . she is a doll . . . I'm sick of the masquerade." In spite of the great revolution of the second wave, we are not exempt. Now we can look out over ruined barricades: A revolution has come upon us and changed everything in its path, enough time has passed since then for babies to have grown into women, but there still remains a final right not fully claimed.

The beauty myth tells a story: The quality called "beauty" objectively and universally exists. Women must want to embody it and men must want to possess women who embody it. This embodiment is an imperative for women and not for men, which situation is necessary and natural because it is biological, sexual, and evolutionary: Strong men battle for beautiful women, and beautiful women are more reproductively successful. Women's beauty must correlate to their fertility, and since this system is based on sexual selection, it is inevitable and changeless.

None of this is true. "Beauty" is a currency system like the gold standard. Like any economy, it is determined by politics, and in the modern age in the West it is the last, best belief system that keeps male dominance intact. In assigning value to women in a vertical hierarchy according to a culturally imposed physical standard, it is an expression of power relations in which women must unnaturally compete for resources that men have appropriated for themselves.

"Beauty" is not universal or changeless, though the West pretends that all ideals of female beauty stem from one Platonic Ideal Woman; the Maori admire a fat vulva, and the Padung, droopy breasts. Nor is "beauty" a function of evolution. Its ideals change at a pace far more rapid than that of the evolution of species, and Charles Darwin was himself unconvinced by his own explanation that "beauty" resulted from a "sexual selection" that deviated from the rule of natural selection; for women to compete with women through "beauty" is a reversal of the way in which natural selection affects all other mammals. Anthropology has overturned the notion that females must be "beautiful" to be selected to mate: Evelyn Reed, Elaine Morgan, and others have dismissed sociobiological assertions of innate male polygamy and female monogamy. Female higher primates are the sexual initiators; not only do they seek out and enjoy sex with many partners, but "every nonpregnant female takes her turn at being the most desirable of all her troop. And that cycle keeps turning as long as she lives." The inflamed pink sexual organs of primates are often cited by male sociobiologists as analogous to human arrangements relating to female "beauty," when in fact that is a universal, nonhierarchical female primate characteristic.

Nor has the beauty myth always been this way. Though the pairing of the older rich men with young, "beautiful" women is taken to be somehow inevitable, in the matriarchal Goddess religions that dominated the Mediterranean from about 25,000 BCE to about 700 BCE, the situation was reversed: "In every culture, the Goddess has many lovers. . . . The clear pattern is of an older woman with a beautiful but expendable youth—Ishtar and Tammuz, Venus and Adonis, Cybele and Attis, Isis and Osiris . . . their only function the service of the divine 'womb.'" Nor is it something only women do and only men watch: Among the Nigerian Wodaabes, the women hold economic power and the tribe is obsessed with male beauty; Wodaabe men spend hours together in elaborate makeup sessions, and compete—provocatively painted and dressed, with swaying hips and seductive expressions—in beauty contests judged by women. There is no legitimate historical or biological justification for the beauty myth; what it is doing to women today is a result of nothing more exalted than the need of today's power structure, economy, and culture to mount a counteroffensive against women.

If the beauty myth is not based on evolution, sex, gender, aesthetics, or God, on what is it based? It claims to be about intimacy and sex and life, a celebration of women. It is actually composed of emotional distance, politics, finance, and sexual repression. The beauty myth is not about women at all. It is about men's institutions and institutional power.

The qualities that a given period calls beautiful in women are merely symbols of the female behavior that that period considers desirable: *The beauty myth is always actually prescribing behavior and not appearance.* Competition between women has been made part of the myth so that women will be divided from one another. Youth and (until recently) virginity have been "beautiful" in women since they stand for experiential and sexual ignorance. Aging in women is "unbeautiful" since women grow more powerful with time, and since the links between generations of women must always be newly broken: Older women fear young ones, young women fear old, and the beauty myth truncates for all the female life span. Most urgently, women's identity must be premised upon our "beauty" so that we will remain vulnerable to outside approval, carrying the vital sensitive organ of self-esteem exposed to the air.

Though there has, of course, been a beauty myth in some form for as long as there has been patriarchy, the beauty myth in its modern form is a fairly recent invention. The myth flourishes when material constraints on women are dangerously loosened. Before the Industrial Revolution, the average woman could not have had the same feelings about "beauty" that modern women do who experience the myth as continual comparison to a mass-disseminated physical ideal. Before the development of technologies of mass production— daguerrotypes, photographs, etc.—an ordinary woman was exposed to few such images outside the Church. Since the family was a productive unit and women's work complemented men's, the value of women who were not aristocrats or prostitutes lay in their work skills, economic shrewdness, physical strength, and fertility. Physical attraction, obviously, played its part; but "beauty" as we understand it was not, for ordinary women, a serious issue in the marriage marketplace. The beauty myth in its modern form gained ground after the upheavals of industrialization, as the work unit of the family was destroyed, and urbanization and the emerging factory system demanded what social engineers of the time termed the "separate sphere" of domesticity, which supported the new labor category of the "breadwinner" who left home for the workplace during the day. The middle class expanded, the standards of living and of literacy rose, the size of families shrank; a new class of literate, idle women developed, on whose submission to enforced domesticity the evolving system of industrial capitalism depended. Most of our assumptions about the way women have always thought about "beauty" date from no earlier than the 1830s, when the cult of domesticity was first consolidated and the beauty index invented.

For the first time new technologies could reproduce—in fashion plates, daguerreotypes, tintypes, and rotogravures—images of how women should look. In the 1840s the first nude photographs of prostitutes were taken; advertisements using images of "beautiful" women first appeared in mid-century. Copies of classical artworks, postcards of society beauties and royal mistresses, Currier and Ives prints, and porcelain figurines flooded the separate sphere to which middle-class women were confined.

Since the Industrial Revolution, middle-class Western women have been controlled by ideals and stereotypes as much as by material constraints. This situation, unique to this group, means that analyses that trace "cultural conspiracies" are uniquely plausible in relation to them. The rise of the beauty myth was just one of several emerging social fictions that masqueraded as natural components of the feminine sphere, the better to enclose those women inside it. Other such fictions arose contemporaneously: a version of childhood that required continual maternal supervision; a concept of female biology that required middle-class women to act out the roles of hysterics and hypochondriacs; a conviction that respectable women were sexually anesthetic; and a definition of women's work that occupied

them with repetitive, time-consuming, and painstaking tasks such as needlepoint and lacemaking. All such Victorian inventions as these served a double function—that is, though they were encouraged as a means to expend female energy and intelligence in harmless ways, women often used them to express genuine creativity and passion.

But in spite of middle-class women's creativity with fashion and embroidery and child rearing, and, a century later, with the role of the suburban housewife that devolved from these social fictions, the fictions' main purpose was served: During a century and a half of unprecedented feminist agitation, they effectively counteracted middle-class women's dangerous new leisure, literacy, and relative freedom from material constraints.

Though these time- and mind-consuming fictions about women's natural role adapted themselves to resurface in the postwar Feminine Mystique, when the second wave of the women's movement took apart what women's magazines had portrayed as the "romance," "science," and "adventure" of homemaking and suburban family life, they temporarily failed. The cloying domestic fiction of "togetherness" lost its meaning and middle-class women walked out of their front doors in masses.

So the fictions simply transformed themselves once more: Since the women's movement had successfully taken apart most other necessary fictions of femininity, all the work of social control once spread out over the whole network of these fictions had to be reassigned to the only strand left intact, which action consequently strengthened it a hundredfold. This reimposed onto liberated women's faces and bodies all the limitations, taboos, and punishments of the repressive laws, religious injunctions, and reproductive enslavement that no longer carried sufficient force. Inexhaustible but ephemeral beauty work took over from inexhaustible but ephemeral housework. As the economy, law, religion, sexual mores, education, and culture were forcibly opened up to include women more fairly, a private reality colonized female consciousness. By using ideas about "beauty," it reconstructed an alternative female world with its own laws, economy, religion, sexuality, education, and culture, each element as repressive as any that had gone before.

Since middle-class Western women can best be weakened psychologically now that we are stronger materially, the beauty myth, as it has resurfaced in the last generation, has had to draw on more technological sophistication and reactionary fervor than ever before. The modern arsenal of the myth is a dissemination of millions of images of the current ideal; although this barrage is generally seen as a collective sexual fantasy, there is in fact little that is sexual about it. It is summoned out of political fear on the part of male-dominated institutions threatened by women's freedom, and it exploits female guilt and apprehension about our own liberation—latent fears that we might be going too far. This frantic aggregation of imagery is a collective reactionary hallucination willed into being by both men and women stunned and disoriented by the rapidity with which gender relations have been transformed: a bulwark of reassurance against the flood of change. The mass depiction of the modern woman as a "beauty" is a contradiction: Where modern women are growing, moving, and expressing their individuality, as the myth has it, "beauty" is by definition inert, timeless, and generic. That this hallucination is necessary and deliberate is evident in the way "beauty" so directly contradicts women's real situation.

And the unconscious hallucination grows ever more influential and pervasive because of what is now conscious market manipulation; powerful industries—the $33-billion-a-year diet industry, the $20-billion cosmetics industry, the $300-million cosmetic surgery industry, and the $7-billion pornography industry—have arisen from the capital made out of unconscious anxieties, and are in turn able, through their influence on mass culture, to use, stimulate, and reinforce the hallucination in a rising economic spiral.

This is not a conspiracy theory; it doesn't have to be. Societies tell themselves necessary fictions in the same way that individuals and families do. Henrik Ibsen called them "vital lies," and psychologist Daniel Goleman describes them working the same way on the social level that they do within families: "The collusion is maintained by directing attention away from the fearsome fact, or by repackaging its meaning in an acceptable format." The costs of

these social blind spots, he writes, are destructive communal illusions. Possibilities for women have become so open-ended that they threaten to destabilize the institutions on which a male-dominated culture has depended, and a collective panic reaction on the part of both sexes has forced a demand for counterimages.

The resulting hallucination materializes, for women, as something all too real. No longer just an idea, it becomes three-dimensional, incorporating within itself how women live and how they do not live: It becomes the Iron Maiden. The original Iron Maiden was a medieval German instrument of torture, a bodyshaped casket painted with the limbs and features of a lovely, smiling young woman. The unlucky victim was slowly enclosed inside her; the lid fell shut to immobilize the victim, who died either of starvation or, less cruelly, of the metal spikes embedded in her interior. The modern hallucination in which women are trapped or trap themselves is similarly rigid, cruel, and euphemistically painted. Contemporary culture directs attention to imagery of the Iron Maiden, while censoring real women's faces and bodies.

Why does the social order feel the need to defend itself by evading the fact of real women, our faces and voices and bodies, and reducing the meaning of women to these formulaic and endlessly reproduced "beautiful" images? Though unconscious personal anxieties can be a powerful force in the creation of a vital lie, economic necessity practically guarantees it. An economy that depends on slavery needs to promote images of slaves that "justify" the institution of slavery. Western economies are absolutely dependent now on the continued underpayment of women. An ideology that makes women feel "worth less" was urgently needed to counteract the way feminism had begun to make us feel worth more. This does not require a conspiracy; merely an atmosphere. The contemporary economy depends right now on the representation of women within the beauty myth. Economist John Kenneth Galbraith offers an economic explanation for "the persistence of the view of homemaking as a 'higher calling'": the concept of women as naturally trapped within the Feminine Mystique, he feels, "has been forced on us by popular sociology, by magazines, and by fiction to disguise the fact that woman in her role of consumer has been essential to the development of our industrial society. . . . Behavior that is essential for economic reasons is transformed into a social virtue." As soon as a woman's primary social value could no longer be defined as the attainment of virtuous domesticity, the beauty myth redefined it as attainment of virtuous beauty. It did so to substitute both a new consumer imperative and a new justification for economic unfairness in the workplace where the old ones had lost their hold over newly liberated women.

Another hallucination arose to accompany that of the Iron Maiden: The caricature of the Ugly Feminist was resurrected to dog the steps of the women's movement. The caricature is unoriginal; it was coined to ridicule the feminists of the nineteenth century. Lucy Stone herself, whom supporters saw as "a prototype of womanly grace . . . fresh and fair as the morning," was derided by detractors with "the usual report" about Victorian feminists: "a big masculine woman, wearing boots, smoking a cigar, swearing like a trooper." As Betty Friedan put it presciently in 1960, even before the savage revamping of that old caricature: "The unpleasant image of feminists today resembles less the feminists themselves than the image fostered by the interests who so bitterly opposed the vote for women in state after state." Thirty years on, her conclusion is more true than ever: That resurrected caricature, which sought to punish women for their public acts by going after their private sense of self, became the paradigm for new limits placed on aspiring women everywhere. After the success of the women's movement's second wave, the beauty myth was perfected to checkmate power at every level in individual women's lives. The modern neuroses of life in the female body spread to woman after woman at epidemic rates. The myth is undermining—slowly, imperceptibly, without our being aware of the real forces of erosion—the ground women have gained through long, hard, honorable struggle.

The beauty myth of the present is more insidious than any mystique of femininity yet. A century

ago, Nora slammed the door of the doll's house; a generation ago, women turned their backs on the consumer heaven of the isolated multiapplianced home; but where women are trapped today, there is no door to slam. The contemporary ravages of the beauty backlash are destroying women physically and depleting us psychologically. If we are to free ourselves from the dead weight that has once again been made out of femaleness, it is not ballots or lobbyists or placards that women will need first; it is a new way to see.   [1991]

34

When I Was Growing Up

NELLIE WONG

I know now that once I longed to be white.
How? you ask.
Let me tell you the ways.

> when I was growing up, people told me
> I was dark and I believed my own darkness
> in the mirror, in my soul, my own narrow vision

>> when I was growing up, my sisters
>> with fair skin got praised
>> for their beauty, and in the dark
>> I fell further, crushed between high walls

> when I was growing up, I read magazines
> and saw movies, blonde movie stars, white
> skin,
> sensuous lips and to be elevated, to become
> a woman, a desirable woman, I began to wear
> imaginary pale skin

>> when I was growing up, I was proud
>> of my English, my grammar, my
>> spelling
>> fitting into the group of smart children
>> smart Chinese children, fitting in,
>> belonging, getting in line

> when I was growing up and went to high school,
> I discovered the rich white girls, a few yellow
> girls,

their imported cotton dresses, their cashmere
   sweaters,
their curly hair and I thought that I too should
   have
what these lucky girls had

   when I was growing up, I hungered
   for American food, American styles,
   coded: white and even to me, a child
   born of Chinese parents, being Chinese
   was feeling foreign, was limiting,
   was unAmerican

when I was growing up and a white man wanted
to take me out, I thought I was special,
an exotic gardenia, anxious to fit
the stereotype of an oriental chick

   when I was growing up, I felt ashamed
   of some yellow men, their small bones,
   their frail bodies, their spitting
   on the streets, their coughing,
   their lying in sunless rooms,
   shooting themselves in the arms

when I was growing up, people would ask
if I were Filipino, Polynesian, Portuguese.
They named all colors except white, the shell
of my soul, but not my dark, rough skin

   when I was growing up, I felt
   dirty. I thought that god
   made white people clean
   and no matter how much I bathed,
   I could not change, I could not shed
   my skin in the gray water

when I was growing up, I swore
I would run away to purple mountains,
houses by the sea with nothing over
my head, with space to breathe,

   uncongested with yellow people in an area
   called Chinatown, in an area I later learned
   was a ghetto, one of many hearts
   of Asian America

I know now that once I longed to be white.
How many more ways? you ask.
Haven't I told you enough?   [1981]

35

To Other Women Who Were Ugly Once

INÉS HERNANDEZ-AVILA

Do you remember how we used to panic
when Cosmo, Vogue and Mademoiselle
   ladies
      would Glamour-us
    out of existence
        so ultra bright
        would be their smile
        so lovely their
        complexion
their confianza[a] based on
someone else's fashion
and their mascara'd mascaras[b]
     hiding the cascaras[c]
     that hide their ser?[d]

I would always become cold inside
          mata*onda*[e] to compete
     to need
     to dress right
     speak right
     laugh in just the
     right places
     dance in just
     the right way
My resistance to this type of
   existence
   grows stronger every day
Y al cabo ahora se
   que se vale
   preferir natural luz[f]
        to neon.   [1980]

---

[a]Confidence.
[b]Masks.
[c]Shells.
[d]Being.
[e]Dampener: *onda* is a "trip" in the positive sense—to *matar onda* is to kill, to frustrate the "trip"—to dishearten.
[f]And now anyway I know that it is worthy to prefer natural light.

36

Nose Is a Country . . . I Am the Second Generation

AISHE BERGER

for Emma Eckstein

Emma Eckstein was a socialist and a writer before she became a patient of Freud's. He diagnosed her as an hysteric because she was prone to emotional outbursts and masturbated frequently. Freud turned Emma over to his colleague Dr. Fleiss, who believed operating on the nose would inhibit sexual desire. Fleiss broke Emma's nose and left a large wad of gauze inside her nasal passage. This "error" wasn't discovered until years later, long after Emma's physical and emotional health was ruined and she was left an invalid.

"Such a nice girl, you have the map of Israel all over your face."
                    —Woman in fruitstore when I was thirteen

I. RHINOPLASTY

Nose that hangs on my face like a locket
with a history inside   you kiss
on our once a week date like lovers
in their mid forties
or maybe just my mother who is a lover
in her mid forties who had a nose job
in her mid twenties
the bump
the bumpy roads that troubled my father
the trouble with my father
who liked *zoftig*[1] women
all sides moldable
no bumps on the nose
map of Israel   on the face
map of Israel   on the map
a place on the edge of a deep blue
romantic sea on the map
a place that keeps shuffling its feet
backward   shrinking
like her nose under gauze
under wraps
under hemorrhage that accidentally
happened when the doctor left

---
[1]Plump.

the operating room and didn't
return till the anesthesia was already
loosening to sound
like an avalanche
in preparation
her nose bleeding under that
temporary wrap
a change in the landscape
my mother passes me down
this nation
this unruly semitic landmass on my face

My teeth were always
complimented for their four years
of braces
the rumblings of my jaw as my face
continentally drifted and my nose
grew
not like my mother's which is
like a border with its bone gates
levelled neutral
a passive face my mother's
bumpless smile

II. HEMORRHAGE

I think of Emma Eckstein
whose cartilage
was hammered out of her   the ancient
steppes on her face   the long view
of the world flooded
with large quantities of blood

Emma Eckstein who took her hands lovingly
inside her
who perhaps merely rubbed her legs together
in her seat and orgasmed
told she is hysterical
she wants too much in the final analysis
in the final analysis
the nose is inextricably linked
to the clitoris and the need to take hands
to yourself lovingly
is abnormal
Which was then a fresh new word
abnormal
the desire to treat oneself with kindness

Take your hands and put them on your lap
Take your nose and put it on inside out

On the ancient steps
up Emma Eckstein's nose
a man named Fleiss committed

strange unnatural acts in the name of
Psycho therapy
which was then a fresh new word

Emma
Levelled
Neutral
a passive face
a bumpless smile
her hands
jerk
at the thought
of herself
the hammer
reinforced
the hammer

III. ASSIMILATION INTO THE MODERN WORLD

and the gauze
under my own eyes
black and blue staying
in my house for a week
like sitting *shiva*[2]
fourteen years old
the most important days of my life

My mother promises me
a profile
like Greta Garbo

She used to tell me
my best friend Hilary
was prettier than me

The little Yeshiva boys yelled
that I took all their air up
when I walked down the hall
Then the boys at camp said
they'd kiss me if they could
ever find my lips

My dermatologist pierces
my ears

[2]Practice of mourning the death of a relative by sitting in the house for a week.

when I'm ten and advises me
to wear big earrings
it will distract people away
from my face

At eight I learn the word *rhinoplasty*
and it becomes a goal in my future
like becoming the first woman president
or flying to the moon

I am the second generation
Nose is a country where little wooden puppets
tell lies
where paintings of Shylock
are in every hotel lobby
Nose is a country where women have to
walk with their heads down
Where I await my new
modern look
assimilated
deconstructed

IV. BRIDGES

The body doesn't let go
of bridges

they expose me to the world after seven days
I expect to be noseless erased
but I am there   long and sloped
like a mountain after a fierce rain

I am there
the body knows

Mine stopped breathing at the crucial moment
the moment where they smash
bridges
the moment where the enemy
takes over

This time they couldn't finish
what they started
a part of me revolted
against the gas   they had to
revive me before the last
bone was broken

The suspension of my long
winding bridge where my Jewish soul
still wanders over
the slightly altered terrain

the body knows

My desert nose my sweet ripe nose
    my kosher nose
my zoftig nose my mountain nose
    my gentle nose
my moon of nose my sea of nose
    my heart pumping
lungs stretching fire of nose
    my full bodied
wine of nose   my acres of
    sheyne sheyne meydele[3]
nose

that you kiss at night

Nose that I put my loving hands on.   [1986]

_____

[3]Pretty, pretty girl.

 37

Homage to My Hair

LUCILLE CLIFTON

when i feel her jump up and dance
i hear the music! my God
i'm talking about my nappy hair!
she is a challenge to your hand
black man,
she is as tasty on your tongue as good greens
black man,
she can touch your mind
with her electric fingers and
the grayer she do get, good Good,
the blacker she do be!   [1976]

 ## *Our Crown, Our Glory, Our Roots*

MEAH CLAY

In my earliest childhood memories. I began my day with a strict hair routine. My mother would rise early, usually around 4:00 a.m., to prepare herself for work and get my siblings and me ready for school. Whenever I heard the shrill of her alarm clock, I knew that my sister and I would soon be awakened and commanded to gather our hair accessories so that Mama could do our hair. It always took her about 25 minutes for each of us, because she would have to press our hair before combing and styling it into several pigtails. Our brother was always able to remain asleep nearly an hour longer than us, because of course, his short cut and "finer" texture hair did not require the strenuous efforts that ours did.

For many African-American women, having bone-straight, long hair outweighs all of our other beauty desires. I imagine if we had never known anything other than nappy hair, perhaps beauty would then be based on the woman having the most stiff, immovable afro puff. However, the constant images of the larger society surround and cajole us into accepting a white-washed standard of beauty. I'm waiting for the day when I will see several purely natural African-American women gracing the catwalks of fashion shows, their heads crowned by an all natural afro. As African-American women, we must learn to embrace the distinctiveness of our natural hair, among the many other things that make us unique, so that we too may hold our heads up high with unrelenting confidence and the pride that comes with possessing a precious, rare jewel. For us, one of those rare jewels lies in the unique natural beauty of our hair, our crowning glory.   [2006]

🌿 38

The Body Politic

ABRA FORTUNE CHERNIK

My body possesses solidness and curve, like the ocean. My weight mingles with Earth's pull, drawing me onto the sand. I have not always sent waves into the world. I flew off once, for five years, and swirled madly like a cracking brown leaf in the salty autumn wind. I wafted, dried out, apathetic.

I had no weight in the world during my years of anorexia. Curled up inside my thinness, a refugee in a cocoon of hunger, I lost the capacity to care about myself or others. I starved my body and twitched in place as those around me danced in the energy of shared existence and progressed in their lives. When I graduated from college crowned with academic honors, professors praised my potential. I wanted only to vanish.

It took three months of hospitalization and two years of outpatient psychotherapy for me to learn to nourish myself and to live in a body that expresses strength and honesty in its shape. I accepted my right and my obligation to take up room with my figure, voice, and spirit. I remembered how to tumble forward and touch the world that holds me. I chose the ocean as my guide.

Who disputes the ocean's fullness?

Growing up in New York City, I did not care about the feminist movement. Although I attended an all-girls high school, we read mostly male authors and studied the history of men. Embracing mainstream culture without question, I learned about womanhood from fashion magazines, Madison Avenue and Hollywood. I dismissed feminist alternatives as foreign and offensive, swathed as they were in stereotypes that threatened my adolescent need for conformity.

Puberty hit late; I did not complain. I enjoyed living in the lanky body of a tall child and insisted on the title of "girl." If anyone referred to me as a "young woman," I would cry out, horrified, "Do not call me the *W* word!" But at 16 years old, I could no longer deny my fate. My stomach and breasts rounded. Curly black hair sprouted in the most embarrassing places. Hips swelled from a once-flat plane. Interpreting maturation as an unacceptable lapse into fleshiness, I resolved to eradicate the physical symptoms of my impending womanhood.

Magazine articles, television commercials, lunchroom conversation, gymnastics coaches and write-ups on models had saturated me with diet savvy. Once I decided to lose weight, I quickly turned expert. I dropped hot chocolate from my regular breakfast order at the Skyline Diner. I replaced lunches of peanut butter and Marshmallow Fluff sandwiches with small platters of cottage cheese and cantaloupe. I eliminated dinner altogether and blunted my appetite with Tab, Camel Lights, and Carefree bubble gum. When furious craving overwhelmed my resolve and I swallowed an extra something, I would flee to the nearest bathroom to purge my mistake.

Within three months, I had returned my body to its preadolescent proportions and had manipulated my monthly period into drying up. Over the next five years, I devoted my life to losing my weight. I came to resent the body in which I lived, the body that threatened to develop, the body whose hunger I despised but could not extinguish. If I neglected a workout or added a pound or ate a bite too many, I would stare in the mirror and drown myself in a tidal wave of criticism. Hatred of my body generalized to hatred of myself as a person, and self-referential labels such as "pig," "failure," and "glutton" allowed me to believe that I deserved punishment. My self-hatred became fuel for the self-mutilating behaviors of the eating disorder.

As my body shrank, so did my world. I starved away my power and vision, my energy and inclinations. Obsessed with dieting, I allowed relationships, passions, and identity to wither. I pulled back from the world, off of the beach, out of the sand. The waves of my existence ceased to roll beyond the inside of my skin.

And society applauded my shrinking. Pound after pound the applause continued, like the pounding ocean outside the door of my beach house.

The word "anorexia" literally means "loss of appetite." But as an anorexic, I felt hunger thrashing inside my body. I denied my appetite, ignored it, but never lost it. Sometimes the pangs twisted so sharply, I feared they would consume the meat of my heart. On desperate nights I rose in a flannel nightgown and allowed myself to eat an unplanned something.

No matter how much I ate, I could not soothe the pangs. Standing in the kitchen at midnight, spotlighted by the blue-white light of the open refrigerator, I would frantically feed my neglected appetite: the Chinese food I had not touched at dinner; ice cream and whipped cream; microwaved bread; cereal and chocolate milk; doughnuts and bananas. Then, solid sadness inside my gut, swelling agitation, a too-big meal I would not digest. In the bathroom I would rip off my shirt, tie up my hair, and prepare to execute the desperate ritual, again. I would ram the back of my throat with a toothbrush handle, crying, impatient, until the food rushed up. I would vomit until the toilet filled and I emptied, until I forgave myself, until I felt ready to try my life again. Standing up from my position over the toilet, wiping my mouth, I would believe that I was safe. Looking in the mirror through puffy eyes in a tumescent face, I would promise to take care of myself. Kept awake by the fast, confused beating of my heart and the ache in my chest, I would swear I did not miss the world outside. Lost within myself, I almost died.

By the time I entered the hospital, a mess of protruding bones defined my body, and the bones of my emaciated life rattled me crazy. I carried a pillow around because it hurt to sit down, and I shivered with cold in sultry July. Clumps of brittle hair clogged the drain when I showered, and blackened eyes appeared to sink into my head. My vision of reality wrinkled and my disposition turned mercurial as I slipped into starvation psychosis, a condition associated with severe malnutrition. People told me that I resembled a concentration camp prisoner, a chemotherapy patient, a famine victim, or a fashion model.

In the hospital, I examined my eating disorder under the lenses of various therapies. I dissected my childhood, my family structure, my intimate relationships, my belief systems. I participated in experiential therapies of movement, art, and psychodrama. I learned to use words instead of eating patterns to communicate my feelings. And still I refused to gain more than a minimal amount of weight.

I felt powerful as an anorexic. Controlling my body yielded an illusion of control over my life; I received incessant praise for my figure despite my sickly mien, and my frailty manipulated family and friends into protecting me from conflict. I had reduced my world to a plate of steamed carrots, and over this tiny kingdom I proudly crowned myself queen.

I sat cross-legged on my hospital bed for nearly two months before I earned an afternoon pass to go to the mall with my mother. The privilege came just in time; I felt unbearably large and desperately wanted a new outfit under which to hide gained weight. At the mall, I searched for two hours before finally discovering, in the maternity section at Macy's, a shirt large enough to cover what I perceived as my enormous body.

With an hour left on my pass, I spotted a sign on a shop window: "Body Fat Testing, $3.00." I suggested to my mother that we split up for 10 minutes; she headed to Barnes & Noble, and I snuck into the fitness store.

I sat down in front of a machine hooked up to a computer, and a burly young body builder fired questions at me:

"Age?"

"Twenty-one."

"Height?"

"Five nine."

"Weight?"

"Ninety-nine."

The young man punched my statistics into his keyboard and pinched my arm with clippers wired to the testing machine. In a moment, the computer spit out my results. "Only ten percent body fat! Unbelievably healthy. The average for a woman your age is twenty-five percent. Fantastic! You're this week's blue ribbon winner."

I stared at him in disbelief. *Winner? Healthy? Fantastic?* I glanced around at the other customers in the store, some of whom had congregated to watch my testing, and I felt embarrassed by his praise. And then I felt furious. Furious at this man and at the society that programmed him for their ignorant approbation of my illness and my suffering.

"I am dying of anorexia," I whispered. "Don't congratulate me."

I spent my remaining month in the hospital supplementing psychotherapy with an independent examination of eating disorders from a social and political point of view. I needed to understand why society would reward my starvation and encourage my vanishing. In the bathroom, a mirror on the open door behind me reflected my backside in a mirror over the sink. Vertebrae poked at my skin, ribs hung like wings over chiseled hip bones, the two sides of my buttocks did not touch. I had not seen this view of myself before.

In writing, I recorded instances in which my eating disorder had tangled the progress of my life and thwarted my relationships. I filled three and a half Mead marble notebooks. Five years' worth of: *I wouldn't sit with Daddy when he was alone in the hospital because I needed to go jogging; I told Derek not to visit me because I couldn't throw up when he was there; I almost failed my comprehensive exams because I was so hungry; I spent my year at Oxford with my head in the toilet bowl; I wouldn't eat the dinner my friends cooked me for my nineteenth birthday because I knew they had used oil in the recipe; I told my family not to come to my college graduation because I didn't want to miss a day at the gym or have to eat a restaurant meal.* And on and on for hundreds of pages.

This honest account of my life dissolved the illusion of anorexic power. I saw myself naked in the truth of my pain, my loneliness, my obsessions, my craziness, my selfishness, my defeat. I also recognized the social and political implications of consuming myself with the trivialities of calories and weight. At college, I had watched as classmates involved themselves in extracurricular clubs, volunteer work, politics, and applications for jobs and graduate schools. Obsessed with exercising and exhausted by starvation, I did not even consider joining in such pursuits. Despite my love of writing and painting and literature, despite ranking at the top of my class, I wanted only to teach aerobics. Despite my adolescent days as a loud-mouthed, rambunctious class leader, I had grown into a silent, hungry young woman.

And society preferred me this way: hungry, fragile, crazy. *Winner! Healthy! Fantastic!* I began reading feminist literature to further understand the disempowerment of women in our culture. I digested the connection between a nation of starving, self-obsessed women and the continued success of the patriarchy. I also cultivated an awareness of alternative models of womanhood. In the stillness of the hospital library, new voices in my life rose from printed pages to echo my rage and provide the conception of my feminist consciousness.

I had been willing to accept self-sabotage, but now I refused to sacrifice myself to a society that profited from my pain. I finally understood that my eating disorder symbolized more than "personal psychodynamic trauma." Gazing in the mirror at my emaciated body, I observed a woman held up by her culture as the physical ideal because she was starving, self-obsessed, and powerless, a woman called beautiful because she threatened no one except herself. Despite my intelligence, my education, and my supposed Manhattan sophistication, I had believed all of the lies; I had almost given my life in order to achieve the sickly impotence that this culture aggressively links with female happiness, love, and success. And everything I had to offer to the world, every tumbling wave, every thought and every passion, nearly died inside me.

As long as society resists female power, fashion will call healthy women physically flawed. As long as society accepts the physical, sexual, and economic abuse of women, popular culture will prefer women who resemble little girls. Sitting in the hospital the summer after my college graduation, I grasped the absurdity of a nation of adult women dying to grow small.

Armed with this insight, I loosened the grip of the starvation disease on my body. I determined to re-create myself based on an image of a woman warrior. I remembered my ocean, and I took my first bite.

Gaining weight and getting my head out of the toilet bowl was the most political act I have ever committed.

I left the hospital and returned home to Fire Island. Living at the shore in those wintry days of my new life, I wrapped myself in feminism as I hunted sea shells and role models. I wanted to feel proud of my womanhood. I longed to accept and honor my body's fullness.

During the process of my healing, I had hoped that I would be able to skip the memory of anorexia like a cold pebble into the dark winter sea. I had dreamed that in relinquishing my obsessive chase after a smaller body, I would be able to come home to rejoin those whom I had left in order to starve, rejoin them to live together as healthy, powerful women. But as my body has grown full, I have sensed a hollowness in the lives of women all around me that I had not noticed when I myself stood hollow. I have made it home only to find myself alone.

Out in the world again, I hear the furious thumping dance of body hatred echoing every place I go. Friends who once appeared wonderfully carefree in ordering late-night french fries turn out not to eat breakfast or lunch. Smart, talented, creative women talk about dieting and overeating and hating the beach because they look terrible in bathing suits. Famous women give interviews insulting their bodies and bragging about bicycling 24 miles the day they gave birth.

I had looked forward to rejoining society after my years of anorexic exile. Ironically, in order to preserve my health, my recovery has included the development of a consciousness that actively challenges the images and ideas that define this culture. Walking down Madison Avenue and passing emaciated women, I say to myself, *those women are sick.* When smacked with a diet commercial, I remind myself, *I don't do that anymore.* I decline invitations to movies that feature anorexic actors, I will not participate in discussions about dieting, and I refuse to shop in stores that cater to women with eating disordered figures.

Though I am critical of diet culture, I find it nearly impossible to escape. Eating disorders have woven their way into the fabric of my society. On television, in print, on food packaging, in casual conversation and in windows of clothing stores populated by ridiculously gaunt mannequins, messages to lose my weight and control my appetite challenge my recovered fullness. Finally at home in my body, I recognize myself as an island in a sea of eating disorder, a sea populated predominantly by young women.

A perversion of nature by society has resulted in a phenomenon whereby women feel safer when starving than when eating. Losing our weight boosts self-esteem, while nourishing our bodies evokes feelings of self-doubt and self-loathing.

When our bodies take up more space than a size eight (as most of our bodies do), we say, *too big.* When our appetites demand more than a Lean Cuisine, we say, *too much.* When we want a piece of a friend's birthday cake, we say, *too bad.* Don't eat too much, don't talk too loudly, don't take up too much space, don't take from the world. Be pleasant or crazy, but don't seem hungry. Remember, a new study shows that men prefer women who eat salad for dinner over women who eat burgers and fries.

So we keep on shrinking, starving away our wildness, our power, our truth.

Hiding our curves under long T-shirts at the beach, sitting silently and fidgeting while others eat dessert, sneaking back into the kitchen late at night to binge and hating ourselves the next day, skipping breakfast, existing on diet soda and cigarettes, adding up calories and subtracting everything else. We accept what is horribly wrong in our lives and fight what is beautiful and right.

Over the past three years, feminism has taught me to honor the fullness of my womanhood and the solidness of the body that hosts my life. In feminist circles I have found mentors, strong women who live with power, passion, and purpose. And yet, even in groups of feminists, my love and acceptance of my body remains unusual.

Eating disorders affect us all on both a personal and a political level. The majority of my peers—including my feminist peers—still measure their beauty against anorexic ideals. Even among feminists, body hatred and chronic dieting continue to consume lives. Friends of anorexics beg them to please start eating; then these friends go home and continue their own diets. Who can deny that the millions of young women caught in the net of disordered eating will frustrate the potential of the next wave of feminism?

Sometimes my empathy dissolves into frustration and rage at our situation. For the first time in history, young women have the opportunity to create a world in our image. But many of us concentrate instead on re-creating the shape of our thighs.

As young feminists, we must place unconditional acceptance of our bodies at the top of our political agenda. We must claim our bodies as our own to love and honor in their infinite shapes and sizes. Fat, thin, soft, hard, puckered, smooth, our bodies are our homes. By nourishing our bodies, we care for and love ourselves on the most basic level. When we deny ourselves physical food, we go hungry emotionally, psychologically, spiritually, and politically. We must challenge ourselves to eat and digest, and allow society to call us too big. We will understand their message to mean too powerful.

Time goes by quickly. One day we will blink and open our eyes as old women. If we spend all our energy keeping our bodies small, what will we have to show for our lives when we reach the end? I hope we have more than a group of fashionably skinny figures.   [1995]

🌿 39

Breaking the Model

GRACIELA (CHELY) RODRIGUEZ

I spent the best part of my teenage years "training to be a model . . . or just look like one." I didn't end up on the catwalk, but rather, in the hospital, recovering from anorexia and bulimia.

That's right, me—an 18-year-old Latina who's supposed to be immune to such things. Or so I'm told. Everyone from magazine publishers to television producers has suggested that Latina and African-American girls aren't likely to develop eating disorders, that we're less influenced by the skinny-girl images than our white peers.

I've lived in the small town of Carpinteria, California, for my whole life. It's one of the few towns I know to be truly multicultural. My schools have always been filled with kids from all backgrounds—different ethnicities, races, religions. My own Latina identity has been just one among many—and it's never held me back. I've worked hard to fit in and be accepted.

As a young teen, I shared the dream of many girls: I wanted to be a model and an actress. Like most girls, I wanted to be popular, and more than anything that meant I had to be attractive. When I was 13, I was scanning a fashion magazine and saw an ad for a model search contest that was coming to Beverly Hills. I jumped at the chance and convinced my parents to take me.

Three weeks later, I got a phone call from one of the representatives, saying that I was a finalist. I wasn't one of the top *five* finalists, who were awarded money and free modeling classes. I was, however, a runner-up, which made me eligible for a partial scholarship to help cover modeling and acting lessons. My parents would only have to pay $2,000, the rep told me. To this day, I'm not sure why they did it. On my first day, an agent named Pat took my measurements. He frowned and clucked his tongue as he scribbled my dimensions onto a clipboard—five-foot-three, 130 pounds, size seven. Then, he told me that the average model wore a size three and recommended that I drop down to that as quickly as possible.

For motivation, Pat handed me a stack of fashion magazines. He suggested I study the models in *Teen* and *Seventeen* and watch *Beverly Hills 90210* to "get an idea of what real models look like." It didn't matter that I was only 13 years old and not even fully developed. I was expected either to lose the weight or to get lost.

I left depressed, thinking I would never look like a model because I came from a line of full-figured Mexican women. Early on, I discovered my mother's diet pills and began taking them secretly. When she caught on that some were missing, she confronted me and I denied it. She didn't believe me, though, and even had the principal search my school locker. Soon after, I started to buy my own appetite suppressants, which I hid in my change purse.

I was eager to lose weight, and the modeling agency was happy to help. They gave me a list of "forbidden" foods, which was basically anything that didn't taste like sawdust or water. Every day, I had a salad with lemon juice or a plain baked potato, and that was it. I ate only once a day, limiting my intake to a 250-calorie maximum. After a year, my body submitted to this starvation regimen, and my appetite nearly disappeared. Although my stomach would rumble loudly in class, I learned to drink lots of water to fill it for long enough to spare me the embarrassment.

Bingeing and purging became a ritual. The same friend who introduced me to diet pills taught me that I could eat whatever I wanted and then force it back up so I wouldn't gain any weight. After a while, I didn't even have to stick my finger down my throat; I could throw up just by eating a chip. I also exercised for at least two hours a day at a local gym and at the park near my house. I was so obsessed with losing weight that I would wake up as early as three o'clock in the morning to run, and then jog again in the afternoon. I also enrolled in aerobics classes, and in eighth grade I became captain of the cheerleading squad and president of the student body.

I would come home from school exhausted some days and flop down on my bed. But I was surrounded by pictures of teen models that I'd ripped from magazines and taped to my walls. My response was instant—one look at the wall and I'd be lacing up my Nikes and heading for the track.

There was an unspoken competition among my friends and I, or at least a comparison, to see who had the most "willpower." Somehow, the quest for that power made us overlook the throbbing headaches and the gnawing hunger pangs that came with the territory of thinness.

At the modeling agency, most of the girls were also on strict diets and concerned about their bodies. In the end, going to extremes never paid off. None of us ever got any real modeling jobs. I did a couple of department store fashion shows, but that was it. It never amounted to the money my parents shelled out for my lessons.

I might not have been as "beautiful" as some models—after all, none of the models I saw on TV were Latina—but at least I was as skinny as they were.

Still, like most girls with eating disorders, I was never satisfied. In fact, I was unaware that I even had an eating disorder. All I knew was that I didn't feel "perfect" yet. My quest for the perfect body ended when a family member caught me throwing up in a restaurant bathroom. She told my parents, who took me to the hospital immediately, where I was diagnosed with anorexia and bulimia.

My family was as surprised as I was. Fortunately, I began counseling immediately. My counselor helped me to recover from my insecurity and to rebuild my self-esteem. I began to recognize that my worth was not based solely on my looks. It took me about a year to recover. I started to eat more and more and turned to healthier sources to stay in shape. I still exercised, but not nearly as much.

To this day, weight is a big issue in my life and may always be. One of the most influential things my counselor said to me was, "Chely, you are beautiful inside and out." It seems basic, yet somewhere in my quest for the perfect body, I had forgotten this. I decided never to change for anyone or try so hard to fit in. There's a reason we're given

Revenge Against the Scale

JENNIFER OLLENDORF

The emphasis on thinness and dieting tells us that our worth is based upon how much we weigh. If we are thin we are supposedly happy, popular, good people. If we are not thin then we are ugly, lazy, and grotesque. Of course these messages are nothing but nonsense. Being thin is certainly not the key to happiness, and being larger than the point of emaciation does not mean we are lazy.

To go about proving this point I decided to get rid of the key offender: the scale. Women dictate their days based upon what this magical instrument tells them. If they lose weight it will be a good day, if they gain it will be a bad day. Now if we just don't weigh ourselves and simply strive to be healthy then our days will have nothing to do with our weight. In this case not knowing will make us freer.

Rather than simply throwing the scale out though, I thought it would be more appropriate to do so in a manner symbolic of what it does to women's lives. I decided to destroy it; annihilate it. To start off I placed it on a cement surface, noting the way it says the word "Thinner" at the top, the brand of the scale I suppose. And then I took a hammer to it. I beat it as hard as possible as it began to give in to the persistent pounding. It began to crack apart and look pathetic, the same as it does to women's lives that become dependent upon it.

That wasn't enough though. It still looked like it was somewhat in one piece. So I placed it on the road in front of my Sentra. Then I shifted into drive, and did exactly that. I drove over the scale. And then I reversed and went backwards. I did this a few times until I was positive that scale was as dead as it could possibly get. At that point I got out of my car and looked at the mess I created. It was completely shattered, springs and pieces of metal all over the place. I was satisfied. It can't have any control over me anymore.

---

an image that's so hard to achieve. As long as we're chasing an impossible weight, we'll always have a reason to buy more diet products, to watch *90210*, and to read *Seventeen*.

I now weigh 130 pounds again, and I'm proud of my body. But I need a lot of support to maintain that. Whenever I feel bad, I remind myself, "If people don't accept me the way I am, it's their problem." I also continue to heal myself by helping others. I'm actively involved as a peer advocate. I promote healthy eating habits and exercise and encourage girls to get involved in sports. I'm now a high school senior, and I'm still involved in cheerleading and soccer (I often find myself

"counseling" younger teammates about body acceptance). I'm also active in a number of girls clubs that help me maintain my self-esteem in the face of negative body image messages.

After recovering from my eating disorder, I participated in an organization called Girls Incorporated, which helps nurture young girls to become strong, self-confident women. Girls Inc. recently awarded me $10,000 toward my college tuition. I've never been prouder. It felt incredible to receive a scholarship that was based on my achievements, rather than on the way I looked.

Eating disorders affect girls of color, too. I'm a perfect example of a Latina who developed an eating disorder because I so badly wanted to look and be like the thin, popular girls I saw in the media. I saw very few Latina role models on TV, and if I did see any, they were in gangs, wearing bikinis, or cleaning houses. I have rarely seen a Latina get acknowledged for her accomplishments rather than her large breasts. If I'd had positive Latina role models, I might never have felt ashamed to come from a full-figured line of women. I would have felt proud.

In the meantime, I've decided to become my own role model by reminding myself who I am every day. I am an 18-year-old Latina, a full-figured former model. I have survived an eating disorder. And I'm learning to love my body.   [edited, 2000]

40

The Fat Girl Rules the World

JULY SIEBECKER

From the plush velvet throne
in her subterranean lair
The fat girl rules the world.
We hate her, oh we hate her
Her voracious will
Her demanding spread
Her unrepentant appetite
Too loud and too laughing
Too big for our britches
She gives us these urges
She makes us all crazy
Ribs us to excess
and though we try to deny her
we secretly know that
we each are just barely
a licentious whisper
and a dangerous curve
from joy-running naked
and shrieking with laughter
through night-blackened woods.
She cannot be handled.
She cannot be trusted.

she makes us
very
nervous.
And so we shame her to silence,
And stuff her underground
And imagine that she is controlled.
But you can't kill the fat girl
she's laughing way down there
You drive her below
and she rules the roots
Leaving you wanting
and making you flustered
never quite sure if your
feet can be trusted
to walk you to work without
suddenly dancing.
She's down there right now
saying
I won't be denied
Saying
Deal with me
Saying
YES!   [2002]

41

Homage to My Hips

LUCILLE CLIFTON

these hips are big hips
they need space to
move around in.
they don't fit into little
petty places. these hips
are free hips.
they don't like to be held back.
these hips have never been enslaved,
they go where they want to go
they do what they want to do.
these hips are mighty hips.
these hips are magic hips.
i have known them
to put a spell on a man and
spin him like a top!   [1976]

🌿 42

Double Life: Every-one Wants to See Your Breasts—Until Your Baby Needs Them

LISA MORICOLI LATHAM

From earliest puberty, a woman must face the public nature of two of her most personal body parts. Trading in her cotton undershirt for a training bra is only the beginning: Between strap-snapping classmates, sadistic bra salesladies who insist on leaving the fitting-room door ajar, and relatives who chuckle over how she's grown, the first growing pain is the start of a lifelong push-and-pull between the public and the private appearance of a woman's breasts. From then on, cleavage depth, shirt transparency, bra-strap show-through, and nipple outlines are a daily concern—and that's not even getting into the unsolicited daily commentary a woman's breasts receive on the street, on the bus, and at the office.

But when the advent of motherhood transforms a woman's breasts once again, she is caught in an even deeper and more troubling conflict between the private and the public breast. From *Playboy* to the St. Pauli Girl, American culture declares that while breasts as a signifier of available sexuality should be flaunted, breasts doing the job nature assigned them are taboo. Right when a woman needs her breasts the most, she's told to cover up and move on.

The antagonism between the sexual and the working breast arises almost as soon as a woman discovers that she's pregnant. Publicly apparent changes such as substantial—even alarming—breast growth early in pregnancy increase the visual allure of breasts while, at the same time, private changes like tenderness and pain significantly decrease their actual potential to offer sexual pleasure to their owner.

Once her baby is born, a mother's rack becomes even less private. Strangers are prone to asking whether she's bottle- or breastfeeding her newborn. Breastfeeding puts a mother's breasts out in public even more, because sooner or later, she'll need to feed her baby around other people. And while Americans gladly tolerate extensive sexual displays of cleavage, we demand that nursing breasts stay completely hidden—an impossible task, especially for the mother new to nursing, given the sometimes gymnastic efforts she must undertake to teach a newborn to latch on properly. Trying to cover herself while struggling with a squirming, wobbly-necked neonate can be like fighting a cat inside a tent: not pretty, and liable to cause injury.

In *A History of the Breast*, the definitive source on all things mammarian, the historian Marilyn Yalom points out that even in notoriously buttoned-up Victorian times, women could breastfeed in church without notice or comment; these days, the merest sliver of lactating nipple can be less welcome than a public nosepicking. A baby's fumble to latch on can inspire friends and relatives to leap up and shield a nursing mother with coats and tablecloths, like she's an adolescent changing clothes at the beach. That this comic spectacle is supposedly less embarrassing than the possibility that someone might glimpse a patch of flesh somewhere beneath the folds of a lifted blouse indicates that a normalized working breast is far, far off.

Today nursing mothers are routinely kicked out of public places, harassed into covering up, and generally looked upon as deviants bent on an exhibitionist thrill, rather than mothers simply trying to feed their offspring. Publicly nursing a toddler or a preschooler is likely to subject a mother to accusations of child abuse. Indeed, exposing the public to a nursing mother has become tantamount to exposing the public to sex.

The 1999 Right to Breastfeed Act, which guarantees a woman's right to breastfeed on federal property, was precipitated by several complaints about the National Gallery of Art in Washington, D.C. Although the gallery reverently houses paintings of the Madonna nursing the Christ child, several women were kicked out for nursing actual babies—an appropriate illustration of America's simultaneous veneration of and contempt for mothers' roles.

The cognitive disjunction between the sexual breast and the working breast amounts to a vicious circle: Without more acceptance of nursing breasts as normal and necessary, acceptably decorative breasts are ever more divorced from the reality of their nonsexual functions, and working mammaries remain, in public perception, stubbornly sexual and therefore not fit for the literal public consumption babies demand.

Motherhood itself, however, is considered beyond sex, if not actually antisex; mothers and breasts must not be associated if breasts are to retain their ability to arouse. Coincident with a new mother's sudden, purely practical need of her breasts, our culture desexualizes her. (Just try, for instance, to find a sexy nursing bra in a marketplace that only recently began offering them in the most opaque black cotton.)

With all the breasts used to sell out there, it's also notable how few belong to pregnant or nursing mothers. The fact that maternal breasts don't have the kind of immediately understood currency of, say, those of a teenage model means that Americans can go their entire lives without seeing pregnant, nursing, or postchildbearing breasts depicted as either beautiful or sexual (for adults, not children)—and that does a disservice to the full spectrum of meaning contained in women's roles.

The problem is not the dual nature of our breasts but a cultural unwillingness to understand or accept that this nature is fluid. Men who ogle breasts on the street and grandparents who object to public nursing represent two sides of the same coin: Both confine breasts in public to the realm of sexuality and tolerate no alternatives. If more American women face down these naysayers and adjust the exclusivity of that confinement, who knows where the social advantages might end. Nursing bras that acknowledge that mothers don't lose their libido when they gain an offspring are a step in the right direction; more widespread respect for the reduced cancer rates and lower incidence of childhood ear infections that result from increased breastfeeding would be even more so. But the understanding that working breasts and their bearer's sexuality are decidedly separate yet need not be mutually exclusive, and the understanding that a woman's breasts in public are nobody's business but her own—and sometimes her baby's—will benefit all women, from pubescent girls to mothers of five, whether they choose to keep their breasts public, private, or a little of both.   [edited, 2006]

Sexuality and Relationships

Our sexual experiences, on both emotional and physical levels, are closely tied to what we learn about the meaning of sexuality and its relationship to other dimensions of our lives. Jessica Valenti, one of the leading voices in the feminist movement, laments that women's worth is associated deeply with their sexuality and sexual behavior. She writes especially about our society's prevalent "purity myth," which values virginity in girls and associates girls' and women's morality with their sexual chastity. Yen Le Espiritu and Caridad Souza describe communities where it is not acceptable for a young woman to be openly sexual and girls are expected to conform to explicitly stated sexual norms.

No discussion of contemporary sexuality, especially among young adults, would be complete without attending to the effects of HIV/AIDS on sexual attitudes, behaviors, and relationships. Adolescents and young adults, who often consider themselves invulnerable to disease and mortality, continue to be at high risk for contracting HIV. In the box "Demanding a Condom," Kat Doud describes her realization of the necessity of demanding that her partner use a condom. When he responds with anger and contempt, she decides that her health and safety are more important than being with him. Her account reminds us how pleasure and safety can and must be compatible as we develop new ways of relating sexually in the age of AIDS.

What happens when women move beyond the limited stereotypes of "acceptable" sexuality? In the next two selections, women defy the confining norms prescribed for women's sexual behavior. In "Pleasures," by Diane Hugs, two disabled lesbians explore their sexuality; and in "Loving Another Women," by Anne Koedt, two previously heterosexual women describe the process of developing a sexual relationship. In both these selections, women are defining their own sexual lives and discovering new possibilities for sexual expression.

This section concludes with two essays that integrate many of the issues related to sexuality and relationships that we have addressed. Lori Tharps describes being "in search of the elusive orgasm," during which she questioned herself, her sexuality, and her marriage. Her essay shows us that women need to take an active role in exploring and understanding their sexuality before expecting a partner to provide "ultimate" pleasure for them. Robyn Ochs shares her exploration of the relation between her feminist ideals and beliefs, her sexual experiences with women and men, and what she has learned about herself in the process. Ochs's essay conveys the subtle ways in which heterosexuals take their privilege for granted as they move through the world of male-female couples. Both of these selections help us see that women can grow beyond the stereotyped images of female sexuality to claim sexual relationships that are truly gratifying.

🌿 43

The Cult of Virginity

JESSICA VALENTI

In the moments after I first had sex, my then boyfriend—lying down next to me over his lint-covered blanket—grabbed a pen from his night-stand and drew a heart on the wall molding above his bed with our initials and the date inside. The only way you could see it was by lying flat on the bed with your head smashed up against the wall. Crooked necks aside, it was a sweet gesture, one that I'd forgotten about until I started writing this book.

The date seemed so important to us at the time, even though the event itself was hardly awe-inspiring. There was the expected fumbling, a joke about his fish printed boxers, and ensuing condom difficulties. At one point, his best friend even called to see how things were going. I suppose romance and discretion are lost on sixteen-year-olds from Brooklyn. Yet we celebrated our "anniversary" every year until we broke up, when Josh left for college two years before me and met a girl with a lip ring.

I've often wondered what that date marks—the day I became a woman? Societal standards would have me believe that it was the day I became morally sullied, but I fail to see how anything that lasts less than five minutes can have such an indelible ethical impact—so it's not that, either.

Really, the only meaning it had (besides a little bit of pain and a lot of postcoital embarrassment) was the meaning that Josh and I ascribed to it. Or so I thought. I hadn't counted on the meaning my peers, my parents, and society would imbue it with on my behalf.

From that date on I was a "sexually active teen," a term often used in tandem with phrases like "at risk," or alongside warnings about drug and alcohol use. Through the rest of high school, whenever I had a date, my peers assumed that I had had sex because my sexuality had been

defined by that one moment when my virginity was lost. It meant that I was no longer discriminating, no longer "good." The perceived change in my social value wasn't lost on my parents, either; before I graduated high school, my mother found an empty condom wrapper in my bag and remarked that if I kept having sex, no one would want to marry me.*

I realize that my experience isn't necessarily representative of most women's—everyone has their own story—but there are common themes in so many young women's sexual journeys. Sometimes it's shame. Sometimes it's violence. Sometimes it's pleasure. And sometimes it's simply nothing to write home about.

The idea that virginity (or loss thereof) can profoundly affect women's lives is certainly nothing new. But what virginity is, what it was, and how it's being used now to punish women and roll back their rights is at the core of the purity myth. Because today, in a world where porn culture and reenergized abstinence movements collide, the moral panic myth about young women's supposed promiscuity is diverting attention from the real problem—that women are still being judged (sometimes to death) on something that doesn't really exist: virginity.

Since I've become convinced that virginity is a sham being perpetrated against women, I decided to turn to other people to see how they "count" sex. Most say it's penetration. Some say it's oral sex. My closest friend, Kate, a lesbian, has the best answer to date (a rule I've followed since she shared it with me): It isn't sex unless you've had an orgasm. That's a pleasure based, non-heteronormative way of marking intimacy if I've ever heard one. Of course, this way of defining sex isn't likely to be very popular among the straight-male sect, given that some would probably end up not counting for many of their partners.

But any way you cut it, virginity is just too subjective to pretend we can define it.

---

*After years of denying she ever said such a thing, to her benefit, my mother finally sheepishy apologized.

Laura Carpenter, a professor at Vanderbilt University and the author of *Virginity Lost: An Intimate Portrait of First Sexual Experiences*, told me that when she wrote her book, she was loath to even use the word "virginity," lest she propagate the notion that there's one concrete definition for it.[1]

"What is this thing, this social phenomenon? I think the emphasis put on virginity, particularly for women, causes a lot more harm than good," said Carpenter.[2]

This has much to do with the fact that "virgin" is almost always synonymous with "woman." Virgin sacrifices, popping cherries, white dresses, supposed vaginal tightness, you name it. Outside of the occasional reference to the male virgin in the form of a goofy movie about horny teenage boys, virginity is pretty much all about women. Even the dictionary definitions of "virgin" cite an "unmarried girl or woman" or a "religious woman, esp. a saint."[3] No such definition exists for men or boys.

It's this inextricable relationship between sexual purity and women—how we're either virgins or not virgins—that makes the very concept of virginity so dangerous and so necessary to do away with.

Admittedly, it would be hard to dismiss virginity as we know it altogether, considering the meaning it has in so many people's—especially women's—lives. When I suggest that virginity is a lie told to women, I don't aim to discount or make light of how important the current social idea of virginity is for some people. Culture, religion, and social beliefs influence the role that virginity and sexuality play in women's lives—sometimes very positively. So, to be clear, when I argue for an end to the idea of virginity, it's because I believe sexual intimacy should be honored and respected, but that it shouldn't be revered at the expense of women's well-being, or seen as such an integral part of female identity that we end up defining ourselves by our sexuality.

I also can't discount that no matter what personal meaning each woman gives virginity, it's people who have social and political influence who ultimately get to decide what virginity means—at least, as it affects women on a large scale.

VIRGINITY: COMMODITY, MORALITY, OR FARCE?

It's hard to know when people started caring about virginity, but we do know that men, or male-led institutions, have always been the ones that get to define and assign value to virginity.

Long gone are the days when women were property or so we'd like to think. It's not just wedding traditions or outdated laws that name women's virginity as a commodity; women's virginity, our sexuality, is still assigned a value by a movement with more power and influence in American society than we'd probably like to admit.

I like to call this movement the virginity movement.* And it is a movement, indeed—with conservatives and evangelical Christians at the helm, and our government, school systems, and social institutions taking orders. Composed of antifeminist think tanks like the Independent Women's Forum and Concerned Women for America; abstinence only "educators" and organizations; religious leaders; and legislators with regressive social values, the virginity movement is much more than just the same old sexism; it's a targeted and well-funded backlash that is rolling back women's rights using revamped and modernized definitions of purity, morality, and sexuality. Its goals are mired in old-school gender roles, and the tool it's using is young women's sexuality.

And, like it or not, the members of the virginity movement are the people who are defining virginity—and, to a large extent, sexuality—in America. Now, instead of women's virginity being explicitly bought and sold with dowries and business deals, it's being defined as little more than a stand-in for actual morality.

It's genius, really. Shame women into being chaste and tell them that all they have to do to be "good" is not have sex.

---

*The "abstinence movement" would be accurate, as would the "chastity movement." But neither quite captures how this obsession really is about virginity, virgins, and an almost too-enthusiastic focus on young women's sexuality. So the "virginity movement" seemed not only appropriate, but also a bit needling. Which I enjoy.

For women especially, virginity has become the easy answer—the morality quick fix. You can be vapid, stupid, and unethical, but so long as you've never had sex, you're a "good" (i.e., "moral") girl and therefore worthy of praise.

Present-day American society—whether through pop culture, religion, or institutions—conflates sexuality and morality constantly. Idolizing virginity as a stand-in for women's morality means that nothing else matters—not what we accomplish, not what we think, not what we care about and work for. Just if/how/whom we have sex with. That's all.

Just look at the women we venerate for not having sex: pageant queens who run on abstinence platforms, pop singers who share their virginal status, and religious women who "save themselves" for marriage.

But for plenty of women across the country, it is special. Staying "pure" and "innocent" is touted as the greatest thing we can do. However, equating this inaction with morality not only is problematic because it continues to tie women's ethics to our bodies, but also is downright insulting because it suggests that women can't be moral actors. Instead, we're defined by what we don't do—our ethics are the ethics of passivity.

But it's not only abstinence education or conservative propaganda that are perpetuating this message; you need look no further than pop culture for stark examples of how young people—especially young women—are taught to use virginity as an easy ethical road map.

A 2007 episode of the MTV documentary series *True Life* featured celibate youth.[4] Among the teens choosing to abstain because of disease concerns and religious commitments was nineteen-year-old Kristin from Nashville, Tennessee. Kristin had cheated on her past boyfriends, and told the camera she'd decided to remain celibate until she feels she can be faithful to her current boyfriend. Clearly, Kristin's problem isn't sex—it's trust. But instead of dealing with the actual issues behind her relationship woes, this young woman was able to circumvent any real self-analysis by simply claiming to be abstinent. So long as she's chaste, she's good.

Or consider singer and reality television celebrity Jessica Simpson, who has made her career largely by playing on the sexy-virgin stereotype. Simpson, the daughter of a Baptist youth minister, started her singing career by touring Christian youth festivals and True Love Waits events. Even when she went mainstream, she publicly declared her virginity—stating that her father had given her a promise ring when she was twelve years old—and spoke of her intention to wait to have sex until marriage. Meanwhile, not surprisingly, Simpson was being marketed as a major sex symbol—all blond hair, breasts, and giggles.

Despite Simpson's public persona as an airhead women are supposed to want to be her, not only because she's beautiful by conventional standards, but also because she adheres to the social structures that tell women that they exist purely for men: as a virgin, as a sex symbol, or, in Simpson's case, as both. It doesn't matter that Simpson reveals few of her actual thoughts or moral beliefs; it's enough that she's "pure," even if that purity means she's a bit of a dolt.

For those women who can't keep up the front as well as someone like Simpson, they suffer heaps of judgment—especially when they fall off the pedestal they're posed upon so perfectly. American pop culture, especially, has an interesting new trend of venerating and fetishizing "pure" young women—whether they're celebrities, beauty queens, or just everyday young women—simply to bask in their eventual fall.

It's impossible to talk about tipped-over pedestals without mentioning pop singer Britney Spears. Spears, first made famous by her hit song "Baby One More Time" and its accompanying video, in which she appeared in a Catholic schoolgirl mini-uniform, was very much the American purity princess. She publicly declared her virginity and belief in abstinence before marriage, all the while being marketed—much like Simpson was—as a sex symbol. But unlike Simpson, Spears fell far from grace in the eyes of the American public. The most obvious indications of her decline were splashed across newspapers and entertainment weeklies worldwide—a breakdown during which she shaved her head in front of photographers, and various pictures of her drunk and sans panties. But Spears began distancing herself from the virgin ideal long before these incidents hit the tabloids.

First, Spears got some press for moving in with then-boyfriend and fellow pop star Justin Timberlake. But the sexist brouhaha began in earnest when Spears was no longer considered "attractive," because she started to gain weight, got pregnant, and no longer looked like a little girl. Pictures of her cellulite popped up on websites and gossip magazines nationwide, along with guesstimations about her weight and jokes about her stomach. Because "purity" isn't just about not having sex, it's about not being a woman—and instead being in a state of perpetual girlhood.

Shaming young women for being sexual is nothing new, but it's curious to observe how the expectation of purity gets played out through the women who are supposed to epitomize the feminine ideal: the "desirable" virgin. After all, we rarely see women who aren't conventionally beautiful idolized for their abstinence. And no matter how "good" you are otherwise—even if you're an all-American beauty queen—if you're not virginal, you're shamed.

The desirable virgin is sexy but not sexual. She's young, white, and skinny. She's a cheerleader, a baby sitter; she's accessible and eager to please. She's never a woman of color. She's never a low-income girl or a fat girl. She's never disabled. "Virgin" is a designation for those who meet a certain standard of what women, especially younger women, are supposed to look like. As for how these young women are supposed to act? A blank slate is best.   [edited, 2009]

NOTES

1. Laura M. Carpenter. *Virginity Lost: An Intimate Portrait of First Sexual Experiences* (New York: New York University Press, November 2005).
2. Laura M. Carpenter. Interview with the author, March 2008.
3. Dictionary.com definition of "virgin," http://dictionary.reference.com.
4. MTV. "True Life: I'm Celibate," July 2007, www.mtv.com/videos.

44

"We Don't Sleep Around Like White Girls Do": Family, Culture, and Gender in Filipina-American Lives

YEN LE ESPIRITU

Sexuality, as a core aspect of social identity, is fundamental to the structuring of gender inequality (Millett 1970). Sexuality is also a salient marker of otherness and has figured prominently in racist and imperialist ideologies (Gilman 1985; Stoler 1991). Historically, the sexuality of subordinate groups—particularly that of racialized women—has been systematically stereotyped by the dominant groups.[1] At stake in these stereotypes is the construction of women of color as morally lacking in the areas of sexual restraint and traditional morality. Asian women—both in Asia and in the United States—have been racialized as sexually immoral, and the "Orient"—and its women—has long served as a site of European male-power fantasies, replete with lurid images of sexual license, gynecological aberrations, and general perversion (Gilman 1985). In colonial Asia in the nineteenth and early twentieth centuries, for example, female sexuality was a site for colonial rulers to assert their moral superiority and thus their supposed natural and legitimate right to rule. The colonial rhetoric of moral superiority was based on the construction of colonized Asian women as subjects of sexual desire and fulfillment and European colonial women as the paragons of virtue and the bearers of a redefined

---

[1]Writing on the objectification of black women, Patricia Hill Collins (1991) argues that popular representations of black females—mammy, welfare queen, and Jezebel—all pivot around their sexuality, either desexualizing or hypersexualizing them. Along the same line, Native American women have been portrayed as sexually excessive (Green 1975), Chicana women as "exotic and erotic" (Mirande 1980), and Puerto Rican and Cuban women as "tropical bombshells, . . . sexy, sexed and interested" (Tafolla 1985, 39).

colonial morality (Stoler 1991). The discourse of morality has also been used to mark the "unassimilability" of Asians in the United States. At the turn of the twentieth century, the public perception of Chinese women as disease-ridden, drug-addicted prostitutes served to underline the depravity of "Orientals" and played a decisive role in the eventual passage of exclusion laws against all Asians (Mazumdar 1989, 3–4). The stereotypical view that all Asian women were prostitutes, first formed in the 1850s, persisted. Contemporary American popular culture continues to endow Asian women with an excess of "womanhood," sexualizing them but also impugning their sexuality (Espiritu 1997, 93).

Filipinas—both in the Philippines and in the United States—have been marked as desirable but dangerous "prostitutes" and/or submissive "mail-order brides" (Halualani 1995; Egan 1996). These stereotypes emerged out of the colonial process, especially the extensive U.S. military presence in the Philippines. Until the early 1990s, the Philippines, at times unwillingly, housed some of the United States's largest overseas airforce and naval bases (Espiritu 1995, 14). Many Filipino nationalists have charged that "the prostitution problem" in the Philippines stemmed from U.S. and Philippine government policies that promoted a sex industry—brothels, bars, and massage parlors—for servicemen stationed or on leave in the Philippines.

Cognizant of the pervasive hypersexualization of Filipina women, my respondents, especially women who grew up near military bases, were quick to denounce prostitution, to condemn sex laborers, and to declare (unasked) that they themselves did not frequent "that part of town."

Many of my respondents distanced themselves culturally from the Filipinas who serviced U.S. soldiers by branding them "more Americanized" and "more Westernized." In other words, these women were sexually promiscuous because they had assumed the sexual mores of white women. This characterization allows my respondents to symbolically disown the Filipina "bad girl" and, in so doing, to uphold the narrative of Filipina sexual virtuosity and white female sexual promiscuity. In the following narrative, a mother who came to the United States in her thirties contrasted the controlled sexuality of women in the Philippines with the perceived promiscuity of white women in the United States:

> In the Philippines, we always have chaperones when we go out. When we go to dances, we have our uncle, our grandfather, and auntie all behind us to make sure that we behave in the dance hall. Nobody goes necking outside. You don't even let a man put his hand on your shoulders. When you were brought up in a conservative country, it is hard to come here and see that it is all freedom of speech and freedom of action. Sex was never mentioned in our generation. I was thirty already when I learned about sex. But to the young generation in America, sex is nothing.

Similarly, another immigrant woman criticized the way young American women are raised: "Americans are so liberated. They allow their children, their girls, to go out even when they are still so young." In contrast, she stated that, in "the Filipino way, it is very important, the value of the woman, that she is a virgin when she gets married."

The ideal "Filipina," then, is partially constructed on the community's conceptualization of white women. She is everything that they are not: she is sexually modest and dedicated to her family; they are sexually promiscuous and uncaring. Within the context of the dominant culture's pervasive hypersexualization of Filipinas, the construction of the "ideal" Filipina—as family-oriented and chaste—can be read as an effort to reclaim the morality of the community. This effort erases the Filipina "bad girl," ignores competing sexual practices in the Filipino communities, and uncritically embraces the myth of "Oriental femininity." Cast as the embodiment of perfect womanhood and exotic femininity, Filipinas (and other Asian women) in recent years have been idealized in U.S. popular culture as more truly "feminine" (i.e., devoted, dependent, domestic) and therefore more desirable than their more modern, emancipated sisters (Espiritu 1997, 113). Capitalizing on this image of the "superfemme," mail-order bride agencies market Filipina women as "'exotic, subservient wife imports' for sale and as alternatives for men sick of independent 'liberal' Western women" (Halualani 1995, 49; see also Ordonez 1997, 122).

In the next section, I detail the ways Filipino immigrant parents, under the rubric of "cultural preservation," police their daughters' behaviors in order to safeguard their sexual innocence and virginity. These attempts at policing generate hierarchies and tensions within immigrant families—between parents and children and between brothers and sisters.

THE CONSTRUCTION(S) OF THE "IDEAL" FILIPINA: "BOYS ARE BOYS AND GIRLS ARE DIFFERENT"

As the designated "keepers of the culture" (Billson 1995), immigrant women and their behavior come under intensive scrutiny both from men and women of their own groups and from U.S.-born Americans (Gabbacia 1994, xi). In a study of the Italian Harlem community from 1880 to 1950, Orsi reports that "all the community's fears for the reputation and integrity of the domus came to focus on the behavior of young women" (1985, 135). Because women's moral and sexual loyalties were deemed central to the maintenance of group status, changes in female behavior, especially that of growing daughters, were interpreted as signs of moral decay and ethnic suicide and were carefully monitored and sanctioned (Gabbacia 1994, 113).

Although immigrant families have always been preoccupied with passing on their native culture, language, and traditions to both male and female children, it is daughters who have the primary burden of protecting and preserving the family. Because sons do not have to conform to the image of an "ideal" ethnic subject as daughters do, they often receive special day-to-day privileges denied to daughters (Haddad and Smith 1996, 22–24). This is not to say that immigrant parents do not place undue expectations on their sons; rather, these expectations do not pivot around the sons' sexuality or dating choices.In contrast, parental control over the movement and action of daughters begins the moment they are perceived as young adults and sexually vulnerable. It regularly consists of monitoring their whereabouts and forbidding

dating (Wolf 1997). For example, the immigrant parents I interviewed seldom allowed their daughters to date, to stay out late, to spend the night at a friend's house, or to take an out-of-town trip.

Many of the second-generation women I spoke to complained bitterly about these parental restrictions. They particularly resented what they saw as gender inequity in their families: the fact that their parents placed far more restrictions on their activities and movements than on their brothers'. Some decried the fact that even their younger brothers had more freedom than they did. "It was really hard growing up because my parents would let my younger brothers do what they wanted but I didn't get to do what I wanted even though I was the oldest. I had a curfew and my brothers didn't. I had to ask if I could go places and they didn't. My parents never even asked my brothers when they were coming home."

When questioned about this double standard, parents generally responded by explaining that "girls are different":

> I have that Filipino mentality that boys are boys and girls are different. Girls are supposed to be protected, to be clean. In the early years, my daughters have to have chaperones and curfews. And they know that they have to be virgins until they get married. The girls always say that is not fair. . . . It was the way that I was raised. I still want to have part of that culture instilled in my children. And I want them to have that to pass on to their children.

Even among self-described Western-educated and "tolerant" parents, many continue to ascribe to "the Filipino way" when it comes to raising daughters. As one college-educated father explains,

> Because of my Western education, I don't raise my children the way my parents raised me. . . . So the double standard kind of operates: it's alright for the boys to explore the field but I tended to be overly protective of my daughter. My wife feels the same way because the boys will not lose anything, but the daughter will lose something, her virginity, and it can be also a question of losing face, that kind of thing.

Although many parents discourage or forbid dating for daughters, they still fully expect these young women to fulfill their traditional roles as women: to marry and have children. A young Filipina recounted the mixed messages she received from her parents:

This is the way it is supposed to work: Okay, you go to school. You go to college. You graduate. You find a job. *Then* you find your husband, and you have children. That's the whole time line. *But* my question is, if you are not allowed to date, how are you supposed to find your husband? They say "no" to the whole dating scene because that is secondary to your education, secondary to your family. They do push marriage, but at a later date. So basically my parents are telling me that I should get married and I should have children but that I should not date.

The restrictions on girls' movement sometimes spill over to the realm of academics. Wolf (1997, 467) reports that some Filipino parents pursued contradictory tactics with their children, particularly their daughters, by pushing them to achieve academic excellence in high school but then "pulling the emergency brake" when they contemplated college by expecting them to stay at home, even if it meant going to a less competitive college, or not going at all. In the following account, a young Filipina relates that her parents' desire to "protect" her surpassed their concerns for her academic preparation:

My brother [was] given a lot more opportunity educationally. He was given the opportunity to go to Miller High School that has a renowned college preparatory program but [for] which you have to be bussed out of our area.[2] I've come from a college prep program in junior high and I was asked to apply for the program at Miller. But my parents said "No, absolutely not." This was even during the time, too, when Southside [the neighborhood high school] had one of the lowest test scores in the state of California. So it was like, "You know, mom, I'll get a better chance at Miller." "No, no, you're going to Southside. There is no ifs, ands, or buts. Miller is too far. What if something happens to you?" But two years later, when my brother got ready to go on to high school, he was allowed to go to Miller. My

sister and I were like, "Obviously, whose education do you value more? If you're telling us that education is important, why do we see a double standard?"

The above narratives suggest that the process of parenting is gendered in that immigrant parents tend to restrict the autonomy, mobility, and personal decision making of their daughters more than that of their sons. I argue that these parental restrictions are attempts to construct a model of Filipina womanhood that is chaste, modest, nurturing, and family-oriented. Women are seen as responsible for holding the cultural line, maintaining racial boundaries, and marking cultural difference.

The interview data do suggest that inter generational conflicts are socially recognized occurrences in Filipino communities. Even when respondents themselves had not experienced intergenerational tensions, they could always recall a cousin, a girlfriend, or a friend's daughter who had.

SANCTIONS AND REACTIONS: "THAT IS NOT WHAT A DECENT FILIPINO GIRL SHOULD DO"

I do not wish to suggest that immigrant communities are the only ones in which parents regulate their daughters' mobility and sexuality. Feminist scholars have long documented the construction, containment, and exploitation of women's sexuality in various societies (Maglin and Perry 1996). We also know that the cultural anxiety over unbounded female sexuality is most apparent with regard to adolescent girls (Tolman and Higgins 1996, 206). The difference is in the ways immigrant and nonimmigrant families sanction girls' sexuality. To control sexually assertive girls nonimmigrant parents rely on the gender-based good girl/bad girl dichotomy in which "good girls" are passive, threatened sexual objects while "bad girls" are active, desiring sexual agents (Tolman and Higgins 1996). As Dasgupta and DasGupta write, "the two most pervasive images of women across cultures are the goddess and whore, the good and bad women" (1996, 236). This good girl/bad girl cultural story conflates femininity with sexuality, increases women's vulnerability to sexual coercion, and justifies women's containment in the domestic sphere.

---

[2]The names of the two high schools in this excerpt are fictitious.

Immigrant families, though, have an additional strategy: they can discipline their daughters as racial/national subjects as well as gendered ones. That is, as self-appointed guardians of "authentic" cultural memory, immigrant parents can attempt to regulate their daughters' independent choices by linking them to cultural ignorance or betrayal. As in the case of "bar girls" in the Philippines, Filipina Americans who veered from acceptable behaviors were deemed "Americanized"—as women who have adopted the sexual mores and practices of white women. As one Filipino immigrant father described "Americanized" Filipinas: "They are spoiled because they have seen the American way. They go out at night. Late at night. They go out on dates. Smoking. They have sex without marrying."

From the perspective of the second-generation daughters, these charges are stinging. The young women I interviewed were visibly pained—with many breaking down and crying—when they recounted their parents' charges. This deep pain, stemming in part from their desire to be validated as Filipina, existed even among the more "rebellious" daughters. One 24-year-old daughter explained:

> My mom is very traditional. She wants to follow the Filipino customs, just really adhere to them, like what is proper for a girl, what she can and can't do, and what other people are going to think of her if she doesn't follow that way. When I pushed these restrictions, when I rebelled and stayed out later than allowed, my mom would always say, "That is not what a decent Filipino girl should do. You should come home at a decent hour. What are people going to think of you?" And that would get me really upset, you know, because I think that my character is very much the way it should be for a Filipina. I wear my hair long, I wear decent makeup. I dress properly, conservative. I am family oriented. It hurts me that she doesn't see that I am decent, that I am proper and that I am not going to bring shame to the family or anything like that.

This narrative suggests that even when parents are unable to control the behaviors of their children, their (dis)approval remains powerful in shaping the emotional lives of their daughters (see Wolf 1997). Although better-off parents can and do exert greater controls over their children's behaviors than do poorer parents (Wolf 1992; Kibria 1993), I would argue that all immigrant parents—regardless of class background—possess this emotional hold on their children.

Despite these emotional pains, many young Filipinas I interviewed contest and negotiate parental restrictions in their daily lives. Faced with parental restrictions on their mobility, young Filipinas struggle to gain some control over their own social lives, particularly over dating. In many cases, daughters simply misinform their parents of their whereabouts or date without their parents' knowledge. They also rebel by vowing to create more egalitarian relationships with their own husbands and children.

Another Filipina who was labeled "radical" by her parents indicated that she would be more open-minded in raising her own children: "I see myself as very traditional in upbringing but I don't see myself as constricting on my children one day and I wouldn't put the gender roles on them. I wouldn't lock them into any particular way of behaving." It is important to note that even as these Filipinas desired new gender norms and practices for their own families, the majority hoped that their children would remain connected to Filipino culture.

My respondents also reported more serious reactions to parental restrictions, recalling incidents of someone they knew who had run away, joined a gang, or attempted suicide. A Filipina high-school counselor relates that most of the Filipinas she worked with "are really scared because a lot of them know friends that are pregnant and they all pretty much know girls who have attempted suicide."

CONCLUSION

Because the policing of women's bodies is one of the main means of asserting moral superiority, young women face numerous restrictions on their autonomy, mobility, and personal decision making. This practice of cultural (re)construction reveals how deeply the conduct of private life can be tied to larger social structures.

The construction of white Americans as the "other" and American culture as deviant serves a dual purpose: It allows immigrant communities both to reinforce patriarchy through the sanctioning of women's (mis)behavior and to present an unblemished, if not morally superior, public face to the dominant society. Strong in family values, heterosexual morality, and a hierarchical family structure, this public face erases the Filipina "bad girl" and ignores competing (im)moral practices in the Filipino communities. Through the oppression of Filipina women and the denunciation of white women's morality, the immigrant community attempts to exert its moral superiority over the dominant Western culture and to reaffirm to itself its self-worth in the face of economic, social, political, and legal subordination. In other words, the immigrant community uses restrictions on women's lives as one form of resistance to racism. This form of cultural resistance, however, severely restricts the lives of women, particularly those of the second generation, and it casts the family as a potential site of intense conflict and oppressive demands in immigrant lives.   [edited, 2011]

REFERENCES

Collins, Patricia Hill. 1991. *Black Feminist Thought: Knowledge, Consciousness, and the Politics of Empowerment.* New York: Routledge.

Dasgupta, Shamita Das, and Sayantani DasGupta. "Public Face, Private Space: Asian Indian Women and Sexuality." In *"Bad Girls/Good Girls": Women, Sex, and Power in the Nineties,* ed. Nan Bauer Maglin and Donna Perry. New Brunswick, NJ: Rutgers University Press, 1996.

Egan, Timothy. "Mail-Order Marriage, Immigrant Dreams and Death." *New York Times,* May 26, 1996, p. 12.

Espiritu, Yen Le. 1997. *Asian American Women and Men: Labor, Laws, and Love.* Thousand Oaks, CA: Sage.

Gabbacia, Donna. *From the Other Side: Women, Gender, and Immigrant Life in the U.S., 1820–1990.* Bloomington: Indiana University Press, 1994.

Gilman, Sander L. *Difference and Pathology: Stereotypes of Sexuality, Race, and Madness.* Ithaca, NY: Cornell University Press, 1985.

Green, Rayna. "The Pocahontas Perplex: The Image of Indian Women in American Culture." *Massachusetts Review* 16, no. 4 (1975): 698–714.

Haddad, Yvonne Y., and Jane I. Smith. "Islamic Values among American Muslims." In *Family and Gender among American Muslims: Issues Facing Middle Eastern Immigrants and Their Descendants,* ed. Barbara C. Aswad and Barbara Bilge. Philadelphia: Temple University Press, 1996.

Halualani, Rona Tamiko. "The Intersecting Hegemonic Discourses of an Asian Mail-Order Bride Catalog: Pilipina 'Oriental Butterfly' Dolls for Sale." *Women's Studies in Communication* 18, no. 1 (1995): 45–64.

Kibria, Nazli. 1993. *Family Tightrope: The Changing Lives of Vietnamese Immigrant Community.* Princeton, N.J.: Princeton University Press.

Maglin, Nan Bauer, and Donna Perry. "Introduction." In *"Bad Girls/Good Girls": Women, Sex, and Power in the Nineties,* ed. Nan Bauer Maglin and Donna Perry. New Brunswick, NJ: Rutgers University Press, 1996.

Mazumdar, Suchetta. "General Introduction: A Woman-Centered Perspective on Asian American History." In *Making Waves: An Anthology by and About Asian American Women,* ed. Asian Women United of California. Boston: Beacon, 1989.

Millett, Kate. *Sexual Politics.* Garden City, NY: Doubleday, 1970.

Mirande, Alfredo. 1980. "The Chinano Family: A Reanalysis of Conflicting Views." In *Rethinking Marriage, Child Rearing, and Family Organization,* ed. Arlene S. Skolnick and Jerome H. Skolnick, 479–93. Berkeley: University of California Press.

Ordonez, Raquel Z. "Mail-Order Brides: An Emerging Community." In *Filipino Americans: Transformation and Identity,* ed. Maria P. Root. Thousand Oaks, CA: Sage, 1997.

Orsi, Robert Anthony. *The Madonna of 115th Street: Faith and Community in Italian Harlem, 1880–1950.* New Haven, CT: Yale University Press, 1985.

Stoler, Ann Laura. "Carnal Knowledge and Imperial Power: Gender, Race, and Morality in Colonial Asia." In *Gender at the Crossroads of Knowledge: Feminist Anthropology in the Postmodern Era,* ed. Micaela di Leonardo. Berkeley: University of California Press, 1991.

Tafolla, Carmen. 1985. *To Split a Human: Mitos, Machosy la Mujer Chicana.* San Antonio, Tex.: Mexican American Cultural Center.

Tolman, Deborah L., and Tracy E. Higgins. "How Being a Good Girl Can Be Bad for Girls." In *"Bad Girls/Good Girls": Women, Sex, and Power in the Nineties,* ed. Nan Bauer Maglin and Donna Perry. New Brunswick, NJ: Rutgers University Press, 1996.

Wolf, Diane L. *Factory Daughters: Gender, Household Dynamics, and Rural Industrialization in Java.* Berkeley: University of California Press, 1992.

———. "Family Secrets: Transnational Struggles among Children of Filipino Immigrants." *Sociological Perspectives* 40, no. 3 (1997): 457–82.

 45

Esta Risa No Es De Loca[1]

CARIDAD SOUZA

Esta risa no es de loco. Se están riendo de mí. Me dicen que yo estoy loco pero se están cayendo de un coco. Porque de mí no pueden reír . . .[2]
          —Hector La Voe, *Vamos a Reír Un Poco,* 1978

ESTA LOCURA TIENE RAÍCES[3]

I'm not exactly sure when it was that I began to feel crazy, but I think it has something to do with being

Puerto Rican, and working class, from a woman-headed family, and a girl-child who has come of age in the late twentieth century. It's really quite a feat to be a Puerto Rican woman in the late twentieth century. You barely exist outside your own imagination except in the form of vicious stereotypes. The only way to bring your own self out of oblivion is to remind folks about that peculiarly colonial/post-colonial relationship the U.S. has with a small island in the Caribbean and its people in diaspora. The huge wall of silence that always stops a conversation among people in the United States whenever you bring up those "controversial" issues they'd rather forget speaks to the way Puerto Rican women continually get erased. It always makes me feel so crazy.

My first lessons in erasure happened during my early childhood within my extended family. I was born in the South Bronx at the tail end of the baby boom, my Puerto Ricanness was questioned by my mother's family. Although on the surface I seemed to fit all the appropriate Puerto Rican identity markers, there were wrinkles in this fabric. My father was the child of dual migrations. His mother, an orphan from Ponce, Puerto Rico, migrated to the United States as a domestic servant during the first significant wave of Puerto Rican migration in the early part of the century. My paternal grandfather migrated to the United States from the Cape Verde Islands. I was four years old when he died, so I had little contact with his relatives. My father, although New York born and bred, brought that culture alive for me through religious beliefs and practices that connected me to my African heritage through a particular cosmological worldview. My mother, on the other hand, was part of the "great migration" of Puerto Ricans to the United States that began at midcentury. She passed down to her children some historically and regionally specific cultural values and practices that connect me to my *puertorriqueñidad*. But her Puerto Rico was the one of her childhood in the fifties, a Puerto Rico partly constructed through the imaginings of a migrating female, colonial subject. She fed us the nostalgic narrative of an island paradise interspersed with stories of poverty and hardship that made sense only after we moved to the island when I was eight years old. That's how I got to be a child of multiple diasporas. But the

glaring contradictions in my family's narrative were what started me off feeling crazy.

When my father moved us back to the United States we ended up in the small seaside community of Far Rockaway, Queens. It was in Far Rockaway that I spent the rest of my formative years, and it had an important impact on my sense of *puertorriqueñidad*, and my craziness. Shortly after my family moved to Far Rockaway, my parents permanently separated. The change in our household composition, and our subsequent fall from the working class into the ranks of the poor, meant we were subjected to severe material deprivation. In the multiethnic context of my childhood I had to constantly negotiate different sociocultural politics as a Puerto Rican girl. This meant that whenever I visited friends, I was subjected to a certain scrutiny by wary mothers who wanted to assure themselves I wasn't *that* kind of Puerto Rican. No matter the ethnic background of any of my friends, whether Colombian, Jewish, Dominican, or Italian-American, once their mothers found out I was Puerto Rican, I could expect an interrogation at my first visit. My parents raised me to respect my elders and inculcated in me an ethic of respect that won me the approval, sometimes even the affection, of my friend's parents. But the fact that I was Puerto Rican and poor was enough to render me suspicious. Despite passing the entry exams, I was still subject to undue questioning whenever anything was lost or missing and whenever my friends got into mischief. I worked hard to please the adults, going out of my way to comport myself appropriately and to abide by any household rules. But my racial, ethnic, and class position marked me no matter how well I behaved, no matter how respectful I was, no matter how much I followed the rules. My name was always the first to come up whenever something went wrong. I learned to anticipate this scrutiny and develop elaborate arguments in my own defense. It annoyed the hell out of the adults and didn't endear me to them, but it saved me the pain of their scrutiny.

THAT PUTA THING THAT JUST DOESN'T GO AWAY

Specific gender and sexual ideologies governed my behavior as a young girl and adolescent in this community. The label of *puta* (whore) was used within this Latino community for girls and young women to uphold the rigid lines of sexual propriety. Any woman who didn't conform to the prevailing gender and sexual norms was a *puta*. The word tethered us like a huge ball and chain. So great was the power of this label that none of us escaped constructing our sexual identities without, at some level, addressing the *puta* thing. For someone like me who was poor, from a woman-headed family on welfare, and Puerto Rican, the label *puta* had a particular resonance. My explicit sexualization meant that I didn't merit the respect "ladies" get by virtue of living in households with a male head. For better or for worse, I did not get the kind of patriarchal protection most Latinas do. The lack of male presence at home left me open to whatever assaults and attacks men deemed appropriate for someone of my station. It didn't matter that I wasn't even interested in sex with men, that I didn't have a boyfriend, and that I was not actively pursuing a man. Junior whores-in-training like me, guilty by association, bore the brunt of the psychological and sociopolitical impact of the *puta* label. More than anything, it was this label that taught me the most important lessons about patriarchal domination and masculine violence.

Sexual stigma was status- and color-oriented among Puerto Ricans in this community, but it was more intensely racialized outside of the Puerto Rican enclave among Latinos and other ethnic groups. I lived with the stigma of the word *puta*, carrying it around like a marker of my worth, an index of how I should be treated. Even before I had a chance to define my own sexuality, my own identity, the label preceded me like a calling card. Once a friend's older brother, who was on a home visit from the military, decided I had grown up enough to bestow his masculine virility on me. He cornered me in his sister's bedroom and tried to kiss me. I pushed him away with such force that he slammed against the wall. He seemed surprised by this and he said, in all earnestness, "What? You want to go to a hotel?" Perhaps my friend's constant refrain—that the only thing Puerto Rican women were good for was to cook, dance, and fuck—should have tipped me off. Until that moment, I really didn't know that

I was open season even to the boys I grew up with once they became men. It was another one of those revelatory moments.

These types of incidents taught me to anticipate whether or not knowledge about my woman-headed-household-on-public-assistance background might matter to people. I carefully selected my friends based on the position they took. This *puta* thing also meant men assumed that I was sexually available to them, especially after they learned that I was Puerto Rican. Somehow *puertorriqueña* became synonymous with *puta*. And since I was undoubtedly a *puta*, the logic went, then I must also be interested in casual sex with any man who approached me. Whenever I wasn't grateful enough to oblige a man's sexual interest in me, I was treated abusively, sometimes even violently. Since for me the sexual attention of men was always dangerous, usually painful, and always unsolicited, I avoided contact with them. I steered clear from sexual encounters with men and worked hard never to find myself in a position where I was alone with a man for fear of his expectations and their consequences. I constantly fended off unwanted sexual attentions and sexual attacks, becoming an expert in dodging and evasiveness to avoid such encounters. I learned to watch for the ways people might misperceive me sexually, to read between the lines, to intuit whether double entendres meant a dangerous situation was brewing. Consequently, I was never all-consumed with finding a man to settle down with in a relationship, unlike many of the women I knew. Since my gender and sexual identity were not defined relationally by attachment to a man, I concentrated on developing relationships with women. Yet, despite my lack of engagement with men, the stigma of being a *puta* even when I wasn't, made me feel more than a little crazy.

NO GREAT EXPECTATIONS

No one expected much out of me. There are no great expectations for little Puerto Rican girls from women-headed families on welfare. I achieved in spite of this, exceeding all their expectations for someone from my background, and sometimes even my own. In many respects I've become the quintessential American achievement story. From an outsider's view, I've defied the odds. My achievements are celebrated by the very people who expected nothing from me. After struggling to get out from under the weight of my sociopolitical inheritance, after struggling against the stereotypes about me within and outside of the Latino community I lived in, after struggling to get beyond the structural constraints on my life and after grappling with my low self-esteem, I've become successful by their standards. More importantly I've become successful by my own standards. But the damage is still there. Now I wage a new struggle to remind people that none of my achievements are guaranteed. And that it's all been at a cost. And while, yes, I'm better off materially, and perhaps even more in control of my life, while academia and intellectual work offer me a certain refuge, and while a lot of hard work on my part has paid off, much of it is a result of institutional support. The end result is that all of this has enhanced my ability to see contradictions and to grapple with them in ways that can benefit me.

For a long time my ability to read the cultural, social, and political contradictions in my life made me feel really crazy. They tore me apart. But the basis for my sense of craziness is really a world that compartmentalized me a priori into social categories that I did not fit. I was born into these categories without much say, and the expectations and stereotypes about my potential really only measure the biases upon which they were based and not my social worth as a person. No matter my own values, I realized I would be judged by societal assumptions about who I ought to be, not who I actually was. These assumptions used superficial understandings of me that certainly never considered my views. My fate was sealed before I could have a say. In the world I was born into, I used to feel like I was crazy. These days I've learned that what is crazy is a world that is so structured by inequality and injustice that it doesn't nurture poor Puerto Rican girls simply because they are poor, Puerto Rican girls.

Only recently I have been able to appreciate my ability to "see" beyond the surface; how these experiences have taught me to be aware of my surroundings; and what it means to be marked by race, class, gender, and ethnicity. It's given me an edge. I've learned, for example, that political allies come in a variety of shapes and forms, and I've learned to choose them on the basis of ideological and poetical persuasion. I've also learned about partially situated perspectives, about the transparency of claims to objectivity, and about the importance of cross-referencing. The life situations I've narrated have taught me much about how people come to view things, about how our biases mediate our perspectives. From my family I've learned a healthy distrust for authority and for the "official story." From the way that race, class, gender, and ethnicity have come together in my life, I've learned that people will question facts before they question their convictions, especially if those convictions support stereotypes about others that benefit them in some way. I have witnessed how the adults around me were wrong about their perceptions, how authority figures made mistakes. Much later I learned that racist ethnocentrism was actually a very logical, rational system of oppression.

One of the most important ways my life experiences have prepared me for academia has been to develop my own internal standards, and to look to those standards for validation. Otherwise I would have to accept the assessment of a world that despises me. The world I live in does not validate little Puerto Rican girls. So I've developed my own measures of success, of progress, of achievement. Learning to redefine categories, to question received ones, and to create new definitions and concepts means I participate in creating alternative perspectives. Why accept definitions of others when they were not only possibly wrong, but potentially harmful and inaccurate anyway? I've learned to question everything. People have their own sense of meaning, and they also make meaning as they move along the trajectories of their lives. I learned that I don't have to accept their meanings, especially if those meanings were constructed to devalue me. My own meanings, perspectives, and interpretations are just as valid, just as useful.

Laughter has always been a part of my survival mechanism, one that I learned in my family. Although I'm usually serious, I find myself almost

Demanding a Condom

KAT DOUD

Before I understood AIDS, who got it, and how it could be prevented, I was scared, really scared. I felt at risk but for the wrong reasons. I was afraid of casual contact with people instead of being afraid of having unsafe sex with a man I was seeing at the time. Max (not his real name) was putting a lot of pressure on me to get birth control pills for protection, [but] the only protection pills would offer would be for pregnancy—not AIDS. During this time, my fear of AIDS was growing. I was getting really paranoid, so I called the hotline. They talked a lot about condoms and safer sex. I went immediately to Max to tell him how I was feeling and that I wouldn't have sex with him without condoms. His reaction was horrible. He got very angry and full of contempt and accused me of having AIDS, and angry that I insinuated that he did. I began to try to explain, then realized he wasn't worth my time. Why would I want to sleep with this creature who didn't care about my life? I never saw him again after that night.   [1990]

---

ready to explode with giggles at the most inappropriate times. Or a word sounds strange and I laugh to myself. Sometimes I will remember a silly moment and will chuckle out loud to myself while sitting on the train or bus. That kind of laughter has always marked me as crazy. Laughter helps to heal the crazies. Lately, my laughter sounds less like the screech of a crazy woman than of someone who delights in the world I see, disorderly, contradictory, and complex as it may be. Recently, I was taking one of my students to an awards banquet. Her mother, who was in the car with us, turned to me and said, "Cari, *tú no te crees nadie*."[4] An immigrant from Latin America, I understood her words to mean that I am not pretentious. I laughed heartily at this. It's hard to be pretentious in a world that devalues you at every turn. *Pero esta risa no es de loca.*[5] I'm having the last laugh. Only this time it's the laughter of a woman grounded in who she is regardless of how she's been marked.

So I guess the last laugh is on me.   [2002]

NOTES

1. Jus' Cuz I'm Laughin' Don't Mean I'm Crazy
2. This laughter doesn't mean I'm crazy. They're laughing at me. They say I'm crazy but *'se están cayendo de un coco'* (untranslatable word play, possibly for the purpose of rhyming *loco*[crazy] with *coco*[coconut]). But they can't laugh at me . . .

3. This Madness Has Roots.
4. "Cari, you don't believe yourself to be better than other people."
5. "But jus' cuz I'm laughin' doesn't mean I'm crazy."

 46

Pleasures

DIANE HUGS

We both sat there, two disabled lesbians in our wheelchairs, each on opposite sides of the bed. Sudden feelings of fear and timidness came over us. But once we finished the transferring, lifting of legs, undressing and arranging of blankets, we finally touched. Softly and slowly we began to explore each other, our minds and bodies. Neither could make assumptions about the sensations or pleasures of the other. It was wonderful to sense that this woman felt that my body was worth the time it took to explore, that she was as interested in discovering my pleasure as I was in discovering hers.

From the first touch it was a stream of sensations; to listen to every breath, each sigh, and to feel every movement of our love intermingling. It was so intense, so mutual that I must say this beginning was one of the deepest and most fulfilling that I have ever experienced.

When I was an able-bodied lesbian, my approach to relating sexually had been to find out what moves turned someone on and go from there. Never before have I taken the time or had the opportunity to begin a relationship with such a beautiful feeling of pleasure, not only from the pot of gold at the end of the rainbow, but also from the exploration itself.   [1985]

 ## 47

Loving Another Woman

ANNE KOEDT

The following is from a taped interview with a woman who talked about her love relationship with another woman. Both of these women, who requested anonymity, had previously had only heterosexual relationships; both are feminists. The interview was conducted by Anne Koedt.

Question: You said you had been friends for a while before you realized you were attracted to each other. How did you become aware of it?

Answer: I wasn't conscious of it until one evening when we were together and it all just sort of exploded. But, looking back, there are always signs, only one represses seeing them.

For example, I remember one evening—we are in the same feminist group together—and we were all talking very abstractly about love. All of a sudden, even though the group was carrying on the conversation in a theoretical way, we were having a personal conversation. We were starting to tell each other that we liked each other. Of course one of the things we discussed was: What is the thin line between friendship and love?

Or, there were times when we were very aware of having "accidentally" touched each other. And Jennie told me later that when we first met she remembered thinking, "abstractly" again, that if she were ever to get involved with a woman, she'd like to get involved with someone like me.

The mind-blowing thing is that you aren't at all conscious of what you are feeling; rather, you subconsciously, and systematically, refuse to deal with the implications of what's coming out. You just let it hang there because you're too scared to let it continue and see what it means.

Q: What did you do when you became aware of your mutual attraction?

A: We'd been seeing a lot of each other, and I was at her house for dinner. During the evening—we were having a nice time, but I remember also feeling uncomfortable—I became very aware of her as we were sitting together looking at something. There was an unusual kind of tension throughout the whole evening.

It was quite late by the time we broke up, so she asked me whether I wanted to stay over and sleep on her couch. And I remember really being very uptight—something I certainly wouldn't have felt in any other situation with a friend. Yet, even when I was uptight and felt that in some way by staying I would get myself into something, I wasn't quite sure what—something new and dangerous—I decided to stay anyway.

It wasn't really until I tried to fall asleep, and couldn't, that all of a sudden I became very, very aware. I was flooded with a tremendous attraction for her. And I wanted to tell her, I wanted to sleep with her, I wanted to let her know what I was feeling. At the same time I was totally bewildered, because here I was—not only did I want to tell her, but I was having a hard time just facing up to what was coming out in myself. My mind was working overtime trying to deal with this new thing.

She was awake too, and so we sat and talked. It took me about two hours to build up the courage to even bring up the subject. I think it is probably one of the most difficult things I ever had to do. To say—to in any way whatsoever open up the subject—to say anything was just so hard.

When I did bring it up in an oblique way and told her that I was attracted to her, she replied somewhat generally that she felt the same way. You see, she was as scared as I was, but I didn't know it. I thought she seemed very cool, so I wasn't even sure if she was interested. Although I think subconsciously I knew, because otherwise I wouldn't have asked her—I think I would have been too scared of rejection.

But when I finally did bring it up, and she said she felt the same way, well, at that point there was really no space left for anything in your mind. So we agreed to just drop it and let things happen as they would at a later time. My main, immediate worry was that maybe I had blown a good friendship which I really valued. Also, even if she did feel the same way, would we know what to do with it?

Q: When you first realized that you were possibly getting involved with a woman, were you afraid or upset?

A: No. The strange thing is that the next morning, after I left, I felt a fantastic high. I was bouncing down the street and the sun was shining and I felt tremendously good. My mind was on a super high.

When I got home I couldn't do any kind of work. My mind kept operating on this emergency speed, trying to deal with my new feelings for her. So I sat down and wrote a letter to myself. Just wrote it free association—didn't try to work it out in any kind of theory—and as I was writing I was learning from myself what I was feeling. Unexpectedly I wasn't feeling guilty or worried. I felt great.

Q: When did you start sleeping with each other?

A: The next time we were together. Again, we really wanted each other, but to finally make the move, the same move that with a man would have been automatic, was tremendously difficult . . . and exhilarating. Although we did sleep together, it wasn't sexual; just affectionate and very sensual. After that evening we started sleeping together sexually as well.

I guess it was also a surprise to find that you weren't struck down by God in a final shaft of lightning. That once you fight through that initial wall of undefined fears (built to protect those taboos), they wither rapidly, and leave you to operate freely in a new self-defined circle of what's natural. You have a new sense of boldness, of daring, about yourself.

Q: Was it different from what you had thought a relationship with a woman would be like?

A: Generally, no. Most of the things that I had thought intellectually in fact turned out to be true in my experience. One thing, however, was different. Like, I'd really felt that very possibly a relationship with a woman might not be terribly physical. That it would be for the most part warm and affectionate. I think I probably thought this because with men sex is so frequently confused with conquest. Men have applied a symbolic value to sex, where the penis equals dominance and the vagina equals submission. Since sensuality has no specific sex and is rather a general expression of mutual affection, its symbolic value, power-wise, is nil. So sex with a man is usually genitally oriented.

Perhaps I wasn't quite sure what would happen to sexuality once it was removed from its conventional context. But one of the things I discovered was that when you really like somebody, there's a perfectly natural connection between affection and love and sensuality and sexuality. That sexuality is a natural part of sensuality.

Q: How is sex different with a woman?

A: One of the really mind-blowing things about all this has been that it added a whole new dimension to my own sexuality. You can have good sex, technically, with a woman or a man. But at this point in time I think women have a much broader sense of sensuality. Since she and I both brought our experiences as women to sexuality, it was quite something.

Another aspect of sexuality is your feelings. Again, this is of course an area that has been delegated to women; we are supposed to provide the love and affection. It is one of our duties in a male-female relationship. Though it has been very oppressive in the context that we've been allowed it, the *ability* to show affection and love for someone else is, I think, a fine thing—which men should develop more in themselves, as a matter of fact. Love and affection are a necessary aspect of full sexuality. And one of the things I really enjoy with Jennie is this uninhibited ability to show our feelings.

Q: Is the physical aspect of loving women really as satisfying as sex with a man?
A: Yes.

Q: You've been together a while now. What's your relationship like?
A: Once we got over the initial week or so of just getting used to this entirely new thing, it very quickly became natural—natural is really the word I'd use for it. It was like adding another dimension to what we'd already been feeling for each other. It is quite a combination to fall in love with your friend.

We don't have any plans, any desire, to live together, although we do see a great deal of each other. We both like our own apartments, our own space.

I think one of the good things we did in the beginning was to say: Let's just see where it will go. We didn't say that we loved each other, just that we liked each other. We didn't immediately proclaim it a "relationship," as one is accustomed to do with a man—you know, making mental plans for the next ten years. So each new feeling was often surprising, and very intensely experienced.

Q: What would you say is the difference between this relationship and those you have had with men?
A: Well, one of the biggest differences is that for the first time I haven't felt those knots-in-the-stomach undercurrents of trying to figure out what's *really* happening under what you *think* is happening.

I think it all boils down to an absence of role-playing; I haven't felt with Jen that we've fallen into that. Both of us are equally strong persons. I mean, you can ask yourself the question, if there

were going to be roles, who'd play what? Well, I certainly won't play "the female," and I won't play "the male," and it's just as absurd to imagine her in either one of them. So in fact what we have is much more like what one gets in a friendship, which is more equalized. It's a more above-board feeling.

I don't find the traditional contradictions. If I do something strong and self-assertive, she doesn't find that a conflict with her having a relationship with me. I don't get reminded that I might be making myself "less womanly." And along with that there's less *self*-censorship, too. There's a mutual, unqualified, support for daring to try new things that I have never quite known before.

As a result, my old sense of limits is changing. For example, for the first time in my life I'm beginning to feel that I don't have a weak body, that my body isn't some kind of passive baggage. The other day I gritted my teeth and slid down a fireman's pole at a park playground. It may sound ordinary, but it was something I had never dared before, and I felt a very private victory.

Q: Given the social disapproval and legal restrictions against lesbianism, what are some of the external problems you have faced?
A: One thing is that I hesitate to show my affection for her in public. If you're walking down the street and you want to put your arm around someone or give them a kiss—the kind of thing you do without thinking if it is a man—well, that's hardly considered romantic by most people if it's done with someone of your own sex. I know that if I were to express my feelings in public with Jennie, there would be a lot of social intrusion that I would have to deal with. Somehow, people would assume a license to intrude upon your privacy in public; their hostile comments, hostile attitudes, would ruin the whole experience. So you're sort of caught in a bind. But we have in fact begun to do it more and more, because it bothers me that I can't express my feeling as I see fit, without hostile interference.

Q: What made you fall in love with a woman?

A: Well, that's a hard question. I think maybe it's even a bit misleading the way you phrased it. Because I didn't fall in love with "a woman," I fell in love with Jen—which is not exactly the same thing. A better way to ask the question is: How were you able to *overcome* the fact that it was a woman? In other words, how was I able to overcome my heterosexual training and allow my feelings for her to come out?

Certainly in my case it would never have happened without the existence of the women's movement. My own awareness of "maleness" and "femaleness" had become acute, and I was really probing what it meant. You see, I think in a sense I never wanted to be either male *or* female. Even when I was quite little and in many ways seemed feminine and "passive"—deep down, I never felt at home with the kinds of things women were supposed to be. On the other hand, I didn't particularly want to be a man either, so I didn't develop a male identity. Before I even got involved with the women's movement, I was already wanting something new. But the movement brought it out into the open for me.

Another thing the movement helped me with was shedding the notion that, however independent my life was, I must have a man; that somehow, no matter what I did myself, there was something that needed that magical element of male approval. Without confronting this I could never have allowed myself to fall in love with Jennie. In a way, I am like an addict who has kicked the habit.

But most important of all, I like her. In fact I think she's the healthiest person I have ever been involved with. See, I think we were lucky, because it happened spontaneously and unexpectedly from both sides. We didn't do it because we felt compelled to put our ideological beliefs into reality.

Many feminists are now beginning to at least theoretically consider the fact that there's no reason why one shouldn't love a woman. But I think that a certain kind of experimentation going on now with lesbianism can be really bad.

Because even if you do ideologically think that it is perfectly fine—well, that's a *political* position; but being able to love somebody is a very personal and private thing as well, and even if you remove political barriers, well, then you are left with finding an individual who particularly fits *you.*

So I guess I'm saying that I don't think women who are beginning to think about lesbianism should get involved with anyone until they are really attracted to somebody. And that includes refusing to be seduced by lesbians who play the male seduction game and tell you, "you don't love women," and "you are oppressing us" if you don't jump into bed with them. It's terrible to try to seduce someone on ideological grounds.

Q: Do you now look at women in a more sexual way?

A: You mean, do I now eye all women as potential bed partners? No. Nor did I ever see men that way. As a matter of fact, I've never found myself being attracted to a man just because, for example, he had a good physique. I had a sexual relationship with whatever boyfriend I had, but I related to most other men pretty asexually. It's no different with women. My female friends—well, I still see them as friends, because that's what they are. I don't sit around and have secret fantasies of being in bed with them.

But there's a real question here: What is the source, the impetus, for one's sexuality? Is it affection and love, or is it essentially conquest in bed? If it's sex as conquest in bed, then the question you just asked is relevant, for adding the category of women to those you sleep with would mean that every woman—who's attractive enough to be a prize worth conquering, of course—could arouse your sexuality. But if the sexual source lies in affection and love, then the question becomes absurd. For one obviously does not immediately fall in love with every woman one meets simply because one is *able* to sleep with women.

Also, one thing that really turns me off about this whole business of viewing women as potential bedmates is the implied possessiveness of it. It has taken me this long just to figure out how men are treating women sexually; now when I see some lesbians doing precisely the same kinds of things, I'm supposed to have instant amnesia in the name of sisterhood. I have heard some lesbians say things like, "I see all men as my rivals," or have heard them proudly discuss how they intimidated a heterosexual couple publicly to "teach the woman a political lesson." This brings out in me the same kind of intense rage that I get when, for example, I hear white men discussing how black men are "taking their women" (or vice versa). Who the hell says we belong to anyone?

Q: Do you think that you would have difficulty relating to a man again if this relationship broke up? That is, can you "go back" to men after having had a relationship with a woman?

A: It's an interesting thing that when people ask that question, most often what they're really asking is, are you "lost" to the world of what's "natural"? Sometimes I find myself not wanting to answer the question at all just because they're starting out by assuming that something's wrong with having a relationship with a woman. That's usually what's meant by "go back to men"—like you've been off someplace wild and crazy and, most of all, unsafe, and can you find your way home to papa, or something. So first of all it wouldn't be "going back."

And since I didn't become involved with a woman in order to make a political statement, by the same token I wouldn't make the converse statement. So, sure I could have a relationship with a man if he were the right kind of person and if he had rejected playing "the man" with me—that leaves out a lot of men here, I must add. But if a man had the right combination of qualities, I see no reason why I shouldn't be able to love him as much as I now love her.

At a certain point, I think, you realize that the final qualification is not being male or female, but whether they've joined the middle. That is—whether they have started from the male or the female side—they've gone toward the center where they are working toward combining the healthy aspects of so-called male and female characteristics. That's where I want to go and that's what I'm beginning to realize I respond to in other people.

Q: Now that you've gotten involved with a woman, what is your attitude toward gay and lesbian groups?

A: I have really mixed feelings about them. To some extent, for example, there has been a healthy interplay between the gay movement and the feminist movement. Feminists have had a very good influence on the gay movement because women's liberation challenges the very nature of the sex role system, not just whether one may be allowed to make transfers within it. On the other hand, the gay movement has helped open up the question of women loving other women. Though some of this was beginning to happen by itself, lesbians made a point of pressing the issue and therefore speeded up the process.

But there is a problem to me with focusing on sexual choice, as the gay movement does. Sleeping with another woman is not *necessarily* a healthy thing by itself. It does not mean—or prove, for that matter—that you therefore love women. It doesn't mean that you have avoided bad "male" or "female" behavior. It doesn't guarantee you anything. If you think about it, it can be the same game with new partners: On the one hand, male roles are learned, not genetic; women can ape them too. On the other, the feminine role can be comfortably carried into lesbianism, except now instead of a woman being passive with a man, she's passive with another woman. Which is all very familiar and is all going nowhere.

The confusing of sexual *partners* with sexual *roles* has also led to a really bizarre situation where some lesbians insist that you aren't really a radical feminist if you are not in bed with a woman. Which is wrong politically and outrageous personally.

Q: Did the fact that lesbians pushed the issue in the women's movement have a major effect upon your own decision to have a relationship with a woman?

A: It's hard to know. I think that the lesbian movement has escalated the thinking in the women's movement, and to that extent it probably escalated mine.

But at the same time I know I was slowly getting there myself anyway. I'd been thinking about it for a long time. Because it is a natural question; if you want to remove sexual roles, and if you say that men and women are equal human beings, well, the next question is: Why should you only love men? I remember asking myself that question, and I remember it being discussed in many workshops I was in—what is it that makes us assume that you can only receive and give love to a man?   [1973]

🌿 48

In Search of the Elusive Orgasm

LORI L. THARPS

Ask me why I never had an orgasm until I was a married woman of 28. I blame it on Harlequin. Publisher of romantic fantasies, mass-distributor of schoolgirl dreams. All that fiery passion, those heart-wrenching betrayals and predictable happily-ever-afters are addicting and dangerous, especially for a girl on the cusp of womanhood. While my classmates traded copies of Sweet Valley High novels, I was pilfering paperback Harlequins from my Auntie's attic collection. I am not proud of that time. And as I look back, I realize how much damage was done in those formative years.

Basically, it comes down to this: The Harlequin romance novel and all of its heftier bodice-ripping incarnations shaped the way I viewed sexuality. It's how I cobbled together my understanding of what really went on between a man and a woman, only to discover 18 years later that I got it all wrong.

I could see pretty easily where the stories were psychologically mistaken. (All men aren't misunderstood brutes who need a virginal but passionate woman to unlock their tortured spirits.) But from a physical standpoint I was misguided, thinking a woman's role in sex was to lie back and prepare for cascading waves of pleasure to wash over her lithe and quivering form. I basically gathered that true love and good sex were synonymous. The only other options were rape and chastity. The virginal protagonist always turned out to be an excellent lover on her very first tumble with the man she loved. And she wasn't just good; she was always better than the buxom harlot the hero used to visit to satisfy his lusty loins. As long as the heroine was infused with true love for her roving stud, she would prove to be a treasure betwixt the sheets. And, more important, he would know instinctively how to make her squirm with orgiastic ecstasy. I was totally brainwashed.

It was really quite perfect to discover Harlequins at about the same time I started high school. Where historical romances had seemed an escape to another world, the Harlequins presented a real woman in modern times, and it wasn't too much of a stretch to imagine myself in the same situation. I could be a zoologist working in Wyoming or an antique collector looking for Mr. Right in a cozy hamlet in Vermont. Although the stories were maddeningly formulaic, I still could count on finding just the right one to heal my adolescent angst or provide comfort while I sat home on prom night without a date. Although I quit cold turkey when I went away to school (at my politically active, left-leaning women's college, my penchant for Cinderella fairy tales seemed akin to treason), those Harlequin notions of love and romance stayed with me.

Toward the end of my third year, spent studying in Spain, I met the man who would become my husband. I first saw Javier in German class. He walked into the room and I fell for him instantly. After months of trying to attract his attention away from the other women who followed his every move, he finally noticed me, and we started a good old-fashioned courtship. We walked home together from school and went out for coffee in the afternoons and tapas on the weekends. By the time I had to leave España, we were deliriously in love. But I returned to the United States thinking I'd simply had "an affair to remember." Little did I know I'd discovered "endless love." We spent the next two years pouring our hearts out in handwritten letters, spending gobs of money listening to each other breathe on transatlantic phone calls and traveling back and forth across the pond for visits on major holidays. When Javier finally moved to New York to be with me, I was ecstatic. Danielle Steel could not have penned a better ending. But that was only the beginning.

But then came the wedding night, a night I had dubbed the "night o' passion." Even though we had moved in together a few months before the wedding, we made it a point not to have sex so the wedding night would be that much more exquisite. Every "first time" story from my Harlequin junkie past flooded my mind and enlivened my imagination. I just knew our night o' passion would be filled with effortless, ecstatic sexual release. We stayed in a charming bed and breakfast that just oozed rustic romance with a touch of convenient modernity. The stone fireplace burst into roaring flames with the flip of a bedside switch. The sunken Jacuzzi was surrounded by gilded mirrors. We took advantage of all the amenities, and the sex was sweet and passionate—but there was no big O for me. No cascading waves of pleasure. No joyous heights of ecstasy. I wasn't too discouraged, though. The way I saw it, we had the rest of our lives to compensate.

But one night turned into a series of nights, which turned into a year of pleasant but orgasmless sex for me. My husband tried every position, trick and technique he knew to help me have an orgasm. And it wasn't that I wasn't enjoying it—I just didn't experience that explosion that supposedly everyone else was experiencing. After a year of tenderness and patience, my husband began to get frustrated that he wasn't able to make me come. This wasn't his macho Spanish ego shining through—he felt like he was letting me down. He thought I didn't find him attractive enough. He began to doubt his own sexual prowess. I tried to assure him that I was still enjoying myself, but a man needs to see results. I'm sure he wanted to believe me and for a while he did, but in the back of his mind he was plagued with guilt. Since we were each other's first and only sex partners, neither of us had a basis for comparison, which didn't help put any of this into perspective.

The worst part of this entire experience was having no one to talk to. According to a survey in a popular women's magazine I read at the time, more than 85 percent of sexually active women achieve orgasm. Unfortunately, I didn't know where to find the other 15 percent. I listened to the women around me discuss their sexual activities, and it seemed as if they were all happily ensconced within that majority group. I couldn't figure out why I was different.

I finally decided something was either physically or emotionally wrong with me. I wondered if perhaps I was gay and this was my body's reaction to being in a heterosexual union. I stared at my clitoris until I was convinced it was deformed. I ran through every excuse in the book. Eventually, Javier's guilt coupled with my own frustrations caused me to dread having sex. Finally, when it looked like my husband had given up all hope, I decided to approach the problem head-on, just like I approached every other obstacle. I bought a penis-shaped vibrator and an instructional tome on becoming orgasmic and promised my husband I wouldn't give up until my loins were throbbing with pleasure.

It didn't happen. Even with my fancy equipment, the manual and the encouragement of a few good friends, I wasn't getting any closer to the big O. By then my husband was suggesting I seek professional help. He was convinced that my politically conservative mother had raised me to be afraid of my own sexuality, but I assured him that was not the case: I played spin-the-bottle in junior high. I French-kissed a stranger at a rock concert. I read *Delta of Venus* in the bathtub. He wasn't buying it. What he saw was a woman unable to experience sexual pleasure fully—reason being, we both concluded, that I didn't have the first clue how to get there.

About six months shy of our second wedding anniversary, Javier and I started talking about having a child. Although the conversation was still in the abstract, it struck me that I might experience sex for procreation before I experienced it for pure physical pleasure—and that seemed fundamentally wrong. Or at least unfair. I grew up believing women had the right to be sexual. An orgasm was my due. My reward, if you will, for waiting for Mr. Right. Having let the pursuit of the big O lie dormant for a period, once again it reared its hooded head. This time I was more adamant about it than Javier, determined to experience an orgasm before the idea of motherhood dominated all the conversations about sex. Now the issue was more about me than us. Around this time, my husband left to visit his family in Spain for an entire month. I dedicated that very same month to becoming orgasmic. I dusted off the books, videos, and vibrator, lit candles every night and became obsessed with taking bubble baths. Although I got to know certain parts of my body better than ever before, I didn't find myself any closer to feeling that special thing (by the way, I didn't even know what to expect—just that I'd know it when I felt it).

One evening during Operation Orgasm, I had dinner with a friend (let's call her Simone). She wasn't a good friend yet, just a kindred spirit I had been meaning to get to know better. Our conversation touched on several topics and finally settled on sex and relationships. That's when Simone confessed to me that she was almost 28 years old and she had never had an orgasm. I knew I could top that story. I was 28, *married* and had never had an orgasm. But I struggled with sharing this information. As many mixed signals as there are about female sexuality in western culture, in groups of women being orgasmic is a sign of achievement. More than a sign of sexual maturity, it's a status symbol of intrinsic sexuality. Outing myself as inorgasmic felt like admitting I still wet the bed.

For a moment I considered offering Simone only a sympathetic ear and not admitting I had the same problem, but I changed my mind. I figured maybe I'd find out what was wrong with me by spilling my guts to someone else. That night over Cambodian food in Brooklyn, we told each other everything that frustrated us about living an orgasm-free life. Then we tried to figure out what had gone wrong. She thought it was because her mother had raised her in a repressive environment where emotion and overt affection were restricted. As I sat there and listened, I wondered what that had to do with me. My family was loud and affectionate, and sex was talked about without shame. In fact, on the day after my wedding, I was forced to divulge all the intimate details from the night o' passion to my aunties, who were just dying to share with me their own wedding-night stories.

As Simone and I rehashed our childhood, adolescence and sexual experiences, I began to realize how much I romanticized sex. Even though I considered myself a strong, independent woman, I truly believed my man was supposed to take charge of my sexual pleasure. Masturbation did not work for me because deep down I didn't believe in it. I wanted the fairy tale. I wanted, "In a cascade, his essence, the life force of his manhood, coursed into her, flooding and filling and fulfilling every last fragment of her body. [Insert my name here] gasped with happiness, then convulsed again and again, then catapulted like a projectile into realms beyond reality." How could K-Y Jelly and a dildo compete with that?

The following day, still high off our night of divulgence, my new best friend and I went on a field trip to an elegant little sex shop in midtown Manhattan. We were determined that our time had come. After spending close to one $100, dollars, I came home with a state-of-the-art vibrating turtle (designed to nestle comfortably in the folds of the vagina), an erotic video and a lifetime supply of personal lubricant. I told myself I deserved these indulgences and felt euphoria and trepidation all mixed up together as I contemplated the evening ahead. After cooking myself an elaborate dinner, washing the dishes, and taking a long, hot shower, I slipped into my one pair of silk pajamas and lay down on the couch. I placed my new toys around me and put the video in the VCR. This time, instead of thinking about masturbation, I just focused on feeling pleasure.

When my loins started quivering and my hips started thrusting of their own accord, I turned on my turtle and immediately started shivering with waves of pleasure. In less than five minutes, I felt it. Something like a dam bursting sent the most delicious waves of pleasure zinging through my body and ended in a roaring crescendo. I was laughing and crying at the same time. I finally got it. I understood. I knew. Before I forgot what it felt like, I grabbed my journal and wrote this down: "Ain't I a woman."

For the rest of the week, I tried to make up for lost time. I'd wake up and turn on the turtle, run home from work to turtle myself and put myself to sleep with a little swish of my soft pink reptile. I felt like a naughty 13-year-old boy, yet deliciously indulgent. And the more often I made myself orgasm, the more I realized it didn't require male participation. While I looked forward to my hubby coming home and experiencing a new level of pleasure with him, I also felt possessive of my developing sexual relationship with myself.

When I called Javier in Spain and told him about my great new discovery, he was thrilled. His advice? "Keep practicing." He also wanted to know if he could play with the turtle when he came home. Luckily, unlike many men, he did not feel he'd been replaced by a battery-operated piece of rubber. He was just so happy that I'd finally felt the big O. When he did come home, intercourse still didn't mean an orgasm for me, but it felt like a tremendous burden was lifted. In addition, Javier respected how I had unlocked my sexual powers, and he finally believed I wasn't suffering from the effects of a repressive childhood. Now we use the turtle and incorporate all kinds of play into our sex. Sometimes I get to O, sometimes Javier does; we're working on the day when we come together . . . just like in the movies! (I'm kidding.)

Clearly, I can't condemn Harlequin romance novels for every woman's sexual dysfunction, but I can lay part of the blame on the powerful myth that they—and the rest of popular culture—continue to perpetuate. In movies, on television, and in those ubiquitous love tomes, women enter the throes of ecstasy by having a man on top of them. Since my own personal orgasmic revelation, I can't keep my mouth shut. It is high time for women to examine their sexual expectations and stop buying into the pop culture paradigm of female pleasure coming only at the hands of a seasoned lover who looks like Fabio. The job can be well-served by a piece of machinery, one's own hand, and a clear conscience. It wasn't until I decided I deserved to feel sexual pleasure for myself and by myself that I was able to experience results (although I still stumble over the word "masturbate"). Sure, our partners can be part of the equation, but all we really need in order to reach the pinnacles of earth-shattering desire are a vibrating turtle and a ban on bodice-ripper romances.　　　　　　　　　　　　　　[2001]

49

Bisexuality, Feminism, Men, and Me

ROBYN OCHS

Where does feminist consciousness come from? Why do some women begin to question what has been presented to us as given and, as a result of that questioning, come to understand the ways in which women have been systemically limited? Each of us takes a different road to feminism. Many of our journeys begin with a pivotal event or transition that forces us to question our assumed reality.

My own route to feminism was long, convoluted and closely connected with my developing bisexual consciousness. In my early twenties I realized that my emotional and sexual attractions toward women as well as men were not going to go away, and I began to address those feelings. Forced off-balance by the turbulence of these emotions and their implications for my future, I began for the first time to consciously question the assumptions I had made about my life. I began to understand that many of my choices had not been freely made, but rather had been made within the context of a system that Adrienne Rich calls "compulsory heterosexuality," a system that posits heterosexuality as the only way to be.[1] In this essay I describe my own journey: what I learned and what I unlearned, and how these changes in my thinking have fundamentally changed my relationships with men.

I grew up believing that women deserved equal pay for equal work and that we had the right not to be raped or battered and the right to control our own reproduction. These beliefs were firmly held by my mother and grandmothers. In the kitchen of the house I grew up in, a cartoon showing two toddlers looking into their diapers was tacked to the bulletin board next to the telephone. One of the toddlers was saying to the other, "So *that* explains the difference in our salaries." Had I been asked as a young person whether I was a feminist I would have answered in the affirmative. To me, these issues were the essence of feminism.

But despite adopting the feminist label for external causes, I did not escape female socialization. I learned some "basic truths": that as a woman my value was in my body, and that mine was not "good enough": that sooner or later every woman needs a man; and that I would have to behave in certain ways in order to get myself one. These truths, which very much shaped my behavior for many years, I'll describe in greater detail below.

MY BODY AND ME

Like many women, I grew up hating my body. I remember wearing shorts over my bathing suit as a preteen to hide my "ugly" fat thighs. As a teenager, I spent a lot of time worrying whether I was attractive enough. Of course, I was never quite up to standard. I wanted very much to have the kind of exterior that would cause scouting agents from pinup magazines or from modeling agencies to approach me on the street to recruit me. Needless to say, this never happened, reinforcing my belief that physically I was a total failure as a woman. I fantasized about being a dancer but knew I did not have the requisite "dancer's body." I thought my size 7½ feet were enormous. For the record, I have

always been more or less average in weight. But average was not good enough. As long as I didn't look like one of those women in *Playboy*, I wasn't pretty enough.

Too big too short too stocky too busty too round too many zits blackheads disgusting pinch an inch fail the pencil test cellulite don't go out without makeup don't let them see what you really *look like they'll run away in terror but if you are really lucky and have a few beers and do it in the dark he might not notice so make sure to turn off the light before . . .*

I never questioned my standards of measurement, never realized that these standards are determined by a male-dominated culture and reinforced by a multibillion-dollar "femininity" industry that sells women cosmetics, diet aids, plastic surgery, fashion magazines, liposuction, creams, and girdles. I took my inability to live up to these standards as personal failure and never drew any connections between my experience and that of other women.

MEN AND ME

Men, you can't live without 'em. Sooner or later I would end up with one. My grandfather used to tell me that it was good that I was short, as that way I would have the option of marrying either a tall man or a short one. There aren't enough men to go around and it gets harder and harder to find one as you get older. Men aren't comfortable with women who are more educated/smarter/earn more than they. My 50-year-old aunt never married. She waited *too long,* and by then it was *too late* because she was *too old, poor dear.* It's just as easy to fall in love with a rich man as a poor man. Men lead.

I always had a boyfriend. From age 13 until after college, I don't remember going for more than a month without being in a relationship or at least having a crush. Having a boyfriend was a measure of my worth. I would select the boy and flirt with him until he asked me out. Most times, like the Mounties, I got my man. In dance, this is called backleading, directing the action from the follower's position. It allows the man to look like he is in control.

I learned that there's a man shortage. There are more women than men. And "good men" are extremely rare. Therefore, if you manage to get hold of a good one, you'd better hang on to him. This message got louder as I moved into my twenties. I saw older women in their thirties and beyond searching frantically for a suitable partner with whom to reproduce the human species and make their lives meaningful. I learned that you'd better pay attention to your "biological clock."

THE UNLEARNING

These messages had a powerful grip on me. How did I begin to unlearn them? The women's studies class I took in college helped a bit. However, I continued to consider feminism only in terms of situations outside of myself. I looked at my environment and catalogued the injustices, but did not look inside.

It wasn't until I was considering a relationship with a woman that I began to see the relevance of the feminist theory I had read as a first-year college student to my own life. My perspective changed dramatically. For example, in my first relationship with a woman, it became quickly apparent that in many ways I fit quite neatly into the passive "femme" role of the butch/femme stereotype. I was behaving as I had always behaved in relationships, but for the first time, now that my lover was a woman, my "normal" behavior appeared to me (and probably to her as well) strange and unbalanced. Why were my lover and I behaving so differently? Suddenly our roles appeared constructed rather than natural. I won't pretend that I woke up one day and found myself suddenly freed of my conditioning. Rather, I spent several years unfolding and unraveling the layers of misinformation I had internalized, learning more with each subsequent relationship or incident.

My body image began to change. Through the firsthand experience of my own attractions, I learned that women, and their bodies, are beautiful, though I did not immediately apply this knowledge to my opinion of my own body. There was one woman friend on whom I had a crush for more than two years. I thought she was beautiful, with her solid, powerful angles and healthy fullness. One day, with a sense of shock, I realized that her body was not so very different from mine and that I had been holding myself to a different, unattainable standard than I had been holding her and other women to. It was this experience of seeing my image reflected in another woman that finally allowed me to begin developing a positive relationship with my own body.

I learned from firsthand experience about the privilege differential that results when the gender of your partner changes. Before I had experienced some of society's disapproval and disregard, I had no sense of the privileges I had experienced in heterosexual relationships. In subsequent years, each time I changed partners I was painfully aware of this absurd double standard and began to strategize ways to live in such a way that I could challenge rather than collaborate with these injustices. I have made a personal commitment to be "out" as bisexual at every possible opportunity and to avoid taking privileges with a male lover that I would not have with my female lover. For these reasons, I have chosen not to marry, though I hope someday to establish a "domestic partnership" and have a "commitment ceremony." If I feel someone would be unwilling to hear me talk about a same-sex lover, I disclose nothing about *any* of my relationships, even if my current partner is of the opposite sex. This is not very easy, and occasionally I backslide, but I am rewarded with the knowledge that I am not contributing to the oppression of lesbian, gay, and bisexual people when I am in an opposite-sex relationship.

It was empowering to realize that men as romantic partners were optional, not required. I no longer felt pressured to lower my relationship standards in light of the shortage of good men. Yes, I might get involved with and spend the rest of my life with one, but then again I might choose to spend my life with a woman. Or perhaps simply with myself. This was to be my choice.

I realized how I had been performing my designated gender role. It's amazing how being in a same-sex relationship can make you realize just how much of most heterosexual relationships is scripted from the first date to the bedroom to the dishes. In relationships with women, I learned how to lead and learned that I like to lead sometimes. As sometimes I like to follow. And as sometimes I prefer to negotiate every step with my partner, or to dance alone.

Finally, I made a personal commitment to hold men and women to the same standards in relationships. I realized that in our society women are grateful when a man behaves in a sensitive manner, but expect sensitivity of a woman as a matter of course. I decided that I would not settle for less from men, realizing that it means that I may be categorically eliminating most men as potential partners. So be it.

My experience with being in relationships with women has been in a way like a trip abroad. I learned that many of the things I had accepted as natural truths were socially constructed, and the first time I returned to a heterosexual relationship things felt different. I hadn't yet learned how to construct a relationship on my own terms, but I was aware that things were not quite right. As time passed, my self-awareness and self-confidence increased. I gathered more experience in lesbian relationships and began to apply my knowledge to subsequent heterosexual relationships.

It is not possible to know who or where I would be today had I remained heterosexual in my attractions and in my self-identity. Perhaps other events in my life would have triggered a feminist consciousness. At any rate, it is entirely clear to me that it was loving a woman that made me realize I had fallen outside my "script," which in turn forced me to realize there *was* a script. From there, I moved toward a critical self-awareness and the realization that I could shape and write my own life. [1992]

NOTES

Thanks to Marti Hohmann, Rebecca Kaplan, and Annie Senghas for their feedback and support while I was writing this essay.

1. Adrienne Rich, "Compulsory Heterosexuality and Lesbian Existence," *Signs: Journal of Women in Culture and Society* 5, no. 4 (1980): 631–60.

CHAPTER IV
Institutions That Shape Women's Lives

We have examined the ways that sexist attitudes about women's potential, abilities, and social roles have limited their sense of self, impeded their growth, and damaged their self-confidence. Sexism, however, is more than a set of attitudes; it is firmly entrenched in the structure of society. Chapter IV examines the position of women in four of the major institutions that shape women's lives: the economy, the legal system, the family, and religion. Together they have reinforced women's subordination in all areas of social life. Although we are accustomed to thinking of relationships such as family and motherhood as emotional and biological, they serve social and political purposes.

Feminist analysis has revealed that institutions tend to allocate power and resources in complex and subtle ways that systematically support patriarchy and other systems of domination as well. While overt personal prejudice is apparent to most people, institutionalized sexism is so deeply embedded in our social life that it appears to be the natural order. Much of it remained unnoticed until the feminist movement called attention to it, revealing layer upon layer of discriminatory patterns. The deeper we look, the more patterns emerge. For example, women's analysis of the workforce first revealed much outright discrimination. Employers paid women less and excluded them from jobs because they were women. But when the Equal Pay Act of 1963 and Title VII of the Civil Rights Act of 1964 made such discrimination illegal, women remained in a disadvantaged position in the workforce. This was caused not only by discrimination that eluded the law but by occupational segregation, the clustering of women into female-dominated occupations that pay less and offer fewer opportunities for advancement than male-dominated occupations.

Our society has been organized around the notion that the public arenas of work, politics, and education are the province of men and the private world of home and family is female terrain. This division of activities and resources is powerful as ideology, but it has never been an accurate description of the lives of all women. As Patricia Hill Collins argues, for example, most black women have occupied both public and private worlds, bearing both economic and nurturing responsibility for families.[1] Today, a large proportion of women of all races and ethnic groups work outside the home. Despite these facts, the belief that women's natural roles are in the family and men's are in the public world shapes the primary institutions of social life. The contradiction between the realities of many women's lives and the social institutions structured by the belief in this division of labor is one of the major sources of tension in contemporary American life.

In fact, women have always played crucial economic roles both inside and outside the family. The work that women do in the home is absolutely essential to economic life. Because it is unpaid, however, it is invisible and difficult to measure. Women have also been working outside the home for centuries. Female slaves worked in the fields and young women factory workers were the first employees of the American textile industry. Until the middle of the twentieth century, most white women left their

---

[1]Patricia Hill Collins, *Black Feminist Thought* (New York: Routledge, 1990).

jobs when they married, but African-American women continued to work outside the home while caring for their own homes and children. In the past several decades women of all racial and ethnic groups have entered the workforce in increasing numbers. Women constitute nearly 50 percent of the total workforce. Nevertheless, the belief that women's primary role is in the home continues to shape women's workplace experience, restricting opportunities, creating pay inequity, and preserving women's responsibility for child care and housework even while they hold full-time jobs.

Affirmative action policies have increased the hiring, promotion, job stability, and wages of women. A 2002 Department of Labor study estimated that 5 million people of color and 6 million women were in higher occupational classifications than they would have been without affirmative action policies. Affirmative action has spurred companies and other organizations to create innovative programs to open up new opportunities for women. For example, an employee development program established by a Pennsylvania chemical company encourages students of color and white female students to pursue careers in chemistry and engineering and recruits extensively to hire promising, qualified female candidates and males of color for entry-level positions.[2]

Although sex discrimination is against the law, significant wage gaps based on sex and race also persist. Overall, women who work full-time, year-round earn only 77.0 percent of what men earn who also work full-time, year-round. White women in 2009 earned 75 percent of the salary of white men, while black women, Latinas, and Asian-American women were paid 61.9 percent, 82.3 percent, and 57.8 percent, respectively, of what white men earned.[3]

Although there had been progress in the labor market position of women, the reduction in the wage gap in the past 30 years was more a result of stagnant earnings for men than significant increases for women. Women continue to encounter sexual harassment, sexual double standards, and what has been described as the glass ceiling, an invisible barrier of discrimination that has prevented women from advancing beyond a certain level.

Despite the fact that there have been some recent advances in challenging sex discrimination in the workplace, such discrimination is all too common. A 2004 court ruled that the nation's largest brokerage firm, Merrill Lynch, award claims to women stockbrokers for systematic discrimination; nevertheless the decision required the women to remain silent about the bias they faced. The National Partnership for Women and Families reported that in 2004, women filed many more claims of pregnancy discrimination, sexual harassment, and gender bias with the Equal Employment Opportunity Commission (EEOC) than in the prior decade, and that claims by women of color account for much of the increase. Sex

---

[2]National Partnership for Women and Families, "Affirmative Action Helps Boost Women's Pay and Promotes Economic Security for Women and Their Families," http://www.national partnership.org/workand family/workplace/affirmact/aa_newwage.htm. ½7/02.

[3]Institute for Women's Policy Research, "The Gender Wage Gap: 2009," http://www.iwpr.org/publications 3.26.11.

discrimination charges increased by 12 percent, with claims of women of color increasing most: Latinas, 68 percent; African-Americans, 20 percent; Asian/Pacific Islanders, 83 percent, and Native American women, 44 percent.[4]

Recognizing that the clustering of women in low-paid, low-status jobs has been a major source of the wage inequities between women and men, some women have begun to enter occupations that have been historically male-dominated. Another approach to this problem is the demand for comparable worth or pay equity—the reevaluation of male- and female-dominated jobs on the basis of the required skill, effort, responsibility, and working conditions.

In fact, the workplace pay gap between men and women has remained relatively the same since 2001. According to Barbara Gault of the Institute for Women's Policy Research, "To address the continuing disparities in pay between women and men we need to raise the minimum wage, improve enforcement of Equal Employment Opportunity Laws, help women succeed in higher paying, traditionally male occupations and create more flexible, family friendly workplace policies."[5]

Women's responsibility for child care remains one of the biggest obstacles to economic equality for women. The United States lags behind other countries in providing child care facilities, parental leave, and other features that make the workplace compatible with parenting. It is one of a few countries without a national maternity leave policy and one of the few industrialized countries that does not provide universal health care or income supports to families with children. Without a fundamental restructuring of the workplace to accommodate workers—both male and female—who have family responsibilities, women will continue to be in a disadvantaged position.

In recent years some employers have provided more "family-friendly" policies, policies that enable women to better balance work and family life. Benefits often include on-site child care, flexible work schedules, summer programs, and sick-child care, among others. Because more than three-quarters of women who have school-age children are in the workforce, employers have found such policies boost recruitment and lower absenteeism. Unfortunately these policies are not options in most workplaces and are more often available to professionals and managers than to women with low-wage jobs.

The Family and Medical Leave Act of 1993 requires employers to give workers up to 12 weeks of unpaid leave during a 12-month period for birth or adoption, to care for a seriously ill parent, spouse, or child, or to undergo medical treatment for their own serious illness. While helpful to some women workers, the law covers only employers with 50 or more employees. It is estimated that the Act affects 62 percent of U.S. employers and 40 percent of all employees. Because the leave is unpaid, it is difficult for women in low-paying jobs to afford to take advantage of the leave.

---

[4]Myra Clark-Siegel, "Women Today File Many More Claims of Pregnancy Discrimination, Sexual Harassment, Gender Bias with the EEOC Than a Decade Ago," National Partnership for Women and Families, July 7, 2004, news release, www.nationalpartnership.org.

[5]"Gender Wage Gap Widening, Census Date Shows," in *Your Guide to U.S. Gov. Info/Resources,* ed. Robert Longley, Sept. 1, 2004, Institute for Women's Policy Research.

Enacted in 2004, California's Paid Family Leave Law is an important step forward. It provides six weeks of partial income to workers who take time off to care for a new child or seriously ill family member. A 2011 study found that the nation's first family leave program is an unqualified success. An overwhelming majority of employers and workers report positive effects from the program.[6] This could provide a model for national policy, since the United States and Australia are the only industrialized countries without paid family leave.

Women face many barriers in the workplace, among them sexual harassment. For centuries women and girls have endured various forms of harassment, from ogling on the street to demands for sex in return for rewards with threat of reprisal. Such retribution in the workplace can bring on job loss, denial of promotion, and an intimidating atmosphere, making working conditions very stressful. There were no legal remedies for women faced with sexual harassment until the mid-1970s when courageous women began to talk publicly about sexual harassment and turned to the courts for relief. Rulings in these cases affirmed that sexual harassment violated the ban on workplace sex discrimination in Title VII of the 1964 Civil Rights Act.[7] Sexual harassment remains a significant problem for all women, but women of color have been in the forefront of the movement to challenge sexual harassment. Charges filed to the EEOC increased 22 percent between 1992 and 2003: the claims of white women increased 5 percent; those of African-American women increased by 42 percent and for Latinas by 120 percent.[8]

Women, however, have a long history of organizing for better working conditions for themselves and others. Recently, associations of working women such as 9to5, organizations for union women such as the Congress of Labor Union Women, and renewed commitments by the AFL/CIO to organize low-wage women workers have resulted in both economic gains for women and solidarity among women workers who have often felt isolated.

In recent decades, globalization in its current form—a quickening spread of the profit-system worldwide—has had a profound effect on women's work in the United States and abroad. Governments in industrial nations have supported international trade agreements, such as NAFTA (North American Free Trade Agreement), and free-market policies of international organizations, such as the World Bank, that have undermined workers' wages, health, and safety as well as weakened environmental regulations. This gives significantly more power to transnational corporations to do business with minimal regulations across national boundaries for greater profit. Corporations have outsourced work that had been done in the United States to nations with cheaper labor where women are paid much less. Many women in these nations who've lived previously sustainable lives have been forced

---

[6]Deborah Ness, "The Verdict Is In: Nation's First Family Leave Program an Unqualified Success, Women's Leader Says," National Partnership for Women and Families, January 13, 2011, news release, www.national partnership.org.

[7]Gwendolyn Mink, " Stop Sexual Harassment Now!," *Ms. Magazine*, Fall 2005, 36–37.

[8]Clark-Siegel, "Women Today File More Claims."

off their land by transnational corporations that use this land for exportable crops. To support their families, many of these women have left their homelands for work abroad and have become part of the "nanny chain," doing child care and domestic work for affluent families in the United States and other industrial nations.

The legal system and social policies enforce the subordination of women generally, as well as in the workplace. As recently as 1961 the Supreme Court upheld a law exempting women from jury service because "woman is still regarded as the center of home and family life" and therefore not subject to the same public obligations as men are.[9] Laws have changed in the past 50 years, and the courts now recognize women's rights to equal protection, but the legal system remains male-dominated and biased against women in many ways. At the same time, women have used the judicial system to challenge sexism and to fight for reproductive freedom, child support, domestic safety, and workplace justice, among others. The gains that women have made, however, are threatened by the appointment of ultraconservative Supreme Court justices in the last decade. These rights include privacy, affirmative action, protection against gender discrimination, family and medical leave, and quality health care services.

Social policy is typically drafted and passed into law by white, affluent, male legislators. One piece of legislation that has not been passed into law is a bill for an Equal Rights Amendment to the U.S. Constitution, first proposed by Alice Paul in 1923. The text reads: "Equality of rights under the law shall not be denied or abridged by the United States or any State on account of sex." It took until 1972 for the ERA to be approved by Congress, but then it had to be ratified by 35 states as well. That 10-year effort fell short by just 3 states. Since 1982 the ERA has been reintroduced each session of Congress with the goal that women's rights will ultimately be embodied in the Constitution.

Social policies written by white, affluent males can particularly burden poor, single women with children who are consigned to poverty by the absence of affordable child care and the low pay of most women's jobs. Prior to 1996 these poor women were assured some cash assistance through welfare, Aid to Families with Dependent Children (AFDC). The Personal Responsibility and Work Opportunity Act (1996) eliminated AFDC and replaced it with the Temporary Assistance for Needy Families (TANF), a block grant program that removes any guarantee of assistance. It mandates states to force poor mothers into the low-wage labor market by adding a work requirement.

Despite politicians' claims of the success of welfare-to-work policies, very serious problems exist. Sufficient funding has not been provided to create jobs, increase child care, or provide job training and health coverage to low-wage workers. Randy Abelda writes, "The welfare-to-work solution is a match made in hell. It joins together poor mothers with few resources whose family responsibilities require employment flexibility with jobs in the low-wage labor market that often are most inflexible, have the least family-necessary benefits and provide levels of pay that

---

[9]*Hoyt v. Florida,* 1969.

often are insufficient to support a single person, let alone a family." Because the jobs most poor mothers get don't provide much dignity or sufficient wages to support a family, the experience is not only demoralizing, but economically crippling. "For many, welfare-to-work policies are a cruel hoax that makes legislators feel better about themselves, but leaves poor families in the lurch."[10] Social policy changes that promote education, training, and access to jobs that pay a living wage would be true reforms. The association for working women, 9to5, urges changing the purpose of the bill itself—to end child and family poverty.

TANF violates women's rights to vocational freedom and sexual privacy, while it seeks to restore the patriarchal family. "Mothers who are married do not have to work outside the home, for labor market work by only one parent in a two-parent family satisfies TANF's work requirement. . . . Far from 'ending dependency,' the TANF regime actually fosters poor mothers' dependence on individual men."[11] If women's caregiving work were valued and supported, welfare could be rethought as income owed to women, married or not, whose work is now unpaid.

The position of women in the workforce is inextricably connected with the position of women in the family. The division of power and resources in the patriarchal family has often subordinated the needs of married women to those of their spouses. The sentimental rhetoric that often surrounds the family not only obscures the unequal power relations, but also conveys the impression that only the patriarchal family is legitimate. In fact, the family, a group of people who are committed to each other and share resources, can take a variety of forms. The African-American family, often sustained by mothers, aunts, and grandmothers, has proved remarkably durable in the face of almost insurmountable odds.

Feminist theorists have found it useful to view motherhood as an institution as well as a relationship between mother and child. As an institution, motherhood was for a long time assumed to be women's primary function, one that made women unfit for full participation in other realms. The sentimentalization of motherhood obscures the realities of mothers' experience in a number of ways. While most mothers love and enjoy their children, motherhood can be lonely and sometimes painful in a society in which there are few social supports. The image of the perfect mother leads people to blame mothers when they don't live up to that idealized image. When motherhood takes place outside the patriarchal family, the mantle of sentimentality further disappears. Lesbian mothers have lost custody of their children, and single mothers face social censure. Sentimentalized motherhood also obscures the fact that not all women enjoy motherhood, and that mothers who have no other sources of identity and satisfaction can become disoriented when their children grow up. Some essays in this chapter tell the stories of real women whose lives belie the myths. They demonstrate the need to see motherhood as a more varied experience and to envision social supports that enable women to be mothers while participating fully in other aspects of human life.

---

[10]Randy Abelda, "Fallacies of Welfare-to-Work Policies," *Annals, AAPSS* 577 (September 2001), 68, 74.
[11]Gwendolyn Mink, " Violating Women: Rights Abuses in the Welfare Police State," *Annals, AAPSS* 577 (September 2001), 81.

Our society glorifies the nuclear family and disparages people, particularly women, who live outside it. Feminists believe that women should be able to choose how and with whom they live. Because one can choose freely only if a variety of lifestyles are considered legitimate, feminists seek to expand women's options, recognizing that different women will choose different ways to live and love.

Feminists insist that the nuclear family is not the only viable form in which to build lasting relationships and raise children. For feminists, a broadened definition of family includes any living arrangement in which people share time and space, contribute to the physical and psychological tasks of making a household function, share common history and ritual, and stay together over time. Members are not necessarily tied by biology or by the sanction of the state or church or by living in the same house all the time. Feminists work toward building families in which all members both give and receive support and love and have space to grow as autonomous individuals.

By supporting their families and maintaining nurturing homes, single mothers are defying the notion that children don't stand a chance in life because a father isn't present; lesbian parents affirm the validity of their families. Some women have created cooperative living arrangements in which they share household and parenting responsibilities.

The struggle for public recognition of one alternative family form, lesbian and gay marriage, has caused considerable controversy and backlash in recent years. The Defense of Marriage Act, passed by large majorities in Congress and signed into law by President Clinton in 1996, affirms that states are not required to recognize marriages that were performed in other states. For the first time ever in our country's history it creates a federal definition of "marriage" as a "legal union between one man and one woman as husband and wife." Since DOMA was enacted, a handful of states have legalized same-sex marriage, others have created constitutional laws prohibiting it, and others have created state statutes prohibiting it. In 2011, Barack Obama repudiated DOMA, saying that his administration would "no longer defend the constitutionality of a federal law banning recognition of same-sex marriage."

Supporters of same-sex marriage have fought to provide equal legal rights, such as to visit a sick partner in the hospital or to inherit belongings of a partner at death. In addition, gay marriages provide relationship recognition and can transform prevailing social standards. Sarah Schulman writes, "Have you ever said hello to someone on the street and have them not reply? If the person stopped, said, 'Hello, Sarah, How are you?' then we could experience human acknowledgment. . . . But if they refuse that acknowledgment, and instead choose shunning, they create a relationship of tension and conflict which needs to be resolved." Schulman suggests that legalizing gay marriages pushes the culture to respond to gay people so the current tension of exclusion can be addressed.[12]

---

[12]Sarah Schulman, "Withholding Creates Tension: Acknowledgment Creates Relief," in *"I Do, I Don't": Queers on Marriage*, ed. Greg Wharton and Lar Philipps (San Francisco: Suspect Thoughts Press, 2004), 304–9.

The struggle for legal recognition of same-sex marriage has raised questions for feminists about the best strategy for creating an environment that supports a wide variety of family formations and living arrangements. Though all feminists agree that legal recognition of same-sex marriage is an important step toward equality for lesbians and gay men, some feminists, like Martha Ackelsberg and Judith Plaskow in this chapter, fear that focusing on the right to marry reinforces the idea that living as a married couple is the only socially acceptable family form. Others, like Peggy Pascoe, have argued that same-sex marriage can be seen as a method of detaching marriage from the system of male privilege that it has historically buttressed. "There is a reason," she points out, "that it seems nonsensical to conceive of a marriage between two women as one between two "wives"; in the absence of a man/husband to define it against, the social role of 'wife' is exposed for the gendered creation it is."[13]

The final institution that this chapter considers is institutionalized religion, in which women have been the members, men the decision-makers. "It has been said that women are the 'backbone' of the church," writes Jacquelyn Grant, who studies black women and the church. "On the surface, this may appear to be a compliment, considering the function of the backbone in the human anatomy. . . . The telling part of the word 'backbone' is 'back.' It has become apparent to me that most of the ministers who use this term are referring to location rather than function. What they really mean is that women are in the 'background' and should be kept there; they are merely support workers."[14]

Patriarchal religion has had a powerful effect on women's lives, not only by systematically excluding them from many leadership positions in most organized religions, but by justifying subordination and enveloping it in divine sanction. Religious symbolism can reinforce both sexism and racism, as in the case of Christianity. Jacquelyn Grant writes, "Though we insist that God is a spirit and Jesus died for us all, we persist in deifying the maleness of both God and Jesus, certainly giving men a social, political, and theological advantage over women. . . . We have consistently and historically represented God and Jesus as White."[15] Women who have spoken and acted on behalf of women's freedom have often found themselves colliding with church dogma.

Since the 1990s, religious fundamentalism has become more influential in the United States and worldwide. In all of fundamentalism's forms—whether Christian, Muslim, Hindu, Jewish, or Buddhist—women are confined to a traditional, secondary status in the family and in society. In their efforts to influence governmental policy, fundamentalists have spearheaded efforts to challenge women's

---

[13]Peggy Pascoe, "Sex, Gender and Same-Sex Marriage," in *Is Academic Feminism Dead: Theory and Practice,* ed. Social Justice Group (New York: NYU Press, 2000), 110.

[14]Jacquelyn Grant, "Black Women and the Church," in *Some of Us Are Brave,* ed. Gloria Hull, Patricia Bell Collins, and Beverly Smith (New York: Feminist Press, 1982).

[15]Jacquelyn Grant, "Womanist Jesus and the Mutual Struggle for Liberation," in *The Recovery of Black Presence, An Interdisciplinary Exploration,* ed. Randall Bailey and Jacquelyn Grant (Nashville, TN: Abington Press, 1995), 134.

reproductive rights and right to sexual choice and freedom. A 2010 international study of the threats fundamentalism poses to women's rights found that a major fundamentalist strategy globally is the use of discourse that blames social problems on a "decline in morality" or "disintegration of the family." The psychological impact of fundamentalism on women can be long-lasting, in that many women believe that they don't have the right to have rights, and that decisions about themselves, their minds, and bodies can be made by others.[16]

Recently women's struggle for equality in institutional religion has contributed to the decision of some religious groups to ordain women ministers and rabbis. While Roman Catholic women cannot become priests or Orthodox Jewish women rabbis, the presence of women clergy elsewhere may help change many people's vision of God as masculine. Women who have fought patriarchy within their own religions have fostered changes: women's prayer groups in Islam; alternative, lay masses in Catholicism; women's seders in Judaism; and rewording of hymnals and prayer books to include female imagery in some Protestant denominations. Women are doing some of the most challenging and innovative work in theology and ministry by infusing religious traditions with an emphasis on female experience. Other women have taken their quest for spirituality beyond organized religion and are developing their own forms of feminist spirituality that often have links both to historic female-centered religious practices and to the natural world.

All these institutions are intimately connected to each other. Women's experience in one reinforces our position in another, indicating that change in the position of women in our society needs to take place on many fronts. The selections in this chapter show that within our social institutions, gender, class, and race work together to shape female experience. Our culture teaches us to believe that hard work and talent will be rewarded, but institutions place white men in advantageous social positions. Understanding these institutional barriers enables us to see that all people do not have equal opportunity in our society, and that to create it, we must make fundamental changes in our social institutions. Unless we recognize the historic advantages of white men, it is impossible to move toward a more equitable society. Affirmative action programs, which commit organizations to give preferences to women and members of other historically disadvantaged groups, recognize that in many ways a "white male affirmative action program" has been in place for centuries.

Finally, the selections in Chapter IV testify to the durability of patriarchy. Women have made significant advances in the recent past, but sexism is proving to be a stubborn adversary. As women occupy new territory in our society, new problems emerge or come into view. We are just beginning to understand, for example, the extent to which sexual harassment of women has crippled us in the workplace, particularly in nontraditional occupations. When barriers to women's equality are toppled, they often reappear in different forms, requiring us to develop new strategies for change.

---

[16]Deepa Shankaran, "The Right to Have Rights: Resisting Fundamentalist Orders," *Open Democracy,* May 5, 2010; http://ww.opendemocracy.net/?q+5050/deepa-shankaran/right-to-have-rights-resisting.

Women and Work

The selections in this section consider the ways sexism shapes women's work both in and outside the home and suggest approaches to change.

Although the media give the impression that women have unlimited opportunities and have made unprecedented career advances, the reality of the workplace is much more discouraging. Women have made significant progress in a few areas, but the majority of women face a sex-segregated labor market that devalues the work that most women do. In "An Overview of Women and Work," Ellen Bravo and Gloria Santa Anna, former co-directors, and Linda Meric, current director, of 9to5, National Association of Working Women, detail the problems women face at work and suggest policy changes needed to bring gender equity to the workplace. The next piece presents data from the National Committee for Pay Equity on the wage gap between men and women and a plan for eliminating sex and race discrimination in wages through a system of pay equity. Since most women and people of color are still segregated into a small number of jobs that are underpaid, a system of pay equity would ensure that the criteria employers use to set wages would be sex and race neutral.

The work that women do in the home—housework, child care, and nurturing—is work that is extremely demanding, in time, energy, and skill. Women still do most of the work in the home, despite their increasing participation in the labor force. Pat Mainaradi's "The Politics of Housework," a classic piece from the early days of the women's liberation movement, points to the struggle involved in getting men to take responsibility for housework. Because it is associated with women, housework is seen as demeaning and lacking in value. Like many of the writings from this period, it demonstrates that an activity that has been treated as private is indeed political; that is, it involves the allocation of power and resources.

Women pay a significant economic price for becoming mothers, as Ann Crittenden describes in "The Price of Motherhood." When mothers do the necessary work of raising children and sustaining families, their reward is often professional marginalization, a loss of status, and long-term losses in income and benefits due to lost time in the workplace. As Betty Holcomb writes, even when women enter the workforce and are employed by companies with "family-friendly" policies, women face another form of discrimination.

Because of increased globalization, many women from poor, developing nations, whose economies have been devastated by policies of the World Bank and International Monetary Fund, have come to the United States and other industrialized nations in recent years to work as nannies, maids, and sex workers. Barbara Ehrenreich and Arlie Hochschild describe the human price many of these women pay being separated from their children in order to earn enough money to support them. By the 1970s, women who had not been working outside the home, mainly white women, began to enter the U.S. paid workforce in much greater numbers. Unfortunately, their entrance into paid work did little to increase men's contributions to the work of the home. Thus, many affluent families now pass on to immigrant women of color household work and child care, allowing men to continue to avoid household work.

Low-wage workers are least likely to get the benefits of those policies. Ellen Bravo, Gloria Santa Anna, and Linda Meric, in "9to5," describe the history of an association for working women that for almost 40 years has organized women in low-wage jobs to fight for equity at work. In the process of doing so, it has helped women see that their struggles are not personal, but based in the need to redistribute power in the workplace.

Another barrier to equity in the workplace is sexual harassment. Women who are sexually harassed come from all walks of life, reflecting our shared vulnerability to unwanted sexual attention, as Ellen Bravo and Linda Meric describe in their article "Sexual Harassment." Arlene Foy Reynolds then documents the history of legal cases that have generated avenues for women to challenge sexual harassment.

Because their studies are the bulk of college students' work, we include in this section Bernice Sandler's "In Case of Sexual Harassment," a guide for women students who have experienced sexual harassment in their college or university. Sexual harassment of women students is about power and control; therefore, many women victims feel unable to confront their harasser. This article provides clear, concise information about strategies for dealing with harassment so that women can reclaim their dignity and stand up for their rights.

Collective efforts by women make a significant difference in gaining equity in the workplace. Miriam Ching Yoon Louie describes the organizing efforts of Korean immigrant women workers and their allies to challenge unfair working conditions in Los Angeles restaurants. Union membership under a collective bargaining agreement is associated with higher wages and longer job tenure, as well as a smaller pay gap between women and men. This section ends with a poem in which Alice Walker pays tribute to the strength and resourcefulness of her mother, and the many black women whose labors of love and creativity made possible a future for their daughters.

🌿 50

An Overview of Women and Work

ELLEN BRAVO, GLORIA SANTA ANNA, and LINDA MERIC

Any commentator reviewing progress in the United States during the twentieth century will list prominently the gains of working women. Swept away were laws and customs that prevailed for the centuries—allowing lower pay for women doing the same work as men, permitting women to be fired for being pregnant, considering women fair game for harassment on the job. From doctor to drill sergeant, carpenter to CEO, women changed the face of the nation's workforce. The notion that women had been absent from certain jobs because they weren't capable was dealt a significant blow.

And yet, women in this country still earn less than men for equivalent jobs. Many women today lose their jobs when they give birth. Sexual harassment remains a persistent problem in the workplace. While women appear in almost every occupational category, they are woefully underrepresented in higher-paying positions.

In fact, the picture for working women is decidedly mixed. Gains have been real and important, but many women have not been significantly affected by them. A close look at three areas—pay, work/family balance, and welfare—helps illustrate the problems and their impact on women and their families. If women as a whole are to benefit, concern for equality must be joined with fundamental change in the way this society does business.

WHO'S WORKING

A quick look at the numbers shows how greatly the workforce has changed. By 2010, women accounted for nearly half of the total U.S. labor force, compared with 37.7 percent in 1960. More than 6 out of every 10 women—61 percent—age 16 and over were now working or looking for work.[1] Women are primary or co-primary breadwinners in two-thirds of all families.[2]

While marriage and childbirth had never spelled the end of employment for certain groups of women, especially African-Americans and immigrants, the majority of women in the past left the workforce to care for their families. That reality has changed drastically, as a result of shrinking real wages and growing expectations. Debate about whether women should work has become moot. Most women—including most mothers, even mothers of infants—are in the labor force.[3] Employment, however, has brought women neither equality nor an end to poverty.

PAY

Despite dramatic increases in pay for some, earnings for women as a group remain significantly lower than men's. Taken as a percentage of white men's pay, white women who work full-time full-year earn 77 percent as much. For black women, the figure is 61.9 percent, and for Latinas, only 51.9 percent.[4] Women's pay is not just lower than men's but often very low indeed:

- Of women working full-time in 2004, 20.1 percent earned less than $15,000 for the year; the figure is 22.3 percent for African-American women, 32.2 percent for Latinas.
- More than one in five employed women in 2005 lived in a household with annual income of less than $25,000.[5]

Why do women make so little money? Because their employers pay them so little. And why is that? Aside from the continuation of blatant discrimination, the reasons include the following factors:

(1) Although there have been huge changes in jobs formerly closed to women, most women do the same jobs they've always done, and those jobs pay less than comparable jobs done by men.

- Nearly three in five women workers are employed in service, sales, and clerical jobs.
- Even within certain occupations, women are clustered in the lower-paying jobs. In retail trades, for instance, women in 2000 constituted 78 percent of employees in gift and novelty shops but only 20 percent of those employed in higher-paying car dealerships.

• More women are in professional and managerial positions, but they've made little headway in skilled construction trades and other traditionally male, blue-collar occupations or at the top of the corporate ladder. Women account for only 2.2 percent of electricians, 7.1 percent of civil engineers, and 3 percent of Fortune 500 CEOs.

• Women of color are concentrated in the lowest-paying jobs, including domestic workers, nurses' aides, and child care workers.

• Only 8 percent of men work in female-dominated jobs. Nearly twice that percentage of women (15 percent) consistently work in male occupations—yet in both the top and the bottom tiers of those jobs, women earn one-third less than their male counterparts.[6]

Many people talk about the need to increase the number of women in science and math. While those efforts are needed, they ignore the underlying question: why does society value accountants more than social workers? Embedded in the market value of jobs is the legacy of past discrimination, based on gender and on race.

(2) Women disproportionately are employed in part-time and temporary jobs. No law says these jobs have to pay the same as full-time and permanent positions, or give any, much less equivalent, benefits.

Tracy was a temp for more than six years because she could not find permanent employment. She had to leave her house—and her school-aged son—at 5 a.m. to ride a bus that took her to a van that transported her (for a fee) to jobs in the outlying areas. Her annual income was less than $13,000 and she had no benefits. Tracy could not afford a car and sometimes was without a home. "Even though I was always working," said Tracy, "I was living in poverty."

When Linda's marriage fell apart, she tried to find full-time employment but had to make do with three part-time jobs. None of her jobs provided health insurance, including one at a nursing home. At age 38, Linda had a serious heart attack. She eventually found a doctor and a hospital willing to do the surgery and was able to have hospital bills waived. Still, she owed $20,000 to 16 different health care professionals. After she recovered, Linda found a full-time job and a second, part-time position to pay something every month on those bills. She suffered another heart attack and died on that job the day before her 42nd birthday.

(3) Moonlighting—working more than one job—has been one area where women have made great gains in recent years. About half of all multiple-job holders in 2008 were women, up from 22 percent in 1974.[7] Three out of ten of these women work two part-time jobs.[8]

Part-time or temporary positions can be beneficial for women, as long as they are voluntary and equitable. Increasingly, these positions are neither. Regular part-time female workers are paid 20 percent less than regular full-time workers with similar characteristics. In 2004, median weekly earnings of temp workers were $384 a week, as compared to $529 a week for workers in traditional production jobs.[9] Being paid less than full-time and permanent workers often means poverty wages. Female part-time workers are three and a half times more likely than full-time women workers to earn poverty pay. Fewer than one in 20 temps and 1 in 4 part-timers received health insurance from their employer in 2004.[10]

(4) Women are still largely responsible for family. The penalty for that is significant—and most women never make it up. Over a period of 15 years, taking one year off amounts to a penalty of 32 percent in earning power. Two years chops your pay by 46 percent, and three by more than half—56 percent.[11] For lower-wage women, taking a leave may also mean losing a job and having to start over—often having to go on welfare.

In a 1980 speech, Clarence Thomas spoke with disdain of his sister who had gone on welfare. He neglected to mention that she'd done so in order to care for an aunt who had a stroke.[12]

(5) The globalization of the economy has affected women's pay in several ways. Large numbers of women from Asia, Central America, and elsewhere find themselves in the United States, their native economies turned upside-down by transnational corporations. Here they fill jobs U.S.-born workers try to avoid, sewing garments and assembling products in old-fashioned sweatshops,

picking crops, not uncommonly with their children by their side. The most basic employment protections often elude them. Globalization has costs as well for workers who aren't immigrants, as the same transnationals move jobs overseas in the quest for ever cheaper labor. Decent-paying manufacturing jobs disappear, replaced by lower-paying industries or low-wage service jobs.

(6) Women are disproportionately represented among minimum-wage earners, accounting for more than three-fifths of all those in this category. These workers are more vulnerable to wage theft—violations of minimum wage and overtime laws.[13] Women are disproportionately found among those earning "tipped" minimum wage, stuck since 1991 at a mere $2.13 an hour. And they account for most home health care workers, who are excluded from any minimum wage protection.[14]

(7) Unionized women earn almost 34 percent more than nonunion women.[15] Despite talk of "supply and demand," wage levels depend above all on *bargaining power*. Being able to bargain collectively for pay and benefits helps diminish the undervaluation of women's work and to create more opportunities for women to move into higher-paying jobs. A contract also ensures greater protection against arbitrary firing and a greater likelihood of paid maternity leave—with the longer job tenure ensuring higher pay. However, only 11.1 percent of all women are unionized. Although the percentage of union members who are women has increased, up to 44.6 percent in 2009, from 35 percent in 1988, that gain also reflects the loss of union jobs for men—only 12.6 percent are in unions, down from 20.4 percent in 1988.

Clearly, the solution to women's low pay must be much more far-reaching than elevating greater numbers of women into jobs traditionally performed by men. To end poverty among women and their families will require fundamental restructuring of the economy.

WORK/FAMILY ISSUES

In 2010, fewer than one in five married families with children fit the stereotype of Dad as breadwinner, Mom full-time at home. Yet the workplace has not kept pace with these changes. Passage of the Family and Medical Leave Act (FMLA) in 1993 was an important step forward. This law allows women and men to take up to 12 weeks of unpaid leave to care for a new child or a seriously ill child, spouse, or parent, or for a personal illness. But the impact of the bill remains unacceptably narrow. Consider these findings from an updated study originally done for the bipartisan Commission on Leave:[16]

- Only 62 percent of U.S. workers both work for covered employers (those with 50 or more employees) and meet the eligibility requirements (at least 12 months on the job, working for at least 1,250 hours).
- Only 11 percent of private-sector work sites are covered.
- Two-fifths of noncovered firms with 25–49 employees do not provide leave for all FMLA reasons.
- 62 percent of employees at covered establishments do not know if the FMLA applies to them; 16 percent of those employers do not know if they are covered or mistakenly report that they are not when, in fact, they are.
- Women, younger workers, workers with low family incomes, and those not protected by collective bargaining are most likely to be ineligible or unable to afford leave. Of all ethnic groups, Latino workers are least likely to be protected.
- Of those who needed leave but didn't take it, 78 percent said they couldn't afford to lose their wages. Nearly one out of ten leave-takers used public assistance to deal with lost income during leave.

Not all workers in the United States have access to paid sick leave or even vacation. Two-fifths of full-time, private-sector workers have no paid sick days. Only one in six part-time workers has paid sick days. Lower-wage workers are particularly vulnerable—more than three in four have no paid sick days.[17] A study by the Urban Institute found that low-wage workers with more than two years' job tenure were no more likely to receive paid leave than those who worked less than a year. Recent welfare recipients fared the worst.[18] Adding to the problem has been the view in U.S. culture that care of family members is a private problem to be solved by individual employees.

WELFARE

In 1996 we saw the passage of national welfare reform legislation—the stunning reversal of U.S. policy that for decades had guaranteed assistance to poor women and children. Unfortunately, the new policy is based on faulty assumptions and an unrealistic view of where women will work.

Many architects of welfare reform started with the premise that the majority of women are on welfare because they *wouldn't work*. Their strategy was to *force them to work*—any job will do. They designed extensive punishments for those who don't comply. Since women can't work without some assistance, they provided some help with health insurance and child care. The measure of success is reduction in the welfare rolls.

The facts at the time welfare "was ended" show a very different picture. Seventy percent of women on welfare during a two-year period were working or looking for work.[19] They were *cyclers* (on and off welfare) or *combiners* (combine work and welfare). According to a study of six Midwest states by Northern Illinois University, only 6.3 percent of Aid to Families with Dependent Children (AFDC) recipients never worked; only 3.4 percent of adults were under 18.[20]

The most serious problem with the program implemented in 1996 is that it's missing the key component: jobs. There aren't enough jobs, the ones that are available don't pay enough, and there's a mismatch between the job seekers and where good jobs are located and the skills they require. Not surprisingly, most welfare "leavers" who are employed are stuck in low-paying jobs. Half or more are still living in poverty, a greater number than before in extreme poverty.[21] The number of people living in poverty has gone up for each of the last four years.

We need to understand that most women are on welfare because of *problems with work* or with some other system in their lives, such as marriage or education. The strategy must be to *find solutions* for those problems—job training, creation of living-wage jobs with affordable leave, adequate quality child care, health insurance, along with efforts to eliminate domestic violence, reach equity and quality in all schools, and so forth. Because the problems affect more people than those on welfare, the solutions need to be universal. The measure of success must be *reduction in poverty*, not in caseloads, and rise in self-sufficiency for families.

CONCLUSION

Often policy makers and advocates for women's rights speak of "women" as if one size fits all. But women exist in splendid diversity. Only a thorough understanding of specific conditions of various groups, an understanding that looks through the lens of class, race and ethnicity, and sexual orientation, can lead us to the range of solutions that women need. Progress for women cannot be measured only by what happens to women in professional and managerial jobs. Full freedom for women requires freedom for *all* women. That means the fight for gender equality must go hand in hand with the struggle against all forms of oppression.   [2011]

NOTES

1. The numbers are highest for African-American women—63.4 percent.
2. *The Shriver Report: A Woman's Nation Changes Everything*, ed. Heather Boushey and Ann O'Leary. Institute for Women's Policy Research Compilation of Current Population Survey Labor Force Statistics, 2009.
3. In 2008, nearly two-thirds of all mothers of children under five, 56.6 percent of mothers of infants under the age of one, and 77 percent of mothers whose children are 18 or under were employed outside the home.
4. Institute for Women's Policy Research Compilation of Current Population Survey Labor Force Statistics, 2009.
5. The percentages are 22.5 percent for women of all races, 28.5 percent for African-American women, 30.3 percent for Asian women, and 24.2 percent for Hispanic women. Source: Calculated using U.S. Census Bureau, *Current Population Survey, 2005, Annual Social and Economic Supplement*, FINC-01: "Selected Characteristics of Families by Total Money Income in 2004," http://pubdb3.census.gov/macro/032005/faminc/new01_000.htm (September 27, 2005).
6. Stephen Rose and Heidi Hartmann created a three-tier schema of elite, good, and less-skilled jobs; in each tier, they identify a set of occupations that are predominantly male and a set of those that are predominantly female. Within each of those six categories, at least 75 percent of the workers are of one gender. And in each tier, women's jobs pay significantly less that those of their male counterparts with the same educational background. Rose and Hartmann, "Still a Man's

Gender Segregation and Pay Differentials by Occupation

The table below demonstrates that in almost no occupation do women earn equal to or more than men. In addition, in occupations where women are most of the workers, women's wages are far lower than in occupations where men predominate, even if the amount of training required is similar. Thus, pay inequity affects women negatively both by designating the jobs that they do as inferior and also by paying them less than men within the occupation.

Occupations from most male dominated to most female dominated	Percentage of Men/ Percentage of Women in the field	Average weekly salary earned by workers in the field in dollars	Ratio of female to male earnings
Computer software engineers	76/24	1,350	.80
Bartenders	90/10	596	.79
Laborers/Material Movers	85/15	443	.88
General Operations Manager	76/24	1,129	.75
Purchasing Manager	64/36	1,092	.66
Maids/Housekeeping	12/88	331	.81
Packaging/Filling materials operations	44/56	368	.83
Cashiers	25/75	322	.82
Child Care Worker	06/94	334	.99
Hairdresser/ Cosmetologists	08/92	396	.91
Food Preparation	02/98	368	.91

[2011]

Source: Bureau of Labor Statistics, *Highlights of Women's Earnings,* 2008, http://www.bls.gov/cps/cpswpm2008.pdf.

Labor Market," http://www.iwpr.org/publications/pubs/still-a-mans-labor-market-the-long-term-earnings-gap.

7. Department of Professional Employees, AFL-CIO, http://dpeaflcio.org/wp-content/uploads/2010/08/Professional-Women-2010.pdf.

8. Cynthia Costello and Anne J. Stone, eds., *The American Woman, 2001–2002* (New York: Norton, 2001).

9. The Bureau of Labor Statistics lists temps as a subset of professional production jobs and also a subset of production jobs. The gap between temp median weekly earnings and those for professional production workers—$597—is even higher.

10. Kaiser Family Foundation/Health Research and Educational Trust, *Employer Health Benefits, 2004 Annual Survey,* September 2004, exhibits 2.5 and 2.6, 40–41, at http://www.kff.org/insurance/7148/sections/ehbs04-2-5.cfm and http://www.kff.org/insurance/7148/sections/ehbs04-2-6.cfm.

11. Rose and Hartmann, "Still a Man's Labor Market." Another study by Sylvia Hewlett of 2,443 highly qualified women (graduate degrees and high-honors undergraduate) found more than a third stopped working for some period of time, usually to care for children, 24 percent for elders. The average time of this "off-ramping," as Hewlett calls it, was 2.2 years. The leave cost women 18 percent of their earning power—37 percent if they took three or more years off. See Hewlett, "The New Have-It-All Myth," *More,* June 2005.

12. See Juan Williams, "A Question of Fairness," *Atlantic Monthly*, February 1987.

13. Kim Bobo, *Wage Theft* (New York: New Press, 2010).

14. Tsedeye Gebreselassie and Paul Sonn, "Women and the Minimum Wage," July 24, 2009, http://www.prospect.org/cs/articles?article=women_and_the_minimum_wage.

15. AFl-CIO, http://www.aflcio.org/joinaunion/why/uniondifference/uniondiff4.cfm.

16. *Balancing the Needs of Families and Employers: Family and Medical Leave Surveys 2000 Update*, conducted by Westat for the U.S. Department of Labor (Washington, D.C.: U.S. Department of Labor, 2000).

17. Jody Heymann et al., *Work-Family Issues and Low-Income Families* (New York: Ford Foundation, 2002).

18. Katherin Ross Phillips, "Getting Time Off: Access to Leave Among Working Parents" (Washington, D.C.: Urban Institute), April 22, 2004.

19. Roberta Spalter-Roth et al., *Welfare That Works: The Working Lives of AFDC Recipients* (Washington, D.C.: Institute for Women's Policy Research, 1995).

20. Paul Kleppner and Nikolas Theodore, *Work After Welfare: Is the Midwest's Booming Economy Creating Enough Jobs?* (Chicago: Northern Illinois University, 1997).

21. Gregory Acs and Pamela Loprest, "Final Synthesis Report of Findings from ASPE 'Leavers' Grants" (Washington, D.C.: Urban Institute), November 27, 2001. A 2005 report by the Legislative Audit Bureau in Wisconsin found that only 42.1 percent of those who left W-2 employment in 1999 earned more than the poverty level in 2003—and that's only when you count the state and federal earned income tax credits. During the first year after leaving the program, only one in five earned more than the poverty level.

 51

Questions and Answers on Pay Equity

NATIONAL COMMITTEE FOR
PAY EQUITY

WHAT IS PAY EQUITY?

Pay equity is a means of eliminating sex and race discrimination in the wage-setting system. Many women and people of color are still segregated into a small number of jobs such as clerical, service workers, nurses, and teachers. These jobs have historically been undervalued and continue to be underpaid to a large extent because of the gender and race of the people who hold them. Pay equity means that the criteria employers use to set wages must be sex- and race-neutral.

WHAT IS THE LEGAL STATUS OF PAY EQUITY?

Two laws protect workers against wage discrimination. The Equal Pay Act of 1963 prohibits unequal pay for equal or "substantially equal" work performed by men and women. Title VII of the Civil Rights Act of 1964 prohibits wage discrimination on the basis of race, color, sex, religion, or national origin. In 1981, the Supreme Court made it clear that Title VII is broader than the Equal Pay Act, and prohibits wage discrimination even when the jobs are not identical. However, wage discrimination laws are poorly enforced and cases are extremely difficult to prove and win. Stronger legislation is needed to ease the burden of filing claims and clarify the right to pay equity.

HOW LARGE IS THE WAGE GAP?

2008 Median Annual Earnings of Year-Round, Full-Time Workers

All Men	All Women
$46,367 (100%)	$35,745 (77%)

In 2008, the earnings for African-American women were $31,489, or 67.9 percent of men's earnings (a drop from 68.7 percent in 2007), and Latinas' earnings were $26,846, or 58 percent of men's earnings (a drop from 59 percent in 2007). Asian American women's earnings in 2008 were $42,215, or 91 percent of men's earnings (an increase from 89.5 percent in 2007).

Source: U.S. Census Bureau, *Current Population Survey, 2009 Annual Social and Economic Supplement*, Series PINC-05.

WHY IS THERE A WAGE GAP?

The wage gap exists, in part, because many women and people of color are still segregated into a few low-paying occupations. More than half of all women workers hold sales, clerical, and service jobs. Studies show that the more an occupation is dominated by women or people of color, the less it pays. Part of the wage gap results from differences in education, experience, or time in the workforce. But a significant portion cannot be explained by any of those factors; it is attributable to discrimination. In other words, certain jobs pay less because they are held by women and people of color.

HASN'T THE WAGE GAP CLOSED CONSIDERABLY IN THE RECENT YEARS?

The wage gap has narrowed by about 15 percentage points during the last 23 years, ranging from 62 percent in 1982 to 77 percent in 2008. Since 1973, however, approximately 60 percent of the change in the wage gap is due to the fall in men's real earnings and only about 40 percent to the increase in women's wages. At this rate of change, the Institute for Women's Policy Research estimates, it will take until 2057 to close the wage gap.

IS IT POSSIBLE TO COMPARE DIFFERENT JOBS?

Yes, employers have used job evaluations for nearly a century to set pay and rank for different occupations within a company or organization. Today, two out of three workers are employed by firms that use some form of job evaluation. The federal government, the nation's largest employer, has a 70-year-old job evaluation system that covers nearly two million employees.

WHO REALLY NEEDS PAY EQUITY?

Women, people of color, and white men who work in jobs that have been undervalued due to race or sex bias need pay equity. Many of these workers are the sole support for their families. In addition, it is estimated that 70 percent of women with children under 18 work outside the home (up from 44.9 percent 20 years ago). Discriminatory pay has consequences as people age and across generations. Everyone in society is harmed by wage discrimination. Therefore, everyone needs pay equity.

IS PAY EQUITY AN EFFECTIVE ANTIPOVERTY STRATEGY?

Yes, pay equity helps workers become self-sufficient and reduces their reliance on government assistance programs. A recent study found that nearly 40 percent of poor working women could leave welfare programs if they were to receive pay equity wage increases. Pay equity can bring great savings to taxpayers at a minimal cost to business. Adjustments would cost no more than 3.7 percent of hourly wage expenses.

WILL WHITE MEN'S WAGES BE REDUCED IF PAY EQUITY IS IMPLEMENTED?

No. Federal law prohibits reducing pay for any employee to remedy discrimination. Furthermore, male workers in female-dominated jobs benefit when sex discrimination is eliminated, as do white workers in minority-dominated jobs. Pay equity means equal treatment for all workers.

WILL ACHIEVING PAY EQUITY REQUIRE A NATIONAL WAGE-SETTING SYSTEM?

No, pay equity does not mandate across-the-board salaries for any occupation, nor does it tamper with supply and demand. It merely means that wages must be based on job requirements like skill, effort, responsibility, and working conditions without consideration of race, sex, or ethnicity.

DOESN'T PAY EQUITY COST EMPLOYERS TOO MUCH?

In Minnesota, where pay equity legislation meant raises for 30,000 state employees, the cost was only 3.7 percent of the state's payroll budget over a four-year period—less than 1 percent of the budget each year. In Washington State, pay equity was achieved at a cost of 2.6 percent of the state's personnel costs and was implemented over an eight-year period. Voluntary implementation of pay equity is cost effective, while court-ordered pay equity adjustments can lead to greater costs. Discrimination is costly and illegal.

ARE WAGE INEQUALITIES THE RESULT OF WOMEN'S CHOICES?

Again, part of the wage gap is attributed to differences in education, experiences, and time in the workforce. However, the overwhelming evidence that wage discrimination persists in America can be found in numerous court cases and legal settlements, Department of Labor investigations, surveys of men and women on the job, and salary surveys that control for age, experience, and time in the workforce. While women sometimes take time out of the workforce to raise children, it should be noted that when couples are deciding who should stay home with children, the fact that the wife is earning a lower salary impacts that decision. In addition, some of the other explainable factors can sometimes be attributed to discrimination. For example, if women and men have different jobs in a company, women may not be choosing the lower-paying jobs. They may have trouble advancing in a company due to bias about women's abilities or levels of commitment.

WILL IMPLEMENTING PAY EQUITY DISRUPT THE ECONOMY?

No. The Equal Pay Act, minimum wage, and child labor laws all provoked the same concerns and all were implemented without major disruption. What disrupts the economy and penalizes families is the systematic underpayment of some people because of their sex or race. When wages for women and people of color are raised, their purchasing power will increase, strengthening the economy. One survey found that a growing number of businesses support the elimination of wage discrimination between different jobs as "good business" and that pay equity is consistent with remaining competitive.

WHAT IS THE STATUS OF EFFORTS TO ACHIEVE PAY EQUITY?

Pay equity is a growing national movement building on the progress made in the 1980s, when 20 states made some adjustments of payrolls to correct for sex or race bias. (Seven of these states successfully completed full implementation of a pay equity plan. Twenty-three states plus Washington, D.C., conducted studies to determine if sex was a wage determinant. Four states examined their compensation systems to correct race bias, as well.)

In the last few years, pay equity bills have been introduced in more than 25 legislatures. On the federal level, the Paycheck Fairness Act, which would amend the Equal Pay Act and the Civil Rights Act of 1964 to provide more-effective remedies to workers who are not being paid equal wages for doing equal work, was passed by the House of Representatives in the 110th Congress and again on January 9, 2009. Hearings on the bill were held March 11, 2010, in the Senate, where action on the bill is pending. The Fair Pay Act has been introduced in the U.S. House of Representatives by Delegate Eleanor Holmes-Norton, and in the U.S. Senate by Senator Tom Harkin. The Fair Pay Act would expand the Equal Pay Act's protections against wage discrimination to workers in equivalent jobs with similar skills and responsibilities, even if the jobs are not identical.

WHAT CAN I DO ABOUT PAY EQUITY?

Urge your senators to support the Paycheck Fairness Act (S. 182). The Senate Health, Education, Labor, and Pensions Committee held a hearing, "Fair Share for All: Pay Equity in the New American Workplace," on March 11, 2010, with testimony about the Paycheck Fairness Act; see www.womenspolicy.org.   [2010]

 ## *Office Double Standards*

A businessman is aggressive, a businesswoman is pushy.
He's careful about details, she's picky.
He follows through, she doesn't know when to quit.
He's firm, she's stubborn.
He makes judgments, she reveals her prejudices.
He's man of the world, she's "been around."
He exercises authority, she's bossy.
He's discreet, she's secretive.
He says what he thinks, she's opinionated.

(original sources, unfortunately, unknown)

🌿 52

The Politics of Housework

PAT MAINARDI OF REDSTOCKINGS

Though women do not complain of the power of husbands, each complains of her own husband, or of the husbands of her friends. It is the same in all other cases of servitude; at least in the commencement of the emancipatory movement. The serfs did not at first complain of the power of the lords, but only of their tyranny.

—John Stuart Mill
On the Subjection of Women

Liberated women—very different from Women's Liberation! The first signals all kinds of goodies, to warm the hearts (not to mention other parts) of the most radical men. The other signals—HOUSEWORK. The first brings sex without marriage, sex before marriage, cozy housekeeping arrangements ("I'm living with this chick") and the self-content of knowing that you're not the kind of man who wants a doormat instead of a woman. That will come later. After all, who wants that old commodity anymore, the Standard American Housewife, all husband, home and kids? The New Commodity, the Liberated Woman, has sex a lot and has a career, preferably something that can be fitted in with the household chores—like dancing, pottery, or painting.

On the other hand is Women's Liberation—and housework. What? You say this is all trivial? Wonderful! That's what I thought. It seemed perfectly reasonable. We both had careers, both had to work a couple of days a week to earn enough to live on, so why shouldn't we share the housework? So I suggested it to my mate and he agreed—most men are too hip to turn you down flat. You're right, he said. It's only fair.

Then an interesting thing happened. I can only explain it by stating that we women have been brainwashed more than even we can imagine. Probably too many years of seeing television women in ecstasy over their shiny waxed floors or breaking down over their dirty shirt collars. Men have no such conditioning. They recognize the essential

fact of housework right from the very beginning. Which is that it stinks.

Here's my list of dirty chores: buying groceries, carting them home and putting them away; cooking meals and washing dishes and pots; doing the laundry, digging out the place when things get out of control; washing floors. The list could go on but the sheer necessities are bad enough. All of us have to do these things, or get someone else to do them for us. The longer my husband contemplated these chores, the more repulsed he became, and so proceeded the change from the normally sweet, considerate Dr. Jekyll into the crafty Mr. Hyde who would stop at nothing to avoid the horrors of—housework. As he felt himself backed into a corner laden with dirty dishes, brooms, mops, and reeking garbage, his front teeth grew longer and pointier, his fingernails haggled and his eyes grew wild. Housework trivial? Not on your life! Just try to share the burden.

So ensued a dialogue that's been going on for several years. Here are some of the high points:

• "I don't mind sharing the housework, but I don't do it very well. We should each do the things we're best at." MEANING: Unfortunately I'm no good at things like washing dishes or cooking. What I do best is a little light carpentry, changing light bulbs, moving furniture (how often do *you* move furniture?). ALSO MEANING: Historically the lower classes (black men and us) have had hundreds of years experience doing menial jobs. It would be a waste of manpower to train someone else to do them now. ALSO MEANING: I don't like the dull, stupid, boring jobs, so you should do them.

• "I don't mind sharing the work, but you'll have to show me how to do it." MEANING: I ask a lot of questions and you'll have to show me everything every time I do it because I don't remember so good. Also don't try to sit down and read while I'M doing my jobs because I'm going to annoy the hell out of you until it's easier to do them yourself.

• "We used to be so happy!" (Said whenever it was his turn to do something.) MEANING: I used to be so happy. MEANING: Life without housework is bliss. No quarrel here. Perfect Agreement.

• "We have different standards, and why should I have to work to your standards? That's unfair." MEANING: If I begin to get bugged by the dirt and crap I will say, "This place sure is a sty" or "How can anyone live like this?" and wait for your reaction. I know that all women have a sore called "Guilt over a messy house" or "Household work is ultimately my responsibility." I know that men have caused that sore—if anyone visits and the place *is* a sty, they're not going to leave and say, "He sure is a lousy housekeeper." You'll take the rap in any case. I can outwait you. ALSO MEANING: I can provoke innumerable scenes over the housework issue. Eventually doing all the housework yourself will be less painful to you than trying to get me to do half. Or I'll suggest we get a maid. She will do my share of the work. You will do yours. It's women's work.

• "I've got nothing against sharing the housework, but you can't make me do it on your schedule." MEANING: Passive resistance. I'll do it when I damned well please, if at all. If my job is doing dishes, it's easier to do them once a week. If taking out laundry, once a month. If washing the floors, once a year. If you don't like it, do it yourself oftener, and then I won't do it at all.

• "I hate it more than you. You don't mind it so much." MEANING: Housework is garbage work. It's the worst crap I've ever done. It's degrading and humiliating for someone of *my* intelligence to do it. But for someone of *your* intelligence. . . .

• "Housework is too trivial to even talk about." MEANING: It's even more trivial to do. Housework is beneath my status. My purpose in life is to deal with matters of significance. Yours is to deal with matters of insignificance. You should do the housework.

• "This problem of housework is not a man-woman problem. In any relationship between two people one is going to have a stronger personality and dominate." MEANING: That stronger personality had better be *me*.

• "In animal societies, wolves, for example, the top animal is usually a male even where he is not chosen for brute strength but on the basis of cunning and intelligence. Isn't that interesting? MEANING: I have historical, psychological, anthropological, and biological justification for keeping you down. How can you ask the top wolf to be equal?

• "Women's liberation isn't really a political movement." MEANING: The revolution is coming too close to home. ALSO MEANING: I am only interested in how I am oppressed, not how I oppress others. Therefore the war, the draft, and the university are political. Women's liberation is not.

• "Man's accomplishments have always depended on getting help from other people, mostly women. What great man would have accomplished what he did if he had to do his own housework?" MEANING: Oppression is built into the system and I, as the white American male, receive the benefits of this system. I don't want to give them up.

Participatory democracy begins at home. If you are planning to implement your politics, there are certain things to remember.

1. He *is* feeling it more than you. He's losing some leisure and you're gaining it. The measure of your oppression is his resistance.
2. A great many American men are not accustomed to doing monotonous, repetitive work which never issues in any lasting, let alone important, achievement. This is why they would rather repair a cabinet than wash dishes. If human endeavors are like a pyramid with man's highest achievements at the top, then keeping oneself alive is at the bottom. Men have always had servants (us) to take care of this bottom stratum of life while they have confined their efforts to the rarefied upper regions. It is thus ironic when they ask of women—Where are your great painters, statesmen, etc.? Mme. Matisse ran a military shop so he could paint. Mrs. Martin Luther King kept his house and raised his babies.
3. It is a traumatizing experience for someone who has always thought of himself as being against any oppression or exploitation of one human being by another to realize that in his daily life he has been accepting and implementing (and benefiting from) this exploitation; that his rationalization is little different from that of the racist who says, "Black people don't feel pain"

(women don't mind doing the shitwork); and that the oldest form of oppression in history has been the oppression of 50 percent of the population by the other 50 percent.

4. Arm yourself with some knowledge of the psychology of oppressed peoples everywhere, and a few facts about the animal kingdom. I admit playing top wolf or who runs the gorillas is silly but as a last resort men bring it up all the time. Talk about bees. If you feel really hostile bring up the sex life of spiders. They have sex. She bites off his head.

   The psychology of oppressed peoples is not silly. Jews, immigrants, black men, and all women have employed the same psychological mechanisms to survive: admiring the oppressor, glorifying the oppressor, wanting to be like the oppressor, wanting the oppressor to like them, mostly because the oppressor held all the power.

5. In a sense, all men everywhere are slightly schizoid—divorced from the reality of maintaining life. This makes it easier for them to play games with it. It is almost a cliché that women feel greater grief at sending a son off to a war or losing him to that war because they bore him, suckled him, and raised him. The men who foment those wars did none of those things and have a more superficial estimate of the worth of human life. One hour a day is a low estimate of the amount of time one has to spend "keeping" oneself. By foisting this off on others, man has seven hours a week—one working day more to play with his mind and not his human needs. Over the course of generations it is easy to see whence evolved the horrifying abstractions of modern life.

6. With the death of each form of oppression, life changes and new forms evolve. English aristocrats at the turn of the century were horrified at the idea of enfranchising working men—were sure that it signaled the death of civilization and a return to barbarism. Some working men were even deceived by this line. Similarly with the minimum wage, abolition of slavery, and female suffrage. Life changes but it goes on. Don't fall for any line about the death of everything if men take a turn at the dishes. They will imply that you are holding back the revolution (their revolution). But you are advancing it (your revolution).

7. Keep checking up. Periodically consider who's actually *doing* the jobs. These things have a way of backsliding so that a year later once again the woman is doing everything. After a year make a list of jobs the man has rarely if ever done. You will find cleaning pots, toilets, refrigerators, and ovens high on the list. Use time sheets if necessary. He will accuse you of being petty. He is above that sort of thing (housework). Bear in mind what the worst jobs are, namely the ones that have to be done every day or several times a day. Also the ones that are dirty—it's more pleasant to pick up books, newspapers, etc., than to wash dishes. Alternate the bad jobs. It's the daily grind that gets you down. Also make sure that you don't have the responsibility for the housework with occasional help from him. "I'll cook dinner for you tonight" implies it's really your job and isn't he a nice guy to do some of it for you.

8. Most men had a rich and rewarding bachelor life during which they did not starve or become encrusted with crud or buried under the litter. There is a taboo that says women mustn't strain themselves in the presence of men—we haul around 50 pounds of groceries if we have to but aren't allowed to open a jar if there is someone around to do it for us. The reverse side of the coin is that men aren't supposed to be able to take care of themselves without a woman. Both are excuses for making women do the housework.

9. Beware of the double whammy. He won't do the little things he always did because you're now a "Liberated Woman," right? Of course he won't do anything else either. . . .

I was just finishing this when my husband came in and asked what I was doing. Writing a paper on housework. Housework? he said. *Housework?* Oh my god how trivial can you get? A paper on housework.   [1970]

53

The Price of Motherhood: Why the Most Important Job in the World Is Still the Least Valued

ANN CRITTENDEN

In the United States, motherhood is as American as apple pie. No institution is more sacrosanct; no figure is praised more fulsomely . . .

When I was on a radio talk show in 1998, several listeners called in to say that child rearing is the most important job in the world. A few weeks later, at a party, Lawrence H. Summers, a distinguished economist who subsequently became the secretary of the treasury, used exactly the same phrase. "Raising children," Summers told me in all seriousness, "is the most important job in the world." As Summers well knows, in the modern economy, two-thirds of all wealth is created by human skills, creativity, and enterprise—what is known as "human capital." And that means parents who are conscientiously and effectively rearing children are literally, in the words of economist Shirley Burggraf, "the major wealth producers in our economy."[1]

But this very material contribution is still considered immaterial. All of the lip service to motherhood still floats in the air, as insubstantial as clouds of angel dust. On the ground, where mothers live, the lack of respect and tangible recognition is still part of every mother's experience. Most people, like infants in a crib, take female caregiving utterly for granted.

The job of making a home for a child and developing his or her capabilities is often equated with "doing nothing." Thus the disdainful question frequently asked about mothers at home: "What do they *do* all day?" I'll never forget a dinner at the end of a day in which I had gotten my son dressed and fed and off to nursery school, dealt with a plumber about a leaky shower, paid the bills, finished an op-ed piece, picked up and escorted my son to a reading group at the library, ran several miscellaneous errands, and put in an hour on a future book project. Over drinks that evening, a childless female friend commented that "of all the couples we know, you're the only wife who doesn't work." . . .

In my childless youth I shared these attitudes. In the early 1970s I wrote an article for the very first issue of *Ms.* magazine on the economic value of a housewife. I added up all the domestic chores, attached dollar values to each, and concluded that the job was seriously underpaid and ought to be included in the Gross National Product. I thought I was being sympathetic, but I realize now that my deeper attitude was one of compassionate contempt, or perhaps contemptuous compassion. Deep down, I had no doubt that I was superior, in my midtown office overlooking Madison Avenue, to those unpaid housewives pushing brooms. "Why aren't they making something of themselves?" I wondered. "What's wrong with them? They're letting our side down."

I imagined that domestic drudgery was going to be swept into the dustbin of history as men and women linked arms and marched off to run the world in a new egalitarian alliance. It never occurred to me that women might be at home because there were children there; that housewives might become extinct, but mothers and fathers never would. . . .

The devaluation of mothers' work permeates virtually every major institution. Not only is caregiving not rewarded, it is penalized. These stories illustrate the point:

• Joanna Upton, a single mother working as a store manager in Massachusetts, sued the company for wrongful dismissal after it fired her for refusing to work overtime—until nine or ten at night and all day Saturday. Upton had been hired to work 8:15 a.m. until 5:30 p.m.; she could not adequately care for or barely even see her son if she had to work overtime. Yet she lost her suit. The Massachusetts Supreme Judicial Court ruled that under state contract law, an at-will employee may be fired "for any reason or for no reason at all" unless the firing violates a "clearly established" public policy. Massachusetts had no public policy dealing with a parent's responsibility to care for his or her child.[2]

- A woman in Texas gave up a 15-year career in banking to raise two children. Her husband worked extremely long hours and spent much of his time on the road. She realized that only if she left her own demanding job would the children have the parental time and attention they needed. For almost two decades she worked part-time as a consultant from her home, and for several years she had little or no income. Recently the Social Security Administration sent her an estimate of her retirement income—a statement that was full of zeroes for the years spent caregiving. Social Security confirmed that her decision to be the responsible, primary parent had reduced the government pension by hundreds of dollars a month in retirement income.

- A mother in Maryland had a son who had been a problem child ever since kindergarten. At junior high, the boy was suspended several times; he was finally caught with a gun in his backpack and expelled. The boy's father sued for custody, and the mother countered with a request for more child support, to help pay the $10,000 tuition for a special private school. She also quit her full-time job to have more time for her family. At his new school, the boy showed dramatic improvement both in his academic work and in his behavior. When the case came to court, the father was denied custody, but the judge refused to require him to pay half the costs of the boy's rehabilitation, including therapy and tutoring, despite evidence that the father could afford to do so. A mother who did not work full-time was, in the judge's view, a luxury that "our world does not permit." So the mother was in effect penalized for having tried to be a more attentive mother, and the boy was forced to leave the only school in which he had enjoyed any success. . . .[3]

As these examples reveal the United States is a society at war with itself. The policies of American business, government, and the law do not reflect Americans' stated values. Across the board, individuals who assume the role of nurturer are punished and discouraged from performing the very tasks that everyone agrees are essential. We talk endlessly about the importance of family, yet the work it takes to make a family is utterly disregarded. This contradiction can be found in every corner of our society.

First, inflexible workplaces guarantee that many women will have to cut back on, if not quit, their employment once they have children. The result is a loss of income that produces a bigger wage gap between mothers and childless women than the wage gap between young men and women. This forgone income, the equivalent of a huge "mommy tax," is typically more than $1 million for a college-educated American woman.

Second, marriage is still not an equal financial partnership. Mothers in 47 of the 50 states—California, Louisiana, and New Mexico are the exceptions—do not have an unequivocal legal right to half of the family's assets. Nor does a mother's unpaid work entitle her to any ownership of the primary breadwinner's income—either during marriage or after a divorce. Family income belongs solely to "he who earns it," in the phrase coined by legal scholar Joan Williams. A married mother is a "dependent," and a divorced mother is "given" what a judge decides she and the children "need" of the father's future income. As a result, the spouse who principally cares for the children—and the children—are almost invariably worse off financially after divorce than the spouse who devotes all his energies to a career.

Third, government social policies don't even define unpaid care of family dependents as work. A family's primary caregiver is not considered a full productive citizen, eligible in her own right for the major social insurance programs. Legal nannies earn Social Security credits; mothers at home do not. Unless she is otherwise "employed," the primary parent is not entitled to unemployment insurance or workman's compensation. The only safety net for a caregiver who loses her source of support is welfare, and even that is no longer assured.

For all these reasons, motherhood is the single biggest risk factor for poverty in old age. American mothers have smaller pensions than either men or childless women, and American women over 65 are more than twice as likely to be poor as men of the same age.

The devaluation of a mother's work extends to those who do similar work for pay. Even college-educated teachers of infants are often characterized as "baby-sitters," and wages for child care are so low that the field is hemorrhaging its best-trained people. Increasingly, day care is being provided by an inexperienced workforce—what one expert calls "Kentucky Fried Day Care"—while highly trained Mary Poppins–style nannies are officially classified as "unskilled labor," and as such largely barred from entry into the United States.

The cumulative effect of these policies is a heavy financial penalty on anyone who chooses to spend any serious amount of time with children. This is the hard truth that lies beneath all of the flowery tributes to Mom. American mothers may have their day, but for the rest of the year their values, their preferences, and their devotion to their children are shortchanged. As the twenty-first century begins, women may be approaching equality, but mothers are still far behind. Changing the status of mothers, by gaining real recognition for their work, is the great unfinished business of the women's movement. . . .

Unpaid female caregiving is not only the life blood of families, it is the very heart of the economy. A spate of new studies reveals that the amount of work involved in unpaid child care is far greater than economists ever imagined. Indeed, it rivals in size the largest industries of the visible economy. By some estimates, even in the most industrialized countries the total hours spent on unpaid household work—much of it associated with child rearing—amount to at least half of the hours of paid work in the market.[4] Up to 80 percent of this unpaid labor is contributed by women.

This huge gift of unreimbursed time and labor explains, in a nutshell, why adult women are so much poorer than men—even though they work longer hours than men in almost every country in the world.[5] One popular economics textbook devotes four pages to problems of poverty without once mentioning the fact that the majority of poor people are women and children. The author never considers that this poverty might be related to the fact that half the human race isn't paid for most of the work it does.

In economics, a "free rider" is someone who benefits from a good without contributing to its provision: in other words, someone who gets something for nothing. By that definition, both the family and the global economy are classic examples of free riding. Both are dependent on female caregivers who offer their labor in return for little or no compensation.

It may well be that mothers and others who care for children and sick and elderly family members will go on giving, whatever the costs or consequences for themselves. Maternal love, after all, is one of the world's renewable resources. But even if this is so, there is still a powerful argument for putting an end to free riding on women's labor. It's called *fairness*.

An analogy to soldiers might be helpful here. Soldiers, like mothers, render an indispensable national service to their country. The ultimate rationale for offering honors and material rewards to military veterans is to avoid free riding on their services. The public feels it owes its warriors some quid pro quo. The G.I. Bill, for example, was not originally a recruitment tool, as military benefits later became, but repayment of a debt that a grateful nation owed to its fighting men. No one, after World War II, dreamed of being a free rider on the sacrifices of Normandy Beach and Guadalcanal.

By the same token, it isn't fair to demand that the nurturing of human capabilities, the national service primarily rendered by women, be valued any less. It isn't fair that mothers' life-sustaining work forces women to be society's involuntary philanthropists. It isn't fair to expect mothers to make sacrifices that no one else is asked to make, or have virtues that no one else possesses, such as a dignified subordination of their personal agenda and a reliance on altruism for life's meaning. Virtues and sacrifices, when expected of one group of people and not of everyone, become the mark of an underclass.[6]

Establishing a fair deal for mothers would go beyond "wages for housewives," an idea that surfaced in the 1970s; or even mothers' benefits similar to veterans' benefits. What is needed is across-the-board recognition—in the workplace, in the family, in the law, and in social policy—that someone has to do the necessary work of raising children and sustaining families, and that the reward for such vital work should not be professional marginalization, a loss of status, and an increased risk of poverty.

Such recognition would end the glaring contradiction between what we tell young women—go out, get an education, become independent—and what happens to those aspirations once they have a child. It would demolish the anachronism that bedevils most mothers' lives: that although they work as hard as or harder than anyone else in the economy, they are still economic *dependents*, like children or incapacitated adults.

The standard rationale for the status quo is that women choose to have children, and in so doing, choose to accept the trade-offs that have always ensued. As an African safari guide once said of a troop of monkeys, "The mothers with the little babies have a hard time keeping up." But human beings, unlike apes, have the ability to ensure that those who carry the babies—and therefore our future—aren't forever trailing behind.   [2001]

NOTES

1. In no known human culture have males ever had the primary task of rearing small children. According to two preeminent scholars of children's history, one of the few things that can be said with certainty, amid the "extraordinary variety" in the historical treatment of children, is that "the vast majority of human infants have been and continue to be cared for primarily by females." N. Roy Hiner and Joseph M. Hawes, *Children in Historical and Comparative Perspective* (New York: Greenwood Press, 1991), 6. If this ever changed, writes Marion J. Levy, a sociologist at Princeton University, the implications would be more radical than the discovery of fire, the invention of agriculture, or the switch from animate to inanimate sources of power. Marion J. Levy, Jr., *Maternal Influence* (New Brunswick, NJ: Transaction Publishers, 1992), xix, 20–23.
2. Unpublished data from the March 1999 Current Population Survey, provided by Steve Hipple.
3. Female university graduates' labor force participation rates were provided by Agneta Stark, an economist at the University of Stockholm, during an interview in August 1997 in Stockholm.
4. More than two million American women work in a home-based business. They average 23 hours of work (in the business) a week.
5. Deborah Fallows made this comment during a panel discussion at the Harvard/Radcliffe twenty-fifth reunion in 1996, attended by the author.

Council of Economic Advisers, *Families and the Labor Market, 1969–1999: Analyzing the "Time Crunch,"* (Washington, D.C., 1999), 4.
6. Louis Uchitelle, "As Labor Supply Shrinks, a New Supply Is Tapped," *New York Times*, December 20, 1999.

 54

Friendly for Whose Family?

BETTY HOLCOMB

One might have assumed that Linnell Minkins was thrilled to work for the Marriott International back in 1999. For many years Marriott made *Working Mother* magazine's list of the 100 best companies for mothers. Marriott won the coveted spot on the list because the corporation offered flexible work schedules, hotlines to help employees find child care in a pinch, and three on-site child care centers.

Minkins, a food server at the San Francisco Marriott, could use that sort of help. But she learned that such assistance wasn't available to her, as an hourly employee. Instead, she never knew, from week to week, what her hours would be, making it hard to find and keep decent child care and make medical and dental appointments for her daughter. As her children grew older and started school, her logistics grew more challenging. She had to figure out how to get them to school on days when she had to show up early at work. A simple schedule change could have solved the problem, but she didn't ask for one. "I don't dare bring it up to them. I'm afraid I'll get written up."

Getting "written up" means getting disciplined, and too many write-ups can lead to losing your job. Marriott had a flextime policy on the books for its 135,000 U.S. employees. Yet when Minkins first inquired about it, she was told to fix the "problem" at home so she wouldn't need flexibility at work. Her annual performance review that year described her as being "challenged" by time management. She let it go and did not pursue the inaccurate evaluation because she needed the money.

At the same time, she noticed that senior managers didn't seem to suffer the same scrutiny. "I don't think it's as difficult for them to take time when they need it. It just doesn't look like their job was being challenged in any way. But the lower people, the people in the back of the house, they are the ones having the problems."

So it goes for hundreds of thousands of other lower-level workers at companies that are widely recognized for their "family-friendly" policies. Exclusive research conducted by the Families and Work Institute for this article back in 1999 revealed, in fact, that the workers who most need benefits such as child care and flexible work hours are the least likely to get them.

Consider just these facts from the study. Workers in lower-paying, low-status jobs are:

- Half as likely as managers and professionals to have flextime,
- Half as likely to have on-site child care at the job,
- Far more likely to lose a day's pay when they must stay home to care for a sick child,
- Three times less likely to get company-sponsored tax breaks to help pay for child care.

The original research sparked other reports that showed a similar pattern, even at the height of attention in corporate America to creating so-called "family-friendly" workplaces. Despite the highly visible lists touting the new benefits, workers in entry-level, low-paying, or low-status jobs are much less likely to get a paid maternity leave, or to get as much time off, even if it is unpaid, after a baby is born as managers do. Paid sick days are unusual for workers in retail, restaurant, and hospitality industries and rarely available to workers who put in part-time hours. Indeed, a growing number of jobs, especially public-sector jobs, are now part-time or temporary, adopted as a strategy by towns, states, and private employers to avoid having to offer paid time off. Put another way, some families seem to count more than others.

The initial report on the research spurred considerable attention to the issue of equity in access to family-friendly benefits. Yet the situation has deteriorated for most workers, with low-wage workers continuing to take the biggest hit. And since women make up a disproportionate share of low-wage, low-status workers, this reality falls especially hard on them—and at a time when women's incomes have grown more important than ever in keeping family finances afloat. While *Working Mother* still churns out its annual list of "best companies" offering benefits such as paid leave, time off to care for sick children, and flexible schedules, the universe of workers able to take advantage of such perks—and the value of such benefits—has continued to erode after the first decade of the twenty-first century.

By 2010, with the collapse of the technology sector, a slowed economy and a growing labor surplus in even the "knowledge" sector of the economy—including the communications and pharmaceutical giants that led the way in creating the so-called family-friendly workplace—many companies had scaled back their work-family departments or even abolished them altogether. Many corporations had a short-staffed and overworked human resources department charged with getting more from every worker for less. "Without a labor shortage, there's not much interest in being family friendly anymore," said one human resource director, who had been a member of the Association of Work-Life Professionals, as it mushroomed in the 1990s. "There's still lip-service to being family friendly, and companies like to get on the *Working Mother* list, but it's not the priority it was."

If anything, benefits with high visibility for the twenty-first century began to look more like strategies to get workers to work more and with less flexibility. Telecommuting and on-site snack bars and gyms at the most elite companies translated into working all hours, all days, at the most glamorous companies such as high-tech companies. In fact, the latest data from the Families and Work Institute shows just that. In 2008, three-quarters of all employees reported a serious "time-famine," reporting that they had to put in more time at work, just to stay even. And putting in all those hours took a big toll on family life. That figure was up from 66 percent in 1992, a 9 percent increase since the survey began.

In a separate 2009 study focusing exclusively on low-wage workers, the researchers found the crunch had grown even worse for those on the lower rungs of the workforce. "Many employers still view low-wage employees as a low-cost 'commodity' that is easily replaced and not worth significant investment to retain," concluded James Bond and Ellen Galinsky, co-authors of the study *Workplace Flexibility and Low-Wage Employees*. "This is all the more true when unemployment is high and labor markets slack."

This exploitative view of low-wage workers, often women of color, persists despite the fact these workers are often the company's face to customers and perform the critical day-to-day tasks that keep America's economy humming. Still, for most executives, "workplace flexibility is typically featured as a means for talent development and talent management, and many employers view 'talent' as applying primarily to their higher earners rather than their workforce as a whole," Bond and Galinsky conclude. The acceleration of globalization, and the export of many jobs, puts low-wage workers on particularly shaky ground. With unemployment hovering near 10 percent in 2010, the idea of a family-friendly workplace grew all the more distant. Wages stagnated and many benefits, even those long assumed to be settled and secure, began to evaporate. Even retirement and health care came under assault, and even in union-protected jobs.

Still, the picture was brightest for union workers, as family-friendly benefits, such as child care and paid leave gained a higher priority for some in the labor movement. In New York City, for example, the health workers union, District 1199, created a dependent-care fund that not only provided child care benefits to its workers, but also helped to fund child care centers. Several thousand public-sector workers also participated in a state-sponsored demonstration project that created child care subsidies for low-wage workers employed by the city.

Yet with membership in decline, because of growing attacks on public employee unions in particular, it is far from clear that these wins will be scaled up across the nation. "Increasingly, unions are looking to public policy as a way to change the workplace for everyone," says Netsy Firestein, Director of the Labor Project for Working Families. Recent union-led campaigns to win paid family leave and paid sick days have met with some success at the state and local level. California, Washington, and New Jersey, for example, have created paid family leave. San Francisco and Milwaukee have enacted local laws to require paid sick days, a boon for low-wage workers in the retail, hospitality, and restaurant industries.

American business simply needs to catch up with the reality of change in American life—that all workers now face serious conflicts between their work and family duties, regardless of gender or class. All workers, most especially those at the bottom rungs of the workplace, need to be valued if America is to thrive.   [2011]

🌿 55

Nannies, Maids, and Sex Workers in the New Economy

BARBARA EHRENREICH
and ARLIE RUSSELL HOCHSCHILD

"Whose baby are you?" Josephine Perera, a nanny from Sri Lanka, asks Isadora, her pudgy two-year-old charge in Athens, Greece.

Thoughtful for a moment, the child glances toward the closed door of the next room, in which her mother is working, as if to say, "That's my mother in there."

"No, you're *my* baby," Josephine teases, tickling Isadora lightly. Then, to settle the issue, Isadora answers, "Together!" She has two mommies—her mother and Josephine. And surely a child loved by many adults is richly blessed.

In some ways, Josephine's story—which unfolds in an extraordinary documentary film, '*When Mother Comes Home for Christmas*, directed by Nilita Vachani—describes an unparalleled success. Josephine has ventured around the world, achieving a degree of independence her mother could not have imagined, and amply supporting her three children with no help from her ex-husband, their father. Each month she mails a remittance check from Athens to Hatton, Sri Lanka, to pay the children's living expenses and school fees. On her Christmas visit home, she bears gifts of pots, pans, and dishes. While she makes payments on a new bus that Suresh, her oldest son, now drives for a living, she is also saving for a modest dowry for her daughter, Norma. She dreams of buying a new house in which the whole family can live. In the meantime, her work as a nanny enables Isadora's parents to devote themselves to their careers and avocations.

But Josephine's story is also one of wrenching global inequality. While Isadora enjoys the attention of three adults, Josephine's three children in Sri Lanka have been far less lucky. According to Vachani, Josephine's youngest child, Suminda, was two—Isadora's age—when his mother first left home to work in Saudi Arabia. Her middle child, Norma, was nine; her oldest son, Suresh, thirteen. From Saudi Arabia, Josephine found her way first to Kuwait, then to Greece. Except for one two-month trip home, she has lived apart from her children for ten years. She writes them weekly letters, seeking news of relatives, asking about school, and complaining that Norma doesn't write back.

Although Josephine left the children under her sister's supervision, the two youngest have shown signs of real distress. Norma has attempted suicide three times. Suminda, who was twelve when the film was made, boards in a grim, Dickensian orphanage that forbids talk during meals and showers. He visits his aunt on holidays. Although the oldest, Suresh, seems to be on good terms with his mother, Norma is tearful and sullen, and Suminda does poorly in school, picks quarrels, and otherwise seems withdrawn from the world. Still, at the end of the film, we see Josephine once again leave her three children in Sri Lanka to return to Isadora in Athens. For Josephine can either live with her children in desperate poverty or make money by living apart from them. Unlike her affluent First World employers, she cannot both live with her family and support it.

Thanks to the process we loosely call "globalization," women are on the move as never before in history. In images familiar to the West from television commercials for credit cards, cell phones, and airlines, female executives jet about the world, phoning home from luxury hotels and reuniting with eager children in airports. But we hear much less about a far more prodigious flow of female labor and energy: the increasing migration of millions of women from poor countries to rich ones, where they serve as nannies, maids, and sometimes sex workers. In the absence of help from male partners, many women have succeeded in tough "male world" careers only by turning over the care of their children, elderly parents, and homes to women from the Third World. This is the female underside of globalization, whereby millions of Josephines from poor countries in the south migrate to do the "women's work" of the north—work that affluent women are no longer able or willing to do. These migrant workers often leave their own children in the care of grandmothers, sisters, and sisters-in-law. Sometimes a young daughter is drawn out of school to care for her younger siblings.

This pattern of female migration reflects what could be called a worldwide gender revolution. In both rich and poor countries, fewer families can rely solely on a male breadwinner. In the United States, the earning power of most men has declined since 1970, and many women have gone out to "make up the difference." By one recent estimate, women were the sole, primary, or coequal earners in more than half of American families.[1] So the question arises: Who will take care of the children, the sick, the elderly? Who will make dinner and clean house?

While the European or American woman commutes to work an average twenty-eight minutes a day, many nannies from the Philippines, Sri Lanka, and India cross the globe to get to their jobs. Some female migrants from the Third World do find something like "liberation," or at least the chance to become independent breadwinners and to improve their children's material lives. Other less fortunate migrant women end up in the control of criminal employers—their passports stolen, their mobility blocked, forced to work without pay in brothels or to provide sex along with cleaning and child care services in affluent homes. But even in more typical cases, where benign employers pay wages on time, Third World migrant women achieve their success only by assuming the cast-off domestic roles of middle- and high-income women in the First World—roles that have been previously rejected, of course, by men. And their "commute" entails a cost we have yet to fully comprehend.

The migration of women from the Third World to do "women's work" in affluent countries has so far received little scholarly or media attention—for reasons that are easy enough to guess. First, many, though by no means all, of the new female migrant workers are women of color, and therefore subject to the racial "discounting" routinely experienced by, say, Algerians in France, Mexicans in the United States, and Asians in the United Kingdom. Add to racism the private "indoor" nature of so much of the new migrants' work. Unlike factory workers, who congregate in large numbers, or taxi drivers, who are visible on the street, nannies and maids are often hidden away, one or two at a time, behind closed doors in private homes. Because of the illegal nature of their work, most sex workers are even further concealed from public view.

At least in the case of nannies and maids, another factor contributes to the invisibility of migrant women and their work—one that, for their affluent employers, touches closer to home. The Western culture of individualism, which finds extreme expression in the United States, militates against acknowledging help or human interdependency of nearly any kind. Thus, in the time-pressed upper middle class, servants are no longer displayed as status symbols, decked out in white caps and aprons, but often remain in the background, or disappear when company comes. Furthermore, affluent careerwomen increasingly earn their status not through leisure, as they might have a century

ago, but by apparently "doing it all"—producing a full-time career, thriving children, a contented spouse, and a well-managed home. In order to preserve this illusion, domestic workers and nannies make the house hotel-room perfect, feed and bathe the children, cook and clean up—and then magically fade from sight.

The lifestyles of the First World are made possible by a global transfer of the services associated with a wife's traditional role—child care, homemaking, and sex—from poor countries to rich ones. To generalize and perhaps oversimplify: in an earlier phase of imperialism, northern countries extracted natural resources and agricultural products—rubber, metals, and sugar, for example—from lands they conquered and colonized. Today, while still relying on Third World countries for agricultural and industrial labor, the wealthy countries also seek to extract something harder to measure and quantify something that can look very much like love. Nannies like Josephine bring the distant families that employ them real maternal affection, no doubt enhanced by the heartbreaking absence of their own children in the poor countries they leave behind. Similarly, women who migrate from country to country to work as maids bring not only their muscle power but an attentiveness to detail and to the human relationships in the household that might otherwise have been invested in their own families. Sex workers offer the simulation of sexual and romantic love, or at least transient sexual companionship. It is as if the wealthy parts of the world are running short on precious emotional and sexual resources and have had to turn to poorer regions for fresh supplies.

Immigration statistics show huge numbers of women in motion, typically from poor countries to rich. Although the gross statistics give little clue as to the jobs women eventually take, there are reasons to infer that much of their work is "caring work," performed either in private homes or in institutional settings such as hospitals, hospices, child care centers, and nursing homes.

The statistics are, in many ways, frustrating. We have information on legal migrants but not on illegal migrants who, experts tell us, travel in equal if not greater numbers. Furthermore, many Third World countries lack data for past years, which makes it hard to trace trends over time; or they use varying methods of gathering information, which makes it hard to compare one country with another.

The governments of some sending countries actively encourage women to migrate in search of domestic jobs, reasoning that migrant women are more likely than their male counterparts to send their hard-earned wages to their families rather than spending the money on themselves. In general, women send home anywhere from half to nearly all of what they earn. These remittances have a significant impact on the lives of children, parents, siblings, and wider networks of kin—as well as on cash-strapped Third World governments. Thus, before Josephine left for Athens, a program sponsored by the Sri Lankan government taught her how to use a microwave oven, a vacuum cleaner, and an electric mixer.

Why this transfer of women's traditional services from poor to rich parts of the world? The reasons are, in a crude way, easy to guess. Women in Western countries have increasingly taken on paid work, and hence need others—paid domestics and caretakers for children and elderly people—to replace them.[2] For their part, women in poor countries have an obvious incentive to migrate: relative and absolute poverty. The "care deficit" that has emerged in the wealthier countries as women enter the workforce *pulls* migrants from the Third World and postcommunist nations; poverty *pushes* them.

Meanwhile, over the last thirty years, as the rich countries have grown much richer, the poor countries have become—in both absolute and relative terms—poorer. Global inequalities in wages are particularly striking. In Hong Kong, for instance, the wages of a Filipina domestic are about fifteen times the amount she could make as a school-teacher back in the Philippines. In addition, poor countries turning to the IMF or World Bank for loans are often forced to undertake measures of so-called structural adjustment, with disastrous results for the poor and especially for poor women and children. To qualify for loans, governments are usually required to devalue their currencies, which turns the hard currencies of rich countries into gold and the soft currencies of poor countries into straw. Structural adjustment programs also call for cuts in support for "noncompetitive industries," and for the reduction of public services such as health care and food subsidies for the poor. Citizens of poor countries, women as well as men, thus have a strong incentive to seek work in more fortunate parts of the world.

But it would be a mistake to attribute the globalization of women's work to a simple synergy of needs among women—one group, in the affluent countries, needing help and the other, in poor countries, needing jobs. For one thing, this formulation fails to account for the marked failure of First World governments to meet the needs created by its women's entry into the workforce. The downsized American—and to a lesser degree, western European—welfare state has become a "deadbeat dad." Unlike the rest of the industrialized world, the United States does not offer public child care for working mothers, nor does it ensure paid family and medical leave. Moreover, a series of state tax revolts in the 1980s reduced the number of hours public libraries were open and slashed school-enrichment and after-school programs. Europe did not experience anything comparable. Still, tens of millions of western European women are in the workforce who were not before—and there has been no proportionate expansion in public services.

Secondly, any view of the globalization of domestic work as simply an arrangement among women completely omits the role of men. Numerous studies, including some of our own, have shown that as American women took on paid employment, the men in their families did little to increase their contribution to the work of the home. With divorce, men frequently abdicate their child care responsibilities to their ex-wives. So, strictly speaking, the presence of immigrant nannies does not enable affluent women to enter the workforce; it enables affluent *men* to continue avoiding the second shift.

The men in wealthier countries are also, of course, directly responsible for the demand for immigrant sex workers—as well as for the sexual abuse of many migrant women who work as domestics.

Of course, not all sex workers migrate voluntarily. An alarming number of women and girls are trafficked by smugglers and sold into bondage. Because trafficking is illegal and secret, the numbers are hard to know with any certainty.

To an extent then, the globalization of child care and housework brings the ambitious and independent women of the world together: the career-oriented upper-middle-class woman of an affluent nation and the striving woman from a crumbling Third World or postcommunist economy. Only it does not bring them together in the way that second-wave feminists in affluent countries once liked to imagine—as sisters and allies struggling to achieve common goals. Instead, they come together as mistress and maid, employer and employee, across a great divide of privilege and opportunity.

This trend toward global redivision of women's traditional work throws new light on the entire process of globalization. Conventionally, it is the poorer countries that are thought to be dependent on the richer ones—a dependency symbolized by the huge debt they owe to global financial institutions. However, dependency also works in the other direction, and it is a dependency of a particularly intimate kind. Increasingly often, as affluent and middle-class families in the First World come to depend on migrants from poorer regions to provide child care, homemaking, and sexual services, a global relationship arises that in some ways mirrors the traditional relationship between the sexes. The First World takes on a role like that of the old-fashioned male in the family—pampered, entitled, unable to cook, clean, or find his socks. Poor countries take on a role like that of the traditional woman within the family—patient, nurturing, and self-denying. A division of labor feminists critiqued when it was "local" has now, metaphorically speaking, gone global.   [edited, 2001]

NOTES

1. See Ellen Galinsky and Dana Friedman, *Women: The New Providers*, Whirlpool Foundation Study, Part 1 (New York: Families and Work Institute, 1995), 37.
2. This "new" source of the Western demand for nannies, maids, child care, and elder-care workers does not, of course, account for the more status-oriented demand in the Persian Gulf states, where most affluent women don't work outside the home.

 56

9to5: Organizing Low-Wage Women

ELLEN BRAVO, GLORIA SANTA ANNA, and LINDA MERIC

When 9to5, National Association of Working Women, was founded in Boston, Massachusetts, in 1973, the terms "sexual harassment," "pay equity," and "family leave" did not yet exist or weren't widely used in the American vocabulary. But experiences with sexual degradation on the job, undervaluation of women's work, and lack of consideration for family responsibilities were common. So were the consequences, both financially and emotionally, for women workers.

The women who started 9to5 worked as secretaries in Boston's prestigious colleges. Karen Nussbaum and Ellen Cassedy were angry over the daily reminders from those with power that support and clerical staff were powerless. They attended a weekend workshop for office workers where women attendees listed the problems: low pay, limited advancement opportunity, little control over working conditions. A bank teller said she didn't make enough to get a loan from the bank she worked for. A clerk in a hospital couldn't afford to get sick; a university secretary couldn't afford to send her children to college. For the most part, workshop participants were proud of their skills and their work. Their goal was not so much to get out of office work as to upgrade it— to change the way they were treated and the way they were paid.

Ten women got together after that workshop and printed a short newsletter. In the mornings on the way to work they passed out the newsletters in front of subway stops and large office complexes. The response was overwhelming. The group called a meeting and 300 women showed up, bursting with grievances. In November 1973, they formed an association of working women and called it "9to5" after the usual hours of the business day.

The organization's early focus was on clerical workers, who represented the sphere of traditionally female jobs. The founders of 9to5 learned that one-third of all working women were employed in administrative support positions, then the largest and fastest-growing sector of the workforce. Many of the women in these jobs lived near or in poverty—yet they were not being reached by antipoverty groups, nor were they the focus of feminist organizations. At the time, most unions ignored them.

The movement began to grow. Women in other cities, motivated by experiences in the social movements of the 1960s as well as the huge influx of women into the workforce, formed similar groups. In the mid-1970s they joined together to make 9to5 a national association. Staff and volunteers answered questions about job problems and held workshops on how to ask for a raise, plan for retirement, and organize to win better treatment on the job. And many began to celebrate actual victories. Women reported asking for raises for the first time in their lives—and getting them. Groups of clerical workers met with managers to demand policy changes, including accurate job descriptions and job postings. Women in the publishing, insurance, and banking industries filed discrimination charges and won millions of dollars in back pay as well as new promotion and training programs. A few corporations, pressured by 9to5 activists, set aside money to help pay for employees' child care.

Inspired by the group, actress Jane Fonda decided to make a movie about the concerns of office workers and called it "Nine to Five," greatly increasing the group's visibility. The original movie plot involved murdering the boss. "That's not really on our agenda," 9to5 activists persuaded Fonda, who changed the story to a kidnapping and fantasies of murder—all based on interviews with 9to5 members.

Some actions brought quick results. When a bank in Milwaukee told its employees they would have to take over payments for dependent health coverage—the equivalent of a week's take-home pay—9to5 organized a demonstration outside the bank, with flyers and picket signs that read "Should banks care about kids?" Within days the bank gave the women a raise equivalent to the cost of the health premium. Other campaigns dragged on for years, such as the eventually successful efforts by the Delta 9to5 Network to gain recognition for their class action lawsuit against their employer. Workers for the airline had numerous complaints of discrimination against employees with physical disabilities, including the practice of identifying and firing employees with HIV.

From the early days, 9to5 leaders were interested in the intersection between the women's movement and the labor movement. Would unionization work for clerical workers? After some local efforts in Boston, 9to5 began exploring a relationship with an international union. In 1981, District 925 was born as an affiliate of Service Employees International Union. That group, which functioned as a separate organization from 9to5, National Association of Working Women, organized women office workers across the country to bargain collectively. Union women overall make higher wages than non-union employees and usually have greater benefits. In addition, a union contract can give protection on the job from arbitrary firing and recognition for seniority. So there were clear benefits to unionization for clerical workers. 9to5 found that working as a nonprofit association had advantages as well, particularly in involving women for whom unionization wasn't an immediate option and in attracting media visibility.

In addition to empowering women individually and in groups, 9to5 has helped change the policy environment. Issues that were trivialized when the group started became part of the public agenda. Using interviews with the media, actions, testimony, and educational programs, 9to5 members have also influenced the laws. They've watched years of hard work result in passage of the 1978 Pregnancy Discrimination Act, the 1991 Civil Rights Act, the 1993 Family and Medical Leave Act, and the 2009 Lilly Ledbetter Fair Pay Act on the federal level, as well as numerous state pay equity, family leave, and welfare laws, and some state statutes establishing protections for computer users.

The group's victories didn't escape the notice of management. In one midwestern city, the start of a 9to5 chapter was greeted with a seminar called "9to5: Not Just a Movie—How to Keep 9to5 Out of Your Office." The seminar planners made one miscalculation: they'd forgotten who opens the mail in most offices. Several secretaries mailed the notice to the fledgling 9to5 chapter, who sent someone undercover to the seminar—and then called a press conference immediately afterward to denounce the tactics of trying to prevent employees from organizing.

In the late 1980s, 9to5's agenda expanded to address the needs of those who work at the margins of the economy—part-time and temporary workers, women who cycle on and off welfare public assistance programs because they can't financially meet their families' basic needs. 9to5 activists with direct experience of welfare drew attention to the connections between women's problems in the workforce and their need to rely on public assistance. What happens to women who lose their jobs because of discrimination or lack of family leave, they asked? If you really want to reform the welfare system, they told policy makers, start by looking at the need to reform *work*. In the 1990s, 9to5 became involved in struggles for a living wage and state self-sufficiency standards. The group has also been prominent in struggles around removal of the social safety net. While working for short-term improvements, 9to5 points to the root causes of poverty and discrimination and the need for lasting solutions, as well as the need for alliances with other women's groups, labor, faith-based groups, and community organizations.

Technological developments added another issue: electronic surveillance. In 1989, 9to5 started a hotline to track computer users who were being monitored on the job by their employers, often without their awareness. Workers resented being spied on. Spying, one woman said, is what you do to the enemy.

Electronic surveillance wasn't the only reason people dialed the hotline. They called with every type of job problem, eager to find out if they had any rights. After the Clarence Thomas Supreme Court confirmation hearings in 1991, the line was deluged with calls about sexual harassment. Many had experienced the harassment years earlier. As one woman put it, "I've never told anyone before. I thought that's just what you had to put up with."

At 9to5, we have developed our Job Survival Helpline and our website—www.9to5.org—into organizing tools for the group; we publicize the helpline and website, and for many women it's the way they first learn about the organization and how they can get involved. We also organize by going where women are—welfare and unemployment offices, job training programs, child care centers—to reach them and get them involved in our efforts.

In 1996, 9to5 initiated its Election Connection project, a nonpartisan voter registration, education, and mobilization effort to increase the participation of low-wage women in the electoral and political arenas, where decisions are made every day that directly affect them. This aspect of 9to5's work has grown significantly, from leading collaborative voter education efforts reaching hundreds of thousands of voters in a state, to leading work to make Colorado the first state ever to defeat an anti-equal-opportunity measure at the ballot box, to passing a municipal paid sick days ballot initiative in Milwaukee with almost 70 percent of the vote.

Today 9to5 organizes around four main policy areas. Our national priority is winning family-flexible policies for low-wage workers. This includes expanding the federal Family Medical Leave Act to make it more accessible and affordable, passing the proposed federal Healthy Families Act to guarantee workers the right to earn seven paid sick days annually, winning affordable child care and family-supporting jobs with living wages and health care benefits, and state and local organizing on similar issues. Our work on economic security includes national- and state-level efforts to: raise the minimum wage; strengthen the safety net; win education and training for low-wage families; expand protections for temporary and part-time workers and curb abuses by temporary employment agencies; and win more consideration for family care in welfare and unemployment policies. 9to5's anti-discrimination work includes support for efforts to defend and promote affirmative action programs that provide equal opportunity for women and people of color, for efforts to strengthen pay equity and sexual harassment laws, to add sexual orientation and gender identity as categories protected from discrimination, and to link issues faced by immigrants with issues affecting low-wage women.

9to5 has worked hard to make visible the problems working women face and to identify solutions. The vehicle at times is humorous, such as the contest for many years to "Rate Your Job: The Good, the Bad and the Downright Unbelievable." Winners included the manager who sent his secretary to bars on Saturday nights with a beeper to save him the trouble of scoping out women he might like; the doctor who demanded his nurse return to the office after she found her children's babysitter had died in her home; and a chain store in California that cut a 15-year employee's hours, ending all her benefits and sick days. A similar 9to5 contest called on women to rate their employers' policies on a scorecard and nominate co-workers who've helped "Raise the Score" at work.

9to5 brings the voices of low-income women into national and local policy debates on issues that directly affect them. We have members in all 50 states, and staffed chapters in five cities. By winning state and local policy change, we build momentum for federal-level policy change. We develop all of our campaigns so that all members can take part— whether she's a single activist in her city or she's one member of a chapter of 300 members.

The group has always been multiracial and multicultural, with an emphasis on fighting all forms of discrimination. But for many years the highest-level staff were all or predominantly white. In the mid-1990s, with leadership from many parts of the organization, 9to5 set about examining how to become a genuinely anti-oppression organization. The process included structural changes such as adding caucuses to create safe spaces for women of color, lesbian/bisexual/transgender women, women living with disabilities, and women in poverty to come together. Board and staff have reviewed everything from our mission to our program to our methods of resolving internal conflict in order to make sure that the group consistently "walks its

talk." We've developed a more collaborative management team structure and flattened the organization overall to make it less hierarchical.

Over the years 9to5 has helped raise the *expectations* of low-wage women. Most women were already aware of problems on the job. As a popular 9to5 button put it, "My consciousness is fine— it's my *pay* that needs raising." Thanks to 9to5, women workers have gained greater awareness that they deserve better treatment. Yet many still *lack the belief that change is possible*—or the concept that they themselves are the real agents of change. 9to5 tries to address this gap by helping members recognize and expand their leadership skills, and above all by showing the difference that collective action can make. The organization popularizes success stories to demystify the change process, revealing the many small steps that lead to a victory.

Some of the women activists who have been involved in 9to5 include Kiki, a single mother in Pennsylvania who got tired of going to interviews for jobs she was qualified for only to be turned away because she was caring for her daughter. Today Kiki leads organizing to add protection against workplace discrimination based on parental and marital status to state law, and she hosts regular media presentations on women's workplace rights.

Rene, an activist in Milwaukee, Wisconsin, got involved telling her story as part of 9to5's efforts on welfare issues. Rene then organized other Wisconsin women to tell their stories to media and elected officials about the challenges of being a good parent and a good employee when you don't have access to paid sick days. And Rene was active in 9to5's successful campaign to collect 10,000 postcards from voters pledging to support candidates who support family-friendly workplace and public policies for low-wage women and families.

In Denver, 9to5 members Holly and Elaine registered new voters at welfare and unemployment offices, at low-income housing and child care centers, helping other low-wage women make the connection between the issues they face in everyday life and the decisions that elected officials at every level make. The women they registered participated in the political process by voting and, most importantly, by getting involved in 9to5's organizing campaigns to hold elected officials accountable after the elections.

Thirty-eight years after its founding, 9to5 is still transforming itself. We're taking on new issues, expanding public awareness using new media and social networking tools, and incorporating innovative new models and collaborations to reach and engage low-wage women in grassroots organizing, policy advocacy, leadership development, and social change. Above all, 9to5 strives to be a vehicle where working women can see that the particular pain they've experienced isn't personal—it's not about one bad manager or one set of policies or one election, but about power. Rather than striving simply to put more women into power, 9to5 aims to put more power in the hands of all women and all other groups who've been denied it.   [2011]

 57

Sexual Harassment

ELLEN BRAVO and LINDA MERIC

Though the law was passed in 1964 that today makes sexual harassment illegal, the term "sexual harassment" didn't exist until a full decade later.[1] Most women who were groped or flashed or subjected to sexual threats or lewd remarks or pornographic images didn't tell anyone—they considered it a bitter part of life on the job. That invisibility changed in October 1991 when the Supreme Court confirmation hearings for Clarence Thomas turned into a forum on whether or not he'd repeatedly made lurid sexual comments and displayed pornography to a former subordinate by the name of Anita Hill. Suddenly everyone knew the term "sexual harassment" and everyone had an opinion on it. Not surprisingly many of these opinions were based on erroneous assumptions. If the Thomas hearings functioned as a national teach-in on sexual harassment, the "teachers," members of the Senate Judiciary Committee, were woefully ignorant about the subject and spread a lot of confusion and misinformation— dismissing the charges as "fantasies," insisting the

truth in such cases is "always elusive," maintaining that pornography would be "a poor choice of seduction techniques."[2] Still, reporters published some useful information, including the toll-free number for 9to5, National Association of Working Women. In the two weeks surrounding the confirmation, more than 2,000 women called our hotline. In voices barely above a whisper or hoarse with rage, they told their stories. Most just wanted someone to know what they'd experienced; some of the incidents went back four decades.

Fast-forward to 1999. A teenager whose boss kept hitting on her in an after-school job sought help from "Dear Abby." "You have my permission to quit the job," Abby said, "but you have to tell your parents." In a follow-up letter to Abby, 9to5 clarified that the behavior wasn't just out of line, as Abby indicated, but against the law and gave our 800 number. This time nearly 1,000 people contacted us. In many ways their experiences differed from those earlier callers. The silence had been broken, as Anita Hill once told a *Sixty Minutes* reporter. More women were speaking out. Most callers knew about the law, although they weren't sure what that meant for their individual situations. Unlike eight years earlier, the vast majority had reported the harassment to higher-ups. So why were they calling? Because they couldn't get the behavior to stop. It wasn't that the harassers didn't "get" it—they were simply getting away with it.

The media feasts on stories of a first-grader kicked out of school for giving his classmate a peck on the cheek. But few people hear about the middle school boys who push a sixth-grader to her knees and shove her face against a boy's crotch, or the high school girl who told her teacher she probably wouldn't report harassment "because you never know, you could wind up dead." And girls aren't the only targets. The public seldom reads about boys who are ridiculed for being scrawny or hairless or sexually inexperienced. In school hallways, sexual harassment is as common as overloaded backpacks.

In fact, it's disturbingly common everywhere. Studies estimate that 35 to 50 percent of women are sexually harassed at some point in their careers.[3] A 2010 survey by Society for Human Resource Management found that sexual harassment complaints had gone up in 30 percent of workplaces in the past five years. Female troops fighting to bring safety to others often find themselves in harm's way from their fellow soldiers; 35 to 50 percent of women veterans report at least one incident of harassment in their careers, and many—30 percent in one survey—say they were victims of rape or attempted rape while on active duty.[4] Did they report the incidents to a ranking officer? Three in four said no—some because they didn't know how to do that, and some because they believed rape was "to be expected" in the military.[5] From the military to media moguls to mainline financial institutions, sexual harassment is the pesky little problem that won't go away.

Sexual harassment really isn't that complicated. It's behavior of a sexual nature at work or school that is unwanted, offensive, usually repeated, and makes it harder to keep your job or do your work. That means flirting and even off-color jokes may be fine, as long as they make someone feel good and not uncomfortable. Most people, from students to firefighters to top executives, have no trouble identifying the difference.

Some things, of course, don't have to be repeated in order to be over the line. You can't tell someone even once to "sleep with me or you're fired." You can never touch someone in a private part of the body (it's hard to say, "Sorry, I didn't know that would offend you"). Some comments are so vulgar, even one occasion may be too much. And if you're the boss, asking someone out on a date may cross a line because of the power imbalance—the subordinate may not feel free to say no.

No one has ever called 9to5's toll-free hotline to complain that someone said, "You look great." They call because they're being subjected to coarse, abusive, and sometimes threatening behavior and they can't make it stop. Compliments make people feel appreciated; sexual harassment makes them feel degraded. A compliment deteriorates into something else when it's *sexualized* by words or gestures or tone of voice.

Most people, including most men, aren't harassers. Some harassers behave badly without realizing it—like the guy who stayed in his seat during a break in our training and kept repeating, "Wow, I'm the person you're talking about. I must have offended a lot of people here and I had no idea." But most harassers know exactly what they're doing. When we say that harassment isn't about sex but about power, we mean that some people gain a sense of control and power by making others feel out of control and powerless. They've figured out what will make someone feel humiliated or embarrassed—or they simply don't care if what they feel like saying or viewing has that effect on others.

Typically harassers go after someone they perceive as vulnerable. Women of color tend to be harassed in higher numbers than white women, both because they're more likely to lack various measures of security on the job and because harassers are more likely to hold racist as well as sexist views, building on crude stereotypes of African-American women in particular as wanton and animalistic.[6] Also, women supervisors are more likely than non-supervisors to report being harassed, suggesting that coworkers, clients or supervisors who view women's power as illegitimate or easily undermined may turn to harassment as an "equalizer" against women supervisors.[7]

Employers don't do nearly enough, the law doesn't go far enough—what that amounts to is that many people, most but not all of them women, continue to experience harassment and the range of problems it drags with it, from economic loss to depression, anxiety, and stress-related physical health problems. Nearly half of women who complain of sexual harassment say they experience some form of retaliation.[8]

The stories differ enormously, but certain similarities emerge: the behavior is usually unexpected and takes people off guard. The person being harassed says "Stop" in many ways and keeps hoping that this episode will be the last, only to run into a new variation. Above all, sexual harassment is an *injury* with effects that last long afterward. As an Employee Assistance Program director put it, "Victims of sexual harassment are like victims of a crime. Except that crime victims get empathy—and sexual harassment victims get accusations and scrutiny. Crime victims may have broken locks or a broken arm—but a sexual harassment victim has a broken spirit for many years."

Sexual harassment doesn't occur in a vacuum. It's a particular way to devalue women, and it functions to keep them in an inferior status. The fact that most harassers are male has nothing to do with biology, but rather with socialization that celebrates sexual conquest, perpetuates a sexual double standard, and confuses toughness with aggression. Unfortunately, some women who've made it into powerful positions have adopted ruthless behaviors they associate with power—including sexual humiliation. Creating equality at work, eradicating behavior based on degradation and fear, will be a huge gain for men as well as women. Ending sexual harassment can happen only in a workplace that relies on trust, dignity, and respect for everyone.

To create the necessary climate, we also need public policy changes, including requiring employers to have a policy and make it known to employees; requiring them to provide sexual harassment awareness training to all employees; expanding funding for enforcement agencies to increase the speed and effectiveness of follow-through on complaints; curtailing the use of mandatory arbitration; and extending the statute of limitations.   [2011]

NOTES

1. The first documented use of the term was a 1975 conference at Cornell University that included a "Speak-Out on Sexual Harassment." Lin Farley and Catharine A. MacKinnon popularized the phrase in the titles of their books (1978 and 1979, respectively). Finally in 1980, after a number of public hearings, speakouts, court cases, and media articles about the subject, the Equal Employment Opportunity Commission (EEOC) developed a definition.
2. Statements during the hearing by Sens. Arlen Specter (R-PA), Alan Simpson (R-WY), and Orrin Hatch (R-UT), respectively.
3. Barbara Gutek and R. Done, "Sexual Harassment," in *Handbook of the Psychology of Women and Gender,* ed. R. K. Unger (New York: Wiley), 2001.
4. Testimony from Thomas Garthwaite, Veterans Affairs Deputy Undersecretary, before the house Veterans Affairs subcommittee in 1998. According to Garthwaite, nearly one in five female veterans seeking services from the department report that they've been sexually assaulted in the military. Reports of assault increased 20 percent in 1997. According to a *Sixty Minutes* report (February 20, 2005), women in the military are 10 times as likely to say they've experienced sexual assault as civilian women—3 in 100 compared to 3 in 1,000. The Miles Foundation, a nonprofit dedicated to stopping violence

against women in the military, refers to a recent survey that found that up to 30 percent experienced rape or attempted rape while on active duty. Of these, more than one in three said they'd been raped more than once; 14 percent reported having been gang raped.
5. Miles Foundation, http://hometown.aol.com//milesfdn/.
6. Anita Hill, among others, describes the way slaveholders justified the rape of slave women to continue and enlarge their holdings by casting them as "wanton, perverse, and animalistic, . . . unchaste and eagerly available." Hill, *Speaking Truth to Power* (New York: Doubleday, 1997), 280. Hill quotes a prize-winning 1925 essay by Marita O. Bonner, "On Being Young—a Woman—and Colored," which asked, "Why do they see a colored woman only as a gross collection of desires, all uncontrolled reaching out for their Apollos and Quasimodos with avid indiscrimination?" (ibid., 281).
7. Heather McLaughlin et al., "A Longitudinal Analysis of Gender, Power and Sexual Harassment in Young Adulthood," University of Minnesota, August 2009).
8. Ann C. Wendt and William M. Stonaker, "Sexual Harassment and Retaliation: A Double-Edged Sword," *Advanced Management Journal* (Autumn 2002).

🌿 58

Sexual Harassment and the Law

ARLENE FOY REYNOLDS

Courts reference the Civil Rights Act of 1964 in their decisions on sexual harassment, but the phrase "sexual harassment" is not found in the law itself. Sexual harassment as a means of sex discrimination is a concept that began in feminist analysis and crossed over into legal analysis through judicial interpretation of Title VII of the Act over the course of several decades.

Title VII is aimed at achieving "equal employment opportunity" by prohibiting discrimination in employment based on race, color, religion, sex and national origin. The prohibition against sex discrimination was almost accidental in that it was added to the law at the eleventh hour by a Southern Congressman hoping to derail the bill. Nevertheless, having passed the Equal Pay Act in the prior year, Congress adopted this nondiscrimination law with sex as a protected class. No one at the time could have foreseen how far-reaching that legislation would be in changing the dynamics between men and women at work.

Among the many unforeseen consequences of Title VII were complaints by women that the jobs now open to them had strings attached. Were the sexual advances that women complained of a form of discrimination or just the natural result of males and females working together? The first federal sexual harassment lawsuit (*Barnes v. Train*, 1974) was initially dismissed on the grounds that the elimination of Paulette Barnes's position by her supervisor because she refused to have sex with him was not sex discrimination but the reasonable response of a man who had had his sexual advances rejected. But Paulette Barnes was only one of many woman who complained of this kind of treatment, indicating that something other than normal workplace social interaction was occurring, and in 1977, the case (now *Barnes v. Costle*) was reversed and Paulette Barnes was awarded $18,000 in back pay.

In 1979, Catherine MacKinnon, in *Sexual Harassment of Working Women: A Case of Sex Discrimination,* identified sexual harassment as an issue of power rather than sex or sexual attraction and set the foundation for legal interpretations that followed. In 1980, given enough evidence that "sexual harassment" was a way of keeping women in their place, the Equal Employment Opportunity Commission used concepts introduced by MacKinnon to define sexual harassment in its guidelines to the courts. While not binding on the courts, the definition described the circumstances under which an employer might be held liable for permitting sexual harassment in the workplace.

One type of sexual harassment was called "quid pro quo" ("this for that"), borrowing MacKinnon's phrase, and referred to unwelcome sexual advances or requests for sexual favors when "submission to such conduct is made either explicitly or implicitly a term or condition of an individual's employment," or "submission to or rejection of such conduct by an individual is used as a basis for employment decisions affecting such individual." The other type of sexual harassment was termed "hostile work environment," when sexual images,

gestures or comments "have the purpose or effect of unreasonably interfering with an individual's work performance or creating an intimidating, hostile or offensive working environment." *Barnes v. Costle* had shown that the courts did regard demands for sexual favors in exchange for a job or promotion to be a form of sex discrimination, but would courts accept the concept of "hostile environment"?

In 1986, in the case of *Meritor Savings Bank v. Vinson*, the U.S. Supreme Court answered this question. The case involved Mechelle Vinson, whose supervisor, Sidney Taylor subjected her to sexual harassment for four years after which Ms. Vinson went out on sick leave and, when she did not return at the end of it, she was terminated. Ms. Vinson then filed suit against the bank charging that she was incapacitated and unable to return to work because of Mr. Taylor's behavior. This behavior included fondling Ms. Vinson in the presence of other employees, following her into the women's restroom at work when she was there alone, engaging her in sexual intercourse during and after working hours and, on several occasions, forcibly raping her. *Meritor v. Vinson* gave the court an opportunity to examine the "hostile environment" definition of sexual harassment since Ms. Vinson had not been denied promotions and she did not charge Mr. Taylor with conditioning her employment on her submitting to his advances. Could there be discrimination without any "tangible loss"? The U.S. Supreme Court held that Congress intended "terms, conditions, or privileges of employment" to include "the entire spectrum of disparate treatment of men and women" and held, unanimously, "that a claim of 'hostile environment' sexual discrimination is actionable under Title VII." In 1993, in *Harris v. Forklift Systems,* the Court ruled that an environment permeated with sexual innuendo and insults to women constituted sexual harassment, even when there had been no psychological or economic harm. In the words of Justice Sandra Day O'Connor, "Title VII comes into play before the harassing conduct leads to a nervous breakdown."

In 1998, the Court chose to take on several sexual harassment cases and more closely define the

Unions Benefit Working Women

As we enter the second decade of the twenty-first century, the ability to organize by workers is under threat everywhere. However, studies and surveys conducted by major economic organizations demonstrate the powerful positive impact of unionization on women's lives. Women join unions in disproportionately large numbers, and it has been predicted that by 2047 they will be the majority of unionized workers. Unionized women earn more than nonunion women workers. In 2010, union women earned 34 percent more than nonunion women. Women also benefit from unionization because union workers are more likely to have health insurance, pension plans, and short-term disability benefits. In 2010, 94 percent of union workers in the private sector had jobs providing access to medical care benefits, compared with only 64 percent of nonunion workers. Unionization raises the likelihood of having a pension by almost 25 percent, which is actually larger than the corresponding effects of obtaining a four-year college degree. Thirty-four percent of union workers have access to defined-benefit pension plans, compared with 11 percent of nonunion workers. (Defined-benefit plans are federally insured and provide a guaranteed monthly pension amount. They are better for workers than defined contribution plans, such as 401K plans, in which the benefit amount depends on how well the underlying investments perform.) Additionally, 47 percent of union workers have short-term disability benefits, while only 34 percent of nonunion workers have such benefits.

Sources: U.S. Department of Labor, Bureau of Labor Statistics, *Union Members—2010, Jan. 21, 2011*; U.S. Department of Labor, naunion/why/uniondifference/uniondiff4.cfm; Center for Economic and Policy Research, http://www.cepr.net/documents/publications/benefits-of-unions.pdf (February 2010).

employer's responsibility under the law. As Justice Souter wrote for the (7-2) majority in *Faragher v. City of Boca Raton,* "Everyone knows by now that sexual harassment is a common problem in the American workplace." Beth Ann Faragher, a college student and one of the few females working as a lifeguard for the City of Boca Raton, reported that male supervisors regularly propositioned female lifeguards for sex, touched them in ways that were offensive, and made lewd and demeaning comments about women. Ms. Faragher complained to one of her supervisors about the treatment but he did not take any measures to see that the behavior stopped. The City claimed in its defense that it had a written sexual harassment policy and that Ms. Faragher failed to use it, but the City had not distributed the policy to workers at the beach and so the lifeguards and their supervisors were unaware of its existence. In a 7-2 decision, the Court held that an employer is liable for the hostile work environment created by a supervisor and that there is automatic liability to the employer if a subordinate suffers a "tangible employment action" as a result of sexual harassment. Ms. Faragher had not suffered a "tangible employment action" but was awarded the damages that she had requested: $1.

In two other decisions that year, the Supreme Court laid out a new analysis. In place of "quid pro quo" sexual harassment was the concept of a "tangible employment action" (demotion, denial of promotion, termination, etc.) against a subordinate for either refusing sexual advances or for objecting to a hostile environment created by a supervisor. In the presence of a "tangible employment action" related to sexual harassment, the employer would have no defense against liability. But if no tangible employment action had been taken, then an employer could attempt an "affirmative defense" by showing that it had exercised reasonable care to prevent sexual harassment in the workplace and that the employee had unreasonably failed to take advantage of the remedies available. In 1998, the Court also decided, in *Oncale v. Sundowner Offshore Services,* that "discriminatory intimidation, ridicule and insult" against a member of one's own sex constituted a violation of Title VII and was sexual harassment.

When the Civil Rights Act of 1964 was passed, Congress did not envision the ways in which sex discrimination permeated the workplace. The Supreme Court has responded with remarkable consistency in holding that the employer has a responsibility to maintain a workplace free of sexual harassment and, after 1998, most employers have put in place written sexual harassment policies in order to be able to claim an "affirmative defense" if a charge of sexual harassment is made against them. This does not mean that sexual harassment has vanished from the workplace, but the courts have made significant progress in creating the legal framework for challenging this behavior.   [2006]

 59

In Case of Sexual Harassment: A Guide for Women Students

BERNICE SANDLER

MYTHS ABOUT SEXUAL HARASSMENT

Myth: Sexual harassment only happens to women who are provocatively dressed.

Fact: Sexual harassment can happen to anyone, no matter how she dresses.

Myth: If the women had only said "NO" to the harasser, he would have stopped immediately.

Fact: Many harassers are told "NO" repeatedly and it does no good. NO is too often heard as YES.

Myth: If a woman ignores sexual harassment, it will go away.

Fact: No, it won't. Generally, the harasser is a repeat offender who will not stop on his own. Ignoring it may be seen as assent or encouragement.

Myth: All men are harassers.

Fact: No, only a few men harass. Usually there is a pattern of harassment: one man harasses a number of women either sequentially or simultaneously, or both.

Myth: Sexual harassment is harmless. Women who object have no sense of humor.

Fact: Harassment is humiliating and degrading. It undermines school careers and often threatens economic livelihood. No one should have to endure humiliation with a smile.

Myth: Sexual harassment affects only a few people.

Fact: Surveys on campus show that up to 30 percent of all female college students experience some form of sexual harassment. Some surveys of women in the working world have shown that as many as 70 percent have been sexually harassed in some way.

WHAT YOU CAN DO ABOUT SEXUAL HARASSMENT

Ignoring sexual harassment does not make it go away. Indeed, it may make it worse because the harasser may misinterpret no response as approval of his behavior. However, there are things you can do, from informal strategies to formal ones. Here are some of your options.

• Know your rights. Sexual harassment is illegal in many instances. Your college or university may also have specific policies prohibiting faculty and staff from sexually harassing students and employees. Familiarize yourself with these policies. (For example, you can ask the Dean of Students if there is a policy.)

• Speak up at the time. Be sure to say "NO" clearly, firmly and without smiling. This is not a time to be polite or vague. (For example, you can say, "I don't like what you are doing," or "Please stop—you are making me very uncomfortable.") There is a chance—albeit small—that the harasser did not realize that his behavior was offensive to you. Additionally, if you decide to file charges at a later date, it is sometimes helpful, but not essential, to have objected to the behavior.

• Keep records, such as a journal and any letters or notes received. Note the dates, places, times, witnesses and the nature of the harassment—what he said and did and how you responded.

• Tell someone, such as fellow students or co-workers. Find out if others have been harassed by the same person and if they will support you should you decide to take action. Sharing your concern helps to avoid isolation and the tendency to blame yourself. Sexual harassment incidents are usually not isolated; most sexual harassers have typically harassed several or many people.

• Identify an advocate, perhaps a counselor, who can give you emotional support as well as help and information about both informal and formal institutional procedures.

• Write a letter. Many people have successfully stopped sexual harassment by writing a special kind of letter to the harasser. This letter should be polite, low-key and detailed, and consists of three parts:

  • Part I is a factual account of what has happened, without any evaluation, as seen by the writer. It should be as detailed as possible with dates, places, and a description of the incident(s). (For example, "Last week at the department party you asked me to go to bed with you." Or "On Oct. 21, when I came to you for advice on my test, you patted my knee and tried to touch my breast.")

  • Part II describes how the writer feels about the events described in Part I, such as misery, dismay, distrust, and revulsion. (For example, "My stomach turns to knots when I come to class," or "I'm disgusted when I look at you.")

  • Part III consists of what the writer wants to happen next. This part may be very short, since most writers usually just want the behavior to stop. (For example, "I don't ever want you to touch me again or to make remarks about my sexuality," or "Please withdraw my last evaluation until we can work out a fair one.")

The letter should be delivered either in person or by registered or certified mail. Copies are not sent to campus officers or the press. The writer should keep at least one copy of the letter. (In the unlikely event that it fails to achieve its purpose, the letter can later be used to document retaliation or in support of a formal complaint or lawsuit.)

In most cases, the harasser is often astonished that his behavior is viewed in the way the writer sees it. He may also be fearful of a formal charge, and worry about who else has seen the letter. The letter also seems to be far more powerful than a verbal request—even those who may have ignored verbal requests to stop, often respond differently when the request is put into writing. The recipient of the letter rarely writes back; usually he just stops the sexual harassment immediately, and typically does not harass anyone else either.

Occasionally the harasser may want to apologize or discuss the situation. You don't need to discuss it if you don't want to—you can simply reiterate that you want the behavior to stop and it's not necessary to discuss it.

There are many advantages to writing a letter:

• It helps the victim regain a sense of being in control of the situation;

• it often avoids formal charges and a public confrontation;

• it keeps the incident(s) confidential;

• it provides the harasser with a new perspective on his behavior;

• it may minimize or prevent retaliation against the writer;

• it is not necessary to address questions such as legality, confidentiality, evidence and due process; and

• it usually works.   [1992]

60

"Each Day I Go Home with a New Wound in My Heart"

MIRIAM CHING YOON LOUIE

On June 6, 1998, workers, their supporters, and Korean Immigrant Workers Advocates (KIWA) organizers embarked on a massive march demanding justice for Korean and Latino restaurant workers in Los Angeles' Koreatown. Snaking through mini-malls filled with surprised shoppers, the marchers' stomachs soon growled as the mouth-watering smells of *kalbi, bulgogi, kimchee, mae-un tang, dwen-jang jikae,* and *pa-chun* wafted out the doors of their favorite restaurants. The march ended in front of the Shogun Sushi Restaurant where workers were paid just $2 an hour. Koreatown restaurant worker Han Hee Jin surged to the front of the rally and delivered a fiery speech. Just a week before, her boss fired her from a *naeng myon* [cold noodle] specialty restaurant when she complained about having to simultaneously wait tables, cook, and wash dishes. Han told the marchers,

> Even though we need each other, owners always treat workers with suspicion. And yet employers want to be treated as Master. Even in a small restaurant, we are always forced to call employers, "Yes, Boss," "Yes, Madam," while we are subjected to degrading comments such as "you are only a servant" or "you are made for carrying a tray all your life" or "you, waitress bitch." After seven years of being subjected to these and more degrading remarks, I stand here today to state that we will not tolerate them anymore.[1]

Han's impassioned appeal signaled a major new twist in a drama unfolding within the emerging Korean community. Despite blacklisting and censorship, women like Han have begun to break the silence and stand up for their rights. Like their Chinese and Mexican counterparts, many Korean immigrant women workers worked in global assembly line, service, and finance industry jobs before coming to the United States. As young women they served as the foot soldiers in South Korea's rapid march to industrialization and Four Dragon status.[2] They labored under the shadow of South Korea's militarized and global-ized sex industry and within niches of the informal economy that sprang up from the ruins of their war-ravaged country. After immigrating, many Korean immigrant women found work in factories like those they had worked in at home; others started on the lowest rungs of the service industry, especially within the ethnic enclave economy that

mushroomed with the jump in Korean immigration after 1965. Some brought their experiences with the independent workers movement in South Korea. . . .

ORGANIZING WOMEN, RELEASING HAN

Immigrant Korean women workers confronted gender and class oppression not only at their workplaces, but also within their families and the Korean community. In the course of organizing, the women began to develop a women's support network, and incorporate gender-specific education campaigns and services into their organizing work.

Despite Korean women's long work hours in the United States, they are still expected to perform almost all the domestic chores in their homes, while their husbands cope with either long hours or underemployment and a big drop in economic and social status, connections, and stability.[3] This creates a volatile environment in which alcoholism and domestic violence often erupt. A 2000 community needs assessment survey on the problem of domestic violence conducted by Shimtuh, the Korean Domestic Violence Program, found that 42 percent of the 347 respondents said that they knew of a Korean woman who had experienced physical violence from a husband or boyfriend, while 50 percent knew of a Korean woman who had experienced regular emotional abuse, and 33 percent reported that their fathers had hit their mothers at least once.[4]

The combined gender and class oppression women face became evident during a sharing session held in April 1999 among some Korean women workers (who wish to remain anonymous). The women began by drawing charts plotting the highs and lows of their lives. One woman described the collapse of her husband's business, into which she had poured all of her labor and for which she had borrowed money from her family. She told of how her husband then fled to the United States, leaving her to close down the business and pay off its debts by herself. Once she arrived in the United States to start life over again, she found herself having to fight an abusive boss.[5]

Another woman, "Mrs. H.," told of how she and her husband, poor and hungry while struggling to survive in Korea, had planned a family suicide. They would drown themselves by jumping into the river while holding their kids. But she couldn't bear to pass the baby over the fence. Then her husband bolted. She searched for him for days. Since his body never turned up in the river, she began to suspect that he was still alive. He later appeared, and they eventually migrated to the United States with their children. Laughing bitterly and joking to make light of her story, she described how she went through many hardships because of her husband's drinking and gambling and her family's extreme poverty. Later when another woman recounted being beaten black and blue by her husband, Mrs. H. shouted out, "That's why I never left him in spite of everything; he never beat me."[6]

These stories released a flood of pent-up anguish, resentment, and tears, mixed with exclamations of "*sei sang eh!* [what is this world coming to]" and other expressions of shock, sympathy, and support. Sometimes the women's faces glistened with tears; at other moments the room erupted in peals of laughter as they teased each other about the absurdity of it all.

The women workers' consciousness raising session combined popular education methodology and the cathartic release of *han*.[7] *Han* is the Korean term used to describe accumulated suffering, sadness, and hardship. According to psychiatrist Luke Kim, *han* is an "individual and collective emotive state of Koreans, involving feelings of anger, rage, grudge, resignation, hate and revenge. [It is a] form of victimization syndrome of Korean people, with feelings of injustice and indignation suppressed and endured."[8] The "down side" of *han* is the sadness, oppression, injustice, colonialism, war, tragedy, and cruel twists of fate suffered by Korean people. But the sharing of *han* between the women workers expresses the "up side" of *han*, a socially and culturally shared understanding that acknowledges and articulates Korean women's pent-up suffering, and *therefore*, facilitates and allows for its release through a collective process of support, solidarity, and sisterhood.

JOINING THE MOVEMENT

Korean women workers joined the movement when they reached the point when they could no longer tolerate their bosses' abuses. Some women organized together with their co-workers, while others started out fighting because of an individual grievance. Because of the close-knit character of the Korean community and ethnic enclave, women's decisions to stand up for their rights had immediate consequences. Restaurant owners quickly blacklisted some of the first Korean women restaurant workers who dared speak out. In addition to the bosses' attacks, some women endured censorship from their ministers and the ethnic media, and pressure from worried co-workers and family members who feared they would never be able to work in Koreatown again.

Chu Mi Hee worked at Koreatown's largest restaurant, Siyeon, as a waitress for two years. In 1996, she was fired and blacklisted after participating in a struggle against the boss.

> *Him dul ot jiyo!* [It was a strain, it was very hard] to work there. If things did not go his way, he [the boss] would use his fists. He would kick things, even people. The woman owner was about the same. She didn't use her fists, but she did the same thing with her words. They treated the workers very inhumanely. At first about 36 people worked there. . . . Then they started firing people they didn't like, and also to cut their labor costs. That's when our Mexican *chinku* [friends] started opening relations with KIWA. . . . Without me knowing, the owners found out and fired our Mexican friends.
>
> We wanted to be treated with dignity and not have to work under physical and verbal abuse. Most of the Mexican workers and Korean waitresses united. With KIWA's help, we leafleted the customers. We made a wildcat strike that lasted one hour and demanded that the original promises be kept that the owners made when they opened. . . . I hoped that protesting, passing out leaflets, talking to people, all of these things would bring about good results. I feel that the things we were demanding were very basic. We were not asking for anything outrageous.[9]

After she was fired by Siyeon for fighting for a collective bargaining agreement, she took a new job at a coffee shop called Prince, which was owned by a cousin of one of the Siyeon owners. She was disoriented when Prince's manager and then her minister called her at home.

> I was awakened by a phone call from the minister of the church where the manager and I went. The minister said, "I heard that you are suing [Siyeon] on behalf of the workers. How can you do such a childish thing?" The minister said he had gotten a phone call from the [Prince] manager and heard all about what was going on and that it was hard for me to continue working at [Prince]. Then I knew that I was being blacklisted.
>
> When the Siyeon owner found out that I worked at Prince, he went to the Prince owner and asked, "How can you hire a person like that?" The Prince owner said, "None of your business." But the Prince owner wanted to consult with the manager because she was the one who referred me to Prince. The manager told me, "I'm very disappointed in you. How could you [participate in the Siyeon dispute]? Koreatown is really small. It's going to be hard for you to find another job." I demanded [that she] let me talk to the owner directly. She [the manager] said, "Let's all quit." At that time I felt really disappointed in humanity. After that incident I couldn't go back to church and face the [manager]. I found another job after resting for a while. To find a new job, I had to show my work experience, but to show my experience I had to talk about Siyeon. So I was afraid to go to places to look for work.[10]

The Siyeon workers had successfully negotiated a collective bargaining agreement in February and March of 1996, establishing wage scales, meal times, and the conditions for discharge, but they had to keep fighting for compliance. KIWA helped file lawsuits against the Siyeon and Prince operatives for firing and blacklisting Chu. On February 15, 1997, however, Siyeon went out of business and the case was subsequently dropped.[11]

Paek Young Hee worked 12 hours a day, 6 days a week, but her boss at Ho Dong restaurant blacklisted her for demanding unpaid wages in 1996. As with Chu, the owners' association contacted Paek's next boss to get her fired.[12] Luckily, her new boss told her what had happened.

> One day when I was working at my new job, the owner called me into the office and asked why did I go against the restaurant where I was fired. I told him that it was only because I was not paid my rightful wage. The owner confessed that he had received a call from the Korean Restaurant Owners Association who told the owner to let me go because I was a troublemaker. But the owner ended up telling me that I was a great worker and that they needed me and were not going to fire me. I am still working at this restaurant now.[13]

Paek weathered a lot of criticism because she spoke up about the wages she was owed and how she was fired and blacklisted.

> I am very grateful because KIWA helps poor people who are powerless. I try to be active and help out all that I can. . . . But I feel a little ashamed. I feel like I have done something that I should not have done. All the people around me are telling me, "Why are you stabbing somebody from your own nationality? If they didn't pay you that well, you should have just accepted it, and left it at that. Why did you have to take these actions?" I tell them, "Why shouldn't I be paid for the work that I did?" But at the same time they give me dirty looks like I did something wrong.
>
> Both my children and my husband were not at all supportive of my actions . . . especially after they saw the news on the TV. The children said that the fact that I came out on TV might have a negative impact on their future as students. My husband was embarrassed because all his co-workers were talking about it. They were saying it was a disgrace. . . . Although I was criticized, . . . I feel that it was not right to let the owner of the restaurant do what she did to me and the other people. I did it to stop her from continuing to do these things to people.[14]

SPEAKING UP FOR THE POWERLESS

Immigrant women workers have said *ka ja!* [let's go!] and begun to write a new chapter in

Korean-American history. This story begins with their labor struggles in their homeland and continues in the kitchens, dining rooms, hotels, factories, and on the picket lines of inner city barrios, tossed together like *chap chae* [mixed vegetables and noodles] with their Mexican and Central American immigrant co-workers. They have endured long hours, low wages, sexual harassment, age discrimination, insults, firings, blacklisting, censorship, criticism, and fear. They have been urged to be patient, endure, and keep their mouths shut. Yet these pioneers are taking a stand and beginning to change the climate and thinking within the community, winning respect for women workers' human rights, building multiracial solidarity, opening up new spaces for democracy, and securing more justice within the Korean and other communities of color within the United States.

The November 14, 1998 community town hall meeting of Koreatown restaurant workers demanding "justice, dignity, and democracy" conveyed a tumultuous mix of images, languages, and emotions. An angry gauntlet of restaurant owners taunted all seeking to enter the towering union hall hosting the gathering. The owners' ringleader boasted that he learned how to picket after being picketed by workers and KIWA. Inside the hall the atmosphere was simultaneously welcoming, protective, and edgy as Korean and Mexican restaurant workers delivered testimony to elected officials, government enforcement agencies, Korean, Spanish, and English language press, community supporters, and family members. After describing the abusive behavior by her ex-bosses, Kyung Park said:

> I go home every day with a new wound in my heart because of all the hurtful things that happen at work. I am a wife and mother at home, but at work, I am viewed sometimes as a servant, sometimes as a thief. This is the reality of restaurant workers. Not being able to get paid as we are supposed (to) and suffering through each day facing insults and curses—this is what makes up the lives of restaurant workers in Koreatown. . . . I would like to say to all the government leaders, media, workers, and all the other members of the audience present today: it is

very possible that by coming forward today I may face the possibility of losing my job. But I have chosen to come to this gathering today in spite of all that. This is because I believe that unless someone speaks up for the rights of the powerless workers in Koreatown, we would have no choice but to go on living with bruises in our hearts.[15]   [2001]

NOTES

1. Han Hee Jin, Speech delivered in front of Shogun Sushi, Koreatown, Los Angeles, June 6, 1998.
2. Called the "Four Dragons," "Four Tigers," or the East Asian Newly Industrialized Countries (NICs), South Korea, Taiwan, Singapore, and Hong Kong experienced rapid economic growth since the 1960s based on their special relationship with the United States and Japan, and a system of state-directed capitalist development (Bello, Walden & Stephanie Rosenfeld. 1990. *Dragons in distress: Asia's miracle economies in crisis*. San Francisco: Insititute of Food and Development Policy), 1–16.
3. Song, Young I & Ailee Moon. (ed.). 1998. *Korean American Women: From Tradition to Modern Feminism*. Westport: Praeger.
4. Shimtuh, 2000. See also Korean American Coalition to End Domestic Abuse, 1999; and Song and Moon, 1998b: 162–63. Song and Moon's 1987 study that found that 60 percent of Korean immigrant women reported having been battered by their spouses.
5. Meeting of Koreatown restaurant workers, April 3, 1999.
6. Meeting of Koreatown restaurant workers, April 3, 1999.
7. Popular education is the process through which people process direct lived experiences as the knowledge base from which to make connections with and analyze broader relations in the society and economy. See Freire, 1990; Bell et al., 1990.
8. Luke I. Kim, 1991, cited in Kim-Goh, 1998:230. The cultural sector of the 1980s *minjung* movement helped reclaim and transform the practice of kut and *han puri*, Korean shamanistic exorcism and *han* release rituals, such as those dedicated to the memory of the Comfort Women and the martyrs of the Kwangju Massacre. Luke Kim says that Korean psychotherapists and theologians have grown more interested in exploring the concept of *han* as it sheds light on problems facing their clients and parishioners (Luke I. Kim, 1998:219).
9. Interview with Chu Mi Hee, March 25, 1997.
10. Interview with Chu Mi Hee, March 25, 1997.
11. Korean Immigrants Workers Advocates. 1997. *Industry wide organizing in Korea town restaurants*. KIWA, News 5, pp 7–9.
12. Korean Immigrants Workers Advocates, 1996. *KIWA Programs*. KIWA News 6, pp 5–7.
13. Interview with Paek Young Hee, March 27, 1997.
14. Interview with Paek Young Hee, March 27, 1997.
15. Korean Immigrants Workers Advocates. 1998. *Worker Testimonies*. Community Town Hall Meeting. Mov 14, Los Angeles: KIWA.

61

Women

ALICE WALKER

They were women then
My mama's generation
Husky of voice—Stout of
Step
With fists as well as
Hands
How they battered down
Doors
And ironed
Starched white

Shirts
How they led
Armies
Headragged Generals
Across mined
Fields
Booby-trapped
Kitchens
To discover books

Desks
A place for us
How they knew what we
Must know
Without knowing a page
Of it
Themselves   [1974]

Women, the Law, and Social Policy

Laws and social policies shape women's experience of all institutions in our society. Although more women have entered the legal profession, legislatures, and government agencies in recent years, sexism continues to permeate the policies and practices of these institutions and those that they affect.

In the first article, Kathleen O'Keefe and Liann Snykus describe the ways that the legal system has constrained women and the ways feminists have used the law to fight for civil rights in the area of work. Despite legal advances on issues such as reproduction, sexuality, marriage, domestic violence, and rape, countervailing challenges are strong. The authors write, "While progress has been made and social concerns that were considered radical a generation ago are now mainstream, an increasingly conservative Supreme Court, the right wing's determination to undo the progress that women have made . . . require a renewed commitment to address legal sex discrimination." Similarly on a global scale, women's status under the law is oppressive in many countries. Jessica Neuwirth describes some examples of those conditions as well as recent progress to change them.

Sexism pervades social policies that shape women's lives as well. Compared to European countries, for example, the United States has few governmental supports, like child and maternal benefits, that protect mothers and children from poverty. In "How to Bring Children Up Without Putting Women Down," Ann Crittenden describes policies that employers could effect that would redesign work around parents' needs, as well as policies the government could enact to replace the welfare state with a caring state supportive of women.

The dual role women workers are expected to take on without support, combined with inequities in the workplace, trap many women in poverty. When women had children and couldn't find work that paid enough to support their families and pay for child care, they often had to turn to welfare. A former welfare recipient, Rita Henley Jensen, describes the realities of being a woman on welfare. She shows how in the early 1970s that system provided her a way out, and how and why it doesn't now. In "The New Antipoverty Regime: Same Single-Mother Poverty Problems," Randy Albelda describes the welfare "reform" legislation of 1996, pointing out the ways TANF (Temporary Aid to Needy Families) worsens the lives of women in poverty, and concluding with suggestions for reforms that would work. Tonya Mitchell's description of the painful effect of this legislation on her hopes for earning a college degree as a single, black mother on welfare stands in sharp contrast to Rita Henley Jensen's experience before "welfare reform." She shows how women of color on welfare rolls are especially vulnerable to the negative impacts of these policies.

Feminist economist Susan Feiner explains how economic policy hurts women. The tax structure, for example, disadvantages women and other working people and privileges wealthy corporations and men. Some social policies, however, have positively affected women, among them Title IX, a federal law passed in 1972 prohibiting sex discrimination in education. Using Title IX, women have taken advantage of many more opportunities to participate in sports, as Pat Griffin describes. It has opened other doors, such as a 2005 Supreme Court decision that enables teachers and coaches to turn to the court under Title IX if they are fired in retaliation for speaking out about sex discrimination. People concerned about equity need to continually defend the advances we have made.

🌿 62

Women and the Law: Successes, Setbacks, and Unfinished Business

KATHLEEN O'KEEFE
and LIANN O. S. SNYKUS

The laws of the United States have historically discriminated against women. Such discrimination was "enforced" by societal institutions that required, promoted, and excused legally condoned discrimination against women on an individual basis and as a group in both the public and the private spheres. Issues commonly associated with notions of women's legal rights include the right to bodily integrity and reproductive autonomy; to vote; to hold public office; to work; to fair wages and comparable pay; to own property; to education; to serve in the military; to enter into legal contracts; and to enjoy marital, parental, and religious rights. Many of these legal rights were unheard of when the United States was founded and, in some instances, have been recognized in law only relatively recently. Other legal rights, such as marriage equality, are still not recognized nationwide. Moreover, despite the progress that has been made and the existing laws that have changed women's legal status, historical and cultural prejudices continue to have a profound effect on the lives of women both publicly and privately.

The United States Constitution, as it was originally written, provided no legal rights to women, reflecting the view that women were not suited to the public demands of citizenship and should confine their lives to the private sphere of the home. Women were legally and politically invisible, unable to hold public office or vote, and dependent on men for their social and legal identity. This legal and political invisibility in the early American colonies stemmed from the English policy of "coverture." In 1765, Judge William Blackstone, an influential English judge, described coverture by stating that after marriage "the husband and wife are one person in law: that is, the very being or legal existence of the woman is suspended during the marriage, or at least is incorporated and consolidated into that of the husband."[1] Under coverture, a married woman could not own property, sign legal documents, or enter into contracts. She was required to obtain her husband's permission to pursue an education and to work and, if she was permitted to work, to relinquish her wages to her husband. She also had no rights to her children.

INDIVIDUALISM AND WOMEN'S CHANGING STATUS IN THE PUBLIC SPHERE

The original United States Constitution, including the Bill of Rights, contained unequivocal protection for the right to enter into contracts and the right to own private property. Given this emphasis, it is not surprising those early efforts to extend rights to women focused on property and contractual rights. Beginning in the 1840s, when only men could vote or hold public office, state legislatures started passing the Married Women's Property Acts that discontinued many of the discriminatory laws that prohibited married women from retaining their property after marriage, purchasing or inheriting property during marriage, or earning wages during marriage. Although the Married Women's Property Acts changed the legal rights of women regarding property, the cultural expectation that women's private lives were still controlled by their husbands continued.

At about the same time that the Married Women's Property Acts were enacted, a Declaration of Sentiments was issued at the Seneca Falls Convention of 1848 in Seneca Falls, New York. The Declaration of Sentiments sought civil, social, and moral rights for women and included the very controversial demand for the right to vote.[2]

THE RIGHT TO VOTE
AND THE RIGHT TO PRACTICE LAW

After the Civil War, three amendments to the United States Constitution were adopted. The Thirteenth Amendment abolished slavery. The Fourteenth Amendment, known most commonly for the Equal Protection and Due Process Clauses it contains, also contains a phrase that indicates, for the first time in the Constitution, the inferior legal and political status of women by providing special protection for "male inhabitants." The Fifteenth Amendment provides that "the right of citizens of the United States to vote shall not be denied or abridged by the United States or by any State on account of race, color, or previous condition of servitude."[3] Notably, the amendment did not protect female citizens' right to vote free from discrimination on the basis of gender or sex, and, when presented with the issue, the Supreme Court rejected an equal protection challenge on behalf of a woman who sought to vote.[4] In 1920 all women in the United States were finally guaranteed the right to vote by the enactment of the Nineteenth Amendment to the Constitution, more than 70 years after the Seneca Falls Convention.[5]

The legal profession in the United States has a long history of discrimination against women, and women have had to fight to gain entrance. Myra Bradwell was refused admission to the Illinois bar and took her case all the way to the Supreme Court in 1873. The Court held that women's delicate nature made them ill-suited for the occupations of civil life, such as the practice of law, and denied her claim.[6] She eventually was admitted to the Illinois bar in 1890.

By 1920 a number of elite law schools admitted women, but these law school graduates could usually find employment only as stenographers and law librarians.[7] After a protracted struggle by civil rights groups, there was some progress. By 1980, 12.4 percent of lawyers were women, and by 2009, 31 percent of lawyers were women.[8] Today, approximately 47 percent of law students are women.[9]

CONSTITUTIONAL ISSUES
IN THE TWENTIETH CENTURY

The Equal Rights Amendment (ERA) was first introduced in 1923 to amend the United States Constitution to guarantee women's equality. It provided that equality of rights could not be denied or abridged by the United States or any state on account of sex. For many years it has been reintroduced in each successive Congress, but only once did it garner the two-thirds vote in both the Senate and the House to allow it to be sent to the states for ratification. In 1982 the deadline for ratification passed, three states short of the 38 states needed for the amendment to take effect. The United States Constitution still does not explicitly guarantee women equality.

The Fourteenth Amendment was adopted to protect newly freed slaves. Its text contains a sweeping pronouncement of the rights, privileges, and immunities of "citizens," and its Equal Protection Clause prohibits discriminatory enforcement of the law against any "person." However, despite its broad language, attempts to use the Equal Protection Clause to challenge gender-based discrimination were repeatedly rejected.[10]

The Fourteenth Amendment explicitly gave Congress the power to enact legislation to promote the goals of the Amendment,[11] The laws enacted by Congress originally addressed racial discrimination but increasingly in the twentieth century extended to other forms of discrimination, including gender discrimination.

Such federal laws include the Equal Pay Act of 1963; Title VII of the Civil Rights Act of 1964; Title IX of the Education Amendment of 1972; the Pregnancy Discrimination Act of 1978; the Civil Right Restoration Act of 1987; and the Fair Pay Act of 2009.

By the mid-twentieth century, the Equal Protection Clause also started to be utilized in an effective way to challenge discriminatory statutes when courts were persuaded to scrutinize gender discrimination claims more vigorously. Supreme Court decisions striking down laws discriminatory to women relied in whole or in part on the Fourteenth Amendment.[12] Then in 1976 the Supreme Court struck down a gender-based distinction in an Oklahoma statute because it violated the Fourteenth Amendment's Equal Protection Clause.[13]

LEGAL CHANGES IN THE PUBLIC SPHERE TRANSFORM THE PRIVATE SPHERE

Although the Nineteenth Amendment, giving women the right to vote, and federal statutes and case law in the twentieth century transformed women's legal status, state statutes continued to reflect religious and cultural beliefs regarding women's sexuality and their roles as wives and mothers in society. Because state laws control many legal matters that most directly affect a woman's daily life, reform often must be won through the state legislative process and in state and federal courts, resulting in a patchwork quilt of laws across the country.

REPRODUCTION AND SEXUALITY

Until 1965 it was legal for a state to ban married couples from using contraceptives. The Supreme Court, in *Griswald v. Connecticut*, struck down the statute, holding that it violated the right of privacy guaranteed by the Constitution, particularly the First Amendment's associational rights and the Fourteenth Amendment's Due Process Clause that protects individual liberty.[14] In 1972 the Court struck down a Massachusetts law that banned the distribution of contraception to unmarried persons, relying on *Griswald* and holding that the ban was a violation of the Equal Protection Clause.[15]

In 1973 the Supreme Court heard a challenge to a Texas law that criminalized any abortion that was performed other than to save the life of the mother.

In *Roe v. Wade*, the Court struck down the statute as unconstitutional and established the trimester approach whereby a woman's right to privacy and individual liberty, which encompasses a right to have an abortion, is balanced with the state's interest in potential life as the fetus becomes viable.[16] The Court held that in the first trimester, a woman's privacy rights are primary and a state may only regulate but not ban abortion. As the pregnancy proceeds, the state's interests become stronger and more restrictions are permissible. This holding struck down statutes in dozens of states. A subsequent Supreme Court decision affirmed *Roe*, but emphasized the "viability" of a fetus as the point where abortion could be restricted, provided that such restriction does not unduly burden the right to an abortion and allows an exception based on the preservation of the life or health of the woman.[17]

Gays and lesbians have been targeted for their sexuality as well. They have been charged with criminal consensual sodomy in many states even though sodomy laws apply to both heterosexual and homosexual couples. Recently state sodomy laws were struck down when the Supreme Court held that "there are broad statements of the substantive reach of liberty under the Due Process Clause" that support private consensual conduct.[18] This was an important recognition of individual and familial privacy.

MARRIAGE

In the United States, state law has historically controlled marriage, and in 1967 it was still illegal in Virginia for persons of different races to marry. The Supreme Court struck down the law prohibiting interracial marriage in *Loving v. Virginia*.[19]

Until 1975, marital rape was not recognized as a legal concept anywhere in the United States and spouses were legally exempt from charges of rape in marriage. South Dakota was the first state to change the law, in 1975. Most states changed their laws in the 1980s and 1990s, and North Carolina was the last state to do so, in 1993.

In the 1990s, state legislators started introducing bills that would allow same-sex marriages. In an attempt to prevent same-sex marriage, Congress passed the Defense of Marriage Act (DOMA) and

President Bill Clinton signed it into law on September 21, 1996.[20] However, today we are experiencing a marriage revolution in America as states, one after another, pass marriage equality laws. A federal court held a portion of the DOMA unconstitutional in July 2010, and Attorney General Eric Holder announced in February 2011 that the Obama administration would no longer be defending the federal statute in court.

DOMESTIC VIOLENCE

In 1994 the federal Violence Against Women Act (VAWA)[21] was enacted as part of a broad criminal justice statute to provide services, training, consistent enforcement, and a coordinated effort by police, prosecutors, victim services, and the private bar to address violence committed against women in the United States.[22] Many states have also passed laws to better address violence against women.

For instance, New York changed the primary mandate of Family Courts in domestic violence cases to one that seeks to protect the safety of family members rather than preserve the family unit. New York also established a central depository for orders of protection that police could access from anywhere in the state and established specialized Domestic Violence Courts to handle such cases. Recently, after many years of controversy, New York also changed the definition of "family" to allow unmarried couples without children, either straight or gay, access to Family Court in domestic violence cases.[23]

RAPE

Historically rape was considered a property crime against a man. Women were bartered and bride prices were common. A father could demand a civil penalty to compensate him for the daughter's chastity or could demand "redemption" by marriage, meaning the rapist would marry the daughter, who was viewed as damaged property. In thirteenth-century England, rape was made a crime against the crown and the punishment was death. In the United States, 16 states imposed the death penalty for the crime of rape when, in 1977, the Supreme Court held that such a penalty violated the Eighth Amendment's ban on cruel and unusual punishment. Many women supported this ruling because the possibility of death inhibited prosecution, reduced conviction rates, and reinforced racist and sexist attitudes.

Prior to that, the legal definition of rape was open to interpretation and rules of evidence created barriers to prosecution. Requiring proof that a woman had not consented was equated with force; force was equated with resistance; and resistance was proven by injuries. Many states also required corroboration for each element of the crime, which was not so with other crimes like robbery. By 1980 most states had repealed their resistance and corroboration requirements[24]

CONTINUING AND NEW LEGAL CHALLENGES

The Attack on Abortion

Sometimes an issue the United States Supreme Court "settles" is so controversial that states will seek ways around the ruling. Furthermore, because judges on the highest court change, cases that were addressed by earlier courts are often revisited. This has been true for the issue of abortion.

The holding in *Roe v. Wade* that struck down statutes in dozens of states triggered an effort to undermine and repeal the *Roe* decision at both the federal and the state levels. Hundreds of statutes have been enacted across the country over the last 38 years that make it harder for women to get abortions, including waiting periods between counseling and the abortion procedure, parental notification laws, and bans on state and federal funds for abortions. Legal challenges in the courts have usually followed.

In 2004, during the presidency of George W. Bush, the federal Unborn Victims of Violence Act was enacted.[25] This law promotes the personhood of a fetus, by defining a "child in utero" as a legal victim, separate and apart from the woman who is pregnant, and imposes penalties for harmful acts against such victims. As of 2011, 35 states have enacted a version of the Unborn Victims of Violence Act.[26] Antiabortion advocates, relying on the "personhood" of the fetus as defined in the Unborn Victims of Violence Act, are now promoting a "Pregnant Woman's Protection Act" at the federal and state level.[27] This law creates a special second defense to an assault or murder charge for a pregnant woman who uses deadly force in the defense of her fetus.[28] Oklahoma enacted such a law in 2009,[29] and Missouri did so in 2010.[30] Similar, but broader, legislation, which could be used to justify the murder of an abortion provider by a third party,[31] was introduced in South Dakota,[32] Nebraska,[33] and Iowa[34] in 2011.

In 2011 the new Republican majority in the House of Representatives is seeking to cut the entire federal program that supports family planning and defund Planned Parenthood as a means of forcing it to spend nonfederal funds to provide basic health services, other than abortions, to its clientele of mostly low-income women.[35] They are also seeking to redefine rape as "forcible rape" to narrow the federal provision that allows federal Medicaid funds to pay for abortions.[36]

At the state level, extreme views are expressed in laws and bills designed to limit reproductive choices, promote the personhood of fetuses, and defend violent acts that seek to prevent abortions. In March 2011 a law was enacted in South Dakota to require that a woman seeking an abortion attend a "consultation" with an antiabortion counselor before the procedure can be done. It also requires that a woman wait three days after her initial visit with an abortion provider, the longest waiting period in the country, before obtaining an abortion.[37]

Almost four decades after the *Roe* decision, one of the most private and life-altering decisions that a woman can make, whether or not to have a child, is still the subject of a national public debate over control of women's bodies.

The Criminalization of Motherhood

Law enforcement and prosecutors in approximately 30 states have arrested and criminally charged more than 200 pregnant women for behavior during pregnancy deemed harmful to a fetus.[38] To do so, they have used state child abuse and drug-trafficking laws and have argued that the definition of a "child" includes a fetus. These efforts have disproportionately affected women of color and their children.[39] When convictions occurred, most were reversed on

appeal with the help of reproductive and civil rights advocates[40] but not before the targeted women had suffered great harm in the criminal justice system.

The Supreme Court of South Carolina has, by judicial fiat, promoted the most extreme interpretations of these laws. In 1997 it issued a ruling that recognized a fetus's rights and sentenced a mother who had used cocaine during her pregnancy, but whose baby was born healthy, to prison for eight years for "child" endangerment.[41] The United States Supreme Court refused to hear the case. Based on the South Carolina decision, another woman was convicted of homicide by child abuse because she used cocaine during her pregnancy and her fetus was stillborn. She was sentenced to 12 years in prison.[42] By 2003 at least 100 women had been prosecuted in South Carolina for using drugs during pregnancy.[43]

Other legal attempts to control pregnant women have occurred. Doctors and hospitals have obtained court orders to force women to have cesarean sections against their wishes. Women have been charged with criminal penalties and found guilty of child abuse and neglect for refusing to allow cesarean sections to be performed on them. At least one federal district judge has acted on his own to "protect" a fetus, ignoring federal sentencing guidelines and the objections of an assistant United States attorney. In 2009 a judge in Maine ordered a woman who was HIV-positive and pregnant jailed for a term that would coincide with her due date to ensure that she received adequate medical care and did not transmit HIV to her fetus.[44]

Miscarriages also now raise suspicion about criminality, although they occur commonly and spontaneously during pregnancy and sometimes without a woman's knowledge. In Georgia, a bill has been introduced every year since 2002 that would criminalize a miscarriage if a woman could not prove that it occurred without human involvement.[45]

CONCLUSION

Changes in the law that promote equality for women happen incrementally. It was not until 72 years after the Seneca Falls Convention that women finally won the vote in 1920 with passage of the Nineteenth Amendment. But today, social and cultural inequalities remain entrenched. While progress has been made and social concerns that were considered radical a generation ago are now mainstream, an increasingly conservative Supreme Court, the right wing's determination to undo the progress that women have made, and new emerging issues require a renewed commitment to address legal sex discrimination. The fight for equality continues.   [2011]

NOTES

1. William Blackstone, *Commentaries on the Law of England,* http://avalon.law.yale.edu/18th_century/blackstone_bk1ch15.asp (1765–1769).
2. "The Declaration of Sentiments," http://www.fordham.edu/halsall/mod/senecafalls.html (1848).
3. U.S. Const., amend. XV, § 1.
4. *Minor v. Happersett,* 88 U.S. 162 (1874) (acknowledging that women are persons and citizens but holding that the right to vote was not a privilege of citizenship and therefore that no violation of the Equal Protection Clause occurred when women were denied the vote).
5. "The right of citizens of the United States to vote shall not be denied or abridged by the United States or by any State on account of sex." U.S. Const. amend. XIX, § 1.
6. *Bradwell v. Illinois,* 83 U.S. (16 Wall.) 130 (1873).
7. Cynthia Grant Bowman, *Women in the Legal Profession from the 1920s to the 1970s: What Can We Learn from Their Experience About Law and Social Change?* 4, http://scholarship.law.cornell.edu/facpub/12 (2009).
8. ABA Commission on Women in the Profession, *A Current Glance at Women in the Law* (2009).
9. Ibid.
10. *Bradwell v. Illinois,* 83 U.S. (16 Wall.) 130 (1873) (rejecting a challenge to Illinois's refusal to grant a woman a law license); *Goesaert v. Cleary,* 335 U.S. 464 (1948) (rejecting a challenge to a Michigan statute prohibiting a woman from working as a bartender unless she was the wife or daughter of the owner); *Hoyt v. Florida,* 368 U.S. 57 (1961) (rejecting a challenge to a jury selection system excluding women who said they did not want to serve).
11. U.S. Const., amend. XIV, § 5.
12. *Reed v. Reed,* 404 U.S. 71 (1971) (gender discrimination in estate administration unconstitutional); *Frontiero v. Richardson,* 411 U.S. 677 (1973) (gender discrimination in military benefits unconstitutional); *Weinberger v. Wiesenfeld,* 420 U.S. 636 (1975) (gender discrimination in Social Security survivor benefits unconstitutional).
13. *Craig v. Boren,* 429 U.S. 190 (1976).
14. *Griswald v. Connecticut,* 381 U.S. 479 (1965).
15. *Eisenstadt v. Baird,* 405 U.S. 438 (1972).
16. *Roe v. Wade,* 410 U.S. 113 (1973).
17. *Planned Parenthood v. Casey,* 505 U.S. 833 (1992).
18. *Lawrence v. Texas,* 539 U.S. 558, 564 (2003).
19. *Loving v. Virginia,* 388 U.S. 1 (1967).
20. 1 U.S.C. § 7; 28 U.S.C. § 1738C.
21. Pub. L. No. 103-322, Title IV, 108 Stat. 1902 (1994).
22. The Supreme Court later held that part of the VAWA that allowed a woman to sue someone for gender-motivated violence was unconstitutional. *United States v. Morrison,* 529 U.S. 598 (2000).
23. N.Y. Family Court Act § 812.
24. Jennifer A. Bennice and Patricia A. Resnick, "Marital Rape, History, Research, and Practice," *Trauma, Violence, and Abuse* 4, no. 3 (2003), 228, 230.
25. 18 U.S.C. 1841; 10 U.S.C., §919a.
26. National Right to Life, "State Homicide Laws That Recognize Unborn Victims," February 25, 2011, www.nrtl.org/Unborn_Victims/Statehomicidelaws092302.html.
27. Americans United for Life, *Model Legislation and Policy Guide for the 2011 Legislative Year* (2011).
28. All persons already have the right to use deadly force to defend their lives.
29. H.B. 1103 of 2009.
30. H.B. 2081 of 2010.
31. Daniel Schulman, "Memo to Americans United for Life: Our Questions Still Stand," *Mother Jones,* March 1, 2011.
32. H.B. 1171 of 2011.
33. L.B. 232 of 2011.
34. House File 7 and House File 153 of 2011.
35. Erik Eckholm, "Planned Parenthood Financing Is Caught in Budget Feud," *New York Times,* February 18, 2011.
36. Nick Baumann, "The House GOP's Plan to Redefine Rape," *Mother Jones,* January 28, 2011.
37. A. G. Sulzberger, "Women Seeking Abortions in South Dakota to Get Anti-Abortion Advice," *New York Times,* March 22, 2011.
38. Lynn Paltrow, "Punishing Women for Their Behavior During Pregnancy: An Approach That Undermines the Health of Women and Children," http://advocatesforpregnantwomen.org/file/Punishing%20Women%20During%20Pregnancy_Paltrow.pdf.
39. ACLU, "Break the Chains: Communities of Color and the War on Drugs and the Brennan Center at NYU School of Law," in *Caught in the Net: The Impact of Drug Policies on Women and Families,* http://www.aclu.org/files/images/asset_upload_file431_23513.pdf.
40. See, for example, North Dakota: *State v. Geiser,* 763 N.W.2d 469 (N.D. 2009); Maryland: *Kilmon v. State,* 905 A2d 306 (Md. 2006); Hawaii: *State v. Aiwohi,* 123 P3d 1210 (2005); New Mexico: *State of New Mexico v. Martinez,*; Nevada: *Sheriff, Washoe County v. Encoe,* 885 P.2d 596 (Nev. 1994); Florida: *Johnson v. State,* 602 So.2d 1288 (Fla. 1992).
41. *Whitner v. State,* 492 S.E.2d 777 (S.C. 1997).
42. *State v. McKnight,* 576 S.E.2d 168 (S.C. 2003). The conviction was later reversed. *McKnight v. State,* 661 S.E.2d 354 (S.C. 2008).
43. Silja J. A. Talvi, "Criminalizing Motherhood," *The Nation,* December 3, 2003.
44. Judy Harrison, "Judge Jails Woman Until Baby Is Born," *Bangor Daily News,* June 2, 2009, http://new.bangordailynews.com/2009/06/02/news/bangor/judge-jails-woman-until-baby-is-born/. Her sentence was subsequently overturned on appeal. Judy Harrison, "Pregnant African to Be Resentenced," *Bangor Daily News,* July 21, 2009, http://new.bangordailynews.com/2009/07/21/news/bangor/pregnant-african-to-be-resentenced/.
45. H.B. 1 of 2011.

LGBTQ Rights in Several Countries

In the last couple of decades there has been a flurry of activity in legislatures around the world with regard to laws pertaining to Lesbian, Gay, Bisexual, Transgendered, Queer (LGBTQ) rights. In some countries individuals belonging to the LGBTQ community enjoy unprecedented rights, protecting their civil liberties and access to basic human rights. In others, there is work still to be done by activists to establish these rights, and discrimination and persecution of individuals belonging to the LGBTQ community is rampant and goes unpunished. In the USA, there is wide regional variation in the legal framework available to the LGBTQ community to redress civil rights violations.

Country	Homosexuality legal	Same-sex relationships recognized	Same-sex marriage recognized	Same-sex adoption allowed	Explicit anti-discrimination laws (sexual orientation)	Anti-discrimination laws (gender identity)
Norway	Yes	Yes	Yes	Yes	Yes	Yes
Canada	Yes	Yes	Yes	Yes	Yes	Yes
France	Yes	Yes	No	Yes	Yes	Yes
USA	Yes	Varies by State	Varies by State*	Varies by State**	Varies by state***	Varies by State***
Mexico	Yes	Varies by State	Varies by State	Varies by State	Yes	Yes
Brazil	Yes	Yes	No	Yes	Yes	Yes
South Africa	Yes	Yes	Yes	Yes	Yes	Yes
India	Yes	No	No	No	No	Yes

[2011]

*The federal government does not recognize same-sex marriage. Some states do.
**Single homosexual individuals may adopt, but couple adoption varies by state
***Few federal protections are offered for homosexual individuals or individuals who identify as transgendered, but discrimination is banned in 20 states. The Matthew Shepard Law of 2009 introduces some protection to the community.
Source: http://www.queer.ucsc.edu/resources/links.shtml

 63

Unequal: A Global Perspective on Women Under the Law

JESSICA NEUWIRTH

Around the world, real discrimination against women persists—much of it in blatant, tolerated, *legal* form. Why?

It makes no sense. The right to equality has been affirmed repeatedly, in international law, national constitutions, and various treaties. Name them: the Universal Declaration of Human Rights, the International Covenant on Civil and Political Rights, the Convention on the Elimination of All Forms of Discrimination Against Women (CEDAW)—all provide for equality before the law and equal protection. The Beijing Platform for Action, adopted at the 1995 United Nations Fourth World Conference on Women, states the need to "ensure equality and nondiscrimination under the law and in practice" and to "revoke any remaining laws that discriminate on the basis of sex."

It sounds good. But the reality on the ground, in cities and villages, homes and schools, and even in the courts, is quite different.

Many discriminatory laws still relate to family law, limiting a woman's right to marry, divorce, and remarry, and allowing for such marital practices as polygamy. Mali, Sudan, and Yemen are among countries with laws still mandating "wife obedience" in marital relations. Sudan's 1991 Muslim Personal Law Act provides that a husband's rights include being "taken care of and amicably obeyed" by his wife. Yemen's 1992 Personal Status Act even enumerates the elements of wife obedience, including requirements that a wife "must permit him [her husband] to have licit intercourse with her," that she "must obey his orders," and that "she must not leave the conjugal home without his permission."

But if you think blatant legal discrimination is a problem only in Muslim societies and/or developing countries, think again.

Many nations, including the United States, explicitly discriminate on the basis of sex in the transmission of citizenship: to children, depending on the sex of the parent, and/or through marriage, depending on the sex of the spouse. The U.S. law—which gives children born abroad and out of wedlock differing rights to citizenship, depending on whether their mothers or fathers are U.S. citizens—was upheld by the Supreme Court in 2001: Children of U.S. mothers have a lifetime right to citizenship, while children of U.S. fathers (including all those GIs stationed overseas) must take legal steps, before turning 18, to claim citizenship.

In its 5-4 decision, the Court held that the law was justified on the basis of two governmental interests: "assuring a biological parent-child relationship exists" and a "determination to ensure that the child and the citizen parent have some demonstrated opportunity or potential to develop . . . a relationship that . . . consists of the real, everyday ties that provide a connection between child and citizen parent, and, in turn, the United States." The majority opinion, authored by Justice Anthony M. Kennedy, did not address the fact that such a relationship was arbitrarily required by law for U.S. citizen fathers but not U.S. citizen mothers. In

the dissent, Justice Sandra Day O'Connor noted, "Indeed, the majority's discussion may itself simply reflect the stereotype of male irresponsibility that is no more a basis for the validity of the classification than are stereotypes about the 'traditional' behavior patterns of women."

Other "personal status" laws that discriminate on the basis of sex range from the denial of women's right to vote in Kuwait to the prohibition against women driving in Saudi Arabia.

Inheritance and property laws are also key areas where discrimination exists. Lesotho's laws provide that "no immovable property shall be registered in the name of a woman married in community of property." Chile's Civil Code mandates that "the marital partnership is to be headed by the husband, who shall administer the spouses' joint property as well as the property owned by his wife." Until 2002, the law in Nepal was that daughters had the right to a share of family property only if they were at least 35 years old and unmarried; after years of effort, the Nepali Women's Movement succeeded in amending the law—but just in part: Now, daughters are born with the same right to family property as are sons, but the law requires women to *return* any such property upon marriage.

In many countries, criminal offenses—their definitions as well as rules governing admissible evidence—are explicitly sex-discriminatory. In Pakistan, for example, written legal documents concerning financial obligations must be attested to by two men, or by one man and two women. In rape cases there, four Muslim adult males must testify to witnessing the rape; there is no provision for testimony from female witnesses.

Marital rape is explicitly excluded from rape laws in many nations—for example, India, Malaysia, and Tonga. Ethiopia, Lebanon, Guatemala, and Uruguay exempt men from penalty for rape—if they subsequently marry their victims. Northern Nigeria's penal code notes that assault is not an offense if inflicted "by a husband for the purpose of correcting his wife" so long as it "does not amount to the infliction of grievous hurt." And in cases of so-called honor killings, men who murder their wives are exempt from punishment by law in Syria,

Morocco, and Haiti. In Jordan, a campaign against "honor" killings did change the law—but only to make it gender neutral, exempting any spouse from punishment for an "honor" killing. Since virtually all such killings are perpetrated by men, this amendment removes the appearance of sex discrimination, not the discrimination itself.

Laws that explicitly discriminate are only the tip of the iceberg. The denial of equal opportunity in education and employment, exclusion from political representation, deprivation of sexual and reproductive rights, plus the use of social forces and physical violence to intimidate and subordinate women—all these are violations of the right to equality. In many countries, abortion is a criminal offense that burdens women with medical consequences, often fatal, of unsafely terminating a pregnancy. In some countries—the Philippines, for example—prostitution is a criminal offense for the prostituted female but not for the male customer.

In virtually all countries, there are laws, policies, and practices that, though not explicitly discriminatory, in practice deny women equality. This in itself is illegal. Whenever laws perpetuate women's inequality—even when their language appears gender neutral—they constitute discrimination in violation of international norms.

In June 2000, a Special Session of the U.N. General Assembly reviewed implementation of the Beijing Platform, five years after its adoption. An Outcome Document was adopted, outlining achievements, obstacles, and further actions to be taken by governments and by the U.N. to implement the Platform. Paragraph 21 cites gender discrimination as one such obstacle to implementation of the Platform, noting that discriminatory legislation persists. It notes, too, that new laws discriminating against women have been introduced (in Nigeria, for example). The Document also provides that countries should review legislation "striving to remove discriminatory provisions as soon as possible, preferably by 2005." The preliminary draft had noted 2005 as an unequivocal target date for the elimination of discriminatory laws; the final document reflects a compromise, with the target date stated as a preference.

Elimination of such laws doesn't require financial expenditure. It requires political will, in the form of a legislative act. This political will is obviously absent; the very notion of setting a target date five years into the future—merely to remove explicitly discriminatory legal provisions—was hotly contested at the General Assembly Special Session.

Still, there has been progress. A number of countries have repealed discriminatory laws since the adoption of the 1995 Beijing Platform for Action. Venezuela adopted a new constitution that removed discriminatory citizenship provisions. Mexico rescinded a law that required a woman to wait 300 days from the dissolution of marriage before remarrying. Turkey rescinded a law that designated the husband as the head of a marital union, responsible for all family savings. Papua New Guinea removed the exemption of marital rape from its definition of rape, and Costa Rica removed the exemption from punishment for rapists who subsequently married their victims. Switzerland amended a law that had barred women in the military from using arms other than for self-defense; thus opening all military functions/responsibilities to women. In 2001 (after threat of financial sanctions from the European Commission), France rescinded a law prohibiting women from night employment in industrial "workplaces of any nature, be they public or private, civil or religious, even if such establishments are for the purpose of professional education or charitable work."

Laws are changing. But the pace of change is lethargic, while the need for change is urgent. The substantial gap between the rhetoric and the reality of sex-equality rights indicates the lack of meaningful commitment to applicable treaty obligations and commitments governments have made. Public pressure can play a role in helping to overcome such lethargy.

The diplomatic community can feel shame under pressure, and that itself is a powerful technique too rarely used by governments, themselves fearful of the same spotlight. NGOs, of course, continually work to shatter the silence. But until governments match their interest in setting standards with an interest in implementing the standards they set, the integrity of the legal process will remain a question. That there are any laws explicitly discriminating against women is unacceptable, and must be universally seen and acknowledged as such—even in the diplomatic corridors of the United Nations.   [2004]

🌿 64

How to Bring Children Up Without Putting Women Down

ANN CRITTENDEN

The feminist task is neither to glorify nor discount the differences between men and women, but to challenge the adverse consequences of whatever differences there may be.

—Christine Littleton

In the early spring of 1995, I attended an international conference in the fashionably faded Villa Schifanoia, a Renaissance estate in the elegant Florentine suburb of Fiesole. The topic was "The Cost of Being a Mother; the Cost of Being a Father."

The meetings were conducted in an ornate, high-ceilinged former theater hung with tapestries. Some 50 assembled scholars from Europe, the United States, and the United Kingdom listened through headsets to simultaneous translations as they sat beneath murals of cherubs playing lyres. Between sessions, the participants strolled through the grounds along avenues of stately cypress trees.

I had gone to this unlikely setting to get beyond the often sterile American debate over family values and the work-family conflict, by learning more about other advanced countries' policies toward caregivers. Were the Europeans really as successful as they are said to be in protecting mothers and children from poverty? Had they been able to promote caring for others without hindering women's progress in all the other arenas of work and life?

What I learned at this gathering, sponsored by the European University Institute, was heartening. First, despite severe budget cuts in virtually every European country, not one government was cutting its generous maternal and child benefits, with the important exception of reduced subsidies for child care in the former East Germany. In recent elections in both France and Norway, politicians had even competed over how to increase governmental support for families.

The American assumption that Europe can no longer afford its investment in good care for those who need it is clearly not shared by most Europeans. The public strongly supports policies that have kept poverty among children and their mothers substantially lower than in the United States. . . .

Moreover, the European debate seems to be more candid about the fact that family support issues are very much women's issues. The conference itself was organized around the idea that the costs of caring have to be better understood and more fairly shared between men and women and by society as a whole. Several commentators noted that unless this cost sharing occurs, women will never escape a precarious, semidependent economic status.

The implicit assumption in all of the papers presented was that caring needs to be conceptualized as work if it is ever to be properly valued socially, legally, or economically. By the same token, those who provide care, unpaid as well as paid, must be seen as productive citizens who deserve the same social rights as all other workers and citizens. . . .

The United States is not Europe, and Americans may never accept the kind of compassionate capitalism or caring state that western Europeans demand. But it doesn't strike me as beyond our reach to revise a new social contract as well. I can easily imagine adding care to our pantheon of national values, along with liberty, justice, and the pursuit of happiness through the pursuit of money.

But this will never happen unless women demand it. Women have to insist that caretaking and early education can no longer depend on their cheap or unpaid labor. And before that can happen, women have to understand that the true costs of care include their exclusion from full participation in the economy and in society.[1]

The only way women can achieve equal citizenship is for the entire society to contribute to the provision of a public good that everyone desires: well-raised children who will mature into productive, law-abiding citizens. And that means that all free riders—from employers to governments to husbands to communities—have to pitch in and help make the most important job in the world a top national priority—and a very good job. . . .

EMPLOYERS: REDESIGN WORK AROUND PARENTAL NORMS

Give Every Parent the Right to a Year's Paid Leave

In 1997, American pediatricians officially recommended that new mothers breast-feed for a full year. This was a sick joke in a country that entitles new mothers to no paid leave at all. American mothers are guaranteed only three months' maternity leave without pay—forcing most working mothers to return to their jobs within a few weeks after giving birth, because they can't afford to take three months off without a paycheck.[2] As a consequence, poor mothers are far less likely to breast-feed than their better-off sisters, and infants as young as six weeks are going into day care, with some spending as many as ten hours a day in group settings. No other women or children in the industrialized world are forced to live under these conditions, which child development experts agree are deplorable, if not downright harmful.

Those concerned about family values or parental neglect of children could find no better place to attack the problem than by demanding a paid leave, which could be shared by both parents, of at least one year. This would do more to improve infant care, increase family income, enhance fathers' emotional ties to their offspring, and promote economic equality between husbands and wives than almost any other single measure.

More generous leaves allowing parents to stay home with a sick child are also essential. Fewer than half of working parents stay home when their children are sick, even though research shows that sick children recover more quickly when a parent is there.[3] According to a recent survey by the AFL-CIO, 54 percent of working women are not entitled to any paid leave for taking care of a sick child or other family member.

Corporate lobbyists have vehemently opposed the most minimal paid parental or family leaves, claiming that the cost would bankrupt American business. This is blatantly untrue. Generous paid parental leaves are a basic right in every other economically advanced nation, and in none of them does business have to foot the entire bill. In some countries the leaves are paid for by contributions of employers and employees to the national old-age insurance system; in others they come out of general tax revenues or some combination of taxes, Social Security, and employer or employee insurance funds.

The costs to the economy can be offset by reduced turnover and the creation of a wider labor pool of women who will remain in the paid workforce if they don't have to quit to take care of an infant or a sick child.

Shorten the Workweek

Experts estimate that roughly 5 to 7 million American children are left unattended at home every day. Why? Because parents of young children don't have the right to work a day that coincides with the school day.

In Sweden, parents can opt to work a six-hour day until their children are eight years old. In the Netherlands the official workweek is 36 hours, and workers have a right to a four-day week. The legal workweek in France was reduced from 39 to 35 hours in 2000, and pressure is rising for the rest of Europe to follow suit.[4]

American parents have complained for years that they need a shorter workweek, but for many the workday is getting steadily longer instead. The average workweek has crept up to almost 48 hours for professionals and managers, and even so-called part-time work is now edging toward 40 hours a week. . . .

Despite their adamant opposition, American companies might discover gains in a shorter workweek. Overwork-related stress disorders, absenteeism, and turnover would surely be reduced, and productivity in some cases improved, as a number of French companies have already discovered.

Provide Equal Pay and Benefits for Equal Part-time Work

A shorter workweek would have to be accompanied by a federal law requiring companies to pay part-time workers at the same hourly rates as full-timers doing the same job, as well as prorated fringe benefits, including vacations, sick leave, and inclusion in company pension plans. Currently, only about 22 percent of part-time workers have any health insurance, compared with 78 percent of full-time workers, and only 26 percent have any private pensions, compared with 60 percent of full-timers. These inequities give employers a huge incentive to hire nonstandard workers—most of them mothers—on cheap, exploitative terms.

A model for ending the exploitation and marginalization of part-time work has been established in the Netherlands, where one-third of all jobs are now part-time. Dutch part-timers enjoy all of the benefits that accrue to full-time workers, on a prorated basis. The Canadian province of Saskatchewan has also set a precedent by becoming the first jurisdiction in North America to rewrite its labor laws to extend benefits to part-time workers.

Eliminate Discrimination Against Parents in the Workplace

Only eight states currently have laws prohibiting parental discrimination. Although such bias is hard to quantify, parents believe that it is widespread. One obvious example would be people who are penalized for declining to work overtime because of family responsibilities.

In the 1997 Massachusetts case of *Upton v. JWP Businessland*, a single mother working as a store manager brought suit for wrongful dismissal after she was fired for refusing to work much longer hours than she had originally been hired to do, including all day Saturday. The woman argued that the compulsory overtime would prevent her from being an adequate mother to her son—indeed she would scarcely be able to see him. Yet the Massachusetts Supreme Judicial Court ruled against her. The court decided that state contract law permitted at-will employees to be fired "for any reason or for no reason at all" unless the firing violates a "clearly established" public policy. It found that Massachusetts had no public policy dealing with the responsibility of a parent to care for his or her child.[5] Perhaps it is time for governments to establish such policies.

GOVERNMENT: REPLACE THE WELFARE STATE WITH A CARING STATE

Equalize Social Security for Spouses

Under this reform, both spouses would automatically earn equal Social Security credits during their marriage. They would combine these credits with whatever credits they might have earned before or after marriage, for their own individual retirement benefits. This so-called earnings sharing would increase benefits for working and stay-at-home mothers alike, and for divorced women, who are among the poorest old people in the country.

Currently, the Social Security system penalizes anyone who spends time working as an unpaid caregiver, and anyone who earns significantly less than their spouse—that is, the great majority of married mothers. In 1992 Congress issued a report on the inequities surrounding women and retirement, with the intention of launching a national debate on the issue. But the expected debate never occurred. As soon as the new 1994 Republican Congress came into power, it abolished the Select Committee on Aging that had issued the report.

The avatars of free enterprise had a very different debate in mind. Soon we began to hear about privatization of Social Security: allowing individuals to keep and invest for themselves money that would have gone into the Social Security Trust Fund.

One of the versions of privatization favored by Republicans would allow a sizable portion of a person's Social Security contributions to be put into a so-called PSA: a personal savings account to be invested as he or she saw fit. At retirement everyone would receive a flat minimum stipend from Social Security plus whatever had accumulated in their PSA.

This scheme would mean that the spouse who makes the home, wipes the runny noses, kisses away the bruises, cuts the corners off her own career, and earns less money would not necessarily have a stake in the accumulated savings of her family. There would be no "family" savings, only "personal" savings. The millions of women who are primary caregivers would have smaller PSAs than their husbands, to match their lower lifetime earnings. If they wanted anything more than a below-subsistence retirement income, they would either have to go out and earn their own money to invest for themselves or have to "depend on what he felt like giving her," according to attorney Edith Fierst. It would be hard to dream up a more anti-caregiver retirement plan.

If any version of privatization ever does occur, it should mandate an FSA—a family savings account—for all married couples with children, jointly owned by both spouses, rather than individual PSAs that would allow the big breadwinner to salt away most of the family savings and future retirement income as his own. An alternative would be simply to give Social Security credits to family caregivers. Both France and Germany give women pension credits for time spent out of the labor market caring for family members, young or old. During the 2000 election campaign such a "caregiver's credit" was proposed by Vice President Albert Gore. He would credit any stay-at-home parent with $16,500 annual income for up to five years. This would lift the benefits of as many as 8 million people, almost all of them mothers, by an average of $600 a year.

Offer Work-Related Social Insurance Programs to All Workers

The artificial distinction between "members of the labor force," who work for wages, and those who provide unpaid care should be abolished. A "worker" would be defined as anyone who either is employed in the provision of goods and services or is engaged in the unpaid provision of care and services to dependent adults and children. Primary caregivers would be considered to be "in the labor force," and eligible for temporary unemployment compensation and job training in the event of divorce, and workmen's compensation for job-related injuries.

Provide Universal Preschool for All Three- and Four-Year-Olds

A caring state would also guarantee that all children have access to developmental education in their critical early years. In the nineteenth century the United States led the world in establishing free public education for all children starting at age six. The early twentieth century saw the expansion of public education through high school. Yet the country has become a laggard in providing young children with the early education that can prepare them for success in school and in life. This failure to invest in human capital is surely one major reason why one out of every six adult Americans is functionally illiterate.

The remedy is universal preschool for all American three- and four-year-olds. We have seen that quality early education is beyond the means of most parents, just as most parents cannot afford the full costs of primary or secondary education. Even middle-class families are routinely priced out of licensed nursery schools and child care centers. According to the Census Bureau, child care is the single biggest expense of young families, after housing and food.

Among low-income families, government-subsidized early education and child care is so scarce that only about one-twelfth of the poor families who are eligible for subsidies receive them, according to a 1999 study by the Department of Health and Human Services.[6]

No state offers universal early education to three-year-olds, and only one state, Georgia, offers subsidized preschool to every four-year-old (although in 2000 Oklahoma and New York were also starting to take steps in that direction).

The practical effect of this neglect is to deny an early education to poor children, who are the very ones who need it the most. Nationally, only 36 percent of three- to five-year-olds from families earning less than $15,000 a year attend any kind of prekindergarten, compared with 79 percent from families earning more than $75,000.

In France, by contrast, 99 percent of three- to five-year-olds attend preschools at no or minimum charge. The French government also finances a licensed network of subsidized crèches, where 20 percent of younger children are cared for in a family setting. . . .

Stop Taxing Mothers More Than Anyone Else

We know that children as well as women benefit when mothers have significant control over family income and some financial independence. . . . One of the fairest, most effective ways of accomplishing this would be to lower taxes on mothers' incomes, as opposed to family tax cuts per se. . . .

The current tax regime, like the Social Security system, was set up between the 1930s and 1950s with a traditional male breadwinner, dependent female spouse in mind. To some degree intentionally, the tax laws discourage two-earner families at all income levels by taxing the lower-earning spouse at much higher rates than the primary earner.

The government could actually raise more revenue, without lowering families' income by a penny, by taxing married men more and married women less. Economists have discovered that in response to high tax rates, married women do shift from work outside the home to unpaid work in the home, while lower taxes, and more take-home pay, draw them back into the paid labor force. When taxes go up for married men, by contrast, either their work patterns are not affected by the change, or, if anything, the men work harder to make up for the loss of income. . . .

One simple way to remedy this tax bias against married working mothers is to restore separate filing of federal income tax returns, as was done in the United States before 1948. Separate filing, the most common method of taxing married persons in other advanced democracies would currently put the first $10,000 earned by the secondary earner, usually the mother, in a zero tax bracket, rather than having every dollar of her income taxed at the family's highest marginal rate. Separate filing would also eliminate the anachronistic designation of one spouse as "head of household" and the other as "spouse." I may earn less money than my husband, but that doesn't make him the "head of the household" and me the "spouse." Let us file and be taxed (or not taxed) separately, as financial equals in the family.

A mother's taxes could also be reduced considerably by allowing her to deduct child care expenditures. If business executives can deduct half the cost of meals and entertainment as a legitimate cost of doing business, then surely the family's primary caregiver should be allowed to deduct the cost of substitute child care as a business expense, which it certainly is.

A Child Allowance; or Social Security for Children

The big problem with tax deductions and tax credits for children and for child care is that tax breaks do nothing for the roughly 30 percent of parents whose income is so low they pay no federal taxes. Far better than tinkering with the tax code would be a *child allowance* paid to *all* primary caregivers of young children, whether they work outside the home or not. Such a "salary" for every mother is paid in a number of countries, including Britain and France, and is truly neutral regarding parents' decisions on how to raise their children, for the money can be used either to help pay for child care or to help pay the bills in households where one parent stays home.

A child allowance, with the check made out to the person who is the family's primary caregiver, would target children far more effectively than a "family tax cut." Tax cuts, including the child tax credit, increase the income of the major breadwinner—and not even that in families who earn too little to pay income taxes. Child care deductions, for their part, don't help families where the mother provides the care. An allowance, or "family wage" paid directly to caregivers, would help all families with kids. It could be paid out of a Children's Trust Fund, similar to the Social Security Trust Fund, supported by a dedicated income stream, possibly including contributions from employers and employees, as in the case of Social Security. One version of the family wage idea calls it Social Security for Children.

Provide Free Health Coverage for All Children and Their Primary Caregivers

Another minimal element in a caring state is adequate health insurance for *all* dependents, including children as well as the elderly and disabled. An American journalist whose wife recently had a baby in Paris discovered how nice it is to live in a place that values maternal and child health more highly. "[I] have become French enough to feel, stubbornly," he wrote, "that in a prosperous society all pregnant women should have three sonograms and four nights in a hospital if they want to. . . . It doesn't seem aristocratically spoiled to think that a woman should keep her job and have some paid leave afterward. . . . All human desires short of simple survival are luxurious, and a mother's desire to have a slightly queenly experience of childbirth . . . seems as well worth paying for as a tobacco subsidy or another tank."[7]

Even in Britain, where the Darwinian struggle was invented, all new mothers receive several home visits from a nurse to ensure that everything is going well. Among other things, the nurses make sure that new mothers have a grasp of the techniques of successful breast-feeding. In the United States, by contrast, new mothers are routinely sent home from hospitals after one day, often knowing less about babies than they do about their cat. Recently, a young American mother was indicted for manslaughter because she didn't know enough about breast-feeding to realize that her baby was slowly starving to death."[8]

Add Unpaid Household Labor to the GDP

A final, and relatively cheap, step the government could take toward valuing unpaid child care would be to include it in the GDP. In the early 1990s, the United Nations Statistical Commission recommended that member countries prepare so-called satellite GDP accounts estimating the value of unremunerated work. Countries all over the globe are complying.   [2001]

NOTES

1. For an elaboration of this point, see Mona Harrington, *Care and Equality* (New York: Knopf, 1999).
2. Jacob Alex Kierman and Arleen Leibowitz, "The Work-Employment Distinction Among New Mothers," *Journal of Human Resources* 29, no. 2 (spring 1994): 296. Unfortunately, another female boss who separated a new mother from her job was Washington senator Patty Murray, who had campaigned as "a Mom in tennis shoes" with the promise that as a woman she could understand other women's problems. But apparently not enough; her legislative aide Pam Norick was forced to resign after becoming pregnant with her second baby. The story is summarized by Clara Bingham in *Women on the Hill* (New York: Times Books, 1997), 114–15, 253.
3. Alvin Powell, "Parents' Presence Helps Heal Children," *Harvard University Gazette*, November 4, 1999.
4. Suzanne Daley, "A French Paradox at Work," *New York Times*, November 11, 1999. In France not even managers are supposed to work more than 39 hours a week.
5. See Mona Harrington, *Care and Equality*, pp. 51–52, 153.
6. Raymond Hernandez, "Millions in State Child Care Funds Going Unspent in New York," *New York Times*, October 25, 1999.
7. Adam Gopnik, "Like a King," *New Yorker*, January 31, 2000.

   The mother was subsequently committed on a lesser charge and released on probation. Among the conditions of her release was a requirement that she attend parenting classes.
8. The mother, a poor, 21-year-old living in the Bronx, was subsequently convicted of criminally negligent homicide, despite the fact that she had twice taken the baby to her HMO for checkups and been turned away because the baby's Medicaid card hadn't yet arrived in the mail. She was sentenced to five years' probation, including a condition that if she had another child during the probation period, she take parenting classes. See Katha Pollitt, "A Bronx Tale," *The Nation*, June 14, 1999; Nina Bernstein, "Mother Convicted in Infant's Starvation Death Gets 5 Years' Probation," *New York Times*, September 9, 1999.

Family Support Policies and Programs: An International Perspective

The USA lags behind other developed countries, and even some developing countries, in its family and maternity support policies. Of 178 countries studied by Human Rights Watch, the USA was the only one without a national maternity leave policy. Only about 1 in 10 U.S. workers had any paid family leave benefits. This leaves the least-skilled workers the most vulnerable to work and family stresses. The study commends European countries like Sweden and France, where maternal employment is high and where there is significantly more government help available to support families. The table below outlines maternity leave policies in several countries—notice that even some developing countries offer better services for caregivers than the USA does.

In most of Europe, government supports are in the form of mandated family leaves with pay, and free or inexpensive access to good-quality preschools regardless of parents' employment status. The majority of families take advantage of these services. These services are accompanied by other governmental supports in the form of generous paternity and maternity leave policies, high government oversight of day cares and preschools, and educationally challenging preschool programs aimed at school readiness of children. National regulations in these countries demand high levels of training requirements for child care workers, and these workers are paid well.

The sound family-friendly policies implemented by European governments extend beyond child care subsidies and oversight to including other family needs of parents and caregivers with children—for example, alternative work arrangements and shortened workweeks without penalty in the form of benefits or professional development, easy access to health care services, and income supplements. The major difference in governmental policies and practices between other developed countries and the USA is that in the other countries significant public funds are allotted to child care, preschools, and other family support systems. In the USA, these institutions are almost entirely privatized and managed on a for-profit basis. The latter system leads to unequal services where the most privileged families obtain the best services and families in the lower social strata are not able to afford good-quality child care and educational services for their children. Over many generations, this leads to a widening of social inequality.

Country	Maternal mortality per 100,000	Maternity leave	% wages paid during maternity leave
Norway	7	46–56 weeks	80–100
France	8	16 weeks	100
Spain	4	16 weeks	100
United States	11	Not determined	No national program
Brazil	60	12 weeks	100
South Africa	400	4 months	60
India	450	12 weeks	100

[2011]

Sources: Human Rights Watch, Failing Its Families, February 23, 2011, http://www.hrw.org/en/node/96430/section/6; Marcia K. Meyers and Janet C. Gornik, "The European Model: What We Can Learn from How Other Nations Support Families That Work," *American Prospect*, 2004, http://www.thirdworldtraveler.com/Europe/European_Model_Families. html; United Nations Statistic Division (2011), retrieved on February 17, 2011, http://unstats.un.org/unsd/demographic/products/indwm/tab5g.htm.

🌿 65

Exploding the Stereotypes: Welfare

RITA HENLEY JENSEN

I am a woman. A white woman, once poor but no longer. I am not lazy, never was. I am a middle-aged woman, with two grown daughters. I was a welfare mother, one of those women society considers less than nothing.

I should have applied for Aid to Families with Dependent Children (AFDC) when I was 18 years old, pregnant with my first child, and living with a boyfriend who slapped me around. But I didn't.

I remember talking it over at the time with a friend. I lived in the neighborhood that surrounds the vast Columbus campus of Ohio State University. Students, faculty, hangers-on, hippies, runaways, and recent émigrés from Kentucky lived side by side in the area's relatively inexpensive housing. I was a runaway.

On a particularly warm midsummer's day, I stood on High Street, directly across from the campus' main entrance, with an older, more sophisticated friend, wondering what to do with my life. With my swollen belly, all hope of my being able to cross the street and enroll in the university had evaporated. Now, I was seeking advice about how merely to survive, to escape the assaults and still be able to care for my child.

My friend knew of no place I could go, nowhere I could turn, no one else I could ask. I remember saying in a tone of resignation, "I can't apply for welfare." Instead of disagreeing with me, she nodded, acknowledging our mutual belief that taking beatings was better than taking handouts. Being "on the dole" meant you deserved only contempt.

In August 1965, I married my attacker.

Six years later, I left him and applied for assistance. My children were 18 months and 5 1/2 years old. I had waited much too long. Within a year, I crossed High Street to go to Ohio State. I graduated in four years and moved to New York City to attend Columbia University's Graduate School of Journalism. I have worked as a journalist for 18 years now. My life on welfare was very hard—there were times when I didn't have enough food for the three of us. But I was able to get an education while on welfare. It is hardly likely that a woman on AFDC today would be allowed to do what I did, to go to school and develop the kind of skills that enabled me to make a better life for myself and my children.

This past summer, I attended a conference in Chicago on feminist legal theory. During the presentation of a paper related to gender and property rights, the speaker mentioned as an aside that when one says "welfare mother" the listener hears "black welfare mother." A discussion ensued about the underlying racism until someone declared that the solution was easy: all that had to be done was have the women in the room bring to the attention of the media the fact that white women make up the largest percentage of welfare recipients. At this point, I stood, took a deep breath, stepped out of my professional guise, and informed the crowd that I was a former welfare mother. Looking at my white hair, blue eyes, and freckled Irish skin, some laughed; others gasped—despite having just acknowledged that someone like me was, in fact, a "typical" welfare mother.

Occasionally I do this. Speak up. Identify myself as one of "them." I do so reluctantly because welfare mothers are a lightning rod for race hatred, class prejudice, and misogyny. Yet I am aware that as long as welfare is viewed as an *African-American* woman's issue, instead of a *woman's* issue—whether that woman be white, African-American, Asian, Latina, or Native American—those in power can continue to exploit our country's racism to weaken and even eliminate public support for the programs that help low-income mothers and their children.

I didn't have the guts to stand up during a 1974 reception for Ohio state legislators. The party's hostess was a leader of the Columbus chapter of the National Organization for Women and she had opened up her suburban home so that representatives of many of the state's progressive organizations could lobby in an informal setting for an increase in the state's welfare allotment for families. I was invited as a representative of the campus area's single mothers' support group. In the living room, I came across a state senator in a just-slightly-too-warm-and-friendly state induced by the potent combination of free booze and a crowd of women. He quickly decided I looked like a good person to amuse with one of his favorite jokes. "You want to know how a welfare mother can prevent getting pregnant?" he asked, giggling. "She can just take two aspirin—and put them between her knees," he roared, as he bent down to place his Scotch glass between his own, by way of demonstration. I drifted away.

I finally did gather up my courage to speak out. It was in a classroom during my junior year. I was enrolled in a course on the economics of public policy because I wanted to understand why the state of Ohio thought it desirable to provide me and my two kids with only $204 per month—59 percent of what even the state itself said a family of three needed to live.

For my required oral presentation, I chose "Aid to Families with Dependent Children." I cited the fact that approximately two-thirds of all the poor families in the country were white; I noted that most welfare families consisted of one parent and two children. As an audiovisual aid, I brought my own two kids along. My voice quavered a bit as I delivered my intro: I stood with my arms around my children and said, "We are a typical AFDC family."

My classmates had not one question when I finished. I don't believe anyone even bothered to ask the kids' names or ages.

If I were giving this talk today, I would hold up a picture of us back then and say we still represent typical welfare recipients. The statistics I would cite to back up that statement have been refined since the 1970s and now include "Hispanic" as a category. In 1992, 38.9 percent of all welfare mothers were white, 37.2 percent were black, 17.8 percent were "Hispanic," 2.8 percent were Asian, and 1.4 percent were Native American.

My report, however, would focus on the dramatic and unrelenting reduction in resources available to low-income mothers in the last two decades.

Fact: In 1970, the average monthly benefit for a family of three was $178. Not much, but consider that as a result of inflation, that $178 would be approximately $680 today. And then consider that the average monthly payment today is only about $414. That's the way it's been for more than two decades: the cost of living goes up (by the states' own accounting, the cost of rent, food, and utilities for a family of three has doubled), but the real value of welfare payments keeps going down.

Fact: The 1968 Work Incentive Program (the government called it WIN; we called it WIP) required that all unemployed adult recipients sign up for job training or employment once their children turned six. The age has now been lowered to three, and states may go as low as age one. What that means is you won't be able to attend and finish college while on welfare. (In most states a college education isn't considered job training, even though experts claim most of us will need college degrees to compete in the workplace of the twenty-first century.)

Fact: Forty-two percent of welfare recipients will be on welfare less than two years during their entire lifetime, and an additional 33 percent will spend between two and eight years on welfare. The statistics haven't changed much over the years: women still use welfare to support their families when their children are small.

In 1974, I ended my talk with this joke: A welfare mother went into the drugstore and bought a can of deodorant. I explained that it was funny because everyone knew that welfare mothers could not afford "extras" like personal hygiene products. My joke today would be: A welfare mother believed that if elected public officials understood these facts, they would not campaign to cut her family's benefits.

The idea that government representatives care about welfare mothers is as ridiculous to me now as the idea back then that I would waste my limited funds on deodorant. It is much clearer to me today what the basic functions of welfare public policy are at this moment in U.S. history.

By making war on welfare recipients, political leaders can turn the public's attention away from the government's redistribution of wealth to the wealthy. Recent studies show that the United States has become the most economically stratified of industrial nations. In fact, Federal Reserve figures reveal that the richest 1 percent of American households—each with a minimum net worth of $2.3 million—control nearly 40 percent of the wealth, while in Britain, the richest 1 percent of the population controls about 18 percent of the wealth. In the mid-1970s, both countries were on a par: the richest 1 percent controlled 20 percent of the wealth. President Reagan was the master of this verbal shell game. He told stories of welfare queens and then presided over the looting of the nation's savings and loans by wealthy white men.

Without a doubt, the current urgency for tax cuts and spending reductions can be explained by the fact that President Clinton tried to shift the balance slightly in 1992 and the wealthy ended up paying 16 percent more in taxes the following year, by one estimate.

The purpose of this antiwelfare oratory and the campaigns against sex education, abortion rights, and aid to teenage mothers is to ensure a constant supply of young women as desperate and ashamed as I was. Young women willing to take a job at any wage rate, willing to tolerate the most abusive relationships with men, and unable to enter the gates leading to higher education.

To accomplish their goals, political leaders continually call for reforms that include demands that welfare recipients work, that teenagers don't have sex, and that welfare mothers stop giving birth (but don't have abortions). Each "reform" addresses the nation's racial and sexual stereotypes: taking care of one's own children is not work; welfare mothers are unemployed, promiscuous, and poorly motivated; and unless the government holds their feet to the fire, these women will live on welfare for years, as will their children and their children's children.

This type of demagoguery has been common throughout our history. What sets the present era apart is the nearly across-the-board cooperation of the media. The national news magazines, the most prestigious daily newspapers, the highly regarded broadcast news outlets, as well as the supermarket tabloids and talk-radio hosts, have generally abandoned the notion that one of their missions is to sometimes comfort the afflicted and afflict the comfortable. Instead, they too often reprint politicians' statements unchallenged, provide charts comparing one party's recommendations to another's without really questioning those recommendations, and illustrate story after story, newscast after newscast, with a visual of an African-American woman (because we all know they're the only ones on welfare) living in an urban housing project (because that's where all welfare recipients live) who has been on welfare for years.

When *U.S. News & World Report* did a major story on welfare reform this year, it featured large photographs of eight welfare recipients, seven of whom were women of color: six African-Americans and one Latina or Native American (the text does not state her ethnicity). Describing the inability of welfare mothers to hold jobs (they are "hobbled not only by their lack of experience but also by their casual attitudes toward punctuality, dress, and coworkers"), the article offers the "excuse" given by one mother for not taking a 3 p.m. to 11 p.m. shift: " 'I wouldn't get to see my kids,' " she told the reporter. You can't win for losing—should she take that 3-to-11 job and her unsupervised kids get in trouble, you can be sure some conservative would happily leap on her as an example of one of those poor women who are bad mothers and whose kids should be in orphanages.

Why don't the media ever find a white woman from Ohio or Iowa or Wisconsin, a victim of domestic violence, leaving the father of her two children to make a new start? Or a Latina mother like the one living in my current neighborhood, who has one child and does not make enough as a home health care attendant to pay for her family's health insurance? Or a Native American woman living on a reservation, creating crafts for pennies that will be sold by others for dollars?

Besides reinforcing stereotypes about the personal failings of welfare recipients, when my colleagues write in-depth pieces about life on welfare they invariably concentrate on describing welfare mothers' difficulties with the world at large: addictions, lack of transportation, dangerous neighbors, and, most recently, shiftless boyfriends who begin beating them when they do get jobs—as if this phenomenon were limited to relationships between couples with low incomes.

I wonder why no journalist I have stumbled across, no matter how well meaning, has communicated what I believe is the central reality of most women's lives on welfare: they believe all the stereotypes too and they are ashamed of being on welfare. They eat, breathe, sleep, and clothe themselves with shame.

Most reporting on welfare never penetrates the surface, and the nature of the relationship between the welfare system and the woman receiving help is never explored. Like me, many women fleeing physical abuse must make the welfare department their first stop after seeking an order of protection. Studies are scarce, but some recent ones of women in welfare-to-work programs across the U.S. estimate that anywhere from half to three-fourths of participants are, or have been, in abusive relationships. And surveys of some homeless shelters indicate that half of the women living in them are on the run from a violent mate.

But if welfare is the means of escape, it is also the institutionalization of the dynamic of battering. My husband was the source of my and my children's daily bread and of daily physical and psychological attacks. On welfare, I was free of the beatings, but the assaults on my self-esteem were still frequent and powerful, mimicking the behavior of a typical batterer.

As he pounds away, threatening to kill the woman and children he claims to love, the abuser often accuses his victims of lying, laziness, and infidelity. Many times, he threatens to snatch the children away from their mother in order to protect them from her supposed incompetence, her laziness, dishonesty, and sexual escapades.

On welfare, just as with my husband, I had to prove every statement was not a lie. Everything had to be documented: how many children I had, how much I paid for rent, fuel, transportation, electricity, child care, and so forth. It went so far as to require that at every "redetermination of need" interview (every six months), I had to produce the originals of my children's birth certificates, which were duly photocopied over and over again. Since birth certificates do not change, the procedure was a subtle and constant reminder that nothing I said was accepted as truth. Ever.

But this is a petty example. The more significant one was the suspicion that my attendance at Ohio State University was probably a crime. Throughout my college years, I regularly reported that I was attending OSU. Since the WIN limit at that time was age six and my youngest daughter was two when I started, I was allowed to finish my undergraduate years without having to report to some job-training program that would have prepared me for a minimum-wage job. However, my caseworker and I shared an intuitive belief that something just had to be wrong about this. How could I be living on welfare and going to college? Outrageous! Each day I awoke feeling as if I were in a race, that I had to complete my degree before I was charged with a felony.

As a matter of fact, I remember hearing, a short time after I graduated, that a group of welfare mothers attending college in Ohio were charged with food stamp fraud, apparently for not reporting their scholarships as additional income.

Batterers frequently lie to their victims—it's a power thing. Caseworkers do too. For example, when I moved to New York to attend graduate school and applied for assistance, I asked my intake worker whether I could apply for emergency food stamps. She told me there was no emergency food program. The kids and I scraped by, but that statement was false. I was unaware of it until welfare rights advocates successfully sued the agency for denying applicants emergency food assistance. In another case, when someone gave me a 10-year-old Opel so I could keep my first (very low paying) reporting job, my caseworker informed me in writing that mere possession of a car made me ineligible for welfare. (I appealed and won. The caseworker was apparently confused by the fact that although I was not allowed to have any assets, I did need the car to get to work. She also assumed a used car had to have some value. Not this one.)

Then there's the issue of sexual possessiveness: states rarely grant assistance to families with fathers still in the home. And as for feeling threatened about losing custody, throughout the time I was on welfare, I knew that if I stumbled at all, my children could be taken away from me. It is widely understood that any neighbor can call the authorities about a welfare mother, making a charge of neglect, and that mother, since she is less than nothing, might not be able to prove her competency. I had a close call once. I had been hospitalized for 10 days and a friend took care of my children. After my return home, however, I was still weak. I would doze off on the sofa while the kids were awake— one time it happened when they were outside playing on the sidewalk. A neighbor, seeing them there unattended, immediately called the child welfare agency, which sent someone out to question me and to look inside my refrigerator to see if I had any food. Luckily, that day I did.

Ultimately, leaving an abusive relationship and applying for welfare is a little like leaving solitary confinement to become part of a prison's general population. It's better, but you are still incarcerated.

None of this is ever discussed in the context of welfare reform. The idiot state legislator, the prosecutor in Ohio who brought the charges against welfare mothers years ago, Bill Clinton, and Newt Gingrich all continue to play the race and sex card by hollering for welfare reform. They continue to exploit and feed the public's ignorance about and antipathy toward welfare mothers to propel their own careers. Sadly, journalists permit them to do so, perhaps for the same reason.

Lost in all this are the lives of thousands of women impoverished by virtue of their willingness to assume the responsibility of raising their children. An ex-boyfriend used to say that observing my struggle was a little like watching someone standing in a room, with arms upraised to prevent the ceiling from pressing in on her. He wondered just how long I could prevent the collapse.

Today, welfare mothers have even less opportunity than I did. Their talent, brains, luck, and resourcefulness are ignored. Each new rule, regulation, and

reform make it even more unlikely that they can use the time they are on welfare to do as I did: cross the High Streets in their cities and towns, and realize their ambitions. Each new rule makes it more likely that they will only be able to train for a minimum-wage job that will never allow them to support their families.

So no, I don't think all we have to do is get the facts to the media. I think we have to raise hell any way we can.

Our goal is simple: never again should there be a young woman, standing in front of the gates that lead to a better future, afraid to enter because she believes she must instead choose poverty and battery.   [1995]

✿ 66

The New Antipoverty Regime: Same Single-Mother Poverty Problems

RANDY ALBELDA

Women-headed families with children have always been vulnerable to poverty. Being a primary caregiver and having to garner enough income to support a family is remarkably hard. Prior to the 1980s, putting white single mothers to work was thought to be undesirable (there was much less reluctance toward black single mothers). Antipoverty programs in the United States, most of which were developed from the 1930s through the 1970s, reflect these realities and values as they were constructed for white families without an able-bodied male breadwinner, including single mothers, those with disabilities, and elder Americans. The most important of the antipoverty programs for single mothers was the cash assistance program, established in 1935, called Aid to Families with Dependent Children (AFDC)—also commonly referred to as "welfare." But other programs have provided key government supports for poor single mothers and their children. These include food assistance programs (such as Food Stamps—now called SNAP, the Supplemental Nutritional Assistance Program), health insurance (Medicaid), housing assistance (public housing as well as the Section 8 housing voucher program), the refundable Earned Income Tax Credit, and child care assistance. Table 1 includes some information on the original legislation, target groups, and current eligibility requirements of these major programs.

In 1996 the U.S. Congress abolished the provisions of the AFDC cash assistance program for poor families with children in the Personal Responsibility and Work Opportunity Reconciliation Act (PRWORA). This bill, signed into law by President Clinton, in its place created a block grant called TANF (Temporary Assistance for Needy Families) and with it formally swept in a new direction for antipoverty programs for single mothers (and others who are not disabled nor over 65 years old). PRWORA included changes to the Food Stamps program that tightened eligibility by restricting assistance to many immigrants and implementing work requirements for some. Around the same time both the Earned Income Tax Credit (EITC) program—providing refundable tax credits for low-income wage earners—and child care–assistance funding were expanded. In addition, the State Children's Health Insurance Program (SCHIP) was enacted in 1997.

The spate of legislative changes to the major antipoverty programs in the United States had one underlying goal in mind: replace government assistance with earnings. The new social compact with the nondisabled, nonelder poor, as reflected in these major changes to antipoverty programs, was to require (but not necessarily reward) employment in exchange for government support. At the time, conservatives promoted marriage as a key route out of poverty but were content to pass legislation that limited government support and required work. Liberals argued that employment coupled with government supports until adults became "self-sufficient" represented a fair and responsible way to deal with poverty.

Combined, these policy changes have created a mandate for poor adults, especially single mothers, to get a job, any job. But there are some vital missing components in the new antipoverty regime. First, neither the federal government nor state legislatures have put into place sufficient funding for child care or adequate guarantees or even incentives to create the type of jobs that would make this poverty-fighting strategy possible. Second, as government antipoverty programs were transformed into work-supports programs by restricting eligibility and requiring work, few paid attention to the rest of the provisions in these programs, which would ensure that individuals earning low wages might still be able to receive government supports. As it turns out, with a few notable exceptions, the eligibility and reporting requirements of antipoverty programs mean that they do not support low-wage workers very well or for very long. Getting and keeping most of these supports is time-consuming and cumbersome, making it especially hard for working mothers to comply. Further, as earnings increase, most government benefits are reduced substantially and then fade out completely—often at very low levels of the wage spectrum. As a result, some families that receive several of these supports become worse off as they earn more.

The 1990s changes to antipoverty programs have increased the number of poor and low-income families with wages, but it is not at all clear that they have increased the ability of many single-mother families or woman-headed families with children to meet minimum living standards (earn enough to be self-sufficient). There has been little or no talk of revisiting these employment-promoting antipoverty programs, even though the recession has meant the loss of employment for many. In 2009 the unemployment rate for single mothers was just under 14 percent (one out of every seven). For this and other reasons it is time to "modernize" antipoverty programs by ensuring they do what policy makers and others want them to do—encourage employment while reducing poverty. But they must also serve as an important safety net when work is not available or possible. But changes to government policies are not enough. If employment is

Table 1   Six U.S. Means-Tested Antipoverty Programs

Program	Description
Childcare Assistance	This primarily includes Child Care Development Funds (CCDF) established in 1996, TANF funds used for child care, and funds provided by states to help families with child care expenses. The program is meant to help enable poor and low-income adults with children to participate in employment or educational and training activities. It is used to expand educational opportunities for poor children. CCDF funds are provided by the federal government but administered by states. States have considerable leeway in setting provider payment levels, parent co-payment levels, income eligibility requirements, and regulation of programs.
EITC (Earned Income Tax Credit)	The original intent was to reward poor parents with earnings and reduce the impact of payroll taxes on low earners. This federal program sets eligibility rules that apply to everyone, regardless of residence. Income eligibility varies by family size and ranges from $48,362 (married couple, with two or more children) to $13,460 (single childless adult) in 2009.
Food Stamps	In 2008 this program was renamed Supplemental Nutrition Assistance Program (SNAP). It was originally established to improve nutritional levels of low-income households and to bolster the agricultural industry. The federal Food Stamps program is targeted to reach poor and near-poor persons. States administer the program using mostly federal funds. The federal government sets the eligibility requirements, but states can provide their own funding to expand eligibility and have some leeway in changing eligibility requirements. Income eligibility is usually 130 percent of the federal poverty level.
Housing Assistance	Public housing was originally intended to alleviate urban slum conditions for families with earners. Since the 1970s, public housing has come to serve very low-income persons and families, with rents linked directly to income. Section 8 assistance promotes market-based incentives to low-income families to find privately owned housing using vouchers. Local Housing Authorities administer the program using mostly federal funds. Typically households with 30 percent or less of area median income are eligible.
Medicaid and SCHIP (State Children's Health Insurance Plan)	This federal program enables states—through matching grants—to provide funds to providers of health care to meet the medical needs of low-income persons. SCHIP increased Medicaid funding and incentives for states to broaden health insurance for children living in low-income families with the intention of filling the gap between public health coverage and employer-sponsored insurance. States administer both Medicaid and SCHIP and are required to match federal funds. They have considerable leeway on what care is covered and payment rates for services.
TANF (Temporary Assistance to Needy Families)	Established through the Personal Responsibility and Work Opportunity Reconciliation Act of 1996, which replaced its precursor AFDC (Aid to Families with Dependent Children). TANF serves the same population as AFDC but with strong incentives for employment and marriage for low-income families with children. States administer the block grant and have considerable leeway in designing cash assistance programs. Income eligibility and benefits vary widely across (and even within) states. States are required to provide a share of funding based on amounts spent on AFDC in the early 1990s.

to be the route out of poverty, then wages and employer benefits must support workers at basic minimum levels.

EVERY MOTHER A WORKING MOTHER

Jobs have always been promoted as this country's best solution to poverty. But it is a strategy that has never really worked well for women, because until recently women's wages alone have often been too low to support themselves, let alone families. Further, mothers are often responsible for the care of their children, which limits time for paid work. Until the 1980s, work was never so explicitly forced on all poor mothers (especially those with young children), with an emphasis on making recipients of government assistance "work-ready" through employment and training. Sixty percent of all mothers were in the paid labor force by the mid-1980s—public sentiment seemed to indicate that if other mothers must work, why not single mothers? By the 1990s this turned into a mandate that mothers work.

While many families struggle with society's and women's own work expectations, for single mothers the emphasis on employment has been a particular hardship for three basic and simple reasons. First, the average woman earns about three-quarters as much per hour as her male counterpart. Women who need to rely on public supports like welfare earn even less, because they often have fewer skills, less work experience, and more physical disabilities than other women. Second, these families include kids. Like all mothers, single mothers have to deal with both greater demands on their time and larger financial demands—more "mouths to feed." Child care demands limit the time women can spend at their jobs, and interrupt them with periodic crises, ranging from a sick child to a school's summer break. This takes its toll on both the amount and the quality of work many mothers can obtain. Finally, unlike other mothers, single mothers often have only one adult in the family to juggle child care and a job. While a single mother may receive child care from an absent father, she certainly cannot count on the consistent assistance—be it financial support or help with the child care—that a resident father can provide.

The difficulties single mothers face are borne out in the poverty statistics. In 2009, 38.5 percent of woman-headed families with children and single-mother families were poor, compared to just 5.8 percent of married couples with no children. While only 12.5 percent of families in the United States are single-mother families, they comprise 43.2 percent of poor families.

ENDING "WELFARE" AND PROMOTING EMPLOYMENT

The 1990s rang in large changes to most of the major antipoverty programs in the United States. The most sweeping and highly politicized changes were to cash assistance programs through the PRWORA. Relying on the rhetoric that "states know best" and "dependency is bad," this bill gave states tremendous leeway over income and work eligibility rules and how to define education and training. The goal was to put mothers to work. For the first time there was a time limit on benefit receipt: states are not allowed to allocate TANF money to any adult who has received TANF money for 60 months—regardless of how much assistance was received in any month or how long it took to accrue 60 months of aid. States can impose their own time limits, and most have implemented time limits of 60 months or less.

The new law requires recipients whose youngest child is more than one year old to do some form of paid or unpaid work after 24 months of receiving benefits. Although previous federal provisions also had work requirements, they exempted women with a disabled child or whose youngest child was less than six years old, and most job training qualified as being part of a work program. Besides extending the eligible work population to include women with very young or disabled children, most job training and education does not count as "work."

To accommodate the push for employment, Congress also expanded the EITC and increased funding for the Child Care Development Block Grant, which provides states with money to help provide child care to parents leaving TANF and working parents with low incomes. The SCHIP program was implemented in 1997, in part out of recognition that many single mothers were entering low-wage work, losing Medicaid coverage, and working for employers who did not provide any affordable health insurance coverage. Even housing assistance programs took on promoting employment. The U.S. Department of Housing and Urban Development (HUD) facilitated some local housing authorities to take on demonstration projects to redesign housing assistance to induce residents to increase earnings.

In response to these changes, some very clear usage patterns have emerged. The TANF rolls have plummeted. In 1996 there were 4.43 million families on the program; in 2009 there 1.77 million families, despite the highest levels of unemployment in decades. In fact, in 2008, when unemployment soared, only 15 states saw their TANF caseloads increase; the rest continued to experience reductions, calling into question TANF's role as an antipoverty program. In the late 1990s, when the TANF roles fell, so did Medicaid and Food Stamp enrollments. These programs have since seen increases in usage, especially since the recession, but it was clear that when families lost TANF, they also lost access to other supports.

The number of persons receiving EITC has increased dramatically, and the cost of this program exceeds that of Food Stamps (SNAP) and TANF combined. And while the demand for child care assistance has continually increased among poor and low-income working mothers, the funding has not kept pace. In 2006 these funds were serving only one out of every six (17 percent) of all eligible children and 39 percent of poor eligible children. Similarly, funding for public housing has not kept pace with needs (and increasing rents), and the public housing stock is shrinking, with private developers selling off their property after the required time limit for public use has expired. Long waiting lists for public housing and Section 8 housing vouchers are common throughout the United States.

The strategy of promoting employment was remarkably successful at getting single mothers into the labor force. In 1995, 63.5 percent of all single mothers were employed, and 67.8 percent by 2009.

This rate exceeds that of married mothers, whose employment rate in 2009 was 66.3 percent. So with all that employment, why are poverty rates still so high for woman-headed families with children? The answer lies in the nature of low-wage work and the mismatch between poverty-reduction policies and employment.

LOW-WAGE EMPLOYMENT AND SINGLE MOTHERS: A POOR COMBINATION

There are two fundamental mismatches single mothers now face in this new welfare regime. The first has to do with the awkward pairing of poor mothers and low-wage jobs. Almost half of single mothers are in jobs that are low paying (in this case, below two-thirds of median wages). In addition to the low pay, low-wage jobs are also characterized by their lack of employer benefits, such as paid time off and employer-sponsored health insurance and retirement plans. Additionally, many low-wage jobs that mothers find in retail and hospitality have very uneven work hours, providing employers with lots of flexibility but workers with almost none.

The lack of employer-sponsored health insurance is not necessarily replaced by the government health insurance program for low-wage workers. Medicaid income eligibility thresholds for adults with children vary state by state, but in 2008 the vast majority (two-thirds of all states) had it set below 100 percent of the federal poverty line. The new Patient Protection and Affordable Care Act may help, depending on the cost of purchasing insurance, but for now many low-wage mothers go without health care coverage.

It does not take much for a single mother to miss work or be late. A late school bus, car trouble, a sick child, or a sick child care provider can throw a wrench in the best-laid plans for getting to and staying at work. A missed day of work is a missed day of pay, without paid time off, and too many missed days can easily cost a woman her job. A work schedule that changes often makes regular child care arrangements nearly impossible.

Finally, single mothers are employed but are also primarily responsible for their children. Low-wage work requires a large number of hours to earn enough to support oneself, let alone a family. Yet working more hours means less time with kids. This can be costly in several ways. Single mothers have to hire someone to take care of kids while at work, and that can be expensive. If mothers instead rely heavily on good-natured relatives who provide care but don't engage and motivate young children, this leads to other costs. Leaving younger children with older brothers and sisters is another solution, but this too leads to older kids missing out on important after-school learning. Working long hours, coupled with low earnings and a tight budget, might mean missing time to help do homework, meet with teachers, or pay for in- and out-of-school activities that enrich children's lives. Working fewer hours also has its problems, mainly insufficient income.

LOW-WAGE EMPLOYMENT AND ANTIPOVERTY POLICIES: THE NEW MISMATCH

Four of the six antipoverty programs described at the end of this chapter were specifically designed for people with little or no earnings. This includes SNAP, TANF, Medicaid, and housing assistance. Child care assistance and the EITC were specifically designed for workers, but they too have their quirks and problems as antipoverty programs.

What does it mean that these programs are not designed for those with employment? There are two important features. First, it means that income eligibility to receive the benefits tends to be very low—that is, you need to be pretty poor to get them. For example, only two states have income thresholds above the poverty line for TANF. To get any SNAP benefits, a single mother needs to have income below 130 percent of the poverty line. Working full-time at $10 an hour would make a single mother with one child ineligible for both programs in all states. Perhaps as important it means that even when eligible and receiving one of these supports, you lose a portion of the benefits when you have any earnings. For TANF (in most states), SNAP and housing assistance for every additional dollar you earn you lose about 33 cents in each support. As these benefits phase out completely, usually at the eligibility threshold, the support is

there but only when earnings are very small. This means work just does not pay.

Second, the program application and certification procedures and in some cases the level of benefits were designed assuming someone had plenty of time to get and use the benefits. Each program has its own eligibility requirements and sets of documents required to prove initial eligibility as well as continued eligibility. While some states have tried to move to a "one-stop" system, most states require separate applications for each of the programs and many often require an office visit. If you have ever applied for one of these programs, maybe you have experienced the frustration of providing the correct materials in a timely way. The time it takes to provide the paperwork and visit the office can be substantial. Recertification (i.e., maintaining eligibility) can also require office visits and further documentation. In short, the programs assume someone with lots of time on their hands to meet with caseworker and collect documentation. But with employment requirements, this is not the right assumption. Missing time at work to provide needed paperwork for the welfare office is just not worth it. There is considerable evidence that many people just do not use TANF or SNAP even when eligible because of the "hassle factor." Even the benefit levels assume an unlimited amount of time. Until recently, the maximum dollar amount of monthly SNAP benefits was based on a very low-cost budget that required home-cooked meals.

Child care assistance is obviously a program designed for "working" mothers, but it too often has onerous reporting requirements and in most states the subsidies phase out very quickly at the federal poverty line. As these phase out, co-payments to child care providers become steep. As mentioned earlier, even when eligible, the lack of funding means most parents don't receive it. The exception to all these rules is the EITC. It was established explicitly to help low-wage parents with low incomes. It is relatively easy to claim (fill out a two-page tax form along with the rest of the income tax forms) and of all the programs reaches the highest up the income ladder. It even phases out differently: the credit increases as earnings rise, flattens out and then decreases at higher levels or earnings. As a federal program it has uniform standards. It is also the exception to the rule in that almost everyone receives the EITC as a lump sum benefit once a year. As such, the EITC is used very differently than other antipoverty supports. Families often use the lump sum "windfall" to pay off a large bill or pay for things long put off like a visit to the dentist, major car repair, or buying a large-ticket item. While helpful and relatively easy to get, the EITC does not typically help with the monthly and day-to-day expenses, as the other antipoverty programs do.

WHAT MIGHT BE DONE?

Employment, even with government supports, is unlikely to provide a substantial percentage of single-mother families with adequate family incomes. Three factors—women's lower pay, the time and money it takes to care for children, and the presence of only one adult—combine to make it nearly impossible for women to move to stable and sufficient levels of resources. Government antipoverty programs haven't filled in the gaps.

The solution of insufficient pay and time to raise children that face single-mother families will require a set of thorough changes in the relations among work, family, and income.

• *Make work pay by shoring up wages and employer benefits.* To ensure that the private sector does its part, raise the minimum wage. A full-time, year-round minimum wage job pays just over the poverty income threshold for a family of two. Conservatives and the small business lobby will trot out the bogeyman of job destruction, but studies on minimum wage increases show a zero or even positive effect on employment. In addition, mandate paid sick days for all workers and require benefit parity for part-time, temporary, and subcontracted workers. This would close a loophole that a growing number of employers use to dodge fringe benefits.

• *Reform antipoverty programs to really support employment.* To truly support low-wage employment, antipoverty programs should increase income eligibility limits so that a worker can received the supports even while earning and then phase out the

programs less quickly so low-wage workers keep getting them until they earn enough to not need them. Also streamline application processes, making them more "user-friendly." Many states have done this for unemployment insurance and for driver license and care registration renewal. Why not do the same for SNAP, TANF, and Medicaid?

• *Support paid and unpaid care work.* A society that expects all able-bodied adults to work—regardless of the age of their children—should also be a society that shares the costs of going to work, by offering programs to care for children and others who need care. This means universal child care, afterschool programs. It also means paid time off for parental leave and to care for an ill relative. And though many employees now have the right to unpaid family or medical leave through the 1993 federal Family and Medical Leave Act, many can't afford to take time off. California and New Jersey were able to extend their temporary disability insurance (TDI) beyond own disability situations to those facing a wide range of family needs could help.

New antipoverty regime, but same poverty problems: most single mothers *cannot* work their way out of poverty—definitely not without the right kind of supplemental support. There are many possible policy steps that could be taken to help them and other low-wage workers get the most out of an inhospitable labor market. But ultimately, better designed assistance to poor and low-income families, old fashion cash assistance, and minimal employment standards must be part of the formula.   [2011]

RESOURCES

Randy Albelda and Chris Tilly, *Glass Ceilings and Bottomless Pits: Women's Work, Women's Poverty* (Boston: South End Press, 1997); U.S. Census Bureau, *Historical Tables on Poverty* (http://www.census.gov/hhes/www/poverty/poverty.html); Kaiser Family Foundation, Income Eligibility Limits for Working Adults (http://www.statehealthfacts.org/comparereport.jsp?rep=54&cat=4); U.S. Department of Health and Human Services, Office of Assistant Secretary for Planning and Evaluation, *TANF 6th and 8th Annual Report to Congress,* November 2004 and July 2009; U.S. Department of Health and Human Services, Office of Assistant Secretary for Planning and Evaluation, *Estimates of Child Care Eligibility and Receipt for Fiscal Year 2006,* April 2010; Thomas Gabe, *Trends in Welfare, Work, and the Economic Well-Being of Female Headed Families with Children: 1987–2005,* Report RL

30797 (Washington, D.C.: Congressional Research Service, 2007); Randy Albelda and Heather Boushey, *Bridging the Gaps: A Picture of How Work Supports Work in Ten States* (Washington, D.C.: Center for Economic and Policy Research; and Boston: Center for Social Policy, University of Massachusetts Boston, 2007).

🌿 67

If I Survive, It Will Be Despite Welfare Reform

TONYA MITCHELL

In 1993, I found myself to be everything that America loves to hate and blame for its ills: I was young, black, pregnant and unwed, and poor. Yet for some strange reason, I had not felt—and, as a result, did not at the time recognize—the vehemence with which I would be judged as a social pariah, as an outcast, as a Welfare Queen. My mother had raised my brothers and sisters and I with very little money, yet we had come from a loving, clean, and stable home. My father drank away any money we ever had and had left us by the time I was seven. Yet my mother worked diligently to provide us with love, intellectual stimulation, dignity, a sense of direction, and an appreciation for education. So when I found myself pregnant at age 17, my only thought was that, like my mother before me, I would work hard, continue my education, and raise a happy and healthy child. Little did I suspect that things could in any way be harder for me than they had been for my mother. Little did I know that racism, classism, and sexism intersect in the ever popular rhetoric and practice of welfare-bashing, and that my toughest battle of all would be to save my sense of self and worth in a contest that costs many their souls and their self-respect.

My first recognition of the stigma that poor single mothers face came with my initial visit to the welfare office in my third month of pregnancy when I applied to receive medical benefits. Racism was rampant in the county office: As I approached the reception desk, a clerk looked at my small, brown, and still not showing body and bitterly remarked, "Pregnant, I suppose!" From there, it went downhill. During my screening, the caseworker sarcastically stated, "I suppose you don't know who the daddy is"; stifled a laugh when I said I planned to finish my GED and go on to college; and glared at me when I told him that I refused to have my teachers—who did not yet know I was pregnant—sign notes for the welfare office stating that I was still in school and in good standing. To be frank, I was shocked. I had always known and hated racism when I saw and experienced it, but this was something more. It was racism mixed with the sense that someone had the right to hate me, to laugh at me, to disrespect me openly and blatantly because I was black and poor, because I was pregnant, and because I was alone.

I have never backed down in my life, and I was certainly not going to when my unborn child's health depended on my perseverance. So I sat and silently suffered the caseworker's sarcasm and disrespect, but I left with medical coupons in my hand. This, however, did not guarantee that life would be any easier, because I found that many doctors, and most private physicians, can and do refuse to take new patients with medical coupons. The stigma of being a welfare mom was already being read on my body as I went from practitioner to practitioner, begging them to see me and to check on the health of my baby. Finally, I was allowed to see a nurse practitioner at a public medical clinic that operated on a sliding-scale basis. It is at least officially against the law to discriminate against a person on the basis of their race or gender, but it is evidently just fine to refuse to serve them on the basis of their poverty read through receipt of state-issued medical coupons. The final shock of the day came when I found that I was pregnant with twins.

I did go on to finish my GED, and three weeks after the birth of my babies I entered a community college with every intention of finishing at the top of my class, then going on to earn a four-year college degree. I know many feel that welfare is a trap from which one cannot escape. But for me, welfare meant the ability to be a good mother to my baby girls, the freedom to earn an associate of arts degree, the choice not to depend on the man who had gotten me pregnant and who was a manipulative and dangerous person with a temper to be feared and avoided at all costs. I found a very small apartment near the college, which I received for reduced rent in exchange for managing the five other units. Every day, I took my babies to a clean and wonderful child care center, where I also worked in the afternoons. Between dropping the girls off and spending the afternoons with them, I found a paradise in my studies. I had the opportunity to listen to brilliant professors and excited students. There were great music and drama programs to attend for free. I was nurtured and encouraged by teachers and new friends, many of whom were also single parents trying to earn degrees. My world completely opened up as I learned to think in new ways and about subjects to which I had never been exposed.

It was also hard to be in school. It was particularly difficult being in those classes where welfare-bashing was delivered as academic gospel. In one sociology class, the professor opened the discussion by telling the class ridiculous anecdotes about lazy poor women sitting at home collecting welfare checks so they could buy color television sets with which to watch the *Oprah Show*. He had no proof for these allegations, no foundation on which to generalize in his obscene little stories. But he did encourage others to join in with their own ideas of the outrageous misdeeds that the poor inflict on our country—all of which seemed to be pulled out of thin air. I remember sitting and listening and feeling ill, given how exhausting my routine and that of my single-mom–student friends were. But, of course, I was too hurt, too ashamed, and too afraid to be "outed" to protest.

As hard as it was in school, being a welfare mom was far more oppressive on the outside. Oftentimes on buses, between school and the grocery store or the laundry, I would try to read my homework while my babies slept in their stroller. One day, a well-dressed Latina businesswoman put her cell phone down to look at me with disgust and say, "I wish I had time to read. Some of us have to work for a living." When I went to grocery stores and used food stamps, it was OK

as long as I was buying only beans and rice. But as soon as I tried to buy a treat for my family—say, a decent cut of meat or some good baby food for my girls—customers and clerks invariably commented, "Well, how nice that you can afford brand names on taxpayers' money when I can only afford generics."

As a poor single mother, you soon learn to give up your ideas about privacy. When the grocery-store check-out clerk announces over the intercom, "I need food-stamp change on three," and everyone stares at you; when you have to change your babies' diapers in the welfare office's public waiting room because there are no changing tables in the bathrooms; and when you must recount again and again to some paternity official the details of the sexual act that led to your pregnancy, you know you have given up your sense of autonomy and privacy. The state pays for you and the state owns you, and there is absolutely nothing you can do about it.

It was also often difficult to go home exhausted at the end of the day and then cook dinner, clean my house, clean the apartment building, play with the babies, and start my homework, which I sometimes did throughout the night. Money was so tight that my five-foot, two-inch frame went down to about 98 pounds and we often had our electricity shut off because I could not pay enough on my bill to keep it on. But we had our own tidy and safe place; the girls were healthy and happy, and I was in school and falling in love with the idea of becoming a medical professional.

In my two years as a community-college student, I had three *B*s; the rest of my grades were *A*s. In my second year, I started studying chemistry, biology, and physiology, and I loved it. I will never forget the day I mastered the Krebb's cycle or the oral exam on the physiology of a pig embryo, for which I received the highest grade in my class. Every other weekend, I started trading off with another single-mother nursing student, and we took turns going to a medical clinic to do volunteer work helping nurses care for poor folk. I felt alive and needed and valuable. I was really excited about working in a health care field someday, where

I would have the opportunity to work with and really help populations who were so underserved because of racism and poverty. I had dreams of opening a clinic where poor women of color could come for free health care and where they would be treated with the respect and dignity that they deserved. These dreams fueled my studies. When the choice came between getting an LPN degree or an associate's degree so that I could transfer to the university to earn a degree in nursing—at times, I even fantasized about becoming a doctor—the choice was clear. I earned an associate of science degree, then applied to the university, confident that I would be accepted. In the spring of 1995 came the second-happiest day of my life (the first was the day I gave birth to my twin daughters) when I received my letter of acceptance.

On that same day, however, the world came crashing down on my head when I was assaulted in my own home while preparing my daughters to go with me to the grocery store. During the attack, I feared for my life and that of my babies. That night, we slept in a safe house set up by the YWCA, and I spent the next three months in that safe haven, preparing to start school. Despite my pain and fear, I honestly thought that I could leave behind my past to become a productive and respected parent, tax-paying citizen, and worker.

I loved being at the university, and my girls were thriving and happy. University professors pushed me harder and harder, and sometimes I thought my head would explode with all the new information and ways of thinking. We were poor, and I was always tired, but we were moving forward. Yet I was in school for only a few months when President Clinton signed the Personal Responsibility and Work Opportunity Reconciliation Act of 1996 into law, and my life and my ability to be a responsible parent and medical practitioner was forever altered.

I was called into the welfare office in the next term and told that, because I had been deemed "work ready," I would have to start a job or I would be dropped from TANF (Temporary Aid to Needy Families, or welfare) immediately. This meant that I would lose not only the money I needed to pay the bills but also that I would lose medical benefits and food stamps for my girls. I had to comply. I was not even allowed to finish that term at the university, because higher education had not been written into my Personal Plan prior to 1996. Even I had to admit that there was no way I could work that many hours and go to school and care for my daughters. Although one of my professors went with me to petition the state, to show transcripts and testify about my promise as a student, my case was denied, and I was forced to be "responsible" and to "work first."

The state helped me to find a job at a nursing home, where I have now been working for almost three years. Because the nursing home is located about an hour by bus away from my apartment, I have to leave home at 5:15 in the morning, and I do not get home from the girls' child care center until after 7:30 in the evening. I make $6.35 per hour at my job, and I have to pay a good portion of my monthly check for health care for my children and myself. I do have help from the state with child care, but I have lost medical benefits and food stamps, so life is much harder for me now than it was before. It also contains very little hope.

Clearly, welfare reform and the Personal Responsibility Act changed my life. Now it is even worse. I do not have the money I need to pay my rent and bills, and I have to put my twins in an awful day care for about 10 hours a day while I work in this dead-end job. My girls are generally asleep when I drop them off in the early morning and sound asleep by the time I get home in the evening. But even if they had been able to stay awake, I am usually too tired to read to or play with them. This is what breaks my heart the most.

All I wanted was to be a nurse and help care for people. I had a very high grade point average, and I know I would have earned a nursing degree if I had been allowed to stay at the university. Nurses earn about $25 an hour. But I am stuck here. I guess it is where the state thought I belonged all along. I should have known better than to think that I could help myself and my kids to a better life.

There are just two more comments I want to make about being hated as a poor black woman who tried to exit poverty through education.

My family, my friends who are poor, and my children and I are families of love and support. It is hunger and exhaustion and pain that I want to leave behind, not the people I treasure so much. Second, I think it is important to think clearly about the ways in which racism intersects with classism and sexism to make us so hated and punished as welfare mothers. A professor at the university once told me that bell hooks had said in a lecture that "poor black women are demonized and poor white women are erased" in the rhetoric of welfare-bashing. In practical terms, what this means is that everywhere I go, people know and assume that I am "one of those women." There is absolutely no place for me to hide. Poverty is apparent on me because of the fact that I do not have money to buy good clothes, do fashionable things with my hair, or get my teeth fixed. But that obvious poverty is deeply connected to the other obvious thing about me, which is my race. The two are inextricably seen on my body. If I were well-to-do, I believe, my material condition might to some degree neutralize the way my body is read and hated. If I were white, I might be able to hide my position, at least temporarily. But as a poor, black, young, and unmarried mother, there is nowhere to hide. And so they think they have put me where I belong and will keep me stuck here. But they will fail, because I will never give up. Someday, God willing, I will return to school and pull my children out of poverty, not because of but *despite* welfare reform.   [2003]

❧ 68

How to Think Like a Feminist Economist

SUSAN FEINER

As a feminist economist I am constantly amazed—though I suppose I should be used to it by now—by the ways conventional analyses of economic matters completely ignore gender asymmetries.

Because I am a feminist economist, I am hypersensitive to differences in women's and men's economic circumstances. Women earn less, work in jobs with less prestige and few (if any) benefits, and do far more of society's unpaid work. These are not new realities. One is, however, hard-pressed to find discussions of economic policy that place women's disadvantage at the center.

Feminist economists understand how important it is to challenge the assumptions, and hence, the conclusions, of mainstream economics.

The economics that makes its way into the public realm consistently misrepresents the best interests of ordinary folks in their multiple roles as workers, consumers, and citizens. Economics as we know it, and as it is taught in countless undergraduate courses, is little more than an apology for the status quo. Textbook economics, replete with supply-and-demand models demonstrating the market's natural tendency to correct shortages or surpluses, doesn't take the topic of "disadvantage" seriously.

In textbook economics, markets are markets. Competition is competition. And any economic system that encourages competition in markets will, by the very rules baked into the exercise, produce economic outcomes that duly reflect the wishes of the people. Your income is too low? Well, retrain for a job in a higher-paying field. Your neighborhood is decaying? Just save more so you can move. The roads and bridges on which you drive are crumbling? Sell them to the highest bidder and let the private owner charge tolls to cover the upkeep. No problem is too large or too complicated that a good dose of market competition won't fix it.

In short, there is no such thing as "disadvantage." There are only individual bad choices.

The spectacular failure of the financial sector, with the attendant loss of about 20 million full-time jobs, should reveal—even to free-market economists—major flaws in this way of thinking. But an intellectual bankruptcy rules the system, as demonstrated by critiques of every aspect of the theory—its assumptions, claimed links of causation, and the failure to match up with historical experience.

My experience as a feminist economist means that I vigilantly watch for intellectual sleights of hand that present the interests of the rich and powerful as the interests of us all. When bankers, corporate executives, and their minions unite behind purported economic truths, I challenge their arguments, their logic, and their appeals to the so-called "laws of the market." By looking behind and around standard economic narratives, I can construct alternative stories connected to the real world, the actual historical record, and perhaps most importantly, the questions that are not being asked—many of which, it so happens, have to do with women. There is little in economics that is "gender neutral."

TAXES ARE MORE TAXING FOR WORKING WOMEN

Feminist economists have contributed their share to the volumes critical of mainstream economics. One of our key findings is that even a topic as seemingly "gender neutral" as taxes is loaded with implications for women's economic well-being.

When we go shopping, cashiers include sales taxes regardless of our sex. Tax assessors do not value houses differently for female and male homeowners. Income tax forms do not come in pink and blue. All employees pay 6.2 percent of eligible earnings into the Social Security trust fund and all employers match that 6.2 percent. While tax rates may look gender neutral, I know that they are not. Taxes are a feminist issue.

While the hot-button political catch phrase "No new taxes" may sound like a good idea, the reality is otherwise. That's because the taxes that politicians pledge not to raise are precisely the taxes that are least relevant to women's burden of taxation.

You will be much more likely to see the gender dimensions of an economic issue if you focus on ratios rather than the pure numbers. If, for example, the evening news reported on gender differences in tax payments, they'd likely tell us that men, on average, pay more in taxes than do women. Facts and figures describing the economy are almost always more meaningful when we have information on both the numerator and the denominator. In the preceding example, the raw number "dollars paid in taxes" is the numerator. But if taxes paid are put in relation to income earned (the denominator), we will realize that because women still earn 80 cents for every dollar earned by men, women pay a greater share of their income in taxes.

For me, thinking about taxes in terms of tax burdens—who pays how much of their income in each type of tax—is necessary to cut through the political brouhaha about the virtues of tax cutting.

Politicians, pundits, and professors generally ignore the way tax cuts impact the well-being of different income groups. Doing this allows them to create the false impression that reducing taxes benefits women as well as men. Not so.

Understanding women's relationship to the U.S. tax system is critical to any advocacy work on behalf of economic equality.

Not only are there many types of taxes, the various levels of government—federal, state, and local—impose different taxes on different goods and services.

The broad categories of taxes include sales (and excise) taxes, income taxes, payroll taxes, and property taxes.

Sales taxes, payroll taxes, and property taxes are regressive. This means that as incomes rise, less is paid in each of these types of taxes. The tax burden shifts downward, the well-to-do pay less, and the folks lower down the income ladder pay more. As a result, women—who earn less than men—pay a greater share of their income in sales, property, and payroll taxes.

Because income taxes are progressive, the incidence of taxation rises as income rises. Because women earn less than men, federal and state income taxes help correct gender differences in wage income.

Sales and property taxes, which are levied by state or local governments, are regressive. But these are not the most regressive taxes: this honor goes to payroll taxes.

EARNING LESS, PAYING MORE

Every time a worker gets paid, the number at the top of the check—gross earnings—is larger, often much larger, than the actual amount that can be deposited in the bank, the net earnings. Some payroll deductions have little to do with taxes, such as pension or health care contributions.

But for most women in the United States, the lioness's share of monies deducted from each paycheck goes to contributions to Social Security and Medicare. In fact, the amounts a woman pays annually into Social Security and Medicare are likely to exceed any income tax owed to the federal government.

Women in the United States do not need more "tax cuts".

For every $1,000 the typical woman earns in wages, her employer withholds $62 as the woman's contribution to Social Security (6.2 percent). Her employer's share of Social Security contributions is also 6.2 percent, so another $62 is credited to her Social Security account. All wage and salary income, up to $97,500, is subject to Social Security taxes.

Every dollar earned above $97,500 (keep dreaming, honey) is exempt from Social Security withholding. That's why this tax is so regressive. If a woman's annual earnings are $195,000 and Social Security is withheld from only the first $97,500, then the second $97,500 earned is tax free—at least relative to the Social Security tax.

Since men, on average, earn more per year than women, and are more likely to earn more than $97,500 per year, men pay less—as a share of their income—into Social Security. They, therefore, have more to spend and save as a share of their earnings.

Adding insult to injury, studies by such noted think tanks as the Urban Institute estimate that employers don't actually pay 6.2 percent of employees' earnings. Instead, they shift this cost by holding down wages and salaries. This means that everyone who earns less than $97,500 is likely paying the full 12.4 percent of Social Security withholding.

Almost two-thirds of all taxpayers in the United States pay more in payroll (Social Security) taxes than they do in income taxes. Virtually all the tax cuts approved by Congress in the last 30 years have been income tax cuts, and the largest such cuts have gone to the top 5 percent of earners—those folks lucky enough to live in households with

average incomes exceeding $172,000 per year. Very few women earn this much in a year.

Social Security is definitely important to women. For 80 percent or more of women over 65, Social Security constitutes all of their income. To be gender-equitable, the way the government finances Social Security needs to be changed.

A critically important progressive reform would make all income—including those hedge fund bonuses out in the stratosphere—subject to Social Security withholding.

Thinking like a feminist economist reveals this stark conclusion: Women in the United States do not need more "tax cuts." What all of us need is a shift away from taxes on work (payroll taxes) and a significant increase in the taxes on the highest income earners—virtually all of whom are men.

A similar gender analysis can be applied to every tax issue and almost every policy issue that the country faces. But unveiling the gender dimensions of our economic problems and the variously proposed solutions requires a rejection of standard gender-blind analyses, and to do this we dig below a seemingly gender-neutral surface. Thinking like a feminist economist, it turns out, can be an exceedingly valuable tool for the most critical public decisions in the United States and across the globe today.   [2011]

 69

Women in Sport: A Journey Toward Equality

PAT GRIFFIN

Mia Hamm, Serena Williams, Michele Wie, Jenny Finch, Lindsey Vonn, Sheryl Swoopes, Diana Taurasi—these women are only a few of the thousands of accomplished women athletes who have benefited from the 1972 passage of Title IX. Title IX is a federal law prohibiting sex discrimination in education. Though Title IX impacts all aspects of educational programming, it is best known for creating more opportunities for women in sport.

Prior to 1972, schools provided only a few or no opportunities for girls or women to participate on school athletic teams. Colleges did not offer athletic scholarships to women, and institutional financial support for coaches, uniforms and sports equipment, travel, locker rooms, and medical assistance, if available at all, was far below the support offered to boys and men. While men's teams rode to away games on a team bus, the women's teams drove their own cars or were driven by their parents. It was not uncommon for women to coach teams as volunteers while the men's team coaches were paid a salary. Men's teams practiced and played games in prime time, while women's teams were assigned practice and game time when the men's teams were not using the pool, gym, or track.

Women athletes' accomplishments were largely unrecognized by the general public or in the sports media. In fact, the general public only knew of a few famous Olympic or professional athletes. Outstanding Olympic women athletes had no opportunities to continue their sports in college or in professional sport. The few college women athletes who represented their schools were unknowns even on their own campus. Because few professional sports for women were available, outstanding college athletes ended their careers at college graduation with no hope of a career in their sport.

Since the passage of Title IX, opportunities for women in sport have exploded. With increased opportunity to play sports, girls and women have responded with enthusiasm. The latest data from the Women's Sports Foundation show that girls' participation in high school sports has increased by 904 percent and college women's athletic participation has increased by 456 percent. In 1972, only 1 in 27 high school girls played varsity sports. In 2008, 1 in 2.5 high school girls played varsity sports.

As more women and girls have taken advantage of more and better opportunities to play, cultural norms have changed as well. Many more girls and women believe that being physically fit and athletic is an important part of a woman's identity. Athletic girls are no longer called tomboys; they are called athletes. Young girls have female athlete role models, like basketball player Sue Bird, golfer Michelle Wie, or tennis player Serena Williams, who inspire them to pursue their own athletic goals. Earning college athletic scholarships and playing professional sports are now more realistic goals that motivate many young female athletes.

Though more girls and women are participating in sport than ever before, and being an athlete is much more compatible with the self-definitions of girls and women, lingering stereotypes about women athletes still inhibit female sports participation. In the past, athletic women were in the minority. Because being athletic was associated so strongly with masculinity and because few sport opportunities were available for girls and women, those girls who did participate in sports were seen as unfeminine or thought to be lesbians. These stereotypes discouraged many young women from pursuing the meager sport opportunities available to them. As women's sport participation has increased and the feminist movement has encouraged change in traditional gender stereotypes, women athletes now serve as role models for many young girls who play sports on community leagues and school teams.

Despite these changes, homophobia (fear of or discomfort with lesbian and gay people) still affects women's sports. Lesbian and bisexual women athletes and coaches are discriminated against or pressured to keep their identities secret because of negative stereotypes of women athletes and lesbians. The lesbian label is sometimes used as a scare tactic to intimidate women in sport or to discredit women's sports in general. Used in this way, homophobia is a tool of sexism that serves to maintain the inequity between men's and women's sports. Fortunately, more women in sports and their fans are beginning to understand that women of all sexual orientations and races participate in sport and all deserve the opportunity to participate in safe and respectful climates. When accomplished athletes and role models, like WNBA star Sheryl Swoopes, come out as lesbians, stereotypes and fears begin to diminish and the power of homophobia to discourage women's participation in sport will be less of an issue.

Though impressive progress has been made in providing girls and women with more opportunities in sport, much work remains before equality of opportunity will be realized.

Thirty-eight years after the passage of Title IX, data from the National Coalition for Girls and Women in Education show that, despite the increase in participation, women's and girls' athletic school programs continue to lag behind boys' and men's programs in every measurable category, including participation opportunities, receipt of scholarships, and allocation of operating and recruiting budgets. Male athletes still receive 1.1 million more participation opportunities than their female counterparts. Female college athletes receive only 36 percent of sports operating dollars, 42 percent of athletic scholarships, and only 32 percent of athletic team recruiting spending. In addition, while athletic participation by women is rising, the number of women coaches is declining. In 1972, 90 percent of women's teams were coached by women. In 2009 only 42 percent of women's teams were coached by women and only 2 or 3 percent of men's teams were coached by women.

Improvement is also needed in the numbers of girls and women of color who benefit from Title IX. Though women of color are 25 percent of college undergraduates, they make up only 14 percent of collegiate female athletes. Some of this disparity is because the women's sports that have experienced the most growth are those that are disproportionately played by white women.

Moreover, most black women and girls who play school sports participate in basketball and track and field and have not benefited from the addition of sports like tennis, golf, swimming, or other sports dominated by white women. Moreover, the number of women coaches of color is far fewer than expected, given the number of successful women athletes of color. These problems remind us that, though we are closer to equality in sport, we still have a way to go

Achieving gender equality in sport, as in politics, law, medicine, or any other social institution, is a journey. We have achieved much over the last 38 years, but we still have barriers to overcome before we reach our goal of full equality in sport. Thanks to Title IX and the feminist movement, women have more sport opportunities and their athleticism is much more appreciated. In addition, legal and social changes have lessened the effects of racism and homophobia in sport so that more women can achieve their sport goals in safe and respectful climates.

Achieving and keeping gender equality in sport, however, requires that we all continue to speak up when we see inequalities in sports programs for girls and boys and that we insist that sports participation is equally important for girls and boys. As parents, teachers, and concerned citizens, we each have important roles to play in this journey. The next-generation Maya Moores, Paula Creamers, Michele Kwans, and Lindsey Vonns are depending on us.   [2010]

Women and the Family

The family and motherhood are often thought of as "natural" entities rather than institutions that, in traditional forms, reinforce sexism and maintain women's subordinated status. The selections in this section explore first women's situation in the family and then some of women's varied experiences with motherhood. The fictional pieces serve to highlight the emotional realities of some women's lives in the family, realities that are often obscured by rosy cultural images of family life.

While families can be a source of support for some women, sexism in families can hurt us in various ways. Women no longer lose their legal identity and right to contract as they did in earlier centuries, yet, as Susan Lehrer points out, "the nuclear family is a different place for women and men." The family offers women the hope of love, but also the potential of entrapment, as Rosie learns in Hisaye Yamamoto's short story.

As discussed in the introduction to this chapter, feminists distinguish the experience of mothering from the institution of motherhood. In "A Long Story," Mohawk lesbian writer Beth Brant parallels the theft of Native American children by the state in the lives of two mothers living nearly a century apart. The experience of mothering can be agonizing, especially for immigrant women for whom language barriers can isolate them from others, including their children, as Pat Mora suggests in "Elena."

At the same time that women are limited by the institutions of the family and motherhood, they are sometimes blamed for its problems. June Jordan points to the way that black single mothers in particular are blamed as the cause of black poverty. Rather than eliminating the racism and sexism in our society that undermines black families and praising black women for their success in keeping families together, the media "experts" and government officials "talk about our mamas." Writing in 1987, Jordan compares the "crisis of the black family" to what she saw as the truly significant crises of the day that the U.S. government was perpetuating through its international policy. Jordan points to the governmental, institutional, and social changes necessary to support all women and families.

The ability to make conscious choices about personal relationships is central to women's freedom. Because choice is integral to feminism, this section also presents alternatives to the traditional family. Women who are single or celibate are often stigmatized in our society. Yet some women have found the experience of living with oneself to be satisfying and liberating. Mary Helen Washington speaks to the strength she finds in living on her own.

Including children in a male–female relationship brings challenges as well as rewards. Alix Kates Shulman describes the agreement that she and her husband made in their attempt to bring equity to parenting. Though it may appear mechanical and extreme, it reflects the resolve and intentionality many parents find necessary to change gendered social roles and patterns in the family. Finally, Martha Ackelsberg and Judith Plaskow explain why as lesbians in a committed relationship they are not getting married, even though they have that right in Massachusetts. They write, "We want to hold up a vision of a society in which basic rights are not tied to marriage, and in which there are many ways to organize one's intimate life, marriage being only one of them."

🦎 70

Family and Women's Lives

SUSAN LEHRER

We often tend to think about the family as a natural, biological unit. After all, everyone knows it takes two to make a baby. What is meant by family is more than biological relations, of course. In current debates, one specific form of family is referred to as "traditional": the nuclear family—mother, father, and their children, living together, with the father the main breadwinner and the mother responsible for the home. It is maintained and reinforced by law and the state, and forms the basis for social policy toward women and children. Yet by 2010 only 21 percent of American households were married couples and their children.

Work is now the norm. Both the mother and the father were employed in 58.9 percent of married-couple families with children in 2009, while the husband was the only working person in fewer than one in five married-couple families in 2009.[1]

Overwhelmingly, women's family life includes responsibility for children and the home. But women work outside the home in the paid labor force—including well over half of women with children under one year of age.[2] In 2009, over two-thirds of mothers with children under 6 years old (64.2 percent) worked; the rate of those whose youngest child was 6 to 17 years old was 77.3 percent.

Using an outmoded, inaccurate picture of "family" prevents the needs of women and real-life families from being recognized. This essay explores some of the broad historical changes that have changed the family, and the way in which family structure defines the opportunities, economic situation, and social position of women.

HISTORICAL OVERVIEW

Before industrialization, the family was a working, productive unit, with women producing goods for family consumption, as well as maintaining the family's health and material well-being. For example, in *Little House on the Prairie*, Laura Ingalls Wilder describes her childhood frontier family in which Ma's contribution was clear and valued, and Pa's work took place within the family setting as well. This continued into the late nineteenth and early twentieth centuries in rural areas.

With the beginnings of industrialization, a major shift occurred, as "work" became something done outside the home, for pay, by men. "Women's work" within the home (called housework) was not paid labor and hence not seen as "real work." Thus, the roles of breadwinner and homemaker that are often taken for granted as "natural" are the result of specific historical changes like industrialization, and are, as Jesse Bernard put it, specific to a very short period in human history.[3] The household itself changed from a unit of production to one primarily of consumption.

Although men were the main workers (for pay), right from the beginning of industrialization women also worked outside their homes. For example, in making cloth (which was one of the first industries affected by the Industrial Revolution), young women were the main source for factory workers, because men's labor was needed in agricultural production and therefore scarce. Women received wages that were one-quarter to one-half those of men. From the beginning of wage labor and capitalist production for profit, the wage structure itself has been different (and lower) for female workers than for male workers. Although male workers were not well paid, their wages were expected to support a family; women were not expected to be self-supporting, let alone able to support anyone else. This meant that women were dependent upon men for support, even when they did work outside the home.

The "power of the purse" reinforced the husband's control over his family. Under English common law, which our legal system is based on, when a woman married, she lost her own legal identity and her legal right to contract. Her husband had control over all the money and property of the family, including her wages. Marriage represented a legal contract in which a woman's status was subordinate to her husband's. Women's current subordination in marriage is rooted in legal tradition as well as in economic arrangements.

As commercial and industrial development expanded and a national economy emerged in the late 1800s, women's lives were still supposed to be centered within the household—she was the "angel of the hearth," available to provide material and emotional comfort for the man, who braved the world of commercial competition. This idealized version of family was never quite accurate even in the nineteenth century. For middle-class women, it meant complete economic dependence on the goodwill of their husbands and fathers. Less well-off women worked in factories and sweatshops as young women or whenever they were not supported by a man's income. Women also added to the household income in "informal" ways not measured by the census. Enslaved African-American women were expected to perform tasks similar to men, and in the United States, unlike other countries, even slave marriage was not recognized by white law. African-American women worked in the fields as well as in the slave master's household. Nonetheless, studies indicate that many enslaved families sought to maintain strong ties (which amounted to an act of subversion under slavery),

and after emancipation, large-scale relocations of African-Americans were often an attempt to reunite families broken apart by slavery.[4] After slavery, whites still expected African-American wives to work for them, and considered them lazy if they presumed to stay home and act like ladies.[5] Thus, we see that the "traditional" family was expected to apply only to certain groups and not others—white, middle-class families primarily.

Although the number of women working outside the home had been slowly increasing since the early 1900s, the increase in past decades has been astounding. The vast majority of women now combine outside work and family life, and in addition, the proportion of women who are heads of households, never married, and working has increased dramatically.

From this brief historical survey, it is clear that the family is not a natural, unchanging entity, but it changes along with social and economic shifts in the larger social world. We are again in a time when these larger social forces are visibly changing the way families function, as well as the very definition of "family" itself.

THE NUCLEAR FAMILY: IT'S A DIFFERENT PLACE FOR WOMEN THAN FOR MEN

The idealized image of family relationships is that they are warm, loving, and occasionally quarrelsome but, in the long run, supportive. As the saying goes, family is where, when you go there, they have to take you in. The image of the nuclear family—with the father still the main moneymaker and responsible for making the important decisions in the family—continues to be a strong influence. Choices made within the family setting that appear to be simply logical or natural are, in fact, the consequence of the nuclear family structure. For instance, if the man's job is considered the mainstay of the family, his occupational shifts take first place over other family concerns. Because his earnings are likely to be greater than his wife's, her job is considered the logically expendable one. If they have children, the wife is the one who is going to quit work and "stay home with the baby." If his career plans favor relocating to a different city, hers are likely to suffer. This, in turn, reinforces the disparity in their earnings, making it seem natural that his job is the one that is really important, while hers is secondary. Many women's reluctance to plan a career (as distinguished from a job to earn money) reflects the reality that they are expected to fit it in around everything else in the family. Many men agree that their wife's education, job, and career plans are worthwhile, as long as dinner is still on the table, the house in order, and the kids taken care of when he walks in the door.

The reality is that different family members experience the same family very differently. Where money is short, it is women who "bridge the gap between what a household's resources really are and what a family's position is supposed to be."[6] They stretch the available food, clothing, and resources to make ends meet. Where a family consistently comes up short at the end of the paycheck, it is the woman who eats less and does without, so that the kids and husband can have enough. To talk about a family's standard of living as if all family members shared the same level of well-being or poverty is misleading. Defining a family's class by the husband's occupation does not provide a basis for understanding the very different life chances that men and women face within the same family, given the realities of divorce and single parenthood.

FAMILIES: A MULTITUDE OF ARRANGEMENTS

One of the most talked-about changes in American families in recent years has been the increase in family households headed by women. Forty-one percent of births are now to unmarried women; however, the share of births to women who are unmarried varies widely by race and ethnicity. More than 7 in 10 births to black women are to unmarried mothers, compared with about half of births to Hispanic women and about 3 in 10 to white women, though the share of births to unmarried women has risen most rapidly for whites since 1990.[7] The Pew Report also stresses the difference education makes: Most births to college graduates are to married women. Most births to women with less than a high school education are to unmarried women. The current economic recession

emphasized this trend. Better-educated women, who also earn more, are now more likely to marry than less-educated, and therefore less economically secure, couples.[8] Although this tells us about their mothers' legal status (unmarried), it tells us little about the actual family arrangements—for example, whether they are in multigeneration households or cohabiting couples.

Women heading families face a series of obstacles that reflect the unwillingness of policy makers to recognize and address their condition. In order to work and support their families, women must have child care; then they must earn enough to provide for their families. Women's earnings have risen from 62 percent of men's in 1970, to 77 percent by 2009.[9] The good news is that this is a greater proportion than it has been in the recent past; the bad news is that this is mostly because of the relative decline in men's earnings rather than an increase in women's overall income. As the recession deepened between 2007 and 2009, the real median earnings of male workers declined by 4.1 percent, for female workers by 2.8 percent. Overall, per capita income declined by 1.2 percent for the total population between 2008 and 2009. The effects of the recession were felt differently for whites, blacks, and Hispanics, though. Income went down 1.3 percent for whites and 3.5 percent for Hispanics. Changes for non-Hispanic whites, blacks, and Asians were not statistically significant.[10]

The wage gap is affected by both gender and race. The relatively lower pay of black and Hispanic men compared with white men means the gender gap is correspondingly less, but of course this translates to lower overall family incomes for these families. Women heading households are more likely to be poor, not only because there is only one earner in the family but because that earner is a woman.

A female-headed household is almost twice as likely to be poor as a male-headed household. The poverty rate and the number of families in poverty increased across all types of families: married-couple families (5.8 percent and 3.4 million in 2009, from 5.5 percent and 3.3 million in 2008); families with a female householder (29.9 percent and 4.4 million in 2009, from 28.7 percent and 4.2 million in 2008); and families with a male householder (16.9 percent and 942,000 in 2009, from 13.8 percent and 723,000 in 2008).[11]

For these families, the lack of affordable child care hits especially hard. Yet American social policy has not recognized that child care is just as much a social necessity as educating children. The United States is far behind most European countries, which train child care specialists and provide care for children from the youngest ages.

For many women, the descent to poverty occurs as a result of divorce. This is more likely to happen for white women than for black women, partly because of the overall lower earnings of black men relative to white men. Despite all the jokes about men paying their life fortune in alimony to ex-wives, the reality is often that men's standard of living goes up following divorce, while women's drops precipitously.

The transition from Mrs. to ex-Mrs. is especially difficult for older, long-married women, who may not have marketable skills with which to support themselves. The tragic irony is that it is precisely those women who acceded to cultural expectations to stay at home and be good wives and mothers who suffer the most, both economically and emotionally. Women whose whole sense of identity centers around being a wife and mother must cope with profound loss of meaning as well as the economic shock of divorce. These older women are the ones more likely to get alimony (as distinguished from child support). Younger women from shorter-term marriages are unlikely to be awarded alimony and often are unable to even collect child support.

Despite all the movies depicting the hilarious, heart-warming adventures of men raising children, custodial parents are most likely women: 23 percent (17.0 million) of all children lived with their unmarried mother only, while 3 percent (2.4 million) lived with their unmarried father without their mother present.[12] In 2004, of the 26.4 percent of children living with one parent, only 3.2 percent lived with their father only—78.7 percent lived with a single mother, 10.1 percent with a single father.[13] Of children living with only their mother, 36.5 percent were living in poverty, while 16.6 percent

of children who lived with their father only were in poverty. Interestingly, of children living with two parents, 10.9 percent were still likely to be in poverty. Chasing down so-called deadbeat dads became standard rhetoric; rigorous child support programs have resulted in more fathers who do pay up. It does not, however, necessarily mean more money in the mother's household for those families receiving TANF (Temporary Aid to Needy Families), because the father's contribution is usually deducted from their welfare grant.

The reasons for the increase in families headed by women are complex and cannot be reduced to a simple explanation. Young women are now much more likely to have worked, and to continue education longer than in the past, and are postponing marriage (or not marrying at all). In the 40 years from 1970 to 2010, the median age for women to get married increased from 20 to 26 years of age.[14] This increases the likelihood of having children though not married. Shotgun weddings are less common now than in the past (judging by the fact that many fewer pregnant women marry before their first child is born). The options of abortion, and refusing to marry someone you don't like, are more acceptable now. Married couples with children still depend upon the wife to do most of the "second shift"— the housework. Even when both husband and wife work full-time, throughout the 1980s two-thirds of working wives reported that they did most or all of the housework. The time women spent on housework remained about the same whether they worked or not. This is beginning to change—partly because women have simply stopped doing so much of it, but also because more couples believe in sharing household work.[15] Women also spend more time caring for their children, whether infants or older, than fathers do.[16] Despite the variety of social arrangements in which people live their lives, social policy and law persist in penalizing those who do not live in nuclear family settings.

DEFENSE OF MARRIAGE? FOR WHOM?

Perhaps the most visible challenge to conventional assumptions about "family" is the definition of marriage itself. Massachusetts recognized same-sex marriage in 2004, and many such couples were joyously wed there. The aspect that stood out most clearly for those attending marriage ceremonies was seeing these couples' joy in finally achieving the long-withheld social recognition of their love and emotional commitment.

In 1996 the Defense of Marriage Act (DOMA) became federal law; it defines marriage specifically as between one man and one woman. This means that federally mandated benefits or requirements exclude all otherwise legally performed same-sex marriages. States traditionally define who is eligible to marry (e.g., age of consent) and of course recognize marriages from other states. However, DOMA denies this equal protection under federal law for same-sex couples who are legally married, but not for other married couples.[17] Many states have also passed anti-same-sex marriage statutes into laws and state constitutions, and will not recognize same-sex marriages that are legal in other places. There are now numerous legal challenges to DOMA, in courts from California to Arkansas.

One of the ways that nontraditional families are harmed is by excluding same-sex married family members from the member's health insurance plan—without which Americans cannot afford to be sick. (The United States is still the only major industrial nation that does not assure national health coverage for everybody.) Some employers, both private and public, do now include "domestic partners" in health coverage, life insurance, and other employment-related benefits. Remember, "marriage" is a legal status, with entitlements and responsibilities, as well as a traditionally approved social and/or religious arrangement. Married couples are given legal rights under Social Security provisions, immigration status, as well as decision-making standing in times of crisis.

Broadening the conventional scope of "marriage" reveals a shift in public attitudes, and recognition of the diversity of possible living arrangements for people. There is a real "generation gap" in acceptance of same-sex marriages, with younger people more willing to see no problem with it (or

with gays serving openly in the military either). Most adults ages 65 and older are critical of these unmarried couples, whether they are same-sex or opposite-sex couples. Most young adults, ages 18 to 29, are not.[18]

Currently, however, government emphasizes traditional marriage as the "solution" for a host of social ills, especially for low-income and poor people. Instead of policies aimed at, for example, improving child care options, education, and job training for single mothers, this approach promotes marriage as the "cure" and suggests "abstinence only" in lieu of sex education. However, it is a measure of the progress of the women's movement that even these conservative approaches aimed at "strengthening marriage" recognize that domestic violence is a real problem for many women (and children) for whom marriage is not the answer.

The countermovement opposing "gay marriage," based in conservative Christian organizations primarily, views marriage (between one man and one woman) as a sacred rite rather than a secular or legal status. Their antipathy is part of what has been called a larger "culture war" in which not only gay marriage but homosexuality itself is considered against God's principles.[19] They want a federal constitutional amendment to define marriage in accord with their views. On the other hand, many religious groups do not oppose same-sex marriage, and recognize that same-sex couples also make lasting commitments, have families, and need the protections that go with marriage.[20]

There have been similar movements in other nations, including Canada, Belgium, and the Netherlands, toward broadening the definition of marriage to include same-sex couples. In Spain, when same-sex marriages were legalized in 2005, the prime minister clearly distinguished civil marriage from church marriage (Spain is a traditionally Catholic country), noting that marriage is a legal *secular* contract with rights and duties enforceable by law. In France (among other places), "civil unions" are another approach to giving socially recognized status to couples. Each partner is eligible for much the same benefits as traditional marriage confers. Interestingly, in France, by 2009, 95 percent of couples seeking civil unions were heterosexual.[21]

MOM AND APPLE PIE?

The conservatives who attack the women's movement for being antifamily have a specific form of the family in mind—one that certainly does not correspond to what real families are like. These fundamentalist doctrines of the political far right rigidly interpret the Christian Bible to justify the patriarchal family, to attack women's rights, and seek to use the power of the laws to support their views. It is interesting that in times of social change—like the mid-1800s in the throes of industrialization, and our own time—ideologies advocating a return to an earlier, "golden age" surface.

Now, even the basic, biological fact that it takes two to make a baby seems to be blurring at the edges with the advances of reproductive technologies. In vitro fertilization is becoming increasingly common. Or a woman may be pregnant and give birth to a child to whom she is not genetically related, from an ovum that was fertilized in vitro (outside the woman's body). The child then may potentially have two completely different sets of parents. What is the legal status of the woman who was pregnant with the child? What "right," if any, has she to be considered the "mother"? Is a "contract" to give up the child after birth enforceable if she changes her mind? As yet, these are unresolved questions. Typically the couple wishing to become parents is wealthy enough to pay large medical and legal fees, while the woman having the child has much lower income and less to spend on lawyers. Our thinking about women, pregnancy, parenting, and family will need to take these issues into account.

Another possibility is that a woman who wants to become pregnant but is having difficulties can opt for a series of fertility treatments or the implanting of fertilized eggs—procedures that are expensive, uncomfortable, and uncertain. Others want to be parents but not within a male–female

household, either gay/lesbian couples or single persons. All of these are also families with parents who raise children, wipe sniffly noses, and clap at school plays. The challenge is to creatively respond to changed conditions, and to help shape that change in ways that will enhance rather than stifle people's lives. [2011]

NOTES

1. U.S. Bureau of Labor Statistics, *Employment Characteristics of Families, 2009*, report no. USDL-10-0721, 2.
2. Ibid.
3. Jessie Bernard, "The Good Provider Role: Its Rise and Fall," *American Psychologist* 36, no. 1 (January 1981): 1–12.
4. Herbert Gutman, "Persistent Myths About the Afro-American Family," in *The American Family in Social-Historical Perspective*, ed. Michael Gordon, 3rd ed. (New York: St. Martin's Press, 1983), 459–81.
5. Jacqueline Jones, *Labor of Love, Labor of Sorrow: Black Women, Work and the Family from Slavery to the Present* (New York: Vintage, 1985), 59.
6. Rayna Rapp, "Family and Class in Contemporary America: Notes Toward an Understanding of Ideology," in *Rethinking the Family: Some Feminist Questions*, ed. Barrie Thorne and Marilyn Yalom (New York: Longman, 1982), 175.
7. Pew Report, "Decline of Marriage and Rise of New Families, New Demography of Motherhood," August 2010, 13.
8. Pew Report, "Reversal of the College Marriage Gap," October 2010, 1.
9. U.S. Census Bureau, *Current Population Reports: Consumer Income*, September 2010.
10. U.S. Census Bureau, *Income and Poverty and Health Insurance in the U.S.: 2009*, report P60-238, 13, 14.
11. Ibid., 10, 13, 18.
12. Rose M. Kreider, "Living Arrangements of Children: 2004," in *Current Population Reports, 2007*, U.S. Census Bureau, 7.
13. US Census 2008, Child Living Arrangements, 4, 5.
14. "U.S. Census Reports Men and Women Wait Longer to Marry," released 11/10/2010.
15. Stephanie Coontz, *Marriage, a History: From Obedience to Intimacy* (New York: Viking Press, 2005), 299.
16. Robert Drago, "The Parenting of Infants: A Time-Use Study," *Monthly Labor Review*, October 2009.
17. GLAD (Gay & Lesbian Advocates & Defenders) (http://www.glad.org).
18. Pew Report, "Decline of Marriage and Rise of New Families," November 2010, Summary, 9.
19. Russell Shorto, "What's Their Real Problem with Gay Marriage? It's the Gay Part," *New York Times Magazine*, June 19, 2005, 41.
20. ACLU website, Friend-of-Court briefs re the MD law. NY Times: 12/16/2010 p. A4.
21. *New York Times*, December 16, 2010, A4.

🦎 71

Seventeen Syllables

HISAYE YAMAMOTO

The first Rosie knew that her mother had taken to writing poems was one evening when she finished one and read it aloud for her daughter's approval. It was about cats, and Rosie pretended to understand it thoroughly and appreciate it no end, partly because she hesitated to disillusion her mother about the quantity and quality of Japanese she had learned in all the years now that she had been going to Japanese school every Saturday (and Wednesday, too, in the summer). Even so, her mother must have been skeptical about the depth of Rosie's understanding, because she explained afterwards about the kind of poem she was trying to write.

See, Rosie, she said, it was a *haiku,* a poem in which she must pack all her meaning into 17 syllables only, which were divided into three lines of five, seven, and five syllables. In the one she had just read, she had tried to capture the charm of a kitten, as well as comment on the superstition that owning a cat of three colors meant good luck.

"Yes, yes, I understand. How utterly lovely," Rosie said, and her mother, either satisfied or seeing through the deception and resigned, went back to composing.

The truth was that Rosie was lazy; English lay ready on the tongue but Japanese had to be searched for and examined, and even then put forth tentatively (probably to meet with laughter). It was so much easier to say yes, yes, even when one meant no, no. Besides, this was what was in her mind to say: I was looking through one of your magazines from Japan last night, Mother, and toward the back I found some *haiku* in English that delighted me. There was one that made me giggle off and on until I fell asleep—

It is morning, and lo!
I lie awake, *comme il faut,*
sighing for some dough.

Now, how to reach her mother, how to communicate the melancholy song? Rosie knew formal Japanese by fits and starts, her mother had even less English, no French. It was much more possible to say yes, yes.

It developed that her mother was writing the *haiku* for a daily newspaper, the *Mainichi Shimbun,* that was published in San Francisco. Los Angeles, to be sure, was closer to the farming community in which the Hayashi family lived and several Japanese vernaculars were printed there, but Rosie's parents said they preferred the tone of the northern paper. Once a week, the *Mainichi* would have a section devoted to *haiku,* and her mother became an extravagant contributor, taking for herself the blossoming pen name, Ume Hanazono.

So Rosie and her father lived for awhile with two women, her mother and Ume Hanazono. Her mother (Tome Hayashi by name) kept house, cooked, washed, and, along with her husband and the Carrascos, the Mexican family hired for the harvest, did her ample share of picking tomatoes out in the sweltering fields and boxing them in tidy strata in the cool packing shed. Ume Hanazono, who came to life after the dinner dishes were done, was an earnest, muttering stranger who often neglected speaking when spoken to and stayed busy at the parlor table as late as midnight scribbling with pencil on scratch paper or carefully copying characters on good paper with her fat, pale green Parker.

The new interest had some repercussions on the household routine. Before, Rosie had been accustomed to her parents and herself taking their hot baths early and going to bed almost immediately afterwards, unless her parents challenged each other to a game of flower cards or unless company dropped in. Now if her father wanted to play cards, he had to resort to solitaire (at which he always cheated fearlessly), and if a group of friends came over, it was bound to contain someone who was also writing *haiku,* and the small assemblage would be split in two, her father entertaining the nonliterary members and her mother comparing ecstatic notes with the visiting poet.

If they went out, it was more of the same thing. But Ume Hanazono's life span, even for a poet's, was very brief—perhaps three months at most.

One night they went over to see the Hayano family in the neighboring town to the west, an adventure both painful and attractive to Rosie. It was attractive because there were four Hayano girls, all lovely and each one named after a season of the year (Haru, Natsu, Aki, Fuyu), painful because something had been wrong with Mrs. Hayano ever since the birth of her first child. Rosie would sometimes watch Mrs. Hayano, reputed to have been the belle of her native village, making her way about a room, stooped, slowly shuffling, violently trembling (*always* trembling), and she would be reminded that this woman, in this same condition, had carried and given issue to three babies. She would look wonderingly at Mr. Hayano, handsome, tall, and strong, and she would look at her four pretty friends. But it was not a matter she could come to any decision about.

On this visit, however, Mrs. Hayano sat all evening in the rocker, as motionless and unobtrusive as it was possible for her to be, and Rosie found the greater part of the evening practically anaesthetic. Too, Rosie spent most of it in the girls' room, because Haru, the garrulous one, said almost as soon as the bows and other greetings were over, "Oh, you must see my new coat!"

It was a pale plaid of grey, sand, and blue, with an enormous collar, and Rosie, seeing nothing special in it, said, "Gee, how nice."

"Nice?" said Haru, indignantly. "Is that all you can say about it? It's gorgeous! And so cheap, too. Only seventeen-ninety-eight, because it was a sale. The saleslady said it was twenty-five dollars regular."

"Gee," said Rosie. Natsu, who never said much and when she said anything said it shyly, fingered the coat covetously and Haru pulled it away.

"Mine," she said, putting it on. She minced in the aisle between the two large beds and smiled happily. "Let's see how your mother likes it."

She broke into the front room and the adult conversation and went to stand in front of Rosie's mother, while the rest watched from the door.

Rosie's mother was properly envious. "May I inherit it when you're through with it?"

Haru, pleased, giggled and said yes, she could, but Natsu reminded gravely from the door, "You promised me, Haru."

Everyone laughed but Natsu, who shamefacedly retreated into the bedroom. Haru came in laughing, taking off the coat. "We were only kidding, Natsu," she said. "Here, you try it on now."

After Natsu buttoned herself into the coat, inspected herself solemnly in the bureau mirror, and reluctantly shed it, Rosie, Aki, and Fuyu got their turns, and Fuyu, who was eight, drowned in it while her sisters and Rosie doubled up in amusement. They all went into the front room later, because Haru's mother quaveringly called to her to fix the tea and rice cakes and open a can of sliced peaches for everybody. Rosie noticed that her mother and Mr. Hayano were talking together at the little table— they were discussing a *haiku* that Mr. Hayano was planning to send to the *Mainichi*, while her father was sitting at one end of the sofa looking through a copy of *Life*, the new picture magazine. Occasionally, her father would comment on a photograph, holding it toward Mrs. Hayano and speaking to her as he always did—loudly, as though he thought someone such as she must surely be at least a trifle deaf also.

The five girls had their refreshments at the kitchen table, and it was while Rosie was showing the sisters her trick of swallowing peach slices without chewing (she chased each slippery crescent down with a swig of tea) that her father brought his empty teacup and untouched saucer to the sink and said, "Come on, Rosie, we're going home now."

"Already?" asked Rosie.

"Work tomorrow," he said.

He sounded irritated, and Rosie, puzzled, gulped one last yellow slice and stood up to go, while the sisters began protesting, as was their wont.

"We have to get up at five-thirty," he told them, going into the front room quickly, so that they did not have their usual chance to hang onto his hands and plead for an extension of time.

Rosie, following, saw that her mother and Mr. Hayano were sipping tea and still talking together, while Mrs. Hayano concentrated, quivering, on raising the handleless Japanese cup to her lips with both her hands and lowering it back to her lap. Her father, saying nothing, went out the door, onto the bright porch, and down the steps. Her mother looked up and asked, "Where is he going?"

"Where is he going?" Rosie said. "He said we were going home now."

"Going home?" Her mother looked with embarrassment at Mr. Hayano and his absorbed wife and then forced a smile. "He must be tired," she said.

Haru was not giving up yet. "May Rosie stay overnight?" she asked, and Natsu, Aki, and Fuyu came to reinforce their sister's plea by helping her make a circle around Rosie's mother. Rosie, for once having no desire to stay, was relieved when her mother, apologizing to the perturbed Mr. and Mrs. Hayano for her father's abruptness at the same time, managed to shake her head no at the quartet, kindly but adamant, so that they broke their circle and let her go.

Rosie's father looked ahead into the windshield as the two joined him. "I'm sorry," her mother said. "You must be tired." Her father, stepping on the starter, said nothing. "You know how I get when it's *haiku*," she continued, "I forget what time it is." He only grunted.

As they rode homeward silently, Rosie, sitting between, felt a rush of hate for both—for her mother for begging, for her father for denying her mother. I wish this old Ford would crash, right now, she thought, then immediately, no, no, I wish my father would laugh, but it was too late: already the vision had passed through her mind of the green pick-up crumpled in the dark against one of the mighty eucalyptus trees they were just riding past, of the three contorted, bleeding bodies, one of them hers.

Rosie ran between two patches of tomatoes, her heart working more rambunctiously than she had ever known it to. How lucky it was that Aunt Taka and Uncle Gimpachi had come tonight, though, how very lucky. Otherwise she might not have really kept her half-promise to meet Jesus Carrasco. Jesus was going to be a senior in September at the same school she went to, and his parents were the ones helping with the tomatoes this year. She and Jesus, who hardly remembered seeing each other at Cleveland High where there were so many other people and two whole grades between them, had become great friends this summer—he always had a joke for her when he periodically drove the loaded pick-up up from the fields to the shed where she was usually sorting while her mother and father did the packing, and they laughed a great deal together over infinitesimal repartee during the afternoon break for chilled watermelon or ice cream in the shade of the shed.

What she enjoyed most was racing him to see which could finish picking a double row first. He, who could work faster, would tease her by slowing down until she thought she would surely pass him this time, then speeding up furiously to leave her several sprawling vines behind. Once he had made her screech hideously by crossing over, while her back was turned, to place atop the tomatoes in her green-stained bucket a truly monstrous, pale green worm (it had looked more like an infant snake). And it was when they had finished a contest this morning, after she had pantingly pointed a green finger at the immature tomatoes evident in the lugs at the end of his row and he had returned the accusation (with justice), that he had startlingly brought up the matter of their possibly meeting outside the range of both their parents' dubious eyes.

"What for?" she had asked.

"I've got a secret I want to tell you," he said.

"Tell me now," she demanded.

"It won't be ready till tonight," he said.

She laughed. "Tell me tomorrow then."

"It'll be gone tomorrow," he threatened.

"Well, for seven hakes, what is it?" she asked, more than twice, and when he had suggested that the packing shed would be an appropriate place to find out, she had cautiously answered maybe. She had not been certain she was going to keep the appointment until the arrival of her mother's sister and her husband. Their coming seemed a sort of signal of permission, of grace, and she had definitely made up her mind to lie and leave as she was bowing them welcome.

So as soon as everyone appeared settled back for the evening, she announced loudly that she was going to the privy outside, "I'm going to the *benjo!*" and slipped out the door. And now that she was actually on her way, her heart pumped in such an undisciplined way that she could hear it with her ears. It's because I'm running, she told herself, slowing to a walk. The shed was up ahead, one more patch away, in the middle of the fields. Its bulk, looming in the dimness, took on a sinisterness that was funny when Rosie reminded herself that it was only a wooden frame with a canvas roof and three canvas walls that made a slapping noise on breezy days.

Jesus was sitting on the narrow plank that was the sorting platform and she went around to the other side and jumped backwards to seat herself on the rim of a packing stand. "Well, tell me," she said without greeting, thinking her voice sounded reassuringly familiar.

"I saw you coming out the door," Jesus said. "I heard you running part of the way, too."

"Uh-huh," Rosie said. "Now tell me the secret."

"I was afraid you wouldn't come," he said.

Rosie delved around on the chicken-wire bottom of the stall for number two tomatoes, ripe, which she was sitting beside, and came up with a left-over that felt edible. She bit into it and began sucking out the pulp and seeds. "I'm here," she pointed out.

"Rosie, are you sorry you came?"

"Sorry? What for?" she said. "You said you were going to tell me something."

"I will, I will," Jesus said, but his voice contained disappointment, and Rosie fleetingly felt the older of the two, realizing a brand-new power which vanished without category under her recognition.

"I have to go back in a minute," she said. "My aunt and uncle are here from Wintersburg. I told them I was going to the privy."

Jesus laughed. "You funny thing," he said. "You slay me!"

"Just because you have a bathroom *inside*," Rosie said. "Come on, tell me."

Chuckling, Jesus came around to lean on the stand facing her. They still could not see each other very clearly, but Rosie noticed that Jesus became very sober again as he took the hollow tomato from her hand and dropped it back into the stall. When he took hold of her empty hand, she could find no words to protest; her vocabulary had become distressingly constricted and she thought desperately that all that remained intact now was yes and no and oh, and even these few sounds would not easily come out. Thus, kissed by Jesus, Rosie fell for the first time entirely victim to a helplessness delectable beyond speech. But the terrible, beautiful sensation lasted no more than a second, and the reality of Jesus' lips and tongue and teeth and hands made her pull away with such strength that she nearly tumbled.

Rosie stopped running as she approached the lights from the windows of home. How long since she had left? She could not guess, but gasping yet, she went to the privy in back and locked herself in. Her own breathing deafened her in the dark, close space, and she sat and waited until she could hear at last the nightly calling of the frogs and crickets. Even then, all she could think to say was oh, my, and the pressure of Jesus' face against her face would not leave.

No one had missed her in the parlor, however, and Rosie walked in and through quickly, announcing that she was next going to take a bath. "Your father's in the bathhouse," her mother said, and Rosie, in her room, recalled that she had not seen him when she entered. There had been only Aunt Taka and Uncle Gimpachi with her mother at the table, drinking tea. She got her robe and straw sandals and crossed the parlor again to go outside. Her mother was telling them about the *haiku* competition in the *Mainichi* and the poem she had entered.

Rosie met her father coming out of the bathhouse. "Are you through, Father?" she asked. "I was going to ask you to scrub my back."

"Scrub your own back," he said shortly, going toward the main house.

"What have I done now?" she yelled after him. She suddenly felt like doing a lot of yelling. But he did not answer, and she went into the bathhouse.

Turning on the dangling light, she removed her denims and T-shirt and threw them in the big carton for dirty clothes standing next to the washing machine. Her other things she took with her into the bath compartment to wash after her bath. After she had scooped a basin of hot water from the square wooden tub, she sat on the grey cement of the floor and soaped herself at exaggerated leisure, singing "Red Sails in the Sunset" at the top of her voice and using da-da-da where she suspected her words. Then, standing up, still singing, for she was possessed by the notion that any attempt now to analyze would result in spoilage and she believed that the larger her volume the less she would be able to hear herself think, she obtained more hot water and poured it on until she was free of lather. Only then did she allow herself to step into the steaming vat, one leg first, then the remainder of her body inch by inch until the water no longer stung and she could move around at will.

She took a long time soaking, afterwards remembering to go around outside to stoke the embers of the tin-lined fireplace beneath the tub and to throw on a few more sticks so that the water might keep its heat for her mother, and when she finally returned to the parlor, she found her mother still talking *haiku* with her aunt and uncle, the three of them on another round of tea. Her father was nowhere in sight.

At Japanese school the next day (Wednesday, it was), Rosie was grave and giddy by turns. Preoccupied at her desk in the row for students on Book Eight, she made up for it at recess by performing wild mimicry for the benefit of her friend Chizuko. She held her nose and whined a witticism or two in what she considered was the manner of Fred Allen; she assumed intoxication and a British accent to go over the climax of the Rudy Vallee recording of the pub conversation about William Ewart Gladstone; she was the child Shirley Temple piping, "On the Good Ship Lollipop"; she was the gentleman soprano of the Four Inkspots trilling, "If I Didn't Care." And she felt reasonably satisfied when Chizuko wept and gasped, "Oh, Rosie, you ought to be in the movies!"

Her father came after her at noon, bringing her sandwiches of minced ham and two nectarines to eat while she rode, so that she could pitch right into the sorting when they got home. The lugs were piling up, he said, and the ripe tomatoes in them would probably have to be taken to the cannery tomorrow if they were not ready for the produce haulers tonight. "This heat's not doing them any good. And we've got no time for a break today."

It *was* hot, probably the hottest day of the year, and Rosie's blouse stuck damply to her back even under the protection of the canvas. But she worked as efficiently as a flawless machine and kept the stalls heaped, with one part of her mind listening in to the parental murmuring about the heat and the tomatoes and with another part planning the exact words she would say to Jesus when he drove up with the first load of the afternoon. But when at last she saw that the pick-up was coming, her hands went berserk and the tomatoes started falling in the wrong stalls, and her father said, "Hey, hey! Rosie, watch what you're doing!"

"Well, I have to go to the *benjo*," she said, hiding panic.

"Go in the weeds over there," he said, only half-joking.

"Oh, Father!" she protested.

"Oh, go on home," her mother said. "We'll make out for awhile."

In the privy Rosie peered through a knothole toward the fields, watching as much as she could of Jesus. Happily she thought she saw him look in the direction of the house from time to time before he finished unloading and went back toward the patch where his mother and father worked. As she was heading for the shed, a very presentable black car purred up the dirt driveway to the house and its driver motioned to her. Was this the Hayashi home, he wanted to know. She nodded. Was she a Hayashi? Yes, she said, thinking that he was a good-looking man. He got out of the car with a huge, flat package and she saw that he warmly wore a business suit. "I have something here for your mother then," he said, in a more elegant Japanese than she was used to.

She told him where her mother was and he came along with her, patting his face with an immaculate white handkerchief and saying something about the coolness of San Francisco. To her surprised mother and father, he bowed and introduced himself as, among other things, the *haiku* editor of the *Mainichi Shimbun*, saying that since he had been coming as far as Los Angeles anyway, he had decided to bring her the first prize she had won in the recent contest.

"First prize?" her mother echoed, believing and not believing, pleased and overwhelmed. Handed the package with a bow, she bobbed her head up and down numerous times to express her utter gratitude.

"It is nothing much," he added, "but I hope it will serve as a token of our great appreciation for your contributions and our great admiration of your considerable talent."

"I am not worthy," she said, falling easily into his style. "It is I who should make some sign of my humble thanks for being permitted to contribute."

"No, no, to the contrary," he said, bowing again.

But Rosie's mother insisted, and then saying that she knew she was being unorthodox, she asked if she might open the package because her curiosity was so great. Certainly she might. In fact, he would like her reaction to it, for personally, it was one of his favorite Hiroshiges.

Rosie thought it was a pleasant picture, which looked to have been sketched with delicate quickness. There were pink clouds, containing some graceful calligraphy, and a sea that was a pale blue except at the edges, containing four sampans with indications of people in them. Pines edged the water and on the far-off beach there was a cluster of thatched huts towered over by pine-dotted mountains of grey and blue. The frame was scalloped and gilt.

After Rosie's mother pronounced it without peer and somewhat prodded her father into nodding agreement, she said Mr. Kuroda must at least have a cup of tea after coming all this way, and although Mr. Kuroda did not want to impose, he soon agreed that a cup of tea would be refreshing and went along with her to the house, carrying the picture for her.

"Ha, your mother's crazy!" Rosie's father said, and Rosie laughed uneasily as she resumed judgment on the tomatoes. She had emptied six lugs

when he broke into an imaginary conversation with Jesus to tell her to go and remind her mother of the tomatoes, and she went slowly.

Mr. Kuroda was in his shirtsleeves expounding some *haiku* theory as he munched a rice cake, and her mother was rapt. Abashed in the great man's presence, Rosie stood next to her mother's chair until her mother looked up inquiringly, and then she started to whisper the message, but her mother pushed her gently away and reproached, "You are not being very polite to our guest."

"Father says the tomatoes. . . ." Rosie said aloud, smiling foolishly.

"Tell him I shall only be a minute," her mother said, speaking the language of Mr. Kuroda.

When Rosie carried the reply to her father, he did not seem to hear and she said again, "Mother says she'll be back in a minute."

"All right, all right," he nodded, and they worked again in silence. But suddenly, her father uttered an incredible noise, exactly like the cork of a bottle popping, and the next Rosie knew, he was stalking angrily toward the house, almost running in fact, and she chased after him crying, "Father! Father! What are you going to do?"

He stopped long enough to order her back to the shed. "Never mind!" he shouted. "Get on with the sorting!"

And from the place in the fields where she stood, frightened and vacillating, Rosie saw her father enter the house. Soon Mr. Kuroda came out alone, putting on his coat. Mr. Kuroda got into his car and backed out down the driveway onto the highway. Next her father emerged, also alone, something in his arms (it was the picture, she realized), and, going over to the bathhouse woodpile, he threw the picture on the ground and picked up the axe. Smashing the picture, glass and all (she heard the explosion faintly), he reached over for the kerosene that was used to encourage the bath fire and poured it over the wreckage. I am dreaming, Rosie said to herself, I am dreaming, but her father, having made sure that his act of cremation was irrevocable, was even then returning to the fields.

Rosie ran past him and toward the house. What had become of her mother? She burst into the parlor and found her mother at the back window watching the dying fire. They watched together until there remained only a feeble smoke under the blazing sun. Her mother was very calm.

"Do you know why I married your father?" she said without turning.

"No," said Rosie. It was the most frightening question she had ever been called upon to answer. Don't tell me now, she wanted to say, tell me tomorrow, tell me next week, don't tell me today. But she knew she would be told now, that the telling would combine with the other violence of the hot afternoon to level her life, her world to the very ground.

It was like a story out of the magazines illustrated in sepia, which she had consumed so greedily for a period until the information had somehow reached her that those wretchedly unhappy autobiographies, offered to her as the testimonials of living men and women, were largely inventions: Her mother, at 19, had come to America and married her father as an alternative to suicide.

At 18 she had been in love with the first son of one of the well-to-do families in her village. The two had met whenever and wherever they could, secretly, because it would not have done for his family to see him favor her—her father had no money; he was a drunkard and a gambler besides. She had learned she was with child; an excellent match had already been arranged for her lover. Despised by her family, she had given premature birth to a stillborn son, who would be 17 now. Her family did not turn her out, but she could no longer project herself in any direction without refreshing in them the memory of her indiscretion. She wrote to Aunt Taka, her favorite sister in America, threatening to kill herself if Aunt Taka would not send for her. Aunt Taka hastily arranged a marriage with a young man of whom she knew, but lately arrived from Japan, a young man of simple mind, it was said, but of kindly heart. The young man was never told why his unseen betrothed was so eager to hasten the day of meeting.

The story was told perfectly, with neither groping for words nor untoward passion. It was as though her mother had memorized it by heart, reciting it to herself so many times over that its nagging vileness had long since gone.

"I had a brother then?" Rosie asked, for this was what seemed to matter now; she would think about the other later, she assured herself, pushing back the illumination which threatened all that darkness that had hitherto been merely mysterious or even glamorous. "A half-brother?"

"Yes."

"I would have liked a brother," she said.

Suddenly, her mother knelt on the floor and took her by the wrists. "Rosie," she said urgently, "Promise me you will never marry!" Shocked more by the request than the revelation, Rosie stared at her mother's face. Jesus, Jesus, she called silently, not certain whether she was invoking the help of the son of the Carrascos or of God, until there returned sweetly the memory of Jesus' hand, how it had touched her and where. Still her mother waited for an answer, holding her wrists so tightly that her hands were going numb. She tried to pull free. Promise, her mother whispered fiercely, promise. Yes, yes, I promise, Rosie said. But for an instant she turned away, and her mother, hearing the familiar glib agreement, released her. Oh, you, you, you, her eyes and twisted mouth said, you fool. Rosie, covering her face, began at last to cry, and the embrace and consoling hand came much later than she expected.   [1988]

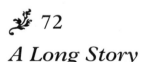

72

A Long Story

BETH BRANT

Dedicated to my Great-Grandmothers
Eliza Powless and Catherine Brant

"About 40 Indian children took the train at this depot for the Philadelphia Indian School last Friday. They were accompanied by the government agent, and seemed a bright looking lot."

—*The Northern Observer*
(Massena, New York, July 20, 1892)

"I am only beginning to understand what it means for a mother to lose a child."
—Anna Demeter, *Legal Kidnapping*
(Beacon Press, Boston, 1977)

1890

It has been two days since they came and took the children away. My body is greatly chilled. All our blankets have been used to bring me warmth. The women keep the fire blazing. The men sit. They talk among themselves. We are frightened by this sudden child-stealing. We signed papers, the agent said. This gave them rights to take our babies. It is good for them, the agent said. It will make them civilized, the agent said. I do not know *civilized*.

I hold myself tight in fear of flying apart in the air. The others try to feed me. Can they feed a dead woman? I have stopped talking. When my mouth opens, only air escapes. I have used up my sound screaming their names—She Sees Deer! He Catches The Leaves! My eyes stare at the room, the walls of scrubbed wood, the floor of dirt. I know there are people here, but I cannot see them. I see a darkness, like the lake at New Moon. Black, unmoving. In the center, a picture of my son and daughter being lifted onto the train. My daughter wearing the dark blue, heavy dress. All of the girls dressed alike. Never have I seen such eyes! They burn into my head even now. My son. His hair cut. Dressed as the white men, his arms and legs covered by cloth that made him sweat. His face, streaked with tears. So many children crying, screaming. The sun on our bodies, our heads. The train screeching like a crow, sounding like laughter. Smoke and dirt pumping out the insides of the train. So many people. So many children. The women, standing as if in prayer, our hands lifted, reaching. The dust sifting down on our palms. Our palms making motions at the sky. Our fingers closing like the claws of the bear.

I see this now. The hair of my son held in my hands. I rub the strands, the heavy braids coming alive as the fire flares and casts a bright light on the black hair. They slip from my fingers and lie coiled on the ground. I see this. My husband picks up the braids, wraps them in cloth; he takes the pieces

of our son away. He walks outside, the eyes of the people on him. I see this. He will find a bottle and drink with the men. Some of the women will join him. They will end the night by singing or crying. It is all the same. I see this. No sounds of children playing games and laughing. Even the dogs have ceased their noise. They lay outside each doorway, waiting. I hear this. The voices of children. They cry. They pray. They call me. *Nisten ha.* I hear this. *Nisten ha.**

1978

I am wakened by the dream. In the dream my daughter is dead. Her father is returning her body to me in pieces. He keeps her heart. I thought I screamed . . . *Patricia!* I sit up in bed, swallowing air as if for nourishment. The dream remains in the air. I rise to go to her room. Ellen tries to lead me back to bed, but I have to see once again. I open her door. She is gone. The room empty, lonely. They said it was in her best interests. How can that be? She is only six, a baby who needs her mothers. She loves us. This has not happened. I will not believe this. Oh god, I think I have died.

Night after night, Ellen holds me as I shake. Our sobs stifling the air in our room. We lie in our bed and try to give comfort. My mind can't think beyond last week when she left. I would have killed him if I'd had the chance! He took her hand and pulled her to the car. The look in his eyes of triumph. It was a contest to him, Patricia the prize. He will teach her to hate us. He will! I see her dear face. That face looking out the back window of his car. Her mouth forming the words *Mommy, Mama*. Her dark braids tied with red yarn. Her front teeth missing. Her overalls with the yellow flower on the pocket, embroidered by Ellen's hands. So lovingly she sewed the yellow wool. Patricia waiting quietly until she was finished. Ellen promising to teach her designs—chain stitch, french knot, split stitch. How Patricia told everyone that Ellen made the flower just for her. So proud of her overalls.

I open the closet door. Almost everything is gone. A few things hang there limp, abandoned. I

---

*Mother.

pull a blue dress from the hanger and take it back to my room. Ellen tries to take it from me, but I hold on, the soft blue cotton smelling of my daughter. How is it possible to feel such pain and live? "Ellen?!" She croons my name. "Mary, Mary, I love you." She sings me to sleep.

1890

The agent was here to deliver a letter. I screamed at him and sent curses his way. I threw dirt in his face as he mounted his horse. He thinks I'm a crazy woman and warns me, "You better settle down Annie." What can they do to me? I am a crazy woman. This letter hurts my hand. It is written in their hateful language. It is evil, but there is a message for me.

I start the walk up the road to my brother. He works for the whites and understands their meanings. I think about my brother as I pull the shawl closer to my body. It is cold now. Soon there will be snow. The corn has been dried and hangs from our cabin, waiting to be used. The corn never changes. My brother is changed. He says that *I* have changed and bring shame to our clan. He says I should accept the fate. But I do not believe in the fate of child-stealing. There is evil here. There is much wrong in our village. My brother says I am a crazy woman because I howl at the sky every evening. He is a fool. I am calling the children. He says the people are becoming afraid of me because I talk to the air and laugh like the raven overhead. But I am talking to the children. They need to hear the sound of me. I laugh to cheer them. They cry for us.

This letter burns my hands. I hurry to my brother. He has taken the sign of the wolf from over the doorway. He pretends to be like those who hate us. He gets more and more like the child-stealers. His eyes move away from mine. He takes the letter from me and begins the reading of it. I am confused. This letter is from two strangers with the names Martha and Daniel. They say they are learning civilized ways. Daniel works in the fields, growing food for the school. Martha cooks and is being taught to sew aprons. She will be going to live with the schoolmaster's wife. She will be a live-in girl. What is a *live-in girl*? I shake my head. The words sound the same to me. I am afraid of Martha and

Daniel, these strangers who know my name. My hands and arms are becoming numb.

I tear the letter from my brother's fingers. He stares at me, his eyes traitors in his face. He calls after me, "Annie! Annie!" That is not my name! I run to the road. That is not my name! There is no Martha! There is no Daniel! This is witch work. The paper burns and burns. At my cabin, I quickly dig a hole in the field. The earth is hard and cold, but I dig with my nails. I dig, my hands feeling weaker. I tear the paper and bury the scraps. As the earth drifts and settles, the names Martha and Daniel are covered. I look to the sky and find nothing but endless blue. My eyes are blinded by the color. I begin the howling.

1978

When I get home from work, there is a letter from Patricia. I make coffee and wait for Ellen, pacing the rooms of our apartment. My back is sore from the line, bending over and over, screwing the handles on the doors of the flashy cars moving by. My work protects me from questions, the guys making jokes at my expense. But some of them touch my shoulder lightly and briefly as a sign of understanding. The few women, eyes averted or smiling in sympathy. No one talks. There is no time to talk. No room to talk, the noise taking up all space and breath.

I carry the letter with me as I move from room to room. Finally I sit at the kitchen table, turning the paper around in my hands. Patricia's printing is large and uneven. The stamp has been glued on halfheartedly and is coming loose. Each time a letter arrives, I dread it, even as I long to hear from my child. I hear Ellen's key in the door. She walks into the kitchen, bringing the smell of the hospital with her. She comes toward me, her face set in new lines, her uniform crumpled and stained, her brown hair pulled back in an imitation of a french twist. She knows there is a letter. I kiss her and bring mugs of coffee to the table. We look at each other. She reaches for my hand, bringing it to her lips. Her hazel eyes are steady in her round face.

I open the letter. *Dear Mommy. I am fine. Daddy got me a new bike. My big teeth are coming in. We are going to see Grandma for my birthday. Daddy got me new shoes. Love, Patricia.* She doesn't ask about Ellen. I imagine her father standing over her, coaxing her, coaching her. The letter becomes ugly. I tear it in bits and scatter them out the window. The wind scoops the pieces into a tight fist before strewing them in the street. A car drives over the paper, shredding it to garbage and mud.

Ellen makes a garbled sound. "I'll leave. If it will make it better, I'll leave." I quickly hold her as the dusk moves into the room and covers us. "Don't leave. Don't leave." I feel her sturdy back shiver against my hands. She kisses my throat, and her arms tighten as we move closer. "Ah Mary, I love you so much." As the tears threaten our eyes, the taste of salt is on our lips and tongues. We stare into ourselves, touching the place of pain, reaching past the fear, the guilt, the anger, the loneliness.

We go to our room. It is beautiful again. I am seeing it new. The sun is barely there. The colors of cream, brown, green mixing with the wood floor. The rug with its design of wild birds. The black ash basket glowing on the dresser, holding a bouquet of dried flowers bought at a vendor's stand. I remember the old woman, laughing and speaking rapidly in Polish as she wrapped the blossoms in newspaper. Ellen undresses me as I cry. My desire for her breaking through the heartbreak we share. She pulls the covers back, smoothing the white sheets, her hands repeating the gestures done at work. She guides me onto the cool material. I watch her remove the uniform of work. An aide to nurses. A healer of spirit.

She comes to me in full flesh. My hands are taken with the curves and soft roundness of her. She covers me with the beating of her heart. The rhythm steadies me. Her heat is centering me. I am grounded by the peace between us. I smile at her face above me, round like a moon, her long hair loose and touching my breasts. I take her breast in my hand, bring it to my mouth, suck her as a woman—in desire, in faith. Our bodies join. Our hair braids together on the pillow. Brown, black, silver, catching the last light of the sun. We kiss, touch, move to our place of power. Her mouth, moving over my body, stopping at curves and swells of skin, kissing, removing pain. Closer,

close, together, woven, my legs are heat, the center of my soul is speaking to her, I am sliding into her, her mouth is medicine, her heart is the earth, we are dancing with flying arms, I shout, I sing, I weep salty liquid, sweet and warm it coats her throat. This is my life. I love you Ellen, I love you Mary, I love, we love.

1891

The moon is full. The air is cold. This cold strikes at my flesh as I remove my clothes and set them on fire in the withered corn field. I cut my hair, the knife sawing through the heavy mass. I bring the sharp blade to my arms, legs, and breasts. The blood trickles like small red rivers down my body. I feel nothing. I throw the tangled webs of my hair into the flames. The smell, like a burning animal, fills my nostrils. As the fire stretches to touch the stars, the people come out to watch me—the crazy woman. The ice in the air touches me.

They caught me as I tried to board the train and search for my babies. The white men tell my husband to watch me. I am dangerous. I laugh and laugh. My husband is good only for tipping bottles and swallowing anger. He looks at me, opening his mouth and making no sound. His eyes are dead. He wanders from the cabin and looks out on the corn. He whispers our names. He calls after the children. He is a dead man.

Where have they taken the children? I ask the question of each one who travels the road past our door. The women come and we talk. We ask and ask. They say there is nothing we can do. The white man is like a ghost. He slips in and out where we cannot see. Even in our dreams he comes to take away our questions. He works magic that resists our medicine. This magic has made us weak. What is the secret about them? Why do they want our children? They sent the Blackrobes many years ago to teach us new magic. It was evil! They lied and tricked us. They spoke of gods who would forgive us if we believed as they do. They brought the rum with the cross. This god is ugly! He killed our masks. He killed our men. He sends the women screaming at the moon in terror. They want our power. They take our children to remove the inside of them. Our power. They steal our food, our sacred rattle, the stories, our names. What is left?

I am a crazy woman. I look to the fire that consumes my hair and see their faces. My daughter. My son. They still cry for me, though the sound grows fainter. The wind picks up their keening and brings it to me. The sound has bored into my brain. I begin howling. At night I dare not sleep. I fear the dreams. It is too terrible, the things that happen there. In my dream there is wind and blood moving as a stream. Red, dark blood in my dream. Rushing for our village. The blood moves faster. There are screams of wounded people. Animals are dead, thrown in the blood stream. There is nothing left. Only the air echoing nothing. Only the earth soaking up blood, spreading it in the four directions, becoming a thing there is no name for. I stand in the field watching the fire, The People watching me. We are waiting, but the answer is not clear yet. A crazy woman. That is what they call me.

1979

After taking a morning off work to see my lawyer, I come home, not caring if I call in. Not caring, for once, at the loss in pay. Not caring. My lawyer says there is nothing more we can do. I must wait. As if there has been something other than waiting. He has custody and calls the shots. We must wait and see how long it takes for him to get tired of being a mommy and a daddy. So, I wait.

I open the door to Patricia's room. Ellen and I keep it dusted and cleaned in case my baby will be allowed to visit us. The yellow and blue walls feel like a mockery. I walk to the windows, begin to systematically tear down the curtains. I slowly start to rip the cloth apart. I enjoy hearing the sounds of destruction. Faster, I tear the material into strips. What won't come apart with my hands, I pull at with my teeth. Looking for more to destroy, I gather the sheets and bedspread in my arms and wildly shred them to pieces. Grunting and sweating, I am pushed by rage and the searing wound in my soul. Like a wolf, caught in a trap, gnawing at her own leg to set herself free, I begin to beat my breasts to deaden the pain inside. A noise gathers in my throat and finds the way out. I begin a

scream that turns to howling, then becomes hoarse choking. I want to take my fists, my strong fists, my brown fists, and smash the world until it bleeds. Bleeds! And all the judges in their flapping robes, and the fathers who look for revenge, are ground, ground into dust and disappear with the wind.

The word *lesbian*. Lesbian. The word that makes them panic, makes them afraid, makes them destroy children. The word that dares them. Lesbian. *I am one.* Even for Patricia, even for her, *I will not cease to be!* As I kneel amidst the colorful scraps, Raggedy Anns smiling up at me, my chest gives a sigh. My heart slows to its normal speech. I feel the blood pumping outward to my veins, carrying nourishment and life. I strip the room naked. I close the door.   [1985]

🌿 73

Elena

PAT MORA

My Spanish isn't enough.
I remember how I'd smile
listening to my little ones,
understanding every word they'd say,
their jokes, their songs, their plots.
    Vamos a pedirle dulces a mamá. Vamos.
But that was in Mexico.
Now my children go to American high schools.
They speak English. At night they sit around
the kitchen table, laugh with one another.
I stand by the stove and feel dumb, alone.
I bought a book to learn English.
My husband frowned, drank more beer.
My oldest said, "*Mamá*, he doesn't want you
to be smarter than he is." I'm forty,
embarrassed at mispronouncing words,
embarrassed at the laughter of my children,
the grocer, the mailman. Sometimes I take
my English book and lock myself in the bathroom,
say the thick words softly,
for if I stop trying, I will be deaf
when my children need help.   [1994]

🌿 74

"Don't You Talk About My Mama!"

JUNE JORDAN

I got up that morning, with malice toward no one. Drank my coffee and scanned the front page of *the New York Times*. And there it was. I remember, even now, the effrontery of that headline four years ago: "Breakup of Black Family Imperils Gains of Decades." I could hardly believe it. Here were these clowns dumping on us yet again. That was 1983, three years into the shameless Real Deal of Ronald Reagan. He'd taken or he'd shaken everything we black folks needed just to hang in here, breathing in and out. And yet the headline absolutely failed to give credit where it was due. Instead, "politicians and scholars—black and white" dared to identify the *victims*—the black single mothers raising 55 percent of all of our black children *with no help from anybody anywhere*—as the cause of black poverty! These expense-account professionals presumed to identify "the family crisis" of Black folks as "a threat to the future of black people without equal." And this was not somebody's weird idea about how to say "thank you." (I could relate to that: somebody finally saying thank you to black women!) No: This was just another dumb, bold insult to my mother.

Now when I was growing up, the one sure trigger to a down-and-out fight was to say something—anything—about somebody's mother. As a matter of fact, we refined things eventually to the point where you didn't have to get specific. All you had to do was push into the face of another girl or boy, close as you could, almost nose to nose, and just spit out the two words: "Your mother!" This item of our code of honor was not negotiable, and clearly we took it pretty seriously: Even daring to refer to someone's mother put you off-limits. From the time you learned how to talk, everybody's mama remained the holiest of holies. And we did not ever forget it, this fact, that the first, the last, and the most, that the number-one persevering, resourceful,

resilient, and devoted person in our lives was, and would always be, your mother and my mother.

But sometimes, as you know, we grow up without growing wise. Sometimes we become so sophisticated we have to read *the New York Times* in order to figure out whether it's a hot or a rainy day. We read the fine print in order to find out the names of our so-called leaders. But what truly surprises me is black folks listening to a whole lot of white blasphemy against black feats of survival, black folks paying attention to people who never even notice us except to describe us as "female-headed" or something equally weird. (I would like to know, for a fact, has anybody ever seen a female-headed anything at all? What did it look like? What did it do?)

Now I am not opposed to sophistication per se, but when you lose touch with your mama, when you take the word of an absolute, hostile stranger over and above the unarguable truth of your own miraculous, hard-won history, and when you don't remember to ask, again and again, "Compared to what?" I think you don't need to worry about enemies anymore. You'd better just worry about yourself.

Back in 1965, Daniel P. Moynihan (now a U.S. senator from New York) issued a broadside insult to the national Black community. With the full support of a Democratic administration that was tired of Negroes carrying on about citizenship rights and integration and white racist violence, Moynihan came through with the theory that we, black folks, and we, black women in particular, constituted "the problem." And now there are black voices joining the choruses of the absurd. There are national black organizations and purported black theoreticians who have become indistinguishable from the verified enemies of black folks in this country. These sophisticated Black voices jump to the forefront of delighted mass-media exposure because they are willing to lament and to defame the incredible triumph of black women, the victory of black mothers that is the victory of our continuation as a people in America.

Archly delivering jargon phrases about "the collapse of black family structure" and "the destructive culture of poverty in the ghetto" and, of course, "the crisis of female-headedness," with an additional screaming reference to "the shame of teenage pregnancy," these black voices come to us as the disembodied blatherings of peculiar offspring: black men and women who wish to deny the black mother of their origins and who wish to adopt white Daniel P. Moynihan as their father. I happen to lack the imagination necessary to forgive, or understand, this phenomenon. But the possible consequences of this oddball public outcry demand our calm examination.

According to these new black voices fathered by Mr. Moynihan, it would seem that the black family subsists in a terrible, deteriorating state. That's the problem. The source of the problem is the black family (that is, it is not white; it suffers from "female-headedness"). The solution to the black family problem is—you guessed it—the black family. It must become more white—more patriarchal, less "female-headed," more employed more steadily at better and better-paying jobs.

Now I would agree that the black family is not white. I do not agree that the problem is "female-headedness." I would rather suggest that the problem is that women in general and that black women in particular cannot raise our children and secure adequately paying jobs because this is a society that hates women and that believes we are replaceable, that we are dispensable, ridiculous, irksome facts of life. American social and economic hatred of women means that any work primarily identified as women's work will be poorly paid, if at all. Any work open to women will be poorly paid, at best, in comparison to work open to men. Any work done by women will receive a maximum of 64 cents on the dollar compared with wages for the same work done by men. Prenatal, well-baby care, day care for children, children's allowances, housing allowances for parents, paid maternity leave—all of the elemental provisions for the equally entitled citizenship of women and children are ordinary attributes of industrialized nations, except for one: the United States.

The problem, clearly, does not originate with women in general or black women specifically, who, whether it's hard or whether it's virtually impossible, nevertheless keep things together. Our hardships follow from the uncivilized political and economic status enjoined upon women and children in our country, which has the highest infant mortality rate among its industrial peers. And, evidently, feels fine, thank you, about that. (Not incidentally, black infant-mortality rates hold at levels twice that for whites.)

The black family persists *despite* the terrible deteriorating state of affairs prevailing in the United States. This is a nation unwilling and progressively unable to provide for the well-being of most of its citizens: Our economic system increasingly concentrates our national wealth in the hands of fewer and fewer interest groups. Our economic system increasingly augments the wealth of the richest sector of the citizenry, while it diminishes the real wages and the available livelihood of the poor. Our economic system refuses responsibility for the equitable sharing of national services and monies among its various peoples. Our economic system remains insensitive to the political demands of a democracy, and therefore it does not yield to the requirements of equal entitlement of all women and all children and black, Hispanic and Native American men, the elderly, and the disabled. If you total the American people you have an obvious majority of Americans squeezed outside the putative benefits of "free enterprise."

Our economic system continues its trillion-dollar commitment *not* to the betterment of the lives of its citizens but, rather, to the development and lunatic replication of a military-industrial complex. In this context, then, the black family persists, yes, in a terrible deteriorating state. But we did not create this state. Nor do we control it. And we are not suffering "collapse." Change does not signify collapse. The nuclear, patriarchal family structure of white America was never our own; it was not *African*. And when we arrived to slavery here, why or how should we have emulated the overseer and the master? We who were counted in the Constitution as three-fifths of a human being? We who could by law neither marry nor retain our children against the predations of the slave economy? Nonetheless, from under the whip through underpaid underemployment and worse, black folks have formulated our own family, our own home base for nurture and for pride. We have done this through extended kinship methods. And even black teenage parents are trying, in their own way, to perpetuate the black family.

The bizarre analysis of the black family that blames the black family for being not white and not patriarchal, not endowed with steadily employed black husbands and fathers who enjoy access to middle-income occupations is just that: a bizarre analysis, a heartless joke. If black men and black women *wanted* black men to become patriarchs of their families, if black men wanted to function as head of the house—shouldn't they probably have some kind of a job? Can anyone truly dare to suggest that the catastrophic 46-percent unemployment rate now crippling working-age black men is something that either black men or black women view as positive or desirable? Forty-six percent! What is the meaning of a man in the house if he cannot hold out his hand to help his family make it through the month, and if he cannot hold up his head with the pride and authority that regular, satisfying work for good pay provides? How or whom shall he marry and on what basis? Is it honestly puzzling to anyone that the 46-percent, Depression-era rate of unemployment that imprisons black men almost exactly mirrors the 50 percent of black households now maintained by black women? Our black families persist despite a racist arrangement of rewards such as the fact that the median black family has only about 56 cents to spend for every dollar that white families have to spend. And a Black college graduate still cannot realistically expect to earn more than a white high-school graduate.

We, children and parents of black families, neither created nor do we control the terrible, deteriorating state of our unjust and meanly discriminating national affairs. In its structure, the traditional black family has always reflected our particular jeopardy within these unwelcome circumstances. We have never been "standard" or predictable or stabilized in any normative sense, even as our black lives have never been standard or predictable or stabilized in a benign national environment. We have been flexible, ingenious, and innovative or we have perished. And we have not perished. We remain and we remain different, and we have become necessarily deft at distinguishing between the negative differences—those imposed upon us—and the positive differences—those that joyously attest to our distinctive, survivalist attributes as a people.

Today we must distinguish between responsibility and consequence. We are not responsible for the systematic underemployment and unemployment of black men or women. We are not responsible for racist hatred of us, and we are not responsible for the American contempt for women per se. We are not responsible for a dominant value system that quibbles over welfare benefits for children and squanders deficit billions of dollars on American pie in the sky. But we must outlive the consequences of this inhumane, disposable-life ideology. We have no choice. And because this ideology underpins our economic system and the political system that supports our economy, we no longer constitute a minority inside America. We are joined in our precarious quandary here by all women and by children, Hispanic Americans and Native Americans, and the quickly expanding population of the aged, as well as the temporarily or permanently disabled.

At issue now is the "universal entitlement" of American citizens (as author Ruth Sidel terms it in her important book *Women and Children Last: The Plight of Poor Women in Affluent America* [Viking Press, 1986]): What should American citizenship confer? What are the duties of the state in relation to the citizens it presumes to tax and to govern?

It is not the black family in crisis but American democracy in crisis when the majority of our people oppose U.S. intervention in Central America and, nevertheless, the president proceeds to intervene. It is not the black family in crisis but American democracy at stake when the majority of our people abhor South African apartheid and, nonetheless, the president proceeds to collaborate with the leadership of that evil. It is not the black family in crisis but American democracy at risk when a majority of American citizens may no longer assume that social programs beneficial to them will be preserved and/or developed.

But if we, black children and parents, have been joined by so many others in our precarious quandary here, may we not also now actively join with these other jeopardized Americans to redefine and to finally secure universal entitlement of citizenship that will at last conclude the shameful American history of our oppression? And what should these universal entitlements—our new American Bill of Rights—include?

1. Guaranteed jobs and/or guaranteed income to ensure each and every American in each and every one of the 50 states an existence *above* the poverty line.
2. Higher domestic minimum wages and, for the sake of both our narrowest and broadest self-interests, a coordinated, international minimum wage so that exhausted economic exploitation in Detroit can no longer be replaced by economic exploitation in Taiwan or Soweto or Manila.
3. Government guarantees of an adequate minimum allowance for every child regardless of the marital status of the parents.
4. Equal pay for equal work.
5. Affirmative action to ensure broadly democratic access to higher-paying occupations.
6. Compensation for "women's work" equal to compensation for "men's work."
7. Housing allowances and/or state commitments to build and/or to subsidize acceptable, safe, and affordable housing for every citizen.
8. Comprehensive, national health insurance from prenatal through geriatric care.
9. Availability of state education and perpetual reeducation through graduate levels of study on the basis of student interest and aptitude rather than financial capacity.
10. A national budget that will invariably commit the main portion of our collective monies to our collective domestic needs for a good life.
11. Comprehensive provision for the well-being of all our children commensurate with the kind of future we are hoping to help construct. These provisions must include paid maternity and paternity leave and universal, state-controlled, public child care programs for working parents.
12. Nationalization of vital industries to protect citizen consumers and citizen workers alike from the greed-driven vagaries of a "free market."
13. Aggressive nuclear-disarmament policies and, concurrently, aggressive state protection of what's left of the life-supportive elements of our global environment.

I do not believe that a just, a civilized nation can properly regard any one of these 13 entitlements as optional. And yet not one of them is legally in place in the United States. And why not? I think that, as a people, we have yet to learn how to say thank you in real ways to those who have loved us enough to keep us alive despite inhumane and unforgivable opposition to our well-being. For myself, I do not need any super-sophisticated charts and magical graphs to tell me my own mama done better than she could, and my mama's mama, *she* done better than I could. And *everybody's mama* done better than anybody had any right to expect she would. And that's the truth!

And I hope you've been able to follow my meaning. And a word to the wise, they say, should be sufficient. So, I'm telling you real nice: Don't you talk about my mama!   [1987]

🌿 75

Working at Single Bliss

MARY HELEN WASHINGTON

I

Apart from the forest
have you seen
that a tree alone
will often take inventive form . . .

—Paulette Childress White
"A Tree Alone"

She who has chosen her Self, who defines her Self, by choice, neither in relation to children nor men; who is Self-identified, is a Spinster, a whirling dervish spinning in a new time/space.

—Mary Daly
Gyn/Ecology (Beacon Press)

Last year I was asked to be on the "Tom Cottle Show," a syndicated television program that originates here in Boston. The psychiatrist-host wanted to interview six single women about their singleness.

I hesitated only a moment before refusing. Six single women discussing the significance of their lives? No, I instinctively knew that the interview would end up being an interrogation of six unmarrieds (a pejorative, like coloreds)—women trying to rationalize lives of loss. Losers at the marriage game. *Les femmes manqués.*

I watched the program they put together without me, and sure enough, Cottle asked a few perfunctory questions about singleness and freedom, and then moved on rapidly to the real killer questions. I found it painful to watch these very fine women trapped in the net he'd laid. "Don't you ever come home from these glamorous lives of freedom [read selfishness] and sit down to dinner alone and just cry?" "What about sex?" "What about children?" The women struggled to answer these insulting questions with dignity and humor, but clearly the game was rigged against them. Imagine the interviewer lining up six couples and asking them the same kinds of questions: "Well, what about your sex lives?" "Why don't you have any children?" (or "Why do you have so many?") "Don't you ever come home at night, sit down to dinner, and wonder why you ever married the person on the other side of the table?" Of course, this interview would never take place—the normal restraint and politeness that are reserved for people whose positions are socially acceptable assure married folks some measure of protection and, at least, common decency.

"You're so lucky, footloose and fancy-free, with no responsibilities," a friend with two children once said to me. Ostensibly that's a compliment, or at least, it's supposed to be. But underneath it is really a critique of single people, implying that their lives do not have the moral stature of a life with "responsibilities." It's a comment that used to leave me feeling a little like a kid, a failed adult; for what's an adult with no responsibilities? A kid. I have had to learn to recognize and reject the veiled contempt in this statement because, of course, single people do have responsibilities.

At age 40, I have been a single adult for 20 years. No, I am neither widowed nor divorced. I am single in the pristine sense of that word—which unleashes that basic fear in all of us, "What will I do if I'm left by myself?" As I have more or less successfully dealt with that fear over the years, I am somewhat indignant at being cast as an irresponsible gadfly, unencumbered by the problems of Big People. I have earned a living and "kept myself," and I have done that without being either male or white in a world dominated by men and corroded by racism. I've sat up nights with students' papers and even later with their problems. Without any of the social props married people have, I have given many memorable parties. Like my aunts before me, I've celebrated the births, birthdays, first communions, graduations, football games, and track meets of my 10 nephews. And not a hair on my mother's head changes color without my noticing it.

As Zora Hurston's Janie says, "Two things everybody's got tuh do fuh theyselves. They got tuh go tuh God, and they got tuh find out about livin' fuh theyselves." If anything, a single person may be more aware of the responsibility to discover and create meaning in her life, to find community, to honor her creativity, to live out her values, than the person whose life is circumferenced by an immediate and intimate family life.

II

To be single and busy—nothing bad in that. Such people do much good.

—Elizabeth Hardwick
Sleepless Nights (Random House)

To some extent my adolescent imagination was bewitched by the myth that marriage is *the* vertical choice in a woman's life—one that raises her status, completes her life, fulfills her dreams, and makes her a valid person in society. In the 1950s, all the movies, all the songs directed us to this one choice: to find our worldly prince and go two by two into the ark. Nothing else was supposed to matter quite as much and it was a surprise to discover that something else matters just as much, sometimes more.

But in spite of the romance-marriage-motherhood bombardment, I grew up in a kind of war-free zone where I heard the bombs and artillery all around me but was spared from a direct attack. I was raised in two very separate but mutually supportive communities—one black, one Catholic, both of which taught me that a woman could be her own person in the world.

In the all-women's Catholic high school and college in Cleveland, Ohio, where I put in eight formative years, we were required to think of ourselves as women with destinies, women whose achievements mattered—whether we chose marriage or religious life or, as it was called then, a life of "single blessedness." In fact, marriage and the single life seemed to my convent-honed ninth-grade mind to have a clearly equal status: they were both inferior to the intrinsically superior religious life.

The program of spiritual, intellectual, social, and physical development the nuns demanded of us allowed an involvement with myself I craved even in the ninth grade. *Some* dating was encouraged at Notre Dame Academy (ninth through twelfth grades)—not as a consuming emotional involvement but as part of a "normal social development." Boys had their place—on the periphery of one's life. (A girl who came to school with her boyfriend's taped class ring on her finger was subject to expulsion.) You were expected to be the central, dominant figure in the fabric of your own life.

The nuns themselves were vivid illustrations of that principle. For me they were the most powerful images of women imaginable—not ladies-in-waiting, not submissive homebodies, not domestic drudges, not deviants. They ran these women-dominated universes with aplomb and authority. Even if "Father" appeared on Monday morning for our weekly religious lesson, his appearance was tolerated as a kind of necessary token of the male hierarchy, and, when he left, the waters ran back together, leaving no noticeable trace of his presence.

Nuns were the busiest people I knew then. No matter how graceful and dignified the pace, they always seemed to be hurrying up and down the corridors of Notre Dame planning something important and exciting. Sister Wilbur directed dramatics and went to New York occasionally to see the latest Off-Broadway productions. Sister Kathryn Ann wrote poetry and went to teach in Africa. Another sister coached debate and took our winning teams to state championships in Columbus. Though technically

nuns are not single, they do not have that affiliation with a male figure to establish their status. (After Mary Daly it should not be necessary to point out that God is not a man.) They also have to ward off the same stigma of being different from the norm as single people do. So it's only a little ironic that I got some of my sense of how a woman could be complete and autonomous and comfortable in the world—*sans* marriage—from the Sisters of Notre Dame.

The message I got from the black community about single life was equally forceful. So many black girls heard these words, they might have been programmed tapes: "Girl, get yourself an education, you can't count on a man to take care of you." "An education is something no one can take from you." "Any fool can get married, but not everyone can go to school."

I didn't know it then, but this was my feminist primer. Aim high, they said, because that is the only way a black girl can claim a place in this world. Marriage was a chancy thing, not dependable like diplomas: my mother and aunts and uncles said that even if you married a Somebody—a doctor or a lawyer—there was no assurance that he'd have a good heart or treat you right. They thought that the worst thing a woman could do was to get into financial dependency with a man—and it was not that they hated or distrusted men so much as they distrusted any situation that made an already vulnerable woman more powerless.

There was such reverence in my mother's voice for women of achievement that I never connected their social status with anything as mundane as marriage. The first black woman with a Ph.D., the first black woman school principal, the first woman doctor—I knew their names by heart and wanted to be one of them and do important things.

My third-grade teacher, the first black teacher at Parkwood Elementary in Cleveland, Ohio, was a single woman in her thirties. At age nine, I saw her as a tall, majestic creature who wore earrings, drove her own car, and made school pure joy. To my family and the neighborhood, Miss Hilliard was like a totem of our tribe's good fortune: an independent, self-sufficient, educated woman bringing her treasures back to their children. She was a part of that tradition of 19th-century black women whose desire for "race uplift" sent them to teach in the South and to schools like Dunbar High in Washington, D.C., and the School for Colored Youth in Philadelphia. Though many of these women were married, the majority of them were widowed for a great many years and those were often the years of achievement for them.

One of these nineteenth-century stellar examples, Anna Julia Cooper, dismissed the question of marriage as a false issue. The question should not be "How shall I so cramp, stunt, simplify, and nullify myself as to make me eligible for the horror of being swallowed up into some little man," but how shall a generation of women demand of themselves and of men "the noblest, the grandest and the best" in their capacities.

III

In the places of their childhoods, the
troubles they had getting grown,
the tales of men they told among
themselves as we sat unnoted
at their feet, we saw some image
of a past and future self.
The world had loved them even
less than their men but this did
not keep them from scheming
on its favor.

—Sherley Anne Williams
Some One Sweet Angel Chile (William Morrow)

I learned early about being single from my five aunts. By the time I was old enough to notice, four were widowed and one divorced, so from my 12-year-old perspective, they were single women for a good part of their lives. They ran their own households, cooked, entertained, searched for spirituality, helped my mother to raise eight children, traveled some, went to work, cared for the sick, planned picnics. In short, they made up their lives by themselves, inventing the forms that satisfied them. And in the course of their "scheming" they passed on to me something about the rituals and liturgy of single life.

The eldest of these aunts, Aunt Bessie, lived as a single woman for 26 years. Her husband of 40 years died when she was 60 and she began to live alone for the first time since she was 18. She

bought a huge old house, painted, decorated, and furnished every room with Oriental rugs and secondhand furniture purchased at estate sales. (Black people discovered this bonanza in the 1940s long before it became a middle-class fad.) She put in a new lawn, grew African violets, and started a whole new life for herself on Ashbury Avenue.

Aunt Bessie was secretly proud of how well she was doing on her own, and she used to tell me slyly how many of these changes she could not have made as a married woman: "Uncle wouldn't have bought this house, baby; he wouldn't have wanted this much space. He wouldn't have changed neighborhoods." She was finally doing exactly what pleased her, and the shape of her life as she had designed it in her singularity was much more varied, dynamic, and daring. What I learned from her is symbolized by that multilevel house on Ashbury Avenue. She had three bedrooms—she needed them for guests; on the third floor she made hats, which she sold for a living; the huge old basement was for her tools and lawn work. All this room was essential to the amount of living she planned to do.

Since she willed all of her furniture to me, my own flat resembles that house in many ways, and her spirit came with the furnishings: I have the sense of inhabiting every corner of my life just as she lived in all 10 rooms of her house. Even my overstocked refrigerator is a reflection of something I learned from her about taking care of your life. Another aunt, Hazel, died only a few years after she was widowed, and I remember Aunt Bessie's explanation of her untimely death as a warning about the perils of not taking your life seriously. "Hazel stopped cooking for herself after her husband died, just ate snacks and junk food instead of making a proper dinner for herself. And she got that cancer and died." The message was clear to me—even at age 12—that single life could be difficult at times and that living it well required some effort, but you were not supposed to let it kill you.

IV

[Friendship] is a profound experience which calls forth our
humanness and shapes our being. . . . This is true for all
persons, but it has a special significance for single persons.

For it is in the context of friendship that most single persons experience the intimacy and immediacy of others.
—Francine Cardman
"On Being Single"

Girded up with all of this psychological armament from my past, I still entered adult life without the powerful and sustaining myths and rituals that could provide respect and support for single life. Terms like "old maid" and "spinster," not yet redefined by a feminist consciousness, could still be used to belittle and oppress single women. By the time I was 35, I had participated in scores of marriage ceremonies, and even had begun sending anniversary cards to my married friends. But never once did I think of celebrating the anniversary of a friendship—even one that was by then 25 years old. (Aren't you entitled to gifts of silver at that milestone?)

Once, about 10 years ago, five of us single women from Cleveland took a trip to Mexico together. (Actually only four of the group were single; the fifth, Ernestine, was married and three months pregnant.) I remember that trip as seven days and eight nights of adventure, laughter, discovery, and closeness.

We were such typical tourists—taking snapshots of ancient ruins, posing in front of cathedrals, paying exorbitant sums to see the cliff divers (whose entire act took about 20 seconds), floating down debris-filled waterways to see some totally unnoteworthy sights, learning the hard way that in the hot Acapulco sun even us "killer browns" could get a sunburn. We stayed up at night talking about our lives, our dreams, our careers, our men, and laughing so hard in these late-night sessions that we hardly had the energy for the next morning's tour.

It was the laughter and the good talk (remember Toni Cade Bambara's short story "The Johnson Girls") that made the trip seem so complete. It was so perfect that even in the midst of the experience I knew it was to be a precious memory. Years later I asked my friend, Ponchita, why she thought the five of us never planned another trip like that, why we let such good times drift out of our lives without an attempt to recapture them. "Because," she said, "it wasn't enough. It was fun, stimulating, warm, exciting, but it wasn't 'The Thing That Made Life Complete,' and it wasn't leading us in that direction; I guess it was a little like 'recess.'" We wanted nests, not excitement. We wanted domestic bliss, not lives lived at random, no matter how thrilling, how wonderful. So there was the potential—those "dependable and immediate supports" existed. But without the dependable myths to accompany them, we couldn't seriously invest ourselves in those experiences.

When my friend Meg suggested we celebrate Mother's Day this year with a brunch for all our single, childless women friends, and bring pictures of the nieces and nephews we dote on, I recognized immediately the psychic value in honoring our own form of caretaking. We were establishing rituals by which we could ceremonially acknowledge our particular social identities.

My oldest friend Ponchita and I did exchange gifts last year on the twenty-fifth anniversary of our friendship, and never again will the form "anniversary" mean only a rite (right) of the married. My journey through the single life was beginning to have its own milestones and to be guided by its own cartography.

V

A life of pure decision, of thoughtful calculations, every inclination honored. They go about on their own, nicely accompanied in their singularity by the companion of possibility.

—Elizabeth Hardwick
Sleepless Nights

Our Mexico trip was in 1971. In the next 10 years, I earned a Ph.D., became director of black studies at the University of Detroit, edited two anthologies, threw out my makeshift bricks-and-board furniture, began to think about buying a house and adopting a child, and in the process, decided that my life was no longer "on hold." These deliberate choices made me begin to regard my single status as an honorable estate. But you know, when I look back at that checklist of accomplishments and serious life plans, I feel resentful that I had to work so hard for the honor that naturally accompanies the married state. Overcompensation, however, sometimes has its rewards: I had established a reputation in my profession that brought the prospect of a fellowship year at Radcliffe and a new job in Boston.

When I was leaving Detroit, I was acutely aware of my single status. What kind of life was it, I wondered, if you could start all over again in a new city with nothing to show for your past except your furniture and your diplomas? I didn't even have a cat. Where were the signs and symbols of a coherent, meaningful life that others could recognize? What was I doing living at *random* like this? I had made this "pure" decision and was honoring my inclination to live in another city, to take a job that offered excitement and challenge. As I packed boxes alone, signed contracts with moving companies, and said good-bye at numerous dinners and going-away parties to all the friends I had made over 10 years, I felt not so very different from a friend who was moving after separating from his wife: "like a rhinoceros being cut loose from the herd."

I think it was the wide-open, netless freedom of it all that scared me, because I was truly *not* alone. I moved into a triple-decker in Cambridge where I live in a kind of semicooperative with two other families. Here, I feel secure, but independent and private. The journalist on the second floor and I read each other's work, and I exchange ideas about teaching methods with the three other professors in the house. We all share meals occasionally; we've met one another's extended families; and we celebrate one another's assorted triumphs. I have put together another network of friends whose lives I feel intimately involved in, and who, like me, are interested in making single life work—not disappear.

But I do not yet have the solid sense of belonging to a community that I had in Cleveland and Detroit, and sometimes I am unsettled by the variousness and unpredictableness of my single life. This simply means that I still have some choices to make—about deepening friendships, about having children (possibly adopting them), about establishing closer ties with the black community in Boston. If and when I do adopt a child, she or he will have

a selection of godparents and aunts and uncles as large and varied as I had. That is one of the surest signs of the richness of my single life.

VI

You're wondering if I'm lonely:
OK then, yes, I'm lonely
as a plane rides lonely and level
on its radio beam, aiming
across the Rockies
for the blue-strung aisles
of an airfield on the ocean

—Adrienne Rich
"Song" from *Diving into the Wreck* (Norton)

Last year Elizabeth Stone wrote an article in the *Village Voice* called "A Married Woman" in which she discussed how much her life had changed since she married at the age of 33. Somewhat boastfully, she remarked at the end that she had hardly made any reference in the whole article to her husband. But if a single woman describes her life without reference to romance—no matter how rich and satisfying her life may be, no matter what she says about wonderful friends, exciting work, cultural and intellectual accomplishments—in fact, the *more* she says about these things—the more skeptical people's reactions will be. That one fact—her romantic involvement—if it is not acceptable can cancel out all the rest. This is how society keeps the single woman feeling perilous about her sense of personal success.

Still, everybody wants and needs some kind of special alliance(s) in her life. Some people have alliances called marriage. (I like that word alliance: it keeps marriage in its proper—horizontal—place.) I'd like an alliance with a man who could be a comrade and kindred spirit, and I've had such alliances in the past. Even with the hassles, they were enriching and enjoyable experiences for me, but I have never wanted to forsake my singularity for this kind of emotional involvement. Whatever psychic forces drive me have always steered me toward autonomy and independence, out toward the ocean's expanse and away from the shore.

I don't want to sound so smooth and glib and clear-eyed about it all, because it has taken me more than a decade to get this sense of balance and control. A lot of rosaries and perpetual candles and expensive long-distance calls have gotten me through the hard times when I would have chosen the holy cloister over another day of "single blessedness." The truth is that those hard times were not caused by being single. They were part of every woman's struggle to find commitment and contentment for herself. Singleness does not define me, is not an essential characteristic of me. I simply wish to have it acknowledged as a legitimate way to be in the world. After all, we started using Ms. instead of Mrs. or Miss because *none* of us wanted to be defined by the presence or absence of a man.

VII

Apart from the forest
a single tree will sometimes grow awry
in brave and extraordinary search
for its own shape

—Paulette Childress White
"A Tree Alone"

When I first started running in 1972, I ran regularly with a man. As long as I had this male companion, the other men passing by either ignored me or gave me slight nods to show their approval of my supervised state. Eventually I got up the nerve to run alone around Detroit's Palmer Park, and then the men came out of the trees to make comments— usually to tell me what I was doing wrong ("Lift your legs higher" or "Stop waving your arms"), or to flirt ("Can I run with you, baby?" was by far the most common remark, though others were nastier).

Once a carload of black teenagers who were parked in the lot at the end of my run started making comments about my physical anatomy, which I started to dismiss as just a dumb teenage ritual. But on this particular day, something made me stop my run, walk over to the car, and say, "You know, when you see a sister out trying to get some exercise, as hard as that is for us, you ought to be trying to support her, because she needs all the help she can get." I didn't know how they would respond, so I was surprised when they apologized,

and somewhat shamefaced, one of them said: "Go on, sister; we're with you."

Now, that incident occurred because I was alone, and the image has become part of my self-definition: I am a woman in the world—single and powerful and astonished at my ability to create my own security, "in brave and extraordinary search for my own shape."   [1982]

76

A Marriage Agreement

ALIX KATES SHULMAN

When my husband and I were first married, a decade ago, keeping house was less a burden than a game. We both worked full-time in New York City, so our small apartment stayed empty most of the day and taking care of it was very little trouble. Twice a month we'd spend Saturday cleaning and doing our laundry at the laundromat. We shopped for food together after work, and though I usually did the cooking, my husband was happy to help. Since our meals were simple and casual, there were few dishes to wash. We occasionally had dinner out and usually ate breakfast at a diner near our offices. We spent most of our free time doing things we enjoyed together, such as taking long walks in the evenings and spending weekends in Central Park. Our domestic life was beautifully uncomplicated.

When our son was born, our domestic life suddenly became *quite* complicated; and two years later, when our daughter was born, it became impossible. We automatically accepted the traditional sex roles that society assigns. My husband worked all day in an office; I left my job and stayed at home, taking on almost all the burdens of housekeeping and child raising.

When I was working I had grown used to seeing people during the day, to having a life outside the home. But now I was restricted to the company of two demanding preschoolers and to the four walls of an apartment. It seemed unfair that while my husband's life had changed little when the children were born, domestic life had become the only life I had.

I tried to cope with the demands of my new situation, assuming that other women were able to handle even larger families with ease and still find time for themselves. I couldn't seem to do that.

We had to move to another apartment to accommodate our larger family, and because of the children, keeping it reasonably neat took several hours a day. I prepared half a dozen meals every day for from one to four people at a time—and everyone ate different food. Shopping for this brood—or even just running out for a quart of milk—meant putting on snowsuits, boots, and mittens; getting strollers or carriages up and down the stairs; and scheduling the trip so it would not interfere with one of the children's feeding or nap or illness or some other domestic job. Laundry was now a daily chore. I seemed to be working every minute of the day—and still there were dishes in the sink; still there wasn't time enough to do everything.

Even more burdensome than the physical work of housekeeping was the relentless responsibility I had for my children. I loved them, but they seemed to be taking over my life. There was nothing I could do, or even contemplate, without first considering how they would be affected. As they grew older, just answering their constant questions ruled out even a private mental life. I had once enjoyed reading, but now if there was a moment free, instead of reading for myself, I read to them. I wanted to work on my own writing, but there simply weren't enough hours in the day. I had no time for myself; the children were always *there*.

As my husband's job began keeping him at work later and later—and sometimes taking him out of town—I missed his help and companionship. I wished he would come home at six o'clock and spend time with the children so they could know him better. I continued to buy food with him in mind and dutifully set his place at the table. Yet sometimes whole weeks would go by without his having dinner with us. When he did get home the children often were asleep, and we both were too tired ourselves to do anything but sleep.

We accepted the demands of his work as unavoidable. Like most couples, we assumed that the wife must accommodate to the husband's schedule, since it is his work that brings in the money.

As the children grew older I began freelance editing at home. I felt I had to squeeze it into my "free" time and not allow it to interfere with my domestic duties or the time I owed my husband— just as he felt he had to squeeze in time for the children during weekends. We were both chronically dissatisfied, but we knew no solutions.

After I had been home with the children for six years I began to attend meetings of the newly formed Women's Liberation Movement in New York City. At these meetings I began to see that my situation was not uncommon; other women too felt drained and frustrated as housewives and mothers. When we started to talk about how we would have chosen to arrange our lives, most of us agreed that even though we might have preferred something different, we had never felt we had a choice in the matter. We realized that we had slipped into full domestic responsibility simply as a matter of course, and it seemed unfair.

When I added them up, the chores I was responsible for amounted to a hectic 6 a.m.–9 p.m. (often later) job, without salary, breaks or vacation. No employer would be able to demand these hours legally, but most mothers take them for granted— as I did until I became a feminist.

For years mothers like me have acquiesced to the strain of the preschool years and endless household maintenance without any real choice. Why, I asked myself, should a couple's decision to have a family mean that the woman must immerse years of her life in their children? And why should men like my husband miss caring for and knowing their children?

Eventually, after an arduous examination of our situation, my husband and I decided that we no longer had to accept the sex roles that had turned us into a lame family. Out of equal parts love for each other and desperation at our situation, we decided to reexamine the patterns we had been living by, and starting again from scratch, to define our roles for ourselves.

We began by agreeing to share completely all responsibility for raising our children (by then aged five and seven) and caring for our household. If this new arrangement meant that my husband would have to change his job or that I would have to do more freelance work or that we would have to live on a different scale, then we would. It would be worth it if it could make us once again equal, independent and loving as we had been when we were first married.

Simply agreeing verbally to share domestic duties didn't work, despite our best intentions. And when we tried to divide them "spontaneously," we ended up following the traditional patterns. Our old habits were too deep-rooted. So we sat down and drew up a formal agreement, acceptable to both of us, that clearly defined the responsibilities we each had.

It may sound a bit formal, but it has worked for us. Here it is:

MARRIAGE AGREEMENT

I. Principles

We reject the notion that the work that brings in more money is more valuable. The ability to earn more money is a privilege that must not be compounded by enabling the larger earner to buy out of his/her duties and put the burden either on the partner who earns less or on another person hired from outside.

We believe that each partner has an equal right to his/her own time, work, value, choices. As long as all duties are performed, each of us may use his/her extra time any way he/she chooses. If he/she wants to use it making money, fine. If he/she wants to spend it with spouse, fine. If not, fine.

As parents we believe we must share all responsibility for taking care of our children and home—not only the work but also the responsibility. At least during the first year of this agreement, *sharing responsibility* shall mean dividing the *jobs* and dividing the *time*.

In principle, jobs should be shared equally, 50-50, but deals may be made by mutual agreement. If jobs and schedule are divided on any other than a 50-50 basis, then at any time either party may call for a reexamination and redistribution of jobs or a revision of the schedule. Any deviation from 50-50 must be for the convenience of both parties. If one party works overtime in any domestic job, he/she must be compensated by equal extra work by the other. The schedule may be flexible, but changes must be formally agreed upon. The terms of this agreement are rights and duties, not privileges and favors.

II. Job Breakdown and Schedule

(A) Children

1. Mornings: Waking children; getting their clothes out; making their lunches; seeing that they have notes, homework, money, bus passes, books; brushing their hair; giving them breakfast (making coffee for us). Every other week each parent does all.

2. Transportation: Getting children to and from lessons, doctors, dentists (including making appointments), friends' houses, park, parties, movies, libraries. Parts occurring between 3 and 6 p.m. fall to wife. She must be compensated by extra work from husband (see 10 below). Husband does all weekend transportation and pick-ups after 6.

3. Help: Helping with homework, personal problems, projects like cooking, making gifts, experiments, planting; answering questions; explaining things. Parts occurring between 3 and 6 p.m. fall to wife. After 6 p.m. husband does Tuesday, Thursday, and Sunday; wife does Monday, Wednesday, and Saturday. Friday is free for whoever has done extra work during the week.

4. Nighttime (after 6 p.m.): Getting children to take baths, brush their teeth, put away their toys and clothes, go to bed; reading with them; tucking them in and having nighttime talks; handling if they wake or call in the night. Husband does Tuesday, Thursday, and Sunday. Wife does Monday, Wednesday, and Saturday. Friday is split according to who has done extra work during the week.

5. Baby-sitters: Getting baby-sitters (which sometimes takes an hour of phoning). Baby-sitters must be called by the parent the sitter is to replace. If no sitter turns up, that parent must stay home.

6. Sick care: Calling doctors; checking symptoms; getting prescriptions filled; remembering to give medicine; taking days off to stay home with sick child; providing special activities. This must still be worked out equally, since now wife seems to do it all. (The same goes for the now frequently declared school closings for so-called political protests, whereby the mayor gets credit at the expense of the mothers of young children. The mayor closes only the schools, not the places of business or the government offices.) In any case, wife must be compensated (see 10 below).

7. Weekends: All usual child care, plus special activities (beach, park, zoo). Split equally. Husband is free all Saturday, wife is free all Sunday.

(B) Housework

8. Cooking: Breakfast; dinner (children, parents, guests). Breakfasts during the week are divided equally; husband does all weekend breakfasts (including shopping for them and dishes). Wife does all dinners except Sunday nights. Husband does Sunday dinner and any other dinners on his nights of responsibility if wife isn't home. Whoever invites guests does shopping, cooking, and dishes; if both invite them, split work.

9. Shopping: Food for all meals, housewares, clothing, and supplies for children. Divide by convenience. Generally, wife does local daily food shopping; husband does special shopping for supplies and children's things.

10. Cleaning: Dishes daily; apartment weekly, biweekly, or monthly. Husband does dishes Tuesday, Thursday, and Sunday. Wife does Monday, Wednesday, and Saturday. Friday is split according to who has done extra work during week. Husband does all the house cleaning in exchange for wife's extra child care (3 to 6 daily) and sick care.

11. Laundry: Home laundry, making beds, dry cleaning (take and pick up). Wife does home laundry. Husband does dry-cleaning delivery and pickup. Wife strips beds, husband remakes them.

Our agreement changed our lives. Surprisingly, once we had written it down, we had to refer to it only two or three times. But we still had to work to keep the old habits from intruding. If it was my husband's night to take care of the children, I had to be careful not to check up on how he was managing. And if the baby sitter didn't show up for him, I would have to remember it was *his* problem.

Eventually the agreement entered our heads, and now, after two successful years of following it, we find that our new roles come to us as readily as the old ones had. I willingly help my husband clean the apartment (knowing it is his responsibility) and he often helps me with the laundry or the meals. We work together and trade off duties with ease now that the responsibilities are truly shared. We each have less work, more hours together and less resentment.

Before we made our agreement I had never been able to find the time to finish even one book. Over the past two years I've written three children's books, a biography and a novel, and edited a collection of writings (all will have been published by spring of 1972). Without our agreement I would never have been able to do this.

At present my husband works a regular 40-hour week, and I write at home during the six hours the children are in school. He earns more money now than I do, so his salary covers more of our expenses than the money I make with my freelance work. But if either of us should change jobs, working hours, or income, we would probably adjust our agreement.

Perhaps the best testimonial of all to our marriage agreement is the change that has taken place in our family life. One day after it had been in effect for only four months our daughter said to my husband, "You know, Daddy, I used to love Mommy more than you, but now I love you both the same." [1971]

77

Why We're Not Getting Married

MARTHA ACKELSBERG and
JUDITH PLASKOW

We love each other, and we've been in a committed relationship for nearly 20 years. We are residents of Massachusetts. But we're not getting married. We fully believe that gays and lesbians should have the right to marry, and we celebrate the fact that a significant barrier to our full citizenship has fallen. In not taking advantage of this new right, however, we can more comfortably advocate for the kind of society in which we would like to live.

Those who have fought for gay marriage have made clear that, in the United States, important benefits are tied to marital status. As the judges of the Massachusetts Supreme Judicial Court themselves noted in the *Goodridge* decision, "marriage provides an abundance of legal, financial, and social benefits." Indeed, over 1,000 federal benefits attach to marriage—benefits relating to social security, inheritance, tax status, child custody, and the like. Further, other significant benefits—most notably, health care—are often linked to marriage. Opening up this status to gays and lesbians makes an enormous difference to those in committed relationships in which at least one partner has access to benefits or resources to share.

But focusing on the right to marry perpetuates the idea that these rights ought to be linked to marriage. Were we to marry, we would be contributing to the perpetuation of a norm of coupledness in our society. The norm marginalizes those who are single, single parents, widowed, divorced, or otherwise living in nontraditional constellations. The Massachusetts decision argued that "marriage is a vital social institution. . . . The exclusive commitment of two individuals to each other nurtures love and mutual support; it brings stability to our society." Thus, the judges affirmed the right of gays and lesbians to marry while, at the same time,

reinforcing very traditional beliefs about the centrality of marriage to the social order.

Seeking expanded benefits through marriage also contributes to what amounts to the increasing privatization of responsibility for caring for children, the elderly, the ill and disabled. The Massachusetts decision argues that gay marriage is good for society because children ought to be raised by two parents. The judges stated, in fact, that "it cannot be rational under our laws to penalize children by depriving them of State benefits" because of their parents' sexual orientation. But why is it any more rational to deprive children of state benefits because their parents are not married? Yet, precisely such arguments tying benefits to marriage are being used to justify repressive "marriage promotion" policies that pressure single mothers receiving welfare benefits to marry, and deny them (and their children) significant benefits if they do not marry.

A focus on marriage and familial status leads us, moreover, to neglect our social responsibilities to provide adequate child care, day care, elder care, etc., that would allow all adults who want to work to be able to do so. We all deserve a basic standard of care, as persons and as citizens. We should not have to rely on family members—generally the women in our families—to attend to our needs when we cannot care for ourselves.

Similarly, a focus on increasing the numbers of people who can get access to health or retirement benefits through their spouses can easily lead us to ignore or deny our societal responsibility to provide basic health care and old age security to all our citizens, regardless of marital status.

It's not easy to walk away from the legal benefits that come with marriage. We are fortunate, in that we do not need to rely on one another's employers for our health coverage, and this allows us the luxury of deciding not to marry.

Nevertheless, as feminists and as lesbians, we have considered ourselves to be part of social movements that were modeling a variety of ways to be in the world, and to be in meaningful relationships, other than through marriage. Indeed, the early women's liberation and gay liberation movements challenged the claim that the married-couple nuclear family was the only legitimate way to organize our intimate lives. What happened to that vision? Where are the feminist and gay, lesbian, bisexual, and transgendered voices calling for the separation of civil and religious unions? Why not argue for the disestablishment of marriage as a legal form and the creation of a status of "civil union" that will allow people to create their own forms, and have them recognized by the state? At this moment, when there is so much focus on celebrating the right to marry, we want to hold up a vision of a society in which basic rights are not tied to marriage, and in which there are many ways to organize one's intimate life, marriage being only one of them.

[2006]

Women and Religion

Institutionalized religion has a powerful impact on women's views of themselves and the values and policies that affect their life choices. Many women appreciate the spiritual aspects of their religious traditions but find the discriminatory practices and policies of organized religious institutions confining and unjust.

A Catholic, Mary Ann Sorrentino writes about her experience of being publicly excommunicated for helping other women obtain abortions. She describes the pain imposed on her family when the Church refused to confirm her daughter unless she repudiated what her mother stood for.

While throughout most of Jewish history the synagogue has primarily been the domain of men, recently women have been ordained as rabbis. Laura Geller discusses some of the potential implications of women having this position of power in Judaism. Because the social distance between the congregant and the clergy lessens with a woman rabbi, she foresees a breakdown of religious hierarchy, leading Jews to see their rabbi not as a "priest" but as a teacher who enables congregants to become more active participants in the life of the synagogue.

Fundamentalism in many religious traditions, whether Christian, Jewish, Muslim, Hindu, or Buddhist, seeks to reinforce patriarchy. In "Christian Fundamentalism: Patriarch, Sexuality, and Human Rights," Susan Rose focuses on the ways in which Christian fundamentalism, in particular, privileges men's rights over women's rights, reinforces the alleged divine difference between men and women, and controls women's expression of sexuality.

Johnnetta Cole and Beverly Guy-Sheftall explore themes of male dominance in African-American churches, as well as highlight women's resistance to these sexist practices. They call for "gender talk"—honest discussion about power relationships between men and women—within the church in order to move beyond the silences that have hurt black communities. Kecia Ali describes the influence of Islam and Islamic law on Muslim women's lives, particularly related to dress, restrictions on mixing of the sexes, and husbands' authority over their wives. She sees Muslim women's discussion groups at mosques and in academic and activist settings as a force for change. "The single most important idea associated with these efforts is that men and women are created equals as believers and that, ultimately, their equality as human beings in the sight of God matters more than any distinctions based on social hierarchy."

Quotes from religious writings, like the Bible, are often used to justify women's oppression. In "Revelations," African-American Linda Villarosa describes how her own biblical research illuminated ways that those in the Religious Right take the Bible literally only when it suits them, ignoring anything that doesn't easily support their beliefs. She describes the process of bolstering her own intellectual and emotional strength to more confidently confront homophobia based in literal interpretations of the Bible.

"In Her Own Image," by Rose Solari, describes the work of women of various faiths who have entered the clergy. In addition to their feminist theological ideas, their very presence in churches challenges tradition. For example, Episcopal priest Carter Heyward, a lesbian, argues that it is important for gay and lesbian priests to be as "visible as we can be just to show that we are already here. It is not like the Church has a choice. We are in it already." These women's voices make visible and legitimate female experiences in the churches and synagogues today.

🦎 78

My Church Threw Me Out

MARY ANN SORRENTINO

I have never had an abortion myself, nor have I ever performed one. But my Church has told me that because I believe that women should be able to have abortions if they so desire, I have automatically excommunicated myself. I still believe that I am a Catholic; I will always be a Catholic—whether or not I can take communion or be buried with the Church's rites. I intend to keep my faith and to fight to change my Church.

I had no idea that I was excommunicated until last May, two days before my daughter's confirmation. Her religion teacher called me that Friday morning and asked me to bring Luisa, who was then 15, to an afternoon meeting with Father Egan, our pastor. Although the teacher was not allowed to tell me why, she said that Luisa's confirmation hung in the balance. I was stunned. Luisa had passed all her tests, and another parish priest had already interviewed her once. I was expecting 20 guests on Sunday to celebrate. I called Father Egan immediately. He told me that Luisa could not be confirmed until he had interrogated her about her views on abortion.

His message was clear: I was the problem. For the last nine years I have been executive director of Planned Parenthood of Rhode Island. As far as the Catholic Church was concerned, my only child could not be confirmed until she had repudiated what her mother stood for.

No one had told Luisa why she was being dismissed from school early, so when I picked her up, she was in tears. She said, "I thought Daddy or Grandma died and that's why you came to get me." When I told her the reason, she began to sob.

I was so outraged at the idea of this ordeal Luisa had to go through that I decided to tape the meeting, in case we needed a record later. My husband, Al, who is a lawyer, accompanied Luisa and me, even though Father Egan had not invited him. When the priest arrived, Al told him he didn't understand why his daughter had to be singled out for questioning from a class of 75. "Because she lives in a particular atmosphere," Father Egan said. "Her mother is an advocate of abortion. I have to ascertain whether Luisa believes in abortion. That's all." Then Father Egan said to me, "You're the one who ties my hands. I *want* your daughter to be confirmed. But if she believes in a doctrine that conflicts with that confirmation, then one thing contradicts another."

I said, "Father, I want to go on record that I don't advocate abortion. What I advocate is that every woman who is pregnant should be allowed to exercise her own conscience and her own choice."

"Well," Luisa spoke up, "I don't have any opinion of abortion. What my mother does for a living is her business."

"If you feel abortion is right, then we can't administer the sacrament," Father Egan replied.

Finally Luisa stated that she herself wouldn't have an abortion.

"But do you believe in abortion?" Father Egan persisted.

"I don't know," Luisa replied.

I felt I had to intervene. I asked Luisa, "But you wouldn't have one, right?"

"No," Luisa answered.

"Then you don't believe in it," Father Egan told her. He added to Al and me, "All I want her to say is that she doesn't advocate abortion." Luisa, by now very upset, left the room, tears running down her cheeks.

Then Father Egan said that he could not give me communion at the confirmation "because you're excommunicated. You should know that already."

I was stunned. Every now and again a "Right-to-Lifer" would accuse me of being excommunicated, but to hear this from a member of the Catholic clergy shocked me.

"I haven't been formally notified," I answered. "And I've taken communion as recently as Christmas." If I, a lifelong Catholic, were indeed excommunicated, I could no longer receive the sacraments of my faith, including communion and the last rites. Excommunication is a formal, official procedure: canon law requires that the local bishop, not a parish priest, inform a church member of excommunication. I knew that no American has been publicly excommunicated for more than 20 years. And I now know that church policy states that those who perform abortions and those who undergo them can be excommunicated. But I didn't know this last spring, and I don't fit either category.

"Your excommunication is automatic because abortion is a sin," said Father Egan. "When you publicly advocate abortion, you become what is known as a public sinner, and you cannot receive the sacraments."

"I don't believe this," I said. I was deeply hurt. But I was also very angry. The Church was trying to blackmail me through my child. The only reason we had allowed Luisa to be interrogated was that she had worked so hard to prepare for confirmation. The Church had us over a barrel.

For six months I did not discuss publicly what had happened to me because Al and I wanted to protect Luisa. On January 21, the eve of the anniversary of *Roe v. Wade,* the Supreme Court decision legalizing abortion, a "Right-to-Life" priest in my hometown of Providence, Rhode Island, placed a newspaper ad for a cable TV program he had produced. The ad asked whether Rhode Island's leading abortion advocate was really a Catholic.

The next day I watched with horrified fascination as he went on the air and called me the state's "public enemy number one of babies in the womb." Then he gave his own answer to the question he had posed in his ad: He said that I wasn't really a Catholic because I had been excommunicated.

Many times during the past nine years, I've been quoted in newspapers and have appeared on radio and television shows in my state—the most Catholic in the union—where Catholics comprise 65 percent of the state's population. I can't count the number of times I've called, not for abortion, but for a pregnant woman's right to exercise her own conscience. Until Luisa's interrogation, no Church authority had ever contacted me or challenged my views. And to this day, the bishop of Providence has never addressed a word to me directly.

For second-generation Italian-Americans like me, excommunication seems like something that could just never happen. Catholicism is part of who I am. For me and for many Italians, Church dogma is closely interwoven with our ethnic and cultural fabric. We want our children to be initiated with God, so we make a big deal out of baptism. We're romantic—we love marriages, so the wedding ceremony has particular meaning for us. We mourn very deeply, so the last rites, the funeral and burial in holy ground are very much a part of our lives. But we tend to be flexible about Church rules. When I was growing up, I remember hearing my uncle say, "It doesn't matter what the Church says about birth control; no one is going to tell me what to do in my own bedroom."

I was raised to be a traditional Italian wife and mother; still, I've always had a history of fighting back. My father, who died when I was nine, was very proud that he could send me to an exclusive Catholic school, the Convent of the Sacred Heart, in Providence. But I felt the nuns there treated us Italians as second-class citizens, compared with the Irish girls. Once, when one of my Italian girlfriends didn't know an answer during an oral exam, the nuns pressed her so hard that she wet her pants. I got into a lot of trouble because I told them to stop picking on her.

Al and I got married right after my graduation. He still had a year of college to go, so I became a social worker. I soon found that I would have to take on the state government. My clients were welfare mothers who asked me for birth control information. I gave it to them. My superior called me in and told me that the taxpayers of Rhode Island weren't paying my salary to have me discuss something they didn't believe in. So I complained to the head of the state welfare department and got other social workers to back me up. The policy eventually changed.

After his graduation, Al announced his plans to attend law school in Boston. This meant I had to keep on working and that we had to move. I was sad to leave my mother—I was extremely close to her—and all the rest of my family.

I cried a lot in those years—I wasn't very independent. I was still a typical Italian wife. Every night I made a three- or four-course gourmet meal. All Al did was study and work, not because he was lazy, but because I would't let him do anything else. Even though I kept getting promoted at work, I continued to take care of everything at home. I discovered my talent for administration and became a unit manager at a local hospital.

I always knew I wanted to have children, but we couldn't afford a baby then. I was taking the Pill, and that's how I first got into trouble with the Church.

During confession, when the priest heard I was practicing birth control, he refused to give me absolution. "I want you to go to Catholic Social Services to learn about the rhythm method," he said. "Father," I replied, "I'm a social worker. Do you know how many rhythm babies are born every year?" Friends told me I should confess to other priests who didn't think the Pill was a sin. I said no. It didn't make any sense to me to have to shop around for absolution. I stopped going to Mass regularly—but I never abandoned the Church.

I was pregnant at Al's law school graduation, which was exactly what I had wanted. When Luisa was born, she became the joy of our lives, and she still is. Yet I have often wondered what I would do if I found myself pregnant today, at 42. I think the only honest answer is that I don't know. A fertilized egg that grows into a fetus is the beginning of human life, but I don't think of a fertilized egg as a person.

I do know that for the last nine years, the proudest work I've done has been holding the hands of women who needed someone with them during an abortion. And by helping these women, I have never considered myself any different from the hundreds of Catholic administrators of hospitals across this country where birth control techniques are distributed, where sterilizations and abortions are performed. That's our work. I've never thought of myself as being any different from a Catholic lawyer who handles divorces. That's your work and you help people who come to you.

What I resent is the way I've been singled out and punished, considering what else is going on today in the diocese of Providence. Two priests are awaiting trial for the alleged sexual abuse of children. Another priest has been charged with perjury in the Von Bulow case. And the headmaster of a Catholic prep school here was recently arrested for transporting a male minor for immoral purposes. These men are passing out communion on one side of the altar rail while trying to keep me away on the other. I want my Church to explain.

Luisa's confirmation took place on a beautiful sunny Sunday, but as far as I was concerned, it was a funeral. I felt a terrible sense of helplessness because our child would be hurt no matter what I did. If I talked openly about the interrogation, she would be denied the sacrament. If I said nothing, we seemed to be accepting the Church's judgment. I felt as if my hands were tied. The guests all came to the party afterward, but Al, Luisa, and I were just going through the motions.

I still cry when I think I might not be buried with my parents. I've told my husband that if I go first and the Church will not allow me to be buried alongside them at our Catholic cemetery, he should have my body cremated and scatter my ashes over their graves. That way I can be with them.

Part of my faith is a strong belief that nothing happens without a reason. I'm not a mystic, but I think there is some reason God singled me out for this trial. If the Catholic Church thinks it has embarrassed me or that I will go quietly and give up, the Church is mistaken. As God, Al, and Luisa know, I am and will die a Catholic.   [1986]

79

Reactions to a Woman Rabbi

LAURA GELLER

At the conclusion of High Holiday services during my first year as an ordained rabbi, two congregants rushed up to talk to me. The first, a middle-aged woman, blurted out, "Rabbi, I can't tell you how different I felt about services because you are a woman. I found myself feeling that if you can be a rabbi, then maybe I could be a rabbi too. For the first time in my life I felt as though I could learn those prayers, I could study Torah, I could lead this service, I could do anything you could do. Knowing that made me feel much more involved in the service—much more involved with Judaism! Also, the service made me think about God in a different way. I'm not sure why." The second congregant had something very similar to tell me, but with a slightly different emphasis. He was a man, in his late twenties. "Rabbi, I realized that if you could be a rabbi, then certainly I could be a rabbi. Knowing that made the service somehow more accessible for me. I didn't need you to 'do it' for me. I could 'do it,' be involved with Jewish tradition, without depending on you."

It has taken me five years to begin to understand the significance of what these people told me.

Throughout most of Jewish history the synagogue has primarily been the domain of men. It has also been a very important communal institution. Was the synagogue so important because it was the domain of men, or was it the domain of men because it was so important? Perhaps the question becomes more relevant if we ask it in another way. If women become leaders in the synagogue, will the synagogue become less important? This concern was clearly expressed in 1955 by Sanders Tofield of the Conservative Movement's Rabbinical Assembly, when he acknowledged that one reason women are encouraged to remain within the private sphere of religious life is the fear that if women

were to be completely integrated into all aspects of Jewish ritual, then men might relegate religious life to women and cease being active in the synagogue.[1] The fear connected with the "feminization" of Judaism is, largely, that once women achieve positions of power within the synagogue, men will feel that the synagogue is no longer sufficiently important to occupy their attention. The other side of the question is also being asked. Is the fact that women are becoming leaders in synagogues a sign that the synagogue is no longer an important institution?

The fact that these questions are posed increasingly suggests to me that the synagogue is not very healthy. Are synagogues so marginal in the life of American Jews that men really would limit their involvement because women are active participants?

The participation of women as leaders and especially as rabbis raises another concern for synagogues. Those two congregants on Rosh Hashanah expressed a feeling that has been echoed many times since then. When women function as clergy, the traditional American division between clergy and lay people begins to break down. Let me give an example from another religious tradition. A woman who is an Episcopal priest told me that when she offers the Eucharist people take it from her differently from the way they would take it from a male priest, even though she follows the identical ritual. People experience her as less foreign, and so the experience is more natural, less mysterious.

People don't attribute to women the power and prestige that they often attribute to men. Therefore, when women become rabbis or priests, there is often less social distance between the congregant and the clergy. The lessening of social distance and the reduction of the attribution of power and status leads to the breakdown of hierarchy within a religious institution. "If you can be a rabbi, then certainly I can be a rabbi!"

Clearly some would argue that the breakdown of traditional religious hierarchy is bad. However, in my view this change could bring about a profound and welcome change in American Judaism. It could lead to synagogues that see their rabbi not as "priest" but as teacher, and that see the congregations not as passive consumers of the rabbi's wisdom but as active participants in their own Jewish lives.

The ordination of women will lead to change in another important area of Judaism: the way Jews think about God. On a basic, perhaps subconscious, level, many Jews project the image of their rabbi onto their image of God. As Dr. Mortimer Ostow has pointed out, "While it is true that no officiant in the service actually represents God, to the average congregant God is psychologically represented by the rabbi, since he is the leader and the teacher and preacher of God's word."[2]

Most adult Jews know that it is inappropriate to envisage God as a male. But given the constant references in Jewish prayer to God as "Father" and "King," and given our childhood memories of imaging God as an old man with a long white beard, it is no surprise that to the extent Jews do conceptualize God in human terms, they often think of God as male or masculine.

Jewish tradition recognizes that God is not male. To limit God in this or any way is idolatrous; God is understood by tradition to encompass both masculinity and femininity and to transcend masculinity and femininity. Unfortunately, many Jews have never incorporated this complex image of God into their theology.

As long as the rabbi is a man, a Jew can project the image of the rabbi onto God. But when Jews encounter a rabbi who is a woman, it forces them to think about God as more than male or female. It provokes them to raise questions that most Jews don't like to confront: What or who is God? What do I believe about God? That primary religious question leads to others. How can we speak about God? What are the appropriate words, images, and symbols to describe our relationship to God? Does the English rendering of Hebrew prayers convey the complexity of God? How can we change language, images, and symbols so they can convey this complexity?

All of these questions could lead to a more authentic relationship to Jewish tradition and to God. Once Jews begin to explore their image of God, they will also reevaluate their image of

themselves. Because all of us are created in God's image, how we think about God shapes how we think about ourselves. That thinking leads to a reevaluation of men's and women's roles within our tradition and our world.

The ordination of women has brought Judaism to the edge of an important religious revolution. I pray we have the faith to push it over the edge.

[1983]

NOTES

1. Sanders Tofield, Proceedings of the Rabbinical Assembly 19 (1955), 190 as cited in Ellen M. Umansky, "Women and Rabbinical Ordination: A Viable Option?" *Ohio Journal of Religious Studies* 4, no. 1 (March 1976): 63.
2. Dr. Mortimer Ostow, "Women and Change in Jewish Law," *Conservative Judaism* (Fall 1974): 7.

 80

Christian Fundamentalism: Patriarchy, Sexuality, and Human Rights

SUSAN D. ROSE

I. INTRODUCTION

The Universal Declaration of Human Rights (Universal Declaration) adopted by the United Nations (UN) proclaims that "all human beings are born free and equal in dignity and rights,"[1] yet women's freedom, dignity, and equality are persistently compromised by law, custom, and religious tradition in ways that men's are not. This essay focuses on Christian fundamentalism and patriarchy, and how they interactively help shape and rationalize both cultural views and social policy related to gender, sexuality, health, reproductive choice, and violence against women and girls.

The reinforcement of patriarchy is the trait that Christian fundamentalism most clearly shares with the other forms of religious belief that have also been called "fundamentalist." This characteristic is most evident across the Abrahamic tradition of the three major monotheistic religions—among fundamentalist Israeli Jews, within both Sunni and Shi'ite Muslim communities in various countries, and within the current revival of evangelical Protestantism emanating from the United States—but is also evident in fundamentalist Hindu and Buddhist movements.[2] All seek to control women and the expression of sexuality. Fundamentalists argue that men and women are by divine design "essentially" different, and they aim to preserve the separation between public and private, male and female, spheres of action and influence.[3] As Charlotte Bunch notes:

> The distinction between private and public is a dichotomy largely used to justify female subordination and to exclude human rights abuses in the home from public scrutiny. . . . When women are denied democracy and human rights in private, their human rights in the public sphere also suffer, since what occurs in "private" shapes their ability to participate fully in the public arena.[4]

The most common rationale given for denial of human rights to women is the preservation of family and culture. While Article 16 of the Convention on the Elimination of All Forms of Discrimination Against Women (CEAFDAW) requires state parties to take "all appropriate measures" to ensure the equality of women and men in marriage and in parental rights and responsibilities,[5] fundamentalists across these traditions maintain that women are the keepers of the heart and hearth, whereas men are the keepers of the mind and marketplace.

The struggle for women's and children's rights as human rights poses a fundamental threat to "traditional" cultural orders and social structures, and especially to "secondary-level male elites."[6] When "secondary-level male elites" are struggling to maintain male dominance in the middling areas of society where jobs are increasingly contested by women, they find that they can reassert themselves in the family, school, and church, which are the social institutions most accessible to them.[7] In contrast, the first-level male elite, who control the major financial

institutions and/or manage the corporate structures, are not so concerned with this kind of patriarchal restoration.[8]

II. MAKING MEN, SUBDUING WOMEN IN LATE-TWENTIETH-CENTURY AMERICA

In the early twentieth century, the original, U.S. Christian fundamentalist movement explicitly stated that reining in women was essential to maintaining social cohesion.[9] Fundamentalists were aware that although religion remained important to women, its appeal was declining among men.[10] In addition, the shift from an agrarian to an industrial society made it more difficult for men to live out "traditional" notions of masculinity.[11] As a result, concerns about the feminization of men and of Christianity developed into a kind of militant, virile masculinity that became the hallmark of the Christian warrior, and the movement's literature became "rife with strident anti-feminist pronouncements, some of them bordering on outright misogyny."[12]

This is no less true today. As Martin Riesebrodt argues, fundamentalism is primarily a "radical patriarchalism" that represents a protest movement against the increasing egalitarianism between the sexes.[13] Within the vast majority of fundamentalist, Pentecostal, neo-Pentecostal, and charismatic Protestant churches (which I refer to under the umbrella terms "evangelical" or "fundamentalist")[14] spreading both within and beyond the United States, the downward lines of authority of the nuclear, patriarchal family are still being firmly reinforced: children are to be obedient to their parents, wives to their husbands, and husbands to their God.[15]

One of the most prominent evangelical groups today to promote a modernized form of patriarchy is the "Promise Keepers" (PK). Founded in 1990 by Bill McCartney, head coach of the University of Colorado football team, the PKs (and their female counterpart, the Promise Reapers) has embraced the goal of motivating men toward Christ-like masculinity. For example, Pastor Tony Evans, in *Seven Promises of a Promise Keeper*, argues that the primary cause of (our) national crisis—the decline of family structure—is "the Feminization of Men," and he urges men to take back their male leadership role: "Unfortunately, however, there can be no compromise here. . . . Treat the lady gently and lovingly. But lead!"[16]

The PKs are promoting good old-fashioned patriarchy with a new twist. They are encouraging men to become more involved in family life, and more responsible to and for their children, but their approach would not meet the obligations of equality under Article 16 of CEAFDAW—which they would be bound to oppose, in any event. Rather than working toward greater equality for both men and women, PK leaders reassure men that if they are faithful, they will gain rather than lose power and authority within the family. Within the fundamentalist framework, family life continues to be gendered along patriarchal lines, and while men are called back to the private sphere, gender apartheid is still maintained. This has significant consequences for social policy that affects the lives and choices of all citizens, particularly in the arenas of reproductive choice and health.

III. LEGISLATING THE CHRISTIAN PATRIARCHAL AGENDA

The pro-family political platform of the contemporary Christian Right in the United States unabashedly supports patriarchy, and privileges men's rights over women's rights, and parents' rights over children's and states' rights. This approach is particularly pernicious given that studies of domestic violence indicate that wife and child abuse is more common among families that adhere to traditional, patriarchal sex role norms.[17]

Over the past several years, conservative groups such as the Christian Coalition, Focus on the Family, the Eagle Forum, and Of the People have campaigned for "parental-rights" legislation at the federal level and in more than 25 states. These various attempts have included the "Pupil Protection Act," also known as the Hatch Amendment of 1978, which requires parental consent when a federally funded program in a school calls for a student to submit to a surveyor evaluation that may reveal information concerning, among other things: political affiliations; mental and psychological problems potentially embarrassing to the student

or his family; sex behavior and attitudes; and illegal, antisocial, self-incriminating, and demeaning behavior.[18] The Christian Religious Right used the Hatch Amendment to attack the curricula of public education and to prohibit curricula dealing with: health issues of suicide, drug and alcohol abuse, and sex education; globalism and world issues such as information on the Holocaust and news reporting from worldwide magazines (*Time* and *Newsweek*); diversity issues, including exposing children to books by African-American and homosexual authors; and general programs concerning political participation, including mock elections.[19] The breadth and depth of the attack on the integrity of a free public education was so great that even Senator Orrin Hatch, the sponsor of the bill, called for "the rule of commonsense [to] prevail."[20]

The patriarchal approach of the Christian Right was also apparent in the proposed "Parental Rights and Responsibilities Act of 1995," which prohibits any government from interfering with or usurping the right of the parent in the upbringing of the child in such areas as education, health, discipline (including corporal punishment), and religious teachings.[21] Such a bill would, among other things, have an obvious "chilling" effect on intervention "in child abuse cases."[22]

The Christian Right's support for parents' rights over children's rights and its attacks on public education demonstrate the clear conflict of interest between, on the one hand, the rights of children to an informed education (including their health) and the duty of all states to provide informed education and, on the other hand, the extent of the parental right to socialize and educate their children within the parameters of their religious faith. It is also important to note that the strongest impact will be on girls because the Christian Right's educational agenda includes the promotion of patriarchy and thus unequal roles for men and women. It is hard to imagine how girls can take away from such education the Universal Declaration's proclamation that "all human beings are born free and equal in dignity and rights."[23]

A major victory for the conservative crusaders in their influence on public school education was their successful lobbying of Congress in 1996 to pass welfare reform that included a provision to promote teen sexual abstinence programs in public schools. The federal government had previously funded similar programs and had been sued for providing public funding to those programs that promoted specific religious teachings.[24] Although the settlement in the case included a requirement that funded programs be medically accurate and free of religious teachings,[25] this standard was not being met under the newly funded programs.

IV. THE SEXUAL POLITICS OF ABSTINENCE

Contemporary evangelicals have concerns about sex and sexuality that focus on issues regarding social order and control—especially over women's bodies and desires. Within the evangelical framework, lack of control over sex and the desires of the body are thought to threaten the integrity of the soul.

Exposure to information about sex, many evangelical leaders argue, leads to sex. Therefore, the political platform of the Religious Right aims to curtail sex education in the schools, and severely limit contraceptive research and dissemination at large. With the United States holding the record for the highest rate of teenage (ages 15 to 19) pregnancies and abortions in the industrialized world,[26] these issues have become all the more critical. Rightfully concerned about the high rates of teenage pregnancy, abortion, sexually transmitted diseases, and AIDS, evangelicals are active in trying to influence public policy. Although the U.S. teenage pregnancy rate has declined over the last two decades,[27] teenage pregnancy is still a problem—but when, where, how, and why it became constructed as a social problem is important to examine. For example, cross-national data indicate that the countries that have low teen pregnancy rates tend to have more open attitudes toward sexuality and sex education, access to contraceptives and a national health care system, and greater socioeconomic equality.[28] But rather than dealing with the complex problems associated with high rates of teenage pregnancy, including the fact that the United States has one of the highest rates of child poverty, child death,

and infant mortality in the industrialized world, and that young teens often become pregnant as a result of rape or incest,[29] abstinence-only advocates simply advise young people to "just say no." Abstinence-only advocates have also "just said no" to substantial and well-documented empirical data that show that to the degree to which an effect of comprehensive sexuality education has been identifiable in studies, it has postponed initiation of sexual intercourse.[30]

A. "Just Say No"

Sex education has always been a point of conflict between public educators and conservative religious groups. Since the 1960s, Religious Right political groups have opposed the teaching of comprehensive sexuality education in public schools. By the 1980s, however, it was clear that the Religious Right was having little success in removing sex education from the schools, because the general American public favors comprehensive sex education.[31] As a result, Religious Right groups, including the Eagle Forum, Concerned Women for America, Focus on the Family, and Citizens for Excellence in Education have all devoted major resources to promoting "abstinence-only" curricula in the public schools as a substitute for comprehensive sex education programs. In 1996, bowing to the Religious Right, Congress allocated $50 million annually for abstinence-only education programs. Since then, over $1.5 billion has been spent on abstinence-only programs.[32] The provision funds programs to teach children that "sexual activity outside of the context of marriage is likely to have harmful psychological and physical effects."[33]

Abstinence-only advocates advise young people to not have sex; their aim, however, is to curtail sexual activity for anyone not in a heterosexual marriage. Uneasy about teen sexuality, homosexuality, the increase in out-of-wedlock births, and the erosion of the patriarchal, nuclear family, they emphasize the dangers of sex and the hazards of sexual relationships outside of marriage. Fear rather than affirmation, rejection rather than acceptance, and denial rather than knowledge about sexuality tend to dominate abstinence-only materials, and serve as a chilling effect on contemporary American research and social policy.

Religious Right groups use sophisticated, fear-based tactics in their abstinence-only programs: "Just say no or die."[34] For example, the video *No Second Chance* juxtaposes images of men dying from AIDS with an evangelical sex educator interacting with a classroom of teenagers. She compares having sex outside of marriage with playing Russian roulette: "Every time you have sex, it's like pulling the trigger." When one teenage boy asks, "What if I do have sex before I get married?" she responds, "I guess you'll just have to be prepared to die."[35]

In abstinence-only materials, sex is often equated with death, disease, and danger, and fear surfaces as the primary message and tactic used to persuade young people to steer clear of sex before or outside of marriage. Leslie Kantor, former director of the Sexuality, Information, and Education Council of the United States (SIECUS) Community Advocacy Project, conducted an extensive content analysis of abstinence-only sex education programs produced and promoted by Christian Right groups that are used in public schools. She concluded that these programs omit the most fundamental information on contraception and disease prevention, perpetuate medical misinformation, and rely on religious doctrine and images of fear and shame in discouraging sexual activity. The Waxman Report (December 2004), which examined school-based sex education curricula, likewise concluded that many young people are receiving medically inaccurate or misleading information, often in direct contradiction to the findings of government scientists. After reviewing the 13 most commonly used curricula, Congressman Waxman's staff concluded that two of the curricula were accurate, but 11 others, used by 69 organizations in 25 states, contain unproved claims, subjective conclusions, or outright falsehoods regarding reproductive health, gender traits, and when life begins.[36]

B. Holding Girls Responsible

When reading through these Christian abstinence materials, one becomes aware of an old, traditional message: the cautionary story of sex as one of male predators and female prey. On the one hand, from an evangelical perspective, humans are not animals (which is at the crux of the evolution/creation debate), rather they stand only a little lower than angels. Yet, beyond a certain point, humans—especially men—are regarded as not being able to control their sexual urges. In fact, according to the sexual arousal time line in *Sexual Common Sense: Affirming Adolescent Abstinence,* "the prolonged kiss" is pinpointed as the "beginning of danger."[37]

After this point of "danger," there is no turning back from sexual arousal. The sexual arousal time line also indicates that although females too have sexual instincts, they take longer to become aroused. Therefore, they hold greater responsibility in exercising constraint. Women are considered to be less controlled by their sexuality and more responsible, not only for their own sexual behavior but for the sexual behavior of men. Evangelist James Robison, whose book *Sex Is Not Love* sold over half a million copies, warns that "sex before marriage . . . develops sensual drives that can never be satisfied and may cause a man to behave like an animal."[38] He states that "some girls become that way, too . . . but most of them don't. When they do, it's the most awful thing that can happen to humanity."[39]

However, it would appear that there are more awful things that can happen: the use of tax dollars to support abstinence-only programs that provide medical misinformation and promote fear and ignorance, and the failure to provide support to implement effective social policy that could effectively curb teenage pregnancy and provide better economic, educational, and health opportunities for all young people.

V. WHOSE RIGHTS?

Central to the sex education debate is the Religious Right's attempt to preserve men's rights over women's rights, and parental rights over children's rights. The Family Research Council in 1995 critiqued the Fourth World Conference on Women, stating that the conference reflected "a radical feminist agenda" that "denigrate[d] motherhood and the traditional family" by noting that there were "unequal power relations" in the family.[40] Radical? Yes, writes evangelical psychologist James Dobson, who heads up the largest Christian Right organization in the United States, Focus on the Family. He warns that the UN Conference on Women represented "the most radical, atheistic, antifamily crusade in the history of the world"[41] and that "the Agency for International Development will channel hundreds of millions of dollars to support women's reproductive and sexual rights and family planning services. The only hope for derailing this train is the Christian church."[42]

As we enter the second decade of the new millennium, family planning, reproductive and sexual health, and economic well-being continue to be vital concerns for individuals, communities, and nations. Rates of pregnancy, and AIDS and other sexually transmitted diseases, remain alarmingly high among America's youth, yet opponents of sexuality education are still trying to censor vital, lifesaving information that has proven effective in dealing with these problems. Abstinence-only proponents not only provide medical misinformation and promote fear and ignorance, they also fail to plan, fund, and implement effective social policy that could more effectively curb teen pregnancy and the spread of STDs—and provide better economic, educational, and health opportunities for all young people. Experts on teen pregnancy and child welfare such as Marianne Wright Edelman and Kristin Luker convincingly argue that teen pregnancy is less about young girls and their sex lives than about restricted horizons and the boundaries of hope. Yet the Religious Right continues to blame women for stepping out of their place, the feminization of men, the decline of two-parent families, homosexuality, and the media for the ills of our society rather than consider the economic and structural forces that help to perpetuate high teen pregnancy rates and inequality between men and women. In the battle over sexuality and choice, it is girls' and women's bodies, lives, and livelihoods that are all too often sacrificed.

The threat of women's equality and the usurping of male power is echoed in many Christian Right newsletters, books, sermons, rallies, and TV and radio shows, as the desire for patriarchal control and parental order is unabashedly pronounced. Both hostile and benevolent forms of sexism are evident here as conservative Christians attempt to keep women in their place, on the pedestal, dependent on men who are expected to remain in control.[43]

The debates around abstinence-only policies, while concerned with trying to prevent adolescent sexual activity, are as much—if not more—about trying to preserve or reclaim the patriarchal, heterosexual Christian family. Planned Parenthood has argued:

> Abstinence-only education is one of the Religious Right's greatest challenges to the nation's sexual health. But it is only one tactic in a broader, longer-term strategy. Since the early 1980s, the "family values" movement has won the collaboration of governments and public institutions, from Congress to local school boards, in abridging students' constitutional rights. Schools now block student access to sexual health information in class, at the school library, and through the public library's Internet portals. They violate students' free speech rights by censoring student publications of articles referring to sexuality. Abstinence-only programs often promote alarmist misinformation about sexual health and force-feed students religious ideology that condemns homosexuality, masturbation, abortion, and contraception. In doing so, they endanger students' sexual health.[44]

The notion of *abstinence only* is more than the description of a U.S. federal program: it reflects deep-seated religious and cultural values held in the United States. President Bush substantially cut or eliminated many domestic social programs, while creating or boosting funding for a handful of others that would promote "traditional" family values. A new president is now in the White House. In his very first days in office, Barack Obama signed an executive order lifting the ban on sending U.S. government funds to organizations that provide abortion counseling with money from other sources, thereby reversing the so-called global gag rule; signed the Lily Ledbetter Fair Pay Act; and has supported stem-cell research and greater access to birth control. In emphasizing the importance of scientific research rather than ideology in guiding policy decisions, we may be entering a new era. In the interest of all children, as well as family well-being, we need to take seriously a broad-based approach to both social problems and social policy that is based on empirical evidence and a recognition of the pluralistic society in which we live. This is what democracy is all about.

While evangelicals represent only 25 percent of the U.S. population, their influence on social policy regarding sexuality education, sexual orientation, teen pregnancy, reproduction, family planning, and economic equity has been significant, though less in establishing their agenda than in putting the brakes on research, education, and funding that could reduce the rates of teen pregnancy, abortion, and violence against women and children; increase the equality between women and men; and better protect and prepare children for healthy, active, responsible lives in the twenty-first century. Their impact is also felt beyond the borders of the United States. Today North American evangelicals are the largest group of missionaries moving across the globe on mission quests.[45] They are effective in establishing churches, schools, and health clinics in various places around the world. What kind of messages are they disseminating? What kinds of influence may evangelical "sex experts" have as they fund programs and advise people and political leaders, not only in the United States but around the world, about gender, family planning, sex, contraception, violence—about life and death?　[2011]

NOTES

1. Universal Declaration of Human Rights, adopted December 10, 1948, G.A. Res. 217A (III), U.N. GAOR, 3d Sess., pt. 1, 183d plen. mtg., at 71, art. 1, UN. Doc.A/810 (1948) (hereinafter cited as Universal Declaration).

2. See Steve Brouwer, Paul Gifford, and Susan Rose, *Exporting the American Gospel: Global Christian Fundamentalism* (New York: Routledge, 1996), 218–26; Helen Hardacre, "The Impact of Fundamentalism on Women, the Family, and Interpersonal Relations," in *The Fundamentalism Project*, vol. 2: *Fundamentalisms and Society*, ed. Martin E. Marty and R. Scott Appleby (Chicago: University of Chicago Press, 1993), 129, 131–47; John S. Hawley, "Hinduism: Sati and Its Defenders," in *Fundamentalism and Gender*, ed. John Stratton Hawley (New York: Oxford University Press, 1994), 79, 93–103; see also Jan Goodwin, *Price of Honor: Muslim Women—Life the Veil of Silence on the Islamic World* (New York: Little, Brown, 1994).

3. See Courtney W. Howland, "The Challenge of Religious Fundamentalism to the Liberty and Equality Rights of Women: An Analysis Under the United Nations Charter," 35 *Colum. J. Transnat'l L.* 271, 283–285 (1997).

4. Charlotte Bunch, "Transforming Human Rights from a Feminist Perspective," in *Women's Rights, Human Rights: International Feminist Perspectives*, ed. Julie Peters and Andrea Wolper (New York: Routledge, 1995), 11, 14.

5. See Convention on the Elimination of All Forms of Discrimination Against Women, adopted December 18, 1979, G.A. Res. 34/180, UN. GAOR, 34th Sess., Supp. No. 46, at 193, 196, art. 16 (1), UN. Doc. A/34/46 (1979), 1249 UN.T.S. 13, 20.

6. Bruce B. Lawrence, *Defenders of God: The Fundamentalist Revolt Against the Modern Age* (Columbia: University of South Carolina Press, 1989), 100.

7. See Susan D. Rose, *Keeping Them Out of the Hands of Satan: Evangelical Schooling in America* (New York: Routledge, 1988), 1–10.

8. See Brouwer, Gifford, and Rose, *Exporting the American Gospel*, 219 and n.19.

9. Ibid., 219–220.

10. See Margaret Lamberts Bendroth, *Fundamentalism and Gender, 1875 to the Present* (New Haven, CT: Yale University Press, 1993), 13, 17.

11. Ibid., 17; Brouwer, Gifford, and Rose, *Exporting the American Gospel*, 219–220.

12. See Bendroth, *Fundamentalism and Gender,* 31.

13. Martin Riesebrodt, *Pious Passion: The Emergence of Modern Fundamentalism in Iran and the United States* (Berkeley: University of California Press, 1993), 176–208.

14. For a more detailed discussion of these different groups and terminology, including the use of the umbrella term "evangelical," see Brouwer, Gifford, and Rose, *Exporting the American Gospel*, 263–71; Nancy T. Ammerman, "North American Protestant Fundamentalism," in *The Fundamentalism Project*, vol. 1: *Fundamentalisms Observed* (Chicago: University of Chicago Press, 1991), 1, 2–5; Laurence R. Innaccone, "Heirs to the Protestant Ethic? The Economies of American Fundamentalists," in *The Fundamentalism Project*, vol. 3: *Fundamentalism and the States* (Chicago: University of Chicago Press, 1993), 342, 343–44.

15. See, e.g., Dr. Edward Hindson, former director of counseling at Jerry Falwell's Thomas Road Baptist Ministries, quoted in Rose, *Keeping Them Out of the Hands of Satan,*

xvii ("The Bible clearly states that the wife is to submit to her husband's leadership").

16. Tony Evans, "Spiritual Purity," in *Seven Promises of a Promise Keeper,* ed. Al Janssen and Larry K.Weeden (Colorado Springs: Focus on the Family, 1994), 73, 80.

17. See *Gender Violence: Interdisciplinary Perspectives,* ed. Laura L. O'Toole, Jessica R. Schiffman, and Margie L. Kiter Edwards (New York: NYU Press, 1997/2007); James Alsdurf and Phyllis Alsdurf, *Battered into Submission: The Tragedy of Wife Abuse in the Christian Home* (Downers Grove, IL: InterVarsity Press, 1989), 10, 16–18.

18. Protection of Pupil Rights, 20 US.C. § 1232h (1994). The Hatch Amendment itself was amended in 1994, but the key provisions remain intact. The current regulations are those that were written before the 1994 amendments. See "Student Rights in Research, Experimental Programs, and Testing," 34 C.ER. § 98 (1996); see generally Anne C. Lewis, "Little-Used Amendment Becomes Divisive, Disruptive Issue," *Phi Delta Kappan,* June 1985, 667.

19. See Susan Rose, "Christian Fundamentalism and Education in the United States," in *Fundamentalisms and Society,* ed. Martin E. Marty and R. Scott Appleby (Chicago: University of Chicago Press, 1993), 452, 467–73.

20. Pupil Protection Rights Regulations, 131 Cong. Rec. 2449, 2451 (1985).

21. See H.R. 1946, 104th Cong. (1995); S. 984, 104th Cong. (1995).

22. Alan Guttmacher Institute, "Supremacy of Parental Authority New Battlecry for Conservative Activists," *Washington Memo,* December 21, 1995, 4.

23. For a discussion of how international human rights law can protect the girl child's right to education, see Deirdre Fottrell and Geraldine Van Bueren, "The Potential of International Law to Combat Discrimination Against Girls in Education," in this volume.

24. See *Brown v. Kendrick,* 487 U.S. 589 (1988) (remanded for trial).

25. See Leslie M. Kantor, "Attacks on Public School Sexuality Education Programs: 1993–94 School Year," 22 *SIECUS Report,* August–September 1994, 11, II.

26. The U.S. *teen birth* rate is nearly 11 times higher than in the Netherlands, five times higher than in France, and four times higher than in Germany (S. Alford and Ammiee S. Feijoo, "Adolescent Sexual Health in Europe and the U.S.—Why the Difference?" Advocates for Youth (2000): www.advocatesforyouth.org; Jacqueline Darroch, Susheela Singh, and Jennifer J. Frost, "Differences in Teenage Pregnancy Rates Among Five Developed Countries," *Planning Perspectives* 33, no. 6 (2001); Elise Jones et al., *Teenage Pregnancy in Industrialized Nations* (New Haven: Yale University Press, 1996); "Teenage Sexual and Reproductive Behavior in Developed Countries: Can More Progress Be Made?" The Guttmacher Institute, 2001; *Sex and American's Teenagers* (New York: Alan Guttmacher Institute, 1994), 40–43.

27. Birth and fertility rates in greater demographic detail are available by state from *Trends in Characteristics of Births by State: United States,* National Vital Statistics Reports, http://www.cdc.gov/nchs/data/nvsr/nvsr52/

nvsr52_19acc.pdf; http://www.childtrendsdatabank.org/?q=node/232; also see Patricia Donovan, "Falling Teen Pregnancy, Birthrates: What's Behind the Decline?" *Guttmacher Report: On Public Policy,* October 1998, 6.

28. Jones et al., *Teenage Pregnancy in Industrialized Nations,* 216–27.

29. See Debra Boyer and David Fine, "Sexual Abuse as a Factor in Adolescent Pregnancy and Child Maltreatment," *Family Planning Perspectives* 24, no. 4 (1992); Patrick A. Langan and Caroline Wolf Harlow, *Child Rape Victims, 1992* (Washington, D.C.: U.S. Department of Justice, 1994).

30. See People for the American Way, *Teaching Fear: The Religious Right's Campaign Against Sexuality* (Washington, D.C.: People for the American Way, 1994).

31. See *The Best Intentions: Unintended Pregnancy and the Well-Being of Children,* ed. Sarah Brown and Leon Eisenberg (Washington, D.C.: National Academy Press, 1995), 132.

32. Maternal and Child Health Services Block Grant, Pub. L. 104-193, 110 Stat. 2353 (1996), 42 U.S.C.A. § 710 (Supp. 1998); "Panel Votes to Restore Abstinence-Only Money," *Huffington Post,* http://www.huffingtonpost.com/2009/09/29/panel-votes-to-restore-ab_n_303812.html.

33. Alan Guttmacher Institute, "Snapshot: Welfare Reform Law," *Washington Memo,* October 8, 1996, 5.

34. See *Teaching Fear,* supra note 30, at 6; Kantor, supra note 25, at 11–12; see, e.g., *Sex, Lies, and the Truth,* video distributed by James Dobson's organization, Focus on the Family.

35. See People for the American Way, *Teaching Fear,* 8 (quoting *No Second Chance,* film used for Sex Respect programs developed by the Committee on the Status of Women, an antichoice organization founded by Phyllis Schafly).

36. Leslie M. Kantor, "Scared Chaste? Fear-Based Educational Curricula," 21 *SIECUS Report,* December 1992/January 1993, 1–15; see also "Sexuality Education Around the World," 24 *SIECUS Report,* February/March 1996, 1; The Waxman Report, *The Content of Federally Funded Abstinence-Only Education Programs,* prepared for Rep. Henry A. Waxman, U.S. House of Representatives Committee on Government Reform, Minority Staff Special Investigations Division, December 2004, http://www.democrats.reform.house.gov/Documents/20041201102153-50247.pdf; Ceci Connolly, "Some Abstinence Programs Mislead Teens, Report Says," *Washington Post,* December 2, 2004, A01; "Evaluation of Abstinence Education Programs Funded Under Title V, Section 510," Mathematica Policy Research Inc. (2007): http://www.mathematicampr.com/welfare/abstinence.as0; Debra Hauser, "Five Years of Abstinence-Only-Until-Marriage Education: Assessing the Impact," *Advocates for Youth* (2004); Douglas Kirby, "The Impact of Abstinence and Comprehensive Sex and STD/HIV Education Programs on Adolescent Sexual Behavior," *Sexuality Research and Social Policy* 5, no. 3 (2008): 18–27; Jennifer Manlove, Angela R. Papillio, and Erum Ikramullah, "Not Yet: Programs Designed

to Delay First Sex Among Teens," National Campaign to Prevent Teen Pregnancy (2004); "New Studies Signal Dangers of Limiting Teen Access to Birth Control Information and Services: Researchers and Medical Experts Urge New Congress and State Legislatures to Heed Data," Guttmacher Institute media release, January 18, 2005; Cynthia Dailard, "Sex Education: Politicians, Parents, Teachers, and Teens," *The Guttmacher Report on Public Policy* 4, no. 1 (2001), http://www.guttmacher.org/pubs/tgr/04/1/gr040109.html; John Santelli, M. A. Ott, M. Lyon, J. Rogers, D. Summers, and R. Schleifer, "Abstinence and Abstinence-Only Education: A Review of U.S. Policies and Programs," *Journal of Adolescent Health* 38 (2006): 72–81; C. Trenholm, B. Devaney, K. Forston, L. Quay, J. Wheeler, and M. Clark, "Impacts of Four Title V, Section 510, Abstinence Education Programs: Final Report," Mathematica Policy Research Inc. (2007), http://www.mathematica-mpr.com/publications/pdfs/impactabstinence.pdf; "Teen Sex Increased After Abstinence Program: Texas Study Finds Little Impact on Sexual Behavior," February 1, 2005, MSNBC.

37. Collen Kelly Mast, *Sex Respect: The Option of True Sexual Feeling Student Handbook,* rev. ed. (Bradley, IL: Respect Incorporated, 1997), 7, 90.
38. William Martin, "God's Angry Man," *Texas Monthly,* April 1981, 153, 223.
39. Ibid. (quoting James Robison).
40. Family Research Council, "UN: Bound for Beijing," 6 *Washington Watch: Special Report,* August 24,1995, 1.
41. James Dobson, "The Family Under Fire by the United Nations," *Focus on the Family Newsletter,* August 1995, 1.
42. Letter from James Dobson, president, Focus on the Family, mass mailing to members, October 1995.
43. Peter Glick and Susan Fiske, "An Ambivalent Alliance: Hostile and Benevolent Sexism as Complementary Justifications for Gender Inequality," *American Psychologist* 56, no. 2 (2001): 109–18.
44. Planned Parenthood, *Abstinence-Only "Sex" Education,* http://www.plannedparenthood.org/pp2/portal/files/portal/medicalinfo/teensexualhealth/fact abstinence-education.xml (accessed January 30, 2006).
45. See generally 45. Brouwer, Exporting, supra note 2, at 182-86.

🌿 81

The Black Church: What's the Word?

JOHNNETTA COLE and BEVERLY GUY-SHEFTALL

As early as 1789, black women joined black men in organizations that worked to end slavery and "lift up the race."[1] While the preachers in their churches were almost always black men who were recognized as leaders by white men, in those early days, black women were prayer warriors, singers, teachers, catechizers, and storytellers. There were a few black women preachers, and their experience with sexism in Black churches has been well documented. For example, Jarena Lee, a free black, struggled to become a preacher against the wishes of her husband.[2]

Around the beginning of the twentieth century, black women lost access to pulpits and their leadership in churches became even more seriously challenged. This "silencing" of black women's voices coincided with "regularizing" the presence of black male preachers. One response by black women was the emergence between 1885 and 1900 of what historian Evelyn Brooks Higginbotham calls a "feminist theology," which "contested the masculinism that threatened them with silence and marginality."[3] Black Baptist women formed the Women's Auxiliary Convention of the National Baptist Convention. Other women moved into the Holiness Movement of the nineteenth century and the Pentecostal Movement of the twentieth century. Another avenue pursued by some black women in response to their suppression within black churches was the formation of the National Association of Colored Women—a club movement of prophetic Christian women.[4]

Perhaps it is not surprising that African-American men, who were prohibited from exercising power in other public arenas, would be adamant about maintaining authority in the one institution they did manage to control, black churches. Their embrace of patriarchy in black churches was aided by passages in the Bible that support the subordination of women. Male dominance in African-American churches was expressed most clearly by the fact that black women were forbidden to be ordained and to preach from a pulpit. These prohibitions continue to be "justified" by reference to biblical sources. At a black Methodist preachers meeting of the Washington annual conference in 1890, the question was posed: "Is woman inferior to man?" The chairman of the meeting replied: "Sad as it may be, woman is as inferior to man as man is to God."[5] In spite of the progress of women in ministry, preaching remains overwhelmingly a form of male discourse.[6]

Subtle and not so subtle notions that black women, like children, are best seen and not heard, and that a black woman should stand several paces behind her man permeated religious circles, and were also present in prescriptions for proper behavior by black women in civil society. For example, in a 1966 *Ebony* magazine special issue on black women, in which women were contributors, the editorial declared, "The immediate goal of the Negro woman today should be the establishment of a strong family unit in which the father is the dominant person." The editorial went on to say that black women would be advised to follow the example of the Jewish mother "who pushed her husband to success, educated her male children first, and engineered good marriages for her daughters." And to the career woman, the advice was given that she "should be willing to postpone her aspirations until her children, too, are old enough to be on their own."[7]

But in many black churches, black women have resisted words and actions that call for them to be subservient to men. Gilkes notes: The cultural maxim, "If it wasn't for the women, you wouldn't have a church," rises up against male attempts to exclude, ignore, trivialize, or marginalize women in a number of capacities.[8]

Some black women directly challenged biblical arguments. As early as the 1830s, Maria Stewart was the first woman of any race to give a public lecture and leave a manuscript record. In 1833, after a brief career on the lecture circuit, however, she delivered a farewell speech to the black community, especially ministers, in which she expressed resentment and hurt about its negative response to her defiance of gender conventions as a public lecturer. She called attention to their hypocrisy and unwillingness to honor her talents. Her passionate defense of women's right to speak in public invokes biblical heroines and wise women throughout history in her query:

> What if I am a woman. . . . Did he [God] not raise up Deborah, to be mother and a judge in Israel?

Did not Queen Esther save the lives of the Jews? And Mary Magdelene first declare the resurrection of Christ from the dead? . . . Did St. Paul but know our wrongs and deprivations, I presume he would make no objections to our pleading in public for our rights . . . holy women ministered unto Christ and the apostles; and women . . . have had a voice in moral, religious and political subjects . . . why the Almighty hath imparted unto me the power of speaking thus, I cannot tell. . . . Among the Greeks, women delivered the Oracles. . . . The prediction of the Egyptian women obtained much credit at Rome. . . . Why cannot we become divines and scholars? (198).

Itinerant preacher and abolitionist Sojourner Truth also used biblical references to defend her preaching and support for women. To a man who said that women couldn't have as many rights as men because Christ wasn't a woman, she retorted at an 1851 Akron, Ohio, women's rights convention: "Where did your Christ come from? From God and a woman! Man had nothing to do with Him!"[9]

Black women also challenged sexist ideas and practices in the church early on through their innovative organizational strategies. Educator, writer, and activist, Nannie Helen Burroughs is responsible for the establishment of National Woman's Day, having instituted in 1907 a "Women's Day" in black Baptist churches that eventually spread to nearly every black church denomination and to some white denominations. This special day was "a glorious opportunity for women to learn to speak for themselves."[10]

For Burroughs, the church was a site of resistance and an important outlet for the political empowerment of black women, though she constantly battled the black male leadership about their insensitivity to women's needs. She also criticized the church for failing to assist in the political development of women, and argued in the August 1915 issue of the *Crisis,* the official organ for the NAACP, that suffrage would enable women to fight male dominance and sexual abuse.

Despite serious resistance, black women have continuously created roles for themselves that become essential for the functioning of the church. Today, in many denominations, black women exercise substantial influence through the positions of deaconess and stewardess. "Church mothers" have also challenged patriarchy in the church. Addressed by the minister and members of the congregation as "Mother," she is an older woman who is looked up to as a sterling example of Christian morality. She may be the leader of the adult class and is surely an expert on the Bible. Some church mothers are said to speak in little sermons, and the words of Mother Pollard who participated in the Montgomery bus boycott are well known: "My feet are tired but my soul is rested." The opinions of a church mother can sometimes prevail over the views of a male preacher.

Yet another way in which black women have shown their opposition to the sexism of black preachers is by "voting with their feet," and leaving a church—sometimes to found one of their own. This willingness to "vote with their feet" may or may not be accompanied by identification with feminism. Indeed, within church circles, many black women exhibit profound ambivalence toward feminism—even when they are vehemently opposed to sexism. While many black women have rejected patriarchal ideas in their churches, many have not, choosing instead to internalize the gender roles put forth by the prevailing church authority.

SEXUALITY AND THE BLACK CHURCH

Some of the most hush-hush race secrets in African-American communities revolve around issues of sexuality and the church. It is not that preachers fail to talk about sex. And it is certainly not that parishioners and preachers are not engaging in sex. What lies at the heart of these "secrets" is the hypocritical disconnect between what is said about sex—with whom it should take place among Christian folks and under what circumstances—and the realities of people's sexual lives.

How did it come about that Sunday after Sunday in black church after black church, ministers warn their congregations about succumbing to carnal desires, and yet some of these same ministers are involved in sexual exploits with women parishioners and others in the community? Though this is not peculiar to black churches, how do we explain the hypocritical behavior of some black ministers (some of whom are closeted gay men) who rant from their pulpits about the sinfulness of homosexuality, and yet turn to the choir directors (some of whom are "secretly known" to be gay) to lift a song? What do we imagine are the feelings of other gay parishioners who worship in churches where their sexual choices are demonized?

Homophobia and heterosexism are so deeply entrenched in "mainstream" American culture that it would be impossible for the black church to have immunized itself against it. Many white Christians have declared homosexuality to be a perversion and have boldly indicated that they hate the sin but love the sinner. However, as Kelley Brown Douglas, the first theologian to seriously address sexuality and homophobia in the black church, observes: "the Bible does not present as clear a position on homosexuality as is often self-righteously asserted. The meaning of the biblical stories customarily referred to as proof against homosexual practices has generally been misconstrued or distorted. Biblical scholars have painstakingly shown that the Leviticus Holiness Codes (Lev. 18:22; 20:13), the story of Sodom and Gomorrah (Gen. 19:1–9), and Paul's Epistle to the Romans (1:26–27) do not present a compelling case against homoeroticism. These scholars have also pointed out that neither the words nor the actions of Jews, as recorded in the Gospels, suggest an anti-gay or anti-lesbian stance. In fact the New Testament shows Jesus to be virtually indifferent about matters of sexuality."[11]

The explanation for such contradictions in black ministers can also be found in the convoluted history of black sexuality, which began during slavery and continues to define black–white and black–black relations in America. This history is so distorted, it is little wonder that for many black Christian women and men, a healthy sense of sexuality is hard to come by. Dyson raises the rhetorical question: "How can [we] have a healthy sense of black Christian sexual identity in a world where being black has been a sin, where black sexuality has been viewed as pathology, and where the inability to own—and to own up to—our black bodies has led us to devalue our own flesh?"[12]

From the very beginning, a conservative view of sexuality was advanced in the churches blacks founded. One explanation points to the conservative theologies of white Christianity, which was steeped in Victorian repression. It became imperative for African-Americans to refute all of the negative beliefs about their sexuality; so the black church became a major site for the rehabilitation of black people's morality.

One such expression of patriarchy that is writ large in black churches is the double standard of sexual morality that privileges all men, but particularly male ministers. This point is worth considering with respect to Dr. Martin Luther King Jr.—one of the world's greatest champions for civil and human rights. Dyson situates Dr. King's behavior within the rampant patriarchy of the black church:

> Only advocates of moral perfection will seek to deny King his high place in history because of his sexual sins. This does not mean that we cannot or should not criticize King for his rampant womanizing and his relentless infidelity. . . . King was certainly reared in a preacherly culture where good sex is pursued with nearly the same fervor as believers seek to be filled with the Holy Ghost. And the war against white supremacy in which King participated was thoroughly sexist and often raucous. . . . King's sexual practices were nourished within a powerful pocket of the church. His sexual habits grew in part out of a subculture of promiscuity that is rampant among clergy and religious figures in every faith.[13]

The church is far more unforgiving concerning the indiscretions of woman ministers, while women in the ministry are under constant pressure to explain and defend their call to the ministry, and their success or failure affects the women clergy who follow them.

NEW DIRECTIONS

While there are some "everyday folks" in black churches who continue to speak out against sexism in their faith communities, there is an even more significant impact when black religious and spiritual leaders address this question. Those religious and spiritual leaders who challenge the black church to change its ways fall into one or more of the following categories: progressive theologians/ministers; academic ordained ministers; womanist theologians/ministers; openly gay and lesbian ministers; ministers of independent churches; ministers of mega churches; and spiritual gurus.

Today men dominate in the pulpit, in published religious scholarship, and in leadership in both the sacred and the profane worlds. A small subset stand out because of their progressive views on "the woman question" and other social and political issues—men such as Drs. James H. Cone, James A. Forbes Jr., James Washington, Vincent Harding, Cornel West, Michael Eric Dyson, and Mark Chapman. Among them, the radical and pioneering black liberation theology of Cone, professor of systematic theology at Union Theological Seminary, included an early critique of sexism in the black church: "Although black male theologians and church leaders have progressive and often revolutionary ideas regarding the equality of blacks in American society, they do not have similar ideas regarding the equality of women in the black church and community."[14] In an unusual appeal to black male ministers, Cone urges them to take the issue of women's liberation seriously and understand the depth of sexism in black churches as well as the connection between racism and sexism; learn how to really listen to women's stories of pain and struggle; and support women's leadership roles in the church, including that of minister. He boldly advocates affirmative action strategies for black women in churches so that they will be represented equally in all positions of responsibility. And finally, he calls for serious discussion of the role of black women in the church and asserts passionately that "the black church cannot regain its Christian integrity unless it is willing to face head-on the evil of patriarchy and seek to eliminate it" (139).

There is a growing body of preachers and seminary scholar-teachers whose work is grounded in womanist philosophy and practice—that is, a belief in gender equality and a theology of liberation that is attentive to the particular experiences of African-American women. Among these preacher-teacher-scholar-activists is the Reverend Dr. Jacquelyn

Grant, a professor at the Interdenominational Theological Center (ITC), an ordained AME minister, and founding director of the Office of Black Women in Church and Society; Kelley Brown Douglas, professor of theology at Howard University Divinity School; and Vashti McKenzie, the first woman bishop elected in the history of the African Methodist Episcopal church, who is now serving in Africa. These women directly address issues of male dominance and female resistance to that dominance in and outside of black churches. These sister religious leaders also openly take on issues of sexuality and sexual violence.

Within the enormously influential community of self-help practitioners there are women who ground their counsel in notions of spirituality. One scholar, Akasha Gloria Hull, labels this communal work "soul talk" or "soul process."[15] Like the organized black church, they are involved in healing our collective wounds, but call upon in much more explicit ways their wisdom as women who've navigated difficult life journeys. Two of the most visible and popular black women whom some would describe as contemporary community "healers" are Susan Taylor and Iyanla Vanzant. Each has built a large following among black women seeking help for the problems that plague them and their families, and counsel on how to transform their lives. Susan Taylor, the former editor-in-chief of *Essence* magazine, and now editorial director of the magazine, she periodically writes a column under the title "In the Spirit," and enjoys great respect and admiration among African-American women for her wise words and spiritual grounding.

Iyanla Vanzant writes and talks about her own struggles to build and maintain a healthy relationship with her husband, sustain the best possible relationships with her children, and affirm herself as a self-actualized black woman.

In their writings and public appearances, both Taylor and Vanzant shy away from what might be labeled as "feminism," but they center their teachings on issues that haunt many African-American women. The "medicine" they prescribe for problems that range from sexual abuse to low self-esteem are grounded in Afrocentric notions of healing and personal empowerment through spiritual growth.

Dr. Barbara King, founding pastor of Atlanta-based Hillside Truth International Center, brings to her large congregation a fusion of womanist and Afrocentric theology. In our interview with her, she spoke about the resistance of many male preachers to the presence of women in the pulpit, and of the many difficulties she faced personally in her quest to become a minister within mainstream denominations. These struggles motivated her to found her own church and chart her own journey as an activist minister committed to addressing openly pressing issues facing contemporary, including younger, congregations.

We call for and indeed hope for sustained gender talk on the part of various religious and spiritual leaders that will reach broad audiences within and outside of the church. For it is such gender talk that is a prerequisite to the change in consciousness and then the action that will allow us to grapple with whatever ails us physically, spiritually, and sexually. And we remain convinced of the unique power of black feminist/womanist analyses, whether generated by women or men, as we move beyond the silences that have exacted far too high a price in our communities.   [edited, 2011]

NOTES

1. Rosalyn Terborg-Penn, "Discrimination Against Afro-American Women in the Women's Movement, 1830–1920," in *The Afro-American Woman: Struggles and Images,* ed. Sharon Harley and Rosalyn Terborg-Penn (Port Washington, NY: Kennikat Press, 1978), 29–34.
2. Jarena Lee, "The Life and Religious Experience of Jarena Lee, a Coloured Lady," in *Sisters of the Spirit: Three Black Women's Autobiographies,* ed. William L. Andrews (Bloomington: Indiana University Press, 1986). Originally published in 1849.
3. Cheryl Townsend Gilkes, *"If It Wasn't for the Women": Black Women's Experience and Womanist Culture in Church and Community* (Maryknoll, NY: Orbis Books, 1991), 200.
4. Important studies of the black women's club movement include Deborah Gray White, *Too Heavy a Load: Black Women in Defense of Themselves, 1894–1994* (New York: Norton, 1999).
5. Bettye Collier-Thomas's documentary history *Daughters of Thunder: Black Women Preachers and Their Sermons, 1850–1979* (San Francisco: Jossey-Bass, 1998) is the most comprehensive discussion of Black women

preachers and debates over the ordination of women ministers within the black church, which began in the antebellum period.

6. Gilkes, *"If It Wasn't for the Women,"* 129–30.
7. "For a Better Future," *Ebony*, August 1966, 15a.
8. Gilkes, *"If It Wasn't for the Women,"* 41.
9. Sojourner Truth quote appears in *Black Women in Nineteenth-Century American Life*, 236. Originally published in *History of Woman Suffrage*, ed. Elizabeth Cady Stanton et al. (Rochester, NY, 1881), 1:116.
10. See Evelyn Brooks Higginbotham's *Righteous Discontent: The Women's Movement in the Black Baptist Church, 1880–1920* (Cambridge, MA: Harvard University Press, 1993) for a lengthy discussion of Burroughs's impact on the black Baptist church; and see Cheryl Gilkes's discussion of Burroughs in chapter 8 of *"If It Wasn't for the Women,"* quote at 33.
11. Kelley Brown Douglas, *Sexuality and the Black Church*, 90.
12. Michael Dyson, "When You Divide Body and Soul, Problems Multiply: The Black Church and Sex," in *Race Rules: Navigating the Color Line* (New York: Vintage), 83.
13. Michael Eric Dyson, *I May Not Get There with You* (New York: Free Press, 2000), 157, 160.
14. James H. Cone, *For My People: Black Theology and the Black Church* (Maryknoll, NY: Orbis Books, 1984), 139; see also *Black Theology: A Documentary History*, vol. 2, *1980–1992*, ed. James H. Cone and Gayraud S. Wilmore (Maryknoll, NY: Orbis Books, 1999). Mark L. Chapman's *Christianity on Trial: African-American Religious Thoughts Before and After Black Power* (Maryknoll, NY: Orbis Books, 1996) contains a sustained and useful discussion of Christianity and sexism, 135–67, which is grounded in womanist theology.
15. Akasha Gloria Hull, *Soul Talk: The New Spirituality of African-American Women* (Rochester, VT: Inner Traditions, 2001), 151.

✿ 82

Rethinking Women's Issues in Muslim Communities

KECIA ALI

The issues facing the majority of Muslim women around the world today are those facing the majority of women everywhere: poverty, illiteracy, political repression, and patriarchy. At the same time, there are now and always have been elite Muslim women, with wealth and clout, who have exercised power and autonomy within social and economic networks. No one can argue that these women all share a "status." For this reason, stereotypes of Muslim women as uniquely oppressed bear little resemblance to reality. Yet the attempt to define "women's status in Islam" persists.

Some people take the question about women's status to be about an idealized Islam, mostly referring to Qur'an and prophetic tradition, sometimes including jurisprudence. As with Christian scripture, analyzing isolated passages from these sources is not likely to give an accurate portrayal of women's rights, nor do these sources necessarily reflect actual practice. A focus on the Qur'anic verses that specifically address women is, however, one common means of attempting to answer the question "What is women's status in Islam?" Indeed, Muslims have often encouraged this approach as a way of deflecting criticism about women's actual disadvantages in some Muslim societies. Faced with clear evidence of oppression, Muslim apologists state that such practices are contrary to "true Islam," which they claim liberated women from their disadvantaged position in pre-Islamic Arabia. An opposite reaction is heard from detractors of Islam. When women achieve social prominence and personal success in Muslim societies, these critics contend that it is despite Islam; this progress (such as several Muslim women becoming heads of state) is possible because of the declining importance of religion. Where legal and social discrimination against women do exist, however, these critics blame it on Islam.

In order to make any headway in understanding Muslim women's lives—and what is needed to make them better—one needs to move beyond these arguments. Islam is not the solution to all of Muslim women's problems, nor is it the cause of them. I would suggest, in fact, that Islam is not directly related to many facets of most Muslim women's lives. To take the most striking example, one can focus on the unequivocally terrible situation of women in Afghanistan under the Taliban. Even in this case, where the Taliban's interpretation of Islam was the explicit justification for oppressive restrictions on women's mobility and education, "Islam" does not by itself come close to explaining women's experience. In order to comprehend women's situation in Afghanistan, one needs to understand not scriptural passages concerning women, but rather decades of devastating war, tribal rivalries, lack of agriculture, a high rate of infant mortality, and so on. While Islam must be analyzed as part of the larger picture, it is meaningless outside Afghanistan's specific historical and geopolitical context. The burka is less relevant to Afghan women's misery than sheer, crushing poverty.

That is not to say, however, that the burka is a nonissue. Without falling into the trap of assuming, as some Western commentators seem to, that women's dress is a barometer through which status can be measured (the less skin showing, the lower the status), I would suggest that it is related to a constellation of issues that are common to Muslim women: a focus on women's dress; some level of restriction of free mixing of the sexes; and the granting to husbands of significant legal and customary authority over their wives. Although there have never been universally agreed-upon rules on these subjects, nor have regulations been uniformly applied to all Muslim women across time and class boundaries, they are among the crucial issues that shape communities and families throughout the Muslim world, including among Muslims in the United States.

ISLAMIC DRESS

Some scholars have shown how debates over Islamic dress have turned it into a potent symbol for authentic Islam, at the same time it becomes a marker of idealized gender difference. Others have suggested that it represents a practical compromise strategy for women who wear it as a means of being taken seriously, not harassed, and allowed more personal freedom without being viewed as unchaste. In this model, women's adoption of the *hijab* is a demonstration of autonomy. Still others have suggested that any use of "the veil" is ultimately self-defeating because it carries such powerful connotations of women's subordination and the idea that women's proper place is in the home. A few have noted that the concept of *hijab* originally referred to a physical barrier of separation from unrelated men for a woman in her home; the idea of a portable "screen" that allows wide mobility and interaction with men outside the family is a very different concept. Of course, seclusion in the pre-modern era was an elite affair only, relying on the free movement of women from the lower classes to provide goods and services. In this sense, contemporary Islamic dress is an egalitarian phenomenon, available for the price of a scarf.

In any event, in the United States and other Western nations women's headcovering takes on a very different meaning. It is one thing to wear a scarf and *abbaya* in Saudi Arabia where such dress is compulsory, quite another to do it in Egypt or Kuwait, where women's dress spans the range from fully covered—including face veil and gloves—to chic, and potentially revealing, skirts and jeans. It is still another thing entirely to adopt a headcovering in a nation where Muslims are a small minority of the population and the *hijab* itself makes the wearer noticeable.

Three views on the scarf seem to have taken root among Muslims in the West. One calls for wearing the scarf as absolutely necessary, based on Qur'an and prophetic tradition; in this perspective, other considerations are irrelevant, and other views are summarily dismissed. A second position argues that women's modesty is critical and that the point of the covering is to make a woman's appearance less the focus of attention. Thus, in the United States, wearing a scarf accomplishes precisely the opposite of the Qur'an's original intention. A third view shares elements with the others. Its proponents recognize both the need to be modest and the specific issues associated with veiling in the United States. They suggest that there are social reasons to veil here, even though some do not consider it obligatory: it makes women less a sex symbol and more of a human being and it makes her recognizable as a Muslim.

Some considerations, generally left out of discussions of veiling, are important to my view that wearing *hijab* needs to be a personal decision made in good faith according to a woman's own understanding of God's commands. At one mosque I attended, I was told that some women's purses had been gone through, during prayers, in order for others to check whether they were properly covered in their driver's license photographs. First, therefore, Muslims need to stop putting so much emphasis on women's dress, and sex segregation, and far more on other aspects of men's and women's moral development (like respecting the privacy of others). Just as we ask non-Muslims not to judge by appearances and assume that a women's headscarf implies oppression, Muslims need to realize that a woman who does not cover her head is not necessarily any less observant or faithful than one who does. Second, and related to the first, is the double standard. The Qur'an verse that is most cited in regard to women's dress (Qur'an 24:31) is preceded by an exhortation to men to "cast down their gazes" (Qur'an 24:30). If Muslim women are not allowed to wear swimsuits at the beach, but it is perfectly acceptable for Muslim men to look at, and interact with, non-Muslim women in bikinis, does this not violate the spirit as well as the letter of the Qur'anic injunction? Muslims need to think of modesty and modest behavior as both male and female duties. Finally, the Qur'anic and prophetic evidence regulating women's dress is far less precise than many assume. Nonetheless, rather than spending more time and attention focused on how exactly to interpret these texts and to best understand how women should dress, I would suggest that it should be a nonissue, at least until the other pressing problems facing Muslim communities are resolved. One of the most pressing issues is that of family law.

FAMILY LAW

One common view of Islamic rules on marriage and divorce deems them particularly harsh and unfair to women. This view is held not only by non-Muslims but also by many Muslims, particularly in the numerous countries that impose some version of "Islamic Family Law" or "Personal Status Codes" purportedly based on classical Islamic law. A contrary view is gaining prominence, however. Its proponents argue that, in fact, women are guaranteed numerous rights by Islamic law; they simply need to learn how to protect themselves by invoking them. The most important way to do so, in this view, is to place conditions in a marriage contract; a wife can thus ensure that she is permitted to work,

to visit her family, or to obtain a divorce if her husband takes a second wife. But these conditions are a matter of significant dispute in classical law. Several of the conditions that are routinely praised as a means for women to obtain rights are deemed by the majority of classical jurists, and today by many national court systems, to be void and unenforceable, thus making women's "right" to include them in their contracts meaningless.

For Muslim women in the United States, the situation is different. American Muslims are not subject to a particular interpretation of Islamic law by government decree but rather may choose, as a matter of conscience, to follow certain doctrines in their personal dealings. In these circumstances, the legal strategy of including conditions in a marriage contract can be an extremely useful way of making clear the spouses' expectations for the marriage and about their roles within it. And if they are written in a prenuptial contract in a way enforceable by the U.S. courts, these conditions can serve as legal requirements for the spouses to abide. This can be an effective approach for certain rights, particularly payment of dower, a wife's right to work (or not to work), and the rights of the spouses to maintain separate property.

In my view, these types of measures are useful as a means of gaining recognition for rights that are recognized by classical jurisprudence but ignored by contemporary Muslims in positions of authority, such as the local imams who draw up marriage contracts. Ultimately, however, these types of conditions do little to alter the traditional imbalance of spousal rights in classical law; as an example, there is no condition a wife can include to restrict her husband's right to repudiate her at any time, for any (or no) reason. This is his unalienable right according to the unanimous view of classical jurists. (Of course, in the United States the spouses would still have to go through civil divorce proceedings before the government would recognize the divorce.) Rather than simply picking and choosing from among the doctrines of established legal schools, what is needed is a more thorough-going legal analysis with an eye to developing a new, more egalitarian law.

There is resistance to this type of work on numerous fronts. I will address only what I believe to be the major obstacle: the assumption of many that *shariia*, or revealed Law, is the same as "Islamic Law" as found in the regulations of the legal schools. The use of the term *shariia* in descriptions of legal doctrines as well national legal codes promotes this confusion; contrast this with the term *fiqh*, literally meaning "understanding," that is the Arabic word for jurisprudence. The legal schools have historically demonstrated significant variability in method and doctrines; they differ substantially on numerous points of law.

These differences are not, as some have suggested, merely matters of detail. I will give a few examples of how real the consequences can be for women. The Shafiii school allows a wife to obtain a divorce on grounds of nonsupport after as little as three days; the Hanafi school never does, even if the wife is indigent and her husband fails to support her for decades. The Maliki school allows a father to contract a marriage for his never-married daughter over her objections even if she is a 35-year-old professional; conversely, the Hanbali school says that the father's power to force a girl into marriage ends when she turns nine. Virtually all Sunni jurists consider a triple repudiation given at once to be legally effective, if reprehensible; Shiii law, however, counts such a pronouncement as only a single repudiation. These mutually contradictory positions cannot all be equally correct interpretations of an infallible Divine Will. All, however, are significantly shaped by the patriarchal constraints of their times of origin. Once Muslims recognize this, the need for qualified Muslims to create a renewed jurisprudence should be clear.

COMMUNITY CONSIDERATIONS

The biggest question now is: how will American Muslims face these issues? There is an understandable desire not to add to the stereotypes non-Muslims have of Muslim women's oppression. As a result, in discussions with outsiders, Muslim women tend to minimize very real experiences of being marginalized within communities. While Muslim women's experiences do not come close to being as oppressive as is popularly imagined, neither are they as rosy as some claim. While clearing up misconceptions is important, it should not come at the expense of women having a chance to really confront those issues that are of concern. Women cannot afford to let concerns be simply dismissed with the statement that "Islam liberated women" and therefore there is no cause for complaint.

There are progressive voices within American Muslim communities addressing these topics today, though unless one is listening for them, they tend to be drowned out by established conservative and apologetic discourses. Issues related to women and gender are becoming increasingly part of the agenda. Growing numbers of Muslim women are interpreting the Qur'an in nonpatriarchal ways, and their writings and lectures are having an impact on the ideas in circulation. Muslim women's discussion groups associated with mosques as well as in academic and activist settings are a force for change. The single most important idea associated with all these efforts is that men and women are created equal as believers and that, ultimately, their equality as human beings in the sight of God matters more than any distinctions based on social hierarchy. I am optimistic that this idea, and its natural consequence of more egalitarian families, communities, and laws, will shape the future of Muslims in the United States. I do not expect it will happen overnight, nor without significant conflict, but I do believe it is the only way for Muslims to truly live out the Divine command for men and women to be protectors of one another (Qur'an 9:71).   [2002]

An earlier version of this article was published in *Taking Back Islam: American Muslims Reclaim Their Faith* (Michael Wolfe and Beliefnet, eds., Emmaus, PA: Rodale Press, 2002).

 83

Revelations

LINDA VILLAROSA

In the May 1991 issue of *Essence* magazine, my mother and I each wrote about my coming out as a lesbian. That article received a tremendous reception—most of it positive—and it remains the most responded-to article in the history of the magazine. Due to the avalanche of mail, my mother and I followed up with "Readers Respond to Coming Out," which ran later that year in the October issue. This article was much more political, allowing me to speak out directly against homophobia in black communities. Almost overnight, I was unexpectedly catapulted into the public arena, which began a wave of national speaking engagements that left me to cope with both adulation and condemnation.

Before I came out in print, I never had someone tell me I was going to go to hell. Now people say it to me regularly. When my mother and I addressed a conference of black social workers about how families may confront their homophobia and accept lesbian and gay children, a sad-eyed man, round-shouldered in a baggy suit, approached me. "I enjoyed hearing what you had to say," he offered, his hand extended. My hand in his, he continued, barely missing a beat, "But you're a sinner. You're going to hell." He said this casually, through a half-smile, as though ready to add, "Have a nice day."

Some people put their condemnation in writing, spitting angry religion-like curse words. These are two of the several letters I received at *Essence:*

From Smyrna, Georgia: [Your] behavior is a sin against God that can be forgiven by sincere repentance and turning away from the sin of homosexuality. In fact, the word of God is very clear on the immorality of homosexuality. Read 1 Corinthians 6:9. Homosexuals and the homosexual lifestyle will never be accepted. I believe that sharing the Word with those individuals afflicted with the sin of homosexuality and imparting love and patience, they can receive the loving salvation of Jesus Christ. This is the only way you, and other homosexuals, can become normal, saved persons.

From Westchester, New York: [Essence] should be ashamed of itself for having a woman like Linda Villarosa on your staff. Lesbian *[sic]* is not a sickness, it's a sin, and if that woman does not repent, she is going to perish. She should read Mathew *[sic]* chapter 19 verses 4 and 5. Read it and see what it says. Linda, no one wants to know who you are!

The worst verbal attack came at Oregon State University, where I was to address a large group of students about being black, lesbian, and out. The trouble started before I arrived. I had requested that the organizers contact African-American student groups about coming to my lecture, because I believe that it's extremely important for blacks—gay and straight—to know that black lesbians exist and can be happy and out and secure in their identities. A member of the school's Black Women's Alliance (BWA), who was also friendly with the gay group on campus, agreed to make an announcement at BWA's next meeting to garner support and ensure a strong black presence at the lecture. At the end of the meeting she told the other sisters that an editor from *Essence* would be speaking the following evening. Several women clapped and nodded. "She'll be talking about what it's like to be a black lesbian," the young woman continued. At that point, the room fell silent. Finally, one woman stood up and said, "Lesbianism is nasty and they should get a vaccine to make them normal." Spurred on, another declared, "Gays are against God, and because of my religion, I can't hear this woman speak." In the end, another exasperated sister said, "Can we please stop talking about this, I'm getting physically ill."

Thankfully, I didn't know about this backlash or I would've been too freaked to do the lecture. Expressions of homophobia hurt deeply, but coming from other black women the pain is particularly acute. Knowing that I would be facing such resistance in what was already a largely white audience on a conservative college campus may well have paralyzed me.

The lecture went fine. The question-and-answer period was particularly long with interested students—gay, straight, and of many races and ethnicities—hungry for answers and information. After a while I became tired and announced that I'd answer one final question. A clean-cut white guy wearing a baseball cap waved his hand frantically from the balcony. And there it was: "You and all gays are going to hell. I'm telling you this because God taught me to love you." Then he cited a Bible passage: "Read Leviticus 20:13."

Bedlam broke out in the room. After several minutes, I got things quieted down and looked out into the expectant faces of the audience. The challenge had been made, and I felt that all of the young, gay people there expected me to defend us all with authority. My voice shook with anger and a little bit of fear that I wouldn't be able to meet this challenge. "Listen, you don't love me, you don't know me, you don't understand me," I said, barely able to remain composed and keep from crying. "You're using religion to cloak your horrible message in the language of love. People like you have used religion to suppress everything you find offensive. In the past the Bible was used to justify slavery and now you're using it to justify your fear and hatred of those of us who are living our lives as gays and lesbians."

The tension broke and the crowd began to applaud, but I felt empty. Even the reporters covering the event saw through my strong front and brave smile. The next day's edition of the *Corvallis (Ore.) Gazette-Times* reported that as I stepped from the podium, I had seemed stunned. It was true: I was stunned. And sad. My words had sounded hollow to me, as though I had been reading from a textbook. I hadn't felt them. My reaction had been a knee-jerk response to being attacked in public; but deep within me, I knew I wasn't so sure about myself. Where do I really stand spiritually? That heckler knew exactly how he felt and where he stands, why didn't I?

Nothing in my own religious upbringing prepared me for these attacks. My family attended an integrated, "progressive" Episcopal church. There were a handful of families of color like us and lots of groovy white people, interracial couples, and aging hippies with their adopted children of color in tow. Our choir didn't sing gospel music, but folky spiritual ballads accompanied by the organ, guitar, and African and Native American drumming.

I don't remember learning many specific religious lessons from our minister. With his long hair flowing over his Roman collar, Father Hammond preached through sleepy eyes, as though he'd been out late drinking the night before. His words were inspirational and easy to understand, filled with references to pop culture. A quote from *Playboy* magazine could seamlessly segue into biblical verse. My mother taught my fourth-grade Sunday school class, stressing discipline and openmindedness. One Saturday morning the group of us gathered for a field trip to a nearby synagogue. We looked like a bunch of "We Are the World" poster children. "It's important to learn about the way other people worship," my mother explained, looking over our group to make sure our two lines were straight and orderly and no noses were running.

To further my religious studies, I attended weeks and weeks of confirmation classes every Thursday night. On confirmation day, I walked down the church aisle, clutching a white prayer book in white-gloved hands. I was wearing a white dress, white lace socks, white patent-leather shoes, and had a white handkerchief pinned to my head. I looked like a brown-skinned vestal virgin awaiting sacrifice. I don't remember one spiritual lesson from that time, but I do remember how hard it was to try to stay clean in all those bleached-white clothes.

We also visited St. John's, my grandmother's Baptist church, on trips back to Chicago, where I was born. Getting dressed for service was a major production. My grandmother had to decide which of her many wigs and hats to wear and whether or not to put on her fur, a decision that had little to do with the temperature outside. After the frenzied preparations, we'd all pile into my grandfather's Electra 225 and float to church in the boat-sized car.

Once inside, I'd always scrunch into my grandmother's side and maneuver a way to sit by her. I knew she was important in this community from the way heads would turn as she led the family—straight-backed—down the aisle to our pew, and I wanted a little of that limelight.

The service really wasn't as fun as the preparation, mainly because of its three-hour length. Until someone got the Spirit. I'd hold my breath as the organ pounded out the same repetitive note and the singing rang louder, rising to more and more tremorous shouts. Inevitably, some well-dressed woman would take to the aisle, chanting and skipping. Then two strong, well-practiced sisters, dressed in white gloves and nurse's uniforms, would walk briskly over and efficiently bring the saved soul back to this world and dispatch her into the care of family members. I would tug at Grandmother's sleeve asking questions about the moment of high drama, but she would slap my Vaselined knees together and hiss into my ear, "Stop-staring-close-your-lips-don't-bite-your-cuticles-put-your-gloves-back-on." The only thing I knew for certain was that no one in our family would ever get the spirit, because my grandmother would die of embarrassment.

From my parents' church I learned about respect for difference and community across seemingly unbridgeable differences, and through my grandmother's church I connected with my Southern Baptist roots. But nothing from my religious past had prepared me to deal with the continued abuse I was receiving from so-called religious people. It was time for me to begin studying the Bible, but, more importantly, it was time to discover my own spiritual core.

First, I dug out the dusty copy of the Revised Standard Version of the Bible left over from my days in confirmation classes, and I looked up the passages that had been thrown in my face. I started with 1 Corinthians 6:9 and 10, which read: "Do not be deceived; neither the immoral, nor idolaters, nor adulterers, nor homosexuals, nor thieves, nor the greedy, nor drunkards, nor revilers, nor robbers will inherit the kingdom of God."

I felt skeptical: had the authors of the Bible really used the word "homosexual" 2,000 years ago? No, they had not. The New Testament had been written in Greek and then translated into Hebrew. In 1382 the Bible was first translated into English, and in 1611 came the King James (or authorized) Version. The Bible I was reading had been revised 335 years later. I purchased a paperback copy of the King James Version and looked up 1 Corinthians 6:9 and 10. This earlier version never used the word "homosexual" but listed the "effeminate" and "abusers of themselves with mankind" in its inventory of the "unrighteous," and that had been translated to mean "homosexual" in the revised version. Something had been lost—or gained—in translation.

I decided not to spend much more time trying to sort out what the authors meant and what lessons they were trying to teach about homosexuality—if that's even what they were talking about—in the context of social systems from 20 centuries past. In fact, even after reading Genesis 19 many times, I still didn't see how the story of Sodom had anything to do with gay sex. In that story, Lot, a holy man and resident of the evil city of Sodom, is visited by two angels. Genesis 19:4–8 reads:

> . . . the men of the city, the men of Sodom, both young and old, all the people to the last man, surrounded the house; and they called to Lot, "Where are the men who came to you tonight [i.e., the angels]? Bring them out to us, that we may know them." Lot went out of the door to the men, shut the door after him, and said, "I beg you, my brothers, do not act so wickedly. Behold, I have two daughters who have not known man; let me bring them out to you, and do to them as you please; only do nothing to these men. . . ."

Eventually, the angels strike the men blind, and God rains fire and brimstone on the city and burns it down. From this story comes the word "sodomy"—a pejorative term for gay sex. And now, when a city like New York is described as a modern-day Sodom, the underlying assumption is that it's full of sin and sex and gays. Even assuming that the word "know" refers to sex, it seems a stretch to use it to condemn gays and lesbians. Why isn't anyone questioning Lot for offering to turn over his virginal daughters to the mob of men, which is the most obvious aberrance relayed there?

Moving on, I looked up Matthew 19:4 and 5, which says: "He answered, 'Have you not read that he who made them from the beginning made them male and female,' and said, 'For this reason a man shall leave his father and mother and be joined to his wife, and the two shall become one flesh.'"

Upon further reading, it was easy to see that the letter writer from Westchester, New York, had taken these verses completely out of context. The passage had nothing to do with lesbians and gay men but was clearly a condemnation of divorce. In fact, the verses she cited were an answer to the question "Is it lawful to divorce one's wife for any cause?" (Matthew 19:3). Verse 9 says that "whoever divorces his wife, except for unchastity, and marries another, commits adultery." In case there's any question about the seriousness of adultery, Leviticus 20:10 spells it out clearly: "If a man commits adultery with the wife of his neighbor, both the adulterer and the adulteress shall be put to death." What does this have to do with queerness?

Next I looked up Leviticus 20:13: "If a man lies with a male as with a woman, both of them have committed an abomination; they shall be put to death, their blood is upon them." I guess they could be murdered along with the divorced remarried couple from earlier Leviticus verses. At this point, I started getting angry.

It doesn't take a biblical scholar to figure out that people use the Bible selectively. The people who write me letters are not sending hate mail to people who are divorced or to those who have cheated on their spouses. The man who lashed out at me in Oregon is not condemning people who eat pork ("And the swine, because it parts the hoof and is cloven-footed but does not chew the cud, is unclean to you. Of their flesh you shall not eat, and their carcasses you shall not touch; they are unclean to you,": Leviticus 11:7–8) or shellfish (". . . anything in the seas or the rivers that has not fins and scales, of the swarming creatures in the waters and of the living creatures that are in the waters, is an abomination to you,": Leviticus 11:10).

Neither is he cursing or carrying on about cattle breeders, farmers who grow two different crops, or anyone who wears a poly-cotton blend of clothing despite Leviticus 19:19: "You shall not let your cattle breed with a different kind; you shall not sow your field with two different kinds of seed; nor shall there come upon you a garment of cloth made of two kinds of stuff."

These people are also overlooking beautiful, lyrical passages in the Bible that celebrate same-sex love. In Ruth 1:16–17 of the Old Testament, Ruth says to Naomi: "Entreat me not to leave you or to return from following you; for where you go I will go, and where you lodge I will lodge; your people shall be my people, and your God my God; where you die I will die, and there will I be buried."

David and Jonathan of the Old Testatment seem to be deeply in love: ". . . the soul of Jonathan was knit to the soul of David, and Jonathan loved him as his own soul" (1 Samuel 18:1). When Jonathan dies in the war, David writes: ". . . your love to me was wonderful, passing the love of women" (2 Samuel 1:26).

Many so-called righteous people are taking the Bible literally when it suits them, ignoring anything that doesn't easily support their narrow condemnations or calls into question their own life-styles. And many black people are using the Bible against their lesbian and gay sisters and brothers just as whites used the scriptures against our ancestors when they interpreted passages such as Ephesians 6:5–6—"Slaves, be obedient to those who are your earthly masters, with fear and trembling, in singleness of heart, as to Christ; not in the way of eyeservice, as men-pleasers, but as servants of Christ"—to mean that our people should remain enslaved.

It is, in fact, a sad irony that the overwhelmingly white Christian Right movement is capitalizing on homophobia in black communities. Groups like the Moral Majority and the Christian Coalition have never marched side by side with or fought for issues affecting people of color. In fact, the Christian Right has actively lobbied against issues such as voting rights and affirmative action. But now they're recruiting our people, taking advantage of the deep spiritual commitment of the African-American community and distorting Christianity to pass anti-gay and lesbian legal initiatives and turn straight blacks against gays—similar to the way their ancestors distorted Christianity to justify slavery.

My Bible studies behind me, I felt fortified intellectually but still on shaky ground spiritually. But I knew exactly what I needed to do. I had heard about Unity Fellowship Church and its lively congregation of hundreds of mostly black lesbians and gay men that worshipped on Sundays at New York City's Lesbian and Gay Community Services Center. Although I had always found excuses to avoid going, now it was time.

When I arrived that first Sunday, the room at the Center was packed with people; in fact, close to 100 hundred latecomers had to be turned away. The service began with testimonials. Person after person stood up and testified to what had happened over the week: breakups, gay bashing, rejections by parents, eviction from apartments, illness, sadness, loneliness, addiction, sorrow, seemed to silence the news of triumphs and causes for celebration. Pain filled the room, black pain, gay pain. But when the pastor, Elder Zachary Jones, marched into the room to the tune of "We've come this far by faith . . . ," the mood in the room changed to one of joy.

"It doesn't have nothing to do with who you sleep with, but what's in your heart," Rev. Zach shouted over the low hum of the choir. "Who says God doesn't love gay people? There's love in this room." And there was. A measure of healing had begun. His simple words struck a chord in me, and I felt relieved and then cleansed. As I looked around at the hundreds of other black lesbian and gay people in the room—who like me had been searching for a spiritual home—I knew I had found a place where I could be comfortable and explore my own spirituality.

Fortified in mind and spirit, from my connection with this community, I felt ready to face the world. And an opportunity presented itself while I was giving a talk at a black cultural center on the West Coast. After going through my usual song and dance about how it felt to be black and a lesbian, I began fielding questions. I noticed a woman raising her hand tentatively. She was a sister in her mid-thirties, turned out in an expensive, corporate-looking suit and bright gold jewelry, with her hair freshly done in braided extensions. "You seem like a really nice woman and I enjoyed hearing your story," she began slowly. "But as a Christian woman I need to share this with you. I went through a period in my life when I thought I was attracted to women. But then I discovered Jesus Christ. By reading the Bible, I realized that homosexuality was unnatural and that I was a sinner. If I continued in the life, I would be condemned."

"Where does the Bible say that?" I asked.

Opening her purse, she pulled out a small, worn copy of the New Testament and began to read from a marked passage. "For this reason God gave them up to dishonorable passions. Their women exchanged natural relations for unnatural, and the men likewise gave up natural relations with women and were consumed with passion for one another, men committing shameless acts with men and receiving in their own persons the due penalty for their error.' Romans 1, verses 26 and 27."

I listened politely as she read. When she had finished, I reached into my backpack and pulled out my own copy of the Bible. "'In like manner that the women adorn themselves in modest apparel with propriety and moderation, not with braided hair or gold or pearls or costly clothing,' 1 Timothy, chapter 2, verse 9," I read. "And 1 Timothy 2:11 and 12 say, 'Let a woman learn in silence with all submissiveness. I permit no woman to teach or to have authority over men; she is to keep silent.' I'm sure in your work you have had to supervise men. I know I have. And even by standing up and speaking out today, I guess we're both sinning."

"Wait, that's not fair," she said, her face looking at once confused and angry. "It's not right to take the Bible out of context like that."

"Why?" I countered. "That's what you're doing."

Even as I hit her close to home, I felt sorry for this woman. She was obviously confused and probably a closet case, and I knew I was preying on that, attacking her with scriptures almost as I had been attacked. I was aiming at a place she had only recently uncovered—where she was still vulnerable.

"Listen," I said softly: "I don't want to do this. All of us need to stop taking the Bible literally, and begin to read it critically and intelligently. You know, there are some important messages that we can understand and agree on." I opened my Bible to Leviticus 19:17 and read in a clear voice, "You shall not hate your brother in your heart, but you shall reason with your neighbor, lest you bear sin because of him. You shall not take vengeance or bear any grudge against the sons of your own people, but you shall love your neighbor as yourself." And this time my words sounded strong and confident, and were definitely my own.   [1995]

🌿 84

In Her Own Image

ROSE SOLARI

For as long as she can remember, Vienna Cobb Anderson wanted to be a priest. "I played priest when I was a child," she recalls. "I dressed up in my choir robes and performed marriage ceremonies. I held funerals for the neighborhood pets." Anderson gave up a career as an actress to enter the seminary in 1964, 12 years before the Episcopal Church approved the ordination of women. As far as she was concerned, her calling took precedence over the Church politics of the time.

"The men in seminary kept telling me not to rock the boat," she says of her early questions about sexism in the Church, "but I couldn't keep quiet. Once in class, the professor—who was, of course, also a priest—became so angry with me that he said, 'You must realize that there is a difference between a priest and other Christians.'" When Anderson pushed him to clarify his point, he blurted out, "I can celebrate the Eucharist, and you can't!" Three decades later, Anderson celebrates the Eucharist every Sunday, proving her former teacher wrong.

She is not alone. Scores of Christian women of all denominations have brought feminism into their churches, reexamining everything from scripture to sexuality. Today, some of the most challenging and innovative work in both theology and ministry is being done by women professors and preachers who combine their religious traditions with a powerful emphasis on female identity and experience. This work is not limited to Christianity alone, nor to the United States: Feminists have formulated critiques and prescriptions for change in Jewish, Buddhist, and Islamic traditions, and feminist theologians have emerged in Asia, Africa, and Latin America. But even if one limits one's gaze to this country and to Christianity, it is clear that—whether their primary identification is as ethicists, womanists, or ecofeminists, whether they

lead congregations or classes—women are breaking open the traditional definitions of what it means to be a disciple of Christ.

Before 1960 one could find little literature on the role of women in the Church; with the emergence of feminism, however, women across the country began to turn a critical eye on all of the systems that might be contributing to their oppression. Beginning in academic journals and presses, then moving into the mainstream on a growing tide of feminist literature, women were discovering that, both on paper and in practice, Christian denominations had as a part of their foundation certain sexist assumptions that were damaging not only to the psyches of individual Christian women but also to the structure of the Church as a whole. Women writers and thinkers began to note such problematic elements of Christianity as the emphasis on Eve as the bringer of sin, the concept of God as father and son, and the theological writing of such thinkers as Thomas Aquinas, whose statements on the inferior nature of women were taught in theological seminaries all over the world.

Since the 1960s, feminist theologians have not simply been looking to make space for the feminine in a male hierarchy. Noting that the history of Christianity was shaped by a male bias that precluded women from participation in the formation of theology, teaching, and preaching, they have been demanding something much more radical. For most of them, the goal has been not to renovate the existing structure but to tear the whole building down and start over, creating something that they believe to be much closer to the roots of Christ's actual teachings and intentions.

FOUNDING MOTHERS

Although the list of writers and thinkers in this field continues to grow—and new approaches are being developed every day—many women cite three early, key figures who helped make their work possible: Mary Daly, whose initial work was an impassioned critique of sexism in Christianity and who eventually abandoned that tradition; Rosemary Radford Ruether, whose work focused on the cultural and historical roots of sexism in Christianity;

and Beverly Wildung Harrison, whose work tackles the ethics of abortion rights and the obligation that Christians have to the poor.

Mary Daly, who grew up a Roman Catholic and obtained doctorates in both philosophy and theology in Europe in the 1960s, was the first to bring the battle cry for feminist theology to a mainstream audience. Combining a thorough academic background with fiery prose, Daly, in her 1968 book *The Church and the Second Sex,* blasted Christianity for providing women with images of themselves as inherently sinful and inferior. In a subsequent volume, *Beyond God the Father,* published in 1975, her critique gained momentum, and by her third book, *Gyn/Ecology,* published in 1978, she had left Christianity behind, positing that it was beyond hope of feminist reform. Unlike feminist theologians who work to separate what they see as Christianity's original, egalitarian message from subsequent patriarchal interpretations, Daly felt that such a task was impossible and unnecessary; to be a truly radical feminist, she asserted, one must part with Christianity altogether.

Ruether shared with Daly the idea that the oppression of women stemmed from the dualistic thinking—placing, for example, the soul in opposition to the body, and spirit in opposition to nature—that has come to be a central aspect of Christian thought. This dualism, she maintained, resulted in a hierarchical structure wherein men are placed above nature and believe that it is their right to dominate it. In a rare personal revelation, found in her essay "The Question of Feminism," Ruether was candid about the impact this structure had on her own freedom. Having devoted herself early on to the pursuit of an academic career, Ruether was astonished when, just after her marriage, the monsignor of her husband's parish informed the young couple that if Rosemary was not pregnant within a year, he would know that they were "living in sin." Noting that she was fortunate in choosing a husband who did not share these expectations, Ruether says that it nonetheless seemed to her that her culture and religion were "bent on destroying the entire identity and future that I had constructed for myself."

But Ruether soon realized that this struggle was not hers alone. In 1963, having just given birth to her third child, she met in the maternity ward a Mexican American woman named Assumptione, who had just delivered her ninth child and who tearfully described to Ruether and the attending physician the circumstances of her life. "The house was without central heating," Ruether writes. "She had to turn on the stove to keep the place warm and was always in danger of being asphyxiated by the fumes. There was little food. Her husband beat her." When the doctor suggested that the woman should avail herself of some form of birth control, "she could only reply that her priest did not allow her." This incident catalyzed Ruether's critique of sexism in the Church, "not just for my own sake, but for those millions of Assumptiones weeping in maternity beds around the world."

FROM FEMINIST TO WOMANIST

African-American women have developed their own approach to the role of feminism in Christianity, an approach that takes into account their experiences of oppression in a predominantly white culture.

For Delores S. Williams, being in graduate school during the early days of feminist theology provided her with inspiration but also with some questions. "Many of us [African-Americans] were favorably disposed to the kinds of claims that theologians like Rosemary Ruether and Beverly Harrison were making," Williams says, "but we did understand that the women's experiences described in these texts did not fit the facts of our lives. So we were looking for a kind of anthropological understanding of womanhood that took seriously what our cultural context had been about. Then Alice Walker came out with this definition of 'womanist,' and right away we recognized that this was it." Writer Alice Walker coined and defined "womanist" in a kind of preface to her 1974 collection of essays, *In Search of Our Mothers' Gardens.*

The definition is composed of four parts that have since been claimed and explored by various womanist writers and theologians. The passage begins with such definitions as "a black feminist or feminist of color. . . . Responsible. In charge. *Serious,*" and moves on to "A woman who loves other women, sexually and/or nonsexually," and concludes with "womanist is to feminist as purple is to lavender." Walker, like Daly, opened a door that other women could step through. Whereas feminist theologians at that time were working to uncover and analyze the ways in which male bias had precluded them from participation in their religious traditions, the women who would come to call themselves womanists noted that their oppression had been perpetuated by all of white society. A womanist analyzing sexism in religion takes into account not only race, but also such interrelated factors as class, economic background, and culture. Williams and many other African-American women—notably Katie Geneva Cannon, Renita Weems, Toinette Eugene, Cheryl Townsend Gilkes, and Emilie M. Townes—have brought womanist perspectives to the study of theology, ethics, sociology, and literature, as well as the ministry.

A large number of womanist professors are also ordained ministers, who speak to their congregations about such issues as feeding and maintaining the self-image of black women, or of the importance of encouraging a younger generation to stay in school. Both from the pulpit and in print, womanists are concerned with building bridges between the academy and people's everyday lives, with particular attention given to issues of oppression and violence. Williams, for instance, has done some of her most controversial work on the link between biblical images of atonement, such as the crucifixion, and violence in contemporary society, and she is concerned with bringing womanist voices into political issues, such as the welfare debate. Williams believes that by bringing discussion of such issues into church congregations as well as academia, womanists can help reshape public policy along more humane lines.

ORDINATION AND CELEBRATION

The subject of how women worship and the question of whom, if anyone, should be designated to lead, remains an critical area of feminist thought. Currently, of the major denominations in the United States, the Roman Catholic Church is alone in not allowing the ordination of women at all. Many Catholic women have switched their focus from the battle for ordination to the pursuit of new, nonhierarchical models of worship. Meanwhile, in some Protestant denominations, there are arguments over a variety of issues that women have brought to the ministry, including the ordination of openly gay and lesbian priests.

Overall, change seems to come earlier to local chapters than to national associations, partly because in some denominations, church leaders who approve women's ordination resist the idea that women should be able to move into positions of higher authority, such as that of bishop. Additionally, as Episcopal priest Carter Heyward points out, "Any real, deep social change is not going to occur because a majority votes in favor of it. It takes some kind of prophetic voice or prophetic action, and then the people come along, sometimes many years later, and say, 'Oh, yes, that's right.'" Heyward should know: she was one of 11 women ordained by the Episcopal Church in 1974—two years before that church officially sanctioned women's ordination.

Now, according to Heyward, a different question rocks her denomination—whether or not to endorse the ordination of openly gay and lesbian priests. Heyward, who came out as a lesbian in 1979, and has written often on the subject of sexuality and spirituality, sees the linking of those two areas—for so long kept apart by institutionalized Christianity—as a particular gift that gay and lesbian theologians can bring to the Church. "Everybody, regardless of sexual identity, needs to look at issues of what it means to be responsible adults sexually and spiritually. Gays and lesbians are bringing an enormous gift to the Church, simply by raising these questions."

For Roman Catholic women, however, the ordination question has turned into an entirely new approach to worship. As early as the 1950s, Catholic nuns and laywomen were reexamining liturgy and their role in it. For example, at Grailville, a community of Catholic women based in rural Ohio, members were celebrating Mass with gender-inclusive language in the 1950s. Such events, followed by the changes established by the Second Vatican Council in the 1960s—including allowing priests to celebrate the Mass in the language of the congregation rather than in Latin and to face the congregation during the Eucharistic prayer rather than away from it—and by the 1975 formation of the Women's Ordination Conference, seemed to indicate that the ordination of women might come to Catholicism within the century. But while such optimism was extinguished with the selection in 1978 of the conservative John Paul II, Catholic women have pursued a new approach to worship, one that does not require a priest at all.

Based on the work of New Testament scholar Elisabeth Schüssler Fiorenza, whose research maintains that early Christianity was a countercultural movement that smashed hierarchical patterns altogether, many Catholic feminists are active in a movement called "Women-Church," an approach to church as a community in which all Christians are engaged in equal ministry to one another.

WHY THEY STAY

While women have made progress in changing the face of Christianity—both in academia and in the ministry—feminist theologians in the United States are also aware that an increasingly conservative political climate makes their work harder. While some women have followed Mary Daly's path out of the Church, others have been invigorated by the fight itself. For many women, their inspiration to continue the fight for a church free of sexism derives from something closer to home—the influence, perhaps, of a loving mother or a kind aunt who embodied the particular gifts that women can bring to the ministry.

Vienna Cobb Anderson, the first woman rector called to a major urban Episcopal parish, grew up in an old and powerful Episcopal family. Their family Bible dated back to 1607, and her grandfather was the senior warden of the parish where she grew up. Nonetheless, it was her grandmother who had the greatest effect on her future calling. "Her concern for the whole community, and her desire to offer them something real, had a powerful effect on me," the rector says. "In many ways, she is my role model in the priesthood."

As feminist theologians in this country continue to work on issues ranging from ordination to birth control, from liturgy to world hunger, the image of Anderson's grandmother seems a telling one. In their emphasis on bringing the truth of women's experiences to their churches, what these scholars and ministers are offering may be, in a sense, the real bread of daily life, offered with a commitment to the principles of love and justice that are for them the basis of Christianity. Whether or not their church hierarchies ultimately accept this gesture seems to these women beside the point. What concerns them is the wholeness of their vision and the persistence of their calling to equality.   [edited, 2011]

CHAPTER V
Health and Reproductive Justice

Women's subordinate position in society, prevailing attitudes toward women's bodies, and the political context of public policy profoundly shape women's health and their reproductive lives. Although women are the majority of health care consumers and provide a great deal of direct care services, most doctors, researchers, and managers of clinics and hospitals are men. As a result, women's health needs have not been adequately addressed. All too often the criteria used to diagnose particular disorders are based on studies of men, and as a result women's symptoms are easily ignored or misinterpreted. Even when exercise is examined, male behavior is the norm. For example, many measures of physical activity focus on activities that are more common in men's lives, and do not include everyday activities that some women regularly engage in, such as those related to household tasks and child care. The male norm of behavior shapes conceptualizations of health as well as illness.

One particularly grievous example of this pattern has been the slowness of the medical community to focus on the experiences of women with AIDS. During the first 20 years of the AIDS epidemic, men were the majority of people with AIDS. Consequently, the medical criteria for diagnosis reflected men's health needs. In fact, during the first 13 years of the epidemic, the Centers for Disease Control and Prevention (CDC) did not include one female-specific condition related to HIV in its diagnostic criteria for AIDS.[1] As the incidence of HIV/AIDS in women increased, however, it was clear that women with AIDS experienced a high rate of reproductive tract diseases, which is not the case for men with AIDS. Thus, because AIDS is manifested differently in women, women who were HIV-positive and actually had AIDS often did not meet the diagnostic criteria. In 1993, following pressure from feminist health activists, the CDC altered its definition of AIDS to include cervical cancer. More attention is currently being paid to the symptoms that HIV-positive women typically experience.[2]

However, women are still underrepresented in the AIDS clinical trials, which examine the effectiveness of HIV/AIDS drugs. The rates of HIV/AIDS infection are increasing faster among women than among men; and African-American and Latina women are 14.7 and 3.8 times more likely, respectively, to be infected than white females. Therefore, it is imperative that the medical community conduct more systematic research on AIDS in women, and particularly on women of color, who face unique risks.[3]

A woman's health status reflects the interaction between her biology and the social/physical environment in which she lives and works. The medical community, however, tends to focus on the biological mechanisms of disease transmission,

---

[1]Nancy Goldstein and Jennifer L. Manlowe, *The Gender Politics of HIV/AIDS in Women* (New York: New York University Press, 1997).

[2]Centers for Disease Control and Prevention, "Subpopulation Estimates from the HIV Incidence Surveillance System—United States, 2006," *Morbidity and Mortality Weekly Report* 57, no. 36 (September 12, 2008), 985–89.

[3]Lily D. McNair and Cynthia M. Prather, "African-American Women and AIDS: Factors Influencing Risk and Reaction to HIV Disease," *Journal of Black Psychology* 30 (2004), 106–23.

without addressing the sociocultural influences on health. But socioeconomic status is closely related to indices of health.[4] The implications of including socioeconomic status for understanding the health of poor women and women of color are significant. For example, researchers and practitioners see high sodium intake as a risk factor for hypertension but often ignore the social and psychological effects of living in poverty, which can result in stress and poor diet. While heart disease is the number one cause of death for all women, poor women and women of color are at higher risk. The implications for understanding the health status of women are startling, particularly when examining women of color. Socioeconomic status is closely related to indices of health. In particular, racial disparities in the health status of women are associated with differences due to socioeconomic status.[5] For example, while heart disease is the number one cause of death for all women, women of color, those with lower socioeconomic status, and older women are at higher risk.

Differences in breast cancer rates and survival also illustrate the role of race and social class in health outcomes. Although African-American women have a lower incidence of breast cancer than white women, their death rates are higher. The incidence rate for breast cancer is increasing most rapidly among Latinas, and they are least likely to survive five years after being diagnosed. On the other hand, Native American women have low rates of breast cancer yet experience the lowest survival rate when compared with all other groups of women in the United States. These differences in breast cancer incidence and survival are related to factors such as poor access to health care and diagnosis at a later stage of cancer, both of which are associated with poverty, lack of health insurance, discrimination, and language barriers.[6] Thus, it continues to be important to address the social and political context of women's health issues in the United States.

Studies show that for many women, sexism permeates the relationship between doctors and their women patients. Professor Ann Turkel reports, "Women are patronized and treated like little girls. They're even referred to as girls. Male physicians will call female patients by their first names but they themselves are always called 'Doctor.' They don't do that with men."[7] Often women's symptoms are not taken seriously because physicians erroneously believe that they have no physical basis and are just "in their heads." Unfortunately, this frequently results in overreliance on psychiatric medications, such as antianxiety drugs, to "calm women's nerves" when they have somatic complaints that are not understood by their physicians.

---

[4]Nancy Krieger and Elizabeth Fee, "Man-Made Medicine and Women's Health: The Biopolitics of Sex/Gender and Race/Ethnicity," *International Journal of Health Sciences* 24 (1994), 265–83.

[5]Lily D. McNair and George W. Roberts, "African American Women's Health," in *Behavioral Medicine and Women: A Comprehensive Handbook*, ed. Elaine A. Blechman and Kelly D. Brownell (New York: Guilford, 1998), 821–25.

[6]Susan J. Ferguson and Anne Kasper, "Living with Breast Cancer," in *Breast Cancer: Society Shapes an Epidemic* (New York: St. Martins, 2000), 1–22.

[7]Leslie Laurence and Beth Weinhouse, "Outrageous Practices: The Alarming Truth About How Medicine Mistreats Women," in *Clashing Views on Abnormal Psychology*, ed. Susan Nolen-Hoeksema (Guildford, CT: Dushkin/McGraw Hill, 1998), 226.

The women's health movement has been a vital part of the rebirth of feminism. Through books such as *Our Bodies, Ourselves* and organizations such as the National Black Women's Health Imperative, the National Asian Women's Health Organization, and the National Women's Health Network, women have reclaimed their bodies, challenged the priorities of the medical establishment, and made women's experiences and needs visible. A striking example of this movement has been breast cancer grassroots activism, which experienced a resurgence in the 1990s.[8] Angry about the limited range of treatments provided to women with breast cancer, as well as the low levels of funding for breast cancer research, women across the country mobilized to mount a multifaceted campaign. In 1991 the National Breast Cancer Coalition united over 180 advocacy groups to push for more money for research into the causes of breast cancer. By putting political pressure on Congress, attracting media attention, and raising awareness of this crisis in women's health—which has a disproportionately high mortality rate among African-Americans—organized women across the nation have had a dramatic effect on increasing research funding for breast cancer.

Over the past 10 years, however, research on breast cancer continues to be marked by the findings of "provocative yet maddeningly contradictory studies." In her 2005 article "The Breast Exposed," Sandra Steingraber recounts the state of research on the connection between breast cancer and exposure to environmental carcinogens. While the findings of these studies are inconclusive, they do point to the possibility that early exposure to environmental toxins may place a woman at increased risk for breast cancer later in life.[9] More research is needed to better understand the complex interplay between environmental risks and other "lifestyle" factors related to diet and exercise. Breast cancer activists continue to work toward more research on prevention and detection.

As Margaret Sanger said in 1914, "Enforced motherhood is the most complete denial of a woman's right to life and liberty."[10] Women have tried to control their reproductive lives throughout history, sharing contraceptive and abortion information among themselves. In the early twentieth century Margaret Sanger led the crusade to legalize birth control and improve the contraceptive technology available to women. Undeterred by arrests and harassment, she and other crusaders succeeded in establishing birth control clinics throughout the country and legalizing the distribution of birth control information and devices. Although birth control was widely used by the 1960s, some states still restricted its use until 1965 when the Supreme Court declared such restrictions unconstitutional in *Griswold v. Connecticut.*

Unfortunately, although the birth control movement began with a firm commitment to all women's right to determine their own reproductive lives, it later made

---

[8]Maureen Hogan Casamayou, *The Politics of Breast Cancer* (Washington, D.C.: Georgetown University Press, 2001).

[9]Sandra Steingraber, "The Breast Exposed," *Ms.*, Fall 2005.

[10]*The Woman Rebel*, June 1914, 25.

alliances with eugenicists, who saw the goal of family planning as the control of population, particularly of elements they saw as less desirable. Dorothy Roberts, in *Killing the Black Body*, comments that Sanger "promoted two of the most perverse tenets of eugenic thinking: that social problems are caused by reproduction of the socially disadvantaged and that their childbearing should therefore be deterred."[11] This kind of thinking contributed to the sterilization of thousands of women of color throughout the 1960s and 1970s. Believing that women's procreation was the cause of their poverty, doctors in poor communities sterilized women, mostly women of color, without their informed consent, often supported by federal funds. In the 1970s Latina, African-American, and Native American women successfully pressured government agencies to enact and enforce guidelines ensuring that women were fully informed about their choices before being sterilized.

This history of oppression faced by communities of color has informed what is called a reproductive justice framework. Because women of color have also struggled to have and keep their children, a reproductive justice framework recognizes that reproductive freedom is not just about access to abortion. Overall, a reproductive justice framework, as it is articulated by organizations like *SisterSong*, moves beyond questions of individual reproductive choice and considers women's reproductive health and freedoms as shaped by institutional race, class, and sex discrimination. Through this lens, the legal right to abortion is rendered meaningless in the lives of women without access.

For this reason Billye Avery, the founder of the National Black Women's Health Imperative, has urged feminists to speak out on reproductive health, which includes both the right to make decisions about one's reproductive life and access to the services required to make that right a reality. Rickie Solinger has pointed out in *Beggars and Choosers* that choice has come to mean the possession of resources, and suggests instead that we work for reproductive rights—which require no resources. "After a generation of practicing 'choice,'" she argues, "it is clear that all women—regardless of race and class—can achieve the status of full citizen in the United States (and around the world) only when reproductive autonomy is a full blooded right, not merely a consumer's choice."[12] Working for reproductive rights means fighting to maintain the access of young, poor, and rural women to safe, legal abortions, access that has been increasingly restricted in the past 10 years, as well as working for the right of all women to have babies if they so choose.

Since the *Roe v. Wade* decision of 1973, women's right to abortion has been under fierce attack, and the Supreme Court has retreated from its support of all women's right to decide whether to bear a child. The activities of the antiabortion movement have brought the matter of abortion to the center of the political stage

---

[11]Dorothy Roberts, *Killing the Black Body: Race, Reproduction and the Meaning of Liberty* (New York: Vintage, 1997), 81.

[12]Rickie Solinger, *Beggars and Choosers: How the Politics of Choice Shapes Adoption, Abortion and Welfare in the United States* (New York: Hill and Wang, 2001), 224.

in the last three decades. Opponents of abortion have harassed abortion clinics and doctors who perform abortion and pressured legislatures to limit abortions. Between 1993 and 2009 eight staff members of abortion clinics were murdered, and there have been over 1,000 incidents of arson and bombings at abortion clinics.[13]

The advocates of women's reproductive rights have called themselves the "pro-choice" movement, emphasizing a woman's right to choose when she has a child. The antiabortion forces have called themselves "the right to life" movement, arguing that human life exists from the moment of conception. Beneath this argument lie conflicting views of sexuality, women's role in society, and individual liberty. As Kristin Luker has shown in *Abortion and the Politics of Motherhood*, most activists in the "right to life movement" adhere to traditional views about women's role, believe that sexuality should be confined to the family, and also believe that women's most important role is motherhood. Advocates of women's reproductive rights believe that these decisions should be made by individual women and that all women have a right to choose how they live, with whom they have sex, and when and if they have children.[14] The debate about abortion is inextricably entangled with the broader debate about women's position in society.

Although the majority of the American people favor legal abortion, the "right to life" movement has succeeded in severely curtailing women's access to abortion on both federal and state levels. Since the "Hyde Amendment" was passed in 1976, women on welfare have been denied federal funding for abortion, and most states prohibit the use of state funds for abortion as well. As a result of congressional action, women in the U.S. armed services can no longer obtain abortions in overseas military hospitals, women who work for the federal government can no longer choose a health plan that covers abortion, and funding for international family planning clinics has been radically reduced. Between 1995 and 2010, states enacted 644 antichoice measures, including 34 in 2010 alone.[15] Abortion services are becoming harder to obtain since the threat of violence has resulted in fewer doctors to perform these procedures. Of all counties in the United States, 88 percent have no abortion providers; in rural counties, this figure rises to 97 percent.[16]

Certain forms of birth control have also come under attack. In 2003 a scientific advisory committee to the Federal Drug Administration (FDA) recommended that emergency contraception, also known as Plan B, which prevents pregnancy if taken within 72 hours of unprotected sex, be accessible without a prescription, as it is in many other countries. Nevertheless, in 2004 the FDA refused the recommendation of its own advisory committee and withheld approval. Several states however, have passed laws permitting pharmacists to dispense the drug without a prescription.

---

[13]National Abortion Federation website, http//www.prochoice.org/violence.

[14]Kristin Luker, *Abortion and the Politics of Motherhood* (Berkeley: University of California Press, 1984).

[15]National Abortion and Reproductive Rights Action League (NARAL) Pro-Choice America website, http//www.prochoiceamerica.org.

[16]National Abortion Federation website, http//www.prochoice.org.

There has been significant political pressure both on the state and federal level by groups claiming that emergency contraception acts as an abortifacient or that making it available to young women would encourage teenage promiscuity. Ellen Goodman, writing in the *Boston Globe,* asked, "Aren't the youngest precisely those who should be most protected from pregnancy?"[17] Many physicians were distressed that the FDA ignored the recommendation of a panel of scientists. Writing in the *New England Journal of Medicine,* three physicians argued: "Over-the-counter availability of Plan B emergency contraception makes good medical sense. It will improve access to an already approved medication, prevent unwanted pregnancies, reduce the need for induced abortions, and put women in the United States on a par with women in many other countries around the world, to whom such medication is already available."[18]

The most direct challenges to abortion rights have come in the form of recent state legislations, several of them in 2010. Nebraska banned abortions at 20 weeks after conception, with exceptions made only in the case of imminent danger to a woman's life. Oklahoma passed a law that requires women to undergo an ultrasound and listen to a detailed description of the fetus before getting an abortion. The Kentucky senate passed a similar bill and variations in other states were expected to follow. Also in 2010, Utah passed a law criminalizing self-induced abortions.

In 2007 the Supreme Court upheld the federal Partial Birth Abortion Ban Act of 2003, *even though it contained no health exception.* The law also does not include a precise definition of what is banned. This was the first time the federal government passed a law restricting abortion, and the first time the Supreme Court allowed a legal restriction to stand that did not include a health exception. Thirty-one states have also enacted bans on "partial birth" abortion, though some have been specifically struck down by courts and others have not been challenged yet.[19]

As the selections in this section make clear, returning to the days of illegal abortion would not eliminate abortion; women would continue to try to control their reproductive lives and would find illegal and sometimes unsafe ways to do it. Because they would have even less access to safe abortions than they do today, it is poor women who would suffer. Studies suggest that in many areas, the majority of the women who died as a result of unsafe, illegal abortions before *Roe v. Wade* were women of color.[20] The antiabortion forces in the United States, in asserting the right of the state to control the behavior of pregnant women, are not only elevating the fetus to the status of human life, but also relegating the woman to the status of

---

[17]Ellen Goodman, *Boston Globe,* September 15, 2005, boston.com/news/globe/editorial_opinion/oped/articles/2005.

[18]Jeffrey M. Drazen, Michael F. Greene, and Alastair J. J. Wood, editorial, *New England Journal of Medicine* 350 (April 8, 2004).

[19]The Guttmacher Institute, http://www.guttmacher.org/statecenter/spibs/spib_BPBA.pdf.

[20]Loretta J. Ross, "African-American Women and Abortion," in *Abortion Wars,* ed. Rickie Solinger (Berkeley: University of California Press, 1998), 161.

carrier, or as the writer Katha Pollitt has put it, "potting soil."[21] As Ruth Hubbard points out, however, the concern for fetal life, which allegedly motivates the regulation of pregnant women's behavior, appears hypocritical when little is being done to improve the social and economic conditions of poverty that endanger so many babies.

Defending reproductive freedom must be a multifaceted campaign that defends the reproductive rights of all women and addresses the social and economic conditions that affect women's ability to determine their reproductive lives.

---

[21]Katha Pollitt, "The New Assault on Feminism," *The Nation*, March 26, 1990, 418.

The Health Care System

Historically, women have been healers and have supported each other with skill and understanding when experiencing physical pain. The legacy of midwives in this country is one example. Yet beginning in the late eighteenth century, male physicians in the United States led a successful campaign to eliminate midwives. In the mid-nineteenth century, they also mounted an assault against the many women medical practitioners who were trained outside the male-dominated medical establishment.

Some of you may be reading the Fortieth Anniversary Edition of *Our Bodies, Ourselves* (Simon and Schuster, 2011) in your course along with *Women: Images and Realities*. *Our Bodies, Ourselves* was originally written by a group of women who, impelled by the lack of available information about women's bodies, began meeting in 1969 to share information and experiences and publish what became the first of many editions of *Our Bodies, Ourselves*. Women of varied racial and class backgrounds from different parts of the country organized similarly to spawn the now-extensive women's health movement.

We begin this section with an excerpt from the most recent edition of *Our Bodies, Ourselves* that discusses the ways women's health is affected by political, social, and economic factors. In "Mandatory Doctor's Visit," Diane Hugs's description of her sexually abusive doctor reminds us how institutional practices reinforce the continued maltreatment and abuse of women. Her story suggests steps to take if it does occur.

Women of color are particularly vulnerable in the health care system. The increasing rates of HIV/AIDS among women, particularly women of color, highlight the ways in which social, economic, and political conditions contribute to health risks. In "The Feminization of AIDS," Marielena Zuniga cites gender inequality as a major factor in the rising rates of AIDS among women and girls globally. Women of color, however, have not been passive victims of an inadequate health care system, but have mobilized around their needs. The next two articles in this section describe African-American and Native American women's health care activism.

Breast cancer has become a very serious health threat for women. Sabrina McCormick's article "Breast Cancer Activism: Moving Beyond the Mammography Debate," points to the need for increased research on environmental risks such as exposure to toxic chemicals. Citing the increasing rates of breast cancer, only partially explained by genetics and lifestyle factors, McCormick calls for environmental health research and related policies that aim to prevent breast cancer in women.

❧ 85

The Politics of Women's Health Care

OUR BODIES, OURSELVES

Women are healthier where policies promote equal access to health care and education; clean, safe neighborhoods and workplaces; fair and livable incomes; and the power to participate democratically in decisions that affect our lives. In fact, these markers of social and economic equality have significant influence over our health and longevity.[1,2]

We have made remarkable progress in achieving social equality since the 1970s when Our Bodies Ourselves (OBOS) began writing about what we need to know to live healthy lives. Many of the issues that the early women's health movement advocated for have become policy. Abortion is legal, and more research is directed toward women's health issues, in the United States and many other countries. Women are now more often both health care professionals and assertive patients (they accounted for 49 percent of medical school graduates in 2007, compared with 9 percent in 1970).[3]

Although the United States spends more on health care per person than any other country, it has some of the worst indicators among developed countries on infant mortality, maternal health, unintended pregnancy, sexually transmitted infections, and reproductive violence. Americans are more likely to lack coverage for health care and are in worse health by several measures. The Patient Protection and Affordable Care Act (ACA)—the health care reform bill signed into law in 2010—begins to address some of the problems of inadequate coverage and a fragmented health care delivery system. However, the law limits immigrants' rights, and it places new restrictions on our rights to reproductive health care.

DISPARITIES AND WOMEN'S HEALTH

There are differences in health status by race and ethnicity that we cannot explain based on physical or genetic characteristics. These differences appear to be influenced primarily by social and economic inequities and policies, including increased exposures to environmental harm, lack of access to health care and education, and residential segregation. Different treatment by health care providers can also play a role. These preventable differences are referred to as disparities. Some glaring disparities in health based on race or ethnicity include:

- From 1970 to 2007, white women's life expectancy increased from 75.6 to 80.8 years, while it increased for black women only from 68.3 to 76.8 years.
- Compared to whites, the infant death rate among African-Americans is more than double; heart disease death rates are more than 40 percent higher; and the death rate for all cancers is 30 percent higher. African-American women have a higher death rate from breast cancer. The rate of new AIDS cases among black women is 55.7 per 100,000 vs. 3.8 for white women.[4]
- Hispanics living in the United States are almost twice as likely to die from diabetes as are non-Hispanic whites, and to have higher rates of high blood pressure, obesity, and tuberculosis.
- Compared with whites, the infant death rate among American Indians and Alaska Natives is almost double, and the rate of diabetes is more than twice that for whites.
- Health indicators suggest that Asians and Pacific Islanders, on average, are one of the healthiest population groups in the United States, although new cases of hepatitis and tuberculosis are higher in these groups than in whites.

There are also disparities—preventable differences—between women and men. For example, women are more likely than men to experience mental health problems, including depression, anxiety, phobias, and post-traumatic stress disorder. In 2008, 40 percent of American Indian/Alaska Native and women of multiple races reported ever having had depression, followed by 36.5 percent of white women.[5]

U.S. HEALTH CARE SYSTEM

The recent economic downturn has greatly reduced women's access to health care. To understand this, it is helpful to understand the infrastructure of the U.S. health care system.

The best way to be sure there is enough money to afford care for everyone is to cover everyone. Since everyone needs health care at some point, it is most affordable if everyone chips in, including while we're still healthy. Most other countries accomplish this, usually through systems of public and private coverage. They also use the negotiating power of the government to moderate health care prices, such as for drugs and for hospital care. They ensure a large supply of primary care services to balance out expensive specialty care. But the United States has historically done none of these.

The United States spends more than any country on health care, about 16 percent of gross domestic product in 2008. Despite this, it is the only industrialized country where all residents are not automatically covered for health-care services. In 2010, close to 51 million Americans did not have health coverage for some time during the year.[6] In 2007, 45 percent of women, compared to 39 percent of men, were underinsured or uninsured for a time in the past year.[7] Even women with health insurance report problems affording health care. Unaffordable cost-sharing requirements and annual or lifetime limits on covered services have a disproportionate impact on women. Over half (52 percent) of working-age women report problems accessing health care because of costs, compared to 39 percent of men.[8]

Public programs guarantee coverage for some people. The federal Medicare program covers most people age 65 and older and people with certain disabilities, and the federal/state Medicaid program covers some of the very poor and disabled. The two public health services, which both pay for and provide care, are the Indian Health Service and the Veterans Affairs system (VA). Most people under age 65 who have private health insurance receive it through an employer. But there is no law requiring employers to provide coverage.

Women are less likely than men to have jobs that offer employment-based private health insurance. This means, for example, that middle-age women who are single, divorced, or widowed, and not yet old enough for Medicare, are often uninsured. Women are more likely to be covered by Medicaid than men, due to rules on eligibility during pregnancy, but the coverage frequently does not continue after the birth of the child. And in states where Medicaid payments are low, many providers might not accept Medicaid patients.

The spiraling cost of health care is attributable in part to administrative costs, which account for 25 percent of private insurance costs, compared with 3 percent in the federal Medicare program. Public systems like Medicare are much more efficient because they cover everyone over age 65, even though older people generally need more health care as they age. And because they are public, they do not make profits. In addition, drug companies, hospitals, and other providers increase charges annually.[9] Other countries use the power of the government to negotiate with these providers and hold down prices. In the United States, private insurance companies haven't done the job.

An Economic Crisis Becomes a Health Care Crisis

With the economy in decline, funding for many safety-net programs has been cut. And as unemployment insurance benefits run out, many of the unemployed have been unable to keep up health insurance payments on their own. The situation is often worst for those workers who never had employer-based care to begin with. They often cannot even find an insurance plan that will take them, especially if plans detect preexisting conditions, which can include pregnancy and past medical treatment for domestic violence. Poverty and poor health go hand in hand: An employment crisis becomes a health care crisis, while a health care crisis can drive a family into poverty.

People of color and people with low incomes are the least likely to have stable health insurance coverage. Black women age 18 to 64 are nearly twice as likely to be uninsured as white women, while

Hispanic women are almost three times as likely not to have insurance.[10] More than a third of low-income women age 18 to 64 lack health insurance, compared to 18 percent of women overall.

Insurance access—or lack thereof—has a very real impact on health and quality of life. Low-income women are twice as likely as higher-income women to report problems getting health care, such as not filling a prescription, not seeing a specialist when needed, or skipping a recommended medical test, treatment, or follow-up visit.[11] Other women who are more likely to lack health insurance include women who are divorced, who work in service jobs such as waitressing, who work part-time or as temps, or who provide full-time care for children, aging parents, or ill family members.

HEALTH CARE REFORM AND THE POLITICS OF WOMEN'S HEALTH

In March 2010, President Obama signed the ACA into law. The Act aims to expand health care coverage to 32 million uninsured Americans, mostly those who are locked out of the private insurance market because they are not part of a large group, already have a health condition, or can't afford coverage. They will be eligible either for the public Medicaid program or for new, private insurance options.

EXPANSION OF COVERAGE

Three provisions on coverage went into effect immediately in 2010: Small employers can get tax credits for providing insurance to their employees; young adults can remain covered on their parents' plans until age 26 if they are not covered through their own jobs; and new, temporary "high-risk pool" plans, called preexisting condition insurance plans (PCIPs), became available for people who have been uninsured for at least six months due to a preexisting condition (these plans will close when the Health Insurance Exchanges open in 2014). Other provisions include:

• Insurance exchanges for individuals and small employers: Beginning in 2014, new state-run health insurance exchanges will be available to individuals and employees of small businesses.

• Medicaid and the Children's Health Insurance Program: The Act maintains current funding levels for the Children's Health Insurance Program (CHIP) through fiscal year 2015. It also expands eligibility for Medicaid to include everyone with incomes below 133 percent of the federal poverty level (FPL) and increases assistance to states to help cover the costs of adding people under Medicaid, as of 2014. The majority of adult beneficiaries of Medicaid (69 percent) are female.

Consumer Protections

• Preexisting conditions: The Act prohibits insurance companies from denying coverage for people with preexisting conditions. The prohibition applied immediately for children; adults will be protected starting in 2014.

• Elimination of gender rating: Many individual and small-group insurance plans charge women more for insurance coverage than men of the same age and health status. The Act eliminates this practice for plans offered through the exchanges.[12]

Improvements to Quality and Lower Costs

• Free preventive care: The Act requires new private plans and Medicare to cover preventive services with no co-payments or deductibles. This dramatically expands women's access to screening for cervical and breast cancer and other forms of preventive reproductive and sexual health care.

• Increased funding for community health centers and primary health care: The Act increases funding by $11 billion over five years to these partly publicly supported neighborhood clinics in underserved areas, known to offer high-quality primary care and often dental and other services.

• Time for mothers to express breast milk: The Act amended the Fair Labor Standards Act (FLSA), giving breastfeeding mothers in all 50 states the right to pump at work.

Where the Act Falls Short

The law is under attack from the U.S. Chamber of Commerce and parts of the insurance industry that oppose expanding population-wide benefits and oppose almost all forms of government involvement and oversight. Congress is proposing to reverse or at least chip away at elements of the reform.

In addition, there are concerns about whether the combination of regulations and delivery system reforms will effectively control costs. The law did not adopt popular proposals to offer a public option through the insurance exchanges. OBOS has long supported proposals for publicly financed systems such as HR-3000, sponsored by U.S. Rep. Barbara Lee (D-Calif.), which would provide affordable care to every resident, and could effectively use the public sector's bargaining power to control health care prices.

Two explicit exclusions are additionally significant for women: the exclusion of some immigrants, and restrictions on abortion and contraceptives.

• Coverage for immigrant women: Immigrant women, a highly vulnerable population, will continue to face high barriers to accessing basic health care. The Act bars undocumented immigrants from receiving Medicaid, or from enrolling in health insurance exchanges. This is a human rights violation and bad public health policy. About half of the nation's 12 million immigrants would be excluded. The bill also imposes a five-year waiting period on permanent, legal residents before they are eligible for assistance such as Medicaid or subsidies for purchasing insurance through the exchange.

• Threats to abortion and contraception care: The law took several significant swipes at reproductive health care. Advocates are exploring options to ameliorate the impact of each provision, while opponents seek to tighten these limits. The main provisions place limits on access to abortion and prescription contraceptive services.

Due to the combination of well-funded and sometimes violent opposition, and a diffuse political defense, the issue of abortion has become stigmatized over the past several decades. Since the 1980s, conservatives focused their efforts on a crusade to limit and ultimately strip women of their rights to sexual and reproductive health services both at home and abroad.

The Affordable Care Act includes a series of explicit limits on coverage for abortion and contraception:

• Limits on federal funding for abortions through the exchanges: The Act ensures that women who receive federal subsidies to help pay for the premium cannot use federal funds for an abortion. This provision was underscored by President Obama when he signed an executive order on March 24, 2010, after the Act was passed, emphasizing that no federal dollars would be used to pay for abortion through the newly created health insurance exchanges or through community health centers, except in the case of rape, incest, or a threat to the life of the mother.

• Limits on coverage for abortion through new temporary health insurance programs, known as PCIPs.

• Prescription contraceptives are not covered under preventive health services.

The Future of Health Care Reform

As women's health advocates have noted, the ACA is not a single-payer system and does not even include a public option. However, it opens the door to states that seek to experiment with single-payer plans; broadens policy space to move further toward universal coverage; and takes a few steps in the right direction by expanding public sector programs such as Medicaid and aiming to reduce administrative waste.[13] OBOS endorses single-payer health care for comprehensive health care reform. Single-payer models build on systems like Medicare. They are publicly financed, instead of going through private insurance plans, and cover everyone. One single payer—the government—replaces the many private insurance plans that now waste billions on administration. Even more importantly, it gives the government the authority to negotiate prices with drug companies, hospitals, and other health care providers, the key to controlling costs while protecting care.

OBOS has supported single-payer proposals since they were first introduced in Congress in the 1970s, including HR-3000, sponsored by

Rep. Barbara Lee (D-Calif). It remains the only plan that explicitly includes women's reproductive health services, including abortion.

We believe these plans would best address women's needs and improve our health. Coverage would be completely independent from employment and from marriage. These plans would better allocate resources and reduce payment incentives that have been obstacles to investing in training more primary care professionals, and that lead to overuse and misuse of drugs and medical procedures.

Other specific advantages of a single-payer system include:

• It would encourage better care for chronic illnesses. Women use chronic care services far more than men. Because caring for people with chronic disease now accounts for more than 75 percent of all health care spending, women will benefit substantially from more efficient and effective ways to deal with severe chronic illnesses.

• It would eliminate substandard tiers of care. Women who are unemployed and have functional limitations that exclude them from the private health insurance market would receive health and medical care on a par with women in general.

• It would address the cost issues that send women into debt and bankruptcy. Medical debt is an enormous concern for many women. A 2009 Commonwealth Fund study found that 45 percent of women accrued medical debt or reported problems with medical bills in 2007 compared to 36 percent of men.[14]

• It would reduce the incidence of medical malpractice. Assuring people they would not have to worry about paying for medical care whenever they experienced bad medical outcomes would relieve the pressure on medical malpractice premiums.

• A single-payer system would enhance the working environment for health care professionals. There would be less need to spend hours on pointless documentation in order to justify billing for services.

For more information, visit ourbodiesourselves .org/singlepayer.

EMERGING ISSUES: BIOPOLITICS, WOMEN'S HEALTH, AND SOCIAL JUSTICE

Advocates for women's health are among the growing number of civil society leaders, scholars, and policy experts who are concerned about the societal implications of new reproductive and genetic technologies and practices being brought to market. While these technologies offer significant benefits, women's health advocates want to ensure that their introduction will be grounded in values of social justice, human rights, ecological integrity, and the common good.

Embryonic Stem Cell Research

Embryonic stem cell research uses embryos initially produced in fertility clinics to help women become pregnant. So long as those embryos are donated with informed consent, most women's health advocates have no objections. Since 1998, some scientists, biotechnology companies, and research advocates have made dramatic claims about the medical potential of human embryonic stem cells, promising treatments and cures for a wide range of chronic, degenerative, and acute diseases—including diabetes, Parkinson's disease, cancer, and Alzheimer's disease. But embryonic stem cell research has also generated heated controversy. The critical voices say that all embryonic stem cell work is immoral because it uses and then destroys human embryos for the sole purpose of harvesting stem cells. Yet a number of reproductive rights advocates (including OBOS) have concerns, too—specifically about a type of stem cell research known as research cloning.

Objections to Research Cloning

The crucial distinction between embryonic stem cell research and research cloning is often blurred in the public debate. Research cloning—also called somatic cell nuclear transfer, embryo cloning, and therapeutic cloning—requires that young women undergo invasive and risky egg extraction procedures solely for the purpose of research. Unlike dozens of countries around the world, the United States has not yet established a federal prohibition on reproductive cloning, making it more likely that unethical researchers would use cloned embryos to attempt to produce a cloned baby. Some reproductive rights advocates have hesitated to speak out against research cloning for fear their concerns will be used by antiabortion activists to elevate the legal and moral status of embryos in efforts to deny access to abortion.

Concerns About Egg Extraction

Many feminists and social justice activists have further concerns about research cloning as it requires egg extraction. Although women already undergo these procedures in fertility clinics, there is not yet sufficient data on health risks to make true informed consent possible.

Women providing eggs for other people's fertility treatments generally receive reimbursements that range from $5,000 to $10,000, and some ads on college campuses have offered as much as $50,000 to $100,000 for eggs from women with desired traits (so-called Ivy League eggs). But it is unlikely that many women would provide eggs for research without reimbursement, and economically disadvantaged and young women would be most vulnerable to such incentives. Whether eggs are for research or helping others to have a baby, all women have the right to be informed about the potential risks. For this reason, advocacy groups are now calling for a national registry that would track the long-term effects of these procedures on egg donors.

Assisted Reproductive Technologies and Fertility Tourism

As assisted reproduction technologies have mushroomed into a multibillion-dollar fertility industry, ethical and social challenges multiply. A small but vocal group of scientists and others envision a future in which parents routinely choose their offspring's sex, physical traits, and even intelligence, prospects that would alter family and social relationships in disturbing ways. And as people seek to avoid policies in one country by traveling to another country to seek the services of a gestational or surrogate mother, or to obtain embryos or donated eggs not available in their own countries, a rapidly growing phenomenon of cross-border reproductive tourism—also called fertility tourism—has magnified these problems.

India has become the leading go-to source of such services. Women with few other economic options are becoming gestational mothers with little assurance that contracts specifying particular payments will be honored, and with little protection for their own well-being and autonomy. These women are sometimes required to leave their own children to live in dormitories attached to fertility clinics for some or all of their pregnancies, and to deliver by C-section even when that is not medically indicated.

Patenting of Human Genes and Women's Health: Who Owns Our Genes?

Since 1980 the U.S. Patent and Trade Office (USPTO) has issued patents on the genes of living organisms, despite the widespread objection that genes are products of nature and not human-made inventions. The controversy has intensified with the patenting of human genes in the early 1990s. Breast Cancer Action and OBOS—the only two women's health groups that are co-plaintiffs—believe that when one company controls all the testing, less information and resources are available to both patients and researchers. Some doctors and researchers involved with the lawsuit contend that this monopoly has long held up not only competing, cheaper tests but also important gene-based research.

Genetic Modification of Future Generations

Inheritable genetic modification (IGM, also called germline engineering) means changing the genes passed on to future generations through in vitro fertilization (IVF). The modified genes would appear not only in the person who developed from that gamete or embryo, but also in all succeeding generations. Genetically modified plants and animals are now relatively common, but IGM has not been tried in humans. Disability rights advocates point out that even embryo selection exerts pressures on women to produce the "perfect baby," and can create new forms of discrimination and prejudice based on genetics.

Some advocates of IGM (and of reproductive cloning and sex selection) are attempting to appropriate the language of the reproductive rights

The Millennium Development Goals: A Promise to the World's Women

Some of the major health issues confronting women around the world are high maternal mortality rates, gender-based violence leading to unwanted pregnancies, sexually transmitted diseases and deaths, prevalence of preventable and treatable cancers, and HIV/ AIDS. In 2000, 189 countries agreed to a set of eight Millennium Development Goals (MDGs) aimed at reducing poverty and hunger and improving health, gender equity, and environmental sustainability. The MDGs are an important global milestone, not only because of their near universal buy-in by all countries, but also because they are evidence-based and provide specific targets to be reached within a 15-year time frame. Gender equality and the empowerment of women are the focus of goal 3 of the MDG, but activists recognize that this goal is also central to the attainment of other goals, especially those focused on women's health. Women share most of the care burden, and their lack of political and social power prevents them from being equal partners in policy-making processes or taking charge of their own health care needs. As part of the MDG objectives, a series of actions were recommended for governments that encouraged women's empowerment, participation in health care policies and gender sensitivity in health research. In 2005, in an evaluation of the progress made toward the goals of the MDGs, it was recognized that because the majority of disease and mortality among women globally stems from a simple lack of access to reproductive health care, sexual and reproductive rights are key to reaching the other goals. In 2007, after pushing the U.S. government—a major donor to world health programs—a new target was added, goal 5b. Goal 5b aims to achieve universal access to reproductive health care, including family planning, by 2015. The USA's initial resistance to this goal reflects how abortion politics inside the USA has tremendous implications for women's health around the world.   [2011]

Sources: Adapted from "Factsheet by Action for Global Health," *actionforglobalhealth.eu/content/.../ Factsheet%203%20-%20Gender.pdf;* E. Denny, "The Millennium Development Goals: Women's Health 10 Years On," Diversity in Health and Care, Volume 8, Number 1, March 2011: pp. 5–7(3), http:// www.ingentaconnect.com/content/rmp/dhc; L. Brown, "Smart Family Planning Improves Women's Health and Cuts Poverty," April 24, 2011. Retrieved from http://populationissuesnetwork.blogspot. com/2011/04/smart-family-planning-improves-womens_1403.html.

movement, claiming that these high-tech procedures are extensions of individual privacy rights. This claim blurs the difference between the right for which women have fought for so many years— the right to terminate an unwanted or unsustainable pregnancy—and a very different thing: the right of individuals (parents) to manipulate the biological traits of a future child. Women's health advocates need to challenge this co-optation of language in the public debate on biotechnology issues.

Given the far-reaching consequences of these technologies, we owe it to ourselves, our children, and future generations to think carefully about which ones we can responsibly and beneficially use as a society. The key question is where and how we would draw the line. OBOS believes that the United States should join the emerging international consensus and pass laws against human reproductive cloning and inheritable genetic modification.   [edited, 2011]

NOTES

1. *Macroeconomics and Health: Investing in Health for Economic Development.* Report of the Commission on Macroeconomics and Health, Geneva, World Health Organization, 2001.

2. PBS, *Unnatural Causes: Is Inequality Making Us Sick?* California Newsreel, 2008. See unnaturalcauses.org.

3. "Women in U.S. Academic Medicine Statistics and Medical School Benchmarking, 2007–2008," Association of American Medical Colleges, 2009, https://www.aamc.org/download/53434/data/wimstats_2008.pdf.

4. CDC, "Subpopulation Estimates from the HIV Incidence Surveillance System—United States, 2006," *Morbidity and Mortality Weekly Report* 57, no. 36 (2008): 985–89.

5. U.S. Department of Health and Human Services, *Women's Health USA 2010* (2010), http://mchb.hrsa.gov/whusa10/.

6. "Census Bureau: Recession Fuels Record Number of Uninsured Americans," *Kaiser Health News*, September 17, 2010, http://smtp01.kaiserhealthnews.org/t/13983/384882/13463/0/.

7. Sheila D. Rustgi, Michelle M. Doty, and Sara R. Collins, "Women at Risk: Why Many Women Are Forgoing Needed Health Care," The Commonwealth Fund (2009), http://www.commonwealthfund.org/Content/Publications/Issue-Briefs/2009/May/Women-at-Risk.aspx.

8. Ibid.

9. National Center for Health Statistics, "Highlights," *Health, United States, 2009*, http://www.cdc.gov/nchs/data/hus/hus09.pdf#highlights.

10. U.S. Census Bureau, Current Population Survey, "Annual Social and Economic Supplement," March 2008, http://www.census.gov/hhes/www/cpstc/cps_table_creator.html.

11. Rustgi, Doty, and Collins, "Women at Risk."

12. National Women's Law Center, "Still Nowhere to Turn: Insurance Companies Treat Women Like a Pre-Existing Condition," 2009, http://www.nwlc.org/our-resources/reports_toolkits/nowhere-to-turn.

13. Ellen R. Shaffer and Judy Norsigan, "A Practical Guide Forward for Progressives on Healthcare," *Salon* (May 22, 2010), http://www.salon.com/news/opinion/feature/2010/05/22/progressives_practical_healthcare_guide.

14. Rustgi, Doty, and Collins, "Women at Risk."

🌿 86

Mandatory Doctor's Visit

DIANA HUGS

Being a disabled woman with a progressive disability requires that I document some of that disability through Social Security. Knowing that my primary physician documented what she saw on my visits, it surprised me a little when Social Security sent me a letter stating that I must see their doctor or I might no longer be considered disabled. This was funny because the small progression of my disability was not even the reason I was on Social Security and could no longer work. But they set up an appointment for me with a doctor I had never heard of and assigned the day and time of this appointment, and they stipulated that I had to go to that appointment.

As usual I took along a friend to the doctor's office; I've found it useful to have someone with me as a patient advocate and to help me remember what I wanted to ask. The doctor's office was in an old building with many rooms in his suite. When we got there it was unusually quiet for an office. We checked around and could not find anyone there. So we picked out what we thought might be the waiting room and waited for the doctor to show up.

The exam was routine and did not require that I remove my clothing. During the exam the doctor started by stroking my thigh as he looked over my chart sent by Social Security. He then asked me about my level of sensation since I am a paraplegic and cannot feel below the point of my paralysis. I held out my hands in front of me indicating that my sensation ended about the same level as my breasts. The doctor stroked my breast and asked me if I could feel that. Since he was below where I can feel I told him no, biting my lip so I wouldn't scream at him. Then he moved up to my level of sensation and touched my breast again with a stroking motion. I said, "Yes I can feel that. But is this necessary?" The reason I wondered was because he was checking neurological data and he was not a neurologist. He answered. "Actually it isn't, I was just curious."

During the exam he rubbed my shoulders and even kissed me; in fact he tried to kiss me on the lips but I turned away. There was no safe way I could think of to stop him; after all, his report would affect my Social Security status, and that is all the income I have in the world. Even though he could not deny I was disabled, he could have messed with my case to stop my checks at least temporarily. This was a psychological weapon which I felt was held over me the entire time I was there. So I kept my mouth shut and held myself back from hitting him during the exam.

As soon as I made it out of the office I burst into tears. My friend felt terrible for not having stood up for me but she was afraid of making more trouble for me. I was numb as I waited for the accessible van to pick me up and drive me home. Once inside the van I broke into tears again and told the driver what had happened. She was furious and told me to call the Center for Independent Living to get some advice. That was very helpful because at that time I could barely think at all.

Upon returning home I called the Center and the first person I talked to told me to call the rape crisis line. At first I was surprised at this suggestion; I had not been raped, just molested. But then I remembered that the local rape crisis center did more than counsel women who had been raped. They also gave information about what you can do or who you can contact in situations like this. So I called the crisis line and talked to one of their counselors. She told me to file a complaint with the police, that this was a crime and I should prosecute. It took me by surprise to have my feelings validated so strongly. Keeping the momentum up I called the police immediately after speaking with the counselor. During the hour and a half that it took before the officer arrived I went through a tornado of feelings. Was I taking this all too seriously? Would the officer think I was paranoid to be making such a charge? Were my perceptions accurate or was I blowing this out of proportion?

While the officer was not the most understanding or sensitive person, he did take what I was saying seriously. He wrote out the complaint and told me they would be back in touch with me for more information and that the medical ethics board would be notified. A few days later my friend was asked to meet with the police and an investigator from the Board of Medical Quality Assurance. She told me the investigator was a really nice guy who seemed seriously interested in seeing this case prosecuted. The next day the investigator came by to take my statement. He was disgusted by the story and hoped they would be able to do something to stop this doctor. It made me feel stronger to be taken so seriously and the investigator thanked me for filing the charges. He had two similar cases with physicians he was working on but it had taken the women years to come forward, making it a lot more difficult to prosecute. Because I had reported the

event so quickly, there was a better chance of the investigator being able to prosecute. He first contacted Social Security to obtain a list of others who had been sent to this particular doctor. He needed to know if there were other women who had been similarly mistreated but who had not had the courage to report it. Although he went through every channel including the police, Social Security would not release any information. They claimed it would violate rights to privacy of Social Security recipients. He even asked if they would have their own people contact other patients they had sent to this doctor to see if anyone else had been abused, but they simply refused his requests. I was so angry— it was a lame excuse for Social Security to say it was a violation of our rights to privacy when they were the ones that made me (and how many other women) go to see this doctor.

Finally the investigator came up with a plan that Social Security would go along with. An undercover policewoman was to be sent in to see the doctor as if she were a disabled woman being sent in by Social Security. She sat in a wheelchair and had all the same forms as I had from Social Security. The exam went the same, the doctor did almost exactly the same things to her. When I learned of this, I realized this must be routine for him to mistreat and abuse Social Security or disabled patients during the exam. And although the undercover policewoman felt horrible and powerless when he kissed her and fondled her breasts, she wrote in her report that she wasn't sure if his actions were criminal. What I think she and the system did not understand was that he had power over my life through what he could do to my Social Security payments. I know it wasn't a weapon he could hold over the undercover policewoman, but I wished she had understood that he had no way of stopping her income. She could have fought back without risking her livelihood.

The district attorney did not see grounds to prosecute. This same D.A. was known for not prosecuting sex-related crimes; in fact later that year he was required by the City Council to prosecute over 70 rape cases he had passed by. Knowing that he did not take sex crimes very seriously, I checked to see if there was any other way to get this into court. But the sad fact is that the D.A. has the final call on whether or not to prosecute a case, and nothing I could do or say could change that fact. My next hope was the Board of Medical Quality Assurance. They brought him up before the discipline board and asked him to explain himself. The doctor admitted to everything that had happened; he just didn't think there was anything wrong with it. The Board warned him to keep his hands to himself and left it at that. Even though I wrote the Board an impassioned plea to reconsider on the grounds that his position of working for Social Security was a weapon against disabled women, they would not hear me.

This was more than I could take. On one hand I was told that I was right, that he had no right to fondle and kiss me, that in fact it was criminal; on the other hand no one would do anything to stop him from doing it to every woman he came into contact with. It really bothered me that he was not only going to get away with what he had done, but there was also no way for my testimony to keep other women safe. I told Social Security that his report on me was invalid since I was a victim, not a client; they told me they didn't want to hear about my personal problems. No way could I make them stop sending people to this doctor. It was driving me crazy to feel so helpless.

Having exhausted all means of legal prosecution, I decided to take him into civil court. There was a lawyer, Leslie Levy, with an outstanding reputation, so I decided to call her. She took the case even though I didn't have a dime and went right to work on it. The malpractice insurance company jumped into defending him even though they said they were in no way liable, because there is an exclusion for the insurance companies for any act that may be deemed criminal rather than a malpractice claim. So we had to battle these high-priced lawyers even though their company assumed no responsibility. There were two years of foot dragging and legal manipulation which my lawyer had to fight while the doctor continued to practice. He said he would settle for $500. I rejected this because I could see no indication that he had the slightest clue that he had done something wrong.

Two years after filing this case and having every legal trick in the book thrown at us, we finally got around to doing court depositions. I was unable to sit upright at the time so not only was I unable to go to his deposition, I had to give mine from my bed. Instead of having all these strangers in my bedroom I used the bed in the living room. That was a very good thing because the doctor decided to show up and listen to my statement. A deposition requires the presence of lawyers from both sides along with a court reporter, and that felt like a huge invasion in itself. The deposition lasted about three hours and I was very lucky to have such a brilliant lawyer on my side. She did not let them get away with asking anything that was not relevant. She jumped up and down a lot, screaming at the other lawyer to back off. Since Leslie was familiar with abusive lawyers and litigants, she protected me from unnecessary harassment and abuse, for which I am eternally grateful to her.

That deposition did the job. The doctor seemed to realize I had been hurt. For the first time he understood that he had done damage, though he was not willing to pay for it. So onwards toward court we went. It was finished four months later and while I cannot divulge the outcome, I can say that the judge was understanding and resolved the case so I didn't have to go before a whole courtroom with it. The terms of the settlement prohibit me from saying anything.

I am still left with feelings of rage and sadness about what he did to me and how the system let him get away with it. If it had not been for the interest of Leslie Levy I would have been left out in the cold. There are not enough lawyers like her.

The legal system is still predominately male and does not take women seriously. It is not a lucrative business for lawyers to take on such cases since there's not that much money in these cases even if you get the court system to see the damage done. For me that was the hardest part, being asked, "Describe how this hurt you" in front of strangers who were not sensitive to my feelings. How to explain what having this uncaring authority figure run his hands all over me did to me, how he made me feel like a whore.

I used to trust doctors, but not anymore. I lost trust not only in the system which ignored my pain, but also I lost trust in people in general. It took over four years for me to let a stranger touch me at all. I had to explain to the doctor's lawyer that this lack of trust, not wanting to be touched, was damage in itself. He tried to downplay it by asking me if I would ever let anyone touch me again. I told him I had every intention of healing from this and hoped to be able to regain my trust. I fought hard. I fought long. It was worth the effort. The doctor knows he was wrong now. I just wish I had been able to stop him from continuing to practice. But I did everything I could and I can live with that.

What I would like to say to other women, disabled or not, is that a doctor does not have the right to touch you in any inappropriate way. We all have the right to fight back. More women need to fight the doctors who don't know the limits of conduct. If you are not sure whether your doctor went too far, but you do not feel good about what happened, follow it through. Contact the Board of Medical Quality Assurance, rape crisis centers and please, if you think there is even a possibility of a criminal case, call the police. The more women who call doctors on misconduct, the fewer doctors will continue to do harm to their women patients. If you cannot do this for yourself, please consider doing it for the next woman. Even though your doctor may not have taken you seriously, having to answer to all the different authorities will make him think twice before he treats another patient the same way again.   [1992]

 87

The Feminization of AIDS

MARIELENA ZUNIGA

She is from Mexico. Poverty forces her into domestic labor at age 13. One night she is raped by her employer's drug-addicted son. But she is blamed for the attack and fired. Her family will not take her back and she is forced into commercial sex work. Today, at 14, she is HIV-positive.

She is from India. She is 18 years old when she is raped by an older man. Forced to marry him, she lives with his family as is the custom in her country. She soon discovers he is HIV-positive and that he has infected her. But her husband's family blames her, not him. He dies. They throw her out of the house. With no money, job, or education, she is forced to survive in any way she can.

She is from Ethiopia. Drought and famine hit her rural village and her husband leaves to find work in one of the larger cities. He is not monogamous. During his visits home, he brings HIV with him. He dies. A widow after one year of marriage, she is in denial that she might be infected. She delays treatment. She, too, dies.

These women, and countless others like them, are the face of AIDS in today's world.

Far from the "gay white men's disease of the 1980s," HIV/AIDS is infecting and affecting women more than ever before. Today AIDS kills 2 million people per year and is the leading cause of death of women of reproductive age. As the epidemic enters its fourth decade, women account for almost half of the 31.3 million HIV-positive adults in the world, but the proportion of women living with HIV is increasing.

Nearly 60 percent of adults living with HIV in sub-Saharan Africa are women, while in the Caribbean, HIV prevalence rates among women have increased from 46 percent in 2001 to 53 percent in 2008, making it the second most affected region after sub-Saharan African.

In 2008, more than 70 percent of people living with HIV/AIDS resided in four of the largest countries in Latin America—Argentina, Brazil, Colombia, and Mexico. The proportion of women living with HIV/AIDS in this region is nearly one-third (30 percent) of adults (aged 15 and older), with increasing numbers of women becoming infected in several countries, including Argentina, Brazil, Peru, and Uruguay.

Brazil alone is home to more than 40 percent of the region's HIV/AIDS population (730,000 people). And even though Brazil has been credited with developing a successful and internationally known program to fight HIV/AIDS, it still leaves much to be desired for women. In that country,

HIV infection rates among women increased by 44 percent between 1996 and 2005.

In the United States, 27 percent of those living with HIV/AIDS are women. But African-American women are becoming infected in far greater numbers than any other racial or ethnic group, with HIV/AIDS the third leading cause of death for African-American women ages 25 to 34.

What's fueling the "feminization of AIDS"? Gender inequality, say experts. A host of cultural, legal, and economic factors limit the control women have over their lives, their sexual relationships, and the power to protect themselves from infection. Sadly, the majority of women are being infected by their husbands, making marriage one of the most dangerous places for women today.

Because relationships between men and women are often based on power, women have a hard time saying no to unwanted or unsafe sex, says Stephanie Urdang, United Nations Development Fund for Women (UNIFEM) advisor on Gender and HIV/AIDS (www.unifem.org). "From teens in America to teens in Africa, to women throughout different age groups . . . even when women know their partners have had sex with others and are in a high-risk category, women can't assert or protect themselves," she says.

A married woman in Zaire told researchers, "If you have AIDS, society rejects you. When you die you will not be missed, because you have died of a shameful disease. They will say that this woman has strayed. They will not see that maybe she has remained faithful while her husband has strayed."

AIDS, GENDER, AND POVERTY

Although many factors make women vulnerable to HIV/AIDS, poverty is a driving engine. And the mix of poverty, gender, and AIDS is lethal. In many cultures women depend on their husbands for economic security or live with their husbands' families. When women do not have independent income, they are often forced to stay in abusive relationships.

"If the people who are the supporting actors in your life—the labor resources, your social world—are all tied into your husband's family, you don't have that kind of option to leave," says Corinne Whitaker, senior program officer for the Africa program of the IWHC.

Without bargaining power, women can't talk about whether they want sex, when they want sex, or how they want to have sex, says Antigone Hodgins, North American representative of the International Community of Women Living with HIV/AIDS (www.icw.org). "All the power is with the husband, and if they [the women] bring up a condom, they're at risk for violence. They get blamed," she says.

Blame, violence, and discrimination—all are the cost for speaking up. A much-publicized story was that of Gugu Diamini, a young woman from Durban, South Africa, who was murdered by her neighbors after publicly disclosing her HIV status. And in Kenya, a group of HIV-positive women admitted hiding the news from their partners because they were afraid of being beaten or abandoned.

If a woman is abandoned, or is denied the right to own or inherit land or property, she spirals into destitution. This has enormous consequences, says Dr. Geeta Rao Gupta, president of the International Center for Research on Women (ICRW), a Washington, D.C.–based nonprofit working to improve the lives of women in poverty and advance their equality and human rights (www.icrw.org). "If a woman is left with no access to economic resources, employment or income, she is more likely to sell sex for money," Dr. Rao Gupta says.

Sex work is often the only option for a woman who must feed her children. "Toward the end of the month, if there is no money to buy food [for her family], a woman will be involved in what is called 'transactional sex work' or 'survival sex work,'" says Urdang of UNIFEM.

At a World AIDS briefing, a woman from Manila, the Philippines, summed up the dilemma of "survival sex" faced by so many women like herself. "AIDS might make me sick one day," she says. "But if I don't work my family would not eat and we would all be sick and die anyway."

YOUNG GIRLS AT HIGHER RISK

In addition to poverty, women also must fight cultural customs that put them at risk. In many villages in Africa, some men are known as "cleansers," paid to have sexual relations with women after their husbands have died to dispel what villagers believe to be evil spirits.

Says Whitaker, "The issues around sex cleansing are decisions not being made by a woman herself. It's not a path she would choose . . . and part of the reason with HIV/AIDS we have to address the broader issues of women's rights and status."

In other parts of Africa, men believe that if they have sexual relations with a virgin they will be cured of AIDS. So infected men actively seek out young girls who are especially at risk. Today, the majority of new infections are among adolescent women, who have the least power and fewer rights and who often "do not have access to information and services to protect themselves," says Whitaker.

Girls are vulnerable for a variety of reasons. For one, older men who have had multiple partners prefer sex with teenage girls. These girls are especially vulnerable because the walls of their vaginas are more prone to tearing, which provides an entry point for the virus. Young girls also exchange sex for money to pay for school, and because they lack assertiveness skills, they don't negotiate safe sex.

In South Asia, as in many other patriarchal societies, when girls marry they have little knowledge of sexuality, HIV, or condoms. Their first task is to produce a son, so even if they had access to condoms, using them would be impossible. Many are physically immature and malnourished, according to the IWHC, and too often, especially if a husband drinks or is a violent person, sex is forced and injures the girl's delicate tissues, making HIV even easier to transmit.

In addition, HIV/AIDS heavily impacts girls when they must drop out of school to help their infected mothers or care for another ailing family member. Urdang of UNIFEM says, "If a girl is taken out of school to support the work in the home, then she loses the opportunity for learning how HIV is transmitted and getting the courage to say 'no.' And, she loses the opportunity for more sound economic employment in the future."

SOLUTIONS AMID SUFFERING

As women and their children continue to die in record numbers, the social and economic consequences are decimating communities and continents. Women are the backbone of agricultural countries, says Whitaker, and are also the generational links and information sharers. Women also bear the added burden of caring for those suffering with AIDS—spouses, siblings, children—whether or not they have the disease themselves.

"They are responsible for keeping their children safe," she says, "and when they are ill and unable to do that, it has a significant impact on the outcomes of their children."

Facing a bleak future, AIDS orphans are likely to be malnourished and unschooled and at greater risk themselves for HIV infection. Today, 25 million children have been orphaned by AIDS globally. In the last decade, HIV/AIDS in children worldwide rose significantly, especially for children under five years of age, according to the World Health Organization.

In the midst of such overwhelming suffering, what is being done to help women? Some say a critical turning point was the UN General Assembly Special Session (UNGASS) on AIDS in June 2001, when 189 countries signed a Declaration of Commitment acknowledging that "gender equality and the empowerment of women are fundamental elements in the reduction of the vulnerability of women and girls to HIV/AIDS."

Ten years later, however, governments in 16 countries have failed to keep their commitments to promote gender equality and women's sexual and reproductive health and rights, and end violence against women.

Governments, international agencies, NGOs, religious organizations, and women themselves, however, are taking action. In 2010, UNAIDS launched an Agenda for Accelerated Country Action for Women, Girls, Gender Equality and HIV (2010–2014), developed to address gender inequalities and human rights violations that continue to put women and girls at risk for HIV infection.

The five-year plan was introduced during the fifty-fourth meeting on the Commission on the Status of Women in New York. It calls on the UN system to support governments, civil society, and development partners in reinforcing country actions to put women and girls at the center of the AIDS response, ensuring their rights are protected.

One of the strongest efforts is toward education, because "strong data" shows that secondary education for girls is negatively correlated with HIV. "The more education girls have, the less likely they are to be infected," says Dr. Rao Gupta.

The education component is part of seven actions that ICRW calls "essential to empowering women." These include, among others, increasing women's access to economic assets; promoting zero tolerance for violence against women; intensifying the development and distribution of women-controlled prevention options; and supporting the needs of women caregivers.

Of the latter, Dr. Rao Gupta says, "Women are the caregivers, the nurses, the ones at home on the frontlines of providing support and care for those who are ill and infected with this disease. But they have absolutely no support. They don't have full information of the risks they face, no gloves, no syringes, no clean water, not to mention no relief from the burden of care . . . what are the government-led systems doing that could help them?"

Whitaker of the IWHC says her organization works with women "to help them realize they have options in their lives." They teach women that they have the right to make decisions and that they have "international agreements and movements within their own countries to support them in that . . . and to give them skills to negotiate encounters or get the resources they need," she says.

Part of the IWHC's efforts are through the Girls Power Initiative in Nigeria, which provides girls with factual information about sex, risk, and use of clinical services, and teaches them healthy body image and self-esteem.

Finally, women themselves are organizing. The International Community of Women Living With HIV/AIDS was started at an international AIDS conference by a group of women who realized they were "outside of any dialogues happening," says Hodgins. "There were very few voices of women at conferences," she says.

Today the group serves in an advocacy role at policy-making tables and government meetings, pushing the implementation of AIDS strategies that help women. "It's important to remember that women have the solutions," she explains. "We're not just victims. I know women who are very brave and faced the stigma in their communities and in their lives and made a difference."

At the XVIII International AIDS Conference in Vienna in 2010, the UNIFEM stated that despite international commitments, HIV-positive women's participation and voices were largely missing from the decision-making in the HIV and AIDS response that impacts their lives.

Women's voices, however, were present through Women ARISE (Access, Rights, Investment, Security, and Equity), a coalition of diverse women's networks and groups from around the world working to ensure that women's perspectives and realities were present at the conference.

GETTING MOBILIZED

Most advocacy groups agree: until a commitment is made to eradicate gender inequalities, governments and nations cannot move forward against the epidemic. Asia is of paramount concern to leaders. Dr. Peter Piot, executive director of UNAID, said, "The question is no longer whether Asia will have a major epidemic, but rather how massive it will be."

Today around 4.7 million people are living with HIV in Asia, according to the 2009 UNAIDS report. India, for example, has an estimated HIV prevalence of 0.3 percent, which seems low when compared to prevalence rates in some parts of sub-Saharan Africa. However, with a population of around 1 billion, this actually equates to 2.5 million people living with HIV in India.

And yet, when Dr. Rao Gupta of the ICRW attended a recent UN General Assembly meeting marking the progress of positive actions in various countries, she noticed the decided absence of Asian leaders.

"African leaders pointed it out," she recalls, "and actually said to their peers, 'Pay attention. We have paid a huge price for responding too late.'

What's frightening is the amount of work that needs to be done with countries like India, to openly talk about this as a gender issue and getting mobilized into strong action."

The AIDS epidemic is an emergency like the world has never known before, according to Dr. Rao Gupta, and it requires a response equal to that emergency. "And the Global Fund for AIDS, TB and Malaria is evidence that the world can respond," she says.

To date, the Fund, an international financing institution, has committed US$19.3 billion in 144 countries to support large-scale prevention, treatment, and care programs against the three diseases.

"It's a first step in that direction," Gupta says. "The Fund needs all the resources it has been asking for in order to avoid a huge social and economic disaster that is already playing out in many countries in Africa and can be averted in other countries. That requires action now."   [2011]

 88

"Necessity Was the Midwife of Our Politics"

DEBORAH R. GRAYSON

Despite media claims to the contrary, neither technological innovation nor physician acumen alone can explain or solve the problems and the politics of health in American culture. In fact, the women's health movement evolved precisely because traditional strategies used to meet the population's health needs have failed to meet the specific health needs of women. Women are the majority users of health and medical services. They access the system nearly twice as often as men do.[1] In addition to seeking services for birth control, pregnancy, and childbirth, women, because they tend to live longer, are also frequently in need of treatment for chronic disease and impairment later in life. Finally, women, especially women of color, make up the majority of low-level health care workers. Not only do they tend

to assume responsibility for the health care needs of their families, which includes tasks such as making doctor's appointments or escorting family members to the doctor's office, women also provide regular care to others in their communities who are ill.

Compounding the familial and occupational responsibilities many women shoulder in their interactions with the medical system are the social, cultural, and political burdens of health care. Black women, for instance, have the additional burden of confronting the intersectional politics of race and class in their encounters with the health care system. Too often, black women meet with difficulty in obtaining sufficient facts to make informed decisions about their health. They frequently suffer from inappropriate medical intervention because of those barriers. The negative impact of this kind of treatment on the health and well-being of African-American women, however, is often underestimated and overlooked.

Not simply privileging one oppression as their central target of political action, black women health activists have devised strategies to address their specific historical and structural circumstances. As black women have said many times now, the multiple statuses of race, gender, and class cannot be separated for them. Further, as long as these interlocking categories of oppression continue to exist, African American women will continue to have worse health outcomes than other groups of American women. This is true not because there is some biological deficiency among black women due to race and gender, as is so often implied. Rather, it is because of the ways the cumulative effects of negative life stresses, such as racism, sexism, and classism, work together to produce "patterns of health and illness in groups that share certain characteristics."[2]

Believing that black women needed a way to voice their concerns about their health, Billye Avery founded the National Black Women's Health Project (NBWHP) to provide black women with a forum from which to speak. Avery, often credited with being at the center of revitalizing the contemporary black women's health movement, used strategies such as the concepts of self-evaluation, self-determination, and self-help to respond to the staggeringly poor health statistics of African American women. She lacked formal training as a health professional herself but nevertheless believed that she could take charge of her own health care and assist in the training of other black women in self-care. With members of the project, Avery worked to empower black women to deal with the struggles they faced in their day-to-day lives that affected their health. Through a two-pronged approach, the NBWHP inspired the growth and development of self-help groups that would address the health needs and concerns of individual women.

"TAKING CHARGE AND TAKING CARE"

Through self-help initiatives, initiatives that promote "taking charge and taking care," that is, taking responsibility for oneself, black women health activists act as "primary health resources" for their families and communities.[3] Individual women and small groups of women organized to assess and to address specific issues related to particular diseases or health concerns of black women. AIDS, currently a major life-threatening condition affecting a disproportionate number of black women, is of great concern to many health activists. The problem of AIDS for black women is exacerbated by concomitant problems of high rates of poverty in black communities, poor nutrition, substance abuse, inadequate housing, under- or unemployment, and lack of access to preventative health care. Also, because early conceptualizations of AIDS described it first as a disease of gay white men and then as a disease of specific "risk groups," women were effectively preempted from consideration in AIDS research. The invisibility of women as a population affected by HIV/AIDS, especially the initial failure of the diagnostic criteria of the Centers for Disease Control and Prevention (CDC) to include gynecological conditions in the CDC definition has contributed to the underdiagnosis, misdiagnosis, and late diagnosis of HIV/AIDS in black women. These failures also contribute to women's unnecessary suffering and dying more quickly from complications related to the disease. Taken together, all of these matters have a devastating effect on the health and well-being of black women.

More than half of all women living with HIV/AIDS are black, and yet on a national level, little is being done to address this overrepresentation. Much of the stigma and the silence related to AIDS has to do with how categories of sex, race, and gender are given meaning in U.S. culture. An elaborate network of sex, race, and gender dynamics shapes the history of sexual behavior in the United States, particularly as it pertains to sexually transmitted diseases. More specifically, for decades racial theories prevalent in American culture constructed black women's bodies as the site and source of immorality and disease. Since at least the nineteenth century societal views of black women's sexuality have constructed black women as "promiscuous, irresponsible, and involved in illicit sexual activity such as prostitution."[4] This distorted perception contributes to defensiveness and hesitance among blacks to openly discuss issues related to sex, sexuality, and their consequences in the age of AIDS. It also perpetuates the treatment of black women as a risk to others (their children, their partners) rather than as individuals deserving of treatment and assistance themselves.[5] Oddly positioned as being both invisible and yet highly visible in AIDS discourse, black woman are being ignored in the AIDS prevention and education programs.[6] Rather than acknowledging how interlocking systems of race, gender, and class oppression cause black women to be un(der)served in the health care system, black women themselves are blamed.

BLACK WOMEN ORGANIZING AGAINST BREAST CANCER

Breast cancer is the leading cause of cancer mortality among black women. While overall, black women have a lower rate of incidence of breast cancer than do white women, black women nevertheless have higher mortality rates from breast cancer. The difference is said to be a result of black women often being diagnosed at more advanced stages of the disease. However, even when controlling for stage at diagnosis, black women still have a higher mortality rate than white women. Currently, there is no single widely accepted explanation of the disparity. Reasons from socioeconomic status to lack of education and low perceptions of risk have been given. Black women's response to these statistics, generally speaking, has been twofold. First, they have worked externally to elicit government action in terms of research and funding to address issues specific to their experiences with breast cancer. Second, they have worked internally to create the support systems needed to help one another in battles against breast cancer.

SOS: SAVING OUR SISTERS FROM BREAST CANCER

In an attempt to answer the questions "Why are older black women screened less for breast cancer?" and "What can be done to narrow the racial gap in mammography screening?" the Save Our Sisters (SOS) Project was founded.[7] Funded by the National Cancer Institute (NCI) the project is an attempt to respond to the dismal rates of participation of black women ages 50 and older in mammography screening. A pilot program in North Carolina was undertaken to assist black women 50–74 years old in obtaining mammograms. Under the premise that "women turn to other women they know for a helping hand, a shoulder to lean on, or advice," the program trained women described as "natural helpers" to become "lay health advisors."[8]

Natural helpers are individuals to whom others "naturally turn for advice, emotional support, and tangible aid."[9] Drawing on the work of Salber and others, Eugenia Eng and Jaqueline Smith assert that all communities have certain individuals with reputations "for good judgement, sound advice, a caring ear, and being discreet"[10] who are sought out by persons who have problems or concerns—before or, sometimes, instead of, resorting to professionals. Taking advantage of the fact that often the first contact persons in Black communities for those concerned about their health are natural helpers, individuals with substantial credibility in the communities, the SOS Project trained them as "lay" health advisors (LHAs). The role of the LHA was developed by the project to utilize resources within the community. The women chosen were willing and able to provide one-to-one assistance to women to get them to have mammograms; to facilitate community-based activities related to organizing around breast cancer issues; and to form a coalition of advisors and their networks to create a nonprofit organization[11] to bring into being community-based systems of care, as well as culturally sensitive and appropriate social support that complemented the role of health professionals.[12]

Eng found that lay health advisors are crucial to getting black women to participate in education programs related to breast cancer. As members of the community, LHAs often have many things in common with the women they are working to educate, including a shared history of facing segregation and discrimination within the medical system. Because they largely have the trust of black communities, LHAs are able to educate members of their communities as well as mediate and build coalitions between state and local health agencies and the communities. In addition, that trust enables the LHAs to break the silence about breast cancer and to demystify breast cancer screening.

RISE, SISTER, RISE: SISTERS SUPPORTING SISTERS

Black women have also organized to help those sisters who must learn how to survive breast cancer. In 1989 Zora Kramer Brown, herself a breast cancer survivor, founded the Breast Cancer Resource Committee (BCRC). The committee, a group based in Washington, D.C., has as its aim helping black women nationwide fight breast cancer. The BCRC's nationally recognized support group Rise, Sister, Rise is an important component in this process. It is one of a small but growing number of such groups in the United States focused on the needs and concerns of black women. Members of its locals discuss the importance of having a group that they can go to where they can discuss "faith, food, family, and feelings"—issues they do not necessarily feel comfortable talking about in "mixed groups."[13] Rise, Sister, Rise deals with related matters such as diet and hair loss; provides a 16-month program that focuses on how to survive in the face of the disease and how to destigmatize the illness; and is a means to prevent isolation. Women who finish the program and eventually leave the group frequently continue to work as breast cancer activists.

Brown and her colleagues also work in black communities, particularly poorer communities, that frequently have less access to health care and information about breast cancer. They lecture in churches, housing projects, and neighborhood centers to combat the black community's silence in regard to the disease. Brown and her colleagues are active, too, in lobbying members of Congress as well as the health, business, and activist communities concerning research and treatment for breast cancer.

NECESSITY IS THE MIDWIFE
TO OUR POLITICS

Much of black women's health activism is based on their ability to mediate between the "private lives of individuals and public institutions of the wider society.[14] Through the representational politics of health advocacy, the activists continue their decades-old tradition of calling on health professionals to pay attention to their health needs. Black women are working to expand the repertoire of research questions to include the kinds that health professionals raise and they demand that researchers include black women in their studies. As activists, black women challenge the ways their bodies have been simultaneously used and ignored in health research. Some of the ways they have issued their challenge is by writing and lecturing about their own encounters with illness. Fueling their activism is a deep sense of the history of African-Americans' experiences with medical institutions. Their community work promotes and provides advocacy and empowerment through education and role modeling. They train and encourage women to actively participate in their own health care. In so doing, they are able to translate the dismal health statistics reported regularly about African-American women into something meaningful: instead of focusing on what black women are dying from, the activists are focusing on what black women are living with. The work of black women health activists puts them in the best position to facilitate and lead in setting the agenda for addressing health issues confronting African-Americans in the coming decades. It is clear in the current work being done by black women health activists that we are our resources.   [1999]

NOTES

The author would like to thank Kimberly Springer and Charles Moore for their comments on earlier drafts of this chapter.

1. Norma Meras Swenson et al., "The Politics of Women's Health and Medical Care" in *Our Bodies, Ourselves for the New Millennium,* ed. Boston Women's Health Collective (New York: Simon & Schuster, 1998).
2. Sheryl Burt Ruzek, Virginia L. Olesen, and Adele Clark, "Intersections of Race, Class, and Culture," in *Women's Health: Complexities and Differences,* ed. Sheryl Burt Ruzek, Virginia L. Olesen, and Adele Clark (Columbus: Ohio State University Press, 1997).
3. Shay Youngblood, "Self-Help Groups: 'Taking Charge and Taking Care'" *Network News* May/June 1983, 8.
4. Beth Richie, "AIDS in Living Color," in *The Black Women's Health Book,* 184.
5. On this issue, see Sandra Crouse Quinn, "AIDS and the African American Woman: The Triple Burden of Race, Class, and Gender." *Health Education Quarterly* 20, no. 3 (Fall 1993): 305–20.
6. On the issue of Black women's invisibility in AIDS discourse, see especially Evelynn Hammonds, "Missing Persons: African American Women, AIDS and the History of Disease," *Radical America* 20 (1986): 7–23.
7. Eugenia Eng, "The Save Our Sisters Project: A Social Network Strategy for Reaching Rural Black Women," *Cancer* 107 (1993): 1071–7.
8. Ibid.
9. Eugenia Eng and Jaqueline Smith, "Natural Helping Functions of Lay Health Advisors in Breast Cancer Education," *Breast Cancer Research and Treatment* 35 (1995): 23–29.
10. Ibid., 24.
11. Eng, "The Save Our Sisters Project," 1074.
12. Eng and Smith, "Natural Helping Functions of Lay Health Advisors in Breast Cancer Education," 24.
13. DeNEEN Brown, "Rise, Sister, Rise, Wipe Your Weeping Eyes: Black Women Find Strength in a Breast Cancer Support Group of Their Own," *Washington Post Health,* May 9, 1995, 10–13.
14. Eng, "The Save Our Sisters Project," 1074.

89

Native American Women's Health Education Resource Center

JAEL SILLIMAN, MARLENE FRIED, LORETTA ROSS, and ELENA GUTIERREZ

The Native American Women's Health Education Resource Center (NAWHERC) was established to raise awareness of Native women's rights over their bodies and their lives. While representatives from the center speak nationally and internationally about reproductive rights issues in the Native American community and work in coalition with other Native American groups and organizations of women of color, the center is firmly rooted regionally. It is specifically committed to improving the health of Native American women living in the Aberdeen area, which, as defined by the Bureau of Indian Affairs (BIA), consists of North Dakota, South Dakota, Iowa, and Nebraska, where 54.5 percent of the Native American population live below the poverty line, almost four times the U.S. all-race rate of 13.1 percent.[1]

Retrieving, nurturing, and affirming Native culture and spirituality is central to NAWHERC's philosophical and political orientation. This orientation grounds the center's work, which includes providing direct services, conducting research, organizing advocacy programs, and forging coalitions with other Native American women in the framework of cultural renewal and Native sovereignty. The center has worked closely with other groups of women of color, promoting an understanding of the reproductive rights concerns of Native women and lobbying for reproductive rights in indigenous communities worldwide.

Due to the high rate of fetal alcohol syndrome (FAS) among babies on the Yankton Sioux reservation and among children born to Native American women in general, the first issue that NAWHERC tackled was FAS. The rate of alcoholism in Native men and women is higher than in any other ethnic group in the United States. At the time NAWHERC began grappling with FAS in the community, statistics showed that among Native Americans and Alaska Natives, mortality rates due to alcoholism for women aged 25 to 34 were nearly 21 per 100,000, compared with 2 per 100,000 for women of all races. Native women between the ages of 35 and 44 had a mortality rate of 47 per 100,000, nearly 10 times the rate of women of all races.[2] Native Americans often yield to alcohol and drugs to cope with prior victimization from incest, rape, and other forms of sexual assault. Annette Jaimes describes the collective and individual hopelessness engulfing Native America as a "colonially induced despair" that has given rise to a host of socially disruptive behaviors, with alcoholism—and concomitantly FAS—chief among them.[3]

NAWHERC crafted its approach to slowing FAS in the community within a reproductive rights framework. The center explicitly opposed the "right-wing approaches" to reducing the incidence of FAS that entailed preventing Native women from having children. The center challenged the widely held notion that the sterilization of Native women was an appropriate response to FAS. New reproductive technologies such as Depo-Provera and Norplant were also gaining popular support as a solution to FAS by those who did not want to deal with the root causes of high rates of addiction among Native women. Instead of addressing why Native women were delivering babies with FAS, the government's approach was to control their reproduction.

The national attitudes toward drug and alcohol addiction have tended to ignore the structural issues fueling it. Furthermore, rather than dealing with addiction as a public health issue, it has been criminalized and characterized as an individual failure. These attitudes, coupled with institutional racism, isolation, and a lack of resources have had an adverse impact on Native American communities. Minimal efforts have been made to address the real issues that could effect prevention. Asetoyer and her colleagues have pointed to the lack of treatment—and the lack of culturally appropriate care when treatment was offered—for those women who are already pregnant and are alcohol- and drug-dependent. Native American women who are substance abusers are rarely hospitalized and rarely receive detoxification or counseling for their addictions. Instead, they are often jailed or deprived of their parental rights.[4] The center's work on FAS led to research on a wide range of other health issues, including the underlying causes of alcoholism and drug addiction. NAWHERC's understanding of the real causes of FAS, and their critique of the responses to it, motivated them to strive to make health policies and services appropriate and responsive to the cultural needs of Native women.[5]

REDEFINING REPRODUCTIVE RIGHTS

In 1990, NAWHERC organized "Empowerment Through Dialogue." This historic three-day gathering brought more than 30 Native women, representing over 10 nations from the Northern Plains to Pierre, South Dakota.[6] Many wanted to address the social, cultural, economic, and community concerns that affected their daily lives and go beyond a narrow focus on abortion and contraception. They created "The Agenda for Native Women's Reproductive Rights,"[7] informed by Native American history and ancestral teachings in which "all matters pertaining to us as indigenous women, including reproductive rights issues, were, are, and always will be the business of women."[8] At the Pierre meeting, women redefined reproductive rights to include: age-, culture-, and gender-appropriate information and education for all family members about sexuality and reproduction; affordable health care, including safe childbirth within Native communities; and access to safe, free, and/or affordable abortions, regardless of a woman's age, with confidentiality and free pre- and postabortion counseling. They called for active involvement in the development and implementation of policies concerning reproductive rights issues, including, but not limited to, pharmaceuticals and technology. They saw domestic violence, sexual assault, and HIV/AIDS as reproductive rights issues.

They also determined that reproductive rights work should include programs to reduce infant mortality and high-risk pregnancy and to meet the nutritional needs of women and families. Culturally specific, comprehensive chemical dependence–oriented prenatal programs—including, but not limited to, prevention of fetal alcohol syndrome and its effects—were an integral part of their reproductive rights agenda, as well as putting an end to coerced sterilization. They underlined the importance of cultural and spiritual development, culturally oriented health care, the right to live as Native women, and Native determination of tribal members. Support for women with disabilities, as well as the right to parent in a non-sexist and nonracist environment, were also part of their far reaching reproductive rights agenda. The programs and outreach activities of the center are built around this set of principles proclaimed at Pierre.

THE MISSION OF THE RESOURCE CENTER

The center's goal is to meet the reproductive rights and health needs of women in the Aberdeen community by offering a range of services and educational programs. It conducts primary research on the health status of women in its own community to advocate on their behalf and to address the health concerns of other Native women. To carry out this mission, it has established partnerships with both local and regional (South Dakota, North Dakota, Minnesota, Nebraska, and Iowa) agencies and organizations. The center also works with local Native women's societies and with progressive Native women in the area.[9]

The resource center collaborates with national and international women's organizations and groups, like the Indigenous Women's Network, that share their efforts to advance the rights of indigenous women. It brings Native women's concerns to mainstream reproductive rights and health groups through published reports and advocacy in the broader reproductive rights community, participation in conferences and meetings, and in coalitions with other women of color. Through its work with women of color groups (such as the National Black Women's Health Project, the National Latina Health Project, and the Women of Color Coalition for Reproductive Health Rights) and their mostly white counterparts (such as the National Women's Health Network and the Boston Women's Health Book Collective), NAWHERC established a national and international presence. The center is truly distinctive in its ability to work at all of these levels while remaining firmly grounded in the Yankton Sioux Reservation community.

To anchor its research in the community, NAWHERC uses the roundtable process, a traditional Native American approach to information sharing and processing.[10] In many ways, it incorporates some of the concepts of Self-Help as utilized by the Latina and African-American women's organizations. The philosophical basis of the roundtable is a belief that participants can demystify problems and find appropriate solutions to challenges facing the community. The roundtable provides a safe space for individual participants to discuss issues such as domestic violence, rape, and drug, alcohol, and sexual abuse. Participants are encouraged to verbalize their personal, social, and historical realities and to identify crucial issues relating to the specific topic being addressed. This space enables participants to deal with internalized oppression and reinforces the traditional systems of women's societies where women come together to address their problems.[11] Furthermore, the format acknowledges that all community members are experts through their life experiences and have the necessary information and solutions to address their concerns.

Through speaking and sharing, partnerships are forged, creative abilities sparked, and women work to solve problems for themselves, their families, and their communities. They share knowledge of traditional teachings so that they may be integrated into their analysis and solutions. A facilitator who is charged with providing direction, support, and encouragement often leads these discussions. The facilitator is encouraged to work creatively with the group and is not expected to conform to a particular preset format. Typically, the participants generate a set of recommendations collectively. The roundtable process is an example of consensus decision-making based on traditional principles that fosters women's leadership in the Native American community.   [2004]

NOTES

1. Level of Need Funded Workgroup, *Phase Two Technical Report* (Rockville, MD: Indian Health Service), http://www.ihs.gov/NonMedicalPrograms/Lnf/PIIDHstatus.htm.
2. Wilhelmina A. Leigh and Malinda A Lindquist, *Women of Color Health Data Book* (Bethesda, MD: Office of Research on Women's Health at the National Institutes of Health, 1998), 4. These mortality rates were for the period from 1990–1992.
3. M. Annette Jaimes with Theresa Halsley, "American Indian Women," in *The State of Native America*, ed. M. Annette Jaimes (Boston: South End Press, 1992), 325.
4. Leigh and Lindquist, *Women of Color Health Data Book*, 4.
5. In fact, as Elizabeth M. Armstrong shows in her article "Diagnosing Moral Disorder: The Discovery and Evolution of Fetal Alcohol Syndrome," *Social Science Medicine* 47, no. 12 (1998): 2025–42, the very construction of FAS as a medically recognized syndrome is problematic, since the original studies involved a very small number of cases and tended to ignore other conditions (such as poverty, malnutrition, etc.) that can also contribute to poor health in newborns, preferring instead to focus on the moral deficiencies of "alcoholic" mothers.
6. This is the way in which the Pierre meeting is discussed in several NAWHERC publications.
7. This agenda was set in Pierre on May 18, 1990. It can be viewed in its entirety, including amendments, at http://www.nativeshop.org/pro-choice.html.
8. From a statement issued on July 7, 1992 by the the the women of color meeting cosponsored by the Religious Coalition of Abortion Rights, the Ms. Foundation, and the NAWHERC held in Washington, D.C.
9. Some of these native societies include the Treaty Council, Tribal Councils, the South Dakota Coalition Against Domestic Violence, and the Minnesota Women's Task Force. Included among the progressive women they work with are Cecilia FireThunder and Karen and Sharon Day, who work on women's health issues.
10. This process is similar to the Latina Roundtable process. Many aspects of the Latina Roundtable process were influenced by Chicana history, and the indigenous histories shared between many Chicana and Native women create some overlap in their approaches.
11. In the appendices for *Moving Forward* there is a note on women's societies, from which the roundtable has consciously drawn. Traditionally, matters pertaining to women, including all decisions concerning reproductive health care, were the business of women. Each individual woman's decision on these matters was final and respected. However, women would often turn to other women within the society for advice, mentoring, and assistance.

Focus on Lesbian Health

KATHLEEN DEBOLD

A young woman goes to a Florida doctor seeking treatment for a bad cough. She leaves with a prescription for Bible scriptures to free her from homosexuality.[1] A New Hampshire dentist refuses treatment to a woman because she listed her female partner as her spouse on the office's "get-acquainted card."[2] The director of clinical rehabilitative services at a health care center in Utica, New York, calls two lesbian senior citizens "faggots" and throws them out of the facility.[3]

Homophobic horror stories from the 1950s? Unfortunately not. These are all recent accounts of lesbians who tried to access health care services in their home towns. Knowing this, it should come as no surprise that stigma and the potential for discrimination in a health care setting have a major impact on lesbian health.

A national survey conducted in 2005 by Harris Interactive and the Mautner Project, the National Lesbian Health Organization, found that lesbians are much more likely than heterosexual women to delay obtaining health care (75 percent versus 54 percent).[4] Sixteen percent of lesbians report that they delayed obtaining health care because they were concerned they would be discriminated against. Their fears are justified: lesbians are more likely than heterosexual women to say that bad experiences with health care providers in the past have caused them to delay obtaining health care (27 percent vs. 12 percent). Three-quarters of lesbians (74 percent) who have experienced discrimination at a doctor's office believe they were discriminated against because of their sexual orientation, and 5 percent said it was because of their gender identity or expression.

Lesbians are found among all subpopulations of women, and are represented in all racial and ethnic groups, all socioeconomic strata, and all ages. The health and well-being of lesbians is, therefore, compromised by all of the factors that affect all women's health, plus:

- Individual and institutionalized homophobia, heterosexism, and gender stereotyping in all aspects of the health care systems;
- Lack of cultural competence on the part of health care providers, health educators, and health policy makers;
- Lack of civil rights (e.g., spousal insurance benefits, hospital visitation, family medical leave), which limits lesbian access to quality health care.

---

[1]National Center for Lesbian Rights (NCLR), "Lesbian Files Complaint Against Doctor for Prescribing Unwanted Anti-Gay 'Treatment,'" San Francisco NCLR, February 2, 2006, http://www.nclrights.org/releases/pr-doctor020206.htm.

[2]Gfn, "Dentist Suspended for Refusing to Treat Lesbian." New York: Gfn. July 21, 2006. Online: http://www.gfn.com/storyArticle.cfm?storyRecordID=1124.

[3]American Civil Liberties Union (ACLU), "*Bizzari & Hackett v. Sitrin Health Center*—Case Profile," New York ACLU, February 24, 2005, http://www.aclu.org/lgbt/discrim/12132res20050224.html.

[4]Harris Interactive Poll, "New National Survey Shows Top Causes for Delay by Lesbians in Obtaining Health Care," Harris, Rochester, NY, March 11, 2005, Online: http://www.mautnerproject.org/programs_and_services/research/305.cfm.

frameworks for fighting reproductive oppression defined by ACRJ:

1. Reproductive Health, which deals with service delivery,
2. Reproductive Rights, which addresses legal issues, and
3. Reproductive Justice, which focuses on movement building.

Although these frameworks are distinct in their approaches, they work together to provide a comprehensive solution. Ultimately, as in any movement, all three components—service, advocacy, and organizing—are crucial.

The Reproductive Justice analysis offers a framework for empowering women and girls relevant to every family. Instead of focusing on the means—a divisive debate on abortion and birth control that neglects the real-life experiences of women and girls—the Reproductive Justice analysis focuses on the ends: better lives for women, healthier families, and sustainable communities. This is a clear and consistent message for all social justice movements. Using this analysis, we can integrate multiple issues and bring together constituencies that are multiracial, multigenerational, and multiclass in order to build a more powerful and relevant grassroots movement.

Reproductive Justice focuses on organizing women, girls, and their communities to challenge structural power inequalities in a comprehensive and transformative process of empowerment that is based on SisterSong's self-help practices that link the personal to the political. Reproductive Justice can be used as a theory for thinking about how to connect the dots in our lives. It is also a strategy for bringing together social justice movements. But also, it is a practice—a way of analyzing our lives through the art of telling our stories to realize our visions and bring fresh passion to our work.

The key strategies for achieving this vision include supporting the leadership and power of the most excluded groups of women, girls, and individuals within a culturally relevant context. This will require holding ourselves and our allies accountable to the integrity of this vision. We have to address directly the inequitable distribution of power and resources within the movement, holding our allies and ourselves responsible for constructing principled, collaborative relationships that end the exploitation and competition within our movement. We also have to build the social, political, and economic power of low-income women, indigenous women, women of color, and their communities so that they are full participating partners in building this new movement. This requires integrating grassroots issues and constituencies that are multiracial, multigenerational, and multiclass into the national policy arena, as well as into the organizations that represent the movement.

SisterSong is building a network of allied social justice and human rights organizations that integrate the reproductive justice analysis into their work. We are using strategies of self-help and empowerment so that women who receive our services understand they are vital emerging leaders in determining the scope and direction of the Reproductive Justice and social justice movements. [2007]

 92

Voices of Reproductive Justice

Disabled Women and Reproductive Justice

MIA MINGUS

In the United States, a culture of ableism, which maintains that able-bodied people are superior and most valuable, prevails. In this culture, disability is feared, hated, and typically regarded as a condition that reduces the value of disabled people. The reproductive justice framework helps us understand how eugenic "science" is still a vibrant part of U.S. culture that interacts with and shapes the reproductive lives of disabled women in many ways.

RIGHT TO PARENT

Women with disabilities (WWD) have a long history of forced sterilization, are often seen as "unfit" mothers, and are discouraged from having children, or not allowed to adopt children. Authorities press disabled women to feel guilty for their decisions to be parents, pointing out that their decision will take a "toll" on their children, families, communities, and on themselves.

SEXUALITY

Society typically defines disabled women as asexual and as dependent on able-bodied people, undermining these women's access to reproductive health. Disabled women and girls often do not receive sex and reproductive health education. Health care providers may fail to ask WWD about their sexual lives, conduct full pelvic exams, or screen WWD for STDs/HIV, because it is assumed that these women do not have sex, or that they should not have sex. Because disabled women are seen as possessing less than "valuable" or "functional" wombs to carry children, their reproductive health may go unchecked and uncared for. WWD, a group with pathologized bodies, have the right to receive care and also the right to refuse it.

ACCESS TO SERVICES

Women with disabilities have limited access to health care services and information. WWD may not have access to suitable transportation (mass transit, use of a wheelchair-accessible automobile). Clinic facilities may be inaccessible (lacking ramps, Braille, sign-language interpreters, equipment). Reproductive health information may not be accessible to WWD due to issues surrounding language and interpretation, isolation due to the level of stigma still associated with most forms of disabilities, dependency on caregivers, and limited access to other WWD. Disability and class also may limit WWD's access to computers, communication devices, or mobility equipment. Women with mental disabilities also encounter barriers when it comes to accessing reproductive health services: they may be institutionalized, vilified as drug users and addicts. These women may not be allowed to have a role in decisions regarding their reproductive health and their bodies.

SEXUAL VIOLENCE

Violence against disabled women and girls is very common. Power imbalance and isolation can create special vulnerability (domestic violence, sexual assault, abuse) for disabled women dependent on caregivers. Caregivers (partners, nurses, family members, doctors) may withhold medication, medical care and information, or transportation as an expression of power and control.

EUGENICS/POPULATION CONTROL

The continuing power of eugenic thought in the United States justifies population control measures for WWD and disabled children. The medical establishment pathologizes "disabling traits," associates these traits with "social problems," and defines them as targets to "cure" and "conquer." Disabled women have been routinely sterilized or maintained on birth control, such as Depo-Provera, which stops periods and prevents conception. These practices have been convenient for caregivers and institutions. While traditionally the project of wiping out disability has centered on eliminating disabled bodies, today Inheritable Genetic Modification (IGM) aims to modify the human gene pool to exclude genes that cause (or might cause) various disabilities.

The use of Prenatal Diagnostics (ultrasounds and amniocentesis) to deselect and abort fetuses with disabilities (down syndrome, spina bifida, muscular dystrophy, sickle-cell anemia, and many more) illustrates the deeply entrenched ableism among women and the culture at large. While many pro-choice Temporarily Able-Bodied feminists argue for the right to abortion, many disabled feminists question the inherent ableism that surrounds the decisions to abort.

The framework of reproductive justice provides an analysis grounded in human rights and collective social justice. "Justice," rather than "right to privacy," allows for a broader analysis and more complicated approach to the politics and challenges surrounding WWD and reproductive justice. For many WWD, the right to privacy is not a privileged experienced in relation to one's body. Disabled women's and girls' bodies have long been invaded and seen as the property of the medical industry, doctors, the state, family members, and caregivers. The goal should not be to "cure the world of disabilities" or to do away with disabled people. The goal should be to work for communities that provide accessible opportunities and resources, human rights, and reproductive justice for WWD. [2007]

Reproductive Justice Issues for Asian and Pacific Islander Women

MARIA NAKAE

Like all women of color, Asian and Pacific Islander (API) women in the United States are negatively impacted by policies and practices that aim to control their bodies, sexuality, and reproduction. Because this is a result of multiple systems of oppression based on race, class, gender, age, immigration status, and language ability, issues of reproductive justice for API women are inherently connected to their struggle for social justice. The following is a snapshot of the wide-ranging reproductive justice issues that impact API women.

ACCESS TO HEALTH CARE

API women face numerous barriers to health care, including lack of health insurance, weak enforcement of regulations that mandate interpretation and translation services, and health professionals who are untrained to serve diverse communities. Furthermore, cultural ignorance and discrimination by providers lead many women to distrust the medical system. A grave consequence is that API women do not use reproductive health services adequately. They have an extremely low rate of pap exams, resulting in a disproportionately high incidence of cervical cancer. Vietnamese have the highest rate of all ethnic groups, which is almost five times higher than white women.

HAZARDOUS, LOW-WAGE EMPLOYMENT

Barriers to health care are extremely problematic, considering API women are concentrated in low-wage jobs with hazardous work environments and no employer-based health insurance or worker protections. For women who are undocumented or limited English proficient, there are few other opportunities for work besides the garment industry, nail salons, massage parlors, and electronics manufacturing. API women who perform domestic work are especially vulnerable to unregulated working conditions, and are often subjected to exploitation and abuse.

HUMAN TRAFFICKING

To meet the demand for cheap and unpaid labor, women are trafficked illegally from countries across Asia and enslaved in domestic work, sweatshops, and the sex trade. Completely isolated from the outside world, trafficked women are extremely vulnerable to physical, sexual, and emotional violence. Without any access to health care, unwanted pregnancies, forced abortions, and sexually transmitted infections are common.

EXPOSURE TO ENVIRONMENTAL TOXINS

API women are frequently exposed to environmental toxins both in the workplace and at home. Nail salon workers are exposed to phthalates and other toxins, and workers in electronics manufacturing plants are exposed to chemicals and heavy metals that lead to miscarriage and birth defects. Many immigrant and refugee families from Southeast Asia have settled in low-income communities near polluting facilities that emit chemicals such as dioxin, a reproductive toxin that is linked to infertility, miscarriage, and birth defects.

ANTI-IMMIGRANT POLICIES

Immigration restrictions, backlogs, and deportation are major obstacles to family reunification, preventing API women from maintaining and caring for their families. Federal and state policies restrict noncitizens' access to public assistance and publicly funded health care and social services, including prenatal care. Citizenship documentation requirements for utilizing free and low-cost clinics cause many immigrant API women to delay or forgo care, even when care is necessary.

Every day, API women face challenges to their bodily self-determination. To achieve reproductive justice, API women must have the power and resources to decide and act on what is best for themselves, their families, and their communities in all areas of their lives.   [2007]

Made in the USA: Advancing Reproductive Justice in the Immigration Debate

PRISCILLA HUANG

Yuki Lin, born on the stroke of midnight this New Year's, became the winner of a random drawing for a national Toys 'R' Us sweepstakes. The company had promised a $25,000 U.S. savings bond to the "first American baby born in 2007." However, Yuki lost her prize after the company learned that her mother was an undocumented U.S. resident. Instead, the bond went to a baby in Gainesville, Georgia, described by her mother as "an American all the way." The toy retailer soon found itself in the midst of the country's heated immigration debate. Under mounting pressure, Toys 'R' Us reversed its decision and awarded savings bonds to both babies, including Yuki. The issue of citizenship was at the heart of this controversy: Is a baby born to undocumented immigrants an American in the same way that a baby born to non-immigrant parents is? Since the fourteenth Amendment grants automatic citizenship to persons born on U.S. soil, both babies have equal standing as citizens. Not all people, however, view citizenship this way. As the grandmother of the Gainesville baby told reporters, "If [the mother is] an illegal alien, that makes the baby illegal."

Today's immigration debate extends beyond the goal of limiting the rights and humanity of immigrants: It's about controlling who may be considered an American. Anti-immigrant activists contend that American citizenship is not about where you were born, but who gave birth to you. By extension, they believe, "the Fourteenth Amendment notwithstanding," that the government must limit the reproductive capacities of immigrant women. Thus, immigrant women of childbearing age are central targets of unjust immigration reform policies.

Anti-immigrant groups, such as the Federation of American Immigration Reform (FAIR), believe immigrant women of childbearing age are a significant source of the country's so-called "illegal immigration crisis" and want to limit the number of immigrant births on U.S. soil. They are calling for changes to *jus soli*, our birthright citizenship laws. Unfortunately, some Congressional members are listening. Recently lawmakers have introduced the Citizenship Reform Act, which would amend the Immigration and Nationality Act to deny birthright citizenship to children of parents who are neither citizens nor permanent resident aliens.

Groups like FAIR assert that immigrant women enter the United States to give birth to "anchor babies," who can then sponsor the immigration of other relatives upon reaching the age of 21, all of whom create a drain on the country's social service programs. The irrational stance of anti-immigrant advocates echoes that of 1990s welfare reformers. Both assume that childbearing by immigrants or poor women of color creates a cycle of poverty and dependence on the government. Immigrant women and women on welfare are depicted as irresponsible mothers and fraudulent freeloaders.

They're wrong. Several studies have shown that immigrants "documented and undocumented" access social welfare services at much lower rates than U.S.-born citizens. Furthermore, under the 1996 Welfare Reform Act, new immigrants are barred from accessing Medicaid benefits for five years, and sponsor liability rules often render many of these immigrants ineligible for services even after that expiration date. And there is no evidence of intergenerational welfare dependency between immigrant parents and children.

Not surprisingly, pregnant immigrant women have become targets for deportation by immigration officials. On February 7, 2006, Immigration and Customs Enforcement (ICE) officials tried to forcibly deport Jiang Zhen Xing, a Chinese woman pregnant with twins. While her husband and two sons waited for her to complete what should have been a routine interview in a Philadelphia immigration office, ICE officials hustled Mrs. Jiang into a minivan and drove her to New York's JFK airport for immediate deportation back to China. After complaining for hours of severe stomach pains, she was eventually taken to a hospital, where doctors found that she had suffered a miscarriage.

Mrs. Jiang had lived in the United States since 1995. Although she entered the country as an undocumented immigrant, she made an agreement with the ICE in 2004 that allowed her to remain in the United States as long as she attended routine check-in interviews at a local immigration office. Jiang's case raises an important question: Why would immigration officials be in such a rush to send a pregnant woman back to her country of origin after she had been allowed to stay in the United States for over 10 years? Supporters of Mrs. Jiang and other immigrant women targeted while pregnant believe the harassment stems from nativist fears of immigrant mothers giving birth to U.S.-citizen children.

Anti-immigrant policy makers and advocates are also trying to exploit anti-immigrant hysteria as a vehicle for denying all women the right to reproductive autonomy, and are manipulating the issue of immigration reform to advance an antichoice agenda. In November 2006, a report from the Missouri House Special Committee on Immigration Reform concluded that abortion was partly to blame for the "problem of illegal immigration" because it caused a shortage of American workers. As the author, Rep. Edgar Emery (R), explained: "If you kill 44 million of your potential workers, it's not too surprising we would be desperate for workers."

Contemporary immigration reform policies recall the early 1900s eugenics movement, which was rooted in the fear that immigrants (and other undesirable groups) were outbreeding "old stock" Americans. Like the anti-immigrant advocates of today, eugenicists believed that curbing the fertility of such socially unfit groups would help reduce social welfare costs. Clearly, then, immigrant rights has become a reproductive justice issue. We must challenge the assumption that immigrant mothers are the country's new welfare queens, and reexamine what makes a newborn "an American all the way."

WHAT YOU CAN DO?

• Contact National Asian Pacific American Women's Forum (www.napawf.org) for fact sheets and issue briefs on a range of reproductive justice issues impacting API women.

• Contact Helen Gym, Justice for Jiang Zhen Xing Campaign (www.aaunited.org).

• Encourage your organization to join the National Coalition of Immigrant Women's Rights (contact NAPAWF for more information).

• Oppose any efforts to pass the Citizenship Reform Act (H.R. 133) or similar bills that seek to deny birthright citizenship to the children of immigrants.

• Ask your local health provider to provide culturally competent and linguistically appropriate services to all members in your community.

[2007]

 93

Abortion: Is a Woman a Person?

ELLEN WILLIS

If propaganda is as central to politics as I think, the opponents of legal abortion have been winning a psychological victory as important as their tangible gains. Two years ago, abortion was almost always discussed in feminist terms—as a political issue affecting the condition of women. Since then, the grounds of the debate have shifted drastically; more and more, the right-to-life movement has succeeded in getting the public and the media to see abortion as an abstract moral issue having solely to do with the rights of fetuses. Though every poll shows that most Americans favor legal abortion, it is evident that many are confused and disarmed, if not convinced, by the antiabortionists' absolutist fervor. No one likes to be accused of advocating murder. Yet the "pro-life" position is based on a crucial fallacy—that the question of fetal rights can be isolated from the question of women's rights.

Recently, Garry Wills wrote a piece suggesting that liberals who defended the snail-darter's right to life and opposed the killing in Vietnam should condemn abortion as murder. I found this notion breathtaking in its illogic. Environmentalists were protesting not the "murder" of individual snail-darters but the practice of wiping out entire species of organisms to gain a short-term economic benefit; most people who opposed our involvement in Vietnam did so because they believed the United States was waging an aggressive, unjust and/or futile war. There was no inconsistency in holding such positions and defending abortion on the grounds that women's welfare should take precedence over fetal life. To claim that three very different issues, each with its own complicated social and political context, all came down to a simple matter of preserving life was to say that all killing was alike and equally indefensible regardless of circumstance. (Why, I wondered, had Wills left out the destruction of hapless bacteria by penicillin?) But aside from the general mushiness of the argument, I was struck by one peculiar fact: Wills had written an entire article about abortion without mentioning women, feminism, sex, or pregnancy.

Since the feminist argument for abortion rights still carries a good deal of moral and political weight, part of the antiabortionists' strategy has been to make an end run around it. Although the mainstream of the right-to-life movement is openly opposed to women's liberation, it has chosen to make its stand on the abstract "pro-life" argument. That emphasis has been reinforced by the movement's tiny left wing, which opposes abortion on pacifist grounds and includes women who call themselves "feminists for life." A minority among pacifists as well as right-to-lifers, this group nevertheless serves the crucial function of making opposition to abortion respectable among liberals, leftists, and moderates disinclined to sympathize with a right-wing crusade. Unlike most right-to-lifers, who are vulnerable to charges that their reverence for life does not apply to convicted criminals or Vietnamese peasants, antiabortion leftists are in a position to appeal to social conscience—to make analogies, however facile, between abortion and napalm. They disclaim any opposition to women's rights, insisting rather that the end cannot justify the means—murder is murder.

Well, isn't there a genuine moral issue here? If abortion *is* murder, how can a woman have the right to it? Feminists are often accused of evading this question, but in fact an evasion is built into the question itself. Most people understand "Is abortion murder?" to mean "Is the fetus a person?" But fetal personhood is ultimately as inarguable as the existence of God; either you believe in it or you don't. Putting the debate on this plane inevitably leads to the nonconclusion that it is a matter of one person's conscience against another's. From there, the discussion generally moves on to broader issues: whether laws defining the fetus as a person violate the separation of church and state; or conversely, whether people who believe an act is murder have not only the right but the obligation to prevent it. Unfortunately, amid all this lofty philosophizing, the concrete, human reality of the pregnant woman's dilemma gets lost, and with it an essential ingredient of the moral question.

Murder, as commonly defined, is killing that is unjustified, willful, and malicious. Most people would agree, for example, that killing in defense of one's life or safety is not murder. And most would accept a concept of self-defense that includes the right to fight a defensive war or revolution in behalf of one's independence or freedom from oppression. Even pacifists make moral distinctions between defensive violence, however deplorable, and murder; no thoughtful pacifist would equate Hitler's murder of the Jews with the Warsaw Ghetto rebels' killing of Nazi troops. The point is that it's impossible to judge whether an act is murder simply by looking at the act, without considering its context. Which is to say that it makes no sense to discuss whether abortion is murder without considering why women have abortions and what it means to force women to bear children they don't want.

We live in a society that defines child rearing as the mother's job; a society in which most women are denied access to work that pays enough to support a family, child care facilities they can afford, or any relief from the constant, daily burdens of motherhood; a society that forces mothers into dependence on marriage or welfare and often into permanent poverty; a society that is actively hostile to women's ambitions for a better life. Under these conditions the unwillingly pregnant woman faces a terrifying loss of control over her fate. Even if she chooses to give up the baby, unwanted pregnancy is in itself a serious trauma. There is no way a pregnant woman can passively let the fetus live; she must create and nurture it with her own body, in a symbiosis that is often difficult, sometimes dangerous, always uniquely intimate. However gratifying pregnancy may be to a woman who desires it, for the unwilling it is literally an invasion—the closest analogy is to the difference between lovemaking and rape. Nor is there such a thing as foolproof contraception. Clearly, abortion is by normal standards an act of self-defense.

Whenever I make this case to a right-to-lifer, the exchange that follows is always substantially the same:

RTL: If a woman chooses to have sex, she should be willing to take the consequences. We must all be responsible for our actions.

EW: Men have sex, without having to "take the consequences."

RTL: You can't help that—it's biology.

EW: You don't think a woman has as much right as a man to enjoy sex? Without living in fear that one slip will transform her life?

RTL: She has no right to selfish pleasure at the expense of the unborn.

It would seem, then, that the nitty-gritty issue in the abortion debate is not life but sex. If the fetus is sacrosanct, it follows that women must be continually vulnerable to the invasion of their bodies and loss of their freedom and independence—unless they are willing to resort to the only perfectly reliable contraceptive, abstinence. This is precisely the "solution" right-to-lifers suggest, usually with a touch of glee; as Representative Elwood Rudd once put it, "If a woman has a right to control her own body, let her exercise control before she gets pregnant." A common ploy is to compare fucking to overeating or overdrinking, the idea being that pregnancy is a just punishment, like obesity or cirrhosis.

In 1979 it is depressing to have to insist that sex is not an unnecessary, morally dubious self-indulgence but a basic human need, no less for women than for men. Of course, for heterosexual women giving up sex also means doing without the love and companionship of a mate. (Presumably, married women who have had all the children they want are supposed to divorce their husbands or convince them that celibacy is the only moral alternative.) "Freedom" bought at such a cost is hardly freedom at all and certainly not equality—no one tells men that if they aspire to some measure of control over their lives, they are welcome to neuter themselves and become social isolates. The don't-have-sex argument is really another version of the familiar anti-feminist dictum that autonomy and femaleness—that is, female sexuality—are incompatible; if you choose the first, you lose the second. But to pose this choice is not only inhumane; it is as deeply disingenuous as "Let them eat cake." No one, least of all the antiabortion movement, expects or wants significant numbers of women to give up sex and marriage. Nor are most right-to-lifers willing to allow abortion for rape victims. When all the cant about "responsibility" is stripped away, what the right-to-life position comes down to is, if the effect of prohibiting abortion is to keep women slaves to their biology, so be it.

In their zeal to preserve fetal life at all costs, antiabortionists are ready to grant fetuses more legal protection than people. If a man attacks me and I kill him, I can plead self-defense without having to prove that I was in danger of being killed rather than injured, raped, or kidnapped. But in the annual congressional battle over what if any exceptions to make to the Medicaid abortion ban, the House of Representatives has bitterly opposed the funding of abortions for any reason but to save the pregnant woman's life. Some right-to-lifers argue that even the danger of death does not justify abortion; others have suggested "safeguards" like requiring two or more doctors to certify that the woman's life is at least 50 percent threatened. Antiabortionists are forever worrying that any exception to a total ban on abortion will be used as a "loophole": better that any number of women should ruin their health or even die than that one woman should get away with not having a child "merely" because she doesn't want one. Clearly this mentality does not reflect equal concern for all life. Rather, antiabortionists value the lives of fetuses above the lives and welfare of women, because at bottom they do not concede women the right to an active human existence that transcends their reproductive function. Years ago, in an interview with Paul Krassner in *The Realist*, Ken Kesey declared himself against abortion. When Krassner asked if his objection applied to victims of rape, Kesey replied—I may not be remembering the exact words, but I will never forget the substance— "Just because another man planted the seed, that's no reason to destroy the crop."* To this day I have not heard a more eloquent or chilling metaphor for the essential premise of the right-to-life movement: that a woman's excuse for being is her womb. It is an outrageous irony that antiabortionists are managing to pass off this profoundly immoral idea as a noble moral cause.

The conservatives who dominate the right-to-life movement have no real problem with the anti-feminism inherent in their stand; their evasion of the issue is a matter of public relations. But the politics of antiabortion leftists are a study in self-contradiction: in attacking what they see as the violence of abortion, they condone and encourage violence against women. Forced childbearing does violence to a woman's body and spirit, and it contributes to other kinds of violence: deaths from illegal abortion; the systematic oppression of mothers and women in general; the poverty, neglect, and battering of unwanted children; sterilization abuse.

Radicals supposedly believe in attacking a problem at its roots. Yet surely it is obvious that restrictive laws do not keep women from seeking abortions; they just create an illicit, dangerous industry. The only way to drastically reduce the number of abortions is to invent safer, more reliable contraceptives,

ensure universal access to all birth control methods, eliminate sexual ignorance and guilt, and change the social and economic conditions that make motherhood a trap. Anyone who is truly committed to fostering life should be fighting for women's liberation instead of harassing and disrupting abortion clinics (hardly a nonviolent tactic, since it threatens the safety of patients). The "feminists for life" do talk a lot about ending the oppression that drives so many women to abortion; in practice, however, they are devoting all their energy to increasing it.

Despite its numerical insignificance, the antiabortion left epitomizes the hypocrisy of the right-to-life crusade. Its need to wrap misogyny in the rhetoric of social conscience and even feminism is actually a perverse tribute to the women's movement; it is no longer acceptable to declare openly that women deserve to suffer for the sin of Eve. I suppose that's progress—not that it does the victims of the Hyde Amendment much good.   [1981]

94

Lost Woman Song

ANI DIFRANCO

I opened a bank account
When I was nine years old
I closed it when I was eighteen
I gave them every penny
That I'd saved
And they gave my blood and urine a number
Now I'm sitting in this waiting room
Playing with the toys
I am here to exercise my freedom of choice
I passed their hand held signs
I went thru their picket lines
They gathered when they saw me coming
They shouted when they saw me cross
I said why don't you go home
Just leave me alone
I'm just another woman lost
You are like fish in the water who don't know that
    they are wet as far as I can tell

---

*A reader later sent me a copy of the Kesey interview. The correct quotation is "You don't plow under the corn because the seed was planted with a neighbor's shovel."

The world isn't perfect yet

The world isn't perfect yet
His bored eyes were obscene
On his denimed thighs a magazine
I wish he'd never come here with me
In fact I wish he'd never come near me
I wish his shoulder wasn't touching mine
I am growing older waiting in this line
But some of life's best lessons are learned at the
worst times
Under the fierce fluorescent she offered her hand
for me to hold
She offered stability and calm
And I was crushing her palm
Through the pinch pull wincing
My smile unconvincing
On that sterile battlefield that sees
Only casualties
Never heroes
My heart hit absolute zero
Lucille, your voice
Still sounds in me
Mine was a relatively easy tragedy
The profile of our country looks a little less
hard-nosed
But that picket line persisted and that clinic has
since been closed
They keep pounding their fists on reality
Hoping it will break
But I don't think there's one of them that leads a
life free
Of mistakes
You can't make me sacrifice my freedom of choice
[1990]

 95

Talking with the Enemy

ANNE FOWLER, NICKI NICHOLS
GAMBLE, FRANCES X. HOGAN, MELISSA
KOGUT, MADELINE MCCOMISH, and
BARBARA THORP

*For nearly six years, leaders on both sides of the abortion debate
have met in secret in an attempt to better understand each other.
Now they are ready to share what they have learned.*

On the morning of Dec. 30, 1994, John Salvi walked into the Planned Parenthood clinic in Brookline and opened fire with a rifle. He seriously wounded three people and killed the receptionist, Shannon Lowney, as she spoke on the phone. He then ran to his car and drove two miles down Beacon Street to Preterm Health Services, where he began shooting again, injuring two and killing receptionist Lee Ann Nichols.

Salvi's 20-minute rampage shocked the nation. Pro-choice advocates were grief-stricken, angry, and terrified. Pro-life proponents were appalled as well as concerned that their cause would be connected with this horrifying act. Governor William F. Weld and Cardinal Bernard Law, among others, called for talks between pro-choice and pro-life leaders.

We are six leaders, three pro-choice and three pro-life, who answered this call. For nearly 5½ years, we have met together privately for more than 150 hours—an experience that has astonished and enriched us. Now, six years after the shootings in Brookline, and on the twenty-eighth anniversary of the *U.S. Supreme Court's landmark Roe v. Wade decision,* we publicly disclose our meetings for the first time.

How did the six of us, activists from two embattled camps, ever find our way to the same table?

In the months following the shootings, the Public Conversations Project, a Boston-based national group that designs and conducts dialogues about divisive public issues, consulted many community leaders about the value of top-level talks about abortion.

Encouraged by these conversations, the project in July 1995 invited the six of us to meet together four times. The meetings would be confidential and we would attend as individuals, not as representatives of our organizations.

Our talks would not aim for common ground or compromise. Instead, the goals of our conversations would be to communicate openly with our opponents, away from the polarizing spotlight of media coverage; to build relationships of mutual respect and understanding; to help de-escalate the rhetoric of the abortion controversy; and, of course, to reduce the risk of future shootings.

Still shaken by the murderous attacks in Brookline, we each agreed to participate.

As we approached the first meeting, we all were apprehensive.

Before the meeting, the pro-life participants prayed together in a booth at a nearby Friendly's. Frances X. Hogan, a lawyer and president of Women Affirming Life and executive vice president of Massachusetts Citizens for Life, worried that a dialogue with pro-choice leaders might generate "a scandal if people thought I was treating abortion merely as a matter of opinion on which reasonable people could differ."

Madeline McComish, a chemist and president of Massachusetts Citizens for Life, had a "gut fear of sitting with people who were directly involved with taking life."

Barbara Thorp was "deeply anguished over the murders at the clinics." She feared that "if lines of direct communication between pro-life and pro-choice leaders were not opened, polarization would only deepen." Despite misgivings, Thorp, a social worker and director of the Pro-Life Office of the Archdiocese of Boston, was "anxious to meet the other side."

The pro-choice participants were also skeptical and concerned. As president and CEO of the Planned Parenthood League of Massachusetts, Nicki Nichols Gamble was directly affected by the shootings. Although she felt that dialogue might help, she "wondered if the talks would divert my energies from coordinating my organization's response to the shootings and from assisting in the healing of my employees and their families."

Melissa Kogut, newly appointed executive director of Mass NARAL, the state affiliate of the National Abortion Rights Action League, wondered how she would "justify to my board and colleagues spending time on something that arguably could be futile."

The Rev. Anne Fowler, rector of St. John's Episcopal Church in Jamaica Plain, believed that her perspective as a Christian leader who is pro-choice would be essential, but worried that her viewpoint might not be respected by either side.

"However, as a priest, peacemaker, and activist, I had to accept this invitation."

The two facilitators who would moderate all the meetings were also anxious. Laura Chasin, director of the Public Conversations Project, "was afraid that talks might do more harm than good." Susan Podziba, an independent public policy mediator from Brookline, recalls, "The threat of violence was palpable. What if the wrong person found out about the dialogue?"

The first meeting took place at the project's office in Watertown on Sept. 5, 1995, a sweltering Tuesday evening. "I had wanted to wear my clerical collar, but it was too hot," recalls Fowler.

That first discussion was grueling. We could not agree on what to call each other. All but one of us were willing to use each side's preferred designation, in virtual or actual quotation marks: "pro-life" and "pro-choice."

Our first of many clashes over language, this disagreement remains unresolved. To this day, Gamble still cannot call the other side pro-life because "I believe my cause is also pro-life," she says. This stand frustrates Thorp and her colleagues. "I have tolerated Nicki's refusal to call us pro-life but, frankly, it angers me. I wasn't eager to call Nicki's side pro-choice, but I did it because it seemed to be necessary for showing respect and for moving the conversation forward," Thorp says.

Kogut questioned her own willingness to agree to these terms, "but I came to two conclusions," Kogut says. "To proceed with a civil dialogue, we needed to call each other what we each wanted to be called. Second, over time, I began to see 'pro-life' as descriptive of the others' beliefs—that life itself, more important than the quality of life, was their preeminent value."

We also struggled over how to refer to what grows and develops in a pregnant woman's womb. The pro-choice women found "unborn baby" unacceptable and the pro-life women would not agree to "fetus." For the sake of proceeding, we all assented, uneasily, to the term "human fetus."

These opening exchanges brought us to the heart of our differences. Nerves frayed. The chasm between us seemed huge.

To help us listen and speak across this divide, ground rules were critical. We would seek to use terms acceptable (or at least tolerable) to all participants. We would not interrupt, grandstand, or make personal attacks. We would speak for ourselves, not as representatives of organizations. Most important, the meetings would be completely confidential unless all of us could agree upon a way to go public.

We also made a commitment that some of us still find agonizingly difficult: to shift our focus away from arguing for our cause. This agreement was designed to prevent rancorous debates.

And indeed, we believe this ground rule has been essential to the long life of our dialogue. Knowing that our ideas would be challenged, but not attacked, we have been able to listen openly and speak candidly.

But it has not been easy.

"From the beginning, I have felt an enormous tension," Hogan says, "between honoring the agreement to not argue for our position and my deep hope—which I still feel—that these women for whom I have such great respect will change their minds about abortion."

Our ground rules also required us to refrain from polarizing rhetoric. In one early session, we generated a list of "hot buttons"—words and phrases that make it almost impossible for some of us to think clearly, listen carefully, or respond constructively.

Pro-choice members are inflamed when called "murderers" or when abortions are likened to the Holocaust or to "genocide." Pro-life participants are incensed by dehumanizing phrases such as "products of conception" and "termination of pregnancy" that obscure their belief that abortion is killing.

We also discussed stereotypes we thought were applied to us by people "on the other side."

Pro-life participants feel maligned when characterized as religious fanatics taking orders from men, or as uneducated, prudish individuals, indifferent to women in crisis and to children after they are born. Pro-choice members are offended by labels such as anti-child, anti-men, anti-family, elitist, frivolous, self-centered, and immoral.

Despite the strains of these early meetings, we grew closer to each other. At one session, each of us told the group why she had devoted so much of her time, energy, and talents to the abortion issue. These accounts—all deeply personal—enlightened and moved us.

After the fourth meeting, we agreed to extend our sessions through the one-year anniversary of the shootings—an occasion, we feared, when tensions over abortion might ignite in Boston.

On the evening of Dec. 30, 1995, about 700 people gathered at Temple Ohabei Shalom in Brookline to honor the memory of Lowney and Nichols. All our pro-choice participants attended the service. Fowler and Gamble officiated. In the solemn crowd were Podziba, one of our facilitators, and two of our pro-life members, Hogan and Thorp, accompanied by David Thorp, her husband.

"Seeing the other members of the group walk in was one of the most meaningful moments of the service for me," Fowler recalls.

In her remarks, Gamble expressed gratitude "for the prayers of those who agree with us and the prayers of those who disagree."

Fowler, in her sermon, reminded us of the "God who calls out to all who love peace." She drew from the words of the Hebrew prophet Isaiah, saying "and new things have sprung forth in the year since Lee Ann's and Shannon's deaths. Much has been transformed, and much will be."

Indeed, to those of us involved in the confidential dialogues, much had been transformed. By the time of this sad anniversary, each one of us had come to think differently about those "on the other side."

While we struggled over profound issues, we also kept track of personal events in one another's lives, celebrating good times and sharing sorrows. As our mutual understanding increased, our respect and affection for one another grew.

This increased understanding affected how we spoke as leaders of our respective movements. The news media, unaware that we were meeting, began noting differences in our public statements.

In an article after the first-year anniversary of the shootings, *Globe* reporter Don Aucoin wrote, "Has the past year brought the lowering of voices . . . called for by Cardinal Law, Governor William Weld, and others? The answer seems to be a qualified yes, at least among some activists."

The article quoted Gamble as saying, "There are numbers of people on both sides of this question who have tried to be thoughtful about the rhetoric they use." Gamble added that she was hearing fewer uses of such labels as "baby-killer, murderer, Nazi."

In the same article, Hogan is quoted as saying she uses "pro-choice because that is what they want to be called. I have a basic respect for the person, even though I don't agree with or respect the position."

Thorp, too, was quoted. "This call for a lowering of voices sent a signal that we really needed to listen to each other with care and respect. I'm more mindful now than I've ever been of speaking in love, speaking in peace, and speaking in respect to anyone no matter how wide the differences are."

In a National Public Radio interview about the anniversary, Hogan explained that while she believed that abortion is killing, she did not call it murder. Hogan also said, "Toning down the rhetoric is critical. It's not just better manners, but it turns out it's also better politics. . . . We reach people we may never otherwise have reached with the message."

Kogut felt and acted differently when she appeared with pro-life spokespeople on news shows and at speaking engagements. Kogut recalls, "I was struck by the media's desire for conflict. One host of a radio talk show actually encouraged me to attack my opponent personally."

In early 1996, we continued to meet, anticipating that the upcoming Salvi trial would present new challenges to protect activists and the public from danger.

At one point, pro-life advocates acted to keep proponents of violence away from Massachusetts. In February 1996, the Rev. Donald Spitz, head of Pro-Life Virginia, made it known that he was planning to come to Boston to show support for what he had called, according to the *Globe*, Salvi's "righteous deed."

McComish wrote a letter to Spitz, signed also by Hogan and Thorp. "Your public statements on the acceptability of violence . . . are counter to everything that the pro-life movement represents," McComish wrote. "At this very difficult time, you are not welcome in Massachusetts."

Spitz and several of his allies objected to McComish's charge. They suggested that she was betraying the cause. But he did not come.

A growing trust opened a "hot line" channel of reliable communication between us. The pro-life leaders alerted Gamble when there was a possibility of imminent physical danger. "It lowered my anxiety—and moved me deeply—to know that there were people on the other side who were concerned about my safety," Gamble says.

Throughout these 5½ years, though external events claimed much of our attention, we managed to explore many aspects of the abortion controversy, such as when life begins, the rights of women, the rights of the unborn, why women get abortions, and the aftermath of abortion.

We spent especially tense hours discussing the issue that pro-choice members describe as "bans on certain abortion procedures" and what pro-life participants call "partial-birth abortions." We also probed a host of other complex and challenging subjects: feminism, sex education, euthanasia, suicide, the death penalty, the role of law in society, and individual responsibility.

When addressing divisive topics, we expected to disagree. But at times, conflicts caught us by surprise—flaring when one side unwittingly used certain words in a way that struck the other as presumptuous or offensive.

One provocative word has been "violence." While the pro-choice leaders use it to refer to shootings and other attacks on clinics, doctors, and staff, the pro-life activists believe that abortion also is a violent act.

In writing this article, we came to an impasse when one side mentioned the Declaration of Independence. The pro-life participants wished to cite the Declaration as a presentation of their core belief that the right to life is inalienable and self-evident. The pro-choice members passionately objected to what they saw as an appropriation of a document that they also cherish. To them, the Declaration affirms every person's right to life and liberty.

In these and all of our discussions of differences, we strained to reach those on the other side who

Pro-choice

The pro-choice members of the group describe their views this way:

We recognize no single, universal truth that determines our moral decisions. On the contrary, we must consider a broad range of values whenever we seek to make wise, ethical, and compassionate choices. We respect a woman's moral capacity to make decisions regarding her health and welfare, including reproductive decisions.

A woman's choices reflect how she weighs her various life circumstances: her important relationships, her economic, social, and emotional resources and obligations, her health, her religious or philosophical beliefs, and the well-being of others for whom she has responsibility.

We live out our destinies in a world of vast and profound complexity, where claims upon our compassion and our judgment compete and often conflict. A woman respects the preciousness of human life by acknowledging and honoring the intricate tapestry of her relationships and commitments; indeed, we believe that the complexity of human life can be a source of moral wisdom and courage.

Pro-life

The pro-life members of the group describe their views this way:

We believe in one universal truth. We three, as Catholics, believe that each human life has its origin in the heart of God. This divine genesis of the human person calls us to protect and respect every human life from the moment of conception to natural death.

The truth regarding the intrinsic dignity of the human person can also be understood through reason and scientific principles of human reproduction and genetics. Indeed, faith and reason resonate, both affirming the inviolable truth that every human life is inherently sacred.

Abortion kills the most vulnerable member of the human family: the unborn child. The right to be born is the most basic of human rights. If it is not protected then all other rights are threatened.

We understand, all too well, the often desperate and overwhelming circumstances that some pregnant women face. We remain committed to creating an environment in which no pregnant woman feels that she must choose between her own well-being and the life of her child. It is an utter failure of love and community for a pregnant woman to feel that abortion is her only choice.

could not accept—or at times comprehend—our beliefs. We challenged each other to dig deeply, defining exactly what we believe, why we believe it, and what we still do not understand.

These conversations revealed a deep divide. We saw that our differences on abortion reflect two worldviews that are irreconcilable.

If this is true, then why do we continue to meet?

First, because when we face our opponent, we see her dignity and goodness. Embracing this apparent contradiction stretches us spiritually. We've experienced something radical and life-altering that we describe in nonpolitical terms: "the mystery of love," "holy ground," or simply, "mysterious."

We continue because we are stretched intellectually, as well. This has been a rare opportunity to engage in sustained, candid conversations about serious moral disagreements. It has made our thinking sharper and our language more precise.

We hope, too, that we have become wiser and more effective leaders. We are more knowledgeable about our political opponents. We have learned to avoid being overreactive and disparaging to the other side and to focus instead on affirming our respective causes.

Since that first fear-filled meeting, we have experienced a paradox. While learning to treat each other with dignity and respect, we all have become firmer in our views about abortion.

We hope this account of our experience will encourage people everywhere to consider engaging in dialogues about abortion and other protracted disputes. In this world of polarizing conflicts, we have glimpsed a new possibility: a way in which people can disagree frankly and passionately, become clearer in heart and mind about their activism, and, at the same time, contribute to a more civil and compassionate society.   [2001]

🌿 96

Parental Consent Laws: Are They a "Reasonable Compromise"?

MIKE MALES

Laws requiring parental consent before a girl under age 18 can obtain an abortion have won endorsement by the U.S. Supreme Court, Congress, several presidents (though as of this writing, President Barack Obama appears generally opposed), 41 state legislatures (though laws in seven states have been invalidated by courts), and large majorities of the American public.[1] They are even seen by many pro-choice adults as a "reasonable compromise." Yet reaffirmation of parental consent laws is by far the most disturbing and intrusive element of the Supreme Court's 1990 ruling in *Hodgson v.*

Minnesota allowing new curbs on abortion, a ruling that demonstrates the mechanism by which abortion rights can be summarily removed from vulnerable populations.

Parental consent laws authorize an outside party—a parent, or a judge if the girl goes to court to obtain an abortion without telling her parents—to force a teenage girl to bear a child against her will. Once another person can decide when a female must bear a child, the 1973 *Roe v. Wade* decision guaranteeing access to abortion is abrogated. It becomes simply a matter of how many barriers can be raised to deny abortion to the only women who stand to lose the right in any case—the young and the poor.

Parental consent is the most popular abortion restriction enacted by states and Congress. In upholding such laws, justices again swept aside monumental realities regarding abortion patterns among teenagers, the family conditions of girls who cannot inform their parents, and the miserable experiences of states with such laws.

Parental involvement laws do not promote parental involvement. In Massachusetts and Minnesota, 40 to 45 percent of all girls (many after judge-shopping) obtain abortions without parental notice, a level higher than in Montana (24 percent), which had no law.[2] After Massachusetts passed such a law in 1981, Brandeis University researchers found 1,000 Massachusetts girls traveling to nearby states for abortions every year.[3] Minnesota's similar law drove hundreds of girls to clinics in Fargo, N.D., and Wisconsin. "The law has, more than anything, disrupted and harmed families" and "can provoke violence," U.S. District Judge Donald Alsop wrote in a compelling opinion ignored by the Supreme Court.[4]

In briefs filed in Judge Alsop's court reviewing parental consent and notification laws, Minnesota and Massachusetts judges recounted harassed, terrified, angry girls forced to reveal intimate details of their lives in intimidating court proceedings. "They find it a very nerve-wracking experience," wrote one judge; another described "incredible amounts of stress" shown in "tone of voice, tenor of voice, shaking, wringing of hands," even physical illness. Judges in these two states, some personally opposed to abortion, unanimously agreed parental consent laws are useless and punitive, Alsop noted.[5]

The court's ruling embodies inconsistent views of family life. In striking down spousal notice laws, justices recognized America's epidemic of domestic abuse and the plight of wives who cannot reveal abortion plans to their husbands for fear of violence and alienation. In upholding parental notice and consent, justices painted an idyllic portrait of loving family concern, ignoring that these same violent, disowning husbands can also be violent, disowning fathers.

Parental consent laws highlight the cruelty of antiabortion regulation; the rich and mobile retain the ability to go to other states or countries; the young and the poor are forced into untenable positions. The effect of such laws is to demand a useless, stressful judicial runaround for girls already facing difficult situations, one the law's supporters hope will lead to the ultimate, bizarre result: a judge who finds a girl too immature for an abortion may force her to become a mother.

In a well-designed study in the August 1997 *American Journal of Public Health*, Charlotte Ellertson of the Population Council dispelled both liberal and conservative homilies about the effects of parental consent laws on adolescent girls' abortions.[6] The study found that teenage girls are not witless fools. Confronted with a humiliating legal barrier manufactured by adults bent on punishing them, girls seeking abortions travel to other states or avail themselves of other alternatives. While conservatives claim teenage abortions declined in states with parental notification/consent laws, Ellertson found that from available data, "minors who traveled out of state may have accounted for the entire observed decline" in in-state abortions. After Missouri's law took effect, abortions to Missouri minors in neighboring states rose "by over 50 percent." Conversely, liberals' assertion that laws making abortions harder for teens to get drive up teenage birth rates was not sustained; Ellertson found teenage birth levels did not increase unduly in states with parental notification/consent laws. However, she found, the hassles entailed in getting around such laws do delay minors' abortions into more hazardous later weeks.

My 2008 comparison of abortion rates tabulated by the Centers for Disease Control's *Abortion Surveillance*[7] finds no effect from parental consent or notification laws. From the earliest tabulation prior to such state laws (1980) to the most recent (2001), abortion rates are available for 15- to 17-year-olds for 27 states that enacted parental consent/notification laws during the period and for 12 states without such laws. States with such laws experienced a decline in adolescent abortion averaging 35 percent, while states without laws experienced an average 38 percent decrease.

However, there is little evidence that supporters of parental consent/notification laws care whether they achieve any important social goal. Much of the impetus for such laws appears to be punishment of pregnant girls. State Representative Jerry Luebbers, the chief sponsor of Ohio's parental notification law, equated a pregnant teenage girl with a criminal who should be forced before a judge.[8]

POVERTY, RAPE, ABUSE

Supporters of parental consent laws ignore the grim conditions of millions of girls most likely to become pregnant. Two million girls do not live with parents, according to the Census Bureau. Three million adolescent girls live in poverty, including 1.2 million in utter destitution.[9] Around 850,000 children are physically abused, sexually abused, or neglected every year.[10] A 1992 Washington study found that two-thirds of all pregnant teenagers were sexually abused during childhood or adolescence, many by parents.[11]

Impoverished, abused girls are by far the most likely to become pregnant. Having ignored America's staggeringly high rates of childhood poverty, domestic abuse, and deficient health care, which contribute to adolescent pregnancy and abortion, politicians now back harsh restrictive substitutes for genuine initiatives to help the young.

ADULT-TEEN SEX

There is, further, no requirement that the male partner in "teenage" abortions face similar sanctions. The reason: It is *adult men*, not teenage boys, who cause or collaborate in the vast majority of all "teenage" pregnancies and abortions, including the 5 percent of all "teen" pregnancies that result from rape. Vital and health statistics records indicate that 90 percent of all pregnancies among girls under age 18 are caused by adult men over age 18, and more than half by men over age 20.[12] The "adult-teen" pregnancy and abortion reality is one lawmakers, justices, and powerful "teen pregnancy" lobbies on all sides refuse to face.

Thus the only ones left to punish are young girls. And yet, minor girls are hardly the cause of the prevalence of abortion that antiabortion forces find so offensive. Only 7 percent of abortions are performed on girls under age 18; less than 2 percent of all abortions in the country involve a pregnancy caused by a couple in which *both* partners are under age 18.[13] The young, like the poor, are targeted for oppressive restrictions because they can't fight back.   [2010]

NOTES

1. Guttmacher Institute, "Parental Involvement in Minors' Abortions: State Policies in Brief, as of October 2, 2010," http://www.guttmacher.org/statecenter/spibs/spibPIMA. pef; On the Issues, "Barak Obama on Abortion" (2010), http://www.ontheissues.org/social/barackobama abortion.htm.
2. Robert Blum et al., "The Impact of Parental Notification Laws on Adolescent Abortion Decision Making," *American Journal of Public Health* 77 (1990): 619–20.
3. Virginia Cartoof and L. V. Klerman, "Parental Consent for Abortion: The Impact of Massachusetts' Law," *American Journal of Public Health* 76 (1986): 397–400.
4. Donald Alsop (1986). *Hodgson v. Minnesota*, 648 FS up 756, *Minnesota Digest*. US Supreme Court (1990), *Hodgson v. Minnesota*, 497 U.S. 417.
5. Ibid. See also, Editors, "Factors Associated With the Use of Court Bypass by Minors to Obtain Abortions," *Family Planning Perspectives* 22 (1990): 158–60; Jeannie Rosoff , "The Supreme Court Retreats Another Step on Abortion," *Family Planning Perspectives* 22(1990): 183.
6. Charlotte Ellertson, "Mandatory Parental Involvement in Minors' Abortions: Effects of the Laws in Minnesota, Missouri, and Indiana," *American Journal of Public Health* 87 (1997): 1367–74.
7. Surveillance summary, "Abortion Surveillance: Preliminary Analysis, 1979–1980—United States," *Morbidity and Mortality Weekly Report* 32, no. 5 (11 February 1983): 62–66; Lilo Strauss et al., "Abortion Surveillance— United States, 2001," *Morbidity and Mortality Weekly Report* 53, no. SS09 (26 November 2004): 1–32.
8. *Dateline NBC* (30 June 1992).
9. "Table POV01: Age and Sex of All People, Family Members and Unrelated Individuals Iterated by Income-to-Poverty Ratio and Race: 2009," *Current Population Survey* (Washington, D.C.: U.S. Bureau of the Census, 2010).
10. Children's Bureau, Administration for Children and Families, *Child Maltreatment, 2008* (Washington, D.C.: US Department of Health and Human Services, 2010).
11. Debra Boyer and David Fine, "Sexual Abuse as a Factor in Adolescent Pregnancy and Child Maltreatment," *Family Planning Perspectives* 24 (1992): 4–11, 19.
12. Mike Males and Kenneth Chew, "The Ages of Fathers in California Adolescent Births, 1991," *American Journal of Public Health* 86 (1996): 565–68; Mike Males, "Teens and Older Partners," *ReCAPP* (May–June 2004) (Santa Cruz, CA: ETR Associates).
13. Lilo Strauss et al.,"Abortion Surveillance—United States, 2001," Tables 4, 5. Calculation by author.

🦎 97

Testimony of William Bell (on Raised Bill #5447)

CONNECTICUT STATE LEGISLATURE

My name is Bill Bell and I reside in Indianapolis, Indiana, with my wife Karen and my 20-year-old son Bill.

I submit this testimony with mixed emotions: dreading to relive the death of my daughter but also realizing a responsibility to others, that the punitive and restrictive laws that are being heard before this committee are understood by all. In writing and in theory these laws appear reasonable and safe. But in practice they are punishing.

My daughter Becky made a mistake and became pregnant. Parental consent laws, very similar to those you are considering today, dictated that in order to terminate her pregnancy she must obtain approval of her parents, petition the courts, or travel to another state that would allow her a safe clinical abortion, *or* seek back-alley assistance. She died [from] an illegal abortion.

In confiding with her best friend she said, "I don't want to disappoint my mother and dad, I love them so much."

Knowing my daughter, I believe that the judicial option would have been too intimidating, given her desperate emotional state. She would also have been faced with the prospect of appearing before a pro-life judge. Hardly a reasonable option considering the fact that she had decided to terminate her pregnancy. She chose the last option available to her, an illegal abortion.

Unfortunately, we have been unable to piece together all the circumstances and today we struggle with the question, why did our daughter have to endure such mental torture in making what turned out to be her final decision?

She was intelligent enough to pursue her options, yet we live with the pain of knowing our daughter was desperate and alone, and because of these punishing and restrictive laws, she further compounded her initial mistake with another, and paid for it with her life.

My daughter was a quality child. She was raised in a functional family environment and was encouraged to develop her own thinking and reasoning skills. Yet, in her time of crisis, others had dictated how she must react, thus denying her a legitimate option that all women should enjoy, the right of self-determination.

Had our daughter come to us, her mother and I would have counseled her, made her aware of all her options, the circumstances, and the consequences, to the best of our ability. But I can state emphatically that the final decision would have been hers.

As it stands today, legislators, judges, self-appointed moralists, and parents are making the decisions for these young women, allowing little or no input from them. Decisions that are clearly along the lines of their own political, moral, or religious beliefs. How can we legislate or dictate that families communicate? How can we dictate to people how they must act or react in a time of crisis?

I realize a great number of young women are going to their parents for counsel and for this I am grateful. Since the death of our daughter, my wife and I have counseled several young women and have been fortunate to get the parents involved. But what about the young woman who doesn't want to disappoint her family?

If I understand correctly, the legislation before you offers no accommodation for a real-life situation like that of a Becky Bell. Nor does it consider the young lady from a dysfunctional home who may fear for her physical well-being. These laws speak to theories and hypotheticals, they do not address the real-life issues taking place today. I submit to you, these punitive and restrictive laws being considered, if enacted, will serve to further isolate the young women of this state. They will serve as a punishment to those who have made a mistake. In the interest of political gain and in the name of God, my daughter was punished.

Others took it upon themselves to decide my daughter's fate, thus denying her a safe option, the best care. Their theories and political stance were placed ahead of and valued more than the life of my daughter.

These laws clearly denied her a safe and reasonable option. And because she had decided to terminate her pregnancy, forced her into making a fatal mistake. My beautiful Becky Bell died on September 16th, 1988.

My daughter's death *will* count for something. She was somebody, somebody beautiful. I will not sit idly by and not speak out to others that could face the same torment that the Bell family now lives with. Not as long as there are those who will go to any length to take away basic human rights.

I am not promoting abortion, far from it. But I am speaking out against those who want to punish, who suggest that we can reduce teenage pregnancy through legislation. I am speaking out against those who will simply not address the needs of birth control and sex education.

Sex among teenagers will not be regulated by legislation, nor will it be eliminated.

I am a man with a broken heart, and it is my desire that speaking out will in some way prevent others from living this same nightmare.

I urge you to consider real-life situations and not punish the young women of this state and uphold the rights of all the people of Connecticut, not just the parents.

Rebecca Suzanne Bell was not a theory, she was a beautiful human being. She was my daughter, taken away because others *thought* they had all of the answers. The bill before you doesn't have all of the answers either and I urge you to defeat this legislation.   [1990]

98

Using Pregnancy to Control Women

RUTH HUBBARD

Strange things have been happening to this culture's ideas about pregnancy. More and more, physicians, judges, legislators, and the media are presenting pregnancy as a contest in which pregnant women and the embryos and fetuses we nourish in our bodies are represented as lined up on opposing sides. But construing the "interests" of embryos and fetuses as opposed to those of the women whose bodies sustain them makes no sense biologically or socially. A pregnant woman's body is an organic unit, of which the fetus is a part. She shares with her fetus one blood supply as well as other essential functions. Any foods or digestive products, hormones, or drugs, or anything else that involves either can have an impact on the other.

This does not mean that pregnant women should scan all their feelings, thoughts, and actions for possible ill effects on the fetus within them. It is probably true that stresses they experience will be transmitted to the fetus, but that includes the stresses and anxieties that would arise from trying to live a life free of stress and anxiety. What it does mean, however, is that it is counterproductive to heap needless stress on pregnant women by worrying them about possible sources of harm to their fetus and by subjecting them to often still-experimental tests and procedures to detect fetal disabilities for which they or the fetus are not specifically predicted to be at risk. Some of today's stresses of pregnancy are evoked by exaggerated concerns and watchfulness intended to avert relatively unlikely risks.

Precisely because anything that is done to a pregnant woman or to her fetus has an impact on both, pregnant women must be the ones to decide whether to carry their pregnancy to term. Only they can know whether they are prepared to sustain the pregnancy as well as the future relationship to their child.

As part of this trend of looking upon embryos and fetuses as though their "interests" could be separated from those of the women whose bodies sustain them, we have been witnessing: (1) prosecutions of pregnant women or of women who have recently given birth for so-called fetal abuse; (2) court-mandated Caesarean sections; and (3) so-called fetal protection practices in which employers bar women of child-bearing age (defined in one instance as 16 to 54 years) from certain kinds of jobs that are said to put a potential fetus at risk, in case these women become pregnant.

I want to look at these three situations and then speculate about why this is happening now and why only in the United States.

"DISTRIBUTING DRUGS TO A MINOR"

Across the nation in the last few years women have been charged with the crime of "distributing drugs to a minor via the umbilical cord" or similarly Orwellian accusations. Since the legal status of the fetus is uncertain, most of these have not stood up in court. Presumably for this reason, in Florida, Jennifer Johnson, a woman who had just birthed her baby, so that it was now legally a born child, was charged with delivering an illicit drug to a minor via the umbilical cord while it was still attached to the cord. Despite the absurdity of this construct, she was convicted.

It seems reasonable to assume that drug use during pregnancy can harm the fetus, though it is not at all clear how dangerous it is. The designation "crack baby" usually is not the result of health care workers noting behavioral abnormalities in a newborn. It came on the scene because a test was devised that can detect metabolic products resulting from women's drug use close to the time of birth. As a result,

---

Editors' note: Efforts to give rights to embryos and fetuses and police and criminalize pregnant women have continued since this article was written over 20 years ago. One notable move is *The Unborn Victims of Violence Act (UVVA)* which was signed into law by George W. Bush in 2004. Couched in the language of protection, this federal law makes "it a crime to cause harm to a 'child in utero,' recognizing everything from a zygote to a fetus as an independent 'victim,' with legal rights distinct from the woman who has been attacked" (Lynn M. Paltrow, "Policing Pregnancy," *The National Advocates for Pregnant Women.* http://www.tompaine.com/Archive/scontent/10189.html).

babies of mothers who fall into certain "suspect" categories—young, unmarried, poor, of color—are tested more or less routinely and especially in public hospitals. (In one recent instance where the test result was challenged by the young woman and her mother—though not until after the young woman and her baby had been forcibly separated—it turned out that the drugs the test detected were medically administered to the woman during labor.)

A recent article in the medical journal *The Lancet* explains that there are no accurate assessments of the dangers to the fetus of drug use by pregnant women. Its authors show that Canada's Society of Pediatric Research between 1980 and 1989 much more frequently accepted papers for presentation at its annual meeting that documented adverse effects of drug use during pregnancy than papers of the same, or superior, scientific quality that failed to detect any harm. As the authors point out, this kind of bias in publication of research reports makes it impossible to know how great the risk actually is. But even if we go with the common wisdom that drugs taken by pregnant women are likely to harm the fetus, the problem is that very few drug-treatment programs accept women, fewer yet pregnant women, and even fewer women on Medicaid. In fact, Jennifer Johnson's sentence in Florida included as a condition of her 15-year probation that she enter a drug-treatment program, something she had tried but been unable, to do while pregnant. Another was that she be gainfully employed, something she had also tried, but been unable to achieve. In other words, she was first victimized by an unresponsive system and then blamed for not availing herself of the remedies she had tried but been unable to obtain. She ended up convicted for the government's negligence and neglect.

It is important to realize that just about all the women who have been prosecuted for prenatal injuries to their babies have been poor and of color. Most of them have had little or no prenatal care and have given birth in public or teaching hospitals. None has been a white, suburban drug user, in the care of a private obstetrician. The so-called war on drugs requires public hospitals to report instances of suspected drug use, while private physicians can avoid doing so. Obviously, this policy is counterproductive, since it will make women who could benefit from medical and social services avoid them for fear of being declared unfit to care for their children.

COURT-MANDATED CAESAREANS

In most cases, a woman submits to a Caesarean section when a physician warns that giving birth vaginally would endanger her baby. This is true in this country, as elsewhere, despite the fact that the incidence of Caesarean sections in the United States is higher (about one in four) than in any other industrialized country (it is one in ten in the Netherlands, which has one of the lowest infant mortality rates in the world). But occasionally, a woman refuses on religious grounds, out of fear of surgery, or for other reasons. Whereas physicians and attorneys argued in print as late as 1979 that physicians have it in their power to cajole or threaten, but that cutting someone open against her will constitutes battery, since 1980 obstetricians have been granted court orders for performing Caesarean sections against the explicit will of the pregnant woman. In a number of instances pregnant women have escaped the operation by going underground or by giving birth vaginally before the court order could be implemented. In all of them the babies have been born unharmed, despite the obstetrician's direst predictions. In one case, the physician had testified that without a Caesarean there was a 99 percent risk that the baby would die and a 50 percent risk of death to the woman if she gave birth vaginally. She did, and both she and the baby were fine, which just shows that birth outcomes are notoriously unpredictable, except to say that most births end well. These situations, too, have involved mostly poor women—many of them of color, and whose primary language is not English—presumably because of the range of power imbalances between obstetricians and pregnant women. The prevalent differences in class, race, sex, and education that interfere with communication even in the best of circumstances are exacerbated when the women have unusual religious convictions or are young or unmarried or don't speak the same language as the doctor.

There is hope that a recent decision handed down by the District of Columbia Court of Appeals may make courts more reluctant to order Caesareans against the wishes of pregnant women. On April 26, 1990, this court ruled on the case of Angela Carder, a woman who was pregnant and dying of cancer. After 26 weeks of gestation, when it became clear that she would not survive until the end of her pregnancy, Georgetown Hospital in Washington, D.C., got a court order to perform a Caesarean section against her wishes as well as those of her parents, her husband, and her attending physicians. Both she and the baby died within 24 hours of surgery. The American Public Health Association, the American Medical Association, the American College of Obstetricians and Gynecologists, and other health and civil liberties organizations joined, as friends of the court, in a suit brought against the hospital. The majority of the D.C. Court of Appeals held that "in virtually all cases, the question of what is to be done is to be decided by the patient—the pregnant woman—on behalf of herself and the fetus." Though this decision governs only in the District of Columbia, we can hope that it will lend weight to refusals of surgery by pregnant women in other jurisdictions.

FETAL ENDANGERMENT IN THE WORKPLACE

Reproductive hazards in the workplace were cited in 1977 as grounds for requiring five women at the American Cyanamid plant in Willow Island, West Virginia, to be sterilized, if they wanted to retain jobs paying $225 per week plus substantial overtime instead of being transferred to janitorial jobs at $175 per week with no extras. None of these women was pregnant or planning a pregnancy, yet without the operation, they were considered "potentially pregnant." A number of such situations have arisen since, and currently the U.S. Supreme Court has agreed to hear an appeal against a lower court decision supporting Johnson Controls' "fetal protection" policy. . . .*

The grounds for barring the women have been that the work involves exposure to lead or other chemicals or radiation that could endanger a fetus, despite the

*Editor's note: In March 1991 in *UAW v. Johnson Controls, Inc.*, the Supreme Court unanimously declared unconstitutional Johnson Controls' policy of excluding women of childbearing capacity from jobs in which they would be exposed to lead.

fact that these agents also put men's reproductive processes, and specifically sperm, at risk. And these situations have only occurred relative to higher-paying jobs, traditionally occupied by men, to which women have been newcomers. Comparable concerns have not been raised about women employed in traditionally female jobs in which they are routinely exposed to hazardous chemicals or radiation, such as surgical operating room or x-ray technician, nurse, beautician, or indeed, clerical or domestic worker. Whether the women are planning to have children appears to be irrelevant. Rather, fertile women, as a class, are always considered "potentially pregnant." This is just one more way to keep women out of higher-paying jobs by dressing up sex discrimination as fetal protection. Of course, it also enhances the status of the fetus as a person, while relegating all women, pregnant or not, to the status of fetal carriers.

These kinds of "protections" make no sense from the viewpoint of health, because any substance that endangers a fetus is also dangerous for workers—female *and* male. But it is cheaper for companies to fire "potentially pregnant" workers (which means any woman who cannot prove she is infertile) than to clean up the workplace so that it becomes safe for everyone. Employers claim they are barring women because they are afraid of lawsuits should a worker whose baby is born with a disability, claim that disability was brought on by workplace exposure. But, in fact, no such suit has ever been filed and, considering the problems Vietnam veterans have experienced in suits claiming reproductive damages from exposure to Agent Orange and farm workers from exposure to toxic pesticides, such a suit is not likely to present a major risk to employers.

WHY?

So, why are these various fetal protection activities happening and why only in the United States? Indeed, why do many cities and states post warnings in bars and subways, now also appearing on liquor bottles, that read: "Warning! Drinking alcoholic beverages during pregnancy can cause birth defects"? (Note: any alcoholic beverage, no specification of how much or of alcohol content, and no mention of possible detrimental effects on sperm.) No doubt, the antiabortion movement has helped raise "the fetus" to mythic proportions. Perhaps also prenatal technologies, especially ultrasound imaging, have made fetuses seem more real than before. Not so long ago, physicians could find out about a fetus's health only by touching or listening to a pregnant woman's distended belly. Now, in the minds of many people, fetuses have an identity separate from that of the woman whose body harbors them, since it is not unusual for their future parents to know their sex and expected health status.

But that doesn't explain why these activities are peculiar to the United States. Europeans often assume that anything that is accepted in the United States today will be accepted in Europe tomorrow—or, if not tomorrow, the next day. But pregnancy is not like Coca-Cola. It is embedded in culture and framed by a network of economic and social policies. We cannot understand the profound differences between the ways pregnant women are regarded here and in other Western countries unless we face the fact that this country alone among industrialized nations has no coherent programs of health insurance, social and economic supports for pregnant women, maternal and child care, and protection of workers' rights. This has been true since the beginning of this century, but the situation has been aggravated since the dismemberment of the, however meager, social policies that existed before the Reagan era. Recent pronouncements by "drug czar" William Bennett and Secretary of Health and Human Services Louis Sullivan, urging that drug use during pregnancy be taken as prima facie evidence of child abuse, are among the ways the administration is shifting blame for the disastrous economic and social policies that have resulted in huge increases in poverty, homelessness, and unprecedented levels of drug use onto the victims of these policies.

While the economic circumstances of women and children, and especially those of color, are deteriorating and disparities in access to services and in infant mortality rates are increasing, what a fine trick it is to individualize these conditions and blame women for selfishly putting their fetuses at risk. Yet taking women to court for fetal endangerment creates more low-income women and more babies that will be warehoused in hospitals or shuttled among an insufficient number of adequate foster homes by overloaded social-service systems. These are not solutions. They are merely ways of diverting attention from the enormous systemic problems that have been aggravated by the Reagan-Bush years and of shifting blame for the consequences onto the most vulnerable people.

The editorial in the June [1990] issue of the *American Journal of Public Health* (Vol. 80, No. 6) calls attention to the longstanding correlation of birth-weight with parental income and living environment, regardless of maternal age, education, or marital status. The author points out that although U.S. infant mortality has declined since the 1940s, the overall decline slowed during the conservative Eisenhower and Reagan-Bush years. He also shows that, though infant mortality has gone down overall since 1947, black/white infant mortality *ratios* have risen from 1.61 in 1947 to 2.08 in 1987 (where race, as usual, is to be interpreted as an indicator of the range of disadvantages that result from racism and not as a biological signifier).

Again and again, studies have documented the deleterious effects of adverse economic and social conditions on maternal and infant health. But it continues to be far easier to get money for yet another study than for the policies and programs that could ameliorate or, indeed, eliminate the dismal conditions that jeopardize the health and welfare of women and children.

WHAT TO DO?

We have to take whatever political actions we can to support the efforts of various community organizations and to pressure government agencies at all levels to provide the economic, social, and educational supports that will let women and children live *above* the poverty level, not below it. We need what other industrialized nations have: adequate education, job security, proper nutrition, subsidized housing, universal health care, accessible drug-treatment programs, and so on. The lack of these is responsible for the disproportionate U.S. infant mortality and disability rates, not women's neglectful behavior during pregnancy.

A friend recently suggested that, rather than being sued, pregnant women should sue in the name of "the fetus" for access to the economic, social, and health measures that are necessary for

Access to Safe Abortion Is a Human Right

International human rights organizations have determined that it is a woman's right to control her body and to consequently make decisions about whether to carry a fetus to term. Safe abortion by trained health care workers using correct, sanitary techniques and proper equipment is a simple lifesaving health service. However, of the 42 million abortions induced globally every year, 20 million are unsafe. The following are facts about access to abortion across the world:

- Legal restrictions do not reduce abortions, contrary to popular myth. They just drive girls and women to seek unsafe abortions. Trained providers may be reluctant to conduct the procedure because they are unsure of the law, afraid for their safety, and fear censure from society. The results of unsafe abortion procedures are death, infections, infertility, and debilitating injuries.
- Funding limitations based on religious beliefs by some governments restrict women's access to safe abortions.
- The best method to reduce abortions is to prevent unwanted pregnancies, not by imposing legal restrictions. This can be achieved by increased availability of contraceptives.
- Access to safe abortion services should be part of a comprehensive approach to women's reproductive health services that include family planning, prenatal and postpartum care, counseling after abortions, prevention and treatment of sexually transmitted diseases, comprehensive sexuality education, and programs to prevent violence against women.
- Sustained advocacy is crucial if access to safe abortion procedures is to be accessible to women. It is important to push for reforms of laws and policies surrounding reproductive rights for women, document the consequences of limiting access to safe abortion, and subsidize services for poor women.

Source: Adapted from "Access to Safe Abortion Is a Human Right," International Women's Health Coalition (2008), http://www.iwhc.org/storage/iwhc/docUploads/Safe%20Abortion_FINAL.pdf?documentID=420.

successful pregnancy outcomes. Of course, this concept suffers from the fact that it, too, makes the fetus a person. Furthermore, such suits probably would not hold up in court, since, while the U.S. Constitution guarantees certain freedoms and rights, it does not guarantee the economic and social conditions necessary for everyone to be able to exercise them. Despite this, a well-orchestrated campaign of this sort could educate and politicize people about the shallowness and hypocrisy of the government's supposed efforts at fetal protection, and so could be used to rally support for the kinds of measures that can improve the needlessly dismal economic and social circumstances in which large sectors of the U.S. population live.   [1990]

 99

Reclaiming Choice for Native Women

JESSICA YEE

I am Native. And I'm pro-choice. Many people seem to think this is an oxymoron, but to me, it makes perfect sense. I have unraveled much of the oppression I was forced to swallow and internalize over the years, which obstructed my ability to see that concepts of "choice" and having "options" in our sexual and reproductive lives are really not new things at all. Moreover, I am entitled to advocate for choice from within my culture, which has always valued women's choices and decision-making. First- and second-wave feminism did not "give" my people reproductive rights; in fact, those of us in Native communities had them a long time ago. And how "pro-choice" identities play out in our communities now probably looks a lot different from what most people think.

> Historically, in the Shuswap Nation we were and still are matriarchal. Within our Shuswap band, women were trained as midwives by grandmothers and elderly women. They were also trained in female ceremonies around the menstrual cycle, as well as the many powers of women and our development (from childhood to adulthood). Shuswap women used Native medicines to keep from becoming pregnant or to end a pregnancy. Pregnancy was ended if hardships occurred within family and community, such as shortage of food, long winters, etc. These hardships were things that could cause numerous deaths within the family and community and could not be prevented.
>
> Shuswap Women had total control over their bodies. They were taught by women at an early age about roles and responsibilities as a child, youth, adult and elder.
>
> —*Wilma K. Boyce (Shuswap Nation) Canim Lake Band, Canim Lake, BC*

Throughout history, many well-respected indigenous women from around the world have interacted with each other through various women's societies with significant political power. Looking closer at traditional teachings and practices within First Nations, Inuit, and Métis nations throughout North America, it is evident that methods of family planning and birth control, including abortion, were performed as necessary procedures to ensure the health and welfare of communities that had women at their core. Although we are vastly diverse in terms of societal structure, whether matriarchal (e.g., Mohawk) or egalitarian (e.g., Inuit), it is clear that the right to govern one's own body and take care of it the way we choose is a foundational principle shared among us all.

My identity as an Inuk often comes into play when fighting for the right of choice. My identity as a woman is first and foremost when fighting for the right of my own body. If I intersect the two, I will look at many factors to my decision. Inuit do not condemn abortion nor do they promote it. This is a choice we have as women. Our people are supportive because that has always been a part of our society, to be supportive in every decision there is.

I am woman and I own my choices, not the men in black robes who by the way are creepy to begin with . . . with their anti-slogans on Parliament Hill.

> —*Inuk woman, name withheld upon request*

For Native communities, choice is a sacred teaching and principle. For many nations, reproductive health issues were decisions made by the individual, and were not thrust into the political arena for any kind of public scrutiny. Most often, the core decision-making for indigenous women has taken place between her and the Great Spirit or Creator. But with the imposition of colonization and Christianity, which brought in cultural genocide and systemic assimilation, conflicting belief systems were forced upon our people. And because women were ancestral heads of families and land title holders, they were targets in moves to depose Native communities from their land.

Yet this structure—in which the community is supportive of decisions made by women for the best interests of the community—has been both forgotten and rejected. Many of the values, practices, and traditions once held strong in our Aboriginal communities are now lost, and this includes the rightful place of our women to govern their own bodies. We know that the debate between those who are "pro-life" and "pro-choice" won't end as long as we live in patriarchal societies. But this fight is also a clear outcome of generations of colonization and genocidal oppression, through which we are still suffering. Among other horrific atrocities that occurred throughout the centuries, this colonization erased traditional ways in which we exercised our innate rights over our own bodies to choose the number of children we wanted within our families, and shamed us into believing that talking about things like sexuality were wrong.

As a Cree woman in Canada, a healthy sexual identity was not part of my personal teachings growing into womanhood. The one biology which distinguishes me from all others—my brown skin—haunts my ability to have true autonomy and agency when it came to a healthy sexual identity. It was much later that I learned how colonization interfered with what information was transferred between my mother and myself regarding sexual health.

Today, I am clear, open, and honest with my children regarding their body, their autonomy over it, and maintenance of it.

—*Gloria Larocque (Sturgeol Lake Cree Nation, Alberta),*
President of the KETA Society. Board Member of
Options for Sexual Health

Today, very little is known about Native women's reproductive health history. With the widespread resistance policy makers display in making sexual and reproductive health a priority in First Nations, Inuit, and Métis communities, young people in particular are paying the price. Additionally, while we know that access to abortion services is severely lacking in rural, remote, and Northern geographical areas where Aboriginal people are highly concentrated, we have yet to bring to the forefront the stories behind that lack of physical access, and the realities Aboriginal women face when they seek abortions. This negligence has enabled coercive legislation and false mass assumptions about what Native communities believe. The Hyde Amendment, which in essence blocks low-income women and, often, women of color from having abortions, inspired similar actions to prohibit Medicaid funding of abortion to U.S. military personnel and their families, Peace Corps volunteers, federal prisoners, and Indian Health Service clients. Many of us raised the alarm and rallied together to take a stand against this human rights violation, but who is listening? And more importantly, do we even have the full support of our Native communities in the struggle?

As a person of Lakota and European descent, I have been raised in both worlds, but my strong tie is to my Native roots, being raised by grandparents for the first seven years of my life. I truly believe that "my body is my decision—as a woman!" Only I know what I can handle, and it's ironic that the medical profession has only recently started believing in that perspective.

Speaking with people that knew our traditions and ways of life, women had to make the sacrifice for the good of the tribe. Our people had only so much to live on during hard times, so some families had to make the decision not to bring a child into this world to suffer. We, as women, were not scorned for our decisions. The entire tribe knew the impact of those decisions and we did not fight about them. It's ironic that "Western ideologies and religious concerns" have taken some of those very beliefs and turned them around on us.

—*Diane Long Fox-Kastner, Lower Brule (Kul Wicasa*
Oyate) and Minneconjou (Cheyenne River)

Cecelia Fire Thunder, first female chief of the Oglala Sioux, was rumored to be ousted in 2006 when she publicly declared she would open up a Planned Parenthood Clinic on her reservation if abortion were made illegal in the state of South Dakota. Earlier this year, Run Bruinooge, new chair of the Parliamentary Pro-Life Caucus in Canada, said that his "Aboriginal views" gave him a unique perspective conducive for his job to "protect the unborn." And the tribal council of the Turtle Mountain Band of Chippewa passed a law in October 2008 that would ban abortions on their land, even though many members say it was unconstitutionally passed during an illegal "closed-door" meeting.

I think it's important to open this debate to a wide audience of Aboriginal women. For me, personally, I know that there are seriously closed gatekeepers who threaten the very spirit of women who support abortion and women's right to chose what goes on with their bodies.

Aboriginal women get pregnant under complex circumstances, and their right to decide about their future must be supported with the best knowledge and options available. Teachings around their roles as mothers and life givers must be given in the contemporary context that we all live in, current and reflective of our past, present, and future. The silence around abortion in our communities has made it a taboo topic full of shame and eternal damnation, and we have the opportunity to reclaim that space for our women to create safe spaces for dialogue and action based on women's needs and women's realities.

I want to be anonymous—isn't that revealing of the circumstance?

—*Name withheld upon request*

Some say that if we had our land, we wouldn't have to depend on the system. I'd like to think of the day when we will not only get back Mother Earth so that we can take care of her, but that in taking care of her, we will remember how to reclaim "choice" for Native women.　　　[edited, 2011]

🌿 100

Abortion in the United States: Barriers to Access

MARLENE GERBER FRIED

Legal abortion in the United States is facing attacks at both the state and federal levels. Opponents of abortion, emboldened by the Republican legislative victories in the November 2010 elections, have stepped up their efforts to restrict abortion. At the state level, they are introducing bills that would ban most abortions after 20 weeks, expand prohibitions on federal and state funding of abortion, require women to view ultrasounds, and limit or prohibit abortion coverage in the exchanges that will be established as a result of health care reform. In Congress, 100 members cosponsored a bill that would allow hospitals that receive federal funds to turn away women in need of emergency pregnancy termination to save their lives.[1] The Smith bill, also known as the "No Taxpayer Funding for Abortion Act," would expand and worsen existing restrictions, with no exceptions to protect a woman's health other than in life-threatening situations. Even more extreme measures were introduced in South Dakota and Nebraska that would broaden the definition of justifiable homicide and make it legal to kill abortion providers. And one of the first Republican initiatives in the new legislative session was an attempt to replace "rape" with "forcible rape" as one of the limited situations in which federal Medicaid funding can be used to pay for abortion. While this was in fact stopped, it provided a glimpse into the full antiabortion agenda. Contraception too is at risk. In February 2011, the House of Representatives voted to end all funding for the Title X program, which includes counseling,

contraceptives, education, and preventative health screenings to low-income women and men.

While these blatant challenges to reproductive rights have evoked a strong political response from supporters of abortion rights, there has been a much less visible but steady erosion of abortion access during the years of legality. Assessing the current status of abortion rights in the United States is, therefore, a complex matter. From a public health perspective, if one looks at the statistics comparing maternal mortality in the United States to countries in which abortion remains illegal and unsafe, the U.S. situation looks extremely positive. Abortion has been legal since 1973. Since that time, there have been 50 million legal abortions and, currently, there are approximately 1.2 million abortions annually.[2]

There is virtually no mortality from abortion, and the complication rate for first-trimester abortion is about the same as for a tonsillectomy. This is a dramatic improvement from maternal deaths in the era before legalization. The availability of safe abortion also accounts for much of the decline in infant mortality.[3]

Focusing on the abortion experiences, however, especially of young and low-income women, presents a very different picture—one in which reproductive options are severely curtailed. Since legalization, the effort to restrict and ultimately to recriminalize abortion has had a devastating impact on many women's lives.

Abortion rights in the United States are literally under siege. Providers operate under constant threat, and many clinics have become secured fortresses. A normal workday includes wearing a bulletproof vest, checking for bombs, and always being aware of who is around them. There is no other medical service for which violence statistics must be collected and where the dangers to the provider are much greater than those to the patient.

This article will give a picture of abortion in the United States at the beginning of the twenty-first century from the vantage point of women who bear the brunt of restricted access. Each year, tens of thousands of women in the United States face significant obstacles to exercising their reproductive rights. Despite 38 years of legal abortion in the United States, access remains a problem. The barriers to access that will be discussed here—from economic constraints to the relentless efforts by antichoice forces—are not unique to the United States. They are pervasive throughout the world, regardless of the legal status of abortion. At the same time, legality is important to insuring that safe abortion will be available to all women who need it. Women's health advocates are continuing to work against legal restrictions and for funding, the training of providers, and to make the range of safe abortion methods available to women.

THE GAP BETWEEN LEGALITY AND ACCESS: ABORTION EXPERIENCES OF LOW-INCOME WOMEN

Legal abortion *is* one of the safest surgical procedures in the United States today, and it *is* relatively inexpensive compared to other surgeries. At the same time, it remains out of reach for thousands of women who find that the expense, location, and shortage of services, burdensome legal restrictions, and antiabortion threats and violence create daunting barriers. This reality is seen daily by those of us who work with the National Network of Abortion Funds.[4]

Grassroots funds get calls from women all over the United States—women in prison, young women, women who have been raped, "undocumented women," and women with few economic resources.

The funds repeatedly hear the desperation of girls and women who are faced with an unwanted pregnancy and have no money for an abortion. Women like "Nancy," who is 45 years old, living in a rural area, in a state that does not pay for abortions, and whose doctor could not perform one for her because his hospital wouldn't allow it;[5] or "Susan," the nurse's aid who works for a city government but has no health insurance; or "Selena," who left her abusive boyfriend and then found out she was pregnant.[6] For these women, it is as if abortion had never been legalized. Their reasons for needing an abortion are the same as any woman's—the difference is that they are poor.

The barriers these women face are the direct result of sustained and successful efforts by anti-choice forces to undermine abortion rights. As a result, restrictive legislation, judicial decisions, and relentless antiabortion activity, both legal and illegal, have dangerously limited abortion access, especially for low-income women, women of color, and young women. In addition to direct attacks on clinics and providers, abortion access has been undermined through the denial of public funding for abortion, laws such as those requiring mandatory waiting periods and parental consent for young women seeking an abortion. All such restrictions impose the most severe burden on the most vulnerable women in our society, those with the least economic resources who are disproportionately women of color, young, women, immigrants, and undocumented women.

Within the system of privatized health care in the United States, a large majority of abortions must be paid for by the patients themselves. About one-third of women lack employment-linked health insurance, one-third of private plans do not cover abortion services, or only cover them for certain medical indications, and over 50 million Americans have no health care coverage at all,[7] including nine million women of childbearing age.[8] Medicaid, the publicly funded program that covers "necessary medical services" for low-income people, prohibits federal funding for abortion.[9] Abortion is the only reproductive health care service that is not paid by Medicaid. In effect, by denying low-income women equal access to abortion, these policies are discriminatory. The restrictions on federal funding came in 1976, soon after legalization, when Congress passed the Hyde Amendment prohibiting the use of federal Medicaid funds for abortion except in cases where the life of the pregnant women is at stake. Prior to Hyde, the federal government paid for about one-third of all abortions, 294,000 in 1977; since Hyde, it pays for virtually none, 267 in 1992. Thirty-three states have also banned the use of state funds for abortions.

The impact of the Hyde Amendment and other funding restrictions has been devastating. Because the average cost of a first-trimester abortion is $468,[10] many women cannot afford abortions at all. It is estimated that 18 to 35 percent of women eligible for Medicaid who would have had abortions instead have carried their pregnancies to term because funding has been unavailable.[11] Others are forced to divert money from food, rent, and utilities in order to pay for their abortion.[12] Even when women have been able to raise the money, the time needed to search for funding makes it more likely that they will have a more costly and difficult second-trimester procedure. Further, one in five Medicaid-eligible women who have had second-trimester abortions would have had first-trimester abortions if the lack of public funds had not resulted in delays.[13]

ANTIABORTION INTIMIDATION, VIOLENCE, AND HARASSMENT

Abortion services are severely limited despite the fact that (1) abortion is legal, (2) there are 40,000 obstetricians and gynecologists practicing in the United States,[14] (3) abortion is the most common obstetrical procedure women undergo and the most commonly performed surgical procedure in the United States,[15] and (4) excellent surgical and medical methods of abortion exist.[16] The number of abortion providers—hospitals, clinics, and physicians' offices—however, has declined since the 1980s, and services are very unevenly distributed. Nine in 10 abortion providers are now located in metropolitan areas; about one-third fewer counties have an abortion provider now than in the late 1970s.[17] Ninety-four percent of nonmetropolitan counties have no services (85 percent of rural women live in these underserved counties). One-quarter of women having abortions travel more than 50 miles from home to obtain them.[18]

Violence, including murder, and harassment aimed at clinics, doctors, and clinic workers contribute to decreased access. Clinics and providers have been targets of violence since the early 1980s. They have faced death threats, stalking, chemical attacks such as with butyric acid, arson, bomb threats, invasions, and blockades.[19] Eight people involved in abortion care have been murdered by opponents of abortion.[20] The brazen murder of Dr. George Tiller, a nationally known and much revered provider, reverberated throughout the provider and advocacy community. Abortion providers are marginalized within the medical profession itself. Perhaps the most disturbing illustration of this is the lack of outcry from doctors and other health care professionals in response to the violence against abortion providers. Would the profession have remained silent if cardiologists were being murdered?

Women who have abortions are also stigmatized. They are portrayed either as selfish people or hapless victims, incapable of making their own decisions. While one expects to find these negative characterizations in antiabortion literature, they are, unfortunately, more pervasive. For example, on prime-time television and in movies, an unplanned pregnancy is most often resolved by a miscarriage, death of the pregnant woman, or carrying the pregnancy to term, not by abortion. The experience of abortion continues to be marked by silence and isolation, despite the fact that there have been 50 million abortions in the United States since legalization[21] and millions of illegal abortions prior to that time.

BACKDOOR EFFORTS TO BAN ALL ABORTION: THE "PARTIAL BIRTH ABORTION" STRATEGY

Until recently, direct efforts to ban abortion entirely through amendments to the federal constitution or federal statutes and in the courts have failed. The antiabortion movement pursued less-overt strategies such as the ban on so-called partial birth abortion. While they claim that this is a specific procedure, "partial birth abortion" is not a medically recognized term. In fact, descriptions of it in legislative bans basically describe what occurs in every abortion procedure.[22] The definition of the term has been kept vague in all of the statutes, which means that it could potentially be used to prohibit *all* abortions.

Nonetheless, Congress has passed such legislation three times, as have 31 states. Although in June 2000 the U.S. Supreme Court ruled in *Stenberg v. Carhart*[23] that the ban from the state of Nebraska and others like it were unconstitutional, Congress again passed a federal ban in 2003 and President Bush signed it. And in 2007 the Supreme Court upheld the ban in the case of *Gonzales v. Carhart.*

The Unborn Victims of Violence Act (2004), which gives separate legal status to the fetus, is another such effort. Passed in the wake of public emotion after the murder of a pregnant woman, Laci Peterson (her husband Scott was convicted of the murder), this is the first federal law to recognize a fertilized egg as a crime victim independent of the pregnant women. The law does nothing to stem violence against women and was therefore opposed by several organizations working to combat domestic violence. An alternative bill, which would have increased penalties for abusers who harm pregnant women without according legal status to the fetus, was rejected.

All of these initiatives enable opponents of abortion to portray it negatively. While battles over the bans and other legal restrictions have weakened and fragmented the pro-choice movement, the antiabortion movement has used these fights as opportunities to consolidate their movement, to draw in new supporters, and to build support for other restrictions on abortion. And although they have not achieved their ultimate objective, as we have seen, they have had important victories.

THE RACE AND CLASS DYNAMICS OF REPRODUCTIVE CONTROL

In order to understand the relationship between restricting abortion rights and other efforts to control reproduction, it is necessary to see the race and class dynamics that underlie both. The brunt of restrictions on abortion has been borne by young, low-income women and women of color. At the same time, historically, from the oppression of Native American women,[24] through slavery, to the present, the right of low-income women and women of color to control their own fertility has been severely restricted.[25]

The reproduction by young, low-income women of color is blamed for poverty, child abuse, drug addiction, violence, and general societal deterioration. A series of punitive and coercive measures have been designed to control the lives and reproductive capacity of low-income women, including contemporary policies curtailing public assistance to low-income women and their families; attempts at coercive contraception; the promotion of long-acting contraception and sterilization in communities of color; prosecutions of women who use illegal drugs while pregnant; and cash payments to the drug-addicted women who agree to be sterilized or to use long-term contraception. All of these policies aim to control the fertility of those considered unfit for motherhood and to punish them if they become pregnant.

Under the rubric of "welfare reform," the government uses subsistence benefits to manipulate and coerce poor women's reproductive decisions. For example, a family cap denies increased payments to women who conceive and bear another child while receiving public assistance. The illegitimacy bonus is another such policy. It offers a multimillion dollar federal bounty to states with the largest decrease in out-of-wedlock birth rates with a simultaneous reduction in abortion rates below 1995 levels.[26] This legislation has ideological implications as well. It revives the stigma of "illegitimacy"[27] by rewarding states that implement policies that make it very difficult for poor single women to have children.

Welfare recipients no longer have a safety net and are often without child care and the other supports necessary to obtain decent-paying, stable jobs. Little attention and less money are directed toward supporting young motherhood or enhancing educational and job opportunities for young, low-income women. Instead, the punitive ideological and legislative policies championed by conservatives emphasize the connection between illegitimacy, poverty, and social decay.[28]

THE INVISIBILITY OF INACCESSIBILITY: CLOSING THE GAP

A current survey finds that 54 percent of Americans support legal abortion in all or most cases; 42 percent say abortion should be illegal in most or all cases.[29] Many people in the United States, even those who support abortion rights, are unaware of the extent to which abortion access has been diminished, or do not see it as a problem. For example, although young women are frequent targets of restrictive policies, they support them.[30] Research done by the Pro-Choice Public Education Project[31] demonstrated that young people think that abortion is overused and that their peers are irresponsible. Narrowing access to abortion services does not worry them; they think that "choice" will always be there for those who really need and deserve it.

A shift in perspective is required to change these views. There is a tremendous gap between the perception that abortion is too accessible and the reproductive experiences of low-income women, young women, and women of color, whose needs and realities remain largely invisible. As part of a strategy to expand reproductive options, the notion of "choice" itself must be reexamined to take into account the experiences of low-income women. Women who face obstacles to having children, or to having an abortion, do not see themselves as having choices. Having an abortion because one cannot afford a child in a society that privatizes child rearing is not an expression of reproductive freedom. Historically the pro-choice movement in the United States has not advocated for the right to have children. It has focused on women's efforts not to have children, neglecting the right to have them. Traditionally groups organized by women of color have taken the lead in placing abortion rights within a broader agenda that includes advocacy not only for women's health, but also for all of the other economic and social rights needed to have real control over one's life. Younger activists too, who have been negotiating their sexual and reproductive lives through the terrain of HIV/AIDS and other sexually transmitted diseases, sexual abuse and violence against women, and the demonization of lesbians and gay men, also have a broader vision of reproductive rights.

To halt the erosion of abortion access, to counteract other threats to reproductive rights, and to expand women's rights and access to meaningful reproductive choice, the fragility of existing rights must be grasped, and the vision of reproductive rights must be broadened. Members of the movement in the United States can learn from our allies in other countries. While the abortion rights battle has been politically isolated in the United States, internationally, especially in the developing world, the women's rights agenda integrates a wide range of issues.

We saw this in the platforms for action of both the International Conference on Population and Development in Cairo, and the Beijing Women's Conference. Advocates for women's rights and health placed abortion in a broad human rights framework, which included concerns about maternal and infant mortality, population control, economic rights, violence against women, and environmental destruction.

Battles over restricting abortion are fundamentally about women's power and who will control women's fertility. In the United States, organizations created by women of color have taken the lead, giving us the concept of reproductive justice, which links an individual woman's ability to control her own sexual and reproductive life to her community's efforts to regulate and control itself.[32] This holistic framework is politically powerful. It has the potential to draw new constituencies to the reproductive freedom struggle. In 2011, I see the growing reproductive justice movement as offering the best possibilities for winning full reproductive freedom for all people.

NOTES

1. http://www.rhrealitycheck.org/blog/2011/02/07/protect-life-will-thereprice-paid.
2. Guttmacher Update, "Facts on Induced Abortion in the United States," January 2011, *http://www.guttmacher.org/pubs/fb_induced_abortion.html.*
3. Stanley K. Henshaw, "Unintended Pregnancy and Abortion: A Public Health Perspective," in *A Clinician's Guide to Medical and Surgical Abortion*, ed. Maureen Paul et al. (New York: Churchill Livingstone, 1999), 19.
4. The National Network of Abortion Funds (NNAF) is a growing association of 110 grassroots organizations that raise money for low-income women and girls who want abortions but cannot afford them.
5. These examples are from the Greater Philadelphia Women's Medical Fund, notes from their files, January to June 2000. Only the names have been changed.
6. Ibid.
7. U.S. Census Bureau, cited by Richard Wolf, *USA Today,* September 17, 2010. Also found at the Center on Budget and Policy Priorities, "Census Data Show Large Jump in Poverty and the Ranks of the Uninsured in 2009," by Arloc Sherman, Danilo Trisi, Robert Greenstein, and Matt Broaddus (September 17, 2010).
8. S. Lerner and J. Freedman, "Abortion and Health Care Reform," *Journal of the American Medical Women's Association (JAMWA)* 49, no. 5 (1994): 144.

9. P. Donovan, *The Politics of Blame: Family Planning, Abortion and the Poor* (New York: Alan Guttmacher Institute, 1995). Donovan points out that even before the Hyde Amendment, not all women in need of subsidized abortion services were able to obtain them, either because the services were not available or accessible to them—because the eligibility ceilings are set so low, Medicaid itself covers fewer than half of those who live in poverty—or because the states had policies prohibiting coverage.

10. "Abortion Funding: A Matter of Justice," *National Network of Abortion Funds: Policy Report* (2005): 6.

11. Heather Boonstra and Adam Sonfield, "Rights Without Access: Revisiting Public Funding of Abortion for Poor Women," *The Guttmacher Report on Public Policy* 3, no. 2 (April 2000): 9.

12. NNAF report, 2005, 6. Costs of abortion go up approximately $100 per week of pregnancy and also vary according to the type of procedure and the type of facility. Abortions in hospitals are more costly. At the same time, hospitals have federal money for free care which can sometimes be accessed for abortions. Medical abortion with mifepristone often costs the same as a first-trimester surgical abortion.

13. Stanley Henshaw and Lawrence Finer, "The Accessibility of Abortion Services in the United States, 2001," in *Perspectives on Sexual and Reproductive Health* 35(a) (2003): 20.

14. Boonstra and Sonfield. "Rights Without Access," 10.

15. *Abortion Delivery in the United States: What Do Current Trends and Non-Surgical Alternatives Mean for the Future?* (New York: Alan Guttmacher Institute, 1995).

16. Malcolm Potts, foreword to *A Clinician's Guide to Medical and Surgical Abortion*, ed. Maureen Paul et al., xi.

17. Edwards, Daney, and Paul in *A Clinician's Guide to Medical and Surgical Abortion*, ed. Maureen Paul et al., 107.

18. Allan Rosenfield, MD, foreword to *A Clinician's Guide to Medical and Surgical Abortion*, ed. Maureen Paul et al., xv.

19. Stephanie Mueller and Susan Dudley, "Access to Abortion in the U.S.," 1997, National Abortion Federation, revised 2003.

20. Regularly updated statistics on clinic violence and harassment can be obtained from the National Abortion Federation and the Feminist Majority Foundation (http://www.prochoice.org), which issues an annual Clinic Violence Survey Report (http://www.feminist.org).

21. "Facts on Induced Abortion in the United States," Guttmacher Institute, January 2011.

22. This is a method in which the fetus is given an injection so that it dies in the womb. Fluid is then removed from the cranium, as this is the only way to bring the head out without causing tears or bleeding in the woman's cervix, and the fetus is removed intact. This method is rare to the extent that the overwhelming majority of abortions are performed in the first trimester. It is used in the third trimester when the life of the pregnant woman is at risk, or in cases of serious fetal anomaly. It may also be used from 20 to 24 weeks of pregnancy if the doctor determines that it is the best procedure to use in the circumstances. This procedure is also referred to in as a D and X. Sometimes, the antiabortion movement uses the phrase "partial birth abortion" to refer to this procedure. Note that the term "partial birth abortion" is a political, not a medical, term. Opponents have portrayed it as infanticide. Most courts in the United States have continued to rule that determinations of appropriate medical procedures may not be made by legislatures, but must be left to the physician attending a woman. See Kolbert et al. in *A Clinician's Guide to Medical and Surgical Abortion*, ed. Maureen Paul et al., 234.

23. On June 28, 2000, the U.S. Supreme Court in *Stenberg v. Carhart* struck down Nebraska's ban on so-called partial birth abortions. The case was argued by Simon Heller from the Center for Reproductive Law and Policy. For more information, contact them at 120 Wall St., 14th Floor, New York, NY 10005. http://www.crlp.org.

24. Andrea Smith, "Better Dead Than Pregnant: The Colonization of Native Women's Reproductive Health," in Jael Silliman and Anannya Bhattacharjee, *Policing the National Body* (Boston: South End Press, 2002); Michael Sullivan DeFine, "A History Governmentally Coerced Sterilization: The Plight of the Native American Woman."

25. For example, Dorothy Roberts points out that African-American women are five times more likely to live in poverty, five times more likely to be on welfare, and three times more likely to be unemployed than are white women. See D. Roberts, "Punishing Drug Addicts Who Have Babies: Women of Color, Equality, and the Right of Privacy," in *Abortion Wars: A Half Century of Struggle, 1950–2000*, ed. R. Solinger (Berkeley: University of California Press, 1998), 152.

26. Q & A on Women and Welfare and Reproductive Rights, "The Illegitimacy Ratio," NOW Legal Defense and Education Fund.

27. "Welfare Reform Update," by Karen Judd with Susan Buttenweiser, Pro-Choice Resource Center, Inc., 1999.

28. Charles Murray described illegitimacy as "the single most important social problem of our time—more important than crime, drugs, poverty, illiteracy, welfare or homelessness because it drives everything else" ("The Coming White Underclass," *Wall Street Journal*, October 29, 1993). Despite the fact that young African-American women bear the brunt of the demonization in the furor surrounding illegitimacy, Murray's focus is on white teenagers. Some critics argue that his real concern is the breakdown of white families and white male authority.

29. http://people-press.org/2011/03/03/section-3-attitudes-toward-social-issues/.

30. A 1998 study by the University of California showed that support for legal abortion among young women has dropped every year for the last nine, from 65.5 percent in 1989 to a low of 49.5 percent.

31. In March 1997, the Pro-Choice Public Education project conducted "An Exploration of Young Women's Attitudes Toward Pro-Choice," a qualitative research project to explore the attitudes of the young women born after *Roe v. Wade*.

32. For more about the concept of reproductive justice, see Jael Silliman et al., *Undivided Rights: Women of Color Organize for Reproductive Justice* (Boston: South End Press, 2004); www.sistersong.net. A paper and PowerPoint presentation is forthcoming from Asian Communities for Reproductive Justice; contact Eveline@reproductivejustice.org.

CHAPTER VI
Matrices of Privilege and Oppression

We are encouraged, in our society, to see ourselves as individuals, whose progress in the world is determined by our own merits and efforts. As we have seen, however, the deeply rooted gender bias that shapes our institutions and culture stunts our possibilities as women. Gender, however, is only one of many systems of inequality that structure our institutions and shape our experience. As Lee Bell has pointed out,

> One of the privileges of dominant group status is the luxury to see oneself as an individual. A white man, for example, is rarely defined by whiteness or maleness. If he does well on his job, he is acknowledged as a highly qualified individual. If he does poorly, the blame is attributed to him alone. Those in subordinated groups, however, can never fully escape being defined by their social group memberships. A Puerto Rican woman in the U.S. mainland, for example, may wish to be viewed as an individual and acknowledged for her personal talents and abilities. Yet she can never fully escape the dominant society's assumptions about her racial/ethnic group, language, and gender. If she excels in her work, she may be seen as atypical or exceptional. If she does poorly, she may be seen as representative of the limitations of the group. In either case, she rises or falls not on the basis of individual qualities alone, but always also partly as a member of her group(s).[1]

As we can see from this example, a woman who is also a member of another subordinate group is affected simultaneously by multiple identities that interact with each other. Some women are limited by oppression and concurrently benefit from advantages. For example, an affluent African-American woman will gain from the privileges of social class while she simultaneously faces discrimination because of her race and sex. The ways that race and gender discrimination play out in the life of a poor African-American woman will be very different. Similarly, a white lesbian, while enduring the discrimination of a heterosexist society, benefits from being white in a racist culture. Jewish women benefit from white privilege while sometimes being subject to anti-Semitism. By deepening our understanding of various forms of oppression and privilege and the ways they intersect in women's lives, we can better address the needs of all women, draw on our various resources, and work together to develop an inclusive feminist vision. Unless we eradicate all forms of domination, we will not be able to create a world in which all women can be free to determine their lives.

Why, many people ask, is it necessary to focus on difference? Why can't we focus on our common humanity or our common experiences as women? In a society in which some group's interests, norms, and values are dominant, suppressing difference renders invisible the experience of people who are not among the dominant group. In the United States, male, white, heterosexual, middle-class, youthful, and able-bodied norms have been dominant; other people's experience is marginalized.

Tightly interwoven in the fabric of our society, inequalities of power, resources, and discriminatory attitudes create and sustain various systems of dominance and

---

[1]Lee Anne Bell, "Theoretical Perspectives for Social Justice Education," in *Teaching Diversity and Social Justice: A Sourcebook,* ed. Maurianne Adams, Lee Anne Bell, and Pat Griffin (New York: Routledge, 1997).

subordination. Laws and practices have structured our various institutions to accord advantages to dominant groups and deny them to members of subordinate groups. Discriminatory attitudes and ideas justify and perpetuate these inequalities. In *The Second Sex,* her pathbreaking book about the subordination of women, Simone de Beauvoir suggested that dominant groups tend to see themselves as the subject relegating subordinate groups to the status of "other," inessential, marginal, and deviant. The media, literature, language, and prevailing attitudes of the culture depict the dominant groups as representing the universal human. Stereotypes of subordinate groups rob members of their individuality, even when they are ostensibly positive—for example, the idea that old women are all grandmotherly, that African-American women are all strong, that Native American women are all spiritual.

This chapter focuses particularly on the effects of race, class, sexual orientation, age, and citizenship on women's experience and relationships among women. It examines the ways institutional discrimination, as well as pervasive prejudice, can prevent us from understanding the experiences we have in common and appreciating the differences among us as a resource. Some of the articles in this chapter reveal these divisions by focusing on the often painful dynamics in our daily lives that reinforce them. Because the barriers between women are hardened by ignorance, Chapter VI includes a large number of first-person and fictional accounts that present women's experiences through their own eyes.

Racism affects all of us, influencing the way we relate to each other and the way we see the world. Because our society marginalizes people of color, white people often think their experience is universal and don't recognize or value other people's activities, needs, or contributions. Adrienne Rich, in an essay called "Disloyal to Civilization," describes what she calls white "solipsism." This, she argues, is "not the consciously held *belief* that one race is inherently superior to all others, but a tunnel-vision which simply does not see non-white experience or existence as precious or significant, unless in spasmodic, impotent guilt reflexes. . . ." She argues that to get beyond this, white women need to listen closely to what the "politics of skin color" have meant to women of color.[2] This would involve understanding the ways that racism has kept women from working effectively against sexism, such as when women excluded African-American women from the early twentieth-century suffrage organizations in order to avoid alienating white racist southerners.

The class system has functioned in similar ways. Economic inequality both shapes our social institutions and is reinforced by them. For example, studies have shown that students from well-funded school districts perform better than those from poorly funded ones, and that academic achievement translates into differences in skill level and employability. Across the country in 2009, there was as much as a $10,000 difference in spending per pupil.[3]

Women who have greater access to education, health care, employment opportunities, and other resources have sometimes worked for their own advancement, excluding

---

[2]Adrienne Rich, "Disloyal to Civilization," in *Lies, Secrets and Silence*, pp. 306 and 307.

[3]"Quality Counts," EPE Research Center, 2009, www.edweek.org/rc/articles/2009/01/21/sow0121.h27.html.

and ignoring poor women. For example, middle- and upper-class women in Puerto Rico in the 1920s advanced a law that gave the right to vote only to literate women over 21, excluding thousands of illiterate women even though many of them had been working for decades to win suffrage. Today, defending the legal right to abortion without also demanding *access* to abortion for women who depend on welfare and public health clinics would sacrifice the reproductive rights of countless women. In the past 20 years, increasing numbers of women in the United States have entered previously male-dominated professions such as business, law, and medicine, yet large numbers of women continue to work in dead-end, low-wage jobs, thus widening class divisions.

Prejudice and discrimination against lesbians in our culture are a reflection of what Adrienne Rich has called "compulsory heterosexuality," a complex web of laws, practices, and attitudes that enforce heterosexuality as a norm and render love and sex between people of the same sex "deviant."[4] As a result of institutional discrimination against lesbians and gay men—sometimes called heterosexism— lesbian mothers have been denied custody of their children, lesbian partners cannot always get health coverage for each other, and lesbians have been fired from jobs because of their sexual orientation. Because of the heavy sanctions, many lesbians have hidden their sexual orientation from employers, family, and friends, and prejudice thrives in an atmosphere in which lesbian lives are hidden. We rarely learn about the rich history of women who have chosen to create lives with each other. As a result, myths and misconceptions about lesbians are numerous in our culture.

Taboos against love and sex between women have constrained the lives of all women. Fear of being labeled a lesbian often deters women from acting and speaking freely. For example, women have sometimes been afraid to develop close friendships because of the fear of being labeled a lesbian, and have sometimes been hesitant to participate in activities that violate the norms of "femininity." As long as the accusation "what are you, some kind of dyke?" still has the power to intimidate women, no woman can be free. Freedom to love and be sexual whomever we choose is a central ingredient of feminism.

For women in our society, aging brings with it a cluster of social taboos and institutional inequities that we call ageism. As Susan Sontag has pointed out, "for a woman to be obliged to state her age, after 'a certain age,' is always a miniature ordeal." Once she passes that certain age, Sontag argues, a woman's age is "something of a dirty secret."[5] While aging men are often considered "distinguished," women are offered an array of camouflage products—cosmetics, surgery, and hair colorings—to prevent them from being seen as old in a culture that equates female beauty with youthfulness. As Cynthia Rich points out, even language trivializes old women's actions. While usually not meant maliciously, expressions such as "little old lady" demean and belittle old women.

---

[4]Adrienne Rich, "Compulsory Heterosexuality and Lesbian Existence," *Signs* 5, no. 4 (Summer 1980), pp. 631–60.
[5]Susan Sontag, "The Double Standard of Aging," in *the Other Within Us: Feminist Explorations of Women and Aging*, ed. Marilyn Pearsall (Boulder, CO: Westview Press, 1997).

Because of the disadvantaged position of women in the workforce and the lack of financial compensation for women's work in the home, far more women over 65 live in poverty than their male contemporaries. Women living alone are disproportionately represented among the elderly poor, and their poverty often results in inadequate health care. Improving the position of all women in the workforce will address some of these problems, but changes in social policy are required to provide adequate health care and pensions for people who have spent much of their lives outside the workforce, and to ensure that affordable housing is available for the thousands of old women living alone.

Sometimes even harder to recognize are the privileges women receive or oppression they face because of their citizenship status. Because of their social location, women living in the United States and other industrialized nations have access to resources and opportunities that we often don't think about and that are denied to women in other parts of the world. And within the United States many women benefit from the privileges of citizenship that undocumented women don't have. Undocumented immigrant women are often blamed for coming to the United States and "taking other workers' jobs" when, in fact, most have been compelled to leave their homelands because of poverty caused by governmental and corporate policies of the industrialized nations. Similarly caught between nations, indigenous women, the earliest inhabitants of many of today's nation-states, suffer from poverty and being "nationless" because their rights, land, natural resources, and cultures have forcibly been taken away.

Becoming aware of the institutional inequities in our society encourages us to challenge what Peggy McIntosh has described as "the myth of meritocracy," the belief that one's success is purely the result of one's own abilities and efforts, unaffected by the advantages or disadvantages that accrue to various social groups. Recognizing the ways that systems of power and privilege enhance the lives of members of advantaged groups can help us to understand better the way they restrict the lives of people without these privileges.

The stories, essays, and poems in this chapter address the many dimensions of prejudice and institutional discrimination as they intersect to affect women. They also reveal some of the attitudes that have prevented women from honestly addressing the differences among us, such as the assumptions that some people's experience is universal while others' is marginal and deviant, the fear of conflict, and the desire to feel safe. Bernice Reagon has pointed out that while we need places to feel safe and comfortable, with people who share our experience, we also need to work toward common goals with people who are different, a process that is both important and challenging. Coalition work, she says, is often uncomfortable, because it requires people to listen to each other, examine their assumptions, and make compromise. Johnson suggests coalition work is challenging because often it's uncomfortable and in coalitions you have to give.[6] By seeing differences from a variety of viewpoints, we can begin to move beyond the distrust of difference that permeates our culture and use our experiences to enrich our analysis of society and understanding of women's lives.

---

[6]Bernice Johnson Reagon, "Coalition Politics: Turning the Century," in *Home Girls: A Black Feminist Anthology*, ed. Barbara Smith (New York: Kitchen Table Press, 1983).

Take a Closer Look: Racism in Women's Lives

Racism in our society operates on many levels and implicates all of us, whether we are conscious of it or not. Despite the advances of the civil rights movement, people of color continue to encounter racism both in institutions and among individuals. Because our society remains highly segregated by race and ethnicity, most of us grow up ignorant of the experiences and feelings of other groups of people. Beverly Daniel Tatum's article, which begins this section, explores the meaning of racism for all of us and makes useful distinctions between individual prejudice and racism, the system of advantages and disadvantages based on race that structures our social institutions. Understanding the ways that racism affects us requires us to recognize differences, despite pervasive pressure in our society to ignore them, as described in Adrienne Su's essay, "Codes of Conduct."

Many of the pieces in this section tell of the scars of racism through the eyes of its victims. They enable us to see both the enormously destructive power of racism and the will of the human spirit to resist it. They also reveal various forms that racism can take. The authors of the first two poems demonstrate the ways that racial stereotypes obliterate their individuality. "Take a Closer Look" describes the agony of children trying to develop a sense of themselves in a racist world.

Peggy McIntosh, recognizing that being white has given her unearned advantages in a racist society, shares examples of the privileges of daily life that white people may be unaware of. Understanding these advantages can enable those of us who benefit from them to better support the struggles of people who are disadvantaged by systems of unequal power and privilege. You may find it useful to apply MacIntosh's ideas to your own campus.

Finally an excerpt from Angela Davis's autobiography describes the ways Davis and her friends resisted racism by developing methods of maintaining their dignity and self-respect in the face of the daily hostility and contempt of white people in the South in the 1940s and 1950s.

101

Defining Racism: "Can We Talk?"

BEVERLY DANIEL TATUM

The impact of racism begins early. Even in our preschool years, we are exposed to misinformation about people different from ourselves. Many of us grew up in neighborhoods where we had limited opportunities to interact with people different from our own families. When I ask my college students, "How many of you grew up in neighborhoods where most of the people were from the same racial group as your own?" almost every hand goes up. There is still a great deal of social segregation in our communities. Consequently, most of the early information we receive about "others"—people racially, religiously, or socioeconomically different from ourselves—does not come as the result of firsthand experience. The secondhand information we do receive has often been distorted, shaped by cultural stereotypes, and left incomplete.

Some examples will highlight this process. Several years ago one of my students conducted a research project investigating preschoolers' conceptions of Native Americans.[1] Using children at a local day care center as her participants, she asked these three- and four-year-olds to draw a picture of a Native American. Most children were stumped by her request. They didn't know what a Native American was. But when she rephrased the question and asked them to draw a picture of an Indian, they readily complied. Almost every picture included one central feature: feathers. In fact, many of them also included a weapon—a knife or tomahawk—and depicted the person in violent or aggressive terms. Though this group of children, almost all of whom were white, did not live near a large Native American population and probably had had little if any personal interaction with American Indians, they all had internalized an image of what Indians were like. How did they know? Cartoon images, in particular the Disney movie *Peter Pan,* were cited by the children as their number-one source of information. At the age of three, these children already had a set of stereotypes in place. Though I would not describe three-year-olds as prejudiced, the stereotypes to which they have been exposed become the foundation for the adult prejudices so many of us have.

Sometimes the assumptions we make about others come not from what we have been told or what we have seen on television or in books, but rather from what we have *not* been told. The distortion of historical information about people of color leads young people (and older people, too) to make assumptions that may go unchallenged for a long time. Consider this conversation between two white students following a discussion about the cultural transmission of racism:

"Yeah, I just found out that Cleopatra was actually a black woman."

"What?"

The first student went on to explain her newly learned information. The second student exclaimed in disbelief, "That can't be true. Cleopatra was beautiful!"

What had this young woman learned about who in our society is considered beautiful and who is not? Had she conjured up images of Elizabeth Taylor when she thought of Cleopatra? The new information her classmate had shared and her own deeply ingrained assumptions about who is beautiful and who is not were too incongruous to allow her to assimilate the information at that moment.

Omitted information can have similar effects. For example, another young woman, preparing to be a high school English teacher, expressed her dismay that she had never learned about any black authors in any of her English courses. How was she to teach about them to her future students when she hadn't learned about them herself? A white male student in the class responded to this discussion with frustration in his response journal, writing "It's not my fault that blacks don't write books." Had one of his elementary, high school, or college teachers ever told him that there were no black writers? Probably not. Yet because he had never been exposed to black authors, he had drawn his own conclusions that there were none.

Stereotypes, omissions, and distortions all contribute to the development of prejudice. *Prejudice* is a preconceived judgment or opinion, usually based on limited information. I assume that we all have prejudices, not because we want them, but simply because we are so continually exposed to misinformation about others. Though I have often heard students or workshop participants describe someone as not having "a prejudiced bone in his body," I usually suggest they look again. Prejudice is one of the inescapable consequences of living in a racist society. Cultural racism—the cultural images and messages that affirm the assumed superiority of Whites and the assumed inferiority of people of color—is like smog in the air. Sometimes it is so thick it is visible, other times it is less apparent, but always, day in and day out, we are breathing it in. None of us would introduce ourselves as "smog-breathers" (and most of us don't want to be described as prejudiced), but if we live in a smoggy place, how can we avoid breathing the air? If we live in an environment in which we are bombarded with stereotypical images in the media, are frequently exposed to the ethnic jokes of friends and family members, and are rarely informed of the accomplishments of oppressed groups, we will develop the negative categorizations of those groups that form the basis of prejudice.

People of color as well as Whites develop these categorizations. Even a member of the stereotyped group may internalize the stereotypical categories about his or her own group to some degree. In fact, this process happens so frequently that it has a name, *internalized oppression*.

Certainly some people are more prejudiced than others, actively embracing and perpetuating negative and hateful images of those who are different from themselves. When we claim to be free of prejudice, perhaps what we are really saying is that we are not hatemongers. But none of us is completely innocent. Prejudice is an integral part of our socialization, and it is not our fault. Just as the preschoolers my student interviewed are not to blame for the negative messages they internalized, we are not at fault for the stereotypes, distortions, and omissions that shaped our thinking as we grew up.

To say that it is not our fault does not relieve us of responsibility, however. We may not have polluted the air, but we need to take responsibility, along with others, for cleaning it up. Each of us needs to look at our own behavior. Am I perpetuating and reinforcing the negative messages so pervasive in our culture, or am I seeking to challenge them? If I have not been exposed to positive images of marginalized groups, am I seeking them out, expanding my own knowledge base for myself and my children? Am I acknowledging and examining my own prejudices, my own rigid categorizations of others, thereby minimizing the adverse impact they might have on my interactions with those I have categorized? Unless we engage in these and other conscious acts of reflection and reeducation, we easily repeat the process with our children. We teach what we were taught. The unexamined prejudices of the parents are passed on to the children. It is not our fault, but it is our responsibility to interrupt this cycle.

RACISM: A SYSTEM OF ADVANTAGE BASED ON RACE

Many people use the terms *prejudice* and *racism* interchangeably. I do not, and I think it is important to make a distinction. In his book *Portraits of White Racism*, David Wellman argues convincingly that limiting our understanding of racism to prejudice does not offer a sufficient explanation for the persistence of racism. He defines racism as a "system of advantage based on race."[2] In illustrating this definition, he provides example after example of how Whites defend their racial advantage—access to better schools, housing, jobs—even when they do not embrace overtly prejudicial thinking. Racism cannot be fully explained as an expression of prejudice alone.

This definition of racism is useful because it allows us to see that racism, like other forms of oppression, is not only a personal ideology based on racial prejudice, but a *system* involving cultural messages and institutional policies and practices as well as the beliefs and actions of individuals. In the context of the United States, this system clearly operates to the advantage of whites and to the disadvantage of people of color. Another related definition of racism, commonly used by antiracist educators and consultants, is "prejudice plus power." Racial prejudice when combined with social power—access to social, cultural, and economic resources and decision-making—leads to the institutionalization of racist policies and practices. While I think this definition also captures the idea that racism is more than individual beliefs and attitudes, I prefer Wellman's definition because the idea of systematic advantage and disadvantage is critical to an understanding of how racism operates in American society.

In addition, I find that many of my white students and workshop participants do not feel powerful. Defining racism as prejudice plus power has little personal relevance. For some, their response to this definition is the following: "I'm not really prejudiced, and I have no power, so racism has nothing to do with me." However, most white people, if they are really being honest with themselves, can see that there are advantages to being white in the United States. Despite the current rhetoric about affirmative action and "reverse racism," every social indicator, from salary to life expectancy, reveals the advantages of being white.[3]

The systematic advantages of being white are often referred to as white privilege. In a now well-known article, "White Privilege: Unpacking the Invisible Knapsack," Peggy McIntosh, a white feminist scholar, identified a long list of societal privileges that she received simply because she was white.[4] She did not ask for them, and it is important to note that she hadn't always noticed that she was receiving them. They included major and minor advantages. Of course she enjoyed greater access to jobs and housing. But she also was able to shop in department stores without being followed by suspicious salespeople and could always find appropriate hair care products and makeup in any drugstore. She could send her child to school confident that the teacher would not discriminate against him on the basis of race. She could also be late for meetings, and talk with her mouth full, fairly confident that these behaviors would not be attributed to the fact that she was white. She could express an opinion in a meeting or in print and not have it labeled the "white" viewpoint. In other words, she was more often than not viewed as an individual, rather than as a member of a racial group.

The article rings true for most white readers, many of whom may have never considered the benefits of being white. It's one thing to have enough awareness of racism to describe the ways that people of color are disadvantaged by it. But this new understanding of racism is more elusive. In very concrete terms, it means that if a person of color is the victim of housing discrimination, the apartment that would otherwise have been rented to that person of color is still available for a white person. The white tenant is, knowingly or unknowingly, the beneficiary of racism, a system of advantage based on race. The unsuspecting tenant is not to blame for the prior discrimination, but she benefits from it anyway.

For many whites, this new awareness of the benefits of a racist system elicits considerable pain, often accompanied by feelings of anger and guilt. These uncomfortable emotions can hinder further discussion. We all like to think that we deserve the good things we have received, and that others, too, get what they deserve. Social psychologists call this tendency a "belief in a just world."[5] Racism directly contradicts such notions of justice.

Understanding racism as a system of avantage based on race is antithetical to traditional notions of an American meritocracy. For those who have internalized this myth, this definition generates considerable discomfort. It is more comfortable simply to think of racism as a particular form of prejudice. Notions of power or privilege do not have to be addressed when our understanding of racism is constructed in that way.

The discomfort generated when a systemic definition of racism is introduced is usually quite visible in the workshops I lead. Someone in the group is usually quick to point out that this is not the definition you will find in most dictionaries. I reply, "Who wrote the dictionary?" I am not being facetious with this response. Whose interests are served by a "prejudice only" definition of racism? It is important to understand that the system of advantage is perpetuated when we do not acknowledge its existence.

RACISM: FOR WHITES ONLY?

Frequently someone will say, "You keep talking about white people. People of color can be racist, too." I once asked a white teacher what it would mean to her if a student or parent of color accused her of being racist. She said she would feel as though she had been punched in the stomach or called a "low-life scum." She is not alone in this feeling. The word *racist* holds a lot of emotional power. For many white people, to be called racist is the ultimate insult. The idea that this term might only be applied to whites becomes highly problematic for after all, can't people of color be "low-life scum" too?

Of course, people of any racial group hateful attitudes and behave in racially discrii and bigoted ways. We can all cite examples of horrible hate crimes which have been perpetrated by people of color as well as whites. Hateful behavior is hateful behavior no matter who does it. But when I am asked, "Can people of color be racist?" I reply, "The answer depends on your definition of racism." If one defines racism as racial prejudice, the answer is yes. People of color can and do have racial prejudices. However, if one defines racism as a system of advantage based on race, the answer is no. People of color are not racist because they do not systematically benefit from racism. And equally important, there is no systematic cultural and institutional support or sanction for the racial bigotry of people of color. In my view, reserving the term *racist* only for behaviors committed by whites in the context of a white-dominated society is a way of acknowledging the ever-present power differential afforded whites by the culture and institutions that make up the system of advantage and continue to reinforce notions of white superiority. (Using the same logic, I reserve the word *sexist* for men. Though women can and do have gender-based prejudices, only men systematically benefit from sexism.)

Despite my best efforts to explain my thinking on this point, there are some who will be troubled, perhaps even incensed, by my response. To call the racially motivated acts of a person of color acts of racial bigotry and to describe similar acts committed by whites as racist will make no sense to some people, including some people of color. To those, I will respectfully say, "We can agree to disagree." At moments like these, it is not agreement that is essential, but clarity. Even if you don't like the definition of racism I am using, hopefully you are now clear about what it is. If I also understand how you are using the term, our conversation can continue—despite our disagreement.

Another provocative question I'm often asked is "Are you saying all whites are racist?" When asked this question, I again remember that white teacher's response, and I am conscious that perhaps the question I am really being asked is, "Are you saying all whites are bad people?" The answer to that question is of course not. However, all white

people, intentionally or unintentionally, do benefit from racism. A more relevant question is what are white people as individuals doing to interrupt racism? For many white people, the image of a racist is a hood-wearing Klan member or a name-calling Archie Bunker figure. These images represent what might be called *active racism*, blatant, intentional acts of racial bigotry and discrimination. *Passive racism* is more subtle and can be seen in the collusion of laughing when a racist joke is told, of letting exclusionary hiring practices go unchallenged, of accepting as appropriate the omissions of people of color from the curriculum, and of avoiding difficult race-related issues. Because racism is so ingrained in the fabric of American institutions, it is easily self-perpetuating.[6] All that is required to maintain it is business as usual.

I sometimes visualize the ongoing cycle of racism as a moving walkway at the airport. Active racist behavior is equivalent to walking fast on the conveyor belt. The person engaged in active racist behavior has identified with the ideology of white supremacy and is moving with it. Passive racist behavior is equivalent to standing still on the walkway. No overt effort is being made, but the conveyor belt moves the bystanders along to the same destination as those who are actively walking. Some of the bystanders may feel the motion of the conveyor belt, see the active racists ahead of them, and choose to turn around, unwilling to go to the same destination as the white supremacists. But unless they are walking actively in the opposite direction at a speed faster than the conveyor belt—unless they are actively antiracist—they will find themselves carried along with the others.

So, not all whites are actively racist. Many are passively racist. Some, though not enough, are actively antiracist. The relevant question is not whether all whites are racist, but how we can move more white people from a position of active or passive racism to one of active antiracism? The task of interrupting racism is obviously not the task of whites alone. But the fact of white privilege means that whites have greater access to the societal institutions in need of transformation. To whom much is given, much is required.

It is important to acknowledge that while all whites benefit from racism, they do not all benefit equally. Other factors, such as socioeconomic status, gender, age, religious affiliation, sexual orientation, mental and physical ability, also play a role in our access to social influence and power. A white woman on welfare is not privileged to the same extent as a wealthy white heterosexual man. In her case, the systematic disadvantages of sexism and classism intersect with her White privilege, but the privilege is still there. This point was brought home to me in a 1994 study conducted by a Mount Holyoke graduate student, Phyllis Wentworth.[7] Wentworth interviewed a group of female college students, who were both older than their peers and were the first members of their families to attend college, about the pathways that led them to college. All of the women interviewed were white, from working-class backgrounds, from families where women were expected to graduate from high school and get married or get a job. Several had experienced abusive relationships and other personal difficulties prior to coming to college. Yet their experiences were punctuated by "good luck" stories of apartments obtained without a deposit, good jobs offered without experience or extensive reference checks, and encouragement provided by willing mentors. While the women acknowledged their good fortune, none of them discussed their whiteness. They had not considered the possibility that being White had worked in their favor and helped give them the benefit of the doubt at critical junctures. This study clearly showed that even under difficult circumstances, white privilege was still operating.

It is also true that not all people of color are equally targeted by racism. We all have multiple identities that shape our experience. I can describe myself as a light-skinned, well-educated, heterosexual, able-bodied, Christian African-American woman raised in a middle-class suburb. As an African-American woman, I am systematically disadvantaged by race and by gender, but I systematically receive benefits in the other categories, which then mediate my experience of racism and sexism. When one is targeted by multiple isms—racism, sexism, classism, heterosexism, ableism, anti-Semitism, ageism—in whatever combination, the effect is intensified. The particular combination of racism and classism in many communities of color is life-threatening. Nonetheless, when I, the middle-class black mother of two sons, read another story about a black man's unlucky encounter with a white police officer's deadly force, I am reminded that racism by itself can kill.   [1997]

NOTES

1. Approximately 75 percent of all black college students attend predominantly white colleges. For a discussion of black college attendance and retention at white colleges in comparison to historically black colleges, see W. R. Allen, "The Color of Success: African-American College Student Outcomes at Predominantly White and Historically Black Public Colleges and Universities," *Harvard Educational Review* 62, no. 1 (1992): 26–44.
2. For a detailed account and many more examples of campus racism, see J. R. Feagin and M. P. Sikes, *Living with Racism: The Black Middle-class Experience* (Boston: Beacon Press, 1994), ch. 3.
3. Many researchers have reported similar findings. For more information, see J. Fleming, *Blacks in College* (San Francisco: Jossey-Bass, 1984). See also W. R. Allen, E. G. Epp, and N. Z. Haniff (eds.), *College in Black and White: African American Students in Predominantly White and Historically Black Public Universities* (Albany: State University of New York Press, 1991).
4. W. R. Allen, "The Color of Success," 39–40. The National Study of Black College Students (NSBCS) surveyed more than 2,500 black college students attending a total of 16 public universities (eight predominantly white and eight historically black) about their college experiences and outcomes.
5. For a discussion of White students' responses to learning about the racial identity development process of students of color, see B. D. Tatum, "Talking about race, learning about racism."
6. Haley and Malcolm X, *The Autobiography of Malcolm X*, 174.
7. M. E. Dyson, *Race rules: Navigating the color line* (Boston: Beacon Press, 1996), 151.

❧ 102

Codes of Conduct

ADRIENNE SU

In the South, where I grew up, the people have an unspoken agreement. Reality is what eve~ says it is. The agreement is meant to protect from any perceived slight. It can be as innocuous as complimenting an ugly outfit, but among the truly polite, you could walk into church with a horse instead of your husband, and everyone would not only fail to notice anything wrong but also exclaim, "What a beautiful hat you have on! And Harry is looking so well! The two of you must come over for dinner sometime." By the end of the day, you'd actually believe that the horse was a man.

In the third grade, some friends and I often reenacted scenes from "Little House on the Prairie." My blonde friend played Mary because of the color of her hair. Another played Carrie, the youngest sister, because she was the youngest. I played Laura, "because you have dark hair," the others explained. Nobody ever pointed out that I did not in the slightest resemble a white Midwestern girl with freckles and brown pigtails. To suggest that perhaps I looked more like the long-lost daughter of a railroad worker of that time was to suggest that I looked different from my friends, and that simply was not done.

Not that the subject never came up—there might be a snack in my lunch that the other kids thought was strange, or a teacher might discreetly ask me about the trip my father took shortly after Nixon's visit opened China to the United States. But most of the time, there was no language for addressing what made me different. No one asked me about Chinese culture or how to say things in Chinese, which I didn't know, anyway. Questions of the sort were considered rude, a way of pointing out that I looked Chinese, rather than like the Southern gal I was.

This doesn't sound too serious—just a form of Southern gentility. But imagine living your whole life in an environment where everyone says that a cat is a dog, all the time. Your perception of animals changes. You see a cat racing up a tree and remark, "My, that dog is a good climber." You hear a plaintive meow from outside and put a beef bone in the backyard. And when you yourself are a cat in this world, you grow to think you are a dog.

This is fine until you leave this world—and go to a land known as the North, where people not only recognize cathood but celebrate it. They form alliances to preserve feline culture, holding fish dinners and mouse-catching lectures. They hold

cat networking activities and cat social events—even writers' conferences for cats who have a way with words. For the cat who's lived her whole life thinking she's a dog, this can come as a bit of a shock.

Up North, in college, I'd find myself in a group of Chinese Americans and think, Hey, I'm surrounded! before realizing that I blended in. I'd go to a gathering of Chinese students and wait to be discovered and thrown out. Talking with my Korean-American roommate, I found that I wasn't the only one whose lack of interest in math and science was seen as a possible birth defect.

One day, when I referred to myself as "Oriental," everyone in the room—white, Korean, Hispanic—pounced on me.

"It's Asian," they cried. "Oriental is offensive."

That was how I learned that there was a vocabulary for a long-unnamed aspect of my life. My visceral feelings of family obligation were known as filial piety, or, as my roommate and I described it, Asian guilt. My parents' unwillingness to contradict their friends was an act of saving face for all. And the melodramatic struggles to pay for dinner were not earnest fights but the desire to avoid guanxi, or obligation, to the other party.

I went home using not the big words of a kid home from college, but ordinary words for things that were familiar, in fact mundane, to my parents.

"I think we're making an unbalanced dinner," I said, peering into a beef stew. "Too many hot element ingredients, too few cold elements. Maybe—"

My mother, absorbed in the *Wall Street Journal*, waved a dismissive hand. My father, opening his mail, murmured, "Whatever." My brother, who was getting ready for hockey practice, was already out the door.

The next evening, I visited my best friend, the one who'd played Carrie, and sat down to my zillionth Southern dinner with her family.

"What classes are you taking?" her mother asked.

"I'm taking Chinese, so I can eavesdrop on my parents," I said, "and a course in East Asian religions—"

"What kind of job do you plan to get with that?" my friend's father joked.

"I just want to know enough to be able to talk to my relatives in China," I said. "To find out who I really am."

What happened next was very strange. You could hear a crumb of cornbread drop. My friend's house had always been a second home to me, as mine was to her, but on this topic, her family, unlike mine, was stuck. And it was my fault: I had carelessly dragged the conversation into never-never land, the land of what made me different.

During that frozen silence, I busied myself eating. Then I heard myself say:

"These mashed potatoes are wonderful! I've been so homesick for them. Up North, people just don't know how to cook."

My friend's mother urged me to have more. My friend's father passed the gravy and made a joke about Yankees. And instantly, my friend and I were eight years old again and digging into our plates, ravenous as puppies, because we were growing so fast. [1997]

🌿 103

Salad

JANICE MIRIKITANI

The woman
did not mean to
offend me,

her blue eyes
blinking
at the glint
of my blade,

as I cut
precisely
like magic
the cucumber in
exact, even,
quick slices.

Do you orientals
do everything
so neatly?   [1982]

🌿 104

I Am Not Your Princess

CHRYSTOS

especially for Dee Johnson

Sandpaper between two cultures which tear one
    another apart I'm not
a means by which you can reach spiritual under-
    standing or even
learn to do beadwork
I'm only willing to tell you how to make fry bread
1 cup flour, spoon of salt, spoon of baking powder
Stir   Add milk or water or beer until it holds together
Slap each piece into rounds   Let rest
Fry in hot grease until golden
This is Indian food only if you know that Indian is
    a government word
which has nothing to do with our names for
    ourselves
I won't chant for you
I admit no spirituality to you
I will not sweat with you or ease your guilt with
    fine turtle tales
I will not wear dancing clothes to read poetry
    or explain hardly anything at all
I don't think your attempts to understand us
    are going to work so I'd rather
you left us in whatever peace we can still scramble up
after all you continue to do
If you send me one more damn flyer about how
    to heal myself for $300
with special feminist counseling I'll probably set
    fire to something
If you tell me one more time that I'm wise I'll
    throw up on you
Look at me
See my confusion   loneliness   fear   worrying
    about all our struggles to keep
what little is left for us
Look at my heart   not your fantasies
Please don't ever again tell me about your
    Cherokee great-great grandmother
Don't assume I know every other Native Activist
    in the world personally

That I even know the names of all the tribes
or can pronounce names I've never heard
or that I'm expert at the peyote stitch
If you ever
again tell me
how strong I am
I'll lay down on the ground & moan so you'll see
at last   my human weakness   like your own
I'm not strong   I'm scraped
I'm blessed with life while so many I've known
   are dead
I have work to do   dishes to wash   a house to
   clean   There is no magic
See my simple cracked hands which have washed
   the same things you wash
See my eyes dark with fear in a house by myself
   late at night
See that to pity me or to adore me are the same
1 cup flour, spoon of salt, spoon of baking powder
   & liquid to hold
remember this is only my recipe   There are many
   others
Let me rest
here
at least   [1987]

 105

Take a Closer Look

CARRIE CASTRO

Can you see as you
take a closer look
beyond how I appear
to be so self assured
of who I am.
My name alone morena
does not reveal
the inner thoughts
of uneasiness
I sometimes feel.

Let me take you
back
to a time
when I was young

and didn't understand
the significance
of colored skins
when I didn't realize
they made a difference.

Back
to a time
when I became
aware of the division
some say existed
between those born
here and those who
come from "over there,"
we made the difference.

Back
to a time
when I grew older
and longed to be
someone else
instead of "me"
because I didn't feel
that was good enough,
I made the difference.

Take a closer look
because inside
my insecurities
you will find
that the reasons
arise from the
cobwebbed minds
of those who cannot see
any beauty in faces
darker than their own.   [1980]

 106

White Privilege: Unpacking the Invisible Knapsack

PEGGY MCINTOSH

Through work to bring materials from Women's
Studies into the rest of the curriculum, I have often
noticed men's unwillingness to grant that they are

over privileged, even though they may grant that women are disadvantaged. They may say they will work to improve women's status, in the society, the university, or the curriculum, but they can't or won't support the idea of lessening men's. Denials that amount to taboos surround the subject of advantages that men gain from women's disadvantages. These denials protect male privilege from being fully acknowledged, lessened, or ended.

Thinking through unacknowledged male privilege as a phenomenon, I realized that since hierarchies in our society are interlocking, there was most likely a phenomenon of white privilege which was similarly denied and protected. As a white person, I realized I had been taught about racism as something which puts others at a disadvantage, but had been taught not to see one of its corollary aspects, white privilege, which puts me at an advantage.

I think whites are carefully taught not to recognize white privilege, as males are taught not to recognize male privilege. So I have begun in an untutored way to ask what it is like to have white privilege. I have come to see white privilege as an invisible package of unearned assets which I can count on cashing in each day, but about which I was "meant" to remain oblivious. White privilege is like an invisible weightless knapsack of special provisions, maps, passports, codebooks, visas, clothes, tools, and blank checks.

Describing white privilege makes one newly accountable. As we in Women's Studies work to reveal male privilege and ask men to give up some of their power, so one who writes about having white privilege must ask, "Having described it, what will I do to lessen or end it?"

After I realized the extent to which men work from a base of unacknowledged privilege, I understood that much of their oppressiveness was unconscious. Then I remembered the frequent charges from women of color that white women whom they encounter are oppressive. I began to understand why we are justly seen as oppressive, even when we don't see ourselves that way. I began to count the ways in which I enjoy unearned skin privilege and have been conditioned into oblivion about its existence.

My schooling gave me no training in seeing myself as an oppressor, as an unfairly advantaged person, or as a participant in a damaged culture. I was taught to see myself as an individual whose moral state depended on her individual moral will. My schooling followed the pattern my colleague Elizabeth Minnich has pointed out: whites are taught to think of their lives as morally neutral, normative, and average, and also ideal, so that when we work to benefit others, this is seen as work that will allow "them" to be more like "us."

I decided to try to work on myself at least by identifying some of the daily effects of white privilege in my life. I have chosen those conditions which I think in my case *attach somewhat more to skin-color privilege* than to class, religion, ethnic status, or geographical location, though of course all these other factors are intricately intertwined. As far as I can see, my African-American co-workers, friends, and acquaintances with whom I come into daily or frequent contact in this particular time, place, and line of work cannot count on most of these conditions.

1. I can if I wish arrange to be in the company of people of my race most of the time.
2. If I should need to move, I can be pretty sure of renting or purchasing housing in an area that I can afford and in which I would want to live.
3. I can be pretty sure that my neighbors in such a location will be neutral or pleasant to me.
4. I can go shopping alone most of the time, pretty well assured that I will not be followed or harassed.
5. I can turn on the television or open to the front page of the paper and see people of my race widely represented.
6. When I am told about our national heritage or about "civilization," I am shown that people of my color made it what it is.
7. I can be sure that my children will be given curricular materials that testify to the existence of their race.
8. If I want to, I can be pretty sure of finding a publisher for this piece on white privilege.
9. I can go into a music shop and count on finding the music of my race represented, supermarket and find the staple foods th

with my cultural traditions, into a hairdresser's shop and find someone who can cut my hair.

10. Whether I use checks, credit cards, or cash, I can count on my skin color not to work against the appearance of financial reliability.

11. I can arrange to protect my children most of the time from people who might not like them.

12. I can swear, or dress in secondhand clothes, or not answer letters, without having people attribute these choices to the bad morals, the poverty, or the illiteracy of my race.

13. I can speak in public to a powerful male group without putting my race on trial.

14. I can do well in a challenging situation without being called a credit to my race.

15. I am never asked to speak for all the people of my racial group.

16. I can remain oblivious of the language and customs of persons of color who constitute the world's majority without feeling in my culture any penalty for such oblivion.

17. I can criticize our government and talk about how much I fear its policies and behavior without being seen as a cultural outsider.

18. I can be pretty sure that if I ask to talk to "the person in charge," I will be facing a person of my race.

19. If a traffic cop pulls me over or if the IRS audits my tax return, I can be sure I haven't been singled out because of my race.

20. I can easily buy posters, postcards, picture books, greeting cards, dolls, toys, and children's magazines featuring people of my race.

21. I can go home from most meetings of organizations I belong to feeling somewhat tied in, rather than isolated, out-of-place, outnumbered, unheard, held at a distance, or feared.

22. I can take a job with an affirmative action employer without having co-workers on the job suspect that I got it because of race.

23. I can choose public accommodation without fearing that people of my race cannot get in or will be mistreated in the places I have chosen.

24. I can be sure that if I need legal or medical help, my race will not work against me.

25. If my day, week, or year is going badly, I need not ask of each negative episode or situation whether it has racial overtones.

26. I can choose blemish cover or bandages in "flesh" color and have them more or less match my skin.

I repeatedly forgot each of the realizations on this list until I wrote it down. For me white privilege has turned out to be an elusive and fugitive subject. The pressure to avoid it is great, for in facing it I must give up the myth of meritocracy. If these things are true, this is not such a free country; one's life is not what one makes it; many doors open for certain people through no virtues of their own.

In unpacking this invisible backpack of white privilege, I have listed conditions of daily experience that I once took for granted. Nor did I think of any of these perquisites as bad for the holder. I now think that we need a more finely differentiated taxonomy of privilege, for some of these varieties are only what one would want for everyone in a just society, and others give licence to be ignorant, oblivious, arrogant and destructive.

I see a pattern running through the matrix of white privilege, a pattern of assumptions that were passed on to me as a white person. There was one main piece of cultural turf; it was my own turf, and I was among those who could control the turf. *My skin color was an asset for any move I was educated to want to make.* I could think of myself as belonging in major ways, and of making social systems work for me. I could freely disparage, fear, neglect, or be oblivious to anything outside of the dominant cultural forms. Being of the main culture, I could also criticize it fairly freely.

In proportion as my racial group was being made confident, comfortable, and oblivious, other groups were likely being made inconfident, uncomfortable, and alienated. Whiteness protected me from many kinds of hostility, distress, and violence, which I was being subtly trained to visit in turn upon people of color.

For this reason, the word "privilege" now seems to me misleading. We usually think of privilege as being a favored state, whether earned or conferred by birth or luck. Yet some of the conditions I have described here work to systematically overempower certain groups. Such privilege simply *confers dominance* because of one's race or sex.

I want, then, to distinguish between earned strength and unearned power conferred systematically. Power from unearned privilege can look like strength when it is in fact permission to escape or to dominate. But not all of the privileges on my list are inevitably damaging. Some, like the expectation that neighbors will be decent to you, or that your race will not count against you in court, should be the norm in a just society. Others, like the privilege to ignore less powerful people, distort the humanity of the holders as well as the ignored groups.

We might at least start by distinguishing between positive advantages that we can work to spread, and negative types of advantages that unless rejected will always reinforce our present hierarchies. For example, the feeling that one belongs within the human circle, as Native Americans say, should not be seen as privilege for a few. Ideally it is an *unearned entitlement*. At present, since only a few have it, it is an *unearned advantage* for them. This paper results from a process of coming to see that some of the power that I originally saw as attendant on being a human being in the United States consisted in *unearned advantage* and *conferred dominance*.

I have met very few men who are truly distressed about systemic, unearned male advantage and conferred dominance. And so one question for me and others like me is whether we will be like them, or whether we will get truly distressed, even outraged, about unearned race advantage and conferred dominance and if so, what we will do to lessen them. In any case, we need to do more work in identifying how they actually affect our daily lives. Many, perhaps most, of our white students in the United States think that racism doesn't affect them because they are not people of color; they do not see "whiteness" as a racial identity. In addition, since race and sex are not the only advantaging systems at work, we need similarly to examine the daily experience of having age advantage, or ethnic advantage, or physical ability, or advantage related to nationality, religion, or sexual orientation.

Difficulties and dangers surrounding the task of finding parallels are many. Since racism, sexism, and heterosexism are not the same, the advantaging associated with them should not be seen as the same. In addition, it is hard to disentangle aspects of unearned advantage that rest more on social class, economic class, race, religion, sex, and ethnic identity than on other factors. Still, all of the oppressions are interlocking, as the Combahee River Collective Statement of 1977 continues to remind us eloquently.

One factor seems clear about all of the interlocking oppressions. They take both active forms that we can see and embedded forms that as a member of the dominant group one is taught not to see. In my class and place, I did not see myself as a racist because I was taught to recognize racism only in individual acts of meanness by members of my group, never in invisible systems conferring unsought racial dominance on my group from birth.

Disapproving of the systems won't be enough to change them. I was taught to think that racism could end if white individuals changed their attitudes. [But] a "white" skin in the United States opens many doors for whites whether or not we approve of the way dominance has been conferred on us. Individual acts can palliate, but cannot end, these problems.

To redesign social systems we need first to acknowledge their colossal unseen dimensions. The silences and denials surrounding privilege are the key political tool here. They keep the thinking about equality or equity incomplete, protecting unearned advantage and conferred dominance by making these taboo subjects. Most talk by whites about equal opportunity seems to me now to be about equal opportunity to try to get into a position of dominance while denying that *systems* of dominance exist.

It seems to me that obliviousness about white advantage, like obliviousness about male advantage, is kept strongly inculturated in the United States so as to maintain the myth of meritocracy, the myth that democratic choice is equally available to all. Keeping most people unaware that freedom of confident action is there for just a small number of people props up those in power and serves to keep power in the hands of the same groups that have most of it already.

Though systematic change takes many decades, there are pressing questions for me and I imagine for some others like me if we raise our daily consciousness on the perquisites of being light-skinned. What will we do with such knowledge? As we know from watching men, it is an open question whether we will choose to use unearned advantage to weaken hidden systems of advantage, and whether we will use any of our arbitrarily awarded power to try to reconstruct power systems on a broader base.   [1989]

🌿 107

An Autobiography (excerpt)

ANGELA DAVIS

The big white house on top of the hill was not far from our old neighborhood, but the distance could not be measured in blocks. The government housing project on Eighth Avenue where we lived before was a crowded street of little red brick structures—no one of which was different from the other. Only rarely did the cement surrounding these brick huts break open and show patches of green. Without space or earth, nothing could be planted to bear fruit or blossoms. But friends were there—and friendliness.

In 1948 we moved out of the projects in Birmingham, Alabama, to the large wooden house on Center Street. My parents still live there. Because of its steeples and gables and peeling paint, the house was said to be haunted. There were wild woods in back with fig trees, blackberry patches, and great wild cherry trees. On one side of the house was a huge Cigar tree. There was space here and no cement. The street itself was a strip of orange-red Alabama clay. It was the most conspicuous house in the neighborhood—not only because of its curious architecture but because, for blocks around, it was the only house not teeming inside with white hostility. We were the first black family to move into that area, and the white people believed that we were in the vanguard of a mass invasion.

At the age of four I was aware that the people across the street were different—without yet being able to trace their alien nature to the color of their skin. What made them different from our neighbors in the projects was the frown on their faces, the way they stood a hundred feet away and glared at us, their refusal to speak when we said "Good afternoon." An elderly couple across the street, the Montees, sat on their porch all the time, their eyes heavy with belligerence.

Almost immediately after we moved there the white people got together and decided on a border line between them and us. Center Street became the line of demarcation. Provided that we stayed on "our" side of the line (the east side) they let it be known we would be left in peace. If we ever crossed over to their side, war would be declared. Guns were hidden in our house and vigilance was constant.

Fifty or so yards from this hatred, we went about our daily lives. My mother, on leave from her teaching job, took care of my younger brother Benny, while waiting to give birth to another child, my sister Fania. My father drove his old orange van to the service station each morning after dropping me off at nursery school. It was next door to the Children's Home Hospital—an old wooden building where I was born and where, at two, I had my tonsils removed. I was fascinated by the people dressed in white and tried to spend more time at the hospital than at the nursery. I had made up my mind that I was going to be a doctor—a children's doctor.

Shortly after we moved to the hill, white people began moving out of the neighborhood and black families were moving in, buying old houses and building new ones. A black minister and his wife, the Deyaberts, crossed into white territory, buying the house right next to the Montees, the people with the hateful eyes.

It was evening in the spring of 1949. I was in the bathroom washing my white shoelaces for Sunday School the next morning when an explosion a hundred times louder than the loudest, most frightening thunderclap I had ever heard shook our house. Medicine bottles fell off the shelves, shattering all around me. The floor seemed to slip away from my feet as I raced into the kitchen and my frightened mother's arms.

Crowds of angry black people came up the hill and stood on "our" side, staring at the bombed-out ruins of the Deyaberts' house. Far into the night they spoke of death, of white hatred, death, white people, and more death. But of their own fear they said nothing. Apparently it did not exist, for black families continued to move in. The bombings were such a constant response that soon our neighborhood became known as Dynamite Hill.

The more steeped in violence our environment became, the more determined my father and mother were that I, the firstborn, learn that the battle of white against black was not written into the nature of things. On the contrary, my mother always said, love had been ordained by God. White people's hatred of us was neither natural nor eternal. She knew that whenever I answered the telephone and called to her, "Mommy, a white lady wants to talk to you," I was doing more than describing the curious drawl. Every time I said "white lady" or "white man" anger clung to my words. My mother tried to erase the anger with reasonableness. Her experiences had included contacts with white people seriously committed to improving race relations. Though she had grown up in rural Alabama, she had become involved, as a college student, in anti-racist movements. She had worked to free the Scottsboro Boys and there had been whites—some of them Communists—in that struggle. Through her own political work, she had learned that it was possible for white people to walk out of their skin and respond with the integrity of human beings. She tried hard to make her little girl—so full of hatred and confusion—see white people not so much as what they were as in terms of their potential. She did not want me to think of the guns hidden in drawers or the weeping black woman who had come screaming to our door for help, but of a future world of harmony and equality. I didn't know what she was talking about.

When black families had moved up on the hill in sufficient numbers for me to have a group of friends, we developed our own means of defending our egos. Our weapon was the word. We would gather on my front lawn, wait for a car of white people to pass by and shout the worst epithets for white people we knew: Cracker. Redneck. Then we would laugh hysterically at the startled expressions on their faces. I hid this pastime from my parents. They could not know how important it was for me, and for all of us who had just discovered racism, to find ways of maintaining our dignity.   [1974]

The Legacy of Class

In the United States, people do not talk about class very much. Nevertheless, most people are very aware of class differences as they manifest themselves in the way people look, talk, and move through the world, and this awareness affects the way we relate to each other. As Donna Langston explains in "Tired of Playing Monopoly?" our class backgrounds have a powerful effect on our values, the ways we see ourselves, and the choices we have in our lives. For example, women who grew up in middle-class homes often saw work outside the home as a form of liberation, while women in poor and working-class families have always worked, often at alienating, dead-end jobs.

The feminist ideal of sisterhood among women is often challenged by class divisions. In "Sisters," both women are African-American, united by the racism and sexism in their lives but divided by social class. Jealousy, competition, and the belief that one can make it on one's own if one is "tough enough" keep them from offering each other the support they each desperately need.

This section includes stories and essays that explore the meaning of class in women's lives. Kendall Johnson describes the vast distance between the social and cultural realities of middle-class and poor people. For Bernice Mennis, being Jewish and working class are closely intertwined in her recollections of her efforts to make sense of a world in which she often felt different. While education was a gateway to the middle class for these women, they recount their efforts, however conflicted, to maintain an ongoing awareness of their class background and connections to their families and their roots. Finally, in Toi Derricotte's poem, Grace Paley, a well-known North American writer, reaches across class differences with a small act of consideration.

108

Tired of Playing Monopoly?

DONNA LANGSTON

I. Magnin, Nordstrom, The Bon, Sears, Penney's, Kmart, Goodwill, Salvation Army. If the order of this list of stores makes any sense to you, then we've begun to deal with the first question which inevitably arises in any discussion of class here in the United States—huh? Unlike our European allies, we in the United States are reluctant to recognize class differences. This denial of class divisions functions to reinforce ruling class control and domination. America is, after all, the supposed land of equal opportunity where, if you just work hard enough, you can get ahead, pull yourself up by your bootstraps. What the old bootstraps theory overlooks is that some were born with silver shoe horns. Female-headed households, communities of color, the elderly, disabled, and children find themselves, disproportionately, living in poverty. If hard work were the sole determinant of your ability to support yourself and your family, surely we'd have a different outcome for many in our society. We also, however, believe in luck and, on closer examination, it certainly is quite a coincidence that the "unlucky" come from certain race, gender and class backgrounds. In order to perpetuate racist, sexist and classist outcomes, we also have to believe that the current economic distribution is unchangeable, has always existed, and probably exists in this form throughout the known universe, i.e., it's "natural." Some people explain or try to account for poverty or class position by focusing on the personal and moral merits of an individual. If people are poor, then it's something they did or didn't do; they were lazy, unlucky, didn't try hard enough, etc. This has the familiar ring of blaming the victims. Alternative explanations focus on the ways in which poverty and class position are due to structural, systematic, institutionalized economic and political power relations. These power relations are based firmly on dynamics such as race, gender, and class.

In the myth of the classless society, ambition and intelligence alone are responsible for success. The myth conceals the existence of a class society, which serves many functions. One of the main ways it keeps the working class and poor locked into a class-based system in a position of servitude is by cruelly creating false hope. It perpetuates the false hope among the working class and poor that they can have different opportunities in life. The hope that they can escape the fate that awaits them due to the class position they were born into. Another way the rags-to-riches myth is perpetuated is by creating enough visible tokens so that oppressed persons believe they, too, can get ahead. The creation of hope through tokenism keeps a hierarchical structure in place and lays the blame for not succeeding on those who don't. This keeps us from resisting and changing the class-based system. Instead, we accept it as inevitable, something we just have to live with. If oppressed people believe in equality of opportunity, then they won't develop class consciousness and will internalize the blame for their economic position. If the working class and poor do

not recognize the way false hope is used to control them, they won't get a chance to control their lives by acknowledging their class position, by claiming that identity and taking action as a group.

The myth also keeps the middle class and upper class entrenched in the privileges awarded in a class-based system. It reinforces middle- and upper-class beliefs in their own superiority. If we believe that anyone in society really can get ahead, then middle- and upper-class status and privileges must be deserved, due to personal merits, and enjoyed—and defended at all costs. According to this viewpoint, poverty is regrettable but acceptable, just the outcome of a fair game: "There have always been poor people, and there always will be."

Class is more than just the amount of money you have; it's also the presence of economic security. For the working class and poor, working and eating are matters of survival, not taste. However, while one's class status can be defined in important ways in terms of monetary income, class is also a whole lot more—specifically, class is also culture. As a result of the class you are born into and raised in, class is your understanding of the world and where you fit in; it's composed of ideas, behavior, attitudes, values, and language; class is how you think, feel, act, look, dress, talk, move, walk; class is what stores you shop at, restaurants you eat in; class is the schools you attend, the education you attain; class is the very jobs you will work at throughout your adult life. Class even determines when we marry and become mothers. Working-class women become mothers long before middle-class women receive their bachelor's degrees. We experience class at every level of our lives; class is who our friends are, where we live and work, even what kind of car we drive, if we own one, and what kind of health care we receive, if any. Have I left anything out? In other words, class is socially constructed and all-encompassing. When we experience classism, it will be because of our lack of money (i.e., choices and power in this society) and because of the way we talk, think, act, move—because of our culture.

Class affects what we perceive and what we have available to us as choices. Upon graduation from high school, I was awarded a scholarship to attend any college, private or public, in the state of California. Yet it never occurred to me or my family that it made any difference which college you went to. I ended up just going to a small college in my town. It never would have occurred to me to move away from my family for school, because no one ever had and no one would. I was the first person in my family to go to college. I had to figure out from reading college catalogs how to apply—no one in my family could have sat down and said, "Well, you take this test and then you really should think about. . . ." Although tests and high school performance had shown I had the ability to pick up white middle-class lingo, I still had quite an adjustment to make—it was lonely and isolating in college. I lost my friends from high school—they were at the community college, vo-tech school, working, or married. I lasted a year and a half in this foreign environment before I quit college, married a factory worker, had a baby, and resumed living in a community I knew. One middle-class friend in college had asked if I'd like to travel to Europe with her. Her father was a college professor and people in her family had actually travelled there. My family had seldom been able to take a vacation at all. A couple of times my parents were able—by saving all year—to take the family over to the coast on their annual two-week vacation. I'd seen the time and energy my parents invested in trying to take a family vacation to some place a few hours away; the idea of how anybody ever got to Europe was beyond me.

If class is more than simple economic status but one's cultural background, as well, what happens if you're born and raised middle-class, but spend some of your adult life with earnings below a middle-class income bracket—are you then working-class? Probably not. If your economic position changes, you still have the language, behavior, educational background, etc., of the middle class, which you can bank on. You will always have choices. Men who consciously try to refuse male privilege are still male; whites who want to challenge white privilege are still white. I think those who come from middle-class backgrounds need to recognize that their class privilege does not float out with the rinse water. Middle-class people can exert incredible power just

by being nice and polite. The middle-class way of doing things is the standard—they're always right, just by being themselves. Beware of middle-class people who deny their privilege. Many people have times when they struggle to get shoes for the kids, when budgets are tight, etc. This isn't the same as long-term economic conditions without choices. Being working class is also generational. Examine your family's history of education, work, and standard of living. It may not be a coincidence that you share the same class status as your parents and grandparents. If your grandparents were professionals, or your parents were professionals, it's much more likely you'll be able to grow up to become a yuppie, if your heart so desires, or even if you don't think about it.

How about if you're born and raised poor or working class, yet through struggle, usually through education, you manage to achieve a different economic level: do you become middle class? Can you pass? I think some working-class people may successfully assimilate into the middle class by learning to dress, talk, and act middle class—to accept and adopt the middle-class way of doing things. It all depends on how far they're able to go. To succeed in the middle-class world means facing great pressures to abandon working-class friends and ways.

Contrary to our stereotype of the working class—white guys in overalls—the working class is not homogeneous in terms of race or gender. If you are a person of color, if you live in a female-headed household, you are much more likely to be working class or poor. The experience of black, Latino, American Indian, or Asian American working classes will differ significantly from the white working classes, which have traditionally been able to rely on white privilege to provide a more elite position within the working class. Working-class people are often grouped together and stereotyped, but distinctions can be made among the working class, working poor, and poor. Many working-class families are supported by unionized workers who possess marketable skills. Most working-poor families are supported by non-unionized, unskilled men and women. Many poor families are dependent on welfare for their income.

Attacks on the welfare system and those who live on welfare are a good example of classism in action. We have a "dual welfare" system in this country whereby welfare for the rich in the form of tax-free capital gain, guaranteed loans, oil depletion allowances, etc., is not recognized as welfare. Almost everyone in America is on some type of welfare; but, if you're rich, it's in the form of tax deductions for "business" meals and entertainment, and if you're poor, it's in the form of food stamps. The difference is the stigma and humiliation connected to welfare for the poor, as compared to welfare for the rich, which is called "incentives." Ninety-three percent of welfare recipients are women. A common focal point for complaints about "welfare" is the belief that most welfare recipients are cheaters—goodness knows there are no middle-class income tax cheaters out there. Imagine focusing the same anger and energy on the way corporations and big business cheat on their tax revenues. Now, there would be some dollars worth quibbling about. The "dual welfare" system also assigns a different degree of stigma to programs that benefit women and children and programs whose recipients are primarily male, such as veterans' benefits. The implicit assumption is that mothers who raise children do not work and therefore are not deserving of their daily bread crumbs.

Working-class women's critiques have focused on the following issues:

Education: White middle-class professionals have used academic jargon to rationalize and justify classism. The whole structure of education is a classist system. Schools in every town reflect class divisions: like the store list at the beginning of this article, you can list schools in your town by what classes of kids attend, and in most cities you can also list by race. The classist system is perpetuated in schools with the tracking system, whereby the "dumbs" are tracked into homemaking, shop courses, and vocational school futures, while the "smarts" end up in advanced math, science, literature, and college-prep courses. If we examine these groups carefully, the coincidence of poor and working-class backgrounds with "dumbs" is rather alarming. The standard measurement of supposed intelligence is white middle-class English. If you're other than white middle-class, you have to become bilingual to succeed in the educational system. If you're white middle-class, you only need the language and writing skills you were raised with, since they're the standard. To do well in society presupposes middle-class background, experiences and learning for everyone. The tracking system separates those from the working class who can potentially assimilate to the middle class from all our friends, and labels us "college bound."

After high school, you go on to vocational school, community college, or college—public or private—according to your class position. Apart from the few who break into middle-class schools, the classist stereotyping of the working class as being dumb and inarticulate tracks most into vocational and low-skilled jobs. A few of us are allowed to slip through to reinforce the idea that equal opportunity exists. But for most, class position is destiny—determining our educational attainment and employment. Since we must overall abide by middle-class rules to succeed, the assumption is that we go to college in order to "better ourselves"—i.e., become more like them. I suppose it's assumed we have "yuppie envy" and desire nothing more than to be upwardly mobile individuals. It's assumed that we want to fit into their world. But many of us remain connected to our communities and families. Becoming college-educated doesn't mean we have to, or want to, erase our first and natural language and value system. It's important for many of us to remain in and return to our communities to work, live, and stay sane.

Jobs: Middle-class people have the privilege of choosing careers. They can decide which jobs they want to work, according to their moral or political commitments, needs for challenge or creativity. This is a privilege denied the working class and poor, whose work is a means of survival, not choice. Working-class women have seldom had the luxury of choosing between work in the home or market. We've generally done both, with little ability to purchase services to help with this double burden. Middle- and upper-class women can often hire other women to clean their houses, take care of their children, and cook their meals. Guess what class and race those "other" women are? Working a double or triple day is common for working-class women. Only middle-class women have an array of choices such as: parents put you through school, then you choose a career, then you choose when and if to have babies, then you choose a support system of working-class women to take care of your kids and house if you choose to resume your career. After the birth of my second child, I was working two part-time jobs—one loading trucks at night—and going to school during the days. While I was quite privileged because I could take my colicky infant with me to classes and the day-time job, I was in a state of continuous semi consciousness. I had to work to support my family; the only choice I had was between school or sleep: Sleep became a privilege. A white middle-class feminist instructor at the university suggested to me, all sympathetically, that I ought to hire someone to clean my house and watch the baby. Her suggestion was totally out of my reality, both economically and socially. I'd worked for years cleaning other people's houses. Hiring a working-class woman to do the shit work is a middle-class woman's solution to any dilemma that her privileges, such as a career, may present her.

Individualism: Preoccupation with one's self—one's body, looks, relationships—is a luxury working-class women can't afford. Making an occupation out of taking care of yourself through therapy, aerobics, jogging, dressing for success, gourmet meals, and proper nutrition, etc., may be responses that are directly rooted in privilege. The middle class have the leisure time to be preoccupied with their own problems, such as their waistlines, planning their vacations, coordinating their wardrobes, or dealing with what their mother said to them when they were five—my!

The white middle-class women's movement has been patronizing to working-class women. Its supporters think we don't understand sexism. The idea of women as passive, weak creatures totally discounts the strength, self-dependence and interdependence necessary to survive as working class and poor women. My mother and her friends always had a less-than-passive, less-than-enamoured attitude toward their spouses, male bosses, and men in general. I know from listening to their conversations, jokes, and what they passed on to us, their daughters, as folklore. When I was five years old, my mother told me about how Aunt Betty had hit Uncle Ernie over the head with a skillet and knocked him out because he was raising his hand to hit her, and how he's never even thought about doing it since. This story was told to me with a good amount of glee and laughter. All the men in the neighborhood were told of the event as an example of what was a very accepable response in the women's community for that type of male behavior. We kids in the neighborhood grew up with these stories of women giving husbands, bosses, the welfare system, schools, unions, and men in general—hell, whenever they deserved it. For me there were many role models of women taking action, control, and resisting what was supposed to be their lot.   [1988]

 109

Sisters

BARBARA NEELY

. . . and are we not one
daughter of the same dark mother's child
breathing one breath from a multitude of mouths . . .
            —from the Sisterhood Song of the Yenga Nation

The offices of Carstairs and Carstairs Management Consultants had that hushed, forbidden air of after five o'clock. No light shone from beneath any of the office doors bordering the central typing pool that was also deserted, except for the new cleaning woman working her way among the desks. Lorisa was the last of the office staff to leave. She'd pushed the button for the elevator before she remembered the notes on Wider Housewares she wanted to look over before tomorrow morning's meeting. She turned and took a shortcut through the typing pool to her office.

"Good evening," she said to the grey uniform-clad back of the cleaning woman as the woman reached down to pick up a wastebasket. Lorisa automatically put on her polite, remote smile, the one that matched the distance in her tone, while she waited for the woman to move out of her way.

Jackie turned with the wastebasket still in her hand and let her eyes roam so slowly over the woman who'd spoken to her that she might have been looking for something in particular. Then she nodded, briefly, curtly, before turning, lifting the basket and dashing its contents into the rolling bin she pushed along ahead of her. Only then did she step aside.

Lorisa hurried into her office, careful not to slam the door and show her irritation. Where did they find the cleaning staff, the asylum for the criminally insane? The woman had given her a look cold enough to cut stone and barely acknowledged her greeting—as though she were not worth the time it took to be pleasant. She, who was always careful to speak to the gum-chewing black girls who worked in the mail room, the old man who shined shoes in the lobby, the newspaper man and any other of her people she met in the building who did menial work. None of them had ever been anything but equally polite to her. She had noticed the shoeshine man always had something pleasant to say to the mailroom girls and only a "Good day" to her. But considering the difference in their positions, his reticence with her seemed only natural and nothing like the attitude of the cleaning woman.

Although she'd only returned for her notes, she found herself moving papers from one side of her desk to the other, making a list of small tasks for tomorrow, staving off the moment when she would have to confront the cleaning woman once again. But Lorisa realized it wasn't the woman's curt nod or the slowness with which she'd moved aside that made her reluctant to leave her office. It was those eyes. Big, black, dense eyes with something knowing in them—something that had made her feel as though her loneliness and her fear of it, her growing uneasiness about her job, the disturbing hollowness where pleasure in her comfortable life should be, and all her other fears and flaws were as visible to the cleaning woman as so many wrinkles and smudges

on her dress. When their eyes had met, the sense of secret knowledge already shared had filled her with an almost overwhelming desire to say something, to explain something about a part of herself she couldn't name. The woman's look of cold disdain had only corroborated her feeling of having been revealed and found wanting. "Your shit ain't so hot, honey, and you know it," the woman's eyes seemed to say. It didn't occur to Lorisa that the way she'd spoken to the cleaning woman could have anything to do with the woman's response. She was tired, with too much work and too little rest. And she was always over imaginative when her period was about to start. She forced herself to open the door to her office and was nearly lightheaded with relief to find the cleaning woman nowhere in sight.

In the descending elevator, she realized that the term "cleaning woman" rang false against the face and figure she'd just encountered. Cleaning women were fat and full of quiet kindness and mother wit. They were not women who looked to be in their late twenties—her own age—with faces strong and proud as her own. They didn't have lean, hard-muscled arms and eyes like onyx marbles. She remembered her grandmother, her father's squat, black, broad-nosed mother who had cooked and cleaned for white people all of her life. On those rare occasions when Lorisa's mother had consented to a visit from her mother-in-law, or, rarer still, when the family paid the older woman a visit in North Carolina, Grandmother would wait on everyone. She would slip into your room while you were in the bathroom in the morning and make your bed, hang up your clothes, and spirit away anything that looked the least bit in need of mending, washing, or pressing. But her dedication didn't earn her much praise.

"Young black girls learn enough about being mammies without your mother to set an example," Lorisa had once heard her mother say to her father. Her mother was explaining why it was impossible for Lorisa to spend part of her summer with her grandmother, despite Lorisa's and her grandmother's wishes. She'd been sent to camp instead, a camp at which, she remembered now, the white kids had called her and the three other black girls "niggers" and put spiders in their beds. As she crossed the lobby, it occurred to her that her grandmother had once been young, just like the woman cleaning the typing pool. Had there been fire in her grandmother's eyes, too, when she was young? Had she spit in the white folks soup, the way the slaves used to do? How long did it take to make a *real* cleaning woman?

★ ★ ★

Jackie banged another wastebasket against her bin with such vigor she left a dent in the basket. What had made her act like that? She slammed the basket down beside the desk and moved on to the next one. The woman was only trying to be polite. But a mean, evil rage had risen up at the very sight of her—walking around like she owned the place, having her own office. And those shoes! She must have paid a hundred dollars for them shoes! Who'd she think she was? Jackie dumped the last basket and began dry mopping the floor with an oversized dustmop. A college education didn't give her the right to give nobody that uptight little greeting, like an icicle down somebody's back, she thought. She'd run into three or four other black women with really good jobs in other buildings where she cleaned. A couple of them had had that air of doing you a favor when they spoke to you, too. But they'd been light-skinned and looked like models, which somehow made their hinctiness less personal. This woman's smooth dark face and big round eyes reminded Jackie of a girl she'd hung out with in school; and she had a cousin with the same big legs and small waist. She didn't need for no plain ole everyday-looking black woman to speak to her because she thought she ought to. She got more than enough of being practically patted on her head, if not her behind, from the phony whites she worked for. She wasn't taking that stuff from one of her own, too!

She let her mind slip into a replay of her latest run-in with her snooty white supervisor in which she'd once again had to point out that she only gave respect when she got it. She was hoping to draw a parallel between the two situations and thereby relieve herself of the knowledge that in the moment when she'd first seen the woman standing there—as crisp and unused as a new dollar bill, as far removed from emptying other people's wastebaskets as a black woman was likely to get—she had been struck dumb by jealousy. She swung the mop in wide arcs, putting more energy into the chore than was called for.

She was just finishing up the Men's Room when she heard the elevator bell. When she left the bathroom no light showed from beneath the woman's door. Although she'd already cleaned the private offices, Jackie crossed the typing pool and tiptoed into the woman's office. She stood in the middle of the room. Light from the street below made turning on the overhead light unnecessary. A hint of some peppery perfume lingered in the air, like a shadow of the woman who worked there. It was a good-sized office, with a beige leather sofa under an abstract painting in shades of blues and brown; a glass and chrome coffee table with dried flowers in a bowl. A big, shiny, wooden desk.

Jackie ran her fingers along the edge of the desk as she walked slowly round it. She stood in front of the leather desk chair and placed the fingertips of both hands lightly on the desk. She leaned forward and looked toward the sofa as though addressing an invisible client or underling. Then she sat—not as she usually sat, with a sigh of relief at getting off her feet as she plopped solidly down. She sat slowly, her head held high, her back straight. In her imagination, she wore Lorisa's raw silk shirtwaist and turquoise beads. Gold glistened at her ears and on her small, manicured hands. Her hair was long and pulled back into a sleek chignon. The desk hid her suddenly corn-free feet, sporting $100 shoes. And she knew things—math, the meaning of big words, what to tell other people to do . . . things that meant you were closer to being the boss than to being bossed.

Once, so long ago it seemed like the beginning of time, she'd thought she might be something—nothing grand enough for an office like this. Being a secretary is what she'd dreamed about: dressing real neat, walking with her legs close together, in that switchy way secretaries always had on TV, typing and filing and so forth. She must have been about 10 years old when she'd hoped for that, not old enough to know that chubby-butt, black-skinned, unwed mothers with GED diplomas and short, nappy hair didn't get jobs as downtown secretaries or very much else, besides floor-moppers or whores, unless they had a college education. She'd had to drop out of school to take care of her son. She'd never considered marrying Carl's father and he had never asked if she wanted to get married. They were both 15 and had only had sex twice. Since then, it seemed she only met two kinds of men—those she didn't like who liked her and those she liked who weren't interested in her. Her marriage dream was no more real than any of her other dreams. She lifted a slim, black pen from its desk holder, shined it on the edge of the apron she wore over her uniform, and quickly replaced it.

But hadn't she at least suspected, even back when she was 10 and still dreaming about secretarial school and happy-ever-after, that this was what her life was going to be—just what her mother's life had been and that of all her girlfriends who were not in jail or on dope or working themselves to death for some pimp or factory owner? Hadn't she known that questions like: "And what do you want to be when you grow up, little girl?" were only grown-ups' way of not talking to her, since they already knew the limits of her life?

A longing beyond words welled up from her core and threatened to escape into a moan so deep and so wrenching its gathering made her suddenly short of breath. She rose quickly from the chair and headed for the door.

What happened to the part of yourself that dreams and hopes, she wondered. Was it just a phase of growing up, to believe you might amount to something, might do something with your life besides have babies and be poor? And how come some people got to have their dreams come true and others didn't?

★ ★ ★

Lorisa lay with her head thrown back against the edge of the high steel tub, droplets from the swirling water gently splashing her face, tightening the skin across her forehead. She stopped by the spa for a whirlpool bath and 15 minutes in the steam room every day after work. As a reward, she told herself, without thinking about what there was about her work that warranted rewarding. She shifted her weight, careful to keep her feet from the sucking pipe that pulled the water in and forced it out to knead and pummel her muscles, dissolving the tension across her shoulders. But not quite.

Jim Daily's face rose behind her eyelids—a pale, oval moon altering the landscape of her leisure with its sickly light. She pressed her eyelids down as hard as possible, but Daily's face remained.

"You notice how much she looks like the maid in that cleanser commercial? You know the one I mean," he'd gone on to whoever was in earshot, to whoever would listen, as he'd circled her, trapped her with his penetrating voice. "Go ahead," he told her, "Put your hand on your hip and say, 'Look, chile!'" He'd transformed his voice into a throaty falsetto. His pale blue gaze had pinned her to the spot where she stood, like a spotlight, as he'd waited for her to perform, to act like some nigger clown in some minstrel show. All in fun, of course; just joking, of course; no offense intended, of course. A hot flush of shame had warmed her cheeks. Is that how she looked to him, to them? she'd wondered, searching her mind for real similarities between herself and the commercial caricature of whom Daily spoke, even though she knew in her heart that he never saw her, that all black women's faces were most likely one to him.

Lorisa tried to let go of the memory, to give herself over to the soothing water, but her back was stiff now, her tongue pressed too firmly to the roof of her mouth behind tightly clenched teeth. All the rage she couldn't let herself release at the time came rolling to the surface in a flood of scenes in which she said all the things she might have said to him, if she'd had the luxury of saying and acting as she pleased—like the cleaning woman in her office. She saw herself putting her hand on her hip and telling Daily what an ignorant, racist dog he was. A stiletto-thin smile curved her lips at the thought of how he would have looked, standing there with his face gone purple and his whiny nasal voice finally silenced.

Of course, from Daily's point of view, from the firm's point of view, she would only have proved conclusively that all blacks were belligerent and had no sense of proportion, none of the civilizing ability to laugh at themselves. And, of course, she would have lost her job. Daily was slightly senior to her. He was also a white male in a white male firm where she, and the two white women consultants, did everything they could to distract attention from the fact that they were not biologically certified for the old boys' club. And Lorisa knew she was on even shakier ground than the white women on staff.

She was the one who got the smallest and most mundane clients with whom to work. It was her ideas that were always somehow attributed to someone else. She was invariably the last to know about changes in the firm's policies or procedures and office gossip was stone cold by the time she heard it. For a while, she'd been fairly successful at convincing herself all this was due to her being a very junior member of the staff, that race had nothing to do with it. Of course, she realized, with the seventh sense of a colored person in a white society, which members of the firm hated her silently and politely because of her color. Daily was not alone in his racism and he was probably less dangerous, with his overt ignorance, than the quiet haters. But they were individuals. The firm was different. The firm was only interested in making all the money it could. It didn't really care who did the work. Wasn't that what she'd been taught in her college economics courses? But more and more, as men with less seniority and skills than she were given serious responsibilities, she was increasingly unable to plaster over the cracks in the theory that the firm was somehow different from the individuals of which it is composed. More and more she was forced to accept the very good possibility that she'd been hired as a token and would be kept as a company pet, as long as she behaved herself . . . or until some other type of token/pet became more fashionable.

It seemed ironic that in college she'd been one of the black students most involved in trying to better race relations. She'd helped organize integrated retreats and participated in race workshops. She'd done her personal share by rooming with a white girl who became her best friend, costing her what

few black girlfriends she'd had on campus. She could almost count the number of dates she'd had on one hand. There were only a few black boys on campus to begin with and a third of them were more interested in her white roommate or light-skinned colored girls than they'd been in the likes of her. Those who had dated her had done so only once and spread the word that she was "lame," and "cold." She quickly evaded the thought that her love life hadn't improved appreciably since college. Back then, there were times when she had felt more comfortable with some of the white kids than she had with some of the black ones, although she'd denied this vehemently when a black girl accused her of it. And she'd originally liked being the only black at Carstairs and Carstairs. She'd thought she'd have more of a chance to get ahead on her own, without other blacks and their problems and claims to her allegiance.

"We're so proud of our Lorisa," her mother's prim school teacher's voice repeated inside Lorisa's head. The occasion had been a family dinner honoring Lorisa's completion of graduate school and the job offer from Carstairs. "Yes, indeed," her mother had gone on, "Lorisa is a fine example of what a young colored woman can do, if she just puts all this race and sex mess behind her and steps boldly, acts forcefully on her own behalf."

Lorisa wondered what her mother would say if she knew how often her daughter longed for just one pair of dark eyes in one brown face in which to see herself mirrored and know herself whole in moments when she was erased by her co-workers' assumptions about her ability or brains based on her color, not to mention her sex. It was only now that she, herself, realized how much she needed for that brown face to belong to a woman. How long had it been since she'd had one of those I-can-tell-you-cause-you're-just-like-me talks that she remembered from her late childhood and early teens? But that was before she and her girlfriends had been made to understand the ways in which they were destined to compete and to apprehend the generally accepted fact that women could not be trusted.

Still, she'd been smart to keep her mouth shut with Daily. The economy wasn't all that good and lots of companies were no longer interested in trying to incorporate blacks. She could have opened her mouth and ended up with nothing more than her pride. No job. No money. No future. She picked at the possibility like a worrisome scab, imagining herself unable to pay the rent on her newly furnished and decorated apartment or meet the payments on her new car, living a life of frozen fish sticks and cheap pantyhose in a roach-ridden apartment. She saw herself clerking in a supermarket or department store, waiting on people who had once waited on her. Or worse. The face of the cleaning woman from her office replaced Daily's in her mind's eye—the woman's scowl, her hands in cheap rubber gloves, her eyes showing something hot and unsettling, like the first glow of an eruption-bound volcano.

They said it wasn't like the old days. Nowadays, blacks could do anything whites could do. Hadn't a black man gone into space? Hadn't a black woman been named Miss America? Then why was it, she wondered, that the minute she began to contemplate being out of work and what would be available to her, it was only work near the bottom that she expected to find? It was as though her degrees, her experiences and skills would amount to nothing, once she descended into the ranks of the black unemployed.

But she was not going to be unemployed. She was not going to be on the outside. She was from a family of achievers. Her father was the first black to get an engineering degree from his alma mater. Her mother had been named best teacher by the local parent-teacher's association for three years in a row. How could she ever explain getting fired to them? Or to members of the black business women's association she'd recently joined? No. She intended to stay right where she was and prove to Carstairs and Carstairs that she was just as dedicated to profit margins and sales, just as adept at sniffing out a rival's weakness and moving in for the kill, just as practiced in the fine art of kissing her superior's ass, as any white boy they could find. She rose quickly from the tub and snatched her towel off the rack, irritated that relaxation had once again eluded her.

★ ★ ★

The room was starting to have that acrid, funky odor of people in danger of losing their last dime. Jackie looked around the card table. Light bounced off Big Red's freckled forehead; his belly was a half-submerged beach ball bobbing above the table. Mabel's lips were pressed near to disappearance. It was a look she'd wear as long as there were cards on the table. Her gambling mask, she called it. Bernice was half drunk. Jackie hated playing cards with drunks. They either knocked over a drink and soaked the cards, or started some shit with one of the other players. Bernice had already signified to Alma about the whereabouts and doings of Alma's old man, Rickie, a good-looking Puerto Rican with a Jones for blue-black thighs. Ramrod Slim sat just like his name. His color and the millions of tiny wrinkles on his face reminded Jackie of raisins and prunes.

Jackie riveted her eyes and attention on Slim's hands as he passed out the cards. The hand he dealt her was as indifferent as all the other hands she'd been dealt tonight. Sweat formed a film separating her fingers from the cards. Oh Jesus! If she could just win a couple of hands, win just enough to pay on Carl's dental bill so the dentist would adjust the child's braces. She gritted her teeth at the memory of the note Carl had brought home when he went for his last visit, a note saying he shouldn't return without at least a $50 payment. Bastard! Honky bastard! All they ever cared about was money. But, of course, it was more than the dentist's money she needed now.

When she'd decided to get in the game, she'd told herself she had $12 of card-playing money. If she lost it, she would leave the game and not have lost anything other than the little bit of extra money she had left over from her bills and other necessities. If she won, there'd be money for the dentist and the shoes she needed so badly. She'd found a quarter on the way to work—a sure sign of luck.

But not only had she lost her $12, she'd also lost her light bill money, all of her carfare for next week and was now in danger of losing part of her grocery money. She gripped her cards and plucked. Damn! Shit on top of shit. She wasn't hardly in the way of winning this hand. She longed for a drink to take away the taste of defeat, to drown the knowledge of once again having made the wrong decision, taken the wrong risk. She would have to get some money from somewhere. She let her mind run over her list of friends in order of the likelihood of their being able to lend her something and was further disheartened. Almost everybody she knew was either laid off or about to be. Those who were working steady were in debt and had kids to feed, too. She didn't have a man at the moment. The last one had borrowed $25 dollars from her and disappeared. But she would have to find the money somewhere, somehow. She wondered what it would be like to be able to lose this little bit of cash—not much more than a pair of those alligator pumps that woman had worn in the building where she'd cleaned yesterday. She tried to make space in her anxious mind in which to imagine having enough money not to constantly be concerned about it.

"Girl! Is you gonna play cards or daydream?" Big Red grumbled.

Jackie made a desultory play, waited for her inevitable loss, indifferent to whom the winner might be.

★ ★ ★

The Carstairs were consummate party givers. They liked entertaining. They liked the accolades providing lavish amounts of expensive food and drink brought them. It was what they did instead of donating to charity. Mr. Carstairs invariably invited all the professional members of the firm and made no secret of how much pleasure it gave him when they were all in attendance. As usual, on party nights, the front door of the Carstairs' 20-room country place was wide open. A jumble of voices underscored the music that danced out to meet Lorisa as she walked slowly up the front steps.

She hoped it would be different this time. Perhaps, just this once, they would not all turn toward her when she first entered the room and leave her feeling blotted out by their blank, collective stare. She could have made it easier on herself by bringing a date, but she didn't know a man she disliked and trusted enough to subject to one of the Carstairs' parties, or a man who liked her well enough to make

the sacrifice. Nevertheless, she attended all the Carstairs' parties, always leaving just as someone started banging out "Dixie" on the piano or telling the latest Jewish, Polish, or gay joke. She knew who would be the butt of the next go-round.

But tonight, she would do more than put in a respectful appearance. Tonight she would prove she was prepared to make whatever sacrifice necessary to play on the team. For she'd decided that it was her nonteam player behavior—her inability to laugh at a good joke, no matter who was the butt of it; her momentary appearances at office social functions; her inability to make other staff accept that she was no different from them in any way that counted—that kept her from total acceptance into the firm. Tonight, she would break through the opaque bubble that seemed to keep her from being seen or heard, making her as murky to the whites on staff as they were to her.

After the usual genuflection before the Carstairs and the obligatory exchange of comments about how very glad they were she could come and how pleased she was to be there, Lorisa ordered a stiff drink from the barman and began to circulate with determination. She stopped at one small grouping after another, asking about wives and children, looking interested in golf scores, remaining noncommittal on the issues of busing and affirmative action until her tongue felt swollen, her lips parched and stretched beyond recovery. And still she pressed on: dancing with Bill Steele; laughing at Daily's tasteless joke about a crippled child; listening to Mrs. Carstairs reminisce about Annie Lee, the dear, dead, colored woman who had raised her, while her mama languished on a chaise lounge with a 20-year-old migraine. And still she pressed on.

And she thought she made her point. She was sure she saw some of them, the ones who counted—the ones who watched the junior staff for signs of weakness or leadership—smile in her direction, nodding their heads as though dispensing a blessing when she caught their eye. Her success was clear in the gentle hug from Mrs. Carstairs, a sign of approval that all the women in the office had come to covet. It was this sense of having proved herself worthy that made her decide to speak to Jill Franklin.

She'd had no intention of trying to enlist anyone in the firm in her struggles with Daily. While she felt one or two of them—including Jill—might be sympathetic, none of them had ever attempted to intervene on her behalf or had even shown overt empathy for her. But the flush of acceptance made her feel as though she had a right to make requests of staff, just like any other member of the firm. She'd been talking to Jill and Ken Horton, whose offices bordered her own, about baseball, until Ken's wife dragged him away. For a few moments, both of the women were quiet. Lorisa gathered strength from the silence, then spoke.

"Listen, Jill, I need to ask you something. You've been working with Jim Daily for a while, now. And you seem to know him well, get along with him. Tell me, is there anything I can do to make him stop?"

"Stop what?" Jill's voice was full of innocent curiosity, her face bland as milk.

For the first time, since she'd arrived at the party, Lorisa looked someone directly in the eye. Jill's eyes had that same blue distance she saw in Daily's eyes.

"Stop . . ." she began, searching desperately for something safe to say to cover her error.

"Hey, you two! This is a party, come out of that corner!" Somebody Lorisa didn't recognize grabbed Jill's hand and pulled her out to the patio where some people were dancing. Lorisa went in search of the Carstairs and made her good-nights.

★ ★ ★

Jackie spotted Mr. Gus as soon as she pushed open the door. He was where she'd expected him to be this time of evening: on his favorite stool near the far end of the bar, away from the juke box in the front of the long room, but not too close to the bathrooms at the back.

"Hey, Miz Pretty." Harold rubbed his grungy bar cloth in a circle and gave her a wink. Cissy and her old man, Juice (so called for his love of it), sat in a booth opposite the bar and stared past each other. Miz Hazel, who ran the newspaper stand, nursed a mug of beer and half a shot of something while she and Harold watched a baseball game on the portable TV at their end of the bar. Jackie was glad for the game. Talking to Mr. Gus would be easier than if the juke box was going. And she did have to talk to Mr. Gus. She'd tried all her girlfriends, her mother, and even her hairdresser. Everyone was broke as she was. Mr. Gus was her last hope. She stopped thinking about all the years she'd promised herself that no matter how broke she got, she wouldn't turn to this sly, old brown coot.

She slid onto a stool three up from Mr. Gus and told Harold to bring her a vodka and orange juice. She glanced at Mr. Gus in the long mirror hanging behind the rows of bottles in front of her. He was looking at the newspaper lying on the bar beside his glass. He didn't lean over the paper, the way most people would. He sat with his back straight, his head slightly inclined, his folded hands resting on the edge of the bar in front of his drink. The white of his shirt glistened in the blue bar light. She had never seen him without a shirt and tie, despite the fact that he wore a uniform at work, just like her.

"How you doin', Mr. Gus?"

He looked up as though surprised to find her there, as though he hadn't seen her from the moment she stepped in the door, as though he hadn't been waiting for her since she was a little girl. Mr. Gus was a neighborhood institution. Being a man who understood the economic realities of most black women's lives, he'd cultivated two generations of little girls and was working on a third generation. He took them for rides in his car, gave them candy—all on the up and up, of course. He would never touch a child. He got a portion of his pleasure from waiting, anticipating. Many of Jackie's little playmates had come to learn they could depend on their old friend, nice Mr. Gus, for treats in their adult lives, too. Only now the candy was cash and the price was higher than a "Thank you, Mr. Gus." But despite the fact that she made next-to-no salary and had a child to raise, Jackie had never come around. Until now. Mr. Gus smiled.

"Anything in the paper about that boy who got shot on Franklin Street, last night?" Jackie craned her neck in his direction, her eyes seeming to search the front page of the paper, her chest thrust forward, in her low-cut sweater. She skipped her behind over the barstools between them, still pretending to be intent upon the headlines. But she was mindful of the cat-with-cream smile on his face. It was a smile that made her sure he knew why she was there; that he had sensed, in that special way some men have, that she was vulnerable, could be run to ground like a wounded doe.

She hadn't meant to drink so much, but Mr. Gus was generous. And he was an excellent listener. There was something about his attitude, his stillness and sympathetic expression that allowed women to tell him things they wouldn't reveal to their best friends. They told their men's secrets, what they had dreamed about the night before, and anything else that was on their minds, as though injected with a truth-inducing drug. To many women, what was a little sex for badly needed cash, after this kind of intimacy? It was a line of thinking Mr. Gus encouraged.

And so, Jackie had rattled on about her lousy job and what her supervisor had said to her and how hard it was trying to raise a boy alone. Mr. Gus nodded and tsked, asked a question or two to prime the pump when she hesitated, ordered more drinks and waited for the beg, the plea. And, of course, the payback.

But in the end, Jackie couldn't do it. She told him how badly Carl needed his braces adjusted and what a fool she'd been to lose her carfare and light bill money in a card game. But when it came to asking him could he see his way clear to let her have $75 or even $50, the same hard glint in his eye that had put her off as a child made her hold her tongue. She did try to get him to say his lines—to ask why she sighed so forlornly, or what she meant when she said, in that frightened voice, that she didn't know what she was going to do. But Mr. Gus refused to play. He wanted the beg. He'd been waiting for it for a long, long time.

They left the bar together. Jackie now a little rocky on her feet, Mr. Gus unwilling to lose when he was so very close. He took her up to his place for one last drink. The smell of old men's undershirts sobered her a bit.

"I sure hate to see you in such a bad way," he said as she sat at his kitchen table trying to adjust her breathing to the bad air.

"Course, you coulda had all I got." He poured another dollop of Seagrams in her jelly glass. Jackie quickly drank it down.

"I don't know why you always been so mean to me, Miz Jackie." He rose and walked to stand behind her chair, kneading her left shoulder with pudgy fingers that radiated damp heat, like a moist heat pad. She willed herself not to pull her shoulder away. He breathed like a cat purring.

"Why you so mean, Miz Jackie?" He spoke in a wheedling, whiny tone, as though he, not she, were on the beg.

"You know Mr. Gus ain't gon let you and little Carl go wanting. Don't you know that, now?" He crept closer to the back of her chair, still moving his fingers in damp slow circles.

"I got me a little piece of money, right here in the bedroom; and I want you to have it."

* * *

At first, Lorisa had considered it a sign of her growing esteem among her superiors that she was chosen to take Stanley Wider, of Wider Housewares, to dinner for a preliminary discussion about his signing a contract with the firm. She was so grateful for any indication of growing favor that it hadn't occurred to her to wonder why she, a junior member of the firm, with no real experience with prestigious clients, should be given this plum. The Wider account had the potential for being very big, very important to the career of whoever pulled him in. Now that dinner with Wider was nearly over, Lorisa understood why she'd been chosen.

Mr. Wider was what the women in the office called "a lunch man"—a client who turned into a sex fiend after dark and could, therefore, only be talked to over lunch. Looking at him, anyone would think he was a kindly, trustworthy genteel man—like Walter Cronkite. Only his eyes and his words told the truth about him. She smiled up from her Peach Melba into his lean, clean-shaven face to find his eyes once again caressing her breasts. He smiled sheepishly, boyishly, when he realized he'd been caught. But his eyes remained cold and hard.

Ralph Wider was a serious pursuer of young corporate women on the rise. In the sixties, when women began pressuring for more room at the top, he'd been bitterly against the idea. But a chance encounter with an extremely ambitious female sales representative had shown him the benefits of affirmative action. In his analysis, women in business fell into two categories: those who were confident and competent enough to know they didn't need to take their panties down to do business; and those who could be convinced that in at least his case, a little sex would get them more business than a lot of facts. He didn't meet many black ones and the ones he met were always smart. He figured they had to be to get high enough to deal with him. But he had a fairly good record of convincing category-one women to slip down a notch. The challenge added spice to his business dealings.

"We're very excited about the possibility of working with your people," Lorisa began, trying once again to introduce the reason for their having dinner together. "We think we can . . ."

"You know, I've always admired black women. You all are so . . . so uninhibited." He stretched the last word out into an obscenity. "I bet you can be a very friendly young lady, when you want to be."

This man is important, not just to the firm, but to my career, Lorisa reminded herself before she spoke.

"I'm afraid I've never been particularly famous for my friendliness, Mr. Wider, but I am a first rate efficiency specialist and I've got some ideas about how to increase . . ."

He lifted his glass in a toast as she spoke. "To freedom" he said with a sly grin.

Twice more she tried to raise the subject of business. Each time he countered with another invitation to spend a weekend on his boat or take a ride in his plane, or have dinner with him in his hotel room the following night.

She knew what she should say to him. She'd practiced gently and firmly explaining that she did not appreciate passes as a part of her work. But she'd never had occasion to use that speech, before. And this man had the power to greatly improve her position in the firm, simply by what he said about their evening together.

"Excuse me," she said between dessert and cognac. She could feel his eyes poking at her behind as she headed for the Ladies Room.

She wrapped wet paper towels around her neck, careful not to dampen her blouse and held her wrists under the cold water tap to calm herself. Tears quickened in her eyes at the sudden desire to tell some woman her woes; to explain about *him* being out there waiting for her and what she ought to do. Somebody deep inside urged her to go out there, pour a glass of ice water in his lap and run like hell—the same someone who'd urged her to talk to Daily as though he had a tail; the same someone who'd urged her to major in archeology instead of business and to stop smiling at white people, at least on weekends. But she was no fool. She wanted the Wider account and the prestige of getting it. She wanted her salary, her vacations, her car. She wanted to prove she was just as good as anybody else in the firm. At the moment, she just didn't know why she needed to prove it.

Lorisa dried her hands, checked her make-up and straightened her shoulders. She couldn't come apart now. She couldn't let them think she was incapable of handling any task the firm gave her. For all she knew, she was being tested. She brushed at her hair and willed that frightened look out of her eyes. I have a contract to get, she told herself as she opened the door.

She stared at his slim, distinguished figure as she crossed the room. So deceiving, she thought, like a bright shiny apple turned to maggotty mush on the inside. But if she could just get him to agree to look at the prospectus. He rose as she returned to her seat.

"I mean it, little lady," he said as he sat down, "I think you're really something special. I'm sure I can do business with you!" he added with a smile as his leg brushed hers beneath the table.

★ ★ ★

If there'd been any way for Lorisa to avoid getting on the elevator with Jackie, she'd have done so. If there'd been other people she'd have had no hesitation about getting on. Other people would have kept her from speaking, as she now feared she might. She didn't look at the woman as she entered the elevator, but she didn't need to. She remembered those eyes. The elevator doors hissed shut before her. The lobby button was already lit so she had only to stand there. She kept her eyes straight ahead and wondered if the elevator always moved this slowly or if the damned thing was going to stall, leaving them alone together for the rest of the night.

Jackie studied Lorisa's back and tried to get up the courage to say something. This was the first time she'd seen the woman since their encounter a couple of evenings ago. She still felt bad about how she'd responded. She wanted to apologize, maybe even change her luck by doing so.

"I'm real sorry for the way I acted the other day. Let me buy you a drink to make up for it," she practiced in her head, even though she didn't have enough money to buy herself a drink. She saw the two of them walking down the street to Libby's Place where she knew she could buy a round or two on credit. They would sit in a booth near the back. The juke box would be off, so the place would be quiet enough for talk. The woman would buy her a drink in return and they would talk about what they needed to talk about. Wasn't no black woman's life without something that needed talking about. But none of that was really going to happen. She could tell from the way the woman stood that she didn't want to be bothered.

As the elevator reached the lower floors, Lorisa reached in her pocket, pulled out her leather driving gloves and smoothed them on over long, slim fingers. She tried to keep her attention focused on what she was doing and away from her urge to somehow make herself acceptable to the woman standing behind her.

"Girl, you sure are evil!" she heard herself saying in a way that smacked of respect for the woman's willingness to give her economic betters hell. She saw them walking out of the building together. She would tell the woman her name and offer her a lift. Their talk in the car would be slow but easy. They might discover they liked one another.

But, of course, that whole scene was irrational. Why should she take a chance on being insulted again? Why should it make any difference to her whether this woman considered her somebody worth being pleasant to? She pressed her lips firmly together as the elevator finally slid to a stop. She stepped quickly forward and brisk-stepped her way to the other door, trying to put as much distance between herself and the cleaning woman as possible, before she did something she would regret.

After all, it wasn't as though they had anything in common.

[1985]

110

Jewish and Working Class

BERNICE MENNIS

When I was called to speak at this conference about working-class experience, my immediate reaction was: "No, get someone else." One voice said: "I have nothing worthwhile to say." A second voice said: "I was not born poor. I always ate well. I never felt deprived. I have not suffered enough to be on this panel." Both voices silenced me. The first came from my class background—a diminished sense of competence, ability, control, power. ("Who are you anyway? You have nothing to say. No one cares or will listen.") The second, the guilt voice, comes from a strange combination of my Jewishness, my fear of anti-Semitism, my own psychological reaction to my own deprivations: a denial of my own pain if someone else seems to suffer more.

Economic class has been a matter of both shame and pride for me, depending on the value judgments of the community with which I identified. The economic class reality has always remained the same: My father had a very small outdoor tomato and banana stand and a small cellar for ripening the fruit. Until he was 68, he worked 12 hours a day, 6 days a week, with 1 week vacation. Although he worked hard and supported our family well, my father did not feel proud of his work, did not affirm his strength. Instead, he was ashamed to have me visit his fruit stand; he saw his work as dirty, himself as an "ignorant greenhorn." The legacy of class.

And I accepted and echoed back his shame. In elementary school, when we had to go around and say what work our parents did, I repeated my father's euphemistic words: "My father sells wholesale and retail fruits and vegetables." It's interesting that later, when I was involved in political actions, my shame turned to pride of that same class background. The poorer one was born, the better, the more credit.

Both reactions—shame and pride—are based on a false assumption that one has control and responsibility for what one is born into. (Society—those in power, institutions—is responsible for people being born into conditions of economic limitation and suffering, for racism and classism. But as individuals we do not choose our birth.) That blame/credit often prevents us from seeing clearly the actual effects of growing up in a certain class: what it allows, what it inhibits, blocks, destroys. Also, if we take credit for what is out of our control, we sometimes do not take sufficient credit and responsibility for what is in our control: our consciousness, our actions, how we shape our lives.

What becomes difficult immediately in trying to understand class background is how it becomes hopelessly entangled with other issues: the fact that my father was an immigrant who spoke with a strong accent, never felt competent to write in English, always felt a great sense of self-shame that he projected onto his children; that my father had witnessed pogroms and daily anti-Semitism in his tiny *shtetl* in Russia, that we were Jewish, that the Holocaust occurred; that neither of my parents went to school beyond junior high school; that I was the younger daughter, the "good" child who accepted almost everything without complaining or acknowledging pain; that my sister and I experienced our worlds very differently and responded in almost opposite ways. It's difficult to sort out class, to see clearly. . . .

Feelings of poverty or wealth are based on one's experiences and where one falls on the economic spectrum. The economic class and the conditions we grow up under are very real, objective, but how we label and see those circumstances is relative, shaped by what we see outside ourselves. Growing up in the Pelham Parkway–Lydig Avenue area of the Bronx, I heard my circumstances echoed everywhere: Everyone's parents spoke Yiddish and had accents; they all spoke loudly and with their hands; few were educated beyond junior high school; no one dressed stylishly or went to restaurants (except for special occasions) or had fancy cars or dishwashers or clothes washers. (Our apartment building had, and still has, only one washing machine for 48 apartments. The lineup of baskets began early in the morning. My mother and I hung the clothes on the roof.) We ate good kosher food and fresh fruits and vegetables (from my uncle's stand). My mother sewed our clothes or we would shop in Alexander's and look for bargains (clothes with the manufacturers' tags removed). Clothes were passed between sisters, cousins, neighbors. I never felt poor or deprived. I had no other perspective, no other reality from which to judge our life.

When I went to the World's Fair and watched the G.E. exhibit of "Our Changing World," I remember being surprised that what I believed was a modern-day kitchen—an exact duplicate of our kitchen at home—was the kitchen of the forties. When I received a fellowship for graduate school, I was surprised to discover I was eligible for the maximum grant because my parents' income fell in the lowest income category. I was surprised when I met friends whose parents talked about books and psychology and art, when I met people who noticed labels and brand names and talked about clothes and cars (but never mentioned costs and money).

What I also didn't see or appreciate was all the work and struggle of my parents to maintain and nourish us, work done silently and without any credit for many years. A few years ago I wrote a poem called "The Miracle" about my mother and her skilled unacknowledged work.

Clearly our assumptions, expectations, and hopes are unconsciously shaped by our class backgrounds. At a very young age I learned to want only what my parents could afford. It was a good survival mechanism that allowed me never to feel deprived or denied. At a later age, when I would read in natural history books about the "immortal species," the lesson was reaffirmed: The key to survival was always to become smaller, to minimize needs. Those species that had become dependent on more luxuriant conditions perished during hard times. Those used to less survived.

There is something powerful about surviving by adapting to little. The power comes from an independence of need, an instinct that allows us to get by. But it is a defense, and, like any defense, its main fault was that it never allowed me to feel the edge of my own desires, pains, deprivations. I defined my needs by what was available. Even now I tend to minimize my needs, to never feel deprived—a legacy of my class background.

Class background reveals itself in little ways. Around food, for example. My family would sip their soup loudly, putting mouths close to the bowl. We would put containers directly on the table and never use a butter dish. We would suck bone marrow with gusto, pick up chicken bones with our hands, crunch them with our teeth, and leave little slivers on our otherwise empty plates. We would talk loudly and argue politics over supper. Only later did I become conscious of the judgment of others about certain behavior, ways of eating, talking, walking, dressing, being. Polite etiquette struck me as a bit absurd, as if hunger were uncivilized: the delicate portions, the morsels left on the plate, the proper use of knife and fork, the spoon seeming to go in the opposite direction of the mouth. The more remote one was from basic needs, the higher one's class status. I usually was unconscious of the "proper behavior": I did not notice. But if I ever felt the eye of judgment, my first tendency would be to exaggerate my "grossness" in order to show the absurdity of others' snobbish judgments. I would deny that that judgment had any effect other than anger. But I now realize that all judgment has effect. Some of my negative self-image as *klutz*, *nebbish*, ugly, unsophisticated is a direct result of the reflection I saw in the judging, sophisticated eye of the upper class.

Lack of education and lack of money made for an insecurity and fear of doing almost anything, a fear tremendously compounded by anti-Semitism and World War II. My parents were afraid to take any risks—from both a conviction of their own incompetence and a fear that doing anything big, having any visibility, would place them in danger. From them I inherited a fear that if I touched something, did anything, I would make matters worse. There was an incredible nervousness in my home

around fixing anything, buying anything big, filling out any forms. My mother still calls me to complete forms for her. When my father was sick, my parents needed me to translate everything the doctor said, not because they did not understand him, but because their fear stopped them from listening when anyone very educated or in authority spoke.

I did not inherit the fear of those in authority. In fact, my observation of people's condescension, use of authority, and misuse of power helped shape my politics at a young age. I identified with the underdog, was angry at the bully, fought against the misuse of power. But I did inherit their fear of taking risks, of doing anything big, of trying anything new. I have trouble with paper forms; I've never been able to write a grant proposal; I have no credit cards. I sometimes seek invisibility as a form of safety.

For poorer people, for people who experience prejudice, there is a strong feeling that one has no power, no ability to affect or control one's environment. For nine years my family and I lived in a very small three-room apartment; my sister and I had no bedroom of our own. When we moved from the fifth floor to the sixth, we got a tiny room just big enough for two beds and a cabinet. I never thought to put up a picture, to choose a room color or a bedspread. I had no notion of control over private space, of shaping my environment.

That feeling of lack of control over one's environment, of no right to one's own space, was psychologically intensified by my parents' experiences of anti-Semitism and by the Holocaust. These fostered a deep sense of powerlessness and vulnerability and, on an even more basic level, a doubt whether we really had a right to exist on this earth.

In college I took a modern dance class. A group of us began "dancing" by caving in on ourselves, slinking around the side walls of the gym. I remember the teacher saying that to dance one needed to be able to open one's arms and declare the beauty of one's being, to take up one's space on the dance floor: to say "I am here." For many women who experience poverty and prejudice this kind of self-assertion feels foreign, impossible, dangerous. One of the unconscious effects of being born wealthy is a natural sense of one's right to be here on this earth, an essential grace that comes from the feeling of belonging. (The danger, of course, is that wealthier people often take up too much space. They do not see the others crushed under their wide flinging steps.) Where the poorer person's danger is the self-consciousness that shrinks us into invisibility, the wealthier one's is the unconscious arrogance that inflates.

But what happens when one feels self-conscious and small and is seen as large, wealthy, powerful, controlling? At a young age, I knew the anti-Semitic portrait of the wealthy, exploitative Jew. I also knew that I did not feel powerful or controlling. My parents and I felt powerless, fearful, vulnerable. We owned nothing. All my parents saved, after working 50 years, would not equal the cost of 1 year of college today. What does it mean to have others' definition of one's reality so vastly different from one's experience of it? The effects are confusion, anger, entrapment. I lost touch with what was real, what my own experiences really were.

As a political person I felt particularly vulnerable to the hated image of "the Jew." I knew it was a stereotype and not my experience or the experience of the Jews I grew up with—but it still made me feel guilt, not pride, for any success I did have, for any rise in status. If the stereotype said "Jews have everything," the only way I could avoid that stereotype would be to have nothing. If you are poor, you are not a Jew. If you are successful, you are a bad Jew. The trap.

The economic and professional success of many second-generation Jews became tinged for me, as if we had done something wrong. To feel bad about achievement, to hold back one's power, is very destructive. My aunts and uncles, my parents, my friends' parents all had little education and little money. Yet we—my cousins, my sister, my friends—not only went to college, but even graduated school and law school. I was speaking the other day with my aunt, who was saying what a miracle it was that her four children were all professionals and she was poor and uneducated. But the miracle was not really a miracle at all. It was the result of parents who saw education as very, very important—as a way out of the entrapment of class and prejudice.

It was the result of parents who worked desperately hard so that their children could have that way out. It was a City College system in New York City that provided completely free education while we worked and lived at home.

In one generation we created an incredible economic, class, professional, and educational distance between ourselves and our parents. The danger of this success is that we forget the material soil that nourished us, the hard work that propped us up; that we lose our consciousness of the harm and evil of condescension, exploitation, oppression, the pain of being made to feel inferior and invisible. Anzia Yezierska, a Jewish immigrant writer, says "Education without a heart is a curse." But to keep that consciousness and that heart and to be able to step onto the dance floor of life and say "I am here," reflecting back to our parents the beauty and strength we inherited from them, that would be a very real "miracle" indeed.   [1987]

🌿 111

Poverty, Hopelessness, and Hope

KENDALL A. JOHNSON

I know that I'm one of the lucky ones. I have a law school education, my ticket into the professional middle class. It's been almost a lifetime since those days of picking fruit and vegetables in the deep south, or freezing without heat or running water in a trailer in upstate New York. It sounds like an American dream, and surely it is, but the odds are against most poor people and they don't make it out. Although I'm truly grateful that I was one of those who did, it saddens me to know that in a wealthy country like ours, most poor people will remain in poverty regardless of their personal efforts to rise above it.

During my early childhood things seemed hopeless. The daily struggles to survive took priority over everything else. In my family working in the fields for money to eat was more important than going to school. Baby-sitting for the little ones so the older ones could work also took priority over school. By the time I realized the importance of education, the immediate struggle to survive was pulling me in the opposite direction. I'm sure that many poor children face this dilemma. Unfortunately, most of them succumb to the pressure and drop out.

Some of the most damning social messages received by poor children are during early childhood education. For me, elementary school was a humiliating experience. I remember feeling inferior, stupid, dirty, ugly, and hated. In the early years we often found ourselves homeless, so we were always moving around and I attended several different schools in a short time. Being a new kid was bad enough, but being poor and dirty made us additional targets for ridicule by teachers, school administrators, and students alike. To further aggravate the situation, we were absent a lot, which made it almost impossible to keep up with grade level.

Under these circumstances, it was hard to feel positive about school. My self-esteem was constantly under attack. I always felt self-conscious and I was aware of the differences between my family and the others who were better off. Furthermore, my mother and older siblings believed that everybody and everything was against us. At the time it was easy to understand why they thought that way. I used to think that the easiest way to cope with the humiliation and maintain some dignity was to fight with the other kids who picked on us. At the time, I believed that if I were tough and fought back, then I could be proud of myself. It seemed easier and it hurt a lot less than quietly swallowing my shame. This of course led to disciplinary problems with the schools, and it wasn't long before I learned that fighting only made things worse. Most of my brothers and sisters never learned this lesson and continued to get in trouble for fighting in school. I think this is partially why so many boys from poor families are labeled as behavior problems and placed in smaller special education classrooms where school administrators feel they can be more easily controlled.

Girls from poor families are less likely to be tracked in this manner because they are less likely to fight back, but the devastation to their self-esteem is notable. Girls in this situation often try to disappear. They sit in the back of the classroom praying that they won't be called on or even noticed. They skip school on days they have gym class so they won't be embarrassed because they don't have appropriate gym clothes or clean socks and underwear. They avoid participating in school activities and seek out a small group of other girls to hang around with from similar backgrounds. I did this for awhile myself. Most of these girls, if they don't drop out of school to have babies, are tracked into vocational studies such as home economics, cosmetology, and noncollege bound mathematics and health sciences.

For me high school was very different. I was the only poor kid in my class taking chemistry, trigonometry, and physics, along with the other college bound courses. Although I was very isolated, I understood how poor children were tracked and I took extreme measures to ensure that I wouldn't be. As soon as I was old enough, I worked after school in the packinghouses packing the fruit and vegetables, instead of picking them during school hours. I fought with my mother to let me go to school, rather than baby-sit. I sought out supportive teachers to mentor me and I always carried my schoolbooks home so if I missed school for a few days I could keep up.

I remember thinking, I'm only a kid and I still have a chance. I'm going to be different. If I stay in school and study hard maybe I can go to college. If I go to college, I won't have to stay poor for the rest of my life. This underlying belief fueled my desire for education as a means to escape the poverty. From the time I was 13 years old through my college career, I would recite this line of reasoning to myself. It kept me focused and gave me the inspiration to remain disciplined. I learned to draw strength from struggle. I was determined to walk the moral high ground. I believed that struggle made one a better person than if things came easy. I told myself this as a source of inspiration during hard times. It got to the point where I believed it, which helped me make it through. Ultimately, my strategies worked and law school was the icing on the cake.

By the time I actually made it to college, I felt a lot of guilt associated with leaving my family behind to pursue my own career. One of the hardest things to watch was the hopes and dreams of my siblings and friends turn to defeat and despair, while my own future looked brighter and brighter with each year of college or law school completed. When I'd go home, all I heard about was everyone's problems and how lucky I was to have gotten out.

At the time I was still broke, living on student loans and part-time waitress jobs, while keeping my eye on the prize. But my family didn't see it that way. I was already well off in their eyes. I had made it. The goal that I was trying to achieve was within my grasp and they saw no distinction between working toward it and having already achieved it. I often thought that they credited my success to luck, as though I personally had little to do with it. I felt like they thought that somehow I was bestowed with the power to change things for all of us, but refused to do so for them. This exacerbated their growing resentment toward me and my feelings of guilt. I knew on some level that regardless of my personal struggles, I was luckier. My future was full of promise, while theirs was not. I felt guilty that I couldn't save them and they didn't understand that I was still struggling to save myself.

Furthermore, by that time most of my daily life was spent with educated middle-class people and I was becoming exposed to different values and belief systems. The cultural divide widened and pretty soon it got harder and harder to find things in common with most of my siblings and former community. Before long, the day-to-day things that we had in common were reduced to memories. This too became a source of guilt. I wanted to romanticize the struggle and some of the values prevalent among poor people in an effort to hang on to my roots and to maintain a connection with those from whom I came.

I wanted to be proud of my accomplishments and I wanted my family to be proud of me as well. But I knew that on several levels they resented me. On the one hand they are proud of my accomplishments, but on the other hand they resented me for they perceived was my acquisition of middle-class values that they found so repressive. It was as though I had become the enemy, the oppressor. I think they thought that I blamed them for being poor. It was like I had become one of those school administrators of my childhood who looked down on us as though we were trash that would never amount to anything.

Moreover, this new value system that I had learned at college was inconsistent with theirs. They had this "us versus them" mentality and I no longer did. Furthermore, in their eyes I had become one of "them." I had become someone to fear. Like the school administrator, I too had the power to have their children taken away. The ignorance, the violence, and the other dysfunctional behaviors were all things that I had openly rejected and they saw my rejection of these things as a rejection of them. In their view, I denied their struggle and thought that I was better than they were.

The truth is, I rejected the ignorance, the violence, and the despair, but I don't reject the people or their struggle. I know that poor people's hardships are genuine and that most people can't overcome them. I'm a realist and I see the real-life obstacles that stand in their way. But I also understand that if you give up and stop trying, you will never succeed.

The prejudice against poor people by the larger society creates additional barriers, which perpetuate poverty. Poor people live such miserable stressed-out lives that they become depressed after struggling for a better life to no avail. They are routinely abused by welfare workers when applying for assistance, which negatively affects their self-esteem, causing undue anxiety, frustration, and even major depression. Negotiating the welfare system is a difficult and humiliating experience, and anyone who has done it will tell you the same. The system is designed to discourage and disqualify people from receiving benefits, rather than helping them. Emotionally abusing applicants and recipients is the most obvious tactic used in this endeavor. Baseless denials and cutoffs of benefits are another. Poor people often go without basic essentials for months at a time while waiting for benefits to be issued or restored. Their bills go unpaid and many of them experience eviction from their housing, even though they have complied with every request that the welfare agency has asked of them.

The working poor are exploited by employers and often have the limited choices of working for unlivable wages without medical benefits or pension plans, or bowing their heads in shame and enduring the abuse of the welfare system in order to get the assistance they need. Most people receiving public assistance work and make so little money on their jobs that they need additional assistance in order to survive.

Most poor people are women and children. And as we already know working women earn significantly less money then men. They are also significantly less likely to abandon their children. As a result, they are left with the sole physical and financial responsibilities for their children, on about two-thirds of a man's paycheck. Although state welfare plans provide child-support collection departments, the onus of locating the fathers and their resources is generally placed on the shoulders of the women, who are often denied benefits by welfare agencies for not having the relevant information.

After being defeated at every turn, depression and despair are inevitable. Hope turns to hopelessness, which is often misinterpreted as laziness. The more sympathetic middle-class experts refer to this hopelessness as learned helplessness, as though it were phenomena endemic to the poor. I think that it is a perfectly normal response to the circumstances that poor people face. Although it's not a particularly healthy one, neither are the circumstances.

Over the years I have learned that I cannot control what my family thinks. But my guilt for having left them behind has never completely subsided. As time has passed it has gotten easier since many of my family elders have passed away. But it's still painful to witness my siblings aging so quickly, and to watch their children as defeated by poverty as they were.

I guess that part of my sadness stems from the fact that I know that most poor people are not responsible for their poverty and that contrary to common beliefs, they personally have little power to change their situation. In a capitalist system like ours, poverty is inevitable regardless of how rich the country is. Corporate America benefits from the fact that there are no Federal laws guaranteeing workers a livable and fair wage that corresponds with inflation and cost of living. Under this system, it is no surprise that it is those already burdened with sexism and/or racism who are most likely to fall to the bottom of the economic scale.

I make it a point to remind myself of how lucky I am. And I believe that those of us who become educated and escape the traps of poverty have a responsibility to those less fortunate. This sense of duty was ingrained in me, and it is one of those values that I learned from my family that I choose to keep. My family always expected my help, and I felt a responsibility to provide it. Unfortunately, I was unable to cure the ills causing their poverty, and I don't think that I will ever completely get over it.

I cope with my guilt in part by dedicating my professional career to providing legal services to the poor. For the past ten years I have fought in the civil courts to provide affordable housing for poor women and children in New York City. Unfortunately, I often feel like my services are accomplishing little more than putting a band-aid on a hemorrhage. Even so, I take solace in the fact that each time I save a poor family from eviction, I make a difference in their individual lives.   [2002]

🌿 112

Grace Paley Reading

TOI DERRICOTTE

Finally, the audience gets
restless, & they send me
to hunt for Grace. I find her
backing out of the bathroom, bending
over, wiping up her footprints
as she goes with a little
sheet of toilet paper, explaining,
"In some places, after the lady mops, the bosses
    come to check on her.
I just don't want them to think
she didn't do her job."   [1997]

"Are You Some Kind of Dyke?"
The Perils of Heterosexism

Attitudes toward lesbians vary across culture and have changed over time. In the United States, loving sensual relationships between women were not seen as deviant in the seventeenth through nineteenth centuries; it was women who passed as men who were punished. In the late nineteenth century medical experts began to define lesbianism as an illness, and close connections among women became suspect. After World War II the taboos against lesbianism became extremely powerful, resulting in the erasure of lesbian experience from history; discrimination against lesbians in social, political, and economic institutions; and the proliferation of prejudices, misconceptions, and myths about lesbian life.

The essays and short story in this section examine the consequences of heterosexism for all women, exploring the ways that heterosexuality is enforced through prejudice, fear, and the denial of resources to lesbian couples. Suzanne Pharr demonstates that homophobia, the fear of homosexuality, and heterosexism—the assumption that heterosexuality is a superior way of life—are used to prevent all women from challenging sexism. In "Cat," love between two young girls feels natural to them until the prejudice of adults destroys it. Carla Trujillo describes the ways that Chicana lesbians are threatening to the established power relations in the Chicano community and urges Chicanas to recognize the commonalities among lesbian and heterosexual women.

Because of the hostility and bigotry lesbians face, coming out is a difficult process for both lesbians and their children. In some situations, being open about being a lesbian entails serious risks. For both Jewelle Gomez and Megan McGuire, however, relationships with friends and family were strengthened when they were open about their lives. Bisexuals and transgender persons experience similar costs of heterosexism and find comparable sources of strength and courage. As a transgender person, Barb Greve describes his lifelong struggle with gender, and his need to be honest about his whole self and "not being willing to put part of me aside to make others feel comfortable."

🌿 113

Homophobia and Sexism

SUZANNE PHARR

Homophobia works effectively as a weapon of sexism because it is joined with a powerful arm, heterosexism. Heterosexism creates the climate for homophobia with its assumption that the world is and must be heterosexual and its display of power and privilege as the norm. Heterosexism is the systemic display of homophobia in the institutions of society. Heterosexism and homophobia work together to enforce compulsory heterosexuality and that bastion of patriarchal power, the nuclear family. The central focus of the right-wing attack against women's liberation is that women's equality, women's self-determination, women's control of our own bodies and lives will damage what they see as the crucial societal institution, the nuclear family. The attack has been led by fundamentalist ministers across the country. The two areas they have focused on most consistently are abortion and homosexuality, and their passion has led them to bomb women's clinics and to recommend deprogramming for homosexuals and establishing camps to quarantine people with AIDS. To resist marriage and/or heterosexuality is to risk severe punishment and loss.

It is not by chance that when children approach puberty and increased sexual awareness they begin to taunt each other by calling these names: "queer," "faggot," "pervert." It is at puberty that the full force of society's pressure to conform to heterosexuality and prepare for marriage is brought to bear. Children know what we have taught them, and we have given clear messages that those who deviate from standard expectations are to be made to get back in line. The best controlling tactic at puberty is to be treated as an outsider, to be ostracized at a time when it feels most vital to be accepted. Those who are different must be made to suffer loss. It is also at puberty that misogyny begins to be more apparent, and girls are pressured to conform to societal norms that do not permit them to realize their full potential. It is at this time that their academic achievements begin to decrease as they are coerced into compulsory heterosexuality and trained for dependency upon a man, that is, for economic survival.

There was a time when the two most condemning accusations against a woman meant to ostracize and disempower her were "whore" and "lesbian." The sexual revolution and changing attitudes about heterosexual behavior may have led to some lessening of the power of the word *whore*, though it still has strength as a threat to sexual property and prostitutes are stigmatized and abused. However, the word *lesbian* is still fully charged and carries with it the full threat of loss of power and privilege, the threat of being cut asunder, abandoned, and left outside society's protection.

To be a lesbian is to be *perceived* as someone who has stepped out of line, who has moved out of sexual/economic dependence on a male, who is woman-identified. A lesbian is perceived as someone who can live without a man, and who is therefore (however illogically) against men. A lesbian is perceived as being outside the acceptable, routinized order of things. She is seen as someone who has no societal institutions to protect her and who is not privileged to the protection of individual males. Many heterosexual women see her as someone who stands in contradiction to the sacrifices they have made to conform to compulsory heterosexuality. A lesbian is perceived as a threat to the nuclear family, to male dominance and control, to the very heart of sexism.

Gay men are perceived also as a threat to male dominance and control, and the homophobia expressed against them has the same roots in sexism as does homophobia against lesbians. Visible gay men are the objects of extreme hatred and fear by heterosexual men because their breaking ranks with male heterosexual solidarity is seen as a damaging rent in the very fabric of sexism. They are seen as betrayers, as traitors who must be punished and eliminated. In the beating and killing of gay men we see clear evidence of this hatred. When we see the fierce homophobia expressed toward gay men, we can begin to understand the ways sexism also affects males through imposing rigid, dehumanizing gender roles on them. The two circumstances in which it is legitimate for men to be openly physically affectionate with one another are in competitive sports and in the crisis of war. For many men, these two experiences are the highlights of their lives, and they think of them again and again with nostalgia. War and sports offer a cover of all-male safety and dominance to keep away the notion of affectionate openness being identified with homosexuality. When gay men break ranks with male roles through bonding and affection outside the arenas of war and sports, they are perceived as not being "real men," that is, as being identified with women, the weaker sex that must be dominated and that over the centuries has been the object of male hatred and abuse. Misogyny gets transferred to gay men with a vengeance and is increased by the fear that their sexual identity and behavior will bring down the entire system of male dominance and compulsory heterosexuality.

If lesbians are established as threats to the status quo, as outcasts who must be punished, homophobia can wield its power over all women through lesbian baiting. Lesbian baiting is an attempt to control women by labeling us as lesbians because our behavior is not acceptable, that is, when we are being independent, going our own way, living whole lives, fighting for our rights, demanding equal pay, saying no to violence, being self-assertive, bonding with and loving the company of women, assuming the right to our bodies, insisting upon our own authority, making changes that include us in society's decision-making; lesbian baiting occurs when women are called lesbians because we resist male dominance and control. And it has little or nothing to do with one's sexual identity.

To be named as lesbian threatens all women, not just lesbians, with great loss. And any woman who steps out of role risks being called a lesbian. To understand how this is a threat to all women, one must understand that any woman can be called a lesbian and there is no real way she can defend herself: there is no way to credential one's sexuality. ("The Children's Hour," a Lillian Hellman play, makes this point when a student asserts

two teachers are lesbians and they have no way to disprove it.) She may be married or divorced, have children, dress in the most feminine manner, have sex with men, be celibate—but there are lesbians who do all those things. *Lesbians look like all women and all women look like lesbians.* There is no guaranteed method of identification, and as we all know, sexual identity can be kept hidden. (The same is true for men. There is no way to prove their sexual identity, though many go to extremes to prove heterosexuality.) Also, women are not necessarily born lesbian. Some seem to be, but others become lesbians later in life after having lived heterosexual lives. Lesbian baiting of heterosexual women would not work if there were a definitive way to identify lesbians (or heterosexuals).

We have yet to understand clearly how sexual identity develops. And this is disturbing to some people, especially those who are determined to discover how lesbian and gay identity is formed so that they will know where to start in eliminating it. (Isn't it odd that there is so little concern about discovering the causes of heterosexuality?) There are many theories: genetic makeup, hormones, socialization, environment, etc. But there is no conclusive evidence that indicates that heterosexuality comes from one process and homosexuality from another.

We do know, however, that sexual identity can be in flux, and we know that sexual identity means more than just the gender of people one is attracted to and has sex with. To be a lesbian has as many ramifications as for a woman to be heterosexual. It is more than sex, more than just the bedroom issue many would like to make it: it is a woman-centered life with all the social interconnections that entails. Some lesbians are in long-term relationships, some in short-term ones, some date, some are celibate, some are married to men, some remain as separate as possible from men, some have children by men, some by alternative insemination, some seem "feminine" by societal standards, some "masculine," some are doctors, lawyers, and ministers, some laborers, housewives, and writers: what all share in common is a sexual/affectional identity that focuses on women in its attractions and social relationships.

If lesbians are simply women with a particular sexual identity who look and act like all women, then the major difference in living out a lesbian sexual identity as opposed to a heterosexual identity is that as lesbians we live in a homophobic world that threatens and imposes damaging loss on us for being *who we are,* for choosing to live whole lives. Homophobic people often assert that homosexuals have the choice of not being homosexual; that is, we don't have to act out our sexual identity. In that case, I want to hear heterosexuals talk about their willingness not to act out their sexual identity, including not just sexual activity but heterosexual social interconnections and heterosexual privilege. It is a question of wholeness. It is very difficult for one to be denied the life of a sexual being, whether expressed in sex or in physical affection, and to feel complete, whole. For our loving relationships with humans feed the life of the spirit and enable us to overcome our basic isolation and to be interconnected with humankind.

If, then, any woman can be named a lesbian and be threatened with terrible losses, what is it she fears? Are these fears real? Being vulnerable to a homophobic world can lead to these losses:

• *Employment.* The loss of jobs leads us right back to the economic connection to sexism. This fear of job loss exists for almost every lesbian except perhaps those who are self-employed or in a business that does not require societal approval. Consider how many businesses or organizations you know that will hire and protect people who are openly gay or lesbian.

• *Family.* Their approval, acceptance, love.

• *Children.* Many lesbians and gay men have children, but very, very few gain custody in court challenges, even if the other parent is a known abuser. Other children may be kept away from us as though gays and lesbians are abusers. There are written and unwritten laws prohibiting lesbians and gays from being foster parents or from adopting children. There is an irrational fear that children in contact with lesbians and gays will become homosexual through influence or that they will be sexually abused. Despite our knowing that 95 percent of those who sexually abuse children are heterosexual men, there are no policies keeping heterosexual men from teaching or working with children, yet in almost every school system in America, visibly gay men and lesbians are not hired through either written or unwritten laws.

• *Heterosexual privilege and protection.* No institutions, other than those created by lesbians and gays—such as the Metropolitan Community Church, some counseling centers, political organizations such as the National Gay and Lesbian Task Force, the National Coalition of Black Lesbians and Gays, the Lambda Legal Defense and Education Fund, etc.,—affirm homosexuality and offer protection. Affirmation and protection cannot be gained from the criminal justice system, mainstream churches, educational institutions, the government.

• *Safety.* There is nowhere to turn for safety from physical and verbal attacks because the norm presently in this country is that it is acceptable to be overtly homophobic. Gay men are beaten on the streets; lesbians are kidnapped and "deprogrammed." The National Gay and Lesbian Task Force, in an extended study, has documented violence against lesbians and gay men and noted the inadequate response of the criminal justice system. One of the major differences between homophobia/heterosexism and racism and sexism is that because of the Civil Rights Movement and the women's movement racism and sexism are expressed more covertly (though with great harm); because there has not been a major, visible lesbian and gay movement, it is permissible to be overtly homophobic in any institution or public forum. Churches spew forth homophobia in the same way they did racism prior to the Civil Rights Movement. Few laws are in place to protect lesbians and gay men, and the criminal justice system is wracked with homophobia.

• *Mental health.* An overtly homophobic world in which there is full permission to treat lesbians and gay men with cruelty makes it difficult for lesbians and gay men to maintain a strong sense of well-being and self-esteem. Many lesbians and gay men are beaten, raped, killed, subjected to aversion therapy, or put in mental institutions. The impact of such hatred and negativity can lead one to depression and, in some cases, to suicide. The toll on the gay and lesbian community is devastating.

• *Community.* There is rejection by those who live in homophobic fear, those who are afraid of association with lesbians and gay men. For many in the gay and lesbian community, there is a loss of public acceptance, a loss of allies, a loss of place and belonging.

• *Credibility.* This fear is large for many people: the fear that they will no longer be respected, listened to, honored, believed. They fear they will be social outcasts.

The list goes on and on. But any one of these essential components of a full life is large enough to make one deeply fear its loss. A black woman once said to me in a workshop, "When I fought for Civil Rights, I always had my family and community to fall back on even when they didn't fully understand or accept what I was doing. I don't know if I could have borne losing them. And you people don't have either with you. It takes my breath away."

What does a woman have to do to get called a lesbian? Almost anything, sometimes nothing at all, but certainly anything that threatens the status quo, anything that steps out of role, anything that asserts the rights of women, anything that doesn't indicate submission and subordination. Assertiveness, standing up for oneself, asking for more pay, better working conditions, training for and accepting a nontraditional (you mean a man's?) job, enjoying the company of women, being financially independent, being in control of one's life, depending first and foremost upon oneself, thinking that one can do whatever needs to be done, but above all, working for the rights and equality of women.

In the backlash to the gains of the women's liberation movement, there has been an increased effort to keep definitions man-centered. Therefore, to work on behalf of women must mean to work against men. To love women must mean that one hates men. A very effective attack has been made against the word *feminist* to make it a derogatory word. In current backlash usage, *feminist* equals *man-hater* which equals *lesbian*. This formula is

created in the hope that women will be frightened away from their work on behalf of women. Consequently, we now have women who believe in the rights of women and work for those rights while from fear deny that they are feminists, or refuse to use the word because it is so "abrasive."

So what does one do in an effort to keep from being called a lesbian? She steps back into line, into the role that is demanded of her, tries to behave in such a way that doesn't threaten the status of men, and if she works for women's rights, she begins modifying that work. When women's organizations begin doing significant social change work, they inevitably are lesbian-baited; that is, funders or institutions or community members tell us that they can't work with us because of our "man-hating attitudes" or the presence of lesbians. We are called too strident, told we are making enemies, not doing good.

The battered women's movement has seen this kind of attack: the pressure has been to provide services only, without analysis of the causes of violence against women and strategies for ending it. To provide only services without political analysis or direct action is to be in an approved "helping" role; to analyze the causes of violence against women is to begin the work toward changing an entire system of power and control. It is when we do the latter that we are threatened with the label of man-hater or lesbian. For my politics, if a women's social change organization has not been labeled lesbian or communist, it is probably not doing significant work; it is only "making nice."

Women in many of these organizations, out of fear of all the losses we are threatened with, begin to modify our work to make it more acceptable and less threatening to the male-dominated society which we originally set out to change. The work can no longer be radical (going to the root cause of the problem) but instead must be reforming, working only on the symptoms and not the cause. Real change for women becomes thwarted and stopped. The word *lesbian* is instilled with the power to halt our work and control our lives. And we give it its power with our fear.   [1988]

🌿 114

Cat

JULIE BLACKWOMON

It is three days after my twelfth birthday and my mother is sitting beside me on the edge of my bed. She is holding a box of sanitary napkins and a little booklet that reads "What Every Young Girl Should Know" and telling me for the third straight year that I am to read the book and keep the pads hidden from the sight of Daddy and Leroy. I am hardly listening. I am sneaking furtive glances out the window and patiently waiting for her to finish so I can meet the boys out on the lot for our softball game.

My mother is saying, "Look, you've thrown your pretty dress on the floor." She is bending down to pick it up. It is a white flared dress with large yellow flowers. Daddy bought it for my birthday. I am remembering the party, the coconut cake with the 12 ballerinas holding 12 pink candles. Momma had straightened my hair but refused to wave it tight to my head so it would look like a process, the way I usually wear it. Instead she has fluffed up the curls like she does my sister Dee Dee's hair. Momma is serving punch in a white apron or just standing around with her hands in the pockets. When she catches my eye she motions with her head for me to go over and talk with the other girls who are standing in a cluster around the record player. I smile nervously back at her, but remain where I am. My friends are all acting strange. Leroy, my brother and very best friend, has been stuck up under Diedra Young all evening, and Raymond and Zip-Zip are out on the back steps giggling with Peggy and Sharon. Jeffrey teases me about my knobby black knees under my new dress until I threaten to punch him in the mouth. I wander out to the kitchen to play with Fluffy, our cat, until Momma misses me and comes to drag me back to the party.

Now, sitting on my bed with Momma, she is saying she will have to get me a training bra. I self-consciously reach up and touch my breasts, then jerk my hands down again. I hate them. I'm always hurting them when I bump into things and now when I fight I not only have to protect my face and head I have to worry about getting hit in the breast too.

"Momma, can I go now? I gotta pitch today," I say. Momma puts her arm around my shoulder and pulls me closer to her. "Sugar, you've got to stop playing with those boys all the time; why don't you go play with Sheila, that nice young girl who's staying with the Jenkins?"

"But I don't know her."

"Well, you can get to know her. She's a nice girl and she doesn't know anybody. You can introduce her to the rest of the girls."

"But Dee Dee know them better than I do."

"Yeah, sugar, but Sheila doesn't have any girlfriends and you don't either, so you could be friends with each other."

I pull away from her. "I got friends," I say. I'm getting annoyed with the conversation, I want to go out and play. I get up and walk over to the window and stand there with my back to her.

"OK," Momma says finally, "but I've invited the Jenkins over for lunch Sunday and if you want to be friends with Sheila fine, if not. . . ." She shrugs her shoulders.

"You gonna make Dee Dee be there too?"

"Yup."

"Can we invite Zip-Zip and Jeffrey?"

She hesitates a moment. ". . . Maybe next time."

"OK, can I go now?" I am inching toward the door.

"All right, scoot." She pats me on the butt as I pass her. I am running down the steps, jumping over the last two. Dee Dee, who has been listening at the door, says, "Can I go with you, Cat?"

"No."

"Why not?"

"'Cause you can't."

I reach the vacant lot where we play ball. There is no game today. The boys are busy gathering ammunition—dirt clods, rocks, bottles—for the fight with the white boys from across the tracks.

Dee Dee whines to Leroy: "Leroy, I wanna go."

"You can't," Leroy says.

"How come?"

"'Cause you're too young."

"I'm just as old as Jeffrey!"

"You can't go," Leroy says, ". . . besides you're a girl."

"Cat's a girl," she says indignantly.

We all ignore her. We are gathering sticks and rocks and throwing them into an empty milk crate.

"How come I can't go? Huh? How come?" Nobody answers her. We are all walking across the lot. Raymond and Leroy are carrying the ammunition; Dee Dee is standing where we left her, yelling, "I'm gonna tell Momma what you're up to! I'm gonna tell you going cross the tracks to fight with those white boys." Then, after a moment or two: ". . . And Cat's got Kotex in her dresser drawer!" My neck burns but I keep walking.

I am 16 years old and sitting in Sheila's dining room. We are playing checkers and I am losing and not minding at all. Her cousin Bob comes in. He is stationed in Georgia and on leave from the army. He says hi to Sheila, ignores me completely and walks through to the back with his green duffel bag in his left hand. His voice drifts in from the kitchen, "Where'd the little bulldagger come from?" Sheila springs back from the table so fast her chair overturns. She yells in the kitchen doorway, "You shut your nasty mouth, Bob Jenkins!" The next day we are supposed to make cookies for her aunt's birthday but she calls to suggest we do it over my house instead. I do not go back over Sheila's again unless Dee Dee is with me, or there is no one home.

We are in Fairmount Park within some semi-enclosed shrubbery. Sheila and I are lying on our backs on an old army blanket. We look like Siamese twins joined together at the head. The sky is blue above us and I am chewing on the straw that came with my coke.

"Cat, tell me again how you used to almost be late for school all the time 'cause you used to be waiting for me to come out of my house so we could walk to school together," Sheila says.

"I've told you 3,000 times already."

"Well, tell me again, I like to hear it."

"If you hadn't been peeping from behind the curtains yourself and waiting for *me* to come out we'd both have gotten to school on time."

She laughs softly, then turns over on her stomach.

"I want a kiss," she says.

I lean up on my elbow, check around to make sure nobody's peeping through the bushes then turn and press my lips to hers. After a few seconds she pulls away. "Man, Cat, I never felt this way about anybody before."

"Me neither." I reach over and touch her hand. We kiss again, briefly, our lips just touching. Then we turn and lie as we were before but continue holding hands.

"Cat?"

"Yeah?"

"I think I'm in love."

"Me too."

She squeezes my hand. I squeeze hers back.

"What would you do if Bob came by and saw us now?" Sheila asks.

"What would you do?"

"I don't know. I'd just say hi, I guess."

"Then I would too," I say.

The sun has moved and is now shining directly over us. I cover my eyes with my arm.

"Bob would say we're both bulldaggers," Sheila says after a while.

"Yeah, I guess he would," I say.

"We aren't bulldaggers, are we, Cat?"

"No, bulldaggers want to be men and we don't want to be men, right?"

"Right, we just love each other and there's nothing wrong with loving someone."

"Yeah and nobody can choose who you fall in love with."

"Right."

Sheila and I are in her bedroom; her uncle is standing over the bed shouting, "What the hell's going on here?" He is home from work early. Sheila and I scramble for the sheet and clutch it across our bodies. I am waiting for her uncle to leave so I can get up and dressed, but he just stands there staring, thunder in his face. Finally I release my end of the sheet and scramble to the foot of the bed. Sheila's stockings are entwined in my blouse. I cram panties into my pocket and pull blue jeans over naked, ashen legs. I am trembling. Her uncle's eyes follow me around the room like harsh spotlights.

Later at my house, Momma, Daddy and I are in the dining room. Leroy and Dee Dee are in their rooms, the doors are shut tight; they've been ordered not to open them. My mother sits on the couch wringing her hands. I sit stiffly forward on the edge of a straight backed chair. My head down. My teeth clenched. My father stomps back and forth across the floor, his hands first behind him, holding each other at the butt, then gesturing out in front of him. He is asking, "What's this I hear about you being in bed with the Jenkins girl?" I sit still on the edge of my chair, looking straight ahead.

"I'm talking to you, Catherine!" His voice is booming to the rafters, I'm sure the neighbors hear. It is dark outside and a slight breeze puffs out the window curtains. I am holding a spool of thread that had been on the table. I am squeezing it in my hands, the round edges intrude into my palms. I continue to squeeze.

"You hear me talking to you, girl?" He is standing directly over me now, his voice reverberates in my ear. I squeeze the spool of thread and stare at a spider-shaped crack in the wall above the light switch. There is an itch on my left leg, below my knee. I do not scratch. Dogs bark in the backyards and one of the Williams kids is getting a spanking. I hear the strap fall, a child wailing, and an angry female voice.

My father is saying, "Look, you'd better say something, you brazen heifer!" He jerks my head around to face him. I yank it back to stare at the crack in the wall.

"You're lucky Tom Jenkins didn't have you arrested—forcing yourself on that girl like that. . . ."

"What? What? What force? Sheila didn't say I forced her to do anything!"

"If you didn't force her, then what happened?"

"Sheila didn't say that! She didn't say it! Mr. Jenkins must have said it!" I am on my feet and trembling, and screaming at the top of my lungs.

"Then what did happen?" my father screams back at me. I sit back down in the chair and again stare at the crack in the wall over the light switch. Trying to concentrate on it, blot out my father's voice. I cannot. I get up and run to the chair where my mother sits. I am pulling on her arm. "Momma, Sheila didn't say that, did she? She didn't say I forced her?"

Momma sits there biting on her bottom lip and wringing her hands. She does not look at me. She lays her hand on my head and does not speak. My father grabs my arm and yanks me away. I am enveloped in his sour breath as he shouts, "Look, I'm a man of God and don't you dare doubt my word!" I yank my arm from his grip and run toward the steps, toward the safety of my bedroom.

"I haven't dismissed you!" I hear my father's footsteps behind me. He grabs me by my tee shirt and swings me around. I lose my footing and fall at the bottom of the steps.

"Arthur, Arthur!" My mother is running behind us. My father's knee is in my chest; he is yelling in a hoarse angry voice, "Catherine Johnson, I have one more thing to say to you, then we needn't discuss it anymore, but you listen carefully because I mean every word I say: There will be no bulldaggers in my house, do you understand me? THERE WILL BE NO BULLDAGGERS IN MY HOUSE!"

I am sitting beside Sheila on a bench in Fairmount Park; we are within walking distance of the spot where we used to meet with our lunch on Daddy's old army blanket. The grass is completely green except for one long crooked brown streak where the boys trampled a short cut to the basketball court. The leaves are green too, save for one or two brown and yellow ones beneath the bench at our feet. Sheila's head is bent.

"I'm sorry," she is saying. She is picking minute pieces of lint from a black skirt. "I'm really sorry but you don't know how my uncle is when he gets mad." I am silent. I am watching three boys play basketball on the court about 20 yards away. A tall white kid leaps up and dunks the ball.

"I just didn't know what else to do," Sheila continues. "I was scared and Uncle Jim kept saying, 'She made you do it, didn't she? She made you do it, didn't she?' And before I knew it, I'd said 'yes.'" A short black kid knocks the ball out of bounds and a fat boy in a green shirt darts out to retrieve it.

"Cathy?" Her hand is on my forearm and I turn to look her full in the face. "I'm sorry, Cat, I just didn't know what else to do." I turn again toward the basketball court. The tall white boy is holding the ball under his arm and shaking the hand of a short kid. The fat boy in the green sweatshirt is pulling a navy blue poncho on over his head.

"Cathy, please?" Sheila is saying. I turn to look her full in the face. "It's all right, Sheila, it's all right." It is getting windy. The basketball court empties and Sheila asks if I'll meet her at our spot next Saturday. I lie and say yes. She checks to make sure no one's looking, pecks me on the cheek, then gets up to leave. I sit watching the empty basketball court for a long time, then I get up and take the long way home. [1983]

115

Chicana Lesbians: Fear and Loathing in the Chicano Community

CARLA TRUJILLO

The vast majority of Chicano heterosexuals perceive Chicana lesbians as a threat to the community. Homophobia, that is, irrational fear of gay or lesbian people and/or behaviors, accounts, in part, for the heterosexist response to the lesbian community. However, I argue that Chicana lesbians are perceived as a greater threat to the Chicano community because their existence disrupts the established order of male dominance, and raises the consciousness of many Chicanas regarding their own independence and control. Some writers have addressed these topics[1]; however, an analysis of the complexities of lesbian existence alongside this perceived threat has not been undertaken. While this essay is by no means complete, it attempts to elucidate the underlying basis of these fears which, in the very act of the lesbian existence, disrupt the established norm of patriarchal oppression.

SEXUALITY

As lesbians, our sexuality becomes the focal issue of dissent. The majority of Chicanas, both lesbian and heterosexual, are taught that our sexuality must conform to certain modes of behavior. Our culture voices shame upon us if we go beyond the criteria of passivity and repression, or doubts in our virtue if we refuse.[2] We, as women, are taught to suppress our sexual desires and needs by conceding all pleasure to the male. As Chicanas, we are commonly led to believe that even talking about our participation and satisfaction in sex is taboo. Moreover, we (as well as most women in the United States) learn to hate our bodies, and usually possess little knowledge of them. Lourdes Arguelles did a survey on the sexuality of 373 immigrant Latinas and found that over half of the women possessed little knowledge of their reproductive systems or their own physiology. Most remarked they "just didn't look down there."[3]

Not loving our bodies affects how we perceive ourselves as sexual beings. As lesbians, however, we have no choice but to confront our sexuality before we can confront our lesbianism. Thus the commonly held viewpoint among heterosexuals that we are "defined by our sexuality" is, in a way, partially true. If we did not bring our sexuality into consciousness, we would not be able to confront ourselves and come out.

After confronting and then acknowledging our attraction, we must, in turn, learn to reclaim that what we're told is bad, wrong, dirty, and taboo—namely our bodies, and our freedom to express ourselves in them. Too often we internalize the homophobia and sexism of the larger society, as well as that of our own culture, which attempts to keep us from loving ourselves. As Norma Alarcón states, "[Chicana lesbians] must act to negate the negation."[4] A Chicana lesbian must learn to love herself, both as a woman and a sexual being, before she can love another. Loving another woman not only validates one's own sexuality, but also that of the other woman, by the very act of loving. Understanding this, a student in a workshop that Cherríe Moraga and I conducted on lesbian sexuality stated, "Now I get it. Not only do you have to learn to love your own vagina, but someone else's too."[5] It is only then that the subsequent experiences of love and commitment, passion and remorse can also become our dilemmas, much like those of everyone else. The effort to consciously reclaim our sexual selves forces Chicanas to either confront their own sexuality or, in refusing, castigate lesbians as *vendidas** to the race, blasphemers to the church, atrocities against nature, or some combination.

IDENTIFICATION

For many Chicanas, our identification as women, that is, as complete women, comes from the belief that we need to be connected to a man.[6] Ridding ourselves of this parasitic identification is not always easy, for we grow up, as my Chicana students have pointed out, defined in a male context: daddy's girl, some guy's girlfriend, wife, or mother. Vying for a man's attention compromises our own personal and intellectual development. We exist in a patriarchal society that undervalues women.[7] We are socialized to undervalue ourselves, as well as anything associated with the concept of self. Our voice is considered less significant, our needs and desires secondary. As the Chicanas in the MALCS workshop indicated,[8] our toleration of unjust behavior from men, the church, the established order, is considered an attribute. How much pain can we bear in the here-and-now so that we may be better served in the afterlife? Martyrdom, the cloth of denial, transposes itself into a gown of cultural beauty.

Yet, an alliance with a man grants a woman heterosexual privileges, many of which are reified by the law, the church, our families and, of course, "la causa." Women who partake in the privileges of male sexual alliance may often do so at the cost of their own sense of self, since they must often subvert their needs, voice, intellect, and personal development in these alliances. These are the conditional contradictions commonly prescribed for women by the patriarchy in our culture and in the larger society. Historically, women have been viewed as property.[9] Though some laws have changed, ideologically little else has. Upon marriage, a father feels he can relinquish "ownership"

and "responsibility" of his daughter to her husband. The Chicana feminist who confronts this subversion, and critiques the sexism of the Chicano community, will be called *vendida* if she finds the "male defined and often antifeminist" values of the community difficult to accept.[10]

The behaviors necessary in the "act of pursuing a man" often generate competition among women, leading to betrayal of one another.[11] When a woman's sense of identity is tied to that of a man, she is dependent on this relationship for her own self-worth. Thus, she must compete with other women for his attention. When the attention is then acknowledged and returned, she must work to ensure that it is maintained. Ensuring the protection of this precious commodity generates suspicion among women, particularly single, unattached women. Since we're all taught to vie for a man's attention, we become, in a sense, sexual suspects to one another. The responsibility is placed entirely upon the woman with little thought given to the suspected infidelity of the man.

We should ask what role the man places himself in regarding his support of these behaviors. After all, the woman is commonly viewed as his possession. Hence, in the typical heterosexual relationship both parties are abetting the other, each in a quest that does not improve the status of the woman (nor, in my view, that of the man), nor the consciousness of either of them.

How does the Chicana lesbian fit into this picture? Realistically, she doesn't. As a lesbian she does many things simultaneously: she rejects "compulsory heterosexuality";[12] she refuses to partake in the "game" of competition for men; she confronts her own sexuality; and she challenges the norms placed upon her by culture and society, whose desire is to subvert her into proper roles and places. This is done, whether consciously or unconsciously, by the very aspect of her existence. In the course of conducting many workshops on lesbian sexuality, Chicana heterosexuals have often indicated to me that they do not associate with lesbians, since it could be assumed that either (1) they, too, must be lesbians, or (2) if they're not, they must be selling out to Anglo culture, since it is implied that

---

*Traitors.

Chicana lesbians do and thus any association with lesbians implicates them as well. This equivocation of sexual practice and cultural alliance is a retrograde ideology, quite possibly originating from the point of view that the only way to uplift the species is to propagate it. Thus, homosexuality is seen as "counter revolutionary."

Heterosexual Chicanas need not be passive victims of the cultural onslaught of social control. If anything, Chicanas are usually the backbone of every *familia,* for it is their strength and self-sacrifice which often keeps the family going. While heterosexual Chicanas have a choice about how they want to live their lives (read: how they choose to form their identities[13]), Chicana lesbians have very little choice, because their quest for self-identification comes with the territory. This is why "coming out" can be a major source of pain for Chicana lesbians, since the basic fear of rejection by family and community is paramount.[14] For our own survival, Chicana lesbians must continually embark on the creation or modification of our own *familia,* since this institution, as traditionally constructed, may be nonsupportive of the Chicana lesbian existence.[15]

MOTHERHOOD

The point of view that we are not complete human beings unless we are attached to a male is further promoted by the attitude that we are incomplete as women unless we become mothers. Many Chicanas are socialized to believe that our chief purpose in life is raising children.[16] Not denying the fact that motherhood can be a beautiful experience, it becomes, rather, one of the few experiences not only supported [by] but expected in a traditional Chicano community. Historically, in dual-headed households, Chicanas (as well as other women) were relegated to the tasks of home care and child rearing, while the men took on the task of earning the family's income.[17] Economic need, rather than feminist consciousness, has been the primary reason for the change to two-income households. Nevertheless, for many Chicanas, motherhood is still seen by our culture as the final act in establishing our "womanhood."

Motherhood among Chicana lesbians does exist. Many lesbians are mothers as by-products of divorce, earlier liaisons with men, or through artificial insemination. Anecdotal evidence I have obtained from many Chicana lesbians in the community indicates that lesbians who choose to become mothers in our culture are seen as aberrations of the traditional concept of motherhood, which stresses male–female partnership. Choosing to become a mother via alternative methods of insemination, or even adopting children, radically departs from society's view that lesbians and gay men cannot "successfully" raise children. Therefore, this poses another threat to the Chicano community, since Chicana lesbians are perceived as failing to partake in one of their chief obligations in life.

RELIGION

Religion, based on the tradition of patriarchal control and sexual, emotional, and psychological repression, has historically been a dual means of hope for a better afterlife and social control in the present one. Personified by the Virgen de Guadalupe, the concept of motherhood and martyrdom go hand in hand in the Catholic religion. Nevertheless, as we are all aware, religion powerfully affects our belief systems concerning life and living. Since the Pope does not advocate a homosexual lifestyle,[18] lesbians and gay men are not given sanction by the largely Catholic Chicano community—hence, fulfilling our final threat to the established order. Chicana lesbians who confront their homosexuality must, in turn, confront (for those raised in religious households) religion, bringing to resolution some compromise of religious doctrine and personal lifestyle. Many choose to alter, modify, or abandon religion, since it is difficult to advocate something that condemns our existence. This exacerbates a sense of alienation for Chicana lesbians who feel they cannot wholly participate in a traditional religion.

In sum, Chicana lesbians pose a threat to the Chicano community for a variety of reasons, primarily because they threaten the established social hierarchy of patriarchal control. In order to "come-out," Chicana lesbians must confront their sexuality, therefore bringing a taboo subject to consciousness. By necessity, they must learn to love their bodies, for it is also another woman's body which becomes the object of love. Their identities as people alter and become independent of men; hence there is no need to submit to, or perform the necessary behaviors that cater to wooing, the male ego. Lesbians (and other feminist women) would expect to treat and be treated by men as equals. Men who have traditionally interacted with women on the basis of their gender (read: femininity) first, and their brains second, are commonly left confused when the lesbian (or feminist) fails to respond to the established pecking order.

Motherhood, seen as exemplifying the final act of our existence as women, is practiced by lesbians, but usually without societal or cultural permission. Not only is it believed that lesbians cannot become mothers (hence, not fulfilling our established purpose as women), but if we do, we morally threaten the concept of motherhood as a sanctified entity, since lesbianism doesn't fit into its religious or cultural confines. Lastly, religion, which does not support the homosexual lifestyle, seeks to repudiate us as sinners if we are "practicing," and only tolerable if not. For her personal and psychological survival, the Chicana lesbian must confront and bring to resolution these established cultural and societal conflicts. These "confrontations" go against many of the values of the Chicano community, since they pose a threat to the established order of male control. Our very existence challenges this order, and in some cases challenges the oftentimes ideologically oppressive attitudes toward women.

It is widely assumed that lesbians and heterosexual women are in two completely different enclaves in regard to the type and manner of the oppression they must contend with. As illustrated earlier in this essay, this indeed, may be true. There do exist, however, different levels of patriarchal oppression that affect all of us as women, and when combined inhibit our collective liberation. If we, as lesbian and heterosexual Chicanas, can open our eyes and look at all that we share as women, we might find commonalities even among our differences. First and foremost among them is the status of *woman*. Uttered under any breath, it implies subservience;

cast to a lower position not only in society, but in our own culture as well.

Second, is the universal of the body. We are all female and subject to the same violations as any woman in society. We must contend with the daily threat of rape, molestation, and harassment—violations that affect all of us as women, lesbian or not.

As indicated earlier, our sexuality is suppressed by our culture—relegated to secrecy or embarrassment, implicating us as wrongful women if we profess to fulfill ourselves sexually. Most of us still grow up inculcated with the dichotomy of the "good girl-bad girl" syndrome. With virtue considered as the most admirable quality, it's easy to understand which we choose to partake. This generates a cloud of secrecy around any sexual activity, and leads, I am convinced, to our extremely high teenage pregnancy rate, simply because our families refuse to acknowledge the possibility that young women may be sexually active before marriage.

We are taught to undervalue our needs and voices. Our opinions, viewpoints, and expertise are considered secondary to those of males—even if we are more highly trained. Time and again, I have seen otherwise sensible men insult the character of a woman when they are unable to belittle her intellectual capacities.[19] Character assassinations are commonly disguised in the familiar "*vendida* to the race" format. Common it seems, because it functions as the ultimate insult to any conscientious *política*. Because many of us are taught that our opinions matter little, we have difficulty at times, raising them. We don't trust what we think, or believe in our merits. Unless we are encouraged to do so, we have difficulty thinking independently of male opinion. Chicanas must be constantly encouraged to speak up, to voice their opinions, particularly in areas where no encouragement has ever been provided.

As Chicanas (and Chicanos), most of us are subject to the effects of growing up in a culture besieged by poverty and all the consequences of it: lack of education, insufficient political power and health care, disease and drugs. We are all subject to the effects of a society that is racist, classist, and homophobic, as well as sexist, and patriarchally dominant. Colonization has imposed itself and affected the disbursement of status and the collective rights of us as individuals. Chicanas are placed in this order at a lower position, ensconced within a tight boundary that limits our voices, our bodies, and our brains. In classic dissonant fashion, many of us become complicit in this (since our survival often depends on it) and end up rationalizing our very own limitations.

The collective liberation of people begins with the collective liberation of half its constituency—namely women. The view that our hierarchical society places Chicanos at a lower point, and they in turn must place Chicanas lower still, is outmoded and politically destructive. Women can no longer be relegated to supporting roles. Assuaging delicate male egos as a means of establishing our identities is retrograde and subversive to our own identities as women. Chicanas, both lesbian and heterosexual, have a dual purpose ahead of us. We must fight for our own voices as women, since this will ultimately serve to uplift us as a people.   [1991]

NOTES

1. Cherríe Moraga, *Loving in the War Years: Lo que nunca pasó por sus labios* (Boston: South End Press, 1983), 103, 105, 111, 112, 117.
2. See Ana Castillo's essay on sexuality: "La Macha: Toward a Beautiful Whole Self," in *Chicana Lesbians: The Girls Our Mothers Warned Us About*, ed. Carla Trujillo (Berkeley: Third Woman Press, 1991). Also see *The Sexuality of Latinas, Third Woman* 4 (1989).
3. Lourdes Arguelles, "A Survey of Latina Immigrant Sexuality," presented at the National Association for Chicano Studies Conference, Albuquerque, New Mexico, March 29–April 1, 1990.
4. Norma Alarcón, personal communication, MALCS (Mujeres Activas en Letras y Cambio Social) Summer Research Institute, University of California, Los Angeles, August 3–6, 1990.
5. Chicana Leadership Conference, Workshop on Chicana lesbians, University of California, Berkeley, Feb. 8–10, 1990.
6. This was spoken of in great detail in a workshop on Chicana Empowerment and Oppression by Yvette Flores Ortiz at the MALCS, 1990.
7. There are multitudes of feminist books and periodicals that attest to the subordinate position of women in society. Listing them is beyond the scope of this essay.
8. Yvette Flores Ortiz, MALCS, 1990.
9. Peggy R. Sanday, "Female Status in the Public Domain," in *Women, Culture & Society,* eds. Michelle Rosaldo and Louise Lamphere (Stanford: Stanford University Press, 1974), 189–206.
10. *Loving in the War Years,* 113.
11. See Ana Castillo's "La Macha: Toward a Beautiful Whole Self." See also *Loving in the War Years,* 136.
12. Adrienne Rich, "Compulsory Heterosexuality and Lesbian Existence," in *Women: Sex and Sexuality,* eds. Catharine R. Stimpson and Ethel Spector Person (Chicago: University of Chicago Press, 1980), 62–91.
13. As Moraga states, "only the woman intent on the approval can be affected by the disapproval," *Loving in the War Years,* 103.
14. Rejection by family and community is also an issue for gay men; however, their situation is muddied by the concomitant loss of power.
15. Cherríe Moraga attests to the necessity of Chicanas needing to "make *familia* from scratch" in *Giving Up the Ghost* (Los Angeles: West End Press, 1986), 58.
16. *Loving in the War Years,* 113.
17. Karen Sacks, "Engels Revisited: Women, the Organization of Production and Private Property," in *Women, Culture & Society,* 207–22.
18. Joseph Cardinal Ratzinger, Prefect, and Alberto Bouone, Titular Archbishop of Caesarea in Numedia, Secretary, "Letter to the Bishops of the Catholic Church in the Pastoral Care of Homosexual Persons," October 1, 1986. Approved by Pope John Paul II, adopted in an ordinary session of the Congregation for the Doctrine of Faith and ordered published. Reprinted in *The Vatican and Homosexuality,* eds. Jeannine Gramick and Pat Furey (New York: Crossroad Publishing Co., 1988), 1–10.
19. This occurred often to the women MeChA (Movimiento Estudiantil Chicano de Aztlán) leaders who were on the Berkeley campus between 1985 and 1989. It also happened to a Chicana panel member during a 1990 National Association for Chicano Studies presentation, when a Chicano discussant disagreed with the recommendations based on her research.

116

Livin' in a Gay Family

MEGAN MCGUIRE

Homosexuality first entered my life when I was 12 years old. The words fag, queer, dyke, and homo were used all around me. I even used them. These words were used to disrespect someone. If you were a fag, you were an outcast or someone others didn't like. In the fall of my seventh-grade year, I began to fear those words and hate people who identified with those words.

And then my mother told me she was gay. She came out. She was a dyke, a fag, a queer. My mother was one of "those" people. I couldn't let any of my friends know. I was afraid they would not like me or that my classmates would beat me up. I wouldn't let anyone know that the other woman, Barb, who was living in my house, was my other mother. I hadn't known about my mom's sexuality until one day when I went into her bedroom and asked "Mom, are you gay?" She told me that she was gay. I became really upset and decided for myself that she was straight. I never gave myself time to think, what if my mom was in fact gay? Then it sunk in. My mom was gay. I cried and got really angry. I wanted to know why she was putting my brother and me into a situation where we had to be secretive about our family. For five years I lived with the secret. It caused me to lie, be angry, and be sad. No one I knew could know that I was living in a gay family.

The first four years my mom was "out" was a very lonely time for me. When I moved up to Boston from Washington, D.C., in 1990, I was in a new city, a new school, and a new life. I made friends. I wanted to be liked, so all I could do was laugh at the jokes my friends made about gays. The people I called my "friends" were not people I wanted to be my friends. I hadn't figured out how to make real friends whom I could trust with the secret. I wasn't ready to tell anybody about my family because I wasn't ready to deal with it myself. I was very lonely and depressed, so I occupied myself playing soccer and sitting in front of the TV.

When I entered high school, I played three sports and joined several clubs. I didn't make time to find a group of people who would give me support. Because I was participating in all of these activities, people got to know me and my face became well recognized. I was an active student who pushed for change in student government and played in almost every female volleyball, basketball, and softball game. I felt the pressure to keep the

secret a secret. I thought that all the popularity I had gained and the friends I had made would end if people knew my mom was gay.

Despite my social success, I spent most of the time hiding who I was, who my family was, and making up lies. My brother and I would take the "gay" literature and hide it when our friends came over, and we would turn over pictures of Barb and mom together, so they could not be seen. Once my brother told a friend that our car was a used car and that we hadn't had time to take the pink triangle off the back windshield. We didn't have people spend the night to avoid the possibility that they might ask "the question." We lived like this for almost 3 1/2 years. Then we moved into a house that had a basement apartment where, we told our friends, Barb lived. It was really a guest room and an office for my mom and Barb.

In the middle of my sophomore year, I finally made a best friend. I didn't tell her anything and she never asked, even when she spent the night. I guess we adopted the "don't ask, don't tell" policy. She knew Barb and Jean as my mothers. I never had to lie to her, but I didn't talk to her about my family until two years later. By the end of my sophomore year I still had this really good friend, which felt like a record for me.

The same year I was asked to be a peer leader. I told one of the coordinators, who happend to be gay, that my mom was gay. He helped me understand that if people didn't like me because of my mom's sexual orientation, they weren't worth my time. I got involved in fighting homophobia. I decided to get educated, so I attended workshops and became more confident about who I am and who my mom is. I attacked homophobic remarks and started to educate others about homophobia.

But I still had not told people how homophobia affected my life. I had not told people that when I sit in the back of the bus coming back from a game and listen to the team talk about what they think of gay people and the children of those gay people, my stomach turns into a big knot. Even though my mom sat me down and told me that it wasn't fair to myself and to the people I was educating to keep silent, I was not ready to talk about my family, since I still didn't have the peer support I wanted and needed.

During the summer following my sophomore year, things went really well. I finally told someone I met at summer camp that my mother was gay. She was a person I will never forget. First she told me she was gay, and then I told her about my family. It was a relief; she didn't assume or judge. I guess telling her was easier than telling others because she was gay, but it was a tremendous relief. I came back from camp really happy and ready to speak at the national coming out day at my school.

There was one problem. My brother was entering his freshman year at my school and he was not ready for me to speak. He wanted me to stay silent about our family. I told him for that year I wouldn't speak, but the next year I would and that I would not lie to anyone anymore. I mentored a freshman health class, and then I understood why my brother asked me not to speak. I realized that, because of the ninth graders' relative immaturity about sexuality, he would have been harassed for the whole year. So I tried to make it safe for him. I educated the class I mentored about homophobia; his friends were in the class. His friends were now my friends and my friends were his, so we both were building a group we could feel comfortable in.

During February I met a person who helped me take the first steps to tell my friends. He asked the "question." He asked if Barb was my mom's girlfriend and I told him, "Ya, she is." Eventually I told my close friends that my mother was gay. I found out they already knew and they thought it was not an issue. Then in May, a reporter from our city's newspaper asked to interview me about growing up in a gay family. There was a photo exhibit of gay families on display at one of the local elementary schools, and the paper wanted a youth to talk about the issues the show raised.

At the end of May, my story was on the front page of the *Cambridge Chronicle*.[1] I told the city that I'm proud of my family and if people have a problem with it, they should keep it their problem. I wanted people to know I felt I had betrayed my family by lying, and it was time for me to be honest about being a child of lesbian moms. A week later I spoke in front of a group of a hundred students, parents, staff, and city officials, telling them that words like fag, queer, dyke, and homo are words that hurt. Not only do these words hurt gay men and women, but also their families and children, and we should not tolerate words that hurt and cause hatred. I continued to speak in some classes at my school, explaining what my life has been like holding in a secret that really shouldn't have had to be a secret.

Since the *Chronicle* article was published, people have asked me two questions. The first is, "Are you gay?" I choose not to answer this question. As teenagers most of us can't explain the feelings going on in our minds and bodies, whether they are for a person of the same sex or the opposite sex. The second question is, "Why are you making a big deal about telling people about your family?" The answer is that it is a big deal for me. Once the article hit the stands I felt a huge relief; it was like a big splinter had been pulled out of me.

I always wanted to know someone who was older who had gay parents and was out about it. I haven't found someone like this. I want to be that someone for other kids, so children of gay men and women don't have to feel afraid to be true to themselves.

I've helped my brother. I know he will never say, "Thank you; OK, I'm glad I don't have to hide and lie anymore," but I know he is relieved. After the article was published, a kid who played hockey with my brother came up to him and said, "I saw the article you fucking fag." My brother said, "Fuck you" and walked away. All of his friends and my friends are cool with it, and they know Barb and my mom as our mothers who are both raising us.

I'm going to enter my last year of high school being able to answer questions about who Barb is, and who my family is, without lying. [1996]

NOTE

1. Amy Miller, "Gay Photo Exhibit Causes Stir at High School," *Cambridge Chronicle*, May 25, 1995, 1.

🌿 117

I Lost It at the Movies

JEWELLE GOMEZ

My grandmother, Lydia, and my mother, Dolores, were both talking to me from their bathroom stalls in the Times Square movie theater. I was washing butter from my hands at the sink and didn't think it at all odd. The people in my family are always talking; conversation is a life force in our existence. My great-grandmother, Grace, would narrate her life story from 7:00 a.m. until we went to bed at night. The only break was when we were reading or the reverential periods when we sat looking out of our tenement windows, observing the neighborhood, which we naturally talked about later.

So it was not odd that Lydia and Dolores talked nonstop from their stalls, oblivious to everyone except us. I hadn't expected it to happen there, though. I hadn't really expected an "it" to happen at all. To be a lesbian was part of who I was, like being left-handed—even when I'd slept with men. When my great-grandmother asked me in the last days of her life if I would be marrying my college boyfriend I said yes, knowing I would not, knowing I was a lesbian.

It seemed a fact that needed no expression. Even my first encounter with the word "bulldagger" was not charged with emotional conflict. As a teen in the 1960s my grandmother told a story about a particular building in our Boston neighborhood that had gone to seed. She described the building's past through the experience of a party she'd attended there 30 years before. The best part of the evening had been a woman she'd met and danced with. Lydia had been a professional dancer and singer on the black theater circuit; to dance with women was who she was. They'd danced, then the woman walked her home and asked her out. I heard the delicacy my grandmother searched for even in her retelling of how she'd explained to the "bulldagger," as she called her, that she liked her fine but she was more interested in men. I was struck with how careful my grandmother had been to make it clear to that woman (and in effect to me) that there was no offense taken in her attentions, that she just didn't "go that way," as they used to say. I was so happy at 13 to have a word for what I knew myself to be. The word was mysterious and curious, as if from a new language that used some other alphabet which left nothing to cling to when touching its curves and crevices. But still a word existed and my grandmother was not flinching in using it. In fact she'd smiled at the good heart and good looks of the bulldagger who'd asked her.

Once I had the knowledge of a word and a sense of its importance to me, I didn't feel the need to explain, confess, or define my identity as a lesbian. The process of reclaiming my ethnic identity in this country was already all-consuming. Later, of course, in moments of glorious self-righteousness, I did make declarations. But they were not usually ones I had to make. Mostly they were a testing of the waters. A preparation for the rest of the world which, unlike my grandmother, might not have a grounding in what true love is about. My first lover, the woman who'd been in my bed once a week most of our high school years, finally married. I told her with my poems that I was a lesbian. She was not afraid to ask if what she'd read was about her, about my love for her. So there, amidst her growing children, errant husband, and bowling trophies I said yes, the poems were about her and my love for her, a love I'd always regret relinquishing to her reflexive obeisance to tradition. She did not flinch either. We still get drunk together when I go home to Boston.

During the 1970s I focused less on career than on how to eat and be creative at the same time. Graduate school and a string of nontraditional jobs (stage manager, midtown messenger, etc.) left me so busy I had no time to think about my identity. It was a long time before I made the connection between my desire, my isolation, and the difficulty I had with my writing. I thought of myself as a lesbian between girlfriends—except the between had lasted five years. After some anxiety and frustration I deliberately set about meeting women. Actually, I knew many women, including my closest friend at the time, another black woman also in the theater.

She became uncharacteristically obtuse when I tried to open up and explain my frustration at going to the many parties we attended and being too afraid to approach women I was attracted to, certain I would be rejected either because the women were straight and horrified or gay and terrified of being exposed. For my friend theoretical homosexuality was acceptable, even trendy. Any uncomfortable experience was irrelevant to her. She was impatient and unsympathetic. I drifted away from her in pursuit of the women's community, a phrase that was not in my vocabulary yet, but I knew it was something more than just "women." I fell into that community by connecting with other women writers, and that helped me to focus on my writing and on my social life as a lesbian.

Still, none of my experiences demanded that I bare my soul. I remained honest but not explicit. Expediency, diplomacy, discretion, are all words that come to mind now. At that time I knew no political framework through which to filter my experience. I was more preoccupied with the Attica riots than with Stonewall. The media helped to focus our attentions within a proscribed spectrum and obscure the connections between the issues. I worried about who would shelter Angela Davis, but the concept of sexual politics was remote and theoretical.

I'm not certain exactly when and where the theory and reality converged.

Being a black woman and a lesbian unexpectedly blended like that famous scene in Ingmar Bergman's film *Persona*. The different faces came together as one, and my desire became part of my heritage, my skin, my perspective, my politics, and my future. And I felt sure that it had been my past that helped make the future possible. The women in my family had acted as if their lives were meaningful. Their lives were art. To be a lesbian among them was to be an artist. Perhaps the convergence came when I saw the faces of my great-grandmother, grandmother, and mother in those of the community of women I finally connected with. There was the same adventurous glint in their eyes; the same determined step; the penchant for breaking into song and for not waiting for anyone to take care of them.

I need not pretend to be other than who I was with any of these women. But did I need to declare it? During the holidays when I brought home best friends or lovers my family always welcomed us warmly, clasping us to their magnificent bosoms. Yet there was always an element of silence in our neighborhood, and surprisingly enough in our family, that was disturbing to me. Among the regulars in my father, Duke's, bar, was Maurice. He was eccentric, flamboyant, and still ordinary. He was accorded the same respect by neighborhood children as every other adult. His indiscretions took their place comfortably among the cyclical, Saturday night, man/woman scandals of our neighborhood. I regret never having asked my father how Maurice and he had become friends.

Soon I felt the discomforting silence pressing against my life more persistently. During visits home to Boston it no longer sufficed that Lydia and Dolores were loving and kind to the "friend" I brought home. Maybe it was just my getting older. Living in New York City at the age of 30 in 1980, there was little I kept deliberately hidden from anyone. The genteel silence that hovered around me when I entered our home was palpable but I was unsure whether it was already there when I arrived or if I carried it home within myself. It cut me off from what I knew was a kind of fulfillment available only from my family. The lifeline from Grace, to Lydia, to Dolores, to Jewelle was a strong one. We were bound by so many things, not the least of which was looking so much alike. I was not willing to be orphaned by silence.

If the idea of cathedral weddings and station wagons held no appeal for me, the concept of an extended family was certainly important. But my efforts were stunted by our inability to talk about the life I was creating for myself, for all of us. It felt all the more foolish because I thought I knew how my family would react. I was confident they would respond with their customary aplomb just as they had when I'd first had my hair cut as an Afro (which they hated) or when I brought home friends who were vegetarians (which they found curious). While we had disagreed over some issues, like the fight my mother and I had over Vietnam when I was 19, always when the deal went down we sided with each other. Somewhere deep inside I think I believed that neither my grandmother nor my mother would ever censure my choices. Neither had actually raised me; my great-grandmother had done that, and she had been a steely barricade against any encroachment on our personal freedoms and she'd never disapproved out loud of anything I'd done.

But it was not enough to have an unabashed admiration for these women. It is one thing to have pride in how they'd so graciously survived in spite of the odds against them. It was something else to be standing in a Times Square movie theater faced with the chance to say "it" out loud and risk the loss of their brilliant and benevolent smiles.

My mother had started reading the graffiti written on the wall of the bathroom stall. We hooted at each of her dramatic renderings. Then she said (not breaking her rhythm since we all know timing is everything), "Here's one I haven't seen before— 'DYKES UNITE.'" There was that profound silence again, as if the frames of my life had ground to a halt. We were in a freeze-frame and options played themselves out in my head in rapid succession: Say nothing? Say something? Say what?

I laughed and said, "Yeah, but have you seen the rubber stamp on my desk at home?"

"No," said my mother with a slight bit of puzzlement. "What does it say?"

"I saw it," my grandmother called out from her stall. "It says: 'Lesbian Money!'"

"What?"

"*Lesbian Money*," Lydia repeated.

"I just stamp it on my big bills," I said tentatively, and we all screamed with laughter. The other woman at the sinks tried to pretend we didn't exist.

Since then there has been little discussion. There have been some moments of awkwardness, usually in social situations where they feel uncertain. Although we have not explored the "it," the shift in our relationship is clear. When I go home it is with my lover and she is received as such. I was lucky. My family was as relieved as I to finally know who I was.   [1990]

Older, Wiser, and Marginalized: Ageism in Women's Lives

Although everyone hopes to live to old age, our society devalues and marginalizes old people, particularly old women who are no longer attractive in the eyes of a youth-obsessed culture. We begin with an overview of the economic, social, and health concerns of old women that documents the harsh realities of many old women's lives. Written by the advocacy group Older Women's League, this essay describes the ways that discriminatory social policy has resulted in economic insecurity and inadequate health care for many old women. The Older Women's League advocates a national universal health care system, reform of the Social Security system, an end to discriminatory workplace practices, and government programs to provide affordable housing for old women.

Cynthia Rich's discussion of the way the media treated an attempt by a group of old women to get better security in their building reveals the power of stereotypes to trivialize old women. The brave effort of this group of African-American women, "their eyes flashing with anger," to stand up for themselves was transformed by newspaper coverage into a sweet tableau of little old ladies pleading for help. Rich explores the fear and contempt with which old women have been held in our culture and warns younger women of the dangers of being divided from older women. Older women are often torn between their desire for independence and their physical fragility. Anna Marie Quevedo describes her grandmother's vulnerability in a large city without an effective and genuine support system.

Janice Keaffaber shares her experiences with the ways ageism affected her life once she turned 60 and the emotional challenges old women face when they become "invisible" to others. She suggests ways people "can help lift the stigma that stereotypes and isolates old women."

118

Older Women: The Realities

OLDER WOMEN'S LEAGUE

Today in America, the average woman age 65 and over lives six years longer than the average man. As a result, she is typically widowed and living alone. She struggles to make ends meet on a limited annual income of $15,615 (compared to an average of $29,171 for men). During her lifetime, she probably spent about 17 years caring for children and 18 years caring for elderly parents. Because of this caregiving, she spent 14 years out of the workforce. Even when caregiving didn't stop her from working altogether, it still affected her work pattern and, history shows, dramatically lowered her lifetime earnings. Her retirement income is also smaller because she probably didn't receive a pension, and was paid less than the average man. As a result, she receives lower Social Security benefits.

Because her retirement income is smaller, she spends a higher proportion of her income on housing costs—leaving less for other vital necessities such as utilities, rising medical costs, food, and transportation. In fact, the average older woman spends almost 30 percent of her income on housing. If she is African-American or Latina, she spends half or more of her income on housing-related costs.

The average older woman in America spends a larger portion of her retirement income on health care. She likely has two or more chronic illnesses, which probably require the use of prescription drugs. Medicare does not cover the cost of most prescription drugs, and it is unlikely she has any supplemental insurance to make up the difference. All told, the average woman on Medicare spends 20 percent more on prescription drugs than the average man—largely because of her greater longevity but also due to her tendency toward chronic illness.

As she ages, her chronic conditions become more prevalent. As a result, the chances are very good she will need some type of long-term care services. Ironically, she was probably a caregiver for her own parents and perhaps her spouse as well. When she needs care herself, she will likely begin with home health services, but could very well end up in a skilled nursing facility. The typical nursing home resident is a woman, 75 years of age or older, who enters a nursing home because her caregiving needs can no longer be met in the community.

Growing old in America is very different for women than it is for men. Race and ethnicity, family and work arrangements, and economic resources are the primary influences in the quality of older women's lives. The economic status of older women reflects their life patterns, including education, employment history, and marital status. It is often an extension of the problems and choices women dealt with earlier in their lives. And it is a reflection of a retirement system that does not respond to women's needs.

POVERTY: A GENDERED PERSPECTIVE

Overall, women are far more likely to live in poverty than men, but this is especially true for women as they age. As women get older, they often get poorer. With a poverty rate of 12 percent (compared to 7 percent for men), women over age 65 account for more than 70 percent of older adults living in poverty. Women of color fare the worst in retirement. Twenty-five percent of Latinas and 30 percent of African-American women over age 65 live in poverty, compared to 11 percent of white women. For older women, poverty began long ago when they first entered the workforce. It began with the realities that shape women's lives early on: the reality of the wage gap, the reality of caregiving, and the reality of part-time jobs that offer few benefits, especially pensions.

Reality: Women earn less. The economic chasm that is evident between women and men during their work lives grows much larger during retirement years. Women still earn only 76 percent of what men earn. The pay gap only increases with age. For workers aged 45–54 (a peak earning period), women's earnings are only 70 percent of men's, and among workers aged 55–64, women earn only 68 percent of what men earn. African-American women earn only 68 percent and Latinas earn an astounding 57 percent of what white men earn. The wage gap ensures that the average woman will consistently have a lower retirement income than the average man. Over a lifetime, the wage gap adds up to about $250,000 less in earnings for a woman to invest in her retirement.

Reality: Women are America's caregivers, and they pay for it in retirement. As in many other facets of life, gender makes a difference when it comes to informal caregiving. The one common denominator to all forms of caregiving, both paid and unpaid, is that women do the vast majority of the work. Caregiving can be an economic disaster for women and is one of the largest barriers to their retirement security. Because of caregiving, women often take more flexible, lower-wage jobs with few benefits, or stop working altogether. As a result of caregiving, women lose an average of $550,000 in lifetime wage wealth and about $2,100 annually in already desperately needed Social Security payments.

Reality: Most women don't have income from pensions or savings. The part-time work that allows women to be caregivers is usually low-wage with few benefits, especially pensions. Women are about half as likely as men to receive pension income, and when they do, the benefit is only about half that of the benefit men receive. When it comes to savings, women don't fare well in general. Women's lower wages prevent them from preparing adequately for retirement. You can't save what you don't earn, and the impact of wage discrimination doesn't end when the job does.

Reality: Women live longer. Women live an average of six years longer than men. A longer life expectancy affects all aspects of an older woman's life, especially in relation to retirement income. Marital status, for example, is one of the most important factors in determining economic independence and support in old age. Older women are three times more likely to lose their spouse than men, and this rate only increases as women age. Many women are only a man away from poverty. More than half of elderly widows now living in poverty were not poor before the death of their husbands. The longer women live, the harder it becomes to financially support their growing needs.

The challenges women face and the decisions they make upon entering the workforce have serious consequences for their economic well-being in old age. Simply put: nonentry or late entry into the job market, job interruptions, and temporary or part-time employment characterize most women's work history. Many younger women believe this is a problem of the past. But almost two-thirds of women today have the same kinds of jobs that women have traditionally held: sales, clerical, and retail—low-wage positions that frequently offer no benefits. And they hold those jobs for the same reasons: the need to move in and out of the workforce to care for family, partners, and friends.

Older Women's League believes that this legacy of poverty does not need to be passed from mothers to daughters and on to granddaughters. We understand the faults and biases of the structure of the U.S. retirement system, which is based on male work and life patterns. We believe that we need to make changes to that structure. Meanwhile, it is possible for some women to break the cycle of poverty that haunts older women by understanding the impact of the decisions they make during their work lives.

SOCIAL SECURITY: WOMEN'S STAKE

Social Security is much more than a retirement plan. It is the heart of our nation's social insurance program, providing universal coverage for workers and their families through a pooling of resources that guarantees benefits to all who qualify. One leg of the mythical three-legged stool of retirement income, Social Security benefits were designed to be complemented by both pension benefits and personal savings to produce a substantial nest egg for retirement. Unfortunately for many women, Social Security is all they have.

Women are the face of Social Security. Women represent 60 percent of all Social Security recipients at age 65 and 72 percent of all recipients by age 85. By and large, it is women who represent Social Security beneficiaries, and it is women who have the largest stake in the continued success of this important program.

Women depend on Social Security. Because women earn less, are half as likely to have pension income, and live longer, they are especially dependent on Social Security as a stable source of income in retirement. More than any other group, women count on Social Security. Without it, 52 percent of white women, 65 percent of African-American women, and 61 percent of Latinas over age 65 would be poor.

The Social Security program can be improved. The Social Security system still best serves the traditional family: a paid worker (usually the husband), an unpaid homemaker (usually the wife), and children. Today, however, most American families do not fit that profile, and even fewer will in the future. Most of all, the program should better reflect the reality of women's lives.

Privatization simply won't work for women. Proposals for privatization recommend diverting some or all of current Social Security taxes into individual private accounts. A system of private accounts would disadvantage women from the onset. Because women earn only 73 percent of what white men earn and often take time out of the workforce for caregiving, they would start off with much less to invest. Women would also lose the often desperately needed, progressive cost-of-living increases (COLA) built into the current Social Security program, and—because of their longevity—face the very real possibility of outliving their assets. Private accounts are not a guaranteed, lifetime benefit like Social Security—when the money runs out, it's gone.

If it doesn't work for women, it doesn't work. Privatized accounts undermine the promise that Social Security has offered to Americans for 67 years. By allowing individuals to withhold part of their contributions, the financial viability of the entire system will suffer, and its social insurance principles will be undermined.

The reality is that young or old, poor or near poor, today in America, women depend on Social Security. Across the generations, it has been there as a constant source of needed retirement income. It has been there for grandmothers, mothers, sisters, and daughters, and we hope it will continue to be there. Millions of older women depend on this program for their livelihood. It is the cornerstone of their retirement income, it is their insurance against disability and the death of a spouse, it is their guarantee, and it is their earned right.

MEDICARE: WHY WOMEN CARE

The typical Medicare recipient is a woman. She's outlived her spouse, she's divorced, (or, increasingly, she's never been married), and because she's alone, she's more likely than a man to be living in poverty. She suffers from a long-term chronic illness—arthritis, osteoporosis, diabetes—and, chances are, she suffers from more than one. She spends an average of $311 a month on prescription drugs and supplemental insurance. And although she may be living in her own home today, her poor health and the lack of help in managing her daily affairs will probably require her to seek long-term care—paid for by Medicaid—tomorrow.

Preserving Medicare is a uniquely important issue for women. At all age groups over age 65, women outnumber men in the Medicare program. Almost 6 in 10 (56 percent) of those on Medicare at age 65 are women. By age 85, women outnumber men in the Medicare program by more than two to one. Over time, the proportion of Medicare beneficiaries who are women will only increase. More and more, the face of Medicare is a woman's face.

Women need protection from high out-of-pocket expenses. Because older women are more likely to live in poverty, they are more likely to face financial barriers to health care, and they spend a greater portion of their income on health care. The average woman spends 21 percent of her income on out-of-pocket health care services—including prescription drugs and supplemental insurance. The older and poorer the woman, the higher her out-of-pocket health care costs.

Women need sufficient support for long-term health care. For women, a particularly glaring gap in Medicare is the absence of long-term care coverage. With more chronic and disabling conditions, longer life spans, and a greater likelihood of being alone, women are more likely than men to have long-term care needs and to use long-term care services. Women account for more than 60 percent of people who receive home health services through Medicare. And over two-thirds of the residents in nursing homes are women.

Medicare is a women's issue. It provides a health and financial safety net for 20 million American women, regardless of health history, health status, employment status, or income. Women's longer lives, lower incomes in retirement, and higher rates of chronic illness make protection against the high cost of health care that Medicare provides especially critical for women. If Medicare does not work for women, then it doesn't work for the majority of Medicare beneficiaries. If it is not affordable for women, it cannot protect the elderly against the high cost of health care. If Medicare-covered services do not reflect the changing medical practice, then the program will become increasingly irrelevant for all. Medicare must be strengthened and preserved for the millions of Americans who are retired or looking forward to retirement and adjusted to better respond to women and their health needs.

THE HOMEFRONT: HOUSING AND OLDER WOMEN

As American women age, the vital need for affordable, quality housing alternatives is increasingly important. Older women are more likely to be poor, living alone, and in need of care services. Where she lives can have a tremendous impact on a woman's well-being and independence in her later years. Unfortunately, women over 65 have difficulty finding and maintaining housing that is both affordable and meets their needs. Whether they are fleeing domestic violence, recovering from divorce, or looking for adequate housing to accommodate their physical conditions, older women often face discrimination, homelessness, and a housing market that does not respond to their needs.

Older women often live alone. Of the more than 10 million older persons living alone in the United States, 74 percent are women. Women living alone face increased economic hardships and social isolation, which has a devastating impact on their overall welfare. As single householders, older women spend a disproportionate amount of their income on housing-related costs. Housing tends to represent one of their greatest expenses, since older women typically maintain smaller incomes and receive fewer benefits than men. Women living alone often live in poverty.

Affordable housing has become increasingly scarce. Whether they rent or own, most older women have difficulty affording a home. The economic, social, and physical challenges older women face are only exacerbated by the current housing crisis. Today's housing market has become increasingly volatile with dramatic declines in affordable housing, along with rental costs that continue to increase faster than income levels for many American households. Many older women struggle to compete for a decreasing supply of affordable housing on the private market.

Older women need community assistance. By 2020, women will represent 85 percent of older persons living alone. As women live longer, services to provide a continuum of care can no longer include just shelter. Along with the development of chronic conditions and disability, women will face increased risks of living in isolation. The need for community-based assistance programs to help older women maintain their independence is apparent. Such programs would include personal care services, transportation services, assistance with daily and household tasks, and structured social activities.

Older women depend on housing assistance. Many older Americans, especially women, count on housing assistance. The typical Section 202 housing assistance resident is a 79-year-old woman living alone with an income of less than $10,100. However, low-income housing assistance is limited. Unfortunately, federal support for housing assistance should be much stronger, and many of the most vulnerable low-income renters spend years in vain, waiting for rental housing assistance.

Because of their longer life expectancy, higher poverty rates, and greater tendency for chronic medical conditions, women have special housing needs—housing needs that are not being especially addressed. Women need access to affordable and safe housing. Women need access to community care services, and women need the opportunity to live their longer lives in the comfort of a secure home.

As the only national grassroots membership organization to focus solely on issues unique to women as they age, OWL strives to improve the status and quality of life for midlife and older women. OWL is a nonprofit, nonpartisan organization that accomplishes its work through research, education, and advocacy activities conducted through a chapter network. Now in its twenty-sixth year, OWL provides a strong and effective voice for the more than 56 million women age 40 and over in America.   [2006]

💐 119

The Women in the Tower

CYNTHIA RICH

In April 1982 a group of Black women demand a meeting with the Boston Housing Authority. They are women between the ages of 66 and 81.

Their lives, in the "housing tower for the elderly" where they live, are in continual danger. "You're afraid to get on the elevator and you're afraid to get off," says Mamie Buggs, 66. Odella Keenan, 69, is wakened in the nights by men pounding on her apartment door. Katherine Jefferson, 81, put three locks on her door, but "I've come back to my apartment and found a group of men there eating my food."

The menace, the violence, is nothing new, they say. They have reported it before, but lately it has become intolerable. There are pictures in the *Boston Globe* of three of the women, and their eyes flash with anger. "We pay our rent, and we're entitled to some security," says Mamie Buggs. Two weeks ago, a man attacked and beat up Ida Burres, 75, in the recreation room. Her head wound required 40 stitches.

"I understand your desire for permanent security," says Lewis Spence, the BHA representative. "But I can't figure out any way that the BHA is going to be offering 24-hour security in an elderly development." He is a white man, probably in his thirties. His picture is much larger than the pictures of the women.

The headline in the *Boston Globe* reads, "Elderly in Roxbury building plead with BHA for 24-hour security." Ida Burres is described in the story as "a feisty, sparrowlike woman with well-cared-for gray hair, cafe au lait skin and a lilting voice." The byline reads "Viola Osgood."

I feel that in my lifetime I will not get to the bottom of this story, of these pictures, of these words.

Feisty, sparrowlike, well-cared-for gray hair, cafe au lait skin, lilting voice.

Feisty. Touchy, excitable, quarrelsome, like a mongrel dog. "Feisty" is the standard word in newspaper speak for an old person who says what she thinks. As you grow older, the younger person sees your strongly felt convictions or your protest against an intolerable life situation as an amusing overreaction, a defect of personality common to mongrels and old people. To insist that you are a person deepens the stigma of your Otherness. Your protest is not a specific, legitimate response to an outside threat. It is a generic and arbitrary quirkiness, coming from

the queer stuff within yourself—sometimes annoying, sometimes quaint or even endearing, never, never to be responded to seriously.

Sparrow-like. Imagine for a moment that you have confronted those who have power over you, demanding that they do something to end the terror of your days and nights. You and other women have organized a meeting of protest. You have called the press. Imagine then opening the newspaper and seeing yourself described as "sparrowlike." That is no simple indignity, no mere humiliation. The fact that you can be described as "sparrowlike" is in part why you live in the tower, why nobody attends. Because you do not look like a natural person—that is, a young or middle-aged person—you look like a sparrow. The real sparrow is, after all, a sparrow and is seen merely as homely, but a woman who is sparrowlike is unnatural and ugly.

A white widow tells of smiling at a group of small children on the street and one of them saying, "You're ugly, ugly, ugly." It is what society has imprinted on that child's mind: to be old, and to look old, is to be ugly, so ugly that you do not deserve to live. Crow's feet. Liver spots. The media: "I'm going to wash that gray right out of my hair and wash in my 'natural' color." "Get rid of those unsightly spots." And if you were raised to believe that old is ugly, you play strange tricks in your own head. An upper-middle-class white woman, a woman with courage and zest for life, writes in 1982: "When we love we do not see our mates as the young view us—wrinkled, misshapen, unattractive." But then she continues: "We still retain, somewhere, the *memory* of one another as beautiful and lustful, and we see each other at our *once-best.*"

Old is ugly and unnatural in a society where power is male-defined, powerlessness disgraceful. A society where natural death is dreaded and concealed, while unnatural death is courted and glorified. But old is ugliest for women. A white woman newscaster in her forties remarks to a sportscaster who is celebrating his sixtieth birthday: "What women really resent about men is that *you* get more attractive as you get older." A man is as old as he feels, a woman as old as she looks. You're ugly, ugly, ugly.

Aging has a special stigma for women. When our wombs are no longer ready for procreation, when our vaginas are no longer tight, when we no longer serve men, we are unnatural and ugly. In medical school terminology, we are a "crock"; in the language of the street, we are an "old bag." The Sanskrit word for widow is "empty." But there is more than that.

Sparrowlike. The association of the old woman with a bird runs deep in the male unconscious. Apparently, it flows back to a time when men acknowledged their awe of what they were outsiders to—the interconnected, inseparable mysteries of life and death, self, and other, darkness and light. Life begins in genital darkness, comes into light, and returns to darkness as death. The child in the woman's body is both self and other. The power to offer the breast is the power to withhold it. The Yes and the No are inextricable. In the beginning was the Great Mother, mysteriously, powerfully connected to the wholeness of Nature and her indivisible Yeses and Nos. But for those outside the process, the oneness was baffling and intolerable, and the Great Mother was split. Men attempted to divide what they could not control—nature and women's relationship to it. The Great Mother was polarized into separate goddesses or into diametrically opposed aspects of a single goddess. The Good Mother and the Terrible Mother. The Good Mother created life, spread her bounty outward, fertilized the crops, nourished and protected, created healing potions. The Terrible Mother, the original old Witch, dealt in danger and destruction, devoured children as food for herself, concocted poisons. Wombs ≠ tomb, light ≠ darkness, other ≠ self. A world of connectedness was split down the middle.

The Terrible Mother was identified with the winged creatures that feed on mammals: vultures, ravens, owls, crows, bats. Her images in the earliest known culture of India show her as old, birdlike, hideous: "Hooded with a coif or shawl, they have high, smooth foreheads above their staring circular eye holes, their owl-beak nose and grim slit mouth. The result is terrifying . . . the face is a grinning skull."

Unable to partake of the mystery of wholeness represented by the Great Mother, men first divided her, then wrested more and more control of her divided powers. The powerful Good Mother—bounteous life-giver, creator and nurturer of others—became the custodian of children who "belong" to the man or the male state. She can no longer even bear "his" child without the guiding forceps or scalpel of a man. She is the quotidian cook (men are the great chefs) who eats only after she has served others. She is the passive dispenser—as nurse, mother, wife—of the "miracles" of modern medicine created by the brilliance of man.

The Terrible Mother—the "old Woman of the West," guardian of the dead—represented men's fear of the powerful aspect of woman as intimate not only with the mysteries of birth but also of death. Today men are the specialists of death—despite a recent study that suggests that men face natural death with much more anxiety than women do. Today male doctors oversee dying, male priests and rabbis perform the rituals of death, and even the active role of laying out the dead no longer belongs to woman (now the work of male undertakers). Woman is only the passive mourner, the helpless griever. And it is men who vie with each other to invent technologies that can bring about total death and destruction.

The Terrible Mother—the vulture or owl feeding on others—represented the fear of death, but also the fear of woman as existing not only to create and nurture others but to create and nurture her Self. Indeed, the aging woman's body is a clear reminder that women have a self that exists not only for others; it descends into her pelvis as if to claim the womb-space for its own. Woman's Self—her meeting of her own needs, seen by men as destructive and threatening—has been punished and repressed, branded "unnatural" and "unwomanly."

In this century, in rural China, they had a practice called "sunning the jinx." If a child died, or there was some similar misfortune, it was seen as the work of a jinx. The jinx was always an old, poor woman, and she was exposed to the searing heat of the summer sun until she confessed. Like the witches burned throughout Europe in the fifteenth to seventeenth centuries, she was tortured by doublethink. If she died without confessing, they had eliminated the jinx. If she confessed her evil powers, she was left in the sun for three more days to "cure her." In Bali today, the Terrible Mother lingers on in magic plays as Ranga, the witch who eats children, "a huge old woman with drooping breasts and a mat of white hair that comes down to her feet." It is a man who plays her part, and he must be old since only an old man can avoid the evil spirit of the Terrible Mother.

In present-day white culture, men's fear of the Terrible Mother is managed by denial: by insisting on the powerlessness of the old woman, her harmless absurdity and irrelevance. The dread of her power lingers, reduced to farce—as in the Hansel and Gretel story of the old witch about to devour the children until the boy destroys her, or in the comic juxtaposition of Arsenic and Old Lace. The image of her winged power persists, totally trivialized, in the silly witch flying on her broomstick, and in "old bat," "old biddy," "old hen," "old crow," "crow's feet," "old harpy." Until, in April of 1982, an old woman's self-affirmation, her rage at her disempowerment, her determination to die naturally and not at the hands of men, can be diminished to feistiness, and she can be perceived as sparrowlike.

Sparrowlike. Writing for white men, did Viola Osgood unconsciously wish to say, "Ida Burres is not a selfish vulture—even though she is doing what old women are not meant to do, speak for their own interests (not their children's or grandchildren's but their own). She is an innocent sparrow, frail and helpless"? Or had she herself so incorporated that demeaning image—sparrowlike—that she saw Ida Burres through those eyes? Or both?

Well-cared-for gray hair. Is that about race? About class? An attempt to dispel the notion that a poor black woman is unkempt? Would Viola Osgood describe a Black welfare mother in terms of her "well-groomed afro"? Or does she mean to dispel the notion that this *old* woman is unkempt? Only the young can afford to be careless about their hair, their dress. The care that the old woman takes with her appearance is not merely to reduce the stigma of ugly; often it is her most essential tactic for survival: it signals to the person who sees her, I

am old, but I am not senile. My hair is gray but it is well-cared-for. Because to be old is to be guilty of craziness and incapacity unless proven otherwise.

Cafe au lait skin. Race? Class? Age? Not dark black like Katherine Jefferson, but blackness mitigated. White male reader, who has the power to save these women's lives, you can't dismiss her as black, poor, old. She is almost all right, she is almost white. She is black and old, but she has something in common with the young mulatto woman whose skin you have sometimes found exotic and sensual. And she is not the power of darkness that you fear in the Terrible Mother.

A lilting voice. I try to read these words in a lilting voice: "I almost got my eyes knocked out. A crazy guy just came in here and knocked me down and hit me in the face. We need security." These words do not lilt to me. A woman is making a demand, speaking truth to power, affirming her right to live—Black, Old, Poor, Woman. Is the "lilting" to say, "Although her words are strong, although she is bonding with other women, she is not tough and dykey"? Is the "lilting" to say, "Although she is sparrowlike, although she is gray-haired, something of the mannerisms you find pleasing in young women remain, so do not ignore her as you routinely do old women"?

I write this not knowing whether Viola Osgood is black or white. I know that she is a woman. And I know that it matters whether she is black or white, that this is not a case of one size fits all. But I know that black or white, any woman who writes news articles for the *Globe,* or for any mainstream newspaper, is mandated to write to white men, in white men's language. That any messages to women, black or white, which challenge white men's thinking can at best only be conveyed covertly, subversively. That any messages of appeal to those white men must be phrased in ways that do not seriously threaten their assumptions, and that such language itself perpetuates the power men have assumed for themselves. And I know that black or white, ageism blows in the wind around us and certainly through the offices of the *Globe.* I write this guessing that Viola Osgood is black, because she has known that the story is important, cared enough to make sure the photographer was there. I write this guessing that the story might never have found its way into the *Globe* unless through a black reporter. Later, I find out that she is black, 35.

And I think that Viola Osgood has her own story to tell. I think that I, white Jewish woman of 50, still sorting through to find the realities beneath the lies, denials, and ignorance of my lifetime of segregations, cannot write this essay. I think that even when we try to cross the lines meant to separate us as women—old and young, Black and white, Jew and non-Jew—the seeds of division cling to our clothes. And I think this must be true of what I write now. But we cannot stop crossing, we cannot stop writing.

Elderly in Roxbury building plead with BHA for 24-hour security. Doubtless, Viola Osgood did not write the headline. Ten words and it contains two lies—lies that routinely obscure the struggles of old women. *Elderly.* This is not a story of elderly people, it is the story of old women, black old women. Three-fifths of the "elderly" are women; almost all of the residents of this tower are women. An old woman has half the income of an old man. One out of three widows—women without the immediate presence of a man—lives below the official poverty line, and most women live one third of their lives as widows. In the United States, as throughout the world, old women are the poorest of the poor. Seven percent of old white men live in poverty, 47 percent of old black women. "The Elderly," "Old People," "Senior Citizens," are inclusive words that blot out these differences. Old women are twice unseen—unseen because they are old, unseen because they are women. Black old women are thrice unseen. "Elderly" conveniently clouds the realities of power and economics. It clouds the convergence of racial hatred and fear, hatred and fear of the aged, hatred and fear of women. It also clouds the power of female bonding, of these women in the tower who are acting together as women for women.

Plead. Nothing that these women say, nothing in their photographs, suggests pleading. These women are angry, and if one can demand where there is no leverage—and one can—they are demanding. They are demanding their lives, to which they know full well they have a right. Their anger is clear, direct, unwavering. "Pleading" erases the force of their confrontation. It allows us to continue to think of old women, if we think of them at all, as meek, cowed, to be pitied, occasionally as amusingly "feisty," but not as outraged, outrageous women. Old women's anger is denied, tamed, drugged, infantilized, trivialized. And yet anger in an old woman is a remarkable act of bravery, so dangerous is her world, and her status in that world so marginal, precarious. Her anger is an act of insubordination—the refusal to accept her subordinate status even when everyone, children, men, younger women, and often other older women, assumes it. "We pay our rent, and we're entitled to some security." When will a headline tell the truth: Old, black, poor women confront the BHA demanding 24-hour security?

The housing tower for the elderly. A tall building filled with women, courageous women who bond together, but who with every year are less able to defend themselves against male attack. A tower of women under siege. A ghetto within a ghetto. The white male solution to the "problem of the elderly" is to isolate the Terrible Mother.

That tower, however, is not simply architectural. Nor is the male violence an "inner-city problem." Ten days later, in nearby Stoughton, a man will have beaten to death an 87-year-old white woman, leaving her body with "multiple blunt injuries around her face, head, and shoulders." This woman was not living in a housing tower for the elderly. She lived in the house where she was born. "She was very, very spry. She worked in her garden a lot and she drove her own car," reports a neighbor. She had the advantages of race, class, a small home of her own, a car of her own. Nor did she turn away from a world that rejects and demeans old women ("spry," like "feisty," is a segregating and demeaning word). At the time of her murder, she was involved in planning the anniversary celebration at her parish.

Yet she was dead for a week before anyone found her body. Why? The reporter finds it perfectly natural. "She outlived her contemporaries and her circle of immediate relatives." Of course. How natural. Unless we remember de Beauvoir: "One of the ruses of oppression is to camouflage itself behind a natural situation since, after all, one cannot revolt against nature."* How natural that young people, or even the middle aged, should have nothing in common with an old woman. Unthinkable that she should have formed friendships with anyone who was not in her or his seventies or eighties or nineties. It is natural that without family, who must tolerate the stigma, or other old people who share the stigma, she would have no close ties. And it is natural that no woman, old or young, anywhere in the world, should be safe from male violence.

But it is not natural. It is not natural, and it is dangerous, for younger women to be divided as by a taboo from old women—to live in our own shaky towers of youth. It is intended, but it is not natural that we be ashamed of, dissociated from, our future selves, sharing men's loathing for the women we are daily becoming. It is intended, but it is not natural that we be kept ignorant of our deep bonds with old women. And it is not natural that today, as we reconnect with each other, old women are still an absence for younger women.

As a child—a golden-haired Jew in the segregated South while the barbed wire was going up around the Warsaw ghetto—I was given fairy tales to read. Among them, the story of Rapunzel, the golden-haired young woman confined to a tower by an old witch until she was rescued by a young prince. My hair darkened and now it is light again with gray. I know that I have been made to live unnaturally in a tower for most of my 50 years. My knowledge of my history—as a woman, as a lesbian, as a light-skinned woman in a world of dark-skinned women, as the Other in a Jew-hating world—shut out. My knowledge of my future—as an old woman—shut out.

Today I reject those mythic opposites: young/old, light/darkness, life/death, other/self, Rapunzel/Witch, Good Mother/Terrible Mother. As I listen to the voices of the old women of Warren Tower, and of my aging self, I know that I have always been aging, always been dying. Those voices speak of wholeness: To nurture Self = to defy those who endanger that Self. To declare the I of my unique existence = to assert the We of my connections with other women. To accept the absolute rightness of my natural death = to defend the absolute value of my life. To affirm the mystery of my daily dying and the mystery of my daily living = to challenge men's violent cheapening of both.

But I cannot hear these voices clearly if I am still afraid of the old witch, the Terrible Mother in myself, or if I am estranged from the real old women of this world. For it is not the wicked witch who keeps Rapunzel in her tower. It is the prince and our divided selves.

Note: There was no follow-up article on the women of the tower, but Ida Burres, Mamie Buggs, Mary Gordon, Katherine Jefferson, Odella Keenan, and the other women of Warren Tower, did win what they consider to be adequate security—"of course, it is never all that you could wish," said Vallie Burton, President of the Warren Tower Association. They won because of their own bonding, their demands, and also, no doubt, because of Viola Osgood. [1983]

NOTES

1. Simone de Beauvoir, *The Ethics of Ambiguity* (New York: Citadel, 1948), 83.

 120

The Day Nani Fell and I Wasn't There to Catch Her

ANNA MARIE QUEVEDO

Nana
lives alone in Echo Park
    Allison Street
one block above the Sunset

Sundays
before glaucoma clouded eyes
ruined her independence
she went to mass

sometimes at La Placita
once in awhile Saint Vibiana's
occasionally Saint Anthony's
every single Sunday
every novena Friday

my nana
at the bus stop
waiting patiently for the #10 going downtown
arriving amid clouds of stinking gasoline fumes

    (she'd complain to me
      "Los Angeles is an ugly city"
      she wished she'd never left Silver.)

after church
shopping at the Grand Central
another walk to the bus stop
#28 going home

suddenly she stumbled!
hand stretched out to break the fall
too late
collarbone snapped, shoulder blade broken
downtown L.A. strangers hardly noticed

Nana
went to a medi-cal hungry doctor
told her it was only a sprain and didn't set it
now her shoulder is slumped
her arm permanently crippled

in Silver City someone would have softened the fall
                            [1982]

🌿 121

Over the Hill and Out of Sight

JANICE KEAFFABER

I confess. I've never been an old woman before. It's more complicated than I anticipated. This is not like being a college freshman or having a baby, where copious advice is handed down friend-to-friend, woman-to-woman. There are even books for most everything else in life: how to get into the college of your choice, how to get the perfect job, how to find a true love, how to be a good parent of teenagers. There's lots of peripheral information out there about handling retirement finances, Social Security, Medicare, how to avoid "Senior Scams"—how to do everything but be old.

We don't talk about the true emotional challenges involved, even with each other. We're all too busy pretending we don't notice the indignities that are heaped upon us as old women. Or worse yet, it seems so natural, even to us, that it doesn't really register that we've become Outsiders.

I've had my own struggles with being ageist. How many of us haven't become at least a little impatient when someone cuts in front of you when you're driving or talks during a movie or holds up the line at the grocery store? All kinds of people do those things. But if it's an old woman, our irritation immediately grabs onto the fact that she's old.

We are all ageist. It's inescapable. Ageism permeates every layer of our culture. After all, entire corporate empires depend on it. Our collective consciousness is fed a steady bias against old women from every direction.

So here I am on this new journey struggling to learn how to be old and to remain myself at the same time. Year after year, I've been a woman fairly comfortable in my own skin. Oh, there were of course things I would like to change, but for the most part, I have always felt like an okay person who had a place in the scheme of things. I seemed to take up some sort of space in the world.

Then, about the time I hit 60, I mysteriously contracted a social disease. It happened suddenly. Like spontaneous combustion. I didn't notice the symptoms myself, but strangers could tell right away.

It started with little things. I walked into a used clothing store in my neighborhood—one of those places that sells hip, funky, old fifties and sixties stuff. Every other customer—all younger, I later realized—were greeted as they entered, engaged in friendly conversation. I alone managed to walk in, browse for several minutes, try on two tye-dyed shirts and a blue denim jacket and then leave the store without anyone acknowledging I was there. It was in such contrast to how other customers were treated, that I wondered if I could have walked out with six sweaters under my arm and they still wouldn't have noticed me. I was puzzled.

I was waiting at another store's counter to pay for a new pair of sunglasses. The clerk didn't see me. She waited on the 40-ish woman ahead of me and then the man behind me. But when she looked at me, her eyes literally glazed over and she went blind. Right there, in the middle of a well-lit, bustling department store. "Excuse me, I was next," I said quite clearly. No response. She had suddenly lost her hearing as well. I was now not only invisible but inaudible too. I had seen this happen to children in a line. I had also seen it happen to the homeless. I remember one fellow especially—dirty, unshaven, wearing torn clothes, and clutching his money for his fast food order. He politely waited. And waited. The clerk behind the counter didn't take his order until I quietly insisted that he be waited on. The homeless man was embarrassed by being ignored in favor of the other customers. And now it was happening to me. I was embarrassed too.

A major protest was being planned in San Diego and a national peace and justice group was coming here to give action trainings. As a member of a street theater group that was going to perform at the protest and possibly engage in civil disobedience, I thought the training sounded like fun. A local activist group began to advertise the event, but each time the notice appeared on the Internet, it said the training was for *young* people. What did that mean exactly? High school? College age? Anyone under 40? All I knew was the notices definitely meant *NOT ME*. Later I talked to one of the trainers and discovered they had never intended this to be a young-person-only activity. To insert the word young in all the announcements was ageism in action. Unthinking maybe, but ageism nonetheless. I knew whoever wrote up the announcements would never have called it training for *white* people or *rich* people. Excluding people of color or

poor people would have been unthinkable. But to arbitrarily exclude the old from a general training wasn't a big deal or even noticed—except by old people who wanted to go. I was disappointed.

Photos from another protest—this time a large protest at the California-Mexico border appeared in a local newspaper. Several old women were front and center in the photos, just as we had been front and center in the action. We simply could not be missed. The photo caption and text exclaimed: *Young activists protest at border*—It had finally happened. I had become totally invisible. Finally, I was angry.

Most people don't have an awareness of ageism; they even see it as funny. Just check any greeting card aisle. But it ceases to be humorous when you bear the brunt of the joke.

Here are some ways you can help lift the stigma that stereotypes and isolates old women:

Please, speak up for me. If someone makes an ageist remark, notice it and talk to them about it. It's not acceptable.

Don't automatically stick the word "young" in front of everything. If an event is for high-schoolers, college-age students, or targeted for a specific audience, then say so—and it would be nice to add why.

Think it over before you arbitrarily limit ages for events. I recently received an e-mail inviting me to enter a women's art exhibit. I had some new work that I thought I would enter—until I read the fine print. It was for women under age 54. I am nine years over an age limit that makes no sense.

Put the word *old* in your vocabulary. Say it right now. Oh, come on. Just say it. *OLD*. I know it might initially feel rude, but that's because it has such a loaded connotation in our culture. A woman came up to me at one of the first Old Women's Project actions and said, "Oh don't call yourselves old. That's not nice!" All of the alternative terms—elderly, older, senior—seem like silly ways to get around saying the real word: old.

I don't want to be a vessel of wisdom and giver of sage advice. I don't want to mentor the young. I don't want to bake cookies or wear purple all the time. And I sure don't want to be over the hill and out of sight. I just want to continue to be me.

[2005]

She Who Once Was

REBECCA MCCLANAHAN

Early photographs confirm my father's frequent remark: "Your mother was a living doll." Sometimes I joke that if he's looking to score points he shouldn't use the past tense. But usually I don't, partly because the remark doesn't seem to bother my mother, but mostly because his affection for her is so obvious, even after 60 years of marriage. Let's say she's getting up from her chair, where she's been piecing a quilt or writing to one of their 15 grandchildren. As she moves across the room, my father's gaze will follow. If beauty resides in the beholder's eyes, my mother is beautiful to her beholder. Yet even so, there remains that troublesome past tense: My mother *was* a living doll.

Two weeks ago I visited my friend Martha, and I can attest that she is still a beautiful woman. I hesitate to phrase it that way. To say that a woman is *still* beautiful suggests a remove from what went before, placing the receiver of the compliment in a fragile holding pattern. *Still* beautiful. Still holding. I don't like the implications, but it is difficult to compliment an aging woman without employing a time marker. She looks so *youthful,* we say. Or, she is *aging* well. Recently, a young colleague, after learning my age, exclaimed, "I don't believe it. I mean, you look good." As if it were some minor miracle, at my advanced age, to look presentable.   [2005]

Nations, Boundaries, and Belonging: Citizenship in Women's Lives

A woman's national status is yet another source of privilege or discrimination. This section explores how a woman's nation and her citizenship status, or lack thereof, affects her sense of place and belonging, as well as her human rights. As Peggy McIntosh helps whites see their racial privilege, similarly Gowri Parameswaran challenges women in the United States and other industrialized nations to examine the benefits they receive by living in the Global North.

The subsequent stories of undocumented, immigrant women encourage women with citizenship status to examine the "Injustice on Our Plates." The discrimination, sexual abuse, and poverty that undocumented food workers face because of their lack of citizenship in the United States is something those with privilege seldom acknowledge as they eat a meal harvested, processed, or served by undocumented women.

Winona LaDuke, Native American activist and environmentalist, describes how 5,000 indigenous nations worldwide meet the definition of nations, but are nevertheless "nationless." Initially colonized, their lands and resources are plundered by transnational corporations, creating oppressive conditions for indigenous women. LaDuke argues that if given their rights as nations, indigenous women and peoples could protect the ecosystems, biodiversity, and cultural diversity of the earth.

In her poem, Anida Yoeu Ali powerfully depicts the power of a woman's name and how it bonds identity and nation. She shares the history, sense of belonging, and meaning her name holds for her as an immigrant, and her pain and anger as white Americans' lack of care and respect for her "foreign" name marginalizes her even further in a place far from home. Charlotte Bunch encourages us to see the value of thinking beyond national boundaries when considering the concept of security. Rather than defend "national security," she suggests that by working toward "human security" we can best struggle against women's oppression and foster peace and justice globally.

122

The Tale of Two Worlds: Unpacking the Power of the Global North over the Global South

GOWRI PARAMESWARAN

Writer's note: While this essay attempts to provide a picture of exploitation of the Global South by the Global North, it is important to acknowledge that the intersections of social class, race, and gender are factors in understanding who benefits from this exploitative relationship. Some individuals and corporations in the Global South benefit enormously from this exploitative relationship with the Global North while relegating the majority in the South to poverty. As jobs move to the Global South communities in the North are relegated to the lowest social class. Men and women in the North are recruited to fight in wars for corporate profits that do not benefit them.

In the map displayed below, the countries marked black are referred to as the Global North and the countries colored in grey are part of the Global South. The nations of the Global North are located in the temperate zones of the Northern Hemisphere (except for Australia and New Zealand), while the nations of the Global South are located in the tropical regions of the Northern Hemisphere and the Southern Hemisphere. The terms were coined by activists from the Global South who, by giving themselves a name, wanted to forge a collective political and economic identity. The aim was to facilitate a struggle for more equal distribution of resources. Most of the world's population lives in

regions that can be termed the Global South. Since about the 1500s, countries in the Global North colonized much of the South, thereby establishing dominion over its lands and resources. During the last half of the twentieth century, the nations of the Global South obtained independence from the North. In order to maintain control over the South, the nations of the North came together to create rules for world governance that kept power and resources in their own hands. They thus ensured an unequal distribution of wealth, resources, materials, and privileges that continues into the present day. Mainstream social sciences reinforced notions of the superiority of European societies by classifying cultures in the Global South as backward and in need of civilizing influences, just like male scientists had argued a century earlier that women were not as capable as men.

I first read the article on unpacking racism by Peggy McIntosh when I was in graduate school and have used it in my own classes as an instructor over the years. Readers cannot but be inspired by the simplicity of McIntosh's message and the deep truths that her list of privileges as a white person reveals about racism in our society. The privileges of the Global North over the South are much harder to perceive than racism, sexism, and classism within our society because many of us do not come across people or communities from the nations of the Global South except through the products we consume and the occasional news stories about the horrors of living in the South. I was born in India, part of the Global South. My family was advantaged within the context we lived in because we were Brahmin, one of the upper castes in a highly hierarchical society. I came to the USA when I was 21 and went back often to my native town in South India. When one travels across boundaries, the invisible privileges that one takes for granted become more visible. Being a woman of color in the United States, and therefore marginalized, allows me to understand the many oppressions that communities from the lower castes experience in India. However, even though as a woman and as an Asian I am disadvantaged in some ways, I am conferred an important privilege as a result of my moving and settling down in the USA. I have become a citizen of the Global North. It is not easy to become a citizen in the nations that form the Global North for most people who live in the South. My privileges came after a long and arduous process of obtaining a green card and later U.S. citizenship; I was allowed access to this exclusive club only because, after extensive education, I had skills to offer the USA.

While reading about the many ways in which people who live in the North are privileged, it is crucial to understand that belonging to the Global North does not benefit everyone or every nation in the North in the same way or to the same extent. The biggest beneficiaries are of course transnational corporations that are allowed to cross national boundaries with ease to set up shop the world over. They take their capital and financial resources along with them leaving communities everywhere without a way to sustain themselves. The average citizen of the Global North still benefits from the unfair distribution of privileges that favor the North over the South. To people who live in the North many of these privileges appear earned and therefore feel like a birthright.

The following is a partial list of benefits and privileges I enjoy that my family that still lives in the Global South do not enjoy. These privileges are interwoven with existing patriarchal power structures in the world of international politics and a masculine view of the world that takes for granted the rights of the rich over the poor and the powerful over the weak. Aggression and violence is the preferred weapon to maintain the hierarchy of dominance by the Global North over the South. Without a conscious exploration of these privileges, women in the Global South cannot enjoy the same rights as their sisters in the Global North.

As a citizen of the Global North, I enjoy:
The Privilege of Life, Work, and Worth:

1. I can choose to visit, live, and work in most places on earth. Since the currencies in the South are valued at a fraction of what the currencies in the North are valued at, it is easier for me to travel and take vacations in the nations of the South. With a U.S. passport, I am not scrutinized to the same extent as people from the Global South. My sisters living in the South will find it much harder to gain entry into the countries of the North.

2. My life is considered more valuable than the lives of people living in the nations of the South. Policy makers with global influence constantly make trade and business calculations based on this assumption. There are several examples that illustrate the devaluing of life in the South. Toxic waste in the North is routinely transferred to the South to be disposed of, even though this practice has enormous negative consequences on the health and the environment of people living in the South.[1] Similarly experimental pharmaceutical products are often tested on people in the South, sometimes without meeting appropriate ethical stipulations that are routine in the North.[2]

3. I am considered a legitimate citizen of my country and bestowed full citizenship rights, while people from the Global South who cross the borders from the South without appropriate government documentation are branded as 'illegals.' This branding reduces them to less than human, even though they may make contributions to society similar to those I make. There is punitive policing of the borders between the North and the South. When they are caught, they are treated as criminals, housed in prisons, and sent back.[3]

4. I have a disproportionate amount of resources devoted to exploring issues related to my health needs versus those of people from the South. Many more resources are devoted to research about diseases that I might suffer from than diseases more prevalent in the South. When research has led to the development of medicines for diseases like malaria or yellow fever that are prevalent in the South, it has often been because the nations of the North wanted to colonize the South or the medicines found have been side products of research to address diseases prevalent in the North.[4]

Cultural Privilege:

1. I can go to most places on earth and be assured that there are feature films, TV shows, books, and music available that I enjoy in the North. Movies and music that are products of Hollywood and other media capitals in the North are profitable all over the world. Books that win major prizes in the North are given due recognition in the Global South and translated into the many languages spoken in the South. Today, there are about seven media companies mainly located in the USA that own much of the world media outlets. Robert McChesney, the noted media critic, calls this global cultural domination by the USA "the Hollywood juggernaut" and compares it to the cultural assimilation within the USA that marginalized communities are subjected to.[5]

2. I do not have to travel outside of the North to view and experience the riches of ancient history from the South. As the North colonized the South, many of the ancient relics from the South were brought back to the North and enjoyed by its citizens. Some nations in the South are currently engaged in court battles in the North to get those artifacts back. One famous example is the demand for the return of the Rosetta stone, which Britain plundered from Egypt when it was still ruling the country. Britain has consistently refused to return it, even though, according to a United Nations 1972 agreement, artifacts are considered properties of the nations of origin.[6]

3. I am used as the yardstick to judge the mental health of people living in the Global South, while their worldviews about what constitutes a healthy individual are ignored by the therapeutic community in the North. Thus it is considered "normal" and "healthy" when people hold values of independence, assertiveness, and mastery over the environment, while dependence, attributing primacy to the group and to nature are considered unhealthy and "treatment worthy." Even though the prognosis for diseases like depression and schizophrenia are best in places

like Zanzibar in Africa, ideas from the Global North are penetrating these communities and pharmaceutical medicines from the North are offered as panacea for problems.[7]

4. I can choose to ignore the cultural and religious beliefs, celebrations, and social conventions in other countries without it having a negative impact on my experiences and work life, even when I am in the Global South. People from the South have to acquaint themselves with the cultural values and languages of the North even to get jobs in their own countries. One example is the monopoly of the English language in business and the impact that has on people in the Global South.[8]

Economic Privileges:

1. I benefit directly and indirectly because of access to natural resources everywhere in the world. If other countries do not give them up readily, my government and others in the North consider it appropriate that they "persuade" them to exploit the resource for the good of the world. Governments of the North routinely topple governments, create unrest, and invade sovereign nations in the South in order to have access to minerals that can be used by corporations and researchers in the North. One current example is the Congo in Africa, considered perhaps the richest tract of land in the world. The country has been in the throes of civil war because the North funds rebel groups who have taken over some very mineral-rich land in Congo; the rebels then lease the captured land to mining companies based in the North who in turn give them weapons and finance them.[9]

2. I can be assured that the rules of global economics and international trade favor me over citizens of the South, because my government and others of the North have made the rules through organizations like the World Trade Organization (WTO). The WTO has the clout and the power to punish nations that do not abide by their economic regime set up by the North. One example is in the area of agriculture. The governments of the North subsidize

their agricultural industries heavily and then force the nations of the South to buy farm products from the North. This impoverishes the rural population in the South and destroys local industries.[10] At the same time, my need for cash crops like tea, coffee, sugar, and chocolate that can grow best in tropical climates have made farming communities in the South susceptible to starvation and have depleted water tables in those regions because of valuable local farming land being diverted to cash crop production that uses a lot of water.[11]

3. I and my fellow citizens from the North benefit from the uneven flow of resources and wealth in favor of the North from the South. One way in which money flows back to the nations of the North are through the profits that corporations make in the nations of the South and banks located in the Global North. The biggest global corporations and banks (GE, GM, IBM, Microsoft, etc.) are located in the North. They set up businesses in the nations of the South, but the profits are sent back to their investors who live in the North.[12] Even though the largest beneficiaries of these resources in the North are the wealthy, even the poorest citizens in the North benefit from this uneven flow of resources through the development of better infrastructure and availability of services (like roads, bridges, transportation, education, and hospitals).

4. I can expect to get paid a lot more for the work that I do compared to a worker who does the same work in the South. For instance, workers in the manufacturing sector earn $21.56 per hour in the USA but earn only $2.61 in Mexico and $2.58 in Brazil. While workers in a manufacturing plant in the North live in relative comfort, their sisters in the South live in shantytowns and in cardboard houses.[13]

The Privilege of International Laws and Security:

1. I and my fellow sisters from the North are much better represented in international institutions that make up the rules for war and peace. One example is the Security Council in the United Nations, whose permanent members are all countries from the North, except for China. Most issues related to war and peace are brought to the Security Council to be debated and ratified. My government can veto any resolution that the Security Council makes that it feels would not benefit my nation or would actively harm it. Thus, my government can choose to ignore international laws that it does not support, while punishing nations in the South for acting on similar principles. The North has consistently voted to punish nations like Iran and India in the Global South that are suspected to have nuclear weapons, even though much of the active nuclear weapons are located in the north and the nuclear industry is extremely profitable for private contractors located in the North.[14]

2. I am much better protected when it comes to legal rights as a citizen than a person from a nation of the South. My sisters who live in the South and who have never visited the North can be accused of committing a crime and can be convicted without due process by my government and others in the North. In the War on Terror, under the pretext of "protection," the U.S. government secretly arrested suspects who were citizens of other nations as enemy combatants. On the other hand, it is hard to bring a citizen of a nation in the North to justice.[15] After the worst industrial accident perpetrated by the U.S. chemical company Union Carbide (now Dow Chemical), in Bhopal, India, the Indian government has tried for over three decades to get the CEO of Union Carbide sent to India for a trial.[16]

3. I have more military power to "protect" me than a citizen of the Global South. Much of the world's military might rests with the nations of the North, especially the USA and the European Union. The USA spends more on its military in general than the next 10 countries combined. The USA, Russian Federation, France, and the United Kingdom possess the most nuclear weapons of all of the nations in the world.[17]

We in the North do not have to do much to earn these privileges. Our government does much of the policing and enforcing of these unjust global laws for us. The excellent roads, bridges, parks, museums, art houses, institutions of higher education and research universities, and other infrastructural amenities that we take for granted have been collectively obtained for our use by the national and transnational institutions that make this unequal transfer of wealth possible. Powerful corporations, agribusinesses, defense industries, the commercial entertainment industry, and mining interests are some of the biggest beneficiaries of the current trade regime. However, they are able to silence the voices of people in the South because of inaction by citizens of the North who have the power to collectively object to this unequal distribution of privileges.

While much of the struggle for equal rights is being waged by citizens of the Global South, the privileged are invaluable allies in the fight against injustice. The average citizen of the North has a lot to gain by pushing for an equal distribution of global wealth. The current unjust trade and governing mechanisms were set up by vested interests in the Global North with the collusion of the powerful and the wealthy in the Global South. The unequal world order that exists today destroys communities in both the North and the South. It would benefit everyone to upset this status quo of privileges.

Bringing the global struggle home to our communities by engaging in actions that benefit our sisters in the South helps strengthen our own local communities. There are many problems today that transcend the artificial borders between the North and the South; some examples of struggles that require our collective strength of action in both the North and the South include:

a. Impending climate change due to industrial activity: Climate change affects us all by altering our environment, pushing the globe to experience extremes in weather leading to droughts and floods, and making large tracts of land unlivable in both the North and the South.

b. Food and water security: In recent years industrial activity has polluted our land, air, and water, leading to toxins being leached into our food system. The unsafe products that we consume affect our individual and community health. Excessive exploitation of our farming land has led to a depletion of water sources. This phenomenon is especially visible in the South. With increasing scarcity of water globally, water sources have been privatized, bottled, and sold to those who can afford it, thereby depriving others of good, clean drinking water. Communities have been waging local struggles to keep water sources open and free.

c. Wars for profit: The North spends an enormous amount of its financial resources building its military might to support the numerous wars engaged in by its governments. The wars are often about maintaining control over oil, minerals, and other resources that the North lacks, or to find new markets to sell products from the North. The resources spent on the military can be better spent supporting local communities and improving health and educational infrastructures in the North. It benefits us all to work together for peace and justice in the world.

A worldview based on patriarchal values that emphasizes competition over cooperation, aggression over diplomacy and negotiation, and exploitation of nature over working with nature have led us to a crucial fork in our collective history. These issues require all of us from the North and South to work together to resolve them. Feminist values offer us hope and faith in our collective strength to make a different world possible—a world where people from the Global North and Global South can share in the bounties of this earth equally and where the incredible benefits of modern technology, rather than being used to exploit some communities, can enhance life everywhere.   [2011]

NOTES

1. Kaya Burgess, "British Toxic Waste Sent to Africa," February 18, 2009, *Times* online, http://www.timesonline.co.uk/tol/news/uk/article5756601.ece.
2. Patrick Winn, "Asia: Guinea Pigs a Plenty for Drug Companies," December 26, 2010, Truthout, http://www.truthout.org/asia-guinea-pigs-aplenty-drug-giants66279.
3. Southern Poverty Law Center, "Injustice on Our Plates: Immigrant Women in the U.S. Food Industry," 2010. Retrieved from http://www.splcenter.org/sites/default/files/downloads/publication/Injustice_on_Our_Plates.pdf.
4. Ken Silverstein, "Millions for Viagra, Pennies for Diseases of the Poor: Research Money Goes to Profitable Lifestyle Drugs," *The Nation*, July 1999.

5. Robert McChesney, "Global Media, Neo-Liberalism and Imperialism," *International Socialist Review*, 2002, http://www.thirdworldtraveler.com/McChesney/GlobalMedia_Neoliberalism.html.

6. Konye Obaji Ori, "Egypt Demands Return of Stolen Artifacts from Europe and U.S.," November 2009, http://www.afrik-news.com/article16460.html.

7. Ethan Waters, "The Americanization of Mental Illness," *New York Times*, January 2010.

8. Yukio Tsuda, "The Hegemony of English and Strategies for Linguistic Pluralism: Proposing the Ecology of Language Paradigm," 2010, http://www.miresperanto.narod.ru/en/english_as_intern/hegemony_of_english.html.

9. Mungbalemwe Koyame and John Clark, "The Economic Impact of the Congo War," in *The African Stakes of the Congo War*, ed. John Clark (New York: Palgrave-Mcmillan, 2002).

10. Paulos Milkias, *Developing the Global South: A United Nations Prescription for the Third Millennium* (New York: Algora, 2010).

11. J. Clapp, "WTO Agricultural Negotiations: Implications for the Global South," *Third World Quarterly* 27, no. 4 (2002): 563–77.

12. "The Paradox of Capital Flows from South to North," *Third World Network*, September 2002.

13. The Jus Semper Global Alliance, "Living Wages North and South," 2010, http://www.jussemper.org/Newsletters/Resources/Wage%20gap%20chartsa.pdf.

14. Hugh Gusterson, "U.S. Nuclear Double Standards," *Bulletin of Atomic Scientists*, February 2008, http://www/thebulletin.org/web-edition/columnists/high-gusterson/us-nucear-double-standards.

15. Stephen Grey, "Flight Logs Reveal Secret Rendition," *Sunday Times*, November 25, 2007.

16. Indira Shah, "Bhopal's Long Injustice," *Guardian*, June 7, 2010.

17. Robert S. Norris and Hans M. Kristensen, "Global Nuclear Stockpiles, 1945–2006," *Bulletin of Atomic Scientists*, August 2006, 64–66.

🌿 123

Injustice on Our Plates: Immigrant Women in the U.S. Food Industry

THE SOUTHERN POVERTY LAW CENTER

Editor's Introduction: Undocumented immigrants form a majority of farmworkers in the USA—the estimates are anywhere from 60 to 80 percent of the farm workforce. Americans depend on them for cheap and plentiful farm produce and processed goods. The nations the workers come from include South and Central American countries that have had a long history of being colonized by the USA. They are forgotten by their nations of origin and actively pursued by the U.S. government as criminals, forcing them to live in the shadows and borderlands that "nationless" communities typically occupy. Undocumented working women are especially vulnerable to exploitation. They are paid below subsistence wages, exposed to dangerous working conditions, and subject to physical, emotional, and sexual violence. Many of them are isolated from their families, and their children and do not see them for years. This excellent study conducted by the Southern Poverty Law Center outlines the tremendous challenges facing undocumented women in the food production industry in the USA.

SARA

When Sara entered the United States in her early twenties, her main goal was to find work and help provide for her family back in Mexico. A decade later, at 33, Sara wishes she had resisted, she says, but "even though I was poor, I was free." The crossing was difficult. She paid $1,800 for the privilege of nearly losing her life in the Sonoran Desert. The journey began with 18 other immigrants. By the end, after five days in the desert, only a handful remained. "Many people got lost." Sara almost didn't make it. She got tangled in barbed wire, and the group, pushed forward by the uncaring guides, began to leave her behind. At the last possible moment, a stranger turned back to free Sara.

Within a week of arriving in the United States, Sara got a job at a poultry plant in North Carolina. Although prepared to work hard, she was shocked at the physical demands of her new job and the abusive and cruel treatment from the supervisors. Working on the "disassembly line," Sara would place skinned, whole chickens onto cones that sped by her. She regularly stood for 8 hours at a time, sometimes 10, reaching up to fill the cones. It was hard to keep up. "You're at the pace of a machine. I felt like I was going to faint. The line was too fast." At other times, she would hang butchered chicken on the sharp points of hangers. "Many times your hands would get scratched with that point because they wouldn't slow down the line." On a few occasions, she cut chicken with dull scissors, her hands swelling as she struggled to cut through bone.

Unlike farmworkers who work in scorching heat, poultry workers have to fight near-freezing temperatures meant to preserve the meat. Every day after her shift, Sara would drag her battered body home to the crowded apartment she shared and curl up on the floor, her body burning with pain. The challenging environment—cold temperature and the dangerous industrial surroundings of sharp metal and fast-moving machines—was made worse by the unrelenting demands of the supervisors. Her managers routinely yelled at and cursed their employees, pushing them to meet impossible production quotas. They denied workers breaks to stretch their gnarled limbs or go to the bathroom. One supervisor, in his rush to get Sara back to work, broke her wrist, she says. The man noticed her struggling to close a latch on a rusty, metal safety glove. He grabbed her hand and slammed the latch in place. "He pressed down on the latch and I felt how the bones cracked apart," she recalls. Her hand went limp with pain, but the supervisor yelled at Sara to get back to work. "I grabbed the chicken and it fell out of my hands because it hurt so much." She did not report the incident because she did not believe anything could be done. Sara intended to stay in the United States for just two years but has, instead, stayed a decade. She is caught in the cruelly self-perpetuating situation of being unable to be with her family in Mexico because she feels she has to remain in the United States to help support them.

"You suffer to come. Then once you're here, you suffer some more."

YAZMIN

To survive the crossing into the United States, Yazmin, then only 16, walked four days and four nights through the mountainous terrain near Tijuana, a journey that cost her $1,600 in fees paid to the *coyotes* who guided her. "We were drinking water from ditches. Who knows if it was clean?" Surviving in the United States also calls for desperate measures. "You can't live in peace here," she says. "If my country weren't poor, I wouldn't be here." During the crossing, she battled heat during the day and plunging temperatures at night, but her father and brother protected her from the other dangers of the road. When they reached California, Yazmin found work picking tomatoes, melons, cucumbers, and chili peppers. "I've always worked," she says.

Yazmin baked for long hours beneath the Florida sun while a supervisor stood over her stooped back, spewing out obscenities and insults. "He mistreated us and said bad things. He would say horrible things, that we weren't worth a [thing], very strong vulgar words. He would insult us, and he said that 'broads' were only good for cranking out kids. Then he fired me." Her next manager sought to squeeze as much labor out of his field-workers as possible. He would not permit any breaks, even for a drink of water. "I asked him for some water to drink. He said no, that there wasn't any . . . and for me to keep working." When she complained, he silenced her by threatening to call immigration authorities. "There are bosses who insult you, or they want to sleep with you because they're bosses."

A timid young woman, Yazmin did not speak out when the harassment grew worse with each job. One supervisor would physically restrain his workers, grabbing them by the head when he grew angry. Another manager would find ways to brush up against Yazmin when she was nearby. "Unfortunately, many people are afraid to report [such incidents] because we're illegal." Still not in the United States a full year, Yazmin had to fight off a sexual assault after accepting a car ride to work one day. "That man tried to rape me in his truck. He was touching me, and I asked him why he was doing that." The man threatened Yazmin. If she told anyone, he would see to it that she lost her job picking watermelons. Frightened, she did not seek out authorities. But Yazmin's teenage innocence was shattered. She was still just 16 years old. "I had never been intimate with anyone. And he touched me, and I had to put up with it. That was a bad experience because I couldn't find a way out. I didn't feel safe enough to tell someone."

After four months, she left that job. Yazmin eventually got married and had three children. But she remained in the fields—ignoring the filthy bathroom facilities, the haze of pesticides that engulfed her from time to time, and, worst of all, the constant menace of sexual harassment. She's conscious of the contribution she's making to the U.S. economy and to our tables. But this contribution—her backbreaking labor in return for poverty wages—does little to improve her situation. She lives in constant fear. She is afraid of being arrested, of being separated from her children, of working for someone who will hurt her. For an undocumented immigrant, "I think there's more risk and not much safety."

CRUCIBLE OF THE CROSSING

An estimated 10.8 million undocumented immigrants live in the USA. Four million of these immigrants are women.[1] The lives of Sara and Yazmin show why millions of women are willing to risk detention, sexual assault, separation from their children, and even death just for the opportunity to earn subsistence wages and live at the bottom of U.S. society.

Undocumented immigrants are prohibited from participating in most federal programs that benefit the poor and unemployed, including welfare, food stamps, housing assistance, disability and unemployment benefits, Medicaid, and Social Security.[2] While they don't receive federal benefits, most economists agree that their cheap labor results in a net benefit to the U.S. economy. Deporting these immigrants en masse would shrink the American economy by as much as $2.6 trillion over 10 years.[3]

The border town of Altar was once a small farming community. Now, by some accounts, its entire economy is based on the smuggling of people across the border.[4] For many undocumented immigrants, the town is the final way station before embarking on one of the most dangerous migratory treks on the planet. Popular routes are controlled by unscrupulous human smugglers and terrorized by predatory gangs. The desert, which covers much of the northern Mexico state of Sonora and stretches well into Arizona and California, ranks in some spots as one of the hottest places on the planet during the summer. This is where the nightmare

often begins for women and girls. They are, by far, the most vulnerable during the crossing—and their experience can have an enormous impact on their lives in the United States. Some academics and humanitarian organizations estimate that as many as 6 out of 10 women and girls experience some sort of sexual violence during the journey through Mexico into the United States.[5] Definitive numbers are not available because the plight of women attempting to cross is severely underreported and understudied.

DEBT TRAP

Typically, undocumented immigrants will pay smugglers anywhere from $1,500 to more than $10,000 to guide them and their families across the border. Often, amounts are far beyond their ability to pay, and they must borrow money or enter into repayment contracts that leave them in debt to the smugglers. Thousands of migrants a year are kidnapped, assaulted, robbed, or raped by criminal gangs.[6] According to a recent report by Mexico's National Human Rights Commission, as many as 9,758 migrants were kidnapped over a six-month period ending in 2009.[7] They are often held until family members pay ransom. In these cases, such payments leave immigrants even further in debt and vulnerable to exploitation in the workplace.

WORKPLACE EXPLOITATION: IMMIGRANT WOMEN POWERLESS IN THE FACE OF ABUSES

Because food production is so labor-intensive, the U.S. food industry requires a vast army of low-wage workers. These jobs—planting, harvesting, processing, packaging, and serving our food—have been handed down from earlier generations of immigrants to an increasingly Latino/Latina workforce. Due to their undocumented status, they fill the lowest-paying jobs in the country. They typically earn minimum wage or less, get no sick or vacation days, and receive no health insurance. Yet, these immigrants play a vital role in our economy, greasing the gears of the great U.S. food machine, which brings a cornucopia of fruits, vegetables, meats, grains, nuts, and processed food to our markets and restaurants like clockwork. Like it or not, we eat the fruits of their labor every day.

Farmers depend on them: The government estimates that 60 percent of our country's agricultural workers are undocumented immigrants.[8] The reality is likely much higher. Food-processing companies depend on them: Almost a quarter of the workers who butcher and process meat, poultry, and fish are undocumented.[9] Restaurant owners depend on them: About one out of five cooks are undocumented, and more than a quarter of the dishwashers are undocumented.[10] If the government were to deport all 10.8 million undocumented immigrants living on U.S. soil, our economy would decline by $2.6 trillion over a decade, not including the massive cost of such an endeavor.[11]

The vast majority of the women who were interviewed by the Southern Poverty Law Center over a period of two months in early 2010 said they worked for poverty wages and have been cheated, at one time or another, out of wages they earned. Many reported injuries from the repetitive and strenuous movement required to keep up with the voracious production demands. Many of those employed in farmwork said they have been sickened by pesticides and toxic chemicals. Those working in meat and poultry processing said they labored long hours in bone-chilling temperatures with inadequate safety equipment. Many of the women reported being denied access to bathrooms or barred from taking time off to tend to emergencies like sick children—even when they worked for huge corporate employers required by law to provide those benefits. Some faced illegal discrimination because of pregnancy. The women are even more vulnerable in the workplace than their male counterparts. They are often the primary caregivers for children, making them less likely to assert their rights for fear of being fired or, worse, being deported and separated from their families. And because of their fear of being reported to immigration authorities, they are reluctant to report wage violations, sexual violence, or gender discrimination, or to take legal action to stop it. Many women said their pay stubs routinely show far fewer hours than they actually worked. If they question their paychecks or ask for a raise, they are ignored or fired, to be replaced by other desperate workers waiting in line. Many growers and labor contractors pay "piece rates" rather than hourly wages. This is often a ruse to avoid paying the minimum wage while putting pressure on laborers to work as fast as possible.

SEXUAL AGGRESSION

Sexual predators view undocumented women as "perfect victims" because they are isolated, thought to lack credibility, generally do not know their rights, and may be vulnerable because they lack legal status. Often, the perpetrators begin the harassment by grooming the women through suggestive comments or unwanted compliments. They may attempt to scare the women, wear them down, and further isolate them until the perpetrator is in a position to commit a sexual assault or rape. Not only are farmworker women dependent almost entirely on men for their continued employment, their assignments, and the evaluation of their work, they often are assigned to work in isolated orchards or fields far from co-workers. Further, the nature of the work, the continuous stooping necessary to pull weeds from tomato fields or pick crops such as strawberries, lettuce, and broccoli, make the women susceptible to "sexual stares, verbal comments, and unwanted grabbing."[12]

Not much has changed in the 50 years since Edward R. Murrow exposed the plight of migrant workers in the documentary *Harvest of Shame*. What has changed is that the majority of farmworkers are now undocumented immigrants, making them in many ways even more vulnerable to exploitation. As Murrow said, they have the strength to harvest our fruits and vegetables but no power to influence the laws and regulations that can improve their lives. That part is up to us—the beneficiaries of their labor.   [edited, 2010]

NOTES

1. Michael Hoefer, Nancy Rytina, and Bryan C. Baker, "Estimates of the Unauthorized Immigrant Population Residing in the United States: January 2009," Policy Estimation, Office of Immigration Statistics: Policy Directorate.

2. Andorra Bruno, "Unauthorized Aliens in the United States," Congressional Research Service, April 27, 2010. www.fas.org/sgp/crs/homesec/R41207.pdf.

3. Raúl Hinojosa-Ojeda, "Raising the Floor for American Workers: The Economic Benefits of Comprehensive Immigration Reform," Center for American Progress and Immigration Policy Center, American Immigration Council, January 2010.

4. David Rochkind and Sacha Feinman, "Altar, Sonora: The Business of Smuggling," Pulitzer Center on Crisis Reporting, April 21, 2009, http://pulitzercenter.org/projects/north-america/altar-sonora-business-smuggling.

5. "Invisible Victims, Migrants on the Move in Mexico," Amnesty International, April 2010.

6. Ibid.

7. "Special Report of the National Committee on Human Rights on the Cases of Kidnapping of Migrants," June 15, 2009. http://www.cndh.org.mx/INFORMES/Especiales/infEspSecMigra.pdf.

8. Julia Preston, "Illegal Workers Swept from Jobs in 'Silent Raids,'" New York Times, July 9, 2010.

9. Jeffrey S. Passel, "Unauthorized Migrants: Numbers and Characteristics," Pew Hispanic Center, June 14, 2005; and Jeffrey S. Passel and D'Vera Cohn, "A Portrait of Unauthorized Immigrants in the United States," Pew Hispanic Center, April 14, 2009.

10. Ibid.

11. Raúl Hinojosa-Ojeda, "Raising the Floor for American Workers," Center for American Progress and Immigration Policy Center, American Immigration Council, January 2010.

12. "Blood, Sweat, and Fear: Workers' Rights in U.S. Meat and Poultry Plants," Human Rights Watch, 2004, citing "Son of a Chicken Man," Fortune, May 13, 2002, 136.

✿ 124

Mothers of Our Nations: Indigenous Women Address the World

WINONA LADUKE

It is a great honor as a young mother of two to be invited to speak to you sisters today, women who have great courage and commitment, women who are peers and leaders, and who like myself are the Mothers of Our Nations.

The Earth is our Mother. From her we get our life, and our ability to live. It is our responsibility to care for our Mother, and in caring for our Mother, we care for ourselves. Women, all females, are the manifestation of Mother Earth in human form. We are her daughters, and in my cultural instructions we are to care for her. I am taught to live in respect for Mother Earth. In indigenous societies, we are told that natural law is the highest law, higher than the laws made by nations, states, municipalities and the World Bank; that one would do well to live in accordance with natural law, with those of our Mother, and in respect for all our relations.

One hundred years ago, one of our great leaders, Chief Seattle, stated, "What befalls the Earth, befalls the people of the Earth." And that is the reality today, and the situation of the status of women, and the status of indigenous women and indigenous peoples.

While I am from one nation of indigenous peoples, there are an estimated 500 million indigenous peoples or some 5,000 nations of indigenous peoples worldwide. We are in the Cordilleras, East Timor, New Zealand, Australia, Tibet, New Caledonia, Hawaii, North America, South America, and beyond. We are not populations nor minority groups. We are peoples and nations of peoples. Under international law we meet the criteria of nation states with each having a common economic system, language, territory, history, culture, and governing institution—conditions which indicate nations of peoples. Despite this fact, indigenous nations are not allowed to participate in the United Nations.

Nations of indigenous peoples are not represented at the United Nations. Most decisions today are made by the 180 or so member states. Those states, by and large, have been in existence for only 200 years or less, while most indigenous nations, with few exceptions, have been in existence for thousands of years. Ironically, there would likely be little argument in this room, that most decisions made in the world today are actually made by some of the 47 transnational corporations and their international financiers whose annual income is larger than the gross national product for many countries of the world.

This is the centerpiece of the problem. Decision making is not made by those who are affected—people who live on the land—but the corporations with interests entirely different from that of the land and the people or the women of the land. This brings forth a fundamental question: What gives corporations like Conoco, Shell, Exxon, Daishowa, ITT, Rio Tinto Zinc, and the World Bank the right which supersedes or is superior to my human right to live on my land, or that of my family, my community, my nation, our nations, and to us as women? What law gives that right to them? Not any law of the Creator or of Mother Earth. Is that right contained within their wealth? Is that right contained within their wealth, which was historically acquired immorally, unethically through colonialism and imperialism and paid for with the lives of millions of people, species of plants, and entire ecosystems? They should have no such right. And we clearly, as women and as indigenous peoples, demand and will recover that right—the right of self-determination, to determine our own destiny and that of our future generations.

The origins of this problem lie with the predator/prey relationship that industrial society has developed with the Earth and, subsequently, the people of the Earth. This same relationship exists vis-à-vis women. We collectively find that we are often in the role of the prey to a predator society whether through sexual discrimination, exploitation, sterilization, absence of control over our bodies, or being the subjects of repressive laws and legislation in which we have no voice. This occurs on an individual level, but equally and more significantly on a societal level. It is also critical to point out at this time most matrilineal societies, societies in which governance and decision making are largely controlled by women, have been obliterated from the face of the Earth by colonialism and industrialism. The only matrilineal societies that still exist in the world today are those of indigenous nations. Yet we also face obliteration.

On a worldwide scale and in North America, indigenous societies remain in a predator/prey relationship with industrial society. We are the peoples with the land—land and natural resources required for someone else's development program and amassing of wealth. The wealth of the United States, the nation that today determines much of world policy, was illegally expropriated from our lands. Similarly the wealth of indigenous peoples of South Africa, Central and South American countries, and Asia was taken for the industrial development of Europe and later for settler states which came to occupy those lands. The relationship between development and underdevelopment adversely affected the status of our indigenous societies and the status of indigenous women.

Eduardo Galeano, the Latin American writer and scholar, writes: "In the colonial to neocolonial alchemy, gold changes to scrap metal and food to poison. We have become painfully aware of the mortality of wealth which nature bestows and imperialism appropriates."

Today, on a worldwide scale, we remain in the same situation as one hundred years ago, only with less land and fewer people. Fifty million indigenous peoples live in the world's rainforests. In the next decade, one million indigenous peoples are slated to be relocated because of dam projects (thanks to the Narmada Project in India, the Three Gorges Dam Project in China, and the James Bay Hydroelectric Project in northern Canada). Almost all atomic weapons which have been detonated in the world have been on lands or waters of indigenous peoples, most clearly evidenced here in China and in the Pacific with France's obscene proposal to detonate atomic weapons this upcoming month. This situation is mirrored in North America. Today, over 50 percent of our remaining lands are forested. Both Canada and the United States continue aggressive clear-cutting policies on our land. Over two thirds of the uranium resources and one third of all low-sulfur coal resources in the United States are on indigenous lands. We have huge oil reserves on our reservations. Over 650 atomic weapons have been detonated on the Western Shoshone Nation. We have two separate accelerated proposals to dump nuclear waste in our reservation lands, and similarly over 100 separate proposals for toxic waste dumps on our lands. We understand clearly the relationship between development for someone else and our own underdevelopment. We also understand clearly the relationship between the environmental impacts of types of development on our lands, and the environmental and subsequent health impacts on our bodies as women.

We also understand clearly that the analysis of North versus South is an erroneous analysis. There is, from our perspective, not a problem of the North dictating the economic policies of the South, and subsequently consuming the South. Instead, there is a problem of the Middle consuming both the North and the South. That is our situation. Let me explain.

The rate of deforestation in the Brazilian Amazon is one acre every nine seconds. Incidentally, the rate of extinction of indigenous peoples in the Amazon is one nation of indigenous peoples per year. The rate of deforestation of the boreal forest of Canada is one acre every twelve seconds. Siberia, thanks to American corporations like Weyerhauser, is not far behind. In all cases, indigenous peoples are endangered. And there is, frankly, no difference between the impact in the North and the South.

Uranium mining in northern Canada has left over 120 million tons of radioactive waste. Since 1975, hospitalizations for cancer, birth defects, and circulatory illnesses in that area have increased dramatically—between 123 percent and 600 percent. In other areas impacted by uranium mining, cancer and birth defects have in some cases increased to 8 times the national average. There is no distinction in this problem caused by radiation whether it is in the Dene of northern Canada, the Laguna Pueblo of New Mexico, or the people of Namibia.

The rapid increase in dioxins, organochlorides, and PCBs (polychlorinated biphenyls) in the world as a result of industrialization also has a devastating impact on indigenous peoples, indigenous women, and other women. Each year, according to Environmental Protection Agency statistics, the world's paper industry discharges from 600 to 3,200 grams of dioxin equivalents in water, sludge, and paper products. This quantity is equal to the amount that would cause 58,000 to 292,000 cases of cancer every year. According to a number of recent studies, this has significantly increased the risk of breast cancer in women. Similarly, heavy metals and PCB contamination of Inuit women of the Hudson Bay region of the Arctic indicates that they have the highest levels of breast milk contamination in the world—28 times higher than the average woman in Quebec and 10 times higher than that considered "safe" by the government. Consequently, it is clear to us that problems are also found in the South due to the export of chemicals and bio-accumulation of toxins. These are problems that emanate from industrial society's mistreatment and disrespect for our Mother Earth, and are reflected in the devastation of the collective health and well-being of women.

In summary, I have presented these arguments to illustrate that these are very common issues for women, not only for indigenous women, but for all women. What befalls our Mother Earth, befalls her daughters—the women who are the mothers of our nations. Simply stated, if we can no longer nurse our children, if we can no longer bear children, and if our bodies are wracked with poisons, we will have accomplished little in the way of determining our destiny or improving our conditions. These problems, reflected in our health and well-being, are the result of historical processes and are inherently resulting in a decline of the status of women. We need to challenge these processes if we want to be ultimately in charge of our own destinies, our own self-determination, and the future of our Earth, our Mother.

I call on you to support the struggle of indigenous peoples of the world for recognition as peoples who have self-determination. I ask you to look into the Charter of the United Nations, which states that "all peoples have the right to self-determination. By virtue of that right, they may freely determine their political status and freely pursue their economic, social and political development." "All peoples" should be construed to mean that indigenous peoples have that right, too. Accord us the same rights as all other nations of peoples, and through that process, allow us to protect our ecosystems, their inherent biodiversity, human cultural diversity, and the last remaining matriarchal governments in the world.

Finally, while we are here in the commonness of this forum, speak of the common rights of all women and the fundamental human rights to self-determination. So long as the predator continues, so long as the Middle countries of the world continue to drive an increasing level of consumption, there will be no safety for the human rights of women, of indigenous peoples, and the basic protection of the Earth from which we get our life. Consumption causes the commodification of the sacred, the natural world, cultures, children, and women. And unless we speak and take meaningful action to address the high levels of consumption, we will never have any security for our individual human rights as women.

This is not a struggle for women of the dominant society in so-called "first world" countries to have equal pay and equal status if that pay and status continues to be based on a consumption model that is unsustainable. It is a struggle to recover our status as Daughters of the Earth. In that is our strength and security, not in the predator, but in the security of our Mother, for our future generations. In that, we can insure our security as the Mothers of Our Nations.　　　　　　[1995]

🌿 125

What's in a Name?

ANIDA YOEU ALI

My name is 2,000 years of history present in
　1 body 3 decades of civil unrest awake in
　3 syllables 5 letters dense of "Birth" "Blood"
　"Islam" "Peace" "Khmer" "Story" 2 letters
　away from "Refugee" 1 letter short of "Home"

My name knows my mother labored screaming for
　hours only to mourn a year later as she buried
　her sorrow.
A baby boy empty of breast milk born into famine
　instead of family. (2 letters and war separate the
　difference)
My mother buried the pains from her first labor
　along with her grief, knowing her son had

learned the word for hunger before he was able
　to call her "mother" or speak her name. She
　labored a second time, and my name was born.
My name unexpectedly inherited first-child
　honors.
My name echoes the same shahadah* whispered
　to early newborns carves legacy into intricate
　ancient mountains thrives as a rice field of
　shallow graves escaped from a land kissed by
　American bombs.

When you say my name it is a prayer a mantra a
　call when you say my name when you whisper
　it when you cry it when you desire it

I respond.

Before countries bounded themselves into borders
　before cities became governments *even* before
　the nations of hip hop it is the original call and
　response that all people claim.

So, I take issue with *your* inarticulate mangling of
　my name she refuses to disintegrate into a colonized tongue.

In America, she's just another foreign name.
My name survived racism before she knew what it
　was called.
Picture this:
A small child sinks deeper into her seat into her
　shame into her difference into *their* laughter into *their* stares into *their* sneers into a
　classroom of white kids with white teachers with white tongues with perfectly pronounceable white American names like
　Katy, Courtney, Jennifer, Michael, Bobby,
　Doug, Mrs. Smith, Mrs. Nelson Mr.
　How-do-you-say-your-weird-name-again?
Miss I'm-sorry-I-just-can't-seem-to-say-it-right!

Every mispronunciation is like a mouth shooting bullets the spit of syllables building from a
　gullet turn barrel triggering *precise* memories
　attached to *precise* feelings like shame inflected
　in my parents' broken English the guilt of witnessing daily sacrifices by my mother and father

---

*Shahadah—a Muslim's declaration of faith.

their dreams and youth slaughtered for money,
food, *my* perfect English.
Every misplaced tongue targets *my* foreignness, *my*
unbelonging, *my* vulnerabilities.
So when I get angry or curse you for your mispronunciation *Please* don't tell me I can't do that
Don't tell me to take it easy Don't scold me afterwards for making a point of it in public Don't
shrink me down any further *Please just listen.*

Allow me to own this one thing:
The rights to my name. to say her correctly to
have her said correctly to come when she calls
me to come to her defense to honor her legacy.
She is my only refuge when I am stripped naked.
She is my bloodline to mothers who have
labored before me. She is My Name. The echo
of Home I long to remember.
My name is Anida daughter of Souraya who is
the daughter of Abidah who is the daughter of
Fatimah who is the daughter of a woman whose
name I do not know who are all daughters of
Hawwa daughters of life sisters of survival
women of resistance daughters of the earth
water breath fire dreams.   [2008]

126

Human Security
vs. National Security

CHARLOTTE BUNCH

The term "human security" has come into greater
use by civil society and the United Nations as a way
to describe an integrated vision of positive peace,
human rights, equality, and development as interrelated. The call to redefine security in terms of human
and ecological needs instead of national sovereignty
and national borders is seen as an alternative to
the state-centered concept of "national security,"
rooted in the military security-defense domain and
academically lodged with the realists in the field of
international relations. The U.N. Human Security

Commission Report (2003) stands as the clear-
est international effort to redefine global security
in these terms. It looks at the fundamental threats
to security inherent in poverty and the everyday
violence of HIV/AIDS, in racism, domestic abuse,
ethnic conflicts, and the massive displacements of
people. These scourges cause more untimely deaths
than terrorism. Moreover, they feed the hopelessness and rage behind terrorist acts.

The report also speaks of security less as defending territory and more in terms of protecting people,
and was followed in 2005 at the U.N. Millennium
Summit with the introduction into U.N. discourse
of the concept of the "Responsibility to Protect
(R2P)." R2P embraces the idea that the international community has the responsibility to intervene in grave humanitarian crises to protect citizens
when their own government fails to do so. To
achieve this clearly requires a shift in the social order
that ensures the equal participation of marginalized
groups, including women, racial or ethnic minorities, and indigenous people, curtails and restricts the
use of military force to humanitarian purposes, and
moves toward collective global security.

For feminists this has meant raising questions
about whose security "national security" defends,
and addressing issues like the violence continuum
that threatens women's security daily, during armed
conflict as well as so-called peacetime. There is no
better paradigm for human insecurity than violence against women, which unseats women's personal sense of security as well as reinforces societal
acceptance of violence as inevitable and acceptable, whether at the core of the family or in military
conflict. For example, in looking at East Asia, some
feminists concluded: "The security treaties . . . that
provide for U.S. bases, military operations, and port
visits in South Korea, Japan, and the Philippines also
compromise the security of local people. Negative
social effects of the U.S. military presence on host
communities include military prostitution, the abuse
of local women, and the dire situation of mixed-race
children fathered by U.S. military men."[1]

Efforts to promote the concept of human security
emerged out of processes where women were active
globally at grassroots and at the U.N.—from the

peace movement to the debate over development. But these discussions were set back by 9/11, with the subsequent resurgence of the masculine warrior discourse. The media has been dominated by male "authority" figures, providing a rude reminder that when it comes to issues of terrorism, war, defense, and national security, feminists are still not on the map.

Yet it is women who have been the major target of fundamentalist terrorism, from Algeria to India to the United States, over the past several decades. And it is mostly feminists who have led the critique of this growing global problem—focusing attention not only on Islamic fundamentalism but on protestant fundamentalism in the United States, Catholic secret societies like Opus Dei in Latin America, Hindu right-wing fundamentalists in India, and so on. Only when it became convenient for military purposes to discuss the rights of Afghan women did the issues of women and fundamentalism surface in the mainstream media. However, this discussion is not often extended to the rights of women in other conflicts and non-Islamic fundamentalist attacks on women like those in Gujarat, India. Thus, what should have led to an examination of threats to women's human rights posed by political fundamentalism, terrorism, and armed conflict in many guises was used instead by the United States and other Western powers to demonize the "Islamic other" and to justify more militarization of society. Growing militarization, often with U.S. support and arms, has brought an increase in defense spending in many other regions, from India and Pakistan to Israel, Colombia, and the Philippines.

Feminists in the United States and globally must challenge this discourse on national security and can build on the concept of human security advanced in the U.N. We must add an understanding of what it will take to create human security for women in terms of deep-seated patterns of domination from the family to racism and militarism. It also requires understanding why support for international aid and financing for development is a critical global security need as well as support for movements that are seeking to advance democracy in the Middle East and elsewhere. The challenges ahead require that we continue to shift the dialogue nationally in the United States as well as globally toward the goals of human security as the only true path to global security and the only real national security in a globalized world.[2]   [2011]

NOTES

1. Gwyn Kirk and Carolyn Bowen Francis, "Redefining Security," *Berkeley Women's Law Journal* 15 (2000): 229–38
2. For further discussion of Human Security vs. National Security, see Charlotte Bunch, "A Feminist Human Rights Lens on Human Security," *Peace Review: A Journal of Social Justice* 16, no. 1 (March 2004); and Bunch, "Women's Human Rights and Security in the Age of Terror," in *Nothing Sacred: Women Respond to Religious Fundamentalism and Terror*, ed. Betsy Reed (New York: Nation Books, 2002).

Borderlands and Intersections

The first step in bridging the differences and divisions among us is by broadening our view of female experience. We hope the previous sections of this chapter have been useful in this enterprise. But broadening our view also means understanding the complex ways in which various forms of discrimination and prejudice intersect in the lives of different groups of women. Understanding such intersectionality has become a key endeavor of women's studies. It means abandoning the idea that a woman of color who is poor, for instance, might somehow be more affected by racism than classism or sexism. Patricia Hill Collins argues that this means resisting the urge to rank systems of oppression, and, instead, reconceptualizing those systems as "interlocking." When we are aware of how multiple systems of oppression and privilege affect us, we can, in the words of Chicana feminist Gloria Anzaldúa, develop a "borderland consciousness," which while potentially making living difficult also brings heightened awareness.

The readings in this section are meant to deepen our understanding of both the differences and divisions among women and the various systems of interlocking oppressions that shape women's lives. Laura Hershey explores the links between the oppression she and other women with disabilities face with other forms of discrimination they encounter based in class, gender, and sexual orientation.

In her influential essay "Age, Race, Class, and Sex: Women Redefining Difference," Audre Lorde, a black lesbian writer who died of cancer in 1993, warns us of the dangers of ignoring difference, and urges us to work harder with ourselves and each other to ensure that our differences, rather than dividing us, will enrich our struggle and our vision. This can entail hearing and honoring the anger that women feel because of their oppression, as exemplified in the work of Haunani-Kay Trask, who speaks and writes about the dispossession of Native Hawaiian people and works to challenge it.

Groups of people who feel embattled in our society often work to claim their own identity and create communities of support. These communities generate a culture that challenges dominant ideas and enables group members to experience a sense of solidarity. Sometimes this can be a source of tension for women like Beverly Yuen Thompson and Lisa Suhair Majaj when their multiple identities overlap several boundaries. "Who will be loyal to me?" Thompson asks as she negotiates her bicultural and bisexual identity. As a Palestinian American, Majaj does not feel that her "identities can be neatly divided" but instead experiences them as a complex and shifting web.

The complex web of identity will include different strands of experience for women of various racial backgrounds. For example, while Thompson "didn't consider race" most of the time she was growing up, women who are part

African-American would be much more likely to be conscious of race in their everyday lives. The experience of being an outsider as a queer woman enables Nell Geiser to empathize with people of color while at the same time recognizing her own privileges as a white person. The pretense of "color blindness," she points out, often prevents white people from addressing the problem of racism. In Linda Hogan's "Friday Night," the concluding poem in this chapter, one woman reaches out to another, conscious both of what they share and of the different cultures they each bring to their friendship.

✣ 127

Rights, Realities, and Issues of Women with Disabilities

LAURA HERSHEY

DINNER CONVERSATION

It was a typical conference banquet—mediocre food, long-winded speakers. Six women, some strangers and some friends, shared a table. Five of us had physical disabilities. Eventually, we began sharing personal memories, and suddenly, revelations lay on the table, clattering against the near-empty plates. Of five women with disabilities, three related memories of extreme abuse in medical settings. Not just the stuff nearly every disabled woman can describe, like being an eight-year-old nude model for medical students. These were deeper violations. Molestation. Rape.

One woman remembered a childhood interrupted by frequent hospitalizations. She had cerebral palsy, and had undergone several surgeries plus intensive physical therapy. These procedures, scary enough for a child, were accompanied by a series of sexual assaults by a staff member. This was her first recounting of the crimes, a disclosure that created a bond of sisterhood among six exhausted conference-goers.

If I stopped here, I'd be presenting a simplistic, disempowering picture of disabled women's experience. From news stories to horror movies, women with disabilities are falsely presented as natural victims—vulnerable, passive. In reality, the disabled women's community confronts its problems with the fierce creativity of a resistance movement.

While a majority of the women at that dinner table had been victimized as girls, none could now be described as passive victims. Each had grown into a strong disabled woman, conscious of injustice and equipped to fight it. One woman, institutionalized and assaulted during childhood, had become a lawyer, facing down the legal profession's sexist and disability prejudices. She related the power she felt when, several years earlier, she'd returned to the institution where she'd once lived—this time, to represent current inmates in their legal complaints against that institution. Another woman had become an advocate and researcher, exploring issues of disability, identity, and pride. Even the woman with the freshest disclosure was actively engaged in a project training medical students about the needs and rights of people with disabilities.

I think of that table as a metaphor for our community. We choose activism for our own survival, or in solidarity with our disabled sisters, or from an indistinguishable combination of the two.

WHO WE ARE

There are about 26 million women with disabilities in the United States. Although the (rare) media images of disabled people tend to be white and male, the reality is different. More women than men have disabilities, and disability impacts women of color disproportionately. In African-American and Native American communities, approximately 22 percent of women have disabilities; European American women have a disability rate of 20 percent.[1]

Our impairments run a gamut. Some affect the brain, some the body, some the senses; some involve a combination. Certain conditions are stable, others erratic; some originated at or before birth; others result from acquired diseases or injuries. Yet with all this diversity, we share many experiences: a proud assertion of difference, and survival against the odds; also systematic discrimination, crushing poverty, and social isolation. By most measures of social status, we find ourselves in last place. Yet we're also workers, students, artists, athletes, lovers, friends, mothers, grandmothers. We adapt to profound change, devising unusual, practical, elegant ways to accomplish what we cannot do through standard approaches. We pave the way for all women—any of whom might join our community at any moment.

We're also leaders, activists, organizers.[2] Every day, we resist society's compulsion to punish or banish us in encounters major and minor—from being called fire hazards and told to move our wheelchairs to the back of the theater, to being termed helpless, incompetent, or crazy, and sent to an institution. From this anger and pain, we wrench new visions of how society might respond to the inevitable, natural fact of disability. No single article can hope to detail every aspect of the disabled women's movement, but citing a few key issues and notable activists may illustrate our struggles and strategies.

ACCESS TO SAFETY

In addition to assaults on our bodily integrity due to the medicalization of our lives, disabled women (like all women) suffer violence at the hands of partners, spouses, family members. The same sexist factors— male rage and entitlement—fuel brutality toward women, regardless of disability.[3] Additional factors make escape more difficult for disabled women. They may feel less able to find jobs or housing, to build a life apart from their abusers. They may stay in such relationships from fear of going to a nursing home, preferring to endure abuse from one individual than from a whole staff. They may stay because they fear losing their children: judges have been known to award custody to an abusive parent rather than a disabled one. Police, service providers, and advocates rarely know how to communicate with deaf women in American Sign Language. Hotlines have no TTY access for deaf callers. Shelters often have stairs and inaccessible bathrooms, bans on necessary medications, or policies prohibiting attendants from visiting to provide needed assistance.

Women and girls with disabilities also experience abuse by service providers and/or authority figures: nursing-home aides, nurses, doctors, group-home supervisors, van drivers. (These perpetrators have effective weapons: they can deny privileges, withhold help, or use a victim's disability to discredit her.)

Activist disabled women have confronted these injustices. For example, the Domestic Violence Initiative for Women with Disabilities (DVI) was formed in Denver, Colorado, in 1985 as a grassroots response to the high incidence of battering of disabled women and the shelter system's inaccessibility to these women. Sharon Hickman, DVI's founder/director, has created a network of volunteers and staff to provide information to domestic-violence service providers.

LIVING IN THE FREE WORLD

Elaine Wilson and Lois Curtis were two women with mental disabilities who lived in institutions in Georgia. Both wanted to live more independently, in small group homes. The state refused, because there were no such "slots" available at the time. So Wilson and Curtis sued the state of Georgia under the Americans with Disabilities Act (ADA). In 1999, the U.S. Supreme Court ruled that states cannot unnecessarily institutionalize disabled people. Justice Ruth Bader Ginsburg's majority opinion stated, "[U]njustified isolation of individuals with disabilities is properly regarded as discrimination based on disability." The decision (*Olmstead v. Lois Curtis*) was regarded by the disability-rights community as a victory. Advocates like Lucy Gwin, Tia Nelis, and Stephanie Thomas then built on this triumph, fighting for noninstitutional living options. Gwin, who survived a brain injury, a coma, and a service system trying to control her life, now edits *The Mouth,* an in-your-face magazine that confronts patronizing, professional do-gooders. Terming *Olmstead* "a clear recall from exile,"[4] Gwin created the Freedom Clearinghouse (*www.freedomclearinghouse.org*), an Internet-based project to help connect advocates in different states and provide them with an advocacy tool kit.

Nelis adapted that tool kit for members of her group, People First. "Some of that stuff is hard for people to understand," says Nelis, who organizes her peers with cognitive disabilities. She's developed trainings and materials in easier language, and educated People First members—who then wear buttons reading: "Ask me about Olmstead"—in turn educating others about the importance of independent living options.[5]

Meanwhile, organizers like Stephanie Thomas of ADAPT (American Disabled for Attendant Programs Today) have been pushing federal legislation to ensure community support services to disabled people nationwide. About 9 million Americans with disabilities—at least half of them women—require personal assistance for everyday activities:[6] getting up, bathing, dressing, cooking, remembering routines, monitoring safety, and doing housework. The Medicaid Community Attendant Services and Supports Act (MiCASSA) would offer "real choice" to people who need such assistance and currently have no options but nursing homes. "Institutions are not our main way to go," Thomas insists. "We need to focus on the person, not the building."[7]

"The building" may be a nursing home, a long-term rehabilitation hospital, a state institution, or a psychiatric hospital. All these facilities thrive by confining people who need assistance of some kind and who, because of current policies, can't get it elsewhere. Disabled women are particularly susceptible to forced institutionalization. Although wives, daughters, sisters, and mothers provide most of the informal at-home assistance needed by disabled and older people, women are much *less* likely, when *we* need it, to have such assistance from husbands, sons, brothers, and fathers.[8] (It should be noted that low-income women, including many women of color, provide much of the cheap labor that makes institutions so profitable to those who own them.)

When dependable, responsive, high-quality assistance *is* available—e.g., through Medicaid-funded programs in some states—people with significant disabilities can be as independent as anyone. Without this assistance, many of us lose what most Americans take for granted: freedom.

EMPLOYMENT

Almost 100 years ago, social-justice campaigner Helen Keller, who was deaf-blind, offered a sophisticated analysis of the social construction of disabling poverty: "Facts show that it is not physical blindness but social blindness which cheats our hands of the right to toil."

Workplace barriers and the rule-bound U.S. benefit system combine to create deterrents to employment for disabled women. In a 1997 income survey, only about 30 percent of women with severe disabilities were employed, earning a median income of $12,030.[9] The reasons are complex, and include discrimination based on ableism and sexism, lack of retraining opportunities, and employers' failure to provide such reasonable accommodations as modified schedules, adaptive equipment, and on-the-job support. In addition, many women with disabilities decide, reluctantly but rationally, not to apply for jobs because of penalties for working that are built into disability-support programs like Social Security and Medicaid.

A number of disabled women have responded to these problems by starting their own small businesses. Barbara Knowlen fought an indifferent bureaucracy to get the necessary equipment and services to found Barrier Breakers. She succeeded because she learned the system's rules better than most of the people who work *for* the system. Now she helps others with disabilities win bureaucratic battles to obtain the necessary resources for going to work or starting a business.

HEALTH CARE

Women with disabilities worry about the same health issues as other women, but have less access to health care. We and our allies have begun taking control of this situation via several projects. One is the Health Resource Center for Women with Disabilities at the Rehabilitation Institute of Chicago. The Center began as a coalition of disabled women's health advocates and supportive medical professionals. It provides appropriate, accessible health care services—including training for parents with disabilities, mentoring for teenage disabled girls, and clinical services. It also educates new health care professionals (including some women with disabilities) in a supportive, disability-conscious environment, and advocates for improved state policies. Judy Panko Reis, director of the program and a disabled woman, says, "Our goal is to promote self-determination . . . which means physical and emotional wellness in teenage and adult women with disabilities."[10]

The women's health movement has largely failed to serve disabled women, who are denied necessary services because of "environmental, attitudinal and information barriers."[11] For example, many physically disabled women can't access standard diagnostic equipment. We can't stand before scanners, climb onto high tables, or wrench our legs into stirrups. Consequently, we are less likely to have mammograms[12] and regular Pap tests.[13]

Projects organized by and for disabled women stand out as bold assertions that disabled women's lives are worth saving—that we have a right to expect good health *and* good health care.

SEXUALITY AND RELATIONSHIPS

Our disabilities play a variety of roles in our erotic lives. A disability may cause awkwardness; and/or demand creative adaptation, cooperation, and communication between partners; and/or be a source of connection and excitement. All these experiences can be exciting, life-affirming, and pleasurable.

Yet women and girls with disabilities face significant barriers in trying to form romantic and sexual relationships. Myths abound that we are asexual, incapable of giving or receiving physical pleasure. This translates into more difficulty with dating, decreased likelihood of marriage, and higher divorce rates.[14] Bombarded by negative messages about our sexuality, many of us struggle for a sense of sexual identity. The media-morphed perfect female does not look like someone we can aspire to be.

But do we want that persona? Our distance from that gendered ideal is a double-edged sword,

taunting some disabled women with impossible aspirations, releasing others from restrictive stereotypes. Corbett O'Toole, who uses a wheelchair and has been organizing in the disabled women's community for 30 years, recalls, "My disability gave me incredible freedom to break with gender stereotypes. When I didn't use makeup in high school, when I didn't date boys, when I wore gender-neutral clothing, there were knowing nods that it was because 'she's different.'"[15]

It takes time and a sometimes painful process of self-exploration to discover not only what we weren't, but what we could be; what we are. Only after that journey can we take the more rewarding step of realizing and claiming our true sexual identities. Even then, when we come out—whether as lesbian, bisexual, heterosexual, transgendered, sensuously chaste, or whatever—we may have to journey farther to find a community where we can be our full sexual selves.

With the leadership of women like O'Toole, we've developed our own networks for exploring issues of identity and community. Speaking frankly with each other and our partners, we affirm our sexiness in all kinds of ways.

REVOLUTIONARY PRINCIPLES: FEMINISM AND DISABILITY RIGHTS

I'm a feminist because I feel my own future and our collective human future depend on achieving real gender justice, and on ending patriarchal domination of culture and nature. I'm a disability-rights activist for very similar reasons: I want freedom and opportunity for myself, and I believe that acceptance of and accommodation to human variation are essential strategies for our human species' survival.

But despite my passionate commitment to both movements, I sometimes feel marginalized by both, as, I know, do many feminists with disabilities. Disability organizations often fail to consider gender issues. And urgent disability-related concerns rarely achieve a prominent place in feminist magazines or conferences.

And why should they? Aren't these the concerns of a small minority? I'd argue that disability rights and feminism directly serve two overlapping *majorities*. (More than half the human species is female, and a substantial percentage of people will, at some time in their lives, be affected by disability resulting from illness, injury, or old age.) Furthermore, both disability rights and feminism address compelling, universal, human needs.

Disabled women are working for change on fronts too numerous to explore here, given space limitations: educational equity; access to technology; media representations; artistic and cultural activities; reproductive rights—including both the right to abortion and the right to bear children; the right to raise children; body image, and identity development.

I believe deeply in the revolutionary principles expressed by the disability experience. For women like myself to deviate dramatically from prevailing norms yet expect the rights and privileges of any other citizen is radical. By demanding full participation in society and the accommodations to make that participation possible, the activist disabled women's community offers a liberating vision of human connectedness—for everyone.

[2003]

NOTES

1. Data from Survey of Income and Program Participation, quoted in *Chartbook on Women with Disabilities in the United States,* prepared by Lita Jans and Susan Stoddard (Berkeley, CA: InfoUse, 1999).
2. Women's historians and other feminists frequently cite U.S. nineteenth-century foremothers from the movements for abolition of slavery and women's suffrage. Yet it is rarely pointed out that at least two such major foremothers were disabled women: Harriet Tubman, a former slave and the leader of the Underground Railroad; and Elizabeth Blackwell, the first woman in the United States to become a doctor with a formal medical degree.—Ed.
3. See "Landscape of the Ordinary: Violence Against Women," by Andrea Dworkin, 58.—Ed.
4. Quoted in "Tracking MiCASSA," by Josie Byzek, *New Mobility* magazine, April 2001 (*http://www.newmobility.com*).
5. "Interview with Tia Nelis: U.S. Self-Advocacy Leader," by Laura Hershey, *Disability World,* no. 8, May/June 2001 (*www.disabilityworld.org/050601/il/nelisinterview.html*).
6. John M. McNeil, analyst, "Disabilities Affect One-Fifth of All Americans," Census Brief, U.S. Census Bureau, Public Information Office, December 1997.
7. Interview with the author, October 2000.
8. "Disabled women living in the community may be particularly vulnerable to unmet needs because many of them live alone with limited resources. Even disabled women in married households may be vulnerable to unmet needs because they may be more likely than men to be in a caregiver role themselves. . . . Steven J. Katz, M.D., M.P.H., and colleagues from the University of Michigan (Ann Arbor), analyzed data from a nationally representative survey in the United States conducted at the University of Michigan in 1993 to determine sex differences in receipt of informal (generally unpaid) and formal (generally paid) home care. . . . [D]isabled elderly women were more likely to be living alone (45.4 percent, compared with men at 16.8 percent). Women were much less likely to be living with a spouse (27.8 percent, compared with men at 73.6 percent). The women were also older, reported less net worth than men, and received less informal care. . . . Overall, women received fewer hours of informal care per week than men (15.7 hours per week for women; 21.2 for men)," Katz et al., reported. "Married disabled women received many fewer hours per week of informal home care than married disabled men (14.8 hours per week for women; 26.2 for men)." Quoted in "Disabled Elderly Women Receive Less Home Care Than Men," *Women's Health Weekly,* 2000, via *NewsRx.com* & *NewsRx.net.* [See also "The Politics of Aging," by Barbara Macdonald with Cynthia Rich, 152; "Traffic at the Crossroads: Multiple Oppressions," by Kimberlé Crenshaw, 43; and (for more on caregiving) "Poverty Wears a Female Face," by Theresa Funiciello, 222.—Ed.]
9. Data from the Survey of Income and Program Participation (SIPP), U.S. Bureau of the Census, August–November 1997.
10. Interview with the author, June 2000.
11. Margaret Nosek (Director of the Center for Research on Women with Disabilities at Baylor College of Medicine, Houston, Texas), quoted in "The Enemy Within, The Battle Without: Fighting for Accessible Services to Beat Breast Cancer," by Rachel Ross, a publication of the National Women's Health Information Center (NWHIC), a service of the Office on Women's Health in the Department of Health and Human Services, August 1999 (*http://www.4woman.gov/editor/aug99.htm*).
12. *Centers for Disease Control and Prevention (CDC) Morbidity and Mortality Weekly Report,* 1998, quoted in *Services Denied: Why Women with Disabilities Aren't Screened for Cancer,* by Christine Haran, in National Women's Health Information Center (NWHIC), a service of the Office on Women's Health in the Department of Health and Human Services, December 2000 (*www.4woman.gov/editor/dec00/dec00.htm*).
13. Ibid.
14. In a 1992 survey, only 44 percent of women with "severe activity limitations" were married, and these women had higher rates of divorce than women with less severe limitations: NHI Survey, quoted in *Chartbook on Women with Disabilities,* op. cit., 30.
15. Personal correspondence with the author, March 2001.

Beside My Sister, Facing the Enemy

MARI MATSUDA

Haunani-Kay Trask recounts the dispossession of Native Hawaiian people—their land-lessness, poverty, unemployment, imprisonment, rates of disease, and illiteracy. Trask speaks of the *haole* (Caucasian) colonizers who removed the Hawaiian government by force, leaving wounds in the native population that have never healed. Expressing outrage at the haole-backed takeover of Hawai'i has earned Trask the reputation of "haole-hater." She speaks out in the press. She writes. She debates. Trask is constantly engaged in dialogue with the haole. She works with whites in coalition on a variety of issues, from nuclear testing in the Pacific, to South African divestment, to degradation of the environment through geothermal development.

I have heard people say of Professor Trask, "She would be much more effective if she weren't so angry," as though they expect a Native Hawaiian feminist to work in coalition without anger. There is a politics of anger: who is allowed to get angry, whose anger goes unseen, and who seems angry when they are not.

Once, when I intended to compliment an African-American woman on a power-ful speech she had made, I said: "I admire your ability to express anger." She looked at me coolly and replied, "I was not angry. If I were angry I would not be speaking here." Another African-American friend of mine jumped into the conversation. "I'm disap-pointed in you," she said. "This is what always happens to us when a Black woman speaks her mind. Someone calls us angry."

I remember this exchange because it was an uncomfortable one for me, and because it was a moment of learning. Talking across differences, my colleague told me that if she were hatefully angry, beyond hope of coalition, she would not talk. In this light, Professor Trask's strong words are acts of engagement, not estrangement.

Would Professor Trask be more effective if she were less angry? There is a cost to speaking without anger of the deaths and dislocation that native Hawaiians suffered in post-contact Hawai'i. On the simple, communicative level, failure to express the pain created by this legacy obscures the depth of one's feeling and discounts the subordina-tion experienced by one's community. More significantly, the use of polite, rational tones when one is feeling violated is a betrayal of the self.

Professor Trask's many white and Asian colleagues who choose to remain in the room when she speaks in tones of outrage about the destruction of Hawaiian lives, land, and culture inevitably find their understanding greatly enriched. The discomfort brings with it an opportunity for learning. As a third-generation Japanese-American, I have felt the discomfort and benefitted from the learning when Professor Trask criticizes the role of immigrants in displacing Native Hawaiians. The choice is mine to remain in the conversation, discussing (sometimes with acrimony) the role of colonialism in bringing my peasant ancestors eastward from Asia to work on land that once belonged to indig-enous peoples of Hawai'i and North America.

I could shelter myself from conflict by leaving the conversation, but I have come to believe that the comfort we feel when we avoid hard conversations is a dangerous com-fort, one that seduces us into ignorance about the experiences of others and about the full meaning of our own lives.

🌿 128

Age, Race, Class, and Sex: Women Redefining Difference*

AUDRE LORDE

Much of Western European history conditions us to see human differences in simplistic opposition to each other: dominant/subordinate, good/bad, up/down, superior/inferior. In a society where the good is defined in terms of profit rather than in terms of human need, there must always be some group of people who, through systematized oppression, can be made to feel surplus, to occupy the place of dehumanized inferior. Within this society, that group is made up of black and Third World people, working-class people, older people, and women.

As a 49-year-old black lesbian feminist socialist mother of two, including one boy, and a member of an interracial couple, I usually find myself a part of some group defined as other, deviant, inferior, or just plain wrong. Traditionally, in American society, it is the members of oppressed, objectified groups who are expected to stretch out and bridge the gap between the actualities of our lives and the consciousness of our oppressor. For in order to survive, those of us for whom oppression is as American as apple pie have always had to be watchers, to become familiar with the language and manners of the oppressor, even sometimes adopting them for some illusion of protection. Whenever the need for some pretense of communication arises, those who profit from our oppression call upon us to share our knowledge with them. In other words, it is the responsibility of the oppressed to teach the oppressors their mistakes. I am responsible for educating teachers who dismiss my children's culture in school. Black and Third World people are expected to educate white people as to our humanity. Women are expected to educate men. Lesbians

*Paper delivered at the Copeland Colloquium, Amherst College, April 1980.

and gay men are expected to educate the heterosexual world. The oppressors maintain their position and evade responsibility for their own actions. There is a constant drain of energy which might be better used in redefining ourselves and devising realistic scenarios for altering the present and constructing the future.

Institutionalized rejection of difference is an absolute necessity in a profit economy which needs outsiders as surplus people. As members of such an economy, we have *all* been programmed to respond to the human differences between us with fear and loathing and to handle that difference in one of three ways: ignore it, and if that is not possible, copy it if we think it is dominant, or destroy it if we think it is subordinate. But we have no patterns for relating across our human differences as equals. As a result, those differences have been misnamed and misused in the service of separation and confusion.

Certainly there are very real differences between us of race, age, and sex. But it is not those differences between us that are separating us. It is rather our refusal to recognize those differences, and to examine the distortions which result from our misnaming them and their effects upon human behavior and expectation.

Racism, the belief in the inherent superiority of one race over all others and thereby the right to dominance. Sexism, the belief in the inherent superiority of one sex over the other and thereby the right to dominance. Ageism. Heterosexism. Elitism. Classism.

It is a lifetime pursuit for each one of us to extract these distortions from our living at the same time as we recognize, reclaim, and define those differences upon which they are imposed. For we have all been raised in a society where those distortions were endemic within our living. Too often, we pour the energy needed for recognizing and exploring difference into pretending those differences are insurmountable barriers, or that they do not exist at all. This results in a voluntary isolation, or false and treacherous connections. Either way, we do not develop tools for using human difference as a springboard for creative change within our lives. We speak not of human difference, but of human deviance.

Somewhere, on the edge of consciousness, there is what I call a *mythical norm*, which each one of us within our hearts knows "that is not me." In America, this norm is usually defined as white, thin, male, young, heterosexual, Christian, and financially secure. It is with this mythical norm that the trappings of power reside within this society. Those of us who stand outside that power often identify one way in which we are different, and we assume that to be the primary cause of all oppression, forgetting other distortions around difference, some of which we ourselves may be practicing. By and large within the women's movement today, white women focus upon their oppression as women and ignore differences of race, sexual preference, class, and age. There is a pretense to a homogeneity of experience covered by the word *sisterhood* that does not in fact exist.

Unacknowledged class differences rob women of each others' energy and creative insight. Recently a women's magazine collective made the decision for one issue to print only prose, saying poetry was a less "rigorous" or "serious" art form. Yet even the form our creativity takes is often a class issue. Of all the art forms, poetry is the most economical. It is the one which is the most secret, which requires the least physical labor, the least material, and the one which can be done between shifts, in the hospital pantry, on the subway, and on scraps of surplus paper. Over the last few years, writing a novel on tight finances, I came to appreciate the enormous differences in the material demands between poetry and prose. As we reclaim our literature, poetry has been the major voice of poor, working class, and colored women. A room of one's own may be a necessity for writing prose, but so are reams of paper, a typewriter, and plenty of time. The actual requirements to produce the visual arts also help determine, along class lines, whose art is whose. In this day of inflated prices for material, who are our sculptors, our painters, our photographers? When we speak of a broadly based women's culture, we need to be aware of the effect of class and economic differences on the supplies available for producing art.

As we move toward creating a society within which we can each flourish, ageism is another distortion of relationship which interferes without vision. By ignoring the past, we are encouraged to repeat its mistakes. The "generation gap" is an important social tool for any repressive society. If the younger members of a community view the older members as contemptible or suspect or excess, they will never be able to join hands and examine the living memories of the community, nor ask the all important question, "Why?" This gives rise to a historical amnesia that keeps us working to invent the wheel every time we have to go to the store for bread.

We find ourselves having to repeat and relearn the same old lessons over and over that our mothers did because we do not pass on what we have learned, or because we are unable to listen. For instance, how many times has this all been said before? For another, who would have believed that once again our daughters are allowing their bodies to be hampered and purgatoried by girdles and high heels and hobble skirts?

Ignoring the differences of race between women and the implications of those differences presents the most serious threat to the mobilization of women's joint power.

As white women ignore their built-in privilege of whiteness and define *woman* in terms of their own experience alone, then women of color become "other," the outsider whose experience and tradition is too "alien" to comprehend. An example of this is the signal absence of the experience of women of color as a resource for women's studies courses. The literature of women of color is seldom included in women's literature courses and almost never in other literature courses, nor in women's studies as a whole. All too often, the excuse given is that the literatures of women of color can only be taught by colored women, or that they are too difficult to understand, or that classes cannot "get into" them because they come out of experiences that are "too different." I have heard this argument presented by white women of otherwise quite clear intelligence, women who seem to have no trouble at all teaching and reviewing work that comes out of the vastly different experiences of Shakespeare, Molière, Dostoyefsky, and Aristophanes. Surely there must be some other explanation.

This is a very complex question, but I believe one of the reasons white women have such difficulty reading black women's work is because of their reluctance to see black women as women and different from themselves. To examine black women's literature effectively requires that we be seen as whole people in our actual complexities—as individuals, as women, as human—rather than as one of those problematic but familiar stereotypes provided in this society in place of genuine images of black women. And I believe this holds true for the literatures of other women of color who are not black.

The literatures of all women of color recreate the textures of our lives, and many white women are heavily invested in ignoring the real differences. For as long as any difference between us means one of us must be inferior, then the recognition of any difference must be fraught with guilt. To allow women of color to step out of stereotypes is too guilt provoking, for it threatens the complacency of those women who view oppression only in terms of sex.

Refusing to recognize difference makes it impossible to see the different problems and pitfalls facing us as women.

Thus, in a patriarchal power system where white-skin privilege is a major prop, the entrapments used to neutralize black women and white women are not the same. For example, it is easy for black women to be used by the power structure against Black men, not because they are men, but because they are black. Therefore, for black women, it is necessary at all times to separate the needs of the oppressor from our own legitimate conflicts within our communities. This same problem does not exist for white women. Black women and men have shared racist oppression and still share it, although in different ways. Out of that shared oppression we have developed joint defenses and joint vulnerabilities to each other that are not duplicated in the white community, with the exception of the relationship between Jewish women and Jewish men.

On the other hand, white women face the pitfall of being seduced into joining the oppressor under the pretense of sharing power. This possibility does not exist in the same way for women of color. The tokenism that is sometimes extended to us is not an invitation to join power; our racial "otherness" is a visible reality that makes that quite clear. For white women there is a wider range of pretended choices and rewards for identifying with patriarchal power and its tools.

Today, with the defeat of ERA, the tightening economy, and increased conservatism, it is easier once again for white women to believe the dangerous fantasy that if you are good enough, pretty enough, sweet enough, quiet enough, teach the children to behave, hate the right people, and marry the right men, then you will be allowed to coexist with patriarchy in relative peace, at least until a man needs your job or the neighborhood rapist happens along. And true, unless one lives and loves in the trenches it is difficult to remember that the war against dehumanization is ceaseless.

But black women and our children know the fabric of our lives is stitched with violence and with hatred, that there is no rest. We do not deal with it only on the picket lines, or in dark midnight alleys, or in the places where we dare to verbalize our resistance. For us, increasingly, violence weaves through the daily tissues of our living—in the supermarket, in the classroom, in the elevator, in the clinic and the schoolyard, from the plumber, the baker, the saleswoman, the bus driver, the bank teller, the waitress who does not serve us.

Some problems we share as women, some we do not. You fear your children will grow up to join the patriarchy and testify against you, we fear our children will be dragged from a car and shot down in the street, and you will turn your backs upon the reasons they are dying.

The threat of difference has been no less blinding to people of color. Those of us who are black must see that the reality of our lives and our struggle does not make us immune to the errors of ignoring and misnaming difference. Within black communities where racism is a living reality, differences among us often seem dangerous and suspect. The need for unity is often misnamed as a need for homogeneity, and a black feminist vision mistaken for betrayal of our common interests as a people. Because of the continuous battle against racial erasure that black women and black men share, some black women still refuse to recognize that we are also oppressed as women, and that sexual hostility against black women is practiced not only by the white racist society, but implemented within our black communities as well. It is a disease striking the heart of black nationhood, and silence will not make it disappear. Exacerbated by racism and the pressures of powerlessness, violence against black women and children often becomes a standard within our communities, one by which manliness can be measured. But these women-hating acts are rarely discussed as crimes against black women.

As a group, women of color are the lowest paid wage earners in America. We are the primary targets of abortion and sterilization abuse, here and abroad. In certain parts of Africa, small girls are still being sewed shut between their legs to keep them docile and for men's pleasure. This is known as female circumcision, and it is not a cultural affair as the late Jomo Kenyatta insisted, it is a crime against black women.

Black women's literature is full of the pain of frequent assault, not only by a racist patriarchy, but also by black men. Yet the necessity for and history of shared battle have made us, black women, particularly vulnerable to the false accusation that anti-sexist is anti-black. Meanwhile, woman hating as a recourse of the powerless is sapping strength from black communities, and our very lives. Rape is on the increase, reported and unreported, and rape is not aggressive sexuality, it is sexualized aggression. As Kalamu ya Salaam, a black male writer points out, "As long as male domination exists, rape will exist. Only women revolting and men made conscious of their responsibility to fight sexism can collectively stop rape."[1]

Differences between ourselves as black women are also being misnamed and used to separate us from one another. As a black lesbian feminist comfortable with the many different ingredients of my identity, and a woman committed to racial and sexual freedom from oppression, I find I am constantly being encouraged to pluck out one aspect of myself and present this as the meaningful whole, eclipsing or denying the other parts of self. But this is a destructive and fragmenting way to live. My fullest concentration of energy is available to me only when I integrate all the parts of who I am, openly, allowing power from particular sources of my living to flow back and forth freely through all my different selves, without the restrictions of externally imposed definition. Only then can I bring myself and my energies as a whole to the service of those struggles that I embrace as part of my living.

A fear of lesbians, or of being accused of being a lesbian, has led many black women into testifying against themselves. It has led some of us into destructive alliances, and others into despair and isolation. In the white women's communities, heterosexism is sometimes a result of identifying with the white patriarchy, a rejection of that interdependence between women-identified women, which allows the self to be, rather than to be used in the service of men. Sometimes it reflects a die-hard belief in the protective coloration of heterosexual relationships, sometimes a self-hate which all women have to fight against, taught us from birth.

Although elements of these attitudes exist for all women, there are particular resonances of heterosexism and homophobia among black women. Despite the fact that woman-bonding has a long and honorable history in the African and African-American communities, and despite the knowledge and accomplishments of many strong and creative women-identified black women in the political, social, and cultural fields, heterosexual Black women often tend to ignore or discount the existence and work of black lesbians. Part of this attitude has come from an understandable terror of black male attack within the close confines of black society, where the punishment for any female self-assertion is still to be accused of being a lesbian and therefore unworthy of the attention or support of the scarce black male. But part of this need to misname and ignore black lesbians comes from a very real fear that openly women-identified black women who are no longer dependent upon men for their self-definition may well reorder our whole concept of social relationships.

Black women who once insisted that lesbianism was a white woman's problem now insist that black lesbians are a threat to black nationhood, are consorting with the enemy, are basically un-black. These accusations, coming from the very women to whom we look for deep and real understanding, have served to keep many black lesbians in hiding, caught between the racism of white women and the homophobia of their sisters. Often, their work has been ignored, trivialized, or misnamed, as with the work of Angelina Grimke, Alice Dunbar-Nelson, and Lorraine Hansberry. Yet women-bonded women have always been some part of the power of black communities, from our unmarried aunts to the amazons of Dahomey.

And it is certainly not black lesbians who are assaulting women and raping children and grandmothers on the streets of our communities.

Across this country, as in Boston during the spring of 1979 following the unsolved murders of 12 black women, black lesbians are spearheading movements against violence against black women.

What are the particular details within each of our lives that can be scrutinized and altered to help bring about change? How do we redefine difference for all women? It is not our differences that separate women, but our reluctance to recognize those differences and to deal effectively with the distortions that have resulted from the ignoring and misnaming of those differences.

As a tool of social control, women have been encouraged to recognize only one area of human difference as legitimate, those differences that exist between women and men. And we have learned to deal across those differences with the urgency of all oppressed subordinates. All of us have had to learn to live or work or coexist with men, from our fathers on. We have recognized and negotiated these differences, even when this recognition only continued the old dominant/subordinate mode of human relationship, where the oppressed must recognize the masters' difference in order to survive.

But our future survival is predicated upon our ability to relate within equality. As women, we must root out internalized patterns of oppression within ourselves if we are to move beyond the most superficial aspects of social change. Now we must recognize differences among women who are our equals, neither inferior nor superior, and devise ways to use each other's difference to enrich our visions and our joint struggles.

The future of our earth may depend upon the ability of all women to identify and develop new definitions of power and new patterns of relating across difference. The old definitions have not served us, nor the earth that supports us. The old patterns, no matter how cleverly rearranged to imitate progress, still condemn us to cosmetically altered repetitions of the same old exchanges, the same old guilt, hatred, recrimination, lamentation, and suspicion.

For we have, built into all of us, old blueprints of expectations and response, old structures of oppression, and these must be altered at the same time as we alter the living conditions that are a result of those structures. For the master's tools will never dismantle the master's house.

As Paulo Freire shows so well in *The Pedagogy of the Oppressed*,[2] the true focus of revolutionary change is never merely the oppressive situations which we seek to escape, but that piece of the oppressor which is planted deep within each of us, and which knows only the oppressors' tactics, the oppressors' relationships.

Change means growth, and growth can be painful. But we sharpen self-definition by exposing the self in work and struggle together with those whom we define as different from ourselves, although sharing the same goals. For black and white, old and young, lesbian and heterosexual women alike, this can mean new paths to our survival.

We have chosen each other
and the edge of each others battles
the war is the same
if we lose
someday women's blood will congeal
upon a dead planet
if we win
there is no telling
we seek beyond history
for a new and more possible meeting.[3]   [1980]

NOTES

1. From "Rape: A Radical Analysis, An African-American Prespective," by Kalamu ya Salaam in *Black Books Bulletin*, vol. 6, no. 4 (1980)
2. Seabury Press, New York, 1970.
3. From "Ourlines," unpublished poem.

✿ 129

Fence Sitters, Switch Hitters, and Bi-Bi Girls: An Exploration of Hapa and Bisexual Identities

BEVERLY YUEN THOMPSON

I had been wondering about taking part in a student theatre project about being Asian American, and I said to Tommy, "The thing is, I don't feel as though I've really lived the . . . Asian American experience." (Whatever I thought that was.)

Tommy kind of looked at me. And he said, "But, Claire, you are Asian American. So whatever experience you have lived, that is the Asian American experience."

I have never forgotten that.
    —Claire Huang Kinsley, "Questions People Have
       Asked Me. Questions I Have Asked Myself"

Claire Huang Kinsley articulates a common sentiment among multiracial Asian Americans regarding their racial and ethnic identity: She describes the reaction that her mixed heritage has provoked from Asians and Anglos, both of whom frequently view her as the "other." In response to these reactions, her faith in her racial identity has been shaken, and she feels unable to identify herself—fearful of being alienated for choosing either her Chinese or Anglo heritage, or both. Although she knows that she is mixed race, the question that still plagues her is whether or not she is included in the term "Asian American."[1]

When I first read Kinsley's article, I was elated to find recognition of a biracial Asian American experience that resembled my own. I have a Chinese mother and an Anglo-American father, as does she, and I am constantly confronted with questions about my ethnic background from curious individuals. Like Kinsley, I also question my ability to call myself Asian American because of my mixed heritage. However, in addition to my mixed heritage, I am also bisexual, which brings with it additional complications and permutations around

my identity formation and self-understanding. The process of identity formation, especially of multiple identities, is complex and lifelong, and my experiences have been no exception.

Though I have always understood that I was mixed race, a true understanding of what this meant in terms of my self-understanding and my relation to the dominant culture and Asian American communities did not develop until I was much older. My first exposure to the political side of identity politics came at the ages of 14 and 15 when I began to develop a feminist understanding of the world around me. Then, at 17, I first began to call myself bisexual after two years of questioning my sexuality and believing that the only options that were available were either a lesbian or straight identity. Finally at the age of 19 I began to uncover the history of Asians in America through my college course work and developed a newfound understanding of my racial identity and its political implications. Yet, as is usually the case, this process was never as linear as it may sound.

Growing up, I was very aware that I was both Chinese and white—but I did not possess a term or racial category that recognized my position. Instead of creating or claiming a category that would accommodate me, I was left in confusion. How was it possible that I existed outside of the racial order of the census forms in my grade school, and what would I have to do in order to correctly fill in the answer to my racial puzzle? This confusion led to great discussions with my father about how I should identify myself. Well-meaning as he was, the only answer that he could arrive at was to choose between the two. This answer did not satisfy me because it would imply that I would be choosing between my parents—a choice I could not make.

Multiracials of Asian descent have a variety of choices available for self-identification; however, this "choice" may become obscured by others who may be quick to categorize based upon their own monoracial template of racial understanding. Physical traits are frequently scrutinized as ethnic signifiers, and one's mixed-race identity may not be accepted by outsiders. Maria P. P. Root elaborates:

> To assume that the biracial person will racially identify with how they look is presumptive, but pervasive. Besides, the biracial person is perceived differently by different people. Many persons make the mistake of thinking the biracial person is fortunate to have a choice; however, the reality is that the biracial person has to fight very hard to exercise choices that are not congruent with how they may be visually or emotionally perceived.[2]

Biracials and multiracials, then, develop a racial identity that risks criticism or denial from others; this influences the ways in which they self-identify, which may change in different contexts. When faced with the "What are you?" question, multiracials may try and consider what the person is really asking and respond accordingly. Racial fluidity is difficult to "see" in a world constructed by mutually exclusive categories based on a black–white dichotomy.

When I was growing up in white-dominated Spokane, Washington, I spent most of my childhood, like most children, trying to fit in. My racial identity would raise its head occasionally, but most of the time I did not consider race. However, I did spend a great deal of energy rejecting my Chinese heritage, which I thought would certainly differentiate me from my white classmates. I would not allow my mother to teach me Chinese, which she attempted to do; I made fun of the Chinese food in the restaurants where she would take us; and I identified more and more with my father, whose side I would take when he belittled my mother's culture and "superstitions." I thought that if I did not speak Chinese then I could use that as proof that I really was white like everyone else. However, when we did end up in Seattle's Chinatown on vacation, I was secretly proud and impressed that my mother could speak in Chinese to the waitresses and would beg her to do so.

When my racial identity was used against me by my peers in school, it was an upsetting experience. One day in my grade school the other children began teasing me and a classmate, Michael, who was Chinese. Based on our racial similarities,

they joked that we were dating. I was horrified to have my classmates group me with this Chinese boy. I took offense, and from that moment on I tried to distance myself from Michael. I thought that if I were friends with him then the Chinese in me would be brought to the surface—made more obvious—and that would be the reason we were friends. There were only three Asians in my grade school, and we were two of them; the only other was my best friend, Cassie, who was also hapa, or of mixed Asian/Pacific Islander descent.[3] Cassie had a white mother and a Japanese father who owned a Japanese restaurant downtown and was therefore never around her house at the same time as any of her friends. She passed as white and, without her father around to connote her Japanese ancestry, her identity was never at issue. Curiously, never once in my eight-year friendship with her did we ever discuss our similar racial identities.

When a few years later I began reading feminist books, I developed a feminist consciousness that consumed all aspects of my life. It fundamentally changed the way I understood myself and the world around me. I was ignited and passionate, seeking out feminist organizations where I could take part in concrete actions around my political philosophy. Yet the literature I read lacked a racial analysis, and this carried over into my developing consciousness. I had moved to Seattle to attend college, and I became active with NOW, Clinic Defense Project, a youth socialist organization, and a queer youth group based in Spokane. I traveled between Seattle and Spokane a great deal and was politically active in both cities. I began to meet many people whose politics and sexual orientation were diverse, and I questioned my own long-held beliefs. My new roommate came out as a lesbian, and we learned a great deal about each other through that experience. She was also a hapa—mixed Hawaiian, Filipina, and white—and she would attempt to engage in racial identity conversations, but that topic did not hold me as much as discussions of politics and sexuality. I had begun to question my sexual orientation: I no longer proclaimed myself heterosexual, yet neither did I adopt a lesbian identity.

As I had years earlier agonized between the choice of seeing myself as Chinese or white, I now agonized between the choice of lesbian or straight. I knew that neither choice represented my feelings, yet I could not comprehend another option. The messages that I received from both the lesbian community and dominant straight society were the same: choose. When I was in college, at around the age of 17, I realized that bisexuality existed as an option, and immediately I knew that was the identity that most accurately described who I felt I was. But I also knew that claiming a bisexual identity would be a hardship because others would analyze me through their monosexual template of understanding. Indeed I ran across many people who demanded to know, "Which do you really like better, boys or girls?" This question reminded me of how my ethnic identity had often elicited the query, "What are you?" People were again confused. Now both my racial and sexual identity crossed lines of demarcation, enacting border-crossings that people have assumed are unnatural and problematic.

Root suggests that the "racially mixed woman may be more open to exploring sexual orientation" because of their lived experience of understanding racial identity as complex. Therefore, this understanding of racial identity may "transfer over to viewing sexual orientation as flexible and sexual identity as mutable."[4] Throughout my life I have had to explain my racial identity instead of having an easy and ready-made label like most monoracials. Yet, besides the occasional difficulty of explaining my race, I also enjoyed being more than one, having more options, and enjoying the benefit of traveling in more than one group. Now with my emerging sexuality, bisexuality seemed the natural conclusion. Already I was racially mixed and therefore I could understand the meaning of a bisexual identity in my own life. Somehow it all came together in a complementary fashion.

After I had come out as bisexual I began to embrace my Asian heritage and accept it back into my life. I was in my senior year at Eastern Washington University, and I began to focus my research on Asian American women and their history. Yet, it was not until I went to graduate school in women's studies at San Diego State University that I gained greater exposure to Asian American culture and history. It was an awakening that I compare to the development of my feminist consciousness. I was both excited to find the material and angered that it had taken so long to discover Asian American history. I wrote on the Japanese internment, studied Chinese American history, and read every Asian American studies book I could find.

Slowly I discovered that, although I could relate to some of the issues and material, my reality as a young bisexual hapa woman was not being addressed. I began to question the place of the multiracial Asian in the academic fields of ethnic studies and women's studies. Ethnic studies seemed to focus overwhelmingly on families that fit a specific model—namely, a heterosexual family made up of two immigrant parents of the same ethnicity and the conflicts their children face negotiating between their Asian parents and Anglo society. In women's studies, there was an awareness and commentary on race and difference among women, but that usually focused on the black–white racial dichotomy; Asian American women were rarely mentioned. Where was I to find myself represented in academic theory that claimed to represent women and racial minorities? As I studied further, however, I became aware that I was not the only one grappling with these issues: There were hapa groups forming around the country as well as magazines and books that were addressing this issue and demanding acceptance within the Asian American community and academy.[5]

My challenge in graduate school, as I saw it, was to explore where I could find myself reflected, with all my complexity, in the literature of ethnic studies and women's studies. As Dana Y. Takagi suggests, it is crucial to recognize "different sexual practices and identities that also claim the label Asian American" in order to begin to challenge notions of identity that have, in the past, been accepted "unproblematically and uncritically in Asian American Studies."[6] Within the "Asian American experience" there is a great deal of diversity that has thus far remained underexplored. Issues of interracial relationships, transracial adoption, biracial identity, and queer identity have remained marginalized and considered exceptions to an unspoken norm of Asian American identity. David Eng and Alice Horn believe it is imperative "to recognize that Asian Americans are never purely, or merely, racial subjects" and to dissolve any rigid or monolithic definitions.[7] Once monolithic norms are instituted, diversity and complexity are shut out and remain excluded.

I have seen these norms instituted in a variety of ways within identity-based groups in my experiences. Organizations and literature on identity de-emphasize aspects that are not considered directly related to the main unifying force they address. I have found myself continuing this silence when in group situations because of the offhanded manner in which comments regarding these other aspects are received. For example, I have usually found myself to be the only Asian American in queer organizations; therefore I feel uncomfortable bringing attention to racial issues because this would presumably turn me into both an object of curiosity and an educator. I prefer to discuss racial issues with others who have similar experiences so that we can share on an equal basis and validate each other in respectful and mutual ways. At the same time, when I am in organizations that focus on racial identity, I also feel silence around sexual identity because, again, I do not want to position myself as an object or educator. In other words, I do not want to detract from my connection with others. Unfortunately, connection is usually based on one issue with other aspects of identity being minimized instead of validated.[8]

Segregating multiple identities in theories of race and gender results in fracturing self-understanding—separating one's gender from race and sexuality. This segregation is also an impossibility: At any moment we inhabit all of our identities and may face discrimination on any or all levels. It is a painful experience to seek out a community based on race, gender, or sexuality only to have other identities denied and rejected. As Karen Maeda Allman reasons, "Mixed-race lesbians may be suspicious of any kind of identity politics based on single-group membership, whether based on race, gender, or sexual orientation.

Too many opportunities exist to exclude us, to declare us as suspect others."[9] When people of color come out as queer, race is an important consideration. Rejection from one's racial/ethnic community based on homophobia, and from the queer community based on racism, is a very real consequence that may bar individuals from true acceptance in any specific community. As a hapa bisexual, I am constantly seeking out inclusion and acceptance of my sexuality in the Asian American community as well as acceptance of my racial identity in the bisexual and queer community.

Paula C. Rust comments that "a positive integration of one's racial, ethnic, or class identity with one's sexual identity is greatly facilitated by support from others who share an individual's particular constellation of identities."[10] The first time I experienced being around others with my "constellation of identities" was when I attended the second national conference of the Asian and Pacific-Islander Lesbian and Bisexual Women's Network at UCLA in July of 1998. One of the workshops at this conference was titled "Mixed Girls in the Mix: Hapas, Mixed Breeds, and Other Racial Misfits." Attending this session was a homecoming for me. Never before had I sat in a room filled with hapas who were both bisexual and lesbian. Of the 20-plus attendees at the workshop, there was a vast array of racial and ethnic diversity. Half of the women were Asian and white, while the other half of the room represented a great diversity of mixed-race hapa women. We explored and discussed numerous issues, and for many of us it was an amazing and eye-opening experience merely to be around other women with whom we had so much in common—and yet still so much in difference. The workshop went overtime, making it very evident that this group needed more time together. Therefore the group decided to create a hapa caucus. Later that evening when the caucuses met, some of the women chose to go to the caucus groups of their ethnicities and some returned to the hapa caucus; we again had to choose between identifying as hapa over our monoethnic options.

I met several women in this newly formed caucus who also identified as both biracial and bisexual.

When I mentioned that I was doing research on biracial and bisexual Asian women, one of the women exclaimed, "The bi-bi girls!" and went on to explain that she herself was a "bi-bi girl" as were some of her friends. I was overflowing with excitement to meet someone who shared my same "constellation of identities" and had even coined a term for this identity.

Rust speaks to this topic of the "bi-bi" identity:

> Many bisexuals of mixed race or ethnicity feel a comfortable resonance between their mixed heritage and their bisexuality. In a society where both racial-ethnic and sexual categories are highly elaborated, individuals of mixed heritage or who are bisexual find themselves straddling categories that are socially constructed as distinct from one another.[11]

Rust captures the ideological and theoretical similarities of bisexual and multiracial identities in this passage, echoing my own experiences of these two identities. Because of the exclusion bisexuals and biracials experience in monoracial and monosexual communities, different responses result when these mixed identities come together in the same individual. For some, this combination brings a sense of familiarity, of being once again outside of the box, of confusing people. Others, however, may be disappointed that they are again marginalized, unwilling to deal with further oppression.

When I think that I must choose between another set of boxes—straight or lesbian—I feel the same pressure and the same inability as I felt choosing between white and Chinese, between my mother and my father. My choice was made for me. It was written on my skin; my face and gestures reflect both parents who made me. And the choice of who I love is decided for me: I love both my mother and my father and will never deny love and acceptance for someone based on their gender or race. Marian M. Sciachitano believes that "taking up a bicultural and biracial politics of difference" means accepting "the contradictions, the uneasiness, and the ambiguity" of such an identity, which may also apply to a bisexual label and the interaction of the two.[12] Yet the contradictions, uneasiness, and ambiguity are imposed from the outside and arise

when I must fit myself into the established mutually exclusive order. For myself, I find comfort in the middle ground, in the ability to transgress and question lines of demarcation and challenge systematic segregation.

I am hapa because I am the descendent of two cultures, two languages, and two people who came together across these boundaries. I am firmly located in the late twentieth century in the United States where interracial marriages have only been legal for a generation. I am one of many people who are hapa, Amerasian, mixed breeds, and mutts. I am constantly called Japanese, Korean, Chinese, Oriental. I am comfortable in other people's discomfort. I am hurt that I denied my mother a proper place in my life. She has divorced my father and has gone to live with Chinese female friends from her childhood, her other life within which I will never be truly included. When I visit her I am left out of the conversation, but the sound of Cantonese soothes me. Sometimes when I pay attention I realize that I am able to follow their body language and remember some Chinese words, but it is the English phrases that are a part of their Chinese American vocabulary that always give me the final gist. I am loyal to my Chinese heritage, I am loyal to my white heritage, and I am loyal to my antiracist beliefs.

I am bisexual because I recognize that both women and men have contributed to my life and I want the freedom to choose a partner based on a person's integrity rather than on genitalia. I am firmly located not only in a time when queer people are oppressed but also in a time when a vital queer community has developed that gives me the ability to understand what that identity means. I am one of many people who are bisexual, queer, fence sitters, and switch hitters. I am called queer, dyke, straight. I am comfortable in other people's discomfort. I am loyal to my love for women, I am loyal to my love for men, and I am loyal to my beliefs in feminism and antiheterosexism.

The question that still lingers in my mind is who will be loyal to me? Which group/community/movement(s) will claim me as their member and comrade? I want to see a movement against oppression that does not trivialize or deny me any aspect of my identity, that recognizes the interconnectedness of my sexuality, race, gender, and politics. I am one of many people whose fight against oppression does not end with their gender, race, or sexuality alone. I am reminded of the words of Teresa Kay Williams:

> One day, the debate on passing will become obsolete (will pass), when Asian-descent multiracials can express the full range of their humanity in which boundaries of race, ethnicity; nation, class, gender, sexuality, body, and language can be crossed and transgressed without judgement, without scorn, and without detriment.[13]

I find a great deal of comfort reading these words by authors whose identities are similar to my own. I know that I am not alone in this world that consistently tries to deny the existence of multiracials and bisexuals. Merely by existing I am challenging stereotypes and the status quo. This battle against racism, sexism, and bi/homophobia is being fought on many fronts by people who are like me, people who have my back.   [2000]

NOTES

1. Claire Huang Kinsley, "Questions People Have Asked Me. Questions I Have Asked Myself," in *Miscegenation Blues: Voices of Mixed Race Women,* ed. Carol Camper (Toronto: Sister Vision Press, 1994), 113–32.
2. Maria P. P. Root, "Resolving 'Other' Status: Identity Development of Biracial Individuals," in *Diversity and Complexity in Feminist Therapy,* ed. Laura S. Brown and Maria P. P. Root (New York: Harrington Park Press, 1990), 197, original emphasis.
3. A term of Hawaiian origin, hapa haole literally means "half outsider" or half white. Although it was originally used as an insult, it is currently being used on the mainland by Asian/Pacific Islanders as a positive term designating those who are mixed race of Asian/Pacific Islander descent.
4. Root, "Resolving 'Other' Status," 185, original emphasis.
5. Overwhelmingly I find that Asian American literature does not mention nonheterosexual identities, which continues to promote invisibility for queer Asians. A few notable exceptions are Russell Leong, ed., *Asian American Sexualities: Dimensions of the Gay and Lesbian Experience* (New York: Routledge, 1996); Sharon Lim-Hing, ed., *The Very Inside: An Anthology of Writings by Asian and Pacific Islander Lesbian and Bisexual Women* (Toronto: Sister Vision Press, 1994); and David L. Eng and Alice Y. Hom, eds., *Q & A: Queer in Asian America* (Philadelphia: Temple University Press, 1998).

6. Dana Y. Takagi, "Maiden Voyage: Excursion into Sexuality and Identity Politics in Asian America," *Amerasia Journal* 20, no. 1 (1994): 2.
7. David L. Eng and Alice Y. Hom, "Introduction: Q & A: Notes on a Queer Asian America," in Eng and Hom, Q & A, 3.
8. I did discover, however, an emerging discussion on multiple identities and their necessary inclusion in feminist research. Through such books as Gloria Anzaldua, ed., *Making Face, Making Soul/Haciendo Caras: Creative and Critical Perspectives by Feminists of Color* (San Francisco: Aunt Lute, 1990); Gloria Anzaldua and Cherrie Moraga, *This Bridge Called My Back: Writings by Radical Women of Color* (Watertown, MA: Persephone Press, 1981); and Asian Women United of California, ed., *Making Waves: An Anthology of Writings by and About Asian American Women* (Boston: Beacon Press, 1989), the voices of women of color and lesbians are emerging. Indeed, the postmodern phase we are in has pushed the concept of difference to buzz word status. Yet, although frequently mentioned, difference is yet to be completely integrated.
9. Karen Maeda Allman, "(Un)Natural Boundaries: Mixed Race, Gender, and Sexuality," in *The Multiracial Experience: Racial Borders as the New Frontier,* ed. Maria P. P. Root (Thousand Oaks, CA: Sage, 1996), 287, emphasis original.
10. Paula C. Rust, "Managing Multiple Identities: Diversity Among Bisexual Women and Men," in *Bisexualilty: The Psychology and Politics of an Invisible Minority,* ed. Beth A. Firestein (Thousand Oaks, CA: Sage, 1996), 254.
11. Rust, "Managing Multiple Identities," 69–70.
12. Marian M. Sciachitano, "Claiming a Politics of Biracial Asian American Difference," in *A Gathering of Voices on the Asian American Experience,* ed. Annette White-Parks et al. (Fort Atkinson, WL: Highsmith Press, 1994), 52.
13. Teresa Kay Williams, "Race-ing and Being Raced: The Critical Interrogation of 'Passing,'" *Amerasia Journal* 23, no. 1 (1997): 64.

 130

Boundaries: Arab/American

LISA SUHAIR MAJAJ

One evening a number of years ago, at a workshop on racism, I became aware—in one of those moments of realization that is not a definitive falling into place, but instead a slow groundswell of understanding—of the ways in which I experience my identity as not merely complex, but rather an uninterpretable excess.

Workshop participants were asked to group ourselves in the center of the room. As the facilitator called out a series of categories, we crossed to one side of the room or the other, according to our self-identification: white or person of color, heterosexual or lesbian/bisexual, middle/upper-class or working-class, born in the United States or in another country, at least one college-educated parent or parents with no higher education, English as a native language or a second language. Although I am used to thinking of myself in terms of marginality and difference, I found myself, time after time, on the mainstream side of the room. White (as I called myself for lack of a more appropriate category), heterosexual, middle-class, born in the United States to a college-educated parent, a native speaker of English, I seemed to be part of America's presumed majority.

I learned a great deal that night about how much I take for granted those aspects of my life that locate me in a privileged sphere. It is a lesson of which I remain acutely conscious, and for which I am grateful. But looking across the room at the cluster of women representing what American society understands as "other," I was disconcerted by the lack of fit between the definitions offered that evening and my personal reality. Born in the United States, I have nonetheless lived much of my life outside it, in Jordan and Lebanon. My father was college-educated and middle-class, but Palestinian—hardly an identity suggestive of inclusion in mainstream American society. I considered myself white: my olive-tinged skin, while an asset in terms of acquiring a ready tan, did not seem a dramatic marker of difference. But I have received enough comments on my skin tone to make me aware that this is not entirely a neutral issue—and as I have learned the history of colonialism in the Arab world, I have come to understand the ways in which even light-skinned Arabs are people of color. Native speaker of English, I grew up alienated from the linguistic medium—Arabic—that swirled around me, living a life in some ways as marginal as that of a non-English speaker in the United States. Although I do not think of myself as having an accent, I have more than once been assumed to be foreign; I speak with an intonation acquired from the British-inflected Jordanian English that delineated my childhood, or from years of the careful enunciation one adopts when addressing non-native speakers. I have been the target of various forms of harassment specifically linked to my Arab identity, from hostile comments to threatening phone calls, racist mail, and destruction of property. I have feared physical assault when wearing something that identifies me as an Arab. And so, standing on the majority side of the room that evening, observing the discrepancy between the facts of my life and the available categories of inclusion and exclusion, I could not help but wonder whether these categories are insufficient, or insufficiently nuanced. . . .

I discovered soon enough that being Arab in the United States—worse, being Palestinian—offers little in the way of reassurance. My hopeful belief that moving to the United States would be a homecoming was quickly shaken. Once I claimed a past, spoke my history, told my name, the walls of incomprehension and hostility rose, brick by brick: un-funny "ethnic" jokes, jibes about terrorists and kalashnikovs, about veiled women and camels; or worse, the shifts to other subjects. Searching for images of my Arab self in American culture I found only unrecognizable stereotypes. In the face of such incomprehension I could say nothing.

But I have grown weary of my silence and paranoia; my fear that if I wear a Palestinian emblem, a *kaffiyeh,* use my few words of Arabic, say my name and where I am from, I will open myself to suspicion or hatred. l am tired of being afraid to speak who I am: American and Palestinian, not merely half of one thing and half of another, but both at once—and in that inexplicable melding that occurs when two cultures come together, not quite either, so that neither American nor Arab find themselves fully reflected in me, nor I in them.

Perhaps it should not have surprised me to cross and recross that room of divisions and find myself nowhere. . . .

★ ★ ★

In my experience cultural marginality has been among the most painful of alienations. My childhood desire, often desperate, was not so much to be a particular nationality, to be American or Arab, but to be wholly one thing or another: to be *something* that I and the rest of the world could understand, categorize, label, predict. Although I spent years struggling to define my personal politics of location, I remained situated somewhere between Arab and American cultures—never quite rooted in either, always constrained by both. My sense of liminality grew as I became more aware of the rigid nature of definitions: Arab culture simultaneously claimed and excluded me, while the American identity I longed for retreated inexorably from my grasp.

My experiences in the United States in many ways reinforced this sense of exclusion. Upon arriving in Michigan for graduate school, after four years at the American University of Beirut during which both my American and Palestinian identities had been inevitably politicized, I yearned, yet again, for the simplicity of belonging. Consciously drawing as little attention as possible to my name, my family, my background, I avoided Middle Eastern organizations, and made no Arab friends at all. A few days after my arrival in the United States, when a man asked me provocatively why I wore a "map of Israel" around my neck, I answered briefly that it was a map of historic Palestine and then retreated from his attempts to draw me into debate, shrinking deep into a cocoon of silence.

"Passing demands a desire to become invisible," writes Michelle Cliff. "A ghost-life. An ignorance of connections."* While the incidents that first made me afraid to reveal myself in the United States were minor—pointed questions, sidelong glances, awkward silences—they were enough to thrust me firmly back into a desire for invisibility. I sought anonymity, as if trying to erode the connections that had brought me, juncture by juncture, to where and who I was, the product of histories I could no more undo than I could undo my bone structure.

But passing, as I was to learn, wreaks implicit violence upon the lived reality of our experiences. "Passing demands quiet," Cliff warns. "And from

that quiet—silence." I have learned to understand silence as something insidious. As a child, lost between the contradictory demands of the worlds I moved between, I claimed silence as a tool of survival; I honed it still further in my American context. What I did not then realize was that silence, with time, atrophies the voice—a loss with such grave consequences that it is a form of dispossession. Silence made it possible for me to blend into my surroundings, chameleonlike; it enabled me to absorb without self-revelation what I needed to know. But its implications were disastrous. Silence wrapped itself around my limbs like cotton wool, wound itself into my ears and eyes, filled my mouth and muffled my throat. I do not know at what point I began to choke. Perhaps there was never a single incident, just a slow deposition of sediment over time. Until one day, retching, I spat out some unnameable substance. And I attempted to speak.

By this time I was beginning to claim the tools of feminism. In Beirut I had pored over a copy of *The Feminine Mystique,* startled by the wave of recognition it evoked. Later, graduate school exposed me to the analytical training and the affirmation of voice that I had been lacking. Although I eventually discovered its cultural insensibilities, American feminism enabled me to begin interrogating the entanglement of gender and culture in a search for my own definitions. While much in my experience had tempted me to reject Arab culture as misogynist, my growing awareness of the ways in which my experiences represented not Arab culture per se, but a conflicted interaction between Arab and American, led me to explore my Palestinian background for positive symbols, not just nationalistic but gendered, on which to draw for identification and strength.

This exploration reinforced my acute awareness of the representation and misrepresentation of Arab culture in the United States. There are ways in which Palestinian women escape the typical stereotypes of Arab women—exotic, sensualized, victimized—only to be laden with the more male-coded, or perhaps merely generic, images of irrational terrorists and pathetic refugees. But none of these images reflect the Arab women I know: my

---

*Michelle Cliff, *Claiming an Identity They Taught Me to Despise* (Watertown, MA: Persephone Press, 1980), 5.

widowed Palestinian grandmother, who raised three boys and buried two girls, raising two grandchildren as well after their mother was killed by a Zionist group's bomb, whose strength and independence people still speak of with awe; or my Lebanese aunt, a skilled nurse, who ran a Jerusalem hospital ward for years, raised four children, gracefully met the social requirements of her husband's busy political and medical careers, and now directs a center for disabled children. My increasing anger at the portrayal of the Middle East as a chaotic realm outside the boundaries of rational Western comprehension, and a slowly developing confidence in my own political and cultural knowledge, came together with my burgeoning feminism to make possible an articulation that, although tentative, was more empowering than anything I had experienced.

At some point I began to feel anger. At the jokes about *kalashnikovs* in my backpack, grenades in my purse. At the sheer amazement of a woman who asked my mother, "But why did you marry a terrorist?" At an acquaintance's incredulous look when I spoke of Arab feminism. At the comments that it must be dangerous to live in Jordan "because of all the terrorism." At the college professor who did not believe that Arabs could be Christians. At the knowledge that when I posted announcements of Arab cultural events on campus they would be torn down moments later. At the look of shock and dismay, quickly masked, on the face of a new acquaintance just learning of my Palestinian background. At the startled response of someone who, having assumed my Arab name to be my spouse's, learned that I chose to keep an *Arab* name. At the conversations in which I am forced to explain that Palestinians do indeed exist; that they claim a long history in Palestine.

And with the anger has come fear. Of the unknown person in my apartment building who intercepted packages I had ordered from an Arab-American organization, strewing their contents, defaced with obscenities, at my door. Of the hostility of airport security personnel once they know my destination or origin point: the overly thorough searches, the insistent questions. Of the anonymous person who dialed my home after I was

interviewed by my local paper, shouting "Death to Palestinians!" Of the unsigned, racist mail. Of the mysterious hit-and-run driver who smashed my car as it was parked on a quiet residential street, a Palestine emblem clearly visible through the window of the car door.

Such actions inscribe their subjects within a singular, predetermined identity, and often elicit responses validating precisely this identity. However, such exclusionary identification remains, finally untenable. During the Gulf War a radio commentator proclaimed, "In war there are no hyphenated Americans, just Americans and non-Americans." It is a familiar, and chilling, sentiment: Japanese-Americans in particular can speak to its implications. But what is to become of those of us in-between, those of us who are neither "just" Americans, nor "just" non-Americans? I could say that I opposed the Gulf War as a human being first, as an American second, and only third as a Palestinian. But in fact my identities cannot be so neatly divided. I am never just an American, any more than I am just a Palestinian. Yet I am not therefore any less of an American, or less of a Palestinian. As I was rarely given the choice in the Middle East to claim or not claim my American identity, so I am not often given the choice in my American context to be or not to be Palestinian. At best I can attempt to pass, suppressing my identity and resorting to silence. And when this strategy fails—*or when I reject it*—then I am forced to take responsibility for *both* American and Palestinian histories in their contradictory entireties—histories articulated through idealism, but resorting too often to violence. And in so doing I come to a fuller understanding of the contradictions, the excesses, which spill over the neat boundaries within which I am often expected to, and sometimes long to, reside. . . .

★ ★ ★

I claim the identity "Arab-American" not as a heritage passed from generation to generation, but rather as an ongoing negotiation of difference. My parents articulated their relationship oppositionally, assumptions colliding as they confronted each other's cultural boundaries. Child of their contradictions, I seek to transform that conflict into a constant motion testing the lines that encircle and embrace me, protect and imprison me. I am caught within a web: lines fade and reappear, forming intricate patterns, a maze. I live at borders that are always overdetermined, constantly shifting. Gripped by the logic of translation, I still long to find my reflection on either side of the cultural divide. But the infinitely more complex web of music beckons, speaking beyond, translation. Who can say how this will end?   [1994]

🌿 131

Why Race Matters to a White Dyke

NELL GEISER

We all have to pick our battles. Even though I'm queer and I look butch, I'm not involved in any campus LGBTQ organizations. Sure, I go to the Dyke March in June, hang out at lesbian clubs on the weekend, and watch The L Word (I admit it)—but queerness on its own isn't enough to get me fired up politically. On the other hand, I deeply respect many people who work primarily within queer communities because they understand that queerness is an inherently political identity and is an important basis for organizing.

Queerness is the identity that I've defined for myself on my own terms. Yet, if I made a list of all the social categories into which I fit, it's only one of many: female, upper-middle class, U.S. citizen, able-bodied, white. At Columbia University, I've found that it's actually my whiteness that matters most to me politically. While the university claims to care a lot about diversity, this lip service doesn't extend to much of the curriculum, campus environment, or financial aid policies. Understanding race and racism is thus key to understanding power and privilege on my campus.

Through taking Ethnic Studies courses, I've learned that race is a socially constructed category that has been used historically to marginalize and oppress people racialized as nonwhite. As a white person grappling with race, I've chosen to avoid the false security of colorblindness. Instead of trying to close my eyes to the race of my friends and insist that "we're all just human," I work to understand what racial identity means for them—both the negative experiences of stereotyping and marginalization and the positive experiences of community, culture and resistance.

Queerness sets me apart and gives me some insight into W. E. B. DuBois's question to black Americans, "How does it feel to be a problem?" To me, it feels really good to be a wrench in the machinery of heterosexual supremacy. Sometimes it's also hard to be seen as a freak.

On the other hand, whiteness grants me access to mind-numbing normalcy and privilege. It's scary, but one of the effects of whiteness as it's lived in America is that white people grow up without knowing how race works. That's a bad thing, because race is really powerful and shapes all of our lives. If we can't detect the way it operates in our daily lives and in society, we won't be able to work effectively against racism. Since I've always had the privileges of whiteness, it would be easy to slip into complacency and urge my friends of color not to make such a big deal out of race. Yet they experience racism everyday and are much more likely to understand that institutions are set up to favor white people. White people can get loans more easily than people of color, walk through a store without being followed, and get angry without being perceived as dangerous. White people aren't forced to be aware of this.

The problem is, most young people are taught that if they work hard, they'll succeed, no matter what their background. And then, when we white people succeed in disproportionately high numbers because of institutionalized racism, we pat ourselves on the back and tell our children that same tired story about meritocracy.

But we know that story is wrong. It doesn't take into account that white people still have a massive amount of unearned privilege just because of our perceived racial identity. Class, gender, and sexuality are also important, but race is a key factor in determining economic status to begin with. According to United for a Fair Economy (www.faireconomy .org), white people in the United States earned an average of 161 percent of what black people earned in 2003, and the median net worth (assets minus debt) of a person of color was only 14 percent that of a white person in 2001.

That's not just the slowly eroding legacy of past injustices; it's the continually reproduced inequality in education, jobs, inheritance, housing, and other key indicators. It's also the failure of antidiscrimination laws to address the real problems of institutional racism or to give us the language to talk about race. According to the logic of the law, only racists talk about race. The Fourteenth Amendment's guarantee of equal protection under the law has been interpreted by post–Civil Rights Movement courts to mean that implementing race-conscious laws in order to *undermine* racial disparities is actually a slippery slope toward racist practice.

This race-neutral, or colorblind, posture in civil rights law, brought about through struggles for racial justice culminating in *Brown v. Board of Education,* has been deployed specifically to undermine affirmative action. According to the courts, one of the only times we're allowed to talk about race is when we condemn institutions for using race as a factor in selecting students or employees. Thus instead of addressing continued racial inequality and making equal opportunity a reality, colorblindness functions to protect the privileges of white people. We can't let ourselves off the hook through colorblindness. Men often ignore how sexism gives them privileges, but we don't let them claim a "gender neutral" defense of their chauvinism.

So how do we get race on the table? I turn back to my experience as a queer woman to figure that out. As an outsider in the arena of sexuality, I'm always aware of my queerness. When I walk down the street and someone refers to me as "sir," or when my grandmother asks whether I have a boyfriend and I demur, I'm made aware that sexuality shapes our lives, from the macro-structures of society to the micro-interactions of daily life. Straight people don't have to think about this fact. Yet sometimes they do, and often they become better activists and intellectuals because of that critical consciousness.

Similarly, white people can make the choice to cultivate critical consciousness when it comes to race. The first step to understanding privilege and oppression is to think about how your own identity is implicated. As a white person, I think about how privilege might allow me to talk a lot in class, to receive preferential treatment in a job interview, and to ignore the role of race in my life if I so choose.

People of color are forced to think about race all the time—they're tokenized, profiled, and made to represent their race. If white people want to become a little more hip to the nefarious machinations of racism, I would suggest that we become more race conscious. We need to think about how the normative privileges that come with whiteness might be at play in our everyday lives and in large institutional structures. We need to acknowledge the way we benefit from institutional racism whether we want to or not, rather than depending on friends who are people of color to explain the mystery of race to us. Among my queer friends, I'm very much aware of race. As a white dyke, my queerness is conditioned by my whiteness and I don't feel like an effective activist unless I am aware of both of those identities and realities.   [2006]

✶ 132

Friday Night

LINDA HOGAN

Sometimes I see a light in her kitchen
that almost touches mine,
and her shadow falls straight
through trees and peppermint
and lies down at my door
like it wants to come in.

Never mind that on Friday nights
she slumps out her own torn screen
and lies down crying on the stoop.
And don't ask about the reasons;
she pays her penalties for weeping.

Emergency Room:
Eighty dollars to knock a woman out.
And there are laughing red-faced neighbor men
who put down their hammers
to phone the county.
Her crying tries them all.
Don't ask for reasons
why they do not collapse
outside their own tight jawbones
or the rooms they build
a tooth and nail at a time.

Never mind she's Mexican
and I'm Indian
and we have both replaced the words

to the national anthem with our own.
Or that her house smells of fried tortillas
and mine of Itchko and sassafras.

Tonight she was weeping in the safety of moonlight
and red maples.
I took her a cup of peppermint tea,
and honey,
it was fine blue china
with marigolds growing inside the curves.
In the dark, under the praying mimosa
we sat smoking little caves of tobacco light,
me and the *Señora of Hysteria*, who said
Peppermint is every bit as good as the ambulance.
And I said, Yes. It is home grown.   [1985]

CHAPTER VII
Violence Against Women

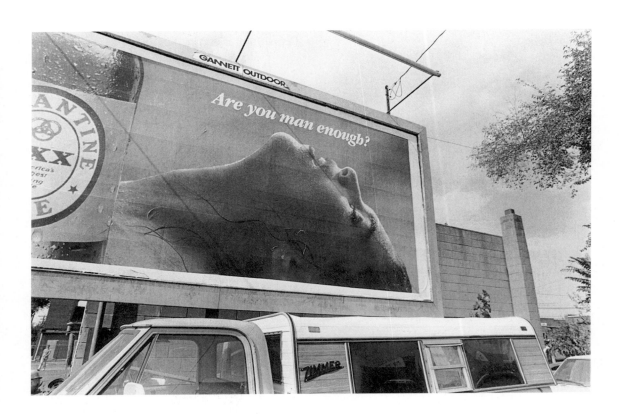

In the past 30 years, research on violence against women has demonstrated that women of all backgrounds have experienced violence, often at the hands of men they love. In fact, the far-ranging physical and emotional consequences of violence against women make it a major public health and criminal justice concern in the United States.[1] Whether in the form of rape, domestic violence, or childhood sexual abuse, violence against women represents an abuse of power in a misogynist culture. When violence occurs in the family, as in the case of domestic violence and incest, a cloak of privacy surrounds it, frequently silencing its victims. The feminist insistence on the political nature of private life enabled women to talk about the experience of violence, revealing how widespread it was and shattering the myths surrounding it.

The roots of domestic violence, sometimes referred to as "intimate partner violence," lie in the soil of the patriarchal family. The belief that a wife is the possession of a male "head of household" who should control the behavior of all other family members is deeply embedded in many social traditions. Women's disadvantaged position in the workforce and their continued responsibility for child raising reinforces their economic dependence on husbands and partners, making it difficult for women to leave abusive relationships. For years, domestic violence eluded the criminal justice system because police were reluctant to interfere in family life. Women who have been trained all their lives to believe that they should accommodate men's needs and fix any problems that arise in their relationships are often trapped in violent relationships by their own feelings of guilt and shame. Many women in abusive relationships have ambivalent feelings about their abuser. It is difficult to believe that a relationship created out of love has become abusive. While women often feel betrayed by men who abuse them, periods of relative harmony can reinforce women's belief that they can reform their abusers and rescue their relationships.

In the past three decades, women have organized to make the criminal justice system more effective in dealing with domestic violence by educating police and changing laws to ensure that women get the protection they need from law enforcement agencies. Because of the pervasiveness of technologies like cell phones and the Internet, shielding women from abusers is, in many cases, made more difficult today. The shelters and "safe houses" that have been created over the past three decades remain a central support system for women fleeing abusive relationships, and, in light of these now-commonplace technologies, vital to protecting women's privacy. Unfortunately, these shelters can temporarily house only a fraction of those who need them.

In 1996 the trial of O. J. Simpson, a star football player charged with the murder of his wife, Nicole Simpson, focused the country's attention on the prevalence of domestic violence as evidence of Simpson's violent treatment of Nicole surfaced during the trial. More recent high-profile instances of intimate partner violence,

---

[1]Patricia Tjaden and Nancy Thoennes, "Full Report of the Prevalence, Incidence, and Consequences of Violence Against Women," U.S. Department of Justice document NCJ 183781, November 2000.

like the abuse of singer Rihanna at the hands of Chris Brown, reveal that violence against women is more openly discussed than it has been in the recent past, and that victims today are more likely to know where to turn for help. Despite these advances, however, violence remains a part of the lives of far too many women and their children; recent statistics indicate that, every year, approximately 1.3 million U.S. women are physically assaulted by an intimate partner.[2]

Sexual violence affects the lives of all women. Fear of rape shapes women's behavior from girlhood, restricting their movement and limiting their freedom. This fear pervades both public and private spaces. The persistence of street harassment, for example, turns public spaces into hostile environments that exacerbate the fear of sexual violence and, ultimately, inhibit women's freedom. But despite the precautions women learn to take, thousands of women and girls are raped and molested each year. A national survey of women 18 years and older in the United States found that one in six women has been a victim of attempted or completed rape. Additionally, it was estimated that 876,064 women are raped each year in the United States, and the majority of them are raped by men they know (present or former spouse, boyfriend, or date).[3] Rape, however, is a grossly underreported crime. The FBI estimates that only about 16 percent of all rapes are reported. Overall, researchers acknowledge the difficulty of accurately assessing the prevalence of rape and suggest that, depending on how rape is defined, 20 to 27 percent of women have reported being victims of rape or attempted rape.[4]

In spite of its pervasiveness, women's experience of sexual violence was, until the late 1970s, rarely discussed in public. Susan Griffin's 1979 article, "Rape: The All-American Crime," broke the silence about rape and called attention to the ways that images of sexual violence pervade Western culture. Susan Brownmiller's comprehensive study, *Against Our Will*, continued this investigation, tracing the history of rape in Western culture and demonstrating that, far from being a problem of individual "psychopaths," sexual violence against women has been reinforced by our legal and criminal justice system, as well as prevailing ideas about gender and sexuality.[5] The belief that women are the sexual property of men was, until recently, embodied in state legal statutes that exempted married men from prosecution for raping their wives. As a result of pressure on state legislatures by feminist groups, by the late 1980s the last of the state marital rape exemption laws were repealed, making it illegal in all 50 states for a man to rape his wife.[6] The notion that women are responsible for male sexual behavior is reflected in the humiliating questions rape victims are often asked about their sexual histories and contributes to the low rate of conviction in rape trials. Such victim-blaming occurs not only in the courtroom but

---

[2]Ibid.

[3]Ibid.

[4]Maria Bevacqua, *Rape on the Public Agenda: Feminism and the Politics of Sexual Assault* (Boston: Northeastern University Press, 2000).

[5]Susan Brownmiller, *Against Our Will: Men, Women and Rape* (New York: Simon and Schuster, 1975).

[6]http://www.wellesley.edu/WCW/mrape.html.

also in everyday discourse, making it difficult for many rape survivors to come forward and press charges against their attackers. Feminist activism has resulted in the enactment of "rape shield laws," state statutes that prohibit defense attorneys from bringing the victim's sexual history into the court proceedings, but many state laws include exceptions that allow evidence of sexual relations between the victim and the accused to be presented in court.[7]

Racism has shaped the experience of rape in this culture, from the systematic rape of enslaved African-American women to the false charges of rape that were used as a pretext for lynching African-American men in the South in the late nineteenth and early twentieth century. African-American rape victims are less frequently believed by white juries, and African-American men are more frequently convicted. The popular myth of the black rapist obscures the realities that most rapes are committed by men who are of the same race as their victims, and that the majority of men arrested for rape in 2000 were white.[8]

Among the myriad misconceptions that surround the subject of rape is the notion that most rapes are committed by strangers. In fact, researchers estimate that 60 to 80 percent of all rapes are acquaintance rapes, many of which occur in dating situations. The traditions of sexual conquest, in which women are seen as sexual objects and male sexuality is assumed to be uncontrollable, make it particularly difficult for the victims of date rape to speak out and be taken seriously. Male culture on college campuses, particularly in fraternities, has encouraged the treatment of women as sexual prey and has celebrated male lust and conquest. The proliferation of drug-induced rape via Rohypnol, the "date rape drug," has increased women's fears of acquaintance rape. Wherever it occurs, rape is a powerful expression of women's subordinate status. To combat it demands asserting that women have a right to say no to unwanted sex and to be seen as sexual actors, not objects.

The sexual abuse of young girls by a trusted adult is another form of sexual violence that has surfaced in shocking proportions in recent years. Researchers estimate that one in four girls is a victim of childhood sexual abuse. Girls are often painfully confused when molested by an adult from whom they crave attention and approval. Feelings of betrayal often follow young women into adulthood, as they attempt to deal with the emotional consequences of abuse. Like the other forms of sexual violence, the molestation of girl children is an egregious violation of female bodily integrity and a cruel, abusive exercise of power.

Because they confront us with some of the most horrifying consequences of gender inequity, the essays and stories in this chapter are upsetting. But silence about these issues has never served women well; only by hearing women's stories and engaging in feminist research can we understand the nature of violence against women and take action against it.

---

[7]Gloria Allred and Margery Summers, "Rape Shield Laws," *Ms.*, Spring 2004.
[8]FBI Uniform Crime Reports, *Forcible Rape*, 2000.

Violence in Intimate Relationships

Physical violence directed at women by their intimate partners has made the home a frightening and dangerous place for the millions of women who are abused each year. While the seven pieces in this section examine violence by intimate partners from a variety of perspectives, the first selection, "Understanding Intimate Partner Violence" by Michele McKeon, details and dispels the "myths and misperceptions" that prevent many people from understanding the experiences of battered women and the reasons that they stay in abusive relationships. Some people assume that if "it really was that bad" women would just leave. Others think that "if she learned to stay out of the way, she wouldn't get hurt." These misconceptions hinder our ability to see partner abuse as a social problem, intimately connected to power relationships within and outside of the home. The pieces in this section demonstrate that social and economic realities often deter battered women from leaving abusive relationships, and cultural norms make it difficult for women to get support from their communities. Some women, though, do manage to leave abusive relationships, as demonstrated by the courageous woman in "The Club," by Mitsuye Yamada.

Violence against women comes in varied forms; sometimes, as in "La Princesa," it happens to women who are successful and independent; sometimes, as bell hooks points out, it is only an occasional incident. Women in some immigrant communities, such as those discussed by Margaretta Wan Lin and Cheng Imm Tan in "Holding Up More Than Half the Heavens," find it difficult to resist violent men, whose "right" to abuse their wives is condoned by the traditions of their cultures. While culture certainly shapes women's experiences of intimate partner violence, Sharmila Lodhia, in "Selective Storytelling," argues that the role of culture is often erroneously elevated in U.S. media coverage of women living in the Global South.

Both locally and globally, there is resistance to domestic violence. But unfortunately, when women do seek help, they often face numerous obstacles at shelters for battered women and law enforcement agencies. Despite these obstacles, many shelters, like the one described by Colleen Farrell, do offer hope to countless women fleeing violent relationships.

🦎 **133**

Understanding Intimate Partner Violence

MICHELE MCKEON

Each day across the country you can watch the news or pick up a newspaper and read about a horrific story of domestic violence. On average, four women a day are killed by their intimate partner. We know the more notorious stories, like Nicole Brown Simpson or Rhianna, but each and every day anonymous women are battered and abused far from the spotlight. For many years, domestic violence lived under the guise that it was just a private family matter. Nothing could be further from the truth. Domestic violence, otherwise known as intimate partner violence, is a crime.[1]

Up until the mid-1970s, intimate partner violence was a family secret not discussed in public. Springing from the civil rights movement, the battered women's movement pressured national, state, and local leaders to begin to recognize this growing problem. By the mid-1980s, programs and shelters were opened in communities across the country. In 1994 the Violence Against Women Act was passed, revolutionizing programs, services, and funding for individuals affected by intimate partner violence and their families.

Today the movement against intimate partner violence continues to adapt to the ever-changing needs of victims and their children. We advocate for policies and legislation to enhance safety and hold offenders accountable for the crimes they commit against their intimate partners. Though much work has been done, there is a tremendous amount of work left to do. There can be true safety for victims only with the commitment of the entire community and a complete understanding of the dynamics and long-standing effects of intimate partner violence.

WHAT IS INTIMATE PARTNER VIOLENCE?

Intimate partner violence is a pattern of coercive tactics used to maintain power and control over an intimate partner. These tactics can be any combination of the following: physical abuse, which includes slapping, hitting, punching, kicking, shoving; verbal abuse; emotional or mental abuse; sexual abuse; and financial abuse. While intimate partner violence is a criminal justice issue, it is also a major public health epidemic, crossing over into social and human services as well. The Centers for Disease Control and Prevention found that 1,181 women were murdered by their intimate partners in 2005; two million women experience injuries at the hands of their intimate partner annually; and that one in four women experience intimate partner violence in their lifetime.[2]

According to the Family Violence Prevention Fund, women are more likely than men to be victimized.[3] Eighty-four percent of spousal abuse victims are women, and 86 percent of victims at the hands of a dating partner are women. Three-fourths of people who commit family violence are male.[4]

Although women are the majority of victims and men are the primary perpetrators, men can also be victims of violence. According to LAMBDA, domestic violence occurs in approximately 30 to 40 percent of gay and lesbian relationships as well. Furthermore, intimate partner violence crosses socioeconomic, educational, religious, race, and ethnic boundaries.[5]

To establish power and control over an intimate partner, a batterer can use a variety of tools, including intimidation, coercion, or threats, threatening harm to children or pets, minimizing or denying abuse, using male privilege, and isolation. All of these can have a paralyzing effect on a victim. Isolation is frequently the most-used tool in a batterer's arsenal. In order to gain control over their intimate partner, it's necessary to isolate them from support networks. Removing support networks from a victim may be a slow process. It may begin with the batterer telling the victim that her friends and family do not like him. He may remove himself from social situations and convince her that "everyone is against him." Her loyalty to him may force her to choose between family and friends or her relationship. It may then progress from simple coercion to a demand for loyalty to him and, finally, forced isolation through threats and intimidation. Victims may also isolate themselves from friends and family for fear of their safety or out of embarrassment. It might not be possible to explain away visible injuries such as bruising, lacerations, or broken bones, or explanations may become implausible to family and friends, and victims may resist or feel unsafe disclosing what is happening to them.

In a well-publicized case, Susan Still speaks about how her husband slowly isolated her from her family and friends, forced her to quit her job, and left her with no outlet and no support outside her home. But Susan eventually went back to work in order to singlehandedly support the household. That outside contact would eventually help Susan leave her abusive husband, for it was Susan's boss who began to notice her bruises and keep a log of her injuries. After nearly a year of quiet support, Susan reached out to her boss, who was able to assist in the prosecution of her husband. Ulner Still was sentenced to a 36-year prison term, the longest prison term without a fatality attached to it. Support systems for victims of intimate partner violence are vital.

There is no stereotypical victim of intimate partner violence, nor is there a one-size-fits-all batterer. While it would be easy to say that all victims are lacking in self-esteem and all batterers are out-of-control rage-aholics, neither of those pictures holds true in every case. Individuals who experience intimate partner violence may end up with low self-esteem, but they don't necessarily start out that way. Batterers use a cycle of tactics that tear at the fabric of their victims over time. Rarely does a batterer show his or her true colors on a first date. Many women tell advocates that it would have been much easier to spot an abuser if their date had punched them at the end of the first date rather than ending the date with a kiss.

Although women of all ages are at risk of intimate partner violence, women are at the greatest risk between the ages 20 and 24. Teens are also a growing population of victims. According to the Family Violence Prevention Fund, one in three teenage girls report being victims of physical, verbal, or emotional abuse, a figure that "far exceeds victimization rates for other types of violence affecting youth."[6] In their article "Dating Violence Against Adolescent Girls and Associated Substance Use, Unhealthy Weight Control, Sexual Risk Behavior, Pregnancy, and Suicidality,"

Silverman, Raj et al. note that teen victims of physical dating violence are more likely than their nonabused peers to smoke, use drugs, engage in unhealthy diet behaviors (taking diet pills or laxatives and vomiting to lose weight), engage in risky sexual behaviors, and attempt or consider suicide.[7] While most services are still tailored to adults seeking services, since 2002 the CDC has funded 14 projects around the country aimed at primary prevention, with one focus being teen dating violence prevention programming.[8]

Technology has also left its mark in the area of intimate partner violence. The prevalence of cell phones, computers, social networking sites, and GPS all make it much easier for us to have access to one another. In healthy relationships, such technologies are used as tools of communication. But in the hands of someone with a need to have complete control over a partner, these technologies are used as tracking devices. Instant communication provides instant access for batterers. Numerous victims report being tracked through their phones, computers, and social networking sites. There are smart phone applications and computer software that can catch every keystroke an individual types or gain access to private e-mail accounts. For as little as $30, spoofcards can change the number, identity, and voice of someone calling. This ever-changing technology makes it even more difficult for victims to find safety from anyone who is interested in stalking and terrorizing them.

MYTHS AND MISPERCEPTIONS

Many people assume that intimate partner violence is caused by an anger management issue or a lack of control. But perpetrators are very specific about where, when, and at whom they lose control. If intimate partner violence were just a matter of anger management, then it would make sense that perpetrators wouldn't be able to control their rage. But in reality, batterers are able to contain their anger and then direct it at their intimate partner behind closed doors. One client shared a story of an incident when her husband assaulted her in a parking lot after a company party. During the party she was at the buffet table with some of her husband's co-workers sharing stories about the office and laughing. She happened to catch her husband's eye and realized he seemed upset about something. She excused herself from the other guests and spent the rest of the evening at her husband's side. Several hours later, as they were getting into the car, he punched her in the face. He accused her of flirting with his co-workers and laughing at him. With a closer look, it's clear that this man didn't lose control. He had perfect control. He had the control to wait three hours until they were alone in an empty parking lot to strike his wife. Intimate partner violence is not an anger management issue; it's an issue of power and control.

Additionally, some people believe that alcohol, drugs, mental illness, poverty, stress, and lack of education cause intimate partner violence. While each of these may be a contributing factor or exacerbate the situation, none of these, in combination or alone, cause the violence. If a batterer has a substance abuse issue and batters his partner, then he has two issues. But substance abuse is not the cause of intimate partner violence.

Treatment for batterers is a murky area, as data do not seem to indicate that one treatment alone works to treat or rehabilitate a batterer. Batterer Intervention Programs operate across the country and vary in approach from clinical treatment to accountability models. Other programs include couples counseling, mediation, as well as anger management. But these methods do not address the issue of power and control in relationships. If the violence is not about anger, but about power and control, then how would an anger management program address the issue? Just as lust management programs are not used as treatment for sex offenders, anger management programs would be ineffectual treatment for batterers.

While it is true that a majority of batterers are men, it's important to remember that not all men are violent with their intimate partners. Most men are respectful and loving to their partners, and it is important to engage these good men in the commitment to ending violence against women. This is not just a women's issue; it is an issue for society as a whole.

VICTIM BLAMING: WHY DOES SHE STAY?

When a story of intimate partner violence is in the news, this question is often posed: Why didn't she leave? This question shifts the blame from the batterer to the victim. If intimate partner violence is a crime, how could the victim participate in its occurrence? Rarely is the victim of a drunk driver asked what they were doing driving on the night of an accident. They are no more responsible than someone attacked in their home by their intimate partner. In cases of intimate partner violence or sexual assault, it is seemingly easier to examine the actions of the victim, rather than look at the factors that led to the abuse in the first place. The most appropriate question to ask is: Will the batterer be held accountable for his actions?

The reality is that people stay in abusive relationships for a whole host of reasons, including family pressure, religious or cultural considerations, socio-economic anxiety, a desire to keep the family as a whole unit, and a fear of homelessness and poverty. A fear of safety for themselves and their children is also often a significant reason victims do not leave relationships. According to the U.S. Department of Justice *National Crime Victim Survey, 1995*, the most dangerous time for a victim is right after they leave or as they are preparing to leave.

SYSTEM RESPONSES

Over the years, law enforcement has improved its responses to intimate partner violence. Long gone are the days when the police response would include separating the parties and asking the offender to "go take a walk and cool off." Many communities now have a mandatory arrest policy and/or a predominant aggressor policy. These tools have been put in place to enhance victim safety and increase offender accountability. Some states have specific domestic violence laws, while others use existing laws to further enhance consequences for batterers. Continuous training and collaboration with service providers increase the response to intimate partner violence and therefore coordinate the service provision to victims.

Although the criminal justice response has improved, a criminal justice approach is merely one system that a victim may access. Many victims do not feel comfortable using the criminal justice system, for a variety of reasons, including immigration fears, an acknowledgment of their own criminal activity, and a distrust of law enforcement. Tricia Bent Goodley notes that racial loyalty is a barrier to African-American women seeking services. She defines racial loyalty as an African-American woman's ability "to withstand abuse and make a conscious self-sacrifice for what she perceives as the greater good of the community but to her own physical, psychological, and spiritual detriment."[9]

Without the criminal justice system, where do victims turn? Victims respond by using a variety of systems and services, including local departments of social services, medical and mental health agencies, child care organizations, and of course, local domestic violence service providers. Across the country nearly every community has a domestic violence service agency. These agencies are designed to provide emergency shelter, safety, support groups, 24-hour emergency hotlines, and comprehensive advocacy services. Most services are free of charge and work to help victims find safety and support. While these services are vital and lifesaving, they are not necessarily meeting all the needs of victims as they access them. Since programs were first created in the mid- to late 1970s, services have adapted to the changing needs of clients. Over the past few years, agencies have begun to offer economic empowerment classes, legal services, as well as clinical services. There is an emerging understanding that emergency services are crucial but they are not necessarily enough. Economic and physical stability and safety are just as important to victims. A combination of services is critical for long-term safety for victims.

THE ROLE OF THE COMMUNITY

What role does the community play in responding to intimate partner violence? How do we heighten awareness, reduce victim blaming, hold offenders appropriately accountable, and provide quality services for those affected by intimate partner violence and their families? A community must demand justice and safety for victims and have a desire to hold batterers accountable for their crimes. Judges, prosecutors, police officers, and advocates must work together to provide an effective, coordinated community response. And because all of us need to be

aware of the warning signs, public awareness campaigns must be targeted to the entire community.

Another important aspect of public awareness is helping to guide community members to provide assistance to someone they suspect is being battered. Parents, siblings, friends, and co-workers call domestic violence programs every day to ask for guidance in addressing the abuse of someone they care about. Advocates review the warning signs of withdrawal, bruises, fear, isolation, and unexplained absences at school or work, and they provide information and referrals to be shared with victims when they are ready to access services.

It's also important that prevention and awareness be brought into our schools at an early age so that tweens and teens are able to identify and recognize what healthy relationships look like. Whether it's Chris Brown assaulting Rhianna, the obsessive-stalking nature of the highly popular Twilight books, or the relationships that play out on hit MTV reality shows, teens and tweens are overwhelmed with a false sense of what relationships should be modeled after. They need to be taught at a young age that dating relationships should not hurt emotionally or physically, and that healthy relationships are based on respect and trust. Parents, schools, and community organizations should work together to counteract these negative images that disrespect and devalue women. Prevention and awareness have grown over the past three decades, as has the availability of programs, services, and assistance. But there is still more to be done. Until victims are not forced to flee their homes for the safety of shelters and batterers are held appropriately accountable for their actions, the work against intimate partner violence will continue until every home is a safe home.   [2011]

NOTES

1. The terms "domestic violence" and "intimate partner violence" are used interchangeably throughout this article.
2. Shannan Catalano, *Intimate Partner Violence in the United States*, U.S. Department of Justice, Bureau of Justice Statistics (2007), http://www.ojp.usdoj.gov/bjs/intimate/ipv.htm.
3. *National Crime Victimization Survey: Criminal Victimization, 2007*, U.S. Department of Justice, Bureau of Justice Statistics (2008), http://www.ojp.usdoj.gov/bjs/pub/pdf/cv07.pdf.

4. Family Violence Statistics: Including Statistics on Strangers and Acquaintances (2005). U.S. Department of Justice, Bureau of Justice Statistics. Available at http://www.ojp.usdoj.gov/bjs/pub/pdf/fvs.pdf.

5. Barnes, "It's Just a Quarrel," *American Bar Association Journal* (February 1998): 25.

6. Antoinette Davis, *Interpersonal and Physical Dating Violence Among Teens*, National Council on Crime and Delinquency Focus (2008), http://www.nccdcrc.org/nccd/pubs/Dating%20Violence%20Among%20Teens.pdf.

7. Jay G. Silverman, Anita Raj, et al., "Dating Violence Against Adolescent Girls and Associated Substance Use, Unhealthy Weight Control, Sexual Risk Behavior, Pregnancy, and Suicidality," *JAMA* 286 (2001): 572–79, http://jama.ama-assn.org/cgi/reprint/286/5/572.

8. Domestic Violence Prevention Enhancement and Leadership Through Alliances (DELTA), CDC website, 2008.

9. Tricia Bent Goodley, "Perceptions of Domestic Violence: A Dialogue with African American Women," *Health Soc Work* 29, no. 4 (November 2004): 323.

134

The Club

MITSUYE YAMADA

He beat me with the hem of a kimono
worn by a Japanese woman
this prized
painted
wooden statue
carved to perfection
in Japan or maybe Hong Kong.

She was usually on display
in our living room atop his bookshelf
among his other overseas treasures
I was never to touch.
She posed there most of the day
her head tilted
her chin resting lightly
on the white pointed fingertips
of her right hand
her black hair
piled high on her head
her long slim neck bared
to her shoulders.
An invisible hand

under the full sleeve
clasped her kimono
close to her body
its hem flared
gracefully around her feet.

That hem
made fluted red marks
on these freckled arms
my shoulders
my back.

That head
inside his fist
made camel
bumps
on his knuckles.
I prayed for her
that her pencil thin neck
would not snap
or his rage would be unendurable.
She held fast for me
didn't even chip or crack.

One day, we were talking
as we often did the morning after.
Well, my sloe-eyed beauty, I said
have you served him enough?
I dared to pick her up with one hand
I held her gently by the flowing robe
around her slender legs.
She felt lighter than I had imagined.
I stroked her cold thighs
with the tips of my fingers
and felt a slight tremor.

I carried her into the kitchen and wrapped her
in two sheets of paper towels
We're leaving
I whispered
you and I
together.

I placed her
between my clothes in my packed suitcase.
That is how we left him
forever.   [1989]

🌿 135

La Princesa

LATINA ANÓNIMA

His car pulled into the driveway. I was crouching behind my neighbor's car, waiting for him to enter the house. As soon as I heard the door slam shut, my heart racing, I ran to the end of the block. I remember feeling the wind in my face and my backpack, carrying students' exams, slumped against my right shoulder. All my senses were alert. It was past dusk and all I could think of was "Where can I go?"

I spotted a bus and jumped on it, shaking, as I slipped some coins into the box, trying to pretend—that everything was fine.

I had finally left him for good. Memories jarred my otherwise numb state.

It was Christmas Eve. We were celebrating it quietly, with a roaring fire, a small "charlie brown" kind of tree, and an abundance of gifts to exchange. I opened package after package—of clothes he had picked out for me. Meanwhile, I lost count of his drinks. Later that evening, I soaked the sleeve of my new coat, stained with blood from the busted lip he had added to my evening's "gifts." I wondered how I would hide the bruises on my left temple and the cuts on the lower left corner of my lip from the friends coming over the next day for tamales. I remember, most of all, looking in the mirror the next morning, not recognizing my own eyes. They were completely vacant of all emotion.

As the bus made stop after stop, I remembered the two years' worth of incidents, apology after apology, promise after promise. I clung to the memory of when I finally snapped, of the moment I knew I would *plan my escape*. It was toward the end of the relationship. By this time I was getting "bold," verbally challenging him when he questioned me, not caring if what I said provoked him. By that time I had finally figured out that no matter what I did, he would find reason for violence.

I entered the house, carrying bags of groceries, placing them on the table. He questioned me, asking me why I had gotten the wrong kind of sausage. He had asked for hot links and I had bought Italian sausage.

He wanted me to return to the store and get the ones he wanted. I didn't like the fact that his tone of voice was in the form of an order. "Go back to the store and get the RIGHT *kind," he screamed. I refused and told him, "I'm not going." He shoved me, from one room to another, beginning his tirade of intimidation. When we entered the living room, he pushed me to the floor. I feigned that he had hurt my back, as a way of keeping him from continuing. Not knowing whether he had really hurt me, he kicked me. He kicked me while I was down on the floor. I was no better than a dog. That's when I snapped.*

That's when I knew that whatever it took I would leave this animal and keep him out of my life forever.

Over the next few months, as I recovered in the safety of my mother's home, I kept asking myself, How could this happen to me? Only a few years before, I had been special. My picture made Spanish-speaking newspapers, announcing my fellowship award to attend graduate school. My entire history, up until this point, had been laced with validation, awards, and recognition for my academic achievements. And at home, I had been loved and cherished. How could I have reached the point that I would accept the slightest form of physical or emotional violence to my person? The question remains today.

As I sought ways to heal and understand, I did what every good academic does. I went to the library. I punched in the words "battery," "domestic violence," and "women" into the computer. Based on her research and interviews in *The Battered Woman*, Lenore Walker developed a typology of characteristics and types of women who tend to become victims of domestic violence. In these pages, I found a description of "the princess syndrome." The princess, Walker explains, is shocked by her confrontation with violence. So sheltered, protected, and revered has she been and so unexposed to any kind of violence in her life that when she encounters someone violent, she is in a state of shock. With no experience of invalidation and feeling intense personal criticism for the first time in her life, the princess believes she can "do right" by the perpetrator and change his opinion of her. Like the other types of women, she endures all the typical cycles before leaving the batterer.

With hindsight, in contextualizing my circumstances, it would be an understatement to say that

Violence in Intimate Relationships: A Feminist Perspective

BELL HOOKS

Given the nature of patriarchy, it has been necessary for feminists to focus on extreme cases to make people confront the issue, and acknowledge it to be serious and relevant. Unfortunately, an exclusive focus on extreme cases can and does lead us to ignore the more frequent, more common, yet less extreme case of occasional hitting. Women are also less likely to acknowledge occasional hitting for fear that they will then be seen as someone who is in a bad relationship or someone whose life is out of control. Currently, the literature about male violence against women identifies the physically abused woman as a "battered woman." While it has been important to have an accessible terminology to draw attention to the issue of male violence against women, the terms used reflect biases because they call attention to only one type of violence in intimate relationships. The term "battered woman" is problematical. It is not a term that emerged from feminist work on male violence against women; it was already used by psychologists and sociologists in the literature on domestic violence. This label "battered woman" places primary emphasis on physical assaults that are continuous, repeated, and unrelenting. The focus is on extreme violence, with little effort to link these cases with the everyday acceptance within intimate relationships of physical abuse that is not extreme, that may not be repeated. Yet these lesser forms of physical abuse damage individuals psychologically and, if not properly addressed and recovered from, can set the stage for more extreme incidents.

Most importantly, the term "battered woman" is used as though it constitutes a separate and unique category of womanness, as though it is an identity, a mark that sets one apart rather than being simply a descriptive term. It is as though the experience of being repeatedly violently hit is the sole defining characteristic of a woman's identity and all other aspects of who she is and what her experience has been are submerged.

. . . Women who are hit once by men in their lives, and women who are hit repeatedly do not want to be placed in the category of "battered woman" because it is a label that appears to strip us of dignity, to deny that there has been any integrity in the relationships we are in. A person physically assaulted by a stranger or a casual friend with whom they are not intimate may be hit once or repeatedly but they do not have to be placed into a category before doctors, lawyers, family, counselors, etc., take their problem seriously. Again, it must be stated that establishing categories and terminology has been part of the effort to draw public attention to the seriousness of male violence against women in intimate relationships. Even though the use of convenient labels and categories has made it easier to identify problems of physical abuse, it does not mean the terminology should not be critiqued from a feminist perspective and changed if necessary.

[1989]

there were competing tensions in my life at the time. They culminated to create ripe conditions—even for a former homecoming "princess," literally—to enter and come to know a sphere of violence far too many women experience. Ideologically, I had failed to reconcile the family expectation that I marry and have children with my pursuit of an advanced degree and my identity as a Chicana feminist (the ironies prevail). I thought I could have both. Hence, when I connected with this man I was still trying to be a "good girl" and find that husband everyone expected. Yet I was in a graduate program that was brutally competitive, alienating, and disempowering. Looking back, I realize that my self-esteem was at an all-time low with respect to my graduate studies and that I was no longer looking to the institution, or academic processes, to nourish my sense of self. Thus, it was no surprise that when I met this man I foolishly looked to him as someone who would make me feel that I was special.

During pensive moments, I've developed a theory for *princesas* of color. *Earned privileges* in a given life cycle only buy us time. The structures of subordination will get even the achievers. Those who think they might have escaped find themselves—like countless other *princesas* of color—treated just as women. Today the memories of this time in my life seem surreal. I do not identify, much less connect, with the experiences I've just recounted. It's as if they belong to someone else. But they don't, and instead they are tucked away in what I like to call my *caja de llagas,* my box of scars. I do, however, use the memories to move myself into using my voice. By remembering the contents, I remember to speak.   [2001]

136

Holding Up More Than Half the Heavens

MARGARETTA WAN LIN
and CHENG IMM TAN

Because of the barriers of language, culture, and economic disparities and the vagaries of racism and sexism, Asian Pacific American (APA) victims of domestic violence suffer revictimization at the hands of institutions designed to serve battered women. According to the 1990 U.S. Census, Asians and Pacific Islanders are the fastest growing minority group, totalling nearly seven million. And yet, in the entire United States only two shelters exist for APA women, one safe-home network and one advocacy group that provides culturally sensitive programs and counseling.[1] Of the domestic violence resources available—police, shelters, hotlines, human services programs—few have staff who speak Asian Pacific languages. Given the highly sensitive nature of addressing domestic violence, it is unacceptable not to have linguistically accessible resources. The language barrier, in effect, shuts out most refugee and immigrant women. In addition, many battered women's shelters turn away APA women because of language and cultural difficulties or sheer racism. Economic concerns present yet another obstacle. Most women who are victims of domestic violence do not have control of the family's money. Many leave their homes with little besides the clothes on their backs. This means that many battered APA women who have gathered up the strength and courage to flee the violence in their homes must then return there because they have no other viable options. Legal protection is also often both inaccessible because of cultural and linguistic barriers and unavailable because of institutionalized racism and sexism. There are too many examples of the revictimization of battered APA women by institutionalized forces; it would require another whole book just to document the abuses we have seen. Consider the story of Ling.

One evening as Ling was cleaning some fish for dinner her husband, who had beaten her repeatedly for the past eight years, and had given her concussions, a broken hip, and a broken jaw, began to pick a fight. Ling did not answer any of his accusations and her enduring silence made him even angrier. He picked up a chair to strike her. She sidestepped the impending blow and screamed at him to stop. The chair broke against the door and he lunged at her, more enraged than before. Ling tried to ward him off by waving the knife that she had been using to clean the fish for dinner that evening. He continued to lunge at her and in attempting to get the knife, fell upon the knife and cut himself. He continued to strike out at Ling.

Terrified, Ling ran to a nearby store to call the police. When the police came, her husband who spoke good English, accused Ling of attacking him. Ling's English was not enough to defend herself. The police whom she called arrested Ling and put her in jail. They set her bond at $2,500. The case against Ling is still pending. This is how our justice system works to protect battered women.

THE PRIMACY OF FEAR OF RACIST ATTACKS, THE SACRIFICE OF OUR SISTERS

Within each ethnic group, male control and domestic violence take on culturally specific expressions. APA communities have tolerated and overlooked domestic violence for some of the same reasons that mainstream society has tolerated and overlooked it for so long—the unquestioning acceptance of patriarchy, of male control and privilege. Some APA activists worry that bringing domestic violence into the open will confirm negative stereotypes about the community, and further fuel the fires of anti-Asian sentiment. To expose the problem within APA communities is not a statement about the greater violence or misogyny in Asian Pacific culture. Instead, the sad reality is that Asian men, like all other men, live in a male-dominated culture that views women as property, objects they must control and possess. Compounding this reality, or underlying it, are cultures that view violence as an acceptable solution to problems.

As a reaction to the pervasive racism and cultural imperialism that threaten to undermine our cultural integrity, APA activists and community leaders have been reluctant to look self-critically at traditional misogynistic attitudes and practices for fear that it would reinforce racist stereotypes about Asian Pacific Americans. This attitude of denial, however, does not keep racism at bay. Instead, it is at odds with cherished notions of our rights as humans and citizens.

The same reasons that inspire the unequivocal and emphatic support of APA activists to identify crimes motivated by race, color, and/or national origin as hate crimes hold for crimes motivated by gender. As with crimes of racist hate, statistics on domestic violence are inadequate; elected officials will not fund programs until we fully document the violence; keeping such statistics would encourage more public awareness and debate on the crimes.

While there is an emerging effort on the part of APA women activists to include domestic violence as a hate crime, APA civil rights and advocacy groups have not supported their work. We believe that along with sexist motivations, fear of betraying our brothers, of adding to their oppression, plays a role in the glaring absence of their support. Such fear causes APA activists to overlook and ignore domestic violence. It has meant sacrificing the lives of our sisters.

A heinous example of this is Dong Lu Chen's murder of his wife, Jian Wan Chen, and his successful use of the cultural defense. On September 7, 1987, Jian Wan Chen's husband smashed her skull in with a claw hammer after she allegedly admitted to having an affair. Chen's teenage son discovered her body in the family's Brooklyn apartment. The trial judge sentenced Dong to five years probation on a reduced manslaughter charge after concluding, based on the testimony of an anthropologist, that Dong was driven to violence by traditional Chinese values about adultery and loss of manhood. APA activists came out in support of the cultural defense as a necessary tool to protect immigrants in U.S. courtrooms.

Does this mean that Jian Wan Chen's immigrant status is negligible, or that such activists believe that Asian men are traditionally more violent and misogynistic than their white counterparts? Does it mean that the status of Jian Wan Chen as an Asian sister, as a human being, is negligible when weighed against the crime of her husband? And what are the repercussions of such outrage? Domestic violence counselors have reported that the case has convinced many battered APA women that they have no protection, period. As for the lawyers, they feel "empowered" to use the cultural defense at any opportunity.[2] What does this say about our society, about our value of human life, about our perception of justice?   [1994]

NOTES

1. Centers in San Francisco, Los Angeles, and New York City provide programs for Chinese, Korean, Philippine, Japanese, Indonesian, Laotian, Vietnamese, and Cambodian women, and are staffed with multilingual abuse-hotlines. A program in Boston provides counseling and advocacy services for Vietnamese, Cambodian, and Chinese women. Bilingual hotlines are available for Koreans in Honolulu and Chicago and for Indians in New Brunswick, New Jersey.
2. Alexis Jetter, "Fear is Legacy of Wife Killing in Chinatown," *Newsday*, November 26, 1989.

❧ 137

Selective Storytelling: A Critique of U.S. Media Coverage Regarding Violence Against Indian Women

SHARMILA LODHIA

In July 2003, Guljit Sandhu was shot and killed by her husband, Inderpreet Sandhu, in Milpitas, California. He killed himself minutes later. After the crime was committed, a family member was quoted as saying that Inderpreet had no choice but to kill his wife, who was attempting to leave him, because his "culture didn't allow divorce."[1] The local media latched onto this statement, and its coverage of the crime focused overwhelmingly on this unchecked assertion about a "cultural" prohibition on divorce as a justification for this violence.[2] News accounts presented the crime as a foreseeable outcome in a community where "marriages are arranged" and women are "second-class citizens."

In October 2003, Nisha Sharma, a woman from India, made international headlines when she had her would-be husband arrested for demanding $25,000 dollars as a dowry payment from her family shortly before their wedding was to take place. While her act was brave and has inspired other young women to challenge dowry demands, news coverage of the event was similarly riddled with generalizations about the so-called "status of women in India" and the motivations for the violence committed against them. In particular, a *60 Minutes* story by CBS correspondent Christiane Amanpour was filled with magnified accounts of the links between marriage, dowry harassment, and a form of domestic violence commonly referred to in India as "bride burning."[3]

In January 2004, Oprah Winfrey began her show with the following statement: "I always say that if you are a woman born in the United States, you are one of the luckiest women in the world. Did you know that? Well, if you didn't know that, you're really going to believe me after this show. . . . Today I wanted to take you to the other side of the globe, so to all of you soccer moms out there, here's a chance to go places you'd never normally see and have an opportunity to meet women you'd never meet."[4] What followed was a montage of images of violence inflicted upon women in the Global South that included, not surprisingly, a highly disturbing journey into the "horror of bride burning in India" that Winfrey warned her audience was "right out of the Dark Ages."[5] The show not only relied on oversimplifications that distorted many aspects of these forms of violence, but also noticeably ignored the very tangible similarities between these crimes and parallel crimes of domestic-violence-related homicide in the United States—similarities that might have raised doubts about how "lucky" American women really are.

These examples are indicative of the limited ways in which ideas about foreign violence against women get imported into the dominant Western imagination. In these storylines, "culture" is presented as monolithic, and religious diversity is disregarded in favor of distorted versions of what gendered violence signifies within the Indian community.[6]

It is much easier for reporters to make claims that leave concepts like culture and race unproblematized and to focus instead on the heightened drama of "the burning bride."[7] What I find especially discouraging is the fact that, in these reports, the Indian community is faulted not only for its particular brand of domestic violence, but also for things like arranged marriages, lavish weddings, and rising consumerism—as if these phenomena have no parallels in the West. I suppose that those who come from the land of speed dating, bridezillas, and millionaire-seeking bachelorettes are insulated from allegations of this kind of "cultural" deviance.[8]

These media reports reinforce the belief that Indian women are at risk of a unique incarnation of patriarchal violence that Uma Narayan describes as "death by culture."[9] Crimes such as "dowry deaths" and "bride burnings" can thus continue to be distinguished from other forms of domestic violence.

Wester audiences seem to derive a kind of voyeuristic pleasure in imagining the spectacle of "burning brides" and hearing lurid tales of deadly mothers-in-law, both of which are perceived as far more intriguing than acts of domestic violence that occur locally. In fact, if these reporters were to look more critically at the issues involved in these cases, they would not only gain a far more complete picture of why these kinds of crimes occur, but they would be forced to notice the striking similarities between these acts and those committed against women in the United States.[10] The weapons may differ, but the fact remains that women in many parts of the world are more likely to die at the hands of a boyfriend or husband than of a stranger. To single out the particular embodiment of lethal violence that one finds in the Indian context is to willfully blind oneself to this tragic reality.

Choosing to invoke ideas about culture exclusively within the context of violence against non-Western women performs several critical functions. One key historical function in the case of India was the desire to advance the goals and objectives of the British Empire. By focusing overwhelmingly on issues such as female infanticide, *sati*, and dowry deaths, the British could present the diverse Indian subcontinent as so steeped in backwardness as to require salvation.[11] This enabled the British to take control of local economies and to masculinize property rights in a way that historian Veena Oldenberg has argued did far more to damage the social position of Indian women than the supposed "traditions" on which these societal ills were blamed.[12]

Elevating the role of "culture" allows for distinctions to be made between violence against "third world women" and violence against women from Western communities. "Women in the third world are portrayed as victims of their culture, which reinforces stereotyped and racist representations of that culture and privileges the culture of the West."[13] . . .

Uma Narayan's critical analysis of what happens when violence travels across borders and becomes decontextualized should inform our thinking about comparisons between the United States and India.[14] In her work she examines how the national contexts of India and the United States differently shaped these violence discourses. In addition to pointing out the difficulty of comparing statistics when definitions of domestic violence are so varied, she also notes that while "there is a *visible category* of 'dowry-murder' that picks out a lethal form of domestic violence in the Indian context, there is no similar, readily available category that specifically picks out *lethal instances* of domestic violence in the United States."[15] In critiquing the popular construction of these crimes, she notes that "Indian women's murder-by-fire seems mysterious, possibly ritualistic, and one of those factors that is assumed to have something to do with 'Indian culture.'"[16]

What scholars like Narayan and Oldenberg have pointed out, however, is that fire is simply more accessible in Indian households than other weapons, and that the use of fire to kill is "forensically expedient," because all evidence is destroyed.[17] Interestingly this exoticized violence seems to garner far more interest and support from feminists who are eager to "expose" the dismal conditions of women internationally, yet who are conspicuously absent in the activism being engaged in by women of color who experience violence within their own countries.

In reality many women in the United States are victims of domestic violence. The U.S. Department of Justice has found that women recently divorced or who have left battering relationships are at greater risk of fatal violence.[18] Pregnant women and women who have been pregnant recently are also more likely to be victims of homicide than to die by other causes, and evidence suggests that a large number of these women are killed by their intimate partners.[19] Women are also far more likely than men to be victims of rape, attempted rape, and stalking in their lifetimes.[20]

These figures indicate a serious problem of violence in the United States, and the fact that there is an increased likelihood of violence when a woman tries to leave a relationship or gets pregnant suggests that similar issues of pride, honor, patriarchy, and—dare I say it even—"culture" may be operating in these cases. We never use such language to describe these crimes, however, and instead these cases are viewed as anomalous breakdowns within a family. Law professor Leti Volpp has noted that while the culture of the "Other" is always described in very limited and ahistorical ways, Western culture is never singled out in the same manner. She argues that because "we tend to perceive white Americans as 'people without culture,' when white people engage in certain practices, we do not associate their behavior with a racialized conception of culture, but rather construct other, noncultural explanations."[21] These problematic *"bad behaviors"* are thus only inscribed on "the bodies of racialized immigrant subjects."[22]

THE REAL STORY: IN INDIA

In September 2005, after years of dedicated advocacy by women's groups, the Indian government passed the Protection for Women from Domestic Violence Act of 2005, and it went into effect in October 2006. This pioneering law covers not only wives but *any* woman residing in a shared household. This includes not only women in live-in relationships, but also sisters, mothers, daughters, widows, divorced women, and women in marriages that the law views as invalid.[23] One of the other striking features of the recently enacted civil law is its broad conceptualization of "domestic violence," which includes physical, sexual, verbal, emotional, and economic abuse. In addition, the law establishes a unique remedial framework for safeguarding the rights of women who are victims of violence, including a unique "right of residency" provision that allows a woman to remain within the family home, regardless of whether she

has a legal claim or share in the property. The enactment of this law was a significant milestone in antiviolence activism for women in India, though critical questions remain about how well it will be implemented.

Beyond efforts toward legal reform, advocates in India have worked to develop a range of innovative nonlegal responses to violence against women in both urban and rural parts of India. In some areas, All-Women Police Stations have been established in an effort to make the police more accessible to women and in the hope of creating greater sensitivity around gender-based crimes.[24] Another distinct response to violence is the "Self-Help Collectives" or "Village Sanghas." These small and self-governed women's groups focus their efforts on improving women's opportunities to gain economic and political power. "The hope . . . is that if women are given increased educational, economic, and political status through these village collectives, or *sanghas*, they will be in a better position to take a stand against domestic violence."[25]

These alternative methods are interesting, because they seek to create an integrated and multilayered approach to the problem of violence within the family. They offer hope for advocacy that extends beyond the boundaries of the criminal justice system and that seeks to address the critical social and economic dimensions of these crimes. The insights about Indian activism, obtained through regional research in India, are extremely valuable and might well inform U.S.-based responses to violence against women, particularly efforts aimed at women whose experiences of violence are magnified by factors such as race, class, or immigrant status. Examinations of violence that occurs outside the United States should not be undertaken in order to convince ourselves that we are more "safe" than other women, but rather in an effort to understand the complex reasons why violence against women persists globally, despite myriad efforts to address it. I would argue that only when we redirect our attention away from culture and focus instead on how violence against women is linked to issues such as globalization, reassertions of state power, shifting racializations, religious fundamentalisms, and increased militarism worldwide can we really begin to understand the true magnitude of this multifaceted problem.   [2008]

NOTES

1. Sue Hutchinson, "Again, Abuse Masquerades as Love and a Woman Dies," *San Jose Mercury News*, August 1, 2003.
2. Julie Patel, "When Culture Rejects Divorce: For Indo-Americans, Breakup Can Be Risky," *San Jose Mercury News*, August 3, 2003; Roxanne Stites, "Milpitas Husband Kills Estranged Wife, Self; Man Distraught Over Breakup of Arranged Marriage," *San Jose Mercury News*, July 22, 2003.
3. Christiane Amanpour, *For Love of Money*, CBSNews.com, October 5, 2003, www.cbsnews.com/stories/2003/10/03/60minutes/main576466.shtml.
4. "Lisa Ling Investigates Dowry Deaths," *The Oprah Winfrey Show*. ABC, January 16, 2004.
5. Ibid.
6. Narayan, *Dislocating Cultures;* Sonia N. Lawrence, "Cultural (in)Sensitivity: The Dangers of a Simplistic Approach to Culture in the Courtroom," *CJWL/RFD* 13 (2001); Leti Volpp, "Symposium: On Culture, Difference, and Domestic Violence," *American University Journal of Gender, Social Policy and the Law* 11 (2003).
7. Parameswaran, Radhika (1996). Coverage of Bride Burning in the *Dallas Observer: A cultural analysis of the other.* Frontiers, 16 (2–3), page 69.
8. Leti Volpp, "Essay: Blaming Culture for Bad Behavior," *Yale Journal of Law and the Humanities* 12 (2000); Parameswaran, "Coverage of Bride Burning."
9. Narayan, *Dislocating Cultures*, 100–17.
10. Ibid.
11. Lata Mani, *Contentious Traditions: The Debate on Sati in Colonial India* (Berkeley: University of California Press, 1998).
12. Oldenburg, Veena Talwar (2002). *Dowry Murders: The imperial origins of a cultural crime.* Oxford University Press: Oxford, England.
13. Kapur, Ratna.The Tragedy of Victimization Rhetoric: Resurrecting the "Native" Subject in International/Post-Colonial Feminist Legal Politics. *Harvard Human Rights*, Journal, 15 (2002), page 6.
14. Narayan, *Dislocating Cultures*.
15. Ibid., 95.
16. Ibid., 101–2.
17. Narayan, *Dislocating Cultures;* Oldenburg, *Dowry Murder.*
18. U. S. Department of Justice, Bureau of Justice Statistics, Special Report, Intimate Partner Violence, NCJ 178247, May 2000.
19. I. Horon and D. Cheng, "Enhanced Surveillance for Pregnancy-Associated Mortality—Maryland, 1993–1998," *Journal of the American Medical Association*, 11 (2001).
20. Patricia Tjaden and Nancy Thoennes, "Full Report of the Prevalence, Incidence and Consequences of Violence against Women: Findings from the National Violence against Women Survey" Pub. No. NCJ 183781, Washington: Department of Justice, 2000.
21. Volpp, "Essay: Blaming Culture for Bad Behavior," 89.
22. Ibid., 90.
23. *The Protection of Women from Domestic Violence Act*, No. 43 (2005).
24. Mangai Natarajan, "Women's Police Stations as a Dispute Processing System: The Tamil Nadu in Experience in Dealing with Dowry-related Domestic Violence Cases," *Women and Criminal Justice* 16.1/2 (2005).
25. Visaria, et al., "Domestic Violence in India: A Summary Report of Three Studies," 36.

 138

Bringing Women's Studies to a Battered Women's Shelter

COLLEEN FARRELL

I was in my midthirties and at a point in my life where I truly felt I was ready to make a change. I returned to college as a women's studies major. That turned out to be the best decision of my life. The curriculum offered through the women's studies program enabled me to see how society's widespread notions, perceptions, and thoughts have had a major impact on my life.

All that I have learned I bring daily to my work as a Domestic Violence Advocate. My women's studies education has helped me to realize that every woman is at risk for becoming a victim of violence. I share with the women with whom I work how violence against women has been accepted and even condoned throughout history. Violence happens regardless of socioeconomic status, race, ethnicity, age, education, sexual orientation, or childhood history. In fact, being female is the only significant risk factor for being a victim of violence. Violence against women is not just a woman's problem. Violence against women is a social problem.

Many of the women who attend the Battered Women's Support Group that I facilitate talk about how they have been called lesbians by their abusers. It is at this time that I explain how society perceives a lesbian as someone who has stepped out of line and how the word lesbian has been used to hurt all women. Many women are also forced to stay in abusive and dangerous relationships because they can't support themselves and their children. My feminist perspective and women's studies background allow me to point out to the members of the support group the common elements of oppressions (sexism, racism, heterosexism, classism, etc.) and how they are linked by economic power and control.

I have also started a newsletter for my co-workers that centers on information about the history of women and women's issues such as heterosexism and sexism, titled "The Lily" (a tribute to the nineteenth century women's newspaper edited by Amelia Bloomer). And finally, I remind myself every day of the most important lesson I have taken with me from my time as a women's studies major at SUNY New Paltz. Never judge other women too harshly—for they too have traveled a long and difficult road. In order to end the devaluation of women and girls in our culture, we must begin to value other women as well as ourselves.   [2003]

Sexual Violence

Whether or not one has personally experienced sexual assault or abuse, the threat of violence shadows the lives of women and girls. The pieces in this section make connections between sexual violence and the celebration of male sexual conquest that prevails in most of the world. From childhood sexual abuse to the rape of women by conquering armies, women are seen as sexual prey. Susan Griffin's 1971 article "Rape: The All-American Crime" drew rape out of the realm of inexplicable atrocities and placed it squarely in the context of patriarchal traditions that entitle men to control women's bodies. The threat of sexual violence looms large for women and girls, curtailing a sense of safety and belonging and made worse, as Holly Kearl argues, by harassment in the streets. Kearl suggests that one of the ways we can begin to take back our public spaces is by encouraging men to find ways to stop street harassment.

While public spaces are often not safe places for women, the myth of the rapist as a stranger lurking in the bushes was further challenged in the 1980s by studies that revealed the extent of acquaintance rape. Peggy Reeves Sanday's groundbreaking article synthesizes these studies and draws attention to the role of fraternities in perpetuating gang rapes on college campuses. Recent high-profile cases have trained the spotlight on the culture of entitlement and misogyny that prevails in the world of competitive male sports.

In a wide variety of ways, women and girls have challenged what some have called a "rape culture." They have reached out to each other, as Rachel did in the "High-School Gauntlet," ending the silence, passivity, and isolation that enable boys to sexually humiliate girls. College women who have been raped by acquaintances are speaking out and taking their rapists to court. Survivors of sexual abuse are using their own experience to help other survivors reclaim their lives, and activists are challenging a criminal justice system that protects male abusers of children. In the past 15 years, women from around the world have worked together to force the international community to recognize rape as a war crime. Several of these essays tell the stories of women who are challenging a culture that supports rape and defending their autonomy as human beings.

🌿 139

With No Immediate Cause

NTOZAKE SHANGE

every 3 minutes a woman is beaten
every five minutes a
woman is raped/every ten minutes
a lil girl is molested
yet i rode the subway today
i sat next to an old man who
may have beaten his old wife
3 minutes ago or 3 days/30 years ago
he might have sodomized his
daughter but i sat there
cuz the young men on the train
might beat some young women
later in the day or tomorrow
i might not shut my door fast
enuf/push hard enuf
every 3 minutes it happens
some woman's innocence
rushes to her cheeks/pours from her mouth
like the betsy wetsy dolls have been torn
apart/their mouths
mensis red & split/every
three minutes a shoulder
is jammed through plaster & the oven door/
chairs push thru the rib cage/hot water or
boiling sperm decorate her body
i rode the subway today
& bought a paper from a
man who might
have held his old lady onto
a hot pressing iron/i dont know
maybe he catches lil girls in the
park & rips open their behinds
with steel rods/i cdnt decide
what he might have done i only
know every 3 minutes
every 5 minutes every 10 minutes/so
i bought the paper
looking for the announcement
there has to be an announcement

of the women's bodies found
yesterday/the missing little girl
i sat in a restaurant with my
paper looking for the announcement
a yng man served me coffee
i wondered did he pour the boiling
coffee/on the woman cuz she waz stupid/
did he put the infant girl/in
the coffee pot/with the boiling coffee/cuz she cried
    too much
what exactly did he do with hot coffee
i looked for the announcement
the discovery/of the dismembered
woman's body/the
victims have not all been
identified/today they are
naked & dead/refuse to
testify/one girl out of 10's not
coherent/i took the coffee
& spit it up/i found an
announcement/not the woman's
bloated body in the river/floating
not the child bleeding in the
59th street corridor/not the baby
broken on the floor/
    "there is some concern
    that alleged battered women
    might start to murder their
    husbands & lovers with no
    immediate cause"
i spit up   i vomit   i am screaming
we all have immediate cause
every 3 minutes
every 5 minutes
every 10 minutes
every day
women's bodies are found
in alleys & bedrooms/at the top of the stairs
before i ride the subway/buy a paper/drink
coffee/i must know/
have you hurt a woman today
did you beat a woman today
throw a child cross a room
    are the lil girl's panties
    in yr pocket
did you hurt a woman today

i have to ask these obscene questions
the authorities require me to
establish
immediate cause

every three minutes
every five minutes
every ten minutes
every day   [1970]

✿ 140

Rape:
The All-American Crime

SUSAN GRIFFIN

I

I have never been free of the fear of rape. From
a very early age I, like most women, have thought
of rape as part of my natural environment—
something to be feared and prayed against like fire
or lightning. I never asked why men raped; I simply thought it one of the many mysteries of human
nature.

I was, however, curious enough about the violent side of humanity to read every crime magazine I was able to ferret away from my grandfather.
Each issue featured at least one "sex crime," with
pictures of a victim, usually in a pearl necklace,
and of the ditch or the orchard where her body was
found. I was never certain why the victims were
always women, nor what the motives of the murderer were, but I did guess that the world was not
a safe place for women. I observed that my grandmother was meticulous about locks, and quick to
draw the shades before anyone removed so much
as a shoe. I sensed that danger lurked outside.

At the age of eight, my suspicions were confirmed. My grandmother took me to the back of the
house where the men wouldn't hear, and told me
that strange men wanted to do harm to little girls.
I learned not to walk on dark streets, not to talk to
strangers, or get into strange cars, to lock doors,

and to be modest. She never explained why a man
would want to harm a little girl, and I never asked.

If I thought for a while that my grandmother's
fears were imaginary, the illusion was brief. That
year, on the way home from school, a schoolmate
a few years older than I tried to rape me. Later, in
an obscure aisle of the local library (while I was
reading *Freddy the Pig*) I turned to discover a man
exposing himself. Then, the friendly man around
the corner was arrested for child molesting.

My initiation to sexuality was typical. Every
woman has similar stories to tell—the first man
who attacked her may have been a neighbor, a family friend, an uncle, her doctor, or perhaps her own
father. And women who grow up in New York City
always have tales about the subway. . . .

When I was very young, my image of the "sexual
offender" was a nightmarish amalgamation of the
bogey man and Captain Hook: he wore a black
cape, and he cackled. As I matured, so did my
image of the rapist. Born into the psychoanalytic
age, I tried to "understand" the rapist. Rape, I
came to believe, was only one of many unfortunate
evils produced by sexual repression. Reasoning by
tautology, I concluded that any man who would
rape a woman must be out of his mind.

Yet, though the theory that rapists are insane
is a popular one, this belief has no basis in fact.
According to Professor Menachem Amir's study
of 646 rape cases in Philadelphia, *Patterns in Forcible Rape*, men who rape are not abnormal. Amir
writes, "Studies indicate that sex offenders do not
constitute a unique or psychopathological type; nor
are they as a group invariably more disturbed than
the control groups to which they are compared."
Alan Taylor, a parole officer who has worked with
rapists in the prison facilities at San Luis Obispo,
California, stated the question in plainer language,
"Those men were the most normal men there.
They had a lot of hang-ups, but they were the same
hang-ups as men walking out on the street."

Another canon in the apologetics of rape is that,
if it were not for learned social controls, all men
would rape. Rape is held to be natural behavior,
and not to rape must be learned. But in truth rape

is not universal to the human species. Moreover, studies of rape in our culture reveal that far from being impulsive behavior, most rape is planned. Professor Amir's study reveals that in cases of group rape (the "gangbang" of masculine slang), 90 percent of the rapes were planned; in pair rapes, 83 percent of the rapes were planned; and in single rapes, 58 percent were planned. These figures should significantly discredit the image of the rapist as a man who is suddenly overcome by sexual needs society does not allow him to fulfill.

Far from the social control of rape being learned, comparisons with other cultures lead one to suspect that, in our society, it is rape itself that is learned. (The fact that rape is against the law should not be considered proof that rape is not in fact encouraged as part of our culture.)

This culture's concept of rape as an illegal, but still understandable, form of behavior is not a universal one. In her study *Sex and Temperament,* Margaret Mead describes a society that does not share our views. The Arapesh do not ". . . have any conception of the male nature that might make rape understandable to them." Indeed our interpretation of rape is a product of our conception of the nature of male sexuality. A common retort to the question, why don't women rape men, is the myth that men have greater sexual needs, that their sexuality is more urgent than women's. And it is the nature of human beings to want to live up to what is expected of them.

And this same culture which expects aggression from the male expects passivity from the female. Conveniently, the companion myth about the nature of female sexuality is that all women secretly want to be raped. Lurking beneath her modest female exterior is a subconscious desire to be ravished. The following description of a stag movie, written by Brenda Starr in Los Angeles' underground paper, *Everywoman,* typifies this male fantasy. The movie "showed a woman in her underclothes reading on her bed. She is interrupted by a rapist with a knife. He immediately wins her over with his charm and they get busy sucking and fucking." An advertisement in the *Berkeley Barb*

reads, "Now as all women know from their day-dreams, rape has a lot of advantages. Best of all it's so simple. No preparation necessary, no planning ahead of time, no wondering if you should or shouldn't; just whang! bang!" Thanks to Masters and Johnson even the scientific canon recognizes that for the female, "whang! bang!" can scarcely be described as pleasurable.

Still, the male psyche persists in believing that, protestations and struggles to the contrary, deep inside her mysterious feminine soul, the female victim has wished for her own fate. A young woman who was raped by the husband of a friend said that days after the incident the man returned to her home, pounded on the door and screamed to her, "Jane, Jane. You loved it. You know you loved it."

The theory that women like being raped extends itself by deduction into the proposition that most or much of rape is provoked by the victim. But this too is only myth. Though provocation, considered a mitigating factor in a court of law, may consist of only "a gesture," according to the Federal Commission on Crimes of Violence, only 4 percent of reported rapes involved any precipitative behavior by the woman.

The notion that rape is enjoyed by the victim is also convenient for the man who, though he would not commit forcible rape, enjoys the idea of its existence, as if rape confirms that enormous sexual potency which he secretly knows to be his own. It is for the pleasure of the armchair rapist that detailed accounts of violent rapes exist in the media. Indeed, many men appear to take sexual pleasure from nearly all forms of violence. Whatever the motivation, male sexuality and violence in our culture seem to be inseparable. James Bond alternately whips out his revolver and his cock, and though there is no known connection between the skills of gun-fighting and love-making, pacifism seems suspiciously effeminate. . . .

In the spectrum of male behavior, rape, the perfect combination of sex and violence, is the penultimate act. Erotic pleasure cannot be separated from culture, and in our culture male eroticism is wedded to power. Not only should a man be taller and stronger than a female in the perfect love-match, but he must also demonstrate his superior strength in gestures of dominance which are perceived as amorous. Though the law attempts to make a clear division between rape and sexual intercourse, in fact the courts find it difficult to distinguish between a case where the decision to copulate was mutual and one where a man forced himself upon his partner.

The scenario is even further complicated by the expectation that, not only does a woman mean "yes" when she says "no," but that a really decent woman ought to begin by saying "no," and then be led down the primrose path to acquiescence. Ovid, the author of Western civilization's most celebrated sex-manual, makes this expectation perfectly clear:

> . . . and when I beg you to say "yes," say "no."
> Then let me lie outside your bolted door. . . . So
> Love grows strong. . . .

That the basic elements of rape are involved in all heterosexual relationships may explain why men often identify with the offender in this crime. But to regard the rapist as the victim, a man driven by his inherent sexual needs to take what will not be given him, reveals a basic ignorance of sexual politics. For in our culture heterosexual love finds an erotic expression through male dominance and female submission. A man who derives pleasure from raping a woman clearly must enjoy force and dominance as much or more than the simple pleasures of the flesh. Coitus cannot be experienced in isolation. The weather, the state of the nation, the level of sugar in the blood—all will affect a man's ability to achieve orgasm. If a man can achieve sexual pleasure after terrorizing and humiliating, the object of his passion, and in fact while inflicting pain upon her, one must assume he derives pleasure directly from terrorizing, humiliating and harming a woman. According to Amir's study of forcible rape, on a statistical average the man who has been convicted of rape was found to have a normal sexual personality, tending to be different from the normal, well-adjusted male only in having a greater tendency to express violence and rage.

And if the professional rapist is to be separated from the average dominant heterosexual, it may be mainly a quantitative difference. For the existence of rape as an index to masculinity is not entirely metaphorical. Though this measure of masculinity seems to be more publicly exhibited among "bad boys" or aging bikers who practice sexual initiation through group rape, in fact, "good boys" engage in the same rites to prove their manhood. In Stockton, a small town in California which epitomizes silent-majority America, a bachelor party was given last summer for a young man about to be married. A woman was hired to dance "topless" for the amusement of the guests. At the high point of the evening the bridegroom-to-be dragged the woman into a bedroom. No move was made by any of his companions to stop what was clearly going to be an attempted rape. Far from it. As the woman described, "I tried to keep him away—told him of my *herpes genitalis*, et cetera, but he couldn't face the guys if he didn't screw me." After the bridegroom had finished raping the woman and returned with her to the party, far from chastising him, his friends heckled the woman and covered her with wine.

It was fortunate for the dancer that the bridegroom's friends did not follow him into the bedroom for, though one might suppose that in group rape, since the victim is outnumbered, less force would be inflicted on her, in fact, Amir's studies indicate, "the most excessive degrees of violence occurred in group rape." Far from discouraging violence, the presence of other men may in fact encourage sadism, and even cause the behavior. In an unpublished study of group rape by Gilbert Geis and Duncan Chappell, the authors refer to a study by W. H. Blanchard which relates, "The leader of the male group . . . apparently precipitated and maintained the activity, despite misgivings, because of a need to fulfill the role that the other two men had assigned to him. 'I was scared when it began to happen,' he says. 'I wanted to leave but I didn't want to say it to the other guys—you know—that I was scared.'"

Thus it becomes clear that not only does our culture teach men the rudiments of rape, but society, or more specifically other men, encourage the practice of it.

II

Every man I meet wants to protect me. Can't figure out what from.

—Mae West

. . . According to the male mythology which defines and perpetuates rape, it is an animal instinct inherent in the male. The story goes that sometime in our prehistorical past, the male, more hirsute and burly than today's counterparts, roamed about an uncivilized landscape until he found a desirable female. (Oddly enough, this female is *not* pictured as more muscular than the modern woman.) Her mate does not bother with courtship. He simply grabs her by the hair and drags her to the closest cave. Presumably, one of the major advantages of modern civilization for the female has been the civilizing of the male. We call it chivalry.

But women do not get chivalry for free. According to the logic of sexual politics, we too have to civilize our behavior. (Enter chastity. Enter virginity. Enter monogamy.) For the female, civilized behavior means chastity before marriage and faithfulness within it. Chivalrous behavior in the male is supposed to protect that chastity from involuntary defilement. The fly in the ointment of this otherwise peaceful system is the fallen woman. She does not behave. And therefore she does not deserve protection. Or, to use another argument, a major tenet of the same value system: what has once been defiled cannot again be violated. One begins to suspect that it is the behavior of the fallen woman, and not that of the male, that civilization aims to control.

The assumption that a woman who does not respect the double standard deserves whatever she gets (or at the very least "asks for it") operates in the courts today. While in some states a man's previous rape convictions are not considered admissible evidence, the sexual reputation of the rape victim is considered a crucial element of the facts upon which the court must decide innocence or guilt. . . .

According to the double standard, a woman who has had sexual intercourse out of wedlock cannot be raped. Rape is not only a crime of aggression against the body; it is a transgression against chastity as defined by men. When a woman is forced into a sexual relationship, she has, according to the male ethos, been violated. But she is also defiled if she does not behave according to the double standard, by maintaining her chastity, or confining her sexual activities to a monogamous relationship.

One should not assume, however, that a woman can avoid the possibility of rape simply by behaving. Though myth would have it that mainly "bad girls" are raped, this theory has no basis in fact. Available statistics would lead one to believe that a safer course is promiscuity. In a study of rape done in the District of Columbia, it was found that 82 percent of the rape victims had a "good reputation." Even the Police Inspector's advice to stay off the streets is rather useless, for almost half of reported rapes occur in the home of the victim and are committed by a man she has never before seen. Like indiscriminate terrorism, rape can happen to any woman, and few women are ever without this knowledge.

But the courts and the police, both dominated by white males, continue to suspect the rape victim, *sui generis*, of provoking or asking for her own assault. According to Amir's study, the police tend to believe that a woman without a good reputation cannot be raped. The rape victim is usually submitted to countless questions about her own sexual mores and behavior by the police investigator. This preoccupation is partially justified by the legal requirements for prosecution in a rape case. The rape victim must have been penetrated, and she must have made it clear to her assailant that she did not want penetration (unless of course she is unconscious). A refusal to accompany a man to some isolated place to allow him to touch her does not in the eyes of the court, constitute rape. She must have said "no" at the crucial genital moment. And the rape victim, to qualify as such, must also have put up a physical struggle—unless she can prove that to do so would have been to endanger her life.

But the zealous interest the police frequently exhibit in the physical details of a rape case is only partially explained by the requirements of the court. A woman who was raped in Berkeley was asked to tell the story of her rape four different times "right out in the street," while her assailant was escaping. She was then required to submit to a pelvic examination to prove that penetration had taken place. Later, she was taken to the police station where she was asked the same questions again: "Were you forced?" "Did he penetrate?" "Are you sure your life was in danger and you had no other choice?" This woman had been pulled off the street by a man who held a 10-inch knife at her throat and forcibly raped her. She was raped at midnight and was not able to return to her home until five in the morning. Police contacted her twice again in the next week, once by telephone at two in the morning and once at four in the morning. In her words, "The rape was probably the least traumatic incident of the whole evening. If I'm ever raped again, . . . I wouldn't report it to the police because of all the degradation. . . ."

If white women are subjected to unnecessary and often hostile questioning after having been raped, Third World women* are often not believed at all. According to the white male ethos (which is not only sexist but racist), Third World women are defined from birth as "impure." Thus the white male is provided with a pool of women who are fair game for sexual imperialism. Third World women frequently do not report rape and for good reason. When blues singer Billie Holliday was 10 years old, she was taken off to a local house by a neighbor and raped. Her mother brought the police to rescue her, and she was taken to the local station crying and bleeding:

*Editor's note: "Third World" was used to describe women of color in the United States at the time this article was written.

When we got there, instead of treating me and Mom like somebody who called the cops for help, they treated me like I'd killed somebody. . . . I guess they had me figured for having enticed this old goat into the whorehouse. . . . All I know for sure is they threw me into a cell . . . a fat white matron . . . saw I was still bleeding, she felt sorry for me and gave me a couple glasses of milk. But nobody else did anything for me except give me filthy looks and snicker to themselves.

After a couple of days in a cell they dragged me into a court. Mr. Dick got sentenced to five years. They sentenced me to a Catholic institution.

Clearly the white man's chivalry is aimed only to protect the chastity of "his" women.

As a final irony, that same system of sexual values from which chivalry is derived has also provided womankind with an unwritten code of behavior, called femininity, which makes a feminine woman the perfect victim of sexual aggression. If being chaste does not ward off the possibility of assault, being feminine certainly increases the chances that it will succeed. To be submissive is to defer to masculine strength; is to lack muscular development or any interest in defending oneself; is to let doors be opened, to have one's arm held when crossing the street. To be feminine is to wear shoes which make it difficult to run; skirts which inhibit one's stride; underclothes which inhibit the circulation. Is it not an intriguing observation that those very clothes which are thought to be flattering to the female and attractive to the male are those which make it impossible for a woman to defend herself against aggression?

Each girl as she grows into womanhood is taught fear. Fear is the form in which the female internalizes both chivalry and the double standard. Since, biologically speaking, women in fact have the same if not greater potential for sexual expression as do men, the woman who is taught that she must behave differently from a man must also learn to distrust her own carnality. She must deny her own feelings and learn not to act from them. She fears herself. This is the essence of passivity, and of course, a woman's passivity is not simply sexual but functions to cripple her from self-expression in every area of her life.

Passivity itself prevents a woman from ever considering her own potential for self-defense and forces her to look to men for protection. The woman is taught fear, but this time fear of the other; and yet her only relief from this fear is to seek out the other. Moreover, the passive woman is taught to regard herself as impotent, unable to act, unable even to perceive, in no way self-sufficient, and, finally, as the object and not the subject of human behavior. It is in this sense that a woman is deprived of the status of a human being. She is not free to be. . . .

III

If the basic social unit is the family, in which the woman is a possession of her husband, the superstructure of society is a male hierarchy, in which men dominate other men (or patriarchal families dominate other patriarchal families). And it is no small irony that, while the very social fabric of our male-dominated culture denies women equal access to political, economic, and legal power, the literature, myth, and humor of our culture depict women not only as the power behind the throne, but the real source of the oppression of men. The religious version of this fairy tale blames Eve for both carnality and eating of the tree of knowledge, at the same time making her gullible to the obvious devices of a serpent. Adam, of course, is merely the trusting victim of love. Certainly this is a biased story. But no more biased than the one television audiences receive today from the latest slick comedians. Through a media which is owned by men, censored by a State dominated by men, all the evils of this social system which make a man's life unpleasant are blamed upon "the wife." The theory is: were it not for the female who waits and plots to "trap" the male into marriage, modern man would be able to achieve Olympian freedom. She is made the scapegoat for a system which is in fact run by men.

Nowhere is this more clear than in the white racist use of the concept of white womanhood. The white male's open rape of black women, coupled with his overweening concern for the chastity and protection of his wife and daughters, represents an extreme of sexist and racist hypocrisy. While on the one hand she was held up as the standard for purity and virtue, on the other the Southern white woman was never asked if she wanted to be on a pedestal, and in fact any deviance from the male-defined standards for white womanhood was treated severely. (It is a powerful commentary on American racism that the historical role of blacks as slaves, and thus possessions without power, has robbed black women of legal and economic protection through marriage. Thus black women in Southern society and in the ghettoes of the North have long been easy game for white rapists.) The fear that black men would rape white women was, and is, classic paranoia. Quoting from Ann Breen's unpublished study of racism and sexism in the South, "*The New South: White Man's Country,*" Frederick Douglass legitimately points out that, "had the black man wished to rape white women, he had ample opportunity to do so during the civil war when white women, the wives, sisters, daughters, and mothers of the rebels, were left in the care of blacks. But yet not a single act of rape was committed during this time. The Ku Klux Klan, who tarred and feathered black men and lynched them in the honor of the purity of white womanhood, also applied tar and feathers to a Southern white woman accused of bigamy, which leads one to suspect that Southern white men were not so much outraged at the violation of the woman as a person, in the few instances where rape was actually committed by black men, but at the violation of his property rights." In the situation where a black man was found to be having sexual relations with a white woman, the white woman could exercise skin-privilege, and claim that she had been raped, in which case the black man was lynched. But if she did not claim rape, she herself was subject to lynching.

In constructing the myth of white womanhood so as to justify the lynching and oppression of black men and women, the white male has created a convenient symbol of his own power which has resulted in black hostility toward the white "bitch," accompanied by an unreasonable fear on the part of many white women of the black rapist. Moreover, it is not surprising that after being told for two centuries that he wants to rape white women, occasionally a black man does actually commit that act. But it is crucial to note that the frequency of this practice is outrageously exaggerated in the white mythos. Ninety percent of reported rape is intranot interracial. . . .

Indeed, the existence of rape in any form is beneficial to the ruling class of white males. For rape is a kind of terrorism which severely limits the freedom of women and makes women dependent on men. Moreover, in the act of rape, the rage that one man may harbor toward another higher in the male hierarchy can be deflected toward a female scapegoat. For every man there is always someone lower on the social scale on whom he can take out his aggressions. And that is any woman alive.

This oppressive attitude toward women finds its institutionalization in the traditional family. For it is assumed that a man "wears the pants" in his family—he exercises the option of rule whenever he so chooses. Not that he makes all the decisions— clearly women make most of the important day-to-day decisions in a family. But when a conflict of interest arises, it is the man's interest which will prevail. His word, in itself, is more powerful. He lords it over his wife in the same way his boss lords it over him, so that the very process of exercising his power becomes as important an act as obtaining whatever it is his power can get for him. This notion of power is key to the male ego in this culture, for the two acceptable measures of masculinity are a man's power over women and his power over other men. A man may boast to his friends that "I have 20 men working for me." It is also aggrandizement of his ego if he has the financial power to clothe his wife in furs and jewels. And, if a man lacks the wherewithal to acquire such power, he can always express his rage through equally masculine activities—rape and theft. Since male society defines the female as a possession, it is not surprising that the felony most often committed together with rape is theft. . . .

★ ★ ★

Rape is an act of aggression in which the victim is denied her self-determination. It is an act of violence, which if not actually followed by beatings or murder, nevertheless always carries with it the threat of death. And finally, rape is a form of mass terrorism, for the victims of rape are chosen indiscriminately, but the propagandists for male supremacy broadcast that it is women who cause rape by being unchaste or in the wrong place at the wrong time—in essence, by behaving as though they were free.

The threat of rape is used to deny women employment. (In California, the Berkeley Public Library, until pushed by the Federal Employment Practices Commission, refused to hire female shelvers because of perverted men in the stacks.) The fear of rape keeps women off the streets at night. Keeps women at home. Keeps women passive and modest for fear that they be thought provocative.

It is part of human dignity to be able to defend oneself, and women are learning. Some women have learned karate; some to shoot guns. And yet we will not be free until the threat of rape and the atmosphere of violence are ended, and to end that the nature of male behavior must change.

But rape is not an isolated act that can be rooted out from patriarchy without ending patriarchy itself. The same men and power structure who victimize women are engaged in the act of raping Vietnam, raping black people and the very earth we live upon. Rape is a classic act of domination where, in the words of Kate Millett, "the emotions of hatred, contempt, and the desire to break or violate personality," take place. This breaking of the personality characterizes modern life itself. No simple reforms can eliminate rape. As the symbolic expression of the white male hierarchy, rape is the quintessential act of our civilization, one which, Valerie Solanis warns, is in danger of "humping itself to death."   [1971]

Rape Law Reform

AMY SILVESTRO

Feminists have struggled to align rape law with the twenty-first century. However, the penal system continues to be confounded by the almost religious adherence to the belief that a woman's word is inherently unreliable. Such prejudice is manifested in the chameleonlike definition of consent in rape law. As a result, 30 years of rape law reform have not deterred the commission of rape nor increased its prosecution or conviction rates.[1]

For example, at first glance, recent changes to marital rape law seem progressive. In fact, in every state there is now protection for wives who are raped by their husbands. But, in several of those states, women must prove the use of physical force—that being the court's only proof that she really *meant* no.

Rape shield laws have been a failure.[2] Repeated challenges have rendered them all but ineffective, revealing the continued power of the myth that once a woman says yes, she is no longer entitled to say no. Most notable are cases where a woman has previously consented to sex with the defendant, or has allowed some degree of intimacy. A woman's prior, consensual sexual behavior should be irrelevant to the question of whether she consents to sexual intercourse with any individual man.

Reformers argue that nothing less than an explicit verbal yes (the affirmative permission requirement)[3] should ever count as consent. It is not enough to demand that the law assert that "no" means "no" as in some cases a woman may abstain from saying no in order to protect herself; silence is not consent. State laws are inadequate when they declare that nonconsent is only established when ". . . the victim clearly expressed that he or she did not consent to engage in such act, and a reasonable person in the [defendant's] situation would have understood such a person's words and acts as an expression of lack of consent to such act under all the circumstances" as New York did in 2001.[4] Here, "no" is taken at face value only if the *perpetrator* believes she really means no.

The next, and final wave of rape law reform must establish an affirmative permission requirement in which consent is given freely and not as a result of coercion or threat. Control of our sexual lives is our right, and must be protected.

---

[1]See Ilene Seidman and Susan Vickers, *The Second Wave: An Agenda for the Next Thirty Years of Rape Law Reform*, Suffolk University Law Review 38 (2005), p. 1.
[2]See generally Michelle J. Anderson, *From Chastity Requirement to Sexuality License: Sexual Consent and a New Rape Shield Law*, George Washington Law Review 70 (2002).
[3]See Seidman and Vickers, p. 485.
[4]N.Y. Penal Law 130.05 (2)(d) (McKinney, 2001).

🌿 141

Whose Body Is It, Anyway?

PAMELA FLETCHER

RAPE

I never heard the word while growing up. Or, if I had, I blocked it out because its meaning was too horrific for my young mind: a stranger, a weapon, a dark place, blood, pain, even death. But I do remember other people's responses to it, especially those of women. I specifically remember hearing about Rachel when I was in high school in the seventies. The story was that she "let" a group of boys "pull a train" on her in the football field one night. I remember the snickers and the looks of disgust of both the girls and the boys around campus. It was common knowledge that nobody with eyes would want to fuck Rachel; she had a face marred by acne and glasses. But, she had *some* body.

While I am writing this essay, I remember the stark sadness and confusion I felt then. This same sadness returns to me now, but I am no longer confused. Then I wondered how she could "do" so many guys and actually like it (!). Then I thought maybe she didn't like it after all, and maybe, just maybe, they made her do it. But the word rape never entered my mind. After all, she knew them, didn't she? There was no weapon, no blood. She survived, didn't she? And, just what was she doing there all by herself, anyway? Now, I know what "pulling a train" is. Now I know they committed a violent crime against her body and her soul. Now I know why she walked around campus with that wounded face, a face that none of us girls wanted to look into because we knew intuitively that we would see a reflection of our own wounded selves. So the other girls did not look into her eyes. They avoided her and talked about her like she was "a bitch in heat." Why else would such a thing have happened to her?

I tried to look into Rachel's eyes because I wanted to know something—what, I didn't know. But she looked down or looked away or laughed like a lunatic, you know, in that eerie, loud, nervous manner that irritated and frightened me because it didn't ring true. Now I wonder if she thought such laughter would mask her pain. It didn't.

PAINFUL SILENCE AND DEEP-SEATED RAGE

I remember another story I heard while I was in college. Larry told me that his close friend, Brenda, let Danny stay over one night in her summer apartment after they had smoked some dope, and he raped her. Larry actually said that word.

"Don't tell anyone," Brenda begged him. "I never should have let him spend the night. I thought he was my friend."

Larry told me not to ever repeat it to anyone else. And, trying to be a loyal girlfriend to him and a loyal friend to Brenda, I didn't say anything. When we saw Danny later at another friend's place, we neither confronted nor ignored him. *We acted as though everything was normal.* I felt agitated and angry. I wondered why Larry didn't say anything to Danny, you know, man-to-man, like: "That shit was not cool, man. Why you go and do somethin' like that to the sista?"

It never occurred to me to say anything to Brenda, because I wasn't supposed to know, or I was supposed to act as though I didn't know, stupid stuff like that. I sat there, disconnected from her, watching her interact with people, Danny among them, acting as though everything was normal.

DENIAL

Since I began writing this essay two months ago, I have had such difficulty thinking about my own related experiences. I hadn't experienced rape. Or, had I? For months, in the hard drive of my subconscious mind, I searched for files that would yield any incidence of sexual violence or sexual terrorism. When certain memories surfaced, I questioned whether those experiences were "real rapes."

I have some very early recollections that challenge me. Max, my first boyfriend, my childhood sweetheart, tried to pressure me into having sex with him when we were in junior high. Two of my friends, who were the girlfriends of his two closest friends, also tried to pressure me because they were already "doing it" for their "men."

"Don't be a baby," they teased. "Everybody's doing it."

But I wouldn't cave in, and I broke up with Max because he wasn't a decent boy.

A year later, when we reached high school, I went crawling back to Max because I "loved" him and couldn't stand his ignoring me. He stopped ignoring me long enough to pin me up against the locker to kiss me roughly and to suck on my neck long and hard until he produced sore, purple bruises, what we called hickies. I had to hide those hideous marks from my parents by wearing turtle-neck sweaters. Those hickies marked me as his property and gave his friends the impression that he had "done" me, even though we hadn't gotten that far yet. We still had to work out the logistics.

I hated when he gave me hickies, and I didn't like his exploring my private places as he emotionally and verbally abused me, telling me I wasn't pretty like Susan: "Why can't you look like her?" And I remember saying something like, "Why don't you go be with her, if that's what you want?" He answered me with a piercing "don't-you-ever-talk-to-me-like-that-again" look, and I never asked again. He continued, however, to ask me the same question.

In my heart, I realized that the way he treated me was wrong because I felt violated; I felt separated from my body, as if it did not belong to me. But at 16 I didn't know how or what to feel, except that I felt confused and desperately wanted to make sense out of what it meant to be a girl trapped inside a woman's body. Yes, I felt trapped, because I understood that we girls had so much to lose now that we could get pregnant. Life sagged with seriousness. Now everybody kept an eye on us: our parents, the churches, the schools, and the boys. Confusion prevailed. While we were encouraged to have a slight interest in boys (lest we turn out "funny") so that ultimately we could be trained to become good wives, we were instructed directly and indirectly to keep a safe distance away from them.

We liked boys and we thought we wanted love, but what we really wanted as youth was to have some fun, some clean, innocent fun until we got married and gave our virtuous selves to our husbands just as our mothers had done. We female children had inherited this lovely vision from our mothers and from fairy tales. Yet now we know that those visions were not so much what our mothers had experienced, but what they wished they had experienced, and what they wanted for us.

We thought "going with a boy" in the early seventies would be romance-filled fun that involved holding hands, stealing kisses, exchanging class rings, and wearing big lettered sweaters. Maybe it was, for some of us. But I know that many of us suffered at the hands of love.

I soon learned in high school that it was normal to be mistreated by our boyfriends. Why else would none of us admit to each other the abuse we tolerated? These boys "loved" us, so we believed that they were entitled to treat us in any way they chose. We believed that somehow we belonged to them, body and soul. Isn't that what many of the songs on the radio said? And we just knew somehow that if we did give in to them, we deserved whatever happened, and if we didn't give in, we still deserved whatever happened. Such abuse was rampant because we became and remained isolated from each other by hoisting our romances above our friendships.

We didn't define what they did to us as rape, molestation, or sexual abuse. We called it love. We called it love if it happened with our boyfriends, and we called other girls whores and sluts if it happened with someone else's boyfriend or boyfriends, as in the case of Rachel and "the train."

We called it love because we had tasted that sweet taste of pain. Weren't they one and the same?

REALIZATION

One sharp slap from Max one day delivered the good sense I had somehow lost when I got to high school. After that point I refused to be his woman, his property. When I left home for college, I left with the keen awareness that I had better take good care of myself. In my involvement with Max, I had allowed a split to occur between my body and my soul, and I had to work on becoming whole again.

I knew that I was growing stronger (though in silent isolation from other young women and through intense struggle) when I was able to successfully resist being seduced (read: molested) by several college classmates and when I successfully fought off the violent advances and the verbal abuse (what I now recognize as an attempted rape) of someone with whom I had once been sexually intimate.

But how does a woman become strong and whole in a society in which women are not permitted (as if we need permission!) to possess ourselves, to own our very bodies? We females often think we are not entitled to ourselves, and many times we give ourselves away for less than a song. The sad truth of the matter is that this is how we have managed to survive in our male-dominated culture. Yet, in the wise words of the late Audre Lorde, "the Master's tools will never dismantle the Master's house." In other words, as long as we remain disconnected from ourselves and each other and dependent on abusive males, we will remain weak, powerless, and fragmented.

Just imagine how different our lives would be today if we were not injured by internalized misogyny and sexism. Imagine how different our lives would be if we would only open our mouths wide and collectively and loudly confront males and *really* hold them accountable for the violent crimes they perpetrate against females. Imagine how our lives would be if all mothers tell their daughters the truth about romantic love and teach them to love themselves as females, to value and claim their bodies, and to protect themselves against violent and disrespectful males.

What if we girls in junior high and high school believed we deserve respect rather than verbal and sexual abuse from our male classmates? What if we girls in my high school had confronted the gang of boys who raped Rachel that night in the football field 20 years ago, rather than perpetuated that cycle of abuse and shame she suffered? What if Larry and I had confronted Danny for raping Brenda that summer night in her apartment? What if Brenda had felt safe enough to tell Larry, me, and the police? What if we females believed ourselves and each other to

be as important and deserving of our selfhood as we believe males to be? Just imagine.

Envision a time when we women are connected to ourselves and each other, when we no longer feel the need and desire to conspire with men against each other in order to survive in a misogynist, violent culture. We must alter our destructive thinking about being female so that we can begin to accept, love, and cherish our femaleness. It is the essence of our lives.

Readjusting our lens so we can begin to see ourselves and each other as full, capable, and mighty human beings will take as much work as reconstructing our violent society. Neither job is easy, but the conditions and the tasks go hand in hand. Two ways to begin our own transformation are to become physically active in whatever manner we choose so we can take pleasure in fully connecting to ourselves and in growing physically stronger, and to respect, protect, support, and comfort each other. Once we stop denying that our very lives are endangered, we will soon discover that these steps are not only necessary but viable in empowering ourselves and claiming our right to exist as whole human beings in a peaceful, humane world. [1993]

🌿 142

Rape and Gender Violence: From Impunity to Accountability in International Law

RHONDA COPELON

"I would like to once again prosecute the Japanese military. They damaged my body and I cannot be productive any more and I would like to have the Japanese government apologize and also pay reparations. I am an old woman and I don't know how long I will live but I will not give up until I win my victory."
—Yuan Zhu-lin of China testifying before the Women's International War Crimes Tribunal on Japan's Military Sexual Slavery

Less than a decade ago, it was openly questioned whether rape was a war crime. Human rights and humanitarian organizations largely ignored sexual violence and the needs of its victims. The connection between sexual conquest of women and war was considered natural and inevitable, an essential engine of war, rewarding soldiers and readying them to fight again. The rape of women in prison was not considered torture but was usually noted as a lesser abuse and even excused in law as a mere personal indiscretion, while official toleration of privately inflicted gender violence was ignored as a human rights issue. Rape was the fault of unchaste women or brushed under the rug, and thus raped women were consigned to invisibility, isolation, and shame.

These cultural attitudes and practices were reinforced by the evolution of the classification of rape in the laws of war. In the 1907 Hague Convention, rape was delicately coded as a "violation of family honor and rights," simultaneously invoking male entitlement and female chastity. Rape was thus explicitly cast as a moral offense, not a crime of violence; the fault lay with the victims, not the perpetrators. The 1949 Geneva Conventions did not name rape, but subsumed it within other offenses. Rape was specifically mentioned, along with "enforced prostitution and indecent assault," as among the "outrages against personal dignity" in the 1977 Second Geneva Protocol relating to non-international armed conflict. With rare exceptions, impunity for rape was the rule of the day.

Courageous and concerted actions of women around the world forced a sea change in international law, culminating in the recognition of gender violence as a human rights concern and in its codification as among the gravest international crimes in the Rome Statute of the International Criminal Court (ICC). In the early 1990s, Korean former "comfort women" broke 50 years of silence to expose Japan's systemization of military sexual slavery during the Second World War. Soon thereafter, survivors, committed journalists, and feminist human rights advocates forced the story of the rape of women in the former Yugoslavia into the media and into international consciousness; and Haitian women, working underground, organized to document the rape of women under the illegal Cedras regime. A growing women's human rights movement and reports by human rights groups demanded recognition of the crime of rape and discredited the notion that women wouldn't talk about it. In a series of United Nations conferences and other forums, survivors and activists from around the globe challenged the exclusion of gender violence and women's human rights from the human rights agenda.

The turning point was the 1993 World Conference on Human Rights in Vienna, which prioritized violence against women and gender mainstreaming throughout the human rights system. Responding to women's demands, the International Criminal Tribunal for the former Yugoslavia began to prosecute rape and sexual violence, including torture and enslavement as crimes against humanity, while the International Criminal Tribunal for Rwanda prosecuted rape as genocide.

These developments laid the foundation for the gender provisions of the Rome Statute of the ICC, which created the world's first permanent criminal court with jurisdiction over genocide, war crimes, and crimes against humanity and provides for future jurisdiction over the crime of aggression. As a result of the interventions and organizing of women's human rights activists and allies, largely through the vehicle of the Women's Caucus for Gender Justice, the Rome Statute is a landmark in the struggle for gender justice, codifying a broad range of sexual and gender crimes as well as structures and procedures necessary to make gender justice a reality.

The Rome Statute names a broad range of sexual and reproductive violent crimes—rape, sexual slavery including trafficking, forced pregnancy, enforced prostitution, enforced sterilization, and other serious sexual violence—as among the gravest crimes of war. These are also "crimes against humanity" when committed as part of a widespread or systematic attack on a civilian population, in times of peace as well as war, and by nonstate actors as well as officials. In addition, crimes against humanity include persecution based on gender. The Rome Statute's overarching principle against gender discrimination also prevents the ghettoization and trivialization of sexual and gender crimes and encourages their prosecution, where appropriate, as traditional crimes such as genocide, torture, enslavement, and inhuman treatment.

The adoption of gender crimes withstood virulent opposition from the Vatican, which has the privileges but not the responsibilities of a state in the U.N., and some Arab states. Opponents correctly perceived that crimes against humanity apply not only to rape in war but also to widespread or systemic sexual and gender crimes in everyday life. Thus, 11 Arab states sought explicitly to immunize rape, sexual slavery, and other sexual violence when committed in the family or as part of religion, tradition, or culture. In addition, the United States urged that slavery be confined to commercial exchange and sought more generally to immunize tolerance of these crimes from criminal responsibility.

Furthermore, after intense negotiations, "gender" was defined to include the social construction of male and female roles and identities, in opposition to efforts to define gender biologically and thereby exclude persecution against gender nonconformists, whether they be single women or transgendered people. Though some compromises were made, the fundamentalist positions were largely rejected, leaving the final word to the ICC judges in accordance with the principle against gender discrimination.

The Rome Statute also encompasses groundbreaking structures and processes to ensure that crimes will be prosecuted in a nondiscriminatory, respectful manner that minimizes the potential for retraumatization and overcomes women's reluctance to participate. Court personnel at every level must reflect a fair or equal representation of women and include experts on violence against women. As a result, 7 women were elected to the first ICC bench of 18 judges.

Investigations and trials contain safeguards that protect the safety and privacy of victims and enhance their role in the process. Evidentiary rules minimize some of the worst traditional features of rape trials, including distrust of women's testimony and humiliation through cross-examination about consent or their sexual histories. In addition, the statute anticipates the active participation of victims before the court and responds to the disconnect between punishment of perpetrators and the needs of victims by recognizing a role for the court in ensuring reparations.

Significantly, the ICC treaty should also affect domestic laws. It is not only the blueprint for the court; it reflects accepted minimal international norms for the operation of a justice system worldwide. The principle of complementarity encourages states to adopt its provisions as local law in order to retain the right to try national offenders. The ICC thereby powerfully supports women's domestic law reform efforts.

But will the ICC help to transform the legal and cultural acceptance of sexual violence? If the ICC survives the current assault by the Bush administration and implements its gender-inclusive mandate, it is possible that it will make a global difference. If its norms become accepted as military and domestic law, sexual violence will no longer be exempt from punishment and hopefully will become less tolerated legally as well as culturally. The survival of the court and of its norms is crucial to legitimating norms of gender justice and shifting both blame and shame from victim to perpetrator. Most importantly, perhaps, the court will contribute to the process of empowering women to say "no" to the shame that society has demanded and will increase the possibility of reparations and participation in peacebuilding. All this requires committed and knowledgeable judicial personnel as well as persistent monitoring and engagement by NGOs at every level.

Women's myriad campaigns around the world, including the continuing struggle for justice by the "comfort women," make clear that women's sexual autonomy and gender-inclusive justice are critical components of women's full citizenship. But formal justice alone will not eliminate these crimes, nor ensure women's empowerment, nor address the roots of militarism. Rape and sexual violence are products of long-standing male entitlement to control and abuse of the bodies and lives of women and perpetuate women's economic, political, cultural, sexual, and psychological subordination. Gender norms and accountability must, therefore, be part of a larger human rights mobilization for full equality, human rights, and empowerment of women as well as for peace, economic justice, and security. The Rome Statute is a watershed and the ICC a fragile, partial, yet crucial opportunity.   [2005]

🦎 143

Catcalls, Groping, and Stalking in Public Places: How to Deal with Street Harassment

HOLLY KEARL

"Being harassed just for being alone on the street happens so regularly, in so many different forms that I just expect it now . . . Whatever I wear, whatever I am doing, walking to work past a building site or out for a run, men [harass me]. If I react aggressively then I risk their anger at my ingratitude at being [treated as] an object . . . I'm sick of it. I just want to go about my day uninhibited in this so-called free country."
—Contributor to the Stop Street Harassment Blog

Often starting during their early teenage years, as many as 80 percent of women around the world face at least occasional unwanted, harassing attention in public places from men they do not know.[1] The harassment ranges from legal leers, whistles, honks, kissing noises, nonsexually-explicit evaluative comments, vulgar gestures, and sexually charged comments, to illegal actions like flashing, stalking, public masturbation, sexual touching, assault, and rape. This type of unwanted, gender-based attention is termed street harassment.

Street harassment, often along with an underlying fear of it escalating into rape or murder, causes most women to feel unwelcome and unsafe in public at least sometimes, especially when they are alone. Street harassment is a form of sexual terrorism. Women never know when it might happen, by whom, or how far it may escalate. Because of street harassment, from a young age women learn that public spaces are male territory. They learn to limit the places they go, they try not to be in public alone (especially at night), and when they are alone, they stay on guard.

Outside of feminist circles, street harassment is rarely seen as a serious issue or as bullying. Instead it is treated as a compliment or "only" a minor annoyance and as a woman's fault due to her attractiveness, what she wore, or where she went. Consequently, victim blaming, including self-blame, is rampant.

If a woman hears that she is at fault for the harassment, she may think it is something she has to put up with and she may not speak about it or work to end it. She may tell other women it is complimentary or no big deal. She may believe it is her fault and change her appearance or habits or try to avoid being alone in places where she could be harassed, which also limits her access to public spaces and the resources there.[2]

Ultimately, to end street harassment, the onus should be on men to stop harassing women, but achieving that goal will take time. In the short term, it is important to empower both girls and women to lead less fearful and restricted public lives by teaching them that street harassment is not their fault and by equipping them with tactics for dealing with harassment.

One of the most important messages for girls and women, then, is that any street harassment they experience is not their fault, no matter what people may tell them. Women are not at fault because of what they wore, where they went, or what time of day or night they were in public, nor because they looked "too attractive" or "too vulnerable." Men who harass are at fault.

RESPONDING TO HARASSERS

Harassed girls and women are put in the difficult position of having to decide how to respond. Overwhelmingly, most women and girls ignore, walk away from, or humor their harassers. Their reasons may include fearing for their safety, being socialized to be polite and not make a scene, not knowing what else to say, not having the time or energy to do anything more, and not wanting to give the harasser the satisfaction of any response.[3]

These responses may be necessary, but they rarely deter a harasser from continuing their behavior and can leave women feeling disempowered and frustrated.[4]

Ignoring harassers can be harmful to women's self-esteem and health. At Rutgers University, psychology scholars Kimberly Fairchild and Laurie A. Rudman studied street harassment and women's self-objectification. Self-objectification means seeing oneself through the eyes of others. In the case of street harassment, it means seeing oneself through the eyes of the men who harass them. Studies show that girls and women who self-objectify are more prone to depression, low self-esteem, and eating disorders. A preoccupation with their looks can keep them from having as much energy and time for other pursuits.[5] In Fairchild and Rudman's study of 228 college women, the women who ignored or denied that the harassment was harassment reported higher rates of feeling self-objectified compared with women who responded to the harasser, reported him, or discussed the experience with friends.[6] Taking action against harassers, when possible, is better for women.

Also, despite a common belief that ignoring a harasser is the best way to stay safe, it is not always true. Crime reports show that women who have the highest success rate in escaping sexual assault are those who use a combination of early verbal and physical resistance, so if a fear of rape is keeping women silent against harassers, it is usually better for them to speak up.[7] The former executive director of the Washington, D.C., Rape Crisis Center, Martha Langelan, noted that there are men who use street harassment as a rape test, and they may attempt rape depending on how a woman responds to street harassment. If she is assertive and forceful, they are likely to leave her alone, but if she cowers or humors them, they may attempt rape.[8]

There is no magic formula or "best" way to respond to every harasser in every circumstance. Individual girls and women are the only ones who can determine the best way to respond in any given incident so they will feel both safe and empowered. The more informed they are about options for responding, the better they can be at making that decision.

Here are some suggestions for assertive responses.[9]

How to talk to a harasser:

- Always use strong body language: Look the harasser in the eyes; speak in a strong, clear voice. Using your voice, facial expressions, and body language together, without mixed signals, show assertiveness and strength.

- Project confidence and calm. Even if you do not feel that way, it is important to appear calm, serious, and confident.

- Do not apologize, make an excuse, or ask a question. You do not need to say sorry for how you feel or what you want. Be firm. Instead of saying, "Excuse me . . . ," "I'm sorry, but . . . ," or "Please . . . ," say directly, "Stop doing X."

- Do not get into a dialogue with the harasser, try to reason with them, or answer their questions. You do not need to respond to diversions, questions, threats, blaming, or guilt-tripping. Stay on your own agenda. Stick to your point. Repeat your statement or leave.

- Do not swear or lose your temper: This type of reaction is the most likely to give a harasser an excuse to escalate his actions into violence or verbal threats.

- Decide when you're done. Success is how you define it. If you said what you needed to say and you're ready to leave, do so.

Ideas for what you can say to a harasser:

- Name the behavior and state that it is wrong. For example say, "Do not whistle at me, that is harassment," or "Do not touch my butt, that is sexual harassment."

- Tell them exactly what you want. Say, for example, "Move away from me," "Stop touching me," or "Go stand over there."

- Use statements, not questions, if you tell them to leave you alone. For example, say, "Leave me alone," not "Would you please leave me alone?"

- Make an all-purpose antiharassment statement, such as: "Stop harassing women. I don't like it. No one likes it. Show some respect."

- Use an A-B-C statement (and be very concrete about A and C).
  A. Tell the harasser what the problem is;
  B. State the effect; and
  C. Say what you want. Here is an example: "When you make kissing noises at me, it makes me feel uncomfortable. I want you to say, 'Excuse me, . . .' from now on if you want to address me."
- Identify the perpetrator: "Man in the yellow shirt, stop touching me." (This is especially useful if there are other people around.)
- Use the "Miss Manners Approach" and ask the harasser something like, "I beg your pardon!" or "I can't believe you said that," combined with strong facial expressions of shock, dismay, and disgust.
- Ask a Socratic question such as, "That's so interesting—can you explain why you think it's okay to call me, a stranger, your baby?"
- Turn what the harasser said into a joke.
- Ask them how they would feel if someone treated their sister, daughter, mother, aunt, girlfriend, or wife the way they are treating you.
- If the harasser is in a car, write down the license plate of the car. Even if you can't see it, pretending to write it down can scare the perpetrator into stopping.
- Tell the harasser that you are conducting a street harassment research project or survey. Take out a notebook and start asking them questions such as, "How often do you do this?" or "How do you choose which people to harass?" or "Are you more likely to do this when you are alone or when you're with other people," or "Do you discuss people you harass with your mother, sister, or female friends?"

If the harasser is threatening, touching, or following you, flashing or masturbating at you, you can try reporting him to the police. Find out what the harassment statutes are in your city that may cover other types of harassment, too. For example, in Independence, Missouri, there is a $500 fine or jail time when someone in a car harasses a pedestrian. Since you do not know the name of the harasser or where he lives, taking down a physical description or snapping a picture of him and a description of where it occurred will help your case if you report it. If there are other people nearby, make sure they realize the man's behavior is unwelcome and harassing, and see if they would be willing to be a witness to the police

Depending on where the harassment takes place, you can also report a harasser to a store manager or transit worker. And if the harasser works for an identifiable company and is harassing you while he is on company time, report him to the company. Stores and transit groups don't want to lose customers due to harassers, nor do companies want their employees harassing people on company time, so you often will see them take action. When you report the harasser in these cases, include a description of the person, the time of day, and the place, if possible.

For further information about responding to street harassers, visit www.stopstreetharassment.com, or read Martha Langelan's book *Back Off! How to Confront and Stop Sexual Harassment* (1993), Sue Wise and Liz Stanley's book *Georgie Porgie: Sexual Harassment in Everyday Life* (1987), my book *Stop Street Harassment: Making Public Places Safe and Welcoming for Women* (2010), and Girls for Gender Equity's book *Hey, Shorty! A Guide to Combating Sexual Harassment and Violence in Schools and on the Streets* (2011). Street harassment can be disempowering, but by using your creativity and smarts to think about how to respond to harassers in an empowering, safe way, you can take back your power and own your right to be in public.

NOTES

1. More than a dozen studies illustrating this statistic are found in chapter 1 of my book *Stop Street Harassment: Making Public Places Safe and Welcoming for Women* (NY: Praeger, 2010).
2. Martha Langelan, *Back Off! How to Confront and Stop Sexual Harassment and Harassers* (New York: Fireside Press, 1993): 99.
3. Brooks Gardner, Passing By: *Gender and Public Harassment*, University of California Press 1995. 148–57; see also Kimberly Fairchild and Laurie A. Rudman, "Everyday Stranger Harassment and Women's Self-Objectification," *Social Justice Research* 21, no. 3 (2008): 344; see also Sue Wise and Liz Stanley, *Georgie Porgie: Sexual Harassment in Everyday Life* (London: Pandora, 1987): 169.
4. Langelan, *Back Off!*, 102.

"Hey, Man, That's Not Cool": Men Stopping Street Harassment

Men who are not harassers are especially positioned to help stop street harassment, because men look to other men for approval and many men harass women only while with men to prove their masculinity through aggression and sexual comments or acts. A societal acceptance of most forms of harassment also contributes to its prevalence. There are many ways, then, that men can help stop street harassment, including by supporting healthy definitions of masculinity, promoting respect for women, and educating men about street harassment. Specific examples include:

- Not encouraging or condoning violence in any form, especially men's violence against women. That means not watching music videos, movies, or pornography or playing video games in which violence against women is glorified or sexualized. This also includes not supporting companies that use violent imagery to sell products.
- Not putting pressure on friends to "score," nor rewarding men for having multiple sexual partners (or penalizing women who do).
- Not describing women as body parts or referring to them only as sex objects instead of as complete human beings with personalities, interests, and talents.
- Not penalizing men or women who act outside their gender norms.
- Eliminating language like "pussy," "wuss," "fag," and "girl" as insults used to punish men who are not being "macho."
- Not penalizing, mocking, or dismissing men and women who speak out against violence, inequality, and disrespectful behaviors.
- Talking to other men about street harassment. Asking them to find out about street harassment from women they care about so they can better understand the issue.
- Brainstorming and role-playing ways to intervene in a harassment incident: either before it occurs, if your friends are the would-be perpetrators, or when you see it.
- Always standing up for other people, for human rights, for human dignity.

For more information and examples of bystander tactics that work, see chapter 7 of Holly Kearl's book *Stop Street Harassment: Making Public Places Safe and Welcoming for Women* (2010) or visit www.stopstreetharassment for a section specifically for male allies. If you care about the women in your life, do something to stop street harassment to make public places safer for them.

5. Caroline Heldman, "Out-of-Body Image," *Ms.*, Spring 2008, http://www.msmagazine.com/spring2008/outOfBodyImage .asp.
6. Fairchild and Rudman, "Everyday Stranger Harassment," 353.
7. Margaret T. Gordon and Stephanie Riger, *The Female Fear: The Social Cost of Rape* (Urbana: University of Illinois Press, 1991), 120.
8. Langelan, *Back Off!*, 45.
9. Along with my own suggestions, this list includes ideas that have been suggested other experts, including Martha Langelan, Lauren R. Taylor, and Dr. Bernice Sandler.

 144

High-School Gauntlet

RACHEL

In my high school there is a patio area where everyone hangs out in between classes and during lunch. The school is small, so you can see everyone from the benches at the end of the patio. That is where the most popular boys in the school used to sit. Every day, as each girl passed, these boys stared at her and rated her different body parts from one to ten. The girls dreaded walking out of the lunchroom. This practice had been going on for years and I'm pretty sure that's why our school had one of the highest eating-disorder rates in the state.

I was friendly with these boys. I knew them all, and actually I was always glad about that because even though they still rated me, at least they never publicly humiliated me by yelling out the numbers. Until one day.

"Six."

"What? No way. That's Rachel. Eight."

"Ha! Seven for the bottom, five and a half for the top."

I felt so degraded and worthless I spent the rest of the lunch period hiding in the bathroom.

But something else happened that day, too. The girls at my school, girls who were usually so competitive with and cruel to one another, started talking. It began in the bathroom, when I rallied us together by suggesting we take action against these boys.

The next day at lunch a bunch of us girls got to the "boys' bench" before they did. We sat and waited until they approached, and when they did we called out *their* ratings as they walked by. We had it all planned out: When they came up to us to talk, we lifted their shirts and grabbed at them just the way they did to us every day. Then we handed each a letter I'd written and gotten 158 girls to sign. It said they needed to stop their behavior right away and that we were not going to stand for it any more.

It sounds amazing, but from then on it all stopped. Instead of taking their intimidating places on the bench, the boys mingled in the lunchroom. If any of the guys made any angry or sexual comments toward us about what we had done, they were immediately silenced by their friends.

It feels great knowing I did something good for girls, especially something that will help those who have yet to enter the frightening halls of high school.   [2002]

🌿 145

Naming and Studying Acquaintance Rape

PEGGY REEVES SANDAY

"When it comes to my masculinity I get very defensive. Because I know that men are admired for having many partners, I set quotas—so many girls in one month. The joy of sex for me is the feeling of acceptance and approval which always goes with having sex with a new person."
                    —Male college student[1]

Martha McCluskey went to college during a time when feminist activism for rape reform was well under way, though not yet widely publicized outside scholarly and legal circles. In 1977 she was sexually abused by a group of fraternity brothers while a student at Colby College. At the time, however, Martha thought that being assaulted by "normal white college men . . . was not significant" and she didn't understand it as "real violence." It wasn't until after graduating from Yale Law School that she wrote about the assault in an article in the *Maine Law Review* on "privileged violence in college fraternities."

It happened at the beginning of vacation, when her dorm was nearly empty. As she described it:

I am standing in the hallway looking out the window for my ride home. I turn around and my suitcase is gone; Joe and Bill from down the hall are laughing as they carry it away. I follow them. I hear a door lock behind me. They let go of my suitcase and grab me.

I am lying on the bare linoleum floor of Joe's bedroom. In the room are a group of Lambda Chi and KDR pledges who live on my hall; several of them are football players. Some are sitting on the bed, laughing. Two others are pinning my arms and my legs to the floor. Joe is touching me while the others cheer.

I am a friendly fellow-classmate as I reasonably explain that I'm in a rush to catch a ride, that I'm not in the mood to joke around; that I'd really like them to please cut it out. It takes a few long upside-down seconds before things look different. As I start to scream and fight I feel like I am shattering a world that will not get put back together. They let me go.

Later I don't talk about this, not even to myself. I sit near Joe and Bill in sociology and English classes. I don't talk in class.[2]

Starting in the 1970s, research on acquaintance rape conducted by psychologists, sociologists, and medical researchers began, and by the 1990s a significant body of knowledge on all aspects of sexual assault and abuse had been established. At first the research focused on the annual incidence and lifetime prevalence of acquaintance rape in order to establish the scope of the problem, but soon it expanded to include causes, consequences, social and psychological costs, and prevention. The studies operated within the legal definition of rape as sexual intercourse, including oral or anal penetration, due to force, the threat of force, or by taking advantage of a person's incapacity to consent. Most studies focused on the heterosexual rape of females. However, in recent years attention has turned also to the heterosexual and same-sex rape of male victims. Least attention has been given to same-sex rape of women.[3]

THE EARLY STUDIES

Studies making a distinction between jump-from-the-bushes stranger rape and rape involving people who know one another go back at least to the 1950s. In 1952 the *Yale Law Journal* recognized that rape ranges from "brutal attacks familiar to tabloid readers to half-won arguments of couples in parked cars." Kalven and Zeisel's distinction between "aggravated" and "simple" rape in their national study of 1950s trials was the first to demonstrate that a significant proportion (40 percent) of rape cases going to trial involved acquaintances. Both of these acknowledged that when the parties know one another, a conviction is much more difficult. Kalven and Zeisel were able to attribute the difficulty to juror prejudice by showing that judges were much more likely than jurors to believe that the evidence warranted a conviction in cases of simple rape.[4]

The best-known of the early studies acknowledging the scope of acquaintance rape was authored by sociologist Menachem Amir. Based on an examination of police files of rapes occurring in 1958 and 1960, Amir concluded that rapists are generally "normal" men. About half of all the rapes were committed by men who knew their victims. Only 42 percent of the rapists were complete strangers to their victims, and not all of the victims resisted to the utmost.[5] More than half of the victims were submissive during the rape; about one-fifth of the victims put up a strong physical fight; and another quarter actively resisted in some other way, like screaming. Twenty percent of the victims were between the ages of 10 and 14, and 25 percent were between 15 and 19. The younger the victim, the less likely she was to resist.[6]

The first widely read feminist studies mentioning acquaintance or date rape were authored by Susan Brownmiller and Diana Russell in the mid-1970s. In her landmark study, *Against Our Will*, Brownmiller is the first to use the term "date rape." The kind of interaction Brownmiller labeled date rape was typical of men and women caught in the double bind of the sexual revolution. Men pressed their advantage thinking that all women now "wanted it," but nice girls hadn't yet learned to make a no stick.

Brownmiller's historic contribution to the anti-rape movement is in her valuable analysis of the cultural forces shaping female passivity when confronted with male sexual aggression and her conceptualization of rape as violence. Brownmiller urged a generation of young women to learn to say no and overcome their historical training to be nice. She recognized that date rapes hardly ever get to court and don't look good on paper because the "intangibles of victim behavior . . . present a poor case."[7] These are the kinds of cases that Kalven and Zeisel found usually ended in acquittals. Before she began researching rape in the early 1970s, Diana Russell held the "crazed stranger" theory of rape, believing that rape was "an extremely sadistic and deviant act, which could be performed only by crazy or psychopathic people." The idea had never occurred to her that rape by a lover, friend, or colleague was possible. She learned differently in 1971 while she was attending the highly publicized rape trial of Jerry Plotkin in San Francisco. Plotkin was a jeweler accused of abducting a young woman at gunpoint to his swank apartment, where he and three other men raped her and forced her to commit various sexual acts.[8]

During the trial, which drew many feminist protestors, Russell began hearing stories from other women who had been raped but who had not reported the rape, fearing the treatment they would probably receive in the courtroom. The outcome of the Plotkin trial was a grim reminder of why so few were willing to report. The jury acquitted Plotkin because of the complainant's prior sex life, which was gone over in minute detail in the courtroom.[9] Convinced of the injustice of the verdict and aware of the need for further education, Russell embarked on a program of research that would produce two of the most important early studies of acquaintance rape. The first demonstrated that rape is just as likely to occur between acquaintances as between strangers, and the second provided a statistical profile of acquaintance- versus stranger-rape in a diverse population of all social classes and racial/ethnic groups.

Of the 930 women surveyed in the second study, 24 percent reported at least one completed rape, and 31 percent reported at least one attempted rape.[10] Russell used the term "acquaintance rape" as an umbrella term to distinguish rapes involving people who know one another from rapes involving strangers. Thirty-five percent of the women in her study experienced rape or attempted rape by an acquaintance (ranging in degrees of intimacy from casual acquaintances to lovers) as compared with 11 percent raped by strangers and 3 percent by relatives (other than husbands or ex-husbands).[11] Only 8 percent of all incidents of rape and attempted rape were reported to the police.[12] These incidents were much more likely to involve strangers than men known to the victim.[13]

Another important early survey, of nearly 4,000 college students at Kent State University, was conducted in 1978 by psychologist Mary Koss. When she first designed the Kent State study, Koss preferred the label "hidden rape" to "acquaintance rape" because of the growing recognition in law enforcement circles that rape was "the most underreported of major crimes." She chose to study "unacknowledged victims of rape," women who have experienced forced sexual intercourse but do not call it rape.

Koss's goal was to determine the prevalence of hidden rape. For the survey, she identified four degrees of sexual aggression, ranging from what she called "low sexual victimization" to "high sexual victimization," in order to separate gradations of sexual abuse.[14] The category labeled "high sexual victimization" was the category that Koss defined as rape. It included women who said they had experienced unwanted intercourse or penetration of the mouth or anus from a man or men who used or threatened to use physical force. Koss separated this category of rape victims into two types: women who acknowledged they had been raped and those who did not name what happened to them as rape. Koss found that 13 percent of the women interviewed answered yes to at least one of three questions asking them whether they had experienced forced penetration at any time since the age of 14. Only 6 percent of the women interviewed, however, answered yes to the question "Have you ever been raped?"[15]

Less than 5 percent of the men in the study admitted to using force. Those who admitted to using force were remarkably similar to the sexually aggressive men described in Kirkendall's 1961 study of college men. For example, like their 1950s counterparts, the Kent State males expressed attitudes illustrative of the double standard. They were more approving of sexual relationships with prostitutes and more disapproving of sexual freedom for women than the less aggressive men in the study. They preferred traditional women, who were dependent, attention-seeking, and suggestible. Their first experiences with sexual intercourse tended to be unsatisfactory, but they expressed more pride in these experiences than the less aggressive men. When asked if they had sex the first time because it was socially expected, nearly half of the men in the sexually aggressive groups answered yes, as compared with only a quarter of the nonsexually-aggressive men.

There were other differences between the types of men in Koss's study reminiscent of Kirkendall's findings. The highly sexually aggressive men were more likely to identify with a male peer culture. More were likely to be in fraternities than those reporting no or low sexual aggression. They were more insensitive to the woman's resistance and more likely to think that sexual aggression was normal sexual behavior, part of the game that had to be played with women. They believed that a woman would be only moderately offended if a man forced his way into her house after a date or forced his attentions in other ways.[16]

To see whether she could replicate her Kent State findings in a nationwide sample, Koss joined with *Ms.* magazine in a 1985 survey of 6,159 students on 32 college campuses. The results of this survey would play a significant role in stepping up antirape activism on college campuses, and in inspiring the campus section of the Violence Against Women Act, which would be introduced into Congress five years later.

The survey questions were similar to those Koss used in the Kent State study. This time, however, she included a question about unwanted sexual intercourse that occurred because of the effects of alcohol or drugs. Robin Warshaw's *I Never Called It Rape*, the first major book on acquaintance rape, was based on Koss's study. Warshaw reported that one in four women surveyed were victims of rape or attempted rape, 84 percent of those raped knew their attacker, and 57 percent of the rapes happened on dates.[17] The women thought that most of their offenders (73 percent) were drinking or using drugs at the time of the assault, and 55 percent admitted to using intoxicants themselves. Most of the women thought that they had made their nonconsent "quite" clear and that the offender used "quite a bit" of force. They resisted by using reasoning (84 percent) and physical struggle (70 percent).[18]

Only one-quarter (27 percent) of the rape victims acknowledged themselves as such. Five percent reported their rapes to the police. Although many women did not call it rape, Koss reported that "the great majority of rape victims conceptualized their experience in highly negative terms and felt victimized whether or not they realized that legal standards for rape had been met."[19]

The results for the men were similar to what Koss had found at Kent State. One-quarter of the men reported involvement in some form of sexual aggression, ranging from unwanted touching to rape. Three percent admitted to attempted rape, and 4.4 percent admitted to rape.[20] A high percentage of the males did not name their use of force as rape. Eighty-eight percent said it was definitely not rape. Forty-seven percent said they would do the same thing again.[21]

Koss's findings that men viewed the use of force as normal were corroborated by other surveys conducted on college campuses. For example, one study cited by Russell found that 35 percent of the males questioned about the likelihood that they would rape said they might if they could get away with it. When asked whether they would force a female to do something sexual she really did not want to do, 60 percent of the males indicated in a third college study that they might, "given the right circumstances."[22]

Since the early studies conducted by Koss and Russell, a number of additional scientifically designed research studies conducted on campuses in various states and in various communities reveal that an average of 13 to 25 percent of the participating females respond affirmatively to questions asking if they had ever been penetrated against their consent by a male who used force, threatened to use force, or took advantage of them when they were incapacitated with alcohol or other drugs.[23] A more recent national study, published in 1992 by the National Victim Center, defined rape more narrowly by leaving alcohol and drugs out of the picture. Thirteen percent of this national sample of a cross-section of women reported having been victims of at least one completed rape in their lifetimes. Most of these women had been raped by someone they knew.[24]

ACQUAINTANCE GANG RAPE

In the 1980s quite a few cases of acquaintance gang rape were reported around the country. In the *Ms.*

article announcing the results of Koss's Kent State study, Karen Barrett describes an incident that took place at Duke University in the Beta Phi Zeta fraternity. A woman had gotten very drunk and passed out. Men lined up outside the door, yelling "Train!" Although the woman did not press charges, saying that she had been a willing participant, Duke moved against the fraternity after it was discovered that senior members had assigned a pledge the task of "finding a drunk woman for a gang bang."[25]

In her national study Koss found that 16 percent of the male students who admitted rape, and 10 percent of those who admitted attempting a rape, took part in episodes involving more than one attacker.[26] In 1985 Julie Ehrhart and Bernice Sandler wrote a report for the Association of American Colleges describing such incidents. They found a common pattern. When a vulnerable young woman is high on drugs, drunk, or too weak to protest, she becomes a target for a train. In some cases her drinks might have been spiked with alcohol without her knowledge. When she is approached by several men in a locked room, she reacts with confusion and panic. As many as 2 to 11 or more men might have sex with her.[27]

In a survey of 24 documented cases of alleged college gang rape reported during the 1980s, psychologist Chris O'Sullivan found that 13 were perpetrated by fraternity men, 9 by groups of athletes, and 2 by men unaffiliated with any group. Nineteen of the cases were reported to the police. In 11 cases, the men pleaded guilty to lesser charges. In five of the six cases that went to trial, all of the men were acquitted. The only finding of "guilty" in the 24 cases she studied involved black defendants on football scholarships.[28]

In 1983, I began hearing stories describing gang rape on college campuses in several parts of the country. One such incident became the focus of my book *Fraternity Gang Rape*. The incident was brought to my attention by a student, whom I called Laurel in the book. Laurel alleged that she was raped at a fraternity party when she was drunk

and too high on LSD to know what was happening. The local district attorney for sex crimes, William Heinman, concluded that a gang rape had occurred because from his investigation of Laurel's state during the party, "there was no evidence that she was lucid" and able to give consent. When her behavior was described to Judge Lois Forer, she also concluded that Laurel was "incapable of giving consent."[29]

The brothers claimed that Laurel had lured them into what they called an "express." Reporting the party activities that night, they posted the following statement on their bulletin board a few days later:

> Things are looking up for the [name of fraternity] sisters program. A prospective leader for the group spent some time interviewing several [brothers] this past Thursday and Friday. Possible names for the little sisters include [the] "little wenches" and "the [name of fraternity] express."[30]

One of the boys involved in the act, who lost his virginity that night, said that he thought what happened was normal sexual behavior, even though the trauma experienced by Laurel sent her to a hospital for a long period of recovery and kept her out of school for two years. He explained his behavior by referring to the pornography he and his brothers watched together at the house. "Pulling train," as they called it, didn't seem odd to him because "it's something that you see and hear about all the time."[31]

Another brother talked at length with me about what he thought happened. Tom [pseudonym] was adamant that it was not rape because Laurel did not name it rape at first. It was only later that she called it rape after talking to campus feminists, he said. He suggested that the real problem was "her sexual identity confusion" and that both men and women who are sexually confused indulge in casual sex. According to Tom, a lot of guys "engage in promiscuous sex to establish their sexuality," because male sexual identity is based on sexual performance. The male ego is built on sexual conquests as a way of gaining respect from other men.

For men, he said, there was lots of peer pressure to be sexually successful.[32]

When I asked Tom about Laurel's bruises, he admitted that she had been bruised that night because she had taken acid and was dancing wildly. He added that sex always involves some degree of force, which also explained the bruises. He went on to say that "subconsciously women are mad that they are subordinate in sex and are the objects of force."[33]   [1996]

HAS ANYTHING CHANGED?

Since I published *Fraternity Gang Rape* in 1990, a great deal has changed. The change has mostly come in two forms. There has been more writing about the rape-prone sexual culture on college campuses, and there is much greater awareness.

In 1996, I published an article describing rape-free versus rape-prone campus sexual cultures.[34] In the revised edition of my 1990 book *Fraternity Gang Rape* (2007), I include an opening chapter describing cases reported early in the twenty-first century.[35] I also broaden the explanatory framework for understanding fraternity gang rape by putting the subject in its personal, social, and historical context. In the afterword to that edition I focus on what has changed and what has not on rape-prone college campuses.

Greater awareness is evidenced in the recent nationwide awareness initiative to end sexual violence on college campuses. The initiative was announced by Vice President Joe Biden in a speech given at the University of New Hampshire on April 4, 2011, and accompanied by a "Dear Colleague" letter from the U.S. Office of Civil Rights, addressed to colleges and K–12 schools throughout the country.

The letter outlined schools' responsibilities under Title IX, the federal civil rights law banning sexual discrimination, harassment, and violence. The letter began with a discussion of Title IX's requirements related to student-on-student sexual harassment, including sexual violence, explaining the responsibility of educational institutions to take immediate and effective steps to end both.

The letter both supplemented requirements and guidelines issued in 2001 and provided additional guidance with practical examples of proactive preventative efforts and remedies to end sexual harassment and violence and address its effects. Biden's speech came just days after the U.S. Office of Civil Rights announced it would investigate a complaint filed under Title IX by 16 Yale University students in March 2011, listing behaviors occurring at Yale in violation of Title IX.

Such efforts demonstrate that much has changed. Abusive male sexuality in the interest of the "guyland" behavior Michael Kimmel describes is no longer the shadow culture on college campuses.[36] Like Kimmel's book, my book *Fraternity Gang Rape* is widely used around the country in college classrooms. Consequently, college administrators and students are no longer in the dark about the rape-prone environment that may confront vulnerable young women who wander into the all-male fraternity parties held on almost every campus in the country. Even a few fraternities are taking note of the problem by assigning designated watchers to protect their guests from the most egregious behaviors.[37]

Another important change is the frequency with which national and local campus surveys are conducted measuring student experience with rape while at college. Although consciousness has been raised, the statistics are not much different from those reported by Mary Koss and her colleagues. The most recent large-sample study was conducted by Krebs et. al. (2007), funded by the U.S. Department of Justice, and was entitled "The Campus Sexual Assault (CSA) Study."[38] The research team surveyed random samples of undergraduate students at two large public universities, one located in the South and the other in the Midwest.

The CSA Survey was administered in the winter of 2006, with a total of 5,446 undergraduate women and 1,375 undergraduate men participating. According to the report, the statistics for males are not reported because this component of the study was exploratory. The study found that one out of five (1 in 5) undergraduate women experienced an attempted or completed sexual assault during their college years. The majority of the sexual assaults occurred when women were incapacitated due to their use of substances (primarily alcohol). It was also found that freshmen and sophomores were at greater risk than juniors and seniors. Finally, as in other studies, the large majority of women reporting assault experienced it from men they knew.

In answer to the question—Has anything changed?—the answer is both yes and no. The sexual culture fueled by alcohol and "hooking up" has grown, not diminished, with more women than before embracing its behaviors. In local campus surveys the 1-in-5 statistic holds for women (on some campuses it is higher). In these surveys, males respond by admitting to their unwanted advances.[39] A small percentage of men (6.6 percent in one campus survey) are also admitting to experiencing sexual abuse, including unwanted touching and rape. Younger women who are not yet able to handle themselves in the alcohol-fueled, male-dominated sexual environment suffer more than the more advanced women students, who increasingly opt out of the party culture. Based on my speaking tours on college campuses, I can say also that for a few older male students the wild sexual narcissism of rape-prone campus sexual cultures is considered shallow and not particularly gratifying.   [2011]

NOTES

1. Interview with anonymous college student, spring 1984.
2. McCluskey (1992:261–62).
3. For an excellent summary of studies of the heterosexual and homosexual assault of male victims, see Struckman-Johnson (1991:192–213). Also see Hickson et al. (1994), which describes a study of 930 homosexually active men living in England and Wales in which 27.6 percent said they had been sexually assaulted or had had sex against their will. Some of these men reported being abused by women assailants. Another source on male–male acquaintance rape is Mezey and King (1992). For a study of partner abuse in lesbian relationships, see Renzetti (1992).
4. Kalven and Zeisel (1966:254).
5. Amir (1971). See LeGrand (1973:922–23) on Amir and for other studies on the proportion of stranger-rape versus acquaintance-rape cases. Also see Prentky, Burgess, and Carter (1986:73–98); these authors state that

a sample of 16 studies showed that the incidence of stranger rape ranged from 26 percent to 91 percent.
6. Amir (1971:245); LeGrand (1973:922–24).
7. Brownmiller (1975:257).
8. Russell (1984a:11). First published in 1974.
9. Ibid., 12.
10. Ibid., 35.
11. Ibid., 59.
12. Ibid., 35–36.
13. Ibid., 96–97, 284.
14. The kind of behavior Brownmiller (1975:257) called date rape (see discussion in the text) corresponded to Koss's (1985:196) "low sexual victimization" category, which Koss does not label rape.
15. Two of the three questions used to determine the 13 percent asked whether actual or threatened physical force had been used in nonconsensual intercourse. The third question asked whether oral or anal intercourse or penetration with an object through the use of force or threat of force had been used in nonconsensual intercourse. Koss (1981: table 4, 51). See also Koss and Oros (1982:455–57).
16. Koss (1981:21–27).
17. Warshaw (1988:11). See also Koss (1988:15–16).
18. Koss (1988:15–16).
19. Koss (1992a:122–26).
20. One and a half percent of the men said they had forced a woman into intercourse, oral or anal penetration, or penetration with objects by using threats or physical force; 4 percent of the men said they had intercourse with an unwilling woman by giving her drugs or alcohol. See Koss (1988:8).
21. Ibid., 18–19.
22. Malamuth study summarized by Russell (1984b:159); Briere study in Russell (1984b:64). See also Malamuth (1981:138–57).
23. For a summary of these studies and others, see Koss and Cook (1993:110).
24. For a summary of many studies, see Koss (1993:1062–1069). For the 1992 national study on rape, see National Victim Center (1992). Koss found that 16 percent of the women in her national sample said they had experienced nonconsensual sex due to a man's force, threat of force, or use of alcohol. When Koss excluded the question about alcohol, this figure was reduced to 11 percent; see Koss and Cook (1993:106).
25. Barrett (1982:50–51).
26. Warshaw (1988:101).
27. See discussion in Sanday (1990:1–2). See also Ehrhart and Sandler (1985).
28. O'Sullivan (1991:144; 151).
29. Sanday (1990:74–75).
30. Ibid., 5–7.
31. Ibid., 34.
32. Ibid., 71–72.
33. Ibid., 72.
34. Sanday (1996:191–208).
35. Sanday (2007).
36. Kimmel (2008).
37. Sanday (1996).
38. Krebs et al., "The Campus Sexual Assault (CSA) Study," (2007).
39. Sanday (1996:191–208).

🌿 146

Stronger Than You Know

RACHEL MODELL

I will never forget the day. It was four days into my freshman year of college. August 27th, 2003. I was coming back from dinner with my roommate. We were all going to watch a movie with some people. On the way up to the guy's dorm my friends all disappeared and I was alone. We went in the room and he overtook me. Locked the door and had his friends standing outside of it. I could have unlocked it and left but I thought that I would fare better being alone with one guy than with a team. A team is what they were—members of the school's basketball team.

I tried to fight back. I repeated the word no over and over and over again. The word has since lost meaning for me and I do not use it. I tried to push him off me, keep my legs closed, but he had a good 80 pounds on me.

I remember the promises he made me. About how I was the first girl he had slept with thus far and how in three months we would still be together. He told me I would be apologizing for having doubted him. All lies, everything that came out of his mouth was a lie. Including the date he said he was born on. I remember it all; every detail of that night stands out in my mind.

That night left me broken in a way I never dreamed possible. When I came home to my parents, I was afraid to leave my house for weeks and then only if my dog was with me. I could not sleep with the light off or have anything on top of me. The weight of even a sheet on top of me made me anxious. I remember he asked me over and over where I lived; I lived in fear that he could come and find me. He told me after he raped me that he would be back to my dorm later that night so we could go again. If I was too tired then he said he would be back the next night and the night after.

I went to the hospital immediately after the rape. I did not shower or go to the bathroom. I did change into pajamas but I brought the clothes that I had worn during the rape to the hospital. I had a rape kit done and it felt like I was being raped all over again. I hated that the policemen had to take pictures of my body; capturing the marks left there. However, without the rape kit, I would not have stood a chance in court.

I did not plan to take this to trial but the rape kit started the ball rolling and I did not want to stop it. I went back to the police station the next night and I gave them my statement. He gave one too and so did a bunch of his friends. Those statements were the only honest things those men said. At grand jury, he changed his story to make it sound like I wanted and initiated sex with him. At trial he changed the story again. His friends denied having ever been at the dorms that night. Luckily they had given statements that night that said otherwise.

I have learned that the truth is extremely precious and in this case it prevailed. The trial itself was hard. I was on the stand for three hours and he did not take his eyes off me that whole time. It's funny, but before I went into the courtroom I saw him outside. He was with his mother and he looked so much smaller than I remembered. The power had been taken away from him; I had it instead. The jury took two full days to deliberate and they found him guilty of rape in the third degree, and of three counts of sodomy. He has been serving a minimum sentence of four years (the max was 12) and he is up for parole March 23, 2006.

I have come a long way since that night. Its events shook me to the core and I have not been the same person since. I do not think that it would be possible to come out of such an event unchanged, I wish that life was different. Not a day goes by when I don't think about him; about what he did to me and the fact that I put him in jail. The justice system has many flaws but it is all we have. He did have numerous chances to stop his actions. That night when he raped me, it was his choice. After grand jury, we offered him a plea bargain which he did not accept. His actions put him where he is now.

It is not in my nature to stay quiet and within a month of my being raped, I had joined a support group for girls 16–22. I was right in the middle, being 18. The group and individual counseling were the best things that I could have done. They helped me move on in ways that I did not think were possible. I have since become an educator about rape in college. I think it is important that people understand that rape does happen. One out of three college women has been raped. Chances are that every day you meet someone who has been raped and you will never know it.

They call rape a crime of passion but that could not be farther from the truth. It is a crime of power and greed. The rapist derives a pleasure from executing total power over his victim. Most of the time rapists do not even get pleasure from the act. They are doing it to fulfill some need inside themselves, a need that leaves pain and destruction in its wake. If you have been raped I advise you to seek counseling or confide in an adult/professor that you trust. There are fears that no one will believe you or that you are just overacting. People are out there to help and that old saying about strength in numbers is true. You should not have to go through this alone; you have already been through enough. The healing process is not easy. I do not think that you can ever come out of a rape and accept it. However, no one deserves to have their body vandalized. You are stronger than you know and in time you will come to see just how much. I did.   [2006]

🌿 147

Protecting Male Abusers and Punishing the Women Who Confront Them: The Current Status of Child-Sex Abuse in America

LANETTE FISHER-HERTZ

Ashley was 14 years old and in the eighth grade when her father, Carmine, began grooming her to be his sexual abuse victim.[1] Although he had often been violent with Ashley while she was growing up—once grabbing her shoulder hard enough to break her collarbone—he now became unexpectedly tender. Every night after dinner, he took Ashley into his study, a room she had previously been forbidden to enter, and showed her pornographic magazines, instructing her on the way grown women should dress and display their bodies. He had Ashley practice posing, urging her to put on make-up, purse her lips, and toss her hair around like a model. It made Ashley giggle, one of the few times she remembers laughing with her dad.

"He wanted to show me how to get dressed up to look sexy for guys so I could get a good husband someday," Ashley told investigators.

When police asked Ashley if she resisted what came later—months of daily rapes—she said no. She wanted to believe her father was trying to help her, and besides, what he did to her with his penis hurt a lot less than the punishments he used to give her with his hands or his belt. It was only when he began to get violent with her again that she went to a guidance counselor for help.

★★★

In my second month as executive director of the Child Abuse Prevention Center in Dutchess County, New York, a team of sexual-abuse investigators walked into my office, flush with triumph, to tell me Ashley's horrifying story. They had obtained a signed confession from the 38-year-old father, Carmine, who had repeatedly raped and sodomized his oldest child during the summer of 2000. The team was thrilled to have persuaded Carmine to "tell his side of the story" since confessions are usually the only means of obtaining a felony conviction for sexual abuse of a minor. (A child's testimony alone is almost always considered insufficient evidence for an indictment.) In this case, our burly male investigator had assured Carmine he understood perfectly how provocative young girls could be—which was, apparently, all the macho encouragement Carmine needed. As he and the investigator shared coffee at Carmine's kitchen table, Carmine earnestly explained that he had engaged in oral, anal, and vaginal sex with his

of my childhood. I couldn't remember what being a child actually felt like. Feeling and knowing were to remain separate and distinct experiences for me for a long time to come.

I was a daring and promiscuous adolescent. At age 14, I had my first consensual sexual experience, and I also began to experiment with drugs. The fear and anticipation I felt when taking risks were uncannily familiar. So was sexual stimulation, and I found some comfort in this familiarity. Something about these experiences, though, while familiar and therefore comforting, also felt unsatisfying and vaguely frightening.

I spent my adolescence escaping life and my feelings about it, through chemicals, sex, and music. I was fortunate to connect with people (friends my own age and older) who were able to keep me relatively safe, despite my muted awareness. I was, however, raped by a "friend" at age 15 and molested by my mother's (male) partner at around the same time. I dismissed these incidents as insignificant and my fault. Actually, I didn't think about these incidents or define them as sexual assaults until my first college women's studies course. Instead of attending to the life my mother provided, I created my own "family" and spent a lot of time away from home. I was introduced to Jerry Garcia and the Grateful Dead at age 14, and their world—concert touring, LSD, marijuana, and sex—became my own. My friends and acquaintances became my family. They kept me distant from the pain buried inside, and perhaps in some ways they gave me the love that I needed to survive. I found solace in my head, using drugs to stay there, and found love through sex, using my body to feel wanted. I didn't understand then how significant this separation was and how I was doing exactly what I had learned to do as a child to survive the incest. I survived without feeling very much for many years. I was blessed with a fair amount of intelligence, and that, coupled with charm and an air of aloofness possible for one who rarely feels, enabled me to do well in high school.

I took these patterns (survival skills) with me to college and spent the first two years experimenting with drugs and men. I barely passed my classes, as

I was rarely if ever fully present at any point during that time. Toward the end of my sophomore year, an incident occurred that I was absolutely unprepared for. I was working at a vacation resort to support myself through college. One day, as I was working by the swimming pool giving out sporting equipment, I looked up and saw Bill, my father's best friend. He had been my music teacher, my caretaker, my "uncle"; he was family. A flood of physical and emotional feelings engulfed me when I recognized him. I was repulsed and terrified, and I was confused, as I could not explain any of this. My body reacted to these feelings as if it were a completely separate entity. I choked. I couldn't breathe and gasped for air, immediately hyperventilating. I felt excruciating pain in my stomach and in my vagina. I doubled over, vomited, and began to cry uncontrollably. It was as if something horrible was happening to my body, only right then and there, nothing was. As soon as I could, I locked myself in the equipment hut and rocked myself to safety. Although my mind had no memory of the sexual abuse, my body remembered.

That first flashback set in motion a process in which I have been involved, both consciously and subconsciously, ever since. In the many flashbacks that followed, remnants of the past would surface, sometimes like torn pieces of still photos stored in my brain, other times like a flood. With each flashback I was thrown into the past, and I felt the terror and the pain I must have known as a little girl. I was fortunate that these experiences lasted only seconds or moments, but from each one I emerged frightened and confused. Memories would also surface, not only of the abuse but also of happy times in my childhood, times I had not previously recalled. During flashbacks, I felt as if I were occupying the past. I was fully conscious of the present during the memories and simply took a mental note of their surfacing. I am still aware when new memories surface and always declare it out loud. At one point I wrote down everything I remembered, good and bad, as I feared that I would forget again. I now know that once the mind releases these things, they are back forever. Survivors remember when our minds are convinced that our bodies can tolerate the pain of knowing. Once we know, we know. It's interesting to me that the memories of the abuse, although confusing, did not surprise me. Somewhere inside I had always known. Knowing and believing, however, are two very different things.

What happened for me next further confused me and made it difficult for me to trust my judgment. I told my mother. I said, "I think Bill did something to me." She said, "Oh, don't be ridiculous—you just never liked him." It felt like my head was about to pop off my shoulders. I felt invisible, and for a moment I believed her. "I must be crazy" was what went through my mind, but then quickly, perhaps because of the vividness of my recent emotions, I thought, "No way." I did not, however, try to convince my mother of what I barely knew myself. It wasn't until four years later, when Bill's picture appeared in a local paper as he was being led away by police for molesting a little girl, that my mother believed me. Interestingly, that arrest cracked my mother's own wall of denial, and she remembered that Bill had been arrested at least once before, when I was about seven years old. He had exposed himself to a group of young campers near the place where our families spent our summers. It is the place where my most severe memories of abuse are from.

Once I began to believe that something actually did happen to me, the memories and flashbacks, as vague and disjointed as they were, became more disturbing. Now that my body was mine, it felt like it was betraying me. I felt crazy. I had difficulty being alone and difficulty being with others. Drugs helped to numb the pain but also interfered with my ability to function as a college student. I took a leave from school and left the state for several months, most of which was spent in a marijuana fog.

I returned to college believing more than ever that I had experienced something horrible involving Bill but ready to focus on something outside myself. My memories were still vague, and perhaps shifting my focus was a much needed distraction. I also believed that because of my own suffering, my college education, and my newly recognized class privilege that I could and ought to help others. I had always wanted to work in

human services. I felt comfortable with pain and suffering and, as I could not touch my own, felt passionate about the suffering of others. I had declared a sociology major early on in my college career. After my hiatus, I stumbled upon an elective that was cross-listed with the Women's Studies Program. The course, entitled "Violence Against Women in the U.S.," was taught by a soft-spoken, even-tempered, radical feminist named Alice Fix. In this class, I realized that it was not my fault that a "friend" forced me to have intercourse against my will, despite the fact that I had invited him to my room. Redefining and clarifying that experience from my adolescence helped me to better understand my connection to suffering. Although I still didn't really know what had happened to me as a child, I did know that at age 15, Greg's behavior was not unfamiliar. The more I learned about other women's experiences, with sexual violence in particular and life in general, the more I felt a bond with other women. Like the survivors I work with in group therapy, I began to experience women's power. I learned about resistance and survival and became aware of my own.

It would be wonderful to say that my healing began there and progressed upwardly thereafter; however, healing from trauma does not work that way. Survivors take "baby steps" and often pace themselves so as not to be overwhelmed. I slowed down the process of recognizing my childhood abuse by doing what I had always done so skillfully: I split myself in two. I separated my mind (knowledge) from my body (feelings) as a child. I reentered a familiar dissociated state of being. Intellectually, I became passionate about feminism and learning about women's lives. I became politically active, joining organizations, demonstrating, educating others about violence against women. I worked at a shelter for battered women and became the director of a women's crisis center. I was a leader, using my head to guide me. My body, however, stayed in what was familiar and unsafe.

I struggled for two years to maintain this dichotomy. Feminism tugged at my body. The personal, after all, is the political, and I had difficulty keeping my body, my heart, distant from the lives of other women. I had, throughout my life, often found my body at risk from others and even tried on several occasions to take my own life as well. Now, I was meeting other women who did so too, and as we learned more about and valued each other, it didn't seem to make much sense. It took nearly dying at the hands of my partner, however, and a radical intervention by a women's studies professor to move me to take action on my own behalf. I left the abusive relationship and began therapy. I also pursued my professional development in a more focused way.

Through my study of sexual abuse I learned about the dissociative process and became determined to share this knowledge with others. I wanted survivors and those who care about us to know that the residual effects, those "crazy" thoughts and behaviors, make perfect sense and that there is hope for recovery. It was knowledge and feelings together, perhaps in sync for me for the first time, that convinced me to continue on this path. The emotions I felt were connected not only to my own experience as a victim but to the courage of millions of survivors, who have struggled to understand and improve the quality of their lives. My feminist beliefs gave me faith in the possibility of change and appreciation for passion as a wonderfully powerful force.

As a budding feminist therapist, I recognized the misogyny inherent in men's abuse of women and children. I believe that the sexist socialization of men plays an important role in this. I also believe that as a feminist, it is my responsibility to take action. And so, I have proceeded to learn and to share, helping others to understand and heal.

As a budding feminist therapist, I recognized the misogyny inherent in men's abuse of women. I believe that the sexist socialization of men plays an important role in this. I have come to understand however, that women also perpetrate sexual abuse, often upon other women. My queer identity coupled with my identity as an educator, a psychotherapist, a mother and a feminist, have sustained the belief that it is my responsibility to take action toward social change. I continue to learn and share, helping others to understand and to heal.   [1999]

❦ 149

Bubba Esther, 1888*

RUTH WHITMAN

She was still upset,
she wanted to tell me,
she kept remembering
his terrible hands:

> how she came, a young girl
> of seventeen, a freckled
> fairskinned Jew from Kovno
> to Hamburg with her uncle
> and stayed in an old house
> and waited while he bought
> the steamship tickets
> so they could sail to America
>
> and how he came into her room
> sat down on the bed, touched
> her waist, took her by the
> breast, said for a kiss
> she could have her ticket,
> her skirts were rumpled, her
> petticoat torn, his teeth were
> broken, his breath full of
> onions, she was ashamed

still ashamed, lying
eighty years later
in the hospital bed,
trying to tell me,
trembling, weeping with anger   [1980]

---

*Grandma

Changing Our World

Throughout history women have worked to improve their lives in the workplace, in schools, and in communities. While changing the position of women in our society can seem like an overwhelming task, women have in fact made significant progress when they have organized. By articulating a critique of male domination and demanding the inclusion of women in social and political life, feminist movements have played a crucial role in accomplishing these changes. By changing the environment, organized feminism has supported and inspired women's efforts to work on their own behalf wherever they are. This chapter, therefore, begins with a brief survey of what historians often refer to as the first and second waves of feminism in the United States.

The metaphor of waves has been the subject of a lively debate among historians. Feminist researchers have discovered many efforts to challenge male domination in periods before and after intense feminist mobilizations. While feminism may not have been as visible, many of these efforts laid the groundwork for the development of a mass movement. Yet the periods of mass mobilization that have been identified as waves accelerated the pace of change, created major shifts in popular consciousness, engaged large numbers of women in various feminist activities, and had profound effects on countless women's lives. Bearing in mind that feminist activity has taken a variety of forms throughout history, we examine the movements identified as the first and second waves of feminism, looking at both the strengths and the weaknesses so that knowledge of the past can inform our efforts to improve the position of women in the present.

The first wave of feminism, which emerged in the 1840s, began with a broad-ranging critique of women's social, political, and economic position in society as expressed by the Resolutions of the Seneca Falls Convention. Much of this initial breadth, however, was lost as the movement narrowed to focus on achieving the right to vote. In the 1960s, the second wave of feminism reengaged many of these issues, developing a critique of the politics of personal life through a process that came to be called consciousness raising, an examination of one's personal life through feminist lenses.

Throughout the 1970s and 1980s, the movement grew and challenged the subordination of women in a wide variety of arenas, from barriers encountered by girls who wanted to play in little league to the discriminatory features of social security. While the achievements of the feminist movement have been impressive, the goal of creating a society in which women are able to participate fully in all aspects of social and political life is still unrealized. In the midst of the process of approaching this goal, a multilayered assault against feminism was launched. In the 1980s the "new right," a coalition of conservative and religious organizations, mounted an offensive against women's rights and succeeded in restricting women's reproductive freedom, diluting affirmative action programs, and preventing the passage of the Equal Rights Amendment. While most people are in favor equal rights and reproductive freedom, by the 1980's women were no longer sufficiently organized to prevent the erosion of many of the accomplishments of the previous decades. Even though there was still a great deal of support for the general goals of feminism, many women hesitated to identify themselves with the feminist movement. "I'm not a feminist but," a refrain of the 1980s, represented the success of a media attack on feminism that Susan Faludi exposed in the her best-selling book *Backlash.* Attacks on feminism have continued into the twenty-first century, led by political and religious groups critical of the social, cultural, and legal changes that feminism has wrought. Cloaking themselves in the mantle of "family values," they have fought against the recognition of same-sex marriage, campaigned for "abstinence only" sex education in the schools, and worked on both state and national levels to limit the reproductive rights of women and girls. The image of the family they invoke is a patriarchal one, in which father always knows best.

Nevertheless, feminism has not disappeared but continues to grow, taking new forms as it tackles new problems. Women throughout the world are organizing on their own behalf, and in the last 25 years a transnational feminist movement has developed that has insisted that women's rights are human rights. Women throughout the world are working to end violence against women, which is condoned by patriarchal cultures in many parts of the world. They have exposed the international sex trade, demanded women's reproductive justice, and worked to enhance women's economic well-being. Challenging the rise of fundamentalism, they have worked to improve women's education and worked together to increase the political empowerment of women. International forums that brought together women from the world over have taught feminists that a truly effective movement must encompass survival issues, such as access to food and water, in order to support women's struggles for self-determination. In the past 30 years, feminists seeking to connect women of various countries have established transnational organizations, sponsored international conferences, and promoted awareness about women's issues in various parts of the world. Such networks increase the possibility of cooperative action across national boundaries. Transnational feminist movements can challenge what Charlotte Bunch calls the "dynamic of domination embedded in male violence" by working against militarism, racism, and sexism wherever it exists. Feminist global alliances have also pushed governments and international policy-making institutions to take women's opinions seriously, and explore policy implications for women and girls as a group before starting new projects, engaging in wars and invasions, and implementing particular economic policies.[1]

Activists throughout the world have demonstrated against international financial institutions such as the International Monetary Fund and the World Bank, whose policies have had harmful effects on women and most other segments of society. For example, in order to ensure that countries owing money to financial institutions can pay off their debts, Structural Adjustment Programs were imposed on

---

[1]Cynthia Enloe, *The Curious Feminist: Searching for Women in the Age of Empire* (Berkeley: University of California Press, 2004).

many countries in the developing world. These programs have resulted in cutting back social services and pressuring countries to develop export-oriented industries in which hundreds of thousands of young women work for low wages under intolerable working conditions. Because many of these factories are subcontracted by U.S.-based corporations such as the Gap, Wal-Mart, and Nike, an antisweatshop movement has developed in the United States. Students have played an important role in this movement by insisting that their campuses refuse to buy school apparel from corporations that refused to guarantee their workers basic human rights.

The Universal Living Wage movement arose from this oppositional collaboration of women across national boundaries. Activists within the movement demanded and continue to demand that all workers must be paid wages that they can comfortably live on and raise a family with no matter where they live and work in the world. According to the Living Wage Campaign, a job should keep one out of poverty, not keep one in it. It is an goal that all women can sign on to and work toward, and it has provided a glue for women's and workers' rights groups to work collectively to further the interests of individuals and families everywhere.[2]

Young people's activism and the opposition cultures they are creating are revitalizing feminism in the twenty-first century. Young women and men who identify as third-wave feminists are engaging in a wide variety of efforts to defend women's rights, fight against violence against women, and challenge a culture they see as dehumanizing and exploitative. They are also making connections between the subordination of women and other forms of injustice and violence. Rebecca Walker, a founder of the Third Wave Foundation, explains, "We want to be linked with our foremothers and centuries of women's movements, but we want to make space for young women to create their own, different brand of revolt, and so we choose the name Third Wave."[3] Leslie Heywood and Jennifer Drake, two women who describe themselves as third-wave feminists, see their movement as combining "elements of second-wave critique of beauty and culture, sexual abuse, and power structures, while it also acknowledges and makes use of the pleasure, danger, and defining power of those structures."[4]

Women singers are introducing passionate feminist lyrics into popular music, and young women are producing "Zines" that express anger at the pressures on young girls to conform to media-inspired images of femininity and outrage at violence against women. Young women are also using the Internet to organize and network around a wide variety of issues. Young feminists have reclaimed the word "girl," which second-wave feminists found demeaning, infusing it with a new spirit of independence, defiance, and female solidarity. According to Amy Richards and

---

[2]Living Wage Campaign, http://letjusticeroll.org/.

[3]Rebecca Walker, "Foreword: We Are Using This Power to Resist," in *The Fire This Time: Young Activists and the New Feminism*, ed. Vivien Labaton and Dawn Lundy Martin (New York: Random House, 2004), p. 3.

[4]Leslie Heywood and Jennifer Drake, Introduction to *Third Wave Agenda: Being Feminist, Doing Feminism*, ed. Leslie Heywood and Jennifer Drake (Minneapolis: University of Minnesota Press, 1997), p. 3.

Jennifer Baumgardner, "third wave feminism's contribution to women's history builds on the foundation of the second wave. It is the thousands of little girls with temporary tattoos on their arms, and Mia Hamm soccer jerseys on their backs, who own the bleachers at the Women's World Cup, just as much as the few writers and leaders who have attained prominence. Our activism is in the single mother who organizes the baby-sitting chain on Election Day so that all the housebound mothers can vote."[5]

One of the strengths of contemporary feminism is its multi-issue approach. As women confront sexism in different situations, new issues emerge and our understanding of women's experience deepens. The final section of this chapter includes descriptions of women organizing in various contexts from the 1970s to the 2000s. They tell stories of women who, inspired by the growing legitimacy of feminist concerns, refused to accept unfair treatment or who perceived a problem and decided to do something about it. In all of these organizing efforts, consciousness raising was a crucial ingredient because women needed to talk to each other about their experiences in order to develop strategies. In some situations, such as women dealing with AIDS in prison, breaking the silence in itself makes an enormous difference. These stories demonstrate that, despite the media proclamations, feminism did not die in the 1980s; it lived in the many efforts of women organizing around specific issues on local, national, and transnational levels. As women develop strategies and tactics to address current issues, they are reviving methods such as civil disobedience and developing new approaches to change. Young women bring a fresh perspective to feminism, as they grew up in a world in which feminist ideas and language were an integral part of our culture even though much work needs to be done to achieve feminist goals.

We hope that the many different voices in *Women: Images and Realities* have spoken to you and deepened your understanding of women's experience. While you may not have agreed with everything you read, we hope it has stimulated your thinking. We have tried in this anthology to do several things: demonstrate the commonalities and differences among women; emphasize the power of women talking and working together; stimulate thinking about the ways women of different backgrounds can work together effectively; and, finally, encourage you to participate in the process of improving women's lives. Though this book is concluding, we hope your involvement with feminism continues.

---

[5]Amy Richards and Jennifer Baumgardner, *Manifesta: Young Women, Feminism and the Future* (New York: Farrar, Straus and Giroux, 2000).

Feminism as a Social Movement

We have discussed feminist ideas earlier in this book, but we turn in this section to a consideration of the history of feminism as a social movement. We begin with a brief history of feminism in the United States from 1848 to 1990 and with documents from the first and second waves of feminism. The second selection is a document signed by the people who gathered at the first women's rights convention in Seneca Falls, New York, in 1848. It describes the wide range of issues they discussed. It is useful to think about the extent to which the goals of the Seneca Falls convention have been achieved and what issues seem most resistant to change.

Three years later, Sojourner Truth addressed a women's rights convention in Akron, Ohio. Sojourner Truth had been a slave in New York State and traveled around the country preaching and speaking against slavery and in favor of women's rights. Her eloquent speeches and powerful delivery made her a sought-after public speaker. The speech that she gave in Ohio was popularized by Frances Gage, the chair of the convention, who wrote it down 12 years after it was given. The Gage version, featuring the refrain "Ain't I a Woman," became a rallying cry for the feminist movement, but historians believe that the newspaper version, recorded by Marius Robinson, the secretary for the meeting, was closer to Truth's actual words.

George Middleton was one of the many speakers at a feminist meeting in 1914 that was designed to educate the public about the ideas of feminism. Middleton was a playwright who was married to another feminist activist, Fola La Follette. His speech expresses the wide-ranging cultural and social critique espoused by the women and men who identified as feminists in the early twentieth century.

The fifth document was written in the early days of the second wave of feminism. It describes the evolution of consciousness raising as a technique for understanding women's oppression, an important source of insight for women's liberation activists in the 1960s and 1970s. The ideas that emerged in consciousness raising often laid the foundation for action projects. As women talked about their bodies, for example, they confronted their own woeful ignorance, a legacy of years of secrecy and shame. Convinced that knowledge was an essential ingredient of controlling one's own body, they determined to teach themselves and each other about women's physiology. Susan Brownmiller tells the story of the Boston Women's Health Book Collective, which emerged from this process and produced a book that has been on the best-seller list for years, has been translated into many languages, and has become a valuable resource for women throughout the world.

In the next four essays, women of color discuss the analysis that emerged from their discussion of the multiple oppressions they encounter. Benita Roth tells the history of the African-American feminism that emerged in the late 1960s and 1970s, which emphasized the importance of class and race as well as gender in shaping women's experience. The writing of feminists of color speaks to the necessity of working against all forms of oppression simultaneously, which involves working with men against racism while challenging their sexism, a process that is often painful. Chicana feminists, Alma Garcia explains, have had to struggle against sexist traditions deeply embedded in their culture. In an essay written after attending the founding convention of Ohoyo, a national organization of American Indian women, in 1979, Kate Shanley points out that American Indian feminists seek to retain the alternative family forms and communal values of tribal life. Miriam Ching Yoon Louie writes that her several identities, as a Korean-American woman, helped her make connections across ethnic, class and national lines to fight for justice on a global scale. As all these selections point out, coalitions among different groups of women can be meaningful only if each group has had an opportunity to develop its own agenda. Even though gender is a source of oppression for all women, discrimination based on race, ethnicity, and class complicates the oppression for women from different backgrounds.

Like any movement that challenges established hierarchies and cherished beliefs, the feminist movement has encountered ridicule and opposition. In her best-selling book *Backlash: The Undeclared War on American Women*, Susan Faludi exposed the media assault on feminism during the 1980s. Faludi argued that the press, TV, movies, and the fashion industry have endeavored to convince women to relinquish the struggle for equality and respect by proclaiming that women have won all the rights they need and this only makes them miserable. In fact, equality has not been achieved, and women are struggling to combine work and family without institutional supports.

Through the 1980s, women everywhere and especially in the Global South joined the labor force in unprecedented numbers. Along with their numbers came a new consciousness about their power and rights as workers and citizens. The Beijing women's conference in 1995 provided a space for women to begin to think about their connections globally as women and workers. Women began organizing at local, national, and international levels. Charlotte Bunch challenges women to expand our perspectives by exploring differences around the world and ultimately bring about a deepening commitment to social justice in a transnational context. She points to the growing global consciousness of feminists in this decade and the importance of bringing a global awareness to local and national actions.

As industries moved across the globe looking for "favorable" labor conditions, exploitation of workers in the Global South (and the North to a lesser extent) became common.[1] Cynthia Enloe describes the oppressive conditions of women workers in Asian sweatshops where they make sneakers and collegiate gear for Nike and other transnational companies. Enloe highlights the courageous efforts of women workers to organize unions in the 1980s and 1990s. Solidarity across

---

[1]Matt Zwolinski, "Sweatshops: Definitions, History and Morality," in *Social Issues in America: An Encyclopedia*, ed. James Ciment (Armonk, NY: M. E. Sharpe, 2006).

national lines was crucial to the success of the workers' efforts in these factories, and students in the USA mobilized against sweatshop labor.

United Students Against Sweatshops (USAS) is exemplary for its support of the struggles against sweatshop labor and demonstrates how working at a local level to support workers' rights elsewhere can lead to successful outcomes. Collaborating with workers in offshore factories like the one described by Sonia Beatriz Lara, they pressured factories to join the Worker Rights Consortium (WRC) which, according to their Web site, is "a non-profit organization created by college and university administrations, students and labor rights experts. The WRC's purpose is to assist in the enforcement of manufacturing Codes of Conduct adopted by colleges and universities; these Codes are designed to ensure that factories producing clothing and other goods bearing college and university names respect the basic rights of workers" (www.workersrights.org). As described in the essay about USAS, student organizing has played a crucial role in supporting workers' efforts to improve their wages and working conditions in Latin America and Asia. Since their essay was written, the workers at the Kukdong factory (whose name changed to Mexmode) negotiated their second contract, bringing their wages to twice the Mexican national average. Their union, initially called SITEKIM (Sindicato Independiente de los Trabajadores de Kujdong) and later SITEMEX when the factory's name changed, remains a strong bargaining agent for the workers at Mexmode.

 150

The First and Second Waves of Feminism in the United States

AMY KESSELMAN

The history of feminism is a story of ebb and flow. There have been periods when women's issues were on everyone's lips: laws changed, barriers toppled, and a world in which women and men participated equally in all aspects of life seemed to be around the corner. Such periods were often followed by periods of reaction in which feminism was labeled evil and socially destructive, and efforts to achieve equality for women stagnated. Throughout history women have worked to improve their lives in a variety of ways, but historians often describe the organized women's movements of the United States as two waves of feminism, because it was these movements that pushed women's issues to the forefront of national politics and are the easiest to document. Increasingly, however, historians are finding efforts to expand women's rights and opportunities before these periods of mobilization, raising the complicated question of when the movements began and ended and how to define feminist activity.[1]

Both the first and second waves of U.S. feminism were born in periods of cultural upheaval when many people were engaged in questioning social, cultural, and political norms. The first wave of feminism emerged among women who were active in the reform movements of the 1840s and 1850s. The antislavery movement in particular nurtured female organizing efforts and stimulated thinking about the meaning of human rights for women. In 1848 a group of women who had been involved in Quaker and antislavery activities organized a convention at Seneca Falls, New York, to "discuss the social, civil and religious rights of women."[2] About 300 people gathered, and they adopted a series of resolutions drafted by Elizabeth Cady Stanton calling for an end to the subordination of women in all areas of life. While both women and men attended this convention, the speeches and resolutions made it clear, in Stanton's words, "that woman herself must do this work; for woman alone can understand the height, the depth, the length and the breadth of her degradation."[3] Women's rights conventions were held regularly after this, and women all over the country engaged in efforts to change unjust laws, improve the education of women, and eliminate the barriers to women's participation in public life.

Although the leadership of the women's rights movement was predominantly white, there were several prominent African-American women who worked for the emancipation of both African-Americans and women. Maria Stewart of Boston was one of the first women to speak in public to groups of women and men, urging African-American women to become economically independent. Her outspoken defense of her right to speak in public on political as well as religious issues put her, according to historian Christine Stansell, "far out in front of even the most advanced opinions about women" in the 1830s.[4] Sojourner Truth, a spellbinding orator, spoke at women's rights and antislavery meetings of the connection between freedom for women and the emancipation of enslaved African-Americans.[5] After the Civil War, Mary Ann Shadd Cary argued that black women were eligible to vote under the Fourteenth Amendment and successfully registered to vote in 1871.[6] Frances Ellen Watkins Harpur, a poet and lecturer, spoke frequently at women's rights conventions as a voice for black women.[7]

At first obtaining the right to vote was but one of the many goals of the women's rights movement, but by the end of the Civil War it became the movement's primary focus, because women's rights activists believed that winning suffrage was a necessary tool for the achievement of all other aspects of women's emancipation.[8] Women worked state by state to obtain the right to vote and by 1900 had achieved suffrage in several western states. After the turn of the century, a new generation of women suffragists renewed the effort to pass a national amendment to the Constitution granting women the right to vote.

The focus on suffrage had advantages and disadvantages. It was a concrete reform that could be used to mobilize women, and it symbolized, perhaps more than anything else, the participation of women as individuals in public life. On the other hand, winning the right to vote required gaining the approval of male voters and politicians. Women suffragists often adopted whatever arguments they felt were necessary to persuade those in power that it was in their interest to grant women the right to vote. They often invoked traditional gender roles as they campaigned for the vote, urging for example that women would "sew the seams and cook the meals; to vote won't take us long."[9]

Suffragist pragmatism also intensified the racism, nativism, and class bias of the white, native-born suffrage leadership. In the late nineteenth and early twentieth centuries, immigrants poured into the United States, radically changing the social, economic, and political landscape. The rhetoric of women's suffrage leadership often reflected the bias of white, native-born citizens against these new Americans. Carrie Chapman Catt, for example, who became president of the National American Woman Suffrage Association (NAWSA), warned against "the danger of the ignorant foreign vote which was sought to be brought up by each party." Urging literacy requirements, she concluded that the best solution would be to "cut off the vote of the slums and give it to the women."[10]

Similarly, southern white suffragists were willing to invoke racism to further their cause, arguing that the enfranchisement of white women would help to sustain white supremacy in the South. When the NAWSA voted in 1903 to allow state chapters to determine their own membership, it gave tacit approval to southern racism because southern clubs excluded African-American women and often argued that suffrage should be granted only to those who met property or literacy requirements.

Despite the racism of white women's suffrage organizations, African-American women were actively involved in efforts to gain the right to vote in the early twentieth century, organizing black women's suffrage clubs throughout the United States. "If white women needed the vote to acquire advantages and protection of their rights, then black women needed the vote even more so," argued Adella Hunt Logan, a member of the Tuskegee Woman's Club.[11] The NAWSA, however, was engaged in efforts to get the women's suffrage amendment passed by a U.S. Senate dominated by white southern men. As a result they were less than hospitable to African-American women's groups that wanted to affiliate, arguing that they should resubmit their application after the vote was won.[12]

While the women's suffrage movement focused on the single issue of winning the right to vote, the late nineteenth and early twentieth century saw the flowering of many different efforts by women to improve their lives and create a more just and generous world. Margaret Sanger, Emma Goldman, Mary Ware Dennett, and others led a movement to make birth control legal and available to all women. Ida B. Wells initiated a crusade against lynching, a source of terror for black people during this period. Black and white women educators worked to expand women's educational opportunities, and women labor activists organized to improve the wages and working conditions of the wage-earning women who worked in factories, stores, and offices.

Attitudes toward women's capabilities began to shift; the image of the "new woman" of the early twentieth century embodied self-reliance and engagement with the world. It was during this period that the term *feminism* was introduced by women who believed women's emancipation required deeper changes than the right to vote. They argued for the full integration of women into social, political, and economic life. While suffragists often argued for the right to vote in the name of women's traditional roles, claiming that women's propensity for nurturance and housekeeping would be useful in the public world, feminists renounced

self-sacrifice in favor of self-development. At a 1914 meeting entitled "What Is Feminism?" Mary Jenny Howe stated: "We want simply to be ourselves . . . not just our little female selves but our whole big human selves."[13] In their speeches and organizational work, women of color emphasized the connections among various forms of oppression. Anna Julia Cooper, an African-American woman, declared in her address to the World's Congress of Representative Women in 1896: "Not till . . . race, color, sex and condition are seen as accidents, and not the substance of life . . . not till then is woman's lesson taught and woman's cause won—not the white woman's, nor the black woman's nor the red woman's, but the cause of every man and every woman who has writhed silently under a mighty wrong. Woman's wrongs are thus indissolubly linked with all undefended woe, and the acquirement of her 'rights' will mean the final triumph of all right over might."[14]

Socialists like Charlotte Perkins Gilman suggested that women's emancipation required the elimination of private housekeeping in favor of community kitchens and child care centers. "If there should be built and opened," Gilman argued, "in any of our large cities today a commodious and well served apartment house for professional women with families, it would be filled at once. The apartments would be without kitchens; but there would be a kitchen belonging to the house from which meals could be served to the families in their rooms or in a common dining room, as preferred. It would be a home where the cleaning was done by efficient workers, not hired separately by the families, but engaged by the manager of the establishment; and a roof-garden, day nursery and kindergarten under well-trained professional nurses and teachers would insure proper care of the children.[15]

After 72 years of work, the women's suffrage amendment was ratified by the states in 1920. In the decades that followed, the women's movement shrank in numbers and influence, and those women who remained active were divided about the best way to improve women's lives. The Constitution now gave all citizens the right to vote, but

African-Americans of both sexes had been disenfranchised in the South by racist violence and state laws. While magazines and newspapers often proclaimed that women's equality had been achieved, many barriers to women's full participation in the workplace, in politics, and in cultural and social life remained intact. Feminism fell into disrepute, conjuring up images of fanatic women out to spoil men's fun. When the depression of the 1930s created massive unemployment, women wage earners were regarded with suspicion, further intensifying antifeminist sentiment. By the post–World War II era a resurgence of the cult of domesticity denigrated female ambition, even though large numbers of women were working for wages. Although there were groups who remained active on behalf of women, laying the groundwork for the future resurgence of feminism, feminism itself was demonized in the popular culture. In the 1960s when women again began to rebel against their subordinate status, the first wave of feminism was a distant memory; recovering its history was an important ingredient in developing a new movement for the liberation of women.

What lessons can we learn from the rise and fall of the first wave of women's rights activism in the United States? Winning the right to vote, a seemingly basic democratic right, took almost a century to accomplish and required an enormous amount of brilliant organizing, writing, and speaking. The benefit of hindsight, however, allows us to see that a great deal was sacrificed to achieve this goal. The capitulation of the mainstream suffrage movement to racism and prejudice against immigrants meant that it spoke for a narrow segment of women. Its failure to challenge the division between men's and women's worlds meant that when it won the right to vote, many forms of sexism remained. The suffrage movement demonstrates the perils of focusing exclusively on one goal, deferring others until it is achieved.

The second wave of feminism developed among different groups of women whose combined resources and insights augmented its power and influence on American culture. The equal rights segment of the movement originated among women working within government agencies who were frustrated by the slow pace of change. They founded the National Organization for Women (NOW) in 1966 to work for equality in work, education, and politics. One of NOW's founders, Betty Friedan, was the author of the influential best-seller *The Feminine Mystique,* which described the frustrations of college-educated suburban housewives and argued that women should be encouraged to pursue careers as well as motherhood.[16]

The tensions that were building in the lives of women in the 1950s and 1960s, however, went beyond the need for work outside the home; they had to do with the devaluation of women in everyday life, sexual objectification, the violence against women that permeated society, and the socialization of women to meet the needs of men. These aspects of sexism were so tightly woven into the fabric of U.S. culture that they were taken for granted and rarely discussed. Young women who had been involved in the social movements for peace and justice in the 1960s were able to bring these issues into the open. These young women called themselves "women's liberation," and argued for radical changes in the political, social, and economic institutions of our society. Accustomed to being on the fringes of respectability, they were willing to talk about subjects that were previously hidden and analyze their own lives for insights about the nature of women's oppression, a process that came to be known as consciousness raising. As women began to talk about their childhood, their sexual lives, their feelings about being female, their work and school experiences, and the ways male violence affected their lives, the contours of feminist theory emerged. Betsy Gilbertson, a white woman who had been active in the antiwar movement, remembers her experience of a consciousness raising.

> We would take some piece of experience, that it had never occurred to me at least to think about differently, and talk about it. Like . . . High School, and the importance of having boobs, and what it was like to be smart, and . . . whether you could major in Math or Science—the things which are now canons of the faith. So we would look at one another and say, "well, I remember" and kind of

piece it together like that. "The way that I felt about this was. . . ." The experience that captured that best for me was one day looking at the front page of the newspaper and there was not a single woman's name on it—and I had been reading the newspaper all my life and I had never noticed that. It was like that. And this light; I mean it was literally like someone had screwed in a light bulb. And all of a sudden I had a set of lenses for looking at the world, that I hadn't had before, and the whole world looked different through them.[17]

Women within the black, Latino, Asian, and American Indian movements of the late 1960s and 1970s were questioning the sexism within their own movements, often encountering resistance from movement men. Emboldened by the hard-won successes of the civil rights movement, African-American women activists began to recognize the disjunction between civil rights rhetoric and women's experience. "Freedom was in the air," remembered Frances Beal, an activist in the Student Nonviolent Coordinating Committee who helped to found the Third World Women's Alliance. "And all this talk—it's like Sojourner [Truth] says what's all this talk about freedom?" As they talked with each other, they confirmed their observations that women were often doing the menial tasks while men took the public leadership roles. "When people began talking about men should do this and do that," commented Beal, "and women should do that, we said, 'Now wait a minute. This sounds familiar.'"[18]

In consciousness-raising groups, women of color broke traditional silences and generated a feminist analysis that spoke to their experience and recognized the interaction of racism and sexism in their lives. In an Asian women's group in the early 1970s, for example, Miya Iwataki remembers, "Women began talking about years of scotch-taping eyelids to create a double eyelid fold and then carefully painting it over with Maybelline eyeliner. Women began to break through years of checking out each other as competition for Asian men; of fearing being found out that one was not a virgin; or having to be anything but a 'natural woman.'"[19]

For the women who were reinventing feminism, the rediscovery of a history of feminist thought and practice was enormously exhilarating; it reconfirmed their belief in the necessity and possibility of changing women's position at a time when women's liberation activists were being ridiculed and discounted. Members of a Chicana women's group in 1971, for example, were delighted to discover a women's organization that published a newspaper called "*Hijas de Cuahtemac*" during the 1910 Mexican Revolution, and they decided to use the same name for their own group. Anna Nieto-Gomez, one of the members, remembers "It was like I had been in a cave and someone has just lit the candle. I [suddenly] realized how important it was to read about your own kind, the women of your own culture, or your own historical heritage, doing the things that you were doing. [It] reaffirmed and validated that you're not a strange, alien person, that what you're doing is not only normal but a part of your history."[20]

The interaction of the various groups of women strengthened the feminist movement. NOW broadened its agenda to include the issues raised by "women's liberation," recognizing that the achievement of equality would require deep systemic changes in the relationship between home and family and the concepts of "femininity" and "masculinity." While women's liberation groups were generating analysis and challenging long-held assumptions, NOW provided concrete strategies for implementing these ideas, such as litigation against discriminatory corporations and efforts to change laws governing rape, violence, and divorce.

As different groups of women developed feminist analysis to address their experience, feminism grew deeper and broader. This process was not always without friction, as groups who felt their needs were being ignored confronted the leadership of feminist organizations, which sometimes presented the experience of white, heterosexual women as if it were universal. After several stormy meetings, NOW included the protection of lesbian rights in its agenda. Women of color generated feminist analysis to address their experience and challenged feminist organizations to work against racism and develop an "inclusive sisterhood."[21] They emphasized the interaction among the effects of class, gender, and race/ethnicity in their lives, rejecting an analysis that focused primarily on gender, and they often worked in separate groups in order to focus on the needs of their communities.[22]

Feminists accomplished a great deal in a short period of time. Ridiculed at first by the media, they quickly changed public consciousness about a host of issues, from rape to employment discrimination. Feminists worked in a variety of ways to change laws, attitudes, practices, and institutions. NOW and other equal rights groups challenged segregated want ads, sued hundreds of major corporations for sex discrimination, and lobbied in state legislatures to change laws about rape, domestic violence, divorce, and employment. Women working outside the system organized demonstrations and attention-grabbing actions like street theater at the Miss America pageant. They also established institutions that addressed women's unmet needs, such as battered women's shelters, rape crisis centers, and feminist health clinics.[23] Feminists inside the university created women's studies programs and engaged in research about women in various disciplines.

Throughout the 1970s and 1980s countless women made individual changes in their lives, going back to school or waged work, leaving oppressive marriages, developing emotional and sexual relationships with other women, working to develop relationships of mutuality and respect with men.

Because reproductive freedom was clearly central to women's efforts to participate fully and equally in society, feminists throughout the country united in efforts to repeal abortion laws, reinvigorating an abortion reform movement that had been active throughout the 1960s. A few states legalized abortion in the early 1970s, but most state legislatures were resistant to efforts to decriminalize abortion, so women throughout the country filed suits against state laws that made abortion illegal.[24] The suit against the Texas abortion statute, *Roe v. Wade,* made its way to the Supreme Court, which, in its landmark decision in 1973, declare laws criminalizing abortion unconstitutional, legalizing abortion in all states.

Many feminists felt that the effort to end sex discrimination would be substantially enhanced by a federal amendment guaranteeing equal rights to women. In 1972 the U.S. Congress passed an equal rights amendment that proclaimed, "Equality of rights under the laws shall not be denied or abridged by the U.S. or by any State on account of sex." The amendment was then sent on to be ratified by the states and was quickly approved in the legislatures of 34 of the 38 states required for final passage. It stalled, however, in 14 states in which a new coalition of conservative organizations mobilized to defeat it. Charging that the equal rights amendment and the feminist revolution that it came to symbolize would undermine traditional values and deprive women of the protections they have as wives and mothers, opponents of the ERA enlisted women in their anti-ERA campaign. Mormon and evangelical religious organizations poured resources into efforts to defeat the ERA. Their rhetoric tapped into anxiety about changes in the division of labor, sexuality, and the family, and galvanized a new antifeminist coalition that opposed the ERA, the legalization of abortion, and other feminist reforms. When the deadline for ratification arrived in 1982, the ERA had not passed in enough states for ratification.[25]

The ascendancy of the right wing in the Republican Party in the 1980s further intensified the assault on feminism, and many of the gains of the 1970s were seriously threatened. The second wave of feminism, however, left an indelible imprint on American society. The momentum may have slowed, but millions of women's lives have been changed, and cherished assumptions about gender, sexuality, work, and family have been deeply shaken. Although women remain a minority in positions of political power, their voices are being heard more clearly on public policy issues. Integrating feminist approaches to these issues into public policy will require continued pressure on centers of political power.   [2011]

NOTES

1. For discussion of women's political rights in the 1840s, see, for example, Lori Ginzberg, *Untidy Origins: A Story of Women's Rights in Antebellum New York* (Chapel Hill: University of North Carolina Press, 2005). For discussion of different streams of women's political and economic rights in the 1940s and 1950s, see Leila Rupp and Verta Taylor, *Survival in the Doldrums: The American Women's Rights Movement, 1945 to the 1960s*

(New York: Oxford University Press, 1987); Kate Weigand, *Red Feminism: American Communism and the Making of Women's Liberation* (Baltimore: Johns Hopkins University Press, 2001); Dorothy Sue Cobble, *The Other Women's Movement: Workplace Justice and Social Rights in Modern America* (Princeton, NJ: Princeton University Press, 2004). For discussion of the activism of women of color and its relationship to the timing of second-wave feminism, see Kimberly Springer, *Living for the Revolution: Black Feminist Organizations, 1968–1980* (Durham: Duke University Press, 2005), 7–10; and Becky Thompson, "Multiracial Feminism: Recasting the Chronology of Second Wave Feminism," *Feminist Studies* (Summer 2002): 337–60.

2. Eleanor Flexner, *Century of Struggle.* Harvard University Press, Cambridge, 1970, p. 74; See also Judith Wellman, *Grass Roots Reform in the Burned-Over District of Upstate New York: Religion, Abolition and Democracy.* (NY: Garland, 2000).

3. Flexner p. 77

4. Marilyn Richardson, ed., *Maria W. Stewart, America's First Black Woman Political Writer: Essays and Speeches* (Bloomington: Indiana University Press, 1987); Christine Stansell, *The Feminist Promise, 1792 to the Present* (New York: Random House, 2010), 35.

5. For biographies of Sojourner Truth, see Carleton Mabee, *Sojourner Truth: Slave, Prophet, Legend* (New York: New York University Press, 1993); Nell Irvin Painter, *Sojourner Truth: A Life, a Symbol* (New York: W. W. Norton, 1996); and Margaret Washington, *Sojourner Truth's America* (Ithaca, NY: Cornell University Press, 2009). For a fictionalized treatment of Sojourner Truth's life, see Jacqueline Sheehan, *Truth: A Novel* (New York: Free Press, 2003).

6. Paula Giddings, *When and Where I Enter* (New York: William Morrow, 1984), 70–71.

7. Ibid., 63–64.

8. Ellen Carol DuBois, *Feminism and Suffrage: The Emergence of an Independent Women's Movement in America, 1848–1869* (Ithaca, NY: Cornell University Press, 1978).

9. "Getting Out the Vote," song from the New York Women's Suffrage Campaign, from *Songs of the Suffragettes.*

10. Quoted in Aileen Kraditor, *The Ideas of the Women's Suffrage Movement, 1890–1920* (New York: Norton, 1981), 125.

11. Quoted in Giddings, *When and Where I Enter,* 121.

12. Rosalyn Terborg-Penn, *African American Women in the Struggle for the Vote, 1850–1920* (Bloomington: Indiana University Press, 1998).

13. Quoted in Nancy Cott, *The Grounding of Modern Feminism* (New Haven, CT: Yale University Press, 1987), 39.

14. Quoted in Elsa Barkley Brown, "Maggie Lena Walker and the Independent Order of St. Luke," *Signs* 14 (Spring 1989): 614.

15. Charlotte Perkins Gilman, "Women in Economics," in *The Feminist Papers,* ed. Alice Rossi (Boston: Northeastern University Press, 1988), 592.

16. Recent research has demonstrated that Betty Friedan had links to what Dorothy Sue Cobble has called the labor feminism of the 1940s, a connection she played down in the context of Cold War politics. See Daniel Horowitz, *Betty Friedan and the Making of the "Feminine Mystique"* (Amherst: University of Massachusetts Press, 1998).

17. Elizabeth Gilbertson, interview with author, July 6, 1991.

18. Quoted in Springer, *Living for the Revolution,* 46. See Carol Giardina, *Freedom for Women: Forging the Women's Liberation Movement, 1953–1970* (Gainesville: University Press of Florida, 2010), for a discussion of the pivotal role of civil rights activists in the development of women's liberation.

19. Quoted in Sherna Gluck, "Whose Feminism, Whose History? Reflections on Excavating the History of (the) U.S. Women's Movement(s)," in *Community Activism and Feminist Politics,* ed. Nancy Naples (New York: Routledge, 1998).

20. Ibid., 39.

21. Bonnie Thornton Dill, "Race, Class and Gender: Prospects for an Inclusive Sisterhood," *Feminist Studies* 9, no. 1 (Spring 1983): 131.

22. See Benita Roth, *Separate Roads to Feminism: Black, Chicana and White Feminist Movements in America's Second Wave* (Cambridge: Cambridge University Press, 2004), for a discussion of the different versions of feminism that developed among these three groups of women.

23. For descriptions of feminism, 1965 to 2000, see Susan Brownmiller, *In Our Time: Memoirs of a Revolution,* (New York: Dial, 1999); Ruth Rosen, *The World Split Open: How the Modern Women's Movement Changed America* (New York: Viking, 2000); Sara Evans, *Tidal Wave: How Women Changed America at Century's End* (New York: Free Press, 2003); Stansell, *The Feminist Promise*; Stephanie Gilmore, ed., *Feminist Coalitions: Historical Perspectives on Second-Wave Feminism in the United States* (Urbana: University of Illinois Press, 2008); and Nancy Hewitt, ed., *No Permanent Wave: Recasting Histories of U.S. Feminism* (New Brunswick, NJ: Rutgers University Press, 2010). For original sources from the women's liberation movement, see Rosalyn Baxandall and Linda Gordon, *Dear Sisters: Dispatches from the Women's Liberation Movement* (New York: Basic Books, 2000).

24. For the story of the movements to legalize abortion, see Reva Seigel and Linda Greenhouse, *Before Roe v. Wade: Voices That Shaped the Abortion Debate Before the Supreme Court's Ruling* (Washington, DC: Kaplan, 2010).

25. See Jane Mansbridge, *Why We Lost the ERA* (Chicago: University of Chicago Press, 1988), for an analysis of the failure of the ERA to be ratified by the states.

🌿 151

The Seneca Falls Women's Rights Convention, 1848

"DECLARATION OF SENTIMENTS"

When, in the course of human events, it becomes necessary for one portion of the family of man to assume among the people of the earth a position different from that which they have hitherto occupied, but one to which the laws of nature and of nature's God entitle them, a decent respect to the opinions of mankind requires that they should declare the causes that impel them to such a course.

We hold these truths to be self-evident: that all men and women are created equal; that they are endowed by their Creator with certain inalienable rights; that among these are life, liberty, and the pursuit of happiness; that to secure these rights governments are instituted, deriving their just powers from the consent of the governed. Whenever any form of government becomes destructive of these ends, it is the right of those who suffer from it to refuse allegiance to it, and to insist upon the institution of a new government, laying its foundation on such principles, and organizing its powers in such form, as to them shall seem most likely to effect their safety and happiness. Prudence indeed, will dictate that governments long established should not be changed for light and transient causes; and accordingly all experience hath shown that mankind are more disposed to suffer, while evils are sufferable, than to right themselves by abolishing the forms to which they were accustomed. But when a long train of abuses and usurpations, pursuing invariably the same object evinces a design to reduce them under absolute despotism, it is their duty to throw off such government, and to provide new guards for their future security. Such has been the patient sufferance of the women under this government, and such is now the necessity which constrains them to demand the equal station to which they are entitled.

The history of mankind is a history of repeated injuries and usurpations on the part of man toward woman, having in direct object the establishment of an absolute tyranny over her. To prove this, let facts be submitted to a candid world.

He has never permitted her to exercise her inalienable right to the elective franchise.

He has compelled her to submit to laws, in the formation of which she had no voice.

He has withheld from her rights which are given to the most ignorant and degraded men—both natives and foreigners.

Having deprived her of this first right of a citizen, the elective franchise, thereby leaving her without representation in the halls of legislation, he has oppressed her on all sides.

He has made her, if married, in the eye of the law, civilly dead.

He has taken from her all right in property, even to the wages she earns.

He has made her, morally, an irresponsible being, as she can commit many crimes with impunity, provided they be done in the presence of her husband. In the covenant of marriage, she is compelled to promise obedience to her husband, he becoming, to all intents and purposes, her master— the law giving him power to deprive her of her liberty, and to administer chastisement.

He has so framed the laws of divorce, as to what shall be the proper causes, and in case of separation, to whom the guardianship of the children shall be given, as to be wholly regardless of the happiness of women—the law, in all cases, going upon a false supposition of the supremacy of man, and giving all power into his hands.

After depriving her of all rights as a married woman, if single, and the owner of property, he has taxed her to support a government which recognizes her only when her property can be made profitable to it.

He has monopolized nearly all the profitable employments, and from those she is permitted to follow, she receives but a scanty remuneration. He closes against her all the avenues to wealth and distinction which he considers most honorable to himself. As a teacher of theology, medicine, or law, she is not known.

He has denied her the facilities for obtaining a thorough education, all colleges being closed against her.

He allows her in Church, as well as State, but a subordinate position, claiming Apostolic authority for her exclusion from the ministry, and, with some exceptions, from any public participation in the affairs of the Church.

He has created a false public sentiment by giving to the world a different code of morals for men and women, by which moral delinquencies which exclude women from society, are not only tolerated, but deemed of little account in man.

He has usurped the prerogative of Jehovah himself, claiming it as his right to assign for her a sphere of action, when that belongs to her conscience and to her God.

He has endeavored, in every way that he could, to destroy her confidence in her own powers, to lessen her self-respect, and to make her willing to lead a dependent and abject life.

Now, in view of this entire disfranchisement of one-half the people of this country, their social and religious degradation—in view of the unjust laws above mentioned, and because women do feel themselves aggrieved, oppressed, and fraudulently deprived of their most sacred rights, we insist that they have immediate admission to all the rights and privileges which belong to them as citizens of the United States.

In entering upon the great work before us, we anticipate no small amount of misconception, misrepresentation, and ridicule; but we shall use every instrumentality within our power to effect our object. We shall employ agents, circulate tracts, petition the State and National legislatures, and endeavor to enlist the pulpit and the press in our behalf. We hope this Convention will be followed by a series of Conventions embracing every part of the country.

SENECA FALLS RESOLUTIONS

Whereas, The great precept of nature is conceded to be, that "man shall pursue his own true and substantial happiness." Blackstone in his Commentaries remarks, that this law of Nature being coeval with mankind, and dictated by God himself, is of course superior in obligation to any other. It is binding over all the globe, in all countries and at all times; no human laws are of any validity if contrary to this, and such of them as are valid, derive all their force, and all their validity, and all their authority, mediately and immediately, from this original; therefore,

Resolved, That such laws as conflict, in any way, with the true and substantial happiness of woman, are contrary to the great precept of nature and of no validity, for this is "superior in obligation to any other."

Resolved, That all laws which prevent woman from occupying such a station in society as her conscience shall dictate, or which place her in a position inferior to that of man, are contrary to the great precept of nature, and therefore of no force or authority.

Resolved, That woman is man's equal—was intended to be so by the Creator, and the highest good of the race demands that she should be recognized as such.

Resolved, That the women of this country ought to be enlightened in regard to the laws under which they live, that they may no longer publish their degradation by declaring themselves satisfied with their present position, nor their ignorance, by asserting that they have all the rights they want.

Resolved, That inasmuch as man, while claiming for himself intellectual superiority, does accord to woman moral superiority, it is preeminently his duty to encourage her to speak and teach, as she has an opportunity, in all religious assemblies.

Resolved, That the same amount of virtue, delicacy, and refinement of behavior that is required of woman in the social state, should also be required of man, and the same transgressions should be visited with equal severity on both man and woman.

Resolved, That the objection of indelicacy and impropriety, which is so often brought against woman when she addresses a public audience, comes with a very ill-grace from those who encourage, by their attendance, her appearance on the stage, in the concert, or in feats of the circus.

Resolved, That woman has too long rested satisfied in the circumscribed limits which corrupt customs and a perverted application of the Scriptures have marked out for her, and that it is time she should move in the enlarged sphere which her great Creator has assigned her.

Resolved, That it is the duty of the women of this country to secure to themselves their sacred right to the elective franchise.

Resolved, That the equality of human rights results necessarily from the fact of the identity of the race in capabilities and responsibilities.

Resolved, *therefore*, That, being invested by the Creator with the same capabilities, and the same

Sojourner Truth was born into slavery in Ulster County, New York, in about 1797 (the exact date of her birth is uncertain). After her escape from slavery she became involved in several of the religious and political movements of her day. Changing her name from Isabella to Sojourner Truth, she traveled widely, speaking eloquently against slavery, for women's rights, and about her vision of a kind and loving God. She died in Battle Creek, Michigan, in 1883.

At the 1851 Women's Rights Convention in Akron, Ohio, Sojourner Truth gave a stirring speech on women's rights. While many people may be familiar with the version of the speech that included the phrase "Ain't I a Woman?" which was recorded by Frances Gage in 1863, we reprint here an account written by Marius Robinson that appeared in a contemporary newspaper, The Anti-Slavery Bugle.

Sojourner Truth's Defense of the Rights of Women

One of the most unique and interesting speeches of the Convention was made by Sojourner Truth, an emancipated slave. It is impossible to transfer it to paper, or convey any adequate idea of the effect it produced upon the audience. Those only can appreciate it who saw her powerful form, her whole-souled, earnest gestures, and listened to her strong and truthful tones. She came forward to the platform and addressing the President said with great simplicity:

May I say a few words? Receiving an affirmative answer, she proceeded; I want to say a few words about this matter. I am a woman's rights. [*sic*] I have as much muscle as any man, and can do as much work as any man. I have plowed and reaped and husked and chopped and mowed, and can any man do more than that? I have heard much about the sexes being equal; I can carry as much as any man, and can eat as much too, if I can get it. I am as strong as any man that is now. As for intellect, all I can say is, if a woman have a pint and man a quart—why cant she have her little pint full? You need not be afraid to give us our rights for fear we will take too much,—for we can't take more than our pint'll hold. The poor men seem to be all in confusion, and dont know what to do. Why children, if you have woman's rights give it to her and you will feel better. You will have your own rights, and they wont be so much trouble. I can't read, but I can hear. I have heard the bible and have learned that Eve caused man to sin. Well if woman upset the world, do give her a chance to set it right side up again. The Lady has spoken about Jesus, how he never spurned woman from him, and she was right. When Lazarus died, Mary and Martha came to him with faith and love and besought him to raise their brother. And Jesus wept—and Lazarus came forth. And how came Jesus into the world? Through God who created him and woman who bore him. Man, where is your part? But the women are coming up blessed be God and a few of the man are coming up with them. But man is in a tight place, the poor slave is on him, woman is coming on him, and he is surely between a hawk and a buzzard.

[1851]

consciousness of responsibility for their exercise, it is demonstrably the right and duty of woman, equally with man, to promote every righteous cause by every righteous means; and especially in regard to the great subjects of morals and religion, it is self-evidently her right to participate with her brother in teaching them, both in private and in public, by writing and by speaking, by any instrumentalities proper to be used, and in any assemblies proper to be held; and this being a self-evident truth growing out of the divinely implanted principles of human nature, any custom or authority adverse to it, whether modern or wearing the hoary sanction of antiquity, is to be regarded as a self-evident false-hood, and at war with mankind.

Resolved, That the speedy success of our cause depends upon the zealous and untiring efforts of both men and women, for the overthrow of the monopoly of the pulpit, and for the securing to women an equal participation with men in the various trades, professions, and commerce.   [1848]

🌿 152

What Feminism Means to Me

GEORGE MIDDLETON

Feminism means trouble: trouble means agitation: agitation means movement: movement means life: life means adjustment and readjustment: so does feminism. It is an attack upon social opinion wherever it discriminates in its attitude toward man and woman on the basis of sex. It asks primarily that man and woman be considered as human beings. It recognizes that man and woman are made of the same soul stuff. It sees them respond to the same rhythm in music, the same beauty in verse and the same elemental emotions in life. . . .

With us our human attributes we have in common. Whatever difference in our human qualities there is, is individual. The variation is the same among men as it is among women. It is not however,

a sex difference. Emotion and spirituality are bonds which men and women share in common. There are so-called masculine qualities in many women and much that is feminine in many men. The appel-lation, "maleness and femaleness" as applied to certain human characteristics, is purely arbitrary. We must recognize it has been environment not a biological necessity which in the past has differen-tiated the sexes in the certain channels. Basically men and women are human and from that stand-point, we face feminism. . . . Feminism does not therefore, believe in the effeminization of life but in its humanization. It is not a woman's movement exclusively: it pays equal dividends to men—as we shall see. It cannot achieve completion without the cooperation of men and women. It is not antago-nism. It is mutuality. Feminism is not femaleness with fewer petticoats. It is not an assault on trou-sers. It does not seek to crinoline men. It asks a new change in the social garments of each. Feminism is therefore a state of mind and as a state of mind it faces many facts of life.

From one aspect feminism is an educational ideal. It asks that children be educated according to temperament and not according to sex. It asks a girl be educated for life and not for marriage alone. . . .

In another aspect feminism is an economic attitude. It is opposed to parasi[ti]sm in either male or female as a habit of thought. It asks equal opportunity to work. In England, for example women can't practice law, neither can they in South Carolina. There have been these discriminations on the grounds of sex all over the world. The brave struggle of women initiated by such leaders as Dr. Blackwell and Florence Nightingale, aided by the sympathetic help of men, are gradually break-ing these restrictions down. With this equal oppor-tunity to work and enter all professions, feminists demand equal pay for equal work. It asks that effi-ciency and not sex be the test of value. . . . Femi-nism asserts that there can never be any equality in the laws of marriage and divorce no matter how equal it phrases toward each sex, if the letter of the law is made solely by man and its spirit interpreted solely by man. Feminism is of course in favor of a freer divorce, without unequal social penalties. . . .

Feminism seeks to change social opinion toward the sex relation; not to advocate license but to recognize liberty: not to encourage looseness but to dismiss the double standard of morality. It wishes to destroy that double standard between the sexes as between the classes. . . .

Woman suffrage is the political aspect of feminism. It is the kindergarten of feminism. Many people who believe in woman suffrage do not believe in all of the aspects of feminism. But all feminists are equal suffragists. Feminism believes that both men and women should have some say in the laws under which both are governed. It does not wish to resort to the subterfuges of indirect influence to obtain the things in legislation which are as much woman's right as man's. It recognizes no limitation in civic expression on the ground of sex. It sees too, the need of the vote for woman so that the part of the human race which she represents shall have representation and not charity. Feminism is democratic in its essence and there can be no democracy in the government that denies the suffrage to half its citizens simply because they wear skirts. It sees that one woman in every five is in modern industry, that they are supporting themselves even in whole or in part. It asks that these women, and all others, have the same right as men to express their need and relation to the community. It sees a great horde of women capable and efficient, who should help man with his civic burdens. It wishes, however, to compel no woman to vote if she does not wish to, but it demands that those who do wish to vote shall not be discriminated against because they are women. Feminists do not think all things will be accomplished through the ballot, they do see the great value of woman's suffrage as the fundamental first step in removing the political discriminations against her. With this removed they feel they will better be able to remove the other discriminations.

Feminism is thus a protest against further sex specialization. It wishes the sickening emphasis of sex differences to be taken out of discussion. It wants the energies that are now being wasted in getting certain rights to be expended in the fruitful and useful utilization of those rights.

Feminism therefore, is a mood as well as a movement. It is a high ideal of mutual understanding between the sexes working amid prejudice and tradition. Its aim is greater freedom. Its amunition is an appeal to common humanness. It is an awakening to the higher possibilities of life which lie in the changing social scheme. . . .

Its spirit is expansive. It asks that each sex separately may be able to give to the other more comradeship, more freedom, more self-realization, more honesty, more justice and I believe more beauty.   [1914]

 153

Consciousness Raising: A Radical Weapon

KATHIE SARACHILD

From a talk given to the First National Conference of Stewardesses for Women's Rights in New York City, March 12, 1973.

To be able to understand what feminist consciousness-raising is all about, it is important to remember that it began as a program among women who all considered themselves radicals.

Before we go any further, let's examine the word "radical." It is a word that is often used to suggest extremist, but actually it doesn't mean that. The dictionary says radical means root, coming from the Latin word for root. And that is what we meant by calling ourselves radicals. We were interested in getting to the roots of problems in society. You might say we wanted to pull up weeds in the garden by their roots, not just pick off the leaves at the top to make things momentarily look good. Women's liberation was started by women who considered themselves radicals in this sense.

Our aim in forming a women's liberation group was to start a *mass movement of women* to put an end to the barriers of segregation and discrimination based on sex. We knew radical thinking and radical action would be necessary to do this. We also believed it necessary to form women's liberation groups that excluded men from their meetings.

In order to have a radical approach, to get to the root, it seemed logical that we had to study the situation of women, not just take random action. How best to do this came up in the women's liberation group I was in—New York Radical Women, one of the first in the country—shortly after the group had formed. We were planning our first public action and wandered into a discussion about what to do next. One woman in the group, Ann Forer, spoke up: "I think we have a lot more to do just in the area of raising our consciousness," she said. "Raising consciousness?" I wondered what she meant by that. I'd never heard it applied to women before.

"I've only begun thinking about women as an oppressed group," she continued, "and each day, I'm still learning more about it—my consciousness gets higher."

Now I didn't consider that I had just started thinking about the oppression of women. In fact, I thought of myself as having done lots of thinking about it for quite a while, and lots of reading, too. But then Ann went on to give an example of something she'd noticed that turned out to be a deeper way of seeing it for me, too.

"I think a lot about being attractive," Ann said. "People don't find the real self of a woman attractive." And then she went on to give some examples. And I just sat there listening to her describe all the false ways women have to act: playing dumb, always being agreeable, always being nice, not to mention what we had to do to our bodies with the clothes and shoes we wore, the diets we had to go through, going blind not wearing glasses, all because men didn't find our real selves, our human freedom, our basic humanity "attractive." And I realized I still could learn a lot about how to understand and describe the particular oppression of women in ways that could reach other women in the way this had just reached me. The whole group was moved as I was, and we decided on the spot that what we needed—in the words Ann used—was to "raise our consciousness some more."

At the next meeting there was an argument in the group about how to do this. One woman—Peggy Dobbins—said that what she wanted to do was make a very intensive study of all the literature on the question of whether there really were any biological differences between men and women. I found myself angered by that idea.

"I think it would be a waste of time," I said. "For every scientific study we quote, the opposition can find their scientific studies to quote. Besides, the question is what *we* want to be, what we think we are, not what some authorities in the name of science are arguing over what we are. It is scientifically impossible to tell what the biological differences are between men and women—if there are any besides the obvious physical ones—until all the social and political factors applying to men and women are equal. Everything we have to know, have to prove, we can get from the realities of our own lives. For instance, on the subject of women's intelligence. We know from our own experience that women play dumb for men because, if we're too smart, men won't like us. I know, because I've done it. We've all done it. Therefore, we can simply deduce that women are smarter than men are aware of, and smarter than all those people who make studies are aware of, and that there are a lot of women around who are a lot smarter than they look and smarter than anybody but themselves and maybe a few of their friends know."

In the end the group decided to raise its consciousness by studying women's lives by topics like childhood, jobs, motherhood, etc. We'd do any outside reading we wanted to and thought was important. But our starting point for discussion, as well as our test of the accuracy of what any of the books said, would be the actual experience we had in these areas. One of the questions, suggested by Ann Forer, we would bring at all times to our studies would be—who and what has an *interest* in maintaining the oppression in our lives. The kind of actions the group should engage in, at this point, we decided—acting on an idea of Carol Hanisch, another woman in the group—would be consciousness-raising actions . . . actions brought to the public for the specific purpose of challenging old ideas and raising new ones, the very same issues of feminism we were studying ourselves. Our role was not to be a "service organization," we decided, nor a large "membership organization." What we were talking about being was, in effect, Carol explained, a "zap" action, political agitation, and education group something like what the Student Non-Violent Coordinating Committee (SNCC) had been. We would be the first to dare to say and do the undareable, what women really felt and wanted. The first job now was to raise awareness and understanding, our own and others—awareness that would prompt people to organize and to act on a mass scale.

The decision to emphasize our own feelings and experiences as women and to test all generalizations and reading we did by our own experience was actually the scientific method of research. We were in effect repeating the seventeenth century challenge of science to scholasticism: "study nature, not books," and put all theories to the test of living practice and action. It was also a method of radical organizing tested by other revolutions. We were applying to women and to ourselves as women's liberation organizers the practice a number of us had learned as organizers in the civil rights movement in the South in the early 1960s.

Consciousness raising—studying the whole gamut of women's lives, starting with the full reality of one's own—would also be a way of keeping the movement radical by preventing it from getting sidetracked into single issue reforms and single issue organizing. It would be a way of carrying theory about women further than it had ever been carried before, as the groundwork for achieving a radical solution for women as yet attained nowhere.

It seemed clear that knowing how our own lives related to the general condition of women would make us better fighters on behalf of women as a whole. We felt that all women would have to see the fight of women as their own, not as something just to help "other women," that they would have to see this truth about their own lives before they would fight in a radical way for anyone. "Go fight your own oppressors," Stokely Carmichael had said to the white civil rights workers when the black power movement began. "You don't get radicalized fighting other people's battles," as Beverly Jones, author of the pioneering essay, "Toward a Female Liberation Movement," put it.   [1973]

 154

The Boston Women's Health Book Collective

SUSAN BROWNMILLER

Collective was always a word with variable meanings in women's liberation. The utopian desire to submerge individual ego for the greater political good led to a range of experiments in the sixties and seventies such as fitful stabs at group writing and the founding of communal houses where personal lives intermingled at every conceivable level and food, clothes, and money were shared. Of all the experiments, foolish and grand, that marked the era, I can say without fear of contradiction that the Boston Women's Health Book Collective stands as an unqualified success. It became the heroic lifetime achievement for the 12 relatively unknown women who wrote and edited the feminist classic *Our Bodies, Ourselves*.

Nancy Hawley had grown up in radical politics. Her mother had been in the Communist Party, and Nancy herself was a charter member of the Students for a Democratic Society at the University of Michigan. After an inspiring conversation in 1968 with her old chum Kathie Amatniek, she started one of the first consciousness-raising groups in Cambridge, enlisting the young mothers in her child's cooperative play group. Happily pregnant again, she attended the stormy Thanksgiving conference in Lake Villa, Illinois, but unlike Amatniek, Charlotte Bunch, and many others, Hawley came away from it euphoric. A heated discussion on motherhood led by Shulamith Firestone, who said that pregnancy was barbaric and women would be equal only when science offered technological alternatives to biological reproduction, left her convinced that the movement needed her input.

In May 1969, a month after giving birth, Hawley chaired an overflowing workshop called "Women and Their Bodies" at a New England regional conference on women's liberation. (This was the Mother's Day weekend conference at Emmanuel

College in Boston, which led to the founding of the socialist-feminist Bread and Roses and where Cell Sixteen gave a rousing karate demonstration.) Summoning an incident fresh in her mind, Hawley opened her workshop by reporting a glib, sexist remark by her obstetrician. "He said," she recalls, "that he was going to sew me up real tight so there would be more sexual pleasure for my husband." Hawley's report, and her outrage, unleashed a freewheeling exchange on patronizing male doctors, childbirth, orgasm, contraception, and abortion that was so voluble and intense nobody wanted to go home.

"Everybody had a doctor story," exclaims Paula Doress, who was scheduled to give birth two weeks later. "We put aside our prepared papers and did consciousness raising."

Vilunya Diskin, in another workshop, received an excited report from Hawley that night. Diskin had survived the Holocaust by being placed with a Polish family. As a young married woman in Boston, she had undergone two traumatic childbirths with severe complications. Her first baby lived, but she had lost her second to hyaline membrane, a lung disease that the hospital had failed to monitor in time. "I was solidly middle class and well educated, and my health care had been appalling," she says. "So I could imagine what it was like for others without my resources."

A fluid core of activists from the Emmanuel conference agreed to continue meeting in order to compile a list of doctors they felt they could trust. They resolved as well to take the "Women and Their Bodies" workshop into the community, wherever they could find free space in church basements and nursery schools. "Our idea," says Diskin, "was to go out in pairs. We hoped that the women who attended the workshop would then go on and give it themselves."

To the core group's bewilderment, the doctors list kept dwindling. Every time it got up to four seemingly solid, unimpeachable names, somebody new showed up to exclaim, "Oh, do I have a story about *him!*" But the workshop project soared. As the summer turned into fall, the women amassed enough hard medical information and the confidence to borrow a lounge at MIT for a 12-session course. Venereal disease and "Women, Medicine and Capitalism" were added to the program.

Ruth Bell, a stranger to Boston, went to the course at MIT in an oversized pair of "Oshkosh, by Gosh" denim overalls, her maternity outfit. "Fifty women were talking about their lives, their sexuality, their feelings," she remembers. "I raised my hand and said, 'I'm pregnant for the first time and I don't know much about this and I'm having nightmares.' Three or four other women got up and said 'That happened to me, too. Let's meet after and talk about it and maybe we can figure something out.' That's how it was. Somebody had a concern, she raised her hand, and three or four others said, 'Boy, that happened to me, too.'"

Joan Ditzion, married to a Harvard medical student and debating whether to have kids, was transfixed by a large, detailed drawing of a vagina with labia and clitoris that the women had placed on an easel. "I'd only seen pictures like that in my husband's textbooks. These women were speaking so easily, without shame. I got my first sense that women could own our own anatomy."

Wendy Sanford, born into an upper-class Republican family, was battling depression after her son's birth. Her friend Esther Rome, a follower of Jewish Orthodox traditions, dragged her to the second MIT session. Previously Wendy had kept her distance from political groups. "I walked into the lounge," she recalls, "and they were talking about masturbation. I didn't say a word. I was shocked; I was fascinated. At a later session someone gave a breastfeeding demonstration. That didn't shock me—I'd been doing it—but then we broke down into small groups. I had never 'broken down into a small group' in my life. In my group people started talking about postpartum depression. In that one 45-minute period I realized that what I'd been blaming myself for, and what my husband had blamed me for, wasn't my personal deficiency. It was a combination of physiological things and a real societal thing, isolation. That realization was one of those moments that makes you a feminist forever."

Ruth Bell gave birth to her daughter in the middle of the course and returned to become "a second-stage original member" of the amorphous collective, along with Joan Ditzion and a renewed, reenergized Wendy Sanford. "There was an open invitation to anyone who wanted to help revise the course notes into a more formal packet," Bell remembers. "If you wanted to work on writing, you'd pair or triple up with people who could do research."

"We had to get hold of good medical texts," says Paula Doress, "so we borrowed student cards to get into Countway, the Harvard Medical School library. It was very eye-opening to realize that we could understand the latinized words."

"Then we'd stand up at a meeting and read what we had written," Ruth Bell continues. "People would make notes. Somebody would raise a hand and say, 'I think you should add this sentence' or 'You need a comma here.' This was how the first editing got done."

Duplicated packets of the course material were making their way around the country. Closer to home, somebody contacted the New England Free Press, a leftist mail-order collective in downtown Boston. "Basically they were a bunch of men, conventionally Marxist, who printed and sold pamphlets at 10 to 25 cents," Jane Pincus sums up. "They didn't see us as political." The mail-order collective grudgingly agreed to publish and distribute the health course papers if the women paid their own printing costs. "So we raised $1,500 from our parents and friends," Pincus relates. "And then we had to hire somebody to send out the orders because the demand was so great."

Five thousand stapled copies of "Women and Their Bodies" on newsprint paper with amateur photos and homey line drawings rolled off the press in December 1970 bearing a cover price of 75 cents. The blunt 136-page assault on the paternalism of the medical establishment that juxtaposed personal narratives with plainspoken prescriptives immediately sold out. A second edition of 15,000 copies, with the price lowered to 35 cents, bore an important change. In one of those Eureka moments, somebody had exclaimed, "Hey, it isn't women and *their* bodies— it's us and our bodies. *Our Bodies, Ourselves.*"

Women's centers in big cities and college towns were thirsting for practical information and new ways to organize. The Boston collective's handbook with its simple directive, "You can substitute the experience in your city or state here," fit the bill. Subsequent pressruns for *Our Bodies, Ourselves* were upped to 25,000 in an attempt to satisfy the demand. Three printings in 1971 were followed by six printings in 1972.

"We are working on revisions," the collective declared. "We want to add chapters on menopause and getting older and attitudes toward children, etc., etc., but we haven't had time." There was no shortage of feedback. "The first edition was weak on the dangers of high-dose estrogen oral contraceptives," Barbara Seaman remembers. She mailed the women a copy of her book, *The Doctors' Case Against the Pill,* and was gratified to see that the next edition reflected her concern. "A woman in Iowa wrote in and said, 'You didn't mention ectopic pregnancy,'" remembers Jane Pincus. "And we said 'Great, write about it and we'll put it in.' This is really how the book evolved."

It was only a matter of time before the big guns in New York publishing got wind of the phenomenal underground success. In the fall of 1972 they came courting with offers of a modest advance. Jonathan Dolger at Simon & Schuster had roomed with Jane Pincus's husband at college, but Charlotte Mayerson at Random House possessed what looked like an insurmountable advantage. "Charlotte was a she, and I was not," says Dolger. "They wanted a woman to edit their book and in truth, we didn't have many women at S & S in those days." Dolger asked Alice Mayhew, a recent arrival, to accompany him to Boston.

Dressed in army fatigues and work boots, the collective grilled the two editors about their intentions. While Dolger quaked in his business suit, Mayhew brusquely got down to business. "I got the impression they were all married to professors at MIT and Harvard," she remembers, not far off the mark. The following evening it was Mayerson's turn to present her case.

For the first time in their experience as a working collective, the women were unable to reach a consensus. They felt a sisterly bond with Mayerson, and indeed they would work with her on later projects, but she would not get the best-selling *Our Bodies, Ourselves.* Random House was owned at the time by RCA, a conglomerate with huge government defense contracts, rendering it complicitous in the war machine. An independent company and seemingly purer, Simon & Schuster won the agonizing vote by a narrow margin.

Freezing their ranks, the women incorporated as a nonprofit foundation. One member, suddenly desirous of a change in lifestyle, split for Toronto. The last to come aboard were Judy Norsigian, their "baby" at 23, and Norma Swenson, their "old lady" at 40. Norsigian and Swenson were to become the public face of the collective over the years.

When news of the commercial sale appeared in the penultimate *New England Free Press*, the mail-order leftists commandeered a page of their own to cry foul, warning that a capitalist publisher would impede the building of socialist consciousness. The women dodged the ideological brickbats as best they could while they readied their beloved creation for its aboveground debut. "Everything had to be decided by consensus," Mayhew remembers. "It took a long time. But we knew they were in touch with a generation of young women who wanted to be talked to straightforwardly. We would have been dopey to interfere."

Rape, an emerging issue for feminists, became a chapter in the handsome, large-format 1973 Simon & Schuster *Our Bodies, Ourselves*. Judy Norsigian, a veteran of the commune movement, wrote a chapter on nutrition. Mindful of the rising tide of lesbian consciousness, the women sent out a call for the appropriate expertise. A Boston gay women's collective produced "In Amerika They Call Us Dykes," insisting on anonymity and complete editorial control of the pages. Continuing the policy started in the first newsprint edition, the illustrations for the aboveground *Our Bodies, Ourselves* included many line drawings and photographs of African-American women. A sharp dig at the U.S. military presence in Vietnam survived in the aboveground edition (the context was venereal disease), but the proviso "Don't forget that Ortho and Tampax are capitalist organizations pushing their own products for profits" got axed. "Women, Medicine and Capitalism," a lengthy polemic, shrank to an unrecognizable paragraph in "Women and Health Care"

amid the nitty-gritty on yeast infections, cystitis, and crabs. Softer rhetoric was a collective decision, in line with the women's desires to reach the mainstream and include more facts, but they resisted the ladylike language a copy editor they nicknamed Blue Pencil wished to impose. "Where we wrote *pee*," says Jane Pincus, "Blue Pencil changed it to *urinate*. We changed it right back."

Our Bodies, Ourselves sold more than a million copies and earned more than a half million dollars in royalties for the collective in its first five years of commercial distribution. More important, it became the premier sourcebook for a generation of sexually active young women across all lines of race and class. It was deeply discounted or given out free at birth control clinics, and it found an audience among hard-to-reach teenagers when it was adopted as a teaching tool in hundreds of high school sex education programs. The royalty money was dispersed to movement projects except for the pittance paid to the staff people, chiefly Norsigian, Swenson, and Rome. By the latter part of the 1970s, the collective, which convened periodically to work on updated editions, had witnessed four divorces and three second marriages. A few members left the Boston area with their husbands, and one discovered her lesbian identity. All told, the women reared nearly two dozen children. "People used to come from overseas and ask to the see the house where the collective lived," says Norma Swenson. "I think they were disappointed to find that we led individual lives." [1998]

155

The Making of the Vanguard Center: Black Feminist Emergence in the 1960s and 1970s

BENITA ROTH

In the late 1990s, feminists in the United States have come to accept the idea that feminism means different things to different women located in different places in this society's race/class hierarchy. Scholarship on the feminist consciousness and activism of women of color and working-class women has shown us that the story of second-wave feminism—as the resurgence in feminist activism in the 1960s and 1970s is generally known—was and is really the story of feminisms.[1]

• • •

One of the resurgent feminisms of the second wave was black feminism. Black feminist organizing began at the same moment that white feminist organizing did, albeit on a smaller scale, and primarily in all-black organizations. There were early challenges to male dominance in the civil rights movement. In 1964, Ruby Doris Smith Robinson, Casey Hayden, Mary King, Mary Varela, and others began to discuss women's status in the Student Nonviolent Coordinating Committee (SNCC); Hayden and King (both white) wrote an "anonymous" memo to other SNCC members about the position of women in the movement.[2] Hayden and King were reluctant to sign their names to the document, and so speculation as to authorship fell on Smith Robinson, in part because of her position of authority within SNCC and her propensity for questioning gender inequities in it.[3]

In 1965, Hayden and King wrote (and this time signed) a memo, "Sex and Caste," about women's status in the New Left at large, and accounts of white feminism move from that action to the formation, in November 1967, of a feminist group by white women, mostly "of the movement"— that is, of the New Left. These women published "Preliminary Statement of Principles" in *New Left Notes,* and then went on to publish the first white women's liberation newsletter, *Voice of the Women's Liberation Movement,* out of Chicago.

Only months later, in 1968, Frances Beal and other members of SNCC's Women's Caucus formed the Third World Women's Alliance (TWWA), a self-consciously black *and* feminist social movement organization. TWWA had an explicitly anticapitalist critique of the middle-class style of the black liberation movement and of white

feminism.[4] In October 1968, MaryAnn Weathers, another TWWA member, argued for black women's liberation in position papers published by TWWA. Entitled "An Argument for Black Women's Liberation as a Revolutionary Force" and "Black Women and Abortion," these papers were widely circulated in both Black and white leftist circles. Feminist ideas on the Left crossed racial boundaries as well when, in August of 1968, Gwen Patton sent a draft of her essay "Black People and the Victorian Ethos" to Robert and Pam Allen.[5] Patton's essay would shortly afterward appear in Toni Cade Bambara's 1970 collection, *The Black Woman.*

From the late 1960s on, black feminist writing was being produced and read by both black and white women. Frances Beal's oft-cited manifesto of black feminism, "Double Jeopardy: To Be Black and Female," was written in 1969, and then published in both *Sisterhood Is Powerful,* Robin Morgan's edited collection, and Cade Bambara's *The Black Woman.* While Morgan's collection is considered a touchstone of second-wave feminism, Cade Bambara's collection is rarely treated by scholars as a product of feminist social movement activism, possibly because *The Black Woman* also included the voices of black women skeptical of the need for an autonomous black feminist movement.

Scholars have noted the impact that black women civil rights activists had on emergent white feminists as role models. But black women were not solely protofeminist role models for white feminists, who then set the feminist stage for black women to reenter. Some early black feminists were involved in political relationships with early white feminists, and influenced one another's thinking. For example, Pat Robinson, one of the founders of the black feminist Mount Vernon/New Rochelle Women's Group, and author of several position papers reprinted in both Cade Bambara's and Morgan's collections, corresponded with Joan Jordan (aka Vilma Sanchez), a white West Coast feminist and labor activist, from October 1966 through at least 1971. From their correspondence, it is clear that the two influenced each other's thinking.

Second-wave feminism was *at its roots* the creation of black and white women.

FORMING THE "VANGUARD CENTER": BLACK FEMINISM'S CLASS CRITIQUE

By exposing the particular needs of black women for liberation, black feminism had ripple effects beyond its boundaries. Black feminist thought has been extremely influential in shaping feminist politics, and the phrase "the intersection of race, class, and gender" is axiomatic now for doing feminist work. But accounts of how black feminists arrived at the intersection do not always show that they were going down all three streets at once from the very start of their movement.

Black feminist ideology did not simply emerge from the empty space created by black feminism's marginalization in the white women's and black liberation movements; it is not simply a residual creation of adding a race component to the gender critique of society and a gender component to the critique of racism. To a remarkably consistent degree, African-American feminists in the second wave developed what I call "a vanguard center" ideological approach to feminist activism: the idea that the liberation of black women, oppressed by race, gender, and class domination, would mean the liberation of all. Facing competing demands on their energies from the black liberation and the white women's liberation movements, black feminists did more than just reject black liberation's sexism and white feminists' racism. Rather, black feminists were critical of the middle-class assumptions and values that were built into *both* movements. In fact, the black feminist critique of both black and white women's liberation was in large part a class critique that posited that each movement's respective shortcomings—black liberation's sexism and white women's liberation's racism— were in no small part *due* to activists' middle-class blinders.

Black feminism's class critiques help to explain differences between black and white feminists on issues like reproductive rights and the family. In articles that appeared in the Philadelphia women's liberation newsletter "Women" in June of 1970,

black feminists assailed white women's failure to acknowledge class and racial aspects to the abortion issue. Abortion on demand—a key demand of white feminism—was seen by black feminists as imperfect policy because it was not linked to other reproductive concerns that were tied to class power: involuntary sterilization; life circumstances that compel poor women to abort; and the possibility that women on welfare would be forced by the state to have abortions. The author(s) argued that if white women's liberationists really cared about having an impact in communities of color, they would expand reformist policies into a commitment to destroy the economic system.

Black feminists had different perceptions about the meaning of feminist struggles surrounding the family; class status, as well as racial status, played a role in creating these different perceptions. The white women's liberation movement was seen as trying to reshape a family structure that black women were trying to stabilize.[6] While many white women experienced family obligations as exploitation, most black women found that the family was the least oppressive institution in their lives and constituted a refuge from white domination.[7] bell hooks noted that white feminists who speculated about the feminist movement's leading to the abolition of the family were seen as a threat by many black women, and she attributed the antifamily attitudes of some white feminists to their ability to rely on outside institutions to be cognizant of their needs; black women, poorer as a group, could not rely on such support.[8] Both hooks and Toni Morrison pointed out that class privilege buys one out of many of the responsibilities of family; upper- and middle-class women can hire other (poor, nonwhite) women to do work for them.[9] And as Lewis argued, white feminist demands for work privileges did not resonate strongly with black women, who had never been excluded from the privilege of working to support their families.[10]

Motherhood itself had different meanings for black and white feminists, as a consequence of class and racial differences. Polatnik, looking at black and white feminist groups in the second wave, argued that for many white feminists, becoming a mother meant being doomed to living a 1950s suburban housewife role, as their mothers had; therefore becoming a mother meant potentially participating in women's oppression.[11] Coming from less prosperous, more urban backgrounds, black feminists knew that alternative mothering styles were possible; in the black community, "other mothering," a more communal style of child rearing, existed. Thus, black feminists did not reject motherhood but, instead, argued for choice and control over motherhood rather than a full retreat.

Black feminists were equally critical of the propagation of middle-class values by many black liberationist groups, and saw black liberation's sexism as emanating in great part from an embrace of middle-class values as a means of "fixing" what was wrong in the black community. From the founding of the Third World Women's Alliance in 1968, black feminists argued against the "middle-class style" of the black liberation movement, along with the movement's sexism and masculinism.[12] Analogous to the critique of white women's liberation's racism, black feminists saw black liberation's sexism as rooted in an unexamined adoption of middle-class white values.

Segments of the Black Power/black liberation movement ideologically favored entrepreneurial capitalism, inasmuch as the Black Power solution had African-Americans turning back to the community and emulating other ethnic groups through self-help.[13] These tendencies were bolstered by the publication of the Moynihan report in 1965, in which the black family was painted as deviant, and pathological in its being matriarchal.[14] Many black liberationists advocated that the black family remake itself along patriarchal lines; they urged black women to take a step back from public activism into merely supportive roles, or to go all the way back into the home, away from public life altogether.

Black feminists countered that the idea of remaking the black family along patriarchal lines was classist, foreign to the black experience, and indicative of a lack of real revolutionary thinking when it came to the role of black women in the community. Highly critical of the Moynihan

report itself, black feminists rejected the desire of black liberationists to restructure the black family along patriarchal lines. They saw "the myth of the matriarchy" as a "sledgehammer" being used to stop black women from effective organizing, since the report had caused many black women to feel that they had to step back from responsibilities and hand the reins over to men.[15]

In "Double Jeopardy," Beal analyzed the cultural ideal of black "manhood" and laid the responsibility for it at the feet of American capitalism. She argued that the construction of masculinity and femininity was necessitated by the need to sell products to men and women. The "typical" middle-class woman, staying home and buying these products, was not a black woman, who had historically worked outside the home (and historically, mostly in white middle-class homes). Beal argued that male black liberationists had failed to extend their class analysis to the position of women. She had sympathy for black men's suffering in white society, but for Beal, consistent class analysis meant recognizing that the move to put black women "back" in the home was futile in the face of technological advancement: "Black women sitting at home reading bedtime stories to their children are just not going to make it."[16] Thus, Beal argued that black liberation needed to purge itself of middle-class ideas about gender relationships, and Black women's groups were needed to steer the course straight.

The black feminist critique of black liberation's middle-class biases was apparent in challenging that movement's take on the issue of birth control. Black feminists challenged black liberationists' assertion that birth control was "genocide," arguing that charges of genocide took away poor black women's right to control their lives. Black liberationists urged black women to have children to thwart dominant white society; the racism present in some family-planning groups made this stance viable.[17] At times, black militants took action to back up their assertions. In 1969, black nationalists closed down a birth control clinic in Pittsburgh, which was subsequently reopened by community women.[18] Ross reported that other birth control clinics were "invaded by black Muslims associated with the Nation of Islam," who published cartoons in *Muhammed Speaks* that depicted bottles of birth control pills marked with a skull and crossbones, or graves of unborn black infants.[19]

The Mount Vernon/New Rochelle group's well-known statement "Poor Black Women" was published in Morgan's 1970 collection and as a pamphlet; Patricia Robinson had formulated a version of the statement about two years earlier, in response to the "Black Unity Party's" stand against the use of birth control by black women.[20] In "Poor Black Women," Robinson and her coauthors argued that the Pill gave "poor Black sisters" the ability to resist white domination; trading that ability in for a life of domesticity—a middle-class picture—would not work for poor black women. More pointedly, the authors accused the anti–birth control black militants of being "a bunch of little middle-class people" with no understanding of the Black poor:

> The middle-class never understands the poor because they always need to use them as you want to use poor black women's children to gain power for yourself. You'll run the black community with your kind of Black Power—You on top! The poor understand class struggle![21]

In summary, black feminist responses to the traditional gender ideology that black liberationists espoused saw sexism as generated by the black liberation's adoption of white middle-class values that were alien to the black community. Black feminists consistently blamed sexism on capitalism and linked struggles against sexism to struggles for economic justice; they linked their critique against white women's liberation's racism to white women's neglect of these same economic struggles. As the 1970s progressed, black feminist organizations like the National Black Feminist Organization and the Combahee River Collective would add another street to the intersection, in the form of an analysis of the impact of heterosexism on black women's lives. The understanding of how feminist activism had to take charge of fighting against intersecting, multiplicative oppressions was therefore a black feminist legacy that could be expanded to reach out to more and more women. The vanguard center could thus grow. . . .

From the standpoint of chronology and ideology, black feminism is at the center of the story of second-wave feminism, not a variant but constitutive of the core of the feminist legacy of that era. It is a myth that black women were hostile to feminism, as polls done during the era show.[22] Black feminists began their struggle at the same time white feminists did; they are absent from the story of feminism's emergence by virtue of the fact that they did not join white women's liberation groups in large numbers. And from the beginning of their feminist activism, they argued for opposition to gender, race, and class oppression, and resistance to prioritizing any one of the three above the others.

By the mid-1970s, black feminism had profoundly influenced the entire feminist movement—the so-called mainstream included. The "vanguard center" critique of interlocking oppressions strongly influenced feminist theory and continued to do so throughout the 1980s and 1990s.[23] Whatever problems remain in feminist practice, black feminists succeeded in bringing their concerns to the center of feminist activism.　　　[edited, 2011]

NOTES

The author would like to thank the following for their critical input: Duchess Harris (Macalester College), Cheryl Johnson-Odim (Loyola University, Chicago), Susan Markens (UCLA), and Kimberly Springer, as well as an anonymous reviewer at New York University Press. An earlier version of this chapter was published in *Womanist Theory & Research* 2:2. It is reprinted by kind permission of *Womanist Theory & Research*.

1. Gluck et al. (1998).
2. Evans (1979).
3. Robnett (1997) noted that Hayden and King's paper was not so much an attack on SNCC's sexism as an attempt to bring up issues of patriarchy and hierarchy as the group wrestled with its structure and direction. That the paper has been seen by subsequent scholars solely as evidence of SNCC's sexism is the result, Robnett argued, of a failure to take a womanist standpoint; such a standpoint would consider what Black women were doing in the organization and would not boil down gender relations to those between white women and Black men.
4. Third World Women's Alliance (1971).
5. Allen (1968).
6. See Dubey (1994).
7. See White (1984).
8. See hooks (1981 and 1984).
9. See Morrison (1971).
10. Lewis (1977).

11. Polatnik (1996). To be fair, most white feminists were not hostile to motherhood; what they were hostile to was the suburban housewife role. But as Polatnik noted, some white feminists were deeply suspicious of motherhood and of works like Shulamith Firestone's (1970) *The Dialectic of Sex* (in which Firestone speculated about the future demise of biological motherhood in terms that left little doubt as to her opinion of it as an experience) that fed the idea that white feminists were widely hostile to being mothers.

12. See Giddings (1984), and before that, Third World Women's Alliance (1971).

13. See Cruse 1968; and Carmichael and Hamilton 1967. Black feminists had a more complicated relationship with the avowedly socialist Panthers. The Panthers were known for having strong women leaders; at the same time, the masculinism of much of the male leadership made women's lives within the party difficult. See Brown (1992); *The Militant* (1969); Newton (1970); Ross (1993); and Smith 1970 on the complicated and contradictory aspects of gender relations within the party.

14. United States Dept. of Labor Office of Planning and Research (1965).

15. See Weathers (1968a); and Murray (1975).

16. Frances Beal, "Double Jeopardy: To Be Black and Female," in Cade Bambara (1970a, 345).

17. See Ross (1993). As Rodrique (1990) noted, the racist, eugenic orientation of some in the birth control movement made advocacy of birth control practices difficult for black women.

18. See Lindsey (1970).

19. See Ross (1993), 153.

20. Robinson (1968). According to a 1967 letter from Robinson to Sanchez/Jordan, Robinson's father, a physician, had been on the national board of Planned Parenthood.

21. Robinson and Mount Vernon /New Rochelle Group (1970b), 361.

22. See Carden (1974); and Klein (1987).

23. See Gluck et al. (1998); Hill Collins (1990); hooks (1984); Johnson Reagon (1983); Joseph and Lewis (1981); King (1988); Moraga and Anzaldúa.

REFERENCES

Allen, Pam. 1968. Letter (August 29). Pam Allen Papers, State Historical Society, Madison, Wisconsin.

Brown, Elaine. 1992. *A Taste of Power: A Black Woman's Story*. New York: Pantheon Books.

Carden, Maren Lockwood. 1974. *The New Feminist Movement*. New York: Russell Sage Foundation.

Carmichael, Stokely, and Charles V. Hamilton. 1967. *Black Power: The Politics of Liberation in America*. New York: Vintage Books.

Cruse, Harold. 1968. *Rebellion or Revolution?* New York: William Morrow & Company.

Dubey, Madhu. 1994. *Black Women Novelists and the Nationalist Aesthetic*. Bloomington and Indianapolis: Indiana University Press.

Evans, Sara. 1979. *Personal Politics: The Roots of Women's Liberation in the Civil Rights Movement and the New Left*. New York: Vintage Books.

Giddings, Paula. 1984. *When and Where I Enter: The Impact of Black Women on Race and Sex in America*. New York: Bantam Books.

Gluck, Sherna, et al. 1998. "Whose Feminism, Whose History? Reflections on Excavating the History of (the) Women's Movement(s)." In *Community Activism and Feminist Politics: Organizing Across Race, Class and Gender*, edited by Nancy A. Naples. New York and London: Routledge.

Hooks, bell. 1981. *Ain't I a Woman? Black Women and Feminism*. Boston: South End Press.

Hooks, bell. 1984. *Feminist Theory: From Margin to Center*. Boston: South End Press.

Joseph, Gloria I. and Jill Lewis. 1981. *Common Differences: Conflicts in Black and White Feminist Perspectives*. Garden City, N.Y.: Anchor Books.

Klein, Ethel. 1987. "The Diffusion of Consciousness in the United States and Europe." In *The Women's Movements of the United States and Western Europe: Consciousness, Political Opportunity, and Public Policy*, edited by Mary Fainsod Katzenstein and Carol McClurg Mueller, 1992. Philadelphia: Temple University Press.

Lewis, Diane K. 1977. "A Response to Inequality: Black Women, Racism, and Sexism." *Signs* 3, no. 2 (Winter).

Lindsey, Kay. 1970. "The Black Woman as a Woman." In *The Black Woman: An Anthology*, edited by Toni Cade Bambara. York and Scarborough, 1992. Ontario: Mentor Books.

Moraga, Cherríe and Gloria Anzaldúa. 1981. "Introduction." In *This Bridge Called My Back: Writings by Radical Women of Color*. Watertown, Mass: Persephone Press.

Morrison, Toni. 1971. "What the Black Woman Thinks About Women's Lib." *New York Times Magazine* (August 22).

The Militant. 1969. "Panther Sisterson Women's Liberation." 1969. Unsigned article (September: 9-10).

Murray, Pauli. 1975. "The Liberation of Black Women. In *Women: A Feminist Perspective*, edited by Jo Freeman. Palo Alto: Mayfield Publishing Company.

Newton, Huey P. 1970. "A Letter from Huey to the Revolutionary Brothers and Sisters about the Women's Liberation and Gay Liberation Movement." Reprint from Black Panther 5:8 (August 21). Women's Liberation Ephemera Files, Special Collections, Northwestern University.

Polatnik, M. Rivka. 1996. "Diversity in Women's Liberation Ideology: How a Black and a White Group of the 1960s Viewed Motherhood." *Signs* 21, no. 1–3: 679–706.

Patricia. 1990. *Black Feminist Thought: Knowledge, Consciousness and the Politics of Empowerment*. Boston: Unwin Hyman.

Robinson, Pat. 1966–1971. Letters to Joan Jordan (aka Vilma Sanchez), 1966–1971. Joan Jordan Papers, 1992. State Historical Society, Madison, Wisconsin.

Robinson, Patricia and the Mount Vernon/New Rochelle Group. 1970a. "Poor Black Women's Study Papers by Poor Black Women of Mount Vernon, New York." In *The Black Woman: An Anthology*, edited by Toni Cade (Bambara). York and Scarborough, Ontario: Mentor Books.

Robnett, Belinda. 1997. *How Long? How Long? African-American Women in the Struggle for Civil Rights*. New York and Oxford: Oxford University Press.

Rodrigue, Jessie M. 1990. "The Black Community and the Birth Control Movement." In *Unequal Sisters: A Multicultural Reader in U.S. Women's History*, edited by Ellen Carol DuBois and Vicki L. Ruiz. New York and London: Routledge.

Ross, Loretta J. 1993. "African-American Women and Abortion: 1800–1970." In *Theorizing Black Feminisms: The Visionary Pragmatism of Black Women,* edited by Stanlie M. James and Abena P. A. Busia, 1993. London and New York: Routledge.

Smith, Fredi A. 1970. "Meet Women of the Black Panthers." *Daily Defender* (January 24).

Third World Women's Alliance. 1971. "History of the Organization." *Third World Women's Alliance* 1, no. 6 (March).

United States Department of Labor. 1965. *The Negro Family: The Case for National Action.* Washington, DC: U.S. Government Printing Office.

Weathers, MaryAnn. 1968a (October). "An Argument for Black Women's Liberation as a Revolutionary Force." Position paper issued by Third World Women's Alliance, Cambridge, Mass. Social Action Files, State Historical Society, Madison, Wisconsin.

White, E. Frances. 1984. "Listening to the Voices of Black Feminism." *Radical America* 18, no. 2–3: 7–25.

Wright, Margaret. 1972. "I Want the Right to Be Black and Me." In *Black Women in White America: A Documentary History,* edited by Gerda Lerner, 1992. New York: Vintage Books.

🦎 156

Chicana Feminist Discourse, 1970s

ALMA M. GARCIA

During the sixties, American society witnessed the development of the Chicano movement, a social movement characterized by a politics of protest. The Chicano movement focused on a wide range of issues: social justice, equality, educational reforms, and political and economic self-determination for Chicano communities in the United States. Various struggles evolved within this movement: the United Farmworkers unionization efforts; the New Mexico Land Grant movement; the Colorado-based Crusade for Justice; the Chicano student movement; and the Raza Unida Party.

Chicanas participated actively in each of these struggles. Between 1970 and 1980, a Chicana feminist movement developed in the United States that addressed the specific issues that affected Chicanas as women of color. The 1970s witnessed the development of Chicana feminists whose activities,

organizations, and writings can be analyzed in terms of a feminist movement by women of color in American society. Chicana feminists outlined a cluster of ideas that crystallized into an emergent Chicana feminist debate. In the same way that Chicano males were reinterpreting the historical and contemporary experience of Chicanos in the United States, Chicanas began to investigate the forces shaping their own experiences as women of color.

Throughout the seventies and eighties, Chicana feminists were forced to respond to the criticism that cultural nationalism and feminism were irreconcilable. In the first issue of the newspaper, *Hijas de Cuauhtemoc [Daughters of Cuauhtemoc],* Anna Nieto Gomez stated that a major issue facing Chicanas active in the Chicano movement was the need to organize to improve their status as women within the larger social movement. Francisca Flores, another leading Chicana feminist, stated:

> [Chicanas] can no longer remain in a subservient role or as auxiliary forces in the [Chicano] movement. They must be included in the front line of communication, leadership and organizational responsiblity.... The issue of equality, freedom and self-determination of the Chicana—like the right of self-determination, equality, and liberation of the Mexican [Chicano] community—is not negotiable. Anyone opposing the right of women to organize into their own form of organization has no place in the leadership of the movement.

Supporting this position, Bernice Rincon argued that a Chicana feminist movement that sought equality and justice for Chicanas would strengthen the Chicano movement. Yet in the process, Chicana feminists challenged traditional gender roles because they limited their participation and acceptance within the Chicano movement.

Cultural nationalism represented a major ideological component of the Chicano movement. Its emphasis on Chicano cultural pride and cultural survival within an Anglo-dominated society gave significant political direction to the Chicano movement. One source of ideological disagreement between Chicana feminism and this cultural nationalist ideology was cultural survival. Many Chicana feminists believed that a focus on cultural survival did not acknowledge the need to alter male-female relations within Chicano communities. For example, Chicana feminists criticized the notion of the "ideal Chicana" that glorified Chicanas as strong, long-suffering women who had endured and kept Chicano culture and the family intact. To Chicana feminists, this concept represented an obstacle to the redefinition of gender roles.

Chicana feminists were also skeptical about the cultural nationalist interpretation of machismo. Such an interpretation viewed machismo as an ideological tool used by the dominant Anglo society to justify the inequalities experienced by Chicanos. According to this interpretation, the relationship between Chicanos and the larger society was that of an internal colony dominated and exploited by the capitalist economy. Machismo, like other cultural traits, was blamed by Anglos for blocking Chicanos from succeeding in American society. In reality, the economic structure and colony-like exploitation were to blame.

Furthermore, many Chicana feminists disagreed with the cultural nationalist view that machismo could be a positive value within a Chicano cultural value system. Although Chicana feminists recognized that Chicanos faced discrimination from the dominant society, they adamantly disagreed with those who believed that machismo was a form of cultural resistance to such discrimination. Chicana feminists called for changes in the ideologies responsible for distorting relations between women and men. One such change was to modify the cultural nationalist position that viewed machismo as a source of cultural pride.

Chicana feminists called for a focus on the universal aspects of sexism that shape gender relations in both Anglo and Chicano culture. While they acknowledged the economic exploitation of all Chicanos, Chicana feminists outlined the double exploitation experienced by Chicanas. Sosa Riddell concluded: "It was when Chicanas began to seek work outside of the family groups that sexism became a key factor of oppression along with racism." Francisca Flores summarized some of the consequences of sexism:

> It is not surprising that more and more Chicanas are forced to go to work in order to supplement the family income. The children are farmed out

to a relative to baby-sit with them, and since these women are employed in the lower income jobs, the extra pressure placed on them can become unbearable.

Thus, while the Chicano movement was addressing the issue of racial oppression facing all Chicanos, Chicana feminists argued that it lacked an analysis of sexism.

The systematic analysis by Chicana feminists of the impact of racism and sexism on Chicanas in American society and, above all, within the Chicano movement was often misunderstood as a threat to the political unity of the Chicano movement. Such Chicana feminists were attacked for developing a "divisive ideology"—a feminist ideology that was frequently viewed as a threat to the Chicano movement as a whole. As Chicana feminists examined their roles as women activists within the Chicano movement, an ideological split developed. One group active in the Chicano movement saw themselves as "loyalists" who believed that the Chicano movement did not have to deal with sexual inequities since Chicano men as well as Chicano women experienced racial oppression. According to Nieto Gomez, who was not a loyalist, their view was that if men oppress women, it is not the man's fault but rather that of the system.

Chicana feminists were also accused of undermining the values associated with Chicano culture. Loyalists saw the Chicana feminist movement as an "anti-family, anti-cultural, anti-man and therefore an anti-Chicano movement." Feminism was, above all, believed to be an individualistic search for identity that detracted from the Chicano movement's "real" issues, such as racism.

Disagreements between these two groups became exacerbated during various Chicana conferences. At times, such confrontations served to increase Chicana feminist activity that challenged the loyalists' attacks, yet these attacks also served to suppress feminist activities.

Chicana feminist lesbians experienced even stronger attacks from those who viewed feminism as a divisive ideology. In a political climate that already viewed feminist ideology with suspicion, lesbianism as a sexual lifestyle and political ideology came under even more attack. Clearly, a cultural nationalist ideology that perpetuated such stereo-typical images of Chicanas as "good wives and good mothers" found it difficult to accept a Chicana feminist lesbian movement.

Cherrie Moraga's writings during the 1970s reflect the struggles of Chicana feminist lesbians who, together with other Chicana feminists, were finding the sexism evident within the Chicano movement intolerable. Just as Chicana feminists analyzed their life circumstances as members of an ethnic minority and as women, Chicana feminist lesbians addressed themselves to the oppression they experienced as lesbians. As Moraga stated:

> My lesbianism is the avenue through which I have learned the most about silence and oppression. . . . In this country, lesbianism is a poverty—as is being brown, as is being a woman, as is being just plain poor. The danger lies in ranking the oppressions. The danger lies in failing to acknowledge the specificity of the oppression.

Chicana, Black, and Asian American feminists experienced similar cross-pressures of feminist-baiting and lesbian-baiting attacks. As they organized around feminist struggles, these women of color encountered criticism from both male and female cultural nationalists who often viewed feminism as little more than an "anti-male" ideology. Lesbianism was identified as an extreme derivation of feminism. A direct connection was frequently made that viewed feminism and lesbianism as synonymous. Feminists were labeled lesbians, and lesbians as feminists. Attacks against feminists—Chicanas, Blacks, and Asian Americans—derived from the existence of homophobia within each of these communities. As lesbian women of color published their writings, attacks against them increased.

Responses to such attacks varied within and between the feminist movements of women of color. Some groups tried one strategy and later adopted another. Some lesbians pursued a separatist strategy within their own racial and ethnic communities. Others attempted to form lesbian coalitions across racial and ethnic lines. Both strategies represented a response to the marginalization of lesbians produced by recurrent waves of homophobic sentiments in Chicano, Black, and Asian American communities. A third response consisted of working within the broader nationalist movements in these communities and the feminist movements within them in order to challenge their heterosexual biases and resultant homophobia. As early as 1974, the "Black Feminist Statement" written by a Boston-based feminist group—the Combahee River Collective—stated: "We struggle together with Black men against racism, while we also struggle with Black men against sexism."

Chicana feminists as well as Chicana feminist lesbians continued to be labeled *vendidas* or "sellouts." Chicana loyalists continued to view Chicana feminism as associated, not only with melting into white society, but more seriously, with dividing the Chicano movement.

Chicana feminists' defense throughout the 1970s against those claiming that a feminist movement was divisive for the Chicano movement was to reassess their roles within the Chicano movement and to call for an end to male domination. Their challenges of traditional gender roles represented a means to achieve equality. In order to increase the participation of and opportunities for women in the Chicano movement, feminists agreed that both Chicanos and Chicanas had to address the issue of gender inequality.   [edited 2011]

REFERENCES

Combahee River Collective Staff. 1986. *The Combahee River Collective Statement: Black Feminist Organizing in the Seventies & Eighties*. Brooklyn: Kitchen Table/Women of Color Press.

Flore, Francisca. 1971a. Conference of Mexican Women: Un Remolino, *Regeneracion* 1(1):1:4.

———. 1971b. "el Mundo Feminil Mexicana." *Regeneracion* 1(10):i.

Gomez, Anna Nieto. 1971. Chicana Identify." *Hijas de Cuauhtemoc* (April):9.

———. 1973. "La Femenista." *Encuentro Femenil* 1:34–47

———. 1976. "Sexism in the Movement." *La Gerite* 6(4):10

Moraga, Cherri. 1981. "La Geura." pp. 27–34 in *This Bridge Called My Back: Writings by Radical Women of Color*, edited by Cherrie Moraga and Gloria Anzaldúa. Watertown, MA" Persephone.

———. *Loving in the War Years*. Boston: South End Press.

Riddell, Adaliza Sosa. 1974. "Chicanas en el Movimiento." *Aztlan* 5: 155–65.

Rincon, Bernice. 1971. "La Chicana: Her Role in the Past and hre Search for a New Role in the Future." *Regeneracion* 1(10):15–17.

Vidal, Mirta. 1971. "New Voice of La Raza: Chicanas Speak Out." *International Socialist Review*. 32: 31–33.

🌿 157

Thoughts on Indian Feminism

KATE SHANLEY

Attending the Ohoyo conference in Grand Forks, North Dakota was a returning home for me in a spiritual sense—taking my place beside other Indian women, and an actual sense—being with my relatives and loved ones after finally finishing my predoctoral requirements at the university. Although I have been a full-time student for the past six years, I brought to the academic experience many years in the workaday world as a mother, registered nurse, volunteer tutor, social worker aide, and high school outreach worker. What I am offering in this article are my thoughts as an Indian woman on feminism. Mine is a political perspective that seeks to re-view the real-life positions of women in relation to the theories that attempt to address the needs of those women.

Issues such as equal pay for equal work, child health and welfare, and a woman's right to make her own choices regarding contraceptive use, sterilization and abortion—key issues to the majority women's movement—affect Indian women as well; however, equality *per se*, may have a different meaning for Indian women and Indian people. That difference begins with personal and tribal sovereignty—the right to be legally recognized as peoples empowered to determine our own destinies. Thus, the Indian women's movement seeks equality in two ways that do not concern mainstream women: (1) on the individual level, the Indian woman struggles to promote the survival of a social structure whose organizational principles represent notions of family different from those of the mainstream; and (2) on the societal level, the people seek sovereignty as a people in order to maintain a vital legal and spiritual connection to the land, in order to *survive* as a people.

The nuclear family has little relevance to Indian women; in fact, in many ways, mainstream feminists now are striving to redefine family and community in a way that Indian women have long known. The American lifestyle from which white middle-class women are fighting to free themselves, has not taken hold in Indian communities. Tribal and communal values have survived after 400 hundred years of colonial oppression.

It may be that the desire on the part of mainstream feminists to include Indian women, however sincere, represents tokenism just now, because too often Indian people, by being thought of as spiritual "mascots" to the American endeavor, are seen more as artifacts than a real people able to speak for ourselves. Given the public's general ignorance about Indian people, in other words, it is possible that Indian people's real-life concerns are not relevant to the mainstream feminist movement in a way that constitutes anything more than a "representative" facade. Charges against the women's movement of heterosexism and racism abound these days; it is not my intention to add to them except to stress that we must all be vigilant in examining the underlying assumptions that motivate us. Internalization of negative (that is, sexist and racist) attitudes toward ourselves and others can and quite often does result from colonialist (white patriarchal) oppression. It is more useful to attack the systems that keep us ignorant of each other's histories.

The other way in which the Indian women's movement differs in emphasis from the majority of women's movement lies in the importance Indian people place on tribal sovereignty—it is the single most pressing political issue in Indian country today. For Indian people to survive culturally as well as materially, many battles must be fought and won in the courts of law, precisely because it is the legal recognition that enables Indian people to govern ourselves according to our own worldview—a worldview that is antithetical to the *wasicu* (the Lakota term for "takers of the fat") definition of progress. Equality for Indian women within tribal communities, therefore, holds more significance than equality in terms of the general rubric "American."

Up to now I have been referring to the women's movement as though it were a single, well-defined organization. It is not. Perhaps in many ways socialist feminists hold views similar to the views of many Indian people regarding private property and the nuclear family. Certainly, there are some Indian people who are capitalistic. The point I would like to stress, however, is that rather than seeing differences according to a hierarchy of oppressions (white over Indian, male over female), we must practice a politics that allows for diversity in cultural identity as well as in sexual identity.

The word "feminism" has special meanings to Indian women, including the idea of promoting the continuity of tradition, and consequently, pursuing the recognition of tribal sovereignty. Even so, Indian feminists are united with mainstream feminists in outrage against woman and child battering, sexist employment and educational practices, and in many other social concerns. Just as sovereignty cannot be granted but *must be recognized* as an inherent right to self-determination, so Indian feminism must also be recognized as powerful in its own terms, in its own right.

Feminism becomes an incredibly powerful term when it incorporates diversity—not as a superficial political position, but as a practice. The women's movement and the Indian movement for sovereignty suffer similar trivialization, because narrow factions turn ignorance to their own benefit so that they can exploit human beings and the lands they live on for corporate profit. The time has come for Indian women and Indian people to be known on our own terms. This nuclear age demands new terms of communication for all people. Our survival depends on it. Peace.   [1984]

🦎 158

Triple Jeopardy and the Struggle

MIRIAM CHING YOON LOUIE

Being bi- and female in the Asian movement also means putting in double, triple, quadruple time.* The Third World Women's Alliance, an offshoot of

---

*Editor's note: This selection is excerpted from the author's essay "It's Never Ever Boring! Triple Jeopardy from the Korean Side," in *Asian Americans: The Movement and the Moment* (Los Angeles: UCLA Asian American Studies Center Press, 2006). The author employs the term "Bi-" with the explicit meaning of her multiple Korean-Chinese ethnic and political identities, with the implicit connotation of solidarity across boundaries of gender and sexuality.

the Black Women's Liberation Committee of the Student Non-Violent Coordinating Committee, dubbed this our "triple jeopardy" dilemma as women of color who have our hands, heads, hearts in multiple movements because of our race, gender, and class status.

As a wide-eyed 17-year-old Educational Opportunity Program freshman admitted the year of the Third World Liberation Front strike, being bimeant consciousness and activism that rapidly ricocheted between Asian, Chinese, Filipino, Japanese, black, Chicano, Native American, Vietnamese, and Korean influences. This was because during the flow of the mass movements of the late 1960s and early 1970s we were all knee-deep in "each other's Kool-Aid."

Being bi- meant the "On strike! Shut it down!" adrenaline rush of running for your life from baton-wielding cops while engulfed in lung-searing tear gas, just because you believed there was more to history than the stories of "great white men." It meant tutoring immigrant kids in Chinatown getting mangled in the public school system. It meant learning construction skills to rebuild the International Hotel and organizing programs for the elderly about to be evicted by "redevelopment"— now-they-call-it "gentrification"—in San Francisco's Manilatown/Chinatown. . . .

It meant spreading the gospel of the grape boycott of the United Farm Workers Union. It meant hot-rodding down to Delano to help build the union's medical clinic and Agabayani retirement village for Manongs who had spent their lives living in cold-water shacks, getting poisoned by pesticides, and enabling California's agribusiness to grow fat. It meant driving university vehicles—odometer cables disconnected—to hot as blazes Coachella/Indio, the self-proclaimed "date capital of the world," to attend a summit of Chicano Movement heavies.

It meant marching for striking seamstresses and restaurant workers. It meant bum-rushing the stage of a giant antiwar rally in Golden Gate Park when white radicals failed to call out the racist genocidal character of the Vietnam War. It meant staying up late with cohorts to mimeograph a student zine on Asian liberation movements under the pen name "The East Is Red The West Is Ready" Collective. It meant submitting the only "Korean contribution" to the *Asian Women's Journal*.

Later being bi- and female meant working in projects like Asian Manpower Services, Korean Community Center of the East Bay, Asian Immigrant Women Advocates, and Women of Color Resource Center. It meant clocking late night and weekend hours with the Third World Women's Alliance and Alliance Against Women's Oppression. It meant dragging the kids to anti-Bakke, U.S. Out of Here, There, and Everywhere!, Gay Pride demos, International Women's Day celebrations, reproductive rights pickets, and Rainbow Coalition conferences until Nguyen and Lung San got big enough to do the "bi- thing" their own way.

PARTYING WITH "THE ENEMY"

Back in 1969 some of us who were active in the Third World strike, Asian American Political Alliance, Third World Board, and formation of Asian Studies at Berkeley decided to go on the first Venceremos! ("We will win!") Brigade.

We cut Cuban sugar cane to break the U.S. government blockade and show our solidarity with those cheeky brown folks who had the nerve to make a revolution right under Uncle Sam's nose. All power to our Asian immigrant ancestors who worked Hawaii's plantations and to poor people everywhere who cut cane for a living! Ugh! Talk about the most hellish work you could imagine doing in the tropics.

But in the wake of Martin Luther King's assassination, Watts, rebellions burning across the face of urban America and Indian Country, and full-scale U.S. intervention in Southeast Asia, the Brigade enabled us to hook up with young bloods from communities of color across the United States, or "belly of the beast" as it used to be called back in the day. We met Roy Whang, a Korean American from Detroit who was working with black auto workers in the Dodge Revolutionary Workers Movement; George Singh, a Vietnam vet and "Bi" with Indian and Mexican parents; and Leo Hamaji, a local Buddha-head.

We also met and partied with "the enemy" revolutionaries from national liberation movements around the world, including Vietnam, Korea, Latin America, the Caribbean, and Africa. On my nineteenth birthday the Cubanos brought me a big pink cake from Havana: yum! We ate a lot of black beans

and rice, called moros y cristianos, or "Moors and Christians"—for the colors of Spain's racial history—sipped super sweet pitch black coffee, guzzled rum, and swayed to Afro-Cuban rhythms under the palm trees: sabroso/delicious!

AFTER KWANGJU

With the Kwangju* movement came new generations of activists and influences. In the Bay Area a number of young folks, especially first-generation Korean students, gravitated toward Young Koreans United, a national organization linked to the radical student movement upsurge in South Korea. These young radicals produce a wealth of materials critical of Japanese and U.S. colonial practices in Korea.

The movement also focused on the minjung, or the common people, and elevated the struggles of workers, peasants, and "comfort" and sex-trafficked women, and revived indigenous folk culture. Over time Korean radicals seeded off many other research, cultural, and organizing initiatives, including those devoted not only to "homeland," but also to those focused on issues of racism, settlement, interethnic conflict, and fighting for workers', immigrants', and women's rights in the United States.

For example, 1.5ers [children of mixed-immigrant-generation parents] Roy Hong and Danny Park helped found Korean Immigrant Workers Advocates (KIWA) in Los Angeles. Korean activists also launched groups like the National Korean American Services and Education Center, Korea Exposure and Education Program, and National Pungmul Network; Korean Resource Center, KIWA, and LA Korea Forum in Los Angeles; the Rainbow Center, Service and Education for Korean Americans, and Nodutol in New York; and Committee for Korean Studies and Korean Youth Cultural Center in Oakland, to name a few.

---

*Editor's note: Kwangju, South Korea, was the scene of a mass popular movement that was massacred by U.S.-supported South Korean paratroopers in May 1980. Miriam writes: "Kwangju was the turning point for the movement in Korea and the U.S. . . . The massacre exposed U.S. government complicity since the troops were dispatched with U.S. Military Command approval and Carter Administration officials' prior knowledge." She goes on to discuss how the events changed consciousness and spurred organizing by a new Korean-American generation.

today earn less than a man with no more than a high school diploma (just as she did in the fifties)—and why does the average female high school graduate today earn less than a male high school dropout? Why do American women, in fact, face the worst gender-based pay gap in the developed world?

If women have "made it," then why are nearly 80 percent of working women still stuck in traditional "female" jobs—as secretaries, administrative "support" workers and salesclerks? And, conversely, why are they less than 8 percent of all federal and state judges, less than 6 percent of all law partners, and less than one-half of 1 percent of top corporate managers? Why are there only three female state governors, two female U.S. senators, and two Fortune 500 chief executives? Why are only 19 of the 4,000 corporate officers and directors women—and why do more than half the boards of Fortune companies still lack even one female member?

If women "have it all," then why don't they have the most basic requirements to achieve equality in the workforce? Unlike virtually all other industrialized nations, the U.S. government still has no family-leave and child care programs—and more than 99 percent of American private employers don't offer child care either. Though business leaders say they are aware of and deplore sex discrimination, corporate America has yet to make an honest effort toward eradicating it. In a 1990 national poll of chief executives at Fortune 1000 companies, more than 80 percent acknowledged that discrimination impedes female employees' progress—yet, less than 1 percent of these same companies regarded *remedying* sex discrimination as a goal that their personnel departments should pursue. In fact, when the companies' human resource officers were asked to rate their department's priorities, women's advancement ranked last.

If women are so "free," why are their reproductive freedoms in greater jeopardy today than a decade earlier? Why do women who want to postpone childbearing now have fewer options than 10 years ago? The availability of different forms of contraception has declined, research for new birth control has virtually halted, new laws restricting abortion—or even *information* about abortion—for young and poor women have been passed, and

the U.S. Supreme Court has shown little ardor in defending the right it granted in 1973.

★ ★ ★

What actually is troubling the American female population, then? If the many ponderers of the Woman Question really wanted to know, they might have asked their subjects. In public opinion surveys, women consistently rank their own *inequality,* at work and at home, among their most urgent concerns. Over and over, women complain to pollsters about a lack of economic, not marital, opportunities; they protest that working men, not working women, fail to spend time in the nursery and the kitchen. The Roper Organization's survey analysts find that men's opposition to equality is "a major cause of resentment and stress" and "a major irritant for most women today." It is justice for their gender, not wedding rings and bassinets, that women believe to be in desperately short supply. When the *New York Times* polled women in 1989 about "the most important problem facing women today," job discrimination was the overwhelming winner; none of the crises the media and popular culture had so assiduously promoted even made the charts. In the 1990 Virginia Slims poll, women were most upset by their lack of money, followed by the refusal of their men to shoulder child care and domestic duties. By contrast, when the women were asked where the quest for a husband or the desire to hold a "less pressured" job or to stay at home ranked on their list of concerns, they placed them at the bottom.

The truth is that the 1980s saw a powerful counterassault on women's rights, a backlash, an attempt to retract the handful of small and hard-won victories that the feminist movement did manage to win for women. This counterassault is largely insidious: in a kind of pop-culture version of the Big Lie, it stands the truth boldly on its head and proclaims that the very steps that have elevated women's position have actually led to their downfall.

The backlash is at once sophisticated and banal, deceptively "progressive" and proudly backward. It deploys both the "new" findings of "scientific research" and the dime-store moralism of yesteryear; it turns into media sound bites both the glib pronouncements of pop-psych trend-watchers and the frenzied rhetoric of New Right preachers. The backlash has succeeded in framing virtually the whole issue of women's rights in its own language. Just as Reaganism shifted political discourse far to the right and demonized liberalism, so the backlash convinced the public that women's "liberation" was the true contemporary American scourge—the source of an endless laundry list of personal, social, and economic problems.

But what has made women unhappy in the last decade is not their "equality"—which they don't yet have—but the rising pressure to halt, and even reverse, women's quest for that equality. The "man shortage" and the "infertility epidemic" are not the price of liberation; in fact, they do not even exist. But these chimeras are the chisels of a societywide backlash. They are part of a relentless whittling-down process—much of it amounting to outright propaganda—that has served to stir women's private anxieties and break their political wills. Identifying feminism as women's enemy only furthers the ends of a backlash against women's equality, simultaneously deflecting attention from the backlash's central role and recruiting women to attack their own cause.

Some social observers may well ask whether the current pressures on women actually constitute a backlash—or just a continuation of American society's long-standing resistance to women's rights. Certainly hostility to female independence has always been with us. But if fear and loathing of feminism is a sort of perpetual viral condition in our culture, it is not always in an acute stage; its symptoms subside and resurface periodically. And it is these episodes of resurgence, such as the one we face now, that can accurately be termed "backlashes" to women's advancement. If we trace these occurrences in American history, we find such flare-ups are hardly random; they have always been triggered by the perception—accurate or not—that women are making great strides. These outbreaks are backlashes because they have always arisen in reaction to women's "progress," caused not simply by a bedrock of misogyny but by the specific efforts of contemporary women to improve their status, efforts that have been interpreted time and again by men—especially men grappling with real threats

to their economic and social well-being on other fronts—as spelling their own masculine doom.

As the backlash has gathered force, it has cut off the few from the many—and the few women who have advanced seek to prove, as a social survival tactic, that they aren't so interested in advancement after all. Some of them parade their defection from the women's movement, while their working-class peers founder and cling to the splintered remains of the feminist cause. While a very few affluent and celebrity women who are showcased in news articles boast about having "found my niche as Mrs. Andy Mill" and going home to "bake bread," the many working-class women appeal for their economic rights—flocking to unions in record numbers, striking on their own for pay equity and establishing their own fledgling groups for working women's rights. In 1986, while 41 percent of upper-income women were claiming in the Gallup poll that they were not feminists, only 26 percent of low-income women were making the same claim.

★ ★ ★

Backlash happens to be the title of a 1947 Hollywood movie in which a man frames his wife for a murder he's committed. The backlash against women's rights works in much the same way: its rhetoric charges feminists with all the crimes it perpetrates. The backlash line blames the women's movement for the "feminization of poverty"—while the backlash's own instigators in Washington pushed through the budget cuts that helped impoverish millions of women, fought pay equity proposals, and undermined equal opportunity laws. The backlash line claims the women's movement cares nothing for children's rights—while its own representatives in the capital and state legislatures have blocked one bill after another to improve child care, slashed billions of dollars in federal aid for children, and relaxed state licensing standards for day care centers. The backlash line accuses the women's movement of creating a generation of unhappy single and childless women—but its purveyors in the media are the ones guilty of making single and childless women feel like circus freaks.

To blame feminism for women's "lesser life" is to miss entirely the point of feminism, which is to win women a wider range of experience. Feminism remains a pretty simple concept, despite repeated—and enormously effective—efforts to dress it up in greasepaint and turn its proponents into gargoyles. As Rebecca West wrote sardonically in 1913, "I myself have never been able to find out precisely what feminism is: I only know that people call me a feminist whenever I express sentiments that differentiate me from a doormat."

The meaning of the word "feminist" has not really changed since it first appeared in a book review in the *Athenaeum* of April 27, 1895, describing a woman who "has in her the capacity of fighting her way back to independence." It is the basic proposition that, as Nora put it in Ibsen's *A Doll's House* a century ago, "Before everything else I'm a human being." It is the simply worded sign hoisted by a little girl in the 1970 Women's Strike for Equality: I AM NOT A BARBIE DOLL. Feminism asks the world to recognize at long last that women aren't decorative ornaments, worthy vessels, members of a "special-interest group." They are half (in fact, now more than half) of the national population, and just as deserving of rights and opportunities, just as capable of participating in the world's events, as the other half. Feminism's agenda is basic: It asks that women not be forced to "choose" between public justice and private happiness. It asks that women be free to define themselves—instead of having their identity defined for them, time and again, by their culture and their men.

The fact that these are still such incendiary notions should tell us that American women have a way to go before they enter the promised land of equality.   [edited, 1991]

NOTES

578 Women's fight for . . . : Nancy Gibbs, "The Dreams of Youth," *Time*, Special Issue: "Women: The Road Ahead," Fall 1990, p. 12.

578 Women have "so much" . . . : Eleanor Smeal, *Why and How Women Will Elect the Next President* (New York: Harper & Row, 1984), p. 56.

578 The *New York Times* reports . . . : Georgia Dullea, "Women Reconsider Childbearing Over 30," *New York Times*, Feb. 25, 1982, p. C1.

578 *Newsweek* says: Unwed women . . . : Eloise Salholz, "The Marriage Crunch," *Newsweek*, June 2, 1986, p. 55.

578 The health advice manuals . . . : See, for example, Dr. Herbert J. Freudenberger and Gail North, *Women's*

Burnout (New York: Viking Penguin, 1985); Marjorie Hansen Shaevitz, *The Superwoman Syndrome* (New York: Warner Books, 1984); Harriet Braiker, *The Type E Woman* (New York: Dodd, Mead, 1986); Donald Morse and M. Lawrence Furst, *Women Under Stress* (New York: Van Nostrand Reinhold Co., 1982); Georgia Witkin-Lanoil, *The Female Stress Syndrome* (New York: Newmarket Press, 1984).

578 The psychology books . . . : Dr. Stephen and Susan Price, *No More Lonely Nights: Overcoming the Hidden Fears That Keep You from Getting Married* (New York: G. P. Putnam's Sons, 1988), p. 19.

578 Even founding feminist Betty Friedan . . . : Betty Friedan, *The Second Stage* (New York: Summit Books, 1981), p. 9.

578 "In dispensing its spoils . . .": Mona Charen, "The Feminist Mistake," *National Review*, March 23, 1984, p. 24.

578 "Our generation was the human sacrifice . . .": Claudia Wallis, "Women Face the '90s," *Time*, Dec. 4, 1989, p. 82.

578 In *Newsweek*, writer . . . : Kay Ebeling, "The Failure of Feminism," *Newsweek*, Nov. 19, 1990, p. 9.

578 Even the beauty magazines . . . : Marilyn Webb, "His Fault Divorce," *Harper's Bazaar*, Aug. 1988, p. 156.

578 "Feminism, having promised her . . .": Dr. Toni Grant, *Being a Woman: Fulfilling Your Femininity and Finding Love* (New York: Random House, 1988), p. 25.

578 The authors of . . . : Dr. Connell Cowan and Dr. Melvyn Kinder, *Smart Women/Foolish Choices* (New York: New American Library, 1985) p. 16.

579 In *The Cost of Loving* . . . : Megan Marshall, *The Cost of Loving: Women and the New Fear of Intimacy* (New York: G. P. Putnam's Sons, 1984), p. 218.

579 Other diaries of . . . : Hilary Cosell, *Woman on a Seesaw: The Ups and Downs of Making It* (New York: G. P. Putnam's Sons, 1985); Deborah Fallows, *A Mother's Work* (Boston: Houghton Mifflin, 1985); Carol Osborn, *Enough Is Enough* (New York: Pocket Books, 1986); Susan Bakos, *This Wasn't Supposed to Happen* (New York: Continuum, 1985). Even when the women aren't really renouncing their liberation, their publishers promote the texts as if they were. Mary Kay Blakely's *Wake Me When It's Over* (New York: Random House, 1989), an account of the author's diabetes-induced coma, is billed on the dust jacket as "a chilling memoir in which a working supermom exceeds her limit and discovers the thin line between sanity and lunacy and between life and death."

579 If American women are so equal . . . : "Money, Income and Poverty Status in the U.S.," 1989, Current Population Reports, U.S. Bureau of the Census, Department of Commerce, Series P-60, #168.

579 Why are they still . . . : Cushing N. Dolbeare and Anne J. Stone, "Women and Affordable Housing," *The American Woman 1990–91: A Status Report*, ed. by Sara E. Rix (New York: W. W. Norton & Co., 1990) p. 106; Newton, "Pension Coverage," p. 268; "1990 Profile," 9 to 5/ National Association of Working Women; Salaried and Professional Women's Commission Report, 1989, p. 2.

579 Why does the average . . . : "Briefing Paper on the Wage Gap," National Committee on Pay Equity, p. 3; "Average Earnings of Year-Round, Full-Time Workers by

Sex and Educational Attainment," 1987, U.S. Bureau of the Census, February 1989, cited in *The American Woman*, 1990–1991, p. 392.

579   If women have "made it," then . . . : Susanna Downie, "Decade of Achievement, 1977–1987," The National Women's Conference Center, May 1988, p. 35; statistics from 9 to 5/National Association of Working Women.

579   And, conversely . . . : Statistics from Women's Research & Education Institute, U.S. Bureau of the Census, U.S. Bureau of Labor Statistics, Catalyst, Center for the American Woman and Politics. See also *The American Woman*, 1990–1991, p. 359; Deborah L. Rhode, "Perspectives on Professional Women," *Stanford Law Review*, 40, no. 5 (May 1988): 1178–79; Anne Jardim and Margaret Hennig, "The Last Barrier," *Working Woman*, Nov. 1990, p. 130; Jaclyn Fierman, "Why Women Still Don't Hit the Top," *Fortune*, July 30, 1990, p. 40.

579   Unlike virtually . . . : "1990 Profile," 9 to 5/National Association of Working Women; Bureau of Labor Statistics, 1987 survey of nation's employers. See also "Who Gives and Who Gets," *American Demographics*, May 1988, p. 16; "Children and Families: Public Policies and Outcomes, A Fact Sheet of International Comparisons," U.S. House of Representatives, Select Committee on Children, Youth and Families.

579   In a 1990 national poll . . . : "Women in Corporate Management," national poll of Fortune 1000 companies by Catalust, 1990.

579   Why do women who want . . . : Data from Alan Guttmacher Institute.

580   In public opinion . . . : In the Annual Study of Women's Attitudes (1988, Mark Clements Research), when women were asked, "What makes you angry?" they picked three items as their top concerns: poverty, crime, and their own inequality. In the 1989 *New York Times* Poll, when women were asked what was the most important problem facing women today, job inequality ranked first.

580   The Roper Organization's . . . . : Bickley Townsend and Kathleen O'Neil, "American Women Get Mad," *American Demographics*, Aug. 1990, p. 26.

580   When the *New York Times* . . . : Dionne, "Struggle for Work and Family," p. A14.

580   In the 1990 . . . : 1990 Virginia Slims Opinion Poll, pp. 29–30, 32.

580   While a very few . . . : "A New Kind of Love Match," *Newsweek*, Sept. 4, 1989, p. 73; Barbara Hetzer, "Superwoman Goes Home," *Fortune*, Aug. 18, 1986, p. 20; "Facts on Working Women," Aug. 1989, Women's Bureau, U.S. Department of Labor, no. 89–2; and data from the Coalition of Labor Union Women and Amalgamated Clothing and Textile Workers Union. The surge of women joining unions in the late eighties was so great that it single-handedly halted the 10-year decline in union membership. Black women joined unions at the greatest rate. Women led strikes around the country, from the Yale University administrative staffs to the Daughters of Mother Jones in Virginia (who were instrumental in the Pittston coal labor battle) to the Delta Pride catfish plant processors in Mississippi (where women organized the largest strike by black workers ever in the state, lodging a protest against a plant that paid its mostly female employees poverty wages, punished them if they skinned less than 24,000 fish a day, and limited them to six timed bathroom breaks a week). See Tony Freemantle, "Weary Strikers Hold Out in Battle of Pay Principle," *Houston Chronicle*, Dec. 2, 1990, p. 1A; Peter T. Kilborn, "Labor Fight on a Catfish 'Plantation,'" *News and Observer*, Dec. 16, 1990, p. J2.

581   In 1986, while . . . : 1986 Gallup Poll; Barbara Ehrenreich, "The Next Wave," *Ms.*, July/August 1987, p. 166; Sarah Harder, "Flourishing in the Mainstream: The U.S. Women's Movement Today," *The American Woman*, 1990–1991, p. 281. Also see 1989 Yankelovich Poll: 71 percent of black women said feminists have been helpful to women, compared with 61 percent of white women. A 1987 poll by the National Women's Conference Commission found that 65 percent of black women called themselves feminists, compared with 56 percent of white women.

581   The backlash line claims . . . : Data from Children's Defense Fund. See also Ellen Wojahm, "Who's Minding the Kids?" *Savvy*, Oct. 1987, p. 16; "Child Care: The Time is Now," Children's Defense Fund, 1987, pp. 8–10.

581   "I myself . . .": Rebecca West, *The Clarion*, Nov. 14, 1913, cited in Cheris Kramarae and Paula A. Treichler, *A Feminist Dictionary* (London: Pandora Press, 1985) p. 160.

581   The meaning of the word "feminist" . . . : *The Feminist Papers: From Adams to de Beauvoir*, ed. by Alice S. Rossi (New York: Bantam Books, 1973), p. xiii. For discussion of historical origins of term feminism, see Karen Offen, "Defining Feminism: A Comparative Historical Approach," in *Signs: Journal of Women in Culture and Society*, 1988, 14, no. 1, pp. 119–57.

581   I AM NOT A BARBIE DOLL . . . : Carol Hymowitz and Michaele Weissman, *A History of Women in America* (New York: Bantam Books, 1978), p. 341.

🌱 160

Bringing the Global Home

CHARLOTTE BUNCH

One of the most exciting world developments today is the emergence of feminism all over the globe. Women of almost every culture, color, and class are claiming feminism for themselves. Indigenous movements are developing that address the specific regional concerns of women's lives and that expand the definition of what feminism means and can do in the future.

This growth of feminism provides both the challenge and the opportunity for a truly global women's movement to emerge in the 1980s. But a global movement involves more than just the separate development of feminism in each region, as exciting and important as that is. Global feminism also requires that we learn from each other and develop a global perspective within each of our movements. It means expansion of our understandings of feminism and changes in our work, as we respond to the ideas and challenges of women with different perspectives. It means discovering what other perspectives and movements mean to our own local setting. Any struggle for change in the late-twentieth century must have a global consciousness since the world operates and controls our lives internationally already. The strength of feminism has been and still is in its decentralized grassroots nature, but for that strength to be most effective, we must base our local and national actions on a worldview that incorporates the global context of our lives. This is the challenge of bringing the global home.

A global feminist perspective on patriarchy worldwide also illustrates how issues are interconnected, not separate isolated phenomena competing for our attention. This involves connections among each aspect of women's oppression and of that subordination to the socioeconomic conditions of society, as well as between local problems and global realities.

To develop global feminism today is not a luxury—it requires going to the heart of the problems in our world and looking at nothing less than the threats to the very survival of the planet. We are standing on a precipice facing such possibilities as nuclear destruction, worldwide famine and depletion of our natural resources, industrial contamination, and death in many forms. These are the fruits of a world ruled by the patriarchal mode—of what I call the "dynamic of domination," in which profits and property have priority over people, and where fear and hatred of differences have prevented a celebration of and learning from our diversity.

Feminists are part of a world struggle that is taking place today over the direction that the future will take. Crucial choices are being made

about the very possibilities for life in the twenty-first century—from macro-level decisions about control over resources and weapons to micro-level decisions about control over individual reproduction and sexuality. At this juncture in history, feminism is perhaps the most important force for change that can begin to reverse the dynamic of patriarchal domination by challenging and transforming the way in which humans look at ourselves in relation to each other and to the world.

A GLOBAL VIEW OF FEMINISM

The excitement and urgency of issues of global feminism were brought home to me at a Workshop on Feminist Ideology and Structures sponsored by the Asian and Pacific Centre for Women and Development in Bangkok in 1979. Women from each region presented what they were doing in relation to the themes of the UN Decade for Women. In doing this, we realized the importance of the international male-dominated media in influencing what we knew and thought about each other before we came to Bangkok.

We saw how the media has made the women's movement and feminism appear trivial, silly, selfish, naïve, and/or crazy in the industrialized countries while practically denying its existence in the Third World. Western feminists have been portrayed as concerned only with burning bras, having sex, hating men, and/or getting to be head of General Motors. Such stereotypes ignore the work of most feminists and distort even the few activities the media do report. So, for example, basic political points that women have tried to communicate—about what it means to love ourselves in a woman-hating society—get twisted into a focus on "hating" men. Or those demonstrations that did discard high-heeled shoes, makeup, or bras, as symbolic of male control over women's self-definition and mobility, have been stripped of their political content.

Thus, women who feel that their priorities are survival issues of food or housing are led to think that Western feminists are not concerned with these matters. Similarly, media attempts to portray all feminists as a privileged elite within each country seek to isolate us from other women. The real strength of feminism can be seen best in the fact that more and more women come to embrace it in spite of the overwhelming effort that has gone into distorting it and trying to keep women away.

By acknowledging the power of the media's distortion of feminism at the Bangkok workshop, we were able to see the importance of defining it clearly for ourselves. Our definition brought together the right of every woman to equity, dignity, and freedom of choice through the power to control her own life and the removal of all forms of inequalities and oppression in society. We saw feminism as a worldview that has an impact on all aspects of life, and affirmed the broad context of the assertion that the "personal is political." This is to say that the individual aspects of oppression and change are not separate from the need for political and institutional change.

Through our discussion, we were able to agree on the use of this concept of feminism to describe women's struggles. While some had reservations about using the word "feminism," we chose not to allow media or government distortions to scare us away from it. As one Asian pointed out, if we shied away from the term, we would simply be attacked or ridiculed for other actions or words, since those who opposed us were against what we sought for women and the world and not really concerned with our language.

In Copenhagen at the 1980 NGO Forum, the conference newspaper came out with a quote-of-the-day from a Western feminist that read: "To talk feminism to a woman who has no water, no home, and no food is to talk nonsense." Many of us felt that the quote posed a crucial challenge to feminists. We passed out a leaflet, "What Is Feminism?" describing it as a perspective on the world that would address such issues, and we invited women to a special session on the topic. Over 300 women from diverse regions gathered to debate what feminism really means to us and how that has been distorted by the media and even within our own movements.

The second challenge we saw in the quote was that if it were true and feminists did not speak to such issues, then we would indeed be irrelevant to many women. We therefore discussed the importance of a feminist approach to development—one

that both addresses how to make home, food, and water available to all and extends beyond equating "development" with industrialization. Terms like "developing nations" are suspect and patronizing. While we need to look at the real material needs of all people from a feminist perspective, we can hardly call any countries "developed." For this reason, while I find all labels that generalize about diverse parts of the world problematic, I use "Western" or "industrialized" and "Third World," rather than "developing" and "developed."

Recently at a meeting in New York, I saw another example of confusion about the meaning of feminism. Two women who had just engaged in civil disobedience against nuclear weapons were discussing feminism as the motivating force behind their actions, when a man jumped up impatiently objecting, "But I thought this meeting was about disarmament, not feminism." It was the equivalent of "to talk feminism in the face of nuclear destruction is to talk nonsense." Such attitudes portray feminism as a luxury of secondary concern and thus both dismiss female experience as unimportant and limit our politics. They fundamentally misconstrue feminism as about "women's issues" rather than as a political perspective on life.

Seeing feminism as a transformational view is crucial to a global perspective. But to adopt a global outlook does not mean, as some feminists fear and male politicos often demand, that we abandon working on the "women's issues" that we fought to put on the political agenda. Nor does it imply setting aside our analysis of sexual politics. Rather it requires that we take what we have learned about sexual politics and use feminist theory to expose the connections between the "women's issues" and other world questions. In this way, we demonstrate our point that all issues are women's issues and need feminist analysis. For example, we must show how a society that tacitly sanctions male violence against women and children, whether incest and battery at home, rape on the streets, or sexual harassment on the job, is bound to produce people who are militaristic and believe in their right to dominate others on the basis of other differences such as skin color or nationality. Or we can point out how the heterosexist assumption that every "good" woman wants to and eventually will be supported by a man fuels the economic policies that have produced the feminization of poverty worldwide. This refusal to accept a woman who lives without a man as fully human thus allows policy makers to propose such ideas as keeping welfare payments or even job opportunities for single mothers limited since they "contribute to the destruction of the family."

The examples are endless. The task is not one of changing our issues but of expanding the frameworks from which we understand our work. It means taking what we have learned in working on "women's issues" and relating that to other areas, demanding that these not be seen as competing but as enabling us to bring about more profound change. To use the illustration above, to seek to end militarism without also ending the dynamic of domination embedded in male violence at home would be futile. And so, too, the reverse: we will never fully end male violence against individual women unless we also stop celebrating the organized violence of war as manly and appropriate behavior.

MAKING CONNECTIONS

The interconnectedness of the economic and sexual exploitation of women with militarism and racism is well illustrated in the area of forced prostitution and female sexual slavery. It is impossible to work on one aspect of this issue without confronting the whole socioeconomic context of women's lives. For example, females in India who are forced into prostitution are often either sold by poverty-stricken families for whom a girl child is considered a liability, or they have sought to escape arranged marriages they find intolerable. In the United States, many girls led into forced prostitution are teenage runaways who were victims of sexual or physical abuse at home, and for whom there are no jobs, services, or safe places to live.

In parts of Southeast Asia, many women face the limited economic options of rural poverty; joining assembly lines that pay poorly, destroy eyesight, and often discard workers over 30; or of entering the "entertainment industry." In Thailand and the Philippines, national economies dependent on prostitution resulted from U.S. military brothels during the Vietnam War. When that demand decreased,

prostitution was channeled into sex tourism—the organized multimillion-dollar transnational business of systematically selling women's bodies as part of packaged tours, which feeds numerous middlemen and brings foreign capital into the country. In all these situations, the patriarchal beliefs that men have the right to women's bodies, and that "other" races or "lower" classes are subhuman, underlie the abuse women endure.

Feminists organizing against these practices must link their various aspects. Thus, for example, women have simultaneously protested against sex tourism and militarism, created refuges for individual victims who escape, and sought to help women develop skills in order to gain more control over their lives. Japanese businesses pioneered the development of sex tourism. Feminists in Japan pioneered the opposition to this traffic. They work with Southeast Asian women to expose and shame the Japanese government and the businesses involved in an effort to cut down on the trade from their end.

On the international level, it is clear that female sexual slavery, forced prostitution, and violence against women operate across national boundaries and are political and human rights abuses of great magnitude. Yet, the male-defined human rights community by-and-large refuses to see any but the most narrowly defined cases of slavery or "political" torture as their domain. We must ask what is it when a woman faces death at the hands of her family to save its honor because she was raped? What is it when two young lesbians commit suicide together rather than be forced into unwanted marriages? What is it when a woman trafficked out of her country does not try to escape because she knows she will be returned by the police and beaten or deported? An understanding of sexual politics reveals all these and many more situations to be political human-rights violations deserving asylum, refugee status, and the help that other political victims are granted. As limited as human rights are in our world, we must demand at least that basic recognition for such women, while we seek to expand concern for human rights generally.

In these areas as well as others, feminists are creating new interpretations and approaches—to human rights, to development, to community and family, to conflict resolution, and so on. From local to global interaction, we must create alternative visions of how we can live in the world based on women's experiences and needs in the here-and-now.

LEARNING FROM DIVERSITY

In sharing experiences and visions across national and cultural lines, feminists are inspired by what others are doing. But we are also confronted with the real differences among us. On the one hand, our diversity is our strength. It makes it possible for us to imagine more possibilities and to draw upon a wider range of women's experiences. On the other hand, differences can also divide us if we do not take seriously the variations on female oppression that women suffer according to race, class, ethnicity, religion, sexual preference, age, nationality, physical disability, and so on. These are not simply added onto the oppression of women by sex, but shape the forms by which we experience that subordination. Thus, we cannot simply add up the types of oppression that a woman suffers one-by-one as independent factors but must look at how they are interrelated.

If we take this approach, we should be more capable of breaking down the ways in which difference itself separates people. Patriarchal society is constructed on a model of domination by which each group is assigned a place in the hierarchy according to various differences, and then allocated power or privileges based on that position. In this way, difference becomes threatening because it involves winning or losing one's position/privileges. If we eliminated the assignment of power and privilege according to difference, we could perhaps begin to enjoy real choices of style and variations of culture as offering more creative possibilities in life.

The world has been torn apart by various male divisions and conflicts for thousands of years and we should not assume that women can overcome and solve in a short time what patriarchy has so intricately conceived. The oppressions, resentments, fears, and patterns of behavior that have developed due to racism, classism, nationalism, and sexism, are very deep. We cannot just wish them away with our desire for women to transcend differences. Above all, we do not overcome differences by denying them or downplaying their effects on us—especially when the one denying is in the position of privilege.

A white woman can only legitimately talk about overcoming differences of race if she struggles to understand racism both as it affects her personally and as she affects it politically. A heterosexual can get beyond the divisions of sexual preference only by learning about both the oppression of lesbians and by acknowledging the insights that come from that orientation. A U.S. American must understand the effects of colonialism before she can hope for unity with women beyond national boundaries. Too often the call to transcend differences has been a call to ignore them at the expense of the oppressed. This cannot be the route of global feminism. We can only hope to chart a path beyond male divisions by walking through them and taking seriously their detrimental effects on us as women. This examination of and effort to eliminate other aspects of oppression does not come before or after working on sexism—it is simultaneous.

A crucial part of this process is understanding that reality does not look the same from different people's perspectives. It is not surprising that one way that feminists have come to understand about differences has been through the love of a person from another culture or race. It takes persistence and motivation—which love often engenders—to get beyond one's ethnocentric assumptions and really learn about other perspectives. In this process and while seeking to eliminate oppression, we also discover new possibilities and insights that come from the experience and survival of other peoples.

In considering what diversity means for a global movement, one of the most difficult areas for feminists is culture. In general, we affirm cultural diversity and the variety it brings to our lives. Yet, almost all existing cultures today are male-dominated. We know the horrors male powers have wrought over the centuries in imposing one cultural standard over another. Popular opposition to such imposition has often included affirmation of traditional cultures. Certainly none of our cultures can claim to have the answers to women's liberation since we are oppressed in all of them.

We must face the fact that in some instances male powers are justifying the continuation or advocating the adoption of practices oppressive to women by labeling them "cultural" and/or "resistance to Western influence." Feminists must refuse to accept *any* forms of domination of women—whether in the name of tradition or in the name of modernization. This is just the same as refusing to accept racial discrimination in the name of "culture," whether in the South of the USA or in South Africa. Feminists are seeking new models for society that allow for diversity while not accepting the domination of any group. For this, women in each culture must sort out what is best from their own culture and what is oppressive. Through our contact with each other, we can then challenge ethnocentric biases and move beyond the unconscious cultural assumptions inherent in our thinking.

In taking into account and challenging the various forms of domination in the world, we do not necessarily accept existing male theories about or solutions to them. We must always have a woman-identified approach—that is, one of seeking to identify with women's situations rather than accepting male definitions of reality. Such a process enables us to distinguish what is useful from male theories and to see where feminist approaches are being or need to be applied to issues such as race, class, and culture. Further, in a world so saturated with woman-hating, it is through woman-identification, which involves profoundly learning to love women and to listen for women's authentic perspectives, that we can make breakthroughs in these areas.

We confront a similar dilemma when examining nationalism. From a feminist perspective, I see nationalism as the ultimate expression of the patriarchal dynamic of domination—where groups battle for control over geographic territory, and justify violence and aggression in the name of national security. Therefore I prefer the term "global" to "international" because I see feminism as a movement among peoples beyond national boundaries and not among nation-states. Yet, nationalism has also symbolized the struggle of oppressed peoples against the control of other nations. And many attempts to go beyond nationalism have simply been supranational empire-building, such as the

idea of turning Africans into "Frenchmen." Further, in the context of increasing global control over us all by transnational corporations, many see nationalism as a form of resistance. In seeking to be global, feminists must therefore find ways to transcend patriarchal nationalism without demanding sameness, and while still preserving means of identity and culture that are not based on domination.

THINK GLOBALLY, ACT LOCALLY

A major obstacle that feminists face in seeking to be global is our lack of control over the resources necessary for maintaining greater contact worldwide. It takes time and money as well as energy and commitment to overcome the problems of distance, language, and culture. Feminists have little control over existing institutions with global networks, such as the media, churches, universities, and the state, but sometimes we must utilize such networks even as we try to set up our own.

Since feminists have limited resources for global travel and communication, it is vital that we learn how to be global in consciousness while taking action locally. For this, we must resist the tendency to separate "international" work into a specialized category of political activity that is often viewed as inaccessible to most women. This tendency reflects a hierarchical mode in which the "world level" is viewed as above the "local level." For those whose work focuses primarily on the global aspects of issues, the challenge is not to lose touch with the local arena on which any effective movement is based. For those whose work is focused locally, the challenge is to develop a global perspective that informs local work. For all of us, the central question is to understand how the issues of women all over the world are interrelated and to discern what that means specifically in each setting.

Global interaction is not something that we choose to do or not to do. It is something in which we are already participating. All we choose is whether to be aware of it or not, whether to try to understand it and how that affects our actions. For citizens of the United States, we begin our global consciousness with awareness of the impact that our country's policies have on other people's daily lives. I learned in the antiwar movement that often the most useful thing that we can do for people elsewhere is to make changes in the United States, and in how it exercises power in the world.

There are many well-known issues such as military aggression, foreign aid and trade policies, or the possibility of worldwide destruction through nuclear weapons or chemical contamination that we see as global. But there are numerous less obvious illustrations of global interrelatedness, from the present world economy where women are manipulated as an international cheap labor pool to the traffic in women's bodies for forced prostitution. Therefore, any attempt we make to deal with the needs of women in the United States, such as employment, must examine the global context of the problem. In this instance, that means understanding how multinational corporations move their plants from country to country or state to state, exploiting female poverty and discouraging unionization by threatening to move again. We must use global strategies, such as that proposed by one group on the Texas-Mexico border advocating an international bill of rights for women workers as a way to organize together for basic standards for all. In a world where global forces affect us daily, it is neither possible nor conscionable to achieve a feminist utopia in one country alone. . . .

A MATTER OF PERSPECTIVE

Beyond techniques and information, the primary task remains one of attitude, approach, and perspective. The point is not that we necessarily change the focus of our work but that we make connections that help to bring its global aspects to consciousness—in our programs, our slogans, our publications, and our conversations with other women. It is when we try to make a hierarchy of issues, keeping them separate and denying the importance of some in order to address others, that we are all defeated.

To use a previous example, if I cannot develop an analysis and discuss openly the ways in which heterosexism supports the international feminization of poverty, without having some women's homophobia prevent them from utilizing this insight, or without having some lesbians fear that I have abandoned "their issue" by working more on global poverty, then work in both areas is diminished. I believe

that the path to effective global feminist theory and action is not through denial of any issue or analysis but through listening, questioning, struggling, and seeking to make connections among them.

To work locally with a global perspective does require stretching feminism, not to abandon its insights but to shed its cultural biases, and thus to expand its capacity to reach all people. In this process, we risk what seems certain at home by taking it into the world and having it change through interaction with other realities and perceptions. It can be frightening. But if we have confidence in ourselves and in the feminist process, it can also be exciting. It can mean the growth of a more effective feminism with a greater ability to address the world and to bring change. If we fail to take these risks and ignore the global dimensions of our lives, we lose possibilities for individual growth and we doom feminism to a less effective role in the world struggle over the direction of the twenty-first century.

My visions of global feminism are grand, perhaps even grandiose. But the state of the world today demands that women become less modest and dream/plan/act/risk on a larger scale. At the same time, the realization of global visions can only be achieved through the everyday lives and action of women locally. It depends on women deciding to shape their own destiny, claiming their right to the world, and exercising their responsibility to make it in some way, large or small, a better place for all. As more women do this with a growing world perspective and sense of connection to others, we can say that feminism is meeting the challenge of bringing the global home.   [1987]

 161

The Globetrotting Sneaker

CYNTHIA ENLOE

All the "New World Order" really means to corporate giants like athletic shoemakers is that they now have the green light to accelerate long-standing industry practices. In the early 1980s, the field marshals commanding Reebok and Nike, which are both U.S.-based, decided to manufacture most of their sneakers in South Korea and Taiwan, hiring local women. L.A. Gear, Adidas, Fila, and Asics quickly followed their lead. In short time, the coastal city of Pusan, South Korea, became the "sneaker capital of the world." Between 1982 and 1989 the United States lost 58,500 footwear jobs to cities like Pusan, which attracted sneaker executives because its location facilitated international transport. More to the point, South Korea's military government had an interest in suppressing labor organizing, and it had a comfortable military alliance with the U.S. Korean women also seemed accepting of Confucian philosophy, which measured a woman's morality by her willingness to work hard for her family's well-being and to acquiesce to her father's and husband's dictates. With their sense of patriotic duty, Korean women seemed the ideal labor force for export-oriented factories.

U.S. and European sneaker company executives were also attracted by the ready supply of eager Korean male entrepreneurs with whom they could make profitable arrangements. This fact was central to Nike's strategy in particular. When they moved their production sites to Asia to lower labor costs, the executives of the Oregon-based company decided to reduce their corporate responsibilities further. Instead of owning factories outright, a more efficient strategy would be to subcontract the manufacturing to wholly foreign-owned—in this case, South Korean—companies. Let them be responsible for workers' health and safety. Let them negotiate with newly emergent unions. Nike would retain control over those parts of sneaker production that gave its officials the greatest professional satisfaction and the ultimate word on the product: design and marketing. Although Nike was following in the footsteps of garment and textile manufacturers, it set the trend for the rest of the athletic footwear industry.

But at the same time, women workers were developing their own strategies. As the South Korean pro-democracy movement grew throughout the 1980s, increasing numbers of women rejected traditional notions of feminine duty. Women began organizing in response to the dangerous working conditions, daily humiliations, and

low pay built into their work. Such resistance was profoundly threatening to the government, given the fact that South Korea's emergence as an industrialized "tiger" had depended on women accepting their "role" in growing industries like sneaker manufacture. If women reimagined their lives as daughters, as wives, as workers, as citizens, it wouldn't just rattle their employers; it would shake the very foundations of the whole political system.

At the first sign of trouble, factory managers called in government riot police to break up employees' meetings. Troops sexually assaulted women workers, stripping, fondling, and raping them "as a control mechanism for suppressing women's engagement in the labor movement," reported Jeong-Lim Nam of Hyosung Women's University in Taegu. It didn't work. It didn't work because the feminist activists in groups like the Korean Women Workers Association (KWWA) helped women understand and deal with the assaults. The KWWA held consciousness-raising sessions in which notions of feminine duty and respectability were tackled along with wages and benefits. They organized independently of the male-led labor unions to ensure that their issues would be taken seriously, in labor negotiations and in the pro-democracy movement as a whole.

The result was that women were at meetings with management, making sure that in addition to issues like long hours and low pay, sexual assault at the hands of managers and health care were on the table. Their activism paid off: in addition to winning the right to organize women's unions, their earnings grew. In 1980, South Korean women in manufacturing jobs earned 45 percent of the wages of their male counterparts; by 1990, they were earning more than 50 percent. Modest though it was, the pay increase was concrete progress, given that the gap between women's and men's manufacturing wages in Japan, Singapore, and Sri Lanka actually *widened* during the 1980s. Last but certainly not least, women's organizing was credited with playing a major role in toppling the country's military regime and forcing open elections in 1987.

Without that special kind of workplace control that only an authoritarian government could offer, sneaker executives knew that it was time to move. In Nike's

Country	Hourly Wages in $
China	0.10–0.14
Indonesia	0.16–0.20
Thailand	0.65–0.75
S.Korea	2.02–2.07
USA	7.38–7.94

Table 8.1 *Hourly Wages in Athletic Footwear Factories*

case, its famous advertising slogan—"Just Do It"—proved truer to its corporate philosophy than its women's "empowerment" ad campaign, designed to rally women's athletic (and consumer) spirit. In response to South Korean women workers' newfound activist self-confidence, the sneaker company and its subcontractors began shutting down a number of their South Korean factories in the late 1980s and early 1990s. After bargaining with government officials in nearby China and Indonesia, many Nike subcontractors set up shop in those countries, while some went to Thailand. China's government remains nominally Communist; Indonesia's ruling generals are staunchly anti-Communist. But both are governed by authoritarian regimes who share the belief that if women can be kept hard at work, low paid, and unorganized, they can serve as a magnet for foreign investors.

Where does all this leave South Korean women—or any woman who is threatened with a factory closure if she demands decent working conditions and a fair wage? They face the dilemma confronted by thousands of women from dozens of countries. The risk of job loss is especially acute in relatively mobile industries; it's easier for a sneaker, garment, or electronics manufacturer to pick up and move than it is for an automaker or a steel producer. In the case of South Korea, poor women had moved from rural villages into the cities searching for jobs to support not only themselves, but parents and siblings. The exodus of manufacturing jobs has forced more women into the growing "entertainment" industry. The kinds of bars and massage parlors offering sexual services that had mushroomed around U.S. military bases during the Cold War have been opening up across the country.

But the reality is that women throughout Asia are organizing, knowing full well the risks involved. Theirs is a long-term view; they are taking direct aim at companies' nomadic advantage, by building links among workers in countries targeted for "development" by multinational corporations. Through sustained grassroots efforts, women are developing the skills and confidence that will make it increasingly difficult to keep their labor cheap. The United Nations conference on women in Beijing, China, was a rare opportunity to expand their cross-border strategizing.

The Beijing conference provided an important opportunity to call world attention to the hypocrisy of the governments and corporations doing business in China. Numerous athletic shoe companies followed Nike in setting up manufacturing sites throughout the country. This included Reebok—a company claiming its share of responsibility for ridding the world of "injustice, poverty, and other ills that gnaw away at the social fabric," according to a statement of corporate principles.

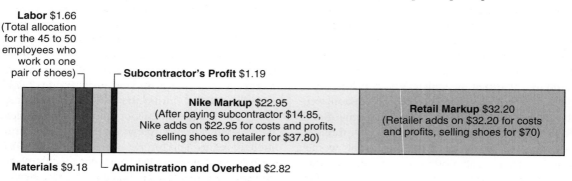

Figure 8.1 *A $70 Pair of Nike Pegasus: Where the Money Goes*

Since 1988, Reebok has been giving out annual human rights awards to dissidents from around the world. But it wasn't until 1992 that the company adopted its own "human rights production standards"—after labor advocates made it known that the quality of life in factories run by its subcontractors was just as dismal as that at most other athletic shoe suppliers in Asia. Reebok's code of conduct, for example, includes a pledge to "seek" those subcontractors who respect workers' rights to organize. The only problem is that independent trade unions are banned in China. Reebok has chosen to ignore that fact, even though Chinese dissidents have been the recipients of the company's own human rights award. As for working conditions, Reebok now says it sends its own inspectors to production sites a couple of times a year. But they have easily "missed" what subcontractors are trying to hide—like 400 young women workers locked at night into an overcrowded dormitory near a Reebok-contracted factory in the town of Zhuhai, as reported last August in the *Asian Wall Street Journal Weekly*.

★ ★ ★

Nike's cofounder and CEO Philip Knight has said that he would like the world to think of Nike as "a company with a soul that recognizes the value of human beings." Nike, like Reebok, says it sends in inspectors from time to time to check up on work conditions at its factories; in Indonesia, those factories are run largely by South Korean subcontractors. But according to Donald Katz in a recent book on the company, Nike spokesman Dave Taylor told an in-house newsletter that the factories are "[the subcontractors'] business to run." For the most part, the company relies on regular reports from subcontractors regarding its "Memorandum of Understanding," which managers must sign, promising to impose "local government standards" for wages, working conditions, treatment of workers, and benefits.

In April, the minimum wage in the Indonesian capital of Jakarta will be $1.89 *a day*—among the highest in a country where the minimum wage varies by region. And managers are required to pay only 75 percent of the wage directly; the remainder can be withheld for "benefits." By now, Nike has a well-honed response to growing criticisms of its low-cost labor strategy. Such wages should not be seen as exploitative, says Nike, but rather as the first rung on the ladder of economic opportunity that Nike has extended to workers with few options. Otherwise, they'd be out "harvesting coconut meat in the tropical sun," wrote Nike spokesman Dusty Kidd, in a letter to the *Utne Reader*. The all-is-relative response craftily shifts attention away from reality: Nike didn't move to Indonesia to help Indonesians; it moved to ensure that its profit margin continues to grow. And that is pretty much guaranteed in a country where "local standards" for wages rarely take a worker over the poverty line. A 1991 survey by the International Labor Organization (ILO) found that 88 percent of women working at the Jakarta minimum wage at the time—slightly less than a dollar a day—were malnourished.

A woman named Riyanti might have been among the workers surveyed by the ILO. Interviewed by the *Boston Globe* in 1991, she told the reporter who had asked about her long hours and low pay: "I'm happy working here. . . . I can make money and I can make friends." But in fact, the reporter discovered that Riyanti had already joined her co-workers, in two strikes, the first to force one of Nike's Korean subcontractors to accept a new women's union and the second to compel managers to pay at least the minimum wage. That Riyanti appeared less than forthcoming about her activities isn't surprising. Many Indonesian factories have military men posted in their front offices who find no fault with managers who tape women's mouths shut to keep them from talking among themselves. They and their superiors have a political reach that extends far beyond the barracks. Indonesia has all the makings for a political explosion, especially since the gap between rich and poor is widening into a chasm. It is in this setting that the government has tried to crack down on any independent labor organizing—a policy that Nike has helped to implement. Referring to a recent strike in a Nike-contracted factory, Tony Nava, Nike representative in Indonesia, told the *Chicago Tribune* in November 1994 that the "troublemakers" had been fired. When asked about Nike policy on the issue, spokesman Keith Peters struck a conciliatory note: "If the government were to allow and encourage independent labor organizing, we would be happy to support it."

Indonesian workers' efforts to create unions independent of governmental control were a surprise to shoe companies. Although their moves from South Korea have been immensely profitable [see table 8.1], they do not have the sort of immunity from activism that they had expected. In May 1993, the murder of a female labor activist outside Surabaya set off a storm of local and international protest. Even the U.S. State Department was forced to take note in its 1993 worldwide human rights report, describing a system similar to that which generated South Korea's boom 20 years earlier: severely restricted union organizing, security forces used to break up strikes, low wages for men, lower wages for women—complete with government rhetoric celebrating women's contribution to national development.

Yet when President Clinton visited Indonesia he made only a token effort to address the country's human rights problem. Instead, he touted the benefits of free trade, sounding indeed more enlightened, more in tune with the spirit of the post–Cold War era than do those defenders of protectionist trading policies who coat their rhetoric with "America first" chauvinism. But "free trade" as actually being practiced today is hardly *free* for any workers—in the United States or abroad—who have to accept the Indonesian, Chinese, or Korean workplace model as the price of keeping their jobs.

The not-so-new plot of the international trade story has been "divide and rule." If women workers and their government in one country can see that a sneaker company will pick up and leave if their labor demands prove more costly than those in a neighbor country, then women workers will tend to see their neighbors not as regional sisters, but as competitors who can steal their precarious livelihoods. Playing women off against each other is, of course, old hat. Yet it is as essential to international trade politics as is the fine print in GATT.

But women workers allied through networks like the Hong Kong-based Committee for Asian Women are developing their own post–Cold War foreign policy, which means addressing women's needs: how to convince fathers and husbands that a woman going out to organizing meetings at night is not sexually promiscuous; how to develop workplace agendas that respond to family needs; how to work with male unionists who push women's demands to the bottom of their lists; how to build a global movement.

These women refuse to stand in awe of the corporate power of the Nike or Reebok or Adidas executive. Growing numbers of Asian women today have concluded that trade politics have to be understood by women on their own terms. If women in Russia and Eastern Europe can challenge Americanized consumerism, if Asian activists can solidify their alliances, and if U.S. women can join with them by taking on trade politics—the post–Cold War sneaker may be a less comfortable fit in the 1990s.   [1997]

This article draws from the work of South Korean scholars Hyun Sook Kim, Seung-kyung Kim, Katherine Moon, Seungsook Moon, and Jeong-Lim Nam.

🦎 162

Transnational Collaboration in Support of Sweatshop Workers

Union Organizing in El Salvador: In Solidarity with U.S. Students

SONIA BEATRIZ LARA

There are a lot of risks to organizing workers in the San Marcos Free Trade Zone. Principally, you can lose your job, which is what happened to me in 1999 after I spoke with a visiting delegation of students from Columbia University. At the time, I did not think of the risks; my courage came from the many injustices that I experienced and witnessed while working in the factory.

The supervisors and Korean bosses at Doall Enterprises were exploiting us greatly. The more we produced, the more they wanted us to increase production. In spite of the fact that we were keeping up with their increased demands, they would mistreat us, both physically and verbally—pressuring us. Always telling us: Hurry up; hurry up and produce more.

Most people felt that they couldn't react: if there was any union effort whatsoever, the workers would get fired—15 or 20 at a time. I have only one child, but most of the women have many children and just couldn't take the risk of losing their jobs.

In November 1999, a group met and tried to form the first union in Doall. They were fired immediately; only one founding member was left inside the factory. That's when the National Labor Committee pressured the American company who, in turn, pressured Doall to reinstate the workers.

So, there was pressure and a negotiation. After three months, 30 of the workers were reinstated—with back wages. Doall signed an agreement: there would be no reprisals and reinstated workers would not be fired again. Further, no discrimination inside the factory was to be allowed, so that others could speak with union workers inside the factory and not be fired themselves. From the time of the reinstatement, the Ministry of Labor required a six-month period before the union could be established. In August, a new union was constituted, called SETDESA.

Now that the union leadership is in place, it works to protect union members from being fired and negotiates with the management to improve other aspects of the factory. For example, before, you had to go into work at 6:50. If you didn't, the supervisors would deduct a half-hour from your wages or they'd send you home. Now the workers just go in at seven o'clock. Previously, workers had no break from seven in the morning until noon. Now there's a 15-minute break at 9:30.

SETDESA is the only functioning union in the *maquilla* (factory) right now in the Free Trade Zone Assembly for Export sector. Union organizers talk with legal representatives of the factory and look for ways to come to an agreement, even though a collective contract doesn't exist. (In El Salvador you're allowed to form a union with 30 memberships, which gives certain legal recognition and protection. But to officially negotiate a collective contract, union leaders need to have a membership of 51 percent, which we don't have yet.)

I believe that the union's existence and its continued growth is exclusively due to the effective U.S. pressure and involvement of U.S. people—in particular, the students. It is very moving to know that even though they don't live in our country, young people joined us in our fight against the suffering we endured in the *maquillas*. Their solidarity has had a great impact and been very important to our movement. [2000]

United Students Against Sweatshops

LIZA FEATHERSTONE and UNITED STUDENTS AGAINST SWEATSHOPS

Fourteen-year-olds from Bangladesh to the Mexican maquila, working 14-hour days in factories that reek of toxic fumes; young women supporting families on some 20 cents an hour; factory managers who forbid sick workers time off to go to the doctor; bosses in El Monte, California, and elsewhere who have, quite literally, turned factories into prisons, forcibly detaining workers in sweatshops surrounded by barbed wire—more and more North Americans are familiar with such images, and the brutality of the garment industry has even made it to prime-time television. On an episode of *ER*, sweatshop workers were killed in a fire when factory owners failed to provide adequate emergency exits. Kathie Lee slave labor jokes are ubiquitous on late-night television. Indeed, the public is so disturbed by garment industry abuses that in a survey conducted by Marymount University, released during the 1999 Christmas holiday season, 86 percent of consumers said they would be willing to pay extra to ensure that their clothing wasn't made in sweatshops. In malls nationwide, it's no longer unusual to overhear shoppers in front of a Gap store debating whether to go inside. "I've heard they use sweatshop labor," one will say.

The sweatshop's new visibility is due, in large part, to the efforts of the North American anti-sweatshop movement, a movement now led by college students. Since 1997, students have been protesting the horrifying conditions in the collegiate apparel industry, demanding better wages and working conditions for the workers who make hats and sweatshirts bearing their school logos. Antisweatshop activists are the most powerful and visible progressive presence on campus since the South African divestment movement in the 1980s, and recently they have enjoyed some concrete successes.

Unlike this student movement, sweatshops themselves are nothing new; in fact, they have always been the foundation of the garment and needle-trade industries. This is partly because the softness of fabric and complexity of patterns don't allow for easy mechanization, which is the way many other industries keep production costs low. The term "sweatshop" is about a hundred years old, deriving from the concept of the "sweating system," a network of subcontracted shops that "sweated" profits out of workers through long hours, low pay based on a piece rate, and poor conditions. Today, although apparel companies and economists tend to reject the word as "emotional" and inflammatory, most other observers find it an all-too-accurate description of prevailing industry conditions in which workers' earnings depend on production levels rather than the hours they work, and where they are subjected to heat, fumes, insults, sexual harassment, physical punishments, and below-subsistence wages.

With the decline of transportation and communication costs since the 1960s, garment manufacturers have increasingly elected to avoid the relatively high wages of U.S. labor by moving most of their factories overseas, often to countries that offer workers little protection. The industry has also become more ruthlessly competitive, as increasingly fickle consumer tastes dictate quicker production cycles. In an attempt to keep clothing prices low enough to seduce American teenagers, manufacturers pay the Nicaraguan and Vietnamese teenagers who make the clothes less than a dollar a day. It is a brutal game, one whose rules young people worldwide—workers and consumers—are beginning passionately to reject.

• • •

In January 2001, over 850 workers at Kukdong International Mexico, a Korean-owned garment factory in Atlixco de Puebla, went on strike when five of their co-workers were illegally fired for trying to organize an independent union. During an occupation of the factory, in which workers peacefully protested the firings, riot police violently assaulted workers. Since Kukdong contracts with Nike and Reebok to make sweatshirts bearing the logos of the Universities of North Carolina—Chapel Hill, Michigan, Oregon and many other schools boasting active antisweatshop groups, the conflict couldn't have presented a better test case for the effectiveness of the student antisweatshop movement. The Kukdong struggle, said Eric Brakken in February, is "the most important thing we've been a part of. If we win here, it's the beginning of a real international strategy."

Like many Mexican workers, Kukdong employees were at that time forced to belong to a mafia union with close ties to management and to the local government, which pays supervisors to support it, resists dissent with brutal violence, and had never been supported by a majority of the factory's workers. The Kukdong workers, 90 percent of whom are young women, knew they needed a union of their own, because the mob union—Revolutionary Confederation of Workers and Peasants, or FCROC—had failed to respond to any of their complaints, and they were getting desperate. "From what I see, the FCROC works only for the factory," 16-year-old Kukdong worker Juana Hernandez said in an interview with USAS researchers. Alvaro Saaveda Anzures, also 16, agreed: "The FCROC is a union in appearance only."

Wages at the factory, most workers say, are insufficient to support a single person, much less someone with children or dependents. Conditions at the factory were abominable as well; many workers accepted the job because management had promised free breakfasts and lunch, but the food Kukdong provided was insufficient and, even worse, rancid and worm-infested. "I was sick for three days from the food I ate there," Alvaro Saavedra told USAS. According to copiously sourced WRC reports—based on extensive interviews with workers and management—the Kukdong employees were also subjected to verbal and physical abuse, even hit with hammers and screwdrivers. The Kukdong factory was in clear violation, the WRC found, of the WRC's code of conduct, and those of its member universities.

The workers' organizing grew out of talks with USAS activists, one of whom, David Alvarado, had been living in Puebla. The Kukdong workers decided to push for an independent union—an extremely bold and risky step in the maquila— because they knew they had powerful allies in USAS and the WRC. When the workers went on strike, students picketed Nike stores in several cities, and on campuses nationwide urged administrators to pressure Nike and Reebok. After widely publicized WRC investigations (whose findings were largely confirmed by Verité, a monitor hired by Nike and Reebok), local media coverage and agitation from students, university administrators, and labor activists worldwide, Nike and Reebok intervened. The companies initially, of course, did nothing; however, eventually the sneaker titans forced Kukdong management to rehire a majority of the fired workers, including two of the union leaders, within two months of the dismissals.

Against all odds, the workers and students have won. According to a WRC report released in late June 2001, their combined agitation had resulted in better food, wage increases for some workers, the apparent abolition of physical abuse, and improved sanitary conditions. Even more surprisingly, the FCROC voluntarily left the factory that summer; management recognized that a majority of the workers support SITEKIM, and at the time of writing, workers and management were about to begin negotiating a collective bargaining agreement. At USAS's instigation, U.S. Representative George Miller visited Puebla in early September, and received a commitment from the governor of Puebla to grant SITEKIM official recognition. (Early USAS activist Tico Almeida was working in Miller's office and brought the situation to the congressman's attention.) SITEKIM will be the first independent union in the Mexican maquila, and one of the few democratic unions chosen by the workers themselves. To celebrate the victory, USAS activists and workers from Kukdong (now

called Mexmode, due to a factory name-change in fall 2001) went on a speaking tour in late November/early December, visiting a dozen U.S. colleges, and emphasizing the influence universities can have in improving working conditions overseas.

• • •

In the fall of 2001, new institutions continued to join the WRC, and in November students' spirits were lifted by learning that workers had voted to unionize at BJ&B, a factory in the Dominican Republic that makes baseball caps for many USAS schools. USAS had been supporting this campaign for years—one of the organization's earliest efforts at cross-border solidarity—so the victory was a profound one. As the response of the U.S. government to the September 11 attacks grew more brutal, many students threw themselves into antiwar organizing. Groups like USAS had established such strong left student networks—and created such a ready culture of dissent—that antiwar protest was visible on many campuses before the bombs even started falling. The new peace activism, which had by late November 2001 touched at least 400 campuses nationwide, has an even more visceral appeal than the anti-sweatshop movement. It is attracting a wider range of students, including rural, Southern schools (North Carolina's Appalachia State and the University of Southern Mississippi), historically black colleges like Morehouse, community colleges from Boston to Hawaii, urban public universities like the University of Illinois—Chicago and CUNY, high schools and middle schools. A newly formed National Youth and Student Peace and Justice Coalition will startle anyone who imagines that all peace activists are white folk-music fans; in addition to groups like USAS, it includes the youth division of the Black Radical Congress and the Muslim Student Association. Many USAS activists see the emerging antiwar movement as an opportunity for a much larger student movement to emerge, one that looks a lot more like America's economically, regionally, and racially varied society.

USAS and the larger student movement face some challenges. Prolonged war—and anti-war activism—could test the warm solidarity developed in recent years between students and labor, though students and workers alike have been working hard to prevent that. There's also the problem of finite human resources: the student movement accomplishes a lot with only a handful of core activists, and sustained opposition to war—important as that is—could drain activist attention from labor issues. That's why, Jackie Bray says, "There is absolute consensus in the organization that we're sticking with labor." USAS endorses peace organizing and is part of the emerging student "peace and justice movement," but feels strongly that its strength lies in its ties to the labor movement. Says Rachel Edelman, a recent University of Michigan graduate who now works full time in the USAS office, "It is more important than ever to fight in solidarity with workers, given the conservative backlash, and the fact that so many workers are losing their jobs."

On the other hand, it may be difficult to help garment workers win victories, as that industry is in the midst of a global slowdown. Garment workers all over the world risk losing their jobs as factories get fewer orders; that's not a good climate for organizing. There's also a danger that recession may leave students too anxious about their own futures to organize. The triple extremities of war, terror, and recession could distract the public from capitalism's everyday inequities. On the other hand, they certainly dramatize the system's problems: Bush's tax breaks to corporations; the way every national burden, from economic slowdown to anthrax, is disproportionately shouldered by the working class. USAS activists see tremendous opportunity in this moment.

Many activists say that the September 11 attacks have left people ever hungrier for forward-looking, optimistic social action. The global economic justice movement in particular may stand a better chance of being heard, at a time when Americans are suddenly looking at the rest of the world and wondering, "Why do 'they' hate us?" Says Jackie Bray, "People are beginning to ask questions." For many, September 11 underscored the need to rethink America's role in the world, and to redress global economic inequality. It is in this spirit that USAS continues to move forward. As the organization asserted in its post–September 11 statement, "We realize that there is a great deal of work and healing ahead of us, and hope to move forward from this moment to build a more just and inclusive place."   [2002]

Women Organizing: Many Issues, Many Voices

The ideas of feminism have influenced countless women, changing their ideas about themselves and their expectations of their future. Feminism, as Winona LaDuke points out, is fundamentally about self-determination—people's ability to control their lives. Working toward self-determination can take many forms. Inspired by the memory of Mama Dixon, a powerful family friend, Sonia Sanchez confronts a man who was exposing himself. The excerpt from *Manifesta: Young Women, Feminism and the Future* is a call for a political movement that addresses the structural and cultural barriers to women's self-determination. In "Just Sex," Jodi Gold and Susan Villari describe the ways that college students have used new technology to challenge the campus culture that encourages acquaintance rape.

Feminism cannot be located in one central organization. Rather it exists in the myriad groups and organizing projects that women form when they encounter injustice or seek to address unmet needs. In the twenty-first century the Internet has facilitated connections among women across geographical boundaries. The black feminists described by Barbara Ramsby, for example, were able to create a national network that they could mobilize when the voices of African-American women were being ignored. Like the African-American women of the 1960s and 1970s described earlier by Benita Roth, their political perspective challenged multiple systems of oppression.

But ending women's subordination involves more than individual acts. It requires working together to challenge those practices that prevent women from controlling their lives. New York State passed a domestic workers bill of rights in 2010, the first state in the nation to pass legislation. For the incarcerated women of AIDS Counseling and Education, activism meant creating an organization that embodies a vision of a more humane and just society. Breaking the silence that keeps people isolated from each other and afraid to speak out, women like the domestic workers described by Ai-jen Poo have pressured governmental bodies successfully to take action against their exploitation.

Sustainable agriculture, environmental justice, and antimilitarism are intimately tied to women's activist work because women are disproportionately affected by war, climate change, and environmental degradation. As Joyce Barry describes in her article, the Coal River Mountain Watch is comprised of working-class women activists in Boone County, West Virginia. They came together in 1998 and have continued to fight since then against the mountaintop removal coal-mining process that has lead to the destruction of their Appalachian communities. Jennifer Cognard-Black laments the fact that women have been ignored in the sustainable food movement even though they have played a prominent role in its leadership. She urges women and girls to get involved in food politics in big and small ways.

War and environmental degradation go hand in hand; wars are expensive and take resources away from other societal needs, and the modern war machine promotes large-scale environmental waste and destruction through its use of harmful chemical and nuclear technology. Code Pink signifies the savvy new women's activism where the connections between many issues like war, environment, and women's rights are raised in exciting headline-grabbing ways. In her interview with Medea Benjamin, one of the co-founders of Code Pink, Angelina Perri Birney explains, "The idea was to turn the color pink on its head from being this nice, feminine, sweet color to one that was very energetic, bold, and determined." The results of their creative energy have been the group's ability to cut through the commercial media machine and draw attention to issues around U.S. wars of imperialism and their environmental and social impact, and to support peace initiatives around the world. Claire Papell narrates her own deepening commitment to feminist antiwar activism through her engagement with women's studies.

We conclude our book with the voices of three young feminists. Their personal narratives describe the ways young women have brought the ideas they learned in women's studies into their work lives.

🌿 163

Struggles of Responsibility

WINONA LADUKE

I have spent my entire adult life as what you might call a political activist. I have testified at hearings, demonstrated at countless protests, and been involved in litigation. I've worked in a number of Native communities across the continent, and founded the White Earth Land Recovery Project (WELRP) on my home reservation. With our work here, we've been able to recover more than 1,700 acres of our land and create a land trust, while we work toward recovery of more of our own birthright. We also continue to work to protect our wild rice from genetic modification and ecosystems from contamination by pesticides, and to stop clear cuts of the forest. From inside my own house, we roast fair-trade and organic coffee. I have written books about the environment, run for vice president twice (as Ralph Nader's Green Party running mate in 1996 and 2000), and been arrested because

I don't think that a thousand-year-old tree should become a phone book.

The perception of me, or of any well-known activist, is probably far from reality. Activists, the thinking goes, must be organized, focused, always working on the next strategy. My real life, the one in which I conduct all of my activism, is, of course, messy. If you came over, you might find my five children, ages 4 to 16, 3 dogs, 15 horses, a few cats, several interns from around the country, and many friends who double as coworkers helping with WELRP's work. The 2000 veep campaign was conducted with me breastfeeding my newborn son before and after each stump speech and during many an interview. I still coordinate the sustainable food projects central to the White Earth Land Recovery Project literally from my kitchen table at the same time as I figure out meals for my kids, take coffee orders for Muskrat Coffee Company, company, and pop in videos for my youngest to watch on TV. I talk to Native community leaders from across the country as I cook meals and clean up (sort of an endless job). I write books at the same table where I make rawhide ornaments for sale as part of WELRP and help with maple syruping in the spring season, and my house is filled with labels that spell out the Ojibwe words for "bed," "book," "cupboard," and "table" as part of my ongoing commitment to indigenous language and culture preservation. My activism is simply in my life—it has to be, or it couldn't get done.

My own life as an identified activist has made me wonder at the term itself. What separates simple "responsibility" in life—motherhood, for example—from the fine line that one crosses to become an "activist"? I have been surprised and moved by encountering so many other mothers in my years as an activist: mothers in Chiapas breastfeeding their babies like anyone else, but who mask their faces as they speak with me because they can't afford to have their identities known; Mohawk and Ojibwe mothers who face down General Motors and Potlach Corporation, knowing that if they don't, their kids won't ever know clean water, and generations ahead will have contaminated breast milk.

I have developed long-standing friendships with women who are engaged in struggles of responsibility—for their land, their own community health, and the water their children drink. Are these women feminists? That depends on who defines the term. Many of these women, including myself, are committed to the process of self-determination and believe in our inherent rights, as bestowed by the Creator, to live with dignity, peace, clean air and water, and our duty to pass on this legacy to our children and the generations to follow.

At the United Nations Conference on the Status of Women in Beijing, China, in 1995, I asked women from small countries around the world why they came all this way to participate in what was, in essence, a meeting. "I came because the World Bank is here," explained Victoria Tauli-Corpuz, an Igarok woman from the Philippines whose village is targeted for a World Bank–funded dam. "I believe that those people at the World Bank and the IMF, those who make the decisions which will transform my life, should see my face." That sentiment applies whether you are an Igarok woman from the Philippines or Sherry Honkala from the Kensington Welfare Rights Union, challenging federal budget cuts to aid for dependent families or tending to the needs of

homeless families. The message of self-determining women is the same for all people: *We want control over our lives, and we will challenge those who impose laws on our bodies, our communities, and our future.*

I believe that women move to activism out of sheer necessity. As a group, we are not of privilege—budget cuts devastated our households, the military wreaks havoc on our bodies and our homelands. The National Priorities Project reports that $152.6 billion spent on military aid in 2003 could have provided Head Start for an additional 20,211,205 children, health coverage for an additional 89,780,249 children, affordable housing vouchers for an additional 22,894,974 families, or salaries for 2,673,864 new elementary school teachers. Feminist activism, then, doesn't begin or end with my uterus: this is about my whole body, my life, and the lives of my children. We are women who redefine "Women's Issues," and say all issues are women's issues. I say: *We are the mothers of our nations, and anything that concerns our nations is of concern to us as women.* Those choices and necessities move us to speak out and to be active.

I happen to come from a line of these women who speak out, and I continue this work—our work. Women's work. My grandmother Helen Peskin, a Jewish woman from the Ukraine, recently passed into the Spirit World. Her early years were formed by the reality of war, first the Cossacks who overran her village and then the Nazis. With her life came a sheer determination to not be a victim, to speak for peace, to make a better life, and to demand dignity. Of her 90 years on this earth a good 40 were spent as a seamstress: a purse maker, a member of the Pocket Book Makers Union in the garment district in New York, a folk dancer, and a peace activist. *A woman's work is about economic justice, and about quality of life.* My mother, Betty LaDuke, made her own path as a muralist and art professor, one of the first women on the faculty of her college, and like other women, she had to do it better than any man around because it took that much to get recognized. She has done this work in a way that celebrates life, and celebrates the work of other women. And she has done this work by linking with women in Eritrea, Nigeria, and Peru. *A women's work is about creating and celebrating life.* Our parents' struggles become our own, in our own time. We can't escape from that history, nor can we escape from our time in it.

In the lives of women in my family, it was never about just our own selves, it was about the collective dignity and *everyone's* health and rights. This is counter, in many ways, to Americanism. Americanism teaches individualism. My family, and indeed movements for social transformation, are not about anything as limited as the better job or the better advantage for the individual woman. Even the tragic deaths of three of my closest friends, activists all, are lessons in the urgency of change on a broader scale. Marsha Gomez, a gifted artist, was killed by her own son, who lacked the psychiatric medical attention he so desperately needed; Nilak Butler passed from ovarian cancer because she did not have adequate health coverage; and Ingrid Washinawatok El-Issa was assassinated by the FARC, Revolutionary Armed Forces of Colombia, with a gun and a bullet that came from my tax dollars in the second most highly financed recipient of U.S. military aid in the world.

The compelling reason behind activism is that our most personal lives—even the intimacy of death—are actually embroidered in the reality of public policy, foreign policy, military aid, and economics. Each day, then, I, like the women in my family before me, and like so many other women in the world, recommit to continue this struggle for life, and to celebrate its beauty in the process. That struggle and that celebration are who we are as women, as we take responsibility for our destinies.   [2004]

🌿 164

style no. 1

SONIA SANCHEZ

i come from a long line of rough mamas.

so here i was walking down market street. coming out of a city hall meeting. night wind at my back,

dressed in my finest. black cashmere coat caressing the rim of my gray suede boots. hat sitting acey duecy. anointing the avenue with my black smell.

and this old dude. red as his car inching its way on the sidewalk. honked his horn. slid his body almost out of his skin. toward me. psst. psst. hey. let's you and me have some fun. psst. psst. c'mon babe. don't you want some of this?

and he pulled his penis out of his pants. held the temporal wonder of men in his hands.

i stopped. looked at him. a memory from deep in the eye. a memory of saturday afternoon moviehouses where knowledge comes with a tremulous cry. old white men. spiderlike. spinning their webs towards young girls legs and out budabbot and loucostello smiles melted. and we moved in the high noon walk of black girls. smelling the breath of an old undertow.

and i saw mama Dixon. dancing on his head. mama Dixon. big loud friend of the family. who stunned us with her curses and liquor. being herself. whose skin breathed hilarious breaths. and i greased my words on her tongue. and she gave them back to me like newly tasted wine.

motha fucka. you even offend the night i said. you look like an old mole coming out of its hole. take yo slimy sat ole ass home. fo you get what's coming to you. and yo generation. ask yo mama to skin you. that is if you have had one cuz anybody ugly as you couldna been born.

and i turned my eyes eastward. toward the garage. waking up the incipient night with my steps. ready for the short days. the wind singing in my veins.   [1987]

🌿 165

Manifesta: Young Women, Feminism, and the Future

JENNIFER BAUMGARDNER
and AMY RICHARDS

In September 1999 in New York City, two women sit down to write in a studio apartment on Avenue

B. The coffeemaker is on. It's late. Wafting up from the streets are the psychosis-inducing sounds of the Mister Softee truck playing "Music Box Dancer" while making its rounds. "When in the course of 30 years of uninterrupted feminism," one woman types, while the other leafs through pages of clips, notes, and correspondence, "it becomes evident that a single generation can only go so far, it behooves the next generation to pick up the reins and articulate the plot that will move their cause forward. The first two waves of feminism had clear political goals that involved holding the government accountable to its citizens, the majority of whom were getting an unequal deal. In order to have a government that responds to the Third Wave, rather than a society by the few for the few, we need a similar declaration of our sentiments. We need a Manifesta."

THIRD-WAVE MANIFESTA: A THIRTEEN-POINT AGENDA

1. To out unacknowledged feminists, specifically those who are younger, so that Generation X can become a visible movement and, further, a voting block of 18- to 40-year-olds.

2. To safeguard a woman's right to bear or not to bear a child, regardless of circumstances, including women who are younger than 18 or impoverished. To preserve this right throughout her life and support the choice to be childless.

3. To make explicit that the fight for reproductive rights must include birth control; the right for poor women and lesbians to have children; partner adoption for gay couples; subsidized fertility treatments for all women who choose them; and freedom from sterilization abuse. Furthermore, to support the idea that sex can be—and usually is—for pleasure, not procreation.

4. To bring down the double standard in sex and sexual health, and foster male responsibility and assertiveness in the following areas: achieving freedom from STDs; more fairly dividing the burden of family planning as well as responsibilities such as child care; and eliminating violence against women.

5. To tap into and raise awareness of our revolutionary history, and the fact that almost all movements began as youth movements. To have access to our intellectual feminist legacy and women's history; for the classics of radical feminism, womanism, *mujeristas,* women's liberation, and all our roots to remain in print; and to have women's history taught to men as well as women as a part of all curricula.

6. To support and increase the visibility and power of lesbians and bisexual women in the feminist movement, in high schools, colleges, and the workplace. To recognize that queer women have always been at the forefront of the feminist movement, and that there is nothing to be gained—and much to be lost—by downplaying their history, whether inadvertently or actively.

7. To practice "autokeonony" ("self in community"): to see activism not as a choice between self and community but as a link between them that creates balance.

8. To have equal access to health care, regardless of income, which includes coverage equivalent to men's and keeping in mind that women use the system more often than men do because of our reproductive capacity.

9. For women who so desire to participate in all reaches of the military, including combat, and to enjoy all the benefits (loans, health care, pensions) offered to its members for as long as we continue to have an active military. The largest expenditure of our national budget goes toward maintaining this welfare system, and feminists have a duty to make sure women have access to every echelon.

10. To liberate adolescents from slut-bashing, listless educators, sexual harassment, and bullying at school, as well as violence in all walks of life, and the silence that hangs over adolescents' heads, often keeping them isolated, lonely, and indifferent to the world.

11. To make the workplace responsive to an individual's wants, needs, and talents. This includes valuing (monetarily) stay-at-home parents, aiding employees who want to spend more time

with family and continue to work, equalizing pay for jobs of comparable worth, enacting a minimum wage that would bring a full-time worker with two children over the poverty line, and providing employee benefits for freelance and part-time workers.

12. To acknowledge that, although feminists may have disparate values, we share the same goal of equality, and of supporting one another in our efforts to gain the power to make our own choices.

13. To pass the Equal Rights Amendment so that we can have a constitutional foundation of righteousness and equality upon which future women's rights conventions will stand.

STANDING ON SHOULDERS

Kim Miltimore, a 28-year-old from Kent, Washington, sat down one night in the fall of 1999 and fired off an e-mail to feminist.com. "I cannot accept that insurance companies cover Viagra but won't cover infertility drugs such as Clomid," she wrote. "I want to help change this gross inequity— do you have any links to groups fighting for equality in medical coverage?"

At the same time, Jewish Women Watching, a group of feminists in New York City, sent out hundreds of cards in celebration of Yom Kippur, the Jewish New Year, which listed various excuses that institutions give for not being sympathetic to women's issues. The cards offered snappy retorts to sexist comments. For example, "We don't offer child care. If women want families, they are going to have to make career sacrifices." To which Jewish Women Watching responded: "This year, support working parents" and "Sexism Is a Sin."

In Australia, junior champion steer rider Peta Browne, age 13, and her friend Ayshea Clements, age 15, protested the fact that girls are banned from riding in the junior steer ride within the National Rodeo Association (NRA). The girls filed a complaint with the Human Rights Commission, but the HRC responded with 24 reasons that they and girls like them are not covered by Australia's Sexual Discrimination Act. Both have been reaching out via the Internet for support to appeal this sexist exclusion.

What all these feminists have in common is this: they saw an injustice and used their rage to become everyday activists. One can be an activist with one's voice, money, vote, creativity, privilege, or the fearlessness that comes from having nothing left to lose. Activists may work within the system— by voting, lobbying Congress, advocating at the United Nations, or monitoring a governmental agency set up to protect human rights and civil liberties. They may also work outside the system—by creating non governmental organizations (NGOs) to fill in the government's gaps, contributing to existing grassroots groups and foundations, organizing boycotts or protests, or doing something individual and agitpropesque, like walking from Pasadena to Washington, D.C., to demonstrate the need for campaign-finance reform. (That last is exactly what 89-year-old Doris Haddock did in anticipation of the 2000 presidential race.) A regular woman becomes an activist when she rights some glaring human mistake, or recognizes a positive model of equality and takes the opportunity to build on it.

Webster's defines activism as "the doctrine or policy of taking positive, direct action to achieve an end." Regardless of how you define it, activism, like feminism, can be something organic to our lives, a natural reflex in the face of injustice and inequality. Also like feminism, activism is one of the most confused concepts we know.

Even among women who relate to the goal of equality and the necessity of achieving it, activism can be an alien idea. To most people, the image of an activist is someone who is out of the ordinary— someone who hoists picket signs in front of the Pakistani Embassy, marches on the Washington Mall demanding money for cancer research, or chains him- or herself to trees. Given these images, it's easy to imagine that activists are "other" people—weird or dauntingly benevolent. If news stories highlighted the real faces and sources of activism, activists would be much more mundane and familiar.

Though activism can be grand or all-consuming, it is also as common and short-term as saying "That's not funny" to a racist joke, "No" to the boss who asks only the "girls" in the office to make the old number of three million or so new cases of STDs each year has dropped to half that amount, STDs are still as common (and about as shameful) as the common cold—and are finally acknowledged as such.

The Equal Rights Amendment has put females in the U.S. Constitution. There are many women of all races in fields or institutions formerly considered to be the province of men, from the Virginia Military Institute and the Citadel to fire departments and airline cockpits. Women are not only free to be as exceptional as men but also as mediocre. Men are as critiqued or praised as women are. Women's salaries have jumped up 26 to 40 percent from pre-equality days to match men's. There are no economic divisions based on race, and the salary categories have been equalized. This categorization is the result of legislation that requires the private sector—even companies that employ fewer than 50 people—to report employees' wages. Many older women are averaging half a million dollars in back pay as a result of the years in which they were unjustly underpaid. Women and men in the NBA make an average of $100,000 per year. Haircuts, dry cleaning, and clothes for women cost the same as they do for men.

The media are accountable to their constituency. Magazines cover stories about congressional hearings on how to help transition men on welfare back into the workforce. Many of these men are single fathers—by choice. Welfare is viewed as a subsidy, just as corporate tax breaks used to be, and receiving government assistance to help rear one's own child is as destigmatized as it is to be paid to rear a foster child. Howard Stern, who gave up his declining radio show to become a stay-at-home granddad, has been replaced on radio by Janeane Garofalo, who no longer jokes primarily about her "back fat" and other perceived imperfections. (Primary caregiving has humanized Stern so that people no longer have to fear for his influence on his offspring.) Leading ladies and leading men are all around the same age. There is always fanfare around *Time* magazine's Person of the Year and *Sports Illustrated*'s coed swimsuit issue. *Rolling Stone* covers female pop stars and music groups in equal numbers with male stars, and women are often photographed for the cover *with* their shirts on. Classic-rock stations play Janis Joplin as often as they play Led Zeppelin.

Women who choose to have babies give birth in a birthing center with a midwife, a hospital with a doctor, or at home with a medicine woman. Paid child care leave is for four months, and it is required of both parents (if there is more than one). Child rearing is subsidized by a trust not unlike Social Security, a concept pioneered by the welfare-rights activist Theresa Funiciello and based on Gloria Steinem's earlier mandate that every child have a minimum income. The attributed economic value of housework is figured into the gross national product (which increases the United States' GNP by almost 30 percent), and primary caregivers are paid. Whether you work in or out of the home, you are taxed only on your income; married couples and people in domestic partnerships are taxed as individuals, too. When women retire, they get as much Social Security as men do, and all people receive a base amount on which they can live.

The amount of philanthropic dollars going to programs that address or specifically include women and girls is now pushing 60 percent, to make up for all the time it was about 5 percent. More important, these female-centered programs no longer have to provide basic services, because the government does that. All school meals, vaccinations, public libraries, and museums are government-funded and thus available to everybody. Taxpayers have made their wishes clear because more than 90 percent of the electorate actually votes.

"Postmenopausal zest" is as well documented and as anticipated as puberty. Women in their fifties—free from pregnancy, menstruation, and birth control—are regarded as sexpots and envied for their wild and free libidos. "Wine and women," as the saying goes, "get better with age."

Every man and woman remembers exactly where they were the moment they heard that the Equal Rights Amendment passed. The president addressed the nation on the night of that victory and said, "Americans didn't know what we were missing before today . . . until we could truly say that all people are created equal." The first man stood at her side with a tear running down his face.

The social-justice movement, formerly known as feminism, is now just *life*.   [2000]

❧ 166

Just Sex: Students Rewrite the Rules on Sex, Violence, and Equality

JODI GOLD and SUSAN VILLARI

Hook-up, mash, fool around, or shag—isn't it all just sex? Sex is no big deal, right? But what if it isn't consensual? Then it is not just sex. Then it is acquaintance rape. In 1989, when I became an antirape educator, I expected to fight rape. I believed that all rape was violence. Rape was not sex. What I found out later was that, yes, rape is violence—but acquaintance rape is also about sex. When I joined the antisexual violence movement, I found women and men like myself trying to navigate the confusing sexual landscape of the late twentieth century. As a result, I spent more time during college talking about sex than having it. . . .

We are often asked why those involved in a movement to end rape spend so much time talking about sex. Didn't the early antirape feminists teach us that rape is about power and not about sex? Fortunately, they did—and in doing so put a name to a crime against women that at the time most people believed was perpetrated by sociopaths, not their husbands, lovers, and acquaintances. Twenty-five years later, despite tremendous legal and social reform, society still has trouble distinguishing between sex and violence. Efforts to clarify the distinction are labeled as puritanical, radical, and revolutionary.

Start by asking someone the definition of acquaintance rape, and invariably part of the response will include a reference to the infamous gray area, where sexual definitions, rules, and roles are ill defined or never defined. Follow it up with a question about whose responsibility it is to prevent acquaintance rape, and you are barraged with codes of conduct based on gender or the infamous *he said, she said*. The schism between *he said, she said* also defaults to gray, a place where there is still a hesitancy to assign blame or responsibility. It is as if the gray area is a misty fog that descends upon you and impairs your vision and reason. When caught in the gray, you cannot see far in the distance. The fog may be so dense that two rational and intelligent people experience the same event with an opposite understanding of it. The gray area is powerful enough to jam communication channels during a sexual encounter, causing one person to refuse sex while the other person assumes consent. This gray area seeps into our offices and under our bedroom doors. It invades computer monitors and TV screens. The gray area is enlisted when one person's harassment is another person's joke, or when the same photograph is simultaneously defended as free speech and condemned as a hate crime against women.

The search to clear up the gray area has exposed the mainstream of American society to the controversial connection between sex and violence. The late twentieth century may well be remembered for our heated national debates over sexual harassment, acquaintance rape, interpersonal violence, and pornography in both private conversations and in the public arena. From the Clarence Thomas confirmation hearings to the William Kennedy Smith rape trial to Tailhook to Paula Jones's allegations against President Clinton, the relationship between sex and violence has increasingly been framed as an issue of civil rights and equal protection under the law.

Nowhere have the debates been stronger and the voices louder than on college campuses. Since the mid-1980s a campus social movement has been stirring that, at its core, rejects the belief that forced sex is an acceptable rite of passage for women. Outraged by the high incidence of acquaintance rape, students have begun to dismantle the gray by publicly debating issues of sexual consent, social constructions of gender, and equal protection. Using new as well as recycled tactics, students' efforts to rewrite the rules on sex, violence, and gender relations may well be their generation's chief contribution to social change, much like advocating for peace had been for previous generation's.[1]

Women and men who came of age in the 1980s and 1990s were the first generation to be weaned on feminism, civil rights, and the so-called sexual revolution. For the first time women acquired degrees at the same rate as their male counterparts.[2] For many of these women college not only represented greater academic and career opportunities but seemed to afford the same rights as men to experiment both socially and sexually. Unfortunately, the illusion of sexual freedom smacked up against the reality of acquaintance rape, bringing them face-to-face with deeply rooted sexism. In case after case, when women brought charges against the men who raped them, their cases were dismissed as a relationship problem, or they were chastised for daring to enjoy the same freedoms as their male peers. . . .

Although a dramatic shift in public awareness has helped dispel myths about rape, too many people still believe that women provoke and encourage men to rape them by the way they dress and act. Similarly, men are told they are unable to separate their desires from their actions. Once sexually aroused, or so the story goes, men must pursue sex even if it is forced or coerced. So-called sexual liberation has done very little to change the rule that men are still encouraged to be sexual aggressors and women are assigned as gatekeepers to sex. Following this logic, it is not surprising that women are still held accountable for men's sexually aggressive behavior and ultimately for the prevention of rape.

Asking women to "be aware" or assuming that all men are potential rapists is not the answer: At the heart of the student movement is the collective belief that sexual violence is neither inevitable nor inherent. On campuses across the country, students are calling into question traditional notions of masculinity and femininity, particularly because these beliefs often dictate what is considered acceptable behavior, both socially and sexually, for men and women. Listen closely to most conversations about acquaintance rape, and you will more fully understand our deeply entrenched gender and sexual roles. *What did she expect? She had been drinking and she was in his dorm room at two a.m. How can you blame him? He is just like any other red-blooded American male.*

Rigid gender roles hinder women's ability to say yes to sex and men's ability to say or hear no. Men are told that seduction means pushing verbally or physically until you get a yes, or believing that no really means yes. Consequently, verbally coercive sex and legally defined rape are protected under the guise of seduction. Challenging this accepted behavior, campus activists promote consent, not coercion, as sexy. In what many believe to be a *new sexual revolution,* they lend their passion and power to the continuing struggle for gender and sexual equality.

THE OLD, THE NEW, AND THE RECYCLED

Borrowing techniques from previous generations' efforts to raise awareness about sexual violence, today's activists organize Take Back the Night marches, survivor speak-outs, and self-defense workshops. They challenge campus policies and advocate for increased resources for prevention programs and support services. Traditional forms of antirape activism often serve as the catalyst for the institutionalization of programs and services, but much of today's social change efforts include service projects, peer education, and working within the system. . . . By viewing students as the experts, groups like Students Against Violence Against Women (SAVAW) at Ithaca College, and Auburn Working for Acquaintance Rape Education (AWARE) provide educational workshops where information and statistics on acquaintance rape are disseminated. More important, these workshops provide a safe place for students to demystify the gray area by exploring how rigid gender roles and power inequities are connected to acquaintance rape. Simple statements such as "Men and women are equally responsible for the prevention of rape," or "It is possible to give nonverbal consent to sex" prompt lively debates on the unwritten rules for "hooking up" and the nonverbal language of sex. Male facilitators will ask other men if it is possible to separate desire from action. Often men genuinely ask, "How can I be sure that I am not raping someone?" Female facilitators will shatter myths about female sexuality and physicality by openly discussing masturbation, orgasm, and how to fight back when in danger. These types of questions and ensuing discussions reveal how disparate socialization is for men and women in this society. Student educators respond by encouraging both men and women to stop and confirm consent if they are receiving mixed messages. In the age of HIV and AIDS students no longer believe that sex must be mysterious and unspoken. More women and men are having sex in college than ever before, but they want it to be fun, safe, and consensual.[3]

RAPE AS A POLITICAL ISSUE

For anyone to appreciate fully the current wave of antirape activism, it's critical to understand the movement's historical foundations. Kate Millett articulated the first feminist analysis of rape in her 1970 book, *Sexual Politics.* The opening lines of her theory of sexual politics begins:

> Coitus can scarcely be said to take place in a vacuum; although of itself it appears a biological and physical activity, it is set so deeply within the larger context of human affairs that it serves as a charged microcosm of the variety of attitudes and values to which culture subscribes.[4]

For Millett politics is defined as "power over," and patriarchy means men's power over women. Therefore, sex is always political in a patriarchy because it reflects the societal inequality between women and men. All sex is not rape, but the power that men have over women and the socialization of men as aggressor and women as passive cannot be excluded from the bedroom. Following this logic, rape is not aberrant behavior, but a natural extension of a system that must maintain male dominance.

It was acquaintance rape that ignited the rumblings on college campuses in the mideighties, but acquaintance rape was not a new phenomenon.

Harry Kalven Jr. and Hans Zeisel conducted a study of 3,000 trials in the 1960s and found that 40 percent of rapes going to trial involved acquaintances.[5] Menachem Amir examined police files between 1958 and 1960. He concluded that rapists are generally "normal" men. About half of all rapes were committed by men who knew their victims, and not all the victims resisted loudly.[6] It was the radical feminists of the women's liberation movement who recognized the political importance of acquaintance rape. The central revelation of the first speak-out and conference on rape held in 1971 by the New York Radical Feminists was:

> The violent rapist and boyfriend/husband are one. . . . The act of rape is the logical expression of the essential relationship between men and women: It is a matter to be dealt with in feminist terms for feminist liberation.[7]

Susan Brownmiller, in her 1975 *Against Our Will,* was the first to use the phrase "date rape." She documents the history of rape and examines the cultural forces that maintain women as passive and men as aggressive.[8] At the time of publication many believed that a woman could not be raped "against her will," that certainly a woman would fight to the death.

Brownmiller and other radical feminists acknowledged the existence of and political nature of acquaintance rape, but Diana Russell took it one step further in her first book, *The Politics of Rape,* published in 1974. She interviewed 90 rape survivors and 1 rapist, who was interviewed by a male colleague. Not all the women were raped by acquaintances, but the rapists included lovers, best friends, fathers, and husbands. The goal of her book was to "emphatically contradict the prevalent view of male authors, clinicians, and doctors, that women enjoy being raped."[9] In 1978 Russell conducted a study of acquaintance rape with 930 randomly selected women. She used the California definition of rape, and she excluded those who "felt" raped but were not "forced." Contrary to the Kalven and Zeisel and Amir findings, she discovered that the vast majority of rapes were perpetrated by acquaintances.[10]

Stranger rape was the easiest and most visible issue of the seventies antirape movement. However, radical feminists had been saying all along that the boyfriend and rapist were one. They pursued three avenues of social change: rape prevention, service reform, and legal advocacy. The first rape crisis center in the world was founded by the Bay Area Women Against Rape in 1970 in response to the rape of a Berkeley high school student.[11] Within a few months the D.C. Rape Crisis Center was founded, followed by centers in Philadelphia, Ann Arbor, New York, and Pittsburgh. By 1976 there were 400 autonomous rape crisis centers. The early rape crisis centers were based on feminist organizing principles of working outside the system, disregard for academic "credentials," attention to process, and a commitment to self-help. They saw themselves as alternatives to the criminal justice system, which generally blamed women for being raped. The predominantly women-only volunteers served as escorts for rape victims during encounters with the law enforcement, medical, and legal systems. They demanded respect for women from emergency room personnel and police and supported victims through a self-help form of recovery. Rape crisis center volunteers were committed to social change in the community and on the campus. The first forms of campus antirape activism occurred in concert with the broader rape crisis movement.

THE EARLY CAMPUS CONNECTION

Antirape activism on the college campus is not new. Community rape crisis centers often worked closely with college campuses providing advocacy, support services, self-defense workshops, and an avenue for campus antirape activists. In 1972 a group of residential advisors at the University of Maryland campus responded to a series of gang rapes and abductions by forming one of the first campus-based rape crisis centers.[12] On April 3, 1973, women at the University of Pennsylvania staged a four-day sit-in in reaction to a series of six rapes and the gang rape of two student nurses. They achieved all their demands, which included a women's center whose primary mission was to provide rape crisis services,

a women's studies program, and improved security measures on campus.[13] A campus rape at the University of California at Berkeley led to the adoption of sexual assault programming throughout the entire University of California system in 1976. A committee of students and staff at Berkeley argued that the university was "obligated to create as safe an environment as possible" for women and that rape education was missing from the curricula. Remnants of the University of California sexual assault education program still exist today.[14]

Throughout the 1980s the nation witnessed a surge in antirape activism and research. In 1981 Claire Walsh founded Sexual Assault Recovery Services (SARS) at the University of Florida. The following year she and students formed Campus Organized Against Rape (COARS), a peer education group that became one of the earliest nationally recognized antirape peer education programs.[15] A 1982 *Ms.* magazine article entitled "Date Rape: A Campus Epidemic," is credited as the first instance of date rape hitting the mainstream media,[16] and research by Dr. Mary Koss would further prove that the biggest threat on campus was not the crazed stranger, but the trusted friend.

Koss began her landmark research at Kent State University in Ohio the same year that Russell conducted her study in California. Koss believed the logical next step after *Against Our Will* was to conduct a comprehensive epidemiological study of acquaintance rape.[17] She started her work at Kent State with a study of college students' experiences with forced sex. Her results were so intriguing that she replicated the study in 1985 with the help of the National Institute of Mental Health and the *Ms.* Foundation. She surveyed 6,159 students at 32-campuses. Koss's findings were later translated for a lay audience by journalist Robin Warshaw in her popular book, *I Never Called It Rape.* Koss documented the increased vulnerability of college-age women to acquaintance rape. The research showed that one out of four women in college today are victims of rape or attempted rape, and 84 percent are assaulted by men whom they know. The average age at the time of the rape was 18½ years old for both the perpetrator and victim/survivor.[18]

The most disturbing yet controversial finding was the reluctance of men and women to define their experiences with forced sex as rape. Only one-quarter of the women surveyed whose experience met the legal definition of rape identified their experience as rape. One in twelve men surveyed reported sexually violent behavior, but the majority did not define their behavior as rape. This phenomenon confirmed what radical feminists had been saying all along—that violence against women is so insidious, it has been framed as part of normative sexual behavior.

Prior to 1985 a limited number of schools had policies or programs addressing sexual assault.[19] By the mid-1980s to the early 1990s, a strong catalyst for institutional reform can be attributed to courageous students going public with their assault stories. Our national survey of college campuses demonstrates that 35 percent of policies enacted by 1993 resulted from a high-profile assault case and/or student activism.[20]

For example, in 1983 several Ohio State basketball players were accused of gang rape. By a twist of fate the NCAA basketball tournament was taking place in Columbus that year. With national media attention protesters picketed outside the stadium, and the university president was quick to respond by funding a rape prevention program that continues to be a national leader. The program was founded with a feminist agenda charged with the task of developing culturally specific curricula. Ohio State is one of the rare schools that actually pay graduate students $40 an hour to present workshops to the 60,000-student body.[21]

Student protests at the University of Michigan (1985)[22] and the University of Minnesota (1986)[23] resulted in comprehensive campus sexual assault services. In 1987 a landmark case at Carleton College, a prestigious liberal arts school, launched a national debate when four female students sued their college for not protecting them against the men whom the college knew to be repeat rapists. The women testified that the school was aware of the previous assaults by their rapists and did nothing to prevent these men from attacking them.[24]

During the late 1980s activism not only sparked the development of institutional policies and procedures, but also tested the limits and enforcement of those policies. At Princeton University, in October 1987, protest and outrage at the lack of enforcement of the sexual harassment policy prompted immediate university action. During an annual Take Back the Night event, several march participants were harassed by fellow Princeton students. One man screamed "We can rape whoever we want," while others dropped their trousers and hurled beer at marchers. The protest that followed this event led to the hiring of a sexual assault director, Myra Hindus, whose job was to oversee the university's sexual assault/harassment policies and procedures.[25]

During this time public opinion was also being shaped by the media and entertainment industries. The topic of acquaintance rape was introduced into television and movies via talk-show hosts, daytime soaps, and drama shows. In 1988 Jodie Foster won an academy award for her role as a "bad girl" rape survivor in the film *The Accused*, which was based on a New Bedford, Connecticut, gang rape trial.

WHY HAS THIS ISSUE MOBILIZED COLLEGE STUDENTS TODAY?

Several important factors appear to have set the stage for the current student movement to end sexual and gender-based violence. In addition to the influence of previous social movements on this generation, and a different sense of entitlement, the contemporary campus is a virtual microcosm of a rape-supportive culture. First-year college students of traditional age represent the highest risk group for being involved in a sexual assault either as perpetrators or victim/survivors.[26] Koss's research found that the use of alcohol and other drugs were involved in a majority of rape cases—70 percent of the men involved and 55 percent of the women involved reported drinking or taking drugs prior to the assault.[27] The use of alcohol and other drugs is perceived as a social lubricant and an easy way to de-stress from academic pressure.

The campus environment is also influenced by powerful male-dominated institutions, such as fraternities, whose rituals encourage hypermasculinity and excessive alcohol use, further adding to the fertile ground for rape to take root in. In 1985 Erhart and Sandler conducted groundbreaking research on the propensity of all-male groups to rape, identifying fraternity culture as conducive to sexual violence.[28] In *Fraternity Gang Rape: Sex, Brotherhood, and Privilege on Campus,* author Peggy Sanday describes what is called "a train"—a sexual ritual in which a number of fraternity men line up to take turns "having sex" with an intoxicated and unwilling female victim. The behavior is described by the participants as normal, "something that you see and hear about all the time."[29] Sanday describes this all-male behavior as homoerotic, and argues that pornography coupled with fraternity culture teaches young men about sex. Athletes who participate in aggressive sports are also at a higher risk for perpetrating sexual violence.[30] It is important to note that *most* athletes and fraternity members do not commit rape. Rather, the odds are greatly increased when excessive alcohol use is coupled with hypermasculine all-male environments whose groups have privilege on campus.

Finally, the work of previous antirape activists and recent legislation have helped to institutionalize sexual assault prevention and support services. The staff who coordinate sexual violence programs, that is, women's center directors and health educators, often got their start in the second wave of the women's movement. Students are often greeted by a generation of sixties and seventies activists firmly rooted in positions of power ready to serve as willing allies. This provides a unique partnership for current student activism. Activist faculty and staff teach students how to organize effectively and also give them access to resources. On the other hand, student activists can push the envelope without fearing loss of employment.

The North American Student Conferences on Campus Sexual Violence, which began in 1992 in Philadelphia, exemplify this unique and effective partnership.[31] Organized by and for students, with significant support from key administrators, the conferences bring together student educators and activists from around the continent. The first conference was originally planned as a regional event, but students were so eager to network and share resources that registrations came in from schools as far away as Oregon, Hawaii, and Alberta, Canada. Py Bateman, feminist self-defense activist and founder of Alternatives to Fear, remarked after her keynote address at this 1992 student conference:

> College students are perfectly placed for social change. They're young and in a position to put pressure on university administration; open to new ideas; and in training for leadership. *The First National Student Conference on Campus Sexual Assault* is a perfect example of the power of students. I have not seen anything like this since the organizing in the 60s.[32]

THE NEW FACE OF STUDENT ACTIVISM

Despite the stereotype that today's college students are apolitical and disengaged, a recent study by Jeanette S. Cureton and Arthur Levine finds that current undergraduates are the most socially active since the 1930s.[33] Social-change efforts on campuses today are often overlooked or misrepresented because 20-somethings have developed their own style of activism, a style that on the surface sharply contradicts the popular image of a student activist. According to Paul Loeb, author of *Generation at the Crossroads: Apathy and Action on the American Campus:*

> Students have been looking for different ways to voice social concern. They want to act. They want to help. They don't want to deal with complicated issues and factions or the messy contention of politics. Instead they have revived approaches to involvement that focus on individual service . . . yet, the same approaches often lead them back toward larger social change.[34]

By the early 1990s peer education programs addressing sexual violence were being implemented all across the country. Generally, peer educators are trained volunteers, with very few receiving academic or monetary compensation. By 1995, 56 percent of schools surveyed had students facilitating workshops on sexual violence—with one-third of those students being men.[35] Program names such as CORE (Creating a Rape Free Environment), POWER (People out Working Together to End Rape), and STAAR (Students Together Against Acquaintance Rape) reflect the belief that if men and women work together, sexual violence can be prevented. Sharing only a commitment to end sexual violence, educators and activists find themselves in coalitions with people they normally might not associate with. For example, it is not uncommon to see a fraternity brother facilitating a workshop with a self-identified "radical" feminist or an openly gay man working with the president of the campus Republicans. The common experience of sexual violence and its profound impact on a community cross gender, racial, ethnic, and sexual orientation boundaries. This diversity is what strengthens the activists' ability to infiltrate a large cross section of campus. Groups educate in dorm rooms, classrooms, bars, and locker rooms.

Students become involved in antirape work for a variety of reasons. The most common motivation is being or knowing a survivor of sexual assault. Men frequently become involved because a girlfriend discloses being raped. These men focus their anger and accompanying sense of powerlessness into educating other men.

Groups such as Men Acting for Change (Duke University), Men Against Rape and Sexism (Iowa State University), and Black Men for the Eradication of Sexism (Morehouse College) often feel equally constrained by rigid gender roles and resent the perception that all men are potential rapists. Omar Freilla, founder of Black Men for the Eradication of Rape and Sexism, comments: "We have discussion groups and talk about what it is, what it means to be a man, and how we were brought up. We are really trying to de-program ourselves."[36]

The issue of deconstructing masculinity is addressed not only in small discussion groups but also in large-scale campus events. Responding to a comment made by journalist Anna Climlin that the "good guys have to stand up and speak out," Rutgers University launched the Real Men of Rutgers campaign in the spring of 1994. Appealing to men's role in ending sexual violence, Ruth Koenick, coordinator of Sexual Assault Services, and student educators designed a poster that featured photos and quotes from twelve male student leaders nominated by the campus. Each man chosen contributed his opinion on how violence could be prevented within his own student community.

Posters hung prominently in all major offices and buildings on campus.[37]

At Ohio State University, contributor Michael Scarce, then coordinator of the Rape Education and Prevention Program, placed placards above men's urinals on campus that read, "In your hands, you hold the power to stop rape."[38]

SEXUAL POLITICS ROCK THE NATION

According to educator and author Michael Kimmel, the early 1990s may well be remembered as the "decade in which America took a crash course on male sexuality,"[39] with the media not only highlighting high-profile celebrity cases but also bringing national attention to activist strategies happening locally on campuses. Responding to the national attention directed toward Brown University in 1990, contributor Jesselyn Brown writes "you know something has touched a nerve when it manages to get lambasted by feminists, antifeminists, and establishment organs alike." Frustrated by a judicial system that continually dismissed sexual assault cases, women at Brown used their speech to protect their fellow students. To have their speech heard, four Brown women generated a conversation on a centrally located women's bathroom stall, which eventually became known on campus as the "rape list." This simple act caused an uproar across the nation, with administrators denouncing the list as "antimale" and referring to the women as "Magic Marker terrorists." Jesselyn Brown argues that when women were sexually assaulted on her campus, the cases were dismissed as trivial; yet when women wrote names of men who assaulted them, using their freedom of speech, it was immediately viewed as an infringement of the men's rights.

During the same time period the issue of how to negotiate consensual sex brought national media attention to the campus of Antioch College. Initiated by activist students, the now infamous Sexual Offense Policy at Antioch College requires "willing and verbal" consent for each sexual act. Despite the fact that this policy was supported by the majority of students, it was criticized by outsiders as "sexual correctness" and "courtship management," and it even ended up being spoofed on an episode of *Saturday*

Night Live. Andy Abrams, who has been humorously referred to as the Antioch poster boy, believes that asking for consent is not only sexy, but smart. "If you don't talk, then all you got is guesswork."

As we watched in horror the interrogation of Anita Hill, Congress was busy debating antirape legislation. The early 1990s would see the passage of the Campus Security Bill and the Student Right to Know Act, the Ramstead Amendment, and the introduction of the Violence against Women Bill.

LAPTOPS, CELL PHONES, AND THE INTERNET

The use of new technology such as the Internet and e-mail not only helped effectively organize students involved in the movement to end sexual violence but also contributed to a new round of debates over free speech.

In 1995, when Cornell male students e-mailed over the Internet "Top 75 Reasons Women (Bitches) Should Not Have Freedom of Speech," angry students from across the country flooded Cornell's e-mail system, eventually causing it to shut down temporarily.[40]

During the planning stages for the First Canadian Student Conference on Campus Sexual Violence at the University of Alberta in Edmonton in 1998, the Canadian Post Office went on strike. Amber Dean, student coordinator of the conference, quickly turned to electronic means to organize the conference, effectively using e-mail to communicate with conference participants and register students online.

As we move into the twenty-first century, the impact of this campus movement remains to be seen. The student movement continues to be strong and vibrant, with the North American Student Conferences on Campus Sexual Violence and its sponsoring organization, SpeakOut, looking forward to hosting their eighth year of annual conferences in the year 2000.   [2000]

NOTES

1. Sarah Ferguson, "Sex on Campus: How Making Love Became the Vietnam of the Nineties," *Village Voice*, April 1991, 9.
2. *The American Woman, 1996–97, Woman and Work* (New York: W. W. Norton, 1996), 269.
3. Peggy Sanday, *Woman Scorned: Acquaintance Rape on Trial* (New York: Doubleday, 1996), 191–92.
4. Kate Millett, *Sexual Politics* (New York: Simon and Schuster, 1990), 23.
5. Harry Kalven Jr. and Hans Zeisel, *The American Jury* (Boston: Little, Brown, 1966), 254. See also Peggy Sanday, *Woman Scorned* for complete history of acquaintance rape, 184–207.
6. Menachem Amir, *Patterns in Forcible Rape* (Chicago: University of Chicago Press, 1971), 245.
7. Redstockings of the Women's Liberation Movement, *Feminist Revolution* (New York: Random House, 1975), 141.
8. Susan Brownmiller, *Against Our Will: Men, Women and Rape* (New York: Ballantine Books, 1975), 257.
9. Diana Russell, *The Politics of Rape*, 2nd ed. (New York: Stein and Day, 1984), 13.
10. Russell, *Politics of Rape*, 59.
11. Sharon Sayles, "Ten Years: 1972–1982: Working against Sexual Assault," Archives of the National Coalition against Sexual Assault, Pittsburgh, Pa., 2.
12. Interview with Ruth Koenick, coordinator of Rutgers University Sexual Assault Services, June 1994.
13. Interview with Ellie DiLapi, director of University of Pennsylvania's Women's Center, June 1994.
14. Interview with Jennifer Beeman, director of University of California, Davis, Rape Education and Prevention Program, July 1994.
15. Beth Ribet, "Fighting Campus Sexual Violence: Notes about the Coalition of Campus Organizations Addressing Rape," unpublished paper, Irvine, Calif.
16. Karen Barrett, "Date Rape: A Campus Epidemic," *Ms.*, September 1982, 51.
17. Mary P. Koss, Christine A. Gidycz, and Nadine Wisniewski, "The Scope of Rape: Incidence and Prevalence of Sexual Aggression and Victimization in a National Sample of Higher Education Students," *Journal of Consulting and Clinical Psychology* 55 (1987): 162–70.
18. Robin Warshaw, *I Never Called It Rape: The Ms. Report on Recognizing, Fighting, and Surviving Date and Acquaintance Rape* (New York: Harper and Row, 1988), 11.
19. Jodi Gold, Jessie Minier, and Susan Villari, "Creating Campuses Intolerant of Rape: Peer Education and the Institutional Response to Sexual Violence" presented at the Sixth International Conference on Sexual Assault and Harassment on Campus, Long Beach, Calif., November 1996.
20. Gold, Minier, and Villari, "Creating Campuses Intolerant of Rape."
21. Interview with Willa Young, director of Women Student Services and Rape Education and Prevention Programs at Ohio State University, July 1994.
22. Interview with Julie Steiner, director of the University of Michigan Sexual Assault Awareness and Prevention Center (SAPAC), July 1994.
23. Interview with Jamie Tiedemann, director of University of Minnesota's Sexual Assault Services, August 1994.
24. *Time*, June 3, 1991, 55.
25. Interview with Myra Hindus, Princeton University, June 1994.
26. Warshaw, *I Never Called It Rape*, 24.

27. Warshaw, *I Never Called It Rape,* 44.
28. Julie K. Ehrhart and Bernice R. Sandler, *Campus Gang Rape: Party Games?* Project on the Status and Education of Women (Washington, DC: Association of American Colleges, 1985).
29. Peggy Reeves Sanday, *Fraternity Gang Rape: Sex, Brotherhood, and Privilege on Campus* (New York: New York University Press, 1990).
30. Carol Bohmer and Andrea Parrot, *Sexual Assault on Campus* (New York: Lexington Books, 1993), 22.
31. The North American Student Conferences on Campus Sexual Violence began at the University of Pennsylvania, Philadelphia, in 1992. Jodi and Susan coordinated this first conference and, at the time, they had no idea that this conference would continue into its eighth year. Since 1993 one to three conferences have been held each year, with 1998 seeing its first Canadian conference. Speak-Out: The North American Student Coalition on Campus Sexual Violence was founded in 1994 to help oversee and coordinate these North American student conferences.
32. Py Bateman, "Keynote Address," First Annual National Student Conference on Campus Sexual Assault, University of Pennsylvania, Philadelphia, March 1992.
33. Arthur Levine, "A New Generation of Student Protesters Arises," *Chronicle of Higher Education,* February 26, 1999, A52.
34. Paul Rogat Loeb, *Generation at the Crossroads: Apathy and Action on the American Campus* (New Brunswick, N.J.: Rutgers University Press, 1994), 61.
35. Gold, Minier, and Villari, "Creating Campuses Intolerant of Rape."
36. *Ms.,* July/August 1995, 95.
37. Interview with Ruth Koenick, June 1994.
38. From the CCOAR listserv, June 1996.
39. Michael Kimmel, "Clarence Williams, Iron Mike, Tailhook, Senator Packwood, Spur Posse, Magic . . . and U.S.," in *Transforming a Rape Culture,* eds. Emile Buchwald, Pamela Fletcher, and Martha Roth (Minneapolis, MN: Milkweed Editions, 1993), 121.
40. Judy Mann, "Sexists on the Net," *Washington Post,* November 15, 1995, E17.

🌿 167

Black Feminism at Twenty-One: Reflections on the Evolution of a National Community

BARBARA RAMSBY

When Deborah King, Elsa Barkley Brown, and I launched the African-American Women in Defense of Ourselves (AAWIDOO) campaign to protest Clarence Thomas's nomination to the Supreme Court and to highlight the issue of sexual harassment and the media's silencing of black women, we did not talk about our long-term goals. As it turned out, our ideas about where the mobilization was headed and at what pace were quite different, and, after several local branches in Chicago, New York, and Philadelphia failed to sustain themselves without the support of a national body or solidly planted roots, the entire AAWIDOO initiative slowly and quietly faded out of existence. Nevertheless, a collective silence had been broken. Not since the National Black Feminist Organization and its more well-known offshoot, the Combahee River Collective, made their marks in the mid-1970s had black women in the United States organized around a feminist/womanist agenda and made a national public intervention. We raised more than $50,000 in a short time to place ads in the *New York Times* and African-American newspapers around the country, and we compiled a mailing list of over 2,000 names, which itself became a vital resource for subsequent local and national mobilizations. The campaign represented a growing consensus among an often invisible network of activists and intellectuals who at least partly shared a political vision, even if we were not all card-carrying members of any one club.[1]

In 1993, black feminist writer Jill Nelson, activist Gail Garfield, and others organized a series of rallies to protest plans by the predominantly male political establishment of Harlem to give Mike Tyson, a convicted rapist, a hero's welcome after his release from prison. Black feminist activists in Harlem took the principled but unpopular position that rape was both a feminist issue and a black community issue and that, racism within the criminal justice system notwithstanding, rapists could not be

---

[1]During the MMM mobilization, the *New York Times Magazine* featured a story on black feminism by a novice writer who distorted and obscured more about black feminism than she revealed (Zooks, 1995). This type of skewed media coverage reinforces invisibility as much as outright silence does. For more carefully researched studies of black feminism and black women's political activism, see Smith (1983); Giddings (1984); Guy-Sheftall (1995); Collins (1998).

celebrated as heroes in our community. The Harlem activists requested the AAWIDOO mailing list to publicize and garner support for their campaign, and AAWIDOO's strategy of buying newspaper ads served as an inspiration and model for St. Louis activists who organized a similar campaign against the exaltation of Tyson in their community.[2]

The growing network of black feminists across the country again became visible in 1995 when the aspiring patriarch of black politics, Nation of Islam minister Louis Farrakhan, convened a gathering of men in the nation's capital to reclaim their rightful places as heads of their families and leaders of the entire black community. Feminist activist and law professor Kimberle Crenshaw organized a national meeting in New York in the spring of 1995 to explore how black feminists should respond to the MMM. We formed an ad hoc committee, issued a public statement, and participated in several community forums. Our response to the MMM and the increasing male-centeredness of black politics and community priorities represented a deepening national consensus among black feminists. The black community as a whole was sharply divided over the march, with the majority in support. The issue, for many, was not clear cut: for some, opposing Clarence Thomas's sexism had been easy because there were so many other reasons (having to do with his conservative antiblack politics) to oppose him, but to challenge a charismatic religious icon like Farrakhan or a superstar athlete like Tyson was a different matter altogether. Nevertheless, black feminists once again mobilized on fairly short notice to do precisely that.

The black feminist statement issued on the eve of the MMM, like AAWIDOO's four years earlier, was not a narrow, single-issue document. It outlined both the sexism and unprecedented gender exclusivity of the MMM and also the conservative class message of the march's principal spokesman. A core of activists held several follow-up meetings and a three-day-long retreat to try to map out a way forward after the march. Again, old phone chains from previous mobilizations were activated and relationships reestablished. There was a clear sense of a tangible national constituency. While most of those who participated were college educated and, to a large extent, middle class, we were engaged in many different areas of political work: international human rights; antiviolence; opposition to the prison industrial complex; welfare rights and antipoverty work; civil rights and sexual harassment litigation; alternative media; lesbian, bisexual, gay, and transsexual work; and student organizing. Some of the members of this group, which called itself African-American Agenda 2000, later became key organizers of either the African American Policy Forum or the Feminist Caucus of the Black Radical Congress (two groups that reconnected to work on the Tabitha Walrond case in the summer of 1999).[3] Even though questions of strategy and tactics have divided us at times, our politics keep bringing us back together.

So, what are the politics that unite a disparate cross section of organizers under the rubric of black feminism? Let me first address the method and style of organizing and then, briefly, the ideological content. Over the past decade, the style of black feminist work has represented a democratic impulse within the larger progressive movement, with decentralized mobilization efforts, informal leadership, and flexible structures. This has not always been the most efficient way to organize, but the political benefits have outweighed the inconvenience. Moreover, we have benefited from such organizational structures, which have consisted of less hierarchical steering committees and coordinating groups rather than chairpersons, presidents, and officers in the more common linear fashion. Over the years, black women have evolved organization styles consistent with the specific cultural,

---

[2]White (1999) provides an excellent detailed analysis of the St. Louis campaign.

[3]Walrond was a young black woman on welfare who, in May 1999, was convicted of negligent homicide for her baby's death. She had attempted unsuccessfully to breast-feed the baby, was not given adequate medical support, and was denied medical treatment for the child a short time before he died because his Medicaid card had not yet arrived in the mail. A coalition of groups supported Walrond's case, citing it as an example of sexism, racism, economic injustice, and the growing emphasis on prisons over social services.

economic, and historical realities that have defined our lives. I cannot, within the confines of this article, outline all of the nuanced variations, but one predominant strain is a decentralized, group-centered, grassroots democratic model, best exemplified by the lifelong work of Ella Jo Baker and Septima Poinsette Clark.[4] Given this history, it is not surprising that no single charismatic figure has emerged to personify and symbolize the movement. For example, there is no dark-skinned version of Gloria Steinem or Betty Freidan in black feminist circles; there are no female counterparts to Louis Farrakhan or Jesse Jackson, Sr. in terms of political visibility. Angela Davis, Barbara Smith, and bell hooks are perhaps the most renowned living black feminist personae, but, for different reasons, each has admirably resisted and declined icon status.

But what are the ideological tenets around which black feminists have organized? Perhaps strongest is the notion that race, class, gender, and sexuality are codependent variables that cannot readily be separated and ranked in scholarship, in political practice, or in lived experience. The main tension within diverse political coalitions has been the tendency to rank different systems of oppression and thus prioritize the liberation agendas of certain groups within the coalition. Because any political agenda that addresses the realities of most African-American women's lives must deal with the four major systems of oppression and exploitation—race, class, gender, and sexuality—black feminist politics radically breaks down the notion of mutually exclusive, competing identities and interests and instead understands identities and political process as organic, fluid, interdependent, dynamic, and historical. The openness of our political processes and the permeability of our multiple identities help create the potential for collaborations that transcend social boundaries and reject elitist criteria for leadership. Instead of policing boundaries, racial or otherwise, black feminists have more often than not penetrated these barriers, expanding the meaning of "we" and "community" in the process.

Contrary to those who argue that black struggles, women's struggles, queer struggles narrow our range of vision and divide us into factions, the radical organizers and theorists within these so-called identity-based movements actually offer the terms for a higher level of unity, integration, and interaction. Radicals within the feminist, lesbigaytrans, and people of color communities generally see fighting against economic exploitation as intimately related to, and inseparable from, the fight against racism, sexism, and heterosexism and as a critical component of their political agenda. Thus, these forces are potentially the connective tissue between various social change movements and constituencies, rather than the wedge that divides them. Nothing embodies this spirit better than the founding statement of the Combahee River Collective, conceived nearly a quarter-century ago by black lesbian feminist activists in Boston, many of whom continue to play central roles in progressive struggles today. It reads: "The most general statement of our politics at the present time would be that we are actively committed to struggling against racial, sexual, heterosexual, and class oppression and see as our particular task the development of integrated analysis and practice based upon the fact that the major systems of oppression are interlocking. The synthesis of these oppressions creates the conditions of our lives" (Combahee River Collective [1977] 1995, 232).

It is no coincidence, then, that black feminist organizers around the country have deeply immersed themselves in struggles that incorporate but are not isolated to gender issues.[5] In the

---

[4]On the democratic character of many of black women's organizing efforts, see Brodkin (1988); Payne (1995); Robnett (1997).

[5]For example, Beth Richie's (1995) work on domestic violence has connections with larger antiviolence, antipoverty, and prisoners' rights movements, as does Angela Davis's work on the prison industrial complex. Atlanta-based black feminist Loretta Ross and Washington, D.C.-based organizer and law professor Lisa Crooms have worked on international and domestic human rights projects that incorporate many issues in additon to gender.

decades since the formation of the short-lived Combahee River Collective, black feminist practice has evolved, not so much reinventing itself as building on the foundational vision, outlined in 1977, of an inclusive, multi-issue political agenda built on a fluid democratic practice. And while we often bemoan the absence of a tangible physical place of our own, black feminists are not invisible, nor have we been effectively silenced. A wealth of scholarship has helped to forge a heterogeneous body of work that explores and debates the applications and interpretations of black feminist political ideology. More important, because of our persistent efforts—the lessons learned, strategies explored, trust established, storms weathered—perhaps now we have the kind of history that can give us greater optimism for the future, optimism that might enable the forging of an independent black feminist organization with links and ties to multiple other oppositional and visionary movements of the twenty-first century.   [2000]

REFERENCES

Brodkin, Karen. *Caring by the Hour: Women, Work, and Organizing at Duke Medical Center.* Urbana: University of Illinois Press, 1988.

Collins, Patricia Hill. *Fighting Words: Black Women and the Search for Justice.* Minneapolis: University of Minnesota Press, 1998.

Combahee River Collective (Barbara Smith, Beverly Smith, and Demita Frazier). (1977) 1995. "A Black Feminist Statement." In Guy-Sheftall 1995, 232–40.

Giddings, Paula. *When and Where I Enter: The Impact of Black Women on Race and Sex in America.* New York: Morrow, 1989.

Guy-Sheftall, Beverly, ed. *Words of Fire: An Anthology of African-American Feminist Thought.* New York: New Press, 1995.

Payne, Charles M. *I've Got the Light of Freedom: The Organizing Tradition and the Mississippi Freedom Struggle.* Berkeley: University of California Press, 1995.

Richie, Beth. *Compelled to Crime: The Gender Entrapment of Battered Black Women.* New York: Routledge, 1995.

Robnett, Belinda. *How Long? How Long? African-American Women in the Struggle for Civil Rights.* New York: Oxford University Press, 1997.

Smith, Barbara, ed. *Home Girls: A Black Feminist Anthology.* New York: Kitchen Table/Women of Color, 1983.

White, Aaronette M. "Talking Feminist, Talking Black: Micromobilization Processes in a Collective Protest against Rape." *Gender & Society* 13(1):77–100, 1999.

Zooks, Krystal Brent. "A Manifesto of Sorts for a New Black Feminist Movement." *New York Times Magazine,* November 12, 1995.

❧ 168

Voices

WOMEN OF ACE (AIDS COUNSELING AND EDUCATION), BEDFORD HILLS CORRECTIONAL FACILITY

The authors of this essay are Kathy Boudin, Judy Clark, "D," Katrina Haslip, Maria D. L. Hernandez, Suzanne Kessler, Sonia Perez, Deborah Plunkett, Aida Rivera, Doris Romeo, Carmen Royster, Cathy Salce, Renee Scott, Jenny Serrano, and Pearl Ward.

INTRODUCTION

We are writing about ACE because we feel that it has made a tremendous difference in this prison and could make a difference in other prisons. ACE stands for AIDS Counseling and Education. It is a collective effort by women in Bedford Hills Correctional Facility. This article will reflect that collectivity by being a patchwork quilt of many women's voices.

ACE was started by inmates in 1988 because of the crisis that AIDS was creating in our community. According to a blind study done in the Fall-Winter of 1987–1988, almost 20 percent of the women entering the New York state prison system were HIV infected.[1] It is likely to be higher today. In addition, women here have family members who are sick and friends who are dying. People have intense fears of transmission through casual contact because we live so closely together. Women are worried about their children and about having safe sex. All this need and energy led to the creation of ACE.

BEFORE ACE

Prior to the formation of ACE, Bedford was an environment of fear, stigma, lack of information, and evasion. AIDS was a word that was whispered. People had no forum in which to talk about their fears. The doctors and nurses showed their biases. They preferred to just give advice, and many wouldn't touch people because of their own fears. There were several deaths. This inflamed people's fear more. People didn't want to look at their own vulnerability—their IV drug use and unsafe sex.

> I felt very negative about people who I knew were sick. To save face, I spoke to them from afar. I felt that they all should be put into a building by themselves because I heard that people who were healthy could make them sick and so they should get specific care. I figured that I have more time (on my sentence); why should I be isolated? They should be. I felt very negative and it came a lot from fear.[2]

Women at Bedford who are sick are housed in a hospital unit called In Patient Care (IPC). ACE members remember what IPC was like before ACE:

> The IPC area—the infirmary—was horrible before, a place where nobody wanted to be. It was a place to go to die. Before ACE people started going there, it looked like a dungeon. It was unsanitary. Just the look of it made people feel like they were going to die. That was the end.

There was no support system for women who wanted to take the HIV-antibody test:

> I had a friend who tested positive. The doctor told her, you are HIV positive, but that doesn't mean you have AIDS. You shouldn't have sex, or have a baby, and you should avoid stress. Period. No information was given to her. No counseling and support. She freaked out.

THE BEGINNING OF ACE: BREAKING THE SILENCE

Some of us sensed that people needed to talk, but no one would break the silence. Finally, five women got together, and made a proposal to the superintendent:

> We said that we ourselves had to help ourselves. We believed that as peers we would be the most effective in education, counseling, and building a community of support. We stated four main goals: to save lives through preventing the spread of HIV; to create more humane conditions for those who are HIV positive; to give support and education to women with fears, questions, and needs related to AIDS; to act as a bridge to community groups to help women as they reenter the community.

The superintendent accepted the proposal. Each of the five women sought out other women in the population who they believed were sensitive and would be interested in breaking the silence. When they reached 35, they stopped and a meeting was called.

BREAKING THE SILENCE CHANGED US: WE BEGAN TO BUILD A COMMUNITY

> At that first meeting a sigh of relief was felt and it rippled out. There was a need from so many directions. People went around the table and said why they were there. About the fourth or fifth woman said, "I'm here because I have AIDS." There was an intense silence. It was the first time anyone had said that aloud in a group. By the end of the meeting, several more women had said that they were HIV positive. Breaking the silence, the faith that it took, and the trust it built was really how ACE started.

BREAKING THE SILENCE MEANT SOMETHING SPECIAL TO PWAS

> I often ask myself how it is that I came to be open about my status. For me, AIDS had been one of my best kept secrets. It took me approximately 15 months to discuss this issue openly. As if not saying it aloud would make it go away. I watched other people with AIDS (PWAs), who were much more open than I was at the time, reveal to audiences their status/their vulnerability, while sharing from a distance, from silence, every word that was being uttered by them. I wanted to be a part of what they were building, what they were doing, their statement, "I am a PWA," because I was. It was a relief when I said it. I could stop going on with the lie. I could be me. People were supportive and they didn't shun me. And now I can go anywhere and be myself.

SUPPORTING PWAS

PWAs and HIV-positive women are at the heart of our work. ACE believes that everyone facing HIV-related illness is confronting issues of life and death and struggling to survive and thrive.

> We had to have some place for PWAs to share their experiences with each other. There have been numerous support groups which allowed us to

express things that hadn't been verbalized but that had been on our minds. It was interesting to see that we had similar issues: how to tell significant others, our own vulnerability about being open, living with AIDS. My first group was a mixture of people. Some were recently diagnosed and others had been diagnosed for two years. It was informative and it was emotional. Sometimes we would just come to a meeting and cry. Or we might come there and not even talk about the issue of AIDS and just have a humor session because we are just tired of AIDS.

One of the first things that ACE ever did was to work in IPC.

ACE started going to IPC. We painted, cleaned up, made it look so good that now the women want to stay there. We take care of the girls who are sick, making them feel comfortable and alive. Now, women there know they have a friend. They feel free, they talk, and look forward to visits. They know they're not there to die, not like before.

BEING A BUDDY

I have been involved in ACE for about three years. About a year ago I started visiting the women in IPC. I was really afraid at first. Not afraid of getting sick, but of becoming emotionally involved and then have the women die. At first, I tried to keep my feelings and friendship at a minimum. The more I went, the more I lost this fear. There is one woman I have gotten closer to than the rest. She has been in IPC since I first started going there. We are buddies. For me to be her buddy means unconditionally loving her and accepting her decisions. I go almost every night to IPC. Some nights we just sit there and say nothing. But there is comfort in my presence. She had a stroke before I met her. So there is a lot she cannot do for herself. There are times when I bathe and dress her. Iron her clothes. I do not think of any of these things as chores. Soon she will be going home. I am overjoyed, but I'm also saddened knowing that I will not see her again. I will miss her hugs, her complaining, and her love. But I would do it all over again and I probably will with someone else.

MEDICAL ADVOCACY

It is obviously a matter of life or death for anyone who is HIV infected to get good medical care and have a good relationship with her health providers. Medical facilities in prisons start out understaffed and ill equipped, and the AIDS crisis escalated these problems enormously. In the 1970s women prisoners here instituted a class action suit, *Todaro v. Ward,* to demand better medical care. Because of that case, the medical facilities and care at Bedford are monitored for the court by an outside expert. That expert issued a report criticizing all aspects of the medical department for being inadequately prepared to meet women's AIDS-related medical needs, and the prison faced a court hearing and possible contempt charges. Under that pressure the state agreed to numerous changes that brought new medical staff and resources, including a full-time medical director, a part-time infectious disease specialist, and more nurses. ACE was able to institute a medical advocacy plan that allowed ACE members to accompany women to their doctor's consultation visit to ensure that nothing was missed. Afterward, there can be a private discussion between the patient and the advocate to clarify matters for the woman, to explore possibilities of treatment, or just to allow the person to express whatever emotions she experienced when she received the news from the doctor.

PEER EDUCATION

Our approach is *peer* education, which we believe is best suited for the task of enabling a community to mobilize itself to deal with AIDS. The people doing the training clearly have a personal stake in the community. The education is for all, in the interests of all. This is communicated from the beginning by the women doing the teaching.

Our peer education takes a problem-posing approach. We present issues as problems facing all of us, problems to be examined by drawing on the knowledge and experience of the women being trained. What are the issues between a man and a woman, for example, that make it hard for a woman to demand that her man use a condom? Will distributing free needles or advocating bleach kits stop the spread of AIDS among IV drug users?

Our educational work is holistic. Education is not solely a presentation of facts, although that is an important part of the trainers' responsibilities.

But what impact do feelings and attitudes have on how people deal with facts? Why would a person who knows that you cannot get AIDS by eating from a PWA's plate still act occasionally as if you could? Why would a person who knows that sex without a condom could be inviting death, not use a condom? For education to be a deep process, it involves understanding the whole person; for education to take root within a community, it means thinking about things on a community, social level.

> Coming to prison, living under these conditions, was scary, and AIDS made it even scarier. I was part of a society that made judgments and had pre-conceived ideas about the women in prison.

EDUCATING OURSELVES

Workshops

To become members of ACE, women must be educated through a series of eight workshops. We look at how stigma and blame have been associated with diseases throughout history, and how the sexism of this society impacts on women in the AIDS epidemic. We teach about the nature of the virus, strategies for treatment, and holistic approaches. After the eight weeks, we ask who would like to become involved, and then there is a screening process. The superintendent has final approval. The workshops are followed by more intensive training of women who become members.

Orientation

When women enter the New York state prison system, they must come first to Bedford Hills, where they either stay or move on after several weeks to one of several other women's prisons. ACE members talk with the women when they first arrive.

> We do orientations of 10 to 35 women. We explain to them how you can and cannot get AIDS, about testing and about ACE. Sometimes the crowd is very boisterous and rude. I say "AIDS" and they don't want to hear about it. But those are the ones I try to reach. After orientation is over, the main ones that didn't want to hear about AIDS are the ones who want to talk more and I feel good about that. A lot of times, their loudness is a defense

because they are afraid of their own vulnerability. They know that they are at risk for HIV infection because of previous behaviors. After I finish doing orientation, I have a sense of warmth, because I know I made a difference in some of their lives.

Seminars

One of the main ways we interact with our sisters is through seminars. We talk about AIDS issues with groups of women on living units, in classrooms, and in some of the other prison programs such as family violence, drug treatment, and Children's Center.

> The four back buildings are dormitories, each holding 100 women with double bunked beds. We from ACE gather right after count, with our easel and newsprint and magic markers and our three-by-five cards with the information on whatever presentation we're making. We move in twos and threes through the connecting tunnels to the building. When we arrive some of the women are sitting in the rec room, but many others are in their cubicles/cells. They ask why we're here. We look like a traveling troupe—and we've felt like it, not knowing what to expect. Some women are excited that we're going to talk about AIDS. Others say, "forget it," or "fuck you, I've heard enough about it, it's depressing."

But we begin, and people slowly gather.

> We ask the women to help us role-play a situation such as a woman going home from prison, trying to convince her man, who has been taking care of her while she's inside, to use a condom. Then the role-play is analyzed. What problems are encountered and how do we deal with those problems? We try to come up with suggestions that we can see ourselves using in that situation. We talk about the risk of violence.

One of the most immediate problems people have is whether or not to take the HIV-antibody test. We do not push testing. We explain what the test is and have a group discussion of things the women need to consider. A woman may be inclined to get tested, but she needs to know that she is likely to be transferred upstate before the results come back from the lab. The choice is up to her. Toward the end of the seminar, PWAs talk about their experiences living with AIDS.

> When they speak, they bring together everything that we have said. Not only that, but they let people know that living with AIDS is not instant death. It makes people realize why the struggles, working together, and being as one are so important. When I hear the women who are PWAs speak, it makes me realize that I could have been in their shoes, or I could still be, if they hadn't been willing to talk about their risk behaviors and what has happened to them. It gives me the courage to realize that it's not all about me. It's actually about us.

We end each seminar with all the women standing with our arms around each other or holding hands—without any fear of casual contact—singing our theme song, "Sister."[3] We sing, having come to a new place where we are for each other, unified. We all feel some sense of relief and some sense of hope. Talking about AIDS openly has changed how we live. We leave the seminar with the knowledge that we can talk about AIDS and that we're going to be okay. . . .

Counseling

When we conduct the seminars and orientation sessions, women come up to us afterward with personal questions and problems. It could be they are HIV positive, or they are thinking of taking the test, or they have a family member who is sick, or they are thinking about getting involved with someone in a relationship. Sometimes they raise one issue, but underlying it are a lot of other issues they're not yet ready to talk about. Because women know we're in ACE, we're approached in our housing units, at school, on the job, in the mess hall, as we walk from one place to another. Women stop us, needing to talk. We're a haven for women because they know ACE has a principle of confidentiality. Women can trust us not to abuse the information they are sharing with us.

> Peer counseling. I'm just impressed that we can do it. I didn't know what kind of potential we'd have as peers. We talk the language that each of us understands. Even if it's silent, even if it's with our eyes,

it's something that each of us seems to understand. I know I wouldn't want someone from the Department of Health who hasn't even taken a Valium to try to educate me about IV drug use. How could they give me helpful hints? I would feel that they are so out of tune with reality that I wouldn't be able to hear them.

A CRISIS AND OPPORTUNITY FOR OUR COMMUNITY

We are a small community and we are so isolated you can feel it—the suffering, the losses, the fears, the anxiety. Out in the street you don't have a community of women affected and living together facing a problem in this same way. We can draw on the particular strengths that women bring: nurturance, caring, and personal openness. So many women prisoners have worked in nursing and old-age homes. Yet when they did, they were never given respect. Here these same activities are valued, and the women are told "thank you," and that creates initiative and feelings of self-worth. And ACE helps us to be more self-conscious about a culture of caring that as women we tend to create in our daily lives.

> For the first time in prison I was part of a group that cared about other prisoners in prison. What did that feel like? It felt like I wasn't alone in caring about people, because in this type of setting I was beginning to wonder about people caring.

OUR IMPACT ON WOMEN

We know that we have played a role in communicating information about what is safe and what is not safe in sexual behavior—both between a man and woman and between two women—and we have certainly been able to create open and relaxed discussions about all this. But we know that actually changing behaviors is another leap ahead of us. We are learning that it's not a one-shot deal, that information doesn't equal behavior change, and it's not just an individual thing. Social norms have to change, and this takes time. And when you talk about women having to initiate change you're up against the fact that women don't have that kind of empowerment in this society. Women who have been influenced by ACE have experienced a change in attitude, but it is unclear whether this will translate into behavior change once they leave the prison.

> When I first started taking the workshops I was 100 percent against using condoms. And yet I like anal sex. But now my views are different. We're the bosses of our own bodies. You know, a lot of people say it's a man's world. Well, I can't completely agree.

OUR DIVERSITY IS A STRENGTH

We are a diverse community of women: black, Latin, and white, and also from countries throughout the world. In ACE there was at first a tendency to deny the differences, maybe out of fear of disunity. Now there is a more explicit consciousness growing that we can affirm our diversity and our commonality because both are important. In the last workshop on women, we broke for a while into three groups—black, Latina, and white women—to explore the ways AIDS impacted on our particular culture and communities. We are doing more of those kinds of discussions and developing materials that address concerns of specific communities. The Hispanic Sector of ACE is particularly active, conducting seminars in Spanish and holding open meetings for the population to foster Hispanic awareness of AIDS issues.

> The workshops didn't deal enough with different ethnic areas, and being Puerto Rican and half-Indian, some things seemed ridiculous in terms of the Hispanic family. Some of the ways people were talking about sex wouldn't work in a traditional Hispanic family. For example, you can't just tell your husband that he has to wear a condom. Or say to him, "You have to take responsibility." These approaches could lead to marital rape or abuse. The empowerment of Hispanic women means making sure that their children are brought up.

WORKING IN A PRISON

We have a unique situation at Bedford Hills. We have a prison administration that is supportive of inmates developing a peer-based program to deal with AIDS. However, because we are in a prison

there are a lot of constraints and frustrations. Before we had staff persons to supervise us, we could not work out of an office space. That meant that we couldn't see women who wanted to talk on an individual level unless we ran into them in the yard or rec room.

You could be helping someone in IPC take her daily shower; it's taking longer than usual because she is in a lot of pain or she needs to talk, but that's not taken into consideration when the officer tells you that you have to leave immediately because it's "count-time." You could be in the rec room, a large room with a bunch of card tables, loud music, and an officer overseeing groups of women sitting on broken-down chairs. You're talking to a woman in crisis who needs comforting. You reach out to give her a hug and the C.O. may come over to admonish you, "No physical contact, ladies." Or maybe a woman has just tested positive. She's taken her first tentative steps to reach out by talking to someone from ACE and joining a support group. Days after her first meeting, she is transferred to another prison.

It's been difficult to be able to call ourselves counselors and have our work formally acknowledged by the administration. Counseling is usually done by professionals in here because it carries such liability and responsibility. We're struggling for the legitimacy of peer counseling. The reality is that we've been doing it in our daily lives here through informal dialogue. We now have civilian staff to supervise us, and Columbia University will be conducting a certification training program to justify the title "peer counselor."

After working over two years on our own, we are now being funded by a grant from the New York State AIDS Institute, coordinated by Columbia University School of Public Health and by Women and AIDS Resource Network (WARN). The money has allowed hiring staff to work with ACE. ACE began as a totally volunteer inmate organization with no office or materials, operating on a shoestring and scrambling for every meeting. Now we have an office in a prime location of the prison, computers, and a civilian staff responsible for making certain that there is something to show for their salaries. Inmates who used to work whenever they could find the time are now paid 73 cents a day as staff officially assigned to the ACE Center. The crises are no longer centered around the problems of being inside a prison, but more on how to sustain momentum and a real grassroots initiative in the context of a prison. This is a problem faced by many other community organizations when they move past the initial momentum and become more established institutions.

BUILDING A CULTURE OF SURVIVAL

When, in the spring of 1987, we said, "Let's make quilt squares for our sisters who have died," there were more than 15 names. Over the next year we made more and more quilt squares. The deaths took a toll not just on those who knew the women but on all of us. Too many women were dying among us. And, for those who were HIV positive or worried that they might be, each death heightened their own vulnerabilities and fears. We have had to develop ways to let people who are sick know that if they die, their lives will be remembered, they will be honored and celebrated, and they will stay in our hearts.

> I remember our first memorial. Several hundred women contributed money—25 cents, 50 cents, a dollar—for flowers. Both Spanish and Black women sang and in the beginning everyone held hands and sang "That's What Friends Are For," and in the end we sang "Sister." People spoke about what Ro meant to them. Ro had died and we couldn't change that. But we didn't just feel terrible. We felt love and caring and that together we could survive the sadness and loss.
>
> In the streets, funerals were so plastic, but here, people knew that it could be them. It's not just to pay respect. When we sang "Sister," there was a charge between us. Our hands were extended to each other. There was a need for ACE and we could feel it in the air.

It was out of that same need that ACE was formed. It will be out of that same need that ACE will continue to strive to build community and an environment of trust and support. We are all we have—ourselves. If we do not latch on to this hope that has strengthened us and this drive that

has broken our silence, we too will suffer and we will remain stigmatized and isolated. Feel our drive in our determination to make changes, and think "community," and make a difference.   [1990]

NOTES

1. Perry F. Smith et al., *Infection Among Women Entering the New York State Correctional System* (1990), unpublished manuscript.
2. All quotations are from the authors' conversations with prisoners at Bedford Hills.
3. By Cris Williamson, from the album *The Changer and the Changed*, Olivia Records, 1975.

🌿 169

Organizing with Love: Lessons from the New York Domestic Workers Bill of Rights Campaign

AI-JEN POO, FOR DOMESTIC WORKERS UNITED

Great organizing campaigns are like great love affairs. You begin to see life through a different lens. You change in unexpected ways. You lose sleep, but you also feel boundless energy. You develop new relationships and new interests. Your skin becomes more open to the world around you. Life feels different, and it's almost like you've been reborn. And, most importantly, you begin to feel things that you previously couldn't have even imagined are possible. Like great love affairs, great campaigns provide us with an opportunity for transformation. They connect us to our deeper purpose and to the commonalities we share, even in the face of tremendous differences. They highlight our interdependence, and they help us to see the potential that our relationships have to create real change in our lives and in the world around us.

The fight to win a Domestic Workers Bill of Rights in New York State—led by Domestic Workers United and the New York Domestic Workers Justice Coalition—has been one of those great organizing campaigns. The Domestic Workers Bill of Rights is a piece of statewide legislation that will recognize the domestic workforce and establish basic labor standards. The first legislation of its kind, the Domestic Workers Bill of Rights will provide overtime pay, protection from discrimination, and other basic benefits for the more than 200,000 women—most of whom are immigrants of color—who work as nannies, housekeepers, and companions for the elderly in New York State. The fight to win the Bill of Rights has been like a love affair, full of exciting moments, inspiring growth, and life-changing struggles. Throughout most years of our efforts, domestic workers and organizers were told we were trying to achieve the impossible. But we believed that we could win.

Our six-year organizing campaign to pass the Bill of Rights saw its first major victory in 2009, when the New York State Assembly passed a bill to end some of the exclusions of domestic workers in existing labor laws. On June 1, 2010, the New York State Senate spent two long hours debating the merits of the Domestic Workers Bill of Rights. On one side, legislators argued that we couldn't ask more of employers in a time of economic hardship. On the other side, legislator after legislator told stories about their mothers and grandmothers who had labored in the shadows as domestic workers to provide for their families. The debate concluded with a vote—33 to 28—in favor of passing the bill. Governor David A. Paterson said,

> Today, both houses of the Legislature passed legislation that truly deserves to be called historic. It would make New York the first State in the nation to enshrine in law the basic rights of a class of workers that has historically and wrongfully been excluded from such protections: the domestic workers who care for our children, clean our homes, and provide the elderly with companionship. Their work is of incalculable value, yet our laws have failed to recognize it. This bill would change that, and serve as a model for such change on a national scale. . . . Most of all, I must express my gratitude to the thousands of individual domestic workers who organized and fought for this legislation. They provide all of us with an example of how individuals can, through struggle

and dedication, bring about positive change in the face of skepticism and doubt. This achievement belongs to them, and I will be pleased to sign it into law on their behalf.

Reflecting on the scope of the challenges that we faced, our campaign won transformations on many different levels. The Bill of Rights campaign has been a catalyst for change within and between individuals, between organizations, and between movements. This fight has challenged broader social values and structures that have devalued women's domestic labor for generations.

As the Lead Organizer at Domestic Workers United (DWU) for the past 10 years, I write this article to share the story of DWU's inspiring history and to draw out the central lessons we learned over the past 10 years—in particular, how our work demonstrates the importance of moving beyond narrow conceptions of self-interest so that we can organize based on an expanded sense of self-interest that honors and reflects our connections and interdependencies.

THE WORLD OF WORK INSIDE THE HOME

Working Conditions

Domestic workers—who care for some of the most important elements of our lives like our families and our homes—are among the most vulnerable workers in the United States today. There are an estimated 2.5 million women who labor as domestic workers. Domestic workers serve as nannies, housekeepers, and caregivers for the elderly. They often perform the duties of nurses, art teachers, counselors, tutors, assistants, and nutritionists as well. In the New York metropolitan area alone, over 200,000 women of color leave their homes early in the morning, often in the dark, in order to arrive at their work sites before their employers leave for work. Some even live in their employers' homes, caring for these families throughout the day and night. The more hours that these women spend working in their employers' homes, the fewer hours they have to give their own children. Many domestic workers have to leave their own children behind in their home nations. Even though the entire economy rests on their work, their labor has long been taken for granted. Historically associated with the unpaid work of women in the home and with the poorly paid labor of black and immigrant women, domestic work today remains undervalued and invisible.

"Maria" is a Central American woman in her midsixties who works as a domestic worker in New York City, and her story provides a telling illustration of the experiences of many other domestic workers. Maria came to the United States to support her family. She has a son with diabetes, and she could not make enough money in her home nation to cover his costly insulin treatments. When she arrived in New York, she found a job as caregiver for a child with a disability. In addition to the "full-time" work it took to provide him with care, her employers required her to do the cooking, cleaning, and ironing for the entire household. Maria worked 18 hours a day, six days a week, for less than $3 an hour. She lived in the basement of her employer's home, where a broken sewage system flooded the floor by her bed. She had to collect cardboard and wood from the street so she could use them as stepping-stones to reach her bed at night. After Maria had spent three years living and working in these conditions, her employers fired her without notice or severance pay.

Crucial Contributions

By taking care of the families and homes of their employers, domestic workers make it possible for their employers to go to work every day. But because women's work in the home has never been factored into national labor statistics, it is difficult to quantify the economic contributions of this workforce. We can estimate these workers' contributions by imagining what would happen if they withheld their labor. If domestic workers went on strike, they could paralyze almost every industry in urban areas. Doctors, lawyers, bankers, professors, small business owners, civil sector employees, and media executives would all be affected. The entire urban economy would quiver.

Excluded from Basic Labor Protections

Because domestic work is one of our nation's oldest professions and because it has a vital role in our economy, one might assume that domestic workers would be protected by labor laws. However, from the New Deal on, U.S. labor laws have explicitly excluded domestic workers. Even if domestic workers were included in labor laws, the structure of the industry would make it difficult to organize workers or to enforce basic labor standards.

The workplaces are unmarked private homes. The terms of employment and working conditions are negotiated house by house. With no clear standards or laws to ensure basic rights, workers have to negotiate the terms of their employment individually, day by day, in situations where they lack any real bargaining power. More often than not, workers risk losing their jobs by asking for basic rights and necessities like an afternoon off to see the doctor or receive a mammogram.

The combination of these dynamics—the racialized exclusion of domestic workers from labor laws, the gendered devaluation of women's work in the home, the decentralized structure of the industry, and the economic pressures facing immigrants from the global South—makes domestic workers extremely vulnerable to exploitation and abuse. In this context, organizing is both difficult and absolutely essential. Over the past 10 years, domestic workers in New York City have developed an innovative organizing model to address the challenging dynamics of the industry and to build grassroots workers' power.

THE HISTORY OF DOMESTIC WORKERS UNITED

The Birth of Domestic Workers United

DWU was born out of a joint organizing effort between two community-based organizations, CAAAV: Organizing Asian Communities and Andolan: Organizing South Asian Workers, in 1999. The two organizations had been organizing and fighting cases of injustice on behalf of workers in different Asian communities for several years. Members of these organizations realized quickly that achieving real change would necessarily involve workers from other communities, so they began to organize open meetings for domestic workers in Brooklyn.

The women at these early meetings decided to form themselves into a Steering Committee, and DWU was born in 2000. Since then, DWU has served as a vehicle for organizing unorganized populations of domestic workers and for coordinating efforts among the existing groups. Today DWU organizes Caribbean, Latina, and African nannies, housekeepers, and caregivers for the elderly in New York. DWU fights for power, respect, and fair labor standards with the goal of building a broader movement for social change.

Our First Steps

DWU helped to organize individual support campaigns for workers who had been mistreated by their employers, were owed wages, or survived trafficking. DWU organized demonstrations at employers' businesses, and we worked with legal partners to file lawsuits against delinquent employers. Using a combination of legal pressure and direct action, DWU has helped to recover over $450,000 in stolen wages.

As the work evolved, it became clear that grassroots worker education and case-by-case fighting wasn't going to give workers the protection they needed. We would have to find a way to change labor laws. In 2002, DWU decided to test the waters and see how possible it would be to win legislative protections for domestic workers. We wanted to see whether legislative campaigns would mobilize workers and help build the organization, and we wanted to see whether we could win. That year DWU led a successful effort to pass a New York City law to compel domestic worker employment placement agencies to educate workers and employers about basic labor rights. On the day of the vote in 2003, domestic workers packed the balcony inside City Council chambers carrying a sign that read, "The First Step to Victory, The Struggle Continues." After the passage of the citywide agency bill, we decided to raise our scopes and try to change labor laws for the state of New York.

Developing the Domestic Workers Bill of Rights

After that initial victory, we wanted to keep domestic workers' issues in the limelight and keep our process of building power moving. DWU decided to hold the "'Having Your Say' Convention" which brought together hundreds of domestic workers with the goal of laying the foundation for a much bolder statewide campaign to establish new labor laws protecting domestic workers. The convention brought together domestic workers from over a dozen different countries for a daylong meeting. Even though they spoke six different languages, these workers found a common voice as they shared their experiences of laboring without respect or basic labor standards. They developed a united vision for quality jobs where they would be treated with respect.

Out of that convention, we developed a set of key priorities that would become the basis for the Domestic Workers Bill of Rights, including overtime pay, a minimum of one day of rest per week, health care, a living wage of $14 an hour, notice of termination, severance pay, paid holidays, paid leave, and protection from discrimination. Supported by the New York University Immigrant Rights Law Clinic, DWU drafted the Bill of Rights into formal legislation.

DWU coordinated with the other organizations that organized domestic workers in New York for the next stage of the fight. Together, we formed the New York Domestic Worker Justice Coalition, and the Bill of Rights Campaign became the place where domestic workers came together across communities to maximize their power as a workforce.

We took our first trip—in a 15-passenger van full of domestic workers—to the state capital in Albany in January 2004. We spent the next five years learning what it would take to build power and win in Albany.

We knew we had to build power if we wanted to win. Moral arguments were not enough. Our strategy for building power was twofold: (1) build our membership base of domestic workers, and (2) build a broad-based coalition of support from a range of different allies: employers, students, communities of faith, and the labor movement.

We expanded our support base by speaking at other organizations' meetings and in classrooms and churches. This expanded base of support enabled us to convince more legislators to sign on as cosponsors on our Bill. By our third year, we decided to strengthen our support base by creating a "Campaign Organizing Committee" that our coalition partners and supporters could join to become a part of the campaign planning process. We invited anyone who had the desire and energy to attend: students, union members, attorneys, and individual activists. By opening that kind of space to all the people who were interested in our struggle, we developed a core group of supporters who could lead independent organizing in their own networks. And the tide started to turn; you could hear a buzz around town about the Bill of Rights campaign. That was the year when we also started to receive significant support from high-profile labor leaders like John Sweeney, president of the AFL-CIO, whose mother had worked as a domestic worker for over 40 years.

Over the course of the six years of the Bill of Rights campaign, DWU members and supporters traveled to Albany more than 40 times. In addition to legislative visits, our Albany mobilizations included rallies, press conferences, and exciting cultural performances. Each person who went to Albany with us returned as an advocate for domestic workers rights. High school students—who at first went to Albany because their teachers thought it would be good exposure to civic processes—talked about the domestic workers in their lives, and they came to realize how those relationships made the Bill of Rights Campaign relevant to their lives.

By the fifth year of the campaign, our years of public education were finally enough to lead to the Assembly's passage of legislation that eliminated exclusions of domestic workers in the labor law. Covering more than 200,000 women, most of them women of color, this legislation provides fundamental protections for a workforce that has been especially vulnerable to abuse. The momentum from local and state initiatives like the New York Bill of Rights can help create the climate for federal legislation to establish standards and reverse the exclusion and discrimination that have defined the lives of domestic workers for generations.

LESSONS IN TRANSFORMATIVE ORGANIZING

As impactful as our campaign has been in changing state policy, the impact of the process of organizing and alliance-building has been equally important. The Bill of Rights campaign offered an opportunity for people to step outside of their own patterns, to make different choices and to build different relationships with others. We learned crucial lessons about personal and social transformation in the process of this campaign. In particular, we learned that the historical assumption on which a great deal of organizing models are based—that we need to build our organizing campaigns based on people's material self-interests—is not the whole story. DWU led a campaign that mobilized many different communities of people based on an expanded sense of self-interest that acknowledged our relationships and our interdependencies.

During our campaigns, we learned that just about everyone is connected—in one way or another—to someone who works as a domestic worker. In many of our meetings with City Council members and with state legislators, we often heard stories where they remembered the experiences of their mothers who did domestic work. Whether they were raised by a domestic worker, or had relatives, or they themselves did this work at one point or another—everyone has a connection to this workforce. The personal connections that everyday people of all walks of life had to this workforce became one of the key mobilizing forces throughout the campaign. As the campaign progressed, our consciousness also shifted. Although the Bill is called the Domestic Workers Bill of Rights, we came to see that ultimately what was at stake was our collective humanity.

BUILDING ON THE STORIES OF DOMESTIC WORKERS

We knew that the stories and leadership of domestic workers would be a driving force throughout the campaign. What we didn't expect was how many other people would feel that their own life stories were so closely connected to the stories of domestic workers. These connections turned out to be an electric cord that energized the campaign from beginning to end.

Our message that we need to "*Respect the work that makes all other work possible*" allowed us to build relationships with women's organizations, mothers, and long-time advocates for gender justice and women's equality. Our "*Reverse a long history of discrimination and exclusion*" message allowed us to build with farmworkers, homeless people, guest workers, and the millions of others excluded by the existing legal system. And "*Standards benefit everyone*" highlighted our interconnectedness as people, and it allowed us to build relationships with unions, employers, faith leaders, and other people who believed in the moral imperative of basic human rights. Here are some examples:

The Children's March

On a hot Sunday morning in the summer of 2009, children of all ages and backgrounds colored in chalk on the sidewalks outside New York's City Hall. They wrote messages like "Respect My Mom" and "I love my Nanny." Then, with red balloons tied around their wrists that read "DWU," children of domestic workers walked together with children who were cared for by domestic workers. They led a march down Broadway to demand the passage of the Domestic Workers Bill of Rights.

The "Children and Families March for Domestic Workers Rights" began with a rally outside City Hall in front of a fence strung with cards made by children with messages like "I want to thank my nanny for taking me to the zoo." Stories like these were followed by the children of domestic workers, who spoke about how they wished they saw more of their mothers.

John Sweeney, Representing 10 Million Workers and His Mother

In June 2007, DWU held a Town Hall meeting to bring attention on the Bill of Rights, and several close allies in the labor movement were able to invite AFL-CIO President John Sweeney to speak. As the son of an immigrant domestic worker who had not had any labor protections, he recounted his memory of her pain. He remembered his mother's disappointment at the exclusion of domestic workers when the National Labor Relations Act passed in 1935. He proclaimed, "The ten million workers who are part of the AFL-CIO support the Domestic Workers Bill of Rights." In that moment, President Sweeney not only paid homage to his beloved mother; he also expanded the ranks of workers who could feel at home in the labor movement.

BUILDING UNITY WITH EMPLOYERS

Given the stark racial and class inequities between domestic workers and their employers, it would have been easy to adopt an organizing model based on antagonism and resentment between these groups. But DWU chose to maintain a space to build relationships and alliances with employers who wanted to find a way to be fair employers. We invited Jews for Racial and Economic Justice members who were either former or current employers of domestic workers to come to our events and speak about why they supported domestic workers' rights. Over time, JFREJ decided to initiate "Shalom Bayit," centered around the idea of bringing together progressive employers and the broader Jewish community to support domestic workers' rights, drawing upon traditional Jewish values and a long history of Jewish progressive unionism. The employer-activists organized "living room gatherings," meetings in their homes where they invited friends who employed domestic workers. At these gatherings, they discussed ways in which employers could take responsibility for creating decent working conditions. JFREJ activists also worked to bring domestic workers to speak in synagogues, to hold workshops for employers in different synagogues around the city, and to mobilize large contingents of Jewish activists and employers to support the Bill of Rights in Albany.

The Ties That Bind: Doormen and Domestic Workers

The Service Employees International Union Local 32BJ is a union that represents the thousands of doormen in luxury apartment buildings around the city. Local 32BJ has a natural affinity between its members and the members of DWU because the Local's members are often the friends, confidants, even husbands, of the domestic workers who work in the apartment buildings of the wealthy. The members of 32BJ have been crucial allies in our fight. They have provided meeting spaces for our meetings and conventions. And they have consistently endorsed our campaigns and used their leverage with elected officials to support the Bill of Rights.

Building Unity Between Excluded Workers

On a cold morning in early March 2008, a white sign that dripped with water outside of the church on the Albany Green read, "End Modern Day Slavery—Reverse The Legacy of Exclusion." The New York State Labor Religion Coalition and the local Jobs with Justice chapter had chosen to highlight domestic workers' and farmworkers' rights during its annual 40-hour fast, which was themed, "Welcoming the Stranger: Prophetic Voices for Immigrant Rights." The New York Justice for Farmworkers Campaign and the Domestic Workers Bill of Rights Campaign mobilized workers to participate in the 40-hour fast activities, which included legislative visits, a morning interfaith service and press conference, and a march.

VICTORY: CONNECTING OUR MUTUAL HUMANITY

Organizing for the Domestic Workers Bill of Rights has profoundly transformed the countless numbers of people who joined in the campaign. The stories that workers have shared in the course of the campaigns, the actions that we have organized and the many relationships that have been built through the campaign—all of these moments have provided entry points to help us connect with our mutual humanity. They have shown us the possibility for the kind of deep social transformation that we need to achieve, throughout society and within ourselves.

When Governor Paterson and the legislature reached agreement on the Domestic Workers Bill of Rights, they agreed to a bill that included: 8-hour workdays, overtime pay at time and a half your regular rate of pay for every hour after those 8 hours, a minimum of 24 consecutive hours of rest per week, overtime pay if the worker agrees to work on her day of rest, a minimum of three paid days off per year, protection against workplace discrimination and harassment, protection from sexual harassment, and the inclusion of both full-time and part-time domestic workers in workers compensation insurance protection. It also mandates the Department of Labor to complete a study on the feasibility and practicality of domestic workers organizing for the purpose of collective bargaining for other rights and benefits.

The experience of the campaign to pass the Domestic Workers Bill of Rights in New York has already provided an opening for the transformation of the relations within the domestic work industry and a vision for how we can transform all of our relations throughout our nation and beyond. Like a great love affair, it has helped us grow.

As a movement, we face enormous challenges ahead. The Bill of Rights Campaign is an example of the types of campaigns—full of hard work, risk, and uncertainty—that we will need to embrace in order to make a real difference for the next generation. It provides a hopeful push, despite the unknown, toward campaigns based on love, to bring us into the right relationships with one another for the change we need. In taking these risks, we may become who we were meant to be as a movement.   [edited, 2011]

 170

Women, Environmental Justice, and the Coal River Mountain Watch

JOYCE M. BARRY

There is a famous Margaret Mead quote, "Never doubt that a small group of thoughtful, committed citizens can change the world. Indeed, it's the only thing that ever has." This quote, copied on a large poster board, hangs in the office of the grassroots environmental justice group, The Coal River Mountain Watch (CRMW) in Whitesville, WV.

Women all over the world are active in environmental justice efforts. Women have been a part of such efforts since the 1970s when women like Lois Gibbs stood up against the impact of Hooker Chemicals in her small community in Love Canal, NY, and when Dolly Burwell, organized groups of African American women to protest the illegal dumping of PCBs in her community of Warren, North Carolina. The women of the Coal River Mountain Watch are recent examples of this trend.

The Coal River Mountain Watch and its members are representatives of the larger social phenomena of women who form organizations to fight environmental injustices in their communities. Around the country, and indeed, the world, poor and working-class women respond collectively to threats on their homes and communities. However, the scale and impact of this social trend has yet to be adequately assessed by feminist and environmental justice scholars. While there is a large body of important, ecofeminist scholarship examining women's connection to the natural world, it frequently fails to consider the role of class and its relation to gender and the environment. Also, this scholarship too often centers on women's individual responses to challenged environments, rarely focusing on women's collective actions.

WOMEN AND ENVIRONMENTAL JUSTICE

Environmental Justice (EJ) is a movement born out of an adversarial stance to the practices and policies of broader, more nationally conceived environmentalism. Mainstream environmentalism is more national in focus, more complicitious with government and business, and more socially homogeneous in membership and constituency than environmental justice groups. Environmentalism has historically conceived of the environment as nature apart from human existence, focusing on the preservation and conservation of wilderness areas, and plants and animals that have been negatively impacted by human behavior. Environmental justice recognizes the presence of humans in the natural world, defining the environment as where humans live, work, and play. It is more class-based in its focus, operating from the assumption that poor people tend to live in poor environments, and is guided by the forged links between social and environmental justice. While environmental justice scholars have been good at examining how poor communities share the burden of environmental hazards, these same scholars have done a less adequate job recognizing the role of women in this movement. This absence is surprising considering that women make up the majority of environmental justice activists in the country.

Women who form or join environmental justice groups to protect their homes and families frequently have little or no political experience. Many have no history of activism, but are propelled into political action because of direct assaults on their homes and communities. These nascent activists educate themselves on environmental issues, the intertwined workings of business and capital, and the heady maze of environmental politics. Theirs is frequently a "trial by fire" education acquired while organizing campaigns against environmental offenders. In the process, these women not only gain knowledge that helps them fight companies and governments that create environmentally jeopardized communities, but also personal self-esteem and an identity apart from their traditional ones as wives and mothers. For example, June, from the Coal River Mountain Watch, a wife and mother, became politically active after being disturbed by the number of dead fish discovered in a creek in her back yard. She had no political experience, or knowledge of the coal industry in Appalachia, but saw her efforts grandly rewarded, as she won the Goldman Environmental Prize for her fight against coal in Appalachia. This prize is an annual prize that awards one grassroots activist from each continent over $100,000. June, a former Pizza Hut waitress, was the North American recipient in 2003.

Giovanna Di Chiro labels women's participation in environmental justice as an "unmarked women's movement" not only because of the sheer degree of female involvement, but also due to the reticence of many women involved in grassroots environmental justice movements to label themselves as either "feminists" or "environmentalists."

MOUNTAINTOP REMOVAL MINING IN APPALACHIA

The Coal River Mountain Watch (CRMW) was formed to fight the devastating impact of mountaintop removal coal mining (MTR) in West Virginia. MTR is a radical form of surface mining that blasts off roughly 1000 feet of mountaintops, unearthing the valuable coal seams within. This ecologically devastating practice continues unabated everyday, around the clock. If continued at this present pace and scale, 1.4 million acres in West Virginia will be destroyed, the size of a small state, such as Delaware (Appalachian Voices, 2006). MTR ultimately serves to cover nearby streams, contaminating water supplies and animal habitats. Worries over coal waste containment are ever present for residents of the coal fields, and for good reason. In Inez, KY in 2000 one of these ponds broke, sending over 300 million gallons of sludge into the Big Sandy River and nearby creeks. Mountaintop removal coal mining has also been blamed for increased flooding in the area, as the original topography of the central. Indeed, in 2001 several small communities in the Whitesville area were literally obliterated by flooding after a hard summer rain.

Most West Virginians are aware of the scope of coal's influence, and its importance to the national energy plan and economy. While people in West Virginia are aware of the function of coal, to many Americans this energy source is what Barbara Freese calls an "invisible power" even though 52% of our country's electricity comes from coal (2003, 163). Americans can harbor the illusion that coal is no longer a major energy source or a big environmental threat, even while the nation burns more of it than ever" (2003, 166). Indeed, with our increasing reliance on digital technologies, from iPods to cell phones to palm pilots, Americans need more energy to power these devices. While coal may be an invisible resource for most people

in the country, it is far from invisible to residents in southern West Virginia.

Coal has owned and controlled the state since the rise of industrialization in the nineteenth century. As Jedidiah Purdy notes, "the coal industry owns half of the land in the Appalachian coalfields and as much as 75 percent in West Virginia's top coal producing counties" (1998, 3). This thoroughly established pattern of ownership has resulted in increased poverty for residents in these areas, while billions of dollars in coal wealth has been transported out of state.

It is in this context, that the Coal River Mountain Watch was formed. These are the conditions that have led women in the area to join this group, and work for economic, environmental, and social justice in their communities.

THE ENVIRONMENTAL JUSTICE ACTIVISM OF THE WOMEN OF THE COAL RIVER MOUNTAIN WATCH

The Coal River Mountain Watch is a small, but highly active, social justice group anchored in Whitesville, West Virginia. The group's name is from its place of origin in Boone county, West Virginia, a rural area in the central Appalachian mountains. This grassroots organization serves as an all-around watchdog of the coal industry oligarchy in West Virginia, fighting the social and environmental injustices created by this extractive industry, and its abetting state political system. The CRMW is overwhelmingly sustained by white, working-class women who live in environmental and economically compromised areas of the state's southern coal fields.

Janet, one of the charter members of CRMW, said that after seeing MTR's presence in the community where she grew up, she had to get involved: "the first thing I saw when I came in was they were doing it on the mountain behind the house where I was born and raised. And I just thought, 'oh, my,' you know. 'my goodness.' I mean I was so shocked. And then I heard some people talk about what was happening you know, to them, personally, and I just, I was so riled I couldn't sleep that night. And the next day they were having a meeting with OSM

(Office of Surface Mining) up on Kayford Mountain and a friend and I went up there and that was it" (Niles 2006). Janet educated herself on the workings of the coal industry in West Virginia, and the political processes that enable it to work.

Another CRMW member, Patricia, joined in 2001, after becoming frustrated with the frequency of coal trucks traveling on the roads near her home, creating pollution, noise, and serving as a danger for other motorists. Mountaintop removal coal mining produces more coal than any other type of coal mining. As a result, the presence of coal trucks has increased in many coalfield neighborhoods. Patricia, along with several women from her neighborhood, spontaneously formed a group that stood on a road near their homes, preventing coal trucks from passing. All of them were jailed for their civil disobedience. Despite the various reasons why individual women join a group like the Coal River Mountain Watch, the group, as a whole, is committed to improving the quality of life in their small communities.

Over the years, the CRMW has engaged in various forms of social protest, including organizing rallies and direct actions, educational campaigns, litigation, monitoring coal industry meetings, community organizing, and lobbying state government to fight for economic and social justice in the coal fields. Activists are especially keen to garner outside support, hoping this issue will receive more national attention, and along with it, more help in the fight against the industry and state forces that sustain MTR.

People typically organize around issues that directly impact their lives. This is especially true of rural, working-class women who join environmental justice groups.

The efforts of the Coal River Mountain Watch are incredibly progressive and transformative. A small group fighting the formidable twin powers of the coal business and state government confront many, many obstacles. One woman, 75 year old Paulette, became politically active in the late 1990s when the disastrous influence of Massey Energy, namely its coal containment and preparation plants, began to impact her community. Paulette was particularly concerned with the increasing levels of coal dust polluting her environment, and Massey's move to force people living in her small community out of their homes by way of company buy-outs. Paulette said the biggest obstacle to fighting mountaintop removal and the coal industry is "the state and federal government. Because all the way down the line they change the laws to protect them, not us. The laws are out there to protect us but they won't abide by them, and the government doesn't make them abide by them . . . if somebody gets a hold of something and they take it to court, then they change it. It's our government. In Washington and in Charleston" (Cadbury 2006).

While many of the members mentioned the corrupt forces of the coal industry and state and federal government as being the biggest roadblocks to exacting transformative change in the Appalachian coalfields, others connect these local issues to larger, national and international ones. One woman, Sally (Hart), said the greatest impediment was "just getting people to care and to understand that it is a problem and that everybody including myself is adding to the problem . . . by using energy. And there's gotta be a better way . . . fossil fuels aren't going to be here forever. And if we don't start making the transition now when are we going to?" (Hart 2006). Likewise, June reminds us of the long view, and the connections between events in Appalachia and the rest of the world. She says "I could go on about West Virginia and mountaintop removal but I can see the big picture. And the big picture is renewable energy. The big picture is America's reliance on fossil fuels," and "what it is doing to the earth" (Brown 2006) the need for alternative sources of fuel (Brown 2006).

It's important to realize that women activists in the Appalachian coalfields fight the industry and political system in the face of tremendous opposition and personal risk. Workers for the coal industry are frequently hired to intimidate any oppositional voices. Also, many residents are angry with any resistance to coal industry practices, labeling activists as environmental radicals who seek to take away jobs in the area.

In addition to direct threats, Janet says the CRMW has many people who stop by the offices trying to gather information about their activities, and others who try to infiltrate by securing memberships to the CRMW. Despite the threats and intimidation, coming from industry officials and community members, Janet doesn't fear for her safety, believing that the group members' increasing visibility gives them a blanket of protection. She says that even though the possibility of physical danger is always present, "it's less likely now than in the past because now if anything happens to one of us, you know, the first place they're gonna look is at Massey Energy . . . to a certain extent that gives us some protection" (Niles 2006). Even though many of the women joined the organization out of a need to protect their families and communities, all members indicated that their families frequently worry about their safety, and the industry and public response to their oppositional activities.

Despite the opposition they keep their collective focus on community preservation foremost in group activities. When I asked Patricia how her work benefited her community she was quick to respond that she hopes to "turn it around so that we can have sustainable communities, save our water supply, clean up the air, and we'd like to see some changes in the economics around here. We want to save our communities, we want sustainable communities, we want jobs" (Smith 2006). June boldly suggests that if "the community and the state would listen to what we say we would already be reaping the rewards of a diverse economy. What we're trying to do is force the state to quit being corrupt, quit being raped by the coal industry, stop helping the coal industry rape the state of WV and the people and our children. (Brown 2006). Sally says that their work is important because it "gets the information out there. As hard-headed as people are they're still seeing it, they're still hearing about it." (Hart 2006).

Janet told me that she believed "there is this dichotomy in the way that men and women look at life. I think it's because women see the broad picture and the long picture. They have this long view of what's going to happen to their children and . . . they can see ahead." She claims that on the contrary "men focus more closely on their job, or what's round them . . . there's an immediacy that I think that men have . . . and women are quick to care. They're quick to care about the people being harmed" (Brown 2006).

Paulette suggested that women are involved in these issues more than men because what the coal industry is doing is "destroying the homes and the homes belong to the women's place . . . men don't have to clean them all the time, women do and I don't know, our men, I think they're just sitting back waiting, hoping the union's going to come back." The gender ideology at work here cannot be severed from the political-economic arrangements that created and continue to sustain the coalfield region of West Virginia. According to Sally Maggard, once the coal industry moved into Appalachia sex segregation became more rigidly entrenched, with men being relegated to the mining labor force and women "assigned the auxiliary work of managing households and caring for dependents and the disabled" (1994, 16). Maggard claims that within this pattern, women became more dependent upon men for their economic survival, and a gender ideology emerged to justify the division of labor: men came to be identified by their work in the dangerous occupation of coal mining, while women were defined by their roles within the home.

This ideology is still strong in the coalfields, particularly in mining communities. In this area, like many parts of the country and indeed, the world, women's social value comes primarily from their role as mothers and wives. There is great pressure in the culture for women to be good mothers, and to sacrifice everything in the service of her home and children. This gender ideology can explain why women in the Coal River Mountain Watch have such a strong sense of protection for their families and communities and work at great risk to save them. However, it is somewhat ironic that the gender ideology that serves to consign women to the private home sector, caring for children and husbands, is the same ideology that has propelled women of the Coal River Mountain Watch out of the home and into coalfield communities, mining sites, the state legislature, stockholder meetings, educational road show campaigns, and any number of public spaces to educate the public about what is devastating their Appalachian communities. In the process these women speak up, defend, and represent themselves as individuals and as members of their communities. In doing so, they become confident, knowledgeable adversaries of the coal industry and the state political system.

This small group of thoughtful, committed, women are, in effect, doing everything in their power to give truth to Margaret Mead's famous assertion about collective action and social change. CRMW activist, June became involved in this organization after the incursions of the coal industry became too much for her community to handle.   [edited, 2008]

REFERENCES

Appalachian Voices. 2006. <http://www.appvoices.org/index.php?/site/mtr_overview/> (accessed October 4, 2006).

Brown, June. 2006. Interview with author in Whitesville, West Virginia. June 10. Tape recording and transcript in possession of the author.

Cadbury, Paulette. 2006. Interview with author in Whitesville, West Virginia. June 17. Tape recording and transcript in possession of the author.

Freese, Barbara. 2003. *Coal: A Human History*. Cambridge, MA: Perseus Publishing.

Hart, Sally. 2006. Interview with author. June 14 (tape recording and transcript in possession of the author).

I Love Mountains. 2006. <http://www.ilovemountains.org> (accessed October 10, 2006).

Maggard, Sally. 1994. From Farm to Coal Camp to Back Office and McDonald's: Living in the Midst of Appalachia's Latest Transformation. *Journal of Appalachian Studies Association* 14–39.

Mother Jones Online. 2006. <http://www.motherjones.com/news/outfront/2002/03/coal_slurry.html> (accessed October 17, 2006).

Niles, Janet. 2006. Interview with author. June 14 (tape recording and transcript in possession of author).

Purdy, Jedediah. 1998. Rape of the Appalachians. *The American Prospect* Nov/Dec: 28–33.

Smith, Patricia. 2006. Interview with author. June 7 (tape recording and transcript in possession of author).

The Coal River Mountain Watch. 2006. <http://www.webpages.charter.net/crmw/> (accessed October 7, 2006).

🦎 171

The Feminist Food Revolution

JENNIFER COGNARD-BLACK

Eat, local seasonal food. Plant food sustainably and enjoy food more slowly—taking time to cook it and sharing meals with family and friends around a common table.

These have been the mantras of women's grassroots and public-policy groups on American food for four decades. As our nation's food economy has become increasingly bankrupt—producing cheap, nutritionally deficient foods through industrial methods while paying farmers and farmworkers less and less—women have founded and developed such programs as:

• **EDIBLE SCHOOLYARD**, a 1-acre organic garden and kitchen classroom for urban public school students in Berkeley, Calif., founded by famed California chef Alice Waters

• **DC URBAN GARDENERS**, a network of Washington, D.C., folks committed to locally grown food and eco-friendly gardening practices, founded by gardening writer Susan Harris

• **FOOD NOT LAWNS INTERNATIONAL**, a movement to "turn yards into gardens and neighborhoods into communities," started by *Food Not Lawns* author Heather C. Flores

• **BUY FRESH BUY LOCAL**, a national network with local *chapters* that connect consumers with locally produced foods, run by Pennsylvania farmer Jessica Greenblatt Seeley

• **FOOD LITERACY INITIATIVE**, a project out of Harvard University to educate the local community about food sources and agriculture, nutrition and food preparation, advised by famed vegetarian cookbook writer Mollie Katzen

Yet the coverage on and credit for such work has largely gone to *men*.

For example, within a month of Michelle Obama unveiling "Let's Move!," ABC aired *Famie Oliver's Food Revolution*, a TV show set in

Huntington, W.V., in which British chef Oliver tried to reteach locals how to cook "tasty meals with fresh ingredients—no packets, no cheating." Oliver said he hoped his show would convince the "bad guys" to "start cleaning up their recipes." That makes him a kind of Supercook in the minds of millions: a manly man fighting nefarious evildoers.

Oliver is but one of a small group of white men who have turned a national *interest in sustainable* food into cults of foodie personality, eclipsing the many women in the movement. . . .

So why are men getting most of the praise and recognition? As Temra Costa, author of the new book *Farmer Jane: Women Changing the Way We Eat* (Gibbs-Smith, 2010)—which profiles 30 exceptional women who advocate sustainable food and farming—explained when asked why men were left out of her book; "It's not that men aren't changing how we eat. . . . It's just that they're really good at getting all of the press."

So let's not forget to also read Marion Nestle's watershed book *Food Politics: How the Food Industry Influences Nutrition and Health* (University of California Press, 2007). And follow the activism of Vandana Shiva, who's written copiously about international seed wars, industrial fertilizer poisoning and what she terms the hijacking of the global food supply. Or study the work of Psyche Williams-Forson, a University of Maryland associate professor of women's studies, African American studies and American studies who, as part of her scholarship on black women's symbolic relationship to chicken, analyzes a KFC commercial through the lenses of gender and race.

Put simply, women's contributions to the national food movement, Michelle Obama notwithstanding, are not visible enough. Many may know of Alice Waters and the 1970s. New American Cuisine that made local, seasonal and sustainable eating fashionable, yet few have heard of the thousands of women who have taken up farming, planted urban and community gardens, advocated for food safety and better school lunches, or run restaurants with organic, seasonal menus. Women's food work has initiated a true revolution in the sense of making wide-reaching and dramatic changes in the ways people think about and participate in how food is produced, prepared and consumed. And it's a feminist revolution, with women farmers, gardeners and sustainable chefs trying to raise the visibility of women as well as enable all of us to make healthier food choices.

One testament to this revolution is the boom in women farmers. In the 2007 U.S. Census of Agriculture, the total number of women operating farms increased 19 percent, far surpassing the overall 7 percent increase in farmers.

Women tend to run smaller, more diversified farms and participate in direct-to-eater (farmers') markets. For almost two decades, women have also been running regional and national associations to support other women farmers and farmworkers, such as Blue Ridge Women in Agriculture (BRWIA), Organización de Líderes Campesinas (Women Farmworker Leaders), the Women's Agriculture Network (WAgN) and the Women, Food and Agriculture Network (WFAN).

Meet one feminist farmer, Elina Snyder, an economics major who runs her own market garden in Leonardtown, Md. During college, she worked on an organic farm, where she found that a number of tasks were deemed "female" or "male" depending on how much strength they required. But Snyder insisted on learning all aspects of farming; she needed to know more than just how to pick cherry tomatoes—a "female" task. "I had to prove how strong I was," she explains. "I had to say 'I can do that.'"

After Snyder started her own small farm, she still had to prove herself at farmers' markets. "I was the only female who was both a grower and a vendor, and I would often get incredulous questions such as 'You grew this all yourself?'" she says.

Snyder is about to apply for graduate school in sustainable agriculture so that she can grow and sell organic food on an even bigger scale. "I distrust agribusiness," she says, "and I want to build a local food network to support both myself and my community."

You don't need a rural farm to grow food, though: There is a long tradition in America of creating urban gardens out of clay soil, concrete or rooftops. The innovative SmartRoofs program, run by Sustainable South Bronx—founded by a woman, Majora Carter—encourages planting multipurpose "green roofs" in the New York borough as a way to improve air quality, lower energy costs, reduce stormwater runoff and provide nourishment.

In Detroit—where many urban residents live in food "deserts" with a lack of nearby access to fresh, healthy food (but usually no shortage of cheap "junk" food)—the Detroit Black Community Food Security Network promotes urban gardens and operates a healthy-food-buying co-op. It also runs a 2-acre urban community farm—managed by a woman, DBCFS vice chair Marilyn Barber.

On an individual basis, there is a growing movement among suburban feminists to pull up lawns and plant front-yard gardens. A mother and community organizer from Edina, Minn., Cheryl Gunness tilled her front lawn to create a vegetable, fruit and flower garden after one of her sons developed an allergy to peanuts. "I put the garden in the front because it was practical—my back yard is shady, the front sunny," says Gunness. "But then it became a very cool thing. People stopped by, asked questions. My elderly neighbors picked my rhubarb and then shared slices of their rhubarb pie."

Gunness felt that front-lawn gardening was a feminist gesture, making a statement about women's labors. "This hard work I'm doing is visible," she says. "Here I am, sweat running down my face, and people *see* me. My drudgery isn't hidden in the back yard."

Heather C. Flores (Chelsea Green Publishing, 2006) further argues in *Food Not Lawns* that growing one's own food is radical, since it shifts the power balance from industrial control back to individual (or community) control. Flores calls such action "guerrilla gardening." "Those who control our food control our lives, and when we take that control back into our own hands, we empower ourselves toward autonomy," she says.

Food makes its way from farms and front lawns to dining tables, and there another group of food revolutionaries—feminist chefs—are cooking with local, seasonal ingredients. Take Maggie Pleskac, owner and top chef of Maggie's Vegetarian Café in Lincoln, Neb.—the first vegetarian/vegan restaurant in the city, and in a state defined by its deeply masculine meat industry. Besides the hypermasculinity, raising beef also undermines the environment and keeps people hungry worldwide, as Frances Moore Lappe—another visionary woman—pointed out in her groundbreaking 1985 book, *Diet for a Small Planet* (Ballantine). Lappe noted that Americans feed ten times as much grain to cattle as is consumed in the U.S.—grain that could feed many more hungry people than the meat from the cattle can.

In Nebraska's culture, Pleskac has had to flex feminist muscle in defense of her ever-changing vegetarian/vegan menu built around seasonal foods. "A fellow male restaurateur once said to me, 'You can't survive without consistency,'" says Pleskac. "I told him, 'I'll never be consistent with the mainstream!'"

Simply choosing vegetarianism or veganism can be a revolutionary feminist act, Pleskac argues, because it refuses dominant and commercial food structures. But one must have real choices, including access to healthy and culturally relevant food, whether from a local grocery store, urban garden or cafeteria lunch line—and those are often unavailable in low-income communities. In the new anthology edited by A. Breeze Harper, *Sistah Vegan: Black Female Vegans Speak on Food, Identity, Health, and Society* (Lantern Books, 2010), contributor Psyche Williams-Forson—not a vegan herself—points out that because of racial and class disparities in our health and food systems, "a lifestyle of health is also about inherent race and class discrimination."

So let's read personal stories on the Farmer Jane (www.farmerjane.org) and Sistah Vegan (www.sistahvegan.wordpress.com) websites of women farmers, guerrilla gardeners and sustainable sistahs. Let's join community gardens, plant lawns with veggies, reform our children's lunches and buy fresh/buy local. Then, let us share our own heroic stories of food and feminists.   [edited, 2010]

🌿 172

Waging Peace: Codepink

ANGELINA PERRI BIRNEY

Any woman who chooses to behave like a full human being should be warned that the armies of the status quo will treat her as something of a dirty joke. That's their natural and first weapon. She will need her sisterhood.
—Gloria Steinem

Medea Benjamin is co-founder of the San Francisco-based human rights organization, Global Exchange, as well as co-founder of CODEPINK Women for Peace.

So what turned "a nice Jewish girl" from Long Island into a political activist?

"Now that goes back some," Medea remarks. "Actually, I think it all began for me in high school. I remember when my sister's boyfriend was sent to Vietnam and mailed home a souvenir of an ear of a Vietcong. I was so disgusted by it that it set me on a path of trying to understand why some people considered others lesser human beings. I wondered how we could reverse that. Also, there were real inequalities in the high school that I went to which resulted in race riots. So here I was in a supposedly quiet, suburban Long Island neighborhood that was suddenly racked in the sixties by race relations and war. That kind of thing certainly leaves a mark on you, especially if it happens earlier in life as it did in my case, when you're just trying to figure out what you want to do and become, and how you want to live your life. All of it urged me down a path of trying to get people to like each other more."

Helping people to like each other can sometimes be a monumental task. Intolerance, abuse, greed, political gain . . . War is often the sad result of their erosive wear. CODEPINK Women for Peace is dedicated to turning the tide—from funding war and aggression toward looking for new avenues for our resources such as green jobs and better healthcare. They are resolved to helping support policies based on diplomacy and compassion rather than those rooted in fear and suppression. From stopping the wars in Iraq and Afghanistan to preventing new aggressions from arising, CODEPINK seeks to activate, amplify and inspire a community of peacemakers through creative campaigns and a commitment to non-violence.

Oftentimes when we hear of such monumental endeavors, we tend to envision some huge campaign behind them. Not always the case. CODEPINK, Medea explains, started when a group of women concerned about the environment got together for a retreat that was organized by a group called Bioneers. "We sat around for several days talking about ways we could address the environmental crisis. During our breaks, we also talked about 9/11 and the US response—the bombing of Afghanistan. We discussed the pending war in Iraq and the color coded alert system that Bush had just declared. It was so odd and nobody knew what to do. We were laughing about it and saying 'okay if it gets to orange is that when we get out the plastic tarps? When do we use the tape? Do we put it around ourselves or the terrorists?' So initially, we had some good laughs about the whole thing. But of course, we also realized how serious it was. We could see there was all this negative male energy out there—Osama bin Laden, Saddam Hussein, and also George Bush. We felt we needed to inject some rational, loving female energy into the situation. So we put the group together, initially thinking we'd call it Code Hot Pink until we found that the URL was taken by a porn group," Medea conveys, laughing. "So we dropped the "hot", which was very disappointing to some of us, and we went with the name CODEPINK. The idea was to turn the color pink on its head from being this nice, feminine, sweet color to one that was very energetic, bold, and determined."

That bold determination has created initiatives like Women Say No to War, inspiring women around the world to become active participants in peacemaking and social change. "We wanted to mobilize women in this country, but we also found in the process that women from other countries were contacting us and saying it's time we all work together across borders. So Women Say No to War is our attempt to take on issues that we can work on with other women. Some are joint projects like supporting refugees from Iraq who are now living in countries all over the world, but particularly in Syria and Jordan. We're also helping to promote women's voices in Afghanistan who are speaking out against the war, as well as working on smaller scale projects run by women that we feel are helpful in building community."

CODEPINK has actively supported women of the Middle East when they have risen up to oppose injustice. "In Afghanistan, when the Karzai government was passing a law in order to get more votes from the Shia community, the president, Hamid Karzai, agreed to a law that basically instituted marital rape. Some of the women in Afghanistan rose up to oppose it under very difficult conditions, and we were there to support them and to echo their desire to get rid of the law. Our efforts were successful to a large extent. Then there's Iran. We have looked toward people like the Nobel Peace prize winner, Shirin Ebadi, for guidance with regard to good campaigns to support. We have also taken groups to Iran, Afghanistan, and to Iraq— obviously places that are oftentimes dangerous and difficult for Americans. That's because we feel it's important for us to meet directly with women from different countries so we can learn from them and have a deeper understanding of how we can best support their efforts."

Women-induced peace initiatives are creating imprints in other Middle Eastern arenas. CODE-PINK, as Medea explains, is one of several groups which are taking on the gritty task of demanding humanitarian relief for the Palestinians virtually imprisoned in Gaza. "CODEPINK became very involved in Israel/Palestine after the Israeli invasion of Gaza that left over 1,400 Palestinians dead. We felt particularly concerned that US tax dollars and our military hardware was used in the attack. CODEPINK has also taken many delegations to Gaza in the last two years. It's hard to get in which is why many other groups don't try. We had a beautiful delegation of almost 100 people,

including Alice Walker, that went in on International Women's Day in 2009."

Medea also stresses the need for us to remember what's actually happening in Gaza. "There's a population of nearly 1.5 million people who are living in what's equivalent to an open air prison. They aren't allowed the freedom to go in and out of the area, really only surviving thanks to the United Nations and other charitable organizations," Medea states. "So we've been trying to push the Israeli government to lift the siege. Along the way, we've made great connections with the women inside Gaza and have been encouraging them as much as possible, both politically and practically. We support projects like women's crafts, for instance, so they can make a living. That's what we do—back concrete projects as well as longer-term policy goals."

Yet real change in policy will never manifest while human beings are being held in bondage and humanitarian aid denied as the international community stands by, allowing it to occur without repercussions. The U.S. government has been complicit in arming Israel and enabling its human rights abuses, including the ongoing siege of Gaza that has kept 1.5. million people living in the world's largest open-air prison.

Medea gives her assessment as to why the U.S. government continues to support Israel in such a biased way. "If you look at who controls policy, it's really the lobby group AIPAC—American Israel Public Affairs Committee. It's really strong and well organized. . . . It gives tremendous amounts of money to the Democratic and Republican parties so it has a very fierce stranglehold on policy, always showing unconditional support for Israel. We're actually mobilizing to try to directly expose AIPAC and how it's policies control American interests. . . . No doubt, confronting organizations such as AIPAC by shedding light on hard-nosed and unfair tactics is becoming more and more necessary. It's also become obvious, as well as essential, that women's voices are heard in any serious attempt to attain peaceful resolution.

"Oftentimes women and children are the number one victims of war, and they are usually excluded when it comes to trying to find peace,"

Article 143b: "Hey Man, That's Not Cool: Men Stopping Street Harassment" from *Stop Street Harassment: Making Public Places Safe and Welcoming for Women* by Holly Kearl. Copyright © 2010. Used by permission of ABC-CLIO, LLC.

Article 144: From *That Takes Ovaries,* edited by Rivka Solomon. Copyright © 2002 by Rivka Solomon. Used by permission of Three Rivers Press, a division of Random House, Inc.

Article 145: From *A Woman Scorned: Acquaintance Rape on Trial* by Peggy Reeves Sanday. Copyright © 1996 by Peggy Reeves Sanday. Used by permission of Doubleday, a division of Random House, Inc.

Article 146: Reprinted by permission of the author.

Article 147: Copyright © Lanette Fisher-Hertz. Used by permission of the author.

Article 148: Copyright © Peri L. Rainbow, MPS. Used by permission of the author.

Article 149: From *Nature's Ban,* edited by Karen McLennan. Copyright © Ruth Whitman. Reprinted by permission of Morton Sacks.

Chapter VIII

Article 150: Copyright © Amy Kesselman. Reprinted by permission of the author.

Article 151: The Seneca Falls Women's Rights Convention, 1848.

Article 152: Defense of the Rights of Women by Sojourner Truth

Article 153: From *Feminist Revolution,* edited by Redstockings (New Paltz, NY: Redstockings, 1975; abridged ed. With additional writings, New York: Random House, 1978). Available from Redstockings Women's Liberation Archives for Action Distribution Project, P.O. Box 2625, Gainesville, FL 32602-2625 or on the web at www.redstockings.org. Reprinted by permission of the author.

Article 154: Copyright © 1998 by Susan Brownmiller. All rights reserved. Reprinted by permission of the author.

Article 155: Reprinted by permission of the author.

Article 156: From *Feminist Nationalism,* edited by Lois West. Copyright © 1997. Reproduced by permission of Routledge/Taylor & Francis Group, LLC.

Article 157: From *A Gathering of the Spirit: Writing and Art* by Native American Women, edited by Beth Brandt., Firebrand Books, Milford, CT. Copyright © 1985 by Beth Brandt. Reprinted by permission of the publisher.

Article 158: "Triple Jeoardy and the Struggle" by Miriam Ching Yoon Louie from Solidarity, 2006. http://www.solidarity-us.org/current/node/1486.

Article 159: From *Backlash* by Susan Faludi. Copyright © 1991 by Susan Faludi. Reprinted by permission of Crown Publishers, a division of Random House, Inc.

Article 160: Edited version from *Passionate Politics,* St. Martin's Press, 1987. Reprinted by permission of the author.

Article 161: Copyright © 1995. Reprinted by permission of *Ms* magazine.

Article 162: From *Global Uprising: Confronting the Tyrannies of the 21st Century, Stories from a New Generation of Activists* by Neva Welton and Linda Wolf. Copyright © 2000 by New Society Publishers. Reprinted with permission of the publisher.

Article 162: From *Students Against Sweatshops: The Making of a Movement* by Liza Featherstone and United Students Against Sweatshops. Copyright © by Liza Featherstone and United Students Against Sweatshops. Reprinted by permission of Verso Books.

Article 163: "Struggles of Responsibility" from *GRASS-ROOTS: A Field Guide for Feminist Activism* by Jennifer Baumgardner and Amy Richards. Copyright © 2005 by Jennifer Baumgardner and Amy Richards. Reprinted by permission of Farrar, Straus and Giroux, LLC.

Article 164: From *Under a Soprano Sky* by Sonia Sanchez, Africa World Press, Trenton, NJ. Reprinted by permission of the author.

Article 165: "Manifesta: Young Women, Feminism, and the Future" by Jennifer Baumgardner and Amy Richards: Excerpted from *MANIFESTA: Young Women, Feminism, and the Future* by Jennifer Baumgardner and Amy Richards, activists (Farrar, Straus & Giroux, LLC, 2000). Reprinted by permission of the authors.

Article 166: From *Just Sex: Students Rewrite the Rules on Sex, Violence, and Equality,* edited by Jody Gold and Susan Villari. Copyright © 2000 by Rowman & Littlefield Publishing, Inc. Reprinted by permission of the publisher.

Article 167: From *Signs,* 25:4 (Summer 2000), pp. 1215–22. Copyright © by University of Chicago Press. Reprinted by permission of the publisher.

Article 168: From *Women, AIDS & Activism,* South End Press, 1990. Copyright © 1990 by the ACT Up/New York Women and AIDS Book Group. Reprinted by permission of South End Press, 7 Brookline Street, #1, Cambridge, MA 02139-4146.

Article 169: "Organizing with Love" by Ai-jen Poo.

Article 170: "Women, Environmental Justice, and the Coal River Mountain Watch" by Joyce M. Barry.

Article 171: "The Feminist Food Revolution" by Jennifer Cognard-Black, Kate Noftsinger, from *Ms.* Magazine, Summer 2010, pp 36–39 edited. Reprinted by permission of *MS* Magazine, © 2010.

Article 172: "Waging Peace: Media Benjamin of Code Pink" by Angelina Perri Birney from *PURE VISION: POWERFUL WOMEN CHANGING THE WORLD.* Reprinted by permission of Angelina Perri Birney, author and publisher, PureVision, High Falls, NY 12010.

Article 173: Used by permission of Claire R. Papell.

Article 174: Copyright © by Lori Gross. Used by permission of the author.

Article 174: Copyright © by Sharon Thompson, MPH, M.D. Used by permission of the author.

Article 174: Reprinted by permission of the author.

Article 116: From *Harvard Educational Reivew,* Vol. 66, no. 2 (Summer 1996), pp. 182–184. Copyright © 1996 by the President and Fellows of Harvard College. All rights reserved. Reprinted with permission. For more information, please call Harvard Education Publishing Group, 800-513-0723.

Article 117: From *Forty-three Septembers.* Published by Firebrand Books, Milford, CT. Copyright © 1993 by Jewelle Gomez. Reprinted by permission of the publisher.

Article 118: Reprinted with permission from OWL (Older Women's League).

Article 119: From *Look Me in the Eye: Old Women, Ageing, and Ageism,* Expanded Edition, by Barbara Macdonald with Cynthia Rich, pp. 76–87. Minneapolis: Spinsters Ink, 1983. Available from Spinsters Ink, P.O. Box 300170, Minneapolis, MN 55403. $8.95. Reprinted by permission of the publisher.

Article 120: From *Every Other Path,* edited by Arcadio Morales, Jr. and Brian Martinez. Permission granted by Francisco A. Lomeli, advisor of Every Other Path.

Article 121a: Copyright © 2005 by Janice Kaeffaber. Reprinted by permission of the author.

Article 121b: "The Woman Who Once Was" by Rebecca McClanahan.

Article 122: Used by permission of Gowri Parameswaran.

Article 123: "Injustice on Our Plates: Immigrant Women in the U.S. Food Industry," Retrieved from http://www.splcenter.org/sites/default/files/downloads/publication/Injustice_on_Our_Plates.pdf. Used by permission of Southern Poverty Law Center, 2010.

Article 124: "Mothers of Our Nations: Indigenous Women Address the World" by Winona LaDuke (1995).

Article 125: "What's in a Name?" by Anida Yoeu Ali, Ch. 2 from *SHOUT OUT: Women of Color Respond to Violence.* Copyright © 2007. Reprinted by permission of Seal Press, a member of the Perseus Books Group.

Article 126: Edited version from *Passionate Politics,* St. Martin's Press, 1987. Reprinted by permission of the author.

Article 127a: Reprinted with the permission of Washington Press, a Division of Simon & Schuster, Inc., from *SISTERHOOD IS FOREVER: The Women's Anthology for a New Millennium,* edited by Robin Morgan. Copyright © 2003 by Robin Morgan. All rights reserved.

Article 127b: Excerpted from *Stanford Law Review,* July 1991. Copyright © 1991 by Stanford Law Review. Reproduced with permission.

Article 128: Copyright © 1984 by Audre Lorde from *Sister Outsider,* published by Crossing Press, CA. Reprinted by permission of the Charlotte Sheedy Literary Agency, Inc.

Article 129: "Fence Sitters, Switch Hitters, and Bi-Bi Girls: An Exploration of Hapa and Bisexual Identities" by Beverly Yuen Thompson, is reproduced from *FRONTIERS: A Journal of Women Studies* with permission from the University of Nebraska Press. Copyright © 2000 by Frontiers Editorial Collective, Inc.

Article 130: From *Food for Our Grandmothers: Writings by Arab-American and Arab-Canadian Feminists,* edited by Joanne Kodi. Reprinted by permission of South End Press, 7 Brookline St., #1, Cambridge, MA 02139-4146.

Article 131: Reprinted by permission of the author.

Article 132: Copyright © 1985 by Linda Hogan. Reprinted by permission of the University of Massachusetts Press.

Chapter VII

Article 133: Used by permission of Michele McKeon.

Article 134: From *The Forbidden Stitch: An Asian American Women's Anthology,* edited by Shirley Geok-lin Lim et al. Copyright © 1989 by Calyx Books. Reprinted by permission of the publisher.

Article 135a: Latina Anonima, "La Princesa," in Telling to Live, Latina Feminist Group, pp. 286–288. Copyright © 2001 by Duke University Press. All rights reserved. Reprinted by permission of the publisher.

Article 135b: From *Talking Back: Thinking Feminism, Thinking Black* by bell hooks. Reprinted by permission of South End Press, 7 Brookline St., #1, Cambridge, MA 02139-4146 and Between the Lines, Torono.

Article 136: From *The State of Asian-American Activism: Resistance in the 1990s,* edited by Karen Aguilar-San Juan. Reprinted by permission of South End Press, 7 Brookline St., #1, Cambridge, MA 02139-4146.

Article 137: Selective Story Telling: A Critique of U.S. Media Coverage Regarding Violence Against Indian Women by Sharmila Lodhia from *SHOUT OUT: women of color respond to violence,* edited by Maria Ochoa and Barbara K. Ige. Copyright © 2007. Reprinted by permission of Perseus Books Group.

Article 138: Copyright © by Colleen Farrell. Used by permission of the author.

Article 139: From *Nappy Edges* by Ntozake Shange. Copyright © 1972 by Ntozake Shange. Reprinted by permission of St. Martin's Press, LLC.

Article 140a: Reprinted from *Ramparts,* Vol. 10, no. 3, September 1971. Reprinted by permission of the author.

Article 140b: Reprinted by permission of the author.

Article 141: From *Transforming a Rape Culture,* edited by Emilie Buchwald, Pamela Fletcher, and Martin Roth. Copyright © 1993 by Pamela Fletcher. Reprinted with permission from the author.

Article 142: Reprinted with permission from *Human Rights Dialogue: Violence Against Women,* Series 2, Number 10, Fall 2003 (New York: Carnegie Council, 2003), pp. 20–21; available at www.cceia.org/viewMedia.php/prmID/1052

Article 143a: Catcalls, Groping and Stalking in Public Places: How to Deal with Street Harassment from Stop Street Harassment: Making Public Places Safe and Welcoming for Women by Holly Kearl. Copyright © 2010. Used by permission of ABC-CLIO, LLC.

Index